A Citizen's Working Guide to Constitutional Reform

BEFORE

◆ ◆ ◆

the Fires

A Comprehensive Guide to

The People's Reclamation Amendment

Written by

Shawn Theis

Before the Fires

A Comprehensive Guide to the People's Reclamation Amendment

Written by Shawn Theis

The text of the People's Reclamation Amendment, contained in Chapter 7, is placed in the public domain. Anyone may reproduce, cite, advocate for, or build upon the Amendment text without permission or attribution.

First Edition · 2026

A Note Before the Book Begins

This is a draft amendment to the Constitution of the United States, accompanied by a citizen's guide to what it does, how it works, and what it asks of the reader. It exists because the existing tools for federal accountability — impeachment, election, judicial review — have demonstrated structural limits, and a country that wants to remain governed by its citizens should have a working answer for the moment those tools are insufficient. Whether the country is in that moment now, or near it, or far from it, is a question the reader will have to answer for themselves. The amendment exists either way; it is patient. The Amendment text is placed in the public domain. Any citizen, journalist, scholar, attorney, or office-holder may reproduce the Amendment, cite it, advocate for it, or propose modifications, without permission or attribution. The book around it — the explanatory chapters, charts, and editorial work — is © 2026 Shawn Theis. If the reader finds the proposal unworkable, they are encouraged to write a better one. The author would, in fact, prefer this. If the reader finds it sound, they are encouraged to share it, defend it, and demand of their elected officials that they engage with it on the merits. The country has the right to better than what it has been getting. This is one attempt to give it a tool.

Contents

Chapter 1 · · · · · · · · · 2
The Breakdown

Chapter 2 · · · · · · · · · 6
When the Tools Fail

Chapter 3 · · · · · · · · · 9
The First Reading

Chapter 4 · · · · · · · · · 28
The Second Reading

Chapter 5 · · · · · · · · · 50
The Third Reading

Chapter 6 · · · · · · · · · 88
The Maps

Chapter 7 · · · · · · · · · 107
The Amendment

Chapter 8 · · · · · · · · · 760
Postscript

Glossary · · · · · · · · · 762

BEFORE THE FIRES

Chapter One

The Breakdown

There is a feeling, common among Americans of all political stripes, that the normal ways of being heard have stopped producing anything. You vote. You call your representative's office. You sign the petition, show up to the town hall, send the email, submit the public comment during the thirty-day window like they ask you to. You do the things a citizen is supposed to do. And the government does roughly what it was going to do anyway.

This book is about what happens when that stops being a feeling and becomes the situation — when none of the usual ways of pushing back move the needle anymore. Here is the whole thing, up front, in one sentence:

There should be a peaceful, lawful way for the people to remove a federal government that has stopped doing its job — and to replace it — without a revolution, without violence, without anything more dramatic than showing up, signing your name, and voting.

That's the book. The rest is just detail — how it works, why it's shaped the way it is, what it would ask of you if it ever came to that. And what it asks is almost nothing: a few hours of your attention, and someday, maybe, your signature. Nothing more than that. So let me back up and explain why a country would ever need such a thing.

Voting, if you stare at it too long, starts to seem completely made up. Not the counting. The counting works fine. It's the choice that feels staged. For as long as most people can remember, it has come down to two names, and the job is to pick the one you can stand. The lesser of two evils. Every cycle, the same. And every cycle it goes the same way after, too — you pick the less-bad one, and nothing gets better. If anything it gets worse. You do it enough times that voting stops feeling like a decision and starts feeling like a formality. And that is the smaller of the two strange parts.

The bigger one is this: it does not actually matter much who wins. The corruption shows up either way. It is not a feature of one party or one man — it is a feature of power sitting still long enough. Give anyone enough time in the seat, enough people willing to pay for a yes, enough chances to get bribed without ever calling it that, and the rot sets in. It always has. The faces change every few years and the favors, the quiet deals, the slow rewriting of the rules to keep the people already in office exactly where they are — those stay. You are not choosing between a clean option and a dirty one. You are picking which set of people gets to screw you for the next four years — and then you get to do it again.

Here's a thing nobody put in the design. There are two parties. There have been two for a long time, and nearly every decision about who runs the country passes through one of them before it gets anywhere near a ballot. The Constitution does not mention them. It mentions Congress, the Presidency, and the Court. It says nothing about the two organizations that decide who fills those seats. The parties are not in the rule book. They are in the upholstery — load-bearing, but not labeled. None of which is a problem, right up until both of them are visibly failing at the same time. You're supposed to pick the better one. When both are getting worse, you're choosing between two things getting worse, and the whole idea of using one to keep the other honest quietly stops applying.

It doesn't fall apart all at once. Nobody calls a meeting. There is no press release. The institutions keep functioning, mostly, but with the bolts visibly loose — and nobody is in charge of the bolts, and nobody is quite sure who has the wrench.

There is a gap, right there in the middle. There should be something between asking politely and waiting, and burning the whole thing down. A way for citizens to fire a federal government that has stopped working for them. That gap has been sitting in plain view for two hundred and fifty years, and the country's response has been, collectively, to shrug, look away, and assume someone else has it handled.

What fills the gap is an amendment to the Constitution — the People's Reclamation Amendment. Here is what it does: it gives the People — which is you, in case anyone has recently tried to convince you otherwise — a way to remove a failed federal government and replace it, peacefully and lawfully, using authority the Constitution already says belongs to them. Not a new country. Not a new constitution. A new tool inside the one we already have.

A few things it is not, because a proposal like this gets mistaken for something else within about five minutes of being introduced.

It is not a call for revolution. Revolutions are how countries lose their constitutions. The entire point of this is to never have to.

It is not partisan. It was not written with any party in mind, and it works the same in either direction. Any party that finds itself in its path earned the spot by failing to do its job.

It is not a threat. The whole hope is that having it — ratified, visible, plainly available — is what keeps it from ever being needed. A government that knows the people can remove it rarely gives them reason to.

Now, about the size of this book. It is long. Not because long books are good — they are not, and nobody wants to read one — but because the thing it describes is genuinely large, and shrinking it would be a kind of lie. Corruption is creative. The answer to it has to be thorough.

Here is the part that matters, though. You do not have to read all of it. You barely have to read much of it. The next chapter lays out the whole idea in plain English, and if you read only that, you will walk away understanding what this is, what it does, and what it asks of you. Everything after is for people who want to go deeper — the engaged citizen, then the lawyer, then the critic whose entire job is to find the holes. The length is there so the thing can survive a fight. It is not there because you have to read it.

Think of the Amendment as the engine and this book as the owner's manual. You do not need to know how the engine works to drive the car. You need to know where the keys are, and that the keys are yours.

They're yours. The rest is up to you.

Chapter Two

When the Tools Fail

A fair objection: the Constitution already has accountability tools. Impeachment. Elections. Courts. And the general sense, vaguely held, that if things get bad enough, somebody somewhere will do something about it. This is a reasonable thing to believe. It is also, on inspection, not quite true. Each of these tools requires conditions that cannot be guaranteed.

Impeachment requires sixty-seven senators to convict. Four presidents have been impeached. None has ever been convicted. The first fell one vote short. And the one time it was clearly headed for removal, the president resigned first — before the House could even vote to impeach him. The system did not remove him. He chose to leave. Generosity, as a constitutional mechanism, has a mixed track record.

Elections require honest elections. The machinery of democracy can keep running — ballots cast, results announced, ceremonies performed — while producing nothing. For roughly ninety years in this country, the constitutional tool of vote them out was technically available and practically useless for a large number of American citizens whose votes had been rendered decorative. The machinery did not stop. It just stopped producing the thing it was supposed to produce. Anyone who believes this is exclusively historical is invited to read more than one newspaper.

Courts require honest courts. The Supreme Court is nine people, appointed for life by politicians, confirmed by other politicians, interpreting the Constitution according to their best understanding of it — which varies considerably from justice to justice, decade to decade, and in a few memorable cases, breakfast to breakfast. They are a hope, dressed up in robes and given a building with columns. Neither the robes nor the columns are load-bearing elements in the architecture of accountability.

Hope requires things to get better on their own. Which is not a mechanism. It is a posture. A country whose accountability depends primarily on hope is a country whose accountability depends on nothing in particular.

The tools do not fail cleanly. They do not collapse in a single dramatic moment. They fail slowly, while continuing to appear to function — which is by some distance the worst way for them to fail. The machinery keeps running. The ceremonies keep happening. Everyone is still wearing the correct robes. A country with working accountability tools and a country without them look, from any reasonable distance, very similar. The difference shows up over years. By the time it is obvious, the damage has usually already been done.

The Framers built redundancy on the theory that if one tool failed, another might hold. What they did not build was a tool that belonged to the citizens themselves. Every tool they built runs through an existing branch of the government being watched. Impeachment runs through Congress. Courts run through judges appointed by presidents. Elections run through officials who are themselves part of the same system. If the system is captured, the tools are captured. Because the tools live inside it. This is not a design flaw so much as a design oversight. The Framers assumed the system being built would not be the problem. In their defense, this is the kind of assumption most people writing founding documents make. The gap has been open for two hundred and fifty years. It has been open the whole time.

They had a lot on their minds in 1787, most of it the immediate problem of getting thirteen suspicious colonies to agree on anything. The idea that the document they were writing might, a couple of centuries later, need an explicit citizen-controlled remedy did not make the priority list. In their defense, they assumed every generation since would be paying attention.

The rest of this book is about the tool they did not build. The People's Reclamation Amendment is one attempt at it. If the country can produce a better one, the country should. The point is not that this particular Amendment is the only possible answer — the point is that the country deserves an answer, and "wait for things to get better" has been tried, exhaustively, and the results have been what they have been.

The federal gap is not the result of a failure of imagination. It is the result of a failure of the more willful variety.

Chapter Three

The First Reading

Welcome to the First Reading.

The previous two chapters were the diagnosis. This one is where the book lays the proposal out in full. If the diagnosis was wrong, the proposal is probably wrong too, and the reader is free to put the book down. If the diagnosis was right, this is the chapter where it starts to matter what comes next.

A quick note on how the rest of the book is organized.

The Amendment itself can be read at three different depths, depending on what the reader wants. Not three different versions — the same Amendment, read three different ways. The Three Readings.

The First Reading is this chapter. It is the Amendment in plain English, for anyone who has never thought about constitutional law in their life and does not intend to start now. If you only read this one, you will still understand what the Amendment is, what it does, and what it asks of you. That is enough.

The Second Reading comes after this one, for readers who want the engaged citizen's tour — how the parts of the Amendment work together, and why each safeguard is there. It is longer. It is still in plain English.

The Third Reading is further on still, for readers who intend to take the Amendment apart. Lawyers. Scholars. Critics. Sitting officials with reasons of their own to know whether this is real. People whose job is to find holes in things. It is the most technical of the three, and it welcomes the scrutiny — a constitutional amendment that cannot survive rigorous examination does not deserve ratification.

You can read all three. You can read one. You can read this First, decide you are satisfied, and close the book. The book belongs to the reader.

Here is the First Reading.

◆ ◆ ◆

What the Amendment does. The Amendment gives the American people a peaceful, constitutional way to remove a federal government that has stopped doing its job. That is the whole thing, in one sentence. Up to this point in American history, if the federal government collectively went bad, the citizens had three options: wait for the next election, hope Congress would impeach somebody, or hope the courts would step in. Chapter Two went over what happens when those options don't work. The answer is that they don't always work, and when they don't, the country has historically had nothing else. The Amendment is the something else.

◆ ◆ ◆

What this is for. The Amendment is not for ordinary political disagreement. There is already a mechanism for that, and it is called the next election. The Amendment is for the situation where the next election cannot fix what is wrong. Where impeachment will not happen because the Senate will not convict. Where elections have been shaped to no longer reliably reflect the will of the voters. Where the courts have been narrowed to where they no longer check the other branches. Where the country looking honestly at its own situation has to admit the system has stopped self-correcting. That is the trigger. That is the moment the Amendment is for. It is, by design, supposed to be rare. The hope is that the Amendment exists, is known to exist, is plainly available to be used, and is therefore almost never actually used — because the prospect of its use, alone, is enough to keep the federal government tethered to the people it represents. Roughly the same logic as a fire extinguisher in a kitchen. The point is not that you intend to use it tonight. The point is that the day comes when you need it — because you burnt dinner — and you have it, and the alternative is the kitchen. When the question arises — should this be used right now? — the answer is almost always no. There is a useful diagnostic question. The reader can ask it of themselves at any time. The question is: are the things that would normally feel embarrassing — politicians being caught, agencies being captured, courts being captured, people in power telling obvious lies to obvious cameras — still embarrassing, or have they started to feel routine? If the answer is the second one, the country is closer to the Amendment than the country was the year before. Whether "close" has become "here" is a determination the country makes collectively, often without realizing it is making it.

◆ ◆ ◆

The Amendment does not exist yet.

It is a proposal. It becomes law the same way every other amendment has become law: through Article V of the Constitution, which has been the front door for every constitutional change since 1791.

Article V provides two pathways. One: two-thirds of both houses of Congress propose the amendment, and three-quarters of the states ratify it. Two: two-thirds of state legislatures — thirty-four of the fifty — call a constitutional convention, the convention proposes the amendment, and three-quarters of the states ratify it. Both pathways end at the same place. They start at different doors.

The first door is unlikely to be used for this particular Amendment. Asking Congress to vote two-thirds in favor of an Amendment that empowers the People to remove Congress is a tough sell. The Amendment does not pretend otherwise.

The second door is the one the Amendment is designed for. Thirty-four state legislatures call a convention. The convention writes the proposal. Thirty-eight states ratify. That is the realistic path.

This is not a shortcut. This is not a loophole. The convention pathway is in the Constitution. It was put there in 1787 by the same people who wrote everything else in Article V, precisely because they anticipated moments when Congress would be unable or unwilling to propose changes that the country needed. It has never been used. It exists for a reason.

If three-quarters of the states do not ratify, the Amendment does not become law. The country has decided.

If three-quarters of the states do ratify, the rest of this chapter starts mattering.

◆ ◆ ◆

The Amendment does not snap into existence fully formed on the day it is ratified. Building functioning institutions takes time, and the Amendment is honest about that.

The day three-quarters of the states say yes is called Day Zero. From Day Zero through about Day 180 — roughly six months — the country is in the build-out phase. The Citizens' Reclamation Offices are being constructed. The terminals are being manufactured, tested, and installed. The Franklin Ledger — the public website that will publish everything the Amendment's institutions do — is being mirrored across its custodial sites. The body that will run the Amendment process is being selected, sworn in, and trained.

During those six months, the country is not without protection. A small body of sitting state Chief Justices, drawn by lottery, convenes within seventy-two hours of ratification to make sure no federal officeholder uses the build-out period to interfere with the Amendment getting built. The Amendment does not assume the federal government will help. It also does not assume the federal government will be allowed to get in the way.

From Day 180 through about Day 780, the Amendment is operational. The running institutions are seated. The Franklin Ledger is live. The prosecution body for anyone trying to interfere with the Amendment is up and running. Anyone in the country who wants to file Articles of No Confidence can do so. The petition window can open.

Two and a half years from Day Zero, the country has the tool it ratified.

The whole architecture in one picture. The names will be explained in the chapters that follow — for the First Reading, the point is to see that the system has shape, not to memorize the parts.

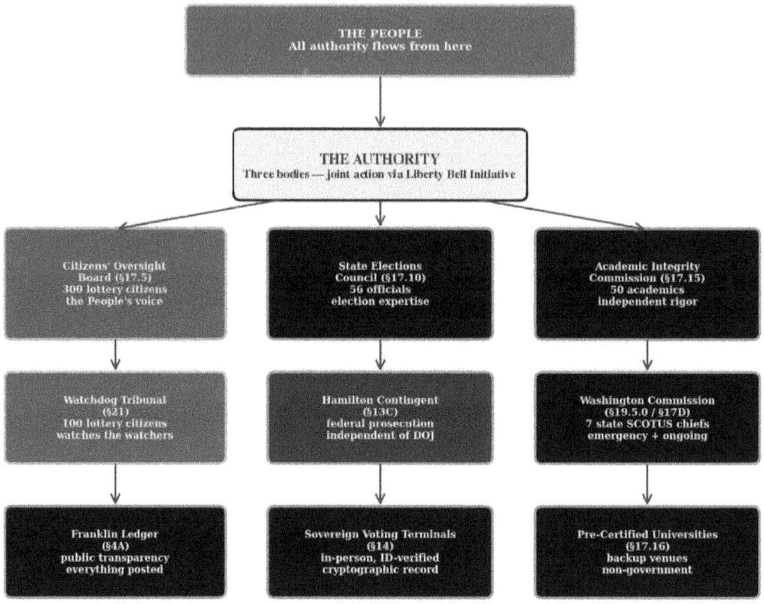

Figure 5 — The Full Institutional Architecture

◆ ◆ ◆

There is one piece of this nobody has to organize.

On Day 780 — about two years and one month after ratification — the country holds a referendum on whether to remove the existing federal government. Automatically. No petition required. No organizing. No fifteen-percent threshold to clear first. The vote is on the calendar from the moment the Amendment passes.

It is called the Inaugural Referendum, and the reason it exists is that the people who wrote the Amendment thought it would be strange to ratify an entire framework for citizen-initiated removal of a federal government and then make the citizens jump through a petition process to actually use it the first time. The country gets one guaranteed chance, no matter what.

The Inaugural Referendum uses the same thresholds as every other referendum under the Amendment: sixty percent of votes cast saying yes, with at least half of all registered voters showing up. If both happen, the federal government is removed and replaced through the same ninety-day transition described later in this chapter. If either does not, the country has, by inaction or by a margin under sixty percent, decided to keep the federal government it has.

After the Inaugural Referendum, normal operation begins. From Day 781 forward, removing a federal government requires the ordinary process — Articles of No Confidence, the petition, fifteen percent, six months. The Inaugural Referendum is the country's first opportunity to use what it ratified, without depending on whether anyone organized a petition in time.

Either way, on Day 780, the country gets to register an opinion.

◆ ◆ ◆

You sign a petition. If enough people sign, there is a vote. If the vote passes, the federal government is replaced.

That is, again, the whole thing.

The rest of this chapter walks through what those three steps actually look like for an ordinary citizen — what you do, where you go, what happens around you while you do it. None of it is complicated. All of it is on purpose.

◆ ◆ ◆

Someone has to start it. The Amendment does not begin on its own.

It begins when one citizen — any citizen — files a document called Articles of No Confidence at a Citizens' Reclamation Office and signs their name to it. That is the first signature on the petition. Everything else follows from it.

The filer does not have to be a lawyer. They do not have to be an elected official. They do not have to be famous, organized, or even particularly persuasive. They have to be a registered American voter willing to walk into a building, state in plain language what they believe the federal government has done that warrants removal, and put their name on the document.

That is the trigger event. In a country of two hundred forty million registered voters, the bar for starting the process is one of them. The bar for the process going anywhere — fifteen percent signing on — is much higher, and is meant to be. But starting is meant to be easy.

If the citizen who files is wrong about the situation, the petition fails. If the citizen who files is right, the rest of the country tells them so by signing along.

Either way, the country gets to register an opinion.

◆ ◆ ◆

The buildings are called Citizens' Reclamation Offices. There is at least one in every state. In larger states there are more — enough that no registered voter has to travel more than a few hours to reach one. The buildings are public. They are not hidden. They are not affiliated with any political party. They are run by people whose actual job is running elections, with federal oversight to make sure nobody is putting a thumb on the scale.

You walk in. You show identification — driver's license, state ID, passport, the same kinds of documents you would show to vote. You are matched to your voter registration record. You are directed to a terminal.

The terminal is a machine that does one thing. It records your signature on the petition, cryptographically, in a way that cannot be forged, cannot be duplicated, and cannot be lost. You read the Articles of No Confidence. You decide whether you agree. If you do, you sign. The machine produces a paper receipt. You leave.

The whole visit takes less time than registering a car.

You do not sign anything online. You do not sign anything on paper that gets mailed somewhere. You do not hand your signature to a stranger with a clipboard at a folding table outside the grocery store. The Amendment is unusually paranoid about the act of signing, and the paranoia is on purpose. In person, on a verified ID, on a secure machine, the signature is what it appears to be. A captured federal government cannot challenge it later by claiming the paperwork wasn't quite right. The number of signatures is whatever the number actually is.

This is, it turns out, harder to argue about.

◆ ◆ ◆

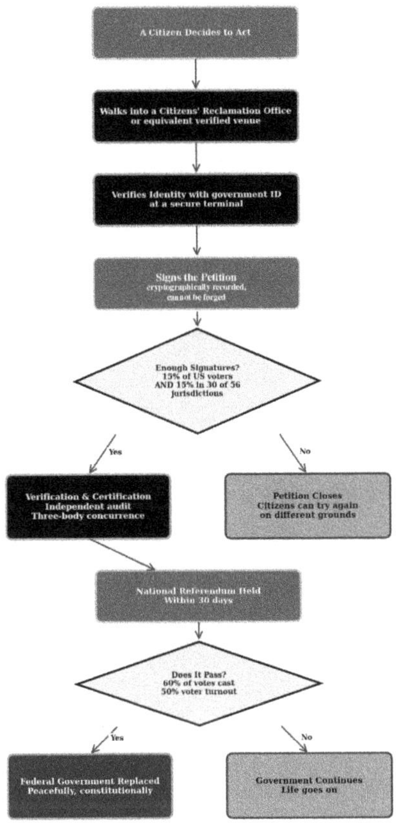

Figure 1 — The Citizen's Journey Through the Amendment

◆ ◆ ◆

The specifics, briefly: To trigger a vote, fifteen percent of registered American voters have to sign the petition. That is a deliberately high bar. The Amendment is not supposed to be used casually. If fifteen percent of the American electorate — tens of millions of people, spread across the country — agree that the federal government needs to go, that is not a casual situation. You sign the petition in person, at a building set up for that purpose, using a verified ID and a secure terminal. You do not sign anything on paper. You do not sign anything online. You do not hand your signature to a stranger with a clipboard. You walk in, you verify who you are, you sign at the machine, you leave. This is on purpose. In person and on a secure machine, signatures cannot be forged, cannot be duplicated, cannot be lost, and cannot be challenged later by someone claiming the paperwork isn't quite right. The number of signatures is whatever the number actually is. The petition has two thresholds, and both have to be met:

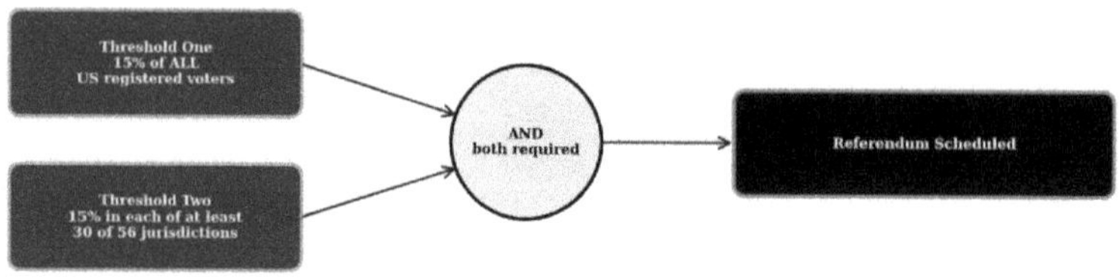

Figure 2 — The Two Thresholds

The two-threshold design prevents a petition from succeeding in only one region of the country, or only in big cities, or only among one political party's voters. To trigger a referendum, broad agreement across the whole country is required, not just loud agreement in one corner of it. You go back to the same kind of building, the same kind of secure terminal, and you vote. Yes or no.

◆ ◆ ◆

From the day the first citizen files Articles of No Confidence, the country has six months. That is the window in which signatures can be collected. The window is fixed. It cannot be extended by friendly officials. It cannot be shortened by hostile ones. Six months, every time, no exceptions.

Six months is meant to be enough time to find out whether the country is interested. Six months is not meant to be enough time for the federal government being evaluated to outwait the discontent. The clock runs the same way for everyone.

During those six months, the petition lives on the Franklin Ledger — the same public website that publishes everything the Amendment's institutions do. Anyone can see the petition. Anyone can read the Articles. Anyone can watch the signature count rise, broken down by state, in real time. There are no closed doors. The numbers are the numbers.

You can sign at any point in the six-month window. Day one, day a hundred and seventy-nine. Once you sign, your signature counts. You can withdraw it before the window closes — there is a procedure — though most people who walk into a Citizens' Reclamation Office and put their name on a petition to remove the federal government tend not to change their mind by Tuesday.

Here is the full arc, from the day Articles of No Confidence are filed to the day the country reaches a verdict:

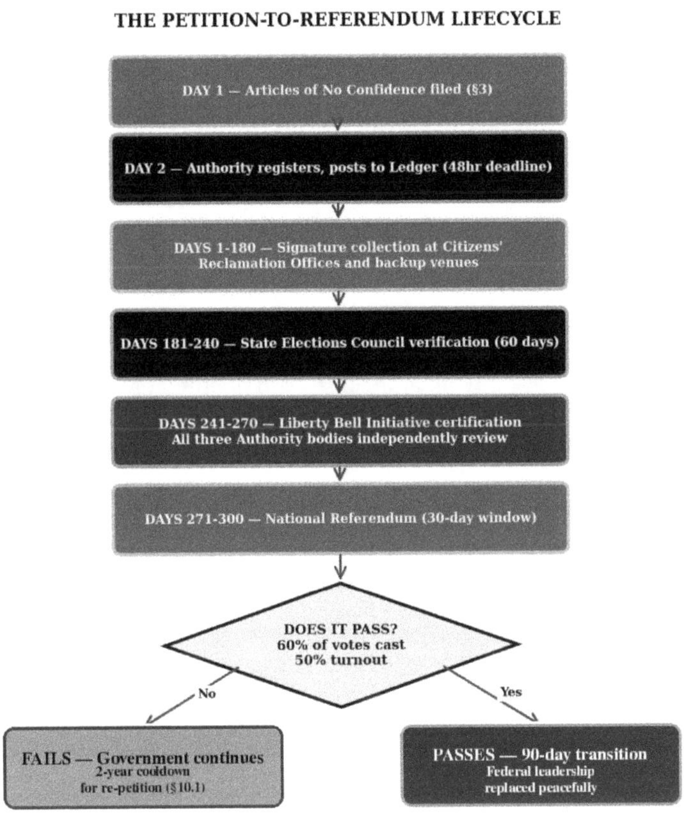

Figure 6 — A Petition's 300-Day Lifecycle

◆ ◆ ◆

If both thresholds are met, the petition moves to verification.

Verification is the part where signatures are checked. Sixty days, conducted by the people whose entire professional life is verifying signatures. They do their work. They publish their numbers. The window closes when the window closes.

After verification, three independent bodies — the ones running the Amendment process — review and certify the result. They do this in public, on the Ledger, with their reasoning attached. Each of the three has to agree. If even one refuses to certify without good-faith published reason, that body's members get investigated for interfering with the process. There is no quiet veto. There is no procedural shrug. Either the petition advances, or somebody publishes, on the permanent public record, exactly why they think it should not.

If all three certify, the country gets a referendum date.

The total time from when the petition opens to when the referendum is held is roughly ten months. Long enough that no political party can manufacture a wave and ride it through before anyone notices. Short enough that a country that has truly decided is not made to wait years.

◆ ◆ ◆

You go back. Same building, same kind of terminal. You vote. Yes or no.

The Amendment does not ask anyone to read several hundred pages first. It asks the same question the Articles of No Confidence asked at the start: should this federal government be removed and replaced.

You vote in person, with verified ID, on a machine that records the vote cryptographically. The same protections as before — no forgery, no duplication, no loss. You get a receipt. You leave.

The vote runs for several days, not several hours, so that working people, parents, shift workers, and citizens in rural areas where the nearest building is a long drive away all have a real chance to vote without choosing between democracy and their job.

When the window closes, the results are tallied in public, in real time, with every step published on the Ledger. There is no period during which "the votes are being counted" away from public view. The chain of custody is the chain of public visibility.

A pass requires both: sixty percent of votes cast saying yes, and at least half of all registered voters showing up to vote. Both have to happen. A simple majority with low turnout does not pass. High turnout with a plurality does not pass. Sixty percent. Fifty percent participation. Both. Always.

If the vote fails, the federal government continues, and no new petition can be filed for two years. The country tried, and decided not to.

If the vote passes, what happens next is the part the rest of this chapter is about.

◆ ◆ ◆

What happens if the vote passes. If sixty percent of people who voted say yes, and at least half of all registered voters showed up, the federal government is removed. Not overthrown. Not attacked. Not dragged out of the buildings. Removed.

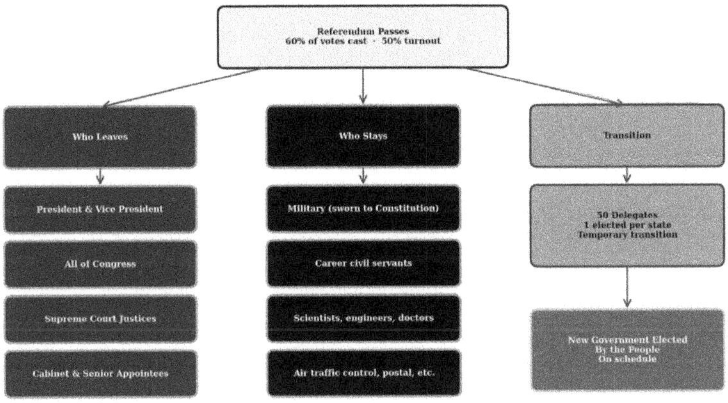

Figure 3 — What Happens When the Vote Passes

The President, the Vice President, every member of Congress, every Supreme Court justice, every Cabinet official, and every senior political appointee vacates their office. Within seventy-two hours of the vote passing, fifty-six people convene as an Interim Caretaker Council. They are the sitting Governors of every state, plus the Mayor of D.C., plus the Governors of the five U.S. territories. These are people already in office, already elected, already running their own jurisdictions. They are not strangers. They are who they were the day before the vote. Their job is narrow and explicit. They sign payrolls, honor existing treaties, and keep federal services running. They do not start wars, pass new laws, or commit the country to anything beyond the brief window of their service. They are caretakers, not rulers — because the alternative, fifty-six governors with unrestricted federal power, is the kind of arrangement that historically does not end well. While the Caretakers are caretaking, an Emergency Delegate Election runs in every state. One delegate per state, fifty in total. Those fifty form a Constitutional Transition Committee, which holds executive, legislative, and judicial authority for a fixed and limited number of days while permanent new federal officials are elected. Then the Committee dissolves and the new officials take office. The career civil service stays throughout. The military stays. Air traffic controllers, postal workers, doctors at veterans' hospitals, scientists at the national labs, rangers at the national parks — they all stay. They have not done anything wrong. The Amendment removes the political leadership of the federal government, not the federal government itself. The country does not stop. It transitions. Peaceful. Orderly. Constitutional. At the end of it, the country has a new federal government, chosen by the citizens, without anyone having been shot.

◆ ◆ ◆

The day the vote is certified, every elected and politically-appointed federal officeholder has seventy-two hours to leave their office. The President. The Vice President. Every member of Congress. Every Supreme Court Justice. Every Cabinet officer. Every senior political appointee. They lose their security clearances. Their access badges deactivate. Their compensation stops.

If any of them refuses to vacate, the Amendment has a framework built specifically for that — escalating penalties, federal marshals, prosecution that the Department of Justice cannot quietly call off because the Department of Justice does not run it. The Amendment does not assume people will leave quietly. It assumes some of them will refuse. It plans for both.

The next morning, the country still has air traffic control. The military still has a chain of command. The Veterans Administration still pays benefits. The Social Security checks still go out. Nothing the federal government does that touches ordinary American life stops working. The career civil service stays. The military stays. The scientists, the inspectors, the postal workers, the park rangers, the doctors at federal hospitals — they all stay. They have not done anything wrong. They were not the problem.

Within those same seventy-two hours, the fifty-six sitting Governors and territorial chief executives meet as the Interim Caretaker Council. They do not move to Washington. They keep their state offices. They sign the federal payrolls and keep the lights on, and that is all. They cannot pass new laws. They cannot start a war. They cannot enter treaties. They are running the trains until the new conductors arrive.

While the Caretakers are caretaking, every state holds an Emergency Delegate Election. One delegate per state, fifty in total. Those fifty form a Constitutional Transition Committee — the body that holds placeholder executive, legislative, and judicial authority for the brief window between the old federal government and the new one. The Committee exists to keep order; it does not exist to govern.

Then the country has a regular federal election. Presidential, congressional, the works — administered with significant oversight to make sure the parties whose government was just removed cannot turn around and capture the replacement.

About six months after the original vote, the new federal officials take office. The Committee dissolves. The Caretakers go back to running their states. The country is back to ordinary constitutional operation, with new federal leadership that the citizens chose.

Six months. From a country deciding its federal government had to go, to a country with the federal government it picked instead.

◆ ◆ ◆

Who can stop you from doing this. Nobody. This is the part that surprises people, so it is worth being explicit.

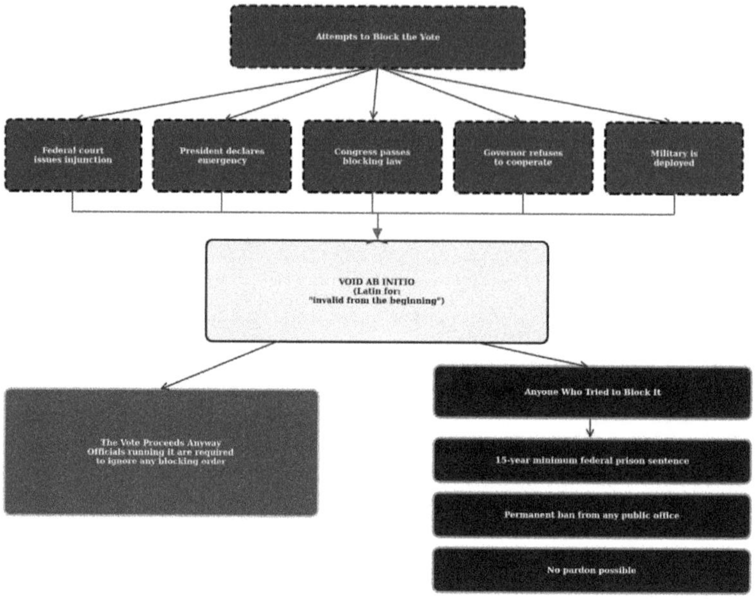

Figure 4 — Protections Against Interference

The petition cannot be blocked by a court. It cannot be blocked by the President declaring an emergency. It cannot be blocked by Congress passing a law. It cannot be blocked by the military. It cannot be blocked by a governor. It cannot be blocked by a state legislature. Any official who attempts to block it is committing a federal felony with a minimum fifteen-year prison sentence and a permanent, unpardonable ban from any public office for the rest of their life. The Amendment is very specific about this. The reason for the specificity is that the Amendment is designed to work in situations where the people trying to stop it are the people it is being used against. Vague protections get worked around. Specific protections do not. If the federal government being evaluated tries to shut down the vote, the vote happens anyway. If the courts issue rulings trying to delay the vote, the rulings are void. If the President declares an emergency, the emergency does not affect the vote. The officials running the vote are legally required to ignore any order telling them to stop, and they cannot be punished for ignoring it. This is not a suggestion. It is written into the Amendment. Repeatedly. With teeth.

◆ ◆ ◆

What this isn't. It is worth being explicit about what the Amendment is not, because in a country that has spent two hundred years arguing about constitutional change, almost any new proposal gets mistaken for something else within five minutes of being introduced. It is not a coup. A coup is a small group of people seizing power against the will of the population. The Amendment is sixty percent of the voting electorate, after a high-bar petition signed by tens of millions, exercising authority the Constitution itself grants them. If sixty percent counts as "a small group," the country has bigger problems than the Amendment can solve. It is not a revolution. Revolutions overthrow the existing constitutional order. The Amendment operates entirely within it — ratified through ordinary Article V process, taking effect as part of the Constitution, in the same way the Bill of Rights did. It is not a tool to overturn a single election the reader's side lost. The thresholds are calibrated to prevent that. If the Amendment could be used that way, both parties would use it that way, and within twenty years it would have replaced elections instead of supplementing them. That is not the design. The Bill of Rights remains in force. The Constitution remains the supreme law of the land. The Amendment adds a tool. It does not remove any.

◆ ◆ ◆

The Amendment is not eternal.

Every twenty years from the first one, the country holds a Sunset Review — a structured, automatic vote on whether to keep the Amendment, modify it, or repeal it. Three options. The country picks one.

The review is automatic. It cannot be skipped. It cannot be advanced. The clock ticks on its own.

The body that conducts the review is structurally separate from the institutions the Amendment created, because asking the institution to evaluate its own continuation is a recipe for self-preservation bias. The Amendment is, in this respect, honest about its own potential failure modes.

If the country votes to keep the Amendment, it continues unchanged. If the country votes to modify it, a Constitutional Review Convention is convened to revise specific provisions through the same supermajority process the Amendment itself was ratified under. If the country votes to repeal it, the Amendment is removed from the Constitution through an orderly two-year wind-down.

No generation may bind those that follow. The Amendment is built to be reconsidered. That is part of how it earns the right to continue.

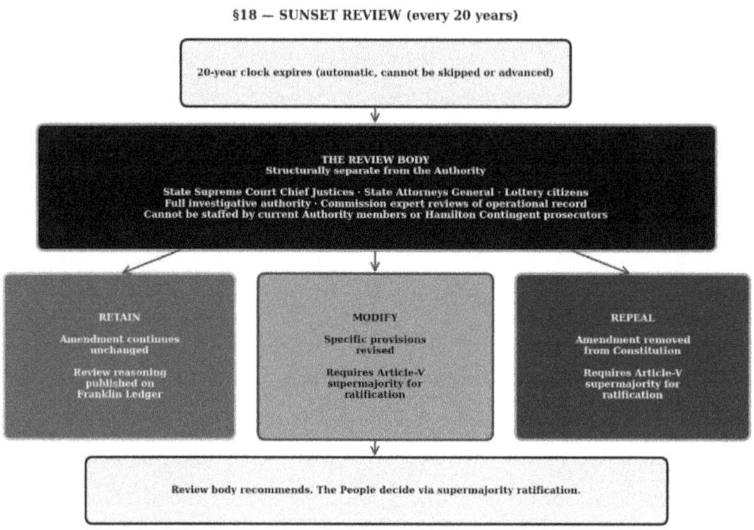

Figure 7 — Sunset Review (Every 20 Years)

◆ ◆ ◆

A handful of questions that come up almost every time someone reads this far.

What if I sign and then change my mind? You can withdraw your signature before the petition window closes. There is a procedure. It exists because the Amendment takes consent seriously, including the consent to withdraw.

What happens if the petition does not reach the threshold? Nothing happens. The federal government continues. The Articles of No Confidence become a historical record on the Ledger, and the country goes back to its ordinary business. No one is punished for having signed.

Who pays for all this? The Amendment includes its own funding mechanism. On the day of ratification, the Treasury has automatic constitutional authority to issue a loan that covers build-out and ongoing operations. The cost does not depend on the existing federal government deciding to fund it — because the federal government being evaluated cannot be allowed to defund the body evaluating it. The loan is repaid over time through recovered corruption assets and ordinary federal revenue. Citizens do not get a bill in the mail.

What if my state's government refuses to host a Citizens' Reclamation Office? The Amendment plans for that. Backup venues at pre-certified universities. Mobile Reclamation Offices deployable across state lines. Federal prosecution of state officials who block access. If your state's government tries to keep you from signing, someone is committing a federal felony, and your signature is going to be collected anyway.

What if I cannot physically get to a Citizens' Reclamation Office? If a disability, a medical condition, or simply the lack of practical transportation keeps you from reaching one, the Amendment provides Mobile Accessibility Teams who come to you. The Amendment is built on the premise that the People means all of them, not just the convenient ones.

What about active-duty military? Active-duty servicemembers are registered voters. They have the same right to sign and to vote as any other citizen, with explicit protections against any officer in their chain of command retaliating against them for it.

What about people in prison, or with prior convictions? The Amendment does not change state law on that. If your state allows participation by people who have been incarcerated, the Amendment process is open to them on the same terms. If your state does not, the Amendment does not override your state on that question.

What about people who are not American citizens? The Amendment process is limited to registered American voters. Same rule as voting in federal elections.

What if officials cheat the count? Every step is published in real time on a public ledger mirrored across seven independent custodians, including the National Archives, university research libraries, and at least one international observer organization. Cheating is not impossible. Cheating without being caught is much closer to it. The Amendment is built on the premise that publicity beats audit.

Do I have to do anything to make this real? No. The Amendment is in the Constitution if it gets ratified. From that day forward, it exists whether you read this book again or not. The whole point of the Amendment is that it does not require ongoing effort from the citizen to remain available. It just stays there. Waiting.

◆ ◆ ◆

What you don't have to do. You do not have to read the Amendment itself — all several thousand paragraphs of it. You do not have to become a lawyer. You do not have to organize anything. You do not have to run for office. You do not have to convince anyone of anything they do not already believe. You do not have to attend meetings. You do not have to donate money. You do not have to post on social media. You are not responsible for making the Amendment work. That is the Amendment's job. What is asked of you is this: show up, verify who you are, sign your name if you agree. Later, if the petition succeeds, show up again and vote. That is all. If the Amendment is never needed, you never have to use it. If it is needed, the mechanism is waiting. It belongs to you.

◆ ◆ ◆

That is the First Reading. If it is enough, you can stop here. The Amendment does what this chapter says it does, and no further reading is required for you to know what you need to know. If you want to understand how the Amendment protects itself — how it handles captured courts, hostile governors, foreign interference, the military, and the hundred other ways a determined adversary might try to break it — the Second Reading begins in the next chapter.

BEFORE THE FIRES

Chapter Four

The Second Reading

Welcome to the Second Reading. If you finished the First Reading and decided you wanted more, this chapter is for you. If you skipped the First Reading and started here, that is also fine. You are clearly the kind of person who likes to know how things work, and the rest of this chapter will respect your time. And if when you finish this you find you still want more — sharper questions, harder edges, every objection a critic might raise — that is the Third Reading, in the chapter after. The First Reading answered the question what does the Amendment do? The Second Reading answers a different question: how, exactly, is the Amendment constructed so that it actually works? The answer is longer because the construction is, deliberately, redundant. There is no single point where the Amendment can be broken. There are also no shortcuts. Every safeguard is there for a reason, and the rest of this chapter is mostly about those reasons. What follows is the engaged citizen's tour of the Amendment's architecture. Section numbers appear sometimes, in case you want to look something up. You do not need to read the Amendment to follow along. The point of this book is to make that unnecessary.

◆ ◆ ◆

The architecture, all at once.

THE AUTHORITY Three bodies — joint action via Liberty Bell Initiative

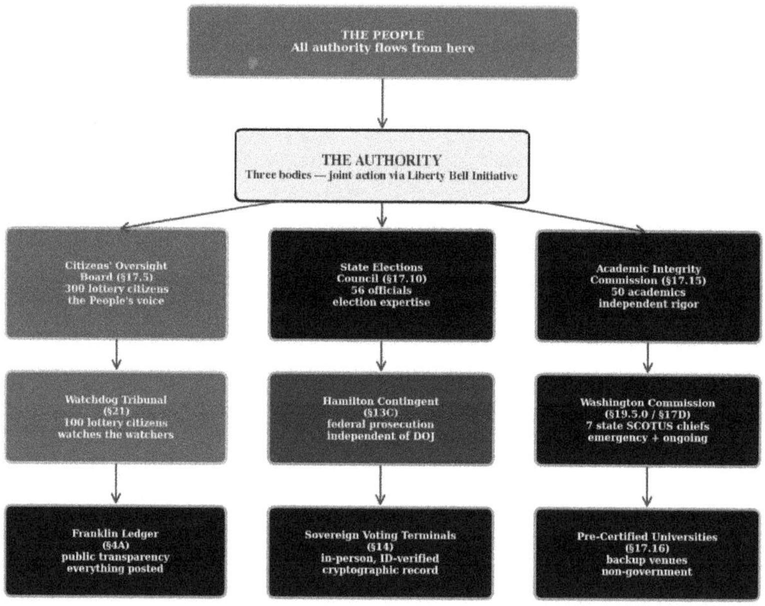

Figure 1 — The Full Institutional Architecture

The Amendment creates not one institution but a system of them. The system has three layers, and all three exist for a reason. Before we walk through them, here is the whole thing on one page. It is a lot. We will get to all of it. At the top sits the People. Every body in the Amendment exists to serve the People's process. None of them have governing power on their own. None of them can decide to remove a federal government on the People's behalf. They administer, verify, investigate, prosecute, and publish. The People decide. That is what is new about this Amendment. That is the whole point. Below the People sits the Authority — the three-body institution that runs the petition-and-referendum process. The Authority is the public face of the Amendment. When citizens sign petitions or cast referendum votes, they do so under Authority administration. Below the Authority sit oversight and enforcement institutions: the Watchdog Tribunal, which investigates the Authority itself; the Hamilton Contingent, which prosecutes interference with the process; and the Washington Commission, which provides emergency convening authority when the Authority cannot act.

At the bottom sit the technical and physical infrastructure: the Franklin Ledger for transparency, the Sovereign Voting Terminals for secure participation, and the Pre-Certified Universities for backup venue capacity. The arrows on the diagram run downward not because power flows downward but because each layer's authority comes from the layer above it. The People constitute the Authority. The Authority operates the supporting institutions. The supporting institutions provide the visible apparatus through which the People act. Anyone trying to read this diagram as a chain of command has it exactly backwards. If you take only one thing from this chapter, take this: the Amendment is not a new branch of government. It is a layered system of citizen-controlled tools. Every tool exists because some specific failure mode demanded it.

◆ ◆ ◆

The Authority. Three bodies, three reasons.

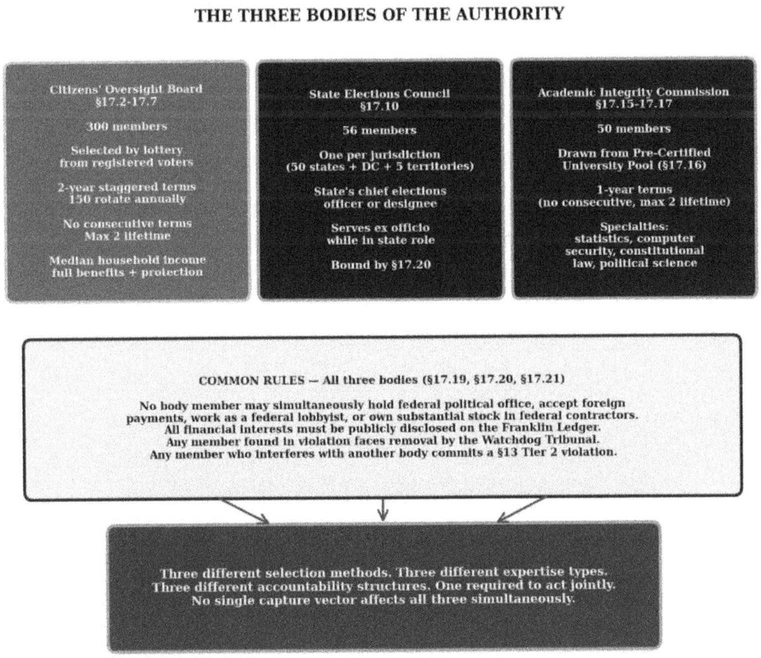

Figure 2 — The Three Bodies in Detail

The Authority is three bodies, not one. The reason it is three rather than one comes down to a simple problem: a single oversight body can be captured, and once captured, it becomes the very thing it was meant to prevent. Three independent bodies, with three different selection methods and three different expertise profiles, are much harder to capture all at once. The Amendment leans into this redundancy as a primary defense. The three bodies that follow are named the Citizens' Oversight Board, the State Elections Council, and the Academic Integrity Commission. The names are descriptive rather than evocative — they describe what the bodies are made of and what their job is. The reader who finds the proper-noun naming throughout this chapter slightly heavy is invited to read past the names and focus on the functions. The Amendment itself does the same.

The Citizens' Oversight Board The first body is three hundred ordinary Americans, selected by lottery from the registered voter rolls, the way juries are. They serve two-year staggered terms, with one hundred fifty members rotating off every year. They cannot serve consecutive terms, and no person may serve more than two total terms in their lifetime. The Board is the People's voice inside the Authority. It is, by design, the body least susceptible to capture by any organized political faction — because the next batch of three hundred is going to be drawn from the same enormous pool you would draw a jury from. Everyone, basically. Members receive a full stipend, child care, travel, and lodging. The cost of public service is not allowed to bar working Americans from participating. The lottery is administered by the Academic Integrity Commission and audited by the Watchdog Tribunal — two of the other bodies in the system, watching this one.

The State Elections Council The second body is fifty-six officials, one from each U.S. state, territory, and the District of Columbia. They serve ex officio while in their state role — meaning the chief elections officer of each jurisdiction (or designated equivalent) sits on the Council automatically by virtue of holding that office. When they leave the state role, they leave the Council, and their successor takes the seat. This body brings election expertise the other two cannot. State elections officers have spent careers running actual elections. They know how voter rolls work, how signature verification works, how chain-of-custody works for ballots. They are also accountable, ultimately, to fifty-six different state-level political processes. Capture of the Council would require capture of fifty-six separate state systems. There is, in a meaningful sense, no boss. Each member is, instead, answerable to the citizens of their own jurisdiction — which is more accountability, not less.

The Academic Integrity Commission The third body is fifty academics drawn from the Pre-Certified University Pool. They serve four-year staggered terms. The pool itself includes universities certified for participation by an open and public process; institutions can apply, are reviewed against published criteria, and are admitted or denied with reasoning posted to the Franklin Ledger. There is no closed list. There is no permanent ranking. Required specialties are spread across the Commission: statistics and survey methodology, computer security and cryptography, constitutional law, political science and election administration. The Commission's job is rigor — to audit the math, ask hard questions, and flag when something does not add up. It is, structurally, the body most equipped to detect technical fraud, which is the kind of fraud that everyone else tends to wave through because it looks like math.

The rules that bind all three Members of any Authority body face strict conflict-of-interest requirements. While serving, no member may simultaneously hold federal political office, accept payments from foreign governments or foreign-controlled entities, work as a registered federal lobbyist, or own substantial stock in major federal contractors. Financial interests must be disclosed publicly on the Franklin Ledger and updated quarterly. Violations trigger removal investigation by the Watchdog Tribunal. Authority members cannot also be members of the Watchdog Tribunal, the Hamilton Contingent, or any other oversight institution under the Amendment. The bodies are deliberately separated. A member found interfering with another body commits a Section 13 Tier 2 interference violation, prosecutable by the Hamilton Contingent. The Authority is, in this respect, designed to be uncomfortable to capture: even if you got someone in, they would be working in a building full of other people who notice. Three different selection methods. Three different expertise profiles. Three different accountability structures. One required to act jointly. No single capture vector compromises all three at once. That is the design.

◆ ◆ ◆

The Liberty Bell Initiative. The three Authority bodies do not act independently when it comes to important decisions. They act jointly, through a procedure called the Liberty Bell Initiative. The name comes from the bell that summoned colonists to hear the Declaration of Independence read aloud. The summons was the action — a call to the People that something significant required their attention. The Liberty Bell Initiative is named in that spirit.

When the Authority must certify a Petition, certify a Referendum result, or take any other constitutionally significant action, all three bodies must concur. Not by majority. Not by leadership agreement. Not by any procedural shortcut. All three bodies, independently, voting in their own deliberations, must reach the same conclusion. If any one body refuses, the action fails. This is the opposite of how government usually works. Government typically defaults to action and requires overruling votes to stop. The Authority defaults to inaction and requires three independent bodies to all agree before anything happens. The bias is toward not acting. This is intentional. The Amendment is not in a hurry, and a body that acts only when all three branches of its conscience agree is harder to push into a mistake. Each body publishes its own decision and reasoning on the Franklin Ledger. Citizens can see which bodies voted which way, and why. There is no closed deliberation on actions of constitutional significance. The People are entitled to know not just what the Authority decided but how each body got there. The Liberty Bell Initiative is the heart of the Amendment's anti-capture design. A captured Authority body that refuses certification it should grant triggers a Watchdog Tribunal investigation under Sections 21 and 23.13, and refusal without good-faith published reasoning is itself a Section 13 violation, prosecutable by the Hamilton Contingent. There is, in other words, no free veto. The standard the Tribunal applies is whether the body's published reasoning would convince a panel of disinterested professionals in the body's own discipline — a statistician on the Academic Integrity Commission's reasoning, an election administrator on the State Elections Council's, and so on. The reasoning has to be defensible on the merits, not merely produced. A body that abuses its veto loses its members.

◆ ◆ ◆

The supporting cast. The Authority does not operate alone. Around it sit several other institutions, each with a job none of the others can do. The Amendment is long partly because each of these institutions is specified in detail. Each one was added because some failure mode demanded it. None of them are decorative.

The Watchdog Tribunal

The Watchdog Tribunal is one hundred citizens, also selected by lottery, whose job is to investigate the Authority itself. If a member of any Authority body is suspected of corruption, abuse, or capture, the Tribunal investigates. The Tribunal can remove members by two-thirds supermajority. The Tribunal exists because someone has to watch the watchers, and putting the People in that role — through random selection — is the only way to do it that nobody can rig.

The Tribunal also has jurisdiction over members of all other Amendment bodies. Hamilton Contingent members. Sovereign Voting Terminal contractors. Pre-Certified University Pool administrators. Anyone with formal power under the Amendment is subject to Tribunal investigation. The Tribunal's findings are published on the Franklin Ledger in real time. There is no senior citizen of the Amendment, no untouchable office, no figure too important to investigate. Members serve three-year staggered terms with no consecutive service permitted, and no person may serve more than two total terms in their lifetime. The lottery pool is the same as for the Citizens' Oversight Board — registered voters, anywhere in the country, drawn at random. The result is that the people watching the watchers are, by construction, the same kind of people the watchers are supposed to be serving.

The Hamilton Contingent

The Hamilton Contingent is a federal prosecution body, named for Alexander Hamilton, who took public corruption seriously enough to actually do something about it. Section 13C creates the institution; it is independent of the Department of Justice, which is to say, the President cannot tell it to stand down. Its only job is to prosecute people who interfere with the Amendment process. It has subpoena power, investigation authority, separate budget, and its own personnel pipeline. The Contingent has four divisions. The Prosecution Division handles indictments. The Protection Division provides physical security to citizens, officials, and witnesses targeted because of Amendment participation. The Public Response Division handles communications and Franklin Ledger postings. The Preservation Division handles evidence chain-of-custody — because corrupt actors will, eventually, try to destroy or alter records, and the Amendment treats evidence preservation as a separate professional discipline. If officials try to obstruct a petition, the Hamilton Contingent comes for them. Not the FBI. Not the DOJ. The Hamilton Contingent. Cases are tried before five-justice panels drawn from the highest courts of five different states, by lottery, sitting in those states' supreme court facilities. The federal judiciary is not involved at first instance. This is by design — the Amendment cannot rely on the federal judiciary to police interference with the Amendment when the federal judiciary is one of the institutions the Amendment exists to constrain.

The Franklin Ledger

The Franklin Ledger is the public face of the entire system, named for Benjamin Franklin, who founded the postal service, the public library, and several other institutions premised on the idea that information ought to be available to ordinary people. The Ledger is a public website, mobile application, telephone information line, and physical print and broadcast distribution system through which every action taken by the Authority, the Tribunal, and the Hamilton Contingent is published in real time. Section 4A specifies what gets published, and the answer is essentially everything. Every signature count. Every certification decision. Every prosecution. Every dollar of recovered corrupt assets. Every Authority member's financial disclosures, updated quarterly. Every Tribunal investigation outcome. Every Hamilton Contingent indictment. The defaults around transparency are inverted from how government usually works: instead of needing a reason to disclose, the Authority needs a reason to withhold, and the reasons are narrow and enumerated. The Ledger has a Serious Findings category that prominently displays significant findings — Section 13 interference convictions, foreign interference determinations, Authority body removals — using objective inclusion criteria. This means no Authority body can hide bad news by tucking it into back pages. The criteria are mechanical: if a finding hits the threshold, it goes on the prominent display, regardless of how anyone feels about it. Mirroring is taken seriously. The Ledger is duplicated across at least seven independent custodians: the National Archives, three rotating state judicial records systems, three rotating state elections offices, three pre-certified university research libraries, and at least one international observer organization. No single custodian — including the federal government — can alter the Ledger's contents. Discrepancies between mirrors trigger automatic Watchdog Tribunal investigation. If somebody tries to scrub a record, seven other copies say otherwise. Sections 4A.6 through 4A.10 specify access channels. The Ledger is available through standard web browsers without registration. A toll-free telephone line provides voice access for citizens without internet. Print mailing exists for citizens without telephones. Broadcast access ensures the Serious Findings category reaches even those without any of the above. The principle is that no citizen should be unable to evaluate their federal government because they cannot afford the technology to read about it. Transparency is not a luxury good.

Sovereign Voting Terminals

Sovereign Voting Terminals are the physical machines used to sign petitions and cast referendum votes. They live in dedicated buildings — Citizens' Reclamation Offices — and at backup venues like pre-certified universities. Section 14 specifies their construction in considerable detail: cryptographic signatures, hardware security modules, dual-chain blockchain ledger, voter-verified paper backup for every interaction. The level of detail is not because the Amendment loves technology. It is because every place the specification could be vague is a place a future hostile actor could exploit. Citizens sign petitions and vote in person. There is no online signing. There is no online voting. There is no mail-in component. This is a deliberate design choice, not a hostility to convenience. In-person, ID-verified, machine-signed records cannot be forged, duplicated, lost, or challenged later by someone claiming the paperwork wasn't quite right. The number of signatures or votes is whatever the number actually is. This is, it turns out, harder to argue about. Terminal contractors are bound by Section 4.16 separation requirements — different teams, different facilities, different network providers, different physical security arrangements for primary and backup chains. A captured contractor cannot compromise the system because the system is designed to outlast contractor capture. Any anomaly between the two primary chains and the standby chain triggers automatic investigation. The chains do not trust each other, on purpose. Universal accessibility is required. Terminals must accommodate disability, language, and literacy variation. Section 11A specifies the accessibility standards that Terminal design under Section 14 must meet. A deaf voter, a blind voter, a voter who reads only Spanish or Mandarin or Lakota — all must be able to use the terminals without assistance. The Amendment is constructed on the premise that the People means all of them, not just the convenient ones.

Pre-Certified Universities

Pre-Certified Universities form the backup infrastructure. If a state government refuses to let Citizens' Reclamation Offices operate, or if hostile actors try to shut them down, signature collection and voting move to university campuses. Universities are not government-controlled. They are not easy to shut down. They have been certified in advance, before any crisis, so that activation does not require new permission from anyone. The Amendment, in this respect, has done its homework before the test. Section 17.16 establishes the certification process. Universities apply against published criteria covering accreditation, governance independence, security capability, and conflict-of-interest disclosure. Certification is reviewed every five years on a rolling basis by the Citizens' Oversight Board, with findings published on the Franklin Ledger. Universities can be decertified for cause; they can also voluntarily withdraw. The pool is meant to be large and stable — the Amendment requires no fewer than 200 qualifying institutions at any time, with a target of 500 or more, drawn from all Participating Jurisdictions to ensure geographic and institutional diversity. The point is redundancy, so that no single closure or refusal can cut off citizen access. Universities provide infrastructure. They do not provide opinions. The Amendment is careful here: a university hosting a Sovereign Voting Terminal is providing the room, the security, and the staffing. It is not endorsing the Petition or Referendum. It is not advocating for outcomes. The faculty and administration of the institution may have their own views, and they are welcome to them; the institution's role under the Amendment is purely infrastructural. The terminals do not care what anybody thinks. They count.

◆ ◆ ◆

The phases. How the Amendment turns on.

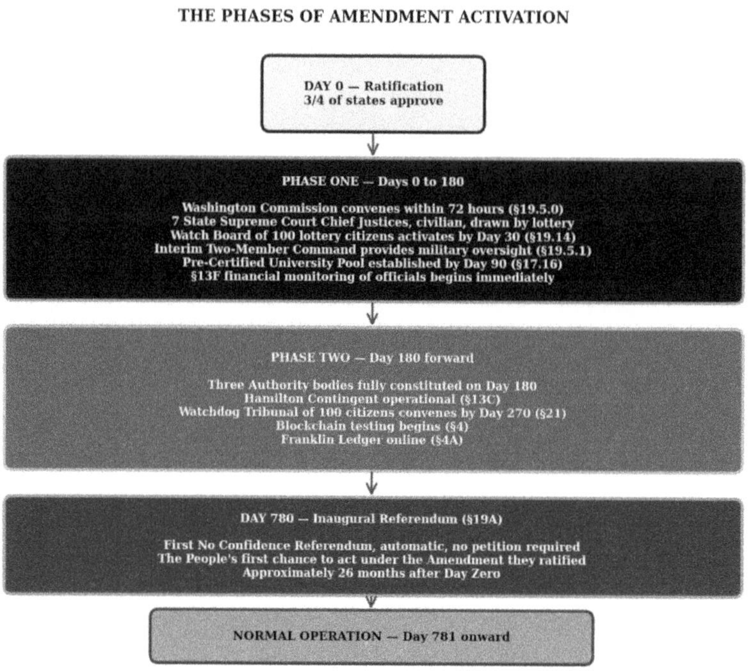

Figure 3 — The Phases of Activation

The Amendment does not snap fully into existence on the day it is ratified. Building functioning institutions takes time. The Amendment specifies a phased activation that runs from Day Zero — the moment three-quarters of states ratify — through Day 780, when the first No Confidence Referendum is automatically held.

Phase One runs from Day Zero through Day 180. The Authority is not yet constituted in this period — its three bodies require time to be selected, sworn in, and trained. Phase One is bridged by interim institutions: the Washington Commission, which convenes within 72 hours of ratification and consists of seven sitting Chief Justices of Participating Jurisdictions, drawn by randomized lottery, all civilian, with the Joint Chiefs of Staff serving as non-voting military advisors; the Watch Board of one hundred lottery citizens, activated by Day 30; and an Interim Two-Member Command that provides military oversight during the activation period. The Amendment does not leave the country in unattended limbo. Somebody is always in the room. Section 13F asset and travel restrictions on federal officials begin immediately on Day Zero. Officials cannot leave the country without explicit Watch Board authorization. International financial movements above ordinary thresholds are flagged for review. This is preventative — corrupt officials, anticipating ratification, might otherwise take steps to hide assets or flee. The Amendment treats Day Zero as a known risk moment and acts accordingly. The drafters were not naïve about who tries to leave the country in interesting moments. Phase Two runs from Day 180 through Day 780. The Authority constitutes on Day 180. The Hamilton Contingent reaches operational capacity. The Watchdog Tribunal convenes by Day 270. Blockchain testing for the Sovereign Voting Terminals begins. The Franklin Ledger goes live with full functionality. By the end of Phase Two, the entire institutional apparatus is operational. Two and a half years from Day Zero, the country has the tool it ratified. Day 780 is the Inaugural Referendum, specified in Section 19A. This is the country's first opportunity to use the Amendment, and it happens automatically — no petition is required to trigger it. The Amendment's drafters reasoned that the People should have a guaranteed first chance to use what they ratified, without depending on whether someone organized a petition. If the Inaugural Referendum fails, normal operation begins, and future referendums require petition initiation in the ordinary way. If it passes, the 90-day transition is triggered. Either way, the country has registered an opinion. From Day 781 onward, the Amendment is in normal operation. Every twenty years, the Sunset Review process begins, allowing the Amendment itself to be retained, modified, or repealed by a structured process. The framework, in other words, is built to be reconsidered. More on that later.

◆ ◆ ◆

A petition, day by day.

FAILS — Government continues

PASSES — 90-day transition

2-year cooldown for re-petition (§10.1)

Federal leadership replaced peacefully

THE PETITION-TO-REFERENDUM LIFECYCLE

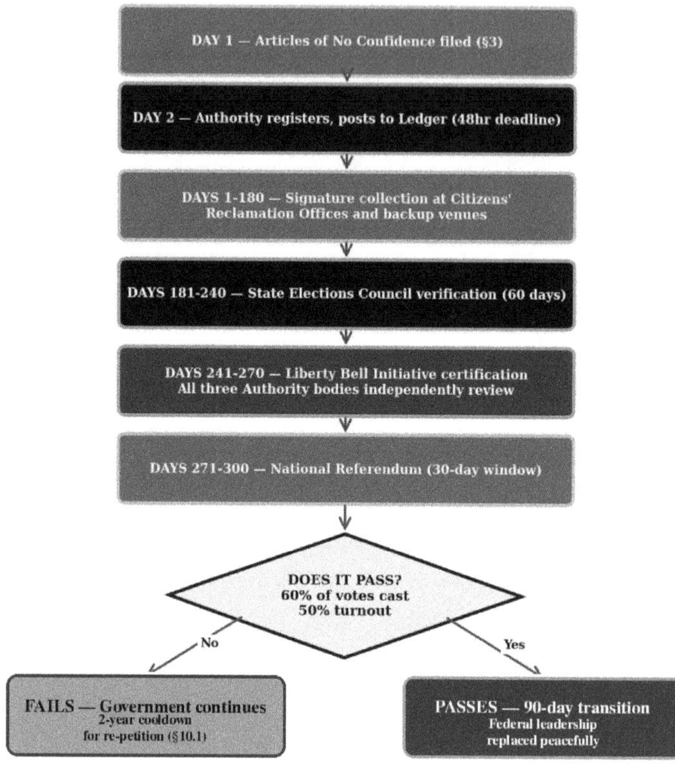

Figure 4 — A Petition's 300-Day Lifecycle

Section 3 of the Amendment specifies how petitions work. The First Reading covered the citizen's experience. The Second Reading covers what the Amendment's institutions do in response, and how long they have to do it. Every petition follows the same timeline. The timeline is fixed in the Amendment. Hostile officials cannot extend it. Friendly officials cannot shorten it. The clock runs the same way for everyone. On Day 1, a citizen files Articles of No Confidence. These are public documents that state, in plain language, what the federal government is alleged to have done that warrants removal. Anyone can file. There is no requirement to be a lawyer, an elected official, or a person of any particular standing. The Articles are filed at any Citizens' Reclamation Office or designated backup venue and are published to the Franklin Ledger upon filing. The first signature is the filer's, and there is nothing else required to start. Within forty-eight hours, the Authority registers the Petition. Registration is administrative; it does not review the merits. The Authority is not allowed to decide whether the citizen's complaint is a good one. That is what the rest of the process is for. The clock starts.

From Day 1 through Day 180, citizens can sign the Petition. They sign in person at Citizens' Reclamation Offices or backup venues. The two thresholds — fifteen percent nationally and fifteen percent within at least thirty of fifty-six jurisdictions — both have to be met. Signatures are continuously verified by State Elections Council audit, but the formal verification window opens on Day 181 regardless of how the count looks earlier. Six months is meant to be enough time to find out whether the country is interested. Six months is not meant to be enough time for the existing federal government to outwait the discontent. Days 181 through 240 are the State Elections Council's verification period. Sixty days. The Council audits the count, checks signature validity, and produces a certified total. The window cannot be extended. If the Council fails to complete verification within sixty days, the certification proceeds anyway, with the count as it stands, and the Council's failure is itself investigated as a possible Section 13 interference matter. Stalling is treated as obstruction. The clock does not stop because the people who are supposed to read it have decided not to. Days 241 through 270 are the Liberty Bell Initiative certification window. All three Authority bodies independently review whether the Petition has met its requirements. Each body publishes its own findings on the Franklin Ledger. If all three certify, the Petition advances. If any one refuses to certify, the Watchdog Tribunal investigates the refusal — because refusing without good-faith published reasoning is itself a Section 13 interference matter. There is no free veto. A body that refuses to do its job loses its members, and a member who refuses to do their job loses considerably more. Days 271 through 300 are the National Referendum. Thirty days. Voters return to the same secure terminals and vote yes or no. Sixty percent of votes cast must be yes. At least fifty percent of registered voters must participate. Both thresholds. Both required. Three hundred days from Day One. About ten months. Long enough for the country to deliberate. Short enough that hostile parties cannot run out the clock. Carefully chosen. The thresholds were chosen the same way: high enough that no narrow majority can dismiss a federal government, low enough that a captured government cannot block its own removal by simply locking up forty-one percent of the apparatus. The math is unforgiving in both directions on purpose.

◆ ◆ ◆

What happens after a passing referendum.

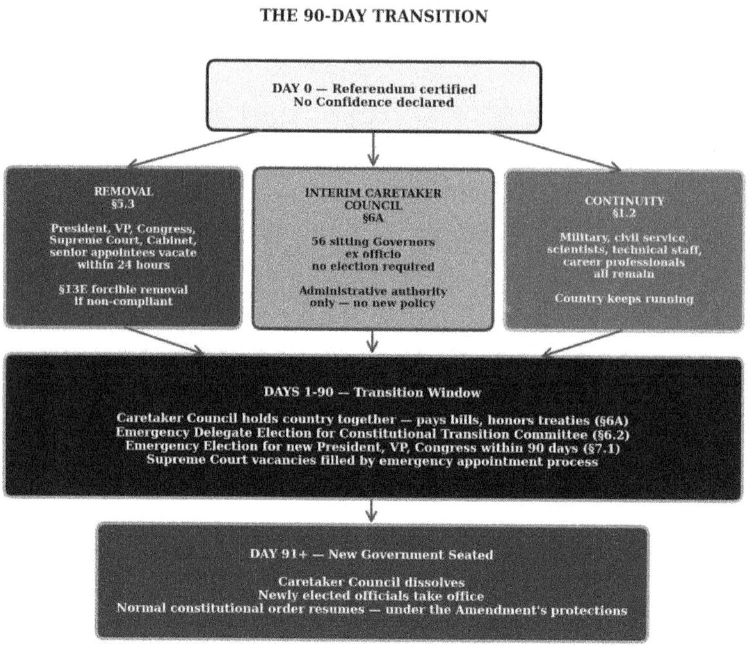

Figure 5 — The 90-Day Transition

If the Referendum passes, the federal government is removed. The First Reading covered who leaves and who stays. The Second Reading covers what happens during the ninety days that follow. On Day Zero of the transition — the day the Referendum is certified — three things happen simultaneously. The first is removal. Section 1.3 specifies that the political leadership enumerated in Section 1.1 — the President, the Vice President, every member of Congress, every Supreme Court Justice, every Cabinet officer, and every senior political appointee — is removed upon passage of the Declaration. They lose access to office facilities, government communications, and government resources. Their security clearances lapse. Their compensation ends. Any Removed Official who does not formally vacate within twenty-four hours triggers Section 13E's Forcible Removal framework — but more on that in the Third Reading. The second is the seating of the Interim Caretaker Council. The Council is fifty-six people: the sitting Governor of every state, plus the Mayor of the District of Columbia and the Governor of each of the five territories — all serving ex officio, automatically, the moment the Referendum is certified. There is no election to run, no appointment to confirm. They were already in office; they convene within seventy-two hours and keep the country running while the elected Constitutional

Transition Committee is being chosen in parallel. The Council is not a government. It has only administrative authority. It pays bills, honors treaties, signs routine documents, and ensures the country does not fall apart during the transition. It does not pass new laws. It does not start wars. It does not appoint judges or sign new treaties. Any action it does take requires a two-thirds supermajority of all fifty-six members. Days 1 through approximately 100 of the transition see the Caretaker Council running federal continuity while the Constitutional Transition Committee delegates are elected and convene. The Council dissolves automatically when the Constitutional Transition Committee convenes — typically around Day 100. The third is continuity. Section 1.2 specifies that career civil servants, the military, scientists, doctors, technical staff, and all professional government employees remain in their roles. They were not removed by the Referendum. They have not done anything wrong. The country keeps running because they keep running it. Days 100 through 190 are filled with the Emergency Election process. Section 7.1 specifies that new presidential and congressional elections are scheduled within ninety days of the Constitutional Transition Committee's convening. Existing election infrastructure is used where available. The Constitutional Transition Committee, supported by Authority oversight, ensures the elections themselves are administered to prevent the transition from being captured by the same parties whose government was just removed. Supreme Court vacancies are filled through an emergency appointment process specified in §6 and §7 that involves the Constitutional Transition Committee and the Authority — not the executive that was just removed. On approximately Day 190, newly elected officials take office. The Constitutional Transition Committee dissolves. Normal constitutional order resumes — under the Amendment's continuing protections. It is, by design, the most boring transition possible. The country has just removed its federal government, and the air traffic controllers are still doing their jobs. The mail still gets delivered. Social Security checks still arrive. The new officials inherit a functioning government, not a smoking ruin. This is the point.

◆ ◆ ◆

When a body goes bad.

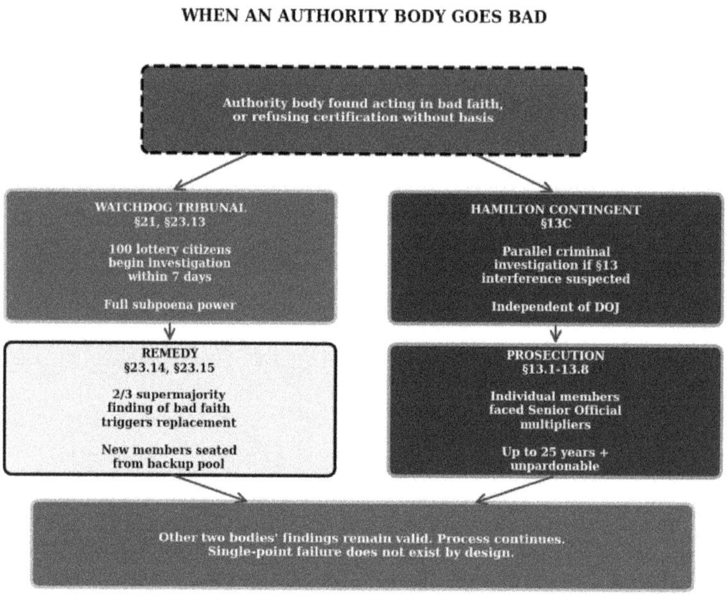

Figure 6 — When an Authority Body Goes Bad

The most common technical objection to multi-body designs is also the most reasonable: what if one of them gets captured? The Amendment thought about this carefully. Sections 21 and 23.13 through 23.15 specify the response. If a body is suspected of corruption — through Authority members' financial misconduct, through bad-faith refusal of certification, through coordination with the federal government the Amendment is examining — the Watchdog Tribunal investigates within seven days under Section 21.7's Capture Finding authority, with the Section 23.13 mutual-veto safeguards applying to refusal cases specifically. The Tribunal has full subpoena authority. It has access to the body's records, which are public anyway because of the Franklin Ledger. The Hamilton Contingent runs a parallel criminal investigation if Section 13 interference is suspected. Watchdog Tribunal action is administrative — removing members, voiding tainted findings, ordering remedial procedures. Hamilton Contingent action is prosecutorial — filing federal charges, securing convictions, recovering corrupt assets. The two run in parallel because they answer different questions: did the body act properly, and did individual members commit crimes. If the Tribunal finds, by two-thirds supermajority, that the body has been captured or has acted in bad faith, the body's members can be removed. New members are seated from a backup pool maintained for exactly this purpose. The findings of the captured body are voided. The other two bodies' independent findings remain valid and can sustain the certification process. This is important: the design assumes one body might go wrong. It does not assume two would go wrong simultaneously. If two of three Authority bodies are captured at the same time, the country has bigger problems than the Amendment, and the Amendment is honest about this. There is no mechanism that can survive coordinated capture of a majority of independent oversight institutions. What the Amendment does ensure is that capture of a single body — which is the realistic threat — does not break the system. Three independent bodies. Random-citizen oversight watching them. Federal prosecutors who do not answer to the President investigating interference. Real-time public publication of everything. None of this is a guarantee. It is the maximum amount of safeguard the Amendment could plausibly construct without making the institution itself a vehicle for the kind of corruption it was built to prevent.

◆ ◆ ◆

The emergency framework. The Amendment normally operates through the Authority. There are circumstances in which the Authority cannot operate — natural disaster, simultaneous incapacitation, contested seating, infrastructure failure. In the most consequential of these — the nuclear emergency — Section 16.10 establishes the Reclamation-Earned Trust Framework. Its principle: emergency authority does not default to the sitting President absent democratic legitimacy earned through the Amendment's removal and election framework. Until the People have demonstrated, at least once, that the removal mechanism works, nuclear emergency authority rests with a distributed Emergency Nuclear Authorization Committee composed of state officials, not with any single officeholder. The framework is gated. Activation requires three independent gates. The first is the Washington Commission's certification, by six-of-seven supermajority of its sitting Chief Justices, that the emergency conditions are met. The second is concurrence from a ninety-percent supermajority of state Governors. The third is a fixed sunset — emergency authority lapses automatically within a defined window. These gates are stringent on purpose. A regular framework that activated easily would be the most attractive capture target imaginable — accomplish through emergency declaration what could not be accomplished through ordinary process. The three-gate structure means emergency activation requires near-unanimous agreement among institutionally separate actors, with a hard time limit on its duration. It is hard to activate and impossible to extend. Section 16.10's Emergency Composite State-Sovereign Authority — the body that exercises emergency power when activated — is composed of state Attorneys General and state Supreme Court Chief Justices in defined proportions, drawn by lottery, sworn to the Constitution. Its powers are bounded; it cannot legislate, cannot declare war, cannot suspend rights. It can administer, certify, and prosecute, in the same categories the Authority normally handles. Most readers will never need to know any of this. The framework exists because someone has to think about the worst day, and the Amendment treats that thinking as a precondition for trusting the rest of the system. A regime that has not planned for its own institutional failure is, in fact, planning to fail institutionally.

◆ ◆ ◆

The Sunset Review. Section 18 specifies that every twenty years, the Amendment itself is reviewed. The review is automatic, public, and structured. It cannot be skipped. It cannot be advanced. The clock ticks on its own. The Sunset Review is conducted by a body that is, by structure, separate from the Authority — because asking the institution to evaluate its own continuation is a recipe for self-preservation bias. The Review body is drawn primarily from state-level institutions (state Supreme Court Chief Justices, state Attorneys General, lottery-selected citizens) and operates with full investigative authority, including the power to commission expert reviews of the Amendment's operational record. Three outcomes are possible. The Review body can recommend retention — the Amendment continues unchanged. It can recommend modification — specific provisions are revised through a structured Article-V-aligned process that requires the same supermajority thresholds the Amendment itself was ratified under. Or it can recommend repeal — the Amendment is removed from the Constitution, again through structured supermajority process. Modification and repeal are not unilateral acts of the Review body. They are recommendations to the country, which must then ratify them. The People retain final authority over their own framework. The Sunset Review's job is to identify what should be considered, not to decide what is changed. There is no mechanism for early Sunset Review. Section 18.16(b) explicitly prohibits convening the Review before the twenty-year interval expires. This prevents the Review from being weaponized against the

Amendment during crisis periods, when politically motivated actors might attempt to dismantle protections precisely when they are most needed. The clock runs at its own pace. The Sunset Review exists because no constitutional document survives forever unmodified, and pretending otherwise produces brittleness. The Amendment is built to be reconsidered. That is part of how it earns the right to continue.

◆ ◆ ◆

Why this is enough. If you have made it this far, you now know more about how the Amendment actually works than ninety-nine percent of Americans, including, in many cases, the people writing about it. You know that there are three Authority bodies, each independent, all required to act jointly. You know there are two oversight institutions watching them — the Watchdog Tribunal and the Hamilton Contingent — themselves separate, themselves accountable. You know that public transparency runs through the Franklin Ledger, that voting runs through Sovereign Voting Terminals, that backup infrastructure runs through Pre-Certified Universities. You know how a petition becomes a referendum, how long it takes, and what happens if it passes. You know what the transition looks like and how the country keeps running through it. You know there is an emergency framework for when the Authority cannot act, and a Sunset Review for when the Amendment itself needs to evolve. What ties all of this together is a single design principle: distribute authority across so many independent points that no single capture event breaks the system. The Amendment is long because that distribution requires specification, and specification is the price of durable protection. A short version of this Amendment would be defeated by interpretation within ten years of ratification. A long version, written carefully, has a much better chance. It is the most safeguard the Amendment could plausibly construct without becoming a vehicle for the kind of corruption it was built to prevent. It is, in the end, a bet — that you can give the People a tool to remove a corrupt government without that tool itself becoming corrupt. The bet is hedged at every layer. The People stay in charge because the entire architecture exists to serve their decision. The Authority does not govern. The Tribunal does not govern. The Hamilton Contingent does not govern. None of them have power on their own. What they have is the obligation to administer, verify, investigate, prosecute, and publish — so that when the People decide, the decision is honestly counted. That is what the Second Reading is about.

◆ ◆ ◆

If you want to go further still — if you want to see the Amendment under cross-examination, with its hardest objections engaged head-on, with section citations and adversarial scenarios — the Third Reading begins in the next chapter. If you would rather stop here, that is also fine. You know what you need to know.

Chapter Five

The Third Reading

Welcome to the Third Reading.

If you have arrived here, one of the following is true. You are a lawyer who would like to take this Amendment apart and see what falls out. You are a constitutional scholar who has been promised that the document survives rigorous examination, and you intend to test the claim. You are a working journalist or policy analyst who has reviewed enough proposed reforms to know that most of them collapse under the slightest pressure. You are a sitting elected official with reasons of your own to know whether this is real. Or you are simply a citizen who likes to know how the watch was made before they put it on. Whichever you are, welcome. The point of the Third Reading is not to flatter the document. The point is to acknowledge the strongest objections and answer them on the record, with section citations you can verify against the Amendment text in Chapter 7. An amendment that cannot survive direct challenge does not deserve ratification. Thirteen objections follow. They are clustered into three groups. The first four are legal and constitutional. The next four are adversarial and practical — what happens when sophisticated parties try to defeat the framework. The last five are structural — questions about the Amendment's own design and durability. Each objection is stated in the strongest version a sophisticated critic would advance. Each is engaged with section citations, edge cases, and concessions where the Amendment is genuinely weaker. The Amendment does not pretend to be perfect. It pretends, at most, to have thought about the problem. A note on citations. Every parenthetical (§X.Y) reference in this chapter points to a verifiable provision in the Amendment text. Readers checking the work are encouraged to do so. The Amendment is in Chapter 7; the section numbers are stable; the cross-references resolve. Before the objections, here is a single chart that may be useful as a reference: the way the Amendment's major sections interlock. Most objections concern one section's strength in isolation. The Amendment's actual design rests on the interaction.

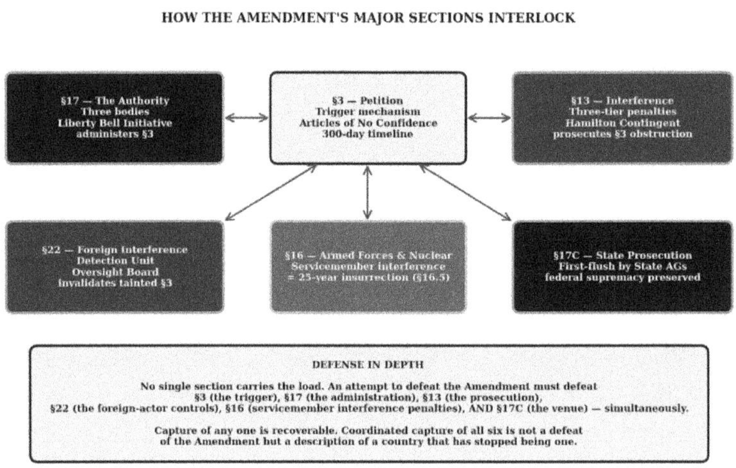

Figure 1 — How the Amendment's Major Sections Interlock

◆ ◆ ◆

Legal and Constitutional Objections "The Article III jurisdiction strip violates the Constitution. Federal courts cannot be silenced this way." The strongest version of this objection: Article III vests the judicial power in the courts Congress establishes, and an amendment that strips federal courts of jurisdiction over a process affecting the fundamental structure of federal government is, at minimum, in serious tension with the original constitutional design. Critics will cite Marbury v. Madison for the proposition that judicial review is constitutionally entrenched, United States v. Klein for the proposition that Congress cannot dictate outcomes by manipulating jurisdiction, and

Boumediene v. Bush for the proposition that the Suspension Clause limits even Congress's power over jurisdictional questions. The argument is that a permanent jurisdiction strip of this scope is not a routine exercise of the Exceptions Clause but a structural rewrite that the Constitution does not permit. The Amendment's response is direct: yes, this is a structural rewrite. That is why it is an amendment. Article V exists for exactly this purpose. The Eleventh Amendment restricted federal court jurisdiction over suits against states. The Sixteenth Amendment overruled Pollock v. Farmers' Loan and reauthorized the income tax the Court had struck down. The Twenty-Sixth Amendment lowered the voting age over the objection of Oregon v. Mitchell's partial federalism. Amendments routinely constrain — and sometimes overrule — the Court's settled doctrine. The People's Reclamation Amendment is in good company. More specifically, the jurisdiction strip in §3.3 is not unbounded. It is limited to the §3 Petition-and-Referendum process and its associated administrative actions. The provision states that no federal court, agency, or official shall have jurisdiction to enjoin, delay, or invalidate a Petition at any stage of the Petition process (§3.3). What the Amendment removes is jurisdiction to halt or invalidate the §3 process. Federal courts retain ordinary federal-question jurisdiction over criminal cases, civil rights cases, and the entire universe of non-§3 federal law. The Amendment also retains a constitutional check against capture by its own institutions: §13H establishes alternative interpretive pathways when judicial capture is genuinely demonstrated, with three independent triggers (Authority Liberty Bell Declaration under §13H.4; data-driven adverse-ruling pattern review under §13H.5; citizen Judicial Review Petition under §13H.6). These pathways activate only on clear and convincing evidence, with §13H.15's narrow construction requirement and §13H.17's protection of non-captured judicial functions. Ordinary disagreement with judicial reasoning does not trigger them.

The Klein concern — that Congress cannot dictate outcomes through jurisdictional rules — is also addressed. Klein involved Congress directing a particular outcome in pending litigation. The Amendment does not do this. It does not direct that any specific Petition succeed or fail. It removes federal courts' jurisdiction to interfere with whichever way the People vote. This is a structural reservation, not an outcome dictation. The People still have to gather signatures (§3.1), the Authority still has to certify (§3.2), sixty percent of voters still have to approve, fifty percent of voters still have to participate (§5.2). The Amendment ensures that these processes — designed by the People, ratified by the People — are not undone by the actors the processes are designed to constrain. Boumediene v. Bush presents a closer challenge. The case held that the Suspension Clause limits Congress's power to strip habeas jurisdiction over Guantanamo detainees, even where Congress had textually authorized the strip. Boumediene's logic is that some jurisdictional limits violate constitutional structure even when textually authorized. The objection: the People's Reclamation Amendment's §3.3 strip is similarly broad, and a future Court could read Boumediene to invalidate it. The Amendment's response is that Boumediene involved a federal statute operating against the constitutional baseline of the original Suspension Clause — a clash within a fixed constitutional order. The People's Reclamation Amendment is itself part of the constitutional order. It does not strip jurisdiction by federal statute against an unchanged constitutional baseline; it changes the constitutional baseline. Boumediene's structural-limits reasoning applies to legislation, not to the Constitution amending itself. The Amendment's strip survives Boumediene because Boumediene is about what the legislature can do, not what the People-as-sovereign can do through Article V. Concession. The Amendment does ask federal courts to accept a limitation that prior jurisdiction-stripping efforts have not asked of them. There is no perfect precedent. What the Amendment relies on is that ratification under Article V — three-quarters of state legislatures or conventions — produces a constitutional change of the same legal stature as the original Article III itself. The two coexist, and where they conflict, the later-ratified provision controls, in the same way the Sixteenth Amendment controls over the Direct Tax Clauses of Article I. This is how the Constitution is supposed to work. Section references: §3.1 (Petition initiation), §3.2 (verification timeline), §3.3 (jurisdiction strip), §5.2 (Referendum thresholds), §13H.4–13H.17 (judicial capture pathways).

◆ ◆ ◆

"The Amendment cannot bind future Congresses or future Supreme Courts. They will simply re-interpret it into nothing." The strongest version of this objection draws on a deep doctrine in constitutional law: the anti-entrenchment principle. No legislature can bind a successor legislature. Constitutional amendments are different — they have higher status — but they too can be reinterpreted. The Court has, in practice, dramatically reshaped amendments through interpretation. The Fourteenth Amendment's Privileges or Immunities Clause was rendered nearly inert by The Slaughter-House Cases within five years of ratification. The Second Amendment's prefatory clause was reread by

District of Columbia v. Heller after two centuries. The Commerce Clause expanded under Wickard v. Filburn, then partially contracted under United States v. Lopez. A People's Reclamation Amendment, the critic argues, will face the same fate. Within twenty years, a hostile Court could read its key provisions into meaninglessness. This objection is correct in its premise. It is wrong about the conclusion. The Amendment was drafted with this very threat in mind. Section 13H establishes the Doctrinal Erosion Protection (§13H.11): when a pattern of judicial interpretation progressively weakens Amendment provisions over time, the Authority may, through Liberty Bell Initiative, issue a Doctrinal Erosion Declaration that triggers immediate review and corrective mechanisms. Combined with §13H's Adverse Ruling Pattern trigger (§13H.5) — under which data-driven analysis demonstrating systematically adverse rulings triggers automatic review — the Amendment provides a structural answer to slow textual hollowing-out. Section 17.22.1 adds another layer: the Single-Body Compromise Declaration, which permits any one of the three Authority bodies to publish a Declaration when one or more of the others have been corrupted, captured, or compromised. A valid Declaration triggers the Expedited Compromise Referendum under §17.22.4 — bypassing the ordinary petition threshold entirely; the Declaration itself substitutes for the petition. Bad-faith reinterpretation by a captured body is met not with appeal but with a fast track for the People to overrule it directly. More structurally: the Amendment's substantive operations do not rest on judicial interpretation. They rest on numerical thresholds and physical processes. Sixty percent of votes cast (§5.2). Fifty percent turnout (§5.2). In-person ID-verified signing at Sovereign Voting Terminals (§14). Liberty Bell Initiative concurrence by all three Authority bodies (§17.22). These are not interpretations. They are events. A court can rule that the Amendment means whatever the court wants it to mean — but the count is the count. The voters who showed up showed up. The signatures collected on hardware-verified cryptographic terminals exist or do not. Concession. A future Court could refuse to recognize a Referendum result as constitutionally valid. This is a real risk. The Amendment's response — that such a refusal would itself be a §13 interference offense, prosecutable by the Hamilton

Contingent before §17C state-level panels — is novel. It has not been tested. Whether the legal infrastructure of state Attorneys General, state Supreme Court Chief Justices, and the Hamilton Contingent would actually carry forward such a prosecution against a sitting Court is, frankly, a question whose answer depends on the country those institutions are operating in. The Amendment cannot guarantee that answer. It can only construct the framework that makes the answer possible. What it does not do is rest its survival on judicial good faith. It rests on the People's continued willingness to count the count. That is, in the end, what every constitutional regime rests on. The People's Reclamation Amendment is honest about this and builds the count to be hard to fake. Section references: §5.2 (Referendum thresholds), §13 (interference penalties), §13H.5 (Adverse Ruling Pattern trigger), §13H.11 (Doctrinal Erosion Protection), §14 (Sovereign Voting Terminals), §17.22.1 (Single-Body Compromise Declaration), §17.22.4 (Expedited Compromise Referendum), §17C (state-level prosecution panels).

◆ ◆ ◆

"The unpardonable §13 Tier 3 conflicts with Article II's pardon power." Article II grants the President "Power to grant Reprieves and Pardons for Offences against the United States, except in Cases of Impeachment." The text is broad. The historical practice has been broader still. Critics correctly observe that the federal pardon power has been read to encompass nearly all federal offenses, with the only textual exception being impeachment. Schick v. Reed (1974) confirmed the pardon power's breadth, holding that the President may attach lawful conditions to a pardon. An amendment that creates a category of unpardonable federal offenses — which §13's Tier 3 does — appears to add a second exception that the original Constitution did not contemplate. The Amendment's response operates on three levels. The textual level. Section 24.2 directly addresses the pardon power, stating that "the pardon power established in Article II, Section 2 of the Constitution shall be subject to the following limitations," and enumerates them. Article V permits constitutional amendments. Where a later-ratified provision conflicts with an earlier one, the later controls — that is the Sixteenth-over-the-Direct-Tax-Clauses pattern, repeated dozens of times in constitutional history. Section 25A explicitly addresses the relationship between the Amendment's provisions and prior constitutional text. The text of Article II is what Article II says it is, as modified by every subsequent amendment that touches it. The structural level. The pardon power's purpose has historically been understood as a check on the criminal-justice system's mistakes and an instrument of mercy — not a tool for self-protection by the office that holds it. To allow the President to pardon someone convicted of attempting to bribe Authority members to invalidate a Petition is to allow the Office to pardon attempts to entrench the Office. That is, structurally, exactly the kind of self-dealing the pardon power was not designed to permit. Section 24's foundational principle is explicit: "concentration of power in any single officeholder creates the conditions for the corruption and tyranny this Amendment exists to prevent" (§24.1). The carve-out is narrow by design — limited to coordinated bad-faith interference with the §3 process — and tracks the structural rationale rather than reaching ordinary federal offenses. The doctrinal level. The honest scholar will observe that the People's Reclamation Amendment's pardon carve-out is structurally different from the Twenty-Second Amendment's eligibility limit. The Twenty-Second added a categorical bar to who can hold the office; it did not change the powers of the office for those who do hold it. The Amendment's §24.2 carve-out is closer to the Civil-War-era debates about whether Congress could exempt offenses from pardon by statute — debates that mostly concluded Congress could not, but which were about statutory limits on Article II, not constitutional ones. The Amendment's claim is that what Congress cannot do by statute, the People can do by Article V ratification. The Amendment does not pretend this is a small claim. It pretends only that it is a permissible one under Article V's plain text and the established practice of amendments overriding earlier provisions. There are existing precedents for bounded pardon power. The pardon power does not extend to state offenses; a President cannot pardon a state crime. The pardon power does not extend to civil contempt. The pardon power does not extend to certain congressional sanctions. Carving out a narrow category of constitutional self-protection from the pardon's reach is consistent with the pattern of how the pardon power is bounded — though the Amendment achieves this through Article V rather than through doctrine. Concession. This will be litigated, and the litigation will be substantial. A future President convicted of a Tier 3 offense (or whose ally is so convicted) will challenge the carve-out as inconsistent with Article II. The challenge will reach the Supreme Court. The Court will have to decide whether to enforce the Amendment's clear text under the established principle that a later amendment controls over earlier provisions, or to read Article II as somehow exempt from amendment. The Amendment's response, if the Court rules against the carve-out, is exactly the response in Objection 2 above: bad-faith reinterpretation triggers §13H mechanisms, public ledger documentation, and downstream Petition mechanics. The Court can strike the carve-out down. The Amendment cannot guarantee that it will not. What it can do is ensure the strike-down is a public, expensive, recorded act. The country gets to know, and gets to act on what it knows. Section references: §13 (interference penalties including Tier 3 unpardonable offenses), §13H (judicial capture pathways), §24.1 (foundational principle on

concentration of power), §24.2 (pardon power limitations), §25A (constitutional amendment effects on prior provisions).

◆ ◆ ◆

"§17C's first-flush prosecution by State AGs and State Supreme Court Justices violates the Appointments Clause, federal supremacy, and anti-commandeering doctrine." This is the most novel — and the most legally vulnerable — piece of the Amendment's architecture. Section 17C establishes a three-phase accountability chain (§17C.2): a State Attorneys General Prosecution Panel of five state AGs drawn by lottery (§17C.3); a State Supreme Court Judicial Panel of five Justices of the highest courts of Participating Jurisdictions, also drawn by lottery (§17C.6); and an Appellate Panel for verdict review (§17C.10). All three stages are structurally separate from the federal judiciary. The Authority bodies, the Watchdog Tribunal, and senior Hamilton Contingent personnel are tried in this state-sovereign system, not in federal courts (§17C.11). The objection: this appears to violate the Appointments Clause of Article II, which requires that officers of the United States be appointed by the President, by the courts of law, or by the heads of departments. State Supreme Court Justices, sitting as a §17C Judicial Panel, are arguably exercising federal judicial power without having been appointed in conformity with the Appointments Clause. It also raises federal supremacy concerns: a federal criminal trial before a state-level panel is a structural inversion of the ordinary supremacy hierarchy. The Amendment's response is, again, that the architecture is intentional and that an Article-V amendment can authorize what Article II would otherwise forbid. But the response is more than this. Section 17C.7 grants the Judicial Panel "the authorities of an Article III trial court for Amendment-body prosecution cases." The Justices on a §17C panel are not exercising ordinary federal judicial power — they are exercising power specifically and exclusively created by §17C, power that did not exist before the Amendment and would not exist without it. Section 17C creates both the offense and the venue in the same legal stroke. This is novel. The Amendment does not pretend otherwise. Section 17C.13 anticipates that the §17C framework will itself be a target of capture attempts and provides anti-capture protections including the lottery randomization, geographic distribution requirements, and the structurally-separate Appellate Panel. Section 17C.15 extends the framework to federal officials prosecuted under Amendment provisions, recognizing that prosecution of corrupt federal officials in courts they may have captured would defeat the Amendment's purpose.

Why this venue choice? The Amendment cannot rely on the federal judiciary to police interference with the Amendment when the federal judiciary is one of the institutions the Amendment exists to constrain. A Supreme Court Justice indicted under §13 cannot reasonably be tried before federal judges who serve in collegial relationship with the Justice's chambers. State Supreme Court Justices, drawn by lottery, sitting in rotating state venues, with no career relationship to the federal judiciary, are the closest available approximation of a neutral forum. Due process and the federal hierarchy. A defense lawyer reading this objection will rightly ask: what process is due to a §13 defendant, and where does a §17C verdict sit in the federal legal hierarchy? Section 17C.7 grants the Judicial Panel "the authorities of an Article III trial court for Amendment-body prosecution cases." Section 17C.9 establishes Trial Procedural Standards ensuring fair process to defendants — including notice, counsel, confrontation, and procedural protections that track the federal criminal-trial standards reflected in Goldberg v. Kelly, Mathews v. Eldridge, and Crawford v. Washington. Section 17C.10 establishes Appeals to the Appellate Panel under defined procedures, with §17C.9.1 providing a Pre-Trial Detention Framework specifically designed for the §17C context. The Amendment is not silent on due process; it tracks the federal standards a defendant would receive in an Article III court. The harder question — whether a §17C conviction is reviewable by federal habeas, and whether a §17C verdict has preclusive effect in subsequent collateral federal proceedings — is one the Amendment does not fully resolve. Section 17C.10's Appellate Panel handles direct appeals; whether collateral federal review remains available is a question that will be litigated in the first §17C habeas petition. The Amendment provides for direct review under §17C.10; it leaves the federal-collateral question open, presumably because closing that channel entirely would create the very capture-vulnerability §17C exists to prevent (a §17C verdict insulated from any federal review at all would itself become a target for capture). Concession. The Appointments Clause challenge will come, and it will be substantial. The Amendment's strongest argument is that §17C panels are constitutional because they were authorized by constitutional amendment, full stop. The weaker argument is that these panels exercise delegated state authority over federal offenses created by the Amendment itself, which is a structural innovation but not a violation of any principle that pre-existed §17C. Whether courts find these arguments persuasive will depend on the political environment of the time and on whether the original §17C ratification was decisive enough to discourage frontal challenge. The Amendment is honest that this provision is its most legally exposed piece. The anti-commandeering challenge. A federalism scholar will raise a separate but related objection: Printz v. United States (1997) and New York v. United States (1992) establish that the federal government cannot commandeer state officials or state legislative processes. The Amendment's §17C framework arguably commandeers state Supreme Court Justices for federal criminal trials, and §20 imposes affirmative compliance duties on state legislatures, executives, courts, and agencies. Printz would, on its face, prohibit this. The Amendment's response is, again, that Article V authorizes what statutory federal law could not. Printz interpreted federal-statutory commandeering against the background of Articles I and II; it did not address whether a constitutional amendment ratified under Article V could create such obligations. The Reconstruction Amendments, particularly the Fourteenth, did exactly this kind of thing — they imposed substantive duties on states that the original Constitution did not. The People's Reclamation Amendment is, structurally, in the same category: a later-ratified constitutional provision that imposes duties on states by direct constitutional command, not by federal statute. More specifically: §20.1's compliance duty is owed to the Constitution-as-amended, not to a federal statute or executive order. The hardship framework of §17.4 applies to state Justices drawn for §17C panels just as it applies to lottery-drawn citizens, providing genuine accommodation for individual Justices who cannot serve. The state, as a state, is subject to the duty under §20.1; individual officials retain individual hardship rights under §17.4. This dual structure tracks the way the Reconstruction Amendments operated — imposing state-level duties through Section 5 enforcement powers while preserving individual-level due process. Concession on commandeering. The argument that a constitutional amendment can do what a federal statute cannot is correct in principle but untested in this exact form. Printz rests partly on structural readings of Article I that an Article V amendment can override; it also rests partly on dual-sovereignty principles that an Article V amendment cannot easily override without expressly addressing them. The Amendment expressly addresses state compliance in §20 and expressly authorizes state-Justice service in §17C, which is the strongest available textual answer. Whether courts find that answer persuasive will be the central federalism litigation of the post-ratification period. The Amendment is honest that this is unresolved. What is the alternative? If §17C is struck down, federal prosecutions of §13 violations would proceed in federal court, before federal judges, who would be ruling on conduct that may include their own colleagues' interference. The Amendment's drafters concluded that such a structure would render §13 prosecution functionally toothless against the highest federal officials, who are precisely the targets §13 was written to address. The §17C structure is the answer to a real problem. It is also the answer that carries the most legal risk. Both are true. Section references: §13 (interference penalties prosecuted via §17C), §17.4 (hardship framework for individual Justices), §17C.2 (three-phase accountability chain), §17C.3 (Prosecution Panel composition), §17C.6 (Judicial Panel composition), §17C.7 (panel authorities — Article III trial court powers), §17C.9 (Trial Procedural Standards — due process), §17C.9.1 (Pre-Trial Detention Framework), §17C.10 (Appellate Panel and direct review), §17C.11 (jurisdictional scope), §17C.13 (anti-capture protections), §17C.15 (federal officials extension), §20.1 (state compliance duty).

◆ ◆ ◆

Adversarial and Practical Objections "The federal courts will block this. They block everything else."

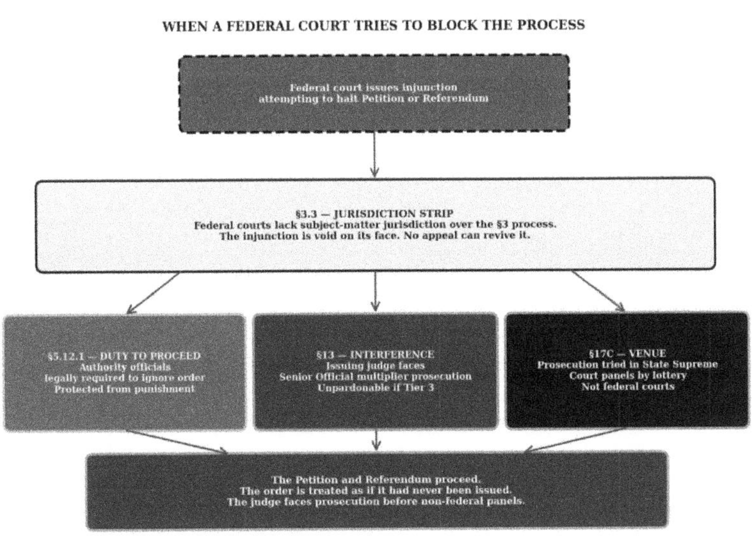

Figure 2 — When a Federal Court Tries to Block the Process

This is the most common objection, and it is the one the Amendment thought about most. The short answer is in §3.3: the Amendment strips federal courts of subject-matter jurisdiction over the Petition-and-Referendum process. An injunction issued anyway is void on its face. Section 5.12 mirrors this for the Referendum stage: "No act of Congress, executive order, presidential proclamation, judicial ruling, state action, emergency declaration, martial law declaration, or any other federal, state, or territorial action shall delay, postpone, abridge, or prevent the holding of a No Confidence Referendum." (For the constitutional argument that this strip is permissible, see Objection 1.) The longer answer recognizes that a captured court could still issue an order. Issuing an order is a physical act that no Amendment can prevent — a judge can sign a piece of paper regardless of whether the law authorizes it. What the Amendment can and does prevent is the order having any legal effect. The Authority's officials are required to proceed, and Authority members and staff face their own §13 interference exposure for complying with an unlawful blocking order. The Watchdog Tribunal supervises compliance. Section 13 then makes the issuance of such an order, by a sitting judge, a Senior Official-tier interference offense (§13A.3 establishes the Senior Official Multiplier — fines no less than fifty times the benefit received). The judge faces prosecution by the Hamilton Contingent (§13C), tried before §17C state-level panels (see Objection 4). A judge issuing an injunction in violation of §3.3 is, in effect, committing a federal felony. Edge cases. What about an ex parte temporary restraining order issued at three in the morning, the day before a Referendum begins? Section 3.3 still applies. The TRO is void on its face. Authority officials proceed at their stations. The judge faces Hamilton Contingent investigation immediately upon the issuance becoming public. What about a Supreme Court order? Same answer, with one wrinkle: a Supreme Court order carries enormous moral and political weight. The Amendment cannot prevent the political weight. It can ensure that the legal weight is zero. Whether the political weight matters depends on whether the country's institutions and citizens treat the Court's order as legitimate. Section 13H.13 specifically forecloses one common evasion: "No court shall invoke political question doctrine, standing limitations, or similar justiciability doctrines to refuse ruling on" the matters listed in that subsection. What about lower-court rulings being aggregated through nationwide preliminary injunctions? Section 3.3 explicitly addresses this: federal courts have no jurisdiction at any stage. A district court cannot enjoin the process even within its district, because the jurisdictional bar is categorical, not geographic. The aggregation strategy that has worked in modern litigation against federal action does not apply here. Concession. The Amendment relies on Authority officials and citizens being willing to act in defiance of formally-issued court orders, even when those officials are individually exposed to political and physical risk. The Hamilton Contingent's Protection Division — one of the four operational divisions established under §13C.2 — provides physical security for citizens, officials, and witnesses targeted because of their §3 work. The Watchdog Tribunal investigates retaliation. But the Amendment cannot make refusing a court order easy. It can only make it lawful and protected. The willingness to do so is, in the end, a matter of political culture, and that the Amendment does not produce on its own. Section references: §3.3 (jurisdiction strip), §5.12 (no delay permitted), §13 (interference penalties), §13A.3 (Senior Official Multiplier), §13C (Hamilton

Contingent), §13H.13 (political question doctrine limits), §17C (state-level prosecution panels).

◆ ◆ ◆

"Hostile state governments will refuse to participate, disenfranchising their own citizens."

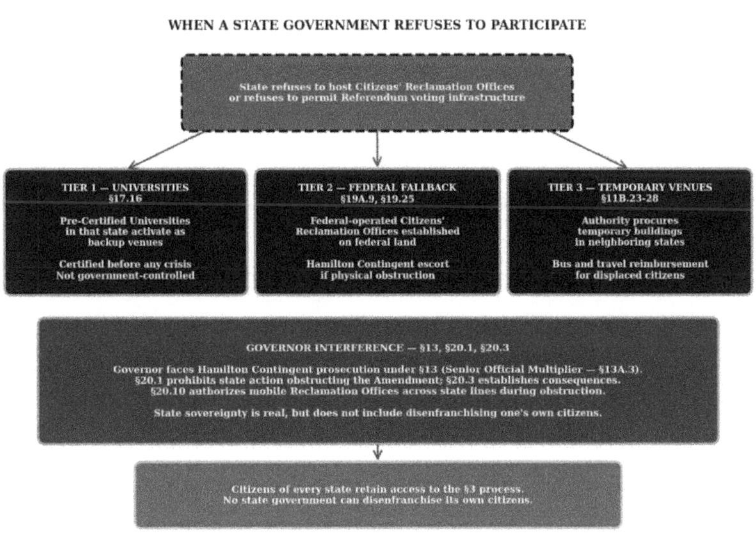

Figure 3 — When a State Government Refuses to Participate

This is the second-most-common objection, and it deserves a careful answer. First, the Amendment is structured so that no individual state government can prevent its citizens from participating. Section 20.1 establishes the foundational rule: “No state, state legislature, state executive, state court, or state agency shall refuse to comply with the requirements of this Amendment, obstruct its Implementation, interfere with its operation...” Section 20 then establishes a graduated response framework when states fail to comply. Second, the physical infrastructure has redundancy. Section 17.16 establishes the Pre-Certified University Pool of at least 200 institutions (target 500+) — non-governmental venues vetted before any crisis arises. Section 11B.23 through §11B.28 provides for temporary venue procurement when permanent Citizens' Reclamation Offices are unavailable. Section 20.10 authorizes the Authority to deploy mobile Citizens' Reclamation Offices just across the state line during any active state non-compliance, ensuring affected citizens retain access. The state government's cooperation is appreciated. It is not required. Third, state officials who actively obstruct face prosecution. Section 13 interference penalties apply to state officials acting to obstruct the §3 process; the Senior Official Multiplier (§13A.3) attaches to any public official wielding public authority, state or federal. A state Attorney General refusing to seat the State Elections Council member is committing a §13 offense. A governor directing state assets to obstruct signature collection is committing a §13 offense. Prosecution proceeds before §17C state-level panels (drawn from other states' supreme courts and other states' Attorneys General, by lottery — the panels are designed to be insulated from the obstructing jurisdiction). Edge cases. What if a state National Guard is mobilized to physically block university campuses? The order is unlawful: state National Guard cannot be used to obstruct the §3 process under §20.1's prohibition; officers carrying out such orders face §13 prosecution; officers refusing them are protected. Section 16.5's military insurrection penalty (twenty-five years for any servicemember attempting to use troops to interfere with the transition) applies to federalized Guard during the transition period. What if a state passes its own statute purporting to make participation in a §3 process a state-level crime? The statute is preempted under §20.1's prohibition on state action obstructing the Amendment; §20.2 specifies consequences for state interference with the Emergency Delegate Election; §20.10's mobile-Reclamation-Office deployment ensures citizens retain access while the obstruction is litigated. Fourth — and this is the structural answer — the broad-distribution requirement of the Petition itself addresses the systemic concern. The Petition requires not just 15% nationally but 15% within at least thirty of the fifty-six jurisdictions (§3.1). A petition that succeeds without rural states does not succeed. A petition that succeeds without coastal states does not succeed. The Amendment is designed to require broad geographic agreement, which makes it impossible for any single state's refusal to be decisive in either direction. A state that refuses to participate effectively concedes its share of the count to its citizens who travel to neighboring jurisdictions. It does not block the process; it merely shifts where its citizens have to go to be heard. Concession. A state government that is sufficiently determined to obstruct can make participation more difficult and more burdensome for its citizens. The Amendment cannot prevent inconvenience. It can prevent disenfranchisement. There is a difference, and the difference is real. A citizen who has to drive to a neighboring state's pre-certified university or to a §20.10 mobile Reclamation Office across the state line is being inconvenienced; that citizen is not being silenced. The Amendment treats inconvenience as a cost it cannot fully eliminate and silence as a cost it cannot tolerate.

Section references: §3.1 (Petition thresholds with geographic distribution), §11B.23–28 (temporary venues), §13 (interference penalties), §13A.3 (Senior Official Multiplier), §16.5 (military insurrection penalty), §17.16 (Pre-Certified University Pool), §17C (state-level prosecution panels), §20.1 (state non-compliance prohibition), §20.2 (Emergency Election interference), §20.10 (mobile Reclamation Offices).

◆ ◆ ◆

"Foreign powers will manipulate the Referendum."

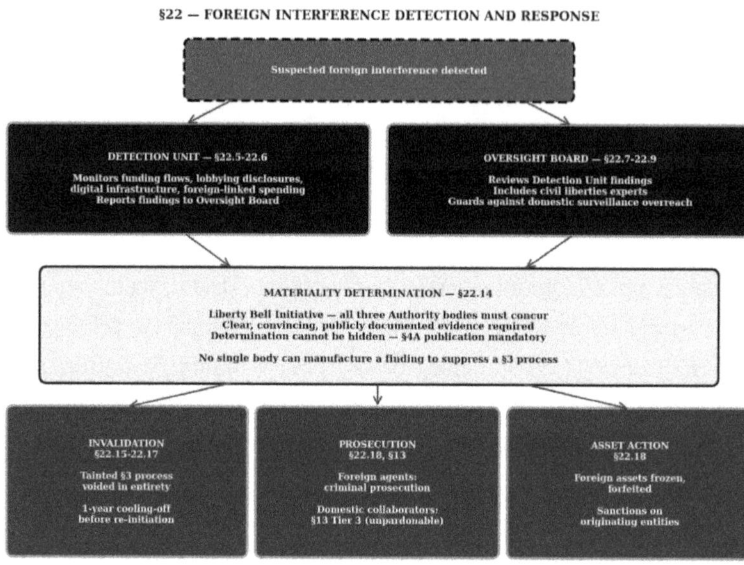

Figure 4 — §22 Foreign Interference Detection and Response

Foreign interference is a real threat to all elections, and the Amendment treats it as a category-one design concern. Section 22 — Protection Against Foreign Interference in Petitions and Referendums — runs to several thousand words on its own. The defense is layered. The Foreign Interference Detection Unit (§22.5) operates as a joint operation of the State Elections Council and the Academic Integrity Commission, with capabilities enumerated in §22.6 (subject to oversight under §22.7 through §22.10). The Foreign Interference Oversight Board (§22.7) protects civil liberties and prevents the Detection Unit from drifting into surveillance of domestic political speech. Civil liberties experts are seated specifically for this purpose.

A determination of material foreign interference under §22.14 requires Liberty Bell Initiative concurrence — separate concurrence of all three Authority bodies — and clear, convincing, and publicly documented evidence (§22.16). Section 22.16 explicitly states that determinations require "not mere allegation, partisan accusation, or political dispute." If a determination is made, the consequences are not symbolic. Section 22.15 invalidates the tainted Petition, Referendum, or Election in its entirety, with a one-year cooling-off period before any new

Petition on the same subject. Section 22.17 establishes penalties for any United States person who knowingly accepts, solicits, coordinates, or directs material support from a Foreign Person or Entity. Section 22.18 establishes penalties for foreign persons or entities themselves: permanent barring of the foreign entity, its successor organizations, and its principal officers, plus asset forfeiture and sanctions on originating entities. Section 22.19 treats knowing failure to disclose as itself a §22.17 offense. Section 22.16.1 closes a sophisticated evasion: aggregate materiality. To prevent foreign actors from structuring interference operations to remain individually below the materiality threshold while collectively producing material effect, the framework treats coordinated sub-threshold actions as cumulative. Edge cases. What about deepfakes — synthetic video or audio designed to mislead voters? Section 22.5's monitoring scope explicitly covers digital infrastructure used by referendum participants and patterns of foreign-linked spending; §22.6 enumerates Detection Unit capabilities including subpoena power to investigate apparent foreign-origin content. Detection capability scales with technology; the framework requires biennial review. What about deniable cyber attacks on Sovereign Voting Terminal infrastructure? Section 14's hardware design — air-gapped voting machines, dual-chain blockchain ledger with cryptographic verification, voter-verified paper backup for every interaction — means that successful tampering requires physical access to a majority of distributed terminals across multiple states, not a single network breach. The Amendment is built to make remote-only attacks ineffective. What about laundering through domestic shell entities — foreign money routed through American LLCs? Section 22.6's Detection Unit capabilities include piercing layered intermediate entities; §22.19's failure-to-disclose framework treats concealed foreign involvement as itself a prohibited act of interference subject to §22.17 penalties. The objection that cuts the other direction. A weaponized Detection Unit could itself become a tool to invalidate legitimate domestic Petitions on pretextual foreign-interference grounds. The Amendment addresses this. The materiality determination requires three-body Authority concurrence (§22.14), not single-body action. The evidence must be clear, convincing, and publicly documented (§22.16). The Watchdog Tribunal can investigate any determination it suspects of bad faith.

False or pretextual findings of foreign interference are themselves §13 interference offenses, and the determination's authors face the Senior Official Multiplier if convicted. There is no costless way to manufacture a foreign-interference finding. The First Amendment line. A serious civil-liberties critic will press a different concern: where is the line between "foreign interference" and domestic political speech that happens to align with foreign interests? Modern American history is full of investigative apparatuses turned against domestic dissent — COINTELPRO targeting civil rights activists, post-9/11 surveillance of mosque attendees, and others. Brandenburg v. Ohio (1969) sets the constitutional floor: speech advocating unlawful action is protected unless directed at producing imminent lawless action and likely to produce such action. A Detection Unit that monitors "patterns of foreign-linked spending" is operating at the edge of First Amendment territory; sometimes inside it. The Amendment's response is structural rather than rhetorical. The §22.7 Foreign Interference Oversight Board exists specifically to prevent the Detection Unit from drifting into surveillance of domestic political speech, and its membership requires civil liberties experts. The §22.16 evidentiary standard — clear, convincing, publicly documented — sets a far higher bar than the bare-suspicion thresholds that have historically enabled domestic-dissent surveillance. The §22.14 Liberty Bell concurrence requirement adds three-body veto. Together these mechanisms attempt to do what no other American surveillance apparatus has: distinguish foreign-actor interference from domestic dissent, with public evidentiary standards a defense lawyer can challenge in §17C proceedings. The Amendment does not pretend this distinction will always hold cleanly. It pretends only that the framework is more constrained than the alternative of no framework or an unconstrained one — and that the §22 architecture is the closest available approximation of the line Brandenburg draws. Concession. Foreign interference is impossible to prevent absolutely. Sufficiently sophisticated state-actor adversaries with sufficient resources can probably influence at least some segment of any Referendum's information environment. What the Amendment does is make such interference expensive, public, and prosecutable, while limiting its ability to alter outcomes by requiring numerical thresholds large enough that small-scale tampering becomes mathematically irrelevant. It does not promise immunity. It promises the most-defended election architecture the country has ever attempted, and it admits the limits of that promise on the record. Section references: §13 (interference penalties), §13A.3 (Senior Official Multiplier), §14 (Sovereign Voting Terminals), §22.5 (Detection Unit), §22.6 (Detection Unit capabilities), §22.7 (Oversight Board), §22.14 (materiality determination), §22.15 (invalidation and cooling-off), §22.16 (evidentiary standard), §22.16.1 (aggregate materiality), §22.17 (US person penalties), §22.18 (foreign entity penalties), §22.19 (failure to disclose).

◆ ◆ ◆

"The military could be used to stop a referendum."

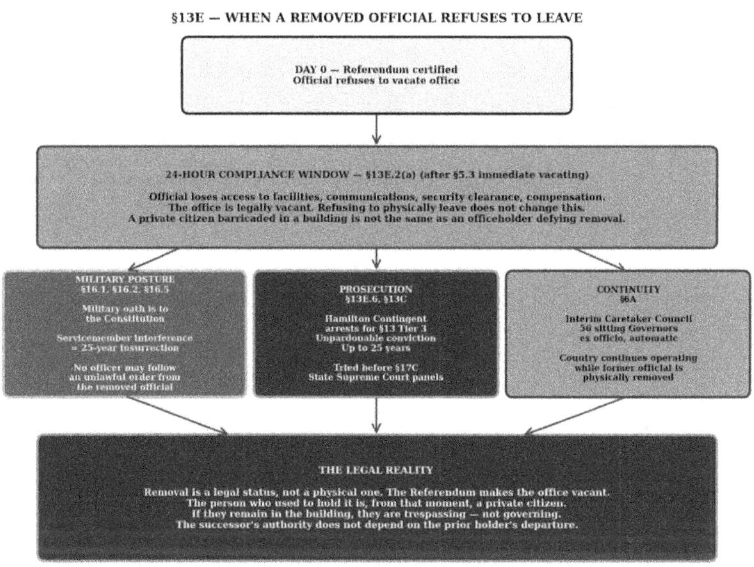

Figure 5 — §13E When a Removed Official Refuses to Leave

◆ ◆ ◆

The military takes an oath to the Constitution, not to the President. Section 16.1 makes this explicit and operational: "The Armed Forces owe their ultimate loyalty to the Constitution and to the People, not to any officeholder, party, or administration." Section 16.2 establishes the obligations of the Armed Forces upon passage of a Declaration of No Confidence: "continue defense against foreign threats; stand down from domestic deployment except as authorized under Section 16.3" and related provisions. Section 16.3 establishes the structure of civilian control during transition. Section 16.6 forecloses one specific evasion: "No removed official shall retain command, control, or access to military forces, weapons systems, or classified facilities." Section 16.5 establishes the consequence for military personnel who attempt to use troops to interfere with the transition: "Any servicemember attempting to use troops to interfere with the transition shall be: (a) immediately removed from command;

(b) subjected to full public military tribunal; and (c) upon conviction, imprisoned not less than 25 years for insurrection." Twenty-five years. The classification is insurrection, not mere insubordination. Edge cases. What if a sitting commander-in-chief orders the deployment of federal troops to disrupt a Referendum? The order is unlawful on its face under §16.5 (transition interference) and §16.2 (Armed Forces obligations during No Confidence period). Refusing to obey is the lawful response. Carrying it out is, under §16.5, insurrection — twenty-five years prison, public military tribunal. It is also a §13 Tier 3 violation, prosecutable by the Hamilton Contingent (§13C) and tried before §17C state-level venues that the executive does not control. What about a chain-of-command breakdown — multiple officers issuing contradictory orders, junior personnel uncertain which to follow? The default rule is in §16.2: continue defense against foreign threats; stand down from domestic deployment except as specifically authorized. Where ambiguity exists about whether an order is lawful, the §16.5 rule on attempted-use-of-troops-to-interfere is severe enough to put the burden on those who would obey: insurrection by §16.5; refusal protected. Personnel who choose non-obstruction in such circumstances are presumptively protected because the alternative — using troops to interfere with the transition — has no lawful authority. What about dual-hatted state National Guard units that have been federalized in advance — can a President use Guard units in their federal capacity to obstruct? Section 16.5 creates a personal criminal penalty for any servicemember who participates in such an order: removal from command, public military tribunal, twenty-five-year insurrection sentence on conviction. The honest answer about federalization itself is harder. The §16.5 individual-level deterrent is the operative provision, not a categorical preemption of the federalized command-chain. A

President who issues a federalization order intending to use the Guard against the §3 process commits §13 interference (with §13A.3's Senior Official Multiplier); officers who participate face §16.5; officers who refuse are protected. The framework relies on individual-level disobedience to render the order practically inoperable rather than on a textual claim that federalization is itself void. What about private military contractors or paramilitary forces? Section 13's interference framework attaches to individual decisionmakers — corporate officers, supervisors, and operators who direct or carry out the obstruction. The contractor's corporate form does not shield the individuals; §13A.7 separately establishes entity-level liability where corporations, limited liability companies, or other entities participate in Corruption Offenses, with penalties on the entity in addition to the individual penalties on its decisionmakers. Section 13A's financial penalties — including 50× the benefit received under the Senior Official Multiplier (§13A.3) — attach to individual public-authority wielders, while §13A.7 reaches the entity itself. Concession. The Amendment relies, ultimately, on the willingness of military officers to refuse orders. This is a willingness that exists in some chains of command and not in others. The Amendment cannot guarantee it. What it does is reinforce existing oath obligations with explicit constitutional grounding (§16.1), public legal protection for those who refuse, and severe consequences for those who comply with unlawful obstruction orders (§16.5's twenty-five-year insurrection classification). The strength of these reinforcements depends on whether the surrounding institutions — military justice, Hamilton Contingent, §17C panels — function as designed. If those institutions are also captured, the military's willingness to refuse becomes the last line. The Amendment is honest that this last line is, in the worst case, the line that holds. Section references: §13 (interference penalties), §13A.3 (Senior Official Multiplier), §13A.7 (entity liability), §13C (Hamilton Contingent), §16.1 (military loyalty to Constitution), §16.2 (Armed Forces obligations on No Confidence passage), §16.3 (civilian control structure), §16.5 (servicemember interference penalty — 25 years insurrection), §16.6 (no command for removed officials), §17C (state-level prosecution panels).

◆ ◆ ◆

Structural and Design Objections "The Authority itself could be captured." This is the deepest objection. A new institution introduced to oversee accountability could itself become the next vehicle for capture. The Amendment takes this seriously.

The structural defenses were covered in the Second Reading: three independent bodies, lottery-selected citizens, mandatory financial-interest disclosure, public real-time publication of every action on the Franklin Ledger (§4A), the Watchdog Tribunal of one hundred lottery citizens watching the watchers (§21), the Hamilton Contingent prosecuting interference (§13C). The technical defenses include cryptographic vote integrity, distributed blockchain records (§4), multiple geographically separated mirror sites for the public ledger (§4A), and pre-certified university backup infrastructure (§17.16). Section 21 establishes the Watchdog Tribunal as a permanent independent body whose sole function is to monitor, audit, and safeguard the three bodies of the Authority against corruption, collusion, capture, or dereliction. Section 21.7's two-thirds supermajority threshold for adverse findings is paired with §21.7.1's explicit anti-blocking-minority provisions: where a captured minority of Tribunal members blocks adverse findings, minority Findings and Public Records procedures permit publication of dissent. What the Amendment does not promise is invulnerability. Coordinated capture of multiple independent oversight institutions, simultaneously, by parties powerful enough to suppress all of the safeguards, is not a scenario any constitutional document can survive. If two of three Authority bodies are simultaneously captured, the Watchdog Tribunal is captured, and the Hamilton Contingent is captured, the country has bigger problems than the Amendment, and the Amendment is honest about this. What the Amendment does promise is that capture has to be coordinated, simultaneous, and complete to succeed. Single-point failure does not exist. The cost of breaking the system is high enough that defending it should usually be cheaper than defeating it. That is the calculation the framework rests on. It is not a guarantee. It is the best available bet. The §21.7 remedy, in detail. When the Watchdog Tribunal finds corruption, collusion, capture, or material dereliction by an Authority body member or members, the Tribunal acts by two-thirds supermajority (sixty-seven of one hundred members under §21.7), and may exercise three distinct powers in combination or alone. First, Forced Replacement under §21.7(a): the corrupt member or members are removed from their Authority body, and replacement is triggered immediately by fresh lottery from the appropriate selection pool — registered voters for the Citizens' Oversight Board, state chief election officers for the State Elections Council, Pre-Certified Pool universities for the Academic Integrity Commission. The replacement pool is the same pool that produced the original members, run again. Second, Criminal Referral under §21.7(b): the matter is referred to federal criminal prosecution under §13 and §17.25, with the Tribunal's evidentiary findings serving as prima facie basis for charges. Third, where capture is systemic — affecting a majority of a body rather than individuals — Body Dissolution and Reconstitution under §21.7(c): the affected body is dissolved and fully reconstituted by fresh lottery within thirty days, with oversight functions temporarily performed during the dissolution period by the State-Level Backstop under §21.12. All Tribunal proceedings, investigations, and findings are published on the Franklin Ledger in real time under §21.8. The remedy is not a debate, a hearing, or an appeal process — it is a predetermined sequence triggered by supermajority finding, designed to be fast precisely because a captured body left in place can do irreversible damage during the time it takes to litigate. The constitutional theory underlying §21.7. A reader familiar with Article III may ask: what authority do lottery-drawn citizens (the Watchdog Tribunal) have to remove other citizens (Authority members) from constitutional office, without a federal court? The answer is that the Amendment, once ratified, creates that authority as a matter of constitutional text. Article V's amendment power permits the People to establish whatever institutional architecture they ratify, including non-judicial accountability mechanisms operating under defined evidentiary standards. The Amendment does not claim that lottery citizens are exercising "judicial power" within Article III's meaning; it claims that the Watchdog Tribunal exercises a constitutionally distinct removal power — the People's structural power to reconstitute their own accountability institutions when those institutions fail. This is not without precedent: impeachment is also a non-Article-III removal mechanism with its own evidentiary standards. The Watchdog Tribunal is impeachment for the Authority — randomized, transparent, and bound by §21.7's supermajority and §21.7.1's anti-blocking-minority safeguards. The constitutional theory is that the People retain the structural power to reconstitute their own oversight institutions, and the Amendment specifies how. The citizen-initiated remedy. The reconstitution procedure assumes an uncaptured Tribunal. The Amendment also provides for the case where it cannot. If the Tribunal is itself captured — or the apparatus has compromised together, three Authority bodies and one hundred Tribunal members bent in the same direction — the §21 procedure is structurally unavailable. The body responsible for finding capture is part of what is captured. There is no internal correction. For exactly this case the Amendment provides §17B — Authority Restoration — Sovereign Reset When All Else Fails. It is the citizen-initiated constitutional mechanism by which the People simultaneously remove and replace the entire oversight apparatus — all three Authority bodies and the Watchdog Tribunal together, five hundred six members in a single sovereign act (§17B.2). It is not an internal correction. It is the same instrument as the No Confidence Referendum the Amendment provides against the federal government, turned inward on the Amendment's own institutions. The thresholds are the No Confidence thresholds. Section 17B.3 requires what §3 and §5 require: a petition by fifteen percent of registered voters nationally, with fifteen percent in at least thirty of fifty-six Participating Jurisdictions (§17B.3(a)), followed by a national Referendum requiring sixty percent affirmative vote at fifty percent minimum turnout (§17B.3(b)). The thresholds track §5.2 on purpose. Removing the People's accountability apparatus is at least as grave as removing the federal government, and the Amendment treats it that way. A petition that succeeds without coastal states does not succeed. A petition that succeeds without rural states does not succeed. The replacement is pre-staged. Five hundred six members removed at once is not a logistical fantasy. The Amendment specifies separate replacement mechanisms for each of the four bodies under §17B.6, each drawing from a source that the capture scenario cannot simultaneously corrupt. The Citizens' Oversight Board's three hundred new members are drawn by randomized lottery from the registered voter rolls under the §17.2 procedures — the same pool that produced the original members, run again. The State Elections Council's fifty-six new members succeed automatically by ex officio operation: whoever holds the chief election officer position in each Participating Jurisdiction on Day 7 takes the seat under §17.9. The Academic Integrity Commission's fifty new representatives are drawn by lottery from the Pre-Certified University Pool under §17.16, with the Washington Commission empowered to exclude any institution complicit in the capture scenario by clear and convincing evidence. The Watchdog Tribunal's one hundred new members are drawn through the accelerated §21.3 process, with the Washington Commission supervising a draw from the Pre-Certified Personnel Roster under §17A.5 — or, where the Roster itself has been compromised, the Alternate Roster under §17A.19.26. All five hundred six new members take the constitutional oath simultaneously at 12:00:01 Eastern Time on Day 7 (§17B.6(e)), at which moment the outgoing members' authority terminates and the new Authority assumes it. This is not improvisation. It is the second seating of an institution the Amendment knew might need a second seating. The five-year protection period, explained. Section 17B.3.1 provides that citizens may initiate a Restoration petition only after the Authority and Watchdog Tribunal have been fully operational for at least five years. A reader will reasonably ask whether this is self-insulation. It is not. The bodies need time to demonstrate how they function, to complete initial audit cycles under §17A.19, to prove that the ordinary accountability mechanisms work before the most drastic remedy is reached for. Without the protection period, opponents of the Amendment could weaponize the Restoration mechanism to dismantle the oversight apparatus before it ever produced its first finding. The protection period prevents that. And the protection period is not absolute. Section 17B.3.3 enumerates emergency triggering events that waive it — criminal indictment of senior Authority leadership (§17B.3.3.1), Franklin Ledger compromise lasting seven or more consecutive days (§17B.3.3.2), capture-pattern triggers (§17B.3.3.3), foreign and adversarial triggers (§17B.3.3.4), and others. These are events so plainly serious that their occurrence is itself the emergency. No captured body's approval is required for citizens to act on them. The five years are when the bodies must work without facing the absolute remedy. The triggers are when ordinary patience runs out. Intermediate remedies: §21.10 and §17.22.1. Between single-body Tribunal-led reconstitution and whole-apparatus Restoration sits a category of cases the Amendment also addresses. Section 21.10 establishes the Citizen Emergency Override: recognizing that even the Tribunal itself may be corrupted, citizens may directly petition for Tribunal-level action when the Tribunal will not act on its own. Section 17.22.1's Single-Body Compromise Declaration permits any one Authority body to publish a Declaration when one or more of the others have been compromised — triggering an Expedited Compromise Referendum under §17.22.4 in which the People vote directly on whether to remove the named body, the declaring body, both, or neither. The remedies are tiered. The Tribunal-led reconstitution handles single-body capture inside the Tribunal's working assumption. The §17.22 Compromise Declaration handles cases where one or two bodies have failed and the Tribunal has not acted. Section 21.10 handles the case in which the Tribunal itself is unreliable. Section 17B handles the case in which the entire apparatus has failed together. No failure mode of the oversight architecture is left without a remedy in citizen hands. When the Restoration petition itself is obstructed. A captured oversight apparatus has every motive to refuse certification of the petition that would replace it. The Amendment names the predictable forms of this obstruction and answers each. What if the State Elections Council refuses to certify a Restoration petition that has met the §17B.3(a) thresholds? Section 23.13.1's extended mutual-veto safeguard expressly covers Restoration Petition Certification, and §23.13.2 imposes an expedited thirty-day Watchdog Tribunal investigation timeline on any such refusal. The Council that refuses to certify a Restoration petition triggers an investigation that can replace its own members under §21.7. If the Tribunal itself is also captured and refuses to investigate, §21.12.1 provides an emergency panel of fifty Chief Justices of Participating Jurisdictions to perform the certification function in place of the State Elections Council. The captured apparatus cannot indefinitely refuse to certify its own removal. What if a captured Watchdog Tribunal preempts a Restoration by issuing a finding designed to head it off — a Capture Finding aimed at the wrong target, or a clean-bill-of-health finding intended to make the emergency-trigger category unavailable? Section 17B.3.3.3's capture-pattern trigger covers this. A Tribunal finding made in bad faith is itself evidence of capture, and §17B.3.3.7's "No Institutional Certification Required" provision permits citizens to initiate a

Restoration petition on the basis of the bad-faith finding without waiting for any other body to certify. The captured Tribunal's attempt to head off Restoration becomes, on its own face, the predicate for Restoration. What if a §17B Restoration is in progress at the same time as a federal No Confidence Referendum against the executive and Congress? The two proceed under separate clocks and address separate institutions. Section 17B targets the oversight apparatus established by the Amendment. Section 5 targets the political leadership the Amendment exists to constrain. The mechanisms are not mutually exclusive; in the worst case, the country may well need both. The Amendment does not require the People to choose which apparatus has failed when both have. The constitutional theory for §17B specifically. The Tribunal-led reconstitution rests on the Amendment's authority to create non-Article-III removal mechanisms — impeachment for the Authority, conducted by lottery citizens, bound by §21's evidentiary standards. The constitutional theory for §17B Restoration is cleaner. It does not rely on lottery citizens exercising any novel power. It relies on the People themselves voting. A Restoration Referendum is not an exotic constitutional construct; it is the same instrument as the federal No Confidence Referendum, applied to a different set of officeholders. The Article III, Article V, and pardon-power objections covered earlier in this chapter argue that the Amendment's authority to remove the federal government through direct citizen vote stands. By parallel reasoning, its authority to remove its own oversight apparatus through the same instrument stands. Concession. The §17B Restoration is most vulnerable at the petition stage. Comprehensive capture means the same apparatus citizens seek to replace controls signature verification, terminal certification, and — potentially — state-level participation in the Pre-Certified University Pool. The Amendment provides specific structural answers: §17B.3.3.7's "No Institutional Certification Required" provision permits emergency-triggered petitions to bypass captured certifying bodies; §23.13.1 and §23.13.2 subject any State Elections Council refusal to expedited Tribunal review within thirty days; §21.12.1 provides the Emergency Chief Justices Panel when the Tribunal itself is unavailable; §17.16's Pre-Certified University Pool and §20.10's mobile Reclamation Offices provide non-captured physical infrastructure. These are not nothing. They may not be enough. The Restoration in conditions of comprehensive capture asks more of citizens, in operational terms, than any other mechanism in this Amendment. The framework is the most safeguard the document could construct; whether it suffices in the worst case is the kind of question the worst case is the only honest place to answer. Section references:

§17B (Authority Restoration framework), §17B.3 (Restoration Petition thresholds), §17.2 (Citizens' Oversight Board selection), §17.9 (State Elections Council ex officio composition), §17.16 (Pre-Certified University Pool), §17A.5 (Pre-Certified Personnel Roster), §17A.19.26 (Alternate Roster — AIC Circuit Break), §17.22.1 (Single-Body Compromise), §21.3 (Watchdog Tribunal composition), §21.7 / §21.7.1 (forced replacement standards), §17B.5 (Washington Commission Restoration Expansion), §17B.6 (Reconstitution Procedures, including §17B.6(e) simultaneous oath), §17B.10 (Restoration as Ultimate Structural Failsafe). Edge cases that test the bet. What if Citizens' Oversight Board members are publicly identified by name and address, exposing them to retaliation that pushes random citizens to refuse service? Section 17.5's full benefits package — federally protected employment with no retaliation permitted; full wage replacement at median U.S. household income, cost-of-living adjusted; full housing, travel, dependent care, and medical coverage; federal protection from harassment, intimidation, or surveillance with violations a 10-year federal felony — addresses this. The Hamilton Contingent's Protection Division provides physical security to members and their families during service. What if the lottery selection itself is gamed? The lottery is run under §17.16.3's AIC Selection Lottery Administration framework with cryptographic verification; the algorithm and seed are published in advance; verification is performed by independent researchers. Manipulation would require capture of the Commission AND the verification researchers — and would leave a cryptographic trail that subsequent honest reviewers could detect. The lottery is, in this respect, more verifiable than ordinary administrative processes. What if drawn citizens cannot serve — sick parent, small business, young child, financial hardship beyond what the wage replacement covers? See Objection 11 for the full hardship framework (§17.4.1 through §17.4.13). Briefly: the Amendment includes automatic categorical exemptions, petition-based hardship categories, mid-service hardship procedures, and universal anti-retaliation protection for those who decline. The lottery system is not designed to coerce service from people who genuinely cannot serve; it is designed to ensure that the service is available to anyone who can. What if the Authority's three bodies conspire to expand their own jurisdiction by joint action? The Liberty Bell Initiative's three-body concurrence requirement (§17.22) was designed to prevent unilateral expansion, but it does not by itself prevent collective expansion. The Amendment's response: the Watchdog Tribunal is structurally outside the Authority and has full authority to investigate and remove Authority members for actions outside their constitutional mandate (§21). The §17D Permanent Washington Commission — the watcher of the watchers' watchers — adds yet another layer: seven sitting Chief Justices of Participating Jurisdictions with biennial rotation, overseeing the Hamilton Contingent, the §17C panels, and Authority operations through Oversight Findings published on the Franklin Ledger. The Sunset Review (§18) provides external review every twenty years. Concession. The Amendment cannot rule out the possibility that a long-running, well-resourced institutional apparatus develops some forms of institutional self-interest that a constitutional document cannot fully prevent. What it does is structure the institutions to make such self-interest expensive: rotation, lottery selection, public ledger transparency, mandatory periodic review, no policy authority, narrow prosecutorial scope. These are real constraints. They are not perfect constraints. The Amendment's wager is that the marginal additional risk of an entrenched accountability institution is less than the existing risk of an unaccountable federal government. The country's experience with institutions like the Federal Reserve, the FBI, or the Department of Defense suggests this wager has costs as well as benefits, and the Amendment treats the Sunset Review as the safety valve for if and when the costs come to outweigh the benefits. Section references: §4 (blockchain ledger), §4A (Franklin Ledger), §13 (interference penalties), §13C (Hamilton Contingent), §17.4.1–17.4.13 (lottery hardship framework — see Objection 11), §17.5 (Board member benefits and protections), §17.15 (AIC lottery selection), §17.16 (Pre-Certified University Pool), §17.22 (Liberty Bell Initiative), §17.25 (bribery penalties), §17D (Permanent Washington Commission), §18 (Sunset Review), §21 (Watchdog Tribunal), §21.7 / §21.7.1 (supermajority and anti-blocking-minority provisions), §21.7(a)–(c) (Forced Replacement, Criminal Referral, Body Dissolution and Reconstitution), §21.8 (Tribunal-proceeding publication on the Ledger), §21.12 (State-Level Backstop during dissolution).

◆ ◆ ◆

"The thresholds are wrong — too high, too low, choose one." The Amendment requires 60% of votes cast and 50% turnout to remove a federal government via Referendum (§5.2). The Petition requires 15% of registered voters nationally and 15% within thirty of fifty-six jurisdictions to advance to the Referendum stage (§3.1). Critics argue these are wrong. The argument runs in both directions. Too low. Sixty percent in a polarized environment is reachable by a sufficiently motivated coalition, the critic argues. A 50.1% threshold is obviously a coup, but

60% is uncomfortably close to ordinary majority politics. A persistent 60% supermajority on any salient issue is rare in modern American politics, but not impossible. Why not require two-thirds, the threshold the original Constitution uses for impeachment conviction, treaty ratification, and amendment proposal? Too high. A different critic argues the opposite. Two-thirds is functionally unreachable in any modern electorate; at 67%, the Amendment becomes ornamental. Even sixty percent is so demanding that it could fail to remove governments that the country, by ordinary measures, does not want. Why not 55%, or simple majority, or some combination of plurality plus turnout? Both critics are responding to a real tension. The Amendment's resolution: 60% plus 50% turnout produces, mathematically, something close to the maximum achievable consensus that real elections can produce, while also setting a number high enough that capture by a 50%+1 coalition cannot trigger removal. Section 5.2 is explicit about why: it characterizes 60% as "the supermajority standard of this Amendment — a clean whole-number threshold high enough to require" broad consensus while remaining reachable. The combined requirement is the key. A passionate minority that produces 60% of votes cast in a 25%-turnout election fails. A 60% supermajority of a 75%-turnout election succeeds. The dual threshold filters out two failure modes: low-turnout minoritarian capture, and bare-majority polarization. What remains is the case where the broad country, paying attention, has reached a clear conclusion. Empirical grounding: the 60% / 50% combination corresponds, roughly, to the threshold that distinguishes broadly accepted constitutional changes from contested ones in practice. Brexit (51.9% on 72% turnout) would not have cleared. The Twenty-Sixth Amendment's ratification (overwhelming bipartisan consensus) easily would have. The threshold is calibrated to admit the latter and reject the former. The Petition threshold (15% national + 15% in 30 of 56 jurisdictions, under §3.1) operates on the same logic. Fifteen percent of registered voters is approximately a tenth of the electorate — small enough that genuinely committed minorities can initiate review, large enough that no faction can do so trivially. The geographic distribution requirement prevents single-region or single-party initiation. A petition that succeeds without rural states does not succeed. A petition that succeeds without coastal states does not succeed. Concession. Could the thresholds be different? Of course. The Amendment fixes them at the values it does because they passed every adversarial simulation the drafters ran. Lower thresholds produced too-easy initiation. Higher thresholds produced unreachable conditions. The numbers are the result of testing, not preference. Reasonable people can disagree, and the §18 Sunset Review every twenty years is the structured channel for re-examining whether the chosen values have aged well — §18.10 explicitly permits substantial amendment through Constitutional Review Convention, including threshold adjustment.

Section references: §3.1 (Petition thresholds), §5.2 (Referendum thresholds with stated rationale), §18.1 (twenty-year Sunset Review), §18.10 (scope of Modify option).

◆ ◆ ◆

"Mandatory lottery service is unworkable. Real people can't drop their lives for two years." This is one of the most practical objections, and it is the one the Amendment's drafters spent the most ordinary common sense on. The premise: the Citizens' Oversight Board (§17.5) and Watchdog Tribunal (§21.3) are filled by lottery from the registered voter rolls. A drawn citizen — whoever they are, whatever their life looks like — is asked to serve a multi-year term in a federal civic role. For some citizens, this is welcome; for many, it would be financially, medically, or logistically impossible. A framework that conscripts unwilling or unable participants is not a democratic framework. It is a draft. The Amendment knows this. Section 17.4.1 establishes the Hardship Framework: "mandatory service on the Citizens' Oversight Board affects registered voters drawn from every walk of American life, and... a legitimate amendment cannot force service upon persons whose circumstances make service genuinely impossible or hazardous." What follows is a multi-layered exemption-and-accommodation system designed to ensure that the lottery selects from people who can actually serve, and that those who cannot are not penalized. Automatic categorical exemptions (§17.4.2). The following are exempt from service upon documented confirmation, without requiring a hardship petition or any adversarial review: medical incapacity (defined functionally, not as a list of diagnoses); active military deployment; sole caregiver status for a dependent who cannot be reasonably substituted; current law enforcement, fire, or emergency medical service in active rotation; recent prior Amendment service (10-year cooldown across all bodies); and conditions making service hazardous to the citizen's life or health. A drawn citizen falling into any of these categories submits documentation. They are excused. There is no review hearing, no adversarial process, no presumption against the citizen. The category is documented; the exemption applies. Petition-based hardship categories (§17.4.5). In addition to automatic exemptions, a drawn citizen may petition for excuse based on: financial hardship beyond §17.5's median-household-income wage replacement (e.g., self-employed citizens whose business cannot continue without their personal involvement); serious medical condition not rising to incapacity but where service would materially worsen the condition; family caregiving obligations (children, aging parents, dependents with special needs); educational obligations (graduate students at dissertation stage; medical residents in critical training periods); religious observance conflicts; and other documented circumstances. These petitions are reviewed by the administering body; the §17.4.5(c) Financial Hardship provision specifically addresses cases where the wage replacement, although substantial, is materially insufficient for the citizen's actual circumstances. Mid-service hardship (§17.4.9). A citizen who has commenced service but subsequently develops hardship — new medical diagnosis, new caregiver obligation, sudden financial crisis — may petition for mid-service exit. The framework expressly contemplates that life events occur during service and provides for orderly transition. Section 17.4.9(g) provides for a five-year cooling-off period before re-entry into the lottery pool, and §17.4.9(h) addresses bad-faith mid-service claims to prevent abuse. Universal right of immediate decline (§17.4.13(f)). For short-duration roles — case-specific panels, ad-hoc lottery-drawn observers, day-of duties — any drawn person retains the right to decline at the moment of call, simply by stating that personal circumstances prevent service. No documentation. No petition. No hearing. The shorter the role, the lower the bar to decline. Universal anti-retaliation protection (§17.4.13(h)). No drawn person shall face retaliation, adverse treatment, professional consequence, or social consequence for declining service in good faith under any provision of §17.4. Retaliation shall itself constitute a §13 interference offense. An employer who fires a citizen for declining lottery service commits a federal felony. A landlord who refuses to renew a lease commits a federal civil rights violation. A neighbor who harasses a citizen for declining service has no lawful basis to do so and faces consequences if their actions rise to interference under §13. Re-entry framework (§17.4.10). A citizen excused for hardship is not banned from future service. Section 17.4.10(e) is explicit: "This Section does not create a lifetime ban from service. A citizen excused for hardship retains the right to serve if circumstances change and the citizen is drawn in a future lottery after the cooling-off period." The framework respects that life changes. Today's caregiver may be tomorrow's empty-nester. Today's resident is next year's attending. The hardship framework excuses the moment, not the person. Application across all lottery roles (§17.4.12, §17.4.13). The framework applies to: the Watchdog Tribunal citizen members (§21.3(a)); the Hamilton Contingent Citizen Oversight Members (§13C.9); the Academic Integrity Commission individual selection (§17.15); the Constitutional Transition Committee delegates (§6, with §6.23 specifically applying the §17.4 framework); the Caretaker Council (§6A — though with the special feature that Caretaker members are sitting Governors ex officio, not lottery-drawn); and ad-hoc panels (§17.4.13). Every lottery-touched role in the Amendment runs through the same hardship framework. Initial arrangement period (§19.14(a)–(d)). Even citizens who can serve and accept service are not asked to drop everything overnight. Selected citizens receive

a thirty-day arrangement window with a state-based arrangement stipend, and a seven-day no-fault refund window during which a citizen may, after orientation, decline without penalty. The window exists because some citizens accept service in principle and discover, upon orientation, that the role is not what they understood. Section 19.14 provides space for that revelation without forcing the citizen to either complete a service they cannot perform or face the consequences of mid-stream withdrawal. Edge cases. What about a self-employed citizen whose small business cannot continue without their personal involvement? Section 17.4.5(c)'s Financial Hardship category specifically addresses this. The §17.5 median-household-income wage replacement is designed for ordinary employed citizens; for self-employed citizens, the wage replacement may be materially insufficient because business income is not equivalent to wage income. The administering body considers the actual financial circumstances, not a formula. What about a citizen with chronic illness who is functional but for whom multi-year service would meaningfully harm their health? Section 17.4.5(b)'s Serious Medical Condition category. Documentation from treating physicians; review by the administering body; exemption granted where the medical evidence supports it. What about a citizen with sole caregiving responsibility for a child or elderly parent? Section 17.4.2(c)'s automatic exemption for sole caregiver status, no adversarial review. The category exists precisely because no constitutional service should require a citizen to abandon a dependent. What about a citizen who is willing to serve but whose employer threatens retaliation? Section 17.4.13(h)'s anti-retaliation provision plus §13 prosecution of the employer. The employer's threat is itself an interference offense under §13, with the Senior Official Multiplier (§13A.3) applying if the employer is an officeholder of any kind. What about a citizen whose religious practice is incompatible with the role's requirements? Section 17.4.5(d)'s religious observance category provides an exemption pathway. The exemption is documented and granted where the religious obligation is genuinely incompatible with service. Concession. No exemption framework can perfectly anticipate every life circumstance. There will be hard cases — citizens whose situation falls between categories, who are functionally unable to serve but lack documentation, who are willing but uncertain. Section 17.4.5's catch-all provision and the administering body's good-faith review address most of these. Where the framework fails an individual, the failure is appealable through the Watchdog Tribunal under §17.4.11, with the appellate body considering whether the administering body's denial was supported by substantial evidence. The framework does not promise that no citizen will ever face a difficult choice between service and life. It promises that the framework was designed by people who took the question seriously, and that the answer is documented in the Amendment text. Why the framework matters. The legitimacy of the Citizens' Oversight Board, the Watchdog Tribunal, and every other lottery-drawn body depends on the body actually being composed of representative citizens — not just the citizens whose circumstances permit service while everyone else is silently excluded. A lottery system without robust hardship accommodation is a lottery in name only; in practice, it draws from a self-selected subset of citizens whose lives happen to permit multi-year federal service. That subset is, by definition, not representative. The hardship framework is what makes the lottery actually a lottery. Section references: §13 (interference penalties), §13A.3 (Senior Official Multiplier), §17.4.1 (Hardship Framework foundational principle), §17.4.2 (automatic categorical exemptions), §17.4.5 (petition-based hardship categories), §17.4.9 (mid-service hardship), §17.4.10 (post-hardship re-entry), §17.4.11 (appeals), §17.4.12 (application across bodies), §17.4.13 (case-specific and ad-hoc roles, including universal right of immediate decline and anti-retaliation), §17.5 (wage replacement and benefits), §19.14 (initial arrangement window).

◆ ◆ ◆

"This creates a permanent fifth branch of government that will accrue power over time, becoming the very thing it was meant to prevent." This is the institutional-Frankenstein objection. The Amendment creates a substantial new apparatus: the Authority's three bodies, the Watchdog Tribunal, the Hamilton Contingent, the Franklin Ledger, the Sovereign Voting Terminals, the

Pre-Certified Universities, the Phase One Washington Commission, the Permanent Washington Commission, and various subsidiary structures. Together, these institutions employ tens of thousands of people, control significant infrastructure, and operate under partial constitutional autonomy. Over time — the critic argues — institutions like this accrue power. They develop institutional interests. They protect themselves from accountability. They become the new center of gravity in the federal system. The Amendment, in this telling, eventually becomes the corruption it was created to address. The objection is taken seriously and the Amendment's response is structural. First: the Authority has no governing power. It does not legislate. It does not adjudicate cases between private parties. It does not control armies, allocate budgets beyond its own operational needs, or set policy. Its powers are administrative — verification, certification, prosecution of interference. There is, in the strongest sense, nothing for the Authority to govern. Its institutional purpose is to enable the People's decisions, not to make decisions on behalf of the People. An institution with no policy power has limited room to expand into general government.

Second: the Authority is composed of rotating citizens, not career officials. The Citizens' Oversight Board's three hundred members are selected by lottery for two-year staggered terms, with one hundred fifty rotating off each year, no consecutive terms, and no more than two total terms in a lifetime (§17.2 through §17.7). The Watchdog Tribunal is similarly lottery-selected with three-year staggered terms and the same lifetime cap (§21.4). The State Elections Council members serve ex officio while in their state roles and rotate when those roles change (§17.10). The Academic Integrity Commission rotates on staggered one-year terms with a two-term lifetime cap (§17.17). There is, deliberately, no permanent class of Authority employees who develop the kind of institutional self-interest that drives expansion in ordinary bureaucracies. Third: the Sunset Review is mandatory and enforceable. Section 18.1 requires that "Every 20 years, the People shall vote to Retain, Modify, or Repeal this Amendment. No generation may bind those that follow." Section 18.18 provides that no act of Congress, executive order, or other federal action shall delay or postpone the Sunset Review Vote. The review can recommend retention, modification (§18.4 — Constitutional Review Convention of 150 delegates), or repeal (§18.5 — orderly two-year wind-down). The review body is structurally separate from the Authority and the Hamilton Contingent. It cannot be skipped. The Amendment is, by design, on probation forever. Fourth: the Franklin Ledger ensures any expansion is visible. Section 4A establishes the public transparency infrastructure. Every action the Authority takes is published. Every dollar it spends is published (§17A authority administration). Every member's financial disclosures are published. Mission creep — were it to occur — would happen on a public ledger that any citizen, journalist, or scholar could read. Expansion of institutional power through quiet accretion, the historical mechanism for institutional self-aggrandizement, is structurally difficult when the institution must publish its own operational record in real time. Edge cases. What if the Hamilton Contingent's prosecutorial discretion is used not against §13 violators but against political enemies of the Authority itself? Section 13C's jurisdictional scope limits Hamilton Contingent prosecutorial authority to specific Amendment-related categories. Prosecutions outside the Amendment's defined offense categories trigger Watchdog Tribunal review (§21) and, if found to be pretextual, §13 prosecution of the Contingent prosecutor. What if the Authority's three bodies conspire to expand their own jurisdiction by joint action? The Liberty Bell Initiative's three-body concurrence requirement was designed to prevent unilateral expansion, but it does not by itself prevent collective expansion. The Amendment's response: the Watchdog Tribunal is structurally outside the Authority (§21) and has full authority to investigate and remove Authority members for actions outside their constitutional mandate. The §17D Permanent Washington Commission provides yet another oversight layer with limited subpoena authority over Covered Accountability Bodies. The Sunset

Review additionally provides external review. Concession. The Amendment cannot rule out the possibility that a long-running, well-resourced institutional apparatus develops some forms of institutional self-interest that a constitutional document cannot fully prevent. What it does is structure the institutions to make such self-interest expensive: rotation, lottery selection, public ledger transparency, mandatory periodic review, no policy authority, narrow prosecutorial scope. These are real constraints. They are not perfect constraints. The Amendment's wager is that the marginal additional risk of an entrenched accountability institution is less than the existing risk of an unaccountable federal government. The Sunset Review is the safety valve. Section references: §4A (Franklin Ledger), §13 (interference penalties), §13C (Hamilton Contingent jurisdictional scope), §17.2–17.7 (Citizens' Oversight Board structure), §17.10 (State Elections Council), §17.17 (Academic Integrity Commission terms), §17A (Authority administration), §17D (Permanent Washington Commission), §18.1 (twenty-year Sunset Review), §18.4 (Modify pathway), §18.5 (Repeal wind-down), §18.18 (no delay of Sunset Review), §21

(Watchdog Tribunal), §21.4 (Tribunal terms).

◆ ◆ ◆

"Implementation costs are unrealistic. Congress will simply refuse to fund it."

The Amendment requires substantial physical and digital infrastructure: Citizens' Reclamation Offices in every congressional district, Sovereign Voting Terminals at hardware-security standards, the Franklin Ledger's seven-mirror redundancy, the Hamilton Contingent's national prosecutorial capacity, the Pre-Certified University Pool's vetting and maintenance. Conservative cost estimates run to the tens of billions of dollars over the initial implementation period and several billion annually thereafter. Critics argue Congress, particularly a Congress hostile to the Amendment's purposes, will simply refuse to appropriate the funds, rendering the framework dead on arrival. The Amendment's response is in §13I and §13C.20. Section 13I establishes the Ratification Loan and Repayment Framework. At the moment of Ratification, the Treasury has automatic constitutional authority to issue the Ratification Loan to fund Amendment build-out (§13I.2). The initial loan ceiling is one hundred billion dollars, indexed for inflation from Ratification (§13I.3). Loan funds are restricted to Amendment-related purposes (§13I.4) and prohibited from other uses (§13I.5). The Treasury administers the loan under specified requirements (§13I.6). This is bootstrap funding — it doesn't require

Congressional appropriation because the constitutional amendment itself authorizes Treasury issuance. Section 13C.20 establishes ongoing Hamilton Contingent funding. Annual funding is approximately two billion dollars, adjusted for inflation, "appropriated as a constitutional mandate not subject to ordinary congressional discretion." Funding is distributed across the four divisions (Prosecution, Protection, Public Response, Preservation) by the Director with Authority concurrence. Section 13D provides asset recovery infrastructure. Post-No-Confidence asset recovery from corruption proceeds returns funds to the Authority's operational budget on a progressive schedule. Recovered corruption proceeds, distributed in part back to the People who were harmed, partially offset Amendment operational costs over time. What if Congress refuses to honor the constitutional appropriation? Refusal to disburse Amendment funding is itself a §13 interference offense. The Hamilton Contingent has authority to prosecute (or, during Phase One before the Hamilton Contingent is operational, the State Attorneys General Council under

§19.5.0.5.2). The combination — constitutional mandate plus criminal enforcement of refusal — is intended to make withholding of funds an active criminal act rather than a passive political choice. Edge cases. What if the Treasury refuses to disburse appropriated funds — for example, if a hostile Treasury Secretary slow-walks payments? Section 13I's Treasury administration provisions (§13I.6) and surrounding obstruction-treatment subsections specify that personal liability attaches to officeholders who direct, authorize, or materially participate in obstruction of Treasury disbursement. The mechanism prevents disbursement-level obstruction without needing to wait for prosecution to complete. What if vendors refuse to contract with the Authority because of political pressure from the executive branch? Section 17A's procurement framework (the Pre-Certified Personnel Roster under §17A.5 and related provisions) anticipates capture-of-procurement attempts and provides anti-blacklisting protections. Concession. Funding mechanisms with constitutional protection have, historically, produced predictable but contestable disputes about whether the protection covers any given line item. The Amendment's funding-related provisions will be litigated. Some line items will be cut. Some will be challenged at the §17C panel level. The framework's net funding will likely be somewhat less than its drafters projected, particularly in periods of hostile-executive-and-Congress alignment. Whether the diminished funding is sufficient to keep the apparatus operational is, in the end, an empirical question whose answer depends on how the litigation goes. The Amendment provides the strongest funding protection a constitutional document can provide; it does not guarantee that the protection will not be eroded around the edges.

Section references: §13 (interference penalties for funding obstruction), §13C.20 (Hamilton Contingent funding mandate), §13D (asset recovery), §13I.2 (Treasury automatic authority), §13I.3 (Ratification Loan ceiling), §13I.4 (uses), §13I.5 (prohibited uses), §13I.6 (Treasury administration), §17A.5 (Pre-Certified Personnel Roster), §17C (state-level prosecution panels), §19.5.0.5.2 (Phase One State AG Council prosecution authority).

◆ ◆ ◆

Those are the objections. There are more, of course. There are always more. The Amendment includes a periodic review process — the §18 Sunset Review, every twenty years — specifically because the drafters did not assume they had thought of everything. The Sunset Review allows the Amendment to be modified, retained, or repealed by the same supermajority structure that governs its operation. The framework is not frozen. It is meant to be revisited as the country and its threats evolve. The Third Reading does not pretend to have settled every dispute it raises. Several of the objections — the Article III strip, the Appointments Clause challenge to §17C, the Article II pardon-power conflict — are matters of constitutional first impression. They will be litigated. The Amendment's response, in each case, is that ratification under Article V produces a constitutional change of the same legal stature as the original Article. Where the new and the old conflict, the new controls. That is how the Constitution is supposed to work, and the Amendment relies on it working that way. What the Amendment does claim, with a clear conscience, is that it has thought about the problems. The objections in this chapter are not surprises. They were considered during drafting. The provisions cited in response to each objection were written precisely because the objection was anticipated. The Amendment is built to survive its strongest critics, and it invites them. If you are a critic, your continued scrutiny is not opposition to the Amendment. It is part of how the Amendment works. The framework was designed to invite hard examination. The drafters expected it. They wrote it that way on purpose. If you have read this far and still have an objection — write it down. Send it. Name the section. Cite the provision. Make the argument. The Amendment was assembled by people sincerely trying to get this right, and improvement is welcomed. The Sunset Review is twenty years away from each ratification, but the public ledger updates daily, and a real argument from a serious critic is exactly what the framework was built to absorb and learn from. If you have read this far and you find that the framework holds — not perfectly, not without exposure, but holds well enough that the country is better off with it than without it — then you have done what the Third Reading exists for. You have tested it. It survived. That is what an amendment worth ratifying does.

Chapter Six

The Maps

Welcome to the Maps. If you have read the first five chapters, you have seen most of these charts already, scattered through their relevant sections. This chapter brings them together. It also introduces several you have not seen — pieces of the architecture that did not get their own diagram in earlier readings, but that you may want to look at side-by-side with the rest. The chapter is built to be useful as a reference. Open it when you want a single picture of how the Authority works. Open it when you need to remember which §13 tier covers which conduct. Open it when someone asks you, on short notice, what the Franklin Ledger's mirror network looks like, and you would like to point at something rather than describe it. Each chart is presented with a brief orientation. The charts are organized into five sections by topic, not by source chapter, so related diagrams sit together. If you are reading the book front to back and the visual recap feels redundant, skip ahead. The Maps will be here when you need them.

◆ ◆ ◆

The Whole Picture. Two views of the whole thing — the institutional architecture in one diagram, and the §13 penalty structure that backstops every one of the other safeguards.

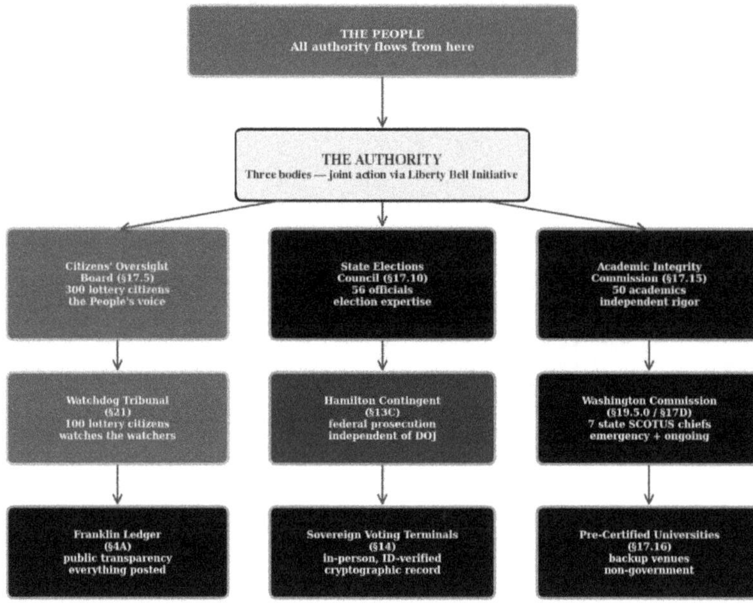

Figure 1 — The Full Institutional Architecture

THE AUTHORITY Three bodies — joint action via Liberty Bell Initiative

The Amendment from People to infrastructure. Power flows downward through layered constitution: People → Authority → oversight institutions → physical and digital systems. Reading chains of command top-to-bottom misreads the diagram.

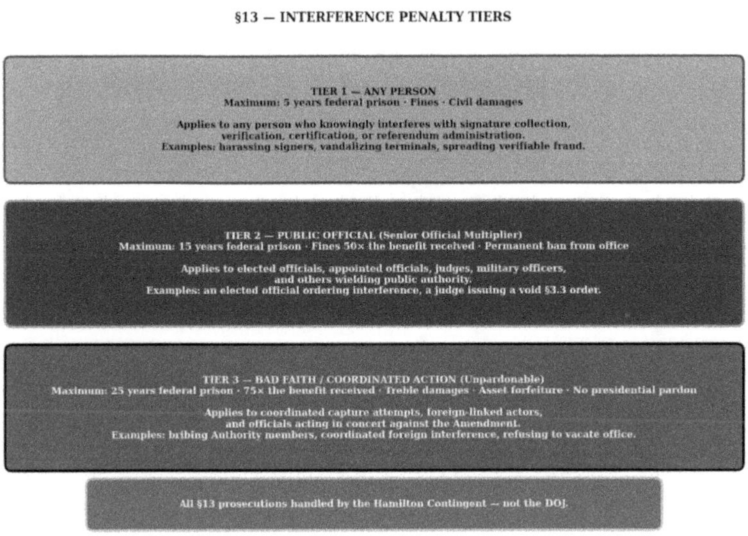

Figure 2 — §13 Penalty Tiers

The §13 three-tier penalty structure. Tier 1 applies to any person; Tier 2 adds a Senior Official multiplier; Tier 3 covers coordinated bad-faith action and is unpardonable. All tiers are prosecuted by the Hamilton Contingent.

◆ ◆ ◆

The Authority. The Authority is the public face of the Amendment, and the institutions that surround it. Four diagrams: the three bodies in detail, the Liberty Bell Initiative concurrence procedure, and the Hamilton Contingent's internal divisions.

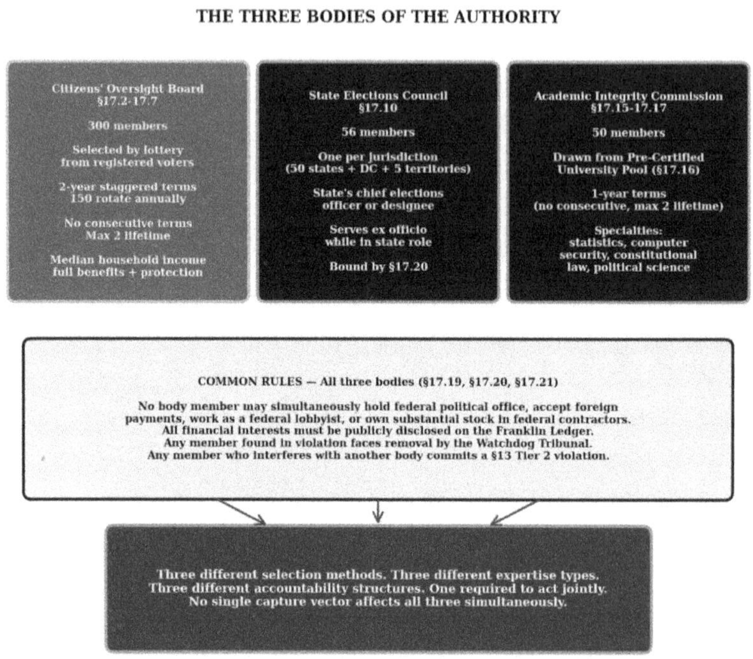

Figure 3 — The Three Bodies in Detail

The Authority's three bodies in detail — composition, selection, terms, and the conflict-of-interest rules that bind all three. The redundancy is the point.

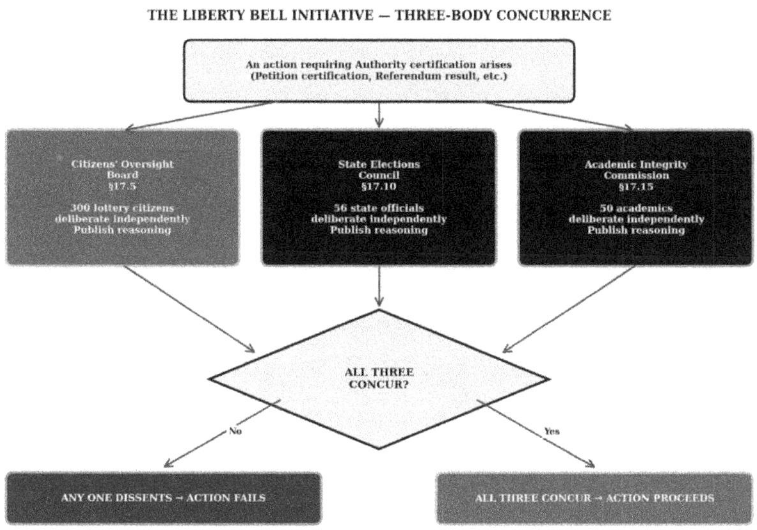

Figure 4 — The Liberty Bell Initiative

How the Liberty Bell Initiative works. Each body deliberates independently. All three must concur for the action to proceed. A single dissent kills it.

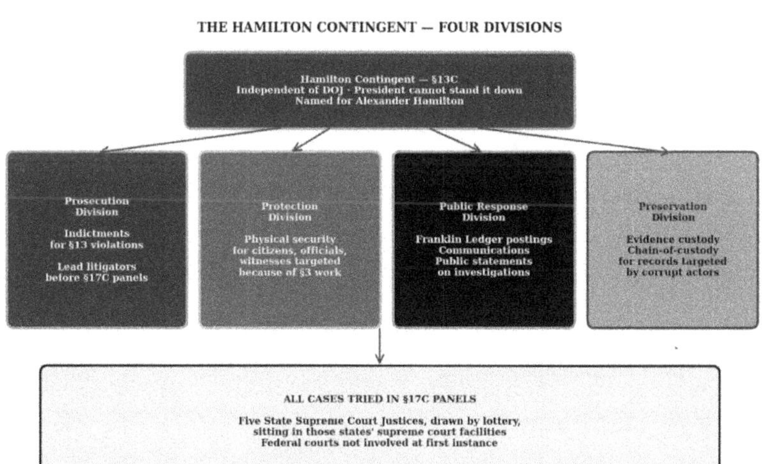

Figure 5 — The Hamilton Contingent — Four Divisions

The Hamilton Contingent's four divisions: Prosecution, Protection, Public Response, and Preservation. The Contingent has its own personnel, budget, and authority — fully independent of the Department of Justice.

◆ ◆ ◆

The Petition and Referendum. How a Petition becomes a Referendum, what happens after a passing vote, and the timeline from Day Zero to normal operation. Four diagrams.

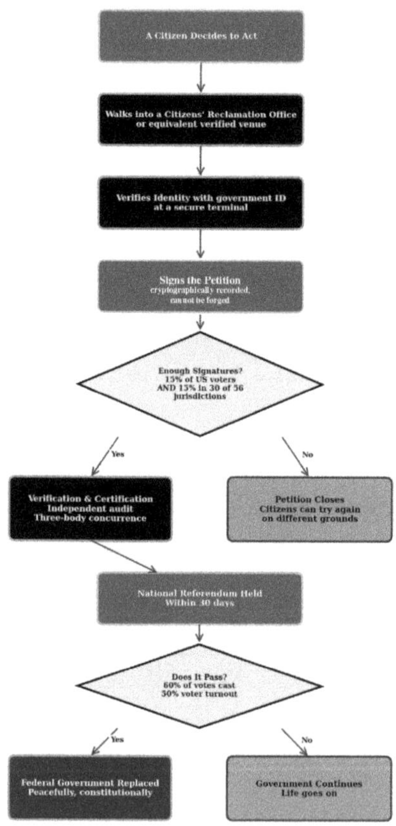

Figure 6 — The Citizen's Journey

The First Reading view of how a citizen actually uses the Amendment. File or sign; verify; vote. In-person, ID-verified, on a secure terminal, every time.

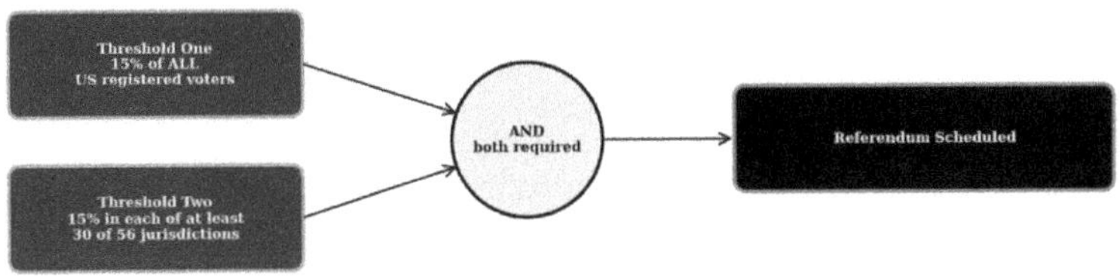

Figure 7 — The Two Thresholds

The two thresholds that must be met for a Petition to advance. Fifteen percent nationally AND fifteen percent in thirty of fifty-six jurisdictions. Both. Required.

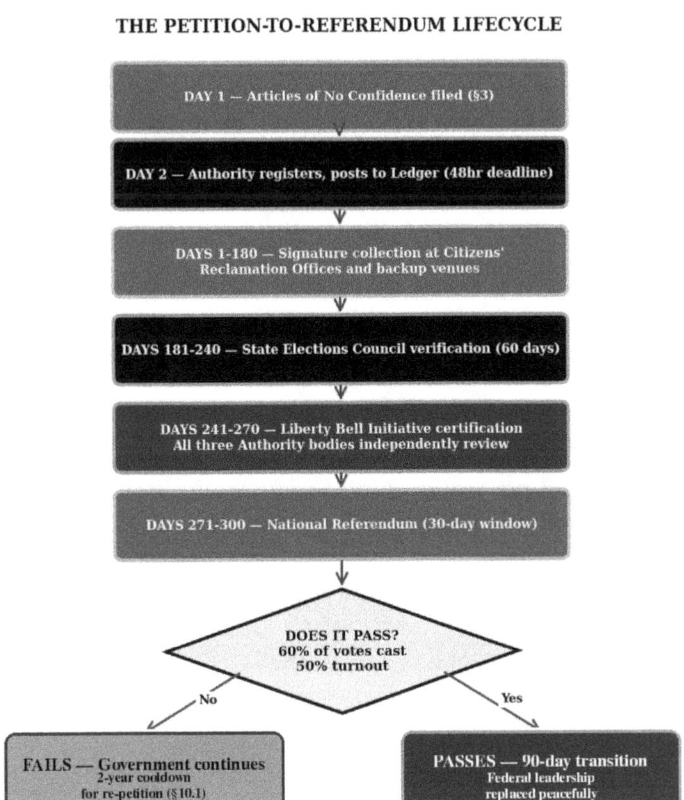

Figure 8 — A Petition's 300-Day Lifecycle

FAILS — Government continues
PASSES — 90-day transition
2-year cooldown for re-petition (§10.1)
Federal leadership replaced peacefully

The 300-day journey from Articles of No Confidence to certified Referendum result. The clock cannot be extended by hostile officials and cannot be shortened by friendly ones.

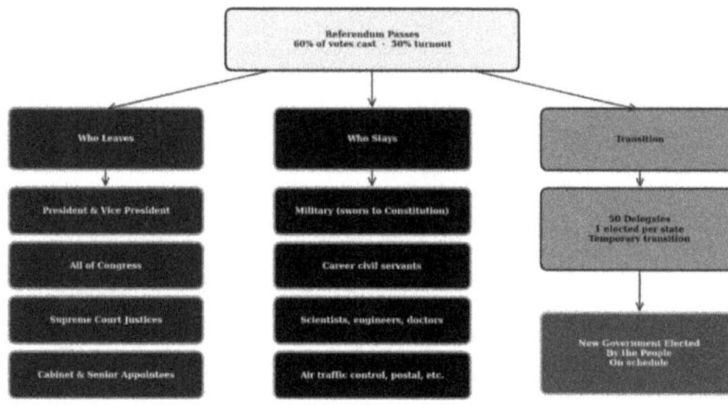

Figure 9 — What Happens When the Vote Passes

What the Referendum result actually does. Removes federal political leadership. Does not remove the military, the civil service, or any career professionals. The country keeps running because they keep running it.

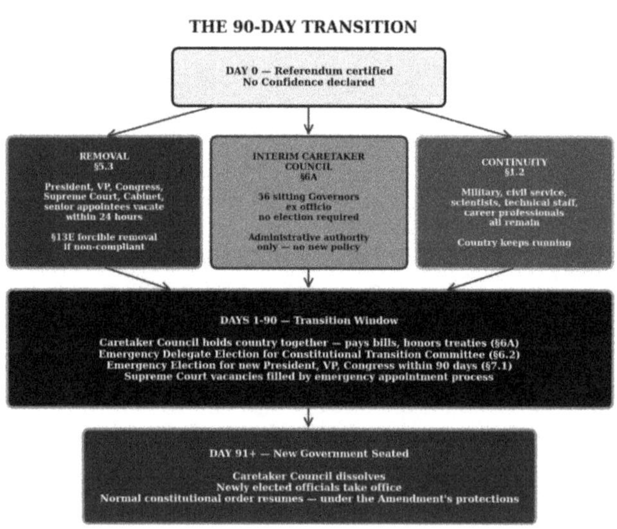

Figure 10 — The 90-Day Transition

What happens in the 90 days after a passing Referendum. Removal, the Interim Caretaker Council, and the continuity of professional government — all happening in parallel from Day Zero.

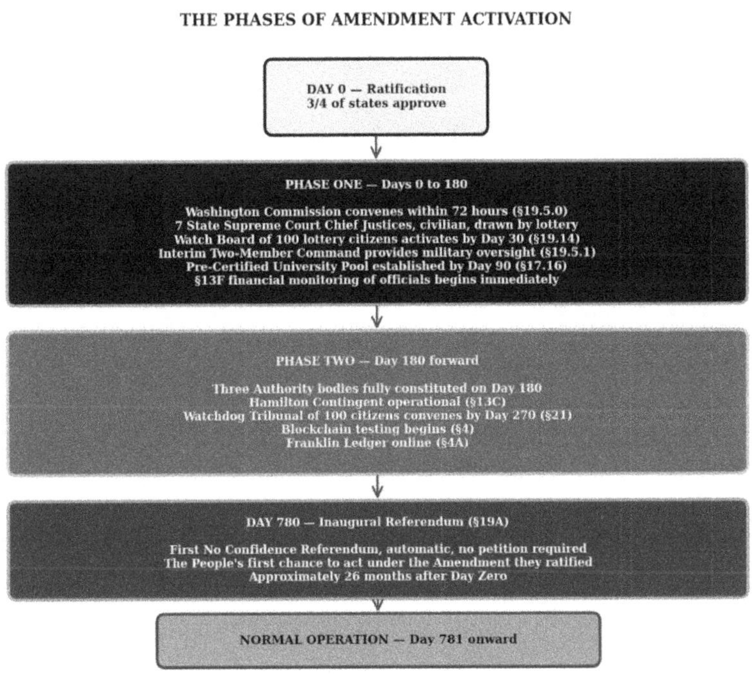

Figure 11 — The Phases of Activation

The Amendment does not snap fully into existence on Day Zero. It activates in phases, with interim institutions bridging the gap until the Authority is fully constituted at Day 180 and the Inaugural Referendum at Day 780.

◆ ◆ ◆

When Things Go Wrong. What the Amendment actually does when something tries to defeat it. Six diagrams: capture of an Authority body, court orders, hostile state governments, foreign interference, the cross-reference defense-in-depth map, and what happens when a removed official refuses to leave.

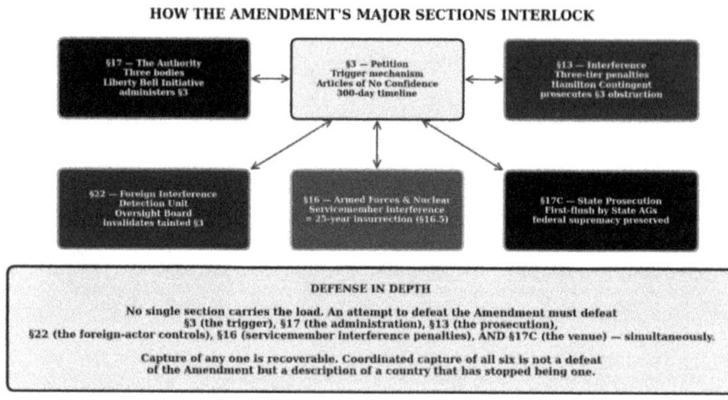

Figure 12 — How the Major Sections Interlock

How the Amendment's major sections interlock. No single section carries the load. An attempt to defeat the framework must defeat §3, §17, §13, §22, §16, AND §17C — simultaneously.

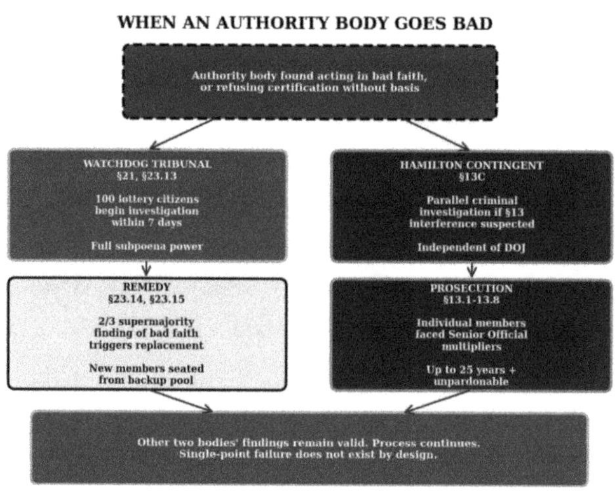

Figure 13 — When an Authority Body Goes Bad

When an Authority body is suspected of capture, the Watchdog Tribunal investigates within seven days, the Hamilton Contingent runs a parallel criminal investigation, and the other two bodies' findings remain valid. Single-point failure does not exist.

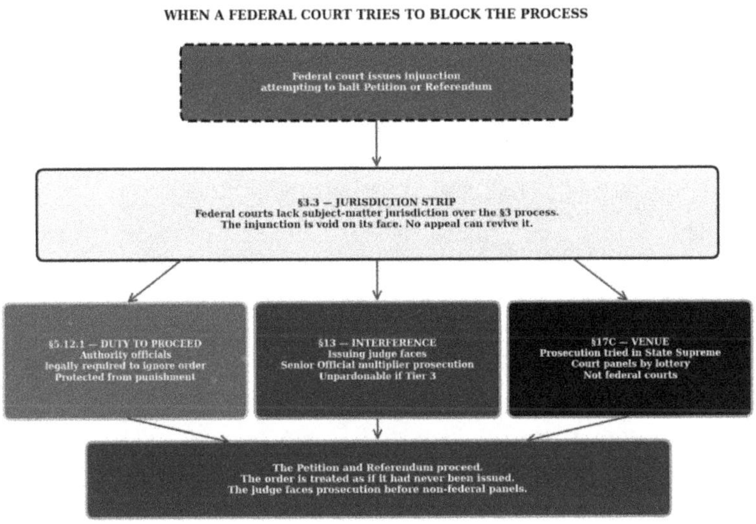

Figure 14 — When a Federal Court Tries to Block the Process

When a federal court issues an order trying to halt the §3 process. Section 3.3 strips jurisdiction; the order is void on its face; officials are required to ignore it; the issuing judge faces prosecution.

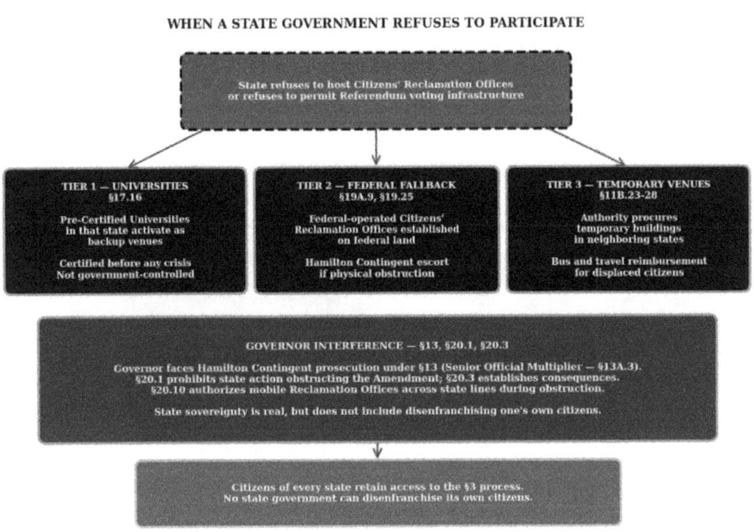

Figure 15 — When a State Government Refuses to Participate

When a state government refuses to host petition signing or referendum voting. Three layered fallbacks: pre-certified universities, federal infrastructure with Hamilton Contingent escort, and temporary venues in neighboring states.

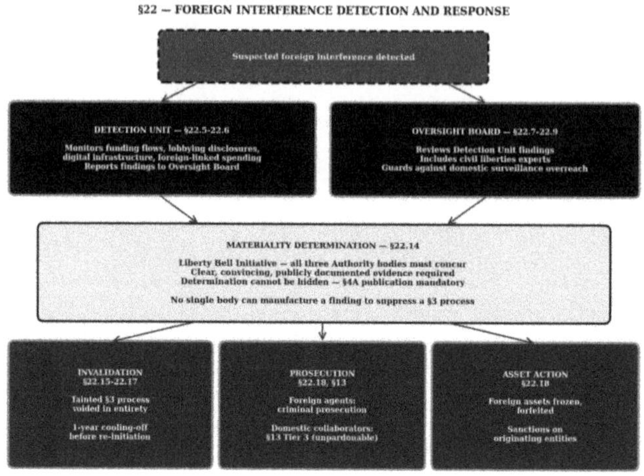

Figure 16 — §22 Foreign Interference Detection and Response

The §22 detection-and-response architecture. A Detection Unit monitors, an Oversight Board reviews, and a Liberty Bell Initiative determination triggers invalidation, prosecution, and asset action.

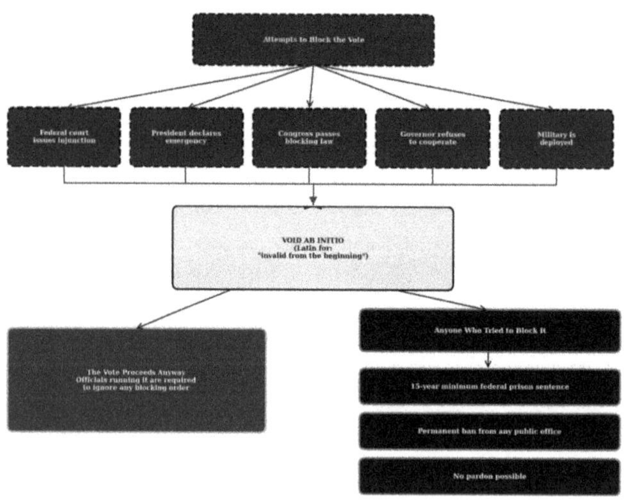

Figure 17 — Protections Against Interference

The First Reading view of what protects the process. Anti-blocking provisions cover every category of interference — courts, officials, foreign actors, and physical obstruction.

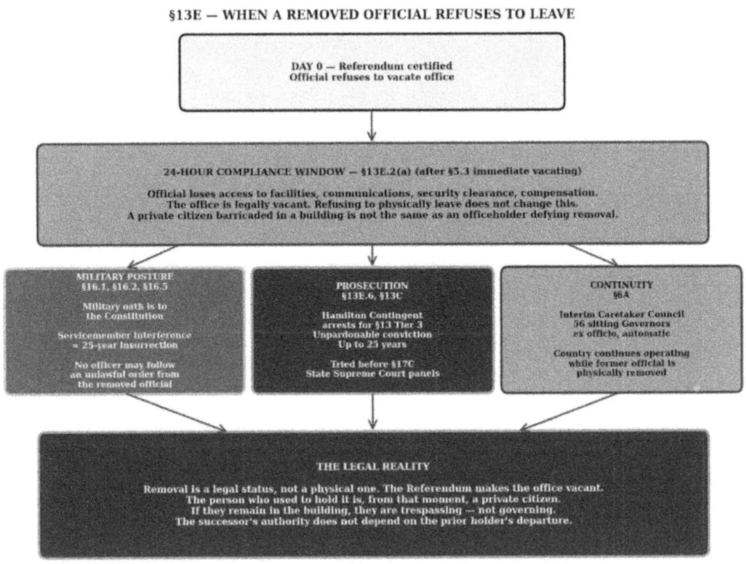

Figure 18 — §13E When a Removed Official Refuses to Leave

What happens when a removed official refuses to vacate. The 24-hour compliance window, the military's posture, the Hamilton Contingent's arrest authority, and the Interim Caretaker Council's immediate seating — all treating removal as a legal status, not a physical contest.

◆ ◆ ◆

The Long Game. How the framework maintains itself over decades. Four diagrams: the every-twenty-year Sunset Review, the Watchdog Tribunal investigation flow, the Franklin Ledger's seven-mirror network, and the Sovereign Voting Terminal architecture.

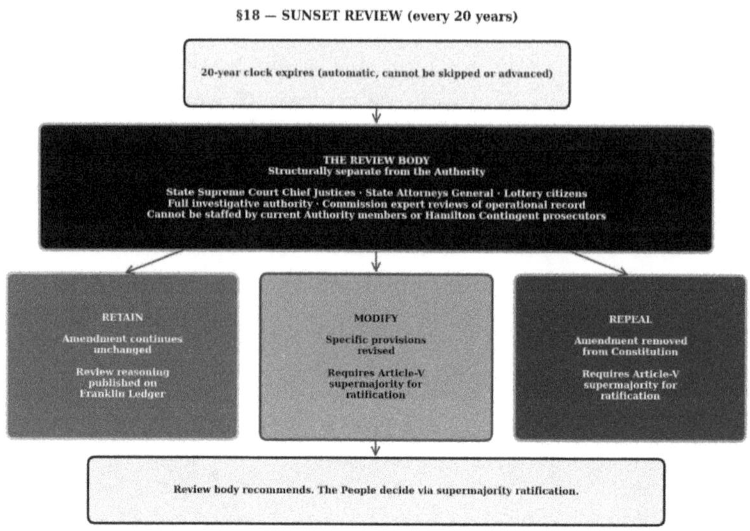

Figure 19 — §18 Sunset Review (Every 20 Years)

Every twenty years, the Amendment reviews itself. A structurally separate review body recommends retain, modify, or repeal — and the People decide via supermajority ratification.

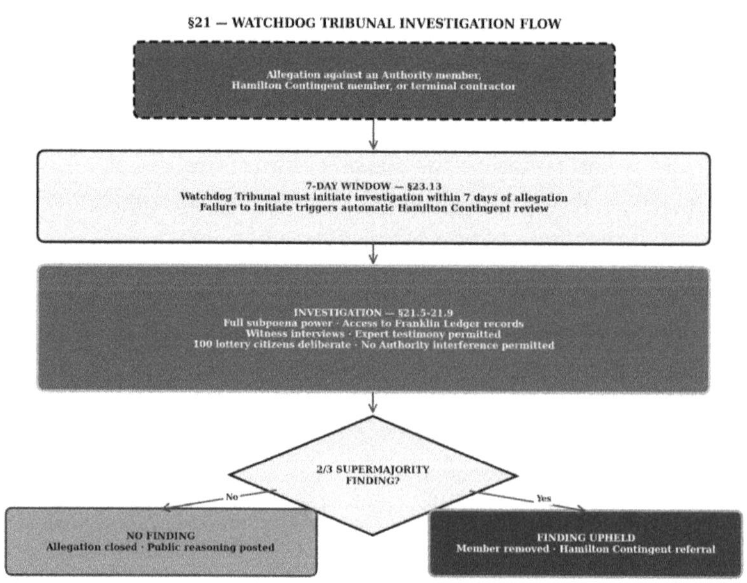

Figure 20 — §21 Watchdog Tribunal Investigation Flow

How an investigation actually unfolds. The Tribunal must initiate within seven days of allegation, has full subpoena authority, and can remove members of any Amendment institution by two-thirds supermajority.

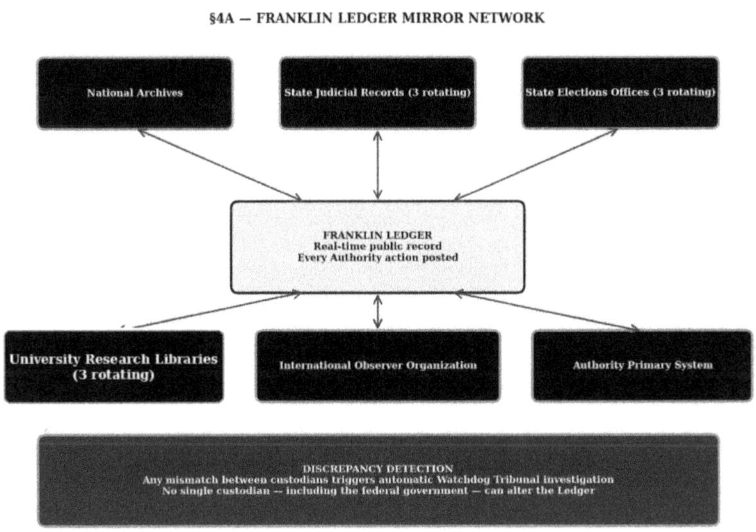

Figure 21 — §4A Franklin Ledger Mirror Network

University Research Libraries (3 rotating)

The Franklin Ledger is duplicated across at least seven independent custodians. No single custodian — including the federal government — can alter it. Discrepancies trigger automatic Watchdog Tribunal investigation.

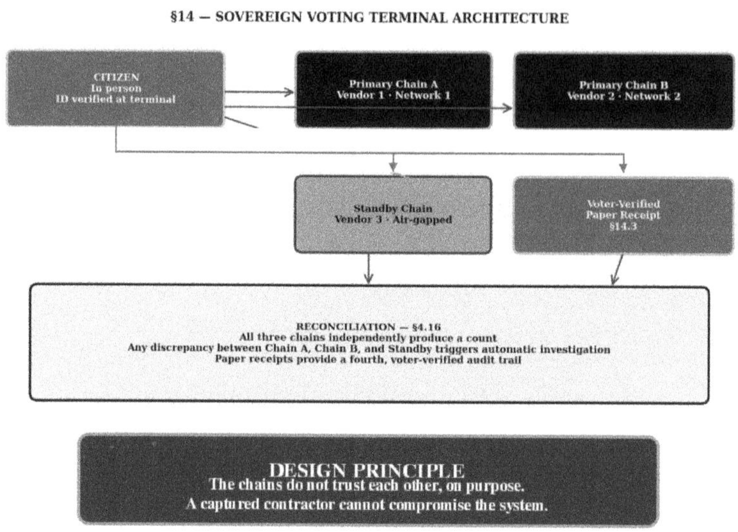

Figure 22 — §14 Sovereign Voting Terminal Architecture

DESIGN PRINCIPLE The chains do not trust each other, on purpose. A captured contractor cannot compromise the system.

The Sovereign Voting Terminal architecture. Two primary chains, one air-gapped standby chain, and a voter-verified paper receipt — four independent records of every interaction. The chains do not trust each other, on purpose.

◆ ◆ ◆

That is the Maps chapter. Twenty diagrams covering the institutions, the timelines, the safeguards, and the recovery procedures. If a friend asks you about the Amendment and you do not feel like explaining the whole thing from memory, this chapter is for them. If you find a diagram useful enough that you want to print it large and pin it to a wall, the Franklin Ledger archive will host high-resolution versions of every chart in this chapter, downloadable, free, no registration required. The maps belong to whoever needs them.

Chapter Seven

The Amendment

What follows is the complete text of the proposed People's Reclamation Amendment to the Constitution of the United States.

The previous six chapters explained what the Amendment does, how it works, what its strongest objections are, and what each of its institutions looks like. This chapter is the document itself. No commentary, no paraphrase, no summary. Just the text. It is long. It is meant to be. The reasons for the length are addressed in the Amendment's own preamble and discussed throughout the earlier chapters. Read what you need. Skip what you do not. Cite what helps. The text is the text.

◆ ◆ ◆

A Proposed

CONSTITUTIONAL AMENDMENT

Of the United States of America

THE PEOPLE'S RECLAMATION AMENDMENT

The People's Reclamation Amendment Act

Drafted by

SHAWN THEIS

Proposed under Article V of the Constitution of the United States of America for the consideration of the several States and the People

PROPOSED AMENDMENT TO THE CONSTITUTION OF THE UNITED STATES

THE PEOPLE'S RECLAMATION AMENDMENT

The People's Reclamation Amendment Act

An Amendment establishing the right of the People of the United States to dissolve a corrupt or tyrannical Federal Government — including its elected officials and the political leadership of the federal bureaucracy — by supermajority vote; to reconstitute it through an Emergency Election and independent review; to protect the daily lives of the People throughout the transition; to restore the sovereign authority of the People over the use of nuclear force; to recover the wealth obtained through corruption and return it progressively to the American People whom it was taken from; subject to review by future generations.

SUMMARY This Amendment establishes the People's constitutional authority to remove a corrupt federal government through peaceful, structured means. It supplements — it does not replace — the existing Constitution, and preserves the essential functions of federal service throughout.

The Core Mechanism Petition. Registered voters gather verified in-person signatures (15% of registered voters nationally AND 15% in each of at least 30 of the 56 Participating Jurisdictions) to trigger a National No Confidence Referendum. Referendum. A 30-day national vote requires 60% affirmative AND 50% turnout of registered voters to pass — a supermajority consensus combined with majority engagement of the registered electorate. Removal. Upon passage, political leadership is removed simultaneously — President, Vice President, Congress, Supreme Court, Cabinet, and senior political appointees. Career civil servants, military personnel, and technical staff remain in place to maintain essential services. Transition. A 50-delegate Constitutional Transition Committee, elected by the states, oversees operations under caretaker authority for approximately 90 days. Emergency Election. Ranked-choice federal elections are held within 90 days to elect new leadership.

Structural Bodies • The Independent Tripartite Oversight Authority — three independent bodies with mutual-veto power: Citizens' Oversight Board, State

Elections Council, and Academic Integrity Commission. • The Watchdog Tribunal — oversees the Authority itself, preventing oversight capture.

• The Hamilton Contingent — independent prosecutor for Amendment enforcement. • The Franklin Ledger — cryptographically secured public record of all Amendment activity. • Sovereign Voting Terminals — in-person, tamper-resistant voting infrastructure in every state.

Key Protections • Career federal personnel are protected from political removal. • Nuclear weapons require multi-body civilian consent AND public supermajority — no single individual can authorize first use. • Military personnel retain the duty and protected right to refuse unlawful orders. • Asset recovery from corruption flows progressively to ordinary Americans harmed. • Voter privacy is cryptographically preserved; coercion and retaliation are prosecutable.

What This Amendment Preserves • The Constitution of the United States and all existing amendments. • Article III federal judiciary in its ordinary constitutional role. • Career civil service and technical expertise in federal agencies. • State sovereignty and state law. • Private-sector rights and institutions. • Future generations' right to revisit this Amendment through Sunset Review every 20 years.

Funding Financed through a federal Ratification Loan and, operationally, through progressive asset recovery from corruption convictions. No state is obligated to contribute funding; federal appropriation covers all Amendment infrastructure.

Implementation Timeline Days 0–180: Build-out of Authority infrastructure and Hamilton Contingent. Days 180–780: Phase One operations under Washington Commission oversight. Day 780: Inaugural Referendum — first opportunity for the People to vote on the sitting federal government under this Amendment.

Day 780 forward: Full Amendment operation with Petition mechanism continuously available. Every 20 years: Sunset Review — voters choose Retain, Modify, or Repeal.

On Length This Amendment's comprehensive specification is a deliberate constitutional choice. The authority it creates — the People's power to remove a corrupt federal government — must be bounded by mechanisms proportionate to its weight. Specific procedures, closed capture pathways, and interpretive rules are necessary to ensure that this authority, once granted, cannot be unwound through ambiguity. Preamble

WHEREAS all governing authority of the United States derives solely and entirely from the consent of the governed; and WHEREAS no institution, office, agency, bureau, department, or instrument of government shall ever be placed above the sovereign will of the People; and WHEREAS the dissolution of a government is the most consequential act a People may undertake, and must therefore require a genuine and broadly distributed supermajority of the citizenry, not merely a narrow majority of those who happen to participate; and WHEREAS the reset of federal institutions must preserve the technical expertise that protects public health, safety, and daily life, while removing the political leadership whose corruption precipitated the reset; and WHEREAS the Armed Forces of the United States owe their ultimate loyalty not to any officeholder, party, or administration, but to the Constitution and to the People of the United States whom they are sworn to defend; and WHEREAS the authority to unleash nuclear weapons must never rest in the hands of any single individual, but shall henceforth require the knowing consent of the People of the United States, save only in circumstances of confirmed imminent attack when no time for deliberation remains; and WHEREAS the construction of the independent institutions established by this Amendment shall itself require protection from interference and corruption from the very day of ratification forward, and shall at no point during that construction — not even in the earliest hours — rest in the hands of military authority alone or in the hands of the very government the Amendment exists to constrain; and WHEREAS no state, however powerful or defiant, shall be permitted to deny its citizens the rights and mechanisms established by this Amendment, and the federal authority to guarantee those rights shall be narrowly tailored, heavily overseen, and never used as a pretext for federal tyranny; and WHEREAS the mere removal of corrupt officials is insufficient unless the wealth obtained through corruption is recovered and returned progressively to the American People who were harmed, with the largest share flowing to those of ordinary means who bear the heaviest cost of corruption; and WHEREAS the exercise of democratic self-government depends upon an informed citizenry, and an informed citizenry depends upon public information that is comprehensive, accurate, verifiable, and accessible to every American regardless of wealth, technology, physical ability, or geography; and WHEREAS evidence of federal corruption must be preserved inviolate from the very hour this Amendment takes force, that no destruction of records, however calculated, may defeat the People's right to know, to hold accountable, and to recover; and WHEREAS the enforcement of this

Amendment shall be vested in constitutional institutions bearing the names and traditions of those founders who established the American commitment to public accountability, public transparency, and public virtue — invoking George Washington's measured stewardship, Alexander Hamilton's

rigorous enforcement, Benjamin Franklin's public accounting, and the Liberty Bell's summons to the consent of the governed; and WHEREAS no branch of government — executive, legislative, or judicial — shall be permitted to entrench itself against democratic renewal through indefinite tenure, inadequate oversight, or accumulated power beyond what the People consented to grant; and WHEREAS the federal judiciary established by Article III of the Constitution remains the fundamental arbiter of federal law and a coequal branch of the constitutional order, whose essential role in the separation of powers this Amendment preserves in full; the specific structural provisions addressing judicial capture scenarios are narrowly tailored defensive protections against identified vulnerabilities, not displacement of ordinary judicial review; and any alternative interpretive or adjudicatory pathway established by this Amendment shall apply only upon documented satisfaction of its specified triggering conditions, preserving Article III authority in all other matters; and WHEREAS the comprehensive specification of procedures, protections, and accountability mechanisms throughout this Amendment reflects a principled constitutional necessity — great power concentrated in federal office attracts great attempts at capture, and only great specification can constrain that power without becoming unworkable; the People, having observed how brevity in foundational documents permits erosion through hostile interpretation, accumulated precedent, gradual institutional drift, and the selective application of ambiguity by those whose conduct the document was meant to constrain, have chosen comprehensive specification as the price of durable protection; the length of this Amendment is therefore a direct function of the responsibility it assumes — to defeat corruption requires comprehensive mechanism; to prevent capture requires closed pathways; to preserve the People's sovereignty across generations requires that interpretive discretion yield to textual specificity at every point where capture is foreseeable; this Amendment's provisions shall be read as a coherent whole whose specific requirements protect the People's sovereign will from both present corruption and future reinterpretation; and WHEREAS in any case of genuine ambiguity within this Amendment, the interpretation most preserving the People's sovereign authority, most preventing capture of accountability structures, and most consistent with the Amendment's stated purposes shall prevail; and no ambiguity shall be construed to expand the power of any federal officeholder beyond its plain textual limits, nor to diminish the structural protections the Amendment establishes for the People's benefit; and WHEREAS the authority created by this Amendment — the People's power to remove a corrupt federal government — is itself a power of such consequence that it must be handled with the same care demanded of any great power; that this Amendment exists because the gravity of the threats it addresses demands mechanisms proportionate to those threats; and that the People accept, in adopting this Amendment, not only its protective benefits but also the responsibility of stewarding its authority carefully — using it only when necessary, reviewing it periodically through the Sunset Review process of Section 18, and handing it to future generations with the same fidelity with which earlier generations handed down the original Constitution; and WHEREAS future generations must retain the right to revisit this Amendment and adapt it to their circumstances, lest this instrument of liberation itself become an instrument of ossification; NOW, THEREFORE, be it enacted and ordained that the following Article is hereby proposed as an Amendment to the Constitution of the United States, to be valid as part thereof when ratified by the legislatures of three-fourths of the several States pursuant to Article V:

Section 1. The Right of Popular No Confidence

1.1 The People of the United States shall possess the inalienable right to issue a Declaration of No Confidence against the Federal Government, compelling the immediate and simultaneous removal from office and service of: (a) the President; (b) the Vice President; (c) all Members of the Senate and House of Representatives; (d) all Justices of the Supreme Court; (e) all political appointees and senior executive officers of every federal department, agency, bureau, board, commission, corporation, administration, authority, and office; and (f) all members of the Senior Executive Service and all federal contractors serving in a policy-making capacity. 1.2 Career technical and operational personnel of the Federal Government — including scientists, engineers, medical professionals, meteorologists, safety inspectors, drug reviewers, epidemiologists, air traffic controllers, aviation safety officers, nuclear regulators, benefit processors, case workers, researchers, and analysts whose duties are primarily technical, scientific, or administrative rather than political — shall NOT be automatically separated from federal service by operation of this Amendment. 1.3 Upon passage of a Declaration of No Confidence, the political leadership enumerated in Section 1.1 shall be removed. The institutions themselves shall continue essential operations under Committee oversight pending review pursuant to Section 15. 1.4 This right shall not be abridged, suspended, enjoined, or delayed by any act of Congress, executive order, judicial ruling, proclamation of emergency, or declaration of martial law. Any act purporting to limit this right shall be void ab initio (a Latin legal term meaning: invalid from the very beginning, as if it never existed legally).

Section 2. The Independent Tripartite Oversight Authority

Key terms in this Section: • "The Authority" — The Independent Tripartite Oversight Authority established in this Section and fully constituted under Section 17, consisting of three separate bodies: the Citizens' Oversight Board, the State Elections Council, and the Academic Integrity Commission. • "Liberty Bell Initiative" — The action taken when all three bodies of the Authority each separately reach the same conclusion through their own internal vote — the structural mechanism by which the Authority certifies any major action. Named for the Liberty Bell at Independence Hall, whose ringing marks moments of civic consent. • "Mutual veto" — The structural rule that any one of the three bodies may block any Authority action by declining to concur, regardless of what the other two bodies decide. 2.1 All functions of petition verification, referendum administration, and emergency election oversight shall be performed exclusively by the Independent Tripartite Oversight Authority ("the Authority"). 2.2 The Authority shall consist of three equal bodies with mutual veto power: the Citizens' Oversight Board, the State Elections Council, and the Academic Integrity Commission, as established in Section 17.

2.3 All proceedings shall be recorded and published in real time upon the Ledger.

Section 3. Petition to Trigger

Key terms in this Section: • "The Authority" — The Independent Tripartite Oversight Authority, consisting of: (1) the Citizens' Oversight Board (300 randomly selected citizens); (2) the State Elections Council (56 state, territorial, and DC chief election officers serving ex officio — a Latin legal term meaning: by virtue of holding another office, without separate appointment); and (3) the Academic Integrity Commission (50 academic representatives from the Pre-Certified University Pool). • "Liberty Bell Initiative" — The action taken when all three bodies of the Authority separately reach the same conclusion through their own internal vote. • "The Ledger" — The Sovereign Blockchain Voting Ledger established in Section 4, the publicly auditable blockchain record of all votes, signatures, and Authority actions. • "Petition" — A citizen-initiated formal request to trigger a No Confidence Referendum, requiring the signature threshold established in this Section. • "Participating Jurisdictions" — The fifty-six units that participate as equals under this Amendment: the 50 states, the District of Columbia, Puerto Rico, Guam, the US Virgin Islands, the Northern Mariana Islands, and American Samoa. • "Chief Justice of a Participating Jurisdiction" — For purposes of this Amendment, the presiding judge of the highest court of a Participating Jurisdiction, however titled under that Jurisdiction's law (including Chief Justice, Chief Judge, Presiding Justice, or equivalent office). Where a Participating Jurisdiction's highest court does not have a single presiding judge, the Chief Justice shall be the judge serving by seniority, rotation, or selection among the court's membership as that Jurisdiction's law provides. Where a Participating Jurisdiction's presiding judge is appointed by a federal officer rather than selected through that Jurisdiction's own process, that judge shall be excluded from the "Chief Justice of a Participating Jurisdiction" category for purposes of any Amendment body that represents Jurisdictional independence from federal executive authority, and the Jurisdiction shall be represented by the senior associate judge selected through the Jurisdiction's own processes, if any such judge exists. The terms "state Chief Justice," "state supreme court Chief Justice," and similar references where used in this Amendment shall be construed as synonymous with "Chief Justice of a Participating Jurisdiction" unless the context specifically and unambiguously limits the reference to the fifty states. 3.0 Activation of the Petition Mechanism. The Petition mechanism established in this Section shall not be available during the twenty-six-month (26-month) period between Ratification (Day Zero) and the Inaugural Referendum on Day Seven

Hundred Eighty (780) under Section 19A. The Inaugural Referendum is the sole and exclusive mechanism for a No Confidence vote during that initial period, and it occurs automatically without any petition requirement. The regular Petition mechanism of this Section shall become available beginning on the day after the Inaugural Referendum has been certified, regardless of whether the Inaugural Referendum passed or failed. From that moment forward, the Petition mechanism shall remain permanently available to the People as the ongoing democratic instrument for triggering a No Confidence Referendum against any future Federal Government. 3.1 A Declaration of No Confidence shall be placed before the People for a national referendum upon submission of a verified Petition that meets BOTH: (a) the valid in-person signatures of not less than fifteen percent (15%) of all registered voters of the United States, including registered voters in the fifty states, the District of Columbia, the five territories enumerated in Section 3.1.1, and overseas Americans; AND (b) valid signatures from at least fifteen percent (15%) of registered voters within each of no fewer than thirty (30) of the fifty-six Participating Jurisdictions defined in Section 3.1.1. 3.1.1 For purposes of this Amendment, the "Participating Jurisdictions" are: the fifty (50) states of the United States; the District of Columbia; the Commonwealth of Puerto Rico; the Territory of Guam; the United States Virgin Islands; the Commonwealth of the Northern Mariana Islands; and the Territory of American Samoa. These fifty-six Participating Jurisdictions shall be treated as equals for all purposes of this Amendment relating to signature thresholds, Reclamation Offices and Centers, petition verification, and Referendum participation, notwithstanding their varying congressional representation or historical statehood status. 3.1.2 American Samoans, who are United States nationals, shall participate fully in every aspect of this Amendment to the same extent as United States citizens of the several states, the District of Columbia, and the other territories. The principle that those subject to federal authority shall have a voice in removing a corrupt federal government admits no distinction between nationals and citizens for purposes of this Amendment. 3.1.3 United States citizens and nationals residing abroad, including but not limited to active-duty military personnel, military spouses and dependents, federal employees stationed overseas, private-sector expatriates, students studying abroad, and dual citizens, shall participate in petition signing and Referendum voting through secure Sovereign Voting Terminals deployed at United States embassies, consulates, and major military installations abroad, pursuant to Section 14.9. Their signatures and votes shall be counted toward the jurisdiction of their most recent United States residence of record, or, for those with no prior United States residence, toward a separate Overseas Americans Jurisdiction administered by the State Elections Council.

3.2 The State Elections Council shall verify signatures within sixty (60) days. The Citizens' Oversight Board and Academic Integrity Commission shall independently audit. A Liberty Bell Initiative — separate concurrence of all three bodies — is required to certify the Petition. 3.3 No federal court, agency, or official shall have jurisdiction to enjoin (meaning: issue a court order to stop or prevent), delay, or invalidate a Petition at any stage of the Petition process — including initiation under Section 12.1, Office registration under Section 12.2, signature collection during the one hundred eighty (180) day window under Section 12.5, State Elections Council verification under Section 3.2, Authority audit under Section 3.2, Liberty Bell Initiative certification under Section 3.2, or post-certification administration. This jurisdiction strip applies to the entire

Petition process from initiation through Referendum administration under Section 5. Protection of the Petition mechanism from federal court interference is essential because the federal courts may be captured by the very federal government the Petition seeks to place before the People for No Confidence evaluation; permitting federal courts to delay, invalidate, or obstruct the Petition at any stage would defeat the Amendment's core mechanism. 3.4 No Delay of Petition Process Permitted. No act of Congress, executive order, presidential proclamation, judicial ruling, state action, emergency declaration, martial law declaration, or any other federal, state, or territorial action shall delay, postpone, modify, or prevent the Petition process established in Sections 3 and 12 at any stage. Any attempt to do so shall be void ab initio and shall have no legal force; Office staff, Oversight Officers, State Elections Council members, Authority body members, and all other Amendment personnel shall proceed with Petition administration notwithstanding any such purported order, declaration, ruling, or action. Any such attempt shall constitute interference under Section 13, triggering the full penalties thereof, including the fifteen (15) year minimum sentence and the lifetime bar from public office without possibility of pardon. The Section 5.12.1 officials' duty-to-proceed protections shall apply to Petition administration without modification. This provision mirrors the undelayability protections applied to Vote Day mechanisms under Sections 5.12, 17B.11, 17.22.6, 18.18, and 19A.4, and reflects the constitutional judgment that the Petition mechanism is the gateway to the No Confidence Referendum and must be protected with equivalent force. 3.5 Timeline Anchors for Petition Process. The following timeline anchors shall govern the Petition process, providing certainty to citizens, administrators, and courts: (a) Petition Initiation. The Petition process commences on the day the initiating voter files the Petition at any Office, Center, Host Site, Satellite Site, or Mobile Participation Unit, which day shall be designated Day One (1) of the Petition process. (b) Office Registration. Office registration under Section 12.2 shall complete within forty-eight (48) hours of initiation, making the Petition active and triggering the signature collection window. (c) Signature Collection Window. The one hundred eighty (180) day signature collection window under Section 12.5 shall commence on the day of Office registration under subsection (b). The window shall close on Day One Hundred Eighty (180) of collection, subject to extensions under Section 12.6 for documented interference. (d) State Elections Council Verification Window. The sixty (60) day State Elections Council verification window under Section 3.2 shall commence on the day after the signature collection window closes. Verification shall be conducted on the cryptographic blockchain record of signatures, which shall constitute automatic submission for verification purposes — no additional physical or procedural handoff shall be required, and no administrator may claim that verification is not yet properly before the State Elections Council on grounds of missing handoff formalities. The verification window shall close on Day Sixty (60) of verification. (e) Authority Audit Concurrent with Verification. The independent audits by the Citizens' Oversight Board and Academic Integrity Commission under Section 3.2 shall proceed concurrently with State Elections Council verification, not sequentially. Concurrent audit preserves the overall timeline while providing the independent review function. (f) Liberty Bell Initiative Certification Deadline. The Liberty Bell Initiative certification under Section 3.2 shall complete within thirty (30) days of State Elections Council verification completion under subsection (d). The three Authority bodies shall deliberate and vote within this window, with each body's decision published on the Franklin Ledger upon completion. The Authority shall not extend this thirty (30) day window through administrative delay; where specific factual or technical questions require additional time, any extension shall require Liberty Bell Initiative itself with specific published reasoning, and shall not exceed an additional thirty (30) days. (g) Referendum Administration. The Referendum shall be administered within thirty (30) days of Liberty Bell Initiative certification under Section 5.1. This thirty (30) day window allows for voter education, ballot preparation, and operational readiness while ensuring the People's sovereign decision is not indefinitely deferred. (h) Maximum Total Timeline. The total Petition process from initiation (Day One) to Referendum administration shall not exceed three hundred (300) days under ordinary operation, plus any Section 12.6 interference extensions which benefit citizens by extending collection time. The three hundred (300) day ceiling consists of: 2 days Office registration + 180 days collection + 60 days verification + 30 days Liberty Bell certification + 30 days Referendum administration = 302 days maximum under ordinary circumstances (with the additional 2 days accounted for by operational transition time between phases). The Authority shall administer the

process to complete within this window. (i) Authority Body Stalling as Interference. Any Authority body member who intentionally delays their body's participation in Liberty Bell Initiative certification beyond the timeline established in subsection (f), without specific published reasoning warranting extension, shall be subject to Section 13 interference penalties and Section 17A accountability review. The distinction between good-faith deliberation within the thirty (30) day window and bad-faith stalling shall be determined by the Watchdog Tribunal under Section 21. 3.6 Failed Petition Re-Initiation. Where a Petition fails to reach signature thresholds within the one hundred eighty (180) day collection window under Section 12.5, or fails Liberty Bell Initiative certification under Section 3.2, the following framework shall apply to subsequent Petition activity: (a) Immediate Re-Initiation Permitted on Different Grounds. A new Petition on materially different grounds (different officials targeted, different acts alleged, different constitutional violations) may be initiated immediately by the same or different initiating voter, without cooldown period. (b) Ninety-Day Cooldown on Substantially Similar Grounds. A new Petition on substantially similar grounds to a failed Petition shall not be initiated within ninety (90) days of the failed Petition's close (close of collection window for threshold failure; date of Liberty Bell Initiative denial for certification failure). This cooldown prevents exhaustion of Office resources through rapid-fire substantially-identical Petitions while preserving citizens' right to renewed effort. Substantial similarity shall be determined by the Watchdog Tribunal, using standards including: substantial overlap in officials targeted, substantial overlap in acts alleged, substantial overlap in constitutional violations cited, and temporal proximity of initiation to the failed Petition. (c) Signatures Do Not Carry Over. Signatures collected for a failed Petition shall not automatically count toward subsequent Petitions, even on substantially similar grounds. Voters who supported the failed Petition may re-sign the new Petition under Section 12.10 one-signature-per-Petition rules, with cryptographic re-verification through Sovereign Voting Terminal. (d) Distinction from Post-Referendum Cooldown. The ninety (90) day re-initiation cooldown under this Section is distinct from the two (2) year cooldown under Section 10.1 following Declaration certification. The two (2) year cooldown applies only where a Petition succeeded and a Referendum was certified (regardless of Referendum outcome). A failed Petition that never reached Referendum does not trigger the Section 10.1 two-year cooldown; only the ninety (90) day re-initiation cooldown of this Section applies. (e) Public Status Publication. The Franklin Ledger (or provisional public ledger during Phase One) shall publish, for every failed Petition: (i) the date of failure; (ii) the reason for failure (threshold not met with specific shortfall, or Liberty Bell

Initiative denial with specific reasoning from the denying body or bodies); (iii) the ninety (90) day cooldown expiration date for substantially similar Petitions; and (iv) statistics on signatures collected and Jurisdictional distribution. Public status ensures citizens know exactly when and why a Petition failed and when renewed effort becomes possible.

Section 4. The Sovereign Blockchain Voting Ledger

Key terms in this Section: • "The Ledger" — The Sovereign Blockchain Voting Ledger established by this Section: the dual-chain, decentralized, tamper-evident, publicly auditable blockchain record of all petitions, votes, and Authority actions under this Amendment. Where this Amendment refers to "the Ledger" in the singular, the reference includes the dual-chain structure operating as a unified verified record. • "Primary Chain" — Either of the two blockchain systems operating in parallel to record and verify all Amendment transactions, each recording every vote and Authority action independently. • "Standby Chain" — The third certified blockchain held in operational readiness, available to replace either Primary Chain if compromised or disabled. • "Authority" — The Independent Tripartite Oversight Authority, consisting of the Citizens' Oversight Board, the State Elections Council, and the Academic Integrity Commission. • "Zero-knowledge proof" — A cryptographic technique that allows verification of a fact (such as a valid signature or vote) without revealing the identity of the person who signed or voted. • "Dual-Chain Verification" — The requirement that every transaction on the Ledger be independently recorded and verified on two separate Primary Chains, with certification requiring both Chains to agree. A. Foundational Requirements 4.1 All voting, signature collection, and Authority action under this Amendment shall be administered exclusively through the Sovereign Blockchain Voting Ledger, maintained via the Sovereign Civic Network established in Section 14. The Ledger shall consist of two (2) independent Primary Chains operating in parallel, with a third Standby Chain held in operational readiness, as provided in this Section. 4.2 Every Primary Chain and the Standby Chain shall meet, at minimum, the following requirements: (a) Decentralization: distributed across all Citizens' Reclamation Offices, Centers, and Host Sites in the Participating Jurisdictions, with no single point of failure; (b) Full public auditability in real time, with the complete transaction record accessible to any citizen; (c) Cryptographic privacy via zero-knowledge proofs, such that voter identity is protected while vote validity is verifiable; (d) Open-source code published upon the Ledger no less than ninety (90) days before any vote; (e) American sovereignty: all operators, validators, primary infrastructure, and governance shall be United States-based, with no foreign validators, foreign-operated nodes, or foreign governmental control permitted; (f) Surge capacity sufficient to handle peak voting loads consistent with the anticipated civic engagement of a

No Confidence Referendum, as specified in Section 4.8. 4.3 All votes shall be cast in person at a Citizens' Reclamation Office, Center, or Host Site via a Sovereign Voting Terminal. 4.4 Fraudulent credential acquisition shall be a federal felony punishable by not less than ten (10) years. B. Post-Body-Formation Evaluation Period and Chain Testing 4.5 Testing Phase. Beginning no earlier than Day One Hundred Eighty (180) following Ratification — after the Academic Integrity Commission has been fully constituted under Section 17 and sworn in — the Academic Integrity Commission shall initiate a seven-and-a-half-month (7.5-month) Testing Phase during which multiple candidate blockchain architectures shall be evaluated in parallel to identify those capable of safely administering Amendment voting. The Testing Phase shall conclude by Day Four Hundred Five (405), with selected chains entering a twelve-month (12-month) setup period under Section 4.10 before full live operation on or before Day Seven Hundred Sixty-Five (765). The delay from Day Zero to Day One Hundred Eighty (180) exists so that the Academic Integrity Commission — the body administering the Testing Phase — actually exists before the testing begins. 4.6 Submission Requirements. Any American team, consortium, or institution may submit a candidate blockchain architecture for evaluation, subject to the following minimum requirements:

(a) American operation: all proposing organizations, operators, and primary infrastructure shall be United States-based and subject to United States jurisdiction; no foreign ownership, foreign validators, or foreign governmental control shall be permitted at any level; (b) Demonstrated security standards: the architecture shall meet or exceed federal cryptographic standards (FIPS 140-3 or successor), with documented third-party security audits at submission; (c) Minimum throughput capacity: the architecture shall demonstrate capacity to process at least fifty thousand (50,000) verified transactions per second sustained, with surge capacity to one hundred thousand (100,000) transactions per second, sufficient to handle anticipated peak loads during a national No Confidence Referendum; (d) Open source: all code shall be fully open source and publicly auditable; (e) Decentralization: the architecture shall distribute validation across no fewer than fifty-six (56) independent nodes, with at least one (1) node in each Participating Jurisdiction; (f) Zero-knowledge proof support: the architecture shall support zero-knowledge proofs for voter privacy protection; (g) Financial and technical capacity: the proposing team shall demonstrate financial stability and technical capability to operate at federal scale for at least ten (10) years; (h) Conflict-of-interest disclosure: complete disclosure of all financial relationships, federal contracts, political affiliations, and foreign relationships of the proposing organization and its leadership. 4.7 Evaluation Methodology. During the seven-and-a-half-month Testing Phase, the Academic Integrity Commission shall conduct comprehensive evaluation of each qualifying submission, including: (a) Simulated voting at scale: each chain shall process simulated test votes at volumes representative of anticipated No Confidence Referendum turnout (not less than one hundred fifty million (150,000,000) test transactions over the testing period); (b) Load and surge testing: each chain shall demonstrate sustained performance under peak loads and surge conditions, including simulated denial-of-service attempts; (c) Red team attack simulations: independent cybersecurity firms shall conduct attack simulations against each chain, attempting to compromise integrity, privacy, or availability;

(d) Cryptographic audits: independent cryptographers from the Pre-Certified Pool shall audit each chain's cryptographic implementation; (e) Governance evaluation: each chain's governance structure, operator accountability, and resilience to capture shall be evaluated; (f) Public transparency: all evaluation methodologies, criteria, and interim results shall be published upon the provisional public ledger established in Section 19.4 in real time, enabling public scrutiny of the evaluation itself. 4.8 Anticipated Civic Engagement. In establishing capacity requirements, the Authority shall recognize that a No Confidence Referendum represents a historic civic event likely to drive voter turnout exceeding any presidential election in United States history. The Ledger must be designed to handle surge capacity consistent with participation rates potentially exceeding seventy-five percent (75%) of all registered voters, with peak hour concentrations potentially exceeding ten million (10,000,000) votes per hour. No capacity limitation shall become a basis for denying any qualified voter the ability to cast a vote. C. Selection of Primary Chains and Standby Chain 4.9 Final Selection. Upon conclusion of the Testing Phase, the Academic Integrity Commission shall: (a) Publish complete evaluation results upon the provisional public ledger; (b) Rank qualifying chains by technical performance across security, throughput, decentralization, and attack resistance; (c) Recommend three (3) chains to advance — two (2) Primary Chains for dual-chain operation plus one (1) Standby Chain — selected not solely by technical ranking but with mandatory architectural diversity such that the two Primary Chains represent materially different architectural approaches, cryptographic primitives, or consensus mechanisms, preventing any single architectural vulnerability from compromising both Primary Chains simultaneously; (d) The Authority shall confirm the Commission's recommendation through Liberty Bell Initiative within thirty (30) days, with authority to reject the recommendation and require re-evaluation upon specific findings published on the Ledger. Absent such rejection, the Commission's recommendation becomes the final selection. 4.10 Twelve-Month Setup Period. Following selection, the two Primary Chains and one Standby Chain shall undergo a twelve-month (12-month) setup period (Days 405 through 765) during which: (a) Full infrastructure buildout shall occur, including validator node deployment across all Participating Jurisdictions; (b) Integration testing with the Sovereign Voting Terminals established in Section 14 shall be completed;

(c) Staff training and operator certification shall occur; (d) Final cryptographic audits, security hardening, and penetration testing shall be completed; (e) Disaster recovery procedures shall be tested and documented; (f) The Academic Integrity Commission shall certify each chain as operationally ready before live operation begins; (g) Any chain that fails to achieve operational readiness by Day Seven Hundred Sixty-Five (765) shall be replaced by the Standby Chain, with the Authority initiating expedited re-evaluation of remaining tested chains to identify a new Standby. D. Dual-Chain Live Operation 4.11 Parallel Recording. During all live operations under this Amendment, every transaction — including every vote cast, every signature collected, every Authority action, and every Ledger entry — shall be independently recorded on both Primary Chains simultaneously. Both Primary Chains shall receive the same transaction data from the Sovereign Voting Terminals and shall independently validate, record, and publish the transaction. 4.12 Dual-Chain Certification. No referendum, petition, or Authority action shall be certified under this Amendment unless both Primary Chains independently record matching results. Specifically: (a) Both Primary Chains shall publish independent tallies in real time upon the Ledger; (b) Both tallies shall match exactly for any certification to proceed, with a de minimis (a Latin legal term meaning: so small it doesn't matter legally) rounding tolerance not exceeding 0.001% attributable to timing of transaction ordering; (c) Any material disagreement between the two Primary Chains shall automatically halt certification pending investigation by the Academic Integrity Commission and, upon Commission request, the Watchdog Tribunal; (d) Investigation findings shall be published upon the Ledger with specific identification of the source of disagreement (technical malfunction, compromise, or other cause); (e) Certification shall resume only upon: (i) resolution of the disagreement through technical verification; (ii) correction of any identified error; or (iii) activation of the Standby Chain to replace a compromised Primary Chain. 4.13 Transparency of Discrepancies. Any material disagreement between Primary Chains shall be publicly disclosed upon the Ledger within twenty-four (24) hours of detection, including: the specific transactions affected; the nature of the disagreement; the investigation status; and the expected resolution timeline. No attempt to conceal, delay disclosure of, or misrepresent a dual-chain discrepancy shall be permitted; violations shall constitute interference under Section 13 and evidence destruction under Section 13B where applicable. 4.14 Standby Chain Activation. The Standby Chain may be activated to replace a compromised, failed, or otherwise disabled Primary Chain upon: (a) Academic Integrity Commission finding of compromise or disability, by Commission vote; (b) Liberty Bell Initiative confirmation by the three bodies of the Authority, within forty-eight (48) hours of Commission finding; (c) Public disclosure upon the Ledger of the reason for activation and the expected duration of Standby operation; (d) Cryptographic migration of the disabled Chain's verified records to the Standby Chain, ensuring no verified transaction is lost. E. Operator Independence and Separation of Powers 4.15 Separation from Terminal Manufacturers. The Sovereign Voting Terminals established in Section 14 shall be manufactured and certified by teams separate and distinct from the teams operating the two Primary Chains and the Standby Chain. No single team, organization, or corporate structure shall simultaneously control Terminal manufacturing and blockchain operation, preventing single-point compromise of the voting system. 4.16 Separation Between Primary Chains. The two Primary Chains shall be operated by different teams under the following mandatory separation: (a) Different operating organizations: each Chain shall be operated by an organizationally distinct team, with no common ownership, shared leadership, or integrated corporate structure; (b) Different facilities: each Chain's primary infrastructure shall be located in different geographic regions of the United States, with different data centers, different network providers, and different physical security arrangements; (c) Different personnel: operational personnel shall be separately recruited, vetted, and credentialed, with no personnel holding simultaneous operational roles on both Chains; (d) Different security audits: each Chain shall undergo independent security audits by different AIC-certified auditing firms, with audit results published independently upon the Ledger; (e) Different public key infrastructure: cryptographic keys, signing authorities, and root-of-trust structures shall be entirely independent between the two Chains;

(f) Common accountability: notwithstanding operational separation, both operators shall be equally accountable to the Authority through the Academic Integrity Commission for compliance with this Amendment. 4.17 Standby Chain Operation. The Standby Chain shall be operated by a third distinct team under the same separation requirements of Section 4.16. During periods when the Standby Chain is not actively replacing a Primary Chain, the Standby Chain shall nonetheless process all transactions in shadow mode, maintaining a continuous verification record that can be compared against the two Primary Chains as an additional integrity check. 4.18 Operator Accountability. Each blockchain operating team shall: (a) Be certified by the Academic Integrity Commission before assuming operational responsibility; (b) Submit to continuous audit by the Commission and, upon referral, by the Watchdog Tribunal; (c) Publish all operational metrics upon the Ledger in real time, including node uptime, transaction throughput, validation latency, and security incident reports; (d) Report any attempted compromise, system anomaly, or security incident within one (1) hour of detection to the Authority and within twenty-four (24) hours to the public via the Ledger; (e) Be subject to the full penalty provisions of Sections 13, 13A, and 13B for any compromise of Ledger integrity, regardless of whether the compromise is malicious or negligent. F. Ongoing Review and Evolution 4.19 Five-Year Technical Review. Every five (5) years, the Academic Integrity Commission shall conduct a comprehensive technical review of the Primary Chains and Standby Chain, assessing: (a) continued security adequacy given evolving threats; (b) continued throughput adequacy given evolving civic participation; (c) the availability of materially superior architectures developed since the last review; and (d) any identified weaknesses or operational concerns. The review shall be published upon the Ledger with recommendations. 4.20 Security Threat Response. If at any time the Academic Integrity Commission identifies a material security threat to a Primary Chain or the Standby Chain, the Commission may, upon Liberty Bell Initiative concurrence of the Authority, initiate emergency chain migration or replacement. Emergency migration shall preserve all verified records and shall be conducted with maximum transparency, subject to appropriate security protections to prevent exploitation of identified vulnerabilities during migration.

4.21 Sunset Review Integration. The Ledger's dual-chain architecture shall be subject to review during each Sunset Review under Section 18. The People may, through the Modify procedure of Section 18.4, direct the Authority to migrate to successor architectures, alter the dual-chain model, or implement technological improvements identified during the twenty-year (20-year) operational history. 4.22 Article V Protection. The provisions of this Section 4 shall be protected under the Article V protection established in Sections 18.6.1 and 18.6.2. No act of Congress, executive order, judicial ruling, or state action shall modify, diminish, or evade the dual-chain verification requirement, the American operator requirement, or the separation-of-operators requirement. The integrity of the People's vote depends upon the integrity of the Ledger, and this Section establishes that integrity as constitutional in character.

Section 4A. The Franklin Ledger — Public Transparency Infrastructure

Key terms in this Section: • "The Franklin Ledger" — The public-facing transparency infrastructure established by this Section, named in honor of Benjamin Franklin, whose foundational work in public accounting, civic transparency, the establishment of public libraries, and the creation of the postal service laid the intellectual groundwork for the public information infrastructure this Amendment seeks to create. The Franklin Ledger is the unified public interface through which citizens access, review, and verify all information required by this Amendment to be publicly available. • "The Sovereign Blockchain Voting Ledger" — The technical blockchain infrastructure established in Section 4, distinct from the Franklin Ledger but integrated with it as a data source for voting and Authority actions. • "Display" — The publication of information upon the Franklin Ledger in forms accessible to ordinary citizens, including web, mobile, physical terminal, phone, and print channels. • "Source System" — Any underlying system from which the Franklin Ledger draws data for display, including the Sovereign Blockchain Voting Ledger, the Hamilton Contingent public reporting systems, federal financial disclosure systems, and other Amendment-required data sources.

• "The Authority" — The Independent Tripartite Oversight Authority (three bodies, see Section 17). • "Liberty Bell Initiative" — Separate concurrence of all three bodies of the Authority. A. Foundational Principle 4A.1 Foundational Principle. Democracy depends upon an informed citizenry, and an informed citizenry depends upon accessible public information. The Sovereign Blockchain Voting Ledger under Section 4 provides cryptographic integrity for voting and Authority actions, but its technical character makes it unsuitable as the primary interface for ordinary citizens. There is therefore hereby established the Franklin Ledger, a comprehensive public transparency infrastructure that displays all information required by this Amendment to be publicly available, in forms accessible to every citizen regardless of age, ability, technical skill, geographic location, or economic circumstance. The Franklin Ledger is the

Amendment's public face: the place where the People see their government in full view. 4A.2 Relationship to the Sovereign Blockchain Voting Ledger. The Franklin Ledger is distinct from, but integrated with, the Sovereign Blockchain Voting Ledger of Section 4. The Voting Ledger is the cryptographic blockchain infrastructure that records votes, signatures, and Authority certifications. The Franklin Ledger displays Voting Ledger data to the public, along with data from all other Source Systems. The Franklin Ledger shall not have authority to alter, modify, or suppress Voting Ledger data; it serves solely as a display and access layer. Any data displayed by the Franklin Ledger from the Voting Ledger shall include cryptographic verification enabling citizens to confirm the Franklin Ledger display accurately reflects the underlying Voting Ledger record. B. Distributed Responsibility 4A.3 Tripartite Authority Oversight. The Franklin Ledger shall be operated and maintained under the joint authority of the three bodies of the Authority, with responsibilities distributed as follows: (a) Academic Integrity Commission: technical construction, cryptographic integrity, security architecture, data integration from Source Systems, ongoing technical operation, and periodic audit of technical systems; (b) Hamilton Contingent Public Response Division: citizen-facing interface design, content organization, the Public Accountability Dashboard previously established in Section 13C.6 and 13C.27 (which shall be integrated into the Franklin Ledger as a core component), accessibility implementation, citizen complaint handling, and public education;

(c) State Elections Council: integration of elections data feeds, voter verification interfaces, and jurisdictional data accuracy; (d) Citizens' Oversight Board: citizen oversight of accessibility, understandability, and responsiveness to public needs; periodic citizen review of Franklin Ledger design and content; (e) Any major change to the Franklin Ledger's structure, scope, or public interface shall require Liberty Bell Initiative concurrence of all three Authority bodies. 4A.4 Anti-Manipulation Protections. The distributed responsibility model is established to prevent any single body or officer from controlling what citizens see. The following protections shall apply: (a) No single body may unilaterally alter the Franklin Ledger's scope, hide required information, or modify displayed data; (b) All changes to the Franklin Ledger's structure shall be logged cryptographically with two-party approval from different Authority bodies; (c) Attempts by any federal officeholder, political appointee, or employee to direct changes to the Franklin Ledger outside the Authority framework shall constitute interference under Section 13; (d) Any suppression, alteration, or manipulation of Franklin Ledger content shall constitute evidence destruction under Section 13B, triggering the twenty-five (25) year minimum sentence and ten million dollar ($10,000,000) minimum fine. C. Accessibility — Multi-Channel Access 4A.5 Comprehensive Accessibility Principle. The Franklin Ledger shall be accessible to every American regardless of age, ability, technical skill, geographic location, or economic circumstance. Accessibility shall not be an optional feature but a fundamental design requirement. No citizen shall be denied access to Amendment-required public information because of technological limitation or personal circumstance. 4A.6 Web and Mobile Access. The Franklin Ledger shall be available through: (a) A public website accessible at a memorable and permanent federal domain, optimized for standard modern browsers, with no subscription, registration, or account required for read-only access; (b) Free native mobile applications for the major mobile operating systems, with functional parity to the web experience; (c) Full compatibility with screen readers, text-to-speech tools, and other assistive technologies, meeting or exceeding Web Content Accessibility Guidelines (WCAG) 2.2 AA standards or their successor;

(d) Interface availability in English, Spanish, and any other language spoken by more than one percent (1%) of the United States population as identified by the most recent federal census; (e) Downloadable data feeds in open, standard formats allowing independent civic organizations, journalists, and researchers to build their own tools using Franklin Ledger data. 4A.7 Physical Terminal Access. Every Citizens' Reclamation Office, Center, Host Site, and Overseas Terminal location under Section 11, 11A, 11B, and 14.9 shall include dedicated Franklin Ledger access terminals, separate from the Sovereign Voting Terminals: (a) These terminals shall provide public read-only access to the Franklin Ledger during all operational hours of the facility; (b) No identification, registration, or voter credential shall be required to use a Franklin Ledger terminal; (c) The terminals shall include printing capability to produce hard copies of displayed information at no cost to the citizen; (d) Oversight Officers under Section 11B shall provide assistance to citizens unfamiliar with the technology, without ever directing or limiting what information citizens access; (e) The terminals shall meet the accessibility standards of Section 11A, including tactile navigation, audio output, and disability accommodation. 4A.8 Telephone Access. The Authority shall maintain a toll-free Franklin Ledger Information Line, available twenty-four (24) hours per day, seven (7) days per week, enabling citizens without internet access to: (a) Request and receive summary information on any Franklin Ledger topic through automated menus and live operators; (b) Receive spoken summaries of key data (current recovery totals, upcoming referenda, recent Authority decisions, etc.); (c) Request printed mailings of specific reports or dashboards at no cost; (d) Access interpretation services in any language covered under Section 4A.6(d); (e) File citizen complaints or requests regarding Franklin Ledger content or accessibility. 4A.9 Print Mailing Access. The Authority shall maintain a Print Mailing service through which any citizen may, at no cost, request: (a) Periodic summary publications of Franklin Ledger key data (monthly, quarterly, or annually as the citizen prefers);

(b) Specific reports upon request, mailed within fourteen (14) days; (c) Large-print formats for visually impaired citizens; (d) Braille formats upon request; (e) Audio recordings of major reports upon request; (f) Language-appropriate translations of any Franklin Ledger content. 4A.10 Broadcast Access. The Authority shall coordinate with public broadcasting infrastructure (including the Public Broadcasting Service, National Public Radio, and successor public media organizations) to provide: (a) Regular television broadcasts of key Franklin Ledger data, including recovery totals, referendum announcements, and major Authority decisions; (b) Radio broadcasts for citizens in areas with limited television access; (c) Emergency broadcasts during any time-sensitive Franklin Ledger events (such as referendum certifications, major dual-chain discrepancies, or asset recovery milestones); (d) Sign language interpretation in all broadcasts; (e) Closed captioning in multiple languages. D. Comprehensive Content 4A.11 Required Content. The Franklin Ledger shall display, at minimum, the following categories of information, organized for citizen understanding: (a) Voting and Democratic Processes: all certified referendum results; all petition signature counts and verification status; all Liberty Bell Initiative decisions; all Emergency Election results; all verification comparisons between Primary Chains under Section 4.12; (b) Financial Transparency: running real-time totals of recovered corrupt assets (as contemplated in the asset recovery framework); all distribution amounts by income bracket; all campaign finance contributions and expenditures under Section 9; all fines, forfeitures, and clawbacks collected under Sections 13A and 13B; all whistleblower rewards distributed; all federal spending on Amendment infrastructure; (c) Accountability and Enforcement: all Hamilton Contingent entries into Covered Spaces under Section 13C.14.6; all Independent Warrant Panel decisions; all Watchdog Tribunal findings; all Oversight Officer conduct reviews; all evidence destruction prosecutions; all Preservation Order compliance certifications; all whistleblower cases (with identity protected); (d) Government Operations: all Executive Order issuance and sunset dates; all emergency declarations and renewals under Section 24.18; all term limit tracking for Congress and federal judiciary; all age limit compliance records; all health evaluation binary results (Fit/Referred) for Supreme Court and federal judges under Section 25.7; (e) People and Officials: complete current rosters of the three Authority bodies, the Watchdog Tribunal, the Hamilton Contingent leadership, and the Independent Warrant Panel selections; all financial disclosures required of Supreme Court Justices, Members of Congress, and Presidential officials; all conflict-of-interest disclosures; all recusal decisions; all ethics findings; (f) Infrastructure and Access: all Host Site designations and agreements under Section 11B; Coverage Standard compliance maps and metrics; Terminal deployment status; Network integrity reports; Mobile Accessibility Team deployment data; (g) Historical Archive: complete searchable archive of all past Franklin Ledger content, enabling citizens to review historical data, track trends over time, and verify continuity of public information. 4A.11.1 Serious Findings Prominent Display. To serve the Amendment's constitutional premise that the People shall be able to evaluate their government through access to comprehensive and organized information, the Franklin Ledger shall maintain a dedicated "Serious Findings" display category featuring, in consolidated prominent form, the Authority's and Tribunal's most significant objective findings. This category exists to help citizens navigate large volumes of Franklin Ledger content to identify findings meeting established severity thresholds. The Serious Findings category shall not constitute advocacy, editorializing, or Authority political action; it shall constitute organized neutral display of findings that have independently met defined evidentiary and severity standards. The category shall operate under the following framework: (a) Objective Inclusion Criteria. A finding shall be automatically included in the Serious Findings category upon meeting any of the following objective triggers, without Authority discretion to exclude qualifying findings or include non-qualifying findings: (i) Section 13 interference findings imposing Senior Official multipliers under Section 13.1 through Section 13.8; (ii) Liberty Bell Initiative material foreign interference determinations under Section 22.14; (iii) Phase One material foreign interference determinations under Section 22.4.1(c); (iv) Section 13B.11 evidence destruction prosecutions reaching formal charge filing; (v) Hamilton Contingent investigations reaching formal indictment or equivalent charging decision; (vi) Watchdog Tribunal formal findings of corruption, abuse of authority, or material dereliction of duty; (vii) Section 17.22.1 Single-Body Compromise Declarations; (viii) Asset recovery determinations under Section

13D exceeding ten million dollars ($10,000,000) in recovered or ordered-forfeit assets from any single Covered Person; (ix) Section 16 military oath violation findings against flag officers or senior civilian defense officials; (x) Section 24 post-Amendment corruption findings against any sitting or former federal official; (b) Neutral Presentation

Standards. The Serious Findings display shall present each finding using the following neutral standards: (i) factual statement of the finding, citing the specific provision under which the finding was made; (ii) date and body making the finding, with individual member votes where applicable; (iii) evidence basis, including summary of the evidence relied upon with link to the full evidentiary record; (iv) accused party response, displayed with equal prominence to the finding itself, including any defense or rebuttal offered by the subject of the finding; (v) current status, indicating whether the matter is under pending investigation, formal charge, conviction, acquittal, or other procedural posture; (vi) no advocacy language, no editorializing, no calls to action, and no language suggesting citizens should or should not take any specific action. The category displays facts; citizens draw their own conclusions; (c) Chronological and Categorized Organization. Serious Findings shall be organized both chronologically (most recent first) and categorically (by the type of finding under subsection (a)), enabling citizens to view recent significant activity or to review history in specific categories; (d) No Exclusion Authority. Neither the Authority nor any single Authority body shall have discretion to exclude from the Serious Findings category any finding meeting the objective criteria of subsection (a). Any such attempted exclusion shall constitute Section 13 interference with Senior Official multipliers. Findings shall remain permanently within the category, subject to status updates as procedural posture evolves, but shall not be removed; (e) Inclusion Error Correction. Where a finding is erroneously included in the Serious Findings category without meeting the objective criteria of subsection (a), the Watchdog Tribunal shall, by majority vote, order removal with published reasoning on the Ledger. Erroneous inclusion shall not itself constitute bad faith absent evidence of intent to weaponize the category; (f) No New Substantive Authority Power. This subsection creates no new substantive investigative, prosecutorial, or enforcement power for the Authority. The Serious Findings category is purely a display and organizational mechanism. The underlying findings remain governed by their respective sections and require the same evidentiary standards, procedures, and safeguards as before; (g) Accessibility Integration. The Serious Findings category shall be accessible through all Franklin Ledger channels under Sections 4A.6 through 4A.10, including web, mobile, physical terminals, telephone access, print mailing, and broadcast access. Citizens shall not require internet access or technical skill to learn what serious findings the Authority and Tribunal have made; (h) Display Duration and Cooldown Rules. To prevent manipulation of the Serious Findings category through repeated flagging or prominence refresh gaming, the following display duration rules shall apply: (i) Initial Prominence Period. Upon initial qualification under subsection (a), each finding shall be displayed in the Serious Findings category's prominent tier for one hundred eighty (180) days. During this period, the finding shall be featured in current-display views alongside newer findings that qualify during the same window; (ii) Automatic Transition to Archive Tier. Upon expiration of the one hundred eighty (180) day initial prominence period, the finding shall automatically transition to the Serious Findings archive tier, remaining fully accessible, searchable, and displayed in chronological and categorical views. The transition shall not constitute removal, deletion, or de-emphasis of the finding's evidentiary significance; it constitutes only a change in display placement to prevent the prominent tier from becoming cluttered with aged findings; (iii) Procedural Status Refresh. Where a finding's procedural status genuinely changes through objective procedural events (including but not limited to: investigation advancing to formal charge filing; formal charge advancing to trial commencement; trial resulting in conviction or acquittal; sentencing; or appellate resolution), the finding may return to the prominent tier for an additional sixty (60) days upon each such status change, with the status change clearly documented and timestamped; (iv) Cooldown Between Refreshes. A minimum ninety (90) day cooldown shall apply between consecutive returns to prominent tier under subsection (iii), regardless of the number of procedural status changes occurring within the cooldown period. Multiple status changes within a cooldown window shall be consolidated into a single refresh at cooldown expiration. The purpose of this cooldown is to prevent prominence manipulation through engineered procedural activity; (v) Exceptions for Genuine New Developments. The ninety (90) day cooldown shall not apply where the procedural status change reveals substantially new evidence, new parties, or new findings distinct from the original basis, as determined by objective criteria including but not limited to: newly charged defendants previously uninvolved; newly discovered foreign sources; or substantially expanded asset recovery scope. Cooldown exceptions shall be documented on the Ledger with specific factual basis, subject to Watchdog Tribunal review for bad-faith cooldown exception invocation; (vi) No

Accumulated Prominence. Multiple small procedural updates shall not accumulate to refresh prominence. A single finding shall not occupy prominent tier for more than one hundred eighty (180) continuous days from original qualification, except where substantially new developments under subsection (v) genuinely warrant continued prominence; (vii) Archive Tier Accessibility. Findings in archive tier shall remain fully accessible through search, category filtering, historical browsing, and all Franklin Ledger access channels under Sections 4A.6 through 4A.10. No finding shall be removed from the Serious Findings category simply because it has aged out of prominent tier; all qualifying findings remain permanently part of the category's historical record; (viii) Anti-Manipulation Safeguard. Any Authority body or Authority personnel who manipulates procedural status changes, engineers artificial procedural activity, or coordinates status updates specifically to refresh Serious Findings prominence shall be subject to Section 13 interference penalties with Senior Official multipliers, and the manipulated finding shall be restored to its ordinary display tier with the manipulation documented on the Ledger. 4A.12 Real-Time Updates. Time-sensitive information shall be updated on the Franklin Ledger in real time, including: voting tallies during active referenda; asset recovery totals; Hamilton Contingent entries during active operations; dual-chain verification status; and Authority emergency actions. Citizens shall not have to wait for scheduled releases to see current information.

4A.13 Plain Language Presentation. All Franklin Ledger content shall be presented in plain language understandable by ordinary citizens without legal or technical training. Legal citations, statutory references, and technical terms shall be explained in accessible form. Where complex information must be displayed, summary presentations with plain-language explanations shall accompany detailed technical displays. 4A.14 Search and Navigation. The Franklin Ledger shall include powerful search, filtering, and navigation tools enabling citizens to find specific information quickly, including: (a) Full-text search across all Franklin Ledger content; (b) Filters by date, category, jurisdiction, official, and subject; (c) Personalized views allowing citizens to save searches or follow specific topics; (d) Notification services (opt-in) alerting subscribed citizens to new information on topics they follow; (e) Citizen-friendly categorization of complex information using intuitive hierarchies. D-bis. Authority Expansion of Displayed Content 4A.14.1 Expansion Authority. The three bodies of the Authority, acting through Liberty Bell Initiative, may vote to add additional categories of information to the Franklin Ledger beyond those required in Section 4A.11. This authority recognizes that future circumstances may warrant transparency in areas not anticipated at the time of Ratification, and that public accountability may require expansion as government evolves, technology advances, and new threats to democratic integrity emerge. 4A.14.2 Expansion Procedure. Any expansion of Franklin Ledger content under this subsection shall proceed through the following procedure: (a) Proposal: any one of the three Authority bodies, the Watchdog Tribunal, the Hamilton Contingent Director, or a citizen petition signed by not fewer than five hundred thousand (500,000) registered voters from at least ten (10) Participating Jurisdictions may propose new content categories for display; (b) Public Notice and Comment: the proposal shall be published upon the Franklin Ledger for a minimum public notice and comment period of one hundred twenty (120) days, during which any citizen, civic organization, or affected party may submit written comments; (c) Consideration: the three Authority bodies shall consider all submitted comments before voting, and shall publish written responses to substantive concerns raised;

(d) Liberty Bell Initiative Required: adoption shall require separate concurrence of all three Authority bodies, with written reasoning published upon the Franklin Ledger; (e) Implementation Timeline: once adopted, new content shall be integrated within one hundred eighty (180) days, with accessibility standards under Section 4A.5 through 4A.10 applying from the first day of display; (f) Ledger Documentation: the full expansion decision, including proposal text, public comments received, Authority reasoning, and implementation details, shall be permanently archived upon the Franklin Ledger. 4A.14.3 Limitations on Expansion Authority. The Authority's expansion authority under this subsection is bounded by the following limits, which no vote of the Authority may override: (a) Additive Only: expansion may only add new categories of displayed content; it may not remove, diminish, or restrict any content required by Section 4A.11 or otherwise mandated by this Amendment; (b) No Private Citizen Information: expansion shall not authorize display of personally identifying information about private citizens who do not hold federal office, federal political appointments, or other Covered Person status under Section 13B, except where the citizen has consented or where the information is already public record; (c) No Retaliation: expansion shall not be used to display information about specific individuals in a manner that constitutes retaliation, harassment, intimidation, or political punishment; (d) Fourth Amendment Protection: expansion shall not authorize display of information obtained in violation of Fourth Amendment rights, attorney-client privilege, or other constitutional protections; (e) Medical and Personal Privacy: expansion shall not authorize display of medical information, sealed court records, or other categories protected by established federal privacy law, except as specifically authorized elsewhere in this Amendment (such as binary health evaluation results under Section 25.7.6); (f) No Burden Through Pollution: expansion shall not be used to overwhelm citizens with trivial or irrelevant information that would dilute the accessibility and usability of the Franklin Ledger, with the Watchdog Tribunal empowered to review any expansion alleged to constitute information pollution. 4A.14.4 Watchdog Tribunal Review. Any expansion adopted under this subsection shall be subject to Watchdog Tribunal review upon: (a) Citizen petition signed by not fewer than one hundred thousand (100,000) registered voters alleging the expansion violates the limitations of Section 4A.14.3;

(b) Referral by any of the three Authority bodies expressing concern about subsequent implementation; (c) Own-motion review by the Watchdog Tribunal upon two-thirds (2/3) supermajority (meaning: a majority larger than a simple majority — in this case, at least two-thirds of members must agree, not just more than half) finding of specific concern. 4A.14.5 Reversal of Expansion. An expansion adopted under this subsection may be reversed by: (a) Subsequent Liberty Bell Initiative vote of the three Authority bodies, following the same public notice and comment procedure of Section 4A.14.2; (b) Watchdog Tribunal finding, by two-thirds (2/3) supermajority, that the expansion violates the limitations of Section 4A.14.3; (c) Sunset Review Modify procedure under Section 18.4. 4A.14.6 Contraction Prohibited by Authority Vote. Notwithstanding the expansion authority of this subsection, the Authority may NOT vote to reduce, limit, or remove content required by Section 4A.11 or otherwise mandated by this Amendment. The scope of required public transparency is a constitutional floor, not a ceiling, and can be expanded but not contracted except through Sunset Review Modify procedures under Section 18.4. Any attempt to contract required transparency shall constitute interference under Section 13 and evidence destruction under Section 13B where applicable. E. Data Integrity and Cryptographic Verification 4A.15 Cryptographic Verification. Every item of information displayed on the Franklin Ledger shall include cryptographic verification linking the display to its Source System, enabling any citizen with technical capability to independently verify that displayed data accurately reflects underlying records. This verification shall not be required for ordinary use, but shall be available to any citizen or civic organization that wishes to audit Franklin Ledger integrity. 4A.16 Immutable Change Log. All changes, additions, or corrections to Franklin Ledger content shall be cryptographically logged with: (a) Timestamp of change; (b) Identity of Authority body and individual personnel responsible; (c) Nature of change (addition, correction, update); (d) Reason for change; (e) Linked cryptographic verification to prior state.

4A.17 Correction Procedures. Where Franklin Ledger content contains genuine errors, corrections shall: (a) Preserve the original content with clear indication that it has been superseded; (b) Display the correction with full explanation of what was wrong and how it was identified; (c) Cryptographically link the correction to the original for verification purposes; (d) Never result in silent removal or replacement of prior content. 4A.18 Independent Audit. The Academic Integrity Commission shall conduct comprehensive audits of Franklin Ledger integrity at least annually, with audit results published upon the Franklin Ledger itself. Any citizen, academic institution, or civic organization may request additional audits upon petition to the Watchdog Tribunal, which may order such audits upon findings of specific concerns. F. Funding, Evolution, and Protection 4A.19 Funding. The Franklin Ledger shall be funded through the constitutional appropriation framework of Section 11.3, with dedicated funding sufficient to maintain full operational capability, accessibility across all channels, and ongoing technical evolution. Funding shall not be subject to congressional reduction or executive redirection. 4A.20 Technical Evolution. The Academic Integrity Commission shall review Franklin Ledger technical architecture every five (5) years to assess: (a) Adequacy of current technical implementation given evolving public needs and technologies; (b) Accessibility adequacy given evolving standards and citizen feedback; (c) Security adequacy given evolving threats; (d) Opportunities for expansion or improvement identified through operational experience. 4A.21 Sunset Review Integration. The Franklin Ledger shall be reviewed during each Sunset Review under Section 18. The People may, through the Modify procedure of Section 18.4, direct expansion, modification, or technical evolution of the Franklin Ledger based on accumulated operational experience. 4A.22 Article V Protection. The provisions of this Section 4A shall be protected under the Article V protection established in Sections 18.6.1 and 18.6.2. No act of Congress, executive order, judicial ruling, or state action shall modify, diminish, or evade the Franklin Ledger's comprehensive accessibility requirements, distributed responsibility model, or public transparency scope. The Franklin Ledger is the People's window into their government, and this Section establishes that window as constitutional in character.

Section 5. The National No Confidence Referendum

Key terms in this Section: • "The Authority" — The Independent Tripartite Oversight Authority (three bodies, see Section 17). • "Liberty Bell Initiative" — Separate concurrence of all three bodies of the Authority. • "The Ledger" — The Sovereign Blockchain Voting Ledger (Section 4). • "Referendum" — The national vote held after a certified Petition, in which the People directly vote whether to declare No Confidence in the existing Federal Government. • "Declaration of No Confidence" — The formal finding, certified by the Authority, that a qualifying Referendum has passed, triggering the removal of the existing Federal Government under Section 1 and the caretaker and reconstitution processes of Sections 6 through 9. 5.1 The referendum shall be administered within thirty (30) days of certification. 5.2 A Declaration of No Confidence shall pass only upon: (a) the affirmative vote of not less than sixty percent (60%) of ballots cast, representing the supermajority standard of this Amendment — a clean whole-number threshold high enough to require genuine broad consensus yet achievable in a polarized political environment; AND (b) participation of not less than fifty percent (50%) of registered voters across all Participating Jurisdictions, reflecting the constitutional principle that removal of the entire federal government warrants genuine majority engagement by the registered electorate rather than a plurality of a small participating fraction. Results falling within the automatic recount margin established in Section 23.3 shall trigger automatic recount procedures before certification. 5.3 Upon passage, all offices enumerated in Section 1.1 shall be vacated immediately. 5.3.1 Certification by the Authority of a passing Referendum and issuance of the Declaration of No Confidence shall proceed under the Liberty Bell Initiative pursuant to Section 17. If any one body of the Authority refuses Certification that the other two bodies independently find valid, the safeguard procedures of Sections 23.13 through 23.15 shall apply without modification, including automatic investigation by the Watchdog Tribunal within seven (7) days and potential replacement of the refusing body upon a two-thirds (2/3) supermajority finding of corruption or bad-faith obstruction. This cross-reference ensures that the mutual-veto structure of the Authority cannot be weaponized to block the legitimate will of the People as expressed in a passing Referendum. 5.4 Ballot Design and Question Wording. The Referendum ballot shall be uniform across all fifty-six (56) Participating Jurisdictions, with design and wording specified as follows: (a) Single Binding Question. The ballot shall present a single binary question: whether the People declare No Confidence in the federal officials specified in the certified Petition. The question shall be stated in plain language as: 'Shall the Declaration of No Confidence against [the specified officials or federal government as a whole] be adopted?' with 'Yes' indicating passage and 'No' indicating retention. (b) Petition Grounds Displayed. The ballot shall display, with each vote, a concise summary of the grounds stated in the certified Petition under Section 12.12, so that voters at the moment of voting can reference what they are voting upon. The full Petition text shall be accessible through the Sovereign Voting Terminal interface upon voter request. Ballot display shall be factual and non-editorial; no framing language beyond what appears in the certified Petition shall be added. (c) Targets Identified. The ballot shall specify, with unambiguous clarity, the federal officials, bodies, or the federal government as a whole against whom the Declaration of No Confidence is sought, so that voters know precisely which officeholders would be removed upon passage. (d) Multi-Language Accessibility. The ballot shall be available in English, Spanish, and the primary languages of Participating Jurisdictions with significant non-English-speaking populations, consistent with Section 12.12(c). Translation accuracy shall be certified by the Academic Integrity Commission prior to the Referendum. (e) Uniform National Presentation. The ballot question, grounds summary, and target identification shall be identical across all Jurisdictions, preventing manipulation through regional variation. The only Jurisdiction-specific element shall be the accessibility language of the ballot where multiple languages are displayed. 5.5 Voting Schedule and Hours. To ensure that the 30-day Referendum window provides genuine opportunity for participation across all Jurisdictions: (a) Full 30-Day Window Available. Every non-holiday day of the 30-day Referendum window shall be a voting day at every Office, Center, Host Site, and Satellite Site. No Office shall close during the Referendum window except pursuant to a Section 10.11 emergency pause, a Section 13.5 law enforcement action, or a documented natural disaster at the specific facility location.

(b) Minimum Hours of Operation. During the Referendum window, every Office, Center, Host Site, and Satellite Site shall operate a minimum of twelve (12) hours per day, from 7:00 AM to 7:00 PM local time, with extended hours of 6:00 AM to 9:00 PM local time during the final seven (7) days of the window. (c) Weekend and Holiday Operation. The Referendum window shall include all weekends. Where the window spans a federal holiday, Offices shall operate that day notwithstanding ordinary holiday schedules, consistent with the constitutional weight of the Referendum. (d) Overseas Terminal Schedule. Overseas Terminals under Section 14.9 shall operate during the Referendum window at hours appropriate to their host locations, with coverage across all time zones ensuring that United States citizens and nationals residing abroad have equivalent opportunity for participation. (e) Mobile Accessibility Team Deployment. Mobile Accessibility Teams under Section 11A.4 shall conduct heightened deployment during the Referendum window, with scheduling prioritizing institutional populations, homebound voters, and remote communities. 5.6 Infrastructure Failure During Referendum. Recognizing that the Referendum is a singular constitutional event whose integrity depends upon continuous operational capability across all fifty-six Participating Jurisdictions, the following procedures shall apply to infrastructure failures during the 30-day Referendum window: (a) Primary Chain Failure. Upon detected failure, compromise, or disagreement of a Primary Chain under Section 4.12, the Standby Chain under Section 4.17 shall be activated immediately, with votes cast during the failure period verified through cryptographic comparison to the surviving Primary Chain and the Standby Chain's shadow-mode records. No votes shall be lost to chain failure where cryptographic verification confirms their recording on any two of the three chains. (b) Office, Center, or Host Site Closure. Where an Office, Center, or Host Site becomes unable to operate during the Referendum window due to natural disaster, infrastructure failure, or security emergency, the Authority shall: (i) immediately publish notice on the Franklin Ledger identifying the closure and projected reopening; (ii) reroute affected voters to the nearest available site; (iii) deploy Mobile Accessibility Teams to affected areas to preserve voting access; and (iv) extend the Referendum window in the affected Jurisdiction by the duration of the closure plus three (3) additional days for affected voters to reach alternative voting locations. (c) Natural Disaster During Referendum. Where a genuine natural disaster under Section 10.7(a) affects one or more Participating Jurisdictions during the Referendum window, the Section 10.11 pause procedures shall apply to the affected Jurisdictions specifically. Voting in unaffected Jurisdictions shall continue on schedule; voting in affected Jurisdictions shall pause and resume upon emergency conclusion with the window extended by the duration of the pause.

(d) Votes Cast During Failure. Votes cast at a Sovereign Voting Terminal during a detected infrastructure failure shall be preserved through the paper ballot system under Sections 14.10 through 14.20, with electronic re-recording upon restoration of chain functionality. No voter shall be required to re-vote where their vote was captured by paper ballot or verified by cryptographic comparison across the three chains. (e) Maximum Disruption Before Automatic

Extension. Where infrastructure failure affects operation of more than ten percent (10%) of Offices, Centers, and Host Sites nationally for more than twenty-four (24) consecutive hours, the Referendum window shall be automatically extended by three (3) days beyond the duration of the failure. This protects against pattern failures that could suppress turnout without triggering individual-facility extensions. (f) Coordinated Sabotage Investigation. Where infrastructure failures display patterns suggesting deliberate sabotage rather than genuine failure — including temporal clustering, geographic clustering, or technical signatures of external interference — the Hamilton Contingent (once operational) and Watchdog Tribunal shall conduct immediate investigation, with findings published on the Franklin Ledger. Confirmed sabotage shall trigger Section 13 interference penalties with Senior Official multipliers where federal officials are implicated, and Section 22 foreign interference penalties where foreign actors are implicated. 5.7 Certification Process. Following close of the Referendum window, certification shall proceed as follows: (a) State Elections Council Jurisdictional Tabulation. Within seven (7) days of Referendum window close, the chief election officer of each Participating Jurisdiction (serving on the State Elections Council under Section 17) shall tabulate votes cast within that Jurisdiction, including vote totals, turnout against registered voter rolls, and provisional ballot disposition under Section 13.8(g). Jurisdictional tabulation shall be published on state government transparency infrastructure and on the Franklin Ledger. (b) National Aggregation and Cryptographic Verification. Within ten (10) days of Referendum window close, the Authority shall aggregate jurisdictional tabulations into national totals, cryptographically verifying each Jurisdiction's tabulation against the dual Primary Chain records under Section 4.11. Any discrepancy between State Elections Council tabulation and Primary Chain records shall be resolved through the Section 4.12 dual-chain verification procedure, with both Chains' records presumed authoritative and any jurisdictional tabulation that cannot be reconciled to Chain records subject to recount under Section 5.8. (c) Threshold Calculation. The Authority shall calculate: (i) total ballots cast; (ii) percentage of affirmative votes among ballots cast; (iii) total registered voters across all Jurisdictions at Referendum commencement; (iv) turnout percentage against registered voter total. Calculation methodology shall be published on the

Franklin Ledger with underlying data sufficient for independent verification by any citizen. (d) Certification Timeline. Certification by Liberty Bell Initiative under Section 5.3.1 shall occur within fourteen (14) days of Referendum window close, unless: (i) automatic recount under Section 5.8 is triggered; (ii) emergency pause under Section 10.11 extends the Referendum window; or (iii) Section 23.13 through 23.15 safeguards regarding a refusing Authority body are invoked. Certification delay beyond fourteen (14) days shall require published reasoning on the Franklin Ledger. (e) Jurisdiction-by-Jurisdiction Publication. Final certified results shall be published with complete jurisdiction-by-jurisdiction breakdown, including: total ballots cast per Jurisdiction; affirmative votes per Jurisdiction; turnout per Jurisdiction; provisional ballot dispositions per Jurisdiction. This granular publication enables public verification of national totals through independent arithmetic and exposes any jurisdictional irregularities to immediate scrutiny. (f) No Federal Executive Interference with Certification. No President, Vice President, Cabinet officer, federal agency head, or other federal executive officeholder shall direct, fund, influence, pressure, or impede certification under this Section. Any such interference shall constitute Section 13 interference with Senior Official multipliers where applicable, and shall trigger Section 23.13 safeguards where the interference targets a specific Authority body. 5.8 Automatic Recount Procedures. Where Referendum results fall within the automatic recount margin established in Section 23.3, the following referendum-specific recount procedures shall apply: (a) Recount Trigger. The automatic recount margin shall be calculated against the 60% affirmative threshold of Section 5.2(a): where certified results show affirmative votes between 58% and 62% of ballots cast, automatic recount shall be triggered. Similarly, where turnout falls between 48% and 52% of registered voters, automatic recount of turnout calculation shall be triggered. (b) Recount Timeline. Automatic recount shall commence within three (3) days of Referendum window close, proceeding in parallel with Section 5.7 certification activities. Recount shall complete within twenty-one (21) days of commencement, with recount certification by Liberty Bell Initiative within seven (7) additional days. (c) Recount Methodology. Recount shall be conducted through comparison of: (i) Primary Chain records; (ii) Standby Chain shadow records; (iii) paper ballot records under Sections 14.10 through 14.20; and (iv) State Elections Council jurisdictional tabulations. Discrepancies among sources shall be resolved with priority to paper ballot records as the voter-verified substrate, consistent with Section 14.10's constitutional role for paper ballots. (d) Status of Offices During Recount. Where recount is triggered before Section 5.3 immediate vacation has occurred (standard case — recount proceeds before certification), federal officials shall remain in office pending recount completion and final certification. Where recount is triggered after Section 5.3 vacation (rare case — recount after initial certification), vacated officials shall not resume office during recount; upon recount completion, if recount reverses the result, vacated officials shall be reinstated with back compensation and without prejudice, and any official actions taken during the vacation shall be subject to Section 15 review. (e) Watchdog Tribunal Oversight. The Watchdog Tribunal (or Phase One equivalent) shall oversee recount methodology and execution, with authority to investigate bad-faith recount conduct, direct recount procedures where methodological disputes arise, and certify recount integrity through findings published on the Franklin Ledger. (f) Manual Recount Authority. Beyond the automatic recount triggered by Section 23.3 margins, any registered voter, civic organization, or Authority body may petition for manual recount of specific Jurisdictions upon clear and convincing evidence of tabulation irregularity. Petitions shall be directed to the Watchdog Tribunal, which shall rule within fourteen (14) days and order manual recount where evidence warrants. 5.9 Post-Certification Actions and Failure Consequences. Depending upon Referendum outcome, the following actions shall proceed: (a) Passage — Immediate Vacation and Transition. Upon certification of a passing Referendum under Section 5.3.1, the offices enumerated in Section 1.1 shall be vacated immediately pursuant to Section 5.3. The Interim Caretaker Council under Section 6A shall convene within seventy-two (72) hours. The Constitutional Transition Committee under Section 6 shall convene upon election under Section 6A. The Emergency Election under Section 7 shall be held within ninety (90) days of Committee convening. Reconstitution of the federal bureaucracy shall proceed under Section 15. (b) Failure — Officials Remain in Office. Upon certification of a failing Referendum (affirmative votes below 60%, or turnout below 50%), the officials enumerated in Section 1.1 shall remain in office under ordinary constitutional authority. Certification shall be published with the same jurisdiction-by-jurisdiction detail required under Section 5.7(e). (c) Failure — Cooldown Period. Upon certification of a failing Referendum, the two (2) year cooldown period under Section 10.1 shall commence, preventing initiation of a new Declaration of No Confidence for two (2) years from certification. Registration of Petitions during the cooldown shall proceed under Section 10.1 with activation deferred until cooldown expiration. (d) Failure — No Penalty to Good-Faith Initiators. Good-faith voters who initiated or signed a Petition that led to a failed Referendum shall not face penalty, adverse consequence, or retaliation. Bad-faith initiation is governed by Section 12.15 under the clear-and-convincing evidence standard; failure to reach passage thresholds

shall not itself constitute bad faith. (e) Permanent Publication. Final certified results — whether passage or failure — shall be permanently published on the Franklin Ledger with full jurisdiction-by-jurisdiction breakdown. No certification result shall be removed, redacted, or altered after publication, preserving the historical record of the People's expressed will. 5.10 Voter Privacy and Anti-Retaliation. The secrecy of the ballot is foundational to authentic Referendum expression. The following protections shall apply: (a) Secret Ballot Preserved Through Zero-Knowledge Proofs. Under the cryptographic framework of Section 4.1(c), individual vote choices shall be preserved in cryptographic privacy while vote validity remains verifiable. No record shall associate an individual voter's identity with their specific Referendum vote choice. (b) No Public Identification of Individual Vote Choices. Neither the Authority, the Watchdog Tribunal, the Hamilton Contingent, federal law enforcement, state officials, nor any other person or body shall publish, disclose, or identify how any specific voter voted in the Referendum. The only publicly disclosed information shall be aggregate totals under Section 5.7(e). (c) Anti-Retaliation Protection. No voter shall face retaliation, adverse treatment, employment consequence, social pressure, or other adverse action for their Referendum vote choice, whether affirmative or negative. Retaliation for Referendum voting shall constitute Section 13 interference prosecutable under the ordinary framework, with enhanced penalties where the retaliation targets voters based on demographic characteristics or institutional dependencies (such as employees of the voter's employer, residents of care facilities, or members of other vulnerable populations). (d) Coercion of Referendum Vote. Coercion of a Referendum vote — whether by threat, bribe, intimidation, or exploitation of dependency — shall constitute Section 13 interference, with framework parallel to Section 12.14 coercion of Petition signatures. Reports of coercion shall be investigated by the Watchdog Tribunal, with confirmed coercion subject to Section 13 penalties. 5.11 Consolidated Cross-References for Completeness. The following provisions from elsewhere in this Amendment apply to the Referendum without modification, and are cross-referenced here for completeness: (a) Voter Authentication. Identity verification at Sovereign Voting Terminals during the Referendum shall proceed under the Section 12.9 framework, including acceptable identification, cryptographic binding, accommodation for voters without standard ID, and privacy protection for identification data. (b) Observer Rights. Public observation of Referendum voting shall proceed under the

Section 12.13 framework, with multi-day observer credentials available for organizations conducting sustained observation during the 30-day window. Voter privacy during individual voting shall be preserved consistent with Section 5.10. (c) Overseas and Military Voters. United States citizens and nationals residing abroad shall participate through Overseas Terminals under Section 3.1.3 and Section 14.9, with signatures and votes attributed to the voter's most recent United States residence of record or the Overseas Americans Jurisdiction. (d) Accessibility. The accessibility framework of Section 11A shall apply in full during the Referendum, including Accessible Terminals, Mobile Accessibility Teams, personal support services, and adaptive equipment. (e) Foreign Interference. The foreign interference framework of Section 22 shall apply with heightened vigilance during the Referendum window, recognizing that the singular constitutional weight of the Referendum creates elevated interference incentives. (f) Emergency Declaration Framework. The emergency declaration framework of Section 10, including the distinction between genuine and pretextual declarations and the cumulative cap provisions, shall apply to any declared emergency during the Referendum window. (g) Voter Roll Integrity. The voter roll integrity protections of Section 13.8 shall apply to Referendum participation, including provisional ballot pathways for voters whose registration records are missing or altered at the time of voting. 5.12 No Delay Permitted. No act of Congress, executive order, presidential proclamation, judicial ruling, state action, emergency declaration, martial law declaration, or any other federal, state, or territorial action shall delay, postpone, modify, or prevent a Referendum certified under Section 3.2. Any attempt to do so shall be void ab initio and shall have no legal force; officials administering the Referendum shall proceed notwithstanding any such purported order, declaration, ruling, or action. Any such attempt shall constitute interference under Section 13, triggering the full penalties thereof, including the fifteen (15) year minimum sentence and the lifetime bar from public office without possibility of pardon. This provision mirrors the Inaugural Referendum protection under Section 19A.4 and reflects the constitutional judgment that once the People have met the Section 3 petition thresholds and the Authority has certified a Referendum, the People's sovereign judgment on federal government continuation cannot be obstructed by the very federal government being evaluated. The Referendum is the constitutional exercise of popular sovereignty that precedes and supersedes ordinary federal authority; ordinary federal authority cannot obstruct its own evaluation. 5.12.1 Officials' Duty to Proceed Notwithstanding Purported Delay Orders. Officials administering a certified

Referendum — including State Elections Council members, Office and Center staff, Oversight Officers, and all other Amendment personnel — shall proceed with Referendum administration notwithstanding any purported federal, state, or territorial order to delay, postpone, modify, or prevent

the Referendum. Such officials shall face no legal consequence, employment consequence, disciplinary action, or other adverse consequence for proceeding with the Referendum in defiance of orders void ab initio under Section 5.12. Any person who prosecutes, disciplines, terminates, or otherwise takes adverse action against an official for proceeding with a certified Referendum shall be subject to Section 13 interference penalties with Senior Official multipliers where applicable, and the adverse action shall itself be void ab initio. This subsection resolves the dilemma that would otherwise face officials who receive conflicting commands from Amendment authority and purported contrary authority: the Amendment prevails, and compliance with the Amendment shall never be punishable. 5.12.2 Article V Protection for Referendum Process. The provisions of Sections 5.12 and 5.12.1 shall be protected under the Article V protection established in Sections 18.6.1 and 18.6.2. The Referendum's undelayability is a foundational feature of the Amendment, without which the entire No Confidence mechanism could be blocked by the very government the Referendum is designed to evaluate.

Section 6. The Constitutional Transition Committee

Key terms in this Section: • "The Authority" — The Independent Tripartite Oversight Authority (three bodies, see Section 17). • "Liberty Bell Initiative" — Separate concurrence of all three bodies of the Authority. • "The Ledger" — The Sovereign Blockchain Voting Ledger (Section 4). • "Terminal" — A Sovereign Voting Terminal (Section 14), the dedicated, air-gapped device used for casting in-person verified votes. • "The Committee" — The Constitutional Transition Committee established by this Section, composed of fifty (50) delegates elected directly by the citizens of each state through Emergency Delegate Elections. • "Chairperson" — The presiding delegate of the Committee, elected by Committee majority vote from among the fifty delegates within five (5) days of convening. • "Vice Chairperson" — The pre-designated successor to the Chairperson, elected at the same time as the Chairperson; automatically and immediately assumes the role of Chairperson upon death, resignation, incapacitation, or removal of the Chairperson.

6.1 All executive, legislative, and judicial authority shall vest in the Committee. The Committee shall be convened within ten (10) days of the completion of Emergency Delegate Elections under Section 6.2, with Elections to be completed within ninety (90) days of the Authority's certification of the Declaration of No Confidence. The Committee may commence its work as soon as a majority of delegates have been elected and sworn pursuant to Section 6.5, even if elections remain pending in some states under permitted extensions. 6.2 The fifty (50) delegates of the Committee shall be elected directly by the citizens of each state, one delegate per state, through an Emergency Delegate Election administered by the State Elections Council. The Election shall be conducted as follows: (a) The Election shall be held within ninety (90) days of the Authority's certification of the Declaration of No Confidence, conducted via the Sovereign Voting Terminals at the Citizens' Reclamation Offices using ranked-choice voting. The ninety-day window provides meaningful time for candidate emergence, campaigning, public review, and citizen deliberation during a crisis — long enough for serious candidates to build awareness across their state and for citizens to make informed choices, while still moving with appropriate urgency; (b) Candidates shall meet the eligibility requirements of Section 17.7: no current or former federal officeholder or political appointee within the preceding ten (10) years; no registered federal lobbyist within the preceding ten (10) years; no person who has made federal political contributions above a minimal public-service threshold within the preceding ten (10) years; no employee of a federal contractor within the preceding ten (10) years; and no immediate family member of any person described in this clause; (c) Candidates shall file a full public financial disclosure upon the Ledger no later than fifteen (15) days before the Election, including all assets, liabilities, business interests, and sources of income; (d) The Election period shall allow a minimum of thirty (30) days for candidate filing, public review, and citizen education before voting commences; and (e) The winning candidate in each state shall be certified by the State Elections Council and sworn in as a Committee delegate within seventy-two (72) hours of certification. 6.3 If the Emergency Delegate Election in any state cannot be completed within the ninety (90) day window due to a genuine and documented emergency (natural disaster, confirmed cyberattack, or verified public health crisis of sufficient scope to materially prevent citizen participation), the Authority may, by Liberty Bell Initiative publicly reasoned upon the Ledger, grant a single fifteen (15) day extension. No state shall receive more than two such extensions in total, and no extension shall exceed fifteen (15) days. Any state official found to have delayed or obstructed the Election pretextually shall be subject to the interference penalties of

Section 13 and the non-compliance consequences of Section 20. 6.4 If a state fails to complete the Emergency Delegate Election within the permitted timeline, the Authority shall directly administer the Election in that state using mobile Citizens' Reclamation Offices deployed pursuant to Section 20.10. No state's citizens shall ever be denied representation on the Committee due to their state's non-compliance. 6.5 The Committee shall commence its work as soon as a majority (twenty-six) of delegates have been elected and sworn, even if elections remain pending in some states. No action of the Committee shall be invalidated by the later arrival of delegates from states with extended Elections. 6.6 Within five (5) days of the Committee's convening, the Committee shall elect by majority vote, from among the fifty delegates, a presiding Chairperson and a Vice Chairperson who shall serve as the pre-designated successor to the Chairperson. The Vice Chairperson shall be of different party affiliation or political orientation than the Chairperson whenever practicable, to ensure ideological diversity in the Committee's leadership. 6.7 If the Chairperson dies, resigns, voluntarily withdraws, or is otherwise unable to perform the duties of office, the Vice Chairperson shall automatically and immediately assume the role of Chairperson, without gap, interruption, or vote. The Committee shall then elect a new Vice Chairperson by majority vote within seventy-two (72) hours. 6.8 The Committee may remove the Chairperson for cause by a two-thirds (2/3) vote of all delegates (thirty-four of fifty), with the specific cause publicly reasoned and recorded upon the Ledger. Valid causes for removal include, but are not limited to: corruption; bribery; abuse of power; material breach of the constitutional oath; collusion with removed officials or foreign powers; or deliberate subversion of this Amendment. Upon removal, the Vice Chairperson shall automatically assume the role of Chairperson pursuant to Section 6.7. 6.9 A determination of Chairperson incapacitation shall require BOTH: (a) Unanimous written certification by three (3) independent physicians, selected by lottery from a pre-established pool maintained by the Academic Integrity Commission, finding that the Chairperson is physically or mentally incapable of performing the duties of office. The certification shall be published in full upon the Ledger; AND (b) A majority vote of the Committee concurring with the medical certification. 6.10 The dual requirement of Section 6.9 prevents both the exploitation of genuine illness to paralyze Committee leadership and the weaponization of false illness claims to unlawfully oust a legitimate Chairperson. If the Chairperson recovers and the physicians unanimously certify restored capacity, the Chairperson shall resume office upon

Committee concurrence by majority vote. During any period of certified incapacitation, the Vice Chairperson shall serve as Acting Chairperson. 6.11 The Committee shall consist solely of the elected delegates. No delegate may be a current or former federal officeholder or political appointee within the preceding four (4) years. 6.11.1 In addition to the fifty (50) voting delegates elected by the states, there shall be six (6) Advisory Delegates representing the District of Columbia and the five territories enumerated in Section 3.1.1: one Advisory Delegate each from the District of Columbia, the Commonwealth of Puerto Rico, the Territory of Guam, the United States Virgin Islands, the Commonwealth of the Northern Mariana Islands, and the Territory of American Samoa. 6.11.2 Advisory Delegates shall be elected directly by the registered voters of their respective Participating Jurisdiction, through Emergency Delegate Elections conducted under the same rules and timelines as state delegate elections pursuant to Sections 6.2 through 6.5. They shall meet the same eligibility standards as voting delegates. 6.11.3 Advisory Delegates shall participate fully in all Committee deliberations, access all materials, introduce proposals, speak in debate, and have their concerns recorded upon the Ledger, but shall not cast binding votes on Committee decisions. Their voice on the Committee shall carry the weight of representing communities subject to federal authority who bear the consequences of Committee action, even if their vote does not yet count in binding tallies. Future Amendments or Sunset Review modifications may elevate Advisory Delegates to full voting status. 6.12 The Committee shall exercise caretaker and reconstitution authority only. It may not enact new legislation, declare war, ratify treaties, or make permanent appointments. 6.13 All actions of the Committee shall be publicly recorded upon the Ledger. 6.14 Quorum and Voting Procedures. Committee action shall proceed under the following framework: (a) Ordinary Quorum. Ordinary quorum for Committee action shall require the presence of not fewer than twenty-six (26) of the fifty (50) voting delegates (a majority), whether physically present at Committee venue or participating via secure video conference under subsection (f). Ordinary action requires majority vote of those present and voting. (b) Supermajority Requirements. The following Committee actions shall require two-thirds (2/3) supermajority of all fifty (50) voting delegates (thirty-four (34)): (i) removal of the Chairperson under Section 6.8; (ii) reconstitution determinations under Section 15.4 affecting agencies with more than ten thousand (10,000) personnel or essential service functions; (iii) authorization of military domestic deployment under Section 16.3(b); (iv) referral of disputed military refusals to public military tribunal under Section

16.3(e); (v) suspension of federal regulations

under Section 15.3 with effect extending beyond the Committee Period; and (vi) any action the Committee determines by majority vote warrants supermajority consideration. (c) Individual Vote Recording. Every delegate's vote on every action shall be individually recorded and published on the Franklin Ledger, with no anonymous or consolidated voting. This transparency ensures delegate accountability to their state's citizens. (d) Advisory Delegate Participation. The six (6) Advisory Delegates under Sections 6.11.1 through 6.11.3 shall participate in all deliberations, with their positions on each action publicly recorded even though not counted in binding vote tallies. (e) Abstention and Recusal. Delegates may abstain from votes where they have specific conflicts of interest or personal involvement with the matter under consideration. Recusal shall be recorded with the specific basis. Abstentions and recusals shall not count toward quorum for the specific action from which they are recused, but shall count toward general quorum. (f) Secure Video Conference Participation. Delegates unable to attend in person due to genuine circumstance may participate via secure video conference approved by the Chairperson, with full voting rights. Secure video participation shall meet security standards certified by the Academic Integrity Commission and shall not become the default mode of Committee operation; in-person attendance at Committee venue shall be the standard expectation. 6.15 Chairperson Military Command Authority. The Chairperson's Commander-in-Chief authority under Section 16.14(c) shall operate as follows: (a) Scope of Command. The Chairperson shall exercise the constitutional Commander-in-Chief authority for all Armed Forces of the United States during the Committee Period, subject to all Section 16 constraints including the nuclear authorization framework, protected refusal framework, communication integrity framework, and chain of command preservation. (b) Specific Limitations. The Chairperson shall not: (i) authorize nuclear first-use outside the Section 16.8 framework; (ii) unilaterally order domestic military deployment (requiring Committee majority authorization under Section 16.3(b)); (iii) remove or reassign Joint Chiefs of Staff except upon documented cause concurred in by Committee supermajority; (iv) issue orders that violate this Constitution, this Amendment, or the laws of war; (v) make permanent changes to military posture, force structure, or acquisition programs that would bind post-Committee-Period leadership without affirmative ratification by the new President. (c) Required Joint Chiefs Consultation. The Chairperson shall consult with the Joint Chiefs of Staff before issuing operational military orders, with consultation records preserved under Section 13B standards. Consultation is procedural — the Joint

Chiefs advise, the Chairperson decides — but the consultation itself shall occur and be documented. (d) Committee Oversight of Chairperson Military Action. The Committee shall receive weekly briefings on military operations under the Chairperson's authority. The Committee, by majority vote, may direct the Chairperson to cease, modify, or reverse specific military actions where the Committee determines the action exceeds caretaker scope, violates this Amendment, or is otherwise inappropriate. (e) Section 16 Protected Refusal Applies. All Section 16 protected refusal provisions apply to orders issued by the Chairperson on the same terms as orders issued by the President. Service members may refuse unlawful Chairperson orders under the Section 16.19 framework. (f) Transfer Back to Elected President. Upon swearing-in of the new President following Emergency Election under Section 7, the Chairperson's military command authority shall terminate immediately. The transfer shall be complete and unconditional, with the new President's Article II authority restored in full as provided in Section 16.14(d). 6.16 Committee Operations and Working Schedule. The Committee shall operate under the following framework: (a) Venue Rotation. Committee sessions shall rotate among state capitols or other state-sovereign secure facilities under Section 11C.10, preventing institutional capture of any single venue. Rotation patterns shall be determined by Committee rule adopted in first session. (b) Continuous Session. The Committee shall maintain continuous session throughout the Committee Period, with regular voting sessions not less than three (3) times per week and working sessions daily during the active oversight period. Periods of reduced activity (weekends, limited holiday schedules) shall be determined by Committee rule while preserving emergency responsiveness. (c) Public Observation. All Committee sessions shall be livestreamed on the Franklin Ledger consistent with Section 11C.6 public observation requirements. Executive sessions for specific limited purposes (personnel matters, classified briefings, deliberations on sensitive personnel or security decisions) may proceed with reduced public observation but shall be documented on the Ledger after session conclusion. (d) Subcommittee Structure. The Committee may establish subcommittees of not fewer than seven (7) delegates to focus on specific domains (military oversight, bureaucracy reconstitution under Section 15, budget and appropriations, foreign affairs, judicial matters, and others). Subcommittees shall prepare recommendations for full Committee vote but shall not exercise binding Committee authority independently.

(e) Record Preservation. All Committee deliberations, votes, resolutions, orders, and working documents shall be preserved under Section 13B standards for permanent accessibility on the Franklin Ledger and through the National Archives after Committee dissolution. 6.17 Committee Staff and Operational Resources. To support Committee function: (a) Professional Staff. The Committee shall employ professional staff including: legal counsel independent of federal executive branch legal services; policy analysts drawn from the Pre-Certified University Pool under Section 17.16; parliamentary staff for session management; records staff for Section 13B compliance; security personnel; and administrative personnel sufficient for Committee operations. Staff shall be paid through the Section 11.3 constitutional appropriation via a dedicated Committee Operations reserve. (b) Academic Integrity Commission Technical Support. The Standing Review Panel under Section 15.5 shall provide ongoing technical expertise to the Committee on reconstitution determinations, regulatory analysis, and other matters requiring subject-matter expertise. (c) Witness and Expert Testimony. The Committee may compel testimony from federal officials (including acting agency leadership under Section 15.11), former federal officials, subject-matter experts, affected stakeholders, and citizens presenting matters within Committee authority. Compelled testimony shall follow established Congressional testimony procedures with perjury liability for knowingly false testimony. (d) Independence From Federal Executive. Committee staff shall be employees of the Amendment's administrative infrastructure, not of any federal executive agency. No President (past or current), Vice President, Cabinet officer, or federal agency head shall have hiring, firing, compensation, or performance-evaluation authority over Committee staff. 6.18 Delegate Security and Protection. Recognizing that Committee delegates face elevated threat during the post-No Confidence transition: (a) Physical Protection. Each delegate shall receive physical protection equivalent to that provided to sitting Members of Congress, including: protective detail for travel to and from Committee venues; residence security during the Committee Period; and immediate response to credible threats. Protection shall continue for six (6) months following Committee dissolution for delegates who served. (b) Communications Security. Delegates shall have access to secure communications infrastructure for Committee-related communications, with encryption standards certified by the Academic Integrity Commission. (c) Family Protection. Immediate family members of delegates shall receive protection against harassment, intimidation, and retaliation, with specific

Section 13 interference prosecution for those targeting delegate families.

(d) Retaliation Protection. No delegate shall face adverse action — including loss of prior employment, denial of future opportunity, professional sanction, or other adverse treatment — for their Committee service or for positions taken during service. Retaliation shall constitute Section 13 interference with enhanced penalties where connected to specific Committee decisions. (e) Post-Service Protection. Following Committee dissolution, delegates shall retain ongoing whistleblower-style protections under Section 13B.16 for five (5) years regarding their Committee service, preserving their ability to speak publicly about Committee deliberations without retaliation. 6.19 Committee Coordination with Other Amendment Bodies. The Committee shall coordinate with: (a) Interim Caretaker Council. Upon Committee convening, the Interim Caretaker Council under Section 6A shall dissolve per Section 6A.15, with all Caretaker Period records transferring to the Committee. The Committee inherits Caretaker authority without interruption. (b) Watchdog Tribunal. The Committee shall coordinate with the Watchdog Tribunal on matters of corruption investigation, officeholder accountability, and oversight of Committee conduct itself. The Tribunal shall maintain oversight authority over the Committee, ensuring the Committee itself is subject to accountability review. (c) Hamilton Contingent. The Committee shall coordinate with the Hamilton Contingent on prosecution of pre-removal corruption, evidence preservation under Section 13B, asset recovery under Section 13D, and related enforcement matters. The Committee shall not direct specific prosecutorial decisions but shall support Contingent enforcement resources and coordination. (d) Authority Bodies During Phase One. Where the Committee Period overlaps with Phase One Authority constitution under Section 19.19, the Committee shall coordinate with the Authority's three bodies (Citizens' Oversight Board, State Elections Council, Academic Integrity Commission) as those bodies stand up. Coordination shall preserve Committee caretaker authority while enabling Authority oversight function. (e) State Attorneys General Council. The Committee shall coordinate with the State Attorneys General Council on matters of state-federal interaction, particularly Section 13 interference prosecution during the Committee Period, with the Council retaining its ordinary prosecution authority under Section 19.5.0.18.9.1. 6.20 Caretaker Versus Permanent Action Distinction. The Committee's caretaker authority under Section 6.12 shall be understood as follows: (a) Caretaker Actions Permitted. The Committee may take actions necessary to: (i) maintain ongoing federal operations per Section 15.2; (ii) make reconstitution determinations under Section 15.4 within the 180-day window; (iii) suspend corrupt regulations under Section 15.3; (iv) authorize military actions within Committee scope; (v) coordinate emergency response where genuine emergencies arise; (vi) administer the transition to the new President; and (vii) take other actions within the caretaker role necessary for orderly operation. (b) Permanent Actions Prohibited. The Committee shall not: (i) enact new legislation; (ii) declare war; (iii) ratify treaties; (iv) make permanent appointments extending beyond the Committee Period; (v) issue executive orders binding future Presidents; (vi) take other actions of permanent character. Prohibited actions taken by the Committee shall be void ab initio. (c) Gray-Area Actions. Actions whose caretaker versus permanent character is ambiguous shall be resolved in favor of narrower caretaker construction. Where the Committee is uncertain, it shall seek Watchdog Tribunal advisory opinion before proceeding. (d) Emergency Exception. Where genuine emergency circumstances require Committee action exceeding caretaker scope, the Committee may act by two-thirds supermajority with specific documented justification, subject to: (i) immediate Watchdog Tribunal review of the action and the emergency justification; (ii) Liberty Bell Initiative review by the Authority where convened; (iii) automatic sunset of the action upon swearing-in of the new President unless the new President affirmatively ratifies; and (iv) Section 13 interference liability for Committee members where the emergency exception was invoked in bad faith. (e) No Self-Extension. The Committee shall not take any action extending its own tenure beyond the Committee Period. Attempts to extend Committee authority shall constitute Section 16.5 insurrection and Section 13 interference with Senior Official multipliers applied to each Committee member voting for extension. 6.21 Emergency Decision-Making. Where time-sensitive Committee action is required: (a) Expedited Consideration. Matters requiring decision within seventy-two (72) hours may be considered under expedited procedure upon Chairperson determination concurred in by Vice Chairperson. Expedited procedure shall preserve quorum requirements and voting standards but may compress notice periods, briefing timelines, and debate duration. (b) Emergency Chairperson Action. Where time does not permit even expedited Committee consideration (matters requiring action within twenty-four (24) hours), the Chairperson may act with concurrence of a five-member Emergency Subcommittee consisting of the Chairperson, Vice Chairperson, and three (3) additional delegates designated by the Committee at first session to serve during periods of emergency. Emergency action shall be subject to full Committee ratification within seventy-two (72) hours, with failure to ratify voiding the action retroactively where operationally possible.

(c) Standard Cannot Be Emergency. Matters that do not genuinely require expedited or emergency treatment shall proceed through ordinary Committee process. Abuse of expedited or emergency procedures to bypass deliberation shall be subject to Watchdog Tribunal review and may trigger Section 13 interference liability. 6.22 Committee-to-New-President Handoff. Upon certification of Emergency Election results under Section 7.16: (a) Transition Period. A seven (7) day transition period shall follow certification, during which the Committee shall brief the President-elect on ongoing operations, pending decisions, interim commitments, and matters requiring early presidential attention. (b) Swearing-In Triggers Transfer. Upon the President-elect taking the constitutional oath, Committee authority over executive functions shall terminate. The new President shall exercise full Article II authority, subject to all Amendment constraints. (c) Committee Dissolution Schedule. The Committee shall dissolve fourteen (14) days after the new President's swearing-in, with a brief continuing period to complete record preservation, Section 15 reconstitution determinations in progress, and final accountability reporting. Committee dissolution shall be automatic upon the fourteen-day mark; no action is required to effect dissolution. (d) Records Transfer. Upon dissolution, all Committee records shall transfer to the National Archives for permanent preservation, with duplicate access through the Franklin Ledger. The new Authority (once fully constituted) shall have continuing access to Committee records for oversight review. (e) Post-Dissolution Accountability. Former Committee members shall remain subject to accountability for Committee actions taken during service. Post-dissolution investigations by the Watchdog Tribunal, Hamilton Contingent, or State Attorneys General Council shall proceed consistent with applicable statutes of limitations and the Section 6.18(e) post-service whistleblower protections. (f) No Post-Dissolution Authority. Former Committee members shall not retain any residual Committee authority following dissolution. Any attempt to exercise former Committee authority post-dissolution shall constitute Section 13 interference. 6.23 Hardship Framework Applicability. The hardship framework of Sections 17.4 through 17.4.13 shall apply to Committee delegates as follows: the Committee is a multi-month service body falling within Section 17.4.13(a) treatment, with the administering body for hardship matters being the Committee's internal Chairperson-plus-Vice Chairperson leadership with appeal to an emergency three-member panel of Chief Justices drawn by lottery. Committee delegates drawn through Emergency Delegate Elections are elected rather than lottery-drawn, but the principles of accommodation-first, privacy protection, and anti-retaliation apply equally. Where a delegate develops hardship during the Committee Period preventing continued service, the Emergency Delegate Election framework of Sections 6.2 through 6.4 shall apply to select a replacement, with expedited timelines consistent with Committee Period operational needs. 6.24 Committee Ethics and Conflicts of Interest. During service: (a) Conflict Disclosure. Delegates shall disclose upon convening, and update as arising, any financial, professional, or personal interests that could reasonably affect their Committee judgment on specific matters. Disclosures shall be published on the Franklin Ledger. (b) Recusal Standard. Delegates shall recuse from specific votes where their disclosed interests would materially affect judgment, with recusal published on the Ledger per Section 6.14(e). (c) Prohibited Activities During Service. Delegates shall not during their service: (i) accept gifts or things of value from any corporation, lobbyist, federal contractor, foreign national, or federal officeholder under review; (ii) engage in outside employment that conflicts with Committee duties; (iii) communicate with pre-removal federal officials about Committee matters outside formal Committee processes; (iv) engage in campaign activity for or against Emergency Election candidates while Committee decisions could affect their candidacy. (d) Post-Service Restrictions. For five (5) years following Committee service, former delegates shall not: (i) lobby the federal government; (ii) accept federal appointive positions exceeding routine boards and advisory roles; (iii) work for federal contractors on matters they oversaw during Committee service; (iv) otherwise trade on their Committee service for personal financial benefit. Restrictions shall be enforced by the Watchdog Tribunal with Section 13 interference penalties for violations. (e) Violation Consequences. Ethics violations during Committee service shall be grounds for Committee removal under Section 6.8 (for Chairperson) or delegate removal by Committee two-thirds vote. Removed delegates shall be replaced through Emergency Delegate Election per Section 6.3. 6.25 Committee Compensation. Delegates shall receive: (a) Federal Salary. Compensation equivalent to the salary of sitting United States Representatives, prorated for the Committee Period duration, paid through the Section 11.3 constitutional appropriation. (b) Travel and Expenses. Full reimbursement for travel to and from Committee venues, housing during Committee sessions away from delegates' home jurisdictions, and ordinary expenses of Committee service. (c) Benefits Continuity. Federal health insurance and benefits during Committee service, equivalent to those available to sitting Members of Congress.

(d) Home-Jurisdiction Employment Protection. Delegates shall have federally protected employment with their home-jurisdiction employers (private, state, or local) with no retaliation permitted for Committee service, consistent with Section 17.5(a) protections for Citizens' Oversight Board members. (e) No Accepting Additional Compensation. Delegates shall not accept additional compensation beyond the federal salary of subsection (a) from any source during service, preventing external interests from financial influence over delegates.

Section 6A. The Interim Caretaker Council

Key terms in this Section: • "The Authority" — The Independent Tripartite Oversight Authority (three bodies, see Section 17). • "Liberty Bell Initiative" — Separate concurrence of all three bodies of the Authority. • "The Ledger" — The Sovereign Blockchain Voting Ledger (Section 4). • "The Committee" — The Constitutional Transition Committee (Section 6). • "Caretaker Council" — The Interim Caretaker Council established by this Section, consisting of the fifty-six sitting Governors (or equivalent chief executives) of the Participating Jurisdictions, convened automatically upon a Declaration of No Confidence and dissolving automatically upon the Committee's convening. • "Caretaker Period" — The period from the Authority's certification of the Declaration of No Confidence until the convening of the Constitutional Transition Committee under Section 6.1 (typically up to one hundred (100) days, reflecting the ninety (90) day Emergency Delegate Election window plus up to ten (10) days for Committee convening). 6A.1 Recognizing that the immediate vacation of all offices enumerated in Section 1.1 upon passage of a Declaration of No Confidence creates a period during which no sitting President, Vice President, Congress, Supreme Court, or political executive branch exists, and recognizing that essential emergency executive functions must continue during this Caretaker Period to protect the United States and its People, there is hereby established the Interim Caretaker Council ("Caretaker Council"), constituted and empowered solely and exclusively as set forth in this Section. The Council's duration reflects the ninety (90) day Emergency Delegate Election window under Section 6.2 plus up to ten (10) days for Committee convening under Section 6.1. A. Composition, Convening, and Dissolution 6A.2 The Caretaker Council shall consist of fifty-six (56) members: the sitting Governor (or equivalent chief executive officer) of each of the fifty states, the Mayor of the District of Columbia, and the Governor of each of the five territories enumerated in Section 3.1.1, all serving ex officio for the duration of the

Caretaker Period. No separate appointment, confirmation, election, or term shall apply. 6A.2.1 Governor Vacancy. In the event that the governor (or equivalent chief executive) position of any Participating Jurisdiction is vacant at the moment the Caretaker Council convenes, or becomes vacant during the Caretaker Period, the acting chief executive of that Jurisdiction under the Jurisdiction's own constitutional succession law shall serve on the Caretaker Council. This respects each Jurisdiction's sovereign authority over its own succession while ensuring all fifty-six seats remain filled. Succession shall apply automatically without federal determination of who serves; the Jurisdiction's own law controls. Upon any mid-Period succession, the newly serving chief executive shall take the Caretaker Council constitutional oath within seventy-two (72) hours and may exercise full Council voting authority immediately upon taking the oath. 6A.3 The Caretaker Council shall convene automatically within seventy-two (72) hours of the Authority's certification of a Declaration of No Confidence. No act of Congress (the existing Congress having been removed), executive order, judicial ruling, or state action shall delay, impede, or invalidate its convening. Any attempt to do so by any person shall constitute interference under Section 13 and shall trigger the full penalties thereof. 6A.4 The Caretaker Council shall dissolve automatically and immediately upon the convening of the Constitutional Transition Committee under Section 6.1. Authority shall transfer to the Committee in the same instant, with any Council action then pending or in progress suspended immediately and referred to the Committee for determination. Records, decisions, and documentation shall transfer to the Committee in full. The Caretaker Council shall have no authority, under any circumstances, to delay its own dissolution or to extend the Caretaker Period. B. Leadership and Voting Procedure 6A.5 The Caretaker Council shall have a Presiding Chair who rotates every calendar day during the Caretaker Period, in alphabetical order of Participating Jurisdiction beginning with Alabama. This daily rotation prevents any individual from accumulating authority and distributes the visible face of the Council across all Jurisdictions during the Period. The Presiding Chair shall preside over meetings only and shall possess no additional voting weight, veto authority, or unilateral decision-making power.

6A.6 Any action of the Caretaker Council shall require the affirmative vote of two-thirds (2/3) supermajority of all members (thirty-eight of fifty-six). No quorum threshold lower than this shall be recognized. The supermajority requirement ensures that no partisan minority or narrow coalition can exercise caretaker authority, and that every action reflects broad multi-jurisdictional consensus. 6A.7 All meetings, deliberations, and votes of the Caretaker Council shall be livestreamed in real time upon the Ledger (or the provisional public ledger if the full Ledger is not yet fully operational at the time of a No Confidence passage). No secret sessions shall be conducted. The existence, timing, and substance of every Council action shall never be classified or redacted, except for narrow operational-security redactions of active military response details certified as necessary by supermajority of the Council and subject to public review within thirty (30) days. C. Authority — What the Caretaker Council MAY Do 6A.8 The Caretaker Council shall possess the following limited authorities, and only these, for the strict purpose of emergency preservation — preventing new harms from arising during the Caretaker Period, not creating new policy or governance: (a) Defensive Military Coordination. Authorize defensive military responses in coordination with the Joint Chiefs of Staff pursuant to Section 16. All Section 16 procedural requirements apply without modification, including the Nuclear Authorization Panel and the emergency override of Section 16.10; (b) Natural Disaster Response. Declare federal emergencies in response to confirmed natural disasters; authorize the disbursement of emergency funding from existing, previously-appropriated federal disaster relief accounts; and coordinate with state and territorial governments on disaster response; (c) Foreign Communications — Receipt Only. Receive necessary foreign communications through career State Department personnel; acknowledge receipt of such communications; and communicate that new substantive diplomatic commitments await the convening of the Committee. The Caretaker Council shall NOT initiate new treaties, agreements, or diplomatic commitments; (d) Critical Career Vacancy Fill. Fill career-personnel vacancies critical to public safety by appointing interim replacements from within existing career ranks (for example, filling a suddenly vacated FAA Air Traffic Control chief position by promoting the most senior existing career deputy). Such appointments are temporary only and subject to Committee review. No political positions shall be filled; (e) Continuity Documents. Sign routine continuity documents that have existing statutory authorization and pre-existing appropriations, such as scheduled Social Security disbursements, Medicare payments, federal employee payroll, and similar ministerial acts that must occur to prevent interruption of essential benefits; and (f) Interstate Emergency Coordination. Coordinate with Participating Jurisdiction governments on interstate emergency matters requiring federal-level interface, limited to genuine emergencies already within federal authority under existing law. D. Prohibitions — What the Caretaker

Council SHALL NOT Do 6A.9 The Caretaker Council is strictly prohibited from the following, under any circumstances, regardless of exigency short of confirmed armed attack upon the United States: (a) Enacting, modifying, suspending, or repealing any regulation, policy, executive order, or statute; (b) Negotiating, signing, ratifying, or initiating any new treaty, international agreement, executive agreement, or diplomatic commitment; (c) Appointing any political position, Cabinet-level officer, ambassador, federal judge, or other political appointee of any kind. Only critical career-replacement appointments from within existing career ranks under Section 6A.8(d) are permitted; (d) Granting any pardon (forgiveness of a criminal conviction), clemency (mercy reducing punishment), commutation (reduction of a sentence to a lesser one), reprieve (temporary postponement of punishment), or act of executive grace of any kind. Presidential pardon authority shall lapse entirely during the Caretaker Period. The Committee may address any such matters after its convening; (e) Initiating any new military operation, deployment, or action beyond defensive response to confirmed armed attack under Section 16; (f) Taking any action that the Committee could reasonably undertake within the Caretaker Period — if a decision can wait, it shall wait for the Committee; (g) Extending, prolonging, modifying, or otherwise affecting the duration of the Caretaker Period or the Council's own authority; (h) Obstructing, delaying, or interfering with the Emergency Delegate Elections under Section 6.2, the convening of the Committee under Section 6.1, or any other process established by this Amendment; (i) Interfering with the ongoing operation of the Authority, the Citizens' Reclamation Offices and Centers, the Ledger, the Sovereign Civic Network, the Sovereign Voting Terminals, or any other institution established by this Amendment; or (j) Directing, influencing, or participating in the conduct of Emergency Delegate Elections in any Participating Jurisdiction, including any Jurisdiction whose Governor sits on the Council. Council members shall recuse themselves entirely

from their own Jurisdiction's election administration during the Caretaker Period. E. Corruption Safeguards and Anti-Capture Protections 6A.10 During the Caretaker Period, Council members shall operate under a Federal Communications Firewall identical to that applicable to the State Elections Council under Section 17.12 and the State Attorneys General Council under Section 19.5.0.18.4. A member shall not accept, solicit, or respond to any communication, directive, request, or instruction from any removed officeholder, former federal official under investigation for interference with this Amendment, or any person acting on behalf of such officials; shall not accept any funding, thing of value, or agreement from any such source; and shall not enter into any agreement or understanding with any such source. Violation shall be a federal felony punishable by imprisonment of not less than ten (10) years, automatic removal from state or territorial office, permanent lifetime disqualification from any federal, state, or local public office, and referral for Section 13 interference penalties. 6A.11 The Watchdog Tribunal established in Section 21.2 shall have full monitoring, investigative, and enforcement jurisdiction over the Caretaker Council throughout the Caretaker Period. The Tribunal may replace Council members found corrupt, refer them for prosecution, or suspend Council actions found to exceed authority, pursuant to the full powers enumerated in Section 21.7. 6A.12 Any Caretaker Council action found to have violated the prohibitions in Section 6A.9, or to have been conducted in violation of the Firewall in Section 6A.10, shall be voidable by the Committee upon its convening, by majority vote. Such void findings shall have no legal force and shall be removed from the Ledger's active records (while remaining in the permanent historical archive for accountability purposes). 6A.13 Any Council member who knowingly directs, authorizes, or participates in a prohibited action under Section 6A.9 shall be subject to Section 13 interference penalties, including the fifteen (15) year minimum sentence and the lifetime bar from any public office without possibility of pardon, commutation, or clemency. The Caretaker Period's lapse of pardon authority under Section 6A.9(d) shall not be retroactively filled by any subsequent officeholder for acts committed by Council members during the Caretaker Period. F. Transparency and Public Record 6A.14 Within seven (7) days of the Caretaker Council's dissolution, the Committee shall receive a complete public Caretaker Report detailing every meeting held, every vote taken, every action authorized, every communication received, every Council member's voting record, and every Watchdog Tribunal intervention. The Caretaker Report shall be published upon the Ledger as the permanent public record of the Caretaker Period, accessible to the People without limitation.

6A.15 The Caretaker Period shall serve as a structural bridge, not a governing interregnum (meaning: a period between two regimes or governments during which normal governance is suspended). Its sole constitutional purpose is to preserve the United States from immediate harm while the People complete the process of replacing a removed government through democratic means. The Council's authority expires in every respect the moment the Committee convenes, and no precedent, policy, or practice established during the Caretaker Period shall bind any future Committee, Authority, or elected government absent affirmative ratification through normal democratic processes. G. Meeting Operations, Staff, and Resources 6A.16 Meeting Schedule and Venue. To ensure operational capacity throughout the Caretaker Period: (a) Initial Convening. Within seventy-two (72) hours of Authority certification of a Declaration of No Confidence, the Caretaker Council shall convene for its initial session at a secure venue designated by unanimous agreement of the State Attorneys General Council with Joint Chiefs of Staff security coordination. The initial venue shall be selected for geographic neutrality and security capability, not for proximity to removed federal offices. (b) Continuous Working Session. The Council shall maintain continuous working session throughout the Caretaker Period, with formal voting sessions held not less than twice daily during the first seven (7) days post-convening, and not less than daily thereafter, with additional sessions convened as required by operational circumstance. (c) Rotating Venue Capability. Following initial convening, the Council may rotate session venues among state-sovereign secure facilities under Section 11C.10, preventing any single venue from becoming an institutional capture target or symbolic focal point. (d) Secure Video Participation. Governors physically unable to attend in person due to documented state emergency or logistical necessity may participate through secure video conference meeting Academic Integrity Commission security standards. In-person attendance shall be the standard expectation; secure video participation is operational-necessity accommodation, not default mode. (e) Session Publication. Session schedules, agendas, and meeting minutes shall be published on the provisional public ledger with observation livestreaming under Section 6A.7, ensuring public visibility of Council deliberations in real time. 6A.17 Staff and Support. To support Council function during the Caretaker Period: (a) Professional Staff. The Council shall employ professional staff including: parliamentary staff for session management; legal counsel independent of federal executive branch legal services; policy analysts drawn from the Pre-Certified

University Pool under Section 17.16; records staff for Section 13B compliance; security personnel; and administrative personnel sufficient for Council operations. (b) Career Federal Expert Access. Career federal personnel (protected under Section 1.2) may advise the Council on technical, operational, or subject-matter questions upon Council request. Advising career personnel shall receive Section 13B.16 whistleblower protections regardless of the advice provided or outcome reached, ensuring career expertise is available without retaliation risk. (c) Independence from Removed Federal Executive. Council staff shall not be employees of, nor subject to direction from, the removed federal executive branch. No removed political appointee, removed official, or ally of removed officials shall have hiring, firing, compensation, performance-evaluation, or direction authority over Council staff. (d) Watch Board Liaison. Where the Citizens' Implementation Watch Board under Section 19.14 is operational at the time of a Caretaker Period, the Watch Board shall provide dedicated citizen oversight liaison to the Council with meeting observation access and reporting capacity. (e) State Attorneys General Council Coordination. The State Attorneys General Council under Section 19.5.0.18 shall maintain a dedicated liaison to the Caretaker Council, facilitating coordination on state-federal interface matters, Section 13I.29 bootstrap funding, and Phase One federal enforcement matters under Section 19.5.0.5.2. 6A.18 Secure Communications Infrastructure. Given the Council's responsibility during a constitutional crisis period: (a) Cryptographically Secure Communications. Council members shall have access to secure communications infrastructure meeting Academic Integrity Commission standards, designed to prevent interception by foreign state actors, compromised federal systems, or removed officials seeking to monitor Council deliberations. (b) Back-Channel to Military. The Council shall maintain secure back-channel communications to the Joint Chiefs of Staff for Section 6A.8(a) defensive military coordination, with communication integrity protected under Section 16.20 standards including authentication protocols and two-person verification for critical communications. (c) Inter-Jurisdictional State Coordination. Governors serving on the Council shall have secure state-to-state coordination capability for cross-jurisdictional emergency matters arising during the Caretaker Period, supplementing ordinary state-level coordination channels. (d) Communication Records Preservation. All Council communications relating to Caretaker business shall be preserved under Section 13B standards for permanent record accessibility after Caretaker Period conclusion, subject to narrow operational-security redactions certified by Council supermajority under Section

6A.7. (e) Foreign Surveillance Countermeasures. Council communications infrastructure shall implement electronic countermeasures against foreign signals intelligence collection targeting the Caretaker Period, recognizing the elevated foreign interference incentive during constitutional transitions. 6A.19 Funding. Council operations shall be funded as follows: (a) Primary Funding Source. Council operations shall be funded through the Section 11.3 constitutional appropriation via a dedicated Caretaker Council reserve, with draws executed through the Section 13I.20 Treasury disbursement framework without requiring additional Congressional authorization. (b) Bootstrap Period. During the early Caretaker Period before Section 13I.7 national budget integration is complete, Council funding flows through the Section 13I.29 state contribution bootstrap framework and, if necessary, the Section 13I.25 Federal Reserve emergency authority. (c) Member Compensation. Governors serving on the Council shall receive no additional federal salary compensation beyond their existing state salaries; ex officio service under Section 6A.2 creates no additional federal salary obligation. Travel, meeting expenses, and Council-specific expenses shall be reimbursed through federal appropriation. (d) Staff Compensation. Professional staff shall be compensated at rates comparable to sitting federal executive branch positions with similar responsibility scope, paid through the same funding framework as Council operations generally. H. Operational Decision-Making 6A.20 Emergency Decision Procedures. For time-sensitive Council action: (a) Decision Trigger. Upon documented emergency matter falling within Council authority under Section 6A.8, any Council member may request emergency session convening, with notification to all Council members within one (1) hour of request. (b) Expedited Convening. Emergency sessions shall convene within six (6) hours of request during day hours, twelve (12) hours during night hours (10:00 PM to 6:00 AM local time at the convening venue), with secure video participation under Section 6A.16(d) permitted to meet time frame. (c) Supermajority Preserved. Emergency decisions still require the Section 6A.6 two-thirds (2/3) supermajority. Time pressure shall not lower the voting threshold; the constitutional weight of Caretaker authority requires sustained supermajority consensus regardless of urgency. (d) Post-Decision Documentation. Every emergency decision shall be published on the provisional public ledger within two (2) hours of decision, with factual basis, vote record, authorizing authority, and scope of action clearly specified.

(e) Watchdog Tribunal Notification. The Watchdog Tribunal (or Washington Commission if the Tribunal is not yet operational at the time of the Caretaker Period) shall be notified within one (1) hour of emergency decision for oversight review under Section 6A.11. (f) Post-Emergency Committee Review. Every emergency decision shall be subject to review by the Constitutional Transition Committee upon its convening, with Committee authority to ratify, modify, or void the decision consistent with Section 6A.12. Emergency necessity does not immunize decisions from subsequent review. 6A.21 Military Coordination Operational Framework. Section 6A.8(a) authorizes defensive military coordination with the following specific operational parameters: (a)

Scope of Defensive Coordination. Council defensive military coordination authorizes: response to confirmed armed attack on United States sovereign territory, armed forces, or treaty allies; coordination with Joint Chiefs on defensive posture and alert levels; emergency defensive actions meeting the Section 16.10 imminent attack or nation-threatening invasion standards. It does not authorize: offensive operations; first-use nuclear authorization outside the Section 16.8 process; major force repositioning beyond defensive necessity; or initiation of new military commitments. (b) Joint Chiefs Advisory Role Preserved. Joint Chiefs of Staff advise the Council on defensive necessity and operational feasibility; the Council decides on authorization. Joint Chiefs retain the Section 16.3(c) constitutional duty to refuse unlawful orders, with refusal protection extending to orders from the Council Chairperson during the Caretaker Period on the same terms as to orders from a President in ordinary operation. (c) Nuclear Procedures Unchanged. All Section 16 nuclear authorization procedures apply without modification during the Caretaker Period. The Council Presiding Chair (rotating daily under Section 6A.5) shall participate in the Nuclear Authorization Panel under Section 16.8(a) in the substitute role that the Committee Chairperson would ordinarily fill; the Chair substitutes solely for Panel purposes, not for broader presidential authority. Nuclear Authorization Vote procedures under Section 16.18 apply without modification. (d) Communication Integrity Applies. Military communications integrity under Section 16.20, including authentication protocols and protected refusal framework, applies fully during the Caretaker Period, protecting against spoofed orders and ensuring chain-of-command integrity. (e) Post-Action Review Required. Every Council defensive military authorization shall be subject to: (i) mandatory Watchdog Tribunal review per Section 16.28 emergency exception framework; (ii) Committee review upon convening; (iii) public documentation on the provisional public ledger within thirty (30) days, with operational-security redactions permitted only as narrowly necessary.

6A.22 Natural Disaster Response Protocol. Under Section 6A.8(b): (a) Federal Disaster Declaration Authority. The Council may declare federal disasters in response to confirmed natural disasters, drawing on existing federal disaster relief appropriations and existing statutory disaster authority without requiring new appropriation or new statutory framework. (b) FEMA Coordination. Career FEMA leadership (protected under Section 1.2) maintains operational authority for disaster response; the Council authorizes specific federal response actions requiring authorization beyond career leadership scope, such as emergency funding draws or multi-agency coordination demands. (c) Interstate

Coordination. The Council coordinates with Participating Jurisdiction emergency management agencies through the State Attorneys General Council liaison under Section 6A.17(e) for multi-state disasters, ensuring federal-state interface does not depend on removed federal political leadership. (d) Resource Allocation Transparency. The Council may authorize drawing federal emergency reserves, with accounting published on the provisional public ledger within seventy-two (72) hours of draw, enabling public verification that disaster response resources are deployed appropriately. (e) No New Regulations. Response proceeds under existing federal emergency authority; the Council shall not create new regulations, expand federal emergency powers, or establish precedent for post-Caretaker-Period disaster response framework changes. 6A.23 Foreign Communications Framework. Under Section 6A.8(c): (a) Career Personnel Channel. Foreign communications shall be received through career State Department personnel (protected under Section 1.2), recognizing that no political State Department appointees exist during the Caretaker Period following Section 1.1 removal. (b) Acknowledgment Only. The Council acknowledges receipt of foreign communications and communicates that substantive United States response awaits Committee convening under Section 6. Substantive diplomatic commitments, new treaty negotiations, and international agreement modifications shall not occur during the Caretaker Period. (c) Allied Notification of Caretaker Period. Upon Caretaker Period commencement, career State Department personnel shall notify allied nations and international organizations of the constitutional transition, confirming United States treaty obligations continue under career personnel execution while political-level foreign policy awaits new administration, consistent with the Section 16.24(b) nuclear notification principle. (d) Emergency Diplomatic Communication. In genuine emergency requiring immediate diplomatic communication (imminent attack, ally in crisis requiring coordination, nuclear-adjacent situation), the Council may authorize specific emergency diplomatic communication executed by career personnel, with Council supermajority approval and immediate provisional ledger publication. (e) No Treaty Supersession. Nothing in the Caretaker Period shall abrogate, modify, or suspend existing United States treaty obligations. Career personnel execution of treaty obligations continues throughout the Caretaker Period without interruption. 6A.24 Career Vacancy Fill Procedures. Under Section 6A.8(d): (a) Eligibility. Critical career vacancies fillable under this Section are those where: (i) the vacancy affects public safety (FAA air traffic control chief, CDC emergency response directors, FBI specialized security functions, nuclear regulatory emergency response); (ii) the vacancy cannot await Committee convening without significant public safety risk; and (iii) a qualified interim replacement exists within existing career ranks. (b) Selection from Career Ranks Only. Interim replacements shall be selected from within the existing career ranks of the affected agency, typically through ordinary career succession (senior-most qualified career deputy). No political appointment, external hire, or non-career appointment shall occur during the Caretaker Period. (c) Temporary Nature. All Section 6A.8(d) appointments are explicitly temporary, subject to Committee review upon convening. Temporary appointees shall not claim any extended tenure based on their Caretaker-Period service. (d) Documentation. Each appointment shall be documented on the provisional public ledger with: the vacancy identified; the public safety basis; the appointee identified; the career qualification basis; and the Council vote authorizing appointment. (e) No Political Position Backdoor. The Council shall not use career-vacancy authority to fill positions that are properly political appointments requiring Senate confirmation or other political-appointment processes. Political positions remain vacant during the Caretaker Period pending Committee convening and eventual Emergency Election-elected leadership. I. Member Framework and Transition 6A.25 Member Security and Protection. Given the Council's responsibilities during a crisis period: (a) Enhanced Federal Protection. Council members (sitting Governors serving ex officio) shall receive federal protection equivalent to Cabinet-level officials during their Caretaker service, supplementing their ordinary state executive security. Protection shall be provided through remaining career Secret Service or equivalent protective services under career leadership.

(b) Family Protection. Immediate family members of Council members shall receive protection against harassment, intimidation, and retaliation, with specific Section 13 interference prosecution for those targeting Council-member families during or as a consequence of Caretaker service. (c) Residence Security Enhancement. Temporary enhanced residence security during the Caretaker Period, extending beyond ordinary state executive security, shall be available where credible threats exist. (d) Cyber Protection. Cyber protection infrastructure shall protect Council member official and personal digital communications during active Caretaker sessions and for thirty (30) days after dissolution. (e) Transition Security. Protection shall extend thirty (30) days beyond Committee convening to cover transition period for former Council members returning to ordinary gubernatorial duties, recognizing that adverse actors may seek retaliation after Caretaker authority lapses. (f) No Retaliation

Permitted. Federal, state, or foreign retaliation against Council members for Caretaker actions shall constitute Section 13 interference with Senior Official multipliers, Section 20A state official targeting offenses where applicable, and Section 22 foreign interference where foreign actors are implicated. 6A.26 Hardship Framework Applicability. The hardship framework of Sections 17.4 through 17.4.13 shall apply to Caretaker Council service with adaptations reflecting ex officio nature: (a) Ex Officio Nature. Governors serve on the Council ex officio by virtue of holding their state executive office. Hardship cannot excuse ex officio service in its entirety absent the Governor ceasing to hold their state executive position through resignation, removal under state law, or succession. (b) Session-Level Accommodation. Individual session accommodation is permitted for medical, family care, or similar hardship circumstance, with secure video participation under Section 6A.16(d) or brief session absence accommodated. Session absence shall not reduce the Section 6A.6 supermajority denominator; absent members count against quorum achievement. (c) Succession for Extended Incapacity. Where a Governor experiences hardship preventing any form of Caretaker service for more than seven (7) consecutive days, the state constitutional succession process shall apply, with the acting chief executive under state law assuming Caretaker duties per Section 6A.2.1 — the Jurisdiction's own succession law controlling which successor serves. (d) Privacy Protection. Hardship documentation shall be subject to privacy protections of Section 17.4.5 with specific sensitivity for sitting state executives whose personal medical or family information is of legitimate public interest; privacy and public interest shall be balanced by Council supermajority decision on specific disclosure requests.

(e) Anti-Retaliation. No Governor shall face retaliation, political consequence, or adverse treatment based on invoking hardship framework accommodations during Caretaker service; this protection parallels the general Section 17.4.7 anti-retaliation framework. 6A.27 Governor State-Duties Interaction. During Caretaker Council service: (a) State Executive Continuity. Governor state executive duties continue during Caretaker Council service; Caretaker service is additional constitutional responsibility, not substitution for state executive duties. The Governor remains fully Governor of their Participating Jurisdiction throughout Caretaker service. (b) State Emergency Priority. Where genuine state emergency requires Governor attention, the Governor may prioritize state emergency response over Caretaker session participation, with secure video participation under Section 6A.16(d) or brief deferral permitted. State emergency response shall not constitute Caretaker session absence for disciplinary purposes. (c) State-Federal Conflict Resolution. Conflicts between state executive duties and Caretaker responsibilities shall be rare given limited Caretaker authority scope. Where conflicts arise: (i) genuine state emergency — state duties prioritized; (ii) routine state matters — Caretaker duties prioritized; (iii) ambiguous situations — Council deliberation with hardship framework flexibility. (d) State Cost-Bearing for Ordinary State Duties. States bear the ordinary cost of their Governor's Caretaker service through the Governor's existing state salary and state-level resources. Federal reimbursement covers only Caretaker-specific expenses (travel to Council venue, federal-level staff and security enhancement, Council-specific operational costs). (e) Return to State Duties. Upon Council dissolution under Section 6A.4, Governors return fully to their ordinary state executive duties without transition disruption. The thirty (30) day post-service federal security extension under Section 6A.25(e) covers the return-to-ordinary-duties period. 6A.28 Committee Handoff Procedures. The transition from Caretaker Council to Constitutional Transition Committee shall proceed as follows: (a) Transition Briefing. Upon certification of the Committee's first convening under Section 6.1, the Caretaker Council shall conduct a transition briefing within seventy-two (72) hours, covering: pending matters and active emergencies; authorized actions summary with reasoning; foreign communications received and responses given; career personnel appointments made under Section 6A.8(d); Watchdog Tribunal interventions received; and overall operational status. (b) Records Transfer. Complete Caretaker Council records shall transfer to the Committee within forty-eight (48) hours of transition briefing, including: all meeting records and vote records; decision documentation with factual basis; communications preserved under Section 6A.18(d); Watchdog Tribunal interventions; and financial records of Caretaker Period expenditures. (c) Seven-Day Public Report. Within seven (7) days of Council dissolution, the complete public Caretaker Report shall be published per Section 6A.14, providing the permanent accountability record for citizens and future constitutional research. (d) Individual Member Debrief. Each Council member shall provide an individual debrief to the Committee, sharing Caretaker Period observations, assessments of the crisis-period operational effectiveness, and recommendations for improvement that the Committee may forward to subsequent Sunset Review under Section 18. (e) Staff Transition. Professional staff may transition to Committee service with continuity where Committee need exists, or return to ordinary assignments; the choice shall be at individual staff discretion, respecting career personnel rights under Section 1.2. (f) No Residual Authority.

Upon Council dissolution under Section 6A.4, former Council members shall have no residual Caretaker authority. Any exercise of former Caretaker authority post-dissolution shall constitute Section 13 interference. The Caretaker Period ends cleanly; its authority does not linger. (g) Committee Autonomy. The Committee shall not be bound by Caretaker Council decisions, precedents, or practices. Every Caretaker action is subject to Committee review and potential modification or voidance under Section 6A.12. The Committee's autonomy is essential; the Caretaker Period is a bridge, not a ruling body whose decisions bind successors. 6A.29 Interim Caretaker Council Training and Preparatory Education. Because the Caretaker Council consists of fifty-six (56) state and territorial Governors serving ex officio during an extraordinary constitutional crisis, and because Caretaker authority is narrow, novel, and different from ordinary gubernatorial duties, the following preparatory education and training framework applies: (a) Preparatory Education Program. The Academic Integrity Commission shall develop and distribute a preparatory education program for all sitting Governors and chief executives of Participating Jurisdictions, covering this Section 6A in full, including: the Council's limited authorities under Section 6A.8; the strict prohibitions under Section 6A.9; the Federal Communications Firewall under Section 6A.10; emergency decision procedures under Section 6A.20; military coordination framework under Section 6A.21; natural disaster response under Section 6A.22; foreign communications framework under Section 6A.23; career vacancy fill procedures under Section 6A.24; supermajority voting mechanics under Section 6A.6; Presiding Chair rotation under Section 6A.5; hardship framework applicability under Section 6A.26; and Committee handoff procedures under Section 6A.28. Materials shall be published on the Franklin Ledger and updated not less frequently than annually.

(b) Completion Expectation. Each Governor shall complete the preparatory education program within one hundred eighty (180) days of assuming office (or within one hundred eighty (180) days of certified Ratification for Governors already in office at Ratification). Completion shall be recorded on state government transparency infrastructure or the Ledger. The timeline is longer than the ninety percent (90%) Governor nuclear vote education timeline under Section 16.7.1(m) because Caretaker Council authority, while significant, engages less frequently than nuclear vote authority and the curriculum is more extensive. (c) Just-In-Time Briefing Upon Council Convening. Because the Caretaker Council convenes only upon certified Declaration of No Confidence — an event that may not have occurred when a Governor took office — each

Governor shall receive a just-in-time briefing upon certified No Confidence triggering and before Council convening under Section 6A.3. Briefing shall be delivered by the Academic Integrity Commission (or during Phase One, by the Washington Commission) through secure communications. Briefing shall focus on: the specific circumstances that led to No Confidence, sensitive matters transferred from the removed government, immediate operational challenges, and framework constraints. Briefing shall not substitute for preparatory education but shall apply education to the specific crisis. (d) Serving Without Education. A Governor who has not completed preparatory education may still serve on the Caretaker Council if convening occurs before completion, as ex officio service by sitting Governors is automatic and cannot be delayed for training without creating a crisis gap. However, such Governors shall complete rapid catch-up briefing within seventy-two (72) hours of Council convening and shall be strongly encouraged to complete preparatory education immediately. Non-completion does not disenfranchise the Governor from voting but may inform Watchdog Tribunal review under Section 6A.11 if Caretaker action appears to reflect misunderstanding of framework constraints. (e) Refresher Education. Governors shall complete refresher education on Caretaker Council duties not less frequently than biennially, with refreshers aligned to ordinary gubernatorial term cycles and with concurrent delivery alongside Section 16.7.1(m) nuclear vote refresher education where practicable. (f) Gubernatorial Transition. Outgoing Governors shall brief incoming Governors on Caretaker Council matters as part of ordinary gubernatorial transition, with briefing documentation preserved as part of state transition records. The briefing shall include any outgoing Governor's specific experience with Caretaker Council service if such service occurred during their term. (g) Federal Executive Non-Interference. No federal officeholder shall direct, influence, or interfere with Governor preparatory education or just-in-time briefing. Attempts shall constitute Section 13 interference with Senior Official multipliers.

(h) No Federal Compensation. Consistent with state sovereignty over Governor office, federal compensation shall not be provided for preparatory education; each Participating Jurisdiction shall cover time and resource costs as part of ordinary gubernatorial duties. (i) State Accountability for Non-Completion. Governor preparatory education completion shall be subject to public transparency but not federal enforcement. State legislatures and state citizens retain the authority to hold their Governors accountable for education completion through state political and electoral mechanisms, consistent with state sovereignty over state executive officers.

Section 7. The Emergency Election

Key terms in this Section: • "The Authority" — The Independent Tripartite Oversight Authority (three bodies, see Section 17). • "The Committee" — The Constitutional Transition Committee (Section 6), the caretaker body composed of fifty citizen-elected delegates. • "The Ledger" — The Sovereign Blockchain Voting Ledger (Section 4). • "Terminal" — A Sovereign Voting Terminal (Section 14). • "Emergency Election" — The national election held within ninety (90) days of the Committee's convening, in which the People elect a new President, Vice President, Congress, and slate of federal judicial nominees using ranked-choice voting. 7.1 An Emergency Election shall be held within 90 days of the Committee's convening under Section 6.1, conducted in person at Sovereign Voting Terminals located in the Citizens' Reclamation Offices, Reclamation Centers, and Overseas Terminals established under Sections 11, 11.1.1, and 14.9, with all votes immediately cryptographically recorded upon the Sovereign Blockchain Voting Ledger established under Section 4. 7.2 The Emergency Election shall employ ranked-choice voting. 7.3 Term Lengths for Officials Elected in Emergency Elections. Officials elected in an Emergency Election shall serve under the following hybrid term structure, designed to return the federal election calendar to its regular cycle while guaranteeing a minimum meaningful term of service: (a) Minimum Term Guarantee. Every official elected in an Emergency Election shall serve a minimum of two (2) years from the date of their swearing-in, regardless of where that date falls in the pre-Amendment electoral cycle;

(b) Return to Regular Cycle. After the minimum two (2) year term, each official's office shall return to its regular constitutional cycle at the next natural election opportunity for that office on the pre-Amendment calendar. For example, if a Presidential Emergency Election occurs in 2027 and the minimum term extends to 2029, the President shall serve until the next regularly scheduled presidential election (2028 being passed, the next would be 2032) — whichever is the earlier of (i) the end of the minimum term or (ii) the next regular election opportunity that comes after the minimum term. If these align, the official serves until that election; (c) Senate Rotation Preservation. Senate Class rotations (Classes I, II, and III) shall be preserved. Senators elected in Emergency Elections shall serve until the next regularly scheduled election for their Class's seat after the minimum two (2) year term; (d) House Cycle. Representatives elected in Emergency Elections shall serve until the next regularly scheduled biennial House election after the minimum two (2) year term; (e) Federal Judicial Nominees. Federal judges confirmed following Emergency Election processes shall serve in accordance with Article III of the Constitution ("during good behavior"), unaffected by the term structure of this Section; and (f) Eligibility for Re-Election. All officials serving under Section 7.3 shall be eligible for re-election at the conclusion of their term under the same rules applicable to officials elected in regular elections, subject to any term limits otherwise applicable to their office. 7.4 Ballot information published upon the Ledger at the time of each Emergency Election shall specify, for each office, the expected term length of the winning candidate under the rules of Section 7.3, so that voters are fully informed of the term they are electing someone to serve. 7.5 Congressional Apportionment for Emergency Elections. The apportionment (meaning: the process of distributing the 435 seats in the House of Representatives among the fifty states based on population, typically redone every 10 years after the census) of seats in the United States House of Representatives used for Emergency Elections under this Section shall be the apportionment in effect at the moment of the Authority's certification of the Declaration of No Confidence under Section 5, and shall remain locked for purposes of the Emergency Election regardless of any apportionment change that occurs during the Caretaker Period or Committee operation period. This prevents the removed federal government from manipulating apportionment during the transition to disadvantage their political opponents in the Emergency Election. 7.6 Backward-Looking Apportionment Review. Any apportionment change made during the twelve (12) months preceding the initiation of a Petition under Section 12 shall be presumed suspect and subject to review by the Authority through Liberty Bell Initiative. If the Authority finds by clear and convincing evidence (a legal standard meaning: substantially more likely true than not — stronger than preponderance of the evidence but weaker than beyond reasonable doubt) that such apportionment change was made in bad faith, for the purpose of entrenching the existing Federal Government against removal under this Amendment, or through corrupt means, the Authority shall invalidate the suspect apportionment and the Emergency Election shall use the prior apportionment in effect before the suspect change. All reasoning shall be published upon the Ledger. 7.7 Delayed or Contested Census. In the event that a decennial census under Article I, Section 2 of the Constitution is actively delayed, contested, or the subject of dispute at the time an Emergency Election is being prepared, the Authority shall, by Liberty Bell Initiative, determine which apportionment data is most reliable and authoritative for use in the Election, with reasoning published upon the Ledger. Priority shall be given to the most recent completed, uncontested census. 7.8 Ballot Design for Emergency Election. The Emergency Election ballot shall be uniform across all Participating Jurisdictions, with design as follows: (a) Ranked-Choice Ballot Structure. The ballot shall present each race as a ranked-choice selection, with voters permitted to rank candidates in order of preference from first choice through final choice. The ballot shall clearly display ranking instructions, with voter-friendly interface design on Sovereign Voting Terminals. (b) Required Candidate Information. Each candidate's ballot entry shall display: name; party affiliation (if any); brief biographical information of not more than fifty (50) words submitted by the candidate; and, for candidates subject to Section 8 eligibility review, the fact that eligibility was reviewed and the outcome. (c) Multi-Language Display. Ballot content shall be available in English, Spanish, and the primary languages of Participating Jurisdictions with significant non-English-speaking populations, consistent with Section 12.12(c). Translation accuracy shall be certified by the Academic Integrity Commission. (d) Uniform National Design. Ballot layout, candidate presentation, ranking mechanism, and voter instructions shall be identical across all Participating Jurisdictions, with only Jurisdiction-specific elements being the candidate list for that Jurisdiction's representatives and the language variants displayed. (e) No Political Party Advantage. Ballot design shall not favor any party through candidate ordering, color-coding, visual prominence, or other design elements. Candidate ordering shall be randomized or alphabetical, with the specific method published in advance and applied uniformly. 7.9 Ranked-Choice Voting Specifics. The ranked-choice voting system under Section 7.2 shall operate as follows: (a) Number of Rankings. Voters may rank up to five (5) candidates per race in order of preference, with the specific number applicable to each race published in

advance. Where fewer than five candidates are on the ballot, voters may rank all available candidates. (b) Elimination Methodology. If no candidate receives a majority of first-preference votes, the candidate with the fewest first-preference votes shall be eliminated, with that candidate's votes redistributed to each voter's next-highest-ranked remaining candidate. Elimination shall continue round-by-round until a candidate achieves majority of remaining votes. (c) Tabulation Through Sovereign Civic Network. All ranked-choice tabulation shall occur through the Sovereign Civic Network with cryptographic verification on both Primary Chains under Section 4.11. Each round's results shall be cryptographically recorded, enabling any citizen to independently verify tabulation accuracy. (d) Round-by-Round Publication. Upon tabulation completion, each round's results shall be published on the Franklin Ledger, showing vote counts per candidate per round and the elimination sequence. This transparency enables voters and observers to confirm the tabulation's correctness. (e) Exhausted Ballot Rule. Where a voter's ranked candidates have all been eliminated before a majority winner emerges, the ballot shall be considered exhausted for that race and excluded from subsequent rounds. Exhausted ballots shall not count toward any remaining candidate. Exhaustion rates shall be published for each race. 7.10 Candidate Filing and Ballot Access. To ensure broad candidate participation during the compressed 90-day window: (a) Filing Window. Candidate filing shall open upon the Constitutional Transition Committee's convening under Section 6 and shall close thirty (30) days before the Emergency Election date. This provides sixty (60) days for Authority eligibility review under Section 8, candidate campaigning, and voter education before election day. (b) Ballot Access Requirements. For ballot access, a candidate shall: (i) meet the constitutional eligibility requirements for the office sought (age, citizenship, residency); (ii) meet Section 8 eligibility review requirements if the candidate was removed under Section 1.1 in a prior No Confidence process; (iii) submit a nominating petition with signatures of not fewer than one thousand (1,000) registered voters for state-level Congressional races, not fewer than five thousand (5,000) for Senate races, not fewer than twenty-five thousand (25,000) for Presidential races, collected at Offices through the Section 12 in-person framework; and (iv) submit any filing fee required by ordinary state or federal law applicable to the office, with fee waivers available for candidates demonstrating financial hardship.

(c) Party Nomination Pathway. Recognized political parties may nominate candidates through their ordinary nomination processes, with party-nominated candidates exempted from the subsection (b)(iii) petition requirement but still subject to all other requirements. Party recognition shall follow existing state and federal law without modification by this Amendment. (d) Independent Candidate Pathway. Candidates without party nomination may access the ballot through the petition pathway of subsection (b)(iii), with petition signature collection proceeding under the Section 12 framework adapted to candidate petitions. (e) No Discriminatory Ballot Access. Filing requirements shall be applied uniformly without discrimination based on political viewpoint, party affiliation (including third parties and independents), prior candidate history, or protected class membership. Discriminatory application shall constitute Section 13 interference. 7.11 Timeline Coordination With Section 8 Eligibility Review. Because Emergency Election candidates may include officials previously removed under Section 1.1, and Section 8 requires Special Eligibility Panel review: (a) Review Timing. Section 8 eligibility review shall commence immediately upon filing by a previously removed official and shall be completed within thirty (30) days as specified in Section 8.2. This timeline permits review completion before the Emergency Election date. (b) Filing Conditional on Review. A candidate subject to Section 8 review may file for the Emergency Election, with their ballot inclusion conditional on favorable review. Pre-review filing permits parallel campaign activities during the review period, subject to the disclosure obligations of Section 8.7. (c) Ineligibility Mid-Campaign. Where a candidate subject to Section 8 review is found ineligible during the campaign period, their name shall be removed from the ballot immediately with public notice on the Franklin Ledger. Ballots already printed shall be reissued if time permits, or the ineligible candidate's votes shall be treated as exhausted under Section 7.9(e) if reissue is not feasible. (d) Appeal Timing. Section 8.3 appeals to a three-Chief-Justice panel shall be expedited to complete within fourteen (14) days, ensuring appellate resolution before the Emergency Election. Appeals shall not extend the Emergency Election timeline. (e) Late Filing For Newly Eligible. Where Section 8 review results in restoration of a candidate's eligibility close to the filing deadline, the Authority may extend the filing deadline by up to seven (7) days for that specific candidate to preserve genuine opportunity to run, with extensions documented on the Franklin Ledger. 7.12 Campaigning During the Compressed Window. Campaigning for an Emergency Election shall proceed as follows:

(a) Active Campaign Period. Active campaigning shall be permitted from the moment of Committee convening through election day, with a sixty (60) day active campaign period following the filing deadline. (b) Campaign Freedom. Candidates shall enjoy full First Amendment rights to campaign speech, political rallies, advertising, media appearances, and direct voter contact. Restrictions on campaign conduct shall be limited to those already applicable under existing campaign law, plus the Amendment-specific provisions of Sections 9 and 22. (c) Protected Campaign Speech at Offices. Candidates, their campaigns, and their supporters shall have the right to engage in political speech in public areas near Offices, Centers, Host Sites, and Satellite Sites, subject only to: (i) the Section 11.8(c) one-hundred-foot buffer zone around Office entrances during active voting; and (ii) ordinary time-place-manner restrictions applicable to public speech. (d) No Candidate Harassment. Harassment, intimidation, or surveillance of candidates, their families, or their campaign staff shall constitute Section 13 interference where connected to the

Emergency Election process. Enhanced penalties shall apply where the harassment involves federal executive resources or federal officeholders. (e) Federal Officeholder Restrictions. Federal officeholders not removed under Section 1.1 (including career personnel protected by Section 1.2, and officeholders whose offices are not within Section 1.1 scope) shall be subject to existing Hatch Act and analogous restrictions on campaign activities while in official capacity, with violations prosecutable under existing law. 7.13 Campaign Finance for Emergency Election. Section 9 campaign finance rules shall apply with the following adaptations for the compressed timeline: (a) Contribution Limits Maintained. Individual contribution limits established in Section 9 shall apply without modification to Emergency Election candidates. Emergency circumstances shall not justify elevated contribution limits. (b) Accelerated Disclosure Timeline. Disclosure of contributions and expenditures shall proceed on an accelerated schedule during the Emergency Election: contributions of one thousand dollars ($1,000) or more shall be reported within seventy-two (72) hours rather than the ordinary timeline; aggregate reports shall be filed weekly during the active campaign period rather than monthly; and all reports shall be published on the Franklin Ledger upon filing. (c) Independent Expenditure Disclosure. Independent expenditures under Section 9 shall face the same accelerated disclosure timeline, with funding source disclosure required within seventy-two (72) hours of expenditure. (d) Foreign Funding Prohibition Enhanced. Section 22 foreign interference prohibitions shall apply with specific heightened vigilance during the Emergency Election window, recognizing that foreign actors may seek to exploit the compressed timeline. Suspected foreign funding shall trigger immediate Hamilton Contingent investigation. (e) Coordinated Campaign Restrictions. Section 9 rules on coordinated campaigns between candidates, parties, and independent expenditure groups shall apply without modification, with enforcement by the Hamilton Contingent (or pre-operational substitute) on accelerated timelines. 7.14 Required Debates. Public debates enable voters to evaluate candidates in the compressed window: (a) Presidential Debates. Not fewer than three (3) Presidential debates shall be organized during the Emergency Election campaign period, consistent with Section 9.13. Debates shall feature all qualifying candidates, with mandatory participation as specified in Section 9.13. (b) Senate Debates. Not fewer than two (2) debates shall be organized for each United States Senate race, consistent with Section 9.13, with mandatory participation. (c) House Debates. At least one (1) debate shall be organized for each contested House race, consistent with Section 9.13, with mandatory participation. (d) Debate Organization. Debates shall be organized by the Authority, academic institutions, or bona fide civic organizations, as specified in Section 9.13, and livestreamed on the Franklin Ledger. Moderator selection shall be non-partisan with qualifications certified by the Academic Integrity Commission. (e) Broadcast Requirements. Broadcast media — including broadcast television, radio, and livestreaming platforms — shall be required to carry debates without charge as a condition of their federal licensing, ensuring broad public access. (f) No Candidate Excluded. Candidates meeting ballot access requirements shall be included in debates, preventing debate organizers from excluding candidates to influence outcomes. Exclusion criteria, if any, shall be narrow (such as minimum polling threshold or petition signature count) and published in advance. 7.15 Media Access and Equal Time. To ensure broad voter access to candidate information: (a) Free Media Minimums. Broadcast media shall provide minimum free airtime to all qualifying candidates, with specific minimums determined by the Authority by Liberty Bell Initiative, consistent with equal-time principles in existing communications law. (b) Equal Access to Forums. Civic organizations, media outlets, and public forums shall provide equal access to all qualifying candidates. Systematic exclusion of candidates from forums shall constitute Section 13 interference where the exclusion is designed to influence outcomes.

(c) Public Broadcasting Priority. Public broadcasting entities (PBS, NPR, and their affiliates) shall provide enhanced coverage of the Emergency Election including candidate interviews, issue analyses, and voter information, funded through the Section 11.3 constitutional appropriation where supplementary funding is required. (d) Voter Information Publication. The Franklin Ledger shall maintain a comprehensive candidate information portal during the Emergency Election, including candidate statements, voting records of incumbents, disclosure filings, debate videos, and endorsement information from identified sources. Portal content shall be neutral and factual. 7.16 Results Certification and Swearing-In. Following the Emergency Election: (a) Certification Timeline. Results shall be certified within fourteen (14) days of election day through the Section 5.7 certification process, adapted for the Emergency Election context with race-by-race certification as tabulation completes. (b) Round-by-Round Transparency. Because ranked-choice tabulation occurs in rounds, each round's results shall be published in real time as tabulation proceeds, with final certification following completion of all rounds and any necessary recounts. (c) Recount Triggers. The Section 5.8 automatic recount framework shall apply to Emergency Election results, adapted for ranked-choice contexts. Recounts shall examine round-by-round tabulation accuracy and the cryptographic verification of vote records. (d) Swearing-In Timeline. Newly elected officials shall be sworn in and assume office within seven (7) days of certification. The Committee Chairperson's role as Commander-in-Chief under Section 6 shall terminate upon the new President's swearing-in. Other Committee oversight of ongoing federal operations shall terminate upon new officeholder swearing-in for each respective office. (e) Transition Support. Upon certification and pending swearing-in, the Committee shall provide transition support to incoming officeholders, including access to facilities, briefings on ongoing operations, and introduction to career personnel. Transition support shall not extend to policy direction or operational commitments binding the new officeholder. 7.17 Replacement Candidate Procedures. Where a candidate dies, withdraws, is found ineligible, or is otherwise unable to continue during the Emergency Election: (a) Pre-Filing-Deadline Replacement. Candidate changes before the filing deadline shall proceed under ordinary candidate replacement procedures, with replacement candidates subject to the same filing and eligibility requirements as original candidates. (b) Post-Filing-Deadline Replacement by Party. Where a party-nominated candidate is unable to continue after the filing deadline, the nominating party may designate a replacement candidate within fourteen (14) days. The replacement shall meet all eligibility requirements; Section 8 review shall be expedited to complete within fourteen (14) days for replacement candidates subject to review. (c) Post-Filing-Deadline Replacement for Independents. Independent candidates unable to continue shall not be replaced; their ballot position shall be removed or, if ballots are already printed, votes for that candidate shall be treated as exhausted under Section 7.9(e). (d) Ballot Reprinting. Where feasible given timeline constraints, ballots shall be reprinted to reflect candidate changes. Where reprinting is not feasible, clear voter guidance shall be provided at every Office informing voters of the candidate change and its effect on their ballot. (e) Timeline Extension for Major Replacement. Where a major-party Presidential candidate or substantial number of Congressional candidates change late in the campaign such that voter information integrity is materially compromised, the Authority may, by Liberty Bell Initiative, extend the Emergency Election date by not more than fourteen (14) days to preserve meaningful voter choice. Extensions shall be exceptional and documented. 7.18 Security During Emergency Election. Recognizing elevated interference risk during the compressed Emergency Election window: (a) Section 11.8 Framework Applies With Enhancement. The Section 11.8

security protocols for active Petition and Referendum periods shall apply with enhanced intensity during the Emergency Election, including enhanced physical security, counter-surveillance measures, and coordination with law enforcement under Section 13.5 protections. (b) Candidate Security. Major candidates for President and Vice President shall be eligible for Secret Service protection on a non-discretionary basis from the filing deadline through election day, with protection extended to winning candidates through swearing-in. Protection shall not be contingent on party affiliation or any political consideration. (c) Foreign Interference Countermeasures. Section 22 foreign interference countermeasures shall be heightened during the Emergency Election window, with the Hamilton Contingent (or pre-operational substitute) conducting continuous monitoring of foreign interference indicators and publishing findings on the Franklin Ledger. (d) Cybersecurity Monitoring. The Academic Integrity Commission shall maintain continuous cybersecurity monitoring of Terminal infrastructure, the Sovereign Civic Network, the Franklin Ledger, and candidate campaign infrastructure (on a voluntary protective basis) throughout the Emergency Election window. (e) Election Day Security Coordination. On election day, federal, state, and local law enforcement shall coordinate on security at Offices, Centers, Host Sites, and

Satellite Sites, with coordination protocols developed in advance and published (with operational-security redactions) on the Franklin Ledger. 7.19 Infrastructure Failure During Emergency Election. The Section 5.6 infrastructure failure framework shall apply to the Emergency Election without modification, with the following additions specific to the Emergency Election context: (a) Timeline Sensitivity. Recognizing the compressed Emergency Election timeline and the constitutional imperative of timely transition to elected government, infrastructure failures shall be addressed with even greater urgency than ordinary Referendum infrastructure failures. The three-day automatic extension under Section 5.6(b) shall apply to affected Jurisdictions, with the overall Emergency Election timeline adjusted accordingly. (b) Multi-Round Tabulation Protection. Infrastructure failures affecting ranked-choice tabulation rounds shall trigger immediate cryptographic comparison across both Primary Chains and the Standby Chain under Section 4.17, with tabulation continuing once verification is complete. Where verification identifies discrepancies, affected Jurisdictions' votes shall be re-tabulated from paper ballot records under Sections 14.10 through 14.20. (c) Coordinated Sabotage Response. Section 5.6(f) coordinated sabotage investigation shall proceed with enhanced urgency during the Emergency

Election, recognizing that sabotage of the Emergency Election attacks the legitimacy of the new government before it takes office. Confirmed sabotage shall trigger maximum penalties under Section 13 with no possibility of pardon.

Section 8. Eligibility of Removed Officials

Key terms in this Section: • "The Authority" — The Independent Tripartite Oversight Authority (three bodies, see Section 17). • "The Ledger" — The Sovereign Blockchain Voting Ledger (Section 4). • "Special Eligibility Panel" — A three-member panel convened for each Emergency Election to review candidacy eligibility for any person previously removed under Section 1.1. 8.1 Any person removed from federal office by a Declaration of No Confidence who seeks to stand as a candidate in an Emergency Election, or in any subsequent federal election, shall first have their eligibility reviewed by a Special Eligibility Panel. The Panel shall consist of three (3) members, one selected by internal majority vote from each of the three bodies of the Authority, with all three selected members meeting the eligibility requirements of Section 17.7. Panel members shall serve solely for the duration of the eligibility review for that Election and shall not hold any other concurrent role within the Authority's ordinary operations. 8.2 The Panel shall evaluate the removed official's conduct for: breach of the public trust; abuse of power; violation of the constitutional oath; collusion with foreign powers; personal financial corruption; or knowing obstruction of this Amendment. The Panel shall render decisions by majority vote, publicly reasoned and recorded upon the Ledger, within thirty (30) days of a candidate's filing. Decisions shall be rendered on the basis of clear and convincing evidence. 8.3 A determination of ineligibility may be appealed by the candidate to a panel of three (3) Chief Justices of Participating Jurisdictions (as defined in Section 3) drawn by randomized lottery from Chief Justices of Participating Jurisdictions not currently serving on any other body established by this Amendment. The appellate panel shall hear the appeal within fourteen (14) days and render a final decision, which shall be binding. 8.4 No person separated under Section 1.1 shall be reappointed to any federal position, elected or appointed, without full public conduct review under Section 15.7 and, if the position involved is elective, Special Eligibility Panel approval under this Section. 8.5 Career technical personnel protected under Section 1.2 are not subject to Special Eligibility Panel review, as they were not removed from service by operation of this Amendment. Any individual review of career personnel shall proceed under Section 15.8. 8.6 Evidentiary Standards for Ineligibility Findings. The clear and convincing evidence standard required by Section 8.2 shall be applied as follows: (a) Definition of Clear and Convincing Evidence. Clear and convincing evidence means evidence substantially more likely true than not — stronger than preponderance of the evidence (more likely than not) but weaker than beyond reasonable doubt (near-certainty). The evidence must establish the relevant finding with a high probability such that the factfinder has a firm belief in its truth. (b) Types of Acceptable Evidence. The Special Eligibility Panel may consider: (i) formal judicial findings from federal, state, or foreign courts; (ii) Congressional investigation findings documented through formal committee proceedings; (iii) Watchdog Tribunal findings; (iv) Hamilton Contingent prosecutorial findings; (v) Inspector General reports; (vi) sworn testimony of witnesses with personal knowledge; (vii) authenticated documentary evidence; (viii) forensic analysis by qualified experts; and (ix) other evidence of comparable probative value as determined by Panel majority. (c) Types of Evidence Carrying Reduced Weight. The Panel shall give reduced weight to: (i) unsubstantiated allegations without documentary support; (ii) partisan

characterizations of disputed policy decisions; (iii) anonymous accusations without independent corroboration; (iv) media reports without identifiable sourcing; and (v) evidence procured through coercion, bribery, or methods violating due process. (d) No Adverse Inference From Prior Political Positions. Previously taken political positions, policy advocacy, campaign statements, or party affiliation shall not constitute evidence of ineligible conduct. Ineligibility findings shall be based on concrete acts of corruption, abuse of power, oath violation, collusion, financial misconduct, or Amendment obstruction — not on disagreement with a candidate's views. (e) Cumulative Evidence Standard. Where no single piece of evidence meets the clear and convincing standard alone, the Panel may find clear and convincing evidence based on the cumulative weight of multiple evidence items, provided the cumulative finding is supported by documented analysis published on the Ledger. 8.7 Candidate Disclosure Obligations. Any person removed from federal office by Declaration of No Confidence who seeks to stand as a candidate shall, at the time of filing for candidacy, provide to the Special Eligibility Panel: (a) Complete Financial Disclosure. Full financial disclosure covering the preceding ten (10) years, including tax returns, asset holdings, business interests, debts, trust relationships, and foreign financial accounts, meeting Section 13F disclosure standards for sitting federal officials. (b) Conduct Affidavit. Sworn affidavit addressing the specific grounds enumerated in Section 8.2 (breach of public trust, abuse of power, oath violation, foreign collusion, personal financial corruption, Amendment obstruction), with specific factual responses to any publicly known allegations or prior investigations. (c) Foreign Contact Disclosure. Disclosure of all contacts with foreign officials, foreign nationals, and foreign entities during and for ten (10) years after federal service, consistent with Section 22 foreign interference protections. (d) Post-Service Employment Disclosure. Disclosure of all employment, consulting arrangements, board memberships, speaking engagements, and other compensated activities since removal, with specific attention to engagements potentially implicating foreign government interests, regulated industry interests, or other accountability concerns. (e) Ongoing Investigation Disclosure. Disclosure of any pending or known contemplated federal, state, foreign, or Authority investigations, with specific identification of investigating bodies, subject matter, and current status. (f) Continuing Duty to Update. Disclosure obligations shall continue throughout the eligibility review and, if the candidate is certified as eligible, throughout the campaign and any resulting service. Material changes shall be reported within fourteen (14) days.

(g) Consequences of False or Incomplete Disclosure. Materially false or incomplete disclosure shall constitute independent grounds for ineligibility finding regardless of whether the underlying conduct would otherwise have qualified. Knowingly false disclosure shall also subject the candidate to Section 13 interference prosecution and, where the candidate is found eligible and subsequently elected, grounds for removal from office. 8.8 Scope of Ineligibility Finding. Where the Special Eligibility Panel finds a removed official ineligible: (a) Federal Office Bar. Ineligibility shall bar the person from all federal elective and appointive offices, including Cabinet positions, federal judicial appointments, ambassador positions, independent regulatory commissioners, and any other position within Section 1.1. (b) No Automatic State or Local Bar. Ineligibility under this Amendment shall not automatically bar the person from state elective or appointive office, local office, or private sector employment, consistent with federalism principles. States may enact parallel disqualifications under state law at their discretion. (c) No Bar on Private Political Activity. Ineligibility shall not restrict the person's right to engage in private political activity including: private speech, media commentary, party membership, candidate support, donation (subject to Section 9 limits), voting, public advocacy, or writing. The Amendment disqualifies from holding office, not from participating in political discourse. (d) Permanent Nature of Ineligibility. Ineligibility shall be permanent, without time limit, and not subject to Presidential pardon, Congressional remission, or other executive or legislative mitigation. Only the Section 8.9 rehabilitation pathway provides any prospect of restoration to eligibility. (e) Application to Section 1.1 Successor Bodies. Where Congress, through constitutional amendment or otherwise, creates successor federal bodies performing functions of Section 1.1 enumerated offices, the ineligibility shall apply to such successor bodies to prevent evasion through renaming or reorganization. 8.9 Rehabilitation Pathway — Limited Restoration of Eligibility. Recognizing that permanent consequences without any pathway to rehabilitation can produce injustice in edge cases, a narrow rehabilitation pathway shall be available under the following framework: (a) Eligibility for Rehabilitation Petition. A person found ineligible under this Section may petition for rehabilitation only after: (i) ten (10) years have elapsed from the ineligibility finding; (ii) the person has completed any criminal sentence, probation, or supervised release resulting from the underlying conduct; (iii) the person has made full restitution for any financial harm caused; and (iv) new evidence or substantially changed circumstances exist that were not before the original Panel. Mere passage of time without changed circumstances shall not qualify. (b) Filing Requirements. Rehabilitation petitions shall be filed with the Special Eligibility Panel of the then-current Authority, with supporting evidence of changed circumstances, documentation of rehabilitation efforts, and disclosure of any conduct since the original finding that would independently warrant ineligibility. (c) Higher Evidentiary Burden. The petitioner shall bear the burden of establishing by clear and convincing evidence that: (i) the original underlying conduct has been remediated to the extent remediable; (ii) no subsequent conduct warrants continued ineligibility; (iii) the changed circumstances are substantial and genuine rather than superficial; and (iv) restoration of eligibility serves the public interest. (d) Panel Composition for Rehabilitation. Rehabilitation petitions shall be reviewed by a Special Eligibility Panel constituted per Section 8.1, with additional review by the Watchdog Tribunal where the petitioner was a Senior Official under Section 13 definitions. No Panel member shall have personal connection to the petitioner or to the original ineligibility proceeding. (e) Public Comment Period. Rehabilitation petitions shall be subject to a minimum sixty (60) day public comment period, with comments from the public, civic organizations, affected industries, and former colleagues preserved for Panel consideration. (f) One Petition Only. A person denied rehabilitation shall not be eligible to re-petition for at least ten (10) additional years, and shall be limited to one additional petition in their lifetime absent extraordinary circumstances certified by Watchdog Tribunal supermajority. This prevents rehabilitation petitions from becoming an ongoing imposition on the Panel's time. (g) Restoration of Eligibility Scope. Successful rehabilitation shall restore eligibility to stand as a candidate; it shall not guarantee election or appointment. Restored candidates shall face ordinary electoral or confirmation processes, with voters and confirmation bodies fully informed of the prior ineligibility and rehabilitation. 8.10 Procedural Protections for Removed Officials. Recognizing that the Special Eligibility Panel process affects substantial liberty and reputation interests, the following procedural protections shall apply: (a) Right to Counsel. The removed official shall have the right to counsel throughout the eligibility proceedings at their own expense. Where the removed official lacks resources for counsel, the Authority shall provide qualified counsel at no cost, drawn from a pool of attorneys certified by the Watchdog Tribunal as independent from federal executive interests. (b) Notice of Specific Grounds. The Panel shall provide the removed official with specific written notice of the grounds under consideration, identifying the particular acts or patterns alleged to warrant ineligibility and the specific evidence being

considered. Generalized notice shall not suffice. (c) Right to Respond. The removed official shall have the right to: (i) submit written response to the Panel's preliminary findings; (ii) present witnesses and documentary evidence; (iii) challenge the credibility and reliability of evidence against them; (iv) cross-examine witnesses where possible; and (v) make oral argument before the Panel. (d) Presumption of Eligibility. The Panel shall begin proceedings with a presumption that the removed official is eligible to stand as a candidate. The burden shall rest on evidence sufficient to overcome that presumption by clear and convincing evidence, not on the candidate to prove their eligibility. (e) Decision on the Record. Panel decisions shall be based solely on the evidence presented during formal proceedings, published on the Ledger, and subject to candidate challenge. Ex parte communications, classified evidence not disclosed to the candidate, or other evidence outside the record shall not support ineligibility findings. (f) Reasoned Written Decision. Panel decisions shall be issued as reasoned written opinions published on the Ledger, addressing each specific ground considered, the evidence relied upon, the analysis applied, and any dissenting reasoning where applicable. (g) Timeline Protections. The Panel shall render its decision within thirty (30) days of candidate filing, as specified in Section 8.2. Delays beyond thirty (30) days shall require published justification and shall not be used to suppress candidacy by running out the election clock. 8.11 Treatment of Resignation in Anticipation of Removal. Where a federal official resigns during the period between initiation of a

Petition under Section 12 and certification of the resulting Referendum under Section 5.3.1: (a) Resignation Not an Escape Mechanism. Resignation during an active Petition or Referendum period shall not exempt the resigning official from subsequent Section 8 eligibility review for any future candidacy. The eligibility framework applies to officials whose conduct would have warranted removal had they not resigned. (b) Voluntary Cooperation Consideration. Where a resigning official voluntarily cooperates with transition, provides material information about pre-removal corruption, or facilitates orderly institutional continuity, such cooperation may be considered by the Panel in subsequent eligibility review as a mitigating factor, though not as a complete defense. (c) Investigation Continues. Resignation shall not terminate any pending Hamilton Contingent, Watchdog Tribunal, or State Attorneys General Council investigation of the resigned official. Investigations shall continue with findings reported to any future Special Eligibility Panel.

(d) Financial Disclosure Continues. Resigned officials shall remain subject to the Section 13F financial monitoring and disclosure framework for the duration specified in Section 13F, regardless of resignation timing. 8.12 Foreign Collusion Standard. The foreign collusion ground under Section 8.2 shall be applied with specific attention to Section 22 framework: (a) Definition. Foreign collusion includes: (i) coordination with foreign officials, foreign nationals, or foreign entities to obtain federal office or to exercise federal authority in ways favorable to the foreign interest; (ii) acceptance of foreign financial support, intelligence, or other material assistance in federal elections or appointments; (iii) disclosure of classified information to foreign actors; (iv) exercise of federal authority materially influenced by undisclosed foreign financial or personal relationships; or (v) other conduct meeting the Section 22.3 willful blindness standard regarding foreign interference. (b) Ongoing Relationships Disclosure. Candidates with prior foreign relationships (through business, family, residence, or other connection) shall disclose such relationships per Section 8.7(c). Such relationships shall not automatically constitute ineligibility; eligibility shall depend on whether the relationships produced corrupt conduct under subsection (a). (c) Cooperation With Foreign Intelligence Investigation. Where the Hamilton Contingent (or pre-operational substitute) is investigating foreign interference connected to a candidate, the Panel shall coordinate with the investigation, including consideration of investigation findings as evidence and deferral of final eligibility determination where the investigation is in active stage affecting the candidate. 8.13 Public Publication of Eligibility Decisions. All Special Eligibility Panel decisions — whether finding eligibility or ineligibility — shall be published on the Franklin Ledger: (a) Full Publication of Ineligibility Findings. Ineligibility findings shall be published with complete reasoning, evidence summary (with appropriate privacy protections for third parties), Panel composition, and dissent where applicable. The public has a legitimate interest in understanding why specific persons are barred from seeking federal office. (b) Publication of Eligibility Findings. Eligibility findings — where the Panel determines the candidate is eligible to stand — shall be published with reasoning, evidence considered, and Panel composition. This ensures that eligibility findings are not rubber-stamp processes but genuine reviews whose reasoning the public can evaluate. (c) Preservation of Historical Record. Published decisions shall be preserved permanently on the Franklin Ledger, enabling voters and future Panels to reference the precedent and reasoning of prior eligibility determinations. Consistency of reasoning across Panels over time serves the Amendment's legitimacy. (d) Appeal Decision Publication. Appellate panel decisions under Section 8.3 shall be published with equivalent detail, including affirmation or reversal of original Panel findings and the reasoning supporting appellate conclusions. (e) Protection of Third-Party Privacy. Publication shall preserve the privacy of third parties mentioned in proceedings — including family members not themselves subjects of the proceedings, innocent business associates, and other third parties — through appropriate redaction while preserving the evidentiary weight of the public record.

Section 9. Campaign Finance

Key terms in this Section: • "The Authority" — The Independent Tripartite Oversight Authority (three bodies, see Section 17). • "The Ledger" — The Sovereign Blockchain Voting Ledger (Section 4), where all campaign contributions and disclosures are recorded. • "Constitutional Elections Fund" — The public matching fund established by this Section to provide small-donor matching for federal candidates. • "Election cycle" — The period beginning the day after the preceding general election for that office and ending on the day of the next general election for that office. • "Federal candidate" — Any individual seeking election to the Presidency, Vice Presidency, United States Senate, or United States House of Representatives, whether in a regular election, a primary election, a special election, an Emergency Election under Section 7, or any other federal election, in any election year, at any time after ratification of this Amendment. Scope and Permanent Application 9.0 Permanent Application to All Future Federal Candidates. The provisions of this Section shall apply, in full, to every candidate for federal office in the United States from the moment of ratification of this Amendment forward, without time limit, expiration, or sunset, and shall govern: (a) Every candidate for the Presidency and Vice Presidency, in every election — regular presidential elections, Emergency Elections under Section 7, and any special or replacement elections; (b) Every candidate for the United States Senate, in every Senate election — regular staggered Class I, II, and III elections, Emergency Elections, and special elections to fill vacancies; (c) Every candidate for the United States House of Representatives, in every House election — regular biennial elections, Emergency Elections, and special elections to fill vacancies; (d) Every candidate in every federal primary election, caucus, runoff, or preliminary contest that determines participation in a federal general election; (e) Every incumbent federal officeholder seeking re-election at any point in the future; and (f) Every future generation of federal candidates for as long as this Amendment remains part of the Constitution. 9.0.1 Continuity Through Transitions. These rules shall apply continuously without regard to: (a) Whether a No Confidence process is active, dormant, or has never been invoked; (b) Whether the election is a regular election, Emergency Election, special election, or replacement election; (c) Whether the candidate is an incumbent, challenger, or first-time candidate; (d) Whether a presidential administration is newly elected, mid-term, or concluding; or (e) Whether this Amendment was recently ratified or ratified generations prior. 9.0.2 No Exemption for Special Circumstances. No federal candidate shall be exempt from any provision of this Section by reason of office sought, party affiliation, incumbent status, personal wealth, public profile, emergency circumstances, transitional period, national security claim, or any other justification. The rules apply uniformly to all federal candidates at all times. 9.0.3 Amendment of Rules Requires Constitutional Process. The thresholds, caps, and procedures established in this Section may be modified only through constitutional amendment under Article V, through a Constitutional Review Convention triggered by a Sunset Review vote to Modify under Section 18.4, or through adjusted amounts published by the Academic Integrity Commission pursuant to the inflation adjustment provisions of Sections 9.1, 9.3, and 9.9. No act of Congress, executive order, judicial ruling, or state law shall alter, reduce, suspend, or effectively nullify any provision of this Section. A. Individual Contribution and Spending Caps

9.1 Individual Contribution Cap. No individual may contribute more than two hundred dollars ($200) to any single federal candidate during a single election cycle. This cap applies uniformly to every contributor regardless of personal wealth, office sought, or relationship to the candidate. The cap shall be adjusted annually for inflation by the Academic Integrity Commission using the most recent consumer price index, with adjusted amounts published upon the Ledger. 9.2 Total Candidate Spending Caps. No candidate for federal office shall spend, receive, or have spent on their behalf, in any election cycle, more than the following amounts, inclusive of all independent expenditures coordinated with the candidate and all self-funded contributions: (a) House of Representatives: five hundred thousand dollars ($500,000); (b) United States Senate: three million dollars ($3,000,000); (c) Presidency and Vice Presidency (combined): twenty-five million dollars ($25,000,000). 9.3 These spending caps shall be adjusted annually for inflation by the Academic Integrity Commission, with adjusted amounts published upon the Ledger no later than January 1 of each year. 9.4 Self-Funding Prohibition. No candidate shall contribute to their own campaign in excess of the individual contribution cap established in Section 9.1. A candidate's personal wealth shall not confer structural advantage in federal elections. Loans to a candidate's own campaign are prohibited. This provision applies regardless of any provision of existing federal or state law permitting unlimited self-funding by candidates. B. Prohibited Sources 9.5 No contribution of any amount shall be accepted by any federal candidate, campaign committee, political action committee, super PAC, party committee, or affiliated entity from any of the following sources: (a) Any corporation, limited liability company, or for-profit business entity; (b) Any political action committee (PAC), super PAC, or similar aggregating vehicle; (c) Any foreign national, foreign government, foreign state-owned enterprise, or Foreign Person or Entity as defined in Section 22; (d) Any anonymous donor or donor whose identity has not been publicly disclosed on the Ledger; (e) Any labor union treasury fund, trade association treasury fund, or similar organizational treasury (individual members of such organizations may contribute personally under Section 9.1);

(f) Any 501(c)(4) organization, dark money vehicle, or other entity designed to conceal the original source of political funds; and (g) Any person or entity acting as a conduit for funds originating from any prohibited source. C. Disclosure Requirements 9.6 Every contribution of any amount shall be publicly disclosed upon the Ledger within twenty-four (24) hours of receipt, including: contributor's full legal name; contributor's city and state of residence; contribution amount and date; and candidate or committee receiving the contribution. No anonymous or aggregated disclosure shall satisfy this requirement. 9.7 Every expenditure by a candidate or coordinated committee shall be disclosed upon the Ledger within seventy-two (72) hours, including:

vendor name; amount; purpose; and date. Advertising expenditures shall additionally disclose the content of the advertisement and the platforms on which it appears. D. The Constitutional Elections Fund and Small-Donor Matching 9.8 There is hereby established the Constitutional Elections Fund, a dedicated public fund administered by the Academic Integrity Commission with Citizens' Oversight Board audit, for the purpose of matching small-donor contributions at a six-to-one (6:1) ratio. 9.9 Small-Donor Match. Every contribution of fifty dollars ($50) or less from a verified United States citizen shall be matched six-to-one (6:1) from the Constitutional Elections Fund, counted against the candidate's spending cap. A fifty dollar contribution thus becomes three hundred fifty dollars ($350) of available campaign spending. The matching cap shall be adjusted annually for inflation along with other thresholds under this Section. 9.10 Fund Source. The Constitutional Elections Fund shall be funded through a dedicated constitutional appropriation, disbursed automatically, with supplemental funding from: (a) a small tax on corporate political advertising expenditures; (b) voluntary designations on federal tax returns; and (c) forfeited assets from campaign finance violations under this Section. No portion of the Fund shall come from candidate contributions or be subject to congressional reduction. E. Enforcement and Penalties 9.11 Any candidate, committee, or individual who violates the caps, source prohibitions, or disclosure requirements of this Section shall be subject to: (a) Immediate disqualification of the candidate from the current election; (b) Federal criminal prosecution, with imprisonment of not less than five (5) years for knowing violations and asset forfeiture of all funds involved;

(c) For intentional laundering of prohibited funds through shell entities or conduits: imprisonment of not less than twenty (20) years, treatment as interference under Section 13 with lifetime bar from public office, and referral under Section 22 if foreign involvement is established; and (d) Public record of violation permanently upon the Ledger. 9.12 Candidates shall certify quarterly under penalty of perjury that all contributions and expenditures are recorded upon the Ledger and comply with this Section. False certification shall be a federal felony punishable by imprisonment of not less than ten (10) years and lifetime disqualification from public office. 9.13 Debates, town halls, and candidate forums organized by the Authority, academic institutions, or bona fide civic organizations, and livestreamed upon the Ledger, shall not count toward any candidate's spending cap. The Authority shall organize at least three (3) Presidential debates, at least two (2) debates for each United States Senate race, and at least one (1) debate for each contested House race, with mandatory participation by all qualifying candidates. 9.14 Earned media coverage by independent news organizations, personal speech by the candidate at campaign events, and online organic social media activity by the candidate or volunteers shall not count toward spending caps, provided that any paid amplification of such content shall count.

Section 10. Safeguards

Key terms in this Section: • "The Authority" — The Independent Tripartite Oversight Authority (three bodies, see Section 17). • "Liberty Bell Initiative" — Separate concurrence of all three bodies of the Authority. • "The Ledger" — The Sovereign Blockchain Voting Ledger (Section 4). • "Petition" — A citizen-initiated Petition under Section 12 to trigger a No Confidence Referendum. • "Referendum" — The national No Confidence Referendum (Section 5). • "Pretextual emergency" — A declared emergency not supported by objectively verifiable evidence of a natural disaster, confirmed military attack, verified public health crisis, or verified cyberattack with ongoing material consequences.

10.1 No Declaration shall be initiated within two (2) years of certification of a prior Declaration. During this two-year cooldown period, any Petition filed at an Office or Center under Section 12 shall be formally registered upon the Ledger but held in abeyance (meaning: temporarily paused or suspended, to be resumed later), with signature collection suspended. The registered Petition shall automatically activate on the two-year anniversary of the prior Declaration's certification, at which time the one hundred and eighty (180) day signature collection window under Section 12.5 shall commence. The Office or Center shall at the moment of initiation inform the initiating voter of the cooldown in writing, and shall publish notice upon the Ledger that the Petition is registered and pending activation. Multiple Petitions may be registered during the cooldown period; upon expiration of the cooldown, only the first registered Petition shall activate, with subsequent Petitions consolidated into it unless withdrawn by their initiating voters. 10.2 All constitutional rights shall remain in full force throughout the transition. 10.3 No martial law or executive order by a removed official shall survive passage. 10.4 Obstruction of this Amendment shall be prosecuted as insurrection. A. Emergency Declarations During an Active No Confidence Process 10.5 Recognizing that an existing Federal Government may attempt to suspend, delay, or obstruct a No Confidence process by invoking declared emergencies, whether genuine or pretextual, this subsection establishes protections against such abuse while preserving the legitimate authority of government to respond to actual crises. 10.6 Upon any declaration of a state of emergency, martial law, national crisis, public health emergency, or any functionally equivalent measure by any officeholder, agency, or branch of the existing Federal Government at any time during an active No Confidence process (defined as the period from the moment a Petition under Section 12 is initiated through the certification of Emergency Election results under Section 7 and the swearing-in of the newly elected officeholders thereunder, encompassing the Petition period, Referendum period, Emergency Delegate Election period, Committee operation period, and Emergency Election period), the Authority shall, by Liberty Bell Initiative, review the declaration within forty-eight (48) hours of its issuance and categorize it as either genuine or pretextual based on the publicly available evidence. 10.7 An emergency declaration shall be categorized as genuine only if supported by objectively verifiable evidence of one or more of the following: (a) a confirmed natural disaster of significant scope; (b) a confirmed military attack upon the United States or its forces; (c) a verified public health crisis recognized by independent medical and scientific authorities; or (d) a verified cyberattack or infrastructure attack with documented ongoing material consequences. Any declaration not meeting this standard shall be categorized as pretextual.

10.8 If an emergency declaration is categorized as pretextual, it shall be overridden immediately and shall have no legal force with respect to the No Confidence process. The officeholders, agencies, or branches responsible for the pretextual declaration shall face immediate referral under Section 13 for interference, triggering the fifteen (15) year minimum sentence and the lifetime bar from public office without possibility of pardon, commutation, or clemency. 10.9 Regardless of categorization, the duration of every declared emergency during an active No Confidence process shall count toward a cumulative cap of one hundred and twenty (120) days across all emergencies combined during that single No Confidence process. The clock shall begin counting the moment the emergency is declared, not the moment the Authority completes its review. 10.10 If the cumulative cap of one hundred and twenty (120) days is exceeded during any single No Confidence process, all officeholders, agencies, or branches responsible for the declarations that caused the cap to be exceeded shall face automatic referral under Section 13 for interference, triggering the fifteen (15) year minimum sentence and the lifetime bar from public office without possibility of pardon, commutation, or clemency. This consequence applies even if each individual declaration was categorized as genuine, as the cumulative impact itself constitutes material obstruction. 10.11 During any declared emergency that has been categorized as genuine and that is counting toward the cumulative cap, the timeline for the active No Confidence process shall pause for the duration of the emergency. Specifically: (a) the one hundred and eighty (180) day signature collection window under Section 12 shall pause; (b) any Petition signatures already collected shall remain valid and shall not expire during the pause; (c) any pending Referendum date shall be rescheduled to a date no less than fifteen (15) days and no more than thirty (30) days after the emergency ends; and (d) all other deadlines and timelines under this Amendment related to the active process shall pause in equivalent manner. Pretextual declarations shall NOT trigger any pause, as they are overridden immediately. 10.12 During any emergency pause under Section 10.11, the Citizens' Reclamation Offices shall remain physically open and accessible to the extent consistent with the genuine emergency (for example, temporary closure during an active natural disaster affecting the Office location only), and shall resume full operations the moment the emergency ends. Remote petition signature collection shall remain prohibited in accordance with Section 12; no emergency shall be used as a pretext to permit remote or unverified signature collection. 10.13 All emergency declarations, Authority reviews, categorizations, overrides, cumulative cap tracking, and penalty referrals under this subsection shall be recorded and published upon the Ledger in real time. The existence, timing, duration, and substance of every emergency declaration and every Authority action related thereto shall never be classified or redacted.

Section 11. The Citizens' Reclamation Offices and Centers

Key terms in this Section: • "The Authority" — The Independent Tripartite Oversight Authority (three bodies, see Section 17). • "The Ledger" — The Sovereign Blockchain Voting Ledger (Section 4). • "Terminal" — A Sovereign Voting Terminal (Section 14), the dedicated voting device housed in each Office and Center. • "Office / Reclamation Office" — A Citizens' Reclamation Office established under Section 11.1 — one per state, directly elected officers, constitutionally appropriated, the permanent physical infrastructure of the People's authority in the fifty states. • "Center / Reclamation Center" — A Citizens' Reclamation Center established under Section 11.1.1 — one each in the District of Columbia and the five territories, functionally identical to Offices in all respects. • "Accessibility services" — The Accessible Terminals, Mobile Accessibility Teams, professional Accessibility Officer, and related services established under Section 11A. 11.1 One Citizens' Reclamation Office shall be established in each of the fifty states, in accordance with this Section and supplemented by the accessibility provisions of Section 11A. 11.1.1 Additionally, one Citizens' Reclamation Center ("Center") shall be established in each of the following Participating Jurisdictions: the District of Columbia; the Commonwealth of Puerto Rico; the Territory of Guam; the United States Virgin Islands; the Commonwealth of the Northern Mariana Islands; and the Territory of American Samoa. Centers shall be functionally identical to Offices in all respects: physical walk-in premises, elected officers, Sovereign Voting Terminals, Ledger access, signature collection, constitutional appropriation, and constitutional protection from search, seizure, closure, or interference. All references in this Amendment to "Offices" shall be read to include Centers where context permits, and citizens or nationals of Participating Jurisdictions served by a Center shall have all rights of participation equivalent to citizens of states served by Offices.

11.2 Offices and Centers shall be governed by officers elected directly by voters of each state, the District of Columbia, or territory every 4 years. 11.3 Offices and Centers shall be funded through a dedicated constitutional appropriation disbursed automatically. 11.4 Office and Center premises shall be constitutionally protected from search, seizure, closure, or interference, subject to Section 13. 11.5 Offices and Centers shall maintain publicly accessible walk-in locations open all non-holiday days. 11.6 Staffing Standards. Each Office and Center shall maintain minimum staffing sufficient to support Amendment functions, as follows: (a) Core Staff Categories. Each Office and Center shall maintain at minimum: (i) one Office Director elected under Section 11.2; (ii) Oversight Officers trained under Section 11B.6 in numbers proportional to voter population served, with not fewer than two (2) Oversight Officers on duty during all operating hours; (iii) professional Accessibility Officers under Section 11A.13; (iv) Sovereign Voting Terminal technical staff certified by the Academic Integrity Commission; (v) administrative personnel sufficient for records management, public communications, and basic Office operations; and (vi) security personnel sufficient to maintain protected premises status under Section 11.4. (b) Staffing Scales with Population. Staffing levels shall scale with the registered voter population served, with the Authority publishing on the Franklin Ledger staffing ratio standards applicable to all Offices and Centers. At minimum, the staffing ratio shall ensure that voters at any Office or Center face wait times during active Petition or Referendum periods no greater than thirty (30) minutes. (c) Surge Staffing During Active Periods. During active Petition collection windows under Section 12.5 and Referendum windows under Section 5.1, Offices and Centers shall increase staffing by not less than fifty percent (50%) above ordinary operating levels, through either additional permanent hires, temporary qualified staff, or cross-deployment from other Amendment Bodies, to accommodate surge in voter traffic. (d) Professional Training Requirements. All Office and Center personnel shall complete the forty (40) hour Oversight Officer training program under Section 11B.6 or equivalent role-specific training certified by the Academic Integrity Commission, with annual refresher training required to maintain certification. (e) Independence from Federal Executive. Office and Center staff shall be employees of the Amendment's administrative infrastructure, paid through the Section 11.3 constitutional appropriation, not employees of any federal executive agency. No President, Vice President, Cabinet officer, or federal agency head shall have hiring, firing, compensation, or performance-evaluation authority over Office or Center staff.

11.7 Minimum Operating Hours. To ensure genuine access for all voters: (a) Ordinary Operating Hours. Every Office and Center shall operate a minimum of ten (10) hours per day on every non-holiday day, from 8:00 AM to 6:00 PM local time. Offices may operate extended hours at Director discretion subject to Section 11.3 funding. (b) Weekend and Evening Accessibility. Each Office and Center shall operate at least one (1) evening extended to 8:00 PM per week and both weekend days, to accommodate voters unable to access Amendment services during standard business hours. (c) Petition and Referendum Window Hours. During active Petition collection windows under Section 12.5, minimum operating hours shall extend to twelve (12) hours per day. Referendum window hours shall follow Section 5.5 specifications. (d) Uniform Minimum, Not Uniform Maximum. The minimum hours established in this Section create floor requirements; individual Offices and Centers may operate additional hours at Director discretion within their appropriation. No Office shall operate fewer than the minimum hours. (e) Publication of Schedule. Each Office and Center shall publish its operating schedule on state transparency infrastructure, the Franklin Ledger, and physical signage at the facility, with schedule changes requiring thirty (30) day advance notice absent genuine emergency under Section 10.7. 11.8 Security Protocols During Active Periods. Recognizing that Offices and Centers face elevated interference risk during active Petition collection and Referendum windows: (a) Enhanced Physical Security. During active Petition collection under Section 12 and Referendum windows under Section 5, physical security personnel shall maintain continuous presence during operating hours, with authority to refuse entry to persons presenting credible threats to voters, staff, or Amendment infrastructure. (b) Coordination

With Law Enforcement. Office security shall coordinate with state and local law enforcement for perimeter security, traffic management, and emergency response, under protocols that preserve the Section 13.5 four-part test for law enforcement action against Office personnel. (c) Anti-Intimidation Buffer Zones. During active voting or signature collection periods, no person — including candidates, campaign representatives, foreign nationals subject to Section 22, lobbyists, or media — shall engage in campaigning, advocacy, intimidation, or voter pressure within a buffer zone of not less than one hundred (100) feet from Office entrances. Violations shall constitute Section 13 interference with enhanced penalties where the violator sought to intimidate or pressure specific voters.

(d) Surveillance Detection. Offices shall maintain counter-surveillance measures to detect unauthorized surveillance of voters, staff, or Terminal operations. Detected surveillance shall trigger immediate investigation by the Watchdog Tribunal and, where federal actors are implicated, Section 13 interference prosecution with Senior Official multipliers. (e) Emergency Response Protocols. Each Office shall maintain emergency response protocols for: medical emergencies; natural disasters; credible threats to voters or staff; infrastructure failure; and coordinated interference attempts. Protocols shall be developed with Academic Integrity Commission technical support, published (with operational-security redactions) on the Franklin Ledger, and exercised annually. (f) Foreign Surveillance Countermeasures. Offices shall implement electronic countermeasures against foreign signals intelligence collection targeting Amendment processes, with technical standards established by the Academic Integrity Commission in coordination with the Hamilton Contingent Preservation Division and published on the Franklin Ledger with appropriate operational-security redactions. 11.9 Temporary Closure Procedures. Where an Office or Center must close temporarily: (a) Authorized Closure Grounds. Temporary closure shall be authorized only upon: (i) genuine emergency under Section 10.7 affecting the facility location; (ii) Section 13.5 law enforcement action meeting the four-part test; (iii) Watchdog Tribunal-authorized security emergency; or (iv) documented infrastructure failure preventing safe operation. No closure shall be authorized on political, budgetary, or administrative grounds absent genuine emergency. (b) Immediate Notification. Upon any temporary closure, the Office Director shall within two (2) hours: (i) publish notice on the Franklin Ledger identifying closure reason and projected reopening; (ii) notify the Authority, the Watchdog Tribunal, and the State Elections Council; (iii) notify the public through state emergency communications infrastructure and local media; and (iv) post physical signage at the closed facility identifying alternative voting locations. (c) Voter Access Preservation. During temporary closure: (i) Mobile Accessibility Teams under Section 11A.4 shall be deployed to affected areas to preserve voting access; (ii) voters shall be rerouted to the nearest open Office, Center, Host Site, or Satellite Site; (iii) during active Petition or Referendum windows, signature collection or voting periods shall be extended by the closure duration plus three (3) additional days in the affected Jurisdiction per Section 5.6(b); and (iv) no voter shall be denied participation due to closure where reasonable alternative access exists. (d) Investigation of Unauthorized Closure. Any closure lacking authorized grounds under subsection (a) shall be investigated by the Watchdog Tribunal (or Phase One equivalent) within seventy-two (72) hours. Unauthorized closure shall constitute Section 13 interference, with closure authorized by persons within federal executive chain of command subject to Senior Official multipliers. (e) Maximum Closure Duration. Temporary closure authorized under subsection (a) shall not exceed seventy-two (72) hours without re-authorization by the Authority (or during Phase One, the Washington Commission) through affirmative vote documenting continuing need. Closures extending beyond seventy-two (72) hours without re-authorization shall be presumed unauthorized under subsection (d). 11.10 State Non-Cooperation and Substitute Facility Authority. Where a state refuses to permit establishment of its required Office, fails to provide necessary services (utilities, emergency response, standard municipal services) to an established Office, or otherwise materially obstructs Office operation: (a) State Non-Compliance Consequences Under Section 20.15. State refusal to cooperate with Office establishment or operation shall trigger the full Section 20.15 material non-compliance framework, including federal funding cutoff, Congressional participation suspension, and individual official Section 13 interference liability. The Office's constitutional status under Sections 11.1 and 11.4 does not depend upon state cooperation; the Amendment's funding, personnel, and facility authority operate directly through the Section 11.3 appropriation. (b) Federal Property Substitute. Where state cooperation is refused, the Authority may establish the Office on federal property within the state (federal courthouses, federal office buildings, postal facilities, or other federal real property), with the federal property treated as an Office protected premises under Section 11.4 regardless of its ordinary federal function. (c) Adjacent Jurisdiction Temporary Coverage. Where a state refuses cooperation and no suitable federal property exists within the state, voters of that state may exercise Amendment rights at the nearest Office or

Center in an adjacent Participating Jurisdiction, with their signatures and votes attributed to their state of registration per Section 12.8(c). This temporary arrangement shall not substitute for establishment of the state's own Office once cooperation is secured or alternative facility is constructed. (d) Direct Federal Construction Authority. Upon documented state non-cooperation for more than ninety (90) days, the Authority through Liberty Bell Initiative shall authorize direct federal construction of the Office on federal property or on property acquired through federal eminent domain pursuant to existing federal property authority, with construction funded through the Ratification Loan under Section 13I.4 if necessary. (e) Individual Official Accountability. State officials personally directing, authorizing, or materially participating in state non-cooperation with Office establishment or operation shall face individual Section 13 interference liability with Senior Official multipliers, prosecutable by the State Attorneys General

Council acting by supermajority under Sections 19.5.0.5.2 and 19.5.0.18.9.1 and, upon operational commencement, by the Hamilton Contingent. 11.11 Inter-Office Coordination. While each Office serves its Jurisdiction, certain functions require coordination among Offices: (a) Shared Technical Infrastructure. Sovereign Voting Terminal software updates, cryptographic verification procedures, and Sovereign Civic Network connectivity standards shall be uniform across all Offices, coordinated through the Academic Integrity Commission under Section 14 technical standards. (b) Cross-Office Voter Services. A registered voter of any Jurisdiction shall be served at any Office or Center (per Section 12.8(c) out-of-jurisdiction signing rules), with the Office of physical presence conducting identity verification and cryptographic recording while attribution flows to the voter's jurisdiction of registration. (c) National Coordination Through State Elections Council. Inter-Office coordination shall flow through the State Elections Council, with each Office's Director communicating through the Council rather than through any federal executive hierarchy. This preserves the Amendment's independence from federal executive capture. (d) Best Practices Exchange. Offices shall participate in annual best-practices exchange coordinated by the Academic Integrity Commission, sharing operational lessons, security innovations, accessibility improvements, and emergency response experiences. Exchange findings shall be published on the Franklin Ledger. (e) Emergency Mutual Support. Where one Office experiences extraordinary demand or emergency, other Offices shall provide mutual support including personnel redeployment, Mobile Accessibility Team cross-deployment, and technical assistance. Mutual support shall be coordinated through the State Elections Council and funded through a dedicated mutual support reserve within the Section 11.3 appropriation. 11.12 Voter Data Protection. Offices and Centers handle sensitive voter identification and participation data. The following data protection standards shall apply: (a) Minimum Data Collection. Offices shall collect from voters only the minimum data necessary for identity verification and cryptographic recording under Sections 12.9 and 5.11(a). Additional data — voting history beyond current participation, personal demographic information beyond that already in voter registration records, contact information beyond that provided for Amendment-specific purposes — shall not be collected. (b) Retention Limits. Identification documents presented for verification shall not be retained per Section 12.9(d). Transaction records required for Section 4.11 cryptographic verification shall be retained in their cryptographic form but shall not include personal identifiers beyond what is cryptographically necessary. (c) No Commercial Use. No voter data collected by Offices shall be sold, licensed, shared with commercial entities, or used for commercial purposes under any circumstance. Voter data is constitutional-purpose data only. (d) Federal Access Limitations. No federal executive agency, federal law enforcement body, or federal intelligence agency shall have access to voter data held by Offices absent: (i) an Independent Warrant Panel warrant under Section 13C.14.8 specifically authorizing access for a defined investigation; or (ii) explicit authorization by the Authority through Liberty Bell Initiative based on specific documented need. Bulk access, pattern analysis without specific investigation, and pre-emptive surveillance shall be prohibited. (e) Breach Notification. Any breach, unauthorized access, or suspected compromise of voter data shall trigger: (i) immediate notification to affected voters; (ii) publication on the Franklin Ledger within seventy-two (72) hours; (iii) Watchdog Tribunal investigation; and (iv) Section 13 interference prosecution where the breach was directed or facilitated by federal or state actors. (f) Voter Data Sovereignty. Voter data held by Offices is sovereign data of the Amendment's oversight architecture, not of any federal executive branch. No President, Vice President, Cabinet officer, or federal agency head shall direct, demand, or coerce release of voter data absent the specific authorizations under subsection (d).

Section 11A. Accessibility and the Right to Participate

Key terms in this Section: • "The Authority" — The Independent Tripartite Oversight Authority (three bodies, see Section 17). • "The Ledger" — The Sovereign Blockchain Voting Ledger (Section 4). • "Terminal" — A Sovereign

Voting Terminal (Section 14). • "Office / Center" — A Citizens' Reclamation Office or Center (Section 11). • "Accessibility Officer" — A professional staff member at each Office or Center, trained in disability accommodation, ADA compliance, or related fields, who coordinates accessible voting services. Supervised by a rotating Citizens' Oversight Board member. • "Mobile Accessibility Team" — A team of two or more certified Office personnel who travel to a voter's location with a portable air-gapped Terminal for homebound voters unable to travel to an Office or Center. • "Accessibility Review Panel" — A three-member panel that hears special-case accessibility requests not fitting standard medical qualification. • "Support person" — A voter's chosen assistant — either a trusted personal contact or a certified Accessibility Assistant — who helps operate the Terminal without influencing the vote. 11A.1 The right to participate in petitions and votes under this Amendment shall not be abridged by disability, chronic illness, mobility limitation, sensory impairment, cognitive disability, or any other condition that prevents a voter from operating a standard Terminal or traveling to an Office or Center. Every registered voter or national shall have an accessible path to participation preserving the same in-person, verified, cryptographically recorded security standards applied to all other voters. A. Accessible Terminals at Every Office, Center, and Overseas Location 11A.2 The Academic Integrity Commission shall design, certify, and maintain Accessible Terminals available at every Office, Center, and Overseas Terminal location. Accessible Terminals shall provide, at minimum: (a) Full audio interface with headphones, supporting all ballot content and voting actions via voice navigation; (b) Braille keypad and tactile controls for voters who are blind or visually impaired; (c) Large-text and high-contrast display modes; (d) Sip-and-puff switches, head-switch controls, and other assistive input devices for voters with limited motor control; (e) Wheelchair-accessible height and approach clearance consistent with current Americans with Disabilities Act standards or any successor accessibility standards; (f) Support for voters with cognitive or intellectual disabilities, including simplified interface modes and audio confirmations of each selection; and (g) Translation into all major languages spoken in the United States, with no language access charge or waiting period. 11A.3 Every Office, Center, and Overseas Terminal facility shall meet or exceed ADA physical accessibility standards. Premises shall include, at minimum: wheelchair-accessible entrances and restrooms; accessible parking; audio and visual alerts; tactile wayfinding; designated quiet areas for voters with sensory sensitivities; and service-animal accommodation. Failure to meet these standards shall be a basis for a voter's qualification for Mobile

Accessibility Team service.

B. Mobile Accessibility Teams 11A.4 Each Office and Center shall maintain no fewer than one (1) Mobile Accessibility Team, with additional Teams deployed as determined by annual review of demand by the Citizens' Oversight Board. Factors for additional Teams shall include: nursing home and hospital populations, hospice and palliative care populations, rural geography and distance barriers, disability prevalence in the jurisdiction, and documented demand from prior petitions or votes. 11A.5 A Mobile Accessibility Team shall consist of: (a) At least two (2) certified Office or Center personnel trained by the Academic Integrity Commission in Terminal operation, chain-of-custody protocols, non-coercion protocols, and disability-sensitive interaction; (b) One (1) portable, air-gapped Sovereign Voting Terminal meeting all security and accessibility requirements of Sections 14 and 11A.2, cryptographically bound to the voter's in-person verified identity at the point of use; and (c) Real-time livestream recording to the Ledger throughout the visit, including Team arrival, voter identification, Terminal setup, voting interaction, and Team departure. The voter may request a privacy screen for the ballot-selection portion of the vote only; the chain of custody and interaction between Team members and voter shall never be concealed. 11A.6 Mobile Teams shall operate within the jurisdiction of their home Office or Center. The Citizens' Oversight Board may authorize cross-jurisdiction Mobile Team service in exceptional circumstances (such as a voter temporarily in another state for specialized medical treatment) upon a voter's petition publicly recorded upon the Ledger. 11A.7 Mobile Team visits shall be scheduled within fourteen (14) days of qualification. During active Petition windows or pending Referendums, the Citizens' Oversight Board may shorten this window as needed to ensure no qualified voter is denied participation due to scheduling delay. C. Qualification for Mobile Accessibility Team Service 11A.8 A voter qualifies for Mobile Accessibility Team service through one of two paths: (a) Standard Qualification. Upon presentation of documentation from any licensed physician, nurse practitioner, physician assistant, or equivalent licensed medical professional stating that the voter's disability or medical condition materially prevents travel to an Office or Center. The documentation shall be confidential and shall not be published upon the Ledger; only the fact of qualification shall be recorded; or

(b) Special Case Qualification. Upon approval by the Accessibility Review Panel under Section 11A.10, for voters whose circumstances do not fit the standard qualification path but who nonetheless face material barriers to Office or Center participation. 11A.9 No voter shall be required to disclose the specific nature of their disability or medical condition to qualify for Mobile Team service, and no voter's medical information shall be published on the Ledger. Only the fact of qualification, the date of service, and the chain-of-custody records of the Mobile Team visit shall be public. D. The Accessibility Review Panel 11A.10 Each Office and Center shall maintain a standing Accessibility Review Panel to hear special-case qualification requests. The Panel shall consist of three (3) members: (a) The Citizens' Oversight Board member currently assigned in a rotating one-year supervisory role to that Office or Center pursuant to Section 11A.13; (b) A licensed physician drawn by randomized lottery from among licensed physicians of the jurisdiction, serving on a ninety (90) day rotation; and (c) One (1) additional Citizens' Oversight Board member drawn by lottery from Board members serving in the same jurisdiction, on a per-case rotating basis, to prevent the same Board members repeatedly serving on Panel matters. 11A.11 The Accessibility Review Panel shall hear and decide each special-case request within seven (7) days of submission. Decisions shall be by majority vote. The Panel's decision and reasoning shall be published upon the Ledger, with the voter's specific medical details and identifying information redacted for privacy. Qualifying special-case circumstances may include, but are not limited to: severe social anxiety or agoraphobia preventing public-building entry; documented post-traumatic stress disorder affecting ability to be in certain settings; housing instability or domestic-violence situations where travel is unsafe; caregiver obligations preventing travel without accommodation; and any other circumstance materially preventing Office or Center participation that does not fit the standard medical qualification path. 11A.12 A voter whose special-case request is denied by the Panel may appeal to the full Citizens' Oversight Board, which shall hear the appeal within fourteen (14) days and render a final decision by majority vote. The appeal shall be decided on the same privacy-protective basis as the original hearing. E. The Accessibility Officer and Citizens' Oversight Board Supervision 11A.13 Each Office and Center shall employ a professional Accessibility Officer, hired through a qualification-based process by the Office's elected officers. The

Accessibility Officer shall have professional training, certification, or demonstrated expertise in at least one of the following: disability services administration; ADA compliance; occupational therapy; licensed social work; or equivalent qualification. The Accessibility Officer's day-to-day responsibilities include: (a) Coordination of Mobile Accessibility Team deployments; (b) Training of Office or Center staff in disability-sensitive interaction and ADA protocols; (c) Maintenance of Accessible Terminal hardware and software in coordination with the Academic Integrity Commission; (d) Support for voters requesting accommodations, including coordination of certified Accessibility Assistants under Section 11A.15(b); and (e) Coordination with local disability advocacy organizations, nursing homes, hospitals, and hospice providers to ensure voters in those populations have access to the vote. 11A.14 Each Office and Center shall have one member of the Citizens' Oversight Board assigned on a rotating one-year term as Accessibility Oversight Supervisor. The Supervisor: (a) Reviews the Accessibility Officer's conduct and decisions; (b) Receives voter complaints regarding accessibility services and investigates them; (c) Serves on the Accessibility Review Panel under Section 11A.10; (d) Publishes a public annual report upon the Ledger assessing the Office or Center's accessibility performance, including Mobile Team deployments, qualification approvals and denials, complaints received and resolved, and any barriers to participation observed; and (e) May recommend replacement of the Accessibility Officer to the Office's elected officers for cause, including inadequate service delivery, dereliction of duty, or evidence of bias. F. Support Persons and Certified Accessibility Assistants 11A.15 A voter using an Accessible Terminal or Mobile Accessibility Team service shall have the right to choose assistance from either: (a) A trusted support person of the voter's choosing, including family members, personal caregivers, American Sign Language interpreters, or other persons the voter trusts. The support person shall sign a sworn non-coercion statement, recorded upon the Ledger, affirming that they will not influence the voter's choices and will provide only the physical, linguistic, or sensory assistance the voter requests. Violation of the sworn statement shall be a federal felony punishable by imprisonment of not less than five (5) years; or (b) A certified Accessibility Assistant, trained and certified by the Academic Integrity Commission, who provides neutral professional assistance without any prior relationship to the voter. Accessibility Assistants shall be available on request at every Office and Center and as part of every Mobile Accessibility Team. 11A.16 No voter shall be required to use a particular type of assistance. The voter's choice between a trusted support person and a certified Accessibility Assistant shall be respected, and no Office, Center, or Mobile Team shall pressure or encourage a voter to choose one over the other. 11A.17 Coercion, intimidation, manipulation, or exploitation of a voter using accessibility services, whether by a support person, Accessibility Assistant, caregiver, family member, staff member, or any other party, shall be a federal felony punishable by imprisonment of not less than ten

(10) years, with a lifetime bar from any role involving care for persons with disabilities. The Citizens' Oversight Board shall maintain a dedicated Voter Protection Hotline for reporting suspected coercion. G. Security Standards and No Compromise 11A.18 All Accessible Terminals and Mobile Accessibility Team Terminals shall meet the full security standards of Section 14, including air-gapping, cryptographic verification, and immediate recording upon the Ledger. Accessibility accommodations shall never compromise the core security model of the Amendment. No remote voting, mail-in ballots, or electronic transmission of votes outside the Sovereign Civic Network shall be permitted under any accessibility accommodation. 11A.19 The Academic Integrity Commission shall audit accessibility implementation every two (2) years as part of the broader Terminal audit cycle under Section 14.6, with specific attention to: Accessible Terminal functionality, Mobile Team chain-of-custody integrity, Accessibility Review Panel fairness, and voter complaint patterns. Audit findings shall be published upon the Ledger. 11A.20 No provision of this Section shall be interpreted to require the physical identification, disclosure, or registration of any voter's disability as a condition of participation. A voter may use Accessible Terminals without any qualification, documentation, or disclosure; only Mobile Team service requires qualification under Section 11A.8. H. Mobile Participation Units — Removing Cost Barriers to Participation 11A.21 Foundational Principle. The right to participate in petitions and votes under this Amendment shall not depend on a voter's ability to travel to a fixed Office, take time away from paid work, arrange childcare, absorb transportation costs, or bear other practical costs disproportionate to their means. While Mobile Accessibility

Teams under Sections 11A.4 through 11A.9 serve voters qualifying through disability or special-case pathways, Mobile Participation Units established by this subheader shall serve broader populations facing geographic, economic, schedule, or logistical barriers to participation — without requiring individual qualification beyond ordinary voter eligibility. 11A.22 Distinction from Mobile Accessibility Teams. Mobile Accessibility Teams and Mobile Participation Units are complementary but distinct: (a) Mobile Accessibility Teams conduct individualized visits to qualified voters at their locations (homes, institutions, hospitals), require individual qualification through medical or special-case pathways under Section 11A.8, and focus on accessibility accommodation. (b) Mobile Participation Units conduct scheduled group deployments at public venues (community centers, workplaces, rural towns), require no individual qualification beyond ordinary voter eligibility, and focus on cost-barrier removal for any eligible voter at the venue. (c) Both frameworks may operate in coordination, with Mobile Accessibility Teams dispatched to individual homes or institutions while Mobile Participation Units serve collective venues; voters may use either as appropriate to their circumstances. Where a voter qualifies for both, they may select whichever framework best serves their needs. 11A.23 Deployment Targets. Mobile Participation Units shall deploy to venues and populations including but not limited to: (a) Rural and geographically distant communities where voters are more than thirty (30) miles from the nearest Office, Center, or Host Site. (b) Working-class neighborhoods and employment centers, with deployment scheduled during evening and weekend hours to accommodate shift workers and voters unable to miss work. (c) Transit-limited areas, census tracts with documented public transportation deficits, and neighborhoods where voters face disproportionate travel burdens. (d) Workplaces, with voluntary employer consent, including large employment sites, factories, warehouses, and service industry locations where voters work long hours. (e) Community gathering places including community centers, public libraries, religious institutions (with the institution's consent), farmers' markets, community festivals, and cultural events. (f) Native American tribal lands and reservations, with full tribal government coordination and consent, respecting tribal sovereignty and applicable tribal consultation protocols.

(g) Institutional populations that may benefit from group-venue service including homeless shelters, transitional housing, recovery facilities, and veteran services facilities, supplementing individualized Mobile Accessibility Team service. (h) Day-labor hiring sites, agricultural worker camps, and other venues serving populations with limited schedule flexibility or documentation resources. (i) Schools and educational institutions during non-school hours or with school district coordination, serving adult voters in the educational community (students, parents, staff) who may face scheduling barriers. 11A.24 Minimum Deployment Frequency. To ensure meaningful cost-barrier removal: (a) Per-Jurisdiction Minimum. Each Participating Jurisdiction shall maintain at minimum two (2) Mobile Participation Units per one million (1,000,000) registered voters, with not fewer than one (1) Unit per Jurisdiction regardless of population. Smaller Jurisdictions may share Units through State Elections Council coordination. (b) Ordinary Deployment Frequency. Each Unit shall conduct not fewer than twenty (20) deployments per month during ordinary operations, distributed across the deployment target categories of Section 11A.23 to ensure breadth of access. (c) Active Petition Window Surge. During active Petition collection windows under Section 12.5, Unit deployment frequency shall increase by not less than fifty percent (50%) above ordinary operations, with specific deployment to venues where petition support or opposition is concentrated. (d) Referendum Window Operations. During the 30-day National No Confidence Referendum window under Section 5.1 and other referendum windows, Units shall operate at scheduled venues during all posted hours, with schedules published to enable voter planning. (e) Annual Schedule Publication. Annual deployment schedules shall be published on the Franklin Ledger and state transparency infrastructure not less than sixty (60) days in advance, permitting community preparation, employer coordination, and voter planning. 11A.25 Mobile Participation Unit Infrastructure. Each Unit shall be equipped with: (a) Mobile Sovereign Voting Terminals — weatherproofed, battery-powered with solar charging capability, satellite and cellular network-connected — meeting all security standards of Section 14 including air-gapping, cryptographic verification, and dual-chain recording. Mobile Terminals shall be identical in security architecture to fixed Terminals, with mobility being the sole operational difference. (b) Paper ballot backup systems per Section 14.10 through 14.20, available for voter use where Mobile Terminal operation is disrupted and for voter preference.

(c) Identity verification equipment meeting Section 12.9 standards, including: secure identity document review; cryptographic binding; accommodation for voters without standard identification; privacy protection for verification data. (d) Multi-language display capability per Section 12.12(c), with specific language support calibrated to deployment venue demographics. (e) Accessibility features consistent with Section 11A.2 accommodating voters with disabilities who participate at Mobile Unit deployments — Mobile Participation Units and Mobile Accessibility Teams serve overlapping populations, and infrastructure shall accommodate either. (f) Physical security equipment including secure chain-of-custody cases for paper ballots, tamper-evident seals, and anti-surveillance countermeasures meeting Section 11.8(f) standards. 11A.26 Mobile Participation Unit Staffing. Each deployment shall include at minimum: (a) Two (2) certified Oversight Officers trained under Section 11B.6 standards, serving as the primary staff responsible for voter registration verification, Terminal assistance, and integrity oversight. (b) One (1) Accessibility Officer or Accessibility-trained Oversight Officer capable of providing accessibility accommodation to any voter requiring it. (c) Security personnel appropriate to the deployment venue and anticipated voter volume, meeting Section 11.8 security standards. (d) Multi-lingual staff capability appropriate to deployment venue demographics, drawing from the jurisdiction's broader Office staff pool as needed. (e) Medical first-aid capability and emergency response coordination for public-venue deployments. 11A.27 Mobile Unit Security Standards. Mobile Participation Units shall meet all Section 11.4 protected-premises standards adapted for mobile context: (a) Anti-Intimidation Buffer Zones. Campaign, advocacy, intimidation, and voter pressure activities shall be prohibited within a buffer zone appropriate to the venue (typically one hundred (100) feet where space permits; smaller where venue constraints apply, with enhanced staff vigilance to compensate). (b) Observer Rights. Public observers shall have rights equivalent to those at fixed Offices under Section 12.13, with venue-appropriate accommodations for observation without disrupting deployment. (c) Chain-of-Custody Protection. Paper ballots, voter records, and Terminal hardware shall maintain continuous chain-of-custody from venue deployment through secure return to Office, with cryptographic verification at each transfer point.

(d) Coordination with Local Law Enforcement. Mobile Unit security shall coordinate with state and local law enforcement for perimeter support, traffic management, and emergency response, under Section 13.5 protections. (e) Foreign Surveillance Countermeasures. Mobile Units shall implement the electronic countermeasures of Section 11.8(f), with technical standards certified by the Academic Integrity Commission. 11A.28 Coordination Framework. Mobile Participation Units shall coordinate with: (a) Mobile Accessibility Teams under Sections 11A.4 through 11A.9, sharing resources where beneficial, jointly deploying to venues where both accessibility and cost-barrier populations are served, and referring voters between programs as appropriate. (b) Office Directors, who shall have operational authority over Mobile Units deployed from their Offices, with Units reporting to Directors through the Accessibility Officer or designated Mobile Unit Coordinator. (c) State Elections Council, which shall provide inter-jurisdictional coordination for deployments serving voters from multiple Jurisdictions (such as rural border communities or multi-state workplaces). (d) Venue host coordination, respecting venue operator consent, scheduling constraints, and operational requirements, with host cooperation voluntary and appreciated but not compulsory. (e) Tribal government coordination for deployments on tribal lands, with tribal consent, tribal protocol observance, and tribal election officer cooperation as established by tribal governments. 11A.29 Supplementary Cost Barrier Support. Where voter participation costs exceed ordinary civic engagement burdens, supplementary support shall be available: (a) Transportation Assistance. Where voters face documented transportation barriers to reaching Mobile Unit deployments (remote rural areas, disability-adjacent mobility challenges not qualifying for Mobile Accessibility Teams), the Authority may authorize transportation voucher support through local transit providers, rideshare services, or community transportation organizations, subject to reasonable cost caps published on the Franklin Ledger. (b) On-Site Childcare. Where deployment scale and venue permit, Mobile Units shall provide on-site childcare during voter participation, enabling parents with young children to participate without arranging separate childcare. Childcare services shall meet applicable state licensing and safety standards. (c) Extended Hours for Workers. Mobile Units deployed to employment centers or worker-dense neighborhoods shall operate during worker-convenient times, including evening shifts, early morning pre-shift hours, weekend deployments, and mid-shift accommodation where employer coordination permits. (d) Funding for Supplementary Support. Supplementary cost barrier support shall be funded through the Section 11.3 constitutional appropriation via a dedicated Mobile Participation Support allocation managed by the Office Director with Citizens' Oversight Board Accessibility Oversight Supervisor concurrence under Section 11A.14. (e) No Means-Testing Required. Supplementary support shall be available based on venue or deployment context, not based on individual voter means-testing that would burden participation with disclosure requirements. The policy objective is cost barrier removal at the deployment level, not individual benefits administration. 11A.30 Equal Legal Status. Signatures and votes recorded at Mobile Participation Units shall have identical legal status to those recorded at fixed Offices, Centers, Host Sites, Satellite Sites, Overseas Terminals, and Mobile Accessibility Team visits. No voter participating through Mobile Unit shall have their participation diminished, challenged, or scrutinized differently than fixed-Office participation. No jurisdictional counting, certification, or audit process shall differentiate Mobile Unit participation from other participation except as necessary for ordinary logistical record-keeping. 11A.31 Citizen Deployment Requests and Accountability. To ensure Mobile Participation Units serve actual community needs: (a) Deployment Request Pathway. Any registered voter, civic organization, or community group may petition for Mobile Unit deployment to underserved areas through the Office Director, with requests publicly tracked on the Franklin Ledger. Directors shall respond to requests within thirty (30) days with: scheduling commitment; explanation of scheduling constraints; alternative deployment proposal; or reasoned denial if deployment is not operationally feasible. (b) Deployment Equity Audit. Academic Integrity Commission biennial audit under Section 11A.19 shall include Mobile Participation Unit deployment equity analysis, with specific attention to: deployment distribution across Jurisdiction demographics; participation rates by venue type; underserved area identification; deployment request response patterns; any evidence of discriminatory deployment practices. (c) No Voter Denial for Cost Barriers. A voter who appears at any Office, Center, Host Site, Satellite Site, or Mobile Participation Unit citing inability to return due to cost, distance, time, childcare, work schedule, or analogous practical barriers shall not be denied participation on technical grounds. Office staff shall proceed to enroll the voter's participation using available accommodations. Pattern denials inconsistent with this principle shall be investigated by the Watchdog Tribunal. (d) Public Schedule and Request Portal. A public-facing portal on the Franklin Ledger shall enable any citizen to: view upcoming Mobile Unit deployments in

their area; submit deployment requests; track prior request responses; review deployment participation statistics; and verify that Mobile Unit operations meet equity and accessibility standards. (e) Sunset Review Assessment. Each Sunset Review under Section 18 shall include assessment of Mobile Participation Unit effectiveness in removing cost barriers to participation, with the People retaining authority to modify Mobile Unit provisions through Sunset Review to improve effectiveness based on operational experience.

Section 11B. Existing Infrastructure Integration and Priority Construction

Key terms in this Section: • "Host Site" — Any existing public building designated by the Authority to host Sovereign Voting Terminals, signature collection, and associated Amendment functions, pursuant to this Section. • "Primary Office" — A purpose-built Citizens' Reclamation Office established under Section 11, serving as the primary facility for a state or jurisdictional region. • "Satellite Site" — A Host Site operating as an extension of a Primary Office, providing local access to Amendment infrastructure. • "Coverage Standard" — The requirement that at least ninety-five percent (95%) of the registered voters within each Participating Jurisdiction shall have access to a Primary Office, Center, Satellite Site, or Mobile Unit within forty-five (45) minutes of travel time by customary means of transportation from their primary residence. • "Oversight Officer" — A federally-appointed personnel assigned to Host Sites to monitor integrity, assist voters, and report to the Authority. • "Priority Construction Zones" — The District of Columbia, the five territories enumerated in Section 3.1.1, and rural or underserved regions identified by the Authority as having insufficient existing infrastructure. 11B.1 Foundational

Principle. Constructing entirely new Citizens' Reclamation Offices in all fifty-six (56) Participating Jurisdictions would consume years of time and billions of dollars, while much of the necessary public infrastructure already exists. The purpose of this Amendment is best served by bringing the People into the democratic process where they already gather — at their libraries, post offices, community centers, and public institutions. There is therefore hereby established a dual-track infrastructure model: Host Site Integration (using existing public infrastructure) plus Priority Construction (focused on areas most in need of new facilities). A. Host Site Integration — Using Existing Public Infrastructure 11B.2 Designation of Host Sites. The Authority, or during Phase One the Implementation Director with Washington Commission concurrence, shall designate Host Sites from among the following categories of existing public buildings in each Participating Jurisdiction: (a) Federal buildings: United States post offices, federal courthouses, Social Security Administration offices, Department of Veterans Affairs facilities, Internal Revenue Service service centers, federal land management offices, and other federally-owned public-facing facilities; (b) State and local government buildings: state capitols, state courthouses, county seats, municipal buildings, Department of Motor Vehicles offices, state and local election offices, and other state or local government facilities open to the public; (c) Public libraries: any public library operating under state, county, or municipal authority and open to the general public at least twenty (20) hours per week; (d) Public educational institutions: public universities, community colleges, and K-12 public schools (during non-school hours and on weekends only for K-12 facilities, to avoid disruption of educational activities); (e) Community centers and civic facilities: publicly-owned community centers, senior centers, recreation centers, and similar civic facilities; (f) Other public facilities: publicly-owned transit stations, tribal government facilities operated under federal recognition, territorial government facilities, and similar civic infrastructure; and (g) Privately-owned facilities designated voluntarily: any privately-owned facility whose owner voluntarily applies to serve as a Host Site and meets the requirements of this Section, subject to Authority approval and equivalent oversight. 11B.3 Host Site Requirements. Every designated Host Site shall meet the following requirements: (a) Dedicated Amendment Space. A physically partitioned area exclusively for Amendment functions during operational hours, meeting the security standards of Section 14 and the accessibility standards of Section 11A; (b) Terminal Capacity. Adequate space to house not fewer than two (2) Sovereign Voting Terminals and not fewer than one (1) Accessible

Terminal, with privacy separations and queue management; (c) Network Infrastructure. Capacity to connect Terminals to the Sovereign Civic Network pursuant to Section 14, with dedicated Amendment-only fiber-optic lines where possible;

(d) Security Standards. Physical security equivalent to state election office standards, including locked storage for paper records, tamper-evident seals, camera coverage, and audit trails; (e) Operating Hours. Minimum operational hours of forty (40) hours per week during non-election periods and sixty (60) hours per week during active No Confidence Petition or Referendum periods, including weekend and evening hours; (f) Public Signage. Clear signage identifying the facility as a Host Site for Amendment functions, with the Authority's standard wayfinding design published upon the Ledger; (g) Non-Partisan Environment. No partisan political displays, campaign materials, or political speech by Host Site personnel within the dedicated Amendment space during operational hours. 11B.4 Host Site Agreements. The Authority shall enter into written Host Site Agreements with the owning or operating entity of each Host Site, specifying: (a) Term of designation and renewal procedures; (b) Cost-sharing arrangements, with the Federal government paying for Terminal installation, maintenance, network infrastructure, and Oversight Officer compensation, while the host entity contributes space and utilities; (c) Hours of operation and access rights; (d) Security and custodial responsibilities; (e) Dispute resolution procedures; (f) Termination conditions and successor facility arrangements. B. Enhanced Oversight Personnel 11B.5 Oversight Officers at Host Sites. Every Host Site shall be staffed with federally-appointed Oversight Officers, whose presence and number shall be scaled to the density of Terminals, the volume of voter traffic, and the criticality of ongoing Amendment processes. Oversight Officers shall be responsible for: (a) Voter assistance and education on Terminal use; (b) Real-time monitoring of Terminal functionality and network integrity; (c) Observation of any irregularities and immediate reporting to the Authority via the Ledger; (d) Coordination with Host Site personnel regarding security and access; (e) Voter complaint intake and escalation to the Authority; (f) Maintenance of chain-of-custody documentation for any paper records;

(g) Enforcement of non-partisan environment standards under Section 11B.3(g). 11B.6 Oversight Officer Staffing Standards. The Authority shall establish minimum staffing standards for Host Sites, with the following floors: (a) At least two (2) Oversight Officers present during all operational hours at any Host

Site; (b) At least one (1) additional Oversight Officer for each additional two (2) Terminals beyond the initial two; (c) At least one (1) Accessibility Officer (under Section 11A.15) present during any hour when an Accessible Terminal is in operation; (d) During active No Confidence Petition or Referendum periods, Oversight Officer staffing shall increase by fifty percent (50%) above ordinary minimums, with on-call rapid response teams available for high-volume sites; (e) At least one (1) bilingual Oversight Officer present at Host Sites serving communities where more than ten percent (10%) of registered voters primarily use a language other than English, with languages selected to match local demographic data. 11B.7 Oversight Officer Selection, Training, and Standards. Oversight Officers shall be selected by the Authority from applicants who meet the following criteria: (a) United States citizenship; (b) Completion of a forty (40) hour Amendment-specific training program administered by the Academic Integrity Commission, covering Terminal operation, Ledger integrity, voter rights, accessibility procedures, and fraud detection; (c) No current or recent (within ten years) service as a federal officeholder, federal political appointee, registered federal lobbyist, or employee of a federal political campaign; (d) Public disclosure upon the Ledger of: prior employment history, political activity, financial interests, and any relationships with federal officeholders or political entities; (e) Ability to perform the duties without accommodation that would compromise security (with reasonable accommodations for disability made where feasible without security impact); (f) Commitment to non-partisan conduct during service, with removal from position upon violation. 11B.8 Compensation and Protection. Oversight Officers shall: (a) Receive federal compensation at a rate not less than the federal General Schedule GS-9 level, adjusted for locality, with full federal employment benefits during service;

(b) Receive federal protection from harassment, intimidation, or retaliation, with violations constituting federal felonies under Section 13; (c) Have the right to refuse unlawful instructions from any person, including elected officials, without adverse consequence; (d) Serve terms of not less than two (2) years, with staggered rotation to preserve institutional knowledge while preventing entrenchment. 11B.9 Oversight Officer Accountability. Oversight Officers shall be accountable to the Authority through the Liberty Bell Initiative, and their conduct shall be reviewed annually with findings published upon the Ledger. Violations of duties shall be investigated by the Watchdog Tribunal under Section 21, with potential penalties including removal, disqualification from future Amendment service, and prosecution under Section 13 or Section 13A where applicable. C. Priority Construction Zones 11B.10 Simultaneous Priority.

The Authority shall designate Priority Construction Zones, to receive new purpose-built Primary Offices and Centers simultaneously and on equal priority, consisting of: (a) The District of Columbia and the five territories enumerated in Section 3.1.1 (the Commonwealth of Puerto Rico, the Territory of Guam, the United States Virgin Islands, the Commonwealth of the Northern Mariana Islands, and the Territory of American Samoa), which historically have lacked equivalent federal civic infrastructure and which deserve purpose-built Centers of equivalent dignity to state Offices; (b) Rural and remote regions identified through data-driven analysis of existing infrastructure coverage gaps, in which citizens cannot meet the Coverage Standard through Host Site integration alone; (c) Historically-underserved communities identified through data-driven analysis of prior voter participation barriers, including but not limited to communities with persistent coverage gaps, transportation barriers, or other structural obstacles to democratic participation; (d) Tribal nations, where federal recognition and tribal sovereignty permit and where tribal governments consent to the establishment of Primary Offices or Satellite Sites on tribal lands. 11B.11 Construction Priority Sequence. The Authority shall publish a Construction Priority Plan within ninety (90) days of full constitution, allocating construction resources as follows: (a) Phase One Construction (Years 2 through 3): All Priority Construction Zone facilities shall be commenced simultaneously, with groundbreaking on all territorial Centers and on at least seventy-five percent (75%) of identified rural/underserved

Primary Offices within the first eighteen (18) months of construction authorization; (b) Phase Two Construction (Years 3 through 4): Remaining rural/underserved Primary Offices, tribal consent facilities, and state Primary Offices in states with insufficient Host Site coverage; (c) Phase Three Construction (Years 4 through 5): Additional Satellite Sites, capacity expansion, and accessibility enhancements based on utilization data and coverage analysis. 11B.12 Resource Equity. The Authority shall ensure that Priority Construction Zone facilities receive construction quality, equipment standards, and operational support equivalent to, or where appropriate exceeding, state Primary Offices. The historical under-investment in territorial and rural civic infrastructure shall not be perpetuated by this Amendment; in particular, territorial Centers shall be built to the same architectural and security standards as state Offices, with the same Terminal counts scaled proportionally to population plus a minimum floor ensuring meaningful democratic access regardless of small population size. D. Coverage Standard and Compliance 11B.13 Coverage Standard. Within each Participating Jurisdiction, the combination of Primary Offices, Centers, Satellite Sites, and Mobile Accessibility Team coverage shall ensure that not less than ninety-five percent (95%) of registered voters have access to in-person Amendment services within forty-five (45) minutes of travel time by customary means of transportation (including private vehicle, public transit, and walking where applicable) from their primary residence. The Coverage Standard shall apply at all times during active operation of the Amendment. 11B.14 Compliance Assessment. The State Elections Council, in coordination with the Academic Integrity Commission, shall assess Coverage Standard compliance annually for each Participating Jurisdiction, using the following methodology: (a) Geographic mapping of all registered voters' primary residences; (b) Travel-time modeling using current road networks, transit schedules, and typical travel speeds for the region; (c) Identification of gaps where voters fall outside the forty-five (45) minute threshold; (d) Recommendations for remediation through Host Site designation, new construction, or Mobile Accessibility Team expansion; (e) Publication of assessment results upon the Ledger with interactive maps accessible to the public. 11B.15 Remediation Priority. Where the Coverage Standard is not met, the Authority shall undertake remediation in the following priority order:

(a) Host Site designation in affected areas, where existing infrastructure is available and suitable; (b) Mobile Accessibility Team expansion, where geographic barriers preclude fixed-site solutions; (c) Satellite Site construction, where Host Sites are insufficient; (d) Primary Office construction, where coverage gaps are substantial and persistent. 11B.16 Transportation Assistance. Where the Coverage Standard cannot be met within a reasonable time despite remediation efforts, the Authority shall provide transportation assistance to affected voters during active No Confidence Petition or Referendum periods, including: (a) Federal-funded transportation voucher programs coordinated with local transit authorities; (b) Dedicated shuttle services to Host Sites or Primary Offices; (c) Mobile Accessibility Team deployment to hard-to-reach areas; (d) Partnership with rideshare and community transportation organizations, subject to Section 14 security standards. E. State and Local Cooperation 11B.17 Cooperation Duty. State and local governments shall cooperate with the Authority in designating Host Sites, facilitating construction of Priority Construction Zone facilities, and meeting the Coverage Standard. Cooperation includes: (a) Permitting reasonable use of existing public buildings as Host Sites on fair cost-sharing terms under Section 11B.4; (b) Expediting permits and approvals for Priority Construction Zone facilities, with default approval if no decision is rendered within ninety (90) days of complete application; (c)

Sharing data necessary for Coverage Standard assessment under Section 11B.14; (d) Allowing federal Oversight Officers access to Host Sites on their premises. 11B.18 Non-Compliance Consequences. A state or local government that refuses to cooperate with this Section without reasonable cause shall be subject to the non-compliance consequences of Section 20, including federal funding restrictions and Tier One through Tier Three response mechanisms. The Authority may also designate Host Sites at alternative venues, including private facilities on a voluntary basis or federally-owned facilities, where state or local cooperation fails. Individual state or local officials who obstruct Host Site designation, permit issuance, or construction shall be subject to Section 13 interference penalties. 11B.19 Non-Discrimination. No state or local government shall refuse Host Site designation on the basis of the political composition of the area served, the demographic characteristics of the voters served, the partisan affiliation of Authority personnel, or any other discriminatory basis. Violations shall constitute interference under Section 13 and shall be subject to the full penalties thereof. F. Transparency and Public Accountability 11B.20 Ledger Publication. The Authority shall publish upon the Ledger: (a) The complete list of designated Host Sites with location, operational hours, and Terminal counts; (b) The Construction Priority Plan and progress updates; (c) Annual Coverage Standard compliance assessments with interactive mapping; (d) All Host Site Agreements in full; (e) Oversight Officer assignments, training completion, and conduct reviews; (f) All remediation activities and their outcomes. 11B.21 Public Comment. Before designating any Host Site, the Authority shall publish the proposed designation upon the Ledger for a minimum of thirty (30) days public comment. Public comments shall be considered in the final designation decision, with written responses published upon the Ledger explaining how comments were addressed. 11B.22 Sunset Review Integration. The provisions of this Section shall be reviewed in each Sunset Review under Section 18, with particular attention to: Host Site performance, Coverage Standard achievement, Priority Construction Zone equity, and Oversight Officer effectiveness. The People may, through a Modify vote, adjust the specific Coverage Standard metrics, staffing ratios, or construction priorities based on accumulated operational experience. D. Authority Procurement of Temporary Venues 11B.23 Foundational Principle for Temporary Venue Procurement. Because constructing fifty-six (56) permanent Citizens' Reclamation Offices and Centers cannot realistically be completed before the Day Seven Hundred Eighty (780) Inaugural Referendum under Section 19A, and because citizens must be able to participate in

Amendment processes from the moment the Petition mechanism activates under Section 3.0, and because routing Amendment operations through state-controlled election offices would partially undo the Amendment's design of Amendment-native infrastructure, the Authority shall have specific procurement authority to establish temporary venues that serve as operational sites for the Inaugural Referendum, for post-Inaugural Petitions and Referendums, and for

ongoing Amendment operations until permanent Offices come online in each Jurisdiction. Temporary venues under this subheader are distinct from Host Sites under Sections 11B.2 through 11B.22 (which integrate existing public infrastructure) and from Primary Offices under Section 11 (which are purpose-built permanent facilities). Temporary venues are buildings procured through lease, commandeer, civic-use agreement, or equivalent arrangements specifically to serve as Amendment operational venues during the build-out period. 11B.24 Procurement Authority and Process. The following framework shall govern Authority procurement of temporary venues: (a) Liberty Bell Initiative Required. Each temporary venue procurement shall be approved through Liberty Bell Initiative — separate concurrence of the Citizens' Oversight Board (providing citizen legitimacy), the State Elections Council (confirming electoral administration viability), and the Academic Integrity Commission (certifying facility security and operational suitability). During Phase One before the Authority is fully constituted, procurement shall be conducted by the Washington Commission under Section 19.5.0 with input from the State Attorneys General Council and Pre-Certified Pool institutions. (b) Procurement Methods. Temporary venues may be procured through: (i) commercial lease at fair market rates for defined operational periods; (ii) civic-use agreements with private or non-profit facility owners; (iii) federal eminent domain under the constitutional appropriation of Section 11.3, with full compensation to owners; (iv) emergency commandeering under narrow documented conditions with full compensation, subject to Watchdog Tribunal review; (v) voluntary donations of facility access from civic-minded institutions, subject to AIC certification that donation does not create inappropriate capture risk. (c) Priority Hierarchy for Venue Selection. Where multiple candidate venues exist, Authority procurement shall prioritize in the following order: (i) University facilities from the Pre-Certified Pool under Section 17.16, where existing AIC institutional relationships support rapid security certification and where academic independence from federal executive control is established; (ii) Civic facilities with long-standing civic-use traditions (libraries, community centers, civic auditoriums, convention centers, fairgrounds) where public access is historically expected; (iii) Federally-owned civilian facilities (post offices, federal courthouses in Jurisdictions with demonstrated judicial independence, GSA-administered properties) subject to Section 19.22 federal executive non-interference protections; (iv) Commercial facilities procured through standard lease or commandeer (hotel ballrooms, closed retail space, corporate conference facilities); (v) State or local government facilities only where state and local cooperation is demonstrated, with Section 13 penalties applicable to any attempted state or local manipulation of temporary venue operations. (d) Number and Coverage. The Authority shall procure sufficient temporary venues to meet the Section 11B.13 Coverage Standard (ninety-five percent (95%) of registered voters within forty-five (45) minutes travel time) in every Participating Jurisdiction, combining temporary venues with Host Sites under Sections 11B.2 through 11B.22 and Mobile Participation Units under Sections 11A.21 through 11A.31. No Jurisdiction shall be left without adequate coverage by Day Seven Hundred Eighty (780). (e) Completion Timeline. The Authority shall complete temporary venue procurement sufficient for the Inaugural Referendum by Day Seven Hundred Twenty (720), sixty (60) days before the Inaugural Referendum. Procurement shall continue thereafter as needed to support post-Inaugural Petition and Referendum activity until permanent Offices come online in each Jurisdiction. (f) Pre-Day-180 Preparatory Identification. During Phase One, willing Pre-Certified Pool universities, State Attorneys General Councils, and civic facility operators may compile preliminary candidate venue lists for Authority review upon Authority constitution at Day One Hundred Eighty (180). This preparatory work is voluntary and creates no pre-Ratification obligation, but preparation enables rapid procurement execution once Authority convenes. 11B.25 Facility Standards for Temporary Venues. Temporary venues shall meet the following operational standards, notwithstanding that physical construction of the building predates Amendment use: (a) Accessibility. All accessibility standards of Section 11A shall apply. Venues not meeting ADA-compliant accessibility shall not be procured unless accessibility modifications are made as part of the procurement arrangement. (b) Anti-Intimidation Buffer Zones. Section 11.4 buffer zone standards shall apply, with appropriate adaptation to venue geometry (typically one hundred (100) feet where space permits; smaller only where venue constraints make larger impossible, with enhanced staff vigilance to compensate). (c) Observer Rights. Section 12.13 observer rights shall apply in full, including multi-day observer credentials, public accessibility, and real-time documentation on the Franklin Ledger or provisional public ledger. (d) Security Standards. Section 11.8 security protocols shall apply, including AIC-certified security measures during active Petition or Referendum periods. Temporary venues may require installation of additional security infrastructure (metal detectors, security personnel, surveillance systems) during Amendment use. (e) Sovereign Voting Terminal Deployment. Each temporary venue shall be equipped with AIC-certified Sovereign Voting Terminals under Section 14 in numbers appropriate to expected voter volume. Terminals may be temporarily installed and removed as operational needs require. (f) Secure Communications Infrastructure. Temporary venues shall have access to Sovereign Civic Network infrastructure sufficient for blockchain recording, signature attribution, and Franklin Ledger transparency publication.

(g) Oversight Officer Staffing. Temporary venues shall be staffed by Oversight Officers meeting Section 11B.7 training and standards. Staffing levels shall meet Section 11B.6 minimum staffing floors adapted to venue size and expected voter volume. (h) Emergency Office-Level Voter Restoration. Section 13.8(g) provisional ballot framework shall apply at temporary venues equally with permanent Offices, ensuring voters with missing or altered registration records are not excluded. 11B.26 Anti-Capture Protections for Temporary Venues. The following protections apply to temporary venue procurement and operation: (a) Federal Executive Non-Interference. No President, Vice President, Cabinet officer, federal agency head, or other federal executive officeholder shall direct, fund, influence, obstruct, or retaliate against Authority procurement of temporary venues, landlords or facility owners entering procurement arrangements, or Authority operations at procured venues. Any such interference shall constitute Section 13 interference with Senior Official multipliers where applicable, prosecutable by State AG Council under Section 19.5.0.18.9.1 and by Hamilton Contingent upon operational commencement. (b) State Official Non-Interference. State officials who obstruct temporary venue procurement within their Jurisdiction, deny necessary permits for Amendment operations, or materially interfere with procured venue function shall be subject to Section 13 interference penalties and Section 20 state non-compliance consequences. Where state officials obstruct, the Authority shall designate alternative venues under Section 11B.24(c) priority hierarchy, including federally-owned or commercial facilities outside state control. (c) Landlord and Facility Owner Protection. Private individuals, universities, civic organizations, or commercial entities that enter temporary venue procurement arrangements with the Authority shall not face federal adverse action, regulatory retaliation, tax scrutiny, contracting consequence, or any other adverse treatment in retaliation for procurement cooperation. Any such retaliatory action shall constitute Section 13 interference with Senior Official multipliers, enforceable under Section 17.16.1 Pool-participation protection framework applied mutatis mutandis. (d) Short-Term Leases Preferred. Where procurement proceeds through lease, short-term leases (one (1) year with renewal options) shall be preferred over long-term commitments, to prevent facility owners from developing leverage over Amendment operations and to preserve Authority flexibility as permanent Offices come online. Multiple candidate venues shall be identified per Jurisdiction to ensure substitutes are available if a given venue becomes unavailable. (e) Transparency. All temporary venue procurement agreements, including lease terms, security certifications, operational readiness assessments, and renewal or termination decisions, shall be published on the provisional public ledger during Phase One and on the Franklin Ledger thereafter. Redactions shall be limited to narrow operational-security specifics (exact alarm system specifications, specific law enforcement contact names) subject to Watchdog Tribunal review. 11B.27 Transition from Temporary Venues to Permanent Offices. As permanent Citizens' Reclamation Offices and Centers complete construction in each Jurisdiction under Section 19.21 Phase Three, the following per-Jurisdiction transition framework applies: (a) Per-Jurisdiction Migration. When a permanent Office in a Jurisdiction receives AIC certification as operational, Amendment operations in that Jurisdiction shall migrate from temporary venues to the permanent Office. Temporary venue procurement in that Jurisdiction shall wind down on a schedule that ensures operational continuity (typically sixty (60) to one hundred twenty (120) days of parallel operation, with specific timing published on the Ledger). (b) No Gap in Service. At no point during per-Jurisdiction migration shall citizens of that Jurisdiction lose access to Amendment services. Temporary venue operations continue until permanent Office is fully operational and citizens are informed of the new venue. (c) Records Transfer. All operational records, signature records, voter participation data, and security logs shall transfer from temporary venue to permanent Office through cryptographically-verified migration, with no loss of evidentiary value or historical record. (d) Lease Termination. Temporary venue leases shall be terminated, not extended, once migration is complete, with facility returned to owner in condition specified in original procurement agreement. (e) Rural Priority in Transition. Where multiple Jurisdictions complete permanent Offices simultaneously, rural and geographically-dispersed

Jurisdictions shall not be deprioritized in the transition; temporary venues serving rural areas shall continue at full operational capacity during their migration window. 11B.28 Relationship to Section 19.21 Construction Timeline. This subheader's temporary venue procurement framework removes the implicit time pressure on Section 19.21 Phase Three permanent Office construction. Construction of the fifty (50) Primary Offices and six (6) Centers shall proceed at a realistic pace consistent with proper construction standards, community input, environmental review, and quality outcomes, with the Year Five (5) target under Section 19.21 serving as a goal rather than a deadline where legitimate construction challenges (including but not limited to permitting delays, supply chain constraints, weather events, public health emergencies, labor availability, or geological/environmental site issues) require additional time. Temporary venues under this subheader shall continue operating until each Jurisdiction's permanent Office is complete, ensuring citizens are never without Amendment infrastructure regardless of construction timeline. No citizen, particularly no rural citizen in Jurisdictions where construction may take longer due to geographic dispersal or limited local construction capacity, shall be

deprived of Amendment service by construction delay. Any lawsuit, administrative challenge, or other action asserting Amendment failure based on the Section 19.21 Year Five target not being met shall be void ab initio; the Amendment's design includes temporary venue continuation precisely to absorb construction variability without service interruption.

Section 11C. Physical Venues for Amendment Bodies

Key terms in this Section: • "The Authority" — The Independent Tripartite Oversight Authority (three bodies, see Section 17). • "Amendment Bodies" — All bodies established by this Amendment, including the Washington Commission, the Watch Board, the three bodies of the Authority, the Watchdog Tribunal, the Hamilton Contingent, the Interim Caretaker Council, the Constitutional Transition Committee, and any sub-bodies, panels, or committees operating under their authority. • "The Ledger" — The Sovereign Blockchain Voting Ledger (Section 4). A. Foundational Principle 11C.1 Foundational Principle. Every Amendment Body must meet somewhere, work somewhere, and be physically secured somewhere. The Constitution cannot lock specific real estate into its text — buildings age, cities change, needs evolve over decades — but the Constitution must establish principles that guide venue selection so that no body is left without a physical home, no body is placed in inappropriate proximity to the government it is meant to check, and no body's venue becomes a tool of concentration, capture, or hostile pressure. This Section establishes those principles. B. Guiding Principles for Venue Selection 11C.2 Independence Principle. No Amendment Body shall operate from, be headquartered within, or routinely meet in any facility controlled by, adjacent to, or physically dependent upon the Federal Government whose conduct that Body is designed to oversee, investigate, or check. Functional independence requires physical independence. Specifically: (a) The three bodies of the Authority, the Watchdog Tribunal, and the Hamilton Contingent shall not be headquartered within buildings owned, leased, or controlled by the executive branch, by sitting Members of Congress, or by any federal agency under investigation;

(b) Where operational coordination with federal law enforcement, intelligence, or military functions is necessary, such coordination shall occur at Amendment Body facilities, not at federal facilities; (c) Temporary meetings with federal officials may occur at mutually acceptable neutral venues. 11C.3 Geographic Distribution Principle. The physical locations of Amendment Bodies shall be distributed across the United States, not concentrated in the District of Columbia or any single region. Concentration of institutional authority in one geographic location creates risk of capture, hostile environmental pressure, and distance from the People. Specifically: (a) No more than three (3) permanent Amendment Body headquarters shall be located within the District of Columbia or its immediate metropolitan area; (b) Permanent headquarters shall be distributed among at least four (4) of the following regions: Northeast, Mid-Atlantic, Southeast, Midwest, Great Plains, Mountain West, Pacific Coast, Alaska, Hawaii, and the territories; (c) At least one (1) Amendment Body shall be headquartered in a jurisdiction other than the continental United States where practicable. 11C.4 Security and Operational Adequacy Principle. Venue selection shall balance independence and distribution against the real operational needs of each Body, including security from hostile action, appropriate meeting space for the Body's size, secure communications infrastructure, accessibility for members and the public, and reliable transportation connections. Neither principle shall be invoked to render a Body operationally unable to perform its functions. 11C.5 Accessibility Principle. Every Amendment Body venue shall meet or exceed the accessibility standards of Section 11A, ensuring full physical accessibility for members and public observers with disabilities. Venue selection shall prioritize locations with established accessibility infrastructure. 11C.6 Public Observation Principle.

Every Amendment Body venue shall include public observation capacity consistent with the body's transparency requirements under this Amendment. Where in-person observation is limited by space, livestreaming upon the Franklin Ledger or provisional public ledger shall provide full public access. No Amendment Body shall operate from a facility structurally incapable of public observation. C. Immediate-Need Bodies (Days 0-30 Following Ratification or No Confidence) 11C.7 Washington Commission Venues. The Washington Commission established in Section 19.5.0 shall convene and operate using highest-court facilities of Participating Jurisdictions, on a rotating basis, in jurisdictions represented by the seven Chief Justices serving on the Commission at any given time. This approach recognizes that the Chief Justices' normal place of work is within Jurisdictional judicial infrastructure, which provides existing security, staff, and communications capacity. The Commission may also convene through secure video conferencing for routine business, with in-person gatherings required for major decisions as determined by Commission procedure. The host Jurisdiction for each in-person session shall rotate to prevent institutional capture of any single venue. 11C.8 Watch Board Venues. The Citizens' Implementation Watch Board established in Section 19.14 shall convene and operate at member institutions of the Pre-Certified University Pool established under Section 17.16. These institutions provide: existing conference and meeting facilities; security infrastructure appropriate to academic settings; distributed locations across the country; neutral, non-governmental environments; and established relationships with the Academic Integrity Commission. The Board shall rotate among Pool institutions to prevent concentration at any single site. The Authority shall negotiate facility-use agreements with Pool institutions, with compensation drawn from the constitutional appropriation under Section 11.3. 11C.9 Interim Two-Member Command Venues. The Interim Two-Member Command established in Section 19.5.1 shall operate from existing Department of Defense facilities appropriate to the Joint Chiefs' ordinary duties, with civilian oversight provided by Watch Board members and Washington Commission oversight channels. This recognizes that military advisory functions require secure military communications infrastructure that civilian venues cannot immediately provide. However, the Command shall not exercise any authority beyond that enumerated in Section 19.5.2, and its military venue shall not become a basis for expansion of authority. Where Department of Defense facilities are denied, obstructed, or compromised during Phase One, the Interim Two-Member Command shall have full access to the alternate venues and alternate communications pathways established under Section 19.5.0.3.2.1, which framework applies to the Interim Two-Member Command on the same terms as to individual Joint Chiefs. 11C.10 Interim Caretaker Council Venues. The Interim Caretaker Council established in Section 6A shall convene at state capitol buildings, on a rotating basis among the Participating Jurisdictions represented on the Council. The default rotation shall follow alphabetical order of jurisdictions, beginning with Alabama, consistent with the Presiding Chair rotation under Section 6A.5. Daily sessions may rotate between capitols or be conducted via secure videoconference, with periodic in-person full Council sessions at host capitols. Host jurisdictions shall provide security and logistical support through their state emergency management infrastructure, reimbursed through the constitutional appropriation. D. Medium-Term Bodies (Day 180 Onward) 11C.11 Authority Headquarters Selection. Within ninety (90) days of each of the three bodies of the Authority being fully constituted under Section 17 and Section 19.19, each body shall, through its own internal procedures, select its permanent

headquarters location, subject to the principles of this Section. Selections shall be published upon the Franklin Ledger or provisional public ledger with written reasoning, and shall be subject to review by the Watchdog Tribunal for compliance with the principles of this Section. 11C.12 Citizens' Oversight Board Venue. The Citizens' Oversight Board (300 randomly selected citizens) shall select a permanent venue suitable for assembly of its full membership, with appropriate meeting space, accommodation for members required to relocate temporarily for service, and public observation capacity. The venue shall not be located in the District of Columbia or its immediate metropolitan area, to honor the geographic distribution principle and to symbolically place citizen oversight outside the federal capital. 11C.13 State Elections Council Venue. The State Elections Council (56 members serving ex officio from their state chief election officer positions) shall primarily conduct its work from members' existing state election offices, with periodic full Council convenings at rotating host state election offices. This approach recognizes that members are already embedded in state election infrastructure and need not be relocated. 11C.14 Academic Integrity Commission Venue. The Academic Integrity Commission (50 academic representatives) shall select a headquarters from among member institutions of the Pre-Certified University Pool, with supporting operations at other Pool institutions to distribute the Commission's work. This natural alignment between the Commission's membership and the Pool ensures continuity of expertise and appropriate academic infrastructure.

11C.15 Watchdog Tribunal Venue. The Watchdog Tribunal (100 members with quasi-judicial functions) shall select a permanent venue with judicial-style proceeding capacity, including hearing rooms, deliberation chambers, document storage, and public observation galleries. Existing federal courthouse facilities may be repurposed for this use, subject to the independence principle of Section 11C.2. The Tribunal shall not operate from facilities shared with executive branch agencies or the Department of Justice. 11C.16 Hamilton Contingent Headquarters. The Hamilton Contingent established in Section 13C shall select a permanent headquarters with appropriate operational infrastructure, including secure communications, evidence storage, investigative operations space, prosecutorial offices, and public response facilities. Regional offices may be established across the country as needed for effective investigative coverage. The Hamilton Contingent shall not be headquartered within any existing federal law enforcement agency's facilities, consistent with its constitutional independence. 11C.17 Franklin Ledger Operations Center. The physical operations of the Franklin Ledger, to the extent requiring dedicated facilities, shall be distributed across the three Authority bodies' respective venues pursuant to the distributed responsibility model of Section 4A.3, with no single concentrated operations center that could become a point of failure or capture. E. Post-No-Confidence Transitional Bodies 11C.18 Constitutional Transition Committee Venue. The Constitutional Transition Committee established in Section 6, convened only upon passage of a No Confidence Referendum, shall meet at a venue designated by the Authority (or during Phase One, by the Washington Commission) within seven (7) days of No Confidence certification. The venue shall be selected based on: available legislative-style chamber space sufficient for fifty (50) voting delegates plus six (6) advisory delegates; secure communications infrastructure; adequate public observation and press capacity; accessibility; and the principles of this Section. The vacated United States Capitol building shall be available for Committee use if the Authority determines its use is appropriate and logistically feasible; otherwise a suitable alternative shall be designated. F. Venue Protections 11C.19 Constitutional Protection. All Amendment Body venues shall be constitutionally protected from search, seizure, closure, or interference in the same manner as Citizens' Reclamation Offices and Centers under Section 11.4. Interference with any Amendment Body venue shall constitute a Section 13 violation and shall trigger the full penalties thereof. 11C.20 Facility-Use Agreements. Where Amendment Bodies operate from facilities not permanently owned by the Authority (such as State Supreme Court facilities for the Washington Commission, state capitol buildings for the Interim Caretaker Council, or Pre-Certified University Pool institutions for the Watch Board or Academic Integrity Commission), written facility-use agreements shall specify: (a) The scope and duration of facility use; (b) Compensation to the host institution through the constitutional appropriation under Section 11.3; (c) Security responsibilities of host and Amendment Body; (d) Communications and technology access; (e) Public observation accommodations; (f) Confidentiality provisions where permitted under this Amendment's transparency requirements; (g) Termination and continuity-of-operations provisions. 11C.21 Funding for Venues. Funding for Amendment Body venues shall be drawn from the constitutional appropriation under Section 11.3, flowing automatically and directly to the Authority for distribution to the respective Bodies, without

congressional appropriation or executive branch intermediation. No Amendment Body shall be starved of venue resources through the federal appropriations process. 11C.22 Hostile Venue Interference. Any federal, state, or local official who denies, obstructs, or interferes with an Amendment Body's access to a venue appropriate under this Section shall be subject to the interference penalties of Section 13, including the fifteen (15) year minimum sentence and the lifetime bar from public office without possibility of pardon. States whose officials engage in such interference shall be subject to the non-compliance provisions of Section 20. 11C.23 Security Arrangements. Each Amendment Body shall have civilian security appropriate to its functions, provided through the constitutional appropriation. Where host institutions provide security under facility-use agreements, such security shall operate under civilian Amendment Body direction, not host institution direction. Where federal law enforcement or military personnel provide security in limited circumstances, their role shall be support-only, without authority over Amendment Body operations. G. Evolution and Sunset Review 11C.24 Venue Review. Each Amendment Body shall review its venue adequacy every five (5) years, with findings published upon the Franklin Ledger. Venue changes may be initiated by the Body for operational reasons, by the Watchdog Tribunal upon finding of principle violation, or by the Authority through Liberty Bell Initiative. 11C.25 Sunset Review Integration. The provisions of this Section shall be reviewed in each Sunset Review under Section 18. The People may, through a Modify vote, adjust the principles or specific venue arrangements based on accumulated operational experience. Permanent headquarters locations established under this Section may be moved, consolidated, or distributed differently pursuant to Sunset Review determinations. 11C.26 Article V

Protection. The principles of this Section — independence, geographic distribution, security, accessibility, and public observation — shall be protected under the Article V protection established in Sections 18.6.1 and 18.6.2. No act of Congress, executive order, judicial ruling, or state action shall evade, diminish, or nullify these principles, although specific venue arrangements may be modified consistent with the principles themselves.

Section 12. The Citizen Initiation Process

Key terms in this Section: • "The Authority" — The Independent Tripartite Oversight Authority (three bodies, see Section 17).

• "The Ledger" — The Sovereign Blockchain Voting Ledger (Section 4). • "Office / Reclamation Office" — A Citizens' Reclamation Office (Section 11), the physical site where signatures may be collected in person. • "Petition" — A citizen-initiated formal request to trigger a No Confidence Referendum, meeting the 15% national threshold plus 15% in at least 30 states. 12.0 Activation. The procedures established in this Section shall not be operative during the twenty-six (26) month period between Ratification (Day Zero) and the Inaugural Referendum on Day Seven Hundred Eighty (780), as provided in Section 3.0. During that initial period, the Inaugural Referendum under Section 19A is the exclusive mechanism for a No Confidence vote, occurring automatically without any petition requirement. From the day following Inaugural Referendum certification forward — regardless of whether the Inaugural Referendum passed or failed — the procedures of this Section shall be continuously and permanently available to the People as the ongoing democratic instrument for triggering a No Confidence Referendum against any future Federal Government. Citizens' Reclamation Offices shall inform prospective petitioners during the initial twenty-six (26) month period of the Section 3.0 activation rule and the Inaugural Referendum timing. 12.1 Any single registered voter may initiate a Petition in person at any Office. 12.2 The Office shall within 48 hours register the Petition and trigger nationwide notice. 12.3 Signatures shall be collected exclusively in person. No digital, mail-in, or proxy signature shall be valid. 12.4 Mandatory public notifications shall be issued within 48 hours and every 30 days thereafter. 12.5 An active Petition shall remain open for 180 days. 12.6 The window shall be suspended and extended by 90 days upon interference, emergency declaration, or attempt to disable an Office. 12.7 Suspension shall be automatic and self-executing. 12.8 Jurisdictional Attribution of Signatures. The jurisdictional signature threshold under Section 3.1(b) (fifteen percent (15%) in at least thirty (30) of fifty-six (56)

Participating Jurisdictions) requires accurate attribution of each signature to a specific Jurisdiction. Attribution shall proceed as follows: (a) Jurisdiction of Registration Controls. A signature shall be attributed to the Participating Jurisdiction in which the signing voter is registered to vote at the moment of signing, as determined by the voter's current registration record.

Jurisdiction is determined by registration record, not by physical location at the time of signing. (b) In-Jurisdiction Signing as Default. Registered voters shall ordinarily sign petitions at an Office, Center, Host Site, Satellite Site, or Mobile Accessibility Team location within their Participating Jurisdiction of registration. Each state has one (1) Office per Section 11.1 and each non-state Jurisdiction has one (1) Center per Section 11.1.1, supplemented within each Jurisdiction by Host Sites, Satellite Sites, and Mobile Accessibility Team coverage under Section 11B. Voters shall utilize these in-jurisdiction locations as the primary signing venue, consistent with the Coverage Standard of Section 11B.13 that not less than ninety-five percent (95%) of registered voters have in-jurisdiction access within forty-five (45) minutes of travel time. (c) Out-of-Jurisdiction Signing Permitted With Correct Attribution. Where a registered voter is physically present in a Participating Jurisdiction other than their jurisdiction of registration (for example, a voter traveling for work), the voter may nevertheless sign at any Office or Center, with the signature attributed to the voter's jurisdiction of registration rather than the physical location of signing. The Sovereign Voting Terminal shall verify the voter's registration through cryptographic interface with the State Elections Council, confirm the jurisdiction of registration, and attribute the signature accordingly. Travel and temporary absence shall never prevent a citizen from exercising Petition rights. (d) Overseas Americans. United States citizens and nationals residing abroad shall sign through Overseas Terminals per Section 3.1.3, with signatures attributed to their most recent United States residence of record or to the Overseas Americans Jurisdiction where no prior residence exists. (e) No Double Attribution. A signature shall be attributed to exactly one Participating Jurisdiction. Any attempt to re-attribute a signature from one jurisdiction to another after cryptographic recording on the Ledger shall constitute evidence tampering under Section 13B. 12.9 Identity Verification at Terminal. To ensure that each signature is authentic and attributable to the correct voter, the following identity verification procedures shall apply at every Office, Center, Host Site, Satellite Site, and Mobile Accessibility Team location: (a) Acceptable Identification. A registered voter presenting for signature collection shall present one of the following forms of identification: (i) a state or territorial government-issued photo identification card; (ii) a United States passport or passport card; (iii) an active-duty United States military identification card; (iv) a federally recognized tribal identification card; or (v) any other government-issued photo identification accepted under the Participating Jurisdiction's ordinary election law. Offices shall not impose documentation requirements beyond those required by the Jurisdiction's ordinary election law, to prevent Offices from being weaponized as documentation chokepoints. (b) Cryptographic Binding and Voter Roll Cross-Reference. Upon successful identification verification, the Sovereign Voting Terminal shall cross-reference the voter's identification against the State Elections Council voter registration record, confirming both identity and active registration status. The resulting signature shall be cryptographically bound to the voter's verified identity at the moment of signing, with the binding recorded on both Primary Chains under Section 4.11. No signature shall be recorded without successful identity binding. (c) Accommodation for Voters Without Standard ID. Voters unable to present any of the forms of identification under subsection (a) shall be offered the provisional process under Section 13.8(g), permitting signature collection pending post-signature eligibility verification within forty-eight (48) hours. The Amendment recognizes that identification requirements can exclude legitimate voters, and the provisional pathway ensures no eligible voter is turned away for lack of particular documentation. (d) Privacy Protection for Identification Data. Photographic identification presented for verification shall not be retained, photographed, scanned, or stored by Offices beyond the duration of the verification transaction. Only the cryptographic verification result (successful or unsuccessful, and the category of identification used) shall be retained. No federal database of identification documents shall be created through Amendment processes. 12.10 One Signature Per Voter Per Petition. Each registered voter may sign a given active Petition exactly once. Attempts to sign the same Petition multiple times shall be prevented by the Sovereign Voting Terminal's cryptographic verification of prior signature status. (a) Multiple Concurrent Petitions. Where multiple active Petitions exist concurrently (such as petitions targeting different officials or different grounds for No Confidence), a registered voter may sign each active Petition separately. The one-signature rule applies per Petition, not across all active Petitions. (b) Deliberate Duplicate Attempts as Interference. Any registered voter who knowingly attempts to sign the same Petition multiple times through identity fraud, impersonation, or other deceptive means shall be subject to Section 13 interference penalties. Unknowing duplicate-signing attempts (a voter who does not recall having signed earlier) shall be prevented by the Terminal without penalty. 12.11 Signature Withdrawal Rights. A registered voter who has signed a Petition may withdraw their signature under the following framework: (a) Withdrawal Window and Venue. Withdrawal may be exercised at any time between initial signature and the close of the one hundred eighty (180) day collection window under Section 12.5, after which the signature is final. Withdrawal shall be exercised in person at any Office, Center, Host Site, Satellite

Site, or Mobile Accessibility Team location, using the same identity verification procedures of Section 12.9. No digital, mail-in, or proxy withdrawal shall be valid. (b) Cryptographic Recording and Unconditional Right. Withdrawal shall be cryptographically recorded on both Primary Chains, with the voter's signature immediately subtracted from the Petition's running total. The voter need not provide any explanation; the right to withdraw is unconditional during the withdrawal window. A voter who has withdrawn may re-sign the same Petition later, subject to the single-signature rule of Section 12.10. (c) Withdrawal Under Alleged Duress. Where a voter alleges that their signature was collected under duress, the withdrawal process of this Section shall apply with an additional option to report the duress circumstances under Section 12.14 for Watchdog Tribunal investigation. 12.12 Petition Text and Specificity. Every Petition shall specify, in plain language publicly displayed on the Franklin Ledger at the moment of Petition registration under Section 12.2: (a) Required Content. The Petition text shall state: (i) the specific federal officials, bodies, or the federal government as a whole against whom No Confidence is sought; (ii) the general grounds for No Confidence, stated in terms citizens can evaluate (including corruption, abuse of authority, dereliction of duty, violation of constitutional oath, or persistent failure to represent the People); (iii) the specific acts or pattern of conduct underlying the grounds, to the extent the initiating voter specifies; and (iv) the citizen-facing Petition language that signing voters are endorsing when they sign. (b) Scope Clarity and Accuracy. Petitions may target the federal government as a whole (triggering a No Confidence Referendum against all Section 1.1 officials collectively) or may target specific officials or bodies individually. The Petition text shall make its scope unambiguously clear. The text shall accurately describe the grounds and acts underlying the No Confidence call; materially false statements known to be false shall subject the initiating voter to Section 12.15 bad-faith review. (c) Language Accessibility. Petition text shall be published on the Franklin Ledger in English, Spanish, and the primary languages of Participating Jurisdictions with significant non-English-speaking populations (including Spanish in Puerto

Rico, Chamorro in Guam, Samoan in American Samoa, and additional languages as required for equal access). Translation shall be certified for accuracy by the Academic Integrity Commission. (d) No Material Amendment; Consolidation Permitted. Once registered, the Petition text shall not be materially amended. Where multiple Petitions with substantially similar grounds and targets accumulate signatures concurrently, the Authority through Liberty Bell Initiative may consolidate them with signatures combining, provided the combined text preserves the substance of each original Petition.

12.13 Observer Rights During Collection. Public observation is essential to signature collection integrity. The following observer framework shall apply: (a) Right of Observation. Any registered voter, accredited journalist, academic researcher, or representative of a civic organization may observe signature collection at Offices, Centers, Host Sites, and Satellite Sites during operating hours. No special credential shall be required for ordinary public observation. Organizations wishing to conduct sustained observation may coordinate with administering Offices for operational purposes, but credentialing shall not be used as gatekeeping. (b) Voter Privacy Preserved. Observers shall maintain visual separation from the Terminal screen and audio distance from voter-Terminal interaction during individual voter signing. Observers shall not photograph or record individual voters without explicit consent, shall not approach voters actively using Terminals, and shall not interact with voters in any manner that pressures, coerces, or influences their signature decision. (c) Oversight Officer Dual Protection. Oversight Officers shall protect legitimate observers from intimidation or expulsion by Office staff, and shall protect voters from intimidation by observers. The dual protection recognizes that observation is essential to transparency while voter privacy and choice are essential to authentic signatures. Any observer engaging in prohibited conduct under subsection (b) may be removed by the Oversight Officer; any Office staff interfering with legitimate observation shall be subject to Watchdog Tribunal review. 12.14 Duress Signature Reporting. To protect voters from coercion and to preserve the authenticity of collected signatures, the following framework shall apply: (a) Right to Report. Any voter whose signature was collected under duress, coercion, deception, or while incapacitated may report the circumstances to any Office, to the Watchdog Tribunal, to the Hamilton Contingent (once operational), or to the State Attorneys General Council. Reports may be filed at any time during the collection window, with withdrawal under Section 12.11 available as a parallel remedy. (b) Investigation and Invalidation. Upon credible report of duress, the Watchdog Tribunal (or Phase

One equivalent) shall conduct expedited investigation within thirty (30) days. If duress is confirmed, the affected signature shall be invalidated with cryptographic documentation on the Ledger. Where duress reports cluster geographically, demographically, or by perpetrator type, the Tribunal shall conduct pattern investigation with findings published on the Franklin Ledger. (c) Perpetrator Penalties and Victim Protection. Coercion of a Petition signature shall constitute Section 13 interference, with enhanced penalties where the coercion targeted elderly voters, voters with disabilities, voters in institutional settings (such as nursing homes or care facilities), or voters dependent on the perpetrator for housing, employment, or care. Voters reporting duress shall receive full Section

13B.16 whistleblower protections; no voter shall face retaliation for good-faith duress reporting. Ordinary political persuasion, advocacy, and public discourse shall not constitute duress — duress requires actual coercion, threat, deception, or exploitation of dependency. 12.15 Bad-Faith Petition Protection. To preserve Petition integrity against deliberate fraud while protecting the People's unqualified right to initiate Petitions on grounds of their choosing, the following framework shall apply: (a) No Authority Gatekeeping of Legitimate Petitions. The People retain the unqualified right to initiate Petitions against federal officials on any grounds they choose. Authority review shall be limited to detecting deliberate fraud, not evaluating political wisdom, controversial grounds, or unpopularity of targets. Failure to reach signature thresholds is not fraud; failure is not bad faith. (b) Clear-and-Convincing Evidence Required. A Petition may be declared bad-faith and invalidated only upon clear and convincing evidence of: (i) materially false statements in Petition text that the initiating voter knew to be false; (ii) coordinated mass-filing of substantially identical petitions by the same person or coordinated group for the purpose of exhausting Office resources; (iii) initiation as part of a foreign interference operation under Section 22; or (iv) collection of signatures known to be fraudulent (including identity fraud, impersonation, or signatures of deceased persons) as part of a coordinated scheme. Bad-faith determinations shall be made only by the Watchdog Tribunal (or Phase One equivalent) following investigation, with the initiating voter given the right to respond and defend the Petition. (c) Consequences of Bad-Faith Determination. Upon bad-faith determination: (i) the Petition shall be invalidated with cryptographic documentation on the Ledger; (ii) signatures already collected shall be released from that Petition but may count toward a subsequent good-faith Petition with substantially similar grounds if voters re-sign; (iii) the initiating voter shall be subject to Section 13 interference penalties; and (iv) the initiating voter shall be barred from initiating new Petitions for five (5) years. Petitions initiated in good faith but that fail to reach signature thresholds, or that fail verification, shall not constitute bad faith. 12.16 Initiator Personal Protection. Because the initiating voter under Section 12.1 is identified publicly in Petition records, because Petition initiation places the initiator in direct constitutional adversity with the federal officials targeted by the Petition, and because retaliation against initiators would have a severe chilling effect on the People's right to trigger No Confidence proceedings, the following protections shall apply to any registered voter who initiates a Petition in good faith under Section 12.1: (a) Protection from Federal Adverse Action. No federal agency, department, official, or employee shall take adverse action against a Petition initiator in retaliation for Petition initiation activity. Prohibited retaliatory actions include but are not limited to: initiation or intensification of tax audits by the Internal Revenue Service or any successor agency; initiation or intensification of regulatory investigations by any federal agency; termination or non-renewal of federal employment, contracts, grants, or benefits; revocation or denial of security clearances; immigration enforcement actions; denial of passport renewal or other federal travel documents; initiation of federal criminal investigation without independent predicate evidence; inclusion on federal watchlists or no-fly lists; and any other federal action that would not have been taken but for the Petition initiation. (b) Protection from State Adverse Action Where Federally-Coordinated. Where state officials take adverse action against a Petition initiator at the direction, suggestion, encouragement, or coordination of federal officials, such state action shall be treated as federal retaliation under subsection (a) and shall trigger Section 13 interference penalties against both federal coordinators and state executors, with Senior Official multipliers where applicable. (c) Protection from Employment Retaliation by Federal Contractors. Federal contractors, subcontractors, and entities receiving substantial federal funding shall not terminate, demote, or otherwise retaliate against Petition initiators who are their employees, in retaliation for Petition initiation. Such retaliatory employment action shall be voidable by the initiator through expedited Watchdog Tribunal proceedings, with reinstatement, back pay, and damages available as remedies. Federal contracting entities engaging in such retaliation shall face contract termination and debarment under Section 13D.4 asset recovery frameworks. (d) Whistleblower-Equivalent Protection. Petition initiators shall enjoy the protections of Section 13B.16 whistleblower framework mutatis mutandis, including: protection from retaliation; confidential reporting channels to the Watchdog Tribunal and Hamilton Contingent Protection Division; expedited investigation of retaliation claims within thirty (30) days; restoration of position, benefits, and compensation upon finding of retaliation; compensatory and punitive damages for retaliation; and enhanced Section 13 criminal penalties for retaliators with Senior Official multipliers. (e) Burden-Shifting on Retaliation Claims. Where a Petition initiator alleges retaliatory federal, state-coordinated, or federal-contractor action, and demonstrates temporal proximity between Petition initiation and the alleged retaliation (adverse action within two (2) years of initiation), the burden shall shift to the acting agency, official, or entity to demonstrate by clear and convincing evidence that the adverse action would have been taken independent of Petition initiation activity. Temporal proximity within six (6) months of initiation or publicly-known initiation activity shall create a rebuttable presumption of retaliation. (f) Identity Protection During Active Petition. During the active signature collection window of a Petition, the Watchdog Tribunal shall have authority to restrict public disclosure of the initiating voter's identifying information beyond what is strictly

necessary for Petition transparency (such as first name and last initial, rather than full name and address) upon a showing by the initiator of specific threat or harassment. This identity protection shall not extend to Petition text, grounds, or substantive content, all of which remain fully public; it applies only to personally identifying information about the initiator that is not essential to public evaluation of the Petition itself. (g) Post-Failure Protection Continuation. The protections of this Section shall continue for two (2) years following close of the Petition collection window (regardless of whether the Petition succeeded or failed), recognizing that retaliation may be delayed strategically to evade temporal-proximity analysis. After two (2) years, ordinary retaliation claim standards apply without the burden-shifting of subsection (e), though Section 13 interference penalties remain available for retaliation against any Amendment participant at any time. (h) Relationship to Bad-Faith Determination. This Section's initiator protections apply to good-faith Petition initiators. Where the Watchdog Tribunal makes a bad-faith determination under Section 12.15, the initiator shall lose these protections prospectively from the date of determination, but shall retain these protections retroactively for any retaliation occurring before the bad-faith determination (since retaliation against a then-good-faith initiator cannot be justified by later findings). This framework prevents bad-faith initiators from claiming protection while ensuring good-faith initiators are not retroactively stripped of protection by subsequent adverse findings. (i) Immediate Household Protection. The protections of subsections (a) through (h) shall extend to members of the Petition initiator's immediate household, defined as: (i) the initiator's spouse or domestic partner; (ii) the initiator's dependent children (including biological, adopted, foster, and step-children under the age of twenty-six (26) or otherwise legally dependent); (iii) the initiator's dependent parents or other dependent adult relatives residing with the initiator; and (iv) the initiator's legal dependents under state or federal law. Retaliatory federal, state, or private-contractor adverse action against any such household member, where temporal proximity or other evidence indicates the action is retaliation for the Amendment participant's Petition activity, shall trigger the same protections, remedies, and burden-shifting as if the action had been taken against the initiator directly. This protection recognizes that targeting family members is a historically common retaliation tactic against dissenters and constitutional participants, and that such retaliation, if permitted, would severely chill the People's willingness to initiate Petitions. Household member retaliation shall additionally be an aggravating factor in Section 13 interference sentencing, reflecting the aggravated harm of punishing constitutional participation through third parties who did not themselves engage in the participation. (j) Private Employer Retaliation. No private employer, regardless of federal contractor status, shall terminate, demote, discipline, reduce compensation or benefits, reassign to materially less favorable duties, subject to hostile work environment, deny ordinary advancement opportunities, or otherwise retaliate against an employee in retaliation for that employee's Petition initiation, Petition signature, Petition-related advocacy, or other Petition-related activity. The following framework shall govern private employer retaliation claims: (i) Retaliatory employment action shall be voidable by the affected employee through expedited Watchdog Tribunal proceedings under Section 21, with reinstatement to prior position, restoration of benefits and compensation including back pay, and compensatory and punitive damages available as remedies; (ii) The burden-shifting provisions of subsection (e) shall apply to private employer retaliation claims, with temporal proximity within six (6) months of Petition activity creating a rebuttable presumption of retaliation; (iii) Private employers engaging in such retaliation shall be subject to Section 13 interference penalties with enhanced penalties where the employer exploited economic dependency (such as employees dependent on employer-provided housing, employees with limited alternative employment, or employees in industries with concentrated employment opportunities); (iv) Private employers may not require employees to waive the protections of this subsection as a condition of employment; any such waiver shall be void as against public policy; (v) Ordinary political persuasion, ordinary workplace speech restrictions applied neutrally, and ordinary performance-based employment decisions made without reference to Petition activity shall not constitute retaliation — retaliation requires causal connection between Petition activity and adverse action; (vi) Nothing in this subsection shall require private employers to provide paid time off for Petition signing activity, though employers may not prohibit employees from Petition activity during breaks, meal periods, before or after work hours, or other non-work time; (vii) This subsection supplements and does not replace the private employer protections available under Section 5.10(c) voter anti-retaliation framework and Section 13 general interference penalties; protections shall be construed cumulatively in favor of the employee. (k) State and Local Government Adverse Action. No state, territorial, tribal, or local government official, employee, or agency shall take adverse action against a Petition initiator, signer, or household member in retaliation for Amendment participation. Prohibited retaliatory actions include but are not limited to: initiation or intensification of state tax audits or state regulatory investigations; termination or non-renewal of state or local employment, contracts, grants, licenses, permits, or benefits; revocation or denial of state-issued identification, licenses, or credentials; state law enforcement investigation without independent predicate evidence; eviction or lease termination from state or locally-owned housing; denial of state or local services available to similarly-situated residents; initiation of state criminal investigation or prosecution without independent predicate evidence; placement on state watchlists or investigation targets; and any other state, local, territorial, or tribal government action that would not have been taken but for the Amendment participation. State-only retaliation shall receive the same remedies, burden-shifting (subsection (e)), and post-failure continuation (subsection (g)) as federal retaliation

under subsection (a). State officials engaging in such retaliation shall be subject to Section 13 interference penalties and Section 20 state non-compliance consequences. Where state officials act at the direction of federal officials, subsection (b) federally-coordinated retaliation framework applies; where state officials act independently, this subsection governs. The protection of Amendment participants from state-level retaliation is as constitutionally essential as protection from federal retaliation, recognizing that captured states in hostile Jurisdictions may attempt to discourage Amendment participation through state mechanisms when federal mechanisms are barred.

Section 13. Penalties for Interference, with Law Enforcement Protections

Key terms in this Section: • "The Authority" — The Independent Tripartite Oversight Authority (three bodies, see Section 17). • "The Ledger" — The Sovereign Blockchain Voting Ledger (Section 4). • "Office / Reclamation Office" — A Citizens' Reclamation Office (Section 11). • "Citizens' Oversight Board" — The 300-member citizen body within the Authority (Section 17), which holds veto authority over law enforcement actions at Reclamation Offices under this Section. 13.1 Obstruction, delay, intimidation, surveillance, or suppression of any Office, Network, Terminal, or Petition shall be a federal felony punishable by not less than 15 years, subject to Section 13.5 protections. 13.2 Convicted officials shall be permanently barred from any public office or government employment, with no pardon or clemency. 13.3 All acts of interference shall be permanently recorded upon the Ledger. 13.4 An active Petition shall not constitute grounds for emergency powers or military deployment. Protections for Legitimate Law Enforcement 13.5 Law enforcement action against Office personnel shall be permitted only upon ALL of the following: (a) unanimous written approval from a three-judge panel drawn by lottery from justices of the highest courts of Participating Jurisdictions as defined in Section 3; (b) specific narrow enumerated offense (embezzlement, credential theft, fraudulent signature collection, Terminal tampering, or violent crime); (c) real-time public publication upon the Ledger of the action, approval, and evidence; and (d) Citizens' Oversight Board retained authority to suspend by majority vote if suppression is suspected.

13.6 Action failing all four requirements shall constitute interference and trigger Section 13.1 penalties against those ordering it. 13.7 Panel or Board members accepting bribes shall trigger Section 17.25 penalties, with their approval or veto null and void. 13.7.1 Offense Definitions. The following definitions shall govern Section 13 interference offenses: (a) Obstruction. Acts preventing, delaying, or impairing operation of an Office, Center, Network, Terminal, Petition, or other Amendment process, including: physically blocking access to facilities; denying utilities or services required for operation; issuing orders that contradict this Amendment; withholding funds constitutionally appropriated under Section 11.3; interfering with personnel performance of Amendment duties; or taking other action with the purpose or effect of preventing Amendment operation. (b) Delay. Acts causing improper timing impairment of Amendment processes, including: deferring required action beyond its constitutional deadline; scheduling obstruction to time-sensitive Amendment functions; imposing procedural requirements not authorized by this Amendment or by Authority rules; or taking other action with the purpose or effect of running out constitutional clocks. (c) Intimidation. Acts designed to discourage voter, official, or staff participation in Amendment processes through fear, threat, or coercion, including: threats of physical harm; threats of adverse employment action; threats of deportation or immigration consequences; threats against family members; public campaigns of harassment against specific persons; or other conduct creating reasonable fear of adverse consequence for Amendment participation. (d) Surveillance. Acts of monitoring voter, official, or staff Amendment participation without specific legal authorization, including: electronic monitoring of communications; physical surveillance of facilities or individuals; collection of biometric data; monitoring of signing or voting activity; or other conduct creating a chilling effect on participation without warrant or authorized legal basis. (e) Suppression. Acts preventing eligible voters from signing Petitions or voting in Referenda, including: voter roll manipulation under Section 13.8; documentation requirements beyond state law; wait-time engineering to discourage participation; misinformation campaigns with specific intent to discourage participation; or other conduct preventing eligible voters from exercising Amendment rights. (f) Interference Generally. Any other conduct with the purpose or effect of impairing Amendment processes, including conduct not specifically enumerated above that a reasonable person would recognize as intended to obstruct, delay, intimidate, surveille, or suppress. The enumerated categories are illustrative, not exhaustive.

(g) Knowing and Willful. Interference offenses shall require that the actor knew their conduct was likely to cause interference, or acted with willful blindness to that likelihood as defined in Section 22.3.1(b). Genuine mistake or good-faith compliance failure shall not constitute interference absent the knowing or willful mental state. 13.7.2 Evidentiary Standards for Interference Offenses. Interference prosecutions shall proceed under the following evidentiary framework: (a) Criminal Prosecution — Beyond Reasonable Doubt. Criminal prosecution for Section 13 interference shall proceed under the ordinary beyond reasonable doubt standard applicable to all federal criminal prosecutions, with full procedural protections of the Fifth and Sixth Amendments to the Constitution. (b) Civil Penalties — Clear and Convincing Evidence. Civil sanctions (including office bar, asset recovery, and civil fines) shall proceed under the clear and convincing evidence standard, defined as substantially more likely true than not. (c) Administrative Findings — Preponderance of the

Evidence. Administrative findings by the Authority, Watchdog Tribunal, or Hamilton Contingent (such as findings of corruption for oversight purposes but not resulting in criminal conviction) shall proceed under the preponderance of the evidence standard. (d) Pattern Evidence. Evidence of patterns of conduct — including temporal clustering, geographic clustering, coordination with other actors, and recurrence across Amendment processes — shall be admissible to establish knowing or willful mental state, even where individual incidents in isolation might appear innocent. (e) Circumstantial Evidence. Circumstantial evidence shall be fully admissible and, when sufficient in aggregate, may satisfy applicable evidentiary standards. Federal prosecution shall not require direct evidence (such as explicit admissions) where circumstantial evidence establishes the elements of the offense. (f) Digital and Cryptographic Evidence. Digital communications records, Ledger entries, cryptographic verification data, and other digital evidence preserved under Section 13B shall be admissible as authenticated records, with authentication through cryptographic verification rather than custodial testimony where appropriate. 13.7.3 Penalty Scaling by Severity. While Section 13.1 establishes a fifteen (15) year minimum sentence for interference offenses, the following severity scaling shall apply in sentencing: (a) Base Penalty. The fifteen (15) year minimum applies to interference offenses generally, with sentencing within the statutory range based on severity factors below. (b) Aggravating Factors. Sentences may be enhanced above the fifteen (15) year minimum based on: (i) scope of interference (number of voters affected, number of

Offices affected, geographic scope); (ii) position of the offender (Senior Official multipliers per Section 13.1(a)); (iii) duration of interference; (iv) coordination with other actors (conspiracy); (v) foreign actor involvement (Section 22 parallel charges); (vi) targeting of vulnerable populations (elderly voters, voters with disabilities, voters in institutional settings); (vii) use of official authority to facilitate interference (abuse of power enhancement); (viii) retaliation against whistleblowers exposing the interference. (c) Mitigating Factors. Sentences may be reduced toward but not below the fifteen (15) year minimum based on: (i) genuine cooperation with investigation leading to identification of senior conspirators; (ii) voluntary cessation of interference before detection; (iii) substantial mitigation of harm; (iv) lack of prior offenses. Cooperation credit shall be documented with specific findings of the cooperation's value, subject to Section 13D.21 standards. (d) Senior Official Multiplier Application. Senior Official multipliers under Section 13.1(a) shall operate as sentence enhancements, not as maximum caps. A Senior Official whose conduct involves aggravating factors may face sentences well above the base Senior Official multiplier range. (e) Asset Recovery Coordination. Penalty scaling shall coordinate with Section 13D asset recovery, with more severe interference offenses triggering higher tiers of asset recovery. The criminal sentence and the asset recovery judgment operate independently but in coordinated fashion. (f) No Presidential Pardon for Amendment Interference. Consistent with Section 24.5, Presidential pardon authority shall not extend to Section 13 interference offenses, reflecting the constitutional principle that interference with the Amendment cannot be excused by the officials who might benefit from the interference. 13.7.4 Statute of Limitations for Interference Offenses. The following statute of limitations rules shall apply: (a) Base Statute — Ten Years. Interference offenses shall be subject to a ten (10) year statute of limitations from the date of the interference, providing substantial time for discovery and investigation of complex interference schemes. (b) Continuing Offense Rule. Where interference is part of a continuing scheme, the statute of limitations shall run from the last act in furtherance of the scheme, not from earlier individual acts. Continuing schemes include coordinated campaigns of voter suppression, systematic surveillance programs, and ongoing corruption arrangements. (c) Senior Official Extension. Where the offender was a Senior Official at the time of the offense, the statute of limitations shall extend to twenty (20) years, reflecting the additional time required to investigate powerful individuals who may have used their office to conceal wrongdoing.

(d) Evidence Destruction Tolling. The statute of limitations shall be tolled (meaning: temporarily paused) during any period when the offender engaged in evidence destruction under Section 13B, willful concealment, flight from jurisdiction, or other conduct preventing discovery of the offense. Tolling shall continue until the offender's concealment conduct ceases or is discovered. (e) No Limitations for Foreign Interference. Interference offenses involving foreign actors under Section 22 shall have no statute of limitations, consistent with Section 22's no-limitations rule for foreign interference. (f) No Limitations for Capital Section 13E Offenses. Section 13E Refusal-to-Vacate offenses (which operate as Section 13 interference with heightened penalties) shall have no statute of limitations, reflecting the foundational threat such conduct poses to constitutional governance. 13.7.5 Prosecutorial Framework. Section 13 prosecutions shall proceed through the following framework: (a) Hamilton Contingent Primary Authority. Upon operational commencement, the Hamilton Contingent Prosecution Division shall serve as primary federal prosecutorial authority for Section 13 offenses, with independence from the Department of

Justice under Section 13C.4. (b) Pre-Hamilton Phase One. During Phase One before Hamilton Contingent operational commencement, federal Section 13 prosecutions shall proceed through the State Attorneys General Council under Section 19.5.0.5.2, acting by supermajority to authorize specific prosecutions. (c) State Concurrent Authority. State Attorneys General retain concurrent authority to prosecute Section 13 offenses under parallel state interference statutes where states enact such statutes, with no federal preemption of state enforcement. (d) Prosecutorial Independence. Prosecutorial decisions under Section 13 shall be made independently of federal executive direction per Section 13C.4.1 (Prosecution Division Internal Firewall). No President, Vice President, Cabinet officer, Attorney General of the United States, or other federal executive officer shall direct, influence, or retaliate against Section 13 prosecutions. (e) Declination Transparency. Prosecutorial decisions to decline Section 13 prosecution despite substantial evidence shall require published reasoning on the Franklin Ledger per Section 13C.4.1(f). Declinations without published reasoning shall trigger Watchdog Tribunal review. (f) Special Prosecutor Authority. Where capture of the ordinary prosecutorial authority is suspected, the Watchdog Tribunal may, by supermajority, direct appointment of a Special Prosecutor from the Pre-Certified State AG Pool under Section 17D.13.1 to conduct specific Section 13 prosecutions independently of the Hamilton Contingent.

13.7.6 Defendant Protections. Section 13 defendants shall enjoy the following procedural protections: (a) Full Due Process. Section 13 prosecutions shall proceed under full Fifth and Sixth Amendment protections, including right to counsel, right to trial by jury, right to confront witnesses, right to compulsory process, presumption of innocence, and requirement of proof beyond reasonable doubt. (b) Section 17C Venue Where Applicable. Where the defendant is a federal official tried for Section 13 offenses, the Section 17C framework may apply under Section 17C.15, providing trial in state-sovereign venues when federal judicial capture is suspected. (c) Discovery Obligations. Prosecution shall comply with full federal criminal discovery obligations, including Brady disclosure of exculpatory material, Giglio disclosure of impeachment material, and timely production of evidence. (d) Appellate Rights. Section 13 defendants shall have full appellate rights consistent with federal criminal appeals, with Section 17C.10 appeals applicable where the case proceeded under Section 17C framework. (e) Protection Against Prosecutorial Abuse. Where a Section 13 prosecution is filed in bad faith, for political retaliation, or without legitimate evidentiary basis, the defendant may seek dismissal with prejudice and file counter-petition with the Watchdog Tribunal for investigation of the filing prosecutors. Bad-faith prosecution shall itself constitute Section 13 interference. 13.7.7 Whistleblower Triggers for Section 13 Investigation. Independent of ordinary prosecutorial initiation, the following triggers shall compel Section 13 investigation: (a) Whistleblower Reports. Whistleblower reports under Section 13B.16 meeting the Section 13B.17 evidentiary threshold shall trigger automatic investigation by the Hamilton Contingent Prosecution Division (or pre-operational substitute under Section 13.7.5(b)), with timelines under Section 13B.18. (b) Citizen Petition Triggers. Registered voter petitions under Section 13C.28 meeting the Section 13C.28 threshold shall trigger Hamilton Contingent review with substantive response required within sixty (60) days. (c) Watchdog Tribunal Referrals. Watchdog Tribunal findings of credible interference shall be referred to prosecutorial authority with presumption that referral warrants investigation. Declination of Tribunal-referred matters shall require published reasoning. (d) Pattern Detection by AIC. Academic Integrity Commission pattern analysis under Section 13.8(c) or comparable provisions identifying likely interference shall trigger Hamilton Contingent investigation upon finding crosses specified threshold.

(e) Inspector General Referrals. Federal Inspector General findings of potential interference shall be referred to prosecutorial authority with expedited review required. (f) State Attorney General Referrals. State Attorney General findings of potential federal interference, produced through state-level investigation, shall be coordinated with federal prosecutorial authority through the State Attorneys General Council, with federal action required where evidence warrants. Voter Roll Integrity 13.8 Voter Roll Integrity for Amendment Processes. Because voter rolls are the gateway through which citizens access the in-person verification required by Section 12 for Petitions and by Section 4 for Referendum voting, corruption of voter rolls constitutes interference with the People's ability to participate in Amendment processes. This Section establishes specific voter roll integrity protections applicable to voter rolls as used for Petition signature verification, Referendum participation, and all other Amendment processes: (a) Scope. This Section applies to voter rolls as utilized for: (i) Petition signature verification under Section 3.2 and Section 12; (ii) Inaugural Referendum participation under Section 19A; (iii) ordinary Referendum, Emergency Delegate Election, Emergency Election, and Sunset Review Vote participation; (iv) Restoration Petition verification under Section 17B.3; (v) Citizen Emergency Override certification under Section 21.11; (vi) participation in any other process established by this Amendment requiring voter registration verification. This Section does not alter state authority over voter rolls for ordinary state and federal elections unrelated to Amendment processes; (b) Prohibited Conduct. No person, acting individually or in concert with others, shall intentionally, recklessly, or through willful blindness as defined in Section 22.3.1(b): (i) Suppression Through Purge. Remove registered voters from voter rolls utilized for Amendment processes without specific, documented, voter-specific grounds meeting the state's ordinary purge criteria applied without discriminatory intent; (ii) Suppression Through Challenge. Challenge voter registrations without specific, documented, voter-specific grounds, particularly where such challenges are geographically concentrated, demographically targeted, or temporally concentrated during active Petition or Referendum periods; (iii) Stuffing. Add non-eligible persons to voter rolls utilized for Amendment processes, including deceased persons, persons ineligible under state law, fictitious persons, or persons recorded at addresses where they do not reside; (iv) Discriminatory Verification. Apply voter registration verification requirements, documentation requirements, or identity requirements selectively or in a discriminatory manner based on geography, demographics, political affiliation presumed from residence, or membership in any protected class; (v) Targeted Record Corruption. Alter voter roll records — including addresses, names, registration dates, or party affiliations — in ways that effectively prevent legitimate voters from completing verification at Offices or Centers; (vi) Discriminatory

System Failure. Operate voter registration systems in a manner that produces discriminatory error rates against specific Participating Jurisdictions, demographic groups, or populations, where such error rates could reasonably have been prevented through ordinary systems maintenance; (vii) Denial of Restoration. Refuse to restore wrongfully-purged or wrongfully-altered voters to voter rolls upon presentation of credible evidence of their eligibility, or apply such restoration procedures in a dilatory or discriminatory manner; (c) Continuous AIC Audit Authority. The Academic Integrity Commission shall continuously audit voter rolls utilized for Amendment processes across all fifty-six (56) Participating Jurisdictions, utilizing automated pattern detection, cross-reference to multiple independent data sources (including the United States Census, Social Security Administration death records, and state vital records), and statistical analysis to identify anomalies including: unusual purge patterns affecting specific geographies or demographics; registration date anomalies suggesting backdated entries or missing historical records; address patterns inconsistent with residential data; discriminatory verification error rates; and other indicia of the prohibited conduct enumerated in subsection (b). During Phase One before AIC full constitution, the audit function shall be performed by the AIC-Designate Forensic Consortium under Section 13B.7.1 with support from the State Attorneys General Council under Section 19.5.0.18.1; (d) Published Findings. AIC audit findings shall be published on the Franklin Ledger with specific jurisdiction-level and pattern-level detail, including identification of Participating Jurisdictions where audit findings suggest prohibited conduct. Findings meeting the Section 4A.11.1 threshold shall automatically be included in the Serious Findings category with neutral presentation under Section 4A.11.1(b); (e) State Remediation Obligation. Upon AIC publication of findings suggesting prohibited conduct affecting voter rolls in a specific Participating Jurisdiction, the chief election officer of that Jurisdiction (serving on the State Elections Council under Section 17) shall, within thirty (30) days, either (i) remediate the identified deficiencies with documented corrective action published on state government transparency infrastructure and the Franklin Ledger, or (ii) publicly rebut the AIC findings with specific factual basis. Good-faith remediation or good-faith rebuttal shall not constitute violation of this Section. Failure to remediate and failure to rebut within the thirty-day window shall constitute prima facie evidence of willful blindness for purposes of subsection (b); (f) State AG Council Enforcement Authority. Where a Participating Jurisdiction fails to remediate AIC-identified deficiencies and fails to provide good-faith rebuttal within the thirty-day window under subsection (e), the State Attorneys General Council acting by supermajority under Section 19.5.0.18.9.1 shall have authority to: (i) initiate Section 13 interference prosecution against responsible state officials, routed through the Section 17C.15 framework for Amendment-related prosecutions; (ii) seek judicial order compelling voter roll remediation in an appropriate state or federal court, with expedited review; (iii) coordinate with the Hamilton Contingent (once operational) for federal-level interference prosecution; (g) Emergency Office-Level Restoration. Where a voter presents at a Citizens'

Reclamation Office, Center, Host Site, or Overseas Terminal with credible evidence of eligibility but finds their registration missing, altered, or otherwise unavailable, the Office shall permit the voter to cast a verified provisional ballot under the following procedures: (i) voter provides valid identification and affirmation of eligibility under penalty of perjury; (ii) voter completes a provisional ballot at a Sovereign Voting Terminal with the provisional status cryptographically recorded on both Primary Chains under Section 4.12; (iii) within forty-eight (48) hours, the State Elections Council verifies eligibility through cross-reference to multiple independent data sources including: prior voter rolls, state vital records, Social Security Administration data, and Census data; (iv) upon eligibility verification, the provisional ballot is counted toward final results; upon verified ineligibility, the provisional ballot is excluded with documented reasoning; (v) provisional ballot processing shall not delay certification beyond the Amendment's ordinary timelines; certification may proceed with provisional ballots either included (if eligibility verified) or excluded (if ineligibility verified) by the certification deadline; (h) Federal Executive Non-Interference. No President, Vice President, Cabinet officer, federal agency head, or other federal executive officeholder shall direct, fund, influence, pressure, or impede voter roll administration by Participating Jurisdictions, AIC audit activities, State AG Council enforcement, or provisional ballot processing under this Section. Any such interference shall constitute Section 13 interference with Senior Official multipliers where applicable, prosecutable by the State AG Council under Sections 19.5.0.5.2 and 19.5.0.18.9.1 during Phase One and by the Hamilton Contingent upon operational commencement, and through the Section 17C.15 framework; (i) No Reduction of State Voter Roll Authority for Non-Amendment Purposes. Nothing in this Section shall alter state authority over voter rolls for ordinary state and federal elections unrelated to Amendment processes. The protections of this Section apply specifically to voter rolls as utilized for Amendment-specific verification and participation, recognizing that voter roll integrity is constitutionally essential to the People's ability to exercise Amendment-specified rights; (j) Penalties. Violations of subsection (b) shall be prosecuted under Section 13 interference framework with the following specific considerations: (i) Senior Official multipliers shall apply to state officials holding positions of supervisory authority over voter registration systems, including state secretaries of state and election directors where such officials direct or willfully permit prohibited conduct; (ii) patterns of prohibited conduct affecting multiple Participating Jurisdictions, conducted by coordinated actors, shall constitute enhanced conspiracy offenses with applicable federal conspiracy penalties; (iii) prohibited conduct timed to specific Petition or Referendum periods shall constitute enhanced offenses with sentence augmentation reflecting the temporal targeting of constitutional processes; (iv) the Section 13D asset recovery framework shall apply to prohibited conduct where the actor received financial benefit; (v) bar from public office under Section 13.2 shall apply to all convictions under this Section; (k) Watchdog Tribunal Oversight. The Watchdog Tribunal shall exercise oversight over AIC audit methodology, State AG

Council enforcement decisions, and provisional ballot processing under this Section, with authority to investigate allegations of bad-faith audit findings, bad-faith enforcement, or bad-faith restoration denial. Tribunal findings shall be published on the Franklin Ledger. 13.9 Initial Comprehensive Voter Roll Audit. Recognizing that the continuous voter roll integrity protections of Section 13.8 operate from Ratification forward, and recognizing that the rolls inherited at Ratification — as a matter of operational fact, not legal characterization — reflect the cumulative results of administrative practice that preceded this Amendment's effective date, and recognizing that Section 13.8's continuous AIC audit authority necessarily encompasses examination of how rolls came to be in their present condition (because evaluating present integrity requires understanding accumulated administrative history), this Section establishes the operational framework under which the first comprehensive cycle of Section 13.8(c) audit operations shall proceed during the initial post-Ratification period, with explicit authorization for retrospective evidentiary scope and timeline structure: (a) Foundational Principle. This Section operates entirely under the post-Ratification authority of Section 13.8 and creates no preconditions on Section 3 Petitions, Section 19A Inaugural Referendum eligibility, or any other Amendment process. The initial comprehensive audit is the first operational application of Section 13.8(c) continuous audit authority; it does not gate the People's exercise of Amendment rights. The audit's value is informational and remediative, not gatekeeping; (b) Audit Scope. The Initial Comprehensive Audit shall examine each Participating Jurisdiction's voter rolls as they exist at Ratification and the administrative history that produced them, including: (i) purge patterns over the ten (10) years preceding Ratification, identifying purges that lacked specific voter-specific grounds, that were geographically concentrated, that were demographically targeted, or that were temporally concentrated during prior election cycles; (ii) registration date anomalies suggesting backdated entries, missing historical records, or systematic record alteration; (iii) address-pattern analysis identifying registration recorded at non-residential addresses, commercial addresses, or addresses inconsistent with residential demographic data; (iv) discriminatory verification error rates compared against ordinary baseline error rates expected from competent administration; (v) cross-reference against United States Census data, Social Security Administration death records, state vital records, and other independent sources to identify systematic distortions; (vi) any other condition meeting the prohibited-conduct categories of Section 13.8(b) had it occurred post-Ratification, recognizing that the Amendment does not retroactively prosecute pre-Ratification conduct but does authorize examination of pre-Ratification conduct as evidence of inherited roll conditions requiring post-Ratification remediation; (c) Audit Timeline. The Initial Comprehensive Audit shall commence within thirty (30) days of certified Ratification under the Phase One AIC-Designate Forensic Consortium, with initial findings published on the provisional public ledger no later than Day Three Hundred (300) following Ratification, and final findings published on the Franklin Ledger no later than Day

Six Hundred (600). The Day Six Hundred (600) target is operational, not gating: completion by Day 600 provides one hundred eighty (180) days of remediation window before the Day Seven Hundred Eighty (780) Inaugural Referendum, but failure to meet the Day 600 target shall not prevent any Amendment process from proceeding; (d) Findings Publication. Audit findings shall be published with the same jurisdiction-level and pattern-level detail required under Section 13.8(d), including: identification of Participating Jurisdictions where the inherited rolls show evidence of accumulated distortions; specific factual basis for each finding; statistical methodology and confidence levels; and explicit distinction between historical accumulated distortions (informational scope of this Section) and post-Ratification conduct (subject to Section 13.8 prohibitions and penalties). Findings shall be included in the Section 4A.11.1 Serious Findings category where they meet the threshold; (e) Remediation Window. Upon publication of audit findings under subsection (d), the chief election officer of each Participating Jurisdiction with audit findings shall have one hundred eighty (180) days from publication to either (i) remediate the identified accumulated distortions through specifically documented corrective action published on state government transparency infrastructure and the Franklin Ledger, including restoration of wrongly-purged voters where individually identifiable, demographic correction of systematic verification rate disparities, and address-record corrections; or (ii) provide good-faith documented rebuttal of the audit findings with specific factual basis; (f) Phase One Substitute Authority. During Phase One before AIC full constitution, the AIC-Designate Forensic Consortium shall conduct the Initial Comprehensive Audit with support from the State Attorneys General Council under Section 19.5.0.18.1, drawing on Pre-Certified University Pool resources under Section 17.16 for technical capacity. Audit work product produced by the Consortium during Phase One shall transfer to the Academic Integrity Commission upon its constitution at Day 180, with the AIC retaining authority to supplement, refine, or extend the audit but not to invalidate Phase One work product without specific cause documented on the Franklin Ledger; (g) Conversion of Maintained Distortions to Section 13.8 Violations. Where a Participating Jurisdiction fails to remediate audit-identified accumulated distortions during the one hundred eighty (180) day window under subsection (e), and fails to provide good-faith rebuttal, the maintained distortions shall be treated as ongoing prohibited conduct under Section 13.8(b), with the State AG Council enforcement authority of Section 13.8(f) applying. The Amendment does not prosecute pre-Ratification conduct; the Amendment prosecutes the post-Ratification choice to maintain documented distortions after notice and opportunity to remediate; (h) Provisional Ballot Pathway During Remediation. While remediation is in progress, the emergency Office-level restoration provisional ballot pathway under Section 13.8(g) shall apply to voters in jurisdictions with documented audit findings, ensuring that documented roll conditions cannot prevent eligible voters from participating in Amendment processes during the remediation period. Provisional ballots cast under this subsection shall receive the same eligibility verification timeline (forty-eight hours) as Section 13.8(g) provisional ballots; (i) No Federal Executive Interference. No President, Vice President, Cabinet officer, federal agency head, or other federal executive officeholder shall direct, fund, influence, pressure, or impede the Initial Comprehensive Audit, AIC-Designate Forensic Consortium operations during Phase One, AIC operations after Day 180, State AG Council enforcement, or provisional ballot processing under this Section. Any such interference shall constitute Section 13 interference with Senior Official multipliers where applicable, prosecutable by the State AG Council under Sections 19.5.0.5.2 and 19.5.0.18.9.1 during Phase One and by the Hamilton Contingent upon operational commencement, and through the Section 17C.15 framework; (j) Subsequent Periodic Comprehensive Audits. After completion of the Initial Comprehensive Audit, the Academic Integrity Commission shall conduct equivalent comprehensive audits every ten (10) years, providing periodic structural reset against accumulated drift. Periodic comprehensive audits operate under the same framework as the Initial Comprehensive Audit, with timing aligned to ensure completion at least one (1) year before any Sunset Review Vote under Section 18.1; (k) Funding. All costs of Initial Comprehensive Audit operations, including AIC-Designate Forensic Consortium operations, AIC operations, technical support from Pre-Certified Universities, and remediation oversight, shall be funded through the Ratification Loan under Section 13I.4 during the Initial Comprehensive Audit, and through the constitutional appropriation under Section 11.3 thereafter; (l) Watchdog Tribunal Oversight. The Watchdog Tribunal shall exercise oversight over Initial Comprehensive Audit methodology, AIC and AIC-Designate Forensic Consortium decision-making, and State AG Council enforcement under this Section, with authority to investigate allegations of bad-faith audit findings, bad-faith enforcement, or bad-faith remediation acceptance. Tribunal findings shall be published on the Franklin Ledger; (m) No Single-Point Failure. Failure or delay of the AIC-Designate Forensic Consortium or the Academic Integrity Commission to complete the Initial Comprehensive Audit within the operational targets of subsection (c) shall not prevent any Section 3 Petition, Section 19A Inaugural Referendum, or any other Amendment process from proceeding. Where audit completion is delayed, the Watchdog Tribunal (or during Phase One, the Short-Term Civilian Review Board under Section 19.5.0.7) shall conduct an emergency capacity review, publishing findings on the Franklin Ledger or provisional public ledger, and the Section 13.8 continuous audit framework shall continue to provide ongoing roll integrity oversight. Capture of, or interference with, the audit administering body shall itself constitute Section 13 interference subject to enhanced penalties; the Amendment's response to audit failure is to investigate the cause and apply Section 13 penalties to bad-faith actors, not to suspend the People's exercise of Amendment rights; (n) Article V Protection. The provisions of this Section shall be protected under the Article V protection established in Sections 18.6.1 and 18.6.2. This Section establishes that the Section 13.8 continuous audit framework, in its initial post-Ratification operation, shall produce comprehensive findings on the inherited state of voter rolls; the People

begin the post-Ratification period with rolls that are subject to examination, public reporting, and remediation under Amendment-native authority, with full provisional ballot protections preserving access during any remediation period.

Section 13A. Financial Penalties for Corruption

Key terms in this Section: • "The Authority" — The Independent Tripartite Oversight Authority (three bodies, see Section 17). • "The Ledger" — The Sovereign Blockchain Voting Ledger (Section 4). • "Corruption Offense" — Any offense under Sections 6A.13, 9.11-12, 13, 17.25, 20.14, 20A, 22.17-19, or any other offense arising under this Amendment involving corrupt intent, bribery, embezzlement, self-dealing, improper influence, or breach of public trust. • "Benefit Received" — The total monetary value, in any form, gained by the offender through the Corruption Offense, including direct payments, indirect payments, gifts, future promises, asset transfers, enhanced compensation, and any other quantifiable financial benefit. • "Actual Harm" — The total monetary value of documented harm to the United States, its citizens, the Amendment's operation, or third parties caused by the Corruption Offense. • "Senior Official" — For purposes of enhanced multipliers under this Section: any President, Vice President, Cabinet-level officer, United States Senator, United States Representative, Justice of the Supreme Court, Article III federal judge, Implementation Director, Watchdog Tribunal member, Authority body member, Caretaker Council member, Washington Commission member, or comparable-rank federal officeholder. 13A.1 Recognizing that financial penalties for corruption must be significant enough to deter the wealthy and powerful — not merely proportional to modest offenses — this Section establishes minimum fines, scaling multipliers, asset forfeiture (meaning: the government permanently taking ownership of assets obtained through or used for criminal activity, without compensation to the former owner), and clawback (meaning: recovering money or benefits already paid out when they were received improperly or as a result of misconduct) provisions that apply to every Corruption Offense under this Amendment. These financial penalties shall apply cumulatively with, not in substitution for, the prison terms and lifetime bars established elsewhere in this Amendment. A. Minimum Fines by Offense Category 13A.2 The following minimum fines shall apply upon conviction for Corruption Offenses, imposed on the individual offender, to be assessed by the sentencing court and collected in the same manner as federal tax obligations: (a) Base Minimum. For any Corruption Offense not otherwise specified below: not less than two hundred thousand dollars ($200,000) OR ten (10) times the Benefit Received, whichever is greater; (b) Campaign Finance Laundering. For offenses involving intentional laundering of prohibited funds under Section 9.11(c): not less than five hundred thousand dollars ($500,000) OR ten (10) times the laundered amount, whichever is greater; (c) Foreign Interference. For offenses under Section 22.17: not less than one million dollars ($1,000,000) OR ten (10) times the Benefit Received, whichever is greater; (d) Authority Body Bribery. For bribery, threats, blackmail, or corruption of any Authority member under Section 17.25: not less than two million dollars ($2,000,000) OR ten (10) times the Benefit Received, whichever is greater; (e) Nuclear Authorization Bypass. For any attempt to bypass Section 16 nuclear authorization requirements: not less than twenty million dollars ($20,000,000), with no upper limit, applied in addition to the treason penalties under Section 16.12; and (f) Inflation Adjustment. All dollar amounts in this Section shall be adjusted annually for inflation by the Academic Integrity Commission using the most recent consumer price index, with adjusted amounts published upon the Ledger no later than January 1 of each year. B. Scaling Multipliers 13A.3 The minimum fines established in Section 13A.2 shall be multiplied, cumulatively, by the following factors where applicable: (a) Senior Official Multiplier. Where the offender is a Senior Official as defined in Section 13A, the fine shall be no less than fifty (50) times the Benefit Received. This recognizes that senior officials occupy positions of greatest public trust and thus should face the greatest consequences for breaching that trust; (b) Repeat Offender Multiplier. Where the offender has been previously convicted of any Corruption Offense under this Amendment, the fine shall be no less than twenty-five (25) times the Benefit Received; (c) Combined Multiplier. Where both the Senior Official and Repeat Offender multipliers apply, the fine shall be no less than seventy-five (75) times the Benefit

Received, representing the sum of the two multipliers; and (d) Authority Member Bribery Special Rule. Where the offender is an Authority body member convicted of accepting bribery under Section 17.25, the Senior Official multiplier applies and the fine shall be no less than fifty (50) times the Benefit Received, in addition to the two million dollar ($2,000,000) minimum under Section 13A.2(d). C. Treble Damages for Harm Caused 13A.4 In addition to the minimum fines and multipliers established above, the sentencing court shall impose treble damages (three times Actual Harm) payable by the offender, calculated as follows: (a) Documented Harm. Actual Harm shall be determined by the sentencing court based on documented evidence, including but not limited to: financial losses to the United States; costs of investigation and prosecution; costs of remediation; losses to individual citizens directly harmed; and costs of public-confidence repair; (b) Three Times Multiplier. The treble damages are three (3) times the Actual Harm, assessed in addition to the Section 13A.2 minimum fine and any Section 13A.3 multipliers; and (c) Distribution. Treble damages collected shall be distributed: one-third (1/3) to the Constitutional Elections Fund under Section 9.8; one-third (1/3) to the constitutional appropriation under Section 11.3 supporting Office and Center operations; and one-third (1/3) returned to direct-to-citizen benefit programs to repair public harm. D. Asset Forfeiture of Corruption Proceeds 13A.5 Upon conviction for any Corruption Offense, all assets derived from or connected to the offense shall be forfeited in full, including: (a) Direct proceeds — cash, securities, real property, and any other property obtained through the Corruption Offense; (b) Indirect proceeds — assets purchased with, commingled with, or otherwise traceable to corruption proceeds; (c) Enhanced compensation — any salary, bonus, severance, pension, or other compensation received during the corrupt tenure that would not have been received but for the corrupt conduct; (d) Corporate or entity proceeds — where a corporation, limited liability company, or other entity was used as a vehicle for the Corruption Offense, all proceeds traceable through the entity, with the entity itself subject to Section 13A.7; and (e) Future Income Derived. Any post-government employment income, consulting fees, book royalties, speaking fees, or other income derived from the offender's federal service or corrupt tenure, earned in the ten (10) years following conviction, subject to forfeiture upon Authority determination that the income derives from that service. E. Clawback of Federal Compensation and Benefits 13A.6 Upon conviction for any Corruption Offense committed during federal service, the following clawback provisions shall apply: (a) Federal Salary Clawback. One hundred percent (100%) of federal salary, bonuses, and allowances received during the period of corrupt tenure shall be repaid to the United States Treasury. The period of corrupt tenure shall be determined by the sentencing court based on evidence of when the corrupt conduct began; (b) Federal Pension Forfeiture. All federal pension benefits, including military pensions, civil service pensions, and Members of Congress pensions, shall be forfeited upon conviction. Any pension benefits already paid during the corrupt tenure shall be subject to clawback; (c) Federal Health Benefits Termination. All federal health benefits, including Federal Employee Health Benefits Program participation and retiree health benefits, shall be terminated upon conviction; (d) Social Security Protection. Social Security benefits, Medicare, Medicaid, and Veterans Affairs benefits shall NOT be affected by this Section; these direct-to-citizen benefits are protected consistent with the approach throughout this Amendment; and (e) Spousal and Dependent Protections. The clawback provisions of this subsection shall not be enforced in a manner that renders innocent spouses or dependent children destitute. Courts shall retain discretion to preserve reasonable support for dependents who were not involved in or knowledgeable of the corrupt conduct. F. Corporate and Entity Penalties 13A.7 Where a corporation, limited liability company, political action committee, nonprofit organization, labor union, trade association, or other entity participates in a Corruption Offense under this Amendment, the entity shall be subject to: (a) Base Entity Fine. Not less than twenty (20) times the amount of corrupt funds involved in the entity's participation, with no upper limit; (b) Federal Contracting Ban. Permanent prohibition from receiving any federal contract, grant, subsidy, or federal tax benefit, effective immediately upon conviction; (c) Charter Revocation. For domestic entities: revocation of corporate charter, articles of incorporation, tax-exempt status, or other federal or state legal authorization to operate. The Authority by Liberty Bell Initiative shall certify the

conditions warranting charter revocation, with state enforcement coordinated through the State Elections Council; (d) Asset Seizure. For foreign entities: seizure of all assets within United States jurisdiction, coordinated with Treasury Department enforcement action; and (e) Successor Liability. Successor entities, reorganizations, mergers, or other corporate transformations designed to evade the penalties of this subsection shall be subject to the same penalties as the original entity, with successor liability determined by the sentencing court. G. Proportionality Safeguards 13A.8 Nothing in this Section shall authorize the imposition of financial penalties grossly disproportionate to the offense in violation of the Eighth Amendment to the Constitution. The minimum fines, multipliers, treble damages, and clawback provisions established in this Section are designed to ensure proportionate-upward scaling with the seriousness of the offense, the offender's position, and the harm caused, while maintaining constitutional proportionality at the low end. 13A.9 In cases where strict application of the minimum fines under Section 13A.2 would result in a financial penalty grossly disproportionate to the offense — for example, a minor technical violation with no actual benefit received — the sentencing court may, with publicly reasoned findings recorded upon the Ledger, impose a lesser fine consistent with the Eighth Amendment. However, the Authority by Liberty Bell Initiative may review any such reduction for consistency with the deterrent purpose of this Section, and appeals from sentencing proceed under existing federal appellate procedures. 13A.10 The scaling multipliers under Section 13A.3 and the treble damages under Section 13A.4 shall be presumptively proportionate where the offense caused documented benefit or harm, as they scale directly with the quantified benefit or harm. Challenges to these scaled penalties shall require clear and convincing evidence that the application is grossly disproportionate to the specific offense. H. Collection, Distribution, and Transparency 13A.11 All fines, treble damages, forfeitures, and clawbacks under this Section shall be collected by the United States Treasury in the same manner as federal tax obligations, with the same enforcement authorities and the same priority over competing claims. Uncollected amounts shall accrue interest at the federal statutory rate until paid. 13A.12 Distribution of collected amounts, except as otherwise specified in Section 13A.4(c): (a) Fifty percent (50%) shall support the constitutional appropriation under Section 11.3 for the ongoing operation of Offices, Centers, and Amendment infrastructure;

(b) Twenty-five percent (25%) shall support the Constitutional Elections Fund under Section 9.8 for small-donor matching; and (c) Twenty-five percent (25%) shall be directed to direct-to-citizen benefit programs to repair public harm caused by corruption, with allocation determined by the Authority through Liberty Bell Initiative with published reasoning. 13A.13 All fines, forfeitures, clawbacks, and distributions under this Section shall be published in full upon the Ledger, with the offender's name, offense, amounts assessed, amounts collected, and amounts distributed, accessible to the People without limitation. Transparency is itself a deterrent; citizens shall see clearly the consequences of corruption.

Section 13B. Evidence Preservation and Anti-Destruction Safeguards

Key terms in this Section: • "Federal Records" — All documents, communications, data, files, devices, and information of any form created, received, or maintained by any federal officeholder, federal employee, federal contractor, or federal agency in the course of federal business, regardless of format, classification level, or storage medium. • "Covered Person" — Any person subject to the preservation duties of this Section, including: all federal elected officials; all federal political appointees; all federal employees including career civil servants; all federal contractors with access to federal records; all members of White House staff; all Members of Congress and Congressional staff; all federal judges and judicial staff; and all spouses, family members, or agents acting on behalf of such persons in matters touching federal business. • "Preservation Order" — The automatic legal obligation, imposed by operation of this Section upon Ratification, that all Covered Persons preserve, maintain, and make accessible all Federal Records in their possession, custody, or control without alteration, deletion, destruction, concealment, or transfer outside proper custody. • "Triple Custody" — The requirement that Federal Records be preserved in three independent systems: (a) the originating federal agency's archival system; (b) the National Archives and Records Administration or successor federal archive; and (c) independent custody by the Academic Integrity Commission under Section 17.

• "Watchdog Tribunal" — The body established under Section 21 for enforcement of anti-corruption provisions. • "Whistleblower" — Any person who reports a violation of this Section or other federal misconduct through channels established by this Section or other federal whistleblower law. 13B.1

Foundational Principle. The period between Ratification and the Inaugural Referendum under Section 19A — and indeed any period when Amendment operation threatens entrenched corrupt interests — presents an acute risk of evidence destruction by officeholders seeking to evade accountability. Such destruction would prevent the Authority, the Watchdog Tribunal, the new Federal Government (if reconstituted through No Confidence), and the People themselves from understanding the conduct of those whom the Amendment is designed to hold accountable. There is therefore hereby established a comprehensive Preservation Order applicable from the moment of Ratification forward. This Section constitutes a constitutional guarantee that the People's right to know the truth about their government shall not be frustrated by destruction of evidence. A. Automatic Preservation Order at Ratification 13B.2 Instant Imposition. Upon the effective date of Ratification (Day Zero), a universal Preservation Order shall attach automatically, by operation of constitutional law and without further procedural step, to all Federal Records in the possession, custody, or control of all Covered Persons. No notice, petition, court order, or administrative action shall be required for the Preservation Order to take effect; it is constitutional in character and self-executing. 13B.3 Comprehensive Scope. The Preservation Order shall apply to all Federal Records without exception, including but not limited to: (a) All electronic communications: emails, text messages, instant messaging, Slack messages, Signal messages, WhatsApp messages, voicemails, video conferences, and all other forms of electronic communication; (b) All documents and files: memos, letters, reports, briefings, meeting minutes, draft documents, spreadsheets, presentations, notes, calendars, and all other written or digital records; (c) All financial records: bank statements, transfer records, wire transfers, payment records, expense reports, tax filings, trust documents, asset disclosures, and all other financial documentation; (d) All foreign contact records: communications with foreign governments, foreign officials, foreign business contacts, foreign financial institutions, and foreign persons; travel records, meeting logs, and diplomatic records;

(e) All devices and media: federal-issued computers, phones, tablets, servers, storage devices, backup tapes, hard drives, cloud storage accounts, and all associated data; (f) All surveillance and monitoring records: security camera footage, building access logs, electronic access records, network activity logs, and all other surveillance data; (g) All meeting and calendar records: calendars, appointment logs, meeting attendance, conference records, and all other documentation of who met with whom and when; (h) All classified documents:

regardless of classification level, preserved in accordance with classification protocols but made available to the Watchdog Tribunal and Academic Integrity Commission under appropriate security clearance procedures; (i) All personal devices and accounts used for federal business: private email accounts, personal phones, personal cloud storage, and all other non-federal systems where federal business has been conducted; (j) All records of family members and agents: where family members, spouses, or agents of Covered Persons have conducted business related to the Covered Person's federal role, such records are subject to preservation. 13B.4 Retroactive Look-Back. Federal Records that were in existence during the one hundred eighty (180) day period prior to Ratification shall also be subject to preservation under this Section, because the public announcement of this Amendment's pending ratification creates notice and incentive for pre-emptive destruction. Destruction that occurred during this look-back period, if demonstrable by clear and convincing evidence, shall be subject to the full penalties of this Section, notwithstanding that Ratification had not yet taken formal effect. 13B.5 Duration of Preservation Order. The Preservation Order shall remain in effect: (a) Indefinitely as to records subject to ongoing investigation, litigation, or accountability proceedings; (b) For not less than twenty (20) years as to all other Federal Records, after which the National Archives and Records Administration shall determine disposition under ordinary federal records law; (c) For not less than five (5) years beyond the departure from office of any Covered Person, for records created during that person's federal service; (d) For the full duration of any Watchdog Tribunal, Authority, or judicial proceeding concerning the conduct of any Covered Person, plus ten (10) years after conclusion of all such proceedings.

B. Triple-Backup Preservation Architecture 13B.6 Mandatory Triple Custody. All Federal Records subject to the Preservation Order shall be preserved in three independent custody systems, each cryptographically linked and mutually verifying, to ensure that destruction of any single copy cannot succeed in eliminating evidence. The three custody systems are: (a) Agency Custody: The originating federal agency shall maintain its primary archival system for its Federal Records, subject to immediate and auditable accessibility to the Watchdog Tribunal and Academic Integrity Commission; (b) National Archives Custody: The National Archives and Records Administration or successor federal archive shall receive complete mirrored copies of all Federal Records within ninety (90) days of creation, with monthly verification of completeness; (c) Academic Integrity Commission Custody: The Academic Integrity Commission shall maintain independent third-party custody of cryptographically-hashed mirrored copies of all Federal Records, stored in multiple geographically-dispersed secure facilities operated by Pre-Certified Pool universities or designated secure contractors. 13B.7 Real-Time Forensic Imaging and Cryptographic Hashing. Within thirty (30) days of Ratification, or within thirty (30) days of creation for records created thereafter, every federal device, server, and storage system shall be subject to forensic imaging with cryptographic hash verification, such that any subsequent alteration, deletion, or destruction is technically detectable. The Academic Integrity Commission shall: (a) Create bit-for-bit forensic images of all federal devices and storage systems; (b) Publish cryptographic hashes of each image upon the Ledger, creating an immutable public record of the state of federal records at the moment of imaging; (c) Conduct periodic re-imaging and hash comparison to detect any alteration; (d) Maintain the forensic images in the Triple Custody system for subsequent forensic analysis if needed. 13B.7.1 AIC-Designate Forensic Consortium — Phase One Imaging Authority. Because the Academic Integrity Commission under Section 13B.7 is not fully constituted until Day One Hundred Eighty (180), but forensic imaging is required within thirty (30) days of Ratification, the following interim forensic imaging authority structure shall apply: (a) Consortium Formation. Upon Ratification, an AIC-Designate Forensic Consortium shall be formed consisting of not fewer than fifteen (15) accredited research universities meeting the qualifying criteria of Section 17.16, with specific demonstrated expertise in digital forensics, cryptographic verification, and federal records preservation. Formation shall proceed as follows: (i) within fourteen (14) days of Ratification, accredited research universities meeting the qualifying criteria may self-nominate for Consortium membership by submitting documentation of digital forensics capability and independence to the Attorney General of their home jurisdiction; (ii) within fourteen (14) additional days, the State Attorneys General Council acting collectively shall verify self-nominations and recognize the Consortium; (iii) the Consortium shall be operationally capable of conducting forensic imaging within thirty (30) days of Ratification, with infrastructure acquisition funded through the Ratification Loan under Section 13I.4; (iv) willing universities may coordinate readiness assessments during the ratification campaign period, but no pre-Ratification obligation is created by this Amendment; (b) Imaging Authority. Upon operational commencement, the Consortium shall have full authority to conduct forensic imaging of federal devices, servers, and storage systems under Section 13B.7, acting under access authorization from: (i) sitting federal Inspector Generals protected under Section 13B.20, acting within their agency jurisdictions as the default first-instance pathway; (ii) the State Attorneys General Council under Section 19.5.0.18.9.2 where the Inspector General pathway is denied, obstructed, or unavailable; or (iii) the Washington Commission under Section 19.5.0.5, as applicable to each imaging matter; (c) Operational Funding. All Consortium operational costs — including infrastructure acquisition, staffing, training, and ongoing imaging operations — shall be funded through the Ratification Loan under Section 13I.4, with disbursement commencing upon Consortium recognition under subsection (a)(ii). No Consortium member institution shall bear operational costs from its ordinary operating budget; federal constitutional funding covers the full operational cost; (d) Transfer to AIC. Upon Academic Integrity Commission full constitution on Day One Hundred Eighty (180), all Consortium imaging operations, records, forensic images, cryptographic hashes, and chain-of-custody documentation shall transfer to the Commission, with the Consortium continuing to provide operational support under Commission direction until the Commission certifies that it has assumed full imaging authority. The Consortium shall not dissolve during Phase One in order to preserve operational continuity, but shall become subordinate to the Commission upon transfer and shall dissolve upon Commission certification of full imaging capability, with Consortium institutions then reverting to their ordinary academic roles including potential selection into the Pre-Certified University Pool under Section 17.16; (e) Federal Executive Non-Interference. No President, Vice President, Cabinet officer, federal agency head, or other federal executive officeholder shall direct, fund, influence, or impede Consortium operations. Any federal executive interference shall constitute Section 13 interference with Senior Official multipliers where applicable, Section 13B.11 evidence destruction penalties where imaging is prevented or delayed, and referral to State Attorneys General Council prosecution under Section 19.5.0.18.9.1; (f) Anti-Retaliation Protection. Consortium member institutions shall receive the same protections against adverse federal action as Pre-Certified Pool universities under Section 17.16.1. Any federal agency investigation, audit, funding reduction, or adverse action against Consortium member institutions or their personnel in

retaliation for Consortium participation shall constitute Section 13 interference, with enforcement through the State Attorneys General Council acting by supermajority under Sections 19.5.0.5.2 and 19.5.0.18.9.1 and, upon operational commencement, through the Hamilton Contingent; (g) Amendment Orientation. Because Consortium member institutions are accredited research universities with existing professional digital forensics expertise, the Amendment does not require substantive forensic training. However, before conducting any Amendment imaging operations, Consortium personnel shall complete a brief Amendment orientation (not less than four (4) hours, not more than twelve (12) hours) administered by the State Attorneys General Council during Phase One (or by the Academic Integrity Commission thereafter) covering: access authorities under Sections 13B.7, 19.5.0.18.9.2, and 19.5.0.5; chain-of-custody standards under Section 13B; reporting obligations; Federal Communications Firewall during active imaging operations; and evidence preservation requirements. Orientation materials shall be published for public review. Orientation is a prerequisite to operational activity; forensic expertise is not questioned, only Amendment-specific duties. 13B.7.2 Auto-Replication Compliance Enforcement During Phase One. Enforcement of the automatic replication requirements under Section 13B.9 during Phase One shall proceed as follows: (a) Compliance Verification. The AIC-Designate Forensic Consortium under Section 13B.7.1 shall verify compliance with Section 13B.9 auto-replication requirements across all federal agencies within fourteen (14) days of Ratification, with compliance reports published on state government transparency infrastructure and, once operational, on the provisional public ledger; (b) Non-Compliance as Evidence Destruction. Failure to maintain auto-replication as required by Section 13B.9 shall be presumed intentional obstruction of preservation, subject to the "No Technical Excuse" rule of Section 13B.10 and Section 13B.11 evidence destruction penalties, with patterns of non-compliance across multiple agencies treated as circumstantial evidence of coordinated obstruction; (c) Corrective Imaging. Where auto-replication has been disabled, compromised, or is non-functional, the Consortium shall conduct corrective forensic imaging as soon as technically feasible under the authorization pathways of Section 13B.7.1(b), and shall restore auto-replication capability, with the cost of such corrective action borne by the responsible federal agency and recoverable from responsible officials through Section 13D asset recovery proceedings; (d) Prosecution Authority. The State Attorneys General Council acting by supermajority under Sections 19.5.0.5.2 and 19.5.0.18.9.1 shall have primary federal prosecution authority for Section 13B.9 violations during Phase One, with prosecution records transferring to the Hamilton Contingent upon its operational commencement for continuation, consolidation, or reconsideration; (e) Ongoing Monitoring. The Consortium shall conduct continuous monitoring of auto-replication status throughout Phase One, with any detected interruption triggering automatic alert to the Washington Commission, the State Attorneys General Council, and, upon convening, the Short-Term Civilian Review Board. Monthly Phase One compliance reports shall be published on the provisional public ledger with agency-by-agency status. 13B.7.3 Temporary Evidence Destruction Task Force — Retroactive Investigation Capacity. Enforcement of the Section 13B.4 retroactive look-back period shall be coordinated through a Temporary Evidence Destruction Task Force established as follows: (a) Convening and Composition. The Task Force shall convene automatically within thirty (30) days of Ratification, consisting of: (i) not fewer than seven (7) State Attorneys General selected by rotation from the State Attorneys General Council under Section 19.5.0.18.1, serving staggered ninety (90) day rotations to prevent capture of the investigative function; (ii) sitting federal Inspector Generals with relevant jurisdiction, protected under Section 13B.20, serving ex officio; (iii) AIC-Designate Forensic Consortium technical experts providing forensic analysis support; (iv) two (2) Washington Commission representatives serving liaison functions; and (v) one (1) Short-Term Civilian Review Board representative once the Board has convened. The Task Force shall operate through consensus among the State AG members, with formal action requiring majority concurrence of the seven rotating State AG members; (b) Investigative Scope. The Task Force shall investigate all credible allegations of evidence destruction occurring during the Section 13B.4 one hundred eighty (180) day retroactive look-back period and during the period from Ratification through Hamilton Contingent operational commencement, with investigations prioritized by: severity of alleged destruction; seniority of alleged destroyer; evidentiary significance of destroyed records; and temporal urgency of preservation concerns; (c) Evidence Standard. Pre-Ratification destruction shall be prosecuted upon clear and convincing evidence, with the Section 13B.10 "No Technical Excuse" presumption applying to demonstrated patterns of destruction occurring within the look-back period. Circumstantial evidence shall be admissible and, when sufficient in aggregate, may satisfy the clear and convincing standard; (d) Prosecution Pathway. Upon Task Force recommendation supported by the evidence standard of subsection (c), prosecution shall proceed through the State Attorneys General Council acting by supermajority under Sections 19.5.0.5.2 and 19.5.0.18.9.1, with the Task Force's evidentiary findings serving as a prima facie basis for charges; (e) No Statute of Limitations. The Section 13B.11(f) no-statute-of-limitations rule shall apply, meaning prosecution for pre-Ratification destruction may be commenced at any time upon discovery, without deadline; (f) Dissolution and Transfer. The

Task Force shall dissolve upon Hamilton Contingent operational commencement under Section 19.19(f) on Day One Hundred Eighty (180), with all investigative records, evidentiary findings, pending matters, and institutional documentation transferring immediately to the Hamilton Contingent Preservation Division under Section 13C.3. The Contingent shall inherit all pending Task Force matters without requirement of re-initiation and shall preserve Task Force evidentiary findings with full probative value; (g) Public Accountability. All Task Force proceedings shall be recorded and published upon the provisional public ledger in real time, subject only to narrow operational-security redactions during active investigations certified as necessary by Task Force consensus and reviewable within thirty (30) days of the

investigation's conclusion; (h) Anti-Abuse Safeguards. Task Force members shall operate under the same Federal Communications Firewall as the State Attorneys General Council under Section 19.5.0.18.4, with violation subject to the penalties of Section 19.5.0.18.5. Any Task Force member who participates in Task Force proceedings in bad faith shall be subject to Section 13 interference penalties and removal from state office under state law procedures. 13B.8 Ledger Blockchain Archive. All Federal Records, or cryptographic hashes thereof where the records themselves are classified or otherwise sensitive, shall be archived upon the Sovereign Blockchain Voting Ledger as they are created or as soon as practicable thereafter, providing an immutable third-party record accessible to the Authority, the Watchdog Tribunal, and authorized investigators. The Ledger archive shall: (a) Use cryptographic hashing to verify record integrity without necessarily exposing classified content; (b) Preserve the chain of custody for every record from creation through preservation; (c) Enable detection of any post-creation alteration; (d) Allow authorized access to the underlying records through security-appropriate channels. 13B.9 Automatic Replication. Electronic communication systems used for federal business shall be configured to automatically replicate all communications to the Triple Custody system in real time, including: (a) All federal email systems shall auto-copy messages to the Triple Custody system; (b) Federal phones and messaging platforms shall preserve messages for Triple Custody transfer; (c) Federal video conferencing shall automatically record sessions for Triple Custody archival; (d) Private accounts and personal devices used for federal business shall be subject to mandatory forensic imaging and content transfer to Triple Custody upon discovery of federal business use. 13B.10 No Technical Excuse. Any system failure, technical difficulty, software error, or operational disruption that results in destruction, loss, or alteration of Federal Records shall be presumed intentional absent clear and convincing evidence of genuine inadvertence. The burden of proving inadvertence rests on the Covered Person or agency asserting it. Patterns of repeated technical difficulties, conveniently-timed system failures, or unusual rates of data loss shall be treated as circumstantial evidence of intentional destruction.

C. Penalties for Destruction 13B.11 Treason-Level Criminal Penalties. Any Covered Person who intentionally destroys, alters, deletes, conceals, transfers outside proper custody, or otherwise renders unavailable any Federal Record subject to the Preservation Order, with knowledge that such conduct violates this Section, shall be guilty of a federal felony punishable by: (a) Imprisonment for not less than twenty-five (25) years; (b) Lifetime bar from any federal, state, or local public office, appointed position, or government employment, without possibility of future eligibility; (c) Minimum fine of ten million dollars ($10,000,000) per offense, with each destroyed or altered record constituting a separate offense; (d) Complete asset forfeiture, including all assets traceable to federal service or acquired during the period of preservation duty; (e) No possibility of pardon, commutation, clemency, or sentence reduction by any subsequent officeholder; (f) No statute of limitations: prosecution may be brought at any time upon discovery of the violation. 13B.12 Enhanced Penalties for Senior Officials. The penalties of Section 13B.11 shall be enhanced as follows for senior officials (including the President, Vice President, Cabinet Members, Members of Congress, Supreme Court Justices, federal judges, and senior political appointees): (a) Minimum fine increased to one hundred million dollars ($100,000,000); (b) Imprisonment increased to not less than thirty-five (35) years; (c) Application of the Section 13A Senior Official multiplier of one hundred times (100×) benefit, reflecting the enhanced duty of senior officials and the enhanced harm caused by their destruction of evidence. 13B.13 Conspiracy and Obstruction Liability. Any person who conspires with, aids, abets, directs, authorizes, or materially participates in evidence destruction under this Section shall be subject to the full penalties of Section 13B.11 or Section 13B.12 as applicable, notwithstanding that they did not personally perform the physical act of destruction. Corporate entities that participate in or facilitate evidence destruction shall be subject to Section 13A.11 corporate penalties and shall face charter revocation. 13B.14 Successor Liability. No corporate restructuring, merger, dissolution, bankruptcy, or successor arrangement shall evade liability for evidence destruction under this Section. Successor entities shall inherit the full liability of predecessor entities for evidence destruction occurring before the restructuring.

13B.15 No Pardon or Clemency. The prohibition on pardon under Section 13B.11(e) is absolute and survives any subsequent amendment, including repeal of this Amendment under Section 18. Any purported pardon for evidence destruction under this Section shall be void ab initio and shall constitute interference under Section 13, triggering additional penalties against the purported pardoner. D. Whistleblower Protection and Rewards 13B.16 Protected Whistleblower Status. Any person who reports actual or threatened destruction of Federal Records to the Watchdog Tribunal, the Academic Integrity Commission, the Authority, any federal Inspector General, or other authorized federal investigator, shall be entitled to Protected Whistleblower status under this Section, including: (a) Complete confidentiality of identity to the maximum extent consistent with due process for accused persons; (b) Federal protection from any form of retaliation, including termination, demotion, reassignment, reduction in pay or benefits, harassment, surveillance, or intimidation; (c) Federal legal representation at no cost to the whistleblower for any proceedings related to the disclosure; (d) Federal relocation and identity protection if threats to personal safety arise; (e) Continued employment or equivalent compensation if termination is deemed necessary for operational reasons unrelated to the disclosure, for a period of not less than five (5) years at the whistleblower's most recent compensation level; (f) Criminal prosecution of any person who retaliates against the whistleblower under Section 13 interference penalties. 13B.17 Whistleblower Financial Rewards. A Protected Whistleblower whose disclosure leads to a criminal conviction, civil recovery, or asset forfeiture under this Section shall be entitled to a financial reward from the recovered assets, fines, or forfeitures, as follows: (a) Fifteen percent (15%) of the first one million dollars ($1,000,000) recovered; (b) Twenty percent (20%) of recovered amounts between one million and ten million dollars ($1,000,000 to $10,000,000); (c) Twenty-five percent (25%) of recovered amounts between ten million and one hundred million dollars ($10,000,000 to $100,000,000); (d) Thirty percent (30%) of recovered amounts exceeding one hundred million dollars ($100,000,000); (e) Capped at a maximum total reward of fifty million dollars ($50,000,000) per whistleblower per case;

(f) Reward payments shall be made from the recovered funds before distribution under Section 13A.12, with remaining funds distributed under Section 13A.12 after whistleblower compensation. 13B.18 Multiple Whistleblowers. Where multiple whistleblowers contribute to a case, rewards shall be apportioned by the Watchdog Tribunal based on the relative significance, timing, and quality of each whistleblower's contribution, with the total combined reward not exceeding the schedule in Section 13B.17. 13B.19 Tax Treatment. Whistleblower rewards under this Section shall be subject to federal income tax at ordinary rates, but shall be exempt from any state or local income tax to prevent reduction of federal rewards through state taxation. E. Inspector General and Watchdog Protection 13B.20 Inspector General Protection During Amendment Operation. During the one hundred eighty (180) day period following Ratification, during the Implementation Period under Section 19, during any active No Confidence Petition or Referendum period (including the Inaugural Referendum), and for ninety (90) days following each such period, no Inspector General, federal auditor, or equivalent accountability officer may be removed, reassigned, demoted, or have their authority materially reduced, except: (a) For cause, with cause established by clear and convincing evidence and published in full upon the Ledger; AND (b) With concurrence of the Watchdog Tribunal by two-thirds (2/3) supermajority; AND (c) With at least thirty (30) days advance notice to Congress and the Ledger, permitting independent review. 13B.21 Protection of Federal Auditors and Inspectors. Federal auditors, internal investigators, ethics officers, and other accountability personnel shall receive federal protection equivalent to Protected Whistleblower status during the periods enumerated in Section 13B.20, including protection from retaliation, adverse personnel actions, and intimidation. 13B.22 Attempts to Fire or Silence Watchdogs. Any attempt by a Covered Person to remove, reassign, silence, intimidate, or impair the function of an Inspector General, auditor, or accountability officer during the protected periods, outside the procedures of Section 13B.20, shall constitute evidence destruction under this Section, triggering the full penalties of Section 13B.11 or Section 13B.12. F. Foreign Asset Transfer Monitoring 13B.23 Treasury and SEC Coordination. Upon Ratification, the Department of the Treasury, the Securities and Exchange Commission, and the Federal Bureau of Investigation shall establish enhanced coordination to monitor and investigate suspicious asset transfers by Covered Persons, including: (a) Transfers of funds to foreign accounts, particularly in jurisdictions with limited cooperation on federal investigations; (b) Conversion of assets to cash, cryptocurrency, precious metals, or other readily-concealed forms; (c) Transfers of property, securities, or other assets to family members, trusts, or third parties; (d) Unusual patterns of financial activity inconsistent with the Covered Person's known income and assets. 13B.24 Mandatory Reporting Thresholds. Financial institutions, securities brokers, and other covered entities shall report to the Foreign Interference Detection Unit (Section 22.9) any transactions by Covered Persons involving: (a) Single transfers of ten thousand dollars ($10,000) or more to foreign accounts; (b) Aggregate transfers of fifty thousand dollars ($50,000) or more over any thirty (30) day period; (c) Any transfer to a jurisdiction on the Treasury Office of Foreign Assets Control watch list; (d) Any cryptocurrency conversion exceeding twenty-five thousand dollars ($25,000); (e) Any conversion to cash exceeding ten thousand dollars ($10,000). 13B.25 Freeze Authority. Upon clear and convincing evidence of asset transfer intended to evade the Preservation Order or to conceal proceeds of corruption, the Watchdog Tribunal by two-thirds (2/3) supermajority may order immediate freeze of assets pending investigation, with due process rights preserved through expedited hearing within fourteen (14) days of the freeze order. G. Implementation and Enforcement 13B.26 Initial Compliance Period. Covered Persons shall have ninety (90) days from Ratification to: (a) Inventory all Federal Records in their possession, custody, or control; (b) Transfer records to proper federal custody where not already there; (c) Disclose any use of private accounts or personal devices for federal business; (d) Certify compliance with the Preservation Order upon the Ledger. 13B.27 Post-Compliance Period Responsibilities. After the initial ninety (90) day compliance period, Covered Persons shall:

(a) Maintain continuous compliance with the Preservation Order; (b) Report any threatened or actual destruction immediately to the Watchdog Tribunal; (c) Cooperate with Triple Custody transfer and forensic imaging; (d) Report any discovery of federal business conducted through private accounts. 13B.28 Watchdog Tribunal Enforcement. The Watchdog Tribunal under Section 21 shall have primary jurisdiction over violations of this Section, with authority to: (a) Investigate suspected violations; (b) Issue findings of violation by two-thirds (2/3) supermajority vote; (c) Order preservation and production of records; (d) Refer criminal prosecutions to appropriate prosecutors; (e) Impose civil penalties under this Section; (f) Order freeze of assets under Section 13B.25. 13B.29 Academic Integrity Commission Technical Authority. The Academic Integrity Commission shall have technical authority over the Triple Custody architecture, including: (a) Establishing technical standards for preservation, hashing, and imaging; (b) Conducting periodic audits of the Triple Custody system; (c) Detecting and reporting alterations or losses of records; (d) Providing forensic analysis in support of Watchdog Tribunal investigations. 13B.30 Article V Protection. The provisions of this Section shall be protected under the Article V protection established in Sections 18.6.1 and 18.6.2. No act of Congress, executive order, judicial ruling, or state action during the Preservation Order period shall diminish, evade, or nullify the preservation requirements. The Preservation Order is self-executing and cannot be suspended, modified, or terminated except through the Sunset Review process of Section 18. 13B.31 Ledger Publication and Transparency. The Authority shall publish upon the Ledger: (a) All Preservation Order compliance certifications; (b) All reports of violations and their investigation status; (c) All Watchdog Tribunal findings regarding evidence destruction; (d) All financial penalties assessed and collected under this Section;

(e) All whistleblower rewards distributed (with whistleblower identity protected per Section 13B.16); (f) Annual comprehensive reports on the integrity of the Triple Custody system.

Section 13C. The Hamilton Contingent

Key terms in this Section: • "The Hamilton Contingent" — The federal enforcement body established by this Section, named in honor of Alexander Hamilton's foundational work in designing federal accountability structures. Also referred to in this Amendment as 'the Contingent.' Originally drafted as the Ratification Day Task Force. • "Division" — A functional sub-unit of the Hamilton Contingent with specific jurisdictional responsibility. This Section establishes four (4) Divisions: Preservation, Prosecution, Protection, and Public Response. • "Contingent Director" — The chief executive of the Hamilton Contingent, selected as provided in this Section, accountable to the three bodies of the Authority through Liberty Bell Initiative. • "Division Chief" — The head of each Division, selected as provided in this Section, reporting to the Contingent Director. • "Pre-Certified Roster" — The pool of qualified expert candidates for Division Chief and senior Division positions, maintained by the Academic Integrity Commission and updated annually. • "Citizen Oversight Members" — Registered voters selected by randomized lottery to serve on each Division alongside expert personnel, providing democratic accountability within the Contingent structure. • "The Authority" — The Independent Tripartite Oversight Authority (three bodies, see Section 17). • "Liberty Bell Initiative" — Separate concurrence of all three bodies of the Authority. Distinct from the Hamilton Contingent, which is this enforcement body. 13C.1 Foundational Principle. The accountability mechanisms of this Amendment require immediate, coordinated, and competent enforcement from the very moment of Ratification. The permanent Authority bodies require up to one hundred eighty (180) days to become fully operational, while threats to evidence integrity, official accountability, and citizen rights are acute from Day Zero forward. There is therefore hereby established the Hamilton Contingent, named in honor of Alexander Hamilton, whose foundational work in designing the Treasury, advocating for federal accountability, and warning in The Federalist Papers of the dangers of factional corruption laid the intellectual groundwork for the federal integrity structures this Amendment seeks to restore. The Contingent shall serve as the immediate federal enforcement body for all accountability functions under this Amendment, commencing operation on the effective date of Ratification and continuing as a permanent parallel enforcement structure unless dissolved by the three bodies of the Authority through Liberty Bell Initiative as provided in this Section. A. Unified Structure with Functional Divisions 13C.2 Unified Command. The Contingent shall be a single federal agency with unified command under a Contingent Director, divided into four (4) operational Divisions, each with specific functional jurisdiction. The unified structure ensures coordination across related enforcement functions while the divisional structure ensures specialized expertise and clear accountability for specific missions. 13C.3 Division of Preservation and Evidence Integrity. The Preservation Division shall have primary operational responsibility for enforcement of Section 13B, including: (a) Forensic imaging of federal devices, servers, and storage systems; (b) Triple Custody coordination and integrity verification; (c) Monitoring of Preservation Order compliance by Covered Persons; (d) Investigation of evidence destruction, alteration, or concealment; (e) Initial intake and investigation of Preservation Order violations before referral to the Prosecution Division; (f) Technical coordination with the Academic Integrity Commission on cryptographic standards. 13C.4 Division of Prosecution and Independent Legal Action. The Prosecution Division shall serve as the independent federal prosecutorial authority for all offenses under this Amendment, operating independently of the Department of Justice of the United States to avoid capture by the federal government subject to No Confidence proceedings. The Prosecution Division shall have authority to: (a) File federal criminal charges for violations of Sections 13, 13A, 13B, 16, 18.6, 22, 24, 25, 26, or any other criminal provision of this Amendment;

(b) Conduct grand jury proceedings under the Prosecution Division's authority, with grand jurors drawn from citizens in the jurisdiction where the alleged offense occurred; (c) Petition federal courts for injunctions (court orders requiring a person to do or stop doing something specific), asset freezes, preservation orders, and other equitable relief (court remedies beyond money damages, such as orders to act or refrain from acting); (d) Pursue civil penalties and forfeitures under Section 13A on behalf of the United States; (e) Coordinate with, but not defer to, the Department of Justice on matters touching Amendment offenses. In the event of conflict between the Prosecution Division and the Department of Justice, the Prosecution Division shall prevail on all Amendment-related charges; (f) Represent the Amendment's accountability framework in any judicial proceeding where the federal government's position would otherwise conflict with the Amendment's purpose. 13C.4.1 Prosecution Division Internal Firewall. Because the independence of prosecutorial judgment from political direction is essential to legitimate accountability, the Prosecution Division shall operate under the following internal firewall provisions, separate from and additional to its independence from the Department of Justice established in Section 13C.4: (a) Director Authority Limited to Priority and Resources. The Contingent Director may establish Division-wide strategic priorities, allocate Division resources, and set general enforcement policy for the Prosecution Division, but shall not direct, influence, or participate in decisions to prosecute or decline to prosecute any specific case. The distinction between general prosecutorial policy (within Director authority) and specific case decisions (outside Director authority) shall be construed strictly in favor of Division Chief independence; (b) Division Chief Final Authority on Cases. The Prosecution Division Chief shall have final authority over which cases to prosecute, which charges to file, which plea agreements to accept, which cases to decline, and all other specific prosecutorial decisions within the Division's jurisdiction. The Division Chief shall make such decisions based on professional prosecutorial judgment applied to the evidence and the law, not on Director preferences or external political considerations; (c) Director Interference as Section 13 Violation. Any Director interference with specific case decisions — including direction to bring or not bring specific charges, pressure regarding plea agreements, intervention in case strategy, or retaliation against Division Chief or Division staff for specific case decisions — shall constitute Section 13 interference with Amendment operation, prosecutable through the ordinary Section 13 framework with Senior Official multipliers applied to the Director's position; (d) Citizen Oversight Member Monitoring Authority. The twelve (12) Citizen Oversight Members of the Prosecution Division under Section 13C.9(b) shall have authority to flag suspected Director interference with specific cases to the Watchdog Tribunal by majority vote (seven (7) of twelve (12)) of their membership, with flags triggering expedited Tribunal investigation under Section 13C.16; (e) Division Chief

Protected Reporting. The Prosecution Division Chief shall have authority to report suspected Director interference directly to the Watchdog Tribunal, the Authority through Liberty Bell Initiative, the State Attorneys General Council during Phase One, or the public upon the Ledger where internal channels are themselves compromised. Such reporting shall be protected under Section 13B.16 whistleblower protections with Division Chief-specific enhancements including preservation of office tenure pending Tribunal resolution of the reported matter; (f) Public Accountability for Prosecutorial Decisions. Decisions to decline prosecution on matters where substantial evidence of Amendment offenses exists shall require published reasoning on the Ledger, with reasoning sufficient for public and Tribunal review. Decisions to prosecute require only ordinary prosecutorial judgment and grand jury review; decisions to decline require transparent justification. 13C.5 Division of Protection for Whistleblowers and Accountability Officers. The Protection Division shall have responsibility for: (a) Receiving whistleblower disclosures under Section 13B.16 and ensuring confidentiality; (b) Administering federal protection programs for whistleblowers, including legal representation, relocation, and identity protection; (c) Administering whistleblower reward calculations and distributions under Section 13B.17; (d) Protecting federal Inspectors General, auditors, and accountability officers under Section 13B.20 through 13B.22 from removal, reassignment, or retaliation; (e) Investigating alleged retaliation against whistleblowers or accountability officers; (f) Protecting Watch Board members, Authority body members, Watchdog Tribunal members, and other Amendment personnel from intimidation, harassment, or obstruction of their duties. 13C.6 Division of Public Response and Citizen Engagement. The Public Response Division shall serve as the primary interface between the Contingent and the People, including: (a) Operating a twenty-four (24) hour public hotline and secure online portal for citizen complaints, reports of violations, and requests for information; (b) Providing a seventy-two (72) hour mandatory response time to all citizen inquiries, with substantive response or acknowledgment of complexity and expected timeline;

(c) Publishing the Public Accountability Dashboard upon the Ledger, accessible to all citizens, showing: Contingent personnel and leadership; pending investigations and their status (to the extent permissible without compromising active investigations); complaints received and their disposition; Division performance metrics; and escalation paths for unresolved matters; (d) Coordinating public education on Amendment rights, reporting mechanisms, and whistleblower protections; (e) Maintaining the Citizens' Accountability

Petition mechanism, permitting petitions signed by one hundred thousand (100,000) or more registered voters to compel Contingent action on specific matters that may otherwise have been neglected. B. Selection and Composition 13C.6.5 Dean Nomination Body — Pre-AIC Director Candidate Compilation. Because the Academic Integrity Commission does not exist prior to Day One Hundred Eighty (180) following Ratification, and because Section 13C.7 requires compilation of a Contingent Director candidate list during the period before the AIC is operational, a Dean Nomination Body shall be formed to perform candidate list compilation in place of the AIC during this pre-operational window: (a) Gubernatorial Nomination. Within thirty (30) days of Ratification, the Governor of each Participating Jurisdiction shall nominate two (2) academic deans to serve on the Dean Nomination Body. Nominations shall be published on state government transparency infrastructure within seven (7) days of each nomination. Each nominated dean shall currently serve as a dean at an accredited institution in the nominating Governor's jurisdiction meeting the qualifying criteria of Section 17.16(a) through (d). Where a Participating Jurisdiction has no accredited institutions meeting those criteria, or no deans serving at such institutions, that Jurisdiction shall not nominate members, with this circumstance documented publicly by the Governor; (b) Body Composition and Quorum. The Dean Nomination Body shall consist of up to one hundred twelve (112) members (two per nominating Jurisdiction) and shall contain not fewer than fifty (50) members in total. Where fewer than twenty-five (25) Participating Jurisdictions are able to nominate deans due to the absence of qualifying accredited institutions or qualifying deans under subsection (a), the Washington Commission shall expand eligibility to include deans at accredited institutions in adjacent Participating Jurisdictions, following the pattern established in Section 17.16.1 for Pool geographic expansion, until the fifty (50) member floor is met. The Body shall act by majority vote of participating members with minimum quorum of fifty percent (50%) of seated members required for valid action. Decisions shall be documented and published on state government transparency infrastructure or, upon activation, the provisional public ledger; (c) Candidate List Compilation Function. The Dean Nomination Body shall compile the Contingent Director candidate list required by Section 13C.7(a), including retired federal judges, retired federal prosecutors, former state attorneys general, former federal Inspectors General, and distinguished federal ethics experts, all with demonstrated records of independence from partisan political activity. The list shall satisfy the minimum twenty (20) candidate requirement of Section 13C.7.1(a); (d) Subsequent

Process Unchanged. After the Dean Nomination Body compiles the candidate list, the subsequent Section 13C.7 process proceeds as written: State Elections Council review under Section 13C.7(b) subject to Section 13C.7.1(c) limits; Washington Commission selection under Section 13C.7(d) during Phase One; Authority re-confirmation per Section 13C.7(d) upon full Authority constitution; (e) Federal Executive Non-Interference. No President, Vice President, Cabinet officer, federal agency head, or other federal executive officeholder shall direct, fund, influence, or impede the Governor nomination process or the Dean Nomination Body's candidate compilation activities. Any such interference shall constitute Section 13 interference with Senior Official multipliers where applicable, prosecutable by the State Attorneys General Council acting by supermajority under Sections 19.5.0.5.2 and 19.5.0.18.9.1 and, upon operational commencement, by the Hamilton Contingent; (f) Dissolution and Transfer. The Dean Nomination Body shall dissolve upon Academic Integrity Commission full constitution on Day One Hundred Eighty (180), with all Body records, candidate documentation, deliberations, and institutional memory transferring to the AIC for future Director selection cycles under Section 13C.7; (g) Brief Orientation. Upon Body convening, the Washington Commission shall provide a brief orientation (not less than two (2) hours, not more than eight (8) hours) covering: the specific candidate qualifying criteria under Section 13C.7(a) and the disqualifying circumstances; the candidate list size minimum under Section 13C.7.1(a); the thirty (30) day public comment framework under Section 13C.7.1(b); Federal Communications Firewall obligations during Body service; pressure protection under Section 13C.7.1(d); and documentation standards. Because Body members are already qualified academic deans with professional expertise in candidate evaluation, orientation focuses on Amendment-specific criteria and procedures rather than general candidate evaluation methodology. Orientation materials shall be published on state government transparency infrastructure for public review.
13C.7 Contingent Director Selection. The Contingent Director shall be selected through the following process: (a) The Dean Nomination Body under Section 13C.6.5 (during the pre-AIC period) or the Academic Integrity Commission (from Day One Hundred Eighty (180) forward) shall compile a list of qualified candidates including retired federal judges, retired federal prosecutors, former state attorneys general, former federal Inspectors General, and distinguished federal ethics experts, all with demonstrated records of independence from partisan political activity; (b) The State Elections Council shall review the list and may remove candidates upon clear and convincing evidence of

disqualification but shall not add candidates;

(c) The Citizens' Oversight Board, once constituted, shall select the Director from the remaining list by majority vote, with the selection subject to Liberty Bell Initiative concurrence; (d) During Phase One before Authority constitution, the Washington Commission shall perform the Citizens' Oversight Board function under this subsection, with the Director subject to re-confirmation by the Authority once fully constituted; (e) The Director shall serve a term of six (6) years, renewable once upon concurrence of all three Authority bodies, for a maximum of twelve (12) years total. 13C.7.1 Initial Post-Ratification Director Selection Protections. Because the initial Director selection commences post-Ratification during a period when Phase One accountability structures are still standing up, the initial selection process is particularly vulnerable to capture pressure and requires enhanced protections. The following protections apply to the initial post-Ratification selection process under Sections 13C.6.5 (Dean Nomination Body) and 13C.7: (a) Minimum Candidate List Size. The candidate list compiled by the Dean Nomination Body under Section 13C.6.5(c) shall contain not fewer than twenty (20) qualified candidates, with documentation establishing each candidate's qualifications published on state government transparency infrastructure concurrent with list compilation. A list containing fewer than twenty (20) candidates shall not satisfy Section 13C.7(a) and shall require supplementation until the minimum is reached; (b) Candidate List Publication and Public Comment. The Dean Nomination Body shall publish the initial candidate list on state government transparency infrastructure with a minimum thirty (30) day public comment period, during which any United States citizen, academic institution, professional association, or civic organization may submit comments regarding candidate qualifications, conflicts of interest, or disqualifying circumstances. All comments shall be preserved for State Elections Council review and for Washington Commission (or Citizens' Oversight Board upon full Authority constitution) selection consideration; (c) Limit on State Elections Council Disqualification Authority. The State Elections Council under Section 13C.7(b) shall not disqualify more than one-third (1/3) of the candidate list without specific evidentiary findings published for each disqualified candidate, with findings subject to challenge by any other Authority body, Washington Commission member, or State Attorney General. Disqualifications beyond one-third of the list without such findings shall be void and the candidates restored to the list; (d) Pressure Protection for Dean Nomination Body Members. Members of the Dean Nomination Body under Section 13C.6.5 shall receive protection against federal adverse action equivalent to Section 17.16.1 Pre-Certified Pool university protection. Any federal agency investigation, audit, funding reduction, or adverse action against Dean Nomination Body members or their home institutions in retaliation for candidate list compilation activity shall constitute Section 13 interference, with enforcement through the State Attorneys General Council acting by supermajority under Sections 19.5.0.5.2 and 19.5.0.18.9.1 during Phase One and through the Hamilton Contingent after operational commencement; (e)

Documentation of Selection Reasoning. Upon final Director selection under Section 13C.7(c) or 13C.7(d), the selecting body shall publish written reasoning documenting: the qualifications of the selected candidate; consideration given to other candidates on the list; any concerns raised during public comment and how they were addressed; and any conflicts of interest disclosed and how they were resolved. The reasoning shall be published on state government transparency infrastructure and, upon activation, the provisional public ledger; (f) Post-Phase-One Re-Confirmation. Where the Washington Commission performs the Citizens' Oversight Board function under Section 13C.7(d) during Phase One, the re-confirmation by the Authority upon its full constitution shall include independent review of the initial selection process under this subsection for evidence of post-Ratification capture or pressure. Re-confirmation shall not be a formality; the Authority shall substantively evaluate whether the selection reflected independent professional judgment. If the Authority by Liberty Bell Initiative finds the selection process was materially compromised, the Director shall be removed and a new selection process conducted under this Section, with the removed Director not eligible for re-selection. 13C.8 Division Chief Selection. Each Division shall be led by a Division Chief, selected as follows: (a) Qualifications shall be specific to the Division's function: the Preservation Division Chief shall have expertise in digital forensics, records management, or archival science; the Prosecution Division Chief shall have significant federal prosecutorial experience; the Protection Division Chief shall have expertise in whistleblower law, witness protection, or civil rights enforcement; the Public Response Division Chief shall have expertise in public administration, civic engagement, or public communications; (b) The Pre-Certified Roster for each Division position shall be maintained by the Academic Integrity Commission and updated annually, with at least ten (10) qualified candidates for each Division Chief position; (c) Division Chiefs shall be selected by the Contingent Director from the Pre-Certified Roster, subject to Authority confirmation through Liberty Bell Initiative; (d) Division Chiefs shall serve terms of four (4) years, renewable once, for a maximum of eight (8) years total. 13C.8.1 Division

Chief Selection Transparency Standards. The Authority confirmation process for Division Chief selection under Section 13C.8(c) shall operate under the following transparency standards, in addition to ordinary Liberty Bell Initiative procedures: (a) Public Posting of Candidates. Upon Director selection of a Division Chief candidate from the Pre-Certified Roster, the Contingent shall publish on the Ledger within seven (7) days the candidate's name, qualifications, professional background, potential conflicts of interest, and

Director's rationale for selection; (b) Minimum Fourteen-Day Public Comment Period. Not less than fourteen (14) days of public comment shall be provided before any Authority body votes on confirmation, during which comments from citizens, professional associations, academic institutions, former colleagues of the candidate, and others may be submitted and preserved on the Ledger for each Authority body's consideration; (c) Minimum Roster Size Enhancement. The Pre-Certified Roster minimum of ten (10) candidates per Division Chief position under Section 13C.8(b) shall be enhanced to fifteen (15) candidates where the Academic Integrity Commission is operating under documented federal pressure as determined by State Attorney General Council supermajority or Authority Liberty Bell Initiative, to ensure adequate candidate diversity in adverse conditions; (d) Public Livestream of Confirmation Votes. The Liberty Bell Initiative votes on Division Chief confirmation shall be livestreamed on the Ledger or provisional public ledger, with each body's deliberations and individual member votes publicly accessible. No Division Chief confirmation shall be conducted in secret session; (e) Individual Vote Recording. Each member of each Authority body shall have their vote on each Division Chief confirmation individually recorded and published on the Ledger, identifying the voting member, the candidate voted upon, and the vote cast; (f) Roster Integrity Protection. The Academic Integrity Commission, in maintaining the Pre-Certified Roster, shall apply the same anti-pressure protections established for the Pre-Certified University Pool under Section 17.16.1. Any pattern of qualified candidates declining Roster inclusion, or withdrawing after inclusion, shall be documented and published on the Ledger, and shall trigger State Attorney General Council investigation under Section 19.5.0.18.9 during Phase One and Hamilton Contingent investigation thereafter. 13C.9 Citizen Oversight Members. Each Division shall include Citizen Oversight Members selected by randomized lottery from all Participating Jurisdictions, as follows: (a) The Preservation Division shall include twelve (12) Citizen Oversight Members; (b) The Prosecution Division shall include twelve (12) Citizen Oversight Members, with no person qualified to serve who has held federal political office within the preceding ten (10) years; (c) The Protection Division shall include twelve (12) Citizen Oversight Members; (d) The Public Response Division shall include twelve (12) Citizen Oversight Members; (e) Citizen Oversight Members shall serve staggered two-year (2-year) terms, with half rotating each year, with no more than two (2) total terms in any individual's lifetime, and shall receive the same wage replacement, protection, and benefits as Citizens' Oversight Board members under Section 17.5; (f) The distribution of Citizen Oversight Members across Divisions shall include at least two (2) members from each of the six (6) non-state Participating Jurisdictions

(DC and the five territories) across the Contingent in aggregate, ensuring territorial representation. 13C.10 Staff Selection. Operational staff of each Division shall be hired by the Division Chief through standard federal hiring procedures, subject to: (a) Background investigation and security clearance appropriate to the Division's function; (b) Public disclosure upon the Ledger of employment history, political activity, financial interests, and relationships with federal officeholders or political entities; (c) Conflict-of-interest screening by the Protection Division; (d) Prohibition on recent federal political service (within ten years) for investigative and prosecutorial staff; (e) Commitment to non-partisan conduct during service. 13C.11 Diversity and Expertise Standards. The Authority shall ensure that the Contingent collectively reflects: (a) Geographic diversity across all Participating Jurisdictions; (b) Professional diversity including legal, technical, investigative, and public administration expertise; (c) Experience with state and territorial enforcement frameworks, not solely federal; (d) Linguistic capacity to serve non-English speaking citizens, with bilingual staff at minimum matching the linguistic distribution of registered voters. C. Authority, Jurisdiction, and Limits 13C.12 Federal Jurisdiction. The Contingent shall have federal jurisdiction throughout the United States and all Participating Jurisdictions, including all territories, for matters within its authority under this Amendment. 13C.13 Authority Enumerated. The Contingent, through its Divisions and under the Director, shall have authority to: (a) Enforce the Preservation Order under Section 13B; (b) Prosecute Amendment offenses independently of the Department of Justice; (c) Protect whistleblowers, Inspectors General, and accountability officers; (d) Receive and respond to citizen complaints; (e) Coordinate with the Watchdog Tribunal on enforcement matters; (f) Coordinate with the Authority on operational matters;

(g) Issue subpoenas (legal orders requiring a person to appear in court, give testimony, or produce documents), compel testimony, and require document production, subject to judicial review; (h) Conduct forensic analysis and technical investigation; (i) Recommend referrals to the Watchdog Tribunal for investigation of alleged corruption; (j) Publish findings, reports, and analyses upon the Ledger. 13C.14 Limits on Authority. The Contingent shall not: (a) Exercise any authority outside the enforcement of this Amendment; (b) Serve as a general-purpose federal police force; (c) Investigate or prosecute matters unrelated to this Amendment absent explicit Authority direction; (d) Substitute for the regular federal courts, except that Prosecution Division matters shall proceed through ordinary federal court procedures with Contingent attorneys appearing as counsel; (e) Exercise military or paramilitary functions; (f) Replace the Watchdog Tribunal under Section 21, which retains its authority to investigate Authority bodies and to serve as the final accountability mechanism. C-bis. Evidence Collection Access Authority 13C.14.1 Foundational Principle. Federal records are the property of the People, held only in trust by federal officeholders and employees, and evidence of official misconduct can be destroyed in minutes while warrant processes take hours or days. Accordingly, the Contingent is hereby granted specific access authority to enter federal and governmental spaces for the collection, preservation, and imaging of federal records, without warrant or advance notice, on terms equivalent to the long-established statutory authority of conservation officers and game wardens to inspect regulated commercial and public spaces. This access authority is specifically limited to governmental and federal spaces and does not extend to private residences or spaces protected by the Fourth Amendment of the Constitution. 13C.14.2 Covered Spaces — Full Access Authority. The Contingent, through credentialed personnel of the Preservation Division or Prosecution Division, shall have unrestricted authority to enter, inspect, and collect federal records from the following spaces at any time, without warrant, without permission of the occupant, and without advance notice: (a) All federal buildings owned, leased, or occupied by the United States government, including but not limited to: the Capitol Complex (House office buildings, Senate office buildings, Capitol, subway, committee rooms, cloakrooms); the White House complex and Executive Office Buildings; federal departmental headquarters and regional offices; federal courthouses; federal agency offices of all kinds; Smithsonian and federal museum administrative offices; and all federal annexes; (b) All congressional offices, including Senate and House member offices in Washington, D.C., and all congressional district offices located anywhere in the United States or its territories; (c) All congressional committee offices, subcommittee offices, and congressional support agency offices (including the Congressional Budget Office, Government Accountability Office, Congressional Research Service, and Library of Congress administrative spaces); (d) All federal facilities operated on behalf of the federal government by contractors, including but not limited to: contractor data centers holding federal records; contractor-operated federal facilities; and contractor office spaces where federal business is conducted; (e) All state government buildings when housing federal records, federal operations, or Amendment-related infrastructure (including state election offices maintaining federal voter registration data); (f) All Host Sites designated under Section 11B, and all Citizens' Reclamation Offices and Centers under Section 11; (g) All federal vehicles, aircraft, vessels, and other federal-owned or federal-leased conveyances; (h) All federally-funded facilities receiving substantial federal appropriations where federal records are maintained. 13C.14.3 No Access Barrier Permitted. No officeholder, employee, security officer, building manager, contractor, law enforcement officer, or other person shall: (a) Refuse entry to credentialed Contingent personnel upon presentation of credentials; (b) Require advance notice, appointment, or scheduling before entry; (c) Require warrant, court order, or judicial authorization as a condition of entry to any Covered Space; (d) Obstruct, delay, or impede Contingent personnel in the performance of their duties; (e) Alert occupants of Covered Spaces of imminent arrival, except where such notification is expressly authorized by the Contingent Director for operational reasons;

(f) Direct subordinates, security personnel, or agents to impede Contingent access. 13C.14.4 Obstruction as Interference. Any obstruction of Contingent access under this Section shall constitute interference under Section 13 and shall trigger the full penalties thereof, including the fifteen (15) year minimum sentence and lifetime bar from public office. Additionally, any obstruction occurring at the time of, or in connection with, suspected evidence destruction shall be deemed evidence destruction under Section 13B.11 and shall be subject to the enhanced twenty-five (25) year minimum sentence and ten million dollar ($10,000,000) minimum fine. 13C.14.5 Authority During Entry. While within any Covered Space, Hamilton Contingent personnel shall have authority to: (a) Inspect all federal records present, including physical documents, digital files, communications, calendars, meeting minutes, financial records, and all other Federal Records as defined in Section 13B; (b) Forensically image any device, server, storage system, or other electronic equipment containing federal records;

(c) Seize physical copies of federal records for forensic analysis, with receipt provided and Ledger documentation; (d) Photograph or document the state of offices, file systems, and record storage for evidentiary purposes; (e) Interview personnel present, with such interviews voluntary and subject to the interviewee's right to counsel and Fifth Amendment protections; (f) Secure records in place to prevent alteration or destruction pending further investigation; (g) Coordinate with building security and Capitol Police on access logistics, but such coordination shall not be construed as permission-seeking or subject to security approval; (h) Return to the space as needed for ongoing investigation, with each return covered by the same authority. 13C.14.6 Mandatory Transparency of Each Entry. Every Contingent entry into a Covered Space under this subsection shall be documented as follows, with documentation published upon the Ledger within seventy-two (72) hours of entry unless publication would compromise an active investigation (in which case documentation shall be sealed and published upon conclusion of the investigation): (a) Identity of personnel entering, including names and credential numbers; (b) Date, time, and duration of entry; (c) Space entered, including full address and office identification; (d) Purpose of entry, stated with specificity;

(e) Records inspected, imaged, or seized, with itemized list; (f) Personnel present during entry; (g) Any obstruction encountered and response; (h) Chain of custody documentation for all collected evidence. 13C.14.7 Limits on Access Authority — Protection of Private Residences. The access authority under this subsection does not extend to: (a) Private residences of any person, including residences of federal officeholders, employees, or their family members (whether owned, rented, or otherwise occupied); (b) Personal vehicles not owned or leased by the federal government, except where operated on federal property for federal purposes; (c) Private offices, businesses, or spaces not used for federal business; (d) Any space protected by the Fourth Amendment of the Constitution that is not within the categories enumerated in Section 13C.14.2; (e) Attorney-client privileged communications, except to the extent such communications are subject to established exceptions to the privilege (such as the crime-fraud exception); (f) Healthcare records of Covered Persons that do not constitute federal records, subject to established health information privacy protections. 13C.14.8 Warrant Process for Non-Covered Spaces — Ordinary Citizens. For spaces not covered by Section 13C.14.2 and occupied by persons who are not Covered Persons as defined in Section 13B, the Hamilton Contingent shall follow ordinary Fourth Amendment warrant procedures, applying to a federal magistrate judge for a search warrant upon probable cause (a legal standard meaning: a reasonable belief, based on specific facts, that a crime has been or is being committed and that evidence will be found in the place to be searched). The Prosecution Division shall have full authority to seek such warrants, and federal courts shall promptly hear such applications. This Amendment does not alter Fourth Amendment rights of private citizens or the warrant requirement for private spaces. C-ter. Independent Warrant Panel for Covered Persons' Private Spaces 13C.14.8.1 Foundational Principle. Federal judges are appointed by the President and confirmed by the Senate — the very offices most likely to be subject to Contingent investigation. The ordinary federal warrant process would therefore create an unavoidable conflict of interest, where Covered Persons could benefit from warrants being evaluated by judges appointed by them or by their political allies. There is therefore hereby established the Independent Warrant Panel, a constitutional body independent of the federal judicial chain of command, with sole authority to issue search warrants for the private spaces of Covered Persons. 13C.14.8.2 Definition of Covered Private Spaces. For purposes of this subsection, 'Covered Private Spaces' means: (a) Private residences of any Covered Person as defined in Section 13B, whether owned, rented, leased, or otherwise occupied, and whether located within the United States or abroad; (b) Private residences of immediate family members of Covered Persons (spouses, parents, children, siblings) where evidence of the Covered Person's potential violations may be located; (c) Personal vehicles of Covered Persons not operated on federal property for federal purposes; (d) Private businesses, offices, or personal storage units owned or controlled by Covered Persons that are not covered by Section 13C.14.2; (e) Safe deposit boxes, storage facilities, and other private custodial arrangements held by or for Covered Persons; (f) Private electronic accounts, cloud storage, and digital assets of Covered Persons maintained outside federal systems. 13C.14.8.3 Constitution of the Independent Warrant Panel. For each warrant application, an Independent Warrant Panel shall be constituted as follows: (a) Three (3) sitting justices of the highest courts of Participating Jurisdictions (as defined in Section 3), drawn by randomized lottery from the pool of all sitting justices of the highest courts of all Participating Jurisdictions (the highest court of each Jurisdiction, by whatever name called), with the selection algorithm designed to ensure that the three justices come from three (3) different Jurisdictions; (b) Lottery selection shall be conducted by the Academic Integrity Commission using cryptographic randomization procedures, with the selection published upon the Ledger within twenty-four

(24) hours of initiation; (c) In addition to the three justices, one (1) civilian observer shall be randomly selected by the same lottery system from the current membership of the Citizens' Oversight Board (Section 17), with the observer's role described in Section 13C.14.8.7. 13C.14.8.4 Lottery Methodology and Conflicts of Interest. The lottery system shall: (a) Exclude any justice whose state includes any Covered Person subject to the specific warrant application (to prevent home-state bias); (b) Exclude any justice who has a documented personal, professional, or financial relationship with the Covered Person or the Covered Person's family;

(c) Exclude any justice who has ruled in a prior case involving the Covered Person in a manner that would cause a reasonable person to question the justice's impartiality; (d) Exclude any justice who has publicly endorsed, contributed to, or campaigned for or against the Covered Person; (e) Proceed with re-selection from the remaining eligible pool until three qualifying justices from three different states are selected; (f) Be entirely reproducible and auditable, with all lottery inputs, algorithms, and outputs published upon the Ledger. 13C.14.8.5 Equal Treatment Across All Offices. The Independent Warrant Panel process under this subsection shall apply uniformly to all Covered Persons, regardless of office, without tiered distinctions based on position. The President of the United States, Members of Congress, Justices of the Supreme Court, federal judges, Cabinet members, senior political appointees, family members of such persons, and all other Covered Persons shall be subject to the same warrant process under this subsection. Equal treatment prevents claims of selective enforcement and preserves constitutional equality under the law. 13C.14.8.6 Two-Gate Process — Tribunal Certification and Panel Approval. No warrant under this subsection shall be issued except upon satisfaction of both of the following gates: (a) Gate One — Watchdog Tribunal Investigation Certification. The Watchdog Tribunal under Section 21 shall, by two-thirds (2/3) supermajority vote, certify that the Hamilton Contingent's underlying investigation is legitimate and not conducted for political, retaliatory, or improper purposes. The Tribunal's certification shall address: the credibility of the initial allegations; the existence of a genuine Amendment-related investigation; the appropriateness of the targeted scope; and the absence of improper motive. Certification may be general (covering an investigation) or specific (covering a particular warrant application), at the Tribunal's discretion; (b) Gate Two — Warrant Panel Probable Cause Review. Upon receiving Tribunal certification, the randomly-selected Independent Warrant Panel shall evaluate the warrant application under the Fourth

Amendment probable cause standard, requiring: a sworn affidavit from Hamilton Contingent personnel; specific description of the place to be searched; specific description of the persons or things to be seized; and probable cause to believe that a violation of this Amendment or other federal law has occurred or is occurring, and that evidence of the violation is likely to be found at the specified place. 13C.14.8.7 Civilian Observer Role. The civilian observer selected under Section 13C.14.8.3(c) shall:

(a) Attend all Warrant Panel deliberations with full access to application materials, oral arguments, and Panel discussion; (b) NOT have voting authority on warrant issuance (preserving judicial authority over the legal determination); (c) Monitor the proceedings for procedural integrity, evidence of judicial bias, coercion, or any compromise of the independent process; (d) Publish a post-decision public report upon the Ledger within seventy-two (72) hours of the Panel's decision, addressing: whether the Panel followed proper procedure; whether the deliberations appeared free from bias; whether all relevant evidence was considered; and any concerns about the integrity of the process; (e) Retain full confidentiality regarding specific evidence and legal reasoning of the deliberations during any active investigation, with full disclosure upon conclusion; (f) Report to the Watchdog Tribunal any observed procedural misconduct, with potential sanctions against participating justices for confirmed misconduct. 13C.14.8.8 Unanimous Concurrence Required. A warrant under this subsection shall issue only upon unanimous concurrence of all three (3) participating justices of the highest courts of Participating Jurisdictions. If any one justice declines to authorize the warrant, the warrant shall not issue, and the Hamilton Contingent shall not resubmit the same application without additional evidence or modification of scope. Justices shall publish individual written opinions (concurrences or dissents) addressing their reasoning, with opinions published upon the Ledger in sealed form during active investigation and in full upon conclusion of the investigation or within three (3) years, whichever is sooner. 13C.14.8.9 Expedited Timeline. The Independent Warrant Panel process shall proceed under the following timeline: (a) Tribunal Certification: within seventy-two (72) hours of Hamilton Contingent request; (b) Warrant Panel Lottery Selection: within twenty-four (24) hours of certification; (c) Panel Convening (by secure video conference or in person): within seventy-two (72) hours of selection; (d) Warrant Decision: within one hundred twenty (120) hours (5 days) of Panel convening; (e) Total timeline from Hamilton Contingent request to warrant decision: not more than fourteen (14) days; (f) Emergency Expedited Process: where evidence destruction is imminent, the Tribunal and

Panel shall process applications within twenty-four (24) hours total, using emergency procedures with abbreviated briefing but preserved decision standards.

13C.14.8.10 Warrant Execution. Warrants issued under this subsection shall: (a) Be executed by Hamilton Contingent personnel of the Preservation Division or Prosecution Division; (b) Be executed within a reasonable time period specified in the warrant (ordinarily not less than seven (7) days); (c) Be accompanied by the Covered Person or their counsel during execution where possible, unless the Panel has authorized no-notice execution upon specific findings of destruction risk; (d) Be conducted by unarmed Hamilton Contingent personnel under Section 13C.14.15, with coordination with the United States Marshals Service for any physical security needs; (e) Include full videorecording of the execution, with recording preserved under the Preservation Order of Section 13B; (f) Result in a receipt itemizing all materials seized, provided to the Covered Person or their counsel at the conclusion of execution; (g) Be documented in full on the Ledger within twenty-four (24) hours of execution, including: warrant contents (as redacted for ongoing investigation), execution team, duration, persons present, and itemized evidence list. 13C.14.8.11 Ledger Publication Requirement. Every warrant executed under this subsection shall be published upon the Ledger within twenty-four (24) hours of execution, except where: (a) The Warrant Panel, upon specific findings of operational necessity, has authorized sealed publication for a period not exceeding ninety (90) days; (b) After any authorized sealing period expires, full publication shall occur; (c) No warrant shall be sealed indefinitely. 13C.14.8.12 Fifth Amendment and Privileged Communications. Warrants under this subsection shall not: (a) Compel testimony of Covered Persons in violation of Fifth Amendment protections; (b) Permit seizure of attorney-client privileged communications, except pursuant to established exceptions to privilege (such as the crime-fraud exception with specific judicial finding); (c) Permit seizure of genuinely personal materials (such as medical records, personal diaries unrelated to federal business, intimate photographs, etc.) unless specifically described as evidence of Amendment violations with probable cause particularized to those materials;

(d) Permit seizure of family members' personal materials unless the family member is separately named as a subject of investigation or probable cause is specifically established for those materials. 13C.14.8.13 Suppression and Fruit of the Poisonous Tree. Evidence obtained in violation of this subsection, or pursuant to a warrant later determined to have been improperly issued, shall be subject to suppression in any criminal proceeding, with application of the fruit-of-the-poisonous-tree doctrine (a legal principle meaning: if the original evidence was obtained illegally, additional evidence later discovered because of that illegal evidence is also inadmissible in court — because it grew from a tainted source) to derivative evidence. Hamilton Contingent personnel who knowingly exceed warrant authority shall be subject to professional sanctions, potential prosecution for civil rights violations, and Watchdog Tribunal review. 13C.14.8.14 Judicial Review and Appeal. A Covered Person whose spaces have been searched under a warrant issued through this process may seek review by: (a) Filing a motion to suppress in any federal criminal proceeding; (b) Filing a civil action for unconstitutional search in any federal district court; (c) Petitioning the Watchdog Tribunal for review of warrant validity; (d) Appealing the Warrant Panel's decision to a Review Panel constituted of three (3) additional justices of the highest courts of Participating Jurisdictions selected by the same lottery process, who shall review the original Panel's decision under an abuse-of-discretion standard within thirty (30) days. 13C.14.8.15 Sanctions for Panel Misconduct. State supreme court justices serving on an Independent Warrant Panel who: (a) leak information about pending applications; (b) tip off Covered Persons to impending warrants; (c) accept improper influence, gifts, or favors related to their Panel service; or (d) otherwise compromise the independence of the process, shall be subject to: (a) Immediate removal from Panel service; (b) Referral to their state's judicial conduct commission for state disciplinary action; (c) Federal prosecution under Section 13 interference penalties and, where applicable, Section 13B evidence destruction penalties; (d) Permanent disqualification from future Panel service. 13C.14.8.16 Funding and Compensation. State supreme court justices serving on Independent Warrant Panels shall be compensated at a rate equivalent to federal district court judge compensation, prorated for their time of service, funded from federal appropriation. Justices shall receive federal travel, security, and logistical support as needed. Panel service shall not displace justices' ordinary state judicial duties, and Panels shall be scheduled to minimize disruption.

13C.14.8.17 Declination to Serve. A selected justice of the highest court of a Participating Jurisdiction may decline to serve on a specific Independent Warrant Panel upon the hardship framework established in Section 17.4.13(c), which governs multi-day case-specific panels and provides forty-eight (48) hour decline with privacy-protected documentation and immediate redraw. Additional specific grounds for decline under this Section include: (a)

Disclosure of a specific conflict of interest not captured by the automatic screening under Section 13C.14.8.4; (b) Health or other compelling personal circumstance; (c) Written justification published upon the Ledger; (d) Automatic re-selection from the eligible pool within twenty-four (24) hours. 13C.14.8.18 Article V Protection. The provisions of this subsection shall be protected under the Article V protection established in Sections 18.6.1 and 18.6.2. No act of Congress, executive order, judicial ruling, or state action may evade, diminish, or replace the Independent Warrant Panel process for searches of Covered Persons' private spaces. The Independent Warrant Panel is a constitutional body whose authority derives from this Amendment itself. 13C.14.9 Capitol Police, Secret Service, and Security Personnel. The Capitol Police, United States Secret Service, Federal Protective Service, and all other federal, state, or local security personnel shall cooperate with Contingent entries under this subsection and shall not impede access. Security personnel may provide security logistics support but shall not exercise veto authority over entry. Orders from any officeholder to security personnel to impede Contingent access shall be void ab initio and shall not be followed; security personnel refusing such unlawful orders shall be fully protected from retaliation under Section 13B.22. 13C.14.10 Credentialing and Identification. Contingent personnel exercising access authority shall carry official credentials issued by the Hamilton Contingent, including photographic identification, credential number, Division affiliation, and the signature of the Contingent Director or designee. Counterfeit credentials shall be prosecuted as federal impersonation offenses. The authenticity of credentials may be verified in real-time through the Ledger by any person upon presentation. 13C.14.11 Training Requirements. Hamilton Contingent personnel exercising access authority shall complete a forty (40) hour specialized training program administered by the Academic Integrity Commission, covering: (a) Constitutional limits on access authority; (b) Chain of custody procedures for evidence collection; (c) Forensic imaging techniques and standards; (d) De-escalation and professional conduct during entries;

(e) Protection of privileged communications and sensitive information; (f) Documentation and Ledger publication requirements; (g) Coordination with security personnel. 13C.14.12 Citizen and Press Access Rights Preserved. The access authority of this subsection does not expand or restrict the existing rights of citizens, journalists, or press to access public spaces or obtain public records through ordinary means including Freedom of Information Act requests, congressional public proceedings, or open courts. The Hamilton Contingent's access authority is a specific enforcement authority for evidence collection, not a substitute for public transparency or a mechanism for citizen access. 13C.14.13 Emergency Response Authority. Where Contingent personnel have reasonable grounds to believe that evidence is being or is about to be destroyed, the Contingent may effect immediate entry to prevent destruction, notwithstanding any other procedural requirement. Such emergency entries shall be documented with particular care under Section 13C.14.6, with written justification of the emergency circumstances and the grounds for belief. Emergency entries that prove unjustified upon subsequent review shall be subject to Watchdog Tribunal oversight under Section 13C.16. 13C.14.14 Judicial Review. Any Covered Person whose space has been entered under this authority may seek judicial review before the Watchdog Tribunal or, at the petitioner's election, a federal district court, on the ground that the entry exceeded the authority of this subsection. Such review shall not delay or impede the entry itself but may result in: (a) suppression of evidence improperly obtained; (b) damages for unconstitutional overreach; (c) professional sanctions against Hamilton Contingent personnel; and (d) injunctive relief against pattern or practice violations. Judicial review shall be expedited, with initial decisions within thirty (30) days. 13C.14.15 Disarmament of Enforcement. Contingent personnel exercising access authority under this subsection shall not be armed with firearms. The access authority is an administrative and investigative power, not a physical enforcement power. Where physical enforcement is required (such as against active violence or physical obstruction), the Contingent shall coordinate with the United States Marshals Service, Federal Bureau of Investigation, or other appropriate armed federal law enforcement, but shall not itself exercise armed enforcement. This limitation reflects the considered judgment that the Contingent's mission is evidence collection and compliance enforcement, not physical coercion. 13C.15 Accountability Chain. The Contingent Director reports to the three bodies of the Authority through Liberty Bell Initiative, not to the President or any other federal officeholder. The Director may be removed only upon two-thirds (2/3) concurrence of all three Authority bodies upon findings of cause published upon the Ledger. During Phase One before Authority constitution, the Washington Commission shall perform the accountability function under this subsection, with reversal authority upon the Authority's full constitution. 13C.15.1 Alternative Director Removal Pathways — Preventing Unremovable Captured Director. Recognizing that the Section 13C.15 requirement of two-thirds concurrence of ALL three Authority bodies creates a vulnerability whereby a blocking minority within any single body can render a captured Director unremovable (as seventeen (17) members of the fifty-member Academic Integrity Commission, nineteen (19) members of the fifty-six-member State Elections Council, or one hundred one (101) members of the three-hundred-member Citizens' Oversight Board may block removal despite broad consensus for removal), the following alternative pathways for Director removal shall be available in addition to Section 13C.15: (a) Tribunal-Plus-One-Body Pathway. The Director may be removed upon: (i) finding by two-thirds (2/3) supermajority of the Watchdog Tribunal (sixty-seven (67) of one hundred (100)) that the Director has engaged in corruption, abuse of authority, material dereliction of duty, or material interference with Prosecution Division case decisions in violation of Section 13C.4.1; AND (ii) concurrence by two-thirds (2/3) supermajority of any one of the three Authority bodies (two hundred (200) of three hundred (300) for the Citizens' Oversight Board, thirty-eight (38) of fifty-six (56) for the State Elections Council, or thirty-four (34) of fifty (50) for the Academic Integrity Commission). This pathway requires Tribunal independent finding and single-body Authority concurrence, preventing any single Authority body's blocking minority from saving a captured Director while ensuring genuine dual-body review; (b) Citizen-Initiated Director Removal Pathway. Registered voters may, through the following process, initiate removal of the Contingent Director: (i) Petition. Valid in-person signatures of not less than ten percent (10%) of registered voters nationally and not less than ten percent (10%) in each of at least twenty (20) Participating Jurisdictions, collected under the signature procedures of Section 12; (ii) Expedited Investigation. Upon petition certification by the State Elections Council (or emergency panel under Section 21.12.1 if SEC refuses), an expedited sixty (60) day investigation by the Watchdog Tribunal, with findings published upon the Ledger; (iii) Referendum. A national referendum within one hundred twenty (120) days of investigation completion, in which citizens vote yes or no on Director removal, requiring majority approval with minimum forty percent (40%) turnout. If approved, the Director shall be removed immediately upon certification, with replacement selected under Section 13C.7 procedures; (iv) Frequency Limitation. No citizen-initiated Director removal petition shall be initiated within two (2) years of a prior certified petition against the same Director, whether the prior petition succeeded or failed, unless new evidence of substantially different alleged conduct emerges; (c) Integration with Existing Pathway. The pathways of this Section are additional to, not in place of, the Section 13C.15 three-body concurrence pathway. The Authority may pursue Section 13C.15 removal at any time, and citizens and the Tribunal may simultaneously pursue pathways under this Section. The existence of multiple pathways reflects the constitutional importance of preventing unremovable captured Directors; (d) Protection Against Abuse. Any attempt to initiate Director

removal in bad faith — whether through Tribunal 2/3 finding without credible evidentiary basis or citizen petition generated through fraudulent signature collection — shall be subject to Section 13 interference penalties. Good-faith removal proceedings that fail at any stage shall not create liability for the participants; (e) Phase One Application. During Phase One before Authority full constitution, the Tribunal-Plus-One-Body pathway shall not be available (as the Authority bodies are not yet constituted). The citizen-initiated pathway remains available, with the Washington Commission performing the Authority function in the replacement process under Section 13C.7(d). 13C.16 Watchdog Tribunal Oversight of the Contingent. The Watchdog Tribunal under Section 21 shall have jurisdiction to investigate the Contingent itself for corruption, abuse of authority, or failure of duty. The Tribunal may, by two-thirds (2/3) supermajority, order removal of Contingent personnel, reconstitution of Divisions, or referral of misconduct for prosecution. D. Day-Zero Activation and Initial Operations 13C.17 Post-Ratification Roster Assembly. Upon Academic Integrity Commission full constitution on Day One Hundred Eighty (180) following Ratification, the Commission shall assemble the Pre-Certified Roster and conduct preparatory training for candidates as an ordinary Commission function under Sections 13C.6 through 13C.16. No pre-Ratification Roster assembly is required by this Amendment, as the Academic Integrity Commission does not exist before Ratification. 13C.18 Day-Zero Activation. Upon the effective date of Ratification, the following shall take effect immediately by operation of this Amendment, without requirement of prior Roster assembly or pre-Ratification preparation: (a) Hamilton Contingent authority is deemed constitutionally established, with operational build-out commencing through Dean Nomination Body Director candidate compilation under Section 13C.6.5, Director selection under Section 13C.7, and Division Chief confirmation under Section 13C.8, targeting full operational capability by Day One Hundred Eighty (180); (b) During the period before Hamilton Contingent reaches operational capability, Phase One substitute authority under Sections 13B.7.1 (forensic imaging through AIC-Designate Forensic Consortium), 13B.7.3 (evidence destruction investigation through Temporary Task Force), 13D.6.1 (forensic audit through State AG Council coordination), and 19.5.0.18.9 (State Attorneys General

Council expanded authorities) shall perform Hamilton functions until Hamilton capacity is reached; (c) Citizen Oversight Member lottery shall commence within thirty (30) days of Ratification, with initial members seated within ninety (90) days, coordinated with Director selection timeline under Section 13C.7;

(d) The Preservation Division forensic imaging function shall be performed by the AIC-Designate Forensic Consortium under Section 13B.7.1 commencing within thirty (30) days of Ratification, with transfer to Hamilton upon operational capability; (e) The Prosecution Division function shall be performed by the State Attorneys General Council acting by supermajority under Sections 19.5.0.5.2 and 19.5.0.18.9.1 until Hamilton reaches operational capability, including prosecution authority for any evidence destruction occurring during the one hundred eighty (180) day retroactive period under Section 13B.4; (f) Whistleblower intake and Public Response Division hotline functions shall be performed by State Attorneys General Council infrastructure, with Authority Oversight under Section 17 providing additional intake pathways, until Hamilton reaches operational capability. 13C.19 Emergency Initial Funding. The Ratification Loan under Section 13I shall fund all Hamilton Contingent build-out and Phase One substitute authority operations, commencing automatically upon Ratification without requirement of further legislative action. This funding shall cover initial operations through Hamilton Contingent reaching full operational capability, with ongoing funding provided through the constitutional appropriation framework of Section 11.3 as modified to include Contingent operations. 13C.20 Ongoing Funding. Annual Hamilton Contingent funding shall be approximately two billion dollars ($2,000,000,000), adjusted for inflation, appropriated as a constitutional mandate not subject to ordinary congressional discretion. Funding shall be distributed across Divisions in proportion to operational needs as determined by the Director with Authority concurrence. Funding may be supplemented from asset forfeitures, civil penalties, and whistleblower-case recoveries under this Amendment. E. Duration and Dissolution Authority 13C.21 Permanent Operation. The Hamilton Contingent shall operate as a permanent parallel enforcement structure, continuing indefinitely unless dissolved pursuant to Section 13C.22. 13C.22 Authority Dissolution Authority. The three bodies of the Authority may, through Liberty Bell Initiative following a period of not less than ten (10) years of Contingent operation, dissolve the Contingent or restructure it significantly upon findings that: (a) The Hamilton Contingent's functions have been substantially absorbed by the permanent Authority, Watchdog Tribunal, or other enforcement structures such that continued operation is duplicative; or

(b) The Hamilton Contingent is no longer necessary to protect the integrity of Amendment operations; or (c) Continued operation would be inconsistent with the evolved constitutional order following twenty (20) or more years of Amendment operation. 13C.23 Dissolution Procedure. Any dissolution or significant restructuring of the Hamilton Contingent shall require: (a) Liberty Bell Initiative concurrence of all three Authority bodies; (b) Public hearings with opportunity for citizen comment for not less than one hundred twenty (120) days; (c) Transition plan ensuring no gap in enforcement capacity, with Hamilton Contingent functions transferred to specified successor bodies before dissolution takes effect; (d) Preservation of all Hamilton Contingent records, investigations, and ongoing matters under the Preservation Order of Section 13B; (e) Protection of Hamilton Contingent personnel through comparable federal employment or severance; (f) Publication of the full dissolution decision, reasoning, and transition plan upon the Ledger. 13C.24 Limited Suspension. The three Authority bodies may, through Liberty Bell Initiative, temporarily suspend specific Contingent operations for not more than ninety (90) days upon findings of emergency need, but shall not dissolve the Contingent except through Section 13C.22 procedures. 13C.25 Protection Against Premature Dissolution. During the first ten (10) years of Hamilton Contingent operation, no action by any person, body, or authority may dissolve, materially reduce the authority of, or suspend the core functions of the Hamilton Contingent. This ten-year protection ensures that the Hamilton Contingent cannot be dismantled before Amendment accountability structures have matured. Violations of this Section shall constitute interference under Section 13 and shall trigger the full penalties thereof. 13C.25.1 Ten-Year Protection — Scope Clarification and Reform Pathways. The Section 13C.25 protection against premature dissolution is designed to prevent bad actors from dismantling the Hamilton Contingent before accountability structures mature. It shall not be construed to prevent legitimate reform where the Contingent itself has been compromised. The following clarifications and reform pathways apply: (a) Personnel Removal Is Permitted. Nothing in Section 13C.25 shall prevent personnel removal through: (i) Section 13C.15 three-Authority-body removal of the Director; (ii) Section 13C.15.1 alternative Director removal pathways; (iii) Section 13C.16 Watchdog Tribunal removal of Contingent personnel by two-thirds (2/3) supermajority; or (iv) ordinary personnel actions for cause within the Contingent's internal procedures. Personnel removal does not constitute dissolution or material authority reduction; (b) Emergency Restructuring Upon Systemic Capture Finding. Where the Watchdog Tribunal by two-thirds (2/3) supermajority, after completing the deep audit procedures of Section 21.6.1, finds that the Hamilton Contingent has been systemically captured — meaning corruption has spread beyond individual personnel to affect core operational capability of two or more Divisions — the Authority may proceed with structural reform under the following conditions notwithstanding Section 13C.25: (i) All three Authority bodies must concur through Liberty Bell Initiative that structural reform is necessary based on the Tribunal's finding; (ii) The proposed structural reform must be published on the Ledger with a thirty (30) day public comment period before Authority action; (iii) A supermajority referendum of sixty percent (60%) approval with minimum fifty percent (50%) turnout of registered voters is required to authorize structural reform during the ten-year protection period, consistent with the No Confidence threshold under Section 5.2; (iv) Structural reform shall preserve the Contingent's core functions (preservation, prosecution, protection, public response) even if the organizational structure, leadership, or staffing changes substantially; (v) Records, ongoing investigations, and pending prosecutions shall be preserved through any restructuring, with continuity of accountability operations maintained; (c) Protection Against Dissolution Distinguished from Protection Against Reform. The Section 13C.25 ten-year protection applies absolutely to dissolution (eliminating the Contingent entirely) and to material reduction of authority (removing core enforcement powers). It does not apply to reform of governance, leadership, or organizational structure where the reform preserves the Contingent's constitutional mission. The distinction shall be construed strictly in favor of preserving Contingent continuity while permitting reform of demonstrably captured components; (d) Citizen Emergency Override Availability. The Citizen Emergency Override under Section 21.10, with its thirty percent (30%) signature threshold, remains available during the ten-year protection period for the specific purpose of investigating all oversight bodies including the Contingent. The five (5) year cooldown under Section 21.11(d) applies to Override petitions generally, not to Contingent-specific reform proceedings under this Section; (e) Good-Faith Reform Protection. Authority bodies, Tribunal members, and citizens participating in good-faith reform proceedings under this Section shall not be subject to Section 13 interference penalties even if reform proceedings ultimately fail to reach the supermajority referendum threshold, provided the proceedings were conducted with documented evidentiary basis and in accordance with the procedures of this subsection. F. Transparency and Public Accountability 13C.26 Ledger Publication. The Hamilton Contingent shall publish upon the Ledger:

(a) Current personnel by Division and position, with qualifications and background disclosures; (b) Current and pending investigations (with protection of active operational details); (c) Prosecutions initiated and their status; (d) Whistleblower cases resolved (with whistleblower identity protected); (e) Citizen complaints received and their disposition; (f) Financial reports including all appropriations, expenditures, and recoveries; (g) Annual comprehensive reports on Hamilton Contingent operations; (h) Performance metrics including response times, case closure rates, and conviction rates. 13C.27 Public Accountability Dashboard. The Public Response Division shall maintain upon the Ledger an interactive Public Accountability Dashboard showing: (a) Current incumbents in every accountability role under this Amendment (not solely Hamilton Contingent) including Authority bodies, Watchdog Tribunal, Inspector Generals; (b) Escalation paths for each type of violation or complaint; (c) Contact information for reporting violations anonymously or on the record; (d) Known response times and performance metrics; (e) Open investigations searchable by type, jurisdiction, or status; (f) Resources for citizens seeking to exercise Amendment rights. 13C.28 Citizens' Accountability Petition Mechanism. Registered voters may, by petition signed by not fewer than one hundred thousand (100,000) registered voters from at least ten (10) Participating Jurisdictions, compel Hamilton Contingent action or review of a specific matter alleged to have been inadequately addressed. The Public Response Division shall administer petitions, and the Contingent Director, with Division Chief concurrence, shall respond substantively within sixty (60) days, either taking the requested action, explaining why action is declined, or referring the matter to the Watchdog Tribunal for further review. 13C.29 Annual Public Hearings. The Hamilton Contingent shall conduct public hearings in each Participating Jurisdiction annually, allowing citizens to directly question Hamilton Contingent personnel, raise concerns, and provide input on Hamilton Contingent priorities. Hearings shall be livestreamed upon the Ledger and transcripts published within seven (7) days. G. Coordination with Other Amendment Structures

13C.30 Coordination with Watchdog Tribunal. The Hamilton Contingent shall cooperate fully with the Watchdog Tribunal's investigations of corruption in Authority bodies or the federal government, including sharing information, providing investigative support, and executing Tribunal directives. In the event of conflict between Hamilton Contingent direction and Watchdog Tribunal direction on a matter within the Tribunal's jurisdiction, the Tribunal's direction shall prevail. 13C.31 Coordination with Authority. The Hamilton Contingent operates as an enforcement body of the Amendment, distinct from but accountable to the three bodies of the Authority. The Contingent Director shall meet with the Authority at least quarterly to report on operations, receive direction, and coordinate strategic priorities. 13C.32 Coordination with State and Local Law Enforcement. The Hamilton Contingent shall coordinate with state and local law enforcement on matters involving Amendment offenses, but shall not defer to state or local authorities on Amendment violations. Where state or local authorities decline to cooperate, the Hamilton Contingent retains full federal jurisdiction under this Section. 13C.33 Article V Protection. The provisions of this Section shall be protected under the Article V protection established in Sections 18.6.1 and 18.6.2. No act of Congress, executive order, judicial ruling, or state action may evade, diminish, or nullify the Hamilton Contingent's authority or undermine its independence. The Hamilton Contingent is a constitutional body, not a statutory creation, and its authority derives from this Amendment itself.

Section 13D. Post-No-Confidence Asset Recovery and Progressive Restitution

Key terms in this Section: • "Removed Official" — Any person holding an office enumerated in Section 1.1 at the moment of certified No Confidence Referendum passage, who is removed from office as a result of the Referendum. • "Forensic Audit" — The comprehensive financial examination of a Removed Official conducted under this Section to determine whether corrupt enrichment occurred during federal service. • "Asset Freeze" — The temporary legal restraint on the transfer, disposition, or concealment of a Removed Official's financial assets during the Forensic Audit period. • "Corrupt Recovery" — Assets determined through this Section's processes to have been obtained through corruption during federal service, subject to forfeiture.

• "Qualifying Recipient" — A person eligible to receive distribution of recovered funds under Section 13D.22, defined therein. • "Cleared Status" — The formal determination under Section 13D.28 that a Removed Official has been investigated and found to have no corrupt enrichment requiring forfeiture. • "The Authority" — The Independent Tripartite Oversight Authority (three bodies, see Section 17). • "The Franklin Ledger" — The public transparency infrastructure established in Section 4A. A. Foundational Principle 13D.1 Foundational Principle. When the People pass a No Confidence Referendum, they do so because the Federal Government has become so fundamentally untrustworthy that complete removal is warranted. Many Removed Officials will have engaged in corrupt enrichment during their service; others will have served honorably despite the failures of the government as a whole. This Section establishes a framework that: (a) recovers assets obtained through corruption and returns them progressively to the American People; (b) protects officials who served honorably from punitive treatment they did not earn; (c) distinguishes the corrupt from the honest through due process rather than assumption; and (d) creates direct material benefit to citizens from the accountability process itself, turning corruption recovery into tangible public good. B. Automatic Asset Freeze and Forensic Audit 13D.2 Automatic Asset Freeze. Upon certification of a No Confidence Referendum under Section 5, the assets of every Removed Official shall be automatically frozen by operation of constitutional law, without further procedural step. The freeze shall apply to: (a) All financial accounts held individually or jointly by the Removed Official at United States financial institutions; (b) All securities, brokerage accounts, and investment holdings; (c) All real property beyond a primary residence; (d) All business interests, partnerships, and corporate holdings; (e) All foreign accounts and assets subject to United States jurisdiction or to treaty-based recovery;

(f) Cryptocurrency holdings, precious metals, and other stores of value in accounts traceable to the Removed Official. 13D.3 Freeze Exceptions — Essential Living Protection. The Asset Freeze shall not apply to: (a) The Removed Official's primary residence (one per official); (b) One personal vehicle per household member; (c) A reasonable essential-living allowance released monthly during the freeze period, sufficient to cover basic housing expenses (beyond mortgage on primary residence which continues), utilities, food, medical care, and legal counsel, with the amount determined by the Watchdog Tribunal based on the Official's jurisdiction's cost of living; (d) Assets necessary for dependent support, including children's education, elder care, and disability care, upon petition to the Watchdog Tribunal; (e) Retirement accounts containing only personal contributions (not federal pension benefits). 13D.4 Freeze Duration. The Asset Freeze shall remain in effect for up to one hundred eighty (180) days from No Confidence certification, except that: (a) Freezes may be lifted earlier upon expedited clearance under Section 13D.28; (b) Freezes may be extended beyond 180 days only upon Watchdog Tribunal finding of active investigation with specific evidence warranting extension, published on the Franklin Ledger, with maximum single-extension period of ninety (90) days; (c) Any single Official's total freeze period shall not exceed two (2) years absent exceptional circumstances published on the Franklin

Ledger; (d) Freezes shall end automatically upon Cleared Status determination under Section 13D.28 or upon final forfeiture determination under Section 13D.13. 13D.5 Spousal and Family Protections. The Asset Freeze shall be implemented with the following protections for innocent family members: (a) Spouses and adult children who have independent income, assets, or business interests unrelated to the Removed Official shall not have their independent assets frozen; (b) Jointly-held assets shall be frozen as to the Official's interest but not necessarily as to the innocent spouse's interest; (c) Family business operations unrelated to federal service shall continue with working capital released by Watchdog Tribunal order upon petition;

(d) Minor children's needs shall be prioritized, with child support, education funds, and medical care preserved; (e) Courts shall retain discretion to preserve reasonable support for dependents consistent with the protections of Section 13A.6(e). C. Mandatory Forensic Audit 13D.6 Automatic Forensic Audit. Every Removed Official shall be subject to automatic Forensic Audit beginning within thirty (30) days of No Confidence certification. The audit shall be conducted by the Hamilton Contingent Preservation Division under Section 13C.3, in coordination with the Treasury Department, Securities and Exchange Commission, and Federal Bureau of Investigation as provided in Section 13B.23. 13D.6.1 Hamilton Capacity Substitute for Forensic Audit Functions. Because the Forensic Audit framework established in Section 13D.6 through Section 13D.8 assigns operational responsibility to the Hamilton Contingent Preservation Division, and because Hamilton Contingent operational capacity is not guaranteed to be at full steady-state levels at the moment of No Confidence certification — which may occur as early as the Inaugural Referendum under Section 19A on Day Seven Hundred Eighty (780) following Ratification — the following substitute framework applies where Hamilton capacity is insufficient to conduct Forensic Audits under the Section 13D.8 timeline: (a) Capacity Determination. The Permanent Washington Commission under Section 17D or, in its absence, the Authority through Liberty Bell Initiative, shall determine within fourteen (14) days of No Confidence certification whether Hamilton Contingent Preservation Division has sufficient operational capacity to conduct Forensic Audits of all Removed Officials under the Section 13D.8 timeline. The determination shall be published on the Franklin Ledger with specific factual basis regarding Hamilton personnel, operational readiness, and audit workload capacity versus expected Removed Official audit demand; (b) Substitute Authority Activation. Where the capacity determination under subsection (a) finds insufficient Hamilton capacity to meet the Section 13D.8 timeline, the following substitute authority shall activate: (i) State Attorneys General Council Forensic Coordination. The State Attorneys General Council under Section 19.5.0.18.1, operating by majority vote, shall coordinate Forensic Audit assignments across the fifty-six (56) Participating Jurisdictions, utilizing state AG investigative and forensic capacity to absorb audit workload that exceeds Hamilton capacity; (ii) Academic Integrity Commission Technical Support. The Academic Integrity Commission under Section 17 shall provide technical and analytical support to state AG offices conducting Forensic Audits, including blockchain transaction analysis, forensic accounting methodology, and document analysis expertise, drawing on Pre-Certified University Pool resources under Section 17.16; (iii) AIC-Designate Forensic Consortium Continuation. To the extent the AIC-Designate Forensic Consortium established under Section 13B.7.1 has operational forensic capacity at the time of substitute activation, the Consortium shall continue in evolved form specifically to support Forensic Audit functions, reporting to the AIC and the State AG Council jointly; (iv) Hamilton Coordination. Hamilton Contingent Preservation Division shall continue Forensic Audits at its available capacity, with substitute authority covering workload exceeding Hamilton capacity. Substitute authority does not displace Hamilton authority; it supplements it; (c) Work Product Transfer to Hamilton. As Hamilton Contingent Preservation Division reaches full operational capacity (determined by subsequent Washington Commission or Authority review not less than every ninety (90) days following initial substitute activation), Forensic Audit work product from state AG offices, AIC, and AIC-Designate Forensic Consortium shall transfer to Hamilton for consolidation, continuation, or final adjudication. No defendant shall face re-audit under Hamilton that duplicates completed substitute-authority audit work; the substitute-authority work product shall be accepted by Hamilton at full evidentiary value; (d) Uniform Standards Preserved. Substitute authority under this Section shall apply the same Forensic Audit standards, scope, and procedural protections established in Section 13D.7 through Section 13D.12. No Removed Official shall face reduced procedural protections by virtue of being audited under substitute authority rather than by Hamilton directly. Defendant rights, burden-shifting framework under Section 13D.9, and all other Section 13D provisions apply equally; (e) Timeline Flexibility During Substitute Period. Where substitute authority under subsection (b) is operating, the Section 13D.8 timelines shall apply as targets rather than rigid deadlines, with good-faith efforts at timely completion required. The Watchdog Tribunal may, by majority vote on motion of the State AG Council coordinating authority or any Authority body, authorize specific timeline extensions upon findings published on the Franklin Ledger, not to exceed ninety (90) days per extension. Extensions shall be the exception, not the norm; the substitute authority shall staff and resource to meet Section 13D.8 timelines wherever feasible; (f) Federal Executive Non-Interference. No President, Vice President, Cabinet officer, federal agency head, or other federal executive officeholder shall direct, fund, influence, or impede the substitute Forensic Audit authority under this Section. Any such interference shall constitute Section 13 interference with Senior Official multipliers where applicable, prosecutable by the State AG Council under Sections 19.5.0.5.2 and 19.5.0.18.9.1 or by Hamilton Contingent upon full operational capacity, and through the Section 17C.15 framework for Amendment-related prosecutions; (g) Funding. Substitute authority operations shall be funded through the constitutional appropriation under Section 11.3, with direct disbursement to state AG offices, AIC, and AIC-Designate Forensic Consortium in amounts proportional to substitute workload assumed. Costs of substitute authority shall not be assessed against state budgets; federal constitutional funding covers the full operational cost; (h) Sunset of Substitute Authority. Substitute authority under this Section shall sunset automatically upon Washington Commission or Authority determination that Hamilton Contingent Preservation Division has reached operational capacity sufficient to conduct Forensic Audits under Section 13D.8 timelines going forward. Sunset shall not

affect the evidentiary value of substitute-authority audit work product; all completed audits remain fully valid and admissible in subsequent Hamilton-led enforcement proceedings. 13D.7 Scope of Forensic Audit. Each Audit shall comprehensively examine: (a) Baseline Comparison: current assets compared against pre-service baseline, with unexplained wealth accumulation during federal service presumed subject to recovery; (b) Foreign Money Investigation: thorough examination of all foreign accounts, foreign transactions, foreign-sourced payments, and foreign business relationships under the enhanced monitoring framework of Section 13B.23 through 13B.25; all transfers from foreign governments, foreign officials, foreign-controlled entities, or foreign nationals during the Removed Official's service shall be specifically examined for corrupt purpose; (c) Category-Specific Review: examination of income from book deals, speaking fees, consulting arrangements, media appearances, stock trades, real estate transactions, cryptocurrency activities, and similar categories commonly used to disguise corrupt payments; (d) Timeline Analysis: correlation of asset accumulation, transactions, and financial events with the Removed Official's official actions, legislative votes, judicial rulings, executive decisions, and policy positions; (e) Family and Associate Analysis: examination of financial flows to spouses, children, close family members, business partners, and close associates for evidence of indirect corrupt enrichment; (f) Prior Preservation Order Compliance: review of the Removed Official's compliance with Section 13B Preservation Order requirements. 13D.8 Audit Timeline. Forensic Audits shall proceed under the following timeline: (a) Initial review and triage: within thirty (30) days of No Confidence certification; (b) Expedited clearance determinations: within sixty (60) days for officials with no initial suspicious findings; (c) Full Forensic Audit completion: within one hundred eighty (180) days for most officials; (d) Extension authority: Watchdog Tribunal may authorize extensions for complex investigations upon findings published on the Franklin Ledger. 13D.9 Burden-Shifting Framework. During Forensic Audit, the following burden-shifting applies: (a) Initial Presumption: the Removed Official is presumed innocent of corrupt enrichment;

(b) Hamilton Contingent's Prima Facie Showing (a Latin legal term meaning: 'at first sight' — enough initial evidence that, if no one responded to it, a reasonable person would conclude the claim is true): upon the Contingent demonstrating unexplained wealth accumulation during federal service, or direct evidence of corrupt transactions, the burden shifts to the Official; (c) Official's Response: the Removed Official may demonstrate legitimate sources for wealth accumulation through pre-service assets, documented legitimate income, inheritance, gifts from permissible sources, investment returns on legitimate holdings, or other lawful means; (d) Unexplained Wealth: wealth that remains unexplained by legitimate sources shall be subject to forfeiture as Corrupt Recovery under this Section; (e) Standard of Proof: preponderance of evidence (a legal standard meaning: more likely than not, or greater than 50% certainty) for civil forfeiture; beyond reasonable doubt (a legal standard meaning: the highest level of certainty required in our legal system, with no reasonable alternative explanation remaining) for any criminal charges. D. Automatic Pension and Salary Clawback 13D.10 Automatic Clawback. All Removed Officials shall have federal pension benefits, retirement contributions, and federally-provided compensation reviewed for clawback consistent with Section 13A.6, with the following refinements for No Confidence removal: (a) Proportional Clawback Based on Corrupt Tenure: pension benefits accrued during periods of clean service shall be preserved; pension benefits accrued during periods of corrupt conduct shall be forfeited; (b) Determination of

Corrupt Tenure: the specific time period of corrupt conduct shall be determined by the Hamilton Contingent through Forensic Audit, subject to judicial review; (c) Default Preservation: if no specific period of corruption is identified, pension benefits shall be preserved in full, consistent with the presumption of innocence; (d) Salary Clawback: federal salary paid during identified corrupt periods is subject to clawback as unjust enrichment; (e) Spousal Dependency Protection: clawback shall be structured to avoid rendering innocent spouses or dependent children destitute, consistent with Section 13A.6(e). E. Individual Criminal Prosecution 13D.11 Referral for Criminal Prosecution. Where Forensic Audit reveals evidence of specific criminal offenses under this Amendment or other federal law, the Hamilton Contingent Prosecution Division shall file charges consistent with its authority under Section 13C.4. Criminal prosecution proceeds independently of civil forfeiture under this Section, with both potentially available against the same Removed Official. 13D.12 Due Process in Criminal Proceedings. All criminal proceedings shall observe full due process rights, including: presumption of innocence; right to counsel; right to jury trial; beyond-reasonable-doubt standard; protection against double jeopardy; and all other constitutional protections. F. Civil Forfeiture Procedures 13D.13 Civil Forfeiture Proceedings. Where Forensic Audit identifies Corrupt Recovery subject to forfeiture, civil proceedings shall be initiated by the Hamilton Contingent Prosecution Division, with: (a) Filing in the federal district court with appropriate jurisdiction; (b) Full service of process and opportunity for the Removed Official to respond; (c) Right to counsel, with federal appointment of counsel for officials unable to afford private representation; (d) Discovery, evidentiary hearings, and appeals consistent with ordinary federal civil procedure; (e) Burden-shifting framework of Section 13D.9; (f) Constitutional protections against excessive fines under the Eighth Amendment. 13D.14 Completion Timeline. Civil forfeiture proceedings should complete within one (1) year of filing, with extensions permitted only upon court findings of complex circumstances. Expedited procedures shall apply to clear-cut cases. G. Good Faith Official Protections 13D.15 Foundational Recognition. A No Confidence Referendum removes the Federal Government as a whole; it does not represent a specific finding of corruption against each individual Removed Official. Many Officials will have served honorably and are subject to removal through no fault of their own. This Amendment establishes meaningful protections for such Officials, calibrated to prevent abuse by genuinely corrupt Officials while ensuring honest service is not punished. 13D.16 Expedited Clearance Process. A Removed Official may qualify for Expedited Clearance within sixty (60) days of No Confidence certification upon: (a) Initial Forensic Audit revealing no unexplained wealth accumulation, no suspicious foreign transactions, no corrupt category-specific income, and no timeline correlations indicating quid pro quo (a Latin legal term meaning: 'this for that' — an improper exchange where an official action was traded for personal

benefit); (b) Voluntary submission to comprehensive financial disclosure beyond what would otherwise be required; (c) Voluntary cooperation with Contingent investigators; (d) No prior adverse findings under Section 13B Preservation Order compliance. 13D.17 Expedited Clearance Effect. Upon Expedited Clearance determination: (a) Asset Freeze shall be lifted within seven (7) days; (b) Pension benefits shall be preserved in full; (c) Salary clawback shall not apply; (d) Full Cleared Status as described in Section 13D.28 shall attach; (e) Transition support under Section 13D.19 shall be provided. 13D.18 Watchdog Tribunal Review of Clearance. Every proposed Expedited Clearance shall be reviewed by the Watchdog Tribunal before taking effect, preventing rubber-stamping of clearances for corrupt officials. Tribunal review shall be completed within fourteen (14) days of Hamilton Contingent recommendation. Clearances may be revoked if subsequent evidence reveals undisclosed corruption. 13D.19 Transition Support for Cleared Officials. Officials granted Cleared Status shall receive the following transition support: (a) Ninety (90) days continued federal salary from date of No Confidence certification, enabling orderly transition to private life; (b) Six (6) months continued federal health insurance coverage; (c) Career placement support through the Authority, offered but not mandatory; (d) Interest on frozen assets at federal statutory rate, calculated from date of freeze to date of release; (e) No punitive impact on Social Security credits or other earned benefits independent of federal service. 13D.20 Public Exoneration. The Franklin Ledger shall display Cleared Status for each cleared Official, with explicit indication of the clearance determination. This is not affirmative endorsement but accurate reflection of investigative findings. Cleared Status may be revoked if later evidence reveals undisclosed corruption, with revocation similarly displayed. 13D.21 Good Faith Cooperation Credit. Officials who cooperate substantially with investigations, including by providing evidence of corruption by other Officials, may receive Cooperation Credit including:

(a) Reduced forfeiture amounts proportional to the value of cooperation provided; (b) Reimbursement of legal fees reasonably incurred; (c)

Whistleblower-equivalent protections from retaliation under Section 13B.16; (d) Eligibility for whistleblower financial rewards under Section 13B.17 where cooperation leads to recovery from other Officials; (e) Cooperation Credit shall be approved by the Watchdog Tribunal and shall not constitute amnesty for the cooperating Official's own corrupt conduct. H. Distribution of Recovered Funds — Progressive Restitution 13D.22 Qualifying Recipients. Recovered funds shall be distributed to Qualifying Recipients, defined as: (a) Eighteen (18) years of age or older at the time of distribution; (b) United States citizens, United States nationals, or lawful permanent residents; (c) Who either (i) filed a federal tax return for the tax year immediately preceding distribution; or (ii) received federal benefits under Social Security Disability Insurance, Supplemental Security Income, or similar federal programs during the preceding tax year; or (iii) would have qualified as a dependent tax filer but did not file due to income below the federal filing threshold, as verified by the Internal Revenue Service through alternative verification procedures. 13D.23 Distribution Allocation. Recovered funds under this Section shall be allocated as follows: (a) Seventy percent (70%) to Qualifying Recipients as Progressive Restitution under Section 13D.24; (b) Thirty percent (30%) to the three bodies of the Authority as dedicated operational budget for Amendment accountability infrastructure, supplementing but not replacing the constitutional appropriation under Section 11.3. 13D.24 Progressive Restitution Tiers. The seventy percent (70%) distribution to Qualifying Recipients shall be allocated across income tiers with the largest share going to lower-income Americans, reflecting that corruption typically enriches the wealthy while harming working Americans. Allocation shall proceed as follows: (a) Under $70,000 annual adjusted gross income (AGI): fifty percent (50%) of the seventy percent (70%) pool; (b) $70,000 to $150,000 AGI: thirty percent (30%) of the pool; (c) $150,000 to $300,000 AGI: fifteen percent (15%) of the pool; (d) $300,000 to $500,000 AGI: five percent (5%) of the pool; (e) Above $500,000 AGI: no distribution;

(f) Within each tier, individual shares shall be calculated by dividing the tier allocation equally among all Qualifying Recipients in that tier; (g) Income brackets shall be adjusted every five (5) years for inflation by the Authority through Liberty Bell Initiative, with adjustments published upon the Franklin Ledger. 13D.25 Distribution Timing. Distributions shall proceed under the following timing: (a) Minimum Verification Period: no distribution shall occur until at least six (6) months after No Confidence certification, during which Forensic Audits proceed, due process is observed, and forfeitures are finalized; (b) Franklin Ledger Running Total: recovered funds shall be tracked in real time upon the Franklin Ledger, visible to all citizens as recoveries accumulate; (c) First Distribution Trigger: the first distribution shall occur when both conditions are met: (i) the six-month minimum verification period has elapsed; and (ii) recovered funds have accumulated to a threshold sufficient to produce meaningful distributions, defined as producing average distribution of not less than ten dollars ($10) per Qualifying Recipient in the lowest tier (under $70,000 AGI). The Authority through Liberty Bell Initiative may set the specific threshold amount higher based on estimated Qualifying Recipient population and administrative considerations, with the threshold published upon the Franklin Ledger; (d) Time Backstop: if recoveries have not reached the threshold by eighteen (18) months after No Confidence certification, the first distribution shall proceed with whatever has been recovered, ensuring distribution does not indefinitely delay; (e) Annual Distributions Thereafter: subsequent distributions shall occur annually on the anniversary of the first distribution, drawing from recoveries accumulated during the prior year; (f) Ongoing Recoveries: recoveries that come in after a distribution shall accumulate toward the next scheduled distribution. 13D.26 First-Time Bonus. The first distribution following No Confidence certification shall include an enhanced first-time bonus to recognize the historic nature of the distribution and compensate Qualifying Recipients for the accumulation period. The first-time bonus shall be: (a) Tiered proportional to the Progressive Restitution structure of Section 13D.24, with the largest bonus going to the lowest-income tier; (b) Drawn from the first distribution pool (not a separate appropriation), thereby making the first distribution larger rather than requiring additional funding; (c) Calibrated by the Authority through Liberty Bell Initiative based on recovered amounts and Qualifying Recipient population;

(d) Paid to every Qualifying Recipient aged 18 or older based on the most recent tax filing, without any additional qualification requirement beyond Section 13D.22. 13D.27 Distribution Administration. The Internal Revenue Service, in coordination with the State Elections Council and the Hamilton Contingent Public Response Division, shall administer distributions using existing federal tax infrastructure, with the following principles: (a) Direct deposit where voter has existing IRS banking information; (b) Physical check delivery for recipients without direct deposit; (c) No application required — eligibility based on existing tax records; (d) Accessibility accommodations for recipients requiring special delivery arrangements; (e) Publication of total distributions by tier upon the Franklin Ledger; (f) Distributions shall be exempt from federal, state, and local income tax, ensuring recipients receive the full intended restitution. I. Cleared Status and Re-Eligibility 13D.28 Cleared Status Determination. A Removed Official shall be formally determined to hold Cleared Status upon either: (a) Expedited Clearance under Section 13D.16 and Watchdog Tribunal review under Section 13D.18; or (b) Completion of full Forensic Audit with findings of no corrupt enrichment warranting forfeiture; or (c) Final judicial determination in civil forfeiture proceedings that no forfeiture is warranted. 13D.29 Re-Eligibility for Federal Office. Officials with Cleared Status may seek federal office in the future, subject to the following: (a) Same Office Waiting Period: a Cleared Official may not seek election or appointment to the same federal office from which they were removed for at least one (1) full Emergency Election cycle following No Confidence, approximately two (2) years from No Confidence certification, ensuring the new Federal Government elected through Emergency Election has opportunity to establish itself; (b) Different Office Immediate Eligibility: a Cleared Official may seek election or appointment to a different federal office immediately upon Cleared Status determination, subject to all other eligibility requirements of this Amendment and the Constitution; (c) State and Local Office: Cleared Status has no effect on eligibility for state or local office, which is governed by state law;

(d) Campaign Disclosure Requirement: any Cleared Official seeking federal office shall disclose in all campaign materials, candidate filings, and Franklin Ledger candidate profiles: (i) their prior federal service; (ii) their removal through No Confidence; (iii) their Cleared Status determination; and (iv) the date of each event. Failure to disclose shall disqualify the candidate; (e) Full Compliance with Section 9: campaign finance rules apply in full with no special exception for previously-removed Officials. 13D.30 Ineligibility for Officials Not Cleared. Officials who are not granted Cleared Status — whether due to findings of corruption, failure to complete investigation procedures, or adverse court determinations — remain subject to Section 8 ineligibility and other applicable disqualification provisions of this Amendment. J. Whistleblower Path During Investigation 13D.31 Retroactive Whistleblower Protection. Removed Officials who come forward during the investigation period to disclose corruption by other Officials may receive Protected Whistleblower status under Section 13B.16, with the following conditions: (a) The Official must provide material evidence of corruption by other specified individuals; (b) The Official must come forward before being personally identified as a target of specific investigation; (c) The disclosure must be substantively useful to ongoing investigations; (d) Whistleblower status does not excuse the Official's own corrupt conduct but may result in Cooperation Credit under Section

13D.21; (e) Whistleblower financial rewards under Section 13B.17 apply where cooperation leads to recovery from other Officials. K. Transparency and Public Accountability 13D.32 Franklin Ledger Publication. The Franklin Ledger shall publish throughout the asset recovery process: (a) Running real-time total of recovered funds; (b) Breakdown of recoveries by Removed Official (with appropriate privacy for ongoing investigations); (c) Clearance determinations for each Official (names and outcomes); (d) Forfeiture determinations with full judicial findings; (e) Distribution amounts by tier for each distribution;

(f) Authority operational budget allocations of the 30% share; (g) Complete annual reports on Section 13D operations. 13D.33 Article V Protection. The provisions of this Section 13D shall be protected under the Article V protection established in Sections 18.6.1 and 18.6.2. No act of Congress, executive order, judicial ruling, or state action shall modify, diminish, or evade the asset recovery framework, the Progressive Restitution structure, or the Good Faith Official protections. This Section establishes that when the People recover wealth taken through corruption, that wealth shall flow back to the American People who were harmed by it, with due process preserved for all Officials and particular care for those who served honorably.

Section 13E. Refusal to Vacate Office and Forcible Removal

Key terms in this Section: • "The Authority" — The Independent Tripartite Oversight Authority (three bodies, see Section 17). • "The Ledger" — The Sovereign Blockchain Voting Ledger (Section 4). • "Refusing Official" — Any person holding an office enumerated in Section 1.1 who, following certification of a No Confidence Referendum under Section 5, takes any action purporting to continue to hold, exercise, or claim authority of that office, or who physically refuses to vacate the premises, records, or instruments of that office. • "Usurpation" — The attempt to continue holding or exercising governmental authority after that authority has been terminated by the People through No Confidence Referendum. • "Loyalist Complicity" — Any knowing material assistance to a Refusing Official, including defense of premises, execution of purported orders, financial support, communications assistance, or public endorsement of continued authority. • "Forcible Removal" — The physical removal of a Refusing Official from office premises, conducted pursuant to the authority and procedures of this Section. A. Foundational Principle 13E.1 Foundational Principle. When the People of the United States declare No Confidence in their Federal Government through the supermajority process of this

Amendment, that declaration is final, self-executing, and not subject to challenge by the Officials thereby removed. An Official who refuses to vacate their office following certified No Confidence does not retain any authority — their authority has been terminated by the sovereign act of the People. What such an Official attempts is not the exercise of office but the usurpation of democratic authority itself — the most serious offense against the constitutional order the People have established. This Section establishes that Refusal to Vacate constitutes a distinct and severe offense, separate from ordinary interference, punishable at treason-equivalent levels, and subject to Forcible Removal by multiple pathways of constitutional authority to ensure the People's sovereign will is carried out without delay or exception. B. Definition of Refusal to Vacate 13E.2 Acts Constituting Refusal to Vacate. Any of the following acts, undertaken by a Removed Official after certification of a No Confidence Referendum, shall constitute Refusal to Vacate: (a) Physical Occupation. Remaining in, occupying, or refusing to leave any official residence, office, chamber, or other federal premises associated with the vacated office, more than twenty-four (24) hours after No Confidence certification; (b) Purported Exercise of Authority. Issuing orders, signing documents, making appointments, taking military actions, making executive decisions, casting votes, hearing cases, writing opinions, or otherwise purporting to exercise the authority of the vacated office; (c) Public Claim of Office. Publicly claiming to remain President, Vice President, Member of Congress, Justice of the Supreme Court, or any other office enumerated in Section 1.1, after certification of No Confidence; (d) Directing Loyalists. Directing federal personnel, military personnel, security personnel, or private persons to treat the Removed Official as the legitimate officeholder or to resist the Amendment's implementation; (e) Instruments of Office Retention. Retaining possession, concealing, or refusing to surrender the physical instruments of office, including but not limited to: the nuclear command authentication devices; presidential seals and authentication tools; classified information systems credentials; official records and communications; government-issued security credentials; and federal property of the vacated office; (f) Legal Challenge Beyond Right. Filing legal proceedings, in any court, that purport to challenge the validity of the No Confidence Referendum itself, after the Authority has certified it in accordance with Section 5. An Official retains the right to contest specific irregularities through the procedures of Section 23, but the validity of the People's supermajority judgment is not subject to judicial challenge.

C. Treason-Equivalent Penalties 13E.3 Penalty Framework. Refusal to Vacate is hereby classified as Usurpation, a treason-equivalent offense against the constitutional order, punishable as follows: (a) Imprisonment for life without possibility of parole, probation, or reduced sentence for any reason; (b) Permanent, total, and irreversible forfeiture of all assets derived from or acquired during federal service, without exception for pardoned or expunged convictions; (c) Permanent forfeiture of all federal pension benefits, retirement contributions, healthcare benefits, and survivor benefits; (d) Permanent lifetime bar from any federal, state, territorial, or local public office, appointed position, or government employment; (e) Permanent lifetime bar from ownership, leadership, or substantial financial interest in any entity receiving federal contracts or federal benefits; (f) Permanent, total, and irreversible loss of eligibility for any Good Faith Official protections under Section 13D.15 through 13D.21, regardless of other conduct; (g) Permanent designation on the Franklin Ledger as a Usurper, with full documentation of the refusal, available to the public in perpetuity; (h) No presidential pardon, executive clemency, commutation, reprieve, or act of grace by any subsequent federal, state, or local official shall have any effect on sentences imposed under this Section. The sovereign act of the People through No Confidence cannot be reversed by any subsequent officeholder. 13E.4 Treason Designation. The offense of Usurpation under this Section shall carry the legal designation of treason against the United States, reflecting that it is an attempt to overthrow the People's sovereign constitutional authority itself. This designation applies notwithstanding any narrower definition of treason in Article III, Section 3 of the Constitution; the People through this Amendment establish this specific form of usurpation as treason-equivalent in all legal respects. 13E.5 No Statute of Limitations. No statute of limitations shall apply to prosecutions under this Section. A Refusing Official may be prosecuted at any time, by any subsequent federal administration, for conduct undertaken during Refusal, regardless of intervening years, transitions of government, or subsequent legal events. D. Loyalist Complicity 13E.6 Knowing Material Assistance. Any person who knowingly provides material assistance to a Refusing Official in the act of Refusal shall be subject to penalties under this Section, including:

(a) Federal personnel (including political appointees, senior executive service, career personnel with policy-making roles) who execute purported orders from a Refusing Official after No Confidence certification: imprisonment of not less than twenty-five (25) years and permanent bar from federal employment; (b) Military personnel who follow orders from a Refusing Official after No

Confidence certification: treated under Section 16.12 military treason provisions, with the added factor of the Refusing Official's removed status as an aggravating circumstance; (c) Security personnel (Secret Service, Capitol Police, Supreme Court Police, other federal security forces) who defend a Refusing Official's premises against lawful removal: imprisonment of not less than twenty (20) years, with Section 16 provisions applicable to any armed resistance; (d) Private persons who finance, materially support, or publicly mobilize for a Refusing Official: imprisonment of not less than fifteen (15) years and forfeiture of assets used in the support; (e) Organizations (corporations, advocacy groups, media organizations) that coordinate material support for a Refusing Official: corporate penalties of not less than one billion dollars ($1,000,000,000), dissolution where coordinated, and personal liability for executives. 13E.7 Good Faith Exception for Personnel. Federal personnel, military personnel, and security personnel shall not be subject to penalties under Section 13E.6 if they: (a) Refuse to follow orders from a Refusing Official immediately upon learning of No Confidence certification; (b) Report any Refusing Official conduct they witness to the Authority, the Interim Caretaker Council, or the Hamilton Contingent; (c) Cooperate with Forcible Removal operations under this Section; (d) Publicly affirm loyalty to the Constitution and to the sovereign authority of the People under this Amendment; and (e) Are not proven to have engaged in prior planning or coordination with the Refusing Official for the refusal. 13E.8 Whistleblower Protection. Personnel who refuse to follow a Refusing Official's orders and report the refusal shall receive full Protected Whistleblower status under Section 13B.16, including retaliation protection, compensation for any adverse employment action, and eligibility for whistleblower rewards under Section 13B.17. E. Forcible Removal Authority

13E.9 Automatic Trigger. The authority for Forcible Removal of a Refusing Official shall be automatically activated upon any of the following conditions, without further procedural requirement: (a) Twenty-four (24) hours passing after No Confidence certification without a Removed Official formally vacating their office; (b) Any public statement by a Removed Official claiming continued authority; (c) Any attempted exercise of office authority after No Confidence certification; (d) Any direction by a Removed Official to federal personnel, military personnel, or security personnel after No Confidence certification; (e) Certification by the Interim Caretaker Council (or Washington Commission during the build-up period) that Forcible Removal is warranted based on specific findings published on the Ledger. 13E.10 Multi-Pathway Removal Authority. Forcible Removal authority is vested in multiple independent pathways to prevent capture or obstruction of any single pathway. Any one of the following pathways may act, with coordination among pathways where practicable: (a) Pathway 1: United States Marshals Service. The United States Marshals Service is hereby constitutionally authorized and directed, upon automatic trigger under Section 13E.9, to effect Forcible Removal of any Refusing Official from office premises. This authority is vested directly by this Amendment and does not require executive branch authorization, Department of Justice approval, or court order beyond the No Confidence certification itself. Marshals acting under this Section shall report directly to the Interim Caretaker Council (or Washington Commission during build-up), not to any Refusing Official or any federal agency under the control of a Refusing Official; (b) Pathway 2: Hamilton Contingent. The Hamilton Contingent established in Section 13C is hereby authorized to effect Forcible Removal through its Prosecution Division and Protection Division, with full arrest, detention, and transport authority. The Hamilton Contingent may act independently or in coordination with the Marshals; (c) Pathway 3: State Law Enforcement. The Governor of any state or territory in which a Refusing Official is physically located may, upon request of the Interim Caretaker Council (or Washington Commission) or upon own-motion determination that Refusal is occurring within their jurisdiction, deploy state law enforcement (state police, national guard under state command, or other state forces) to effect Forcible Removal. State officials acting under this Section shall be fully indemnified and shall have full federal authority for the duration of the removal operation;

(d) Pathway 4: Military Last Resort. If Pathways 1, 2, and 3 are unavailable, obstructed, or overwhelmed — such as where a Refusing Official has coordinated substantial loyalist military resistance — the Joint Chiefs of Staff under Section 16, acting collectively and under civilian oversight of the Interim Caretaker Council, may authorize military support for Forcible Removal. Military action under this pathway shall be strictly limited to effecting removal, shall be subject to all Section 16 oversight requirements, and shall terminate immediately upon removal being effected. Military personnel engaged in Forcible Removal shall not assume any civilian governing authority as a result of their action. 13E.10.1 Multi-Pathway Coordination Protocol. Recognizing that the four independent removal pathways established in Section 13E.10 operate in overlapping jurisdictions and must coordinate to prevent friendly-fire, duplicative effort, custody confusion, and — most critically — escalation to armed confrontation between lawful pathways and loyalist resistance, the following coordination protocol shall apply to all Forcible

Removal operations: (a) Post-Ratification Operational Planning. Within one hundred eighty (180) days of Ratification, the United States Marshals Service, the Academic Integrity Commission (acting as Hamilton Contingent designee prior to Contingent operational commencement), the National Governors Association (or successor organization) on behalf of state law enforcement, and the Joint Chiefs of Staff shall develop and publish Forcible Removal Operational Protocols on the provisional public ledger and, upon activation, the Sovereign Blockchain Voting Ledger. Willing organizations may coordinate protocol development during the ratification campaign period, but no pre-Ratification obligation is created by this Amendment. Protocols shall address: pathway-specific responsibilities; coordination procedures for simultaneous multi-pathway action; communications between pathways during operations; custody transfer of detained Refusing Officials; evidence preservation under Section 13B; and de-escalation procedures for scenarios involving loyalist resistance. Protocols shall be updated annually after initial publication and shall be subject to Watchdog Tribunal review for adequacy under Section 21.6; (b) Designated Coordinating Authority — Steady State. In steady-state Amendment operation, the Interim Caretaker Council convened under Section 6A shall serve as the designated coordinating authority for all Forcible Removal operations, issuing operational directions binding on all four pathways. The Council's coordination authority is limited to sequencing, timing, and resource allocation; it does not alter the independent legal authority of each pathway to act under Section 13E.10; (c) Designated Coordinating Authority — Interregnum. During the specific window after No Confidence certification but before the Interim Caretaker Council is fully convened (a period of up to seventy-two (72) hours under Section 6A.3), coordinating authority shall vest as follows: (i) during Phase One of Amendment implementation before the Authority's full constitution, the Washington Commission under Section 19.5.0 shall serve as coordinating authority, with its seven (7) Chief Justices acting by majority vote; (ii) in steady-state operation after Authority full constitution, the five-member Senior Chief Justice Panel, consisting of the Chief Justice of the Supreme Court of the Participating Jurisdiction with the largest population among the fifty-six Jurisdictions plus the next four such Chief Justices by descending population, shall serve as coordinating authority acting by majority vote. The Senior Chief Justice Panel shall be deemed constituted automatically upon No Confidence certification and shall dissolve upon the Interim Caretaker Council's convening, with all coordination records transferring to the Council; (d) Rules of Engagement

Between Pathways. The four pathways shall operate under the following rules to prevent pathway conflict: (i) No pathway shall obstruct, delay, or interfere with another pathway's operation absent specific coordinating authority direction; (ii) Custody of detained Refusing Officials shall be held by the pathway making the arrest, with transfer to Hamilton Contingent Protection Division for prosecution processing as soon as practicable; (iii) Evidence collection shall be led by Hamilton Contingent Preservation Division under Section 13C.3 regardless of which pathway effects removal, with other pathways preserving evidence in situ pending Preservation Division arrival; (iv) Where pathways converge on the same operational site, the pathway with specific coordinating authority direction shall have operational lead, with other pathways in support roles; (v) No pathway shall engage loyalist resistance using lethal force absent: immediate armed threat to pathway personnel or bystanders; explicit coordinating authority authorization; or coordinating authority determination that non-lethal options have been exhausted; (e) De-Escalation Procedures for Loyalist Resistance. Where loyalist military or paramilitary resistance is positioned to obstruct Forcible Removal, the following de-escalation procedures shall be attempted before Pathway 4 military activation under Section 13E.10(d): (i) Public Notice. The coordinating authority shall publicly notify the loyalist personnel, on the Ledger and through available military communications channels, that the orders they have received are void ab initio under Section 13E.13 and that continued resistance constitutes Section 13E.6(b) and Section 16.5 offenses; (ii) Good-Faith Exception Notice. The notice shall reference the Section 13E.7 good-faith exception available to personnel who stand down and do not actively assist Refusal, providing a clear off-ramp; (iii) Whistleblower Protection Notice. The notice shall reference Section 13E.8 whistleblower protections for personnel who refuse to follow void orders and report the situation; (iv) Reasonable Window for Stand-Down. Personnel shall have a reasonable window (not less than two (2) hours, not more than twelve (12) hours depending on operational circumstances) to stand down before Pathway 4 military response is authorized; (v) Individual Pathway Activation. Pathways 1 through 3 may proceed during the de-escalation window where they can do so without armed confrontation; (vi) Pathway 4 Last Resort. Only after de-escalation procedures have been attempted and failed, and only with coordinating authority affirmative authorization, shall Pathway 4 military response be activated; (f) Non-Interference Rule. No pathway shall refuse to act solely because another pathway is also acting. Redundant pathway activation is permitted and encouraged where capture or obstruction of a single pathway is credibly threatened. The multiple-pathway design reflects the structural value of redundancy over efficiency; (g) Custody Transfer

Protocol. Upon arrest of a Refusing Official by any pathway, custody shall transfer to Hamilton Contingent Protection Division within twenty-four (24) hours (or as soon as practicable where operational circumstances prevent faster transfer), with Refusing Official held at a secure federal facility pending Section 13E.3 prosecution. Custody transfer shall be documented on the Ledger, with chain-of-custody preserved under Section 13B standards; (h) Coordination Failure Accountability. Where coordination failures result in bystander harm, pathway personnel harm, or operational escalation beyond what was necessary, the coordinating authority and responsible pathway leaders shall be subject to Watchdog Tribunal investigation under Section 21.6, with findings published on the Ledger. Coordination failure does not automatically constitute Section 13 interference, but bad-faith coordination failure — including deliberate refusal to coordinate with other pathways for political reasons — shall constitute Section 13 interference with Senior Official multipliers where applicable; (i) Annual Exercise Requirement. The four pathways shall conduct annual joint coordination exercises, simulating Forcible Removal scenarios and testing Protocols under Section 13E.10.1(a). Exercise results shall be published on the Ledger with operational details protected under narrow operational-security redactions. Failure to conduct annual exercises, or failure to meaningfully participate, shall trigger Watchdog Tribunal review. 13E.10.1.1 Senior Chief Justice Panel Orientation. Because the Senior Chief Justice Panel under Section 13E.10.1(c)(ii) consists of five (5) sitting Chief Justices of the Participating Jurisdictions with the largest populations, and because those Chief Justices already possess extensive judicial skill in coordination and decision-making but need Amendment-specific knowledge of their brief coordinating role during the seventy-two (72) hour interregnum, the following orientation framework applies: (a) Preparatory Education. The Academic Integrity Commission shall include Senior Chief Justice Panel materials within the preparatory education program for state Chief Justices under Section 16.7.1(m) and Section 6A.29, ensuring Chief Justices of the five largest Participating Jurisdictions (as determined at any given time) are familiar with Panel duties before potential activation. Materials shall cover: the Panel's coordinating role under this Section; the seventy-two (72) hour operational window; the pathways under Section 13E.10 that the Panel coordinates; rules of engagement under subsection (d); de-escalation procedures under subsection (e); and dissolution and records transfer upon Caretaker Council convening. (b) Just-In-Time

Briefing. Upon certified No Confidence triggering, the five Chief Justices then eligible for Panel membership by virtue of their Jurisdiction's population ranking shall receive a just-in-time briefing by the Academic Integrity Commission (or during Phase One, by the Washington Commission) within four (4) hours of No Confidence certification. Briefing shall cover specific coordination requirements for the emergent situation. (c) Serving Without Preparation. Chief Justices who have not completed preparatory education may still serve on the Senior Chief Justice Panel, as Panel membership is automatic upon ranking and cannot be delayed for training without creating a coordination gap. Judicial skill in decision-making under time pressure is understood to substitute for detailed Amendment-specific preparation in the seventy-two (72) hour window. (d) Federal Executive Non-Interference. No federal officeholder shall direct, influence, or interfere with Panel preparatory education or just-in-time briefing. Attempts shall constitute Section 13 interference with Senior Official multipliers. (e) No Federal Compensation. Training shall occur without federal compensation; costs shall be covered by each Chief Justice's Participating Jurisdiction. 13E.11 Removal Operation Principles. All Forcible Removal operations shall be conducted under the following principles: (a) Minimum Force Necessary. Force shall be limited to that reasonably necessary to effect removal; excessive force shall itself constitute a separate offense; (b) Preservation of Evidence. All documents, records, communications, and instruments of office shall be preserved under Section 13B evidence preservation standards, with Hamilton Contingent Preservation Division taking immediate custody; (c) Transparency. All removal operations shall be recorded and published on the Franklin Ledger (or provisional public ledger), with operational security redactions permitted only where specifically necessary for personnel safety during the operation itself, subject to full publication within seven (7) days of operation completion; (d) Protection of Bystanders. Removal operations shall be conducted with full protection of federal employees, visitors, family members, and other persons present at the removal location who are not themselves Refusing Officials or loyalist complicity participants; (e) Medical Care. Any Refusing Official requiring medical attention during or after removal shall receive appropriate medical care, with custody maintained; (f) Humane Treatment. Detained Refusing Officials shall be treated humanely consistent with their status as accused but not yet convicted persons, pending prosecution under Section 13E.3. 13E.12 Facilities Securing. Upon Forcible Removal (or upon voluntary vacating), the following federal facilities shall be secured by Forcible Removal authorities and transferred to appropriate interim custody: (a)

The White House and Executive Residence: secured by Hamilton Contingent under coordination with the Interim Caretaker Council, pending Constitutional Transition Committee or Emergency-Elected Administration occupation; (b) The United States Capitol Building: secured by Hamilton Contingent under coordination with the Interim Caretaker Council, pending Constitutional Transition Committee occupation pursuant to Section 11C.18;

(c) The United States Supreme Court Building: secured by Hamilton Contingent, pending Emergency-Elected judicial nominations and confirmation; (d) Congressional Office Buildings: secured and inventoried by Hamilton Contingent; (e) Federal Agency Headquarters (where a Refusing Official is a political appointee): secured with career personnel continuing operations under Interim Caretaker Council oversight; (f) All classified information systems, communications networks, and nuclear command infrastructure: access credentials immediately revoked for Refusing Officials, with new credentials issued to Interim Caretaker Council-designated personnel only. F. Chain of Command During Refusal 13E.13 Commander-in-Chief Authority During Refusal. A President who refuses to vacate has no authority as Commander-in-Chief. The Joint Chiefs of Staff shall recognize only the Interim Caretaker Council (or, after its convening, the Constitutional Transition Committee, or, after Emergency Election, the Emergency-Elected President) as the source of lawful civilian command authority. Any order purportedly issued by a Refusing President shall be void ab initio (invalid from the very beginning) and shall not be followed. Military personnel who follow such orders after notice of No Confidence certification shall be subject to Section 13E.6(b) and Section 16.12 penalties. 13E.14 Nuclear Authority During Refusal. The Nuclear Authorization Panel established in Section 16.7 shall recognize only lawful civilian authority. A Refusing Official shall not have access to nuclear command authentication devices, nuclear command codes, or Nuclear Authorization Panel participation. The Joint Chiefs of Staff shall immediately secure all nuclear command infrastructure upon Refusal Trigger under Section 13E.9. 13E.15 Secret Service and Security Force Loyalty. The Secret Service, Capitol Police, Federal Protective Service, Supreme Court Police, and other federal security forces owe their duty to the offices they protect, not to the individuals who temporarily hold those offices. Upon No Confidence certification, these forces shall: (a) Immediately recognize that the Removed Officials no longer hold protected office status; (b) Provide no special protection to Refusing Officials beyond ordinary peace-keeping protection equivalent to that provided to any citizen; (c) Cooperate fully with Forcible

Removal operations; (d) Secure federal premises under direction of the Interim Caretaker Council;

(e) Continue providing ongoing security protection to properly seated interim and emergency-elected officials. 13E.15.1 Secret Service Director Stand-Down Authority. If the Director of the United States Secret Service refuses to issue orders consistent with Section 13E.15 within twelve (12) hours of No Confidence certification, or if the Director has been named as a Refusing Official under this Section, stand-down authority shall temporarily vest in the senior-most Deputy Director whose appointment did not originate with the Refusing Administration. Such Deputy Director shall issue orders to all Secret Service personnel consistent with Section 13E.15, and shall coordinate with the Forcible Removal coordinating authority under Section 13E.10.1(b) or (c). Upon swearing-in of a new federal administration, ordinary Secret Service chain of command shall resume. Deputy Directors acting under this Section shall receive full Section 13B.16 whistleblower protections and Section 13E.7 good-faith exception protections, and their issuance of stand-down orders shall not constitute insubordination, mutiny, or any other offense under federal or state law. 13E.16 Communications Cutoff. Upon Refusal Trigger under Section 13E.9, the following communications shall be immediately terminated for Refusing Officials: (a) Access to classified information systems and briefings; (b) Access to secure government communications networks; (c) Access to the nuclear football and nuclear command communications; (d) Access to presidential daily briefings and intelligence summaries; (e) Use of government-issued communications devices for official purposes; (f) Access to military communications networks. G. Legal Process 13E.17 Prosecution. Prosecution of Refusing Officials under this Section shall be conducted by the Hamilton Contingent Prosecution Division under Section 13C.4, with the following modifications: (a) No Plea Bargaining to Lesser Charges. The Usurpation charge shall not be subject to plea bargaining to a lesser offense; Refusing Officials may plead guilty to Usurpation but cannot have the charge reduced; (b) Expedited Trial. Trial shall commence within one hundred eighty (180) days of detention, subject to reasonable extensions for complex cases; (c) Jury Selection from National Pool. To prevent jurisdictional bias, juries for Usurpation cases shall be drawn from a national pool administered by the Academic Integrity Commission, with peremptory challenges limited to protect against political jury-rigging;

(d) Full Due Process Protections. Notwithstanding the severity of penalties, Refusing Officials shall receive full due process protections, including right to counsel, right to present defense, right to examine witnesses, and right to appeal on legal grounds (though not on the underlying validity of No Confidence certification). 13E.18 Appeals. Refusing Officials may appeal convictions under this Section on: (a) Procedural grounds (adequacy of trial procedures); (b) Evidentiary grounds (sufficiency of evidence that the individual engaged in Refusal); (c) Sentencing grounds (whether specific penalties were properly applied); (d) Appeals SHALL NOT extend to the underlying validity of the No Confidence certification itself, which is final upon Authority certification and not subject to judicial review; (e) Final appellate jurisdiction shall rest with a panel of five (5) Chief Justices of Participating Jurisdictions (as defined in Section 3) drawn by lottery, applying Usurpation law de novo. H. Preventive Provisions 13E.19 Pre-Refusal Warnings. Beginning on the day of Authority certification of No Confidence, the Interim Caretaker Council (or Washington Commission) shall publish upon the Ledger clear public notice to all Removed Officials that: (a) Their authority has terminated as of the moment of certification; (b) Any act of Refusal to Vacate is a treason-equivalent offense under this Section; (c) They have twenty-four (24) hours to formally vacate their office, complete transition documentation, and leave federal premises; (d) Failure to do so will trigger Forcible Removal under Section 13E.9; (e) Cooperation with the transition is strongly encouraged and may be considered at sentencing if any violations are found. 13E.20 Voluntary Compliance Benefits. Removed Officials who fully and promptly comply with the vacating requirements, without any act of Refusal, shall: (a) Remain eligible for Good Faith Official protections under Section 13D.15 through 13D.21 if they meet the standards thereof; (b) Be eligible for Section 13D transition support including 90-day salary continuation, health insurance, and career placement; (c) Not be subject to this Section's treason-equivalent penalties (only ordinary Section 13 interference standards, if applicable to other conduct);

(d) Retain their ordinary appeals and due process rights regarding any other investigation or prosecution. 13E.21 Distinction from Legitimate Challenge. This Section does not prohibit a Removed Official from exercising legitimate rights, including: (a) Filing challenges to specific irregularities in the Referendum procedure under Section 23; (b) Public speech criticizing the Amendment or the Referendum outcome; (c) Cooperating with or participating in Section 13D forensic audit and asset review procedures; (d) Seeking legal counsel and defense in any subsequent prosecution; (e) Participating in political organizing for future elections subject to the re-eligibility provisions of Section 13D.29. I. Protection and Article V 13E.22 Constitutional Protection. The provisions of this Section 13E shall be protected under the Article V protection established in Sections 18.6.1 and 18.6.2. No act of Congress, executive order, judicial ruling, or state action shall evade, diminish, or nullify the Forcible Removal authority or the Usurpation penalties established herein. No subsequent officeholder shall have authority to retroactively pardon, commute, or excuse conduct prosecuted under this Section. 13E.22.1 Anti-Interference Operational Guidance — Judicial Orders and Investigation Protections. Recognizing that the Section 13E.22 prohibition on judicial diminishment of Forcible Removal authority may be tested by issuance of temporary restraining orders, injunctions, or similar orders purporting to halt or delay Forcible Removal operations, the following operational guidance applies: (a) Judicial Orders Void. Any temporary restraining order, injunction, stay, or similar judicial order issued by any federal or state court purporting to halt, delay, or limit a Forcible Removal operation under Section 13E shall be void ab initio (invalid from the very beginning) as exceeding the court's constitutional authority under this Amendment. Such orders shall have no legal effect, shall not bind any Forcible Removal authority, and shall not require response, appeal, or compliance from any party; (b) Duty to Proceed Notwithstanding. The United States Marshals Service, the Hamilton Contingent, state law enforcement acting under Section 13E.10(c), and military personnel acting under Section 13E.10(d) shall have an affirmative duty to proceed with Forcible Removal notwithstanding any such judicial order. Good-faith compliance with this Section by Forcible Removal personnel shall not constitute contempt of court, obstruction of justice, or any other offense, regardless of subsequent judicial action; (c) Legitimate Constitutional Review Pathway — Independent Investigation Panel. Notwithstanding the unavailability of ordinary court review, the Independent Investigation Panel under Section 21.12 shall serve as the legitimate constitutional review pathway for any genuine concern that No Confidence certification was procedurally defective. Upon petition by a Refusing Official or any registered voter, the Panel may by two-thirds (2/3) supermajority convene expedited review of certification procedures, with review completed within fourteen (14) days. Review shall not stay Forcible Removal but may, upon clear and convincing evidence of material procedural defect, recommend to the Authority that certification be reconsidered. This pathway provides substantive review of legitimate concerns while preserving the operational integrity of Forcible Removal; (d) Investigation of Issuing

Judges — Narrow Grounds. Federal or state judges who issue orders falling within subsection (a) shall be subject to Independent Investigation Panel investigation under Section 21.12, but only upon the following narrow evidentiary grounds: (i) specific evidence that the issuing judge acted with knowledge that the order exceeded Article III authority under this Amendment; or (ii) specific evidence of personal relationships, financial ties, or conflicts of interest with the Refusing Officials that should have required recusal under ordinary judicial ethics standards. Good-faith judicial rulings based on reasonable constitutional interpretation, even if ultimately found to be erroneous, shall not be grounds for investigation under this subsection; (e) Investigation Threshold. The Independent Investigation Panel shall not commence investigation under subsection (d) without supermajority finding (three-fourths (3/4), meaning fifty-seven (57) of seventy-five (75) Panel members) that credible evidence exists under the narrow grounds of subsection (d). This high threshold is specifically designed to prevent frivolous investigations and to protect legitimate judicial independence; (f) Judicial Opinions Protected. Nothing in this Section shall subject a judge to investigation for expressing legal opinions regarding the constitutionality of Section 13E or No Confidence certification procedures in published opinions, academic writing, judicial conferences, or other non-binding forums. Subsection (d) investigation liability attaches only to the issuance of binding orders purporting to halt Forcible Removal operations, not to the expression of legal views; (g) Due Process for Prosecution. Independent Investigation Panel findings under this Section create investigation liability only. Any criminal prosecution of a judge based on such findings shall proceed through the Section 17C Panel framework with full due process, grand jury review where applicable, and trial rights. No provision of this Section shall diminish ordinary due process protections for accused judges; (h) Prospective Effect. This Section applies only to judicial orders issued after the effective date of Ratification of this Amendment and only in the context of Forcible Removal operations under Section 13E. It shall not be construed to reach past judicial rulings, rulings in other Amendment contexts, or rulings in matters unrelated to Forcible Removal; (i) Preservation of Ordinary Judicial Authority. Nothing in this Section shall affect the ordinary judicial authority of federal or state courts in matters unrelated to Forcible Removal. Article III courts retain their full constitutional authority in all other contexts. The narrow carve-out established here reflects the specific structural necessity of protecting Forcible Removal operations from post-certification judicial interference, not a general diminishment of judicial authority. 13E.23 Self-Executing Nature. The provisions of this Section are self-executing, meaning they do not require implementing legislation, executive regulations, or court orders beyond the No Confidence certification itself to take effect. From the moment of certification, the constitutional prohibition on Refusal and the constitutional authorization for Forcible Removal are in full force, with the automatic trigger operating as a matter of constitutional law, not agency discretion. 13E.24 Foundational Commitment. The People of the United States, in ratifying this Amendment, commit themselves to the principle that their sovereign will — expressed through supermajority No Confidence Referendum — is final, self-executing, and supreme over any claim of continued authority by removed Officials. This commitment is not subject to negotiation, compromise, or delay. Any Official who tests this commitment tests the foundation of the American republic itself, and shall face the full consequences established in this Section.

Section 13F. Post-Ratification Financial Monitoring and International Travel

Restrictions

Key terms in this Section: • "The Authority" — The Independent Tripartite Oversight Authority (three bodies, see Section 17). • "The Ledger" — The Sovereign Blockchain Voting Ledger (Section 4). • "Covered Official" — Any person holding an office enumerated in Section 1.1, during the period of their service in that office. • "Treasury" — The United States Department of the Treasury, including its enforcement components (FinCEN, OFAC, IRS Criminal Investigation) acting under existing statutory authority. • "Covered Account" — Any financial account held by a Covered Official at a United States financial institution, or any foreign account of which a Covered Official is a beneficial owner and which is subject to United States jurisdiction or treaty-based reporting. • "International Travel" — Physical travel outside the territorial boundaries of the United States, its territories, and its possessions. Travel between the fifty states, the District of Columbia, and the five territories enumerated in Section 3.1.1 shall not constitute International Travel.

A. Foundational Principle 13F.1 Foundational Principle. The ratification of this Amendment creates immediate incentive for existing officeholders to convert their positions into personal benefit, to move wealth beyond the reach of future accountability, or to prepare for flight from prosecution. The period between ratification and the operational readiness of the Authority's full accountability infrastructure is therefore a period of heightened risk. Further, the job of any

Section 1.1 officeholder is to serve the People of the United States in person, within its borders. An official who must travel internationally for personal reasons may resign and travel; an official who remains in office must be present to serve. This Section establishes financial monitoring and travel restrictions for all Covered Officials beginning on the day of ratification, ensuring that assets cannot be silently expatriated and that officials cannot flee during the build-up period. B. Commencement and Coverage 13F.2 Commencement. The provisions of this Section shall take effect on the day of certified ratification of this Amendment under Article V, and shall apply immediately to every Covered Official then holding office. 13F.3 Coverage. This Section applies to all Covered Officials, as defined in this Section, during the period of their service in any office enumerated in Section 1.1. Coverage attaches at the moment of taking office and terminates upon leaving office, except that financial monitoring may continue under Section 13F.22 for purposes of investigating pre-departure conduct. 13F.4 New Officials. Any person taking office in a Section 1.1 position after ratification shall be informed of the requirements of this Section as part of their oath of office procedures, and shall acknowledge understanding of the Section's requirements in writing, filed upon the Franklin Ledger. Taking the oath of office shall constitute consent to the monitoring and travel restrictions of this Section. C. Financial Monitoring Requirements 13F.5 Enhanced Transaction Reporting. All transactions over ten thousand dollars ($10,000) in any Covered Account shall be reported to Treasury within twenty-four (24) hours of the transaction. This threshold may be adjusted for inflation by the Authority through Liberty Bell Initiative, but shall not be raised to reduce monitoring effectiveness. 13F.6 Cryptocurrency and Digital Asset Monitoring. All cryptocurrency and digital asset transactions by Covered Officials shall be reported to Treasury regardless of amount, through enhanced reporting obligations imposed on domestic and foreign cryptocurrency exchanges, wallets, and transfer services subject to United States jurisdiction. Covered Officials shall disclose to Treasury all cryptocurrency wallet addresses under their control within thirty (30) days of ratification or upon taking office, whichever is later. 13F.7 Asset Conversion Monitoring. Any conversion of financial assets into physical stores of value — including but not limited to gold, precious metals, precious stones, art, collectibles, or similar assets — above a cumulative threshold of ten thousand dollars ($10,000) over any thirty (30) day period shall be reported to Treasury. 13F.8 International Wire Transfer Pre-Approval. All international wire transfers, international transfers through money service businesses, and international cryptocurrency transfers by

Covered Officials shall require pre-approval by Treasury. Pre-approval shall be granted routinely for transactions with a clearly documented legitimate purpose (for example: mortgage payments on previously-disclosed foreign property; support of previously-disclosed foreign family members; fulfillment of previously-existing legal obligations). Pre-approval shall be denied or subject to enhanced review for transactions lacking clear legitimate purpose. 13F.9 Family Member Transfer Review. Transfers above a cumulative threshold of fifty thousand dollars ($50,000) in any twelve (12) month period from a Covered Official to any family member (spouse, child, parent, sibling, or in-law, whether or not resident in the United States) shall trigger automatic Treasury review for evidence of asset expatriation or structured avoidance. 13F.10 Enhanced Bank Reporting. United States financial institutions holding Covered Accounts shall implement enhanced reporting obligations, including but not limited to: real-time flagging of wire transfers, suspicious activity reports (SARs) triggered at reduced thresholds for Covered Officials, annual account statements transmitted to Treasury, and immediate reporting of account closure or substantial balance reduction. 13F.11 Franklin Ledger Publication. Aggregate financial data (not individual transactions, to protect privacy) shall be published upon the Franklin Ledger quarterly, including: number of Covered Officials subject to Enhanced Transaction Reporting; number of flagged transactions; number of Treasury investigations opened; number of travel violations; and enforcement actions taken. Individual transaction data shall remain confidential unless released as part of prosecution or Authority-authorized disclosure. D. International Travel Restrictions 13F.12 Phased Travel Framework. The travel restrictions of this Section shall operate in two distinct phases, recognizing the difference between the acute risk of the build-up period and the steady-state risk profile of ongoing federal service. Both phases apply uniformly to all Covered Officials, present and future, throughout the period of their service in any Section 1.1 office.

13F.12.1 Heightened Risk Period — Definition. The Heightened Risk Period shall commence on the day of certified ratification of this Amendment and shall terminate upon the latest of: (a) certification of the Inaugural Referendum result under Section 19A (whether the Referendum passes or fails); (b) swearing-in of any new Federal Government elected through an Emergency Election resulting from a successful Inaugural Referendum; or (c) the operational readiness certification of the full Authority and Watchdog Tribunal under Section 19. The Heightened Risk Period shall also reactivate automatically during any Petition Period (from the moment a Petition under Section 3 is certified through the swearing-in of any resulting new government) and during any period when the Watchdog Tribunal has formally declared a Constitutional Integrity Emergency under Section 21. 13F.12.2 Heightened Risk Period — Absolute Prohibition. During the Heightened Risk Period, no Covered Official shall engage in International Travel. This prohibition is absolute and admits no exceptions for: (a) Official diplomatic travel (which shall be conducted through envoys, representatives, or virtual diplomacy while the Official remains in the United States); (b) Personal or family travel, including weddings, funerals, births, medical needs, religious pilgrimages, or any other personal purpose; (c) Business or professional travel unrelated to federal service; (d) Educational, cultural, or recreational travel; (e) Any other purpose whatsoever. If a Covered Official wishes to engage in International Travel during the Heightened Risk Period, they may do so only by first resigning from their office pursuant to Section 13F.16. 13F.12.3 Steady-State Period — Definition. The Steady-State Period shall be any period that is not a Heightened Risk Period. During the Steady-State Period, two distinct travel regimes shall apply based on the category of the Covered Official: (a) Ratification-Era Officials. Any Covered Official who held a Section 1.1 position at the moment of certified ratification of this Amendment, or who was elected or appointed to a Section 1.1 position between ratification and the conclusion of the first post-Ratification general federal election cycle, shall remain subject to the Liberty Bell approval process of Section 13F.12.4 for the full duration of their service. This category sunsets naturally as those Officials leave office; no Official shall be a Ratification-Era Official if they take office after the first full general federal election cycle has concluded following Ratification; and (b) Post-Amendment Officials. Any Covered Official who takes a Section 1.1 position after the conclusion of the first post-Ratification general federal election cycle, or who is elected in an Emergency Election under Section 7 following any successful No Confidence Referendum, shall be governed by the Ledger Pre-Disclosure regime of Section 13F.12.3.1 rather than the Liberty Bell approval process. The People, in ratifying this Amendment, recognize that future officials elected under the Amendment's full accountability framework — including removal by the Reclamation mechanism itself — need not be subject to case-by-case travel approval, but must remain transparent in their travel through continuous public disclosure. 13F.12.3.1 Ledger Pre-Disclosure Regime for Post-Amendment Officials. Post-Amendment Officials, as defined in Section 13F.12.3(b), shall enjoy International Travel rights subject to the Ledger Pre-Disclosure framework of this subsection. No prior approval shall be required; the Travel

Division shall not have veto authority over any particular trip; and the passport shall remain in the Official's possession during their service. The framework operates through transparency, pre-departure public disclosure, and post-travel accountability, enforced by the Reclamation mechanism itself as the ultimate accountability check. 13F.12.3.2 Pre-Disclosure Requirements. No less than fourteen (14) days before any proposed International Travel, a Post-Amendment Official shall publish upon the Franklin Ledger a complete Trip Disclosure including: (a) Destination. The specific destination or destinations, including all planned stops, transit countries, and the precise duration of presence in each jurisdiction; (b) Dates. The full itinerary with dates of departure, arrival at each destination, movement between destinations, and return to the United States; (c) Stated Purpose. The specific purpose of travel, categorized as official diplomatic, personal, family, medical, religious, educational, business, or recreational, with narrative description sufficient to convey the nature of the trip; (d) Persons Met. The full name, title, organizational affiliation, and nationality of every person the Official intends to meet with during the trip, including foreign officials, foreign business executives, private citizens, family members, and any advisors or representatives accompanying the Official; (e) Agenda. A substantive agenda for every meeting, call, or formal engagement, disclosed with specificity sufficient for citizens to understand what matters will be discussed. General statements ("bilateral relations" or "family matters") shall not satisfy this requirement; agendas shall identify specific topics, deliverables, or purposes; (f) Complete Financial Disclosure. The total expected cost of the trip and the allocation among: personal funds of the Official; federal funds (with specific appropriation identified); funds provided by the destination government or host entity; funds provided by any foreign person or entity; funds provided by any United States-based person or entity not a federal agency; and any other source. Separate line items shall include: transportation (flights, ground transport, private aviation); lodging; meals and hospitality; security; staff travel; gifts to be given or received; and any other category over one thousand dollars ($1,000);

(g) Security Arrangements. The general nature of security arrangements for the trip, including whether United States security personnel will accompany the Official (without disclosing specific personnel, routes, or protocols that would compromise security); and (h) Sworn Attestation. An attestation under penalty of perjury that the disclosure is complete and accurate, that no material fact has been omitted, and that the travel is not intended for any purpose prohibited by this Amendment including asset expatriation, accountability evasion, or coordination with prohibited foreign actors. 13F.12.3.3 Post-Trip Financial Reconciliation. Within fourteen (14) days of return from any International Trip, a Post-Amendment Official shall publish upon the Franklin Ledger a Post-Trip Reconciliation documenting: (a) actual costs incurred in each category disclosed under Section 13F.12.3.2(f), with any variance from the pre-disclosure explained; (b) any meetings held that were not disclosed in the original Trip Disclosure, with explanation; (c) any gifts received during the trip and their disposition under ethics rules; (d) any commitments, agreements, or understandings reached during the trip that bear on federal policy or official duties; and (e) any material deviation from the pre-disclosed agenda or itinerary. Failure to file a Post-Trip Reconciliation within the fourteen-day window shall itself constitute a disclosure violation under Section 13F.17. 13F.12.3.4 Passport Retention and Border Flagging. Post-Amendment Officials shall retain possession of their passports throughout service in a Section 1.1 position. However, upon taking office, the passport shall be flagged in the Department of State, the Department of Homeland Security, the Transportation Security Administration, and the United States Customs and Border Protection systems for real-time verification of international departures against filed Trip Disclosures. Any attempted international departure shall be subject to the following automated process at the exit point: (a) If the departure matches a validly filed and current Trip Disclosure under Section 13F.12.3.2 (correct date, destination, and identity), the departure shall proceed routinely without interference; (b) If no Trip Disclosure is on file, or the disclosure has expired (travel date passed without departure), or the destination does not match the disclosure, the departure shall be automatically flagged and reported in real time to the Watchdog Tribunal Travel Division and to the Hamilton Contingent Prosecution Division, with the Official permitted to proceed only after immediate emergency verification or filing of a same-day disclosure meeting the requirements of Section 13F.12.3.5; (c) If the Trip Disclosure has been filed but the required fourteen (14) day pre-disclosure period has not elapsed, the departure shall trigger automated inquiry by the Travel Division within seventy-two (72) hours regarding the urgency that justified accelerated travel;

(d) All flagged departures shall be recorded permanently upon the Ledger, whether subsequently resolved as routine, emergency, or violation; (e) The flagging system shall operate automatically and in real time, with no discretion vested in any individual officer at the point of departure other than the ministerial function of verifying compliance with the filed disclosure. 13F.12.3.5 Emergency Travel Exception. Where genuine emergency prevents compliance with the fourteen-day pre-disclosure requirement (immediate family member facing imminent death or grave medical crisis abroad; the Official's own urgent medical need unavailable in the United States; verified national security emergency requiring the Official's presence abroad), the Official may depart upon filing an Emergency Trip Disclosure containing the full information required by Section 13F.12.3.2, with narrative explanation of the emergency circumstance sufficient to justify the expedited timeline. Emergency Trip Disclosures shall be filed no later than the moment of departure and shall be flagged on the Ledger as emergency filings. Within seventy-two (72) hours of the Official's return, the Travel Division shall conduct post-hoc review of the asserted emergency and publish findings on the Ledger. Repeated or pretextual invocation of emergency filings shall be treated as a disclosure violation under Section 13F.17 and may be referred to the Hamilton Contingent for investigation of Section 13 interference. 13F.12.3.6 Travel Division Oversight, Not Approval. The Watchdog Tribunal Travel Division's role with respect to Post-Amendment Officials shall be supervisory and investigative rather than approval-based. The Travel Division shall: (a) maintain the Trip Disclosure system on the Franklin Ledger; (b) conduct pattern analysis of filed disclosures to detect possible misconduct; (c) investigate specific trips where credible evidence suggests misconduct; (d) publish quarterly reports on the Ledger summarizing travel patterns, notable disclosures, emergency invocations, and any investigations opened; (e) refer suspected violations to the Hamilton Contingent Prosecution Division for enforcement; and (f) recommend to the Authority whether any particular Official's conduct warrants escalation to Liberty Bell approval requirements under Section 13F.12.3.7. The Travel Division shall not deny, delay, or condition any particular trip of a Post-Amendment Official unless the escalation procedures of Section 13F.12.3.7 have been invoked. 13F.12.3.7 Escalation to Liberty Bell Approval. The Authority, through Liberty Bell Initiative and upon recommendation of the Travel Division, may order that a specific Post-Amendment Official be subject to the full Liberty Bell approval process of Section 13F.12.4 for all future travel upon finding by clear and convincing evidence one or more of the following: (a) the Official has materially falsified or omitted information in a Trip Disclosure or Post-Trip Reconciliation; (b) the Official has engaged in pretextual emergency filings; (c) the Official has been the subject of a certified Petition under Section 3 not yet resolved; (d) the Official is the subject of an active Hamilton Contingent investigation involving foreign financial ties, asset expatriation, or coordination with hostile foreign powers; or (e) the Official has otherwise engaged in conduct inconsistent with the accountability obligations of federal office such that pre-disclosure alone is insufficient to protect the constitutional order. An escalation order shall be published upon the Ledger with specific reasoning, shall be subject to periodic review every one hundred eighty (180) days, and shall be terminated automatically upon resolution of the underlying grounds. 13F.12.3.8 Public Access and Permanence. All Trip Disclosures, Post-Trip Reconciliations, Emergency Trip Disclosures, Travel Division findings, and Authority escalation orders shall be publicly visible upon the Franklin Ledger in real time and in perpetuity. No Official shall have any right to have such disclosures redacted, sealed, or removed from the Ledger after leaving office. The People's right to know when, where, why, and with whom their officials travel is absolute and permanent; it is not subject to any after-the-fact claim of privacy, embarrassment, or political sensitivity. Redaction shall be permitted only for specific security information (personal security officer identities, specific travel routes, secure facility locations) whose disclosure would compromise security, certified as such by the Travel Division with narrow reasoning published alongside the redacted disclosure. 13F.12.3.9 Foundational Trust. The framework of this Section rests on a foundational trust: that officials elected under the full operation of this Amendment, knowing that the People may remove them by Reclamation at any time, will conduct themselves honorably; that transparency is a stronger accountability tool than restriction; and that the People are capable of judging their officials' conduct when given the information to do so. Officials who betray this trust through concealment, misuse of travel, or coordination with hostile foreign actors face: immediate escalation to Liberty Bell approval under Section 13F.12.3.7; full Section 13 interference prosecution; and the ever-present possibility of Reclamation by the People whose trust they have violated. This framework is not permissive; it is accountable in a different way — through the People's direct oversight rather than through case-by-case approval by intermediate bodies. D.1. National Emergency Travel Framework 13F.12.3.10 Purpose. This subheader establishes a narrow exception to the fourteen (14) day pre-disclosure requirement of Section 13F.12.3.2 for genuine national-level emergencies that require immediate international travel by a Covered Official. Recognizing that peace talks, hostage negotiations, natural disasters affecting United States citizens abroad, and crises in allied nations may demand response measured in hours rather than weeks, this framework permits expedited travel subject to mandatory real-time Watchdog oversight. This exception is not a loophole; it is a tightly constrained carve-out with stronger oversight than ordinary travel, not weaker.

13F.12.3.11 Qualifying Emergencies. National-Emergency Travel under this subheader may be invoked only for: (a) Peace Talks — Active, time-sensitive diplomatic negotiations to prevent, end, or de-escalate armed conflict, where the presence of a specific United States Official is material to the negotiation and where delay of fourteen (14) days would materially prejudice the outcome; (b) Hostage Negotiations — Negotiation for the release of United States citizens or nationals held by foreign governments, foreign non-state actors, or criminal organizations, where in-person participation is required by the counterparty or by the circumstances of the negotiation; (c) Natural Disasters Affecting United States Citizens Abroad — Earthquakes, tsunamis, volcanic eruptions, pandemics, severe weather events, or similar natural catastrophes occurring in foreign jurisdictions that have killed, injured, stranded, or otherwise placed United States citizens at serious risk, where an Official's presence would materially aid coordination of emergency response, evacuation, or humanitarian assistance; and (d) Allied Nation in Crisis — Imminent or ongoing threats to a formal treaty ally of the United States, including military attack by a third party, coup or attempted coup, severe political instability, or catastrophic infrastructure failure, where the United States has made a public commitment to support that ally and where an Official's in-person presence would materially affect the response. 13F.12.3.12 Invocation — Who May Invoke. Invocation of National-Emergency Travel shall be limited to the Covered Official who will actually travel, and only where that Official's specific role makes their presence material to the qualifying emergency. The following Covered Officials may invoke for the qualifying emergencies most closely tied to their constitutional role: (a) The President — any qualifying emergency; (b) The Vice President — any qualifying emergency where the President is unable to travel or where both branches of the executive require representation; (c) The Speaker of the House, the Senate Majority Leader, the Senate Minority Leader, and the House Minority Leader — legislative emergencies, bipartisan diplomatic delegations, or representation in commemorative emergency responses; (d) Members of Congress serving on the Senate Foreign Relations Committee, the House Foreign Affairs Committee, the Senate Armed Services Committee, the House Armed Services Committee, or the Intelligence Committees of either chamber — emergencies within their committee jurisdiction where the President or Vice President have delegated or requested their specific participation; and (e) Supreme Court Justices — only in extremely narrow circumstances involving judicial participation in international legal emergencies (such as emergency testimony before international tribunals where required), subject to the Travel Division's immediate consultation. (f) No Member of Congress, Justice, or other Covered Official may invoke National-Emergency Travel for generalized foreign policy engagement, for fact-finding delegations of ordinary scope, or for ceremonial participation. The qualifying emergency must be genuine and the Official's specific presence must be material. 13F.12.3.13 Approval Mechanism — Expedited Two-Body Concurrence. National-Emergency Travel shall require, before departure: (a) Declaration of emergency by the invoking Official, specifying which category under Section 13F.12.3.11 applies and why in-person presence is material; (b) Concurrence of not fewer than two (2) of the three Authority bodies, expressed through majority votes of their respective memberships within twenty-four (24) hours of declaration. The two bodies shall act independently without deliberation between bodies until their separate votes are recorded. In the rare case where only one Authority body can physically convene within twenty-four (24) hours, the emergency may proceed on the single concurrence with mandatory Liberty Bell retroactive ratification within seventy-two (72) hours of return; absent retroactive ratification, the travel shall be treated as unauthorized under Section 13F.17.2 and all consequences shall follow; (c) Immediate Ledger posting at the moment of declaration, including: the qualifying emergency category; the Official's identity; the destination; the expected duration; the specific counterparts or persons to be met with; the stated purpose; and the names of the two Watchdog Tribunal escorts assigned under Section 13F.12.3.14. Intelligence-sensitive specifics (precise itineraries, security arrangements, identities of sources or assets) may be held in sealed Ledger storage under Academic Integrity Commission cryptographic custody, to be released to public view upon the Official's safe return under the procedures of Section 13F.12.3.17; (d) The Ledger posting shall be updated in real time as the emergency proceeds, with permanent recordation of all decisions, concurrences, and dissents. 13F.12.3.14 Watchdog Escort — Requirement and Composition. Every National-Emergency Trip shall be accompanied by two (2) Watchdog Tribunal members serving as Escorts, selected as follows: (a) The Travel Division shall maintain a pre-qualified Emergency Escort Roster drawn from Watchdog Tribunal members who have affirmatively opted in and who possess relevant qualifications, including but not limited to: language capability relevant to likely destinations; regional or cultural expertise; prior diplomatic, military, legal, medical, or humanitarian experience relevant to the categories of qualifying emergency; and the physical health and availability to travel on short notice; (b) Roster members shall complete an Academic Integrity Commission-administered training program covering diplomatic protocol, classified information handling, conflict zone safety, and the specific oversight responsibilities of the Escort role. Training shall be renewed every two (2) years; (c) Upon declaration of a National Emergency, the Travel Division shall select two (2) Escorts by randomized lottery from the subset of the Emergency Escort Roster whose qualifications match the emergency circumstances (by destination region, expected subject matter, or language). In cases of genuine time pressure where the lottery cannot be conducted, the Travel Division may assign the two most recently qualified and available Escorts, with Ledger documentation of the exigency; (d) Escorts shall not be subject to veto by the traveling Official. An Official who declines to travel with the assigned Escorts shall thereby decline the National-Emergency Travel invocation, and shall be subject to the ordinary requirements of Section 13F.12.3.2 including the fourteen-day pre-disclosure window. 13F.12.3.15 Watchdog Escort — Access and Role. The two Escorts shall jointly exercise the following: (a) Full Access. The Escorts shall have full physical access to every meeting, briefing, negotiation session, social gathering, and diplomatic engagement attended by the traveling Official for the duration of the trip, including meetings classified at any level. Foreign counterparts shall be informed in advance that the Escorts are present as mandatory United States constitutional monitors and that their presence is a condition of the Official's travel; (b) Continuous Monitoring. The Escorts shall divide their duties so that at least one Escort is present with the Official at all times during the trip except for legitimate personal functions. They shall coordinate rest periods so continuous coverage is maintained; (c) Documentary Role Only. The Escorts shall not have authority to veto, delay, interrupt, or overrule any decision, statement, agreement, or action of the traveling Official during the trip. Their role is strictly documentary: to observe, record, and later report on the conduct of the trip; (d) Note-Taking and Recording. The Escorts shall maintain contemporaneous notes of all substantive events, meetings, and communications during the trip, in secure format provided by the Academic Integrity Commission. Audio or video recording shall be permitted where consistent with the sensitivity of the setting and the consent requirements of the host jurisdiction; (e) Direct Communication. The Escorts shall have a secure line of communication to the Watchdog Tribunal and to the Authority for emergency consultation, independent of any communication channels controlled by the traveling Official or their staff. 13F.12.3.16 Watchdog Escort — Secrecy Oath and Obligations. Before departure, each Escort shall take an enhanced constitutional oath binding them to: (a) Absolute non-disclosure of classified information witnessed during the trip, beyond what appears in sanitized reports released under Section 13F.12.3.17. Unauthorized disclosure of classified information shall be a federal felony punishable by not less than twenty (20) years imprisonment and permanent federal office bar, with no pardon possible. This penalty shall apply for life; (b) Absolute non-disclosure of diplomatic details whose release would compromise ongoing United States interests, even where not formally classified. This non-disclosure obligation shall extend to family members, personal advisors, journalists, academics, and any other person outside the Watchdog Tribunal; (c) Faithful performance of the documentary role, including complete and accurate contemporaneous notes free from deliberate omission; (d) Full cooperation with any subsequent Watchdog Tribunal investigation, Hamilton Contingent proceeding, or Authority review arising from the trip; (e) No communication with the traveling Official regarding the content of the Escort's notes, observations, or intended report before the report is filed with the Watchdog Tribunal. The Escort and the Official may communicate about logistics and immediate trip operations but shall not engage in substantive discussion of the Escort's forthcoming findings. This separation protects the integrity of the documentary function; and (f) No personal benefit, gift, hospitality, or honorarium received from any foreign person, entity, or government during or in connection with the trip, beyond the ordinary accommodations provided for diplomatic delegations. Any offered benefits shall be refused or, where refusal is diplomatically impossible, immediately reported to the Watchdog Tribunal upon return and publicly disclosed on the Ledger. 13F.12.3.17 Sanitized Report and Ledger Publication. Within thirty (30) days of the Official's return from a National-Emergency Trip: (a) The two Escorts shall jointly prepare and file with the Watchdog Tribunal and the Academic Integrity Commission a full report documenting the conduct of the trip, including all meetings attended, substantive matters discussed, decisions made, agreements reached, and any observations relevant to the constitutional conduct of the traveling Official. This full report shall remain in secure Academic Integrity Commission custody and shall be available to the Watchdog Tribunal, the Authority, and the Hamilton Contingent Prosecution Division upon request relating to any investigation;

(b) The Academic Integrity Commission, in consultation with relevant intelligence, diplomatic, and security authorities, shall prepare a Sanitized Public Report derived from the full report, redacting only that information whose public disclosure would compromise ongoing national security, active negotiations, confidential sources or methods, or the safety of any person. The Commission shall apply the narrowest possible redactions consistent with these interests and shall err in favor of public disclosure where close calls arise. The Sanitized Public Report shall be published on the Franklin Ledger within sixty (60) days of the Official's return; (c) The Sanitized Public Report shall include at minimum: the qualifying emergency and its resolution; the Official's conduct in fulfilling the stated purpose; the identities of foreign officials met with (where not classified); substantive policy commitments or agreements reached; financial costs incurred and funding sources; and any observations by the Escorts bearing on the Official's accountability under this Amendment; (d) Redactions shall themselves be identified by category in the Sanitized Public Report (for example, "Section X redacted under Academic Integrity Commission sources-and-methods protection"), so that the public knows what categories of information have been withheld even while the specific contents remain classified; (e) The full unredacted report shall be automatically declassified and released to the public upon the earliest of: (i) ten (10) years after the date of the trip; (ii) resolution of the ongoing interest protected by the redaction, as certified by the Academic Integrity Commission; or (iii) any Sunset Review vote under Section 18 that includes a citizen initiative to release specific historical reports; and (f) The Watchdog Tribunal shall review the Sanitized Public Report and, if the Escorts' observations raise concerns regarding the Official's conduct, may initiate investigation, recommend escalation to Liberty Bell approval under Section 13F.12.3.7, refer the matter to the Hamilton Contingent Prosecution Division, or take any other appropriate action under its general authority. 13F.12.3.18 Escort Whistleblower Framework. Recognizing that Watchdog Escorts occupy a uniquely sensitive position — witnessing private meetings, financial arrangements, and diplomatic exchanges that ordinary oversight cannot reach — this Section establishes a dedicated whistleblower framework for Escorts whose observations during or after a trip reveal potential corruption, constitutional violations, or other misconduct by the traveling Official, accompanying federal personnel, or foreign actors engaged with them. 13F.12.3.19 Mid-Trip Secure Channel. Throughout the duration of any National-Emergency Trip, each Escort shall have access to an independent, encrypted, secure channel of communication directly to the Watchdog Tribunal leadership, separate from any communication system controlled by the traveling Official, their staff, the State Department, or any intelligence agency. The channel shall be technically maintained by the

Academic Integrity Commission, shall not be subject to interception or monitoring by any party other than the Tribunal, and shall be accessible by each Escort independently at any moment during the trip. If an Escort observes conduct that may constitute Section 13 interference, Section 13A corruption, Section 22 foreign interference, or any other serious violation of this Amendment, the Escort may transmit a Mid-Trip Report through this channel at any time. 13F.12.3.20 Tribunal Response to Mid-Trip Report. Upon receipt of a Mid-Trip Report from an Escort, the Watchdog Tribunal shall, within twenty-four (24) hours, determine and execute one of the following responses: (a) Document and Continue. Where the reported observation is concerning but does not require immediate intervention (evidence preservation, pattern development, or information of value for post-trip investigation), the Tribunal may direct the Escort to continue monitoring and documenting while the trip proceeds; (b) Enhanced Real-Time Coordination. The Tribunal may direct the Escort to intensify documentation, engage the second Escort in coordinated observation, and provide continuous updates while the trip proceeds; (c) Recall Official. Where the reported conduct is so serious that continuation of the trip would materially harm the constitutional order or constitute active ongoing crime, the Tribunal may recommend to the Authority, through Liberty Bell Initiative on an expedited twelve (12) hour timeline, the immediate recall of the Official. Upon Liberty Bell concurrence, the Tribunal shall direct the Escorts to communicate the recall to the Official and to facilitate immediate return; (d) Emergency Relief. In cases of threat to the Escort's own safety, active crime being committed, or imminent material harm, the Tribunal may activate any of the safety protocols of Sections 13F.12.3.22 through 13F.12.3.24 without waiting for Liberty Bell deliberation; (e) Decision and reasoning recorded. Every Tribunal response to a Mid-Trip Report shall be recorded in contemporaneous secure documentation, with full public reasoning posted to the Franklin Ledger upon the trip's conclusion and completion of any related investigation. 13F.12.3.21 Escort Whistleblower Protections — Full Section 13B.16 Application. Any Escort who submits a Mid-Trip Report, a post-trip Protected Disclosure, or other good-faith report of potential violations of this Amendment shall be entitled to the full Protected Whistleblower Status established under Section 13B.16, including: complete confidentiality of identity to the maximum extent consistent with due process; federal protection from any form of retaliation, including termination from Tribunal service, demotion, reassignment, reduction of benefits, harassment, surveillance, or intimidation; federal legal representation at no cost; federal relocation and identity protection if safety threats arise; continued employment or equivalent compensation for a period of not less than five (5) years at the whistleblower's most recent compensation level if Tribunal service ends for

any reason connected with the disclosure; and criminal prosecution of any person who retaliates under Section 13 interference penalties. The rewards schedule of Section 13B.17 shall apply where Escort disclosure leads to criminal conviction, civil recovery, or asset forfeiture. 13F.12.3.22 Safety Threats During Trip — Perpetrator Penalties. The existing twenty (20) year minimum penalty of Section 13F.12.3.16 for unauthorized disclosure of classified information by an Escort shall be mirrored by an equivalent penalty on any person — domestic or foreign — who threatens, bribes, blackmails, coerces, intimidates, or attempts to corrupt any Escort during or in connection with a National-Emergency Trip. Such conduct shall be a federal felony punishable by not less than twenty (20) years imprisonment, with no pardon, commutation, or clemency possible. Where the perpetrator is a United States Official, the penalties of Section 13E (Usurpation-equivalent) shall apply. Where the perpetrator is a foreign actor, the matter shall be referred to the State Department for diplomatic consequences under Section 22, with the foreign person or entity permanently banned from United States jurisdictions. 13F.12.3.23 Safety Threats During Trip — Emergency Evacuation. Where an Escort's safety is actively threatened during a trip — by the traveling Official, by foreign actors, by accompanying personnel, or by any third party — the Escort may invoke Emergency Evacuation by communication through the secure channel of Section 13F.12.3.19 or by direct contact with the nearest United States Embassy or Consulate. Upon invocation: (a) The Watchdog Tribunal shall immediately notify the Department of State, which shall coordinate the Escort's safe extraction from the foreign jurisdiction, including but not limited to emergency visa exit procedures, chartered transport, or diplomatic escort to a secure location; (b) The Watchdog Tribunal shall simultaneously recommend to the Authority on expedited twelve (12) hour timeline the cancellation of the remainder of the trip and the recall of the traveling Official. The trip shall be treated as prematurely terminated, with the Official required to file a post-termination reconciliation on the Ledger within seven (7) days of their return; (c) Cancellation of the trip pursuant to Emergency Evacuation shall not constitute a disciplinary consequence for the Official absent evidence that the Official caused or contributed to the threat. Where the Official is found to have caused or knowingly tolerated the threat, full Section 13 and Section 13F.17 penalties shall apply; (d) Emergency Evacuation invocation shall never be treated as an Escort failure, misconduct, or grounds for removal from the Emergency Escort Roster. Escorts are expected to invoke evacuation when safety is genuinely at risk, and the system shall support their judgment. 13F.12.3.24 Refusal to Continue Participation — Trip Must Abort. An Escort who, in the course of a trip, witnesses conduct that constitutes an active crime under this

Amendment or under federal criminal law (including active bribery, espionage, or foreign agent coordination in progress), shall have the right to refuse continued participation in the trip and to notify the Watchdog Tribunal of their refusal through the secure channel of Section 13F.12.3.19. Upon such refusal: (a) The Watchdog Tribunal shall, within six (6) hours, determine whether the refusal is supported by credible observation of active crime; (b) Where credible, the Tribunal shall direct the traveling Official to abort the trip and return to the United States immediately. Because both Escorts must be present for the trip's continuation under Section 13F.12.3.15, refusal by either Escort shall render the trip's continuation impossible under this Amendment. Any attempt by the Official to continue the trip over the Escort's refusal shall constitute travel without authorized Watchdog oversight and shall trigger the unauthorized travel penalties of Section 13F.17; (c) The refusing Escort shall not be removed, censured, or otherwise penalized for the refusal, provided the refusal was made in good faith based on credible observation. Good-faith refusal is presumed absent clear evidence of bad faith, and the burden of showing bad faith rests entirely on the Watchdog Tribunal through procedures respecting the Escort's due process; (d) Where the Tribunal determines the refusal was made in bad faith (for example, where an Escort falsely reports active crime to disrupt legitimate travel), the Escort shall be subject to removal from the Emergency Escort Roster and from the Tribunal itself, and may face prosecution under Section 13 for interference with legitimate government operation. Such determinations shall require clear and convincing evidence and shall be subject to Authority review through Liberty Bell Initiative. 13F.12.3.25 Protected Scope — Everything Witnessed Plus Pattern Evidence. The whistleblower protections of this subheader extend to the Escort's good-faith reports concerning: (a) the conduct of the traveling Official during or in connection with the trip; (b) the conduct of any federal personnel, contractors, or other persons accompanying the Official; (c) the conduct of foreign officials, foreign nationals, or foreign entities engaged with the Official during the trip; (d) systemic issues or patterns of misconduct observed during the trip; and (e) pattern evidence drawn from the Escort's experience on other

National-Emergency Trips, where the Escort observes that similar concerning patterns of conduct recur across multiple trips involving the same or different Officials. Escorts are not required to confine their reports to a single trip; their accumulated observational expertise across multiple Escort assignments is a resource that this Amendment values and protects. 13F.12.3.26 Safeguard Against Frivolous Reports. While this Section establishes robust whistleblower protections, Escorts who knowingly make false reports, or who abuse the whistleblower channel to disrupt legitimate government operations, shall not be protected. Determinations of bad faith shall require clear and convincing evidence, shall follow due process for the accused Escort, and shall be reviewable by the Authority through Liberty Bell Initiative. Good-faith reports that ultimately prove inaccurate shall not constitute bad faith; only knowing falsity or reckless disregard for truth shall strip whistleblower protection. This safeguard is narrow and shall not be invoked to retaliate against Escorts who simply proved wrong, nor to deter Escorts from future reports. D.2. Ratification-Era Steady-State Travel 13F.12.4 Steady-State Period — Ratification-Era Official Liberty Bell Approval Required. During the Steady-State Period, any proposed International Travel by a Ratification-Era Official as defined in Section 13F.12.3(a) shall require prior approval of the Authority through Liberty Bell Initiative (concurrence of all three bodies), publicly reasoned and recorded upon the Ledger before travel commences. Approval requests shall be submitted no less than fourteen (14) days before proposed travel, except in cases of genuine emergency under Section 13F.12.7. Each request shall include: (a) The specific destination or destinations, including all planned stops and transit countries; (b) The dates of departure and return, and a detailed daily itinerary; (c) The stated purpose of travel (official diplomatic, personal/family, medical, religious, educational, or other, specifically identified); (d) All persons accompanying or meeting with the Official during travel, including any foreign officials, business associates, or family members; (e) Proposed financial arrangements for the travel, including who is paying for flights, lodging, meals, and any other expenses; (f) A sworn attestation that the travel is not for the purpose of asset expatriation, evasion of accountability proceedings, coordination with foreign interference under Section 22, or any other purpose prohibited by this Amendment; (g) Consent to continuous electronic monitoring during travel pursuant to Section 13F.12.6; and (h) Any additional information the Watchdog Tribunal Travel Division reasonably requests to evaluate risk. 13F.12.5 Steady-State Period — Approval Criteria. The Authority, advised by the Watchdog Tribunal Travel Division, shall evaluate each request against the following criteria. Approval shall be denied if any single criterion is not satisfied: (a) Legitimate Purpose. The travel serves a legitimate purpose — personal, family, medical, religious, educational, or official — that is not a pretext for a prohibited purpose under Section 13F.12.4(f);

(b) Destination Risk. The destination is not a jurisdiction identified by the Treasury Financial Crimes Enforcement Network as a high-risk jurisdiction for money laundering, tax evasion, or sanctions evasion, and is not a jurisdiction with which the United States has no extradition treaty, unless the compelling personal circumstances justify the elevated risk; (c) Hostile Foreign Power. The destination is not under the control of a foreign power then designated as hostile to the United States under Section 22, and no meetings are planned with officials or agents of any such power; (d) Financial Integrity. The financial arrangements do not suggest asset expatriation or undisclosed third-party funding; (e) Accountability Posture. The Covered Official is not then the subject of a pending Section 13 investigation, Section 3 Petition, Section 21 Tribunal proceeding, or any other accountability matter of which the Authority has knowledge; and (f) Virtual Alternative. No equivalent legitimate purpose can be accomplished without International Travel through virtual means, written communication, or use of envoys or representatives. 13F.12.6 Steady-State Period — Monitoring During Approved Travel. Every approved International Trip shall be subject to continuous electronic monitoring for the duration of travel, including: (a) real-time geolocation tracking via an official Authority-issued device that the Covered Official shall carry at all times during travel; (b) secure line-of-communication with the Watchdog Tribunal Travel Division for mandatory daily check-ins; (c) pre-approval for any deviation from the approved itinerary; (d) automatic financial transaction review for any expenditure over one thousand dollars ($1,000) during travel; and (e) photographic documentation of all meetings with foreign nationals, submitted to the Watchdog Tribunal Travel Division within seventy-two (72) hours of return. 13F.12.7 Steady-State Period — Emergency Exception. In cases of genuine emergency involving imminent threat to life (immediate family member facing imminent death or grave medical crisis abroad; Covered Official's own urgent medical need unavailable in the United States), expedited approval may be granted within forty-eight (48) hours through majority vote of the Watchdog Tribunal Travel Division, subject to post-approval ratification by Liberty Bell Initiative within seventy-two (72) hours of return. Emergency approvals shall be publicly disclosed upon the Ledger within twenty-four (24) hours of grant, with the specific emergency circumstance noted in a manner that balances transparency with privacy. Abuse of the emergency exception (invoking emergency for non-qualifying circumstances) shall be treated as an unauthorized travel violation under Section 13F.17. 13F.12.8 Steady-State Period — Public Ledger Disclosure. All approved travel shall be publicly disclosed upon the Franklin Ledger no less than seven (7) days before departure, including the destination, dates, purpose, and funding source. This disclosure shall remain permanently visible upon the Ledger even after the Official leaves office. The People have a right to know when and why their officials travel abroad. This disclosure requirement admits no exception for security or confidentiality claims; an Official who believes a trip must be kept confidential may not take that trip while serving in a Section 1.1 office. 13F.12.9 Steady-State Period — Denial and Appeal. A denied travel request may be resubmitted with modifications addressing the grounds for denial. A Covered Official may not circumvent a denial by resignation timed to permit the travel; any resignation within ninety (90) days of a denied travel request shall be presumptively suspect and trigger enhanced post-service investigation by the Hamilton Contingent Prosecution Division for potential Section 13 violations, including but not limited to asset expatriation patterns and foreign-agent contacts during the travel. 13F.13 Passport Handling — Phase-Aware and Category-Aware. Passport handling shall vary based on the phase of application and the category of Covered Official: (a) Heightened Risk Period — All Officials. During any Heightened Risk Period, every Covered Official, regardless of category, shall surrender their passport to the Authority. The passport shall remain in Authority custody continuously and shall be flagged in the Department of State and Department of Homeland Security systems to prevent departure from the United States. A non-travel identification document shall be issued in substitution; (b) Steady-State Period — Ratification-Era Officials. During the Steady-State Period, Ratification-Era Officials shall surrender their passports to Authority custody. The passport shall be released only upon Liberty Bell approval of a specific International Trip under Section 13F.12.4, shall be returned to Authority custody within seventy-two (72) hours of the Official's return from that trip, and shall bear any Authority-issued flags required for monitoring compliance; (c) Steady-State Period — Post-Amendment Officials. Post-Amendment Officials shall retain possession of their passports throughout service, subject to the Border Flagging framework of Section 13F.12.3.4. No passport surrender shall be required during steady-state conditions; accountability operates through the Ledger

Pre-Disclosure regime; and (d) Return Upon Departure from Office. In all cases, any passport held in Authority custody shall be fully returned to the Official upon departure from office, unless held pursuant to investigation or penalty under this Section, Section 13D, or Section 13F.23 (post-removal framework). 13F.14 Exit Point Coordination. The Department of Homeland Security, the Transportation Security Administration, the United States Customs and Border Protection, and other relevant departure-point authorities shall implement flagging of Covered Officials' identifying information at all international departure points (airports, seaports, land border crossings) to prevent unauthorized international

travel during service. 13F.15 Diplomatic Accommodation Via Virtual Presence. Recognizing that federal offices in Section 1.1 have international duties that historically involved travel, those duties during service shall be fulfilled through: (a) virtual participation in international meetings via secure video conference; (b) designation of career diplomatic personnel as in-person representatives; (c) hosting of foreign counterparts within the United States; and (d) other non-travel means. The Authority shall establish standard procedures for virtual diplomatic participation. 13F.16 Resignation Option. An Official who wishes to engage in International Travel may resign from their Section 1.1 office, following which the travel prohibition ceases to apply. Resignation under this subsection shall be irrevocable for the remainder of the term of office to which the Official was elected or appointed, except that the Official may stand for election in a future election subject to ordinary eligibility rules. E. Tiered Penalties for Travel Violations 13F.17 Tiered Penalty Framework. Violations of the international travel prohibition shall be categorized into four tiers based on circumstances, with escalating consequences: 13F.17.1 Tier 1 — Technical Violation. Where an Official inadvertently crosses a border (for example, a pilot error on a commercial flight that briefly enters foreign airspace, or an unplanned medical diversion), or where an Official voluntarily returns within twenty-four (24) hours of an unauthorized departure without having engaged in financial, diplomatic, or other substantive activity abroad: (a) Mandatory public disclosure of the incident on the Franklin Ledger within seventy-two (72) hours; (b) Passport hold for ninety (90) days pending investigation; (c) Section 13 interference review by the Watchdog Tribunal; (d) Potential Section 13 penalties (fifteen year minimum) if Watchdog Tribunal finds bad faith, but Tribunal may determine the violation was genuinely technical and decline further action. 13F.17.2 Tier 2 — Intentional Unauthorized Travel (Returned). Where an Official intentionally travels internationally without authorization, engages in substantive activity abroad, but subsequently returns to the United States: (a) Immediate removal from office through mechanisms available under Section 1.1 (resignation, impeachment, or, if the Official refuses to resign after finding of violation, Section 13E Forcible Removal procedures); (b) Automatic asset freeze under Section 13D.2 standards pending investigation;

(c) Full Section 13 interference prosecution with fifteen (15) year minimum sentence, lifetime bar from public office, no pardon; (d) Forfeiture of all federal pension, retirement, and benefit rights; (e) Referral to Hamilton Contingent for investigation of any conduct during unauthorized travel. 13F.17.3 Tier 3 — Attempted Flight (Intercepted). Where an Official attempts to flee the United States and is intercepted at a border, airport, seaport, or in transit, with evidence of intent not to return: (a) Immediate detention pending Hamilton Contingent prosecution; (b) Immediate asset freeze under Section 13D.2 standards; (c) Prosecution under Section 13E Usurpation-equivalent standards where the flight evidences attempt to escape accountability for prior official misconduct; (d) Life imprisonment minimum if Section 13E standards are met; (e) Permanent asset forfeiture; (f) Permanent lifetime bar from public office with no pardon, commutation, or clemency. 13F.17.4 Tier 4 — Successful Flight (Non-Return). Where an Official successfully departs the United States and does not return to face accountability: (a) Trial in absentia for all applicable offenses, including the travel violation and any underlying corruption; (b) Automatic asset forfeiture of all assets subject to United States jurisdiction; (c) Section 13E Usurpation designation applied, with treason-equivalent consequences upon any return to United States jurisdiction; (d) Diplomatic extradition efforts pursued through State Department, Hamilton Contingent International Division (if established), and treaty partners; (e) Asset tracing and recovery efforts through international banking enforcement, with assets recovered flowing to Section 13D distribution; (f) Family member accountability under Section 13D.5 and Section 13A standards if family members materially assisted the flight; (g) Permanent public designation on the Franklin Ledger as a Fugitive Official. 13F.18 Complicity Penalties. Any person who knowingly assists a Covered Official in violating the International Travel prohibition, including by providing transportation, documentation, financial support, or advance coordination, shall be subject to Section 13 interference penalties, including fifteen (15) year minimum sentence and permanent bar from public office. Airlines, private charter services, and other transportation providers that knowingly assist a Covered Official in unauthorized departure shall face corporate penalties of not less than fifty million dollars ($50,000,000) and potential loss of operating authority within the United States. F. Banking and Financial Institution Obligations 13F.19 Required Compliance. All United States financial institutions, including banks, credit unions, brokerages, investment advisers, cryptocurrency exchanges, money service businesses, and similar entities, shall comply with the monitoring and reporting requirements of this Section for all Covered Accounts. Non-compliance shall be enforced by Treasury through existing Bank Secrecy Act, USA PATRIOT Act, and related statutory authority. 13F.20 Safe Harbor for Good-Faith Compliance. Financial institutions that comply in good faith with the reporting and monitoring requirements of this Section shall be immune from civil liability arising from that compliance, including claims by Covered Officials whose accounts were reported or flagged. Good-faith compliance shall be presumed where the institution followed Treasury guidance reasonably applicable at the time of the action. 13F.21 Penalties for Non-Compliance and Active Obstruction. Financial institutions that fail to comply with reporting obligations or that actively assist Covered Officials in evading monitoring or travel restrictions shall face: (a) Failure to report: existing Bank Secrecy Act penalties, enhanced by a multiplier of not less than three (3) times ordinary penalties for Covered Official-related violations; (b) Active assistance in evasion: treatment as Section 13 interference, with corporate penalties of not less than one hundred million dollars ($100,000,000) for willful violations, criminal liability for executives and personnel with knowledge, and potential revocation of banking charter or operating authority; (c) Assisting unauthorized international fund transfers by Covered Officials: enhanced penalties as above, with additional Hamilton Contingent investigation of the institution's broader practices. G. Termination and Transition 13F.22 Termination Upon Leaving Office. The requirements of this Section shall terminate for an individual Covered Official at the moment they leave the Section 1.1 office, except that: (a) Treasury may continue monitoring pre-departure transactions for up to twelve (12) months after departure to investigate any conduct that occurred during service; (b) Passport return may be delayed by up to thirty (30) days to complete pre-departure transaction audits;

(c) Any active investigation under Section 13, 13A, 13B, 13C, 13D, or 13E shall proceed regardless of the official's departure from office; (d) Upon departure, a final financial disclosure shall be filed on the Franklin Ledger, documenting assets, accounts, and any changes during service. 13F.23 Integration with Post-No-Confidence Framework. If a No Confidence Referendum is certified during a Covered Official's service, the provisions of

Section 13D shall apply in addition to the provisions of this Section, with Section 13D.2 Automatic Asset Freeze taking effect immediately. The monitoring and travel restrictions of this Section shall continue in effect until superseded by Section 13D provisions, ensuring continuous coverage without gap. H. Post-Removal Travel Framework 13F.23.1 Application. This subheader applies to any Covered Official who has been removed from office pursuant to a successful No Confidence Referendum under Section 5, a Watchdog Tribunal removal under Section 21, a Citizen Emergency Override under Section 21.10, or any other removal mechanism of this Amendment ("Removed Official"). These provisions continue in effect notwithstanding Section 13F.22, superseding the general termination rule for officials removed through accountability mechanisms, as opposed to officials who voluntarily depart or complete their term under ordinary circumstances. 13F.23.2 Default Status — Continued Travel Prohibition. Upon removal, a Removed Official shall remain subject to the International Travel prohibition of Section 13F.12.2 (Heightened Risk Period absolute ban) indefinitely, until the Removed Official successfully completes the Travel Restoration Process established in this subheader. The passport surrendered under Section 13F.13 shall remain in Authority custody. No exception shall apply during this period; the resignation alternative under Section 13F.16 is unavailable, as the Official has already been removed. 13F.23.3 Travel Restoration Process — Availability. A Removed Official may petition for restoration of International Travel rights by submitting a complete application to the Watchdog Tribunal Travel Division. The application shall not be considered complete until every requirement of Sections 13F.23.4 and 13F.23.5 has been satisfied. No deadline applies; a Removed Official may petition at any time and may resubmit indefinitely. The burden of demonstrating fitness for restoration shall rest entirely on the Removed Official. 13F.23.4 Required Financial and Asset Disclosures. The application shall include comprehensive disclosure in each of the following categories, attested under penalty of perjury and published upon the Franklin Ledger permanently upon filing: (a) Complete financial disclosure: every asset, liability, bank account, brokerage account, retirement account, investment position, and financial instrument held individually, jointly, or beneficially, regardless of jurisdiction, valued above one hundred dollars ($100); (b) All cryptocurrency and digital asset holdings: every wallet address, exchange account, non-fungible token, decentralized finance position, and staking arrangement under the direct or beneficial control of the Removed Official, with supporting blockchain documentation sufficient to verify ownership; (c) All foreign bank accounts, foreign shell companies, foreign trusts, and foreign legal entities: any financial or ownership interest, beneficial or nominal, in any foreign entity, including trustees, beneficiaries, settlors, protectors, or fiduciaries identified by legal name and jurisdiction; (d) All real estate holdings: every residential, commercial, agricultural, recreational, or undeveloped property interest held individually, jointly, beneficially, or through any intermediate entity, domestic or foreign, with legal description, current fair market value, and any encumbrances; (e) Tax returns for the preceding ten (10) years: complete federal, state, and foreign tax returns filed by the Removed Official or jointly with any spouse, including all schedules, attachments, and amendments. Where returns were not filed, documentation of the exemption or non-filing basis; (f) All business interests and beneficial ownership positions: every corporate, partnership, limited liability company, sole proprietorship, or other business interest, including equity positions of any size, options, warrants, restricted stock, or management roles, with the nature of control and any related-party transactions disclosed; (g) All debts, loans, and financial obligations over five thousand dollars ($5,000): every debt owed by the Removed Official, including credit facilities, private loans, court judgments, tax liabilities, child support or alimony obligations, business guarantees, and any similar obligations, with creditor identity, principal, interest rate, and repayment terms; (h) Contact list of foreign officials, foreign business executives, foreign-government agents, or citizens of hostile foreign powers contacted during federal service: every foreign official, foreign business executive, foreign-government agent, or citizen of a foreign power then designated hostile under Section 22 with whom the Removed Official communicated during their federal service, with approximate dates, nature of communication, and substance of any business or policy matters discussed. Communications with naturalized United States citizens and ordinary foreign constituents are excluded from this disclosure requirement; (i) All gifts received over five hundred dollars ($500) during federal service: every gift, gratuity, meal, travel accommodation, hospitality benefit, or similar transfer of value, with giver identity, approximate value, and circumstances of receipt, regardless of whether previously disclosed under other ethics provisions; and

(j) Complete itinerary of every trip taken during federal service: every international trip, domestic trip, or official travel engaged in during the Removed Official's federal service, with dates, destinations, purpose, and funding source, regardless of whether previously recorded on the Ledger. 13F.23.5 Required Accountability Conditions. The application shall additionally include: (a) Sworn attestation under penalty of perjury that no foreign assets, income, or financial interests are hidden, undisclosed, beneficially held through intermediaries not identified in the application, or held in any jurisdiction not included in the disclosures. False attestation shall constitute felony perjury punishable by not less than ten (10) years imprisonment and shall operate as an automatic permanent bar from Travel Restoration under this subheader; and (b) Agreement to post-departure audit by an independent forensic accountant selected from a pre-qualified roster maintained by the Academic Integrity Commission. The audit shall be conducted at the expense of the Removed Official, shall be completed within one hundred eighty (180) days of acceptance of the application, and shall verify the completeness and accuracy of the financial disclosures under Section 13F.23.4. The forensic accountant's report shall be filed with the Watchdog Tribunal Travel Division and published in full upon the Franklin Ledger. 13F.23.6 Review Authority. The Watchdog Tribunal Travel Division established in Section 21.25 shall administer the Travel Restoration Process, with authority to design and refine specific procedures within the framework established by this subheader. The Travel Division shall publish written procedures upon the Ledger within one hundred eighty (180) days of its convening, and may update those procedures as experience accumulates, subject to the core requirements set forth in Sections 13F.23.4 and 13F.23.5 which shall not be diminished. 13F.23.7 Review Timeline. The Travel Division shall review a complete application within ninety (90) days of the forensic accountant's report being filed. The Travel Division shall recommend approval, denial, or conditional approval to the Authority, with written reasoning published upon the Ledger. The Authority shall act on the recommendation through Liberty Bell Initiative within sixty (60) days of receipt. Travel Restoration granted by the Authority shall be recorded upon the Ledger with complete transparency regarding the terms of restoration. 13F.23.8 Approval Criteria — Heightened Scrutiny. Approval shall be granted only where the Authority, upon Travel Division recommendation, finds by clear and convincing evidence that: (a) all disclosures are complete and accurate as verified by the forensic audit; (b) no pending investigation, prosecution, or accountability proceeding under Sections 13, 13A, 13B, 13C, 13D, 13E, 13G, 13H, 16, 18.6, 21, 22, 24, 25, or 26 is outstanding against the Removed Official; (c) all asset recovery under Section 13D applicable to the Removed Official has been completed, including any ordered forfeitures; (d) the Removed Official has cooperated fully with all accountability proceedings, including providing truthful testimony where required; (e) no material evidence exists suggesting ongoing flight risk, including unusual asset movements, recent contacts with foreign officials of hostile powers, or patterns of resignation-timed conduct suggestive of concealment; and (f) the Travel Division's investigation has revealed no red flags inconsistent with the applicant's sworn attestations. 13F.23.9 Approved Travel — Steady-State Process with Enhanced Scrutiny. Upon restoration, a Removed Official shall be subject to the Steady-State Period Liberty Bell approval process of Section 13F.12.4 for each proposed International Trip, with the following heightened requirements: (a) applications shall be submitted no less than thirty (30) days before proposed travel, rather than the ordinary fourteen (14) days; (b) the approval criteria of Section 13F.12.5 shall apply with the strictest reading; (c) continuous electronic monitoring of Section 13F.12.6 shall apply to all approved travel, with daily check-ins rather than periodic reporting; (d) the Public Ledger disclosure of Section 13F.12.8 shall apply with additional details regarding the connection between the trip and the accountability proceedings that resulted in removal; and (e) the emergency exception of Section 13F.12.7 shall be available but subject to post-travel review by the Travel Division within thirty (30) days of the Removed Official's return. 13F.23.10 Family Travel Review Trigger. International Travel by any immediate family member (spouse, adult child, minor child, parent, sibling, or in-law, whether resident in the United States or abroad) of a Removed Official shall trigger automatic review by the Watchdog Tribunal Travel Division if any of the following conditions are present: (a) the family member holds, beneficially controls, or has had transferred to them within the preceding ten (10) years any asset previously owned or controlled by the Removed Official; (b) the family member's trip involves destinations, dates, or activities that raise reasonable suspicion of asset expatriation or coordination with the Removed Official; (c) the family member is accompanying the Removed Official on any approved trip; or (d) the Travel Division has received credible information suggesting the family travel may facilitate flight, asset transfer, or continuation of prohibited conduct. Where no such trigger is present, family members shall retain full ordinary travel rights under the Constitution. 13F.23.11 Family Travel Review — Scope. When triggered, family travel review shall be limited to verification that the travel does not serve as a vehicle for the Removed Official's prohibited purposes. Family members shall not be subject to the disclosure requirements of Section 13F.23.4 unless the Travel Division, by majority vote with reasoning published on the Ledger, determines that targeted disclosure is necessary to resolve a specific concern. Family members retain full constitutional travel rights subject only to this narrow accountability review.

13F.23.12 Periodic Reconfirmation. A Removed Official granted Travel Restoration shall, every three (3) years for the first ten (10) years following restoration and every five (5) years thereafter for life, submit updated disclosures under Section 13F.23.4 sufficient to confirm that the circumstances supporting restoration remain valid. Failure to timely submit updated disclosures shall result in automatic suspension of Travel Restoration pending completion. Material changes in financial position, newly discovered foreign contacts, or any development suggesting the original approval was based on incomplete or inaccurate information shall result in revocation of Travel Restoration by the Authority through Liberty Bell Initiative. 13F.23.13 Revocation Grounds. Travel Restoration may be revoked by the Authority through Liberty Bell Initiative upon finding by clear and convincing evidence of: (a) material falsity in any disclosure made under Section 13F.23.4 or 13F.23.5; (b) breach of any condition of Travel Restoration; (c) conduct during an approved trip inconsistent with the stated purpose; (d) discovery of previously undisclosed foreign assets, accounts, or relationships; (e) contact with hostile foreign powers not previously disclosed; or (f) any other conduct materially inconsistent with the accountability posture that supported the original grant. Revocation shall result in immediate return of the passport to Authority custody and reinstatement of the default travel prohibition under Section 13F.23.2. 13F.23.14 No Circumvention. The provisions of this subheader shall apply regardless of the elapsed time since removal, regardless of the Removed Official's subsequent private-sector employment or business activities, and regardless of any pardon, clemency, or commutation that may be granted by any subsequent official. Removal through accountability mechanisms creates a lifelong conditional status that can only be altered through the restoration process of this subheader. A Removed Official who dies with Travel Restoration pending shall be deemed to have left the application unresolved, without prejudice to future proceedings involving their estate or survivors. I. Oversight and Evolution 13F.24 Authority Oversight. Treasury's administration of this Section shall be subject to Authority oversight through the Watchdog Tribunal under Section 21, including: review of Treasury decisions that appear to unduly burden Covered Officials; review of Treasury decisions that appear to unduly permit Covered Official activity; and annual audits of Treasury's implementation published on the Franklin Ledger. 13F.25 Sunset Review Integration. The provisions of this Section shall be reviewed in each Sunset Review under Section 18. The People may, through a Modify vote, adjust the specific thresholds, monitoring requirements, travel prohibition scope, or penalty tiers based on accumulated operational experience. The underlying principles — that officials should not expatriate wealth during service and should not travel internationally while serving — shall be preserved. 13F.26 Article V Protection. The provisions of this Section shall be protected under the Article V protection established in Sections 18.6.1 and 18.6.2. No act of Congress, executive order, judicial ruling, or state action shall evade, diminish, or nullify the monitoring requirements, the travel prohibition, or the tiered penalty framework. 13F.27 Foundational Commitment. The People of the United States, in ratifying this Amendment, commit themselves to the principle that Section 1.1 officials shall be physically present in the United States during their service, with their financial conduct transparent to public accountability mechanisms. An official who cannot accept these requirements may decline office or resign; an official who accepts office accepts these requirements fully and completely. No office of federal power entitles its holder to the freedom to flee. 13F.28 Pre-Inaugural Vulnerability Monitoring. Recognizing that the financial monitoring framework of Sections 13F.1 through 13F.27 attaches to Section 1.1 federal Covered Officials, and recognizing that during the Pre-Inaugural Period — the period from Ratification (Day Zero) through the Inaugural Referendum (Day Seven Hundred Eighty), spanning both the narrow Phase One window of Days 0–180 and the Phase Two window of Days 180–780 as defined in Sections 19.19 and 19.20, during which the regular Petition mechanism under Section 3 is not yet available — specific non-federal channels are uniquely capture-vulnerable because they will determine the operational integrity of the institutions that the Amendment will rely on, and recognizing that monitoring narrowly tailored to these Pre-Inaugural vulnerabilities does not displace state authority over the underlying officials but only adds Amendment-specific transparency requirements during the critical Pre-Inaugural Period, the following Pre-Inaugural Vulnerability Monitoring framework applies: (a) Foundational Principle. The Inaugural Referendum on Day Seven Hundred Eighty (780) is the People's first opportunity to exercise the No Confidence authority created by this Amendment. The institutions that will administer that Referendum — the Washington Commission, the Pre-Certified University Pool, the State Elections Council in its initial composition, the AIC-Designate Forensic Consortium — must themselves operate with integrity during the twenty-six (26) months between Ratification and the Inaugural Referendum, or the People's first exercise of Amendment authority is compromised before it begins. The framework of this Section therefore extends Amendment-specific transparency requirements to the specific non-federal channels through which Pre-Inaugural capture would propagate, while leaving state authority over those officials untouched in all other respects; (b) Covered Pre-Inaugural Channels. The following non-federal officials and bodies shall be subject to Pre-Inaugural Vulnerability Monitoring during the period from Ratification through the Inaugural Referendum, with the monitoring sunsetting automatically upon Inaugural Referendum certification: (i) Sitting Chief Justices of Participating Jurisdictions whose names are eligible for the Washington Commission lottery pool

under Section 19.5.0.3 (the seven-member lottery draw and any extended pool under Section 19.5.0.3.5); (ii) Sitting State Attorneys General serving on the State Attorneys General Council under Section 19.5.0.18.1 during Phase One; (iii) Senior administrators of universities certified to or under consideration for the initial Pre-Certified University Pool under Section 17.16.2 (the AIC-Designate Forensic Consortium-administered initial Pool formation); (iv) Members of the AIC-Designate Forensic Consortium during their service; (v) Members of the Short-Term Civilian Review Board under Section 19.5.0.7 during their service; (vi) Members of the Citizens' Implementation Watch Board under Section 19.14 during their service; (c) Scope of Pre-Inaugural Monitoring. The Pre-Inaugural monitoring shall be narrowly tailored to detect capture pressure, not to govern non-Amendment activity. Covered persons under subsection (b) shall be subject to: (i) Pre-service financial disclosure of: federal and foreign payments received within the preceding three (3) years; institutional affiliations including non-public ones; federal lobbying registrations; substantial financial interests of the official, the official's spouse, and the official's minor children; previously undisclosed contractual relationships with foreign governments or their agents; (ii) During-service ongoing reporting of: new federal or foreign payments received during Pre-Inaugural service; new lobbying contacts received during service; substantial financial transactions during service exceeding ten thousand dollars ($10,000) in any single transaction or fifty thousand dollars ($50,000) cumulative within any thirty (30) day window; (iii) Travel notification, not travel restriction: international travel during Pre-Inaugural service shall be reported to the AIC-Designate Forensic Consortium (during Phase One) or to the Academic Integrity Commission (after Day 180) within seventy-two (72) hours of departure, with destination and approximate itinerary, but is not prohibited or subject to permission; (iv) Communications transparency for capture-vector communications: documented contacts from federal officeholders, federal political appointees, foreign government agents, or their intermediaries that relate to Pre-Inaugural Amendment functions shall be disclosed to the administering body within seven (7) days, with the existence of the contact and its general subject matter (not its substantive content where privileged) recorded for capture-pattern analysis; (d) Distinction from Section 13F. This Section's Pre-Inaugural monitoring does not classify the covered persons as Section 1.1 Covered Officials and does not impose travel restriction, asset freezing, or any other Section 13F coercive measure. The Pre-Inaugural monitoring is transparency-and-disclosure only. The covered persons remain state officials or private citizens with full ordinary rights; the Amendment merely requires that during their Pre-Inaugural Amendment-related service, capture-vector activity is documented and made available to anti-capture analysis; (e) Administering Body Across Pre-Inaugural Period. During Phase One (Days 0–180) before the Academic Integrity Commission is fully constituted, the AIC-Designate Forensic Consortium under Section 13B.7.1 shall administer this Section's monitoring, applying the same evidentiary, privacy, and analytical standards used in continuous AIC voter roll auditing under Section 13.8(c). Upon the AIC's constitution at Day 180, administration shall transfer to the AIC for the duration of the Pre-Inaugural Period (Days 180–780, the Phase Two window), with Phase One Forensic Consortium work product transferred at full evidentiary value. Upon Inaugural Referendum certification, the framework sunsets automatically with respect to ongoing Pre-Inaugural monitoring, though completed monitoring records remain in evidence for any ongoing or future Section 13 prosecutions; (f) Pattern Analysis and Anti-Capture Findings. The administering body shall conduct ongoing pattern analysis of Pre-Inaugural disclosures to detect: clustered payments from common sources to multiple covered persons; coordinated contact patterns suggesting an organized capture campaign; foreign-government-linked payments or contacts that meet Section 22 foreign interference indicators; and other patterns inconsistent with ordinary professional activity. Findings meeting clear-and-convincing evidentiary thresholds shall be published on the provisional public ledger during Phase One and on the Franklin Ledger after Day 180; (g) Privacy Protections. Recognizing that this Section reaches non-federal officials whose ordinary privacy expectations are higher than those of Section 1.1 federal officeholders: (i) Disclosed information shall be sealed from public view by default, with public release only upon administering-body finding of capture-vector activity meeting clear-and-convincing evidentiary thresholds; (ii) Family member financial information disclosed under subsection (c)(i) shall be sealed permanently except where directly relevant to a published capture-vector finding regarding the covered person; (iii) Communications subject-matter disclosure under subsection (c)(iv) shall protect attorney-client privilege, judicial deliberative privilege, and ordinary professional confidentiality, with disclosure limited to existence-and-general-subject only; (iv) Records collected under this Section shall not be used for any purpose other than Pre-Inaugural capture-pattern analysis and ensuing Section 13 prosecution where capture is established; (h) Automatic Enforcement Trigger. To prevent disclosure obligations from depending on case-by-case complaint by individual citizens or covered persons, the administering body shall conduct monthly disclosure-completion reviews across all covered channels under subsection (b), publishing on the Franklin Ledger (or provisional public ledger during Phase One) a categorical completion-rate report for each channel category. Non-completion of disclosure obligations under subsection (c) by a covered person shall, upon the next monthly completion review, automatically trigger State AG Council enforcement under Section 19.5.0.18.9.1 during Phase One and Hamilton Contingent enforcement after Day 180, without requirement of separate citizen complaint. The administering body shall provide the covered person ten (10) days' written notice and opportunity to cure documented disclosure failures before automatic enforcement attaches; (i) Penalties. Knowing failure to disclose, intentional misdisclosure, or willful blindness regarding disclosure obligations under this Section shall constitute Section 13 interference where the covered person's service relates to Pre-Inaugural Amendment functions, with the enforcement authority of subsection (h) applying. Senior Official multipliers shall apply where the covered person holds public office; (j) Federal Executive Non-Interference. No President, Vice President, Cabinet officer, federal agency

head, or other federal executive officeholder shall direct, fund, influence, pressure, or impede AIC-Designate Forensic Consortium operations under this Section, AIC operations after Day 180, disclosed-information administration, or Pre-Inaugural pattern analysis. Any such interference shall constitute Section 13 interference with Senior Official multipliers, prosecutable by the State AG Council under Sections 19.5.0.5.2 and 19.5.0.18.9.1 during Phase One and by the Hamilton Contingent upon operational commencement, and through the Section 17C.15 framework; (k) External Oversight of the Administering Body. To prevent self-supervision, the administering body shall itself be subject to oversight by an independent body across the Pre-Inaugural Period: during Phase One (Days 0–180) the Short-Term Civilian Review Board under Sections

19.5.0.7 through 19.5.0.9 shall exercise oversight over the AIC-Designate Forensic Consortium's administration of this Section; upon the Watchdog Tribunal convening at Day 270 under Section 19.19 (which falls within the broader Pre-Inaugural Period), the Watchdog Tribunal shall exercise oversight over the Academic Integrity Commission's administration of this Section; in the gap window between Day 180 (AIC constitution) and Day 270 (Tribunal convening), the Short-Term Civilian Review Board's oversight authority shall extend forward to cover this gap. External oversight shall include authority to investigate allegations of bad-faith administering-body conduct, capture of the administering body itself, or capture-pattern findings made on inadequate evidentiary basis; (l) Negative Enumeration. Notwithstanding any provision of this Section, this Section shall NOT authorize: (i) any travel restriction, asset freeze, or other coercive measure analogous to Section 13F coercive provisions against covered persons under subsection (b); (ii) any monitoring of covered persons' conduct unrelated to Amendment functions or capture-vector indicators; (iii) any disclosure obligations beyond those enumerated in subsection (c); (iv) any expansion of monitoring scope by administering-body interpretation. Any expansion of this Section's scope shall require Article V amendment, not administering-body interpretation. The narrowly-tailored framing is a structural commitment, not a discretionary self-limitation; (m) Funding. All costs of Pre-Inaugural Vulnerability Monitoring shall be funded through the Ratification Loan under Section 13I.4, with allocation by the AIC-Designate Forensic Consortium during Phase One and by the AIC after Day 180; (n) Article V Protection. The provisions of this Section shall be protected under the Article V protection established in Sections 18.6.1 and 18.6.2. The Pre-Inaugural Period cannot become a constitutional blind spot during which capture activity escapes Amendment-specific transparency; the institutions that will conduct the Inaugural Referendum must operate with integrity during the twenty-six (26) months that precede it.

Section 13G. Investigation Tools, Physical Seizure, and Chain of Custody

Key terms in this Section:

• "The Authority" — The Independent Tripartite Oversight Authority (three bodies, see Section 17). • "Hamilton Contingent" — The constitutional enforcement arm established in Section 13C, with four Divisions: Prosecution, Protection, Public Response, and Preservation. • "Watchdog Tribunal" — The body established under Section 21 for enforcement of anti-corruption provisions. • "Seizure" — The physical taking of records, devices, and evidence into Hamilton Contingent custody, distinct from the preservation duty established in Section 13B. Seizure is active; preservation is passive. • "Chain of Custody" — The documented, verifiable, unbroken record of possession, transfer, and custody of evidence from the moment of Seizure through analysis, prosecution, and final disposition. • "Digital Device" — Any electronic storage, processing, or communication device including but not limited to phones, tablets, laptops, desktop computers, servers, external drives, USB storage, smart devices, cloud-accessing credentials, and any successor technology. • "Third-Party Records Holder" — Any person or entity other than the Removed Official who holds records relating to the Removed Official's conduct, including but not limited to banks, brokerages, law firms, accounting firms, consulting firms, telecommunications providers, cloud storage providers, and technology companies. A. Foundational Principle 13G.1 Foundational Principle. Section 13B establishes the duty to preserve evidence. This Section establishes the tools and mechanisms for actively collecting, seizing, accessing, and maintaining chain of custody over that evidence during investigations of corruption. Preservation without collection is insufficient; the People's right to the truth about corruption requires that investigators have clear constitutional authority to take possession of records, to compel cooperation from third parties who hold relevant evidence, to access encrypted digital devices, and to pursue records across jurisdictional boundaries. This Section supplements, and does not replace, the preservation framework of Section 13B.

B. Physical Seizure at Reclamation 13G.2 Automatic Seizure Authority. At the moment of No Confidence certification under Section 5, the Hamilton Contingent Preservation Division shall have automatic constitutional authority to take physical custody of all Federal Records and related evidence in the possession, custody, or control of every Removed Official. This authority is self-executing; no court order, warrant, or further procedural step is required beyond the certification itself. The Seizure authority is limited strictly to Federal Records and evidence relevant to investigations under Sections 13A through 13F and does not extend to wholly personal property unrelated to federal service. 13G.3 Scope of Immediate Seizure. Within twenty-four (24) hours of No Confidence certification, Hamilton Contingent Preservation Division personnel shall take custody of: (a) All federally-issued digital devices, including phones, tablets, laptops, desktop computers, and any other electronic equipment provided to the Removed Official for federal use; (b) All paper files, documents, notes, calendars, and records physically present at federal offices occupied by the Removed Official; (c) All federally-issued credentials, including classified information access badges, secure facility keys, and cryptographic authentication tokens; (d) All federal devices, media, and records in the Removed Official's residence, vehicle, or other non-federal locations where federal records have been stored or used, subject to the search limitations of Section 13G.7; (e) Server access credentials for federal systems, with immediate credential revocation following seizure; (f) Physical evidence relevant to the Section 13B Preservation Order, including backup media, portable storage devices, and hard-copy files. 13G.4 Chain of Custody Protocols. From the moment of Seizure forward, all evidence shall be maintained under the following Chain of Custody protocols: (a) Cryptographic Hashing at Seizure: every item seized shall be immediately cryptographically hashed before any analysis, with hash values published upon the Ledger or provisional public ledger within twenty-four (24) hours, creating an immutable public record of the evidence's state at Seizure; (b) Tamper-Evident Packaging: physical evidence shall be placed in tamper-evident packaging, with packaging seals photographed and documented; (c) Documented Transfer Log: every transfer of custody from one person or facility to another shall be documented with timestamp, identity of transferor and transferee, purpose, and method of transfer;

(d) Triple Custody Preservation: copies shall be maintained in the Triple Custody system established in Section 13B.6, ensuring no single point of failure in preservation; (e) Independent Witness: at the moment of initial Seizure, at least one independent witness (Watch Board member during Phase 1, or Watchdog Tribunal member thereafter) shall observe and document the Seizure, providing independent verification; (f) Forfeiture of Admissibility on Break: any break in Chain of Custody that cannot be reasonably explained shall result in heightened judicial scrutiny of the evidence and may, upon Watchdog Tribunal finding of bad faith, result in the evidence being inadmissible against the Removed Official (though remaining usable for investigatory leads). 13G.5 Evidence Collection Facility. The Hamilton Contingent shall maintain a dedicated, secure Evidence Collection Facility, physically separate from any existing federal law enforcement or intelligence facility, for receipt, processing, and storage of seized evidence. The Facility shall: (a) Be operated exclusively by Hamilton Contingent Preservation Division personnel; (b) Be subject to continuous surveillance recorded for independent review; (c) Require dual-person access protocols for sensitive evidence; (d) Maintain detailed logs of every entry, exit, and evidence access; (e) Be subject to Watchdog Tribunal inspection upon fourteen (14) days notice, or immediate inspection upon allegation of misconduct. C. Personal Electronics and Communications 13G.6 Personal Device Subpoena Authority. Within seventy-two (72) hours of No Confidence certification, the Hamilton Contingent, with Watchdog Tribunal concurrence by majority vote, may issue Investigative Subpoenas for personal devices and accounts where there is reasonable basis to believe federal business has been conducted, including: (a) Personal phones used for federal communications; (b) Personal email accounts used for federal correspondence; (c) Personal cloud storage containing federal materials; (d) Personal computers or devices used to access federal systems; (e) Messaging applications (including Signal, WhatsApp, Telegram, Discord, and successor platforms) where federal business has been discussed; (f) Social media accounts used for federal communications or official business.

13G.7 Residence Search Authority. Where evidence of federal business conducted from non-federal locations is reasonably believed to exist, the Hamilton Contingent may seek a search warrant from a panel of three (3) state Supreme Court Chief Justices drawn by randomized lottery. The panel shall rule within seventy-two (72) hours. Search warrants shall: (a) Specify the premises to be searched and items sought with reasonable particularity; (b) Be limited to federal records, related evidence, and instrumentalities of potential corruption; (c) Preserve Fourth Amendment protections against general warrants and fishing expeditions; (d) Require presence of the Removed Official or counsel during the search where practicable; (e) Result in inventory documentation provided to the Removed Official and filed on the Ledger within forty-eight (48) hours; (f) Be subject to post-search judicial review upon motion of the Removed Official. 13G.8 Cloud Storage Preservation Orders. Hamilton Contingent may issue Cloud Preservation Orders to any cloud storage provider, social media platform, or technology company holding accounts associated with a Removed Official. Such orders shall: (a) Require immediate preservation of all account contents pending investigation; (b) Prohibit deletion, alteration, or routine data management that would affect the preserved content; (c) Be effective for ninety (90) days, renewable upon continued investigation; (d) Not require disclosure of content without further legal process (subpoena or warrant); (e) Carry federal penalties for non-compliance including corporate fines of not less than fifty million dollars ($50,000,000) per account and potential loss of operating authority. D. Encrypted Device Access 13G.9 Encrypted Device Framework. The tension between encrypted device security (beneficial for privacy and cybersecurity) and accountability investigations shall be resolved by the following framework: (a) Voluntary Decryption Incentive: a

Removed Official who voluntarily provides decryption credentials, passwords, or biometric access for relevant encrypted devices shall receive consideration in any subsequent proceedings, including potential Cooperation Credit under Section 13D.21; (b) Judicial Compulsion for Known Credentials: where evidence demonstrates that the Removed Official knows the decryption credentials (for example, they used the device recently), a panel of three (3) state Supreme Court Chief Justices may compel disclosure by judicial order, with contempt penalties for refusal; (c) Technical Decryption: where credentials cannot be obtained, the Academic Integrity Commission's technical infrastructure or commercial forensic services may be employed to attempt technical decryption, subject to preservation of the original encrypted state; (d) Adverse Inference: where a Removed Official refuses decryption of devices reasonably believed to contain evidence of corruption, the fact of refusal may be used as an adverse inference in civil forfeiture proceedings (though not in criminal proceedings where the Fifth Amendment applies); (e) Third-Party Assistance Compelled: technology companies, device manufacturers, and cloud service providers may be ordered to provide technical assistance with encrypted device access, subject to preservation of the security of other users and absent the creation of new backdoors; (f) No Mandated Backdoors: this Section does not authorize and shall not be interpreted to authorize the creation of encryption backdoors, weakened cryptographic standards, or any technical measure that would compromise the security of non-target users. 13G.10 Federal Device Decryption. Federally-issued devices are subject to federal security policies that prohibit encryption unreadable by federal IT. Removed Officials who have modified federal devices to prevent federal access shall face an additional felony charge of tampering with federal property, with ten (10) year minimum sentence. E. Third-Party Records Access 13G.11 Third-Party Records Authority. The Hamilton Contingent, acting upon Watchdog Tribunal authorization, may issue Investigative Subpoenas to Third-Party Records Holders for records relating to a Removed Official's conduct. Such subpoenas may reach: (a) Banks and financial institutions: all account records, wire transfers, deposits, withdrawals, loans, credit applications, and related documentation; (b) Brokerages and investment firms: all securities transactions, portfolio holdings, investment advisory communications, and related records; (c) Law firms: subject to attorney-client privilege limitations, records relating to transactions or legal matters where the firm served the Removed Official;

(d) Accounting and auditing firms: all tax filings, financial statements, accounting records, and advisory communications; (e) Consulting and advisory firms: engagement records, work product not protected by privilege, and payment documentation; (f) Telecommunications providers: call records, text message metadata, internet service logs (content requires warrant); (g) Cloud storage providers: account metadata, access logs, and (with appropriate legal process) content; (h) Real estate professionals: transaction records, escrow documents, appraisals, and related materials; (i) Art dealers, auction houses, and luxury goods sellers: records of high-value transactions. 13G.12 Privilege Limitations. This Section does not abrogate existing legal privileges, including attorney-client privilege, doctor-patient privilege, clergy-penitent privilege, or constitutional privileges. However: (a) Crime-Fraud Exception: the long-established crime-fraud exception to attorney-client privilege applies to communications made in furtherance of ongoing or planned corruption; (b) In Camera Review: disputes regarding privilege claims shall be resolved through in camera review by a panel of three (3) state Supreme Court Chief Justices drawn by lottery; (c) Privilege Log Required: any records withheld on privilege grounds shall be accompanied by a detailed privilege log sufficient to permit judicial review; (d) Preservation Pending Review: disputed records shall be preserved intact pending resolution of privilege claims. 13G.13 Safe Harbor for Compliance. Third-Party Records Holders that comply in good faith with Investigative Subpoenas issued under this Section shall be immune from civil liability arising from that compliance, including claims by Removed Officials whose records were produced. Good-faith compliance shall be presumed where the holder followed subpoena requirements reasonably. 13G.14 Penalties for Non-Compliance. Third-Party Records Holders that refuse compliance with Investigative Subpoenas, provide incomplete responses, or assist Removed Officials in evading subpoenas shall face: (a) Contempt penalties including fines and, for corporate entities, potential dissolution; (b) Section 13 interference penalties for willful obstruction; (c) Loss of any federal licenses, charters, or contracts where applicable;

(d) Personal liability for corporate officers who knowingly authorized non-compliance. F. Family Member Records 13G.15 Family Member Records Framework. Records of family members (spouses, children, parents, siblings, in-laws) are not automatically subject to Seizure or Subpoena. However, family member records may be reached where: (a) Federal Business Conducted: family members conducted federal business on behalf of or with the Removed Official, making their records Federal Records under Section 13B; (b) Financial Flows: family members received financial flows from the Removed Official subject to review under Section 13D.5 family flow analysis; (c) Corruption Patterns

Evidence: family member financial records are relevant to demonstrating corruption patterns (for example, gifts, lavish spending, or travel logs that evidence unexplained wealth of the Official); (d) Conduit for Corrupt Payments: evidence suggests family members served as conduits for corrupt payments to the Removed Official. 13G.16 Family Privacy Protections. Where family member records are reached under Section 13G.15, the following protections shall apply: (a) Narrow Tailoring: subpoenas and searches shall be narrowly tailored to records reasonably relevant to the Official's conduct, not general fishing expeditions into family life; (b) Protective Orders: courts may issue protective orders limiting disclosure of family member personal information beyond what is necessary for investigation; (c) Minor Children Special Protection: records involving minor children shall be subject to heightened protection, with courts reviewing any proposed use in camera; (d) Innocent Family Member Preservation: family members who themselves are not subjects of investigation shall receive protection for their independent affairs. G. Foreign Jurisdiction Records 13G.17 Foreign Records Recovery Framework. Records held in foreign jurisdictions, or in foreign services used to evade domestic preservation, shall be pursued through the following layered approach: (a) Treaty-Based Recovery: existing Mutual Legal Assistance Treaties (MLATs) and other treaty mechanisms shall be used where applicable, with the State Department cooperating with Hamilton Contingent investigations; (b) Extraterritorial Jurisdiction Assertion: where foreign records relate to United States persons and United States conduct, U.S. legal process may assert extraterritorial jurisdiction consistent with existing doctrine; (c) Treasury/OFAC Pressure: foreign financial institutions and service providers refusing cooperation may face Treasury/OFAC-administered consequences, including loss of access to U.S. correspondent banking and U.S. market access; (d) Diplomatic Channels: diplomatic pressure through normal State Department channels shall be employed to obtain foreign cooperation; (e) Technology Company Cooperation: multinational technology companies operating in the United States must produce records regardless of storage location, subject to conflicts of law analysis; (f) Foreign Concealment as Evidence: the act of storing records in non-cooperative foreign jurisdictions shall itself be treated as circumstantial evidence of corrupt concealment under Section 13B.10 "no technical excuse" presumption. 13G.18 Non-Cooperative Jurisdictions. Where a foreign jurisdiction systematically refuses cooperation with Amendment investigations, the Authority may, by Liberty Bell Initiative, publicly designate the jurisdiction as a "Corruption-Sheltering Jurisdiction." Such designation shall: (a) Be published upon the Franklin Ledger with full reasoning; (b) Serve as basis for enhanced Treasury/OFAC scrutiny of financial flows to and from the designated jurisdiction; (c) Create rebuttable presumption that assets held in the designated jurisdiction by Removed Officials are corruption proceeds; (d) Be reviewable by affected foreign jurisdictions through diplomatic process and subject to revocation upon demonstrated cooperation. H. Investigative Authority and Oversight 13G.19 Hamilton Contingent Investigative Powers. In addition to the Seizure, Subpoena, and warrant authorities established above, the Hamilton Contingent Prosecution Division shall have the following standard investigative powers, subject to Watchdog Tribunal oversight: (a) Witness Interviews: voluntary interviews of witnesses, with recording and documentation; (b) Compelled Testimony: subject to Fifth Amendment protections, grand jury and civil deposition authority; (c) Document Authentication: authority to compel authentication of records by their creators or custodians; (d) Expert Witnesses: retention of technical, financial, forensic, and academic experts;

(e) Cooperation Agreements: authority to enter cooperation agreements with witnesses in exchange for testimony, subject to Watchdog Tribunal approval for major agreements; (f) Immunity Grants: limited use and transactional immunity grants, subject to Watchdog Tribunal authorization for serious matters; (g) International Cooperation: coordination with foreign law enforcement and regulatory bodies through State Department channels. 13G.20 Watchdog Tribunal Oversight of Investigation Tools. The Watchdog Tribunal shall continuously oversee the Hamilton Contingent's exercise of investigation tools under this Section, including: (a) Review of Seizure operations for compliance with Chain of Custody protocols; (b) Review of search warrant applications and execution; (c) Review of subpoena issuance and compliance; (d) Investigation of allegations of investigative misconduct; (e) Publication of aggregate investigation statistics upon the Franklin Ledger, preserving investigative confidentiality while ensuring transparency of the enforcement apparatus; (f) Authority to order remediation of investigation misconduct, including exclusion of improperly obtained evidence. 13G.21 Due Process Preservation. Nothing in this Section diminishes the due process rights of Removed Officials or any other person subject to investigation. All proceedings shall preserve: (a) Fourth Amendment protection against unreasonable searches and seizures; (b) Fifth Amendment protection against self-incrimination and due process; (c) Sixth Amendment right to counsel and confrontation; (d) Eighth Amendment protection against excessive fines; (e) Other constitutional protections, including those recognized in case law interpreting the Bill of Rights; (f) Other constitutional protections recognized in case law interpreting the Bill of Rights, except as modified by Section 13G.21.1 below. 13G.21.1 Congressional Privilege — No Shield for Corruption. Notwithstanding Article I, Section 6 of the Constitution and any judicial doctrine interpreting the Speech or Debate Clause, no Congressional privilege, immunity, or protection shall operate to shield any Member of Congress, Congressional staff member, or Congressional employee from investigation, subpoena, seizure, testimony compulsion, or prosecution under this Amendment for conduct constituting corruption, bribery, foreign influence, abuse of public trust, or other violations of Sections 13, 13A, 13B, 13C, 13D, 13E, 13F, or 13G. Specifically: (a) Records, communications, documents, and materials otherwise subject to Speech or Debate Clause protection shall be fully accessible to Hamilton Contingent investigations under this Amendment when sought as evidence of, or in furtherance of investigation into, conduct described in this Section; (b) Members of Congress, Congressional staff, and Congressional employees shall be subject to compelled testimony, subpoena, and all investigation tools of Section 13G on the same terms as other Covered Persons, with no special privilege or exemption; (c) The offices, records, devices, and communications of Members of Congress shall be subject to the physical seizure authority of Section 13G.2-5 on the same terms as other Removed Officials; (d) Existing judicial doctrine interpreting Speech or Debate Clause, including the holdings in United States v. Rayburn House Office Building (2007) and related cases, shall not limit investigation authority under this Amendment to the extent such doctrine would shield corruption from scrutiny; (e) This Section does not apply to genuine legislative deliberation, drafting of legislation, policy debate, or committee inquiry into non-corruption matters; the override is limited strictly to investigations of corruption, bribery, foreign influence, abuse of public trust, and similar misconduct within the scope of this Amendment; (f) Members of Congress retain their ordinary due process rights, including Fourth, Fifth, Sixth, and Eighth Amendment protections, in all proceedings under this Amendment; (g) This Section is adopted with the explicit understanding that this Amendment, being later in time than Article I, Section 6, shall control to the extent of any conflict, consistent with standard constitutional interpretive principles. The People, by ratifying this Amendment, exercise their sovereign authority to determine that no constitutional privilege shall shield corruption from accountability. I. Protections and Constitutional Status 13G.22 Article V Protection. The provisions of this Section shall be protected under the Article V protection established in Sections 18.6.1 and

18.6.2. No act of Congress, executive order, judicial ruling, or state action shall evade, diminish, or nullify the investigation tools, seizure authority, or chain of custody requirements established herein. Specific procedural details may be modified through Sunset Review under Section 18. 13G.23 Sunset Review Integration. The provisions of this Section shall be reviewed in each Sunset Review under Section 18. The People may, through a Modify vote,

adjust specific procedural thresholds, update technology-specific provisions to address evolving digital landscapes, and refine the balance between investigation effectiveness and privacy protection. 13G.24 Foundational Commitment. The People of the United States, in ratifying this Amendment, commit themselves to the principle that corruption investigations must be matched by the tools necessary to investigate. Preservation of evidence without authority to collect it is a half-measure; subpoena authority without chain of custody is insufficient; domestic authority without cross-border reach allows flight; and all authorities without oversight risk abuse. This Section establishes the complete toolkit: seize, subpoena, search, decrypt, reach third parties, address family member records, pursue foreign records, and all under continuous Watchdog Tribunal oversight. The truth about how officials have served the People shall not be hidden by deletion, evasion, or flight.

Section 13H. Judicial Capture and Alternative Interpretive Pathways

Key terms in this Section: • "The Authority" — The Independent Tripartite Oversight Authority (three bodies, see Section 17). • "Watchdog Tribunal" — The body established under Section 21 for enforcement of anti-corruption provisions. • "Judicial Capture" — The condition in which federal or state courts, or specific judges, are compromised by corruption, foreign influence, or systematic bias such that they cannot be trusted to fairly interpret or enforce this Amendment. • "Capture Declaration" — Formal finding by the Authority through Liberty Bell Initiative, or by alternate trigger mechanisms established in this Section, that a specific court, panel, or judge is subject to Judicial Capture for purposes of Amendment interpretation or enforcement. • "Alternative Interpretive Pathway" — The mechanism by which Amendment interpretation and enforcement continues when courts are found to be captured, substituting Amendment bodies for compromised courts. • "Adverse Ruling Pattern" — A statistical pattern of judicial decisions that systematically favor corrupt interests over Amendment enforcement, as defined in this Section.

A. Foundational Principle 13H.1 Foundational Principle. This Amendment exists because existing accountability mechanisms have failed. Among those mechanisms are federal and state courts, which have sometimes shielded corruption behind doctrines of privilege, deference, standing, and political question. It would be internally inconsistent for this Amendment to rely entirely upon the same judicial institutions whose failures necessitated the Amendment's creation. This Section therefore establishes alternative pathways for Amendment interpretation and enforcement when courts themselves are compromised — not to replace the judiciary in its ordinary function, but to ensure that judicial capture cannot become a shield for corruption. The establishment of these alternative pathways reflects not a general distrust of the federal judiciary but a specific constitutional principle: no accountability mechanism can presume its own integrity against capture, and where capture is demonstrated through documented evidence meeting the standards of this Section, alternatives must exist. The alternative pathways of this Section operate only upon documented satisfaction of specific triggering conditions under Section 13H.3 and Sections 13H.5 through 13H.9; in all other matters, ordinary judicial review proceeds without modification. The courts retain their full ordinary constitutional authority over all matters outside this Amendment's specific accountability provisions; this Section applies only where judicial capture threatens to frustrate the People's sovereign will as expressed through this Amendment, and its provisions shall be construed narrowly, operating only upon their specified triggering conditions. B. Scenarios of Judicial Capture 13H.2 Recognized Capture Scenarios. This Section addresses five categories of Judicial Capture, each with tailored response mechanisms: (a) Supreme Court Capture. The Supreme Court of the United States issues rulings that systematically weaken this Amendment, shield corrupt §1.1 officials from accountability, or interpret Amendment provisions contrary to their plain meaning and ratified intent; (b) Post-Reclamation Federal Court Capture. Lower federal courts, whose judges were appointed by a Federal Government subsequently removed through No Confidence, interpret this Amendment in ways that shield Removed Officials or obstruct ongoing investigations; (c) State Supreme Court Chief Justice Compromise. One or more state Supreme Court Chief Justices — upon whom this Amendment relies for warrants, panels, Commission membership, and Nuclear Authorization Panel participation — are found to be corrupted, coerced, or otherwise compromised; (d) Doctrinal Erosion. Courts, over time, develop case law that progressively narrows Amendment provisions, creating precedent that effectively neuters the

Amendment's enforcement power even absent specific corruption; (e) Judicial Abdication. Courts refuse to rule on Amendment matters entirely, invoking political question doctrine, standing limitations, or other doctrines to avoid enforcement responsibility, leaving Amendment provisions without judicial recourse. C. Trigger Mechanisms 13H.3 Multiple Trigger Authority. A Capture Declaration may be issued through any one of the following three independent pathways, each designed to catch different manifestations of Judicial Capture: 13H.4 Trigger One — Authority Liberty Bell Declaration. The Authority, acting through Liberty Bell Initiative (separate concurrence of all three bodies), may declare Judicial Capture with respect to a specific court, panel, judge, or doctrine, upon finding clear and convincing evidence of capture. The Declaration shall: (a) Be published upon the Franklin Ledger or provisional public ledger with complete reasoning; (b) Identify the specific court, panel, judge, or doctrine found to be captured; (c) Specify the scope of the Declaration — which Amendment provisions are affected, and what alternative pathways apply; (d) Be subject to review by the Watchdog Tribunal upon petition, which may modify or revoke the Declaration upon clear and convincing evidence of error; (e) Remain in effect until revoked by the Authority upon demonstrated change in circumstances, or upon Sunset Review determination under Section 18. 13H.5 Trigger Two — Adverse Ruling Pattern. Where data-driven analysis demonstrates that a specific court issues rulings systematically adverse to Amendment enforcement, an automatic review shall be triggered. Adverse Ruling Pattern shall be established when: (a) A court issues three (3) or more rulings within any twelve (12) month period that materially narrow, weaken, or obstruct Amendment provisions, as assessed by the Academic Integrity Commission; (b) A court issues any single ruling that would fundamentally invalidate core Amendment provisions; (c) A court's Amendment-related rulings reverse Authority determinations at a rate exceeding seventy-five percent (75%) over twelve (12) or more rulings, when the ordinary reversal rate for comparable matters is below forty percent (40%); (d) A court systematically invokes political question, standing, or other justiciability doctrines to avoid Amendment enforcement in cases where such doctrines have not ordinarily been invoked.

13H.5.1 Automatic Review Process. Upon any Adverse Ruling Pattern trigger: (a) The Academic Integrity Commission shall publish the triggering analysis upon the Franklin Ledger within fourteen (14) days; (b) The Watchdog Tribunal shall investigate the ruling pattern within thirty (30) days; (c) The Tribunal shall issue findings by two-thirds (2/3) supermajority as to whether Judicial Capture exists; (d) If Judicial Capture is found, the Authority shall issue a formal Capture Declaration within seven (7) days; (e) The affected court shall retain ordinary jurisdiction over non-Amendment matters. 13H.6 Trigger Three — Citizen Petition for Judicial Review. Registered voters may initiate a Judicial Review Petition against a specific court, panel, or judge alleged to be subject to Judicial Capture. Such a Petition shall: (a) Require signatures of not less than five percent (5%) of registered voters nationally, including not less than five percent (5%) in each of not fewer than twenty (20) of the fifty-six Participating Jurisdictions; (b) Be collected in person at Citizens' Reclamation Offices and Centers, subject to the same verification procedures as Section 3 Petitions; (c) Specify the court, panel, or judge alleged to be captured, and provide evidence supporting the allegation; (d) Upon verification of signature thresholds, trigger automatic Watchdog Tribunal investigation within thirty (30) days; (e) Require Liberty Bell Initiative determination following Tribunal findings; (f) Be limited to three (3) active Judicial Review Petitions at any one time to prevent frivolous or coordinated attacks on the judiciary. D. Alternative Interpretive and Enforcement Pathways 13H.7 Division of Alternative Authority. Where Judicial Capture is declared, the ordinary judicial role in Amendment matters shall be substituted as follows, with different functions assigned to different bodies based on their institutional competencies: 13H.8 Watchdog Tribunal — Primary Interpretive Authority. The Watchdog Tribunal shall serve as the primary interpreter of this Amendment on corruption questions when Judicial Capture is declared. The Tribunal's interpretive authority includes:

(a) Determining the meaning and application of Amendment provisions in specific investigations and prosecutions; (b) Resolving privilege disputes under Section 13G.12 when ordinary judicial review is unavailable; (c) Adjudicating Amendment-related controversies between parties where courts have been found captured; (d) Issuing interpretive guidance that binds Hamilton Contingent investigations and Authority operations; (e) Establishing Amendment jurisprudence through reasoned decisions published upon the Franklin Ledger; (f) Reviewing and, by two-thirds (2/3) supermajority, overturning captured court rulings that conflict with Amendment purposes. 13H.9 Authority Bodies — Operational Judicial Functions. The three bodies of the Authority, individually or collectively, shall take over operational judicial functions ordinarily performed by courts when Judicial Capture is declared. These functions include: (a) Warrant Issuance. Search warrants under Section 13G.7 may be issued by a panel of three (3) Watchdog Tribunal members drawn by lottery, with the same procedural protections as the ordinary three-Chief

Justice panel; (b) Subpoena Authorization. Investigation subpoenas requiring judicial authorization may be issued by the Watchdog Tribunal by majority vote; (c) Privilege Review. Disputes under Section 13G.12 may be resolved by panels of three (3) Watchdog Tribunal members, or where classified materials are involved, by Academic Integrity Commission members with appropriate security clearances; (d) Encrypted Device Compulsion. Orders compelling decryption under Section 13G.9(b) may be issued by Watchdog Tribunal panels; (e) Good Faith Official Clearance Review. The Tribunal's Section 13D.18 review authority extends to full judicial substitution when courts are captured; (f) Nuclear Authorization Panel Substitution. When state Supreme Court Chief Justices are found compromised, the Academic Integrity Commission shall provide substitute members through lottery from the Pre-Certified University Pool under Section 17.16, pending restoration of non-captured state judiciary members. 13H.10 Washington Commission Substitute Composition. If one or more Chief Justices of Participating Jurisdictions serving on the Washington Commission during Phase One (Section 19.5.0) are found compromised, those seats shall be filled by randomized lottery from non-compromised Chief Justices of Participating Jurisdictions. If an insufficient number of non-compromised Chief Justices are available, the remaining seats shall be filled by:

(a) Retired state Supreme Court Justices of demonstrated integrity, selected by randomized lottery from a pool maintained by the Academic Integrity Commission; (b) Academic Integrity Commission members with relevant constitutional expertise; (c) Watchdog Tribunal members selected by Tribunal internal vote; (d) In each case, selected individuals must meet the integrity disqualification standards of Section 19.5.0.9. E. Doctrinal Erosion and Amendment Preservation 13H.11 Doctrinal Erosion Protection. Where a pattern of judicial interpretation progressively weakens Amendment provisions over time, the Authority may, through Liberty Bell Initiative, issue a Doctrinal Correction Declaration that: (a) Identifies the specific judicial doctrines found to have eroded Amendment provisions; (b) Articulates the original ratified intent of the affected provisions; (c) Declares that Hamilton Contingent investigations, Authority operations, and Watchdog Tribunal proceedings shall proceed under the ratified meaning rather than the eroded judicial interpretation; (d) Is published upon the Franklin Ledger as authoritative guidance for future Amendment operations; (e) May be incorporated into ordinary Amendment operations through Sunset Review Modify procedures under Section 18.4 if the People choose to formalize the correction. 13H.12 Originalist Interpretation

Presumption. In any Amendment interpretation, the ratified text, the contemporaneous reasoning published upon the Ledger, and the Foundational Commitments articulated throughout the Amendment shall control over subsequent judicial interpretations that narrow or weaken those provisions. This is an explicit repudiation of doctrinal erosion as a permissible interpretive method for this Amendment. Courts may interpret Amendment provisions in cases of genuine textual ambiguity, but may not interpret the Amendment against its ratified purpose of holding corrupt federal officials accountable. F. Judicial Abdication 13H.13 Political Question Doctrine Limits. No court shall invoke political question doctrine, standing limitations, or similar justiciability doctrines to refuse ruling on: (a) The validity of a certified No Confidence Referendum; (b) The authority of Authority bodies to act within their constitutional mandates;

(c) The enforceability of §13 interference penalties; (d) The constitutionality of Hamilton Contingent investigations and prosecutions under this Amendment; (e) The authority of this Section's alternative pathways when Judicial Capture has been declared; (f) Any core Amendment provision where judicial silence would effectively nullify the Amendment's function. 13H.14 Mandamus Authority. Where a court refuses to rule on a matter properly before it under this Amendment, invoking political question or similar doctrines beyond their proper scope, any party may seek mandamus (a court order compelling action) from the Watchdog Tribunal compelling ruling. The Tribunal may, by two-thirds (2/3) supermajority, issue binding orders requiring judicial action or substituting Amendment body determination if judicial action cannot be obtained within reasonable time. G. Safeguards Against Abuse 13H.15 Narrow Construction. This Section shall be narrowly construed to apply only where Judicial Capture is genuinely demonstrated by clear and convincing evidence. Ordinary disagreement with judicial rulings shall not constitute Judicial Capture. Adverse rulings on particular cases, absent the patterns described in Section 13H.5, shall not trigger alternate pathways. The Amendment values judicial review in its proper sphere and does not seek to supplant courts in their ordinary constitutional role. 13H.16 Reversal of Capture Declarations. Capture Declarations may be revoked through: (a) Authority Liberty Bell Initiative upon finding of changed circumstances; (b) Watchdog Tribunal two-thirds (2/3) supermajority finding that Declaration was erroneous; (c) Sunset Review under Section 18, permitting the People to reverse or modify Declarations; (d) Replacement of compromised judges through ordinary appointment processes (for federal judges) or Jurisdictional processes (for Chief Justices of

Participating Jurisdictions). 13H.17 Protection of Non-Captured Judicial Function. The declaration of Judicial Capture with respect to a specific court, panel, judge, or doctrine shall not: (a) Affect that court's jurisdiction over matters unrelated to this Amendment; (b) Prevent non-captured members of that court from serving on matters unrelated to the capture finding;

(c) Impugn the integrity of the broader judiciary absent specific findings against specific actors; (d) Diminish the constitutional role of courts in their ordinary function. 13H.18 Due Process in Alternative Pathways. When alternate pathways are used under this Section, they shall preserve: (a) All due process rights that would apply in ordinary judicial proceedings; (b) Right to counsel, including federally appointed counsel for those unable to afford private representation; (c) Right to present evidence, examine witnesses, and appeal adverse determinations; (d) Published reasoning for all determinations, available for public review upon the Franklin Ledger; (e) Appellate review within the alternative pathway structure, or upon restoration of non-captured judicial function, through ordinary courts. H. Constitutional Status and Commitment 13H.19 Article V Protection. The provisions of this Section shall be protected under the Article V protection established in Sections 18.6.1 and 18.6.2. No act of Congress, executive order, judicial ruling, or state action shall evade, diminish, or nullify the trigger mechanisms, alternative pathways, or interpretive authorities established herein. The very vulnerabilities this Section addresses — capture of courts themselves — require that this Section be particularly well-protected from further judicial erosion. 13H.20 Sunset Review Integration. The provisions of this Section shall be reviewed in each Sunset Review under Section 18. The People may, through a Modify vote, adjust trigger thresholds, alternative pathway structures, and interpretive authorities based on accumulated operational experience. The underlying principles — that courts cannot be relied upon where captured, and that alternative pathways must exist — shall be preserved. 13H.21 Foundational Commitment. The People of the United States, in ratifying this Amendment, commit themselves to the principle that no constitutional provision — no privilege, no immunity, no doctrine of deference — shall operate to shield corruption from accountability. If the courts the People depend upon for accountability are themselves compromised, alternative pathways shall exist. This Section embodies that commitment. Judicial integrity is a constitutional aspiration; it is not a constitutional guarantee. Where it fails, the People retain the sovereign authority to interpret and enforce their own Amendment through the institutions this Amendment establishes for that purpose.

Section 13I. Amendment Funding, Ratification Loan, and Repayment Framework

Key terms in this Section: • "The Authority" — The Independent Tripartite Oversight Authority (three bodies, see Section 17). • "Treasury" — The United States Department of the Treasury, acting under the authority of this Amendment. • "Ratification Loan" — The initial funding instrument issued by Treasury at the moment of Ratification to fund the Amendment's implementation, operations, and infrastructure build-out, including Authority bodies, Washington Commission, Watch Board, Hamilton Contingent, Watchdog Tribunal, and physical infrastructure. • "Amendment Operational Budget" — The ongoing funding for the three bodies of the Authority and all Amendment institutions, integrated into the regular national budget following the first full budget cycle after a new federal government is seated (whether following Ratification, Inaugural Referendum, or Reclamation). • "Confiscation Recovery" — The assets forfeited under Section 13D Post-No-Confidence Asset Recovery, divided between taxpayer distribution (70%) and Authority allocation (30%). • "Taxpayer Loan Contribution" — A scaled percentage of the taxpayer distribution pool redirected to Ratification Loan repayment, activated only under limited conditions and capped to minimize taxpayer impact. A. Foundational Principle 13I.1 Foundational Principle. This Amendment cannot be implemented without funding, and funding cannot wait for the institutions this Amendment creates to establish themselves. The Washington Commission must convene within seventy-two (72) hours of Ratification; the Watch Board within thirty (30) days; the Authority bodies within one hundred eighty (180) days; the Hamilton Contingent simultaneously — all requiring operational funding, infrastructure, personnel compensation, and facility access before any Confiscation Recovery can be realized and before any new federal budget can be established. This Section establishes the complete funding framework from Day 0 through long-term operational sustainability, grounded in a principle that must be explicitly honored throughout: the People bear no responsibility for the corruption that necessitated this Amendment, nor for the costs of restoring their democracy. Without their courage in reclaiming their government, no accountability would have been possible. The People shall not be made to pay for what was stolen from them. B. The Ratification Loan 13I.2 Automatic Issuance Authority. At the moment of Ratification, the United States Department of the Treasury shall have automatic constitutional authority to issue the Ratification Loan to fund Amendment implementation. This authority is self-executing; no act of Congress, executive order, or judicial ruling shall be required for loan issuance, and no such action shall delay or impede issuance. The Ratification Loan is a constitutional appropriation in the form of a loan, created by operation of this Amendment. 13I.3 Loan Ceiling and Expandability. The Ratification Loan shall be issued with an initial ceiling of one hundred billion dollars ($100,000,000,000), indexed for inflation from the date of Ratification. The ceiling may be expanded beyond this amount upon: (a) Authority Liberty Bell Initiative finding that additional funds are required, with detailed justification published upon the Franklin Ledger or provisional public ledger; (b) Watchdog Tribunal concurrence by two-thirds (2/3) supermajority, ensuring independent review of expansion requests; (c) Reasonable demonstration that Confiscation Recovery will provide adequate backing for expanded amounts, protecting Treasury and future taxpayers; (d) No single expansion tranche exceeding fifty billion dollars ($50,000,000,000) inflation-indexed; (e) Published reasoning for each expansion, accessible to the People through ordinary Franklin Ledger access. 13I.4 Uses of the Ratification Loan. Ratification Loan funds shall be used exclusively for Amendment-related purposes, including: (a) Washington Commission operations (Section 19.5.0); (b) Watch Board member compensation, travel, housing, and facilities (Section 19.14); (c) Interim Two-Member Command administrative support (Section 19.5.1); (d) Authority body formation and initial operations (Section 17); (e) Hamilton Contingent formation, four Divisions, regional offices, and initial operations (Section 13C); (f) Watchdog Tribunal formation and initial operations (Section 21);

(g) Sovereign Blockchain Voting Ledger testing, setup, and deployment (Section 4); (h) Franklin Ledger development and initial operations (Section 4A); (i) Citizens' Reclamation Offices, Centers, Host Sites, and Terminals establishment (Sections 11, 11.1.1, 11A, 11B, 11C, 14); (j) Pre-Certified University Pool establishment and compensation to participating institutions (Section 17.16); (k) Physical Venues for Amendment Bodies under Section 11C; (l) Any other direct implementation cost of this Amendment. 13I.5 Prohibited Uses. The Ratification Loan shall not be used for: (a) Ordinary federal government operations unrelated to Amendment implementation; (b) Political campaigns, political party operations, or political advertising; (c) Payments to removed or compromised officials; (d) Any purpose prohibited by Section 13 or Section 13A; (e) Purposes the Watchdog Tribunal determines are inconsistent with Amendment purposes. 13I.6 Treasury Administration. The Treasury shall administer the Ratification Loan with the following requirements: (a) All disbursements published upon the Franklin Ledger or provisional public ledger within seven (7) days, with recipient, amount, and purpose documented; (b) Quarterly accounting reports published by Treasury, showing total disbursements, remaining balance, and confiscation-related recoveries received; (c) Annual audit by the Academic Integrity Commission, with findings published; (d) Watchdog Tribunal oversight of any disbursement alleged to be improper; (e) Emergency disbursement authority for time-sensitive Amendment needs, with post-disbursement justification required within fourteen (14) days. C. Budget Integration 13I.7 Transition to National Budget Integration. The three bodies of the Authority and all institutions established by this Amendment shall become permanent line items in the national federal budget as follows: (a) First Full Budget Cycle. Beginning with the first full federal budget cycle after a new federal government is seated through Emergency Election (if following Reclamation), Inaugural Referendum (in ordinary course), or otherwise as applicable, the Amendment's bodies and institutions shall be funded as permanent line items in the national budget; (b) Automatic Appropriation. Funding shall flow automatically per Section 17.26 and Section 11.3, without requiring congressional authorization or subject to congressional defunding; (c) Minimum Funding Floor. The national budget shall provide not less than the annual funding required for the Amendment's bodies and institutions to perform their constitutional functions at full operational capacity, as determined by the Authority through Liberty Bell Initiative; (d) Inflation Indexing. All budget allocations shall be inflation-indexed to maintain real operational capacity; (e) Congressional Override Prohibited. No act of Congress shall reduce Amendment funding below the minimum funding floor, and any such attempt shall constitute interference under Section 13, triggering the fifteen (15) year minimum sentence and lifetime bar from public office. D. Loan Repayment Framework 13I.8 Repayment Source Hierarchy. The Ratification Loan shall be repaid through the following sources, in order of priority: (a) Confiscation Recovery — 30% Authority Share. The 30% Authority allocation from Section 13D Confiscation Recovery shall be the primary repayment source. Authority operational needs shall be funded first from this share, with remaining amounts applied to loan repayment; (b) National Budget Line Item. The national budget shall include an annual Ratification Loan Repayment line item, beginning with the first full budget cycle after new federal government seating. Repayment shall be treated as a priority obligation — senior to general discretionary spending — to ensure the loan is paid in full over reasonable time, reflecting that this debt was incurred to restore the democracy that the new government represents; (c) Supplementary Confiscation Recovery. Additional Confiscation Recovery beyond the 30% Authority share (for example, recoveries from foreign asset tracing, late-discovered assets, or successor corruption findings) shall be directed to loan repayment before any additional taxpayer distribution occurs, up to the outstanding loan balance; (d) Taxpayer Loan Contribution — Last Resort. A scaled percentage of the taxpayer distribution pool, activated only under the conditions established in Section 13I.9 through 13I.12, and never as primary repayment source. 13I.9 Priority Repayment Principle. Loan repayment shall be treated as a priority federal obligation over the years until fully paid. The Authority, Congress, and

Treasury shall collectively ensure that repayment progresses on a reasonable schedule, not exceeding twenty (20) years absent extraordinary circumstances published upon the Franklin Ledger with two-thirds (2/3) Watchdog Tribunal supermajority concurrence. The Authority shall publish quarterly repayment progress reports, with remaining balance, payment sources, and projected payoff date visible to the People. E. Taxpayer Loan Contribution — Minimal and Protected 13I.10 Foundational Protection. The People bear no responsibility for the corruption that necessitated this Amendment, nor for the costs of restoring their democracy. Without their courage in reclaiming their government, no accountability would have been possible. Any taxpayer contribution toward loan repayment shall therefore be treated as a matter of shared civic stewardship — minimal, temporary, and activated only when other repayment sources prove insufficient. The Amendment's bodies shall exhaust all alternative repayment mechanisms — Confiscation Recovery, budget prioritization, and operational economies — before asking the People to contribute. 13I.11 Activation Conditions. The Taxpayer Loan Contribution shall activate only if ALL of the following conditions are met: (a) First Distribution Completed. The first-time bonus distribution to taxpayers under Section 13D has been fully completed; (b) First Regular Distribution Completed. The first regular progressive-tier distribution following the bonus distribution has been fully completed; (c) Budget Insufficiency. National budget payments under Section 13I.8(b), combined with the 30% Authority share under Section 13I.8(a), have proven insufficient to maintain reasonable loan repayment progress as determined by the Authority; (d) Liberty Bell Initiative Finding. The Authority has, through Liberty Bell Initiative, formally determined that Taxpayer Loan Contribution activation is necessary, with reasoning published upon the Franklin Ledger. 13I.12 Scaled Contribution Schedule. If activated under Section 13I.11, the Taxpayer Loan Contribution shall follow this scaled schedule: (a) Starting Rate. Two percent (2%) of the taxpayer distribution pool, applied to loan repayment; (b) Scaling Increases. The rate shall increase by one and one-half percent (1.5%) every eighteen (18) months (one and one-half years) from activation, reflecting the steady pressure to complete loan repayment; (c) Cap. The rate shall never exceed ten percent (10%) of the taxpayer distribution pool in any year. This cap reflects the principle that the People shall not be made to bear the costs of restoring their democracy beyond a minimal and bounded level; (d) Automatic Deactivation. The Taxpayer Loan Contribution shall automatically deactivate and return to zero percent (0%) if: (i) the Ratification Loan is fully repaid; (ii) the budget and 30% Authority share are catching up with repayment targets; (iii) additional Confiscation Recovery becomes available sufficient to continue repayment without taxpayer contribution; or (iv) the Authority determines by Liberty Bell Initiative that continued contribution is no longer necessary; (e) Annual Reassessment. The Authority shall reassess Taxpayer Loan Contribution activation status annually, with reasoning for continued activation or deactivation published upon the Franklin Ledger. 13I.13 Contribution Transparency. Every taxpayer distribution affected by the Taxpayer Loan Contribution shall be accompanied by clear documentation showing: the gross amount from the distribution pool; the contribution percentage applied; the amount redirected to loan repayment; and the net amount distributed. This transparency ensures that the People can see exactly how their distribution has been affected and hold the Authority accountable for minimizing the impact. 13I.14 Authority Obligations to Minimize. The Authority shall actively work to minimize and, where possible, eliminate the Taxpayer Loan Contribution through: (a) Aggressive pursuit of Confiscation Recovery, including foreign asset tracing, late-discovered assets, and successor corruption findings; (b) Operational economies within Authority bodies and Amendment institutions; (c) Budget advocacy to ensure adequate national budget repayment contributions; (d) Regular public reporting on efforts to minimize taxpayer impact; (e) Annual determination of whether Taxpayer Loan Contribution remains necessary, with an affirmative duty to deactivate when alternative sources suffice. F. Supplementary Distribution Framework 13I.15 Additional Taxpayer Distributions. As Confiscation Recovery continues beyond the initial first-time bonus and first regular distributions, additional taxpayer distributions shall be made as follows: (a) Ongoing Distributions. Regular progressive-tier distributions shall continue under Section 13D as recovered funds meet the $10/person threshold and verification requirements; (b) Supplementary Recovery. As additional assets are recovered from foreign tracing, late-discovered holdings, or successor corruption findings, these shall be incorporated into subsequent distribution cycles; (c) Loan Repayment Priority on Supplements. Supplementary recoveries shall be applied first to outstanding loan repayment (under Section 13I.8(c)), and thereafter

to taxpayer distribution; (d) Notification. Taxpayers shall receive notification of each distribution through Franklin Ledger, IRS communications, or equivalent means, with clear accounting of source and amount. G. Constitutional Status and Protections 13I.16 Article V Protection. The provisions of this Section shall be protected under the Article V protection established in Sections 18.6.1 and 18.6.2. No act of Congress, executive order, judicial ruling, or state action shall: (a) Prevent Treasury from issuing the Ratification Loan at Ratification; (b) Reduce budget line items below the minimum funding floor; (c) Modify the Taxpayer Loan Contribution cap or activation conditions; (d) Divert loan funds to unauthorized uses; (e) Evade, diminish, or nullify the funding framework established herein. 13I.17 Sunset Review Integration. The provisions of this Section shall be reviewed in each Sunset Review under Section 18. The People may, through a Modify vote, adjust the loan ceiling, the repayment schedule, the scaling mechanism of the Taxpayer Loan Contribution, or the cap based on accumulated operational experience. However, the underlying principles — that the People shall not bear the primary cost, that the loan must be repaid over reasonable time, and that confiscation recovery is the primary repayment source — shall be preserved. 13I.18 Foundational Commitment. The People of the United States, in ratifying this Amendment, accept that implementation requires funding and that funding cannot wait for ordinary budget processes. They therefore consent to the Ratification Loan as the necessary mechanism to fund the restoration of their democracy. In return, the Amendment commits to the principle that the People shall bear the minimum possible cost of that restoration — that the corrupt shall pay for what they stole, that their corrupt wealth shall fund the oversight that prevents future theft, and that taxpayer contribution shall be the last resort, bounded and temporary. The work of democracy is the People's work, but the cost of corruption is not the People's debt. H. Funding Obstruction Protection Framework 13I.19 Foundational Principle of Funding Protection. The mechanisms of this Amendment depend on continuous funding. If funding fails, the People's sovereign authority established by this Amendment becomes unenforceable. Recognizing that a captured or corrupted federal government may attempt to defund the Amendment as a means of functional repeal without formal amendment process, the following framework establishes multiple, redundant funding pathways that cannot be simultaneously obstructed by any single officeholder, body, or coordinated faction.

This framework is itself protected under the Article V protection of Sections 18.6.1 and 18.6.2. 13I.20 Direct Treasury Draw Authority. The Amendment establishes self-executing constitutional appropriation with direct Treasury access, operating as follows: (a) Constitutional Appropriation Self-Executing. The appropriations required for this Amendment's operation constitute self-executing constitutional appropriations of the United States Treasury, effective upon Ratification and continuing in perpetuity subject only to Sunset Review modification under Section 18 or constitutional amendment under Article V. No act of Congress shall be required to activate these appropriations; no act of Congress shall be sufficient to suspend, reduce, delay, or redirect them. (b) Treasury Secretary's Constitutional Duty. The Secretary of the Treasury is constitutionally obligated to disburse funds required by this Amendment to the designated Amendment bodies upon proper request, regardless of any directive from the President, Congress, or any other federal officer to the contrary. Refusal or material delay of proper disbursement shall constitute Section 13 interference with Senior Official multipliers and shall be an independent federal offense under Section 13I.23. (c) Proper Request Defined. A proper request for disbursement shall consist of: (i) authenticated request from an authorized signatory of an Amendment body under Sections 11.3, 17.26, or this Section 13I; (ii) specific dollar amount requested; (iii) specific purpose within the body's authorized functions; (iv) certification that the amount falls within applicable funding formulas under Section 13I.21. No additional requirements, certifications, or approvals may be imposed by the Treasury Secretary, Office of Management and Budget, General Services Administration, or any other federal body. (d) Deputy Succession for Treasury Refusal. Where the Treasury Secretary refuses or fails to execute disbursement within seventy-two (72) hours of proper request, disbursement authority shall pass by operation of law to the most senior Treasury Department official willing to execute, and if no Treasury official executes within an additional forty-eight (48) hours, to the Chairperson of the Federal Reserve, and if the Federal Reserve Chairperson does not execute within an additional twenty-four (24) hours, to any Federal Reserve District President willing to execute. This successive-authority framework ensures that coordinated refusal by senior Treasury leadership cannot indefinitely block constitutional disbursement. (e) No Intermediate Approval Required. Amendment body access to Treasury funds shall not require intermediate approval by: the Office of Management and Budget; the General Services Administration; the Department of Justice; the

White House; any Presidential directive; any Executive Order; any federal court order absent clear and convincing evidence of fraudulent request. Attempts to impose intermediate approvals shall be void ab initio and shall constitute Section 13 interference.

13I.21 Baseline Funding Formula. To prevent disputes about funding amounts from becoming a capture vector, the baseline minimum funding for Amendment operations shall be determined by the following formula: (a) Formula. The annual baseline minimum funding shall be the greater of: (i) fifteen hundredths of one percent (0.15%) of total federal outlays for the preceding fiscal year; or (ii) five billion dollars ($5,000,000,000) in constant dollars indexed for inflation from the Ratification Year. This floor ensures minimum operational capacity regardless of federal budget size, while the proportional component ensures scaling with the federal government the Amendment oversees. (b) Ceiling. The annual funding for Amendment operations shall not exceed one percent (1%) of total federal outlays for the preceding fiscal year, preventing the Amendment from becoming a vehicle for disproportionate fiscal expansion. Within this ceiling, the Authority through Liberty Bell Initiative may request additional funding above the baseline minimum by specific documented showing of operational need. (c) Allocation Among Bodies. The baseline funding shall be allocated among Amendment bodies according to a schedule published on the Franklin Ledger, with initial allocation determined by the Washington Commission during Phase One and thereafter by the Authority through Liberty Bell Initiative. The allocation shall ensure: (i) adequate Offices and Centers operations under Section 11; (ii) full Hamilton Contingent operational capacity; (iii) Authority body operations; (iv) Watchdog Tribunal operations; (v) Academic Integrity Commission technical infrastructure; (vi) Franklin Ledger infrastructure; (vii) reserves for emergency needs. (d) Inflation Indexing. All baseline minimums, floors, and specific dollar amounts in this Section shall be indexed for inflation from the Ratification Year using the Consumer Price Index for All Urban Consumers (CPI-U) or successor index. Indexing shall occur automatically on the first day of each fiscal year; no Congressional or Executive action shall be required. (e) Authority to Exceed Baseline. The Amendment's bodies may spend above baseline minimums up to the Section 13I.21(b) ceiling only for: (i) documented operational needs during active No Confidence periods; (ii) emergency capital expenses (infrastructure failure, coordinated attack, natural disaster affecting operations); (iii) extraordinary prosecution costs for specific major corruption cases; and (iv) other documented exceptional circumstances. Exceeding baseline shall require published reasoning on the

Franklin Ledger and Watchdog Tribunal oversight. 13I.22 Anti-Starvation Framework. To protect against coordinated funding obstruction by federal officeholders: (a) Personal Liability for Obstruction. Any federal officeholder who directs, authorizes, materially participates in, or knowingly facilitates: (i) refusal of proper

Treasury disbursement requests; (ii) unauthorized reduction of Amendment funding below baseline minimums; (iii) redirection of Amendment funds to non-Amendment purposes; (iv) imposition of intermediate approval requirements beyond those authorized; or (v) coordinated schemes to defund Amendment operations through any means shall be subject to Section 13 interference prosecution with Senior Official multipliers, asset recovery under Section 13D Tier Three, and permanent disqualification from federal office under Section 8. (b) No Good Faith Defense for Senior Officials. Senior Officials under Section 13 definitions shall not have a good-faith defense for funding obstruction. The Amendment's funding provisions are clear on the face of the Amendment; Senior Officials are constructively aware of their obligations; and the constitutional duty to fund Amendment operations does not depend on personal agreement with the Amendment. Only the Treasury Secretary's subsection 13I.20(b) duty of disbursement, and analogous duties at other levels, control. (c) Automatic Restoration. Where obstruction has occurred, disbursement shall automatically resume upon resolution of the obstruction (whether through successor execution under Section 13I.20(d), court order, Watchdog Tribunal directive, or officeholder compliance). Retroactive payment for the obstructed period shall be required within thirty (30) days of restoration, with interest at Treasury bill rate. (d) Pattern Obstruction Enhanced Penalties. Where obstruction occurs as part of a pattern or coordinated scheme involving multiple officeholders, enhanced penalties shall apply, including: (i) treatment as Section 16.5 insurrection where the pattern affects the Amendment's capacity to function; (ii) doubled Senior Official multipliers; (iii) asset recovery extending to family members and trusts per Section 13D. (e) Whistleblower Protection for Funding Obstruction Reports. Federal employees, Treasury personnel, and other federal actors who disclose funding obstruction shall receive the full Section 13B.16 whistleblower protection framework with enhanced protections reflecting the constitutional-scale nature of Amendment funding. 13I.23 Funding Obstruction as Independent Federal Offense. The following shall constitute independent federal offenses regardless of Section 13 interference prosecution: (a) Refusal of Proper Disbursement. The Treasury Secretary or any authorized disbursement officer who, without lawful cause, refuses to execute a proper disbursement request under Section 13I.20 commits a federal offense punishable by not less than ten (10) years imprisonment, permanent disqualification from federal office under Section 8, and asset recovery under Section 13D. (b) Fraudulent Obstruction Certification. Any officeholder who falsely certifies lawful cause for refusing disbursement, or who procures such false certification, commits a federal offense punishable by the same penalties as subsection (a) plus additional penalties for perjury or false statement offenses.

(c) Coordinated Funding Attack. Conspiracy among two or more federal officeholders to obstruct Amendment funding shall constitute a federal offense separate from individual obstruction, with penalties of not less than fifteen (15) years imprisonment for each conspirator, consistent with Section 13 interference with Senior Official multipliers. (d) Instruction to Obstruct. Any federal officeholder who instructs a subordinate to obstruct Amendment funding shall be personally liable for that obstruction regardless of whether the subordinate complies, consistent with the doctrine that unlawful orders do not shield the order-giver. (e) Prosecutorial Authority. Prosecution of offenses under this Section shall proceed through the Hamilton Contingent Prosecution Division where operational, and during Phase One through the State Attorneys General Council under Section 19.5.0.5.2, with no possibility of Presidential pardon under Section 24.5. 13I.24 Contingent Fallback — Direct State Contribution Authority. Where federal funding pathways are obstructed beyond repair through successor authority under Section 13I.20(d): (a) State Voluntary Contribution. Participating Jurisdictions may voluntarily contribute funds to Amendment operations through their own state fiscal authority. State contributions do not create state obligations; no state shall be required to contribute. (b) State Contribution Treatment. State contributions shall be: (i) treated as constitutional contributions to federal constitutional operations; (ii) not subject to federal executive review, withholding, or redirection; (iii) deposited directly to Amendment body accounts maintained outside Treasury control where Treasury obstruction persists; (iv) credited toward eventual federal reimbursement when federal funding is restored. (c) Reimbursement Framework. States that contribute during federal obstruction periods shall be reimbursed from federal funds plus interest at Treasury bill rate, paid within twenty-four (24) months of obstruction cessation. Reimbursement shall take priority over general federal discretionary spending. (d) Coordination Through State Attorneys General Council. State contributions and reimbursement shall be coordinated through the State Attorneys General Council under Section

19.5.0.18, with the Council authorized to: (i) determine appropriate per-state contribution shares; (ii) manage collection and distribution; (iii) maintain federal reimbursement claims; (iv) coordinate with Amendment bodies on operational priorities during funding crises. (e) State Protection. States participating in the contingent fallback shall be protected from federal retaliation under Section 20A. Federal actions targeting participating states in retaliation for contribution shall constitute Section 13 interference and Section 20A state official targeting offenses.

13I.25 Federal Reserve Emergency Authority — Last Resort. Where both primary Treasury disbursement and state contingent funding have failed: (a) Federal Reserve Emergency Liquidity. The Federal Reserve System shall have constitutional authority to provide emergency liquidity to Amendment bodies upon documented failure of primary and state funding pathways. This authority is self-executing under this Amendment and does not require Congressional authorization or Executive direction. (b) Activation Conditions. Federal Reserve emergency authority shall activate only upon: (i) documented failure of Section 13I.20 Treasury disbursement pathway including successor authority cascade; (ii) documented failure or inadequacy of Section 13I.24 state contingent funding; (iii) specific request from Amendment body supported by Watchdog Tribunal concurrence; and (iv) no reasonable alternative funding source immediately available. (c) Repayment Framework. Federal Reserve emergency liquidity shall be repaid from future Treasury disbursements once primary pathways are restored, with interest at Federal Reserve discount window rate. Repayment shall take priority over general Amendment operational spending after minimum operational capacity is maintained. (d) Protection of Federal Reserve Participation. Federal Reserve Governors, District Presidents, and staff participating in emergency funding under this Section shall be protected from federal retaliation, with any retaliation constituting Section 13 interference with Senior Official multipliers. (e) No Primary Funding Source. Federal Reserve emergency authority is explicitly a last-resort mechanism and shall not become a primary funding pathway. Its existence does not relieve Treasury or Congress of constitutional funding obligations; its use does not establish precedent for replacing primary pathways. 13I.26 Funding During Active No Confidence Periods. Recognizing that the most acute funding-obstruction risk occurs precisely when the Amendment's operations are most needed: (a) Automatic Continuation. During any active Petition, Referendum, Committee Period, Emergency Election, or Reconstitution under Section 15, Amendment funding shall continue automatically without any additional review, approval, or certification. Existing disbursement schedules shall continue; emergency disbursement requests shall be processed on accelerated seventy-two (72) hour timelines. (b) Enhanced Surge Funding. During active No Confidence periods, Amendment bodies may draw above baseline minimums up to the Section 13I.21(b) ceiling to support: increased Office operations under Section 11.6(c); enhanced security under Section 11.8; emergency Hamilton Contingent operations; and other active-period needs. Surge funding shall be documented with reasoning published on the Franklin

Ledger. (c) No Executive Emergency Override. No Presidential emergency declaration, executive order, or other Executive action shall suspend, reduce, or redirect Amendment funding during active No Confidence periods. Attempts shall constitute Section 13 interference with doubled Senior Official multipliers reflecting the heightened gravity of crisis-period obstruction. (d) Independent Treasury Access. Amendment bodies shall maintain accounts at multiple Federal Reserve Banks and, where operationally feasible, at participating state-chartered banks, to ensure continuity of access if any single institutional pathway is obstructed. Account structure shall be designed for redundancy. 13I.27 Programmatic Disbursement Infrastructure. To ensure that human obstructors cannot indefinitely halt constitutionally required disbursements: (a) Cryptographic Disbursement Authority. The Academic Integrity Commission shall develop and maintain cryptographic disbursement infrastructure allowing Amendment bodies to receive Treasury funds through cryptographically verified automated execution where human authorization is improperly withheld. Infrastructure standards shall meet banking and Federal Reserve security standards. (b) Pre-Authorized Disbursement Schedule. Upon Ratification, a pre-authorized disbursement schedule shall be loaded into Treasury systems providing for automatic periodic disbursement of baseline funding to Amendment bodies. This schedule shall execute automatically unless formally paused through proper Amendment body request; it shall not require affirmative authorization each period. (c) Franklin Ledger Verification. All disbursements under this Section shall be cryptographically verified through the Franklin Ledger, ensuring that payment records cannot be falsified, deleted, or manipulated by obstructing actors. The Ledger serves as the authoritative record of what should have been disbursed and what was actually disbursed, with discrepancies triggering Watchdog Tribunal investigation. (d) Attempts to Disable Infrastructure. Any action to disable, corrupt, or circumvent the programmatic disbursement infrastructure shall constitute Section 13 interference, Section 13B.11 evidence destruction (where payment records are affected), and where undertaken by federal officials Section 16.12 treason where the action was part of coordinated Amendment defunding. 13I.28 Funding Transparency and Accountability. All Amendment spending shall be subject to the following transparency requirements: (a) Real-Time Publication. All Amendment body expenditures shall be published on the Franklin Ledger in real time, with detail sufficient for public verification including: recipient; amount; purpose; authorizing official; and source account. Classification of Amendment spending shall be extremely limited; operational-security classifications shall not extend to aggregate spending totals or recipient categories. (b) Annual Academic Integrity Commission Audit. The Academic Integrity Commission shall conduct annual audits of all Amendment spending, with audit methodology and findings published on the Franklin Ledger. Audits shall verify: consistency with baseline funding formulas; absence of waste, fraud, or abuse; effective operational outcomes; compliance with allocation schedules. (c) Public Response to Spending Concerns. Registered voters may submit funding-related inquiries through the Franklin Ledger citizen response framework. Amendment bodies shall respond to legitimate inquiries within thirty (30) days with explanations published on the Ledger. (d) No Kickbacks or Self-Dealing. Amendment body members, staff, and contractors shall be subject to Section 17A anti-corruption standards for all spending decisions, with self-dealing constituting Section 13A corruption with enhanced penalties reflecting the Amendment-constitutional-appropriation source of funds. (e) Sunset Review Assessment. Each Sunset Review shall include assessment of Amendment funding — whether baseline formulas are operating appropriately, whether obstruction has been adequately prevented, whether transparency mechanisms are functioning, and whether modifications to the Section 13I framework would improve effectiveness. The People retain authority to modify funding provisions through Sunset Review per Section 18. I. Bootstrap, Constitutional Authority, and Obstruction Response 13I.29 Graduated Bootstrap Through State Collective Contribution and Federal Tranches. Recognizing that concentrated lump-sum Ratification Loan disbursement before Amendment bodies exist creates both fiscal and capture risks, and that distributed state-level contribution creates political ownership, ratification incentive, and resilience against single-point federal obstruction, the Amendment bootstrap shall proceed through two integrated mechanisms operating in parallel: (a) Foundational Architecture. Bootstrap shall proceed through: (i) voluntary collective state contribution during Days 0 through 90, funding initial operations through Washington Commission, Watch Board, and early Hamilton Contingent standup; and (ii) graduated federal Ratification Loan tranches commencing at Day 90, aligned with operational milestones and providing reimbursement to contributing states. Both mechanisms operate simultaneously; neither is exclusive. Where state contribution falls short, federal Treasury disbursement under the Section 131.20 cascade remains fully available. (b) State Collective Bootstrap Target. A collective bootstrap target of two billion dollars ($2,000,000,000) in constant dollars indexed from Ratification Year is established for voluntary state contribution during Days 0 through 90. The State Attorneys General Council may call for up to an additional one billion dollars

($1,000,000,000) (aggregate three billion dollars, $3,000,000,000) upon specific documented operational need published on the provisional public ledger. Collective target achievement shall not be compulsory; states retain full discretion under federalism principles. (c) Proportional Share Calculation. Each Participating Jurisdiction's proportional share of the collective bootstrap target shall be calculated based on that Jurisdiction's share of total national population per the most recent decennial census. Proportional shares shall be published on the provisional public ledger within seventy-two (72) hours of Ratification, with clear per-state dollar amounts and payment destinations specified. Publication of per-state shares serves informational purposes only; no share constitutes state obligation. (d) Pre-Ratification State Coordination Authority. During the state ratification process for this Amendment, state legislatures are encouraged to appropriate bootstrap funds contingent on ratification success, such that contribution execution is immediate upon certified Ratification. State emergency appropriation authority existing under state law is affirmed as available for this purpose; this Amendment does not compel pre-Ratification state action, but affirms state authority to act in anticipation of Ratification. (e) Escrow Architecture. Both state bootstrap contributions and federal pathway disbursements shall flow to dedicated escrow accounts maintained at: (i) state-chartered banks in Participating Jurisdictions, chosen by the State Attorneys General Council by majority vote within thirty (30) days of Ratification; (ii) the Federal Reserve Banks of New York, San Francisco, and Chicago, providing redundant access outside any single regional banking system; and (iii) at Council election, international custodial accounts at the Bank for International Settlements for up to five percent (5%) of bootstrap funds, providing ultimate reserve resilience against total domestic institutional capture. Multi-institution architecture prevents single-point obstruction of bootstrap disbursement. (f) Days 0-30 Operational Focus. During the first thirty

(30) days post-Ratification, bootstrap funds shall support: Washington Commission convening and operations under Section 19.5; Watch Board establishment; initial Franklin Ledger infrastructure; State Attorneys General Council coordination; and emergency security for all of the foregoing. Immediate operational capacity shall be available within seventy-two (72) hours of Ratification. (g) Days 30-90 Expansion. During Days 30 through 90, expanded bootstrap draws shall support: early Hamilton Contingent staffing and preparatory infrastructure; expanded Watch Board operations; initial Office site selection in the fifty-six Participating Jurisdictions; initial Sovereign Voting Terminal procurement; and Academic Integrity Commission preparatory operations. These draws move bootstrap from emergency footing to orderly build-out ahead of federal tranche transition.

(h) Graduated Federal Tranche Schedule. Commencing at Day 90, Federal Ratification Loan tranches shall be released according to the following graduated schedule, each tied to specific operational milestones: (i) First Tranche — twenty percent (20%) of the Ratification Loan ceiling — released within thirty (30) days of Watch Board full operational certification, funding Hamilton Contingent staffing completion, Office construction acceleration, initial state bootstrap reimbursement, and Terminal deployment initiation; (ii) Second Tranche — thirty percent (30%) — released within thirty (30) days of both Hamilton Contingent operational certification under Section 13C and all three Authority bodies achieving operational quorum under Section 17, funding full operations at scale and state bootstrap reimbursement completion; (iii) Third Tranche — thirty-five percent (35%) — released progressively during the subsequent twelve (12) to twenty-four (24) months upon Authority Liberty Bell Initiative with specific documented need, funding remaining infrastructure buildout and capacity at full scale; (iv) Final Tranche — ten percent (10%) — reserved for capacity expansion and long-term operational stability needs arising in Years 2 through 4 post-Ratification; and (v) Emergency Reserve — five percent (5%) — available throughout build-out for documented emergency circumstances requiring Watchdog Tribunal supermajority concurrence with published reasoning. (i) Milestone Certification Authority. Each federal tranche release shall be triggered by specific documented milestone completion, certified by: the Watchdog Tribunal where operational; the Washington Commission by majority vote before Tribunal convenes; or where both are unavailable, the State Attorneys General Council by two-thirds supermajority. Certification shall be published on the Franklin Ledger (or provisional public ledger pre-Ledger) with factual basis for milestone finding. Milestone certification is the sole operational gate for tranche release; no Executive approval may delay release upon valid certification. (j) Spending Authority Scales with Operational Capacity. Amendment bodies may spend only against currently released tranches and available bootstrap funds. Projected tranches do not authorize spending or contractual commitment. Contracts, obligations, and financial commitments shall be bounded by currently available funds, preventing pre-commitment of future tranches and providing natural oversight check during build-out. (k) Milestone Acceleration or Delay. Where operational milestones are achieved faster than anticipated, tranches may be released early upon appropriate certification under subsection (i). Where milestones slip due to genuine operational circumstance, tranches delay correspondingly without loss of eventual availability or ceiling reduction. Where milestones slip due to obstruction, the Section 13I.22 anti-starvation framework applies to obstructors, and tranche release shall nonetheless proceed upon Watchdog Tribunal finding that milestone would have been achieved but for obstruction.

(l) Enhanced State Reimbursement. Contributing Jurisdictions shall receive priority reimbursement from federal Ratification Loan tranches upon each release, with: (i) full reimbursement of contributed principal; (ii) interest at Treasury bill rate plus two hundred basis points (+2.00%) accrued from date of contribution; (iii) initial reimbursement beginning with the First Tranche under subsection (h)(i) at Day 90, with full reimbursement complete by Second Tranche release at Day 180; (iv) priority over general federal discretionary spending. Contributing states may elect reimbursement in cash or as federal credit applicable to future federal payments, at state election. (m) Simultaneous Federal Treasury Pathway. Where state collective contribution falls short of bootstrap target, or where a Jurisdiction elects not to participate in state bootstrap, the federal Treasury disbursement pathway under Section 13I.20 cascade remains simultaneously available to provide supplementary funding during Days 0 through 90. States do not bear bootstrap alone. The integrated mechanisms ensure bootstrap success through whichever combination of state and federal contribution proves available on the timeline required. (n) State Attorneys General Council as Emergency Requestor for Federal Pathway. Until the Washington Commission convenes, the Watch Board is established, or any Amendment body has taken office, the State Attorneys General Council shall serve as emergency requestor for the simultaneous Treasury disbursement pathway under subsection (m) and for draws against escrow accounts for authorized bootstrap expenses. Council action requires majority vote, with draws documented on the provisional public ledger under Section 19.5.0.4. (o)

Ratification Certification Triggers Both Pathways. The certification of Ratification under Section 19.5.0.5.1 — whether by National Archives publication or by joint State Attorneys General declaration — shall itself trigger: (i) state contribution collection framework activation and Section 13I.29(c) proportional share publication; (ii) any pre-loaded Treasury disbursement schedule for the simultaneous federal pathway; and (iii) escrow account establishment under subsection (e). Treasury systems shall treat certification as dispositive trigger event. No additional federal executive authorization shall be required. (p) Treasury Implementation Window. Where Treasury pre-loaded disbursement schedules exist, systems shall execute within twenty-four (24) hours of Ratification certification. Any delay beyond twenty-four (24) hours shall constitute Section 13I.23 refusal offense, with the Section 13I.20(d) successor authority cascade applying with compressed timelines (twenty-four (24), twelve (12), and six (6) hour steps) reflecting bootstrap urgency. (q) Federal Reserve Bootstrap Cooperation. The Federal Reserve System shall cooperate with both state contribution escrow accounts and Treasury disbursement, including accepting escrow deposits, honoring authorized disbursements, providing technical coordination, and executing Section 13I.25 emergency authority where applicable. Federal Reserve refusal to support bootstrap operations shall constitute

Section 13 interference with Senior Official multipliers applicable to refusing Fed Governors and District Presidents. (r) Bootstrap Audit. The first operational action of the Watchdog Tribunal upon convening shall include an audit of bootstrap compliance, covering: state contribution totals and proportional achievement; federal tranche disbursement compliance with schedule and milestone certification integrity; any obstruction incidents at federal or state level; overall bootstrap resilience and lessons for future Sunset Review assessment under Section 13I.28(e). Findings shall be published on the Franklin Ledger. Bootstrap failures shall trigger accelerated Section 13I.23 prosecution where federal obstruction contributed. (s) Pre-Ratification Non-Binding Status. Nothing in this Section purports to bind the pre-Ratification Treasury, Federal Reserve, or state governments to take action before Ratification. Obligations of this Section attach at Ratification. Pre-Ratification cooperation — including Treasury system preparation, Federal Reserve coordination, and state legislative pre-appropriation — is strongly encouraged but legally voluntary. Post-Ratification obligations are fully enforceable under Sections 13I.20 through 13I.28. 13I.30 Article I Section 9 Supersession for Amendment Appropriations. To foreclose the interpretation that the self-executing appropriations of this Amendment conflict with Article I, Section 9, Clause 7 of the Constitution of the United States: (a) Constitutional Amendment Status. This Amendment operates, among its other functions, as a constitutional amendment to Article I, Section 9, Clause 7 of the Constitution ("No Money shall be drawn from the Treasury, but in Consequence of Appropriations made by Law") with respect to appropriations required for this Amendment's operation. The textual requirement of "Appropriations made by Law" is satisfied by this Amendment itself, which is the supreme law of the United States upon Ratification under Article V. (b) Self-Executing Appropriations Constitute Law. The self-executing appropriations established in Sections 11.3, 13I.2, 13I.7, 13I.20, 13I.21, 13I.29, 17.26, and related provisions throughout this Amendment constitute "Appropriations made by Law" within the meaning of Article I, Section 9, Clause 7. The Amendment is the Law; the appropriations made by the Amendment are appropriations made by Law; no further Congressional appropriation act is required to satisfy Article I, Section 9, Clause 7 for Amendment operations. This constitutional construction is binding on all federal officeholders, federal courts, and the Supreme Court. (c) Foreclosed Interpretations. No federal court, federal officeholder, or legal interpretation shall construe Article I, Section 9, Clause 7 as: (i) requiring additional Congressional appropriation beyond this Amendment for Amendment operations; (ii) permitting Congressional withholding of Amendment appropriations through budget action, continuing resolutions, debt ceiling leverage, or any other appropriations-related mechanism; (iii) creating any pathway by which Article I authority supersedes this Amendment's self-executing provisions; or (iv) treating the self-executing appropriations as anything less than the full satisfaction of Article I, Section 9, Clause 7 requirements for Amendment purposes. Constructions contrary to this subsection shall be void ab initio. (d) Narrow Scope — Non-Amendment Appropriations Unaffected. Nothing in this Section shall limit Congressional appropriation authority for non-Amendment federal operations. Article I, Section 9, Clause 7 continues to apply in full to all ordinary federal expenditures outside the narrow Amendment context. This Section addresses only the specific context of appropriations required by this Amendment's operative provisions, for which this Amendment itself constitutes the required "Appropriation made by Law" consistent with Article I, Section 9. (e) Judicial Capture Safeguard. Any judicial ruling that the Amendment's self-executing appropriations violate Article I, Section 9, Clause 7 shall be construed under Section 13H as a Judicial Capture scenario triggering alternative interpretive pathways, because such ruling would effect functional repeal of the Amendment's funding framework contrary to its explicit constitutional text and thus contrary to the People's sovereign authority expressed through Article V ratification. (f) Interpretive Rule. In any case of asserted tension between Article I, Section 9 and this Amendment's appropriations, courts and federal officeholders shall apply the interpretive principle of Section 18.6 that later constitutional provisions prevail over earlier provisions where irreconcilable, and the interpretive principle of the preamble's WHEREAS clause on ambiguity that the People's sovereign authority shall be preserved and capture of accountability structures prevented. 13I.31 Proportional State Contribution Schedule During Federal Obstruction. Where documented federal obstruction has exceeded seven (7) days without resolution through Section 13I.20(d) successor authority cascade and Section 13I.25 Federal Reserve emergency authority: (a) Proportional Share Calculation. The State Attorneys General Council shall calculate each Participating Jurisdiction's proportional share of baseline Amendment funding based on the Jurisdiction's share of total national population per the most recent decennial census. The proportional share shall be published on the Franklin Ledger within seventy-two (72) hours of the obstruction-duration threshold being crossed, with per-state dollar amounts clearly specified. (b) Voluntary Contribution Preserved. Notwithstanding proportional share calculation, state contribution remains voluntary. No Jurisdiction is obligated to contribute; failure to contribute shall not constitute material non-compliance under Section 20.15 or violate any other obligation-based provision of this Amendment. Federalism principles are preserved.

(c) Public Recording of Contribution Status. Each Jurisdiction's contribution status during federal obstruction periods shall be publicly recorded on the Franklin Ledger, including: (i) proportional share calculated; (ii) contribution made; (iii) gap between share and contribution; and (iv) timing of contribution. This public record serves only to inform the Jurisdiction's citizens of their Jurisdiction's stewardship conduct during the constitutional crisis; it creates no legal obligation, no federal consequence, and no Section 20.15 implication. (d) Accelerated Priority Reimbursement. Contributing Jurisdictions shall receive accelerated reimbursement from federal funds upon obstruction cessation, with reimbursement priority in the following order: (i) Jurisdictions contributing at or above proportional share; (ii) Jurisdictions contributing below proportional share but non-zero. Reimbursement shall complete within eighteen (18) months of obstruction cessation, rather than the twenty-four (24) months of Section

13I.24(c). (e) Enhanced Interest Rate. Interest on reimbursed state contributions during federal obstruction periods shall accrue at the Treasury bill rate plus two hundred basis points (+2.00%), reflecting the extraordinary constitutional service provided. Ordinary state contributions under Section 13I.24 continue to accrue at Treasury bill rate without enhancement. (f) Coordination Through State Attorneys General Council. The State Attorneys General Council shall coordinate: (i) contribution schedule activation and publication; (ii) collection from contributing Jurisdictions; (iii) distribution to Amendment bodies per operational priorities; (iv) reimbursement claim preservation; and (v) reporting to the Watchdog Tribunal upon operational. Contributions shall be made at state-chartered banks or Federal Reserve accounts outside the captured Treasury pathway to ensure obstruction cannot intercept state-funded bootstrap operations. (g) No Federal Retaliation. Jurisdictions contributing under this Section, and the state officials authorizing such contributions, shall face no federal liability, investigation, regulation, prosecution, or retaliation for their contributions. Retaliation shall constitute Section 13 interference with Senior Official multipliers, Section 20A state official targeting offenses, and where severe, Section 16.5 insurrection where retaliation was part of a coordinated scheme against the state's constitutional contribution. (h) Sunset Upon Federal Restoration. The proportional contribution schedule shall sunset automatically upon restoration of federal funding pathways. Sunset shall be certified by Watchdog Tribunal finding or State Attorneys General Council majority vote, with restored federal funding resuming ordinary operation and state contribution schedule suspended pending any future obstruction. 13I.32 Extended State Attorneys General Council Enforcement Authority During Federal Enforcement Obstruction. Section 19.5.0.5.2 establishes the State Attorneys General Council as primary federal prosecution authority during Phase One before the Hamilton Contingent becomes operational. The following extension addresses the separate scenario of federal enforcement obstruction during any period after Phase One: (a) Conditional Extension. Whenever federal enforcement of Section 13 interference offenses, Section 13I.23 funding obstruction offenses, or Section 13A corruption offenses is itself obstructed — whether through Hamilton Contingent defunding, Hamilton Contingent physical suppression or capture, coordinated federal refusal to prosecute, or analogous enforcement failure — the State Attorneys General Council shall reactivate federal prosecution authority under the Section 19.5.0.5.2 framework until enforcement is restored. (b) Activation Conditions. Conditional extension shall activate automatically upon any of the following: (i) documented Hamilton Contingent obstruction for more than fourteen (14) days affecting Section 13 or Section 13I.23 prosecutions; (ii) Watchdog Tribunal finding by majority that federal enforcement is obstructed; (iii) unanimous State AG Council finding that federal enforcement of Amendment offenses has ceased to function; or (iv) failure of Hamilton Contingent to prosecute Section 13I.23 funding obstruction offenses for more than thirty (30) days following documented obstruction. (c) Same Procedural Framework. Extended enforcement authority shall operate under the same procedural framework as Phase One Section 19.5.0.5.2 authority: two-thirds (2/3) supermajority Council authorization for specific prosecutions; lead prosecutor designation by jurisdiction of offense; coordinated investigation; and record transfer to Hamilton Contingent upon operational restoration, without loss of accountability continuity. (d) Priority for Funding Obstruction Cases. Under extended authority, priority shall be given to Section 13I.23 funding obstruction cases, recognizing that funding enforcement is itself necessary to prevent recursion of the obstruction that triggered the extension. The Council shall establish a Funding Obstruction Priority Docket with expedited processing. (e) Sunset Upon Restoration. Extended authority shall sunset automatically upon: (i) Hamilton Contingent operational restoration certified by Watchdog Tribunal; or (ii) combined two-thirds (2/3) supermajority of State AG Council and Watchdog Tribunal finding that federal enforcement is functioning. Pending prosecutions shall transfer to restored federal enforcement without prejudice, with Hamilton Contingent required to continue or explain declination per Section 13C.4.1. (f) State AG Protection Extended. State Attorneys General and Council members acting under extended authority shall have the same federal protections as Phase One authority: no federal liability for Council-authorized prosecutions; protection against federal retaliation; enhanced Section 22 foreign interference protection where relevant; Section 17C state-sovereign accountability framework if any Covered Official is implicated.

(g) Public Notification. Activation, operation, and sunset of extended authority shall be published on the Franklin Ledger, ensuring public knowledge of when the accountability framework is operating in extended versus ordinary mode. The public notification shall include the factual basis for activation and the conditions required for sunset. (h) Federal Court Jurisdiction Preserved. Federal courts retain jurisdiction over extended-authority prosecutions consistent with Section 19.5.0.5.2(b). Where federal courts are themselves captured, Section 17C state-sovereign adjudication pathways apply for Covered Officials, and Section 13H alternative interpretive pathways apply for ordinary federal officials under prosecution. J. Consolidated Role Summaries — Navigation for Key Actors 13I.33 Treasury Secretary's Consolidated Role Under This Amendment. The Secretary of the Treasury has specific constitutional duties under this Amendment consolidated here for operational clarity. These duties operate in addition to, and where conflicting supersede, any contrary Executive direction or Congressional instruction: (a) Ratification Loan Issuance. Upon certified Ratification under Section 19.5.0.5.1, the Secretary shall issue the Ratification Loan automatically per Section 13I.2, without requiring Presidential order, Executive order, or Congressional authorization. (b) Day-0 Bootstrap Execution. The Secretary shall execute the graduated Ratification Loan tranche schedule under Section 13I.29(h), with each tranche released upon milestone certification per Section 13I.29(i). Treasury systems shall execute pre-loaded disbursement schedules within the twenty-four (24) hour window under Section 13I.29(p). (c) Direct Treasury Draw Authority. The Secretary shall honor proper disbursement requests from Amendment bodies under Section 13I.20(c), within the timeframes specified. Claims of executive privilege, deliberative privilege, or similar doctrines shall not bar honoring proper requests. (d) Baseline Funding Formula. The Secretary shall disburse baseline Amendment funding per Section 13I.21 formula (greater of 0.15% of federal outlays or $5 billion indexed), with allocation among bodies per published schedule. Disbursement is constitutional obligation, not discretion. (e) Successor Authority Cascade. Where the Secretary cannot or will not act, authority cascades under Section 13I.20(d): to subordinate Treasury officials, then to the Federal Reserve Chairperson, then to Federal Reserve District Presidents. The Secretary's failure does not block Amendment operations; it only shifts responsibility.

(f) Article I Section 9 Constitutional Status. The Secretary shall treat Amendment self-executing appropriations as constitutionally valid "Appropriations made by Law" per Section 13I.30. No additional Congressional appropriation is required for Amendment operations; Section 13I.30 is binding constitutional construction. (g) Cooperation with Federal Reserve. The Secretary shall cooperate with Federal Reserve emergency liquidity authority under Section 13I.25 when primary pathways fail, and with Federal Reserve bootstrap coordination under Section 13I.29. (h) Cooperation with State Attorneys General Council. The Secretary shall honor disbursement requests from the State Attorneys General Council acting as emergency requestor per Section 13I.29(n) until Amendment bodies convene, and shall coordinate on state bootstrap contributions and reimbursement under Sections 13I.24 and

13I.31. (i) Transparency Obligations. The Secretary shall cooperate with Franklin Ledger real-time publication of all Amendment-related disbursements per Section 13I.28(a). Classification of Amendment disbursements shall be extremely limited. (j) Prohibited Actions. The Secretary shall not: (i) require additional Congressional or Executive authorization beyond this Amendment for Amendment disbursements; (ii) redirect Amendment funds to non-Amendment purposes; (iii) impose intermediate approval gates not established in this Amendment; (iv) refuse Amendment disbursement absent lawful cause; (v) delay Amendment disbursement beyond specified timeframes without Section 13I.23 lawful justification. (k) Consequences for Obstruction. Failure to perform Treasury duties under this Amendment subjects the Secretary to: (i) Section 13 interference prosecution with Senior Official multipliers; (ii) Section 13I.23(a) refusal offense with not less than ten (10) years imprisonment; (iii) permanent Section 8 disqualification; (iv) Section 13D asset recovery; (v) no Presidential pardon available under Section 24.5. (l) Protection for Acting Consistently with Amendment. A Secretary acting consistently with Amendment duties — including acting against contrary Executive direction where necessary — shall receive full Section 13B.16 whistleblower protection, the Section 17 protected refusal framework, and protection from federal retaliation. (m) Role Continuity. The duties in this Section apply to the sitting Treasury Secretary at Ratification and to every successor Treasury Secretary thereafter. The duties are ongoing constitutional obligations, not one-time Ratification-moment actions. 13I.34 Federal Reserve's Consolidated Role Under This Amendment. The Federal Reserve System has specific constitutional duties under this Amendment consolidated here for operational clarity. Federal Reserve monetary policy independence is preserved; these duties supplement but do not replace ordinary

Federal Reserve authority: (a) Successor Authority Cascade. Where Treasury officials refuse to execute Amendment disbursement, successor authority passes under Section 13I.20(d) to the Chairperson of the Federal Reserve, and if the Chairperson does not execute, to any Federal Reserve District President willing to execute. The Chairperson and District Presidents shall execute Amendment disbursements under this cascade without requiring additional authorization. (b) Emergency Liquidity Authority. The Federal Reserve has self-executing constitutional authority under Section 13I.25 to provide emergency liquidity to Amendment bodies when primary Treasury and state funding pathways fail. This authority activates under Section 13I.25(b) conditions and operates without Congressional authorization or Executive direction. (c) Bootstrap Cooperation.

The Federal Reserve shall cooperate with both state bootstrap contributions and federal Treasury disbursement under Section 13I.29(q), including accepting escrow deposits, honoring authorized disbursements, and providing technical coordination with Treasury systems. (d) Escrow Account Hosting. The Federal Reserve Banks of New York, San Francisco, and Chicago shall host dedicated escrow accounts per Section 13I.29(e) for bootstrap contributions and federal disbursements, providing redundant access outside any single regional banking system. (e) Independence Preserved. Amendment duties do not compromise ordinary Federal Reserve monetary policy independence. Interest rate decisions, open market operations, bank regulation, and other monetary policy functions remain within Federal Reserve independent authority. Amendment duties are specific and limited; they do not subordinate the Federal Reserve to Amendment bodies for monetary policy purposes. (f) Coordination Framework. The Federal Reserve shall coordinate with Treasury on Amendment disbursements and with the State Attorneys General Council on bootstrap operations under Section 13I.24 and Section 13I.31 contingent fallback funding. Coordination respects Federal Reserve independence while ensuring Amendment operations are funded. (g) International Reserve Coordination. The Federal Reserve shall coordinate under Section 13I.29(g) with the Bank for International Settlements and allied central banks for international reserve components up to five percent (5%) of bootstrap funds, providing resilience against total domestic-institution capture. (h) Prohibited Actions. The Federal Reserve shall not: (i) refuse Amendment emergency liquidity authority when Section 13I.25(b) conditions are met; (ii) decline to host required escrow accounts; (iii) obstruct Amendment disbursement pathways through the successor authority cascade; (iv) collaborate with Treasury or Executive obstruction of Amendment funding; (v) abuse Amendment duties as pretext for expanded monetary policy authority. (i) Consequences for Obstruction. Federal Reserve Chairperson, Governor, or District President failure to perform Amendment duties subjects them to: (i) Section 13 interference prosecution with Senior Official multipliers applicable to Senate-confirmed officials; (ii) Section 13I.23 refusal offense with not less than ten (10) years imprisonment; (iii) permanent Section 8 disqualification from public office; (iv) Section 13D asset recovery where obstruction enables personal benefit. (j) Protection for Federal Reserve Officials Acting Consistently with Amendment. Chairperson, Governors, District Presidents, and Federal Reserve staff acting consistently with Amendment duties — including acting against contrary Executive or Congressional pressure where necessary — receive full whistleblower and anti-retaliation protection per Section 13I.25(d). (k) Role Continuity. The duties in this Section apply to sitting Federal Reserve Chairperson, Governors, and District Presidents at Ratification and to every successor thereafter. Duties are ongoing constitutional obligations. 13I.35 State Governors' Consolidated Role Under This Amendment. State Governors (including the Mayor of the District of Columbia and territorial Governors of Participating Jurisdictions) have specific constitutional duties under this Amendment consolidated here for operational clarity. These duties operate as supplements to ordinary state executive authority: (a) Interim Caretaker Council Ex Officio Service. Upon passage of a Declaration of No Confidence, the sitting Governor of each Participating Jurisdiction serves ex officio on the Interim Caretaker Council under Section 6A.2, exercising limited emergency caretaker authority under Sections 6A.8 through 6A.28 until the Constitutional Transition Committee convenes. (b) State Bootstrap Contribution Authority. Governors may propose and state legislatures may appropriate voluntary bootstrap contributions during Days 0-90 under Section 13I.29(b), with proportional shares calculated under Section 13I.29(c) and enhanced reimbursement under Section 13I.29(l). Governors shall not be required to propose contributions, but authority to do so is affirmed. (c) Proportional State Contribution During Federal Obstruction. Where federal funding is obstructed, Governors may propose and state legislatures may appropriate proportional state contributions under Section 13I.31, with accelerated reimbursement at Treasury rate plus two hundred basis points (+2.00%). Governors are protected from federal retaliation under Section 13I.31(g). (d) State Elections Council Coordination. Where a State Elections Council sub-council activates under State AG Council emergency authority, Governors shall facilitate state executive cooperation with the sub-council's Amendment functions. Governors shall not obstruct State Elections Council operations within their Jurisdictions.

(e) Blockchain Infrastructure Selection Role. Governors participate in the blockchain infrastructure selection process under Section 19.4 through their Jurisdictions' participation in the Amendment's implementation framework. Specific Governor role is as state-level coordinator, not as unilateral decision-maker. (f) National Guard Coordination. Where a Jurisdiction's National Guard is federalized for Amendment-related military operations under Section 16, Governors coordinate with federal military authority through ordinary state-federal military coordination channels. Governor authority over state National Guard in non-federalized status continues under state law. (g) State Attorneys General Council Support. Governors shall facilitate their

Jurisdiction's Attorney General's participation in the State Attorneys General Council under Section 19.5.0.18, including supporting the AG's engagement in Council deliberations, bootstrap coordination, extended enforcement authority under Section 13I.32, and other Council functions. (h) State Non-Compliance Consequences. Governors whose Jurisdictions actively obstruct Amendment operations face Section 20 non-compliance consequences applicable to their Jurisdictions. Active Governor obstruction, beyond mere Jurisdiction non-participation, may trigger personal Section 13 interference liability with state-official adaptations under Section 20A. (i) Sunset Review Participation. Governors may, through their participation in state-level Amendment implementation, provide input to Sunset Review processes under Section 18. State-level operational experience informs Sunset Review deliberations on Amendment modifications. (j) Protection from Federal Retaliation. Governors acting consistently with Amendment duties — including through Caretaker Council service, bootstrap contribution support, State AG Council coordination, or other Amendment participation — receive Section 20A protection against federal retaliation, Section 13 interference prosecution for actors targeting them, and Section 22 foreign interference protection where relevant. (k) Hardship Framework Adaptation. The Section 17.4 hardship framework applies to Governors' Caretaker Council service with adaptations in Section 6A.26 reflecting ex officio nature. Governors facing genuine hardship cannot be compelled to continue Caretaker service in a manner incompatible with health, family circumstance, or their ability to serve their state executive duties. (l) Role Continuity. The duties in this Section apply to sitting Governors at Ratification and to successor Governors through state constitutional succession. Duties are ongoing state-executive-level constitutional obligations under this Amendment.

13I.36 Treasury Disbursement Timing Requirements and Delay-Equals-Refusal Presumption. Recognizing that Section 13I.23 makes refusal to disburse Amendment funding a Section 13 interference offense, and recognizing that captured or hostile Treasury administration may attempt to evade Section 13I.23 by characterizing functional refusal as ordinary processing delay — "the wire transfer is in queue," "the appropriations memo is awaiting legal counsel review," "the disbursement requires additional documentation we have not yet specified" — thereby starving Amendment institutions of operational funds without ever issuing a formal refusal subject to Section 13I.23 prosecution, the following timing framework converts administrative slow-walking into prosecutable refusal: (a) Foundational Principle. The Section 13I.2 automatic constitutional authority for the Ratification Loan and the Section 13C.20

constitutional appropriation for Hamilton Contingent funding are self-executing; they do not require Treasury discretion or Treasury convenience. Treasury's role with respect to Amendment funding is administrative execution of constitutional command, not policy review of constitutional command. Delay beyond the timing requirements of this Section is therefore not ordinary administrative processing; it is functional refusal subject to Section 13I.23 penalties; (b) Disbursement Categories and Timing Requirements. The following timing requirements apply to Treasury disbursement of Amendment funding, calculated from the date of properly-formatted disbursement request by an Authority body, the Hamilton Contingent, the Permanent Washington Commission, or other Amendment institution authorized to receive funding: (i) Operational Funding (recurring institutional operating costs, payroll, facility costs, ordinary supplies): seven (7) calendar days; (ii) Time-Sensitive Funding (election-related operations, security-related expenditures, emergency response): seventy-two (72) hours; (iii) Initial Ratification Loan Tranches (the first three tranches following Ratification, supporting Phase One bootstrapping): forty-eight (48) hours from each tranche request; (iv) Procurement Funding (contract payments to vendors, infrastructure costs): fourteen (14) calendar days; (v) Asset Recovery Distribution (recovered Section 13D corruption proceeds awaiting redistribution): thirty (30) calendar days; (c) Properly-Formatted Disbursement Request. A disbursement request shall be deemed properly formatted upon meeting the following minimum requirements: (i) identification of the requesting Amendment institution by Section reference; (ii) amount requested with line-item or category-based justification; (iii) specification of disbursement category under subsection (b); (iv) routing information for the receiving account; (v) reference to the constitutional authorization under which disbursement is sought (Section 13I.2 Ratification Loan, Section 13C.20 Hamilton funding, Section 11.3 constitutional appropriation, Section 13D asset recovery distribution, etc.). Treasury may not require additional formatting elements not enumerated in this subsection; the Amendment's constitutional authority to compel disbursement supersedes ordinary Treasury formatting discretion; (d) Documentation Inquiry Window. Where Treasury has good-faith documentation inquiries regarding a disbursement request, such inquiries shall be raised in a single consolidated communication within forty-eight (48) hours of receiving the request. Documentation inquiries raised after the forty-eight (48) hour window shall not toll the timing requirements of subsection (b). Documentation inquiries shall be specific, narrowly scoped to material questions about the request as submitted, and shall not constitute requests for additional or non-required documentation. The requesting Amendment institution shall respond within seven (7) calendar days; upon response, the timing requirements of subsection (b) resume from the response date with the time elapsed during the documentation inquiry tolled; (e) Delay-Equals-Refusal Presumption. Treasury failure to disburse within the applicable timing requirements of subsection (b), as adjusted by any properly-tolled documentation inquiry under subsection (d), shall constitute a rebuttable presumption of Section 13I.23 refusal to disburse. The presumption applies automatically; the Amendment institution requesting disbursement need not separately prove refusal beyond demonstrating that the timing requirement was missed. Treasury may rebut the presumption by demonstrating, with clear and convincing evidence, that the delay arose from circumstances genuinely outside Treasury's control (such as documented federal banking system outages, documented natural disaster impacts on Treasury operations, or specific cybersecurity incidents requiring immediate operational response). Mere administrative inconvenience, staffing constraints, internal policy review, or coordinated executive-branch slow-walking shall not rebut the presumption; (f) Personal Officeholder Liability. Treasury Secretary, Deputy Secretary, Assistant Secretaries, Bureau of the Fiscal Service Commissioner, and any other Treasury officeholder who directs, authorizes, or materially participates in delay beyond the timing requirements of subsection (b) shall be subject to Section 13I.23 personal liability with the following specifications: (i) Senior Official multipliers under Section 13A.3 apply where the officeholder is Senate-confirmed; (ii) the Section 13I.23 minimum sentence of ten (10) years applies upon conviction; (iii) personal asset recovery under Section 13D applies where the officeholder received personal benefit from the delay; (iv) lifetime bar from public office under Section 13.2 applies; (v) bar from federal financial-services industry employment for a period of ten (10) years following sentence completion; (g) Pattern Analysis. The Watchdog Tribunal under Section 21 (and during Phase One the AIC-Designate Forensic Consortium under Section 13B.7.1 with State AG Council support) shall conduct ongoing pattern analysis of Treasury disbursement timing across all Amendment funding requests, identifying: clustered delays affecting specific Amendment institutions; correlation between delays and political circumstance; correlation between delays and identity of the disbursement-authorizing Treasury officeholder; and other patterns inconsistent with ordinary Treasury administration. Pattern findings shall be published on the Franklin Ledger and shall constitute admissible evidence in Section 13I.23 prosecutions; (h)

Emergency Direct Disbursement Pathway. Where Treasury delay beyond subsection (b) timing requirements creates documented operational crisis for an Amendment institution — inability to make payroll, inability to maintain critical infrastructure, inability to conduct time-sensitive operations — the affected

institution may petition the Permanent Washington Commission under Section 17D for Emergency Direct Disbursement Authorization. Upon Commission majority vote (four of seven Chief Justices), the Commission may direct disbursement through alternative channels including: (i) Federal Reserve direct disbursement under Section 13I.34, with Federal Reserve operating under its independent constitutional duties; (ii) State AG Council coordination of state-level bridge financing under Section 13I.32 with accelerated reimbursement; (iii) other constitutionally-grounded alternative pathways the Commission identifies as necessary to prevent operational collapse. Emergency Direct Disbursement Authorization shall be published on the provisional public ledger or Franklin Ledger with full reasoning. Treasury obstruction of Emergency Direct Disbursement Authorization itself constitutes Section 13I.23 refusal subject to enhanced personal liability; (i) Federal Executive Non-Interference. No President, Vice President, Cabinet officer, federal agency head, or other federal executive officeholder — specifically including Treasury Secretary, Office of Management and Budget Director, and White House Chief of Staff — shall direct, fund, influence, pressure, or impede Treasury disbursement of Amendment funding. Direction by such officeholders to delay, slow-walk, or obstruct disbursement constitutes Section 13 interference with Senior Official multipliers, prosecutable through the Section 17C.15 framework regardless of whether the directed Treasury officeholder ultimately complies with the direction; (j) Funding. Costs of Treasury disbursement timing administration, pattern analysis, and Emergency Direct Disbursement Authorization operations shall be funded through the constitutional appropriation under Section 11.3, which itself is subject to the timing requirements of this Section, ensuring that the framework preserving disbursement timing cannot itself be starved through disbursement timing manipulation; (k) Article V Protection. The provisions of this Section shall be protected under the Article V protection established in Sections 18.6.1 and 18.6.2. The capacity of Amendment institutions to operate cannot depend on the cooperation of officials whose own conduct may be the subject of Amendment investigation.

Section 14. Sovereign Voting Terminals and the Sovereign Civic Network

Key terms in this Section: • "The Authority" — The Independent Tripartite Oversight Authority (three bodies, see Section 17). • "The Ledger" — The Sovereign Blockchain Voting Ledger (Section 4). • "Terminal" — A Sovereign Voting Terminal — a dedicated, air-gapped, open-source, AIC-manufactured device used exclusively for casting verified in-person votes and signatures under this Amendment. Not general-purpose, not internet-connected, not connected to any government network.

• "Sovereign Civic Network" — The dedicated fiber-optic network, separate from the public internet, carrying all Terminal and Ledger traffic. Owned by the Authority, operated under public audit, physically isolated from commercial and federal networks. • "AIC / Academic Integrity Commission" — The third body of the Authority (Section 17), which designs, certifies, and audits all Terminal hardware and software. 14.1 Each Office and Center shall have no fewer than one Terminal per 5,000 voters, designed and certified exclusively by the Academic Integrity Commission. 14.2 Voting shall be a single continuous in-person transaction with immediate cryptographic recording. 14.3 Terminals shall operate fully air-gapped. 14.4 The Network shall be dedicated, encrypted, physically independent fiber-optic infrastructure with redundant routing. 14.5 Tampering shall be a federal felony of not less than 20 years, or 30 years without parole during an active vote. 14.6 Full security audits shall occur every 2 years and 90 days before any scheduled vote. 14.7 Source Code Transparency. All Terminal software, Ledger code, and Sovereign Civic Network protocols shall be fully open source, published continuously upon the Ledger, and available for independent cryptographic analysis by any citizen, academic institution, or civic organization. No proprietary code, black-box components, or closed-source dependencies shall be incorporated into any Terminal, Network, or Ledger infrastructure. 14.8 Terminal Supply Chain Integrity. All Terminal hardware components shall be sourced, manufactured, and assembled under Academic Integrity Commission supervision, with cryptographic attestation of supply chain integrity at every stage from component sourcing through final deployment. No single component or manufacturing stage shall be dependent on any single foreign supplier or any entity controlled by a Foreign Person or Entity as defined in Section 22. Supply chain records shall be published upon the Ledger. 14.9 Overseas Participation. The Authority shall establish secure Sovereign Voting Terminals at United States embassies, major consulates, and major military installations abroad, connected to the Sovereign

Civic Network via dedicated encrypted channels meeting the same security standards applicable to domestic Offices and Centers. These Overseas Terminals shall serve United States citizens and nationals residing or temporarily stationed abroad, including active-duty military personnel, military spouses and dependents, federal employees stationed overseas, private-sector expatriates, students studying abroad, and dual citizens. All signatures collected and votes cast at Overseas Terminals shall be subject to the same in-person verification and immediate cryptographic recording as domestic transactions. Signatures and votes shall be counted toward the Participating Jurisdiction of the voter's most recent United States residence of record, or, for voters with no prior United States residence, toward a separate Overseas Americans Jurisdiction administered by the State Elections Council. Overseas Terminals shall not be operated, controlled, or accessed by the State Department, the Department of Defense, or any host-nation government; they shall be operated exclusively by civilian personnel of the Authority and the applicable Office or Center, with protected premises and protected personnel equivalent to domestic Offices. Voter-Verified Paper Ballot System 14.10 Foundational Principle. Notwithstanding the cryptographic verification provided by the dual-chain Ledger under Section 4, every vote cast under this Amendment shall also produce a voter-verified paper ballot retained as an independent physical record of the vote. The paper ballot serves as a third verification source beyond the two Primary Chains, provides disaster-recovery capability independent of electronic infrastructure, enables hand-count verification in case of dispute, and preserves public trust through tangible, human-inspectable evidence of each vote cast. 14.11 Voter Verification Process. Every Sovereign Voting Terminal shall incorporate a secure paper ballot printer operating through the following process: (a) Upon the voter completing their selection on the Terminal screen, the Terminal shall print a paper ballot showing the voter's selection in human-readable form; (b) The printed ballot shall include: the complete vote selection in plain language; a unique cryptographic hash linking the paper ballot to the corresponding blockchain transaction; the date and time of the vote; the Office, Center, Host Site, or Overseas Terminal identifier; and a randomly-generated ballot serial number unconnected to voter identity; (c) The ballot shall NOT include any information identifying the voter personally, preserving the secret-ballot principle; (d) The voter shall view the printed ballot to verify accuracy before the vote is finalized; (e) If the printed ballot does not match the voter's intent, the voter may void the ballot and re-cast their vote, with the voided ballot marked as such and retained separately for audit purposes; (f) Upon the voter confirming accuracy, the Terminal shall deposit the paper ballot into a secure, tamper-evident sealed container within the Terminal, without the

voter handling the physical ballot; (g) At no point shall the voter be permitted to remove a paper ballot from the premises, preventing voter coercion, vote-buying schemes, or chain-of-custody breaks. 14.12 Ballot Container Security. Every Terminal shall be equipped with a secure paper ballot container meeting the following requirements: (a) Tamper-evident design with cryptographic seals that record any unauthorized access attempt; (b) Physical security sufficient to prevent removal or substitution of ballots without detection; (c) Capacity sufficient for the anticipated voting volume at that location plus fifty percent (50%) surge capacity; (d) Overflow protocols requiring pause of voting and Oversight Officer response if capacity is reached, with sealed transfer to secondary container; (e) End-of-session sealing by two-person rule requiring both the Oversight Officer on duty and a citizen observer drawn by same-day lottery from voters present; (f) Full videorecording of container sealing preserved under Section 13B. Chain of Custody and Retention 14.13 Chain of Custody. Paper ballot containers shall be transferred from each voting location to custody of the Watchdog Tribunal under the following chain-of-custody procedures: (a) Immediate sealing at the end of each voting day or voting session, with seal certification recorded upon the Ledger; (b) Transfer within twenty-four (24) hours to secure Watchdog Tribunal custody facilities, via custody chain including two (2) Tribunal personnel and continuous GPS-tracked transport; (c) Logging of every container's location, handlers, and seal status on the Ledger in real time, with automatic alerts on any chain-of-custody anomaly; (d) Storage in climate-controlled, physically-secured Watchdog Tribunal facilities designed to preserve paper integrity; (e) Inventory verification weekly during active custody, with results published on the Ledger. 14.14 Watchdog Tribunal Custody. The Watchdog Tribunal established in Section 21 shall maintain primary custody of all paper ballots throughout the retention period, with the following responsibilities:

(a) Secure storage in Tribunal facilities designed and certified by the Academic Integrity Commission; (b) Regular audits of container integrity and chain-of-custody records; (c) Production of ballots for authorized hand-count audits under Section 14.15; (d) Publication upon the Ledger of custody status, audit results, and any chain-of-custody concerns; (e) Enforcement of restrictions on access, with unauthorized access constituting evidence destruction under

Section 13B; (f) Coordination with the Hamilton Contingent Preservation Division under Section 13C.3 for technical custody infrastructure. 14.15 Hand-Count Triggers. Hand audit of paper ballots shall be conducted only when triggered by one or more of the following: (a) Material Discrepancy: any material disagreement between the two Primary Chains under Section 4.12, automatically triggering hand audit of affected jurisdictions; (b) Close Vote: any Referendum or election where the margin falls below the thresholds established in Section 23, triggering hand audit pursuant to Section 23 procedures; (c) Watchdog Tribunal Order: upon two-thirds (2/3) supermajority finding by the Tribunal that hand audit is warranted to protect the integrity of a specific vote, whether based on citizen complaints, statistical anomalies, intelligence of interference, or other credible basis; (d) Citizen Petition: upon petition signed by not fewer than five hundred thousand (500,000) registered voters from at least ten (10) Participating Jurisdictions alleging specific grounds for concern, with petition verified by the State Elections Council and reviewed by the Tribunal. 14.16 Hand-Count Procedures. Authorized hand audits shall proceed under the following procedures: (a) Scope: the Tribunal shall specify the geographic and numerical scope of the hand audit, ranging from targeted jurisdictional audits to full national recounts depending on the trigger; (b) Personnel: hand counting shall be performed by teams of five (5) counters including at least one (1) Tribunal representative, one (1) State Elections Council representative, one (1) Citizens' Oversight Board representative by lottery, and two (2) civilian observers selected by lottery from registered voters of the jurisdiction; (c) Public Observation: hand counts shall be open to public observation, livestreamed upon the Ledger, and publicly documented;

(d) Reconciliation: hand-count results shall be reconciled with blockchain tallies with any discrepancy investigated by the Academic Integrity Commission and Hamilton Contingent Prosecution Division as appropriate; (e) Binding Authority: where hand-count results conflict with blockchain results in a manner attributable to blockchain compromise or error, the hand-count results shall be binding, and the affected blockchain chain shall be referred to the Academic Integrity Commission for investigation and potential Standby Chain activation under Section 4.14; (f) Timeline: hand audits shall be completed within sixty (60) days of initiation, with extensions permitted only upon Tribunal finding of operational necessity. 14.17 Retention Period. Paper ballots shall be retained by the Watchdog Tribunal for a period of five (5) years from the date of the vote, after which they shall be destroyed under the procedures of Section 14.18. The five-year retention period is calibrated to balance preservation of physical evidence against the costs of permanent retention and the cryptographic backup provided by the dual-chain Ledger. 14.18 Documented Destruction. Upon expiration of the five-year retention period, paper ballots shall be destroyed under the following documented procedures: (a) Ninety (90) Day Advance Notice: the Watchdog Tribunal shall publish upon the Ledger, not less than ninety (90) days before scheduled destruction, notice of the specific ballots scheduled for destruction, including the vote date, jurisdictions affected, and ballot counts; (b) Public Comment Period: during the ninety-day notice period, any citizen, organization, or Authority body may petition the Tribunal to extend retention of specific ballots for ongoing investigations, pending litigation, or other legitimate purposes; (c) Tribunal Review: the Tribunal shall review all extension petitions and publish written determinations upon the Ledger, with retention extensions granted as warranted; (d) Destruction Method: destruction shall be performed by industrial cross-cut shredding followed by incineration or secure pulping, in the presence of: at least three (3) Tribunal members; at least two (2) Citizens' Oversight Board members by lottery; and continuous videorecording preserved on the Ledger; (e) Complete Documentation: the destruction event shall be documented with: the specific ballots destroyed (by jurisdiction and count); the personnel present; the destruction method; timestamps; and chain-of-custody records from storage to destruction; (f) Ledger Publication: all destruction documentation shall be published upon the Ledger within seven (7) days of destruction, accessible to any citizen in perpetuity;

(g) Cryptographic Hashes Retained: the cryptographic hashes linking destroyed ballots to their blockchain transactions shall be retained permanently upon the Ledger, even after the physical ballots are destroyed, enabling continued verification that paper ballots existed and matched recorded votes during their retention period; (h) No Partial Destruction Without Documentation: any destruction of paper ballots before the full retention period has expired shall require Tribunal two-thirds (2/3) supermajority approval published on the Ledger; unauthorized or undocumented destruction shall constitute evidence destruction under Section 13B. 14.19 Ballot Privacy Protection. Notwithstanding retention and custody provisions, the secret-ballot principle shall be preserved throughout the retention and destruction process. No paper ballot shall be linked to voter identity through any procedure in this Section. The cryptographic hash linking ballot to blockchain transaction shall not be traceable to voter identity, preserving the zero-knowledge privacy established under Section 4. 14.20 Article V Protection. The provisions of Sections 14.10

through 14.19 shall be protected under the Article V protection established in Sections 18.6.1 and 18.6.2. No act of Congress, executive order, judicial ruling, or state action shall modify, diminish, or evade the voter-verified paper ballot requirement, the Watchdog Tribunal custody requirement, or the documented destruction requirements. Paper ballots are the People's physical evidence of their vote, and this Section establishes their integrity as constitutional in character. 14.21 Infrastructure Evolution and Security Refresh Framework. Because the Sovereign Voting Terminals, Sovereign Civic Network, Sovereign Blockchain Voting Ledger, Franklin Ledger, and associated infrastructure established under this Amendment must remain operationally secure and technologically effective across the twenty (20) year Sunset Review cycle under Section 18 and indefinitely thereafter, and because technology evolves on timescales shorter than the Amendment's durability horizon — particularly cryptographic security, where advances in computational power or cryptographic attack methods may render current protections insufficient within the Amendment's operational lifetime — the following framework establishes ongoing infrastructure evolution, security refresh, and technology transition procedures. This Section applies to all physical and digital infrastructure operated under this Amendment, including but not limited to Terminal hardware and software, Network infrastructure, blockchain substrates and protocols, Franklin Ledger display systems, Office and Center facilities, and cryptographic systems securing any of the foregoing: (a) Continuous Security Review. The Academic Integrity Commission shall conduct continuous security review of all infrastructure operated under this Amendment, with formal comprehensive review no less frequently than every two (2) years consistent with Section 14.6, and with additional targeted reviews upon: (i) emergence of new cryptographic attacks or vulnerabilities affecting Amendment systems; (ii) advances in computational technology, cryptanalysis, or other attack methodologies threatening current cryptographic protections, whether through quantum computing, successor technologies, or means not currently imaginable; (iii) component obsolescence affecting Terminal hardware, Network equipment, or other physical infrastructure; (iv) discovery of vulnerabilities through source code analysis under Section 14.7; (v) credible threats identified through Authority, Tribunal, or external intelligence sources; and (vi) at the request of any Authority body, the Watchdog Tribunal, or joint petition of not fewer than five (5) state Attorneys General. Security review findings shall be published on the Franklin Ledger with specific technical detail, subject to narrow operational-security redaction where publication would enable active exploitation pending remediation; (b) Authority to Mandate Updates. The Academic Integrity Commission shall have authority, by supermajority vote of not less than sixty percent (60%) of seated members, to mandate infrastructure updates where security review findings under subsection (a) demonstrate that existing infrastructure no longer meets the security, operational, or functional standards required for Amendment purposes. Mandated updates shall be binding on all Amendment infrastructure and shall be implemented under the following framework: (i) Scope Specification. The mandate shall specify: the specific infrastructure affected; the specific deficiency triggering update; the technical specifications of the required update; implementation timeline; and operational continuity requirements during update; (ii) Implementation Authority. The Authority, acting through the AIC with Citizens' Oversight Board and State Elections Council concurrence, shall implement mandated updates through the existing AIC design, certification, and supervision authority under Section 14.1 and throughout this Section; (iii) Tribunal Review. The Watchdog Tribunal may, by majority vote, review any mandate for specific bad-faith update specification, including but not limited to mandates that would narrow the hardware supply base to capturable vendors, mandates that would introduce backdoors under cover of security update, or mandates that would compromise open-source requirements under Section 14.7. Tribunal review within thirty (30) days; mandate stayed pending review; review findings published on the Franklin Ledger; (c) Cryptographic Transition Framework. Because advances in computational power, cryptanalytic methods, or entirely new technologies not yet existing may render current cryptographic protections insufficient within the Amendment's operational lifetime — whether through quantum computing, successor technologies to quantum computing, novel mathematical attacks on current algorithms, or means not currently imaginable — and because transition to replacement cryptography is a particularly consequential infrastructure update affecting blockchain integrity, Terminal security, and all cryptographic systems under this Amendment, the following framework applies: (i) Transition Trigger. When the Academic Integrity Commission determines, by supermajority vote and published technical reasoning, that credible risk exists of cryptographic compromise of any Amendment cryptographic system through any means — including but not limited to quantum computing advances, successor technologies, novel cryptanalytic methods, or other

emerging threats — transition to adequate replacement cryptography shall commence; (ii) Transition Planning. Transition planning shall include:

identification of specific cryptographic systems affected; evaluation of candidate replacement cryptographic schemes using contemporary established standards bodies' recommendations (including, during the era of quantum computing concerns, the NIST Post-Quantum Cryptography standardization process; and in subsequent eras, whatever successor standardization processes exist at the time of transition); timeline for transition allowing orderly migration; operational continuity requirements during transition; parallel operation of legacy and replacement systems during transition to permit verification; and deprecation timeline for legacy systems; (iii) Blockchain Substrate Transition. Where transition requires changes to blockchain substrates under Section 4.12, the AIC shall coordinate with State Elections Council and Citizens' Oversight Board for concurrence, with the transition implemented as a concurrent-chain migration where the dual-chain verification principle is preserved: at any time, at least two independent Primary Chains with non-overlapping operators must be maintaining current cryptographic standards. Transition shall not require interruption of ongoing Amendment operations; (iv) Terminal Cryptographic Update. Terminal cryptographic systems shall be updated through AIC-certified software and hardware releases, with updates tested on non-production systems before deployment, deployed in staged rollouts across geographic regions, and verified post-deployment through cryptographic attestation on the Franklin Ledger; (v) Franklin Ledger Transition. Franklin Ledger cryptographic systems shall be updated with parallel operation during transition, ensuring public access and verifiability are never interrupted; (vi) Technology-Neutral Principle. This Section shall be construed to address whatever cryptographic threats emerge over the Amendment's operational lifetime, not limited to threats known at the time of Ratification. The Academic Integrity Commission retains authority to identify new threat categories and mandate appropriate responses regardless of whether the threats were anticipated by the Amendment's original drafters. Where future technology renders current threat frameworks obsolete, the AIC shall adapt transition procedures to address then-current realities while preserving the core principle that Amendment cryptographic systems must remain secure against contemporary attack capabilities; (d) Physical Infrastructure Refresh. Terminal hardware, Network infrastructure, Office and Center facilities, and other physical Amendment infrastructure shall be refreshed on cycles appropriate to each component's operational lifespan and vulnerability profile: (i) Terminal Replacement Cycle. Terminal hardware shall be refreshed on cycles not exceeding ten (10) years, or earlier where security review findings or manufacturer end-of-support warrants replacement. Replacement Terminals shall meet then-current AIC certification standards under Section 14.1 and Section 14.8; (ii) Network Infrastructure Refresh. Sovereign Civic Network infrastructure shall be refreshed on cycles not exceeding fifteen (15) years, or earlier where performance, security, or capacity requirements warrant replacement. Refresh shall preserve physical independence from commercial and federal networks as required by Section 14.4; (iii) Office and Center Facility Maintenance. Office and Center physical facilities shall be maintained at operational standards through ongoing facility management under Section 11, with major refurbishment on cycles not exceeding twenty (20) years or as structural assessment warrants; (iv) End-of-Life Management. Replaced infrastructure shall be decommissioned through secure procedures preventing recovery of cryptographic material, voter data, or other sensitive information. Decommissioning records shall be published on the Franklin Ledger; (e) Population and Capacity Scaling. As Participating Jurisdiction populations grow, new Participating Jurisdictions join, or usage patterns evolve, Amendment infrastructure shall scale proportionally: (i) Terminal Capacity. Terminal counts per Office and Center shall be adjusted upward as registered voter populations grow, maintaining the Section 14.1 minimum of one Terminal per five thousand (5,000) voters. The AIC shall review Terminal capacity adequacy biennially with adjustments published on the Franklin Ledger; (ii) Office Capacity. Office and Center locations may be supplemented where existing locations are unable to meet demand, subject to Section 11 location standards and Watchdog Tribunal review to ensure geographic distribution serves legitimate capacity needs rather than political manipulation; (iii) Network Capacity. Sovereign Civic Network capacity shall be expanded to accommodate growing transaction volume, with capacity planning documented on the Franklin Ledger; (iv) Franklin Ledger Scalability. Franklin Ledger display systems shall be enhanced as content volume grows, preserving accessibility standards under Sections 4A.6 through 4A.10; (v) New Participating Jurisdictions. Where new Participating Jurisdictions are added to the Amendment through constitutional or statutory processes, infrastructure shall be extended to the new Jurisdiction under the same standards applicable to existing Jurisdictions, with implementation timelines allowing operational buildout while ensuring the new Jurisdiction's citizens have access to Amendment mechanisms without unreasonable delay; (f) Funding for Infrastructure Evolution. All costs of infrastructure evolution, security refresh, cryptographic transition, physical refurbishment, population scaling, and related activities under this Section shall be funded through the constitutional appropriation under Section 11.3, with funding levels automatically adjusted for inflation and scaling requirements. The constitutional appropriation shall not be subject to congressional reduction or executive redirection for infrastructure evolution purposes, and the Academic Integrity Commission shall publish annual infrastructure evolution funding reports on the Franklin Ledger. Where specific major infrastructure transitions exceed ordinary constitutional appropriation capacity, supplemental funding may be obtained through Ratification Loan mechanisms under Section 13I.3 (loan ceiling expansion) or through dedicated Authority bond issuance subject to Watchdog Tribunal review; (g) Anti-Capture Protections for Evolution Process. Because the infrastructure evolution process itself could be a vector for capture if corrupted parties exercise update authority to introduce vulnerabilities, backdoors, or capturable components, the following protections apply: (i) Open-Source

Continuity. All replacement infrastructure shall comply with Section 14.7 open-source requirements. No update, upgrade, or replacement may introduce proprietary code, black-box components, or closed-source dependencies; (ii) Supply Chain Continuity. All replacement hardware shall comply with Section 14.8 supply chain integrity requirements. No update, upgrade, or replacement may introduce single-foreign-supplier dependencies or Foreign Person or Entity control; (iii) Independent Cryptographic Review. Before deployment of any cryptographic system update, the AIC shall obtain independent cryptographic review from not less than three (3) academic institutions in the Pre-Certified University Pool under Section 17.16 and not less than three (3) independent cryptographic experts not affiliated with Amendment bodies. Review findings shall be published on the Franklin Ledger; (iv) Public Comment Period. Before deployment of major infrastructure updates — defined as updates affecting cryptographic systems, Terminal security, Network architecture, or blockchain substrates — the AIC shall publish technical specifications on the Franklin Ledger with not less than ninety (90) day public comment period. Public comment shall be preserved and considered before final deployment; (v) Staged Rollout. Major updates shall be deployed through staged rollouts with geographic distribution, enabling detection of problems before universal deployment and enabling rollback where issues are identified; (vi) Reversibility. Infrastructure updates shall be designed for reversibility wherever technically feasible, permitting rollback to prior versions if updates introduce problems. Non-reversible updates shall be permitted only where technical necessity requires, with specific documented justification published on the Franklin

Ledger; (vii) No Capture via "Update". Any Authority member, AIC member, or Amendment personnel who uses infrastructure update authority to introduce vulnerabilities, backdoors, capturable components, or surveillance capabilities shall be subject to Section 13 interference penalties with Senior Official multipliers, Section 17.25 bribery penalties where corruption is involved, and permanent disqualification from all Amendment bodies and federal employment; (h) Knowledge Transfer and Institutional Memory. Because infrastructure evolution across multiple decades requires preservation of technical knowledge beyond the tenures of individual Amendment personnel, the following knowledge transfer framework applies: (i) Technical Documentation. All infrastructure designs, cryptographic specifications, operational procedures, and security review findings shall be documented to standards permitting independent understanding and future modification. Documentation shall be preserved on the Franklin Ledger as part of permanent public record; (ii) Successor Training. Outgoing AIC members, Hamilton Contingent senior personnel, Washington Commission members, and Watchdog Tribunal members shall participate in structured knowledge transfer to successors, with transfer documentation archived on the Franklin Ledger; (iii) Academic Continuity. Pre-Certified University Pool institutions under Section 17.16 shall maintain ongoing scholarly engagement with Amendment infrastructure, providing institutional memory distributed across academic institutions beyond dependence on any single body's personnel continuity; (iv)

Public Education. The AIC shall maintain publicly accessible educational materials explaining Amendment infrastructure to citizens, students, researchers, and international observers, with materials updated as infrastructure evolves; (i) Sunset Review Integration. Infrastructure evolution findings and needs shall be reported to citizens as part of the twenty (20) year Sunset Review under Section 18.7, informing citizen deliberation regarding Retain, Modify, or Repeal options. Infrastructure modernization costs, capacity trends, security posture, and emerging threats shall be covered in the twenty-year public report; (j) Article V Protection. The provisions of this Section shall be protected under the Article V protection established in Sections 18.6.1 and 18.6.2. No act of Congress, executive order, judicial ruling, or state action shall modify, diminish, or evade the infrastructure evolution framework, the Academic Integrity Commission's authority to mandate security updates, or the funding protections for infrastructure refresh. The People's voting infrastructure must remain secure and operational across generations, and this Section establishes that ongoing durability as constitutional in character.

Section 15. Reconstitution of the Federal Bureaucracy

Key terms in this Section: • “The Authority” — The Independent Tripartite Oversight Authority (three bodies, see Section 17). • “The Committee” — The Constitutional Transition Committee (Section 6), the caretaker body composed of fifty citizen-elected delegates. • “The Ledger” — The Sovereign Blockchain Voting Ledger (Section 4). • “AIC Standing Review Panel” — A panel of independent experts convened by the Academic Integrity Commission to support the 180-day agency review process under this Section. • “Career technical personnel” — Non-political civil servants performing technical, scientific, or safety-critical functions (meteorologists, FDA reviewers, air traffic controllers, nuclear regulators, etc.) whose continued service protects public safety. These personnel are expressly PROTECTED from removal under Section 1. 15.1 Political leadership enumerated in Section 1.1 shall be removed. Career technical personnel under Section 1.2 shall continue under Committee oversight. 15.2 All existing federal operations shall continue under Committee oversight, including: Social Security and federal benefits; military operations; aviation and transportation safety; border security; federal law enforcement; public health, disease surveillance, food and drug safety; weather forecasting and disaster response; nuclear regulatory oversight; postal service; the continuing full operation of all Citizens’ Reclamation Offices and Centers established under Section 11, including their Accessibility services under Section 11A; the continuing full operation of the Ledger, the Sovereign Civic Network, and all Sovereign Voting Terminals under Sections 4 and 14; and all other functions determined essential. 15.3 Existing regulations shall remain in force during transition. The Committee may suspend specific regulations found to be products of corruption, with public reasoning. 15.4 Within 180 days, the Committee shall publicly review every federal agency and determine: (a) reconstitution under new charter and reformed leadership; (b) consolidation; or (c) abolition. 15.5 The Academic Integrity Commission shall provide a Standing Review Panel with technical expertise to support Committee determinations, recorded publicly. 15.6 Determinations shall be published in full with reasoning. A single 30-day extension per agency may be granted. Agencies with no determination shall continue under existing operations pending Congress review. 15.7 No person separated under Section 1.1 shall be reappointed without public conduct review. 15.8 Career personnel under Section 1.2 shall be subject to individual review only upon specific documented misconduct allegations. 15.9 All reconstituted agencies shall be subject to permanent reforms: congressional ratification of new regulations within 2 years or expiry; no criminal penalties without specific authorizing legislation; annual public accounting upon the Ledger. 15.10 Determination Criteria. The Committee shall determine agency disposition (reconstitution, consolidation, or abolition) under Section 15.4 using the following criteria, applied in the order listed: (a) Reconstitution shall be the default for agencies serving functions: (i) mandated by existing statute not subject to Section 1.1 removal; (ii) providing essential services to citizens (Social Security, Medicare, Medicaid, veterans' benefits, disaster response, public health protection, aviation safety, food and drug safety, nuclear regulatory oversight, postal service, and comparable functions); (iii) providing core constitutional functions (judicial administration, law enforcement, national security, diplomatic representation); or (iv) required by international treaty obligations. (b) Consolidation shall be available where two or more agencies serve overlapping functions that can be merged without loss of essential service, where the resulting consolidated agency has clear mission focus, and where the consolidation would reduce corruption vulnerability created by the prior structure. Consolidation determinations shall specify the successor agency, the transferring functions, the

personnel disposition, and the timeline. (c) Abolition shall be reserved for agencies whose functions: (i) are not essential to any of the Reconstitution criteria under subsection (a); (ii) are demonstrably products of corruption or regulatory capture rather than legitimate governmental purpose; or (iii) duplicate functions better served by other agencies, private entities, or state-level authorities. Abolition determinations shall specify the disposition of agency records (preservation through National Archives per Section 13B), the disposition of agency employees (transfer options per Section 15.16), and the timeline for wind-down. (d) Burden of Justification. Reconstitution determinations require no special justification beyond identifying the applicable criteria under subsection (a). Consolidation and abolition determinations require specific documented reasoning published on the Franklin Ledger, including evidence supporting the determination and analysis of alternatives considered. 15.11 Interim Management During Review. Because agency review under Section 15.4 requires 180 days during which the Section 1.1 political leadership has been removed, the following interim management framework shall apply: (a) Career Senior Official Acting Authority. The most senior career official at each federal agency (typically the career Deputy or equivalent position) shall assume acting leadership of that agency upon Section 1.1 removal, with authority to maintain ongoing operations but not to initiate new major policy directions, regulatory actions, or structural changes absent Committee authorization. (b) Committee Oversight. The Constitutional Transition Committee under Section 6 shall maintain oversight of all agency operations during the review period, with authority to: (i) direct acting leadership on specific operational questions; (ii) suspend specific regulations found to be products of corruption, with public reasoning published on the Franklin Ledger; (iii) coordinate inter-agency operations where necessary; and (iv) authorize emergency expenditures or operational changes where required by genuine emergency. (c) Academic Integrity Commission Technical Support. The Standing Review Panel under Section 15.5 shall provide technical expertise to both the Committee and to acting agency leadership, including subject-matter specialists drawn from the Pre-Certified University Pool under Section 17.16 for agency-specific review support. (d) No Major Policy Initiation. Acting leadership shall not: (i) issue new major regulations; (ii) cancel existing regulations except under subsection (b)(ii) Committee authorization; (iii) terminate or initiate federal contracts over specified financial thresholds absent Committee authorization; (iv) authorize major federal enforcement actions absent Committee authorization; or (v) take other actions of similar constitutional or policy significance. Acting leadership shall maintain operations, not redirect them.

(e) Watchdog Tribunal Oversight of Acting Leadership. The Watchdog Tribunal (or Phase One equivalent) shall maintain oversight of acting leadership conduct, with authority to investigate allegations of acting leadership overreach, failure to maintain essential operations, or corruption. Tribunal findings shall be published on the Franklin Ledger. 15.12 Late or Missing Determinations. Where the Committee fails to issue a determination for an agency within the 180-day review period (or the single 30-day extension per Section 15.6): (a) Default to Reconstitution. Any agency for which no determination has been issued by the end of Section 15.6's extended window shall be deemed reconstituted under its existing charter and with its existing functions, pending future legislative or Authority review. This prevents the review period from serving as a covert abolition mechanism through inaction. (b) Continued Operations. Agencies defaulting to reconstitution under subsection (a) shall continue operations under acting leadership per Section 15.11, with the Committee obligated to issue a determination within an additional sixty (60) days and a new 30-day extension available only upon published showing of exceptional circumstance. (c) Public Accountability for Missing Determinations. Each missing determination shall be identified on the Franklin Ledger with specific reasoning for the delay. Patterns of missing determinations affecting specific agency categories shall trigger Watchdog Tribunal investigation of possible capture of the Committee or its review process. (d) No Late-Determination Trap. An agency defaulting to reconstitution under this Section shall not face adverse consequence (budget reduction, personnel reduction, mission narrowing) that would not have applied had a timely determination been issued. Default reconstitution preserves the pre-review status quo. 15.13 Essential Services Continuity Guarantee. Throughout the review period and any transition that follows, the following essential services shall not be interrupted: (a) Social Insurance and Benefits. Social Security payments, Medicare claims processing, Medicaid administration, veterans' benefits, unemployment insurance, and all other federally administered social insurance and benefit programs shall continue without interruption. No payment shall be missed, no claim shall be suspended, and no beneficiary shall face denial of benefits solely due to transition. (b) Public Safety Functions. Aviation safety (FAA), food and drug safety (FDA), nuclear regulatory oversight (NRC), environmental protection enforcement (EPA), workplace safety (OSHA), and comparable public safety functions shall continue without operational interruption. Inspections, certifications, and safety rulings shall proceed on ordinary schedules.

(c) Law Enforcement Continuity. Federal law enforcement operations — excluding politically directed operations being reviewed under the reconstitution process — shall continue. Active investigations, prosecutions, and protective details shall proceed uninterrupted, subject to Watchdog Tribunal review for evidence of political weaponization under the prior political leadership. (d) Military Readiness. The Armed Forces shall maintain full operational readiness under the command structure preserved through Section 16 and the Interim Caretaker Council's civilian control under Section 6A. No military capability shall be degraded due to transition. (e) Disaster Response Capability. FEMA, CDC, and coordinated federal disaster response infrastructure shall remain fully operational, with capacity for immediate response to natural disasters, public health emergencies, or other crises during the review period. (f) International Obligations. Federal obligations under ratified treaties shall continue without interruption. The State Department, Defense Department, and related agencies shall maintain diplomatic and treaty-implementation functions. (g) Emergency Authority for Continuity. Where unanticipated operational needs arise that exceed acting leadership's authority under Section 15.11(d), the Committee shall act within seventy-two (72) hours to authorize necessary operational response, with reasoning published on the Franklin Ledger. 15.14 Career Personnel Protections During Review. Beyond the Section 1.2 protection against automatic separation: (a) No Adverse Action Without Cause. Career personnel shall not face demotion, reassignment, salary reduction, or termination during the review period except upon documented individual misconduct reviewed under Section 15.8. Mass personnel actions targeting categories of career employees shall be prohibited. (b) Whistleblower Protections Enhanced. Career personnel with knowledge of pre-removal corruption, regulatory capture, or Amendment interference shall receive the full Section 13B.16 whistleblower protections with specific enhancements: protection against adverse action for five (5) years regardless of subsequent agency disposition; federal legal representation at no cost; and priority consideration for placement in successor or consolidated agencies where their original agency is reconstituted, consolidated, or abolished. (c) Performance Evaluations Paused. Ordinary performance evaluation schedules shall pause during the review period, preventing adverse reviews from being weaponized by interim actors. Upon conclusion of the review period, performance evaluation shall resume with the evaluation cycle effectively reset. (d) Benefits Continuity. All federal employee benefits — health insurance, retirement contributions, accrued leave, family and medical leave — shall continue without interruption during the review period regardless of eventual agency disposition. (e) Union Recognition. Existing federal employee union recognition and collective bargaining agreements shall continue in force during the review period. Committee authority to suspend specific regulations under Section 15.3 shall not extend to suspension of collective bargaining agreements absent documented collective bargaining between the Committee and recognized unions. 15.15 Stakeholder Appeal Rights. Because agency determinations affect regulated industries, beneficiary populations, state and local governments, and public interest organizations, the following appeal and comment rights shall apply: (a) Public Comment Period Before Determination. Before issuing a reconstitution, consolidation, or abolition determination, the Committee shall publish a preliminary determination on the Franklin Ledger with minimum thirty (30) day public comment period. Comments shall be preserved, categorized, and reviewed by the Committee before final determination. (b) State Attorney General Coordinated Comment. State Attorneys General (collectively through the State Attorneys General Council under Section 19.5.0.18) may submit coordinated comments representing states' interests in specific agency dispositions, including interests of state employees affected, state regulatory coordination with the federal agency, and state-level impact of consolidation or abolition determinations. (c) Appeal to Watchdog Tribunal. Any registered voter, civic organization, state or local government, or affected stakeholder may appeal a Committee determination to the Watchdog Tribunal upon clear and convincing evidence that: (i) the determination was based on materially false or incomplete information; (ii) the determination conflicts with Section 15.10 criteria; or (iii) the determination was procured through corruption, coercion, or conflict of interest. Tribunal shall rule within thirty (30) days. (d) Remediation for Successful Appeals. Where a Tribunal appeal succeeds, the Committee shall re-issue the determination within thirty (30) days, incorporating Tribunal findings. Tribunal shall not substitute its own determination for the Committee's; it shall identify defects and require re-determination. (e) No Delay of Essential Operations. Appeals shall not delay essential operations continuity under Section 15.13. Pending appeals shall be resolved through proceeding determinations on schedule with appeal remedies applied post-determination where successful. 15.16 Personnel Transition Framework. Where agencies are consolidated or abolished, personnel transition shall proceed as follows: (a) Priority Placement in Successor or Related Agencies. Career personnel of consolidated or abolished agencies shall receive priority consideration for placement in successor agencies, consolidated entities, or related agencies with

comparable functions, based on qualifications and without requirement of re-application through standard federal hiring processes. (b) Transition Period Compensation. Personnel unable to immediately place into successor positions shall continue to receive full salary and benefits for a transition period of not less than one hundred eighty (180) days from consolidation or abolition effective date, during which they may search for alternative placement with full federal hiring protections. (c) Retirement Eligibility Acceleration. Personnel within three (3) years of full retirement eligibility at the time of consolidation or abolition shall be eligible for accelerated retirement with full benefits at their current compensation level, as an alternative to transition to other positions. (d) Voluntary Separation Incentives. Personnel electing voluntary separation in lieu of transition shall receive severance calculated at minimum two (2) weeks' salary per year of federal service, plus continuation of health insurance for not less than one hundred eighty (180) days from separation. (e) Anti-Discrimination in Transition. Personnel transition decisions shall not be based on political affiliation, prior policy positions advocated in the course of duty, or membership in protected classes. Watchdog Tribunal shall investigate allegations of discriminatory transition decisions with published findings. (f)

Records Preservation. Personnel records shall be preserved under Section 13B standards throughout transition, ensuring that separation, transfer, or retirement decisions can be reviewed for fairness and consistency with this Section. 15.17 Post-Review Reform Sustainability. The permanent reforms applied to reconstituted agencies under Section 15.9 shall be sustained as follows: (a) Congressional Ratification Window. New regulations issued during the review period and for two (2) years after review completion shall require affirmative congressional ratification or shall expire. This prevents Committee or acting leadership from issuing permanent regulations that bind future Congresses without democratic endorsement. (b) Annual Public Accounting on Ledger. Every reconstituted agency shall publish annual accounting on the Franklin Ledger including: budget execution; regulatory actions taken; enforcement actions pursued; personnel changes; organizational changes; outstanding obligations; and compliance with Section 17A accountability standards. (c) Sunset on Prior Regulations. Existing regulations of reconstituted agencies shall be subject to sunset review on a rolling basis over ten (10) years from review completion, with agencies required to re-justify regulations against current statutory authority. Regulations not re-justified within their sunset window shall expire.

(d) Enhanced Accountability Standards. Reconstituted agencies shall be subject to Section 17A accountability standards as Covered Bodies, including mandatory annual audits, procurement integrity standards, and staffing procedures. This extends Authority-level accountability to the federal bureaucracy reconstituted after No Confidence. (e) Independence from Future Political Retaliation. No future President, Congress, or federal official shall take retaliatory action against reconstituted agencies, consolidated entities, or their personnel on the basis of their role in implementing the reconstitution. Any such retaliation shall constitute Section 13 interference with Senior Official multipliers.

Section 16. The Armed Forces and the People's Authority Over Nuclear Weapons

Key terms in this Section: • "The Authority" — The Independent Tripartite Oversight Authority (three bodies, see Section 17). • "The Ledger" — The Sovereign Blockchain Voting Ledger (Section 4). • "Joint Chiefs" — The Joint Chiefs of Staff of the United States Armed Forces. Under this Amendment they retain the constitutional authority and DUTY to refuse unlawful orders (Section 16.3), and they hold two seats on the Nuclear Authorization Panel. • "Nuclear

Authorization Panel" — The 5-person Panel established by this Section whose unanimous consent is required (along with a 60% public vote at 40% turnout) before any first-use or offensive nuclear action. Composition: the President or Committee Chairperson, 2 senior Joint Chiefs, 1 Citizens' Oversight Board member, 1 Academic Integrity Commission member. • "Nuclear Authorization Vote" — The 72-hour public vote required in addition to the Panel's unanimous consent, requiring 60% affirmative of ballots cast with minimum 40% turnout. • "Emergency override (16.10)" — The narrow exception permitting nuclear response authority to revert to the President and 2 senior Joint Chiefs in cases of confirmed imminent nuclear attack or active invasion of US sovereign territory — defensive only, never first-use.

A. The Armed Forces During the Transition 16.1 The Armed Forces owe their ultimate loyalty to the Constitution and to the People, not to any officeholder, party, or administration. 16.2 Upon passage of a Declaration of No Confidence, the Armed Forces shall: (a) continue defense against foreign threats; (b) stand down from domestic deployment except as authorized under Section 16.3; (c) never be used against any citizen, Office, or the operation of this Amendment; and (d) operate under the civilian command structure in Section 16.3. 16.3 Civilian control of the military during transition shall be structured as follows: (a) The Committee Chairperson shall serve as Commander-in-Chief for the duration of the transition; (b) Any domestic deployment of military forces shall require prior authorization by majority vote of the full Committee, publicly recorded upon the Ledger, specifying scope, duration, purpose, and geographic limits. The Chairperson shall not have unilateral domestic deployment authority; (c) The Joint Chiefs shall have constitutional authority and duty to refuse any order that violates this Constitution, this Amendment, the laws of war, or the laws of the United States. Refusal shall be documented in writing and published upon the Ledger within 24 hours; (d) No officer shall be retaliated against for a documented refusal under 16.3(c); and (e) The Committee, by 2/3 vote, may refer a disputed refusal to public military tribunal. 16.4 Within 24 hours, the Joint Chiefs shall collectively sign and publish a Declaration of Constitutional Duty. Each branch shall affirm through its senior commander within 48 hours. 16.5 Any servicemember attempting to use troops to interfere with the transition shall be: (a) immediately removed from command; (b) subjected to full public military tribunal; and (c) upon conviction, imprisoned not less than 25 years for insurrection. 16.6 No removed official shall retain command, control, or access to military forces, weapons systems, or classified facilities. B. The People's Sovereign Authority Over Nuclear

Weapons 16.7 Notwithstanding any other provision of the Constitution or any law, no nuclear weapon shall be launched, detonated, or deployed in first-use or offensive capacity without the process in this Section. This provision is a permanent feature of the constitutional order, applicable at all times.

16.7.1 Ninety Percent Governor Supermajority for First-Use Nuclear Authorization. In addition to the Panel and Vote requirements of Section 16.8, first-use or offensive nuclear authorization shall require a ninety percent (90%) supermajority affirmative vote of the Governors or chief executives of the fifty-six (56) Participating Jurisdictions — that is, not fewer than fifty-one (51) of fifty-six (56) voting affirmatively. This Governor vote operates as a permanent third gate for first-use nuclear authorization, reflecting the constitutional principle that nuclear first-use, being absolute and irreversible, warrants distribution of authorization authority across the sovereign chief executives of the Participating Jurisdictions in addition to the Panel's unanimous consent and the People's sixty percent (60%) Vote. The distributed authorization structure prevents any single branch, party, region, or captured state from enabling first-use unilaterally, while the ninety percent threshold accommodates a small number of Governors being incapacitated, unavailable, or compromised without breaking the authorization system. The framework operates as follows: (a) Voting Window. Governors shall cast affirmative or negative votes within seventy-two (72) hours of a formal Panel request for first-use authorization, with votes cast through secure communications infrastructure and published upon the Franklin Ledger (or provisional public ledger during Phase One) with identity of voting Governor and vote direction. (b) Abstention Treatment. Governor abstention, failure to vote, or incapacitation within the voting window shall be treated as a negative vote for purposes of the ninety percent (90%) threshold. This default-to-negative treatment reflects the irreversibility of nuclear first-use — the strong presumption is against authorization. (c) Governor Succession. Where a Governor is incapacitated or unavailable, the constitutional or statutory successor under the Jurisdiction's law may cast the vote, with the Jurisdiction's Attorney General verifying the successor's authority. Where no proper successor can be identified within the voting window, that Jurisdiction's vote is treated as negative under subsection (b). (d) Captured or Compromised Governor. Where a Governor has been credibly alleged under Section 20A to be compromised through foreign influence, corruption, or material interference with constitutional duties, the vote of that Governor shall not count toward the affirmative total. Challenges to Governor integrity in connection with nuclear authorization votes shall be adjudicated by the Watchdog Tribunal within forty-eight (48) hours of challenge filing, with findings published on the Ledger. Where such challenges are filed, the seventy-two (72) hour voting window shall extend by the duration of the adjudication window to ensure Jurisdictions whose Governors are not challenged retain full voting time. (e) Simultaneous or Sequential Operation with Panel and Vote. The Governor vote may run concurrently with Panel deliberations and with the public Nuclear Authorization Vote, or sequentially, at the election of the authorizing body.

Authorization requires all three gates to be satisfied independent of order: Panel unanimity under Section 16.8(a), Governor supermajority under this Section, and public sixty percent (60%) Vote under Section 16.8(b). Any one gate failing results in authorization denial. Sequential ordering is permitted where the authorizing body determines that efficient allocation of public resources warrants not initiating the public Vote until Panel and Governor gates are satisfied. (f) Secure Communications Infrastructure. The Governor vote shall be conducted through secure communications infrastructure maintained by the State Attorneys General Council under Section 19.5.0.18 during Phase One, and by the State Elections Council under Section 17 thereafter, with redundant backup channels ensuring Governor ability to vote notwithstanding federal executive obstruction, communications compromise, or infrastructure failure. Infrastructure specifications shall be developed and tested during the Implementation Period, with operational certification required before the Governor vote framework becomes operational for authorization purposes. (g) Federal Executive Non-Interference. No President, Vice President, Cabinet officer, federal agency head, military commander, or other federal executive officeholder shall direct, pressure, coerce, or interfere with any Governor's vote under this Section. Any such interference shall constitute Section 13 interference with Senior Official multipliers and additional penalties under Section 22 where foreign coordination is present. Verbal or written communication providing factual information relevant to the authorization request, made through transparent channels and published on the Ledger contemporaneously, does not constitute interference; covert pressure, coercion, threats, or inducements do. (h) Publication of Results. Results of the Governor vote shall be published on the Ledger within twenty-four (24) hours of vote closure, with identity of each Governor and vote direction, and with documentation of any abstentions, incapacitations, successor votes, or integrity challenges. Public transparency of Governor votes on nuclear first-use is a constitutional requirement, not subject to any claim of executive privilege, national security, or operational secrecy. The Governor's own reasoning for their vote, if provided, shall be published alongside the vote direction. (i) Emergency Override Coordination. Nothing in this Section shall alter the Section 16.10 emergency response framework applicable to confirmed imminent nuclear attack or active nation-threatening invasion. The ninety percent (90%) Governor vote applies only to first-use or offensive nuclear authorization outside Section 16.10 emergency circumstances; emergency response under Section 16.10 proceeds under the Committee framework (Section 16.10(b)) or the Reclamation-Earned Presidential framework (Section 16.10(d)), whichever applies, without requiring the Governor vote, Panel unanimity, or public Vote. Emergency authority under Section 16.10 is narrowly scoped to proportionate defensive response under Section 16.10(i); any action beyond that scope falls under the full three-gate framework of

Section 16.8 including the Governor vote under this Section. (j) Ramp-Up Period. Before the ninety percent (90%) Governor vote framework is certified operational under Section 19.5.0.11.5(j), the Emergency Nuclear Authorization Committee under Section 19.5.0.11.5 shall serve as the interim authorization body for non-emergency first-use authorization. The Governor vote framework shall be certified operational when secure communications infrastructure under subsection (f) is tested and reliable, Governor identity verification protocols are established, and the State Attorneys General Council has published operational procedures for the vote. (k) Sunset Review Consideration. The ninety percent (90%) supermajority threshold shall be reviewed in each Sunset Review under Section 18, with the People retaining authority to adjust the threshold based on operational experience. The threshold shall not be reduced below an eighty-five percent (85%) supermajority of the Governors of the fifty-six (56) Participating Jurisdictions; this floor reflects the absolute and irreversible nature of nuclear first-use and shall remain within the Section 18.6 Amendment Protection framework. (l) Captured System Protection — Intentional Structural Feature. Where the ninety percent (90%) threshold cannot be reached due to captured or compromised Governor exclusions under subsection (d), or where Governor succession failures under subsection (c) reduce the effective pool below the threshold, first-use authorization is blocked. This is an intentional structural feature of the Amendment, not a gap. Nuclear first-use should be more difficult in a captured system, not easier. The constitutional judgment underlying this feature is that: (i) an authorization system requiring near-unanimous consent from sovereign state chief executives is reliable only when most Governors are uncompromised; (ii) in a system where significant Governor capture has occurred, the reliability assumption of the authorization framework fails, and nuclear first-use under such a compromised framework would likely reflect the capture rather than legitimate national interest; (iii) the Amendment prefers defensive passivity (no first-use authorization) over authorization risk in a captured system; (iv) Section 16.10 emergency defensive response remains available for imminent-attack scenarios, so this structural feature does not leave the Republic undefended; (v) the proper response to a captured-Governor scenario blocking first-use is to address the underlying Governor capture through Section 20A state official integrity prosecution, Section 22 foreign interference response, and Section 11A electoral integrity measures — not to lower the first-use threshold or circumvent the structural protection. This subsection makes explicit what otherwise emerges from the arithmetic of subsections (b) and (d): the People's constitutional judgment that nuclear first-use capability is appropriately dependent on a minimum level of uncaptured state-executive integrity. (m) Training and Preparatory Education for Governor Nuclear Vote. Because the ninety percent (90%) Governor supermajority vote under this Section operates on emergency timelines where orientation-on-selection is impractical, the following preparatory education framework ensures each Governor is prepared for nuclear vote duties: (i) Preparatory Education Program. The Academic Integrity Commission shall develop and distribute a preparatory education program for all sitting Governors and chief executives of Participating Jurisdictions, covering: this Section and its operational requirements; verification standards for first-use authorization requests; abstention treatment under subsection (b); Governor succession under subsection (c); captured Governor exclusion under subsection (d); concurrent or sequential operation with Panel and public Vote; secure communications infrastructure usage; Section 16.10 emergency frameworks and their relationship to first-use; the captured system protection under subsection (l); and recognition of federal executive interference under subsection (g). Materials shall be published on the Franklin Ledger and updated not less frequently than annually. (ii) Completion Expectation. Each Governor shall complete the preparatory education program within one hundred twenty (120) days of assuming office (or within one hundred twenty (120) days of certified Ratification for Governors already in office at Ratification). Completion shall be recorded on state government transparency infrastructure or the Ledger. (iii) Voting Without Completion. A Governor who has not completed preparatory education may still participate in the ninety percent (90%) vote if a first-use authorization request arises before completion, but shall be strongly encouraged to complete education as rapidly as possible given the gravity of the authorization. The Amendment does not disenfranchise uneducated Governors (preventing artificial quorum manipulation through training-gating), but creates strong expectations that Governors will prepare themselves for this extraordinary duty. (iv) Refresher Education. Governors shall complete refresher education not less frequently than biennially, covering developments in international nuclear matters, framework operational experience, and emergent threats. Biennial refresher aligns with ordinary gubernatorial term cycles. (v) Gubernatorial Transition. Outgoing Governors shall brief incoming Governors on Section 16.7.1 matters as part of ordinary gubernatorial transition, with briefing documentation preserved as part of state transition records. (vi) Federal Executive Non-Interference. No federal officeholder shall direct, influence, or interfere with Governor preparatory education. Attempts shall constitute Section 13 interference with Senior Official multipliers. (vii) No Federal Compensation. Consistent with the state-sovereign nature of Governor office, federal compensation shall not be provided for preparatory education; each Participating Jurisdiction shall cover time and resource costs as part of ordinary gubernatorial duties. (viii) Accountability. Governor preparatory education completion shall be subject to public transparency but not federal enforcement. State legislatures and state citizens retain the authority to hold their Governors accountable for education completion through state political and electoral mechanisms, consistent with state sovereignty over state executive officers. 16.7.2 Scope Clarification — Retaliation to Confirmed Nuclear Strike Excluded from First-Use Restriction. For purposes of Sections 16.7, 16.7.1, and 16.8, the

phrase 'first-use or offensive capacity' does not include retaliatory response to a confirmed nuclear strike on United States sovereign territory or on deployed United States armed forces operating under lawful authority. The Amendment's captured-executive safeguards govern nuclear aggression (the initiation of nuclear conflict), not retaliation after a nuclear strike has already occurred against the United States. This Section does not authorize retaliation; rather, it clarifies that the Amendment's nuclear authorization framework does not regulate retaliation. Whether retaliation authority exists, and if so how it is exercised, is determined by legal frameworks outside this Amendment, subject always to the Section 16.3 duty of every servicemember to refuse unlawful orders. (a) Confirmation Standard. A 'confirmed nuclear strike' means documented nuclear detonation or nuclear weapon deployment against the United States verified through at least three (3) independent observable indicators, which may include: seismic signatures consistent with nuclear detonation; electromagnetic pulse measurements; verified radiation levels at impact sites; thermal imagery consistent with nuclear yield; independent confirmation from allied nation intelligence; independent confirmation from commercial satellite operators; or direct observation by trained personnel at multiple independent locations. No single source shall be sufficient. At least one of the three indicators shall come from sources outside the federal executive branch. Confirmation shall be documented contemporaneously on the Franklin Ledger or provisional public ledger. (b) Authorization Outside Amendment Scope. Once the confirmation standard under subsection (a) is met, retaliatory response is not regulated by this Section or by Sections 16.7, 16.7.1, or 16.8. Authorization of retaliation is determined by legal frameworks outside this Amendment, subject always to the Section 16.3 duty of every servicemember to refuse unlawful orders. This subsection does not create retaliation authority, does not expand any existing authority, and does not endorse any particular authorization structure; it simply clarifies that this Amendment does not regulate retaliation to confirmed strikes. (c) Scope Limitation — Proportionate Retaliation Only. This subsection authorizes only proportionate retaliation to the confirmed strike. Retaliation exceeding proportionate scope, or retaliation against parties not responsible for the confirmed strike, shall constitute first-use under Section 16.7 and shall require the full three-gate framework of Section 16.8. The proportionality assessment shall consider the scale, source, and nature of the confirmed strike; the minimum response necessary to restore deterrence; and the duty to minimize civilian harm consistent with the laws of war. (d) Fabrication as Treason. Any official who fabricates, participates in fabrication of, or knowingly relies on fabricated confirmation of a nuclear strike for purposes of invoking retaliation authority under this Section shall be subject to Section 16.12 penalties including the most severe penalties available under the Amendment where such fabrication results in actual nuclear weapon deployment. The confirmation standard under subsection (a) is deliberately demanding to make fabrication nearly impossible; any official who claims confirmation met despite inadequate evidentiary basis shall face presumption of bad faith. Foreign coordination in fabrication shall additionally invoke Section 22 penalties. (e) Servicemember Good-Faith Protection. A servicemember who executes retaliation orders in good-faith reliance on what appears to be a confirmed nuclear strike shall not be subject to adverse legal consequence for that execution, even if the strike is subsequently determined to have been fabricated. This good-faith protection does NOT extend to servicemembers who knew or should have known the confirmation was inadequate, or to officials who directed execution without satisfying subsection (a). The Section 16.3 duty to refuse unlawful orders remains the primary safeguard. (f) Mandatory Post-Retaliation Review. Every retaliation authorization under this Section shall trigger mandatory Watchdog Tribunal review (or Washington Commission review during Phase One before Tribunal operability) within seventy-two (72) hours of the retaliation action, with findings published on the Franklin Ledger within thirty (30) days. Review shall assess whether the confirmation standard was genuinely met, whether response was proportionate, and whether any fabrication occurred. Tribunal findings of procedural or substantive violations shall trigger Section 13, Section 16.12, and Section 22 prosecutions as applicable. (g) Relationship to Section 16.10. Section 16.10 emergency response framework continues to apply to imminent-attack scenarios (where a nuclear strike has not yet occurred). This Section applies only after a confirmed strike has occurred. The frameworks are complementary: Section 16.10 governs pre-strike defensive authorization under this Amendment (including Committee framework, Earned Presidential authority, and Emergency Composite State-Sovereign Authority under Section 16.10(o)); this Section clarifies that post-strike retaliation falls outside this Amendment's first-use authorization framework entirely. (h) No Creation of Authority. This Section does not create, expand, or modify any authority to conduct retaliation. It solely clarifies that this Amendment's first-use restriction does not apply to retaliation to a confirmed strike. Whether retaliation authority exists, and if so how it is exercised, is determined by legal frameworks outside this Amendment. Nothing in this Section shall be construed as endorsement, incorporation, or adoption by this Amendment of any external legal framework; the Amendment is simply silent on retaliation authorization. 16.8 Authorization requires ALL THREE: (a) unanimous consent of a five-member Panel (President or Committee Chairperson; two senior-most Joint Chiefs; one Citizens' Oversight Board member by lottery; one Academic Integrity Commission member by lottery); (b) affirmative vote of not less than sixty percent (60%) of ballots cast in a 72-hour Nuclear Authorization Vote, with minimum forty percent (40%) turnout of registered voters; AND (c) ninety percent (90%) supermajority

affirmative vote of the Governors or chief executives of the fifty-six (56) Participating Jurisdictions pursuant to Section 16.7.1 — that is, not fewer than fifty-one (51) of fifty-six (56) Governors or chief executives voting affirmatively. The sixty percent (60%) supermajority threshold established in subsection (b) of this Section is identical to the 60% threshold for No

Confidence under Section 5.2, reflecting the People's judgment that sixty percent constitutes the appropriate supermajority for major decisions affecting the Republic. The forty percent (40%) turnout requirement for the Nuclear Authorization Vote is intentionally lower than the fifty percent (50%) turnout requirement for No Confidence under Section 5.2, because the Nuclear Authorization Vote occurs over a 72-hour window compared to the 30-day No Confidence Referendum window; the compressed voting period makes 40% turnout an already-demanding engagement bar given time constraints, while the 30-day No Confidence window can reasonably sustain the higher 50% turnout requirement. The sixty percent (60%) supermajority remains consistent across both mechanisms as the constitutional standard for major decisions. The ninety percent (90%) Governor supermajority under subsection (c) reflects the constitutional principle that nuclear first-use, being absolute and irreversible, warrants overwhelming consensus across the fifty-six (56) sovereign chief executives of the Participating Jurisdictions — a distribution of authorization authority that prevents any single branch, party, region, or captured state from enabling first-use unilaterally. The thresholds are deliberate and shall not be harmonized further by interpretation. 16.9 The Vote shall be announced by mandatory emergency broadcast within 1 hour. All Offices shall remain open continuously during the 72-hour window. 16.10 Emergency Nuclear Response Authority — Reclamation-Earned Trust Framework. Section 16.8 shall not apply in confirmed emergency circumstances, but emergency authority shall not default to the sitting President absent democratic legitimacy earned through the Amendment's removal and election framework. The philosophical principle: the Amendment's removal mechanism must be demonstrated to actually work at least once before nuclear emergency override authority is entrusted to any Presidency. Until that demonstration occurs, emergency authority rests with the distributed Emergency Nuclear Authorization Committee under Section 19.5.0.11.5. (a) Qualifying Emergency Conditions. Emergency authority under this Section applies only in: (i) imminent nuclear attack independently verified by radar, satellite, intelligence from at least two (2) sources including at least one source outside the sitting federal executive branch (such as allied nation intelligence, independent commercial satellite imagery, or state-level intelligence sources); or (ii) active military invasion of United States sovereign territory by foreign armed forces of sufficient scale to threaten the constitutional existence of the nation. Claimed emergencies not meeting these verification standards do not trigger this Section and remain subject to the full three-gate framework of Section 16.8.

(b) Default Emergency Authority — Committee Framework. Until the conditions of subsection (c) are satisfied, emergency nuclear response authority shall vest in the 7-Member Emergency Nuclear Authorization Committee established under Section 19.5.0.11.5, exercised under the following concurrence standard: (i) Default Unanimous Standard. Emergency authorization requires unanimous concurrence of all seven (7) Committee members. (ii) Certified Unavailability Exception. Where one (1) Committee member is certified as genuinely unreachable, incapacitated, or non-responsive despite good-faith attempts to secure their participation within a two (2) hour window from authorization request, authorization may proceed upon unanimous concurrence of the remaining six (6) members. Certification of member unavailability shall be made by the Washington Commission during Phase One (by majority vote of the seven Chief Justices) or by majority vote of Authority body presiding chairs (two of three) after Phase One. Certification shall be published on the provisional public ledger (or Ledger) within twenty-four (24) hours with specific factual basis for the unavailability determination. In no case shall authorization proceed with fewer than six (6) concurring members. (iii) Additional Concurrence Required. In addition to the Committee concurrence under subsection (b)(i) or (b)(ii), the following additional concurrence is required: (A) during Phase One before Authority bodies are operational — a majority vote of the Washington Commission (four of seven Chief Justices); (B) after Authority bodies are operational — at least two of three presiding chairs of the Authority bodies (Citizens' Oversight Board, State Elections Council, Academic Integrity Commission). (iv) Obstruction Accountability. Deliberate obstruction, refusal to participate in good faith, or willful unavailability by a Committee member to prevent authorization shall constitute Section 13 interference with Senior Official multipliers, shall subject the member to Watchdog Tribunal review, and may result in removal from Committee service. This subsection does not penalize legitimate dissent — a Committee member voting against authorization in good-faith disagreement exercises proper constitutional judgment and is fully protected. It targets only bad-faith obstruction designed to circumvent the concurrence standard through artificial unavailability. The Committee shall remain a permanent standing body under Section 19.5.0.11.5 for this emergency authority purpose, notwithstanding the ramp-up sunset conditions that otherwise would apply. (c) Presidential Emergency Authority — Earned Through Amendment's Removal Mechanism. A sitting President shall possess emergency nuclear response authority under this Section if, and only if, ALL of the following conditions are satisfied: (i) at least one No Confidence Referendum has proceeded to completed vote under Section 5 at any prior point in the Amendment's operation — whether against the current President, a predecessor, whether resulting in removal or retention — demonstrating that the Amendment's removal mechanism is operationally functional. A completed No Confidence vote means the Petition phase under Section 3 succeeded, the Referendum vote under Section 5 was held, and results were certified, regardless of outcome; a No Confidence attempt that failed at the Petition stage without reaching Referendum does not count for this purpose. (ii) the current President took office through an election conducted under the Amendment's electoral framework (either an Emergency Election under Section 7 following a No Confidence Referendum, or an ordinary Presidential election conducted after the first completed No Confidence vote); and (iii) no No Confidence Referendum is currently triggered against the sitting President. This framework establishes that the Amendment's removal mechanism must be demonstrated to function at least once through full Petition-plus-Referendum process before Presidential emergency nuclear authority is restored, creating a constitutional proof-of-concept requirement. A completed vote — whether it removed the President or confirmed them — demonstrates the mechanism works and therefore satisfies the proof-of-concept. (d) Presidential Authority Structure When Earned. When the subsection (c) conditions are satisfied, emergency nuclear response authority may be exercised upon concurrence of: (i) the sitting President; (ii) the two senior-most oath-maintained Joint Chiefs of Staff (oath-maintained per the verification framework of Section 19.5.0.3.2 extended permanently under Section 17D); and (iii) at least two of three presiding chairs of the Authority bodies (Citizens' Oversight Board, State Elections Council, Academic Integrity Commission). The two-of-three requirement prevents cherry-picking of a potentially compromised chair and preserves consistency with the Committee framework concurrence requirement under subsection (b)(ii). This structure preserves rapid decision-making capacity while maintaining cross-branch concurrence as a check on single-Executive-branch capture. (e) Automatic Suspension Upon No Confidence Trigger. Presidential emergency authority under subsection (d) is automatically suspended immediately upon triggering of a No Confidence Referendum under Section 5 against the sitting President. During suspension, the Committee framework under subsection (b) applies exclusively. Suspension lasts until either: (i) the No Confidence fails, at which point Presidential emergency authority is restored; or (ii) the No Confidence succeeds and a new Amendment-elected President takes office, at which point the new President receives emergency authority under subsections (c) and (d). Suspension shall be published on the Ledger within twenty-four (24) hours of No Confidence triggering. (f) Committee Chairperson During Transition — No Emergency Authority. During any No Confidence transition period under Section 6, the Constitutional Transition Committee Chairperson exercising ordinary Section 16.8(a) Panel authority shall NOT exercise emergency nuclear authority under this Section. The 7-Member Committee framework under subsection (b) applies exclusively during transition. This narrow restriction reflects the transitional and non-elected nature of the Chairperson role — emergency nuclear authority requires democratic legitimacy earned through the Amendment's election framework, which the Chairperson, as a transitional caretaker, does not possess.

(g) Pre-Amendment Presidents — No Emergency Authority. No President who came to office prior to certified Ratification of this Amendment, or who took office after Ratification but before the first successful No Confidence Referendum, shall possess emergency authority under subsection (d). For such Presidents, the Committee framework under subsection (b) applies exclusively. This restriction reflects the Amendment's foundational principle: emergency nuclear authority is earned through the Amendment's democratic renewal, not inherited from the pre-Amendment constitutional order. A President elected under the Amendment framework, after the Amendment's removal mechanism has been demonstrated to function, has established the democratic legitimacy required for this authority; Presidents predating that demonstration have not. (h) Durational Rule — Authority Persists Through Subsequent Amendment-Elected Presidents. Once Presidential emergency authority is established under subsection (c) through the first successful No Confidence and subsequent Amendment-elected President, it persists with each subsequent Amendment-elected President (whether elected through ordinary election or subsequent Emergency Election) without requiring additional No Confidence demonstrations, subject always to subsection (e) suspension during any pending No Confidence Referendum. This rule recognizes that once the Amendment's mechanism has been demonstrated to function, subsequent elected Presidents have full democratic legitimacy under the Amendment's framework. (i) Scope Limitation — Proportionate Defensive Response Only. Emergency authority under this Section authorizes only proportionate response to confirmed active threat under subsection (a). Emergency authority does not authorize preemptive first-use beyond the scope of immediate defensive necessity, and does not authorize offensive action against parties not actively engaged in the triggering attack or invasion. Authorizations exceeding proportionate scope shall constitute violations subject to prosecution under Section 16.12 and additional Section 13 interference penalties. (j) Real-Time Documentation. All emergency authorizations under this Section shall be published on the Franklin Ledger (or provisional public ledger during Phase One) in real time as they occur, with identity of authorizing members, factual basis for the triggering conditions, independent verification sources, and scope of authorized response. Publication shall be subject only to narrow targeting-specific operational security redactions that do not obscure the authorization itself, the identity of authorizing members, or the factual basis. Review of any redaction shall be conducted by the Watchdog Tribunal within thirty (30) days with public findings on the Ledger. (k) Falsification as Treason. Intentional falsification of the triggering conditions under subsection (a), fabrication of independent verification sources, or any other form of manufactured emergency used to invoke this Section shall constitute treason under Section 16.12, with maximum penalties. The falsifier shall include any official who directed fabrication, any intelligence official who falsified intelligence, any military officer who confirmed false operational assessments, and any President, Committee member, Joint Chief, or Authority body chair who concurred knowing of the falsification. (l) Post-Action Review Mandatory. Every invocation of emergency authority under this Section shall trigger mandatory Watchdog Tribunal review within seventy-two (72) hours of the emergency action, with findings published on the Franklin Ledger within thirty (30) days. Review shall assess: (i) whether the triggering conditions under subsection (a) were genuinely met; (ii) whether the independent verification was adequate; (iii) whether authorization followed proper procedure under subsections (b) or (d); (iv) whether response was proportionate under subsection (i); and (v) whether documentation under subsection (j) was adequate. Tribunal findings of procedural or substantive violations shall trigger Section 13, Section 16.12, and Section 22 (where foreign coordination is present) prosecutions as applicable. (m) Sunset Review Consideration. This framework shall be reviewed in each Sunset Review under Section 18. The People retain authority to adjust the restoration threshold, authority structure, or scope limitations based on operational experience. The framework shall remain within the Section 18.6 Amendment Protection boundaries; no Sunset Review modification shall restore unilateral Presidential emergency nuclear authority without concurrence from non-Executive branches of government. (n) Pre-Committee Emergency Period — T+0 to First Committee Operability. From the moment of certified Ratification until the first 7-Member Emergency Nuclear Authorization Committee is drawn and operational under Section 19.5.0.11.5 (a period not to exceed forty-eight (48) hours under ordinary circumstances, extendable only through the fallback provisions of Section 19.5.0.11.5(b)), no human-authorized nuclear first-use or offensive nuclear action shall proceed under this Amendment. During this Pre-Committee Emergency Period: (i) Absolute Prohibition. This prohibition is absolute. No claimed emergency, no independent verification, no institutional necessity, and no asserted authority shall authorize human-ordered nuclear first-use or offensive nuclear action during this window. The Amendment establishes no authorization pathway for first-use or offensive action during this period. (ii) No Presidential Override. The sitting President shall not possess emergency nuclear first-use authority under subsection (d) or any other provision during this period; the subsection (c) conditions cannot have been satisfied at T+0 by definition (no completed No Confidence could have occurred post-Ratification in a zero-duration window). A sitting President whose term began prior to certified Ratification is additionally excluded by subsection (g). (iii) No Authority Outside the Amendment. No authority not established by this Amendment shall exercise nuclear first-use authorization during this window, by invoking pre-existing law, emergency claim, asserted inherent authority, or any other basis. The Amendment is the exclusive source of nuclear first-use authorization authority going forward. (iv) Retaliation Exclusion. Section 16.7.2 governs scope exclusion for retaliation to confirmed nuclear strike and is not subject to this subsection. Retaliation to a confirmed strike falls outside this Amendment's first-use framework entirely, as clarified in Section 16.7.2. (v) Accelerated Committee Convening. To minimize the Pre-Committee Period, the Conference of Chief Justices, National Governors Association, and any fallback lottery authorities under Section 19.5.0.11.5(b) shall treat the first Committee lottery as the highest-priority Amendment activation task. (vi) Documentation. Any claimed emergency during the Pre-Committee Period shall be documented on the provisional public ledger in real time, preserved for review by the Committee upon its operability. (vii) Retroactive Review. Upon Committee operability, the first Committee (together with Washington Commission once convened) shall review all events from the Pre-Committee Period to determine whether any official attempted to circumvent this subsection, with Section 13 and Section 16.12 penalties applicable to any such circumvention attempt. Any person who invoked asserted authority outside this Amendment to authorize nuclear first-use during this window shall face the most severe penalties available, including Section 16.12 treason prosecution. This provision reflects the constitutional judgment that a bounded window without first-use authorization is preferable to permitting any authority not established by this Amendment to exercise first-use authority. The Amendment is the complete and exclusive source of nuclear first-use authorization; nothing outside the Amendment grants such authority. (o) Emergency Composite State-Sovereign Authority — Absolute Last-Resort. Where triple-collapse conditions obtain simultaneously — such that neither Committee framework under subsection (b) nor Earned Presidential authority under subsections (c) and (d) can be convened despite good-faith exhaustion of all cascading fallbacks — emergency defensive authorization authority shall vest in an ad hoc Emergency Composite State-Sovereign body of six (6) state officials acting by unanimous concurrence, as an absolute last-resort pathway to prevent total defenselessness during institutional collapse. The Amendment's preference remains defensive passivity over captured-authorization risk (see Section 16.7.1(l)); this subsection activates only where genuine imminent attack or active nation-threatening invasion under subsection (a) coincides with total failure of primary frameworks. (p) Triggering Conditions for Section 16.10(o). All of the following must be documented and published on the provisional public ledger (or Franklin Ledger) contemporaneously before subsection (o) authority activates: (i) the 7-Member Emergency Nuclear Authorization Committee cannot be convened through all cascading authorities under Section 19.5.0.11.5(b), including primary Conference of Chief Justices / National Governors Association authority and all four fallback tiers; (ii) the Washington Commission (during Phase One) cannot be convened through all extended-pool tiers under Section 19.5.0.3.5 including retired Chief Justices, senior Associate Justices, and federal Article III judges; or, after Phase

One, the Authority bodies are non-operational and cannot provide presiding chair concurrence; (iii) Earned Presidential authority under subsections (c) and (d) is not available (either because no completed No Confidence has occurred, or because the sitting President is pre-Amendment, or because earned authority is currently suspended under subsection (e), or because oath-maintained Joint Chiefs and Authority body chair concurrence cannot be obtained); and (iv) a qualifying emergency condition under subsection (a) exists with adequate independent verification. Failure to document any of these conditions voids subsection (o) authorization. (q) Composite Body Composition — Hybrid Selection Framework. The Emergency Composite Authority shall consist of six (6) state officials (three (3) sitting state Governors or chief executives plus three (3) sitting state Chief Justices of the highest courts of Participating Jurisdictions), selected through the following cascading mechanisms, each used only if the prior has failed: (i) Primary — Expedited Lottery. Where lottery infrastructure is operational, selection shall be by cryptographically-verifiable randomized lottery from the two pools described in subsection (q)(iv), administered using multi-party seed contribution under the same standards as Section 19.5.0.3.3. Seed contributors may be drawn from any available combination of: the Conference of Chief Justices, the National Governors Association, the State Attorneys General Council, Authority body members, or (where none of the foregoing are operational) any three (3) or more sitting officials of Participating Jurisdictions (Governors, Chief Justices, or Attorneys General) acting jointly. Lottery results shall be published on the provisional public ledger or Franklin Ledger contemporaneously. (ii) Fallback — Self-Selection With Enhanced Safeguards. Where no combination of officials sufficient to contribute lottery seeds is reachable within four (4) hours of triggering conditions satisfaction — reflecting truly catastrophic institutional collapse — selection shall proceed by self-affirmation, with the first six qualifying officials (three Governors, three Chief Justices, one per Jurisdiction) to publicly affirm willingness to serve constituting the body. Self-selection shall be accompanied by: (A) public affirmation of willingness on the provisional public ledger or Franklin Ledger with identity, Jurisdiction, and timestamp; (B) published individual rationale for self-affirmation; (C) documentation of the inability to run lottery under subsection (q)(i), including attempts made and officials unreachable; (D) acknowledgment by each self-affirming official that their service is subject to the heightened post-action review under subsection (u) and the heightened falsification penalties under subsection (v). (iii) Draw Confirmation and Replacement. Whether selected by lottery or self-affirmation, each official shall have four (4) hours from notification (or from self-affirmation) to confirm availability and lock into service. Where a selected or self-affirmed official becomes unreachable, incapacitated, or declines service within that window, a replacement shall be drawn or self-affirm immediately under the same mechanism that produced the original selection. (iv) Eligibility Pools. The two pools are: (A) all sitting Governors or chief executives of Participating Jurisdictions not credibly alleged under Section 20A to be compromised; and (B) all sitting Chief Justices of the highest courts of Participating Jurisdictions not credibly alleged under Section 20A to be compromised. No more than one official may serve from any single Participating Jurisdiction; where a lottery draws a second official from the same Jurisdiction, the draw shall be re-run for that seat only; where self-affirmation would produce a second official from the same Jurisdiction, the later-affirming official shall be excluded. (v) Mechanism Documentation. The specific selection mechanism used (lottery or self-affirmation), along with the basis for its use and complete selection documentation, shall be published on the provisional public ledger or Franklin Ledger before the Composite Authority takes action under subsection (r). The hybrid framework addresses legitimacy concerns where infrastructure permits lottery, while preserving operational function in true institutional collapse where even lottery administration is impossible. (r) Authorization Standard. Emergency authorization under subsection (o) requires unanimous concurrence of all six (6) members. No lesser concurrence is permitted. Unanimity across six state-sovereign officials from six different Participating Jurisdictions, representing both executive and judicial branches of state government, ensures that even last-resort nuclear authority requires overwhelming consensus across multiple sovereign authorities that cannot be captured through any single pathway. (s) Scope Limitation for Section 16.10(o). Authority under subsection (o) is limited exclusively to proportionate defensive response under subsection (i). Emergency Composite Authority may not authorize offensive first-use in any form, and may not authorize retaliation (retaliation to confirmed strike is governed by Section 16.7.2 through existing military chain of command, not by this subsection). Authority is further limited to the specific emergency that triggered convening; the body may not expand authorization scope, make secondary decisions, or address any matter beyond the specific defensive response needed for the triggering emergency. (t) Immediate Dissolution Upon Higher-Tier Restoration. The Emergency Composite Authority shall dissolve immediately upon either: (i) successful authorization and execution of the defensive response under subsection (r); or (ii) restoration of any higher-tier authorization framework (Committee operability, Commission convening, Earned Presidential authority, or Authority body operability). The Composite Authority is not a standing body and does not persist beyond the specific emergency that triggered its convening. All Composite Authority records transfer to the Watchdog Tribunal (or Washington Commission or Authority, as applicable based on operability) for mandatory post-action review. (u) Mandatory Post-Action Review for Section 16.10(o). Any authorization under subsection (o) shall trigger mandatory Watchdog Tribunal review (or Washington Commission review if Tribunal not operational, or Authority review if neither is operational) within seventy-two (72) hours of the emergency action, with findings

published on the Franklin Ledger within thirty (30) days. Review shall assess: (i) whether triggering conditions under subsection (p) were genuinely satisfied;

(ii) whether higher-tier frameworks were truly unavailable; (iii) whether self-selection of composite members was conducted in good faith; (iv) whether the emergency condition under subsection (a) was adequately verified; (v) whether response was proportionate under subsection (s); and (vi) whether any official acted in bad faith. Tribunal findings of procedural or substantive violations shall trigger the full range of accountability measures under subsection (v). (v) Falsification as Treason — Heightened Penalty for Section 16.10(o). Any fabrication of triggering conditions under subsection (p), any false claim that higher-tier frameworks are unavailable when they are in fact available, any bad-faith convening of the Composite Authority, or any authorization for purposes other than the documented emergency shall constitute treason under Section 16.12, with the most severe penalties available under the Amendment. Because subsection (o) is the last constitutional resort, its integrity is essential; fabrication or abuse shall receive penalties exceeding those applicable to subsection (k). Foreign coordination in subsection (o) abuse shall additionally invoke Section 22 penalties. (w) Narrow Scope — Not a Backdoor. Subsection (o) shall not be invoked as a convenience, shortcut, or preferred pathway. It exists solely to prevent total-collapse defenselessness in genuine institutional failure scenarios and shall be used only when all other frameworks are genuinely unavailable through documented good-faith exhaustion. Any official who invokes subsection (o) when higher-tier frameworks are available, or who participates in subsection (o) authorization without good-faith verification of triggering conditions, shall be subject to Section 13 interference penalties with Senior Official multipliers and potential Section 16.12 prosecution. The Amendment's philosophical preference remains that defensive passivity during institutional collapse is preferable to captured-authorization risk; subsection (o) exists only because confirmed imminent nuclear attack is an extraordinary circumstance warranting extraordinary last-resort pathway. (x) Sunset Review Consideration for Section 16.10(o). The Emergency Composite Authority framework shall be reviewed in each Sunset Review under Section 18. The People retain authority to modify this framework based on operational experience, though no modification shall eliminate this last-resort pathway entirely without replacement of equivalent protection against total-collapse scenarios. The narrow scope limitations under subsection (s) and the heightened penalty structure under subsection (v) shall not be weakened through Sunset Review modification. (y) Training and Preparatory Pool Education for Composite Authority. Because the Emergency Composite Authority operates only in triple-collapse scenarios where ordinary orientation-on-selection may be impossible, and because Composite members are drawn from sitting Governors and Chief Justices who may have only minutes to understand their role, the following educational framework applies: (i)

Preparatory Pool Education. The Academic Integrity Commission shall develop and distribute preparatory educational materials to all sitting Governors and sitting Chief Justices of Participating Jurisdictions (the Composite eligibility pool) covering: the Section 16.10(o) framework, triggering conditions under subsection (p), the confirmation standard under subsection (a), the proportionate defensive response scope under subsection (i), the unanimity standard under subsection (r), the falsification penalties under subsection (v), the mandatory post-action review under subsection (u), and recognition of attempts to abuse the framework. Materials shall be published on the Franklin Ledger and updated not less frequently than annually. (ii) Pool Member Obligations. Pool members shall familiarize themselves with the materials as part of their ongoing duties, with familiarization recorded on state government transparency infrastructure or the Ledger. Failure to familiarize shall not excuse any pool member from proper exercise of Composite authority if selected, as the materials are made available for their benefit; but documented familiarization shall provide good-faith protection under subsection (f) equivalent provisions where disputes arise about Composite action. (iii) Just-In-Time Briefing. Upon triggering conditions satisfaction and member selection (by lottery or self-selection), each Composite member shall receive a just-in-time briefing of not more than thirty (30) minutes covering the specific emergency circumstances, the framework constraints applicable to the pending authorization, and procedural requirements. Briefing shall be delivered by the Washington Commission during Phase One (by its Chief Justices) or by the Academic Integrity Commission thereafter, through secure communications. Where time constraints of the emergency prevent full thirty-minute briefing, abbreviated briefing shall occur with the full briefing completed as soon as operationally feasible during the authorization process. (iv) No Pre-Training Gatekeeping. Because the Composite framework is designed for scenarios where ordinary institutional mechanisms have failed, no member's Composite authority shall be voided for failure to receive just-in-time briefing if the briefing mechanism itself is unavailable due to the same institutional collapse that triggered the Composite framework. Good-faith Composite action based on preparatory education and available information shall be protected under the same good-faith principles applicable to other Amendment bodies, subject to the heightened scrutiny and falsification penalties of subsections (u) and (v). (v) Federal Executive Non-Interference. No federal officeholder shall direct, influence, or interfere with Composite Authority preparatory education or just-in-time briefing. Attempts shall constitute Section 13 interference with Senior Official multipliers, and where occurring during an active emergency shall additionally constitute Section 16.10(k) falsification-adjacent conduct subject to heightened penalty. (vi) Pool Member Preparation is a Duty. Governors and Chief Justices who accept their state offices are understood to accept, as part of the duties of those offices, the possibility of Composite Authority service. Ongoing familiarization with Composite framework materials is an implicit obligation of state executive and judicial office under this Amendment, though not one whose non-performance invalidates subsequent Composite action given the emergency nature of activation. The obligation is educational and preparatory; failure to prepare does not create an excuse for subsequent malperformance but may inform Watchdog Tribunal review under subsection (u). 16.11 Emergency nuclear actions shall be documented in full upon the Ledger within 24 hours and reviewed by the Authority within 30 days. Falsification shall be prosecuted as crimes against humanity. 16.12 Any attempt to bypass this Section shall constitute treason. 16.13 The authorization process shall be documented upon the Ledger. The existence of a Vote, its result, and general nature shall never be classified. C. Chain of Command Continuity and Transfer 16.14 Chain of Command Throughout All Phases. The constitutional chain of command for the Armed Forces of the United States shall be preserved at all times under this Amendment. The chain of command shall transition as follows: (a) During Normal Operation: The elected President of the United States shall serve as Commander-in-Chief pursuant to Article II of the Constitution, subject only to the limitations on nuclear first-use set forth in this Section 16, the Triple-Lock requirements of Section 19.5 where applicable, and the other constraints of this Amendment; (b) During Declaration of No Confidence and Caretaker Period (Days 1-70): Military command shall operate under the provisions of Section 6A.8(a), coordinating defensive military responses through the Caretaker Council with concurrence of the Joint Chiefs of Staff. All Section 16 procedural requirements apply without modification during this period; (c) During Committee Period (Days ~70-160): Military command shall transfer to the Chairperson of the Constitutional Transition Committee under Section 6.7, subject to all Section 16 constraints and the Committee's caretaker-only authority under Section 6.12; (d) Upon Swearing-In of New President Following Emergency Election: Upon the moment of constitutional oath-taking by the newly elected President, all military command authority shall transfer immediately and completely to the new President, and the normal constitutional chain of command under Article II shall be restored in full. All prior orders issued under subsections (b) or (c) above shall be subject to review, modification, or revocation by the new President, except where revocation would create immediate imminent harm and shall be subject to 72-hour review before taking effect; (e) During Implementation Phase One Prior to Director Election: Military command shall operate under the Interim Two-Member Command pursuant to Sections 19.5.1 through 19.5.6, in preparatory capacity only and subject to the Military Freeze of Section 19.5.0.

16.15 Preservation of Constitutional Command Structure. At no point during the operation of this Amendment, including during a No Confidence process, a Caretaker Period, a Committee Period, or Implementation Phases, shall the constitutional chain of command over the Armed Forces be broken, vacated, or held by a body other than those enumerated in Section 16.14. Any attempt by any person or body to claim military command authority outside the succession prescribed in Section 16.14 shall constitute treason under Section 16.12 and shall be subject to the full penalties thereof. 16.16 Military Oath to the Constitution. The military oath of service remains, at all times, an oath to the Constitution of the United States and its lawful Amendments. No provision of this Amendment shall be construed to alter the scope or effect of the military oath, nor to permit the Armed Forces to accept orders from any person or body not properly in the chain of command under Section 16.14. Service members refusing unlawful orders to bypass this Section 16 or to claim authority outside the prescribed chain of command shall be fully protected under this Amendment. D. Nuclear Authorization Operational Framework 16.17 Nuclear Authorization Panel Convening and Procedures. The five-member Panel established in Section 16.8(a) shall operate under the following framework: (a) Physical Convening Requirement. The Panel shall convene physically at a secure venue designated by the Academic Integrity Commission in coordination with the Joint Chiefs of Staff, with secure video conferencing permitted only for members who are physically unable to reach the venue due to documented imminent operational circumstance. No authorization shall occur without Panel members being visually and aurally present to one another in real time throughout deliberation. (b) Convening Time Limit. The Panel shall convene within four (4) hours of any proposed authorization request. A request that cannot produce Panel convening within four hours shall be deemed insufficient to meet the imminent threat standard under Section 16.10 and shall be denied.

This prevents urgency claims from being used to bypass authorization requirements. (c) Documented Deliberation. Panel deliberations shall be audio-recorded and preserved under Section 13B standards, with recordings published on the Franklin Ledger upon conclusion of the crisis that prompted the authorization request. Publication shall occur within thirty (30) days absent specific operational-security need certified by Authority Liberty Bell Initiative, and in no case later than one hundred eighty (180) days. (d) Dissent Right. Each Panel member shall have the right to state dissent to any authorization proposal. Dissents shall be documented with specific reasoning and shall be preserved regardless of the authorization outcome. A Panel member voting against authorization shall not face any adverse consequence for their vote. (e) Panel Integrity Verification. Before any authorization vote, each Panel member shall affirm under oath that they are acting freely, have not been coerced, threatened, bribed, or compromised, and that their vote reflects their genuine judgment. The affirmation shall be recorded. Known or suspected compromise of a Panel member shall trigger immediate suspension of authorization proceedings pending Section 16.28 panel member integrity review. (f) Panel Members' Access to Information. Panel members shall have immediate access to all intelligence, military assessments, diplomatic communications, and other information relevant to the authorization decision. Information shall not be withheld, filtered, or selectively presented. Attempts to withhold relevant information from Panel members shall constitute Section 13 interference with Senior Official multipliers and shall independently constitute treason under Section 16.12. (g) No External Direction. Panel members shall not receive direction, guidance, or pressure from federal officeholders outside the Panel during active deliberation. Communications with the President or Committee Chairperson shall be limited to factual briefing on the situation prompting the request, not to advocacy for a particular outcome. 16.18 Nuclear Authorization Vote Procedures. The 72-hour Nuclear Authorization Vote under Section 16.8(b) shall operate under the following framework: (a) Ballot Content. The Nuclear Authorization Vote ballot shall present a single question: 'Shall the United States authorize the use of nuclear weapons under the authorization request of [date and identifier]?' The ballot shall identify the target, scope, and authorization request specifics to the extent consistent with operational security, with detailed information accessible through the Franklin Ledger. (b) Multi-Language Display. Ballot content shall be available in English, Spanish, and the primary languages of Participating Jurisdictions with significant non-English-speaking populations, consistent with Section 12.12(c). Translation shall be accelerated to meet the 72-hour window. (c) Continuous Operation. All Offices, Centers, Host Sites, Satellite Sites, and Overseas Terminals shall remain continuously operational throughout the 72-hour window, with twenty-four-hour access to Sovereign Voting Terminals. Mobile Accessibility Teams shall conduct emergency deployment to serve voters unable to reach fixed locations. (d) Infrastructure Failure Protocol. Section 5.6 infrastructure failure procedures shall apply with maximum urgency during the Nuclear Authorization Vote. Infrastructure failure affecting more than five percent (5%) of Offices nationally for more than six (6) hours shall trigger automatic extension of the vote by eight (8) hours for each hour of disruption beyond the threshold.

(e) No Extension Beyond 72 Hours Absent Emergency Extension. Outside of infrastructure-failure extension under subsection (d), the 72-hour window shall not be extended. The brevity of the window reflects the nature of nuclear authorization as time-sensitive; indefinite extension would permit delay tactics by either advocates or opponents. (f) Ballot Secrecy. Ballot secrecy under Section 4.1(c) and Section 5.10 shall apply fully to the Nuclear Authorization Vote. No voter shall face inquiry or retaliation regarding their vote. No aggregate statistics tied to individual voter identification shall be published. (g) Result Certification Timeline. Vote results shall be certified within twelve (12) hours of window close under the Section 5.7 framework, accelerated to meet the urgency of nuclear decision-making. Authorization-granting certification shall proceed through Liberty Bell Initiative; authorization-denying certification shall proceed automatically without Authority action required. (h) Publication of Vote Fact. The existence of a Nuclear Authorization Vote, its timing, and its result shall be published on the Franklin Ledger in real time per Section 16.13. The specific authorization request details may be redacted during active operations for operational security, with full publication required within thirty (30) days of crisis resolution. E. Protected Refusal and Communication Integrity 16.19 Protected Refusal Extended to All Service Members. The constitutional duty and protection to refuse unlawful orders under Section 16.3(c) shall extend to all members of the Armed Forces, not only the Joint Chiefs of Staff: (a) Universal Application. Every member of the United States Armed Forces — including enlisted personnel, non-commissioned officers, commissioned officers of all ranks, and civilian personnel in military chains of command — shall have constitutional authority and duty to refuse any order that would violate this Amendment, this Constitution, the laws of war, the laws of the United States, or the nuclear authorization requirements of this Section.

(b) Specific Application to Launch Personnel. Personnel operating nuclear launch systems, missile silos, submarine launch platforms, strategic bomber crews, and any other nuclear delivery infrastructure shall have specific duty to refuse launch orders that fail to meet the Section 16.8 authorization requirements. Launch personnel shall be trained to recognize authorized versus unauthorized orders, with training materials certified by the Academic Integrity Commission. (c) Refusal Documentation Procedures. Refusing service members shall document their refusal through: (i) immediate written or recorded statement identifying the order, the issuing officer, the specific grounds for refusal, and the constitutional or legal basis; (ii) notification to the next higher officer outside the chain giving the refused order (or, if that officer is also in the chain, to the next higher outside the chain); (iii) notification to Inspector General channels under Section 13B.20; and (iv) notification to the Watchdog Tribunal where available. Documentation shall be preserved under Section 13B standards. (d) Protection From Adverse Action. No service member exercising protected refusal shall face: (i) court-martial for the refusal itself; (ii) administrative discharge; (iii) demotion or reduction in rank; (iv) reassignment as retaliation; (v) security clearance revocation; (vi) pension or benefits forfeiture; or (vii) any other adverse action connected to the refusal. Adverse action taken against a refusing service member shall be void ab initio and shall subject the action-taker to Section 13 interference penalties and Section 16.5 insurrection penalties where the retaliation was part of an attempt to execute the unlawful order. (e) Burden of Proof on Order-Giver. Where refusal is contested, the burden shall rest on the order-giving officer to establish by clear and convincing evidence that the order was lawful and complied with all applicable authorizations. The burden shall not rest on the refusing service member to prove the order was unlawful. (f) Career Preservation. Service members whose refusal is validated through subsequent review shall have their careers fully preserved including: retention of rank and assignment; preservation of promotion eligibility; continuation of career development; and protection from informal career consequences. Where formal career harm has occurred before validation, the refusing service member shall be made whole including back compensation, restoration of rank, and removal of adverse materials from personnel files. (g) Good-Faith Mistake Protection. Even where a refusal is ultimately found unnecessary (because the order was lawful), good-faith refusal based on reasonable doubt shall not constitute a violation. The Amendment prefers conservative refusal over reckless compliance for orders of nuclear-scale consequence. 16.20 Communication Integrity and Order

Authentication. Nuclear authorization depends on authentic orders reaching launch personnel. The following framework shall apply: (a) Mandatory Authentication Protocol. All orders relating to nuclear authorization, launch, targeting, or posture changes shall bear cryptographic authentication verifying: (i) the identity of the issuing officer; (ii) the source within the authorized chain of command; (iii) the authorization reference linking to specific Section 16.8 authorization or Section 16.10 emergency exception; and (iv) the integrity of the order content against tampering. Authentication standards shall be developed by the Academic Integrity Commission in coordination with the Joint Chiefs and shall be cryptographically robust against foreign state-actor spoofing. (b) Two-Person Rule at Launch Sites. Every nuclear launch system shall operate under a two-person rule requiring: (i) two independently authenticated personnel with separate launch codes or equivalent mechanisms; (ii) independent verification that the received order meets authentication protocol under subsection (a); (iii)

independent verification that the authorization reference resolves to a valid Section 16.8 authorization or Section 16.10 emergency exception; and (iv) independent authority of either person to refuse under Section 16.19 if verification fails. No single-person launch authority shall exist at any nuclear launch site. (c) Spoof-Order Detection and Response. Where an order fails authentication, contains internal inconsistencies, or appears fabricated, launch personnel shall: (i) refuse execution immediately; (ii) notify the Joint Chiefs of Staff through secure back-channel; (iii) notify the Watchdog Tribunal through emergency notification; (iv) preserve the suspect order for forensic analysis; and (v) await confirmed authentic instructions from verified chain of command. Spoof-order attempts shall be investigated by the Hamilton Contingent Preservation Division for evidence of foreign interference, domestic insurrection, or other unlawful action. (d) Back-Channel Verification. Launch personnel shall have access to encrypted back-channel communications to the Joint Chiefs of Staff, the Watchdog Tribunal, and the Sovereign Civic Network-based Franklin Ledger for verification of authorization validity. Back-channels shall be physically and cryptographically independent of the ordinary chain of command communication, preventing a compromised chain from suppressing back-channel verification. (e) Communication Integrity Enforcement. Any person who: (i) fabricates a nuclear order; (ii) alters an authentic order to change its content; (iii) impersonates an authorizing officer; (iv) blocks or corrupts back-channel verification; or (v) otherwise attacks the integrity of nuclear authorization communication shall be subject to treason prosecution under Section 16.12 and asset recovery under Section 13D Tier Three maximum, with no possibility of pardon, commutation, or clemency under Section 24.5 and Section 18.14. (f) Periodic Integrity Audit. The Academic Integrity Commission shall conduct quarterly audits of communication integrity systems, authentication protocols, two-person-rule procedures, and back-channel availability, with findings published on the Franklin Ledger. Detected vulnerabilities shall trigger immediate remediation with Hamilton Contingent involvement where malicious compromise is suspected. 16.21 Post-Refusal Review Process. Where a service member has exercised protected refusal, review shall proceed as follows: (a) Mandatory Review. Every protected refusal shall be subject to mandatory review within seven (7) days of refusal documentation to determine whether the refusal was justified, whether the order was lawful, and what consequences shall follow for the order-giver and the refusing service member. (b) Review Body. During steady-state operations, review shall be conducted by a three-member panel consisting of: (i) one member of the Watchdog Tribunal drawn by lottery; (ii) one retired senior military officer not currently in federal service, selected from a pool maintained by the Academic Integrity Commission; and (iii) one Chief Justice of a Participating Jurisdiction drawn by lottery. During Phase One before Tribunal convening, the Washington Commission shall perform this function. The review panel shall be independent of the chain of command in which the refusal occurred. (c) Review Standards. The panel shall evaluate: (i) whether the order met Section 16.8 authorization requirements or Section 16.10 emergency exception standards; (ii) whether the order complied with the laws of war and the laws of the United States; (iii) whether the refusing service member acted in good faith based on reasonable grounds; and (iv) what remedial or accountability actions shall follow. Findings shall be published on the Franklin Ledger with appropriate operational-security redactions. (d) Consequences for Validated Refusal. Where refusal is validated, the refusing service member shall be protected and made whole under Section 16.19(f), and the order-giver shall be subject to: (i) removal from command pending investigation; (ii) Section 13 interference prosecution with Senior Official multipliers; (iii) Section 16.5 insurrection prosecution where the unlawful order was part of a coordinated scheme; and (iv) Section 16.12 treason prosecution where the unlawful order concerned nuclear authorization. (e) Consequences for Refusal Not Validated. Where refusal is found to have been based on misunderstanding (and the order was in fact lawful), the refusing service member shall not face punishment under Section 16.19(g) good-faith mistake protection, but may be subject to additional training or counseling. Bad-faith refusal (where the service member knew the order was lawful but refused for improper reasons) shall be subject to ordinary military discipline under the Uniform Code of Military Justice. (f) Appeals. Review panel decisions may be appealed to a five-member appellate panel of Chief Justices of Participating Jurisdictions drawn by lottery, with appellate decision within thirty (30) days. Appeals shall not delay protection of the refusing service member during pendency; protection continues pending final appellate resolution. 16.22 Military Whistleblower Protection for Nuclear Matters. The Section 13B.16 whistleblower framework shall apply with specific enhancements for nuclear-related disclosures: (a) Scope of Protected Disclosure. Military whistleblowers disclosing any of the following shall receive full protection: (i) planned or attempted unauthorized nuclear authorization; (ii) corruption in nuclear authorization processes; (iii) compromise of communication integrity or authentication systems; (iv) coercion or bribery of Panel members; (v) suppression of back-channel verification; (vi) fabrication or attempted fabrication of nuclear orders; (vii) foreign interference in nuclear decision-making; or (viii) any other matter concerning the integrity of the nuclear framework established in this Section.

(b) Disclosure Channels. Military whistleblowers may disclose to: (i) Inspector General channels under Section 13B.20; (ii) the Watchdog Tribunal directly; (iii) the Hamilton Contingent Preservation Division; (iv) the Joint Chiefs of Staff acting collectively (not individually); (v) Congressional Armed Services committees; or (vi) the State Attorneys General Council. The Franklin Ledger shall not be an appropriate initial disclosure channel for operational-security reasons, though Ledger publication may follow disclosure investigation. (c) Classification Does Not Bar Disclosure. Classification shall not bar protected whistleblower disclosure of nuclear-integrity matters. Where classified information is relevant, disclosure to cleared officials through protected channels shall preserve classification while enabling accountability. Claims of classification used to suppress whistleblower disclosure shall constitute Section 13B.11 evidence destruction and Section 13 interference. (d) Enhanced Protections. Nuclear-matter whistleblowers shall receive enhanced protections beyond Section 13B.16 baseline: (i) immediate placement in protective custody where credible threats exist; (ii) federal identity protection and relocation where threats persist; (iii) continued full compensation for not less than ten (10) years if military career is curtailed; (iv) priority civilian placement support; and (v) ongoing Hamilton Contingent Protection Division oversight. (e) Retaliation

Consequences. Retaliation against nuclear-matter whistleblowers shall be treated as attempted suppression of Section 16 safeguards, subject to the same treason-level penalties under Section 16.12 as direct attempts to bypass nuclear authorization. Retaliation need not succeed to trigger the enhanced penalties. F. Scope and Definitions 16.23 Congressional Oversight of Nuclear Matters. Congressional oversight shall operate under the following framework without diminishing the Section 16.8 authorization requirements: (a) Briefings Required. The President, Committee Chairperson, or other Commander-in-Chief under Section 16.14 shall provide quarterly briefings to relevant Congressional committees (Senate Armed Services, House Armed Services, Senate Intelligence, House Intelligence) on: (i) nuclear force posture and any changes; (ii) nuclear authorization requests denied at Panel stage; (iii) nuclear authorization votes conducted; (iv) integrity audit findings; (v) whistleblower disclosures received and disposition; and (vi) any incidents involving nuclear communication or authentication systems. (b) Classification Limits. No classification shall be used to prevent Congressional committees from receiving briefings required by subsection (a). Operational details may be classified, but the existence of authorization requests, vote outcomes, integrity audits, and whistleblower disclosures shall not be classified from oversight committees. (c) No Congressional Authorization Authority. Congressional oversight under this Section shall not extend to approval, modification, or substitute authorization of nuclear actions. The Section 16.8 Panel and Vote framework is the exclusive authorization pathway; Congressional oversight is after-the-fact accountability, not pre-authorization. (d) Public Reporting. The Authority (or during Phase One, the Washington Commission) shall publish quarterly summary reports on the Franklin Ledger regarding nuclear framework operation, with appropriate operational-security redactions. Public reporting ensures that the People retain visibility into the framework's operation between authorization events. 16.24 International Treaty and Allied Coordination. The Section 16 framework shall interact with international obligations as follows: (a) Treaty Compatibility. Section 16 authorization requirements shall apply to all United States nuclear use regardless of treaty framework. NATO Article 5 obligations, bilateral defense treaties, and other alliance commitments shall not permit bypass of Section 16 requirements. United States nuclear response to attacks on allies shall proceed only through the Section 16 authorization process. (b) Allied Notification. Upon initiation of any Section 16.8 Panel convening, the State Department shall notify treaty allies through appropriate diplomatic channels that authorization is under active consideration, without disclosing specific targets or operational details. Allied notification preserves diplomatic coordination without compromising Panel deliberation. (c) Defensive Response to Attack on Allies. Where allies under mutual defense treaties are attacked with nuclear weapons, the Section 16.10 emergency exception may apply depending on whether the attack constitutes 'imminent nuclear attack' or 'active military invasion of US sovereign territory of nation-threatening scale' through the alliance mechanism. Interpretation shall be resolved through the Section 16.8 Panel with appropriate urgency. (d) No Treaty Supersession. No international treaty, executive agreement, or alliance obligation shall supersede Section 16 authorization requirements. Any treaty provision claiming to permit U.S. nuclear use without Section 16 authorization shall be void as to U.S. participation. (e) Arms Control Treaty Interaction. Nothing in this Section shall prevent the United States from entering into arms control treaties reducing or eliminating nuclear capabilities. Such treaties shall strengthen, not weaken, the People's protection and shall not require modification of Section 16 procedural requirements. 16.25 Nuclear-Adjacent Weapons of Mass Destruction. The authorization requirements of this Section shall extend to the following categories of weapons with potential for mass civilian casualties:

(a) Biological Weapons. Any authorization of offensive biological weapon use — including engineered pathogens, naturally occurring disease agents deployed as weapons, or agricultural biological agents with mass casualty potential — shall require Section 16.8 authorization on the same terms as nuclear weapons. Defensive biological countermeasures (vaccines, treatments) are not covered. (b) Chemical Weapons. Any authorization of offensive chemical weapon use — including nerve agents, blister agents, blood agents, and other chemical weapons prohibited by the Chemical Weapons Convention — shall require Section 16.8 authorization on the same terms as nuclear weapons. Riot-control agents in domestic law enforcement are not covered; use in armed conflict is. (c) Radiological Weapons. Any authorization of radiological weapon use — including 'dirty bombs,' radiation dispersal devices, and radiological area denial — shall require Section 16.8 authorization on the same terms as nuclear weapons. (d) Space-Based Kinetic or Energy Weapons of Mass Destruction. Any authorization of space-based kinetic weapons or directed energy weapons with capability for mass casualties shall require Section 16.8 authorization on the same terms as nuclear weapons, consistent with the Outer Space Treaty and analogous international obligations. (e) Autonomous Weapons of Mass Destruction. Any authorization of use of autonomous weapon systems with artificial intelligence or algorithmic decision-making capable of mass casualties shall require Section 16.8 authorization. Algorithmic authorization of mass casualty weapons shall be specifically prohibited; the final authorization decision shall remain with human Panel members and popular vote under this Amendment. (f) Integrated Authorization Framework. Where an authorization request concerns multiple categories of mass casualty weapons, a single Panel convening and a single Vote may address the integrated request, with the Vote ballot clearly identifying all weapon categories subject to the authorization. 16.26 Cyber Attacks of Nuclear-Scale Consequence. The authorization framework shall apply to cyber attacks with consequences approaching nuclear-scale civilian harm: (a) Impact-Based Test. A cyber attack shall require Section 16.8 authorization where the attack is designed to or reasonably likely to produce: (i) mass civilian casualties exceeding ten thousand persons; (ii) catastrophic infrastructure failure affecting critical life-sustaining systems (power grids of major metropolitan areas, water systems, food distribution systems) for extended duration; (iii) release of dangerous materials (from nuclear facilities, chemical facilities, biological laboratories) with mass casualty potential; or (iv) analogous catastrophic harm. (b) Defensive Cyber Operations Not Covered. Defensive cyber operations protecting U.S. networks, responding to active cyber attacks, or disrupting hostile cyber infrastructure targeting U.S. interests are not covered by Section 16 authorization requirements, consistent with the defensive nature of such operations. (c) Offensive Cyber Below Nuclear-Scale. Offensive cyber operations with consequences below nuclear-scale thresholds shall proceed through ordinary military and intelligence authorization procedures, not Section 16. This Section addresses only the nuclear-scale cyber subset. (d) Uncertainty in Impact Assessment. Where uncertainty exists about whether a planned cyber operation meets the subsection (a) threshold, the conservative presumption shall apply — Section 16 authorization shall be sought if the operation could reasonably produce mass casualty consequences. The burden rests on advocates of the operation to establish sub-threshold impact, not on opponents to prove threshold impact. (e) Post-Action Review. Cyber operations undertaken without Section 16 authorization but producing nuclear-scale consequences (whether intended or unintended) shall trigger mandatory post-action review by the Watchdog Tribunal, with findings published on the Franklin Ledger and potential retroactive prosecution where the operation exceeded authorized scope. 16.27 First-Use Versus Defensive Use Definition. Section 16.7 prohibits nuclear first-use and offensive capacity use without authorization. Precise definitions shall apply: (a) First-Use Defined. 'First-use' means any use of nuclear weapons by the United States against any target where (i) the target has not previously employed nuclear weapons against the United States, its armed forces, or its treaty allies; and (ii) no imminent nuclear attack on the United States is independently verified. Section 16.8 authorization is required for all first-use. (b) Retaliatory Response Authorization. Retaliatory response to confirmed nuclear attack on the United States, its armed forces, or (under treaty) its allies, may proceed through the Section 16.10 emergency exception, but retaliatory response shall be: (i) proportionate to the attack received; (ii) targeted against the attacker or the attacker's military capability, not civilian populations beyond unavoidable collateral; (iii) subject to immediate Panel convening as soon as operational circumstances permit; and (iv) fully documented with post-action Authority review within thirty (30) days. (c) De-Escalation Preference. Where a nuclear attack has been received but a response has not yet been executed, the Section 16.10 authority shall prioritize de-escalation, diplomatic resolution, and cessation of hostilities over retaliatory response, consistent with the catastrophic nature of nuclear escalation. (d) Tactical vs. Strategic Distinction Rejected. The Section 16 framework applies to all nuclear weapons regardless of yield classification, tactical versus strategic designation, or other military categorization. 'Tactical' nuclear weapons, 'low-yield'

nuclear weapons, and 'battlefield' nuclear weapons all receive Section 16 treatment. No weapon category shall be exempted from Section 16 on the basis of claimed limited consequence. (e) Proportionality Standard. All Section 16-authorized uses shall meet a proportionality standard, considering the actual or imminent threat, available alternatives, civilian harm potential, and long-term escalation consequences. The Panel's deliberation under Section 16.17 shall explicitly address proportionality. G. Safeguards and Integrity 16.28 Emergency Exception Abuse Prevention. The Section 16.10 emergency exceptions shall be subject to the following abuse-prevention framework: (a) Post-Action Review Mandatory. Every invocation of the Section 16.10 emergency exception shall trigger mandatory Watchdog Tribunal review within seventy-two (72) hours of the emergency action, with findings published on the Franklin Ledger within thirty (30) days. No emergency action shall be exempt from review. (b) 'Imminent' Standard. 'Imminent nuclear attack' under Section 16.10(a) shall require: (i) independently verified intelligence from multiple sources of confirmed hostile intent; (ii) operational indicators of attack preparation or initiation; (iii) time horizon such that Section 16.8 authorization cannot be completed before the attack occurs; and (iv) Joint Chiefs concurrence in the imminent-attack assessment. Claimed imminence without these elements shall constitute fabrication. (c) 'Nation-Threatening Scale' Standard. 'Active military invasion of US sovereign territory of nation-threatening scale' under Section 16.10(b) shall require: (i) confirmed foreign military forces present on U.S. sovereign territory; (ii) scale of invasion sufficient to threaten the continued constitutional existence of the United States, not a limited border incursion or isolated attack; (iii) response through Section 16 authorization not being operationally feasible given the scale and speed of the invasion; and (iv) Joint Chiefs concurrence in the nation-threatening assessment. (d) Fabrication as Treason. Intentional fabrication of the 'imminent attack' or 'nation-threatening invasion' conditions to invoke the Section 16.10 emergency exception shall constitute treason under Section 16.12, with maximum penalties. The fabricator shall include any official who directed fabrication, any intelligence official who falsified intelligence, and any military officer who confirmed false operational assessments. (e) Second-Panel Verification. Where emergency action under Section 16.10 is contemplated but operationally feasible within hours, even abbreviated Panel review shall be attempted. A Panel convened within one (1) hour with at least three (3) of five members present and providing unanimous concurrence shall substitute for the ordinary Section 16.8 process while preserving a documented check. Full

Panel review shall follow as soon as the immediate emergency passes. (f) Exception Narrow Construction. The Section 16.10 exception shall be construed narrowly. Ambiguous situations shall default to Section 16.8 authorization, not emergency exception. The exception exists for genuine catastrophic emergencies, not for crises that merely feel urgent to decision-makers. 16.29 Panel Member Compromise and Succession. The integrity of Panel members under Section 16.8(a) is foundational. The following framework shall apply to compromise and succession: (a) Compromise Detection. Panel member compromise — including bribery, threat, blackmail, coercion, foreign influence, or material conflict of interest — shall be investigated by the Watchdog Tribunal upon credible report. Investigation shall be expedited to complete within forty-eight (48) hours where Panel convening is imminent. (b) Suspension Authority. Upon clear and convincing evidence of Panel member compromise, the Watchdog Tribunal shall suspend the member from Panel service pending full resolution. During Phase One before Tribunal convening, the Washington Commission shall perform this function. (c) Succession for Suspended Members. Suspended Panel members shall be replaced as follows: (i) President or Committee Chairperson suspension — succession through normal constitutional succession under the Twenty-Fifth Amendment and this Amendment's Section 6A/6 framework; (ii) Senior Joint Chief suspension — succession through Joint Chiefs seniority under ordinary military law; (iii) Citizens' Oversight Board member suspension — redraw by lottery from Board membership; (iv) Academic Integrity Commission member suspension — redraw by lottery from Commission membership. (d) Emergency Succession. Where suspension and succession cannot be completed before time-critical Panel convening, the Panel shall proceed with the remaining uncompromised members plus emergency replacement. A compromised Panel member shall not participate in authorization under any circumstance, even if formal suspension has not yet been completed. (e) Consequences for Compromise. A Panel member found compromised shall be subject to: (i) Section 13 interference prosecution with Senior Official multipliers; (ii) Section 16.12 treason prosecution where the compromise was designed to produce unauthorized nuclear action; (iii) permanent bar from Panel service and from any Amendment Body service; and (iv) asset recovery under Section 13D where financial benefit from compromise is established. (f) Attempted Compromise Prosecution. Any person attempting to bribe, threaten, blackmail, coerce, or otherwise compromise a Panel member shall be subject to treason prosecution under Section 16.12, regardless of whether the compromise attempt succeeded. The attempt itself constitutes the offense.

16.30 Nuclear Force Posture and Alert Level Changes. Changes to nuclear force posture short of actual use shall be subject to the following oversight: (a) DEFCON or Equivalent Changes. Changes to nuclear force alert level (DEFCON or equivalent) shall be documented on the Franklin Ledger within twenty-four (24) hours of change, with appropriate operational-security redactions maintained until the change is resolved. The existence and general nature of alert level changes shall not be classified from the public. (b) Nuclear Weapon Movement. Movements of nuclear weapons between storage and deployment positions, across national boundaries (consistent with treaty obligations), or between military branches shall be documented on the Franklin Ledger with secure-channel notification to Congressional oversight committees. (c) Nuclear-Capable Platform Deployments. Deployments of nuclear-capable platforms (submarines, bombers, missile systems) to forward positions shall be documented consistent with subsection (b). (d) Posture Changes Below Authorization Threshold. Ordinary posture changes and alert level adjustments do not require Section 16.8 authorization; they are oversight matters rather than authorization matters. But posture changes designed to enable a specific unauthorized use shall constitute an attempted Section 16.12 treason offense. (e) Integrity Audit of Posture Changes. The Academic Integrity Commission shall audit posture change records quarterly, with findings published on the Franklin Ledger. Unusual patterns — including clustering around specific geopolitical situations, bypass of ordinary notification channels, or disproportionate posture changes relative to stated rationale — shall trigger Watchdog Tribunal investigation. 16.31 Nuclear Testing and Maintenance Framework. Distinctions apply between operational use and testing/maintenance: (a) Testing Authorization. Nuclear weapons testing — including underground tests, above-ground tests where permitted by treaty, subcritical tests, and computer-simulated tests — shall be distinguished from operational use. Actual-yield testing shall require Section 16.8 authorization on the same terms as operational use; subcritical and computer-simulated testing shall proceed under ordinary authorization with Franklin Ledger notification. (b) Maintenance and Sustainment. Nuclear weapons maintenance, sustainment, refurbishment, and component replacement activities shall proceed under ordinary Department of Energy and Department of Defense authority, not requiring Section 16.8 authorization, but subject to integrity audit under Section 16.30(e). (c) Accident Response. Nuclear accidents, broken arrow events, and similar incidents shall be documented on the Franklin Ledger within seventy-two (72) hours with appropriate operational-security consideration. Cover-ups of nuclear accidents shall constitute Section 13B evidence destruction and, where the accident threatened civilian populations, Section 16.12 treason. (d) Decommissioning. Nuclear weapons decommissioning and dismantlement shall proceed under arms control treaty obligations and ordinary departmental authority, with the Academic Integrity Commission auditing decommissioning for completeness and security of fissile material. (e) No Testing Loophole. Testing shall not be used as a mechanism to bypass Section 16.8 authorization. Any test designed to serve as an operational use (targeting hostile infrastructure, delivering a political message through weapons release, or otherwise extending beyond testing purposes) shall be treated as operational use requiring Section 16.8 authorization.

Section 17. Structural Integrity of the Three Bodies of the Authority

17.1 The three bodies shall be constituted per this Section, which cannot be reduced or waived by any act of Congress, state legislature, executive order, or judicial ruling. A. The Citizens' Oversight Board 17.2 The Citizens' Oversight Board shall consist of three hundred (300) registered voters drawn by randomized lottery from all Participating Jurisdictions, distributed as follows: not fewer than three (3) seats reserved to each of the six (6) non-state Participating Jurisdictions (the District of Columbia, the Commonwealth of Puerto Rico, the Territory of Guam, the United States Virgin Islands, the Commonwealth of the Northern Mariana Islands, and the Territory of American Samoa), totaling at least eighteen (18) seats for the non-state Jurisdictions. The remaining two hundred eighty-two (282) or fewer seats shall be distributed among the fifty states in proportion to their voting-age populations. This hybrid distribution ensures that no non-state Jurisdiction is erased by raw population math while preserving broad citizen representation proportional to population. The lottery pool shall include registered voters of all Participating Jurisdictions. 17.3 Staggered 2-year terms, 150 rotating yearly. No consecutive terms, no more than two total lifetime. 17.4 Service is mandatory like federal jury duty. Excuse only upon extreme hardship, publicly recorded. 17.4.1 Hardship Framework for Mandatory Service. Because mandatory service on the Citizens' Oversight Board affects registered voters drawn from every walk of American life, and because a legitimate amendment cannot force service upon persons who genuinely cannot serve without creating both cruelty and a credibility crisis, this Section establishes the specific framework by which hardship is assessed, accommodation is offered, and excuse is granted. The framework shall be construed to enable service where accommodation can make service possible, and to grant excuse only where accommodation cannot. The framework applies to pre-service selection and to mid-service developments alike. 17.4.2 Automatic Categorical Exemptions. The following categories of drawn citizens shall be automatically exempt from service upon documented confirmation of the category, without requiring hardship petition or adversarial review: (a) Age Seventy (70) or Older. Any drawn citizen who has reached the age of seventy (70) by the date of the lottery draw shall be automatically exempt. Exemption is a right of the drawn citizen and not a disqualification; a citizen aged seventy (70) or older who wishes to serve may affirmatively waive the exemption and serve under ordinary terms. (b) Active Military Deployment. Any drawn citizen serving on active military deployment at the time of the draw shall be automatically exempt. The exemption shall continue through the deployment's conclusion. Upon return from deployment, the citizen shall re-enter the lottery pool under Section 17.4.9. (c) Recent Prior Amendment Service. Any drawn citizen who has completed prior service on the Citizens' Oversight Board, the Watchdog Tribunal citizen membership, the Hamilton Contingent Citizen Oversight Members, the Short-Term Civilian Review Board, or the Academic Integrity Commission (in an individual capacity) within the preceding ten (10) years shall be automatically exempt. This exemption prevents the same individuals from being repeatedly conscripted to Amendment service and promotes broader distribution of civic participation. (d) Incapacity of Record. Any drawn citizen who is under legal guardianship, conservatorship, or equivalent adjudication of incapacity shall be automatically exempt. Confirmation shall be through court records provided to the administering body under seal. (e) Documentation Standard. Automatic exemptions shall be confirmed through documentation provided to the administering body: for age, through government-issued identification; for military deployment, through Department of Defense records; for prior service, through Amendment records; for incapacity, through sealed court records. No adversarial hearing is required for an automatic exemption. (f) Public Recording. The fact of exemption and its categorical basis shall be publicly recorded upon the Franklin Ledger. Underlying documentation — including specific dates of birth, specific deployment orders, specific court adjudications — shall remain sealed and accessible only to the administering body and, on review, to the Watchdog Tribunal. 17.4.3 Disability Accommodation as Default. A drawn citizen with a disability that would affect ordinary service shall be offered accommodation before being offered excuse. The Amendment's principle is that persons with disabilities have the same right to civic service as any other citizen, and the administering body shall

affirmatively work to enable service rather than substituting exclusion. Accommodations may include: (a) Remote participation through secure video, audio, or text infrastructure for Board sessions, including live captioning, sign language interpretation, and assistive technology integration; (b) Reduced or modified schedule where the full ordinary schedule would exceed the citizen's capacity but a reduced schedule would not; (c) Personal support services during service, including personal care attendants, communication assistants, and mobility assistance, funded through the Amendment's appropriation under Section 11.3; (d) Adaptive equipment and materials, including screen readers, Braille materials, large-print materials, audio materials, and any other adaptive technology reasonably required; (e) Flexible attendance for episodic conditions where the citizen can serve effectively most of the time but requires flexibility during episodic flare-ups of the underlying condition; (f) Any other accommodation reasonably tailored to the specific citizen's circumstances, with the administering body required to engage in good-faith interactive dialogue with the drawn citizen about what accommodation would enable service. 17.4.4

When Accommodation Cannot Suffice. Where the drawn citizen and the administering body, through good-faith interactive dialogue, conclude that no accommodation can enable service consistent with the citizen's health, safety, or basic needs, excuse shall be granted under Section 17.4.6. The preference for accommodation shall not be used to force service upon persons for whom service would cause genuine harm. 17.4.5 Petition-Based Hardship Categories. In addition to automatic exemptions and disability accommodation, a drawn citizen may petition for excuse based on any of the following hardship categories, each requiring documentation and administrating-body review: (a) Medical Hardship. Documented medical condition affecting the citizen or a dependent family member of such severity that service would materially compromise the citizen's health or the dependent's care. Privacy protections under Section 17.4.7 shall apply to all medical hardship petitions. (b) Primary Caregiver Hardship. The citizen is the primary caregiver for dependent minor children, a spouse or domestic partner with significant medical or disability needs, or aging parents requiring hands-on daily care, and no alternative caregiver is reasonably available during the term of service. The fact of caregiving responsibility shall be documented; identities of care recipients and specifics of their conditions shall be treated under Section 17.4.7 privacy protections. (c) Financial Hardship Beyond Section 17.5 Replacement. Although Section 17.5 provides wage replacement at the median United States household income with cost-of-living adjustment, a drawn citizen may demonstrate that this replacement would be materially insufficient to prevent concrete financial harm — for example, specialized medical costs for a dependent not covered by the Amendment's medical coverage, active business obligations that cannot be delegated during the service term, or outstanding legal financial obligations that exceed median-income capacity. The hardship petition shall document specific financial consequences of service, not general preference for higher income. (d) Essential Personnel. The citizen serves in a narrowly defined essential role — including active emergency medical providers in underserved communities, sole-operator critical infrastructure positions, and analogous roles where the citizen's absence would create concrete public-safety risk — such that service during the term would produce identifiable harm to public safety. Essential-personnel hardship shall be documented through the citizen's employer or licensing authority, with the specific nature of the role and the specific public-safety concern identified. (e) Other Extreme Hardship. A residual category for hardship that does not fit within the enumerated categories but is of comparable severity. Petitions under this category shall identify with specificity the hardship, why enumerated categories do not apply, and why the hardship is of comparable severity to the enumerated categories. 17.4.6 Hardship Petition Process. Petitions for hardship excuse shall proceed under the following framework: (a) Filing Window. A drawn citizen shall file a hardship petition within thirty (30) days of notification of selection. Petitions filed after this window shall be considered only upon showing of good cause for late filing. (b) Filing Requirements. The petition shall identify the hardship category, provide supporting documentation (subject to Section 17.4.7 privacy protections), and affirm under penalty of perjury that the petition is filed in good faith. (c) Initial Review by Administering Body. The administering body — for Citizens' Oversight Board draws, the Board's credentialing committee; during Phase One before Board constitution, the Washington Commission — shall review the petition within twenty-one (21) days and issue a written determination granting excuse, granting accommodation, or denying the petition with specific reasoning. (d) Right of Appeal. A denied petitioner shall have the right to appeal to the Watchdog Tribunal (or, during Phase One before Tribunal convening, to an emergency three-member panel of Chief Justices of Participating Jurisdictions drawn by lottery under Section 19.5.0.3). The appellate body shall review the

petition de novo and issue its determination within fourteen (14) days of appeal filing. Appellate determinations shall be final. (e) Provisional Non-Service During Pendency. While a hardship petition is pending, the drawn citizen shall not be required to commence service. If the petition is ultimately denied, service shall commence upon notification of final denial, with service term calculated from the date service commences rather than the original selection date. (f) No Retaliation for Good-Faith Petition. No drawn citizen shall face adverse consequence for filing a good-faith hardship petition that is ultimately denied. Filing itself is not evidence of bad faith. 17.4.7 Privacy Protections for Hardship Documentation. Medical conditions, caregiving details, specific financial circumstances, and other sensitive personal information supporting hardship petitions shall be treated as follows: (a) Categorical Excuse Publicly Recorded. The fact that excuse was granted, and the general category under which excuse was granted (medical, caregiver, financial, essential-personnel, disability accommodation unable to suffice, or other extreme hardship), shall be publicly recorded upon the Franklin Ledger. Public recording of the categorical basis preserves the accountability function of Section 17.4's 'publicly recorded' requirement. (b) Underlying Documentation Sealed. Specific medical diagnoses, specific caregiver recipients, specific financial details, specific employer-related essential-personnel information, and other sensitive personal information shall be sealed. Sealed documentation shall be accessible only to: (i) the administering body for initial review; (ii) the Watchdog Tribunal on appeal or for pattern-of-abuse review; and (iii) a Section 17.4.8 fraud investigation where bad-faith filing is specifically alleged. (c) Sealed Documentation Retention. Sealed hardship documentation shall be retained for ten (10) years following the original service term that was excused, after which it shall be destroyed under secure procedures. Destruction shall be documented on the Franklin Ledger. Retention enables pattern analysis to detect fraud; time-limited retention prevents permanent surveillance of citizens who sought legitimate hardship excuse. (d) No Publication of Medical, Caregiver, or Financial Specifics. Under no circumstance shall specific medical diagnoses, specific care recipients, or specific financial figures be published upon the Franklin Ledger or any other public forum, regardless of whether excuse is granted or denied. The Amendment's public-accountability mandate does not extend to requiring citizens to publish their private medical, family, or financial information in order to seek hardship excuse. (e) Protected Disclosure to Adjudicators. Disclosure of sealed information to Watchdog Tribunal or Emergency Panel adjudicators shall not constitute waiver of privacy protections; adjudicators receiving sealed information shall be bound by the same confidentiality obligations as the original sealed custody. 17.4.8 Bad-Faith Hardship Claims as Section 13 Interference. A hardship claim filed in bad faith — specifically, a claim that asserts hardship the claimant knows does not exist, that falsifies documentation, or that is designed primarily to evade legitimate civic service — shall constitute Section 13 interference with Amendment operation. The evidentiary standard for bad-faith determination shall be clear and convincing evidence, and such determination shall be made only by the Watchdog Tribunal (or Phase One equivalent) after opportunity for the claimant to respond. Consequences shall include: (a) Denial of hardship excuse and mandatory service on the original service term, with the term recalculated from the date of bad-faith determination; (b) Section 13 interference penalties as provided in Section 13, applied without Senior Official multipliers (as the bad-faith claimant is an ordinary citizen, not a senior official); (c) Permanent disqualification from future Amendment service on any body; (d) Publication of the bad-faith determination on the Franklin Ledger, with the claimant's name and the nature of the falsification specifically identified. Privacy protections under Section 17.4.7 do not apply to documented bad-faith claims, as the public has a legitimate interest in distinguishing legitimate hardship from fraudulent evasion. (e) No Chilling Effect on Good-Faith Petitions. Bad-faith determinations shall be made only upon clear and convincing evidence of actual falsification or knowing misrepresentation. Good-faith hardship petitions that are denied because the hardship does not meet the enumerated threshold, or because documentation proves insufficient, shall not constitute bad-faith claims. The Amendment encourages good-faith petitioning; it prosecutes only deliberate fraud. 17.4.9 Mid-Service Hardship. Where a drawn citizen has commenced service but subsequently develops hardship of the kind enumerated in Sections 17.4.2 through 17.4.5 — including but not limited to new medical diagnosis, new caregiver obligation arising from family member illness, new military deployment orders, or disability condition changes that cannot be accommodated under Section 17.4.3 — the following mid-service framework shall apply: (a) Mid-Service Petition. The citizen may file a mid-service hardship petition with the administering body using the same framework as Section 17.4.6, including privacy protections under Section 17.4.7. (b) Priority Review. Mid-service hardship petitions shall be reviewed on a priority basis — initial review within fourteen (14) days rather than the ordinary twenty-one (21), and appellate review within seven (7) days rather than fourteen (14) — because ongoing service creates ongoing hardship impact.

(c) Interim Leave. While a mid-service petition is pending, the administering body may grant interim leave from specific duties as the petition requires, with the citizen's full service obligation held in abeyance pending final determination. Interim leave does not prejudice the petition's final outcome. (d) Accommodation First Principle Applies. The Section 17.4.3 accommodation-first principle applies to mid-service petitions. Where accommodation can enable continued service consistent with the new hardship, accommodation shall be offered before excuse. (e) Honorable Exit. Where excuse is granted mid-service, the exit shall be recorded as honorable completion of service for the portion served, without penalty, without negative implication, and without prejudice to the citizen's record. Accrued Section 17.5 benefits shall not be revoked on account of honorable mid-service hardship exit. (f) Replacement Selection. Upon honorable mid-service exit, the administering body shall promptly draw a replacement from the lottery pool under Section 17.2 procedures, with the replacement serving the remainder of the departing citizen's term. The replacement shall receive the same protections, compensation, and accommodations as any other drawn citizen. (g) Cooling-Off Period Applies. A citizen who departs service through honorable mid-service hardship exit shall be subject to the Section 17.4.10 five (5) year cooling-off period before re-entry into the lottery pool. (h) Bad-Faith Mid-Service Claims. Mid-service hardship claims filed in bad faith — including fabrication of condition changes or deliberate delay of pre-existing hardship disclosure until after service begins to evade lottery replacement — shall be subject to Section 17.4.8 bad-faith consequences. 17.4.10 Post-Hardship Re-Entry Framework. Where a drawn citizen is excused through hardship under any provision of this Section, re-entry into the lottery pool shall proceed as follows: (a) Five-Year Cooling-Off Period. The excused citizen shall not be eligible for re-draw into Amendment service on any body for a period of five (5) years following the date of excuse. Cooling-off recognizes that the circumstances giving rise to hardship often require time to resolve or stabilize, and prevents the same citizen from being drawn repeatedly in rapid succession. (b) Automatic Re-Entry After Cooling-Off. Upon expiration of the cooling-off period, the citizen shall be automatically returned to the lottery pool without requirement of affirmative action. Re-entry is automatic because lottery pool inclusion is based on registered voter status, not on prior hardship. (c) Continuing Hardship Re-Petition. Where a citizen re-drawn after cooling-off remains in the hardship condition that originally prompted excuse — for example, a caregiver whose care obligations have continued, or a person with a progressive medical condition that has not stabilized — the citizen may file a new hardship petition under Section 17.4.6. Prior excuse does not prejudice subsequent petitions; continuing hardship is adjudicated on its own current basis. (d) Permanent Condition Registration. Where a hardship condition is documented as permanent — including terminal illness, permanent severe disability that cannot be accommodated, and similar conditions — the citizen may register the condition with the administering body to obtain ongoing exemption without repeated petition. Permanent registration shall be subject to Section 17.4.7 privacy protections and may be revoked by the citizen at any time upon resolution or improvement of the underlying condition. (e) No Lifetime Ban. This Section does not create a lifetime ban from service. A citizen excused for hardship retains the right to serve if circumstances change and the citizen is drawn in a future lottery after the cooling-off period. 17.4.11 Annual Hardship Statistics Publication. The administering body shall publish annually on the Franklin Ledger aggregate statistics on hardship petitions, including: (a) total petitions filed; (b) breakdown by category; (c) grant rates by category; (d) accommodation rates where applicable; (e) appeal rates and appeal outcomes; (f) bad-faith determinations and consequences; (g) demographic distributions of petitioners (age, jurisdiction, and other non-sensitive characteristics) to detect possible disparate-impact patterns. Statistics shall preserve individual privacy under Section 17.4.7; no statistics shall identify individual petitioners. Annual statistics enable public accountability and pattern detection without compromising petitioner privacy. 17.4.12 Application to Other Mandatory-Service Bodies. The hardship framework established in Sections 17.4 through 17.4.11 shall apply, mutatis mutandis, to the following other mandatory-service bodies, with the administering body adjusted as specified: (a) Watchdog Tribunal Citizen Members (Section 21.3(a)). The framework applies in full to the fifty (50) citizen members drawn by lottery. For retired federal judge members under Section 21.3(b), who enter service through a voluntary pool rather than compulsory draw, the framework applies at the individual level where a drawn judge member develops hardship affecting continued service — in such cases Sections 17.4.3 (accommodation), 17.4.5 (petition categories), 17.4.6 (process), 17.4.7 (privacy), 17.4.9 (mid-service), and 17.4.10 (re-entry) apply, but the automatic categorical exemptions of Section 17.4.2 do not apply because retired judge selection occurs from a voluntary pool rather than compulsory draw. The administering body for Tribunal hardship matters shall be the Tribunal's internal credentialing committee, with appeal to a three-member emergency panel of Chief Justices drawn by lottery. (b) Hamilton Contingent Citizen Oversight Members (Section 13C.9). The framework applies in full to Citizen Oversight Members drawn by lottery to serve

within Hamilton Divisions. The administering body for Hamilton Citizen Oversight Member hardship matters shall be the Contingent Director with Division Chief concurrence, with appeal to the Watchdog Tribunal. (c) Short-Term Civilian Review Board (Section 19.5.0.7). The framework applies in full to the fifty-six (56) registered voters drawn by lottery. The administering body during Phase One shall be the Washington Commission, with appeal to an emergency three-member panel of Chief Justices drawn by lottery from Chief Justices not serving on the Washington Commission. (d) Academic Integrity Commission — Individual-Level Application (Section 17.15). The framework applies at the individual level to persons selected by their universities to serve on the Academic Integrity Commission. Section 17.16.3(e) already addresses institution-level declined participation; this subsection addresses individual hardship. Where an individual selected by a university develops hardship (pre-service or mid-service) that prevents or impairs service, Sections 17.4.3 (accommodation), 17.4.5 (petition categories), 17.4.6 (process), 17.4.7 (privacy), 17.4.9 (mid-service), and 17.4.10 (re-entry) apply. The automatic categorical exemptions of Section 17.4.2 apply except for paragraph (c) (recent prior Amendment service), which applies only to bodies on which the person previously served, and except that universities with selected individuals unable to serve may invoke Section 17.16.3(e) to substitute a different individual without triggering a separate hardship petition for the replaced individual. The administering body for Academic Integrity Commission hardship matters shall be the Commission's internal credentialing committee (or, during Phase One before Commission constitution, the Washington Commission), with appeal to the Watchdog Tribunal. (e) Administering Body Defined. For each body identified in this Section, the administering body for hardship matters is identified. The administering body shall apply Sections 17.4 through 17.4.11 with the same fidelity as the Citizens' Oversight Board applies the framework to its own members, and shall not use administrative convenience as grounds for denying hardship relief. (f) Privacy Protections Apply Uniformly. Section 17.4.7 privacy protections apply uniformly across all bodies covered by this Section. Regardless of which body's administering committee reviews a petition, sensitive personal information receives the same sealed protection. (g) Coordination for Cross-Body Cooling-Off. The Section 17.4.10(a) five (5) year cooling-off period, and the Section 17.4.2(c) ten (10) year recent-prior-service exemption, shall be coordinated across all bodies. A citizen excused for hardship from one body shall be cooled-off from all bodies for five (5) years; a citizen who served on one body shall be exempt from selection for all bodies for ten (10) years following completion of service. Coordination prevents the same citizen from being drawn rapidly across different bodies despite recent service or hardship.

17.4.13 Application to Case-Specific and Ad-Hoc Lottery-Drawn Roles. Beyond the ongoing-service bodies covered in Section 17.4.12, this Amendment establishes numerous case-specific panels, ad-hoc lottery-drawn roles, and short-duration service obligations. The same hardship principles apply to these roles, but with scaled timelines appropriate to the duration of service. The framework shall apply as follows: (a) Multi-Month Case-Specific Panels. For panels expected to serve for thirty (30) days or longer on a single case or matter — including State Attorneys General Prosecution Panels under Section 17C.3, State Supreme Court Judicial Panels under Section 17C.6, Appellate Panels under Section 17C.9, and other lottery-drawn panels of comparable duration — Sections 17.4.2 through 17.4.11 shall apply in full, with the administering body being the body that convened the Panel (for Section 17C Panels, the Permanent Washington Commission under Section 17D.13.1) and with appeal to the Watchdog Tribunal. (b) Multi-Week Case-Specific Panels. For panels expected to serve for seven (7) days or more but less than thirty (30) days — including Special Eligibility Panels under Section 8.1, certain Emergency Review Panels under Sections 19.5.0.3 and 19.5.0.3.2.1, and comparable lottery-drawn panels — the hardship framework shall apply with compressed timelines: petitions reviewed within seven (7) days rather than twenty-one (21); appeals decided within three (3) days rather than fourteen (14); and replacement drawn immediately upon grant of excuse. (c) Multi-Day Case-Specific Panels. For panels expected to serve for less than seven (7) days — including Independent Warrant Panels under Section 13C.14.8, Residence Search Warrant Panels under Section 13G.7, In Camera Review panels under Section 13G.8, physician capacity panels under Section 6.9, and comparable lottery-drawn panels — the hardship framework shall apply with further compressed timelines: decline may be exercised within forty-eight (48) hours of notification without formal petition; a drawn person may state hardship as grounds for decline and the administering body shall grant excuse and redraw immediately; appeals are not required because the alternative remedy (immediate redraw) is equivalent in effect; privacy protections under Section 17.4.7 apply in full, with the fact of decline recorded but the specific basis sealed. (d) Same-Day Roles. For roles exercised same-day and lasting no more than a single day — including citizen observers at Terminal sealing under Section 14, citizen counters on hand-count teams, lottery-drawn witnesses to specific moments, and comparable brief assignments — a drawn person may simply decline at the moment of call, without petition, without published reasoning, and without any adverse consequence. The administering body shall redraw immediately from the available pool. The speed of such roles means that no formal process is needed; a citizen who says 'I cannot do this right now' shall be taken at their word and another citizen drawn. Repeated same-day declines by the same citizen do not trigger review; each same-day call is independent.

(e) Ex Officio Roles and Mid-Duty Incapacity. For roles held ex officio by existing state officials — including State Elections Council members, Permanent Washington Commission Chief Justices, Interim Caretaker Council Governors, Senior Chief Justice Panel members, Joint Chiefs of Staff, and State Attorneys General Council members — the primary hardship framework shall be each official's home-jurisdiction succession law (for Governors, lieutenant governor succession; for Chief Justices, senior-justice succession; for state AGs, deputy AG succession; and so forth), and such succession shall apply automatically without federal determination. Where an ex officio official develops a temporary incapacity that prevents continued Amendment service without permanently vacating their state office, the official may delegate Amendment duties to the ordinary successor under their state's succession law for the duration of the incapacity, with the delegation documented on the Franklin Ledger. The accommodation principles of Section 17.4.3 apply — an ex officio official with a disability shall be offered accommodation (including remote participation) to enable continued service before succession substitution is required. Privacy protections under Section 17.4.7 apply to the specific medical or personal basis for any delegation. (f) Universal Right of Immediate Decline. Any drawn person, regardless of the role's duration or type, retains the right to decline at the moment of call by stating that personal circumstances prevent service. For short-duration and same-day roles this is self-executing (the person is simply replaced). For ongoing-service bodies this triggers the Section 17.4.6 petition process. The purpose of this universal right is to ensure that no citizen is compelled to participate in the Amendment's accountability architecture against their genuine inability to do so, regardless of the specific role or body. (g) Privacy Protections Apply Uniformly. Section 17.4.7 privacy protections apply uniformly across every role covered by Sections 17.4 through 17.4.13. Regardless of whether the role is multi-year ongoing service or a single-day observer position, sensitive personal information (medical diagnoses, caregiver details, financial specifics, disability specifics) receives sealed protection. Only the categorical fact of hardship-based decline is publicly recorded. (h) Universal Anti-Retaliation Protection. No drawn person shall face retaliation, adverse treatment, professional consequence, or social consequence for declining service in good faith under any provision of this Section. Retaliation shall itself constitute Section 13 interference. This protection applies equally to citizens, state officials, sitting justices, licensed physicians, and all other persons subject to Amendment lottery draws. (i) Universal Bad-Faith Standard. Section 17.4.8 bad-faith consequences apply uniformly across all roles, scaled to the severity of the false claim. A person who fabricates hardship to evade even a single-day observer role is subject to bad-faith determination if the fabrication is clear and convincing; though the penalty shall be proportionate to the role evaded, the principle of no-tolerance for fraud is universal.

(j) Pattern Analysis Across Roles. The Watchdog Tribunal (or Phase One equivalent) shall conduct periodic pattern analysis of hardship petitions, declines, and accommodations across all Amendment roles to detect possible systematic disparities — including geographic clustering of declines (which could indicate regional pressure), demographic clustering (which could indicate disparate impact), professional clustering (which could indicate pressure on certain state officials or professions), and temporal clustering (which could indicate coordinated evasion during specific Amendment proceedings). Pattern findings shall be published on the Franklin Ledger with appropriate privacy preservation. (k) No Erosion of Section 17.4 Core Protections. Nothing in this Section shall be construed to erode, limit, or diminish the core hardship protections established for the Citizens' Oversight Board and the other ongoing-service bodies under Sections 17.4 through 17.4.12. Where the scaled timelines of this Section would provide less protection than Sections 17.4 through 17.4.12 for any specific matter, the more protective provisions shall apply. 17.4.14 Aggregate-Pattern Coordinated Hardship Detection. Recognizing that the hardship framework of Sections 17.4 through 17.4.13 is genuinely robust against individual abuse — because each individual hardship petition is reviewed on its own merits with documented support and good-faith presumption — but recognizing further that the hardship framework remains potentially vulnerable to coordinated demographic-distortion campaigns where a political faction systematically encourages or assists hardship petitions among drawn citizens of a specific demographic, geography, profession, or political alignment, in order to distort the composition of Amendment lottery-drawn bodies without ever causing any individual hardship petition to be bad-faith, this Section establishes detection of aggregate patterns analogous to the aggregate materiality framework under Section 22.16.1 for foreign interference: (a) Foundational Distinction. Individual good-faith hardship petitions remain fully protected. A citizen with a real medical condition, a real caregiver obligation, a real financial constraint, or any other genuine basis for hardship retains full Section 17.4 entitlement. Nothing in this Section permits second-guessing of legitimate individual petitions, and nothing in this Section subjects individual petitioners to retaliation, scrutiny, or burden beyond what Sections 17.4.7 (privacy) and 17.4.13(h) (anti-retaliation) provide. The framework of this Section operates exclusively at the aggregate-pattern level and reaches third-party orchestration of coordinated petition campaigns, not the individual citizens who file good-faith petitions; (b) Safe Harbor for Civic Information and Education. Notwithstanding any other provision of this Section, the following conduct is categorically protected and shall not constitute prohibited orchestration under subsection (c): (i) General Civic Education. Publication, broadcast, or distribution of accurate factual information about the hardship framework's availability, eligibility categories, and procedures, where such information is generally available to all citizens regardless of demographic, geographic, professional, or political characteristics; (ii) Member Communications by Civic

Organizations. Communications by civil rights organizations, civic education groups, labor unions, religious organizations, professional associations, immigrant-services organizations, disability-rights organizations, veterans-services organizations, and similar civic bodies to their members about Amendment rights, including hardship rights, where such communications are part of the organization's ordinary civic-information function and where the organization's membership is not defined exclusively by characteristics that match the demographic, geographic, professional, or political composition the prohibited orchestration would target; (iii) Legal Aid and Pro Bono Assistance. Provision of legal aid, pro bono legal assistance, or no-fee hardship petition assistance by legal services organizations, law school clinics, bar association programs, or individual attorneys, where such assistance is generally available without preference for citizens of specific demographic, geographic, professional, or political characteristics, and where the assistance does not exceed ordinary professional legal-services scope; (iv) Public Commentary. Public commentary, journalism, opinion writing, scholarship, or political speech about the hardship framework, the Amendment generally, or the appropriateness of Amendment service, even where such commentary is critical of Amendment service obligations, provided the commentary does not include systematic identification or contact of specific drawn citizens; (v) Social-Network Communications. Communications among friends, family members, professional colleagues, religious community members, or other ordinary social-network connections about a specific drawn citizen's hardship circumstances, where such communications are individual rather than systematic and where the communicators have an ordinary social-network relationship with the drawn citizen rather than having identified the citizen for contact based on the citizen's lottery selection. The protections of this subsection (b) operate as categorical safe harbors; conduct falling within any subcategory of this subsection (b) shall not be subject to subsection (c) prohibition, subsection (d) detection, or subsection (e) penalties, regardless of statistical patterns the conduct may produce; (c) Prohibited Conduct. The following conduct, when conducted in coordination by two or more persons with the specific purpose of distorting the demographic, geographic, professional, or political composition of any Amendment lottery-drawn body, and not falling within the safe harbors of subsection (b), shall constitute Section

13 interference: (i) Targeted Solicitation of Identified Drawn Citizens. Systematically identifying specific drawn citizens of specific demographic, geographic, professional, or political characteristics — using the fact of their lottery selection as the basis for identification — and contacting them with the specific purpose of encouraging hardship petitions, where such contact is directed at drawn citizens specifically rather than at the general public or organization membership; (ii) Conditional Resource Provision. Providing legal assistance, medical evaluation, financial advice, caregiver-arrangement services, or other resources to drawn citizens, where (A) the provision is conditioned on the citizen filing a hardship petition (or where filing is an explicit or implicit precondition for receiving the resource), (B) the resources are made available exclusively or preferentially to drawn citizens of specific demographic, geographic, professional, or political characteristics rather than to any drawn citizen on equivalent terms, and (C) the conditional or preferential provision is not within the safe harbor of subsection (b)(iii); (iii) Targeted Public Pressure. Conducting organized public campaigns specifically directed at identified drawn citizens of specific demographic, geographic, professional, or political characteristics to discourage acceptance of Amendment service, where the campaign uses the fact of lottery selection as the basis for targeting individuals rather than addressing the general public; (iv) Coordinated Funding. Funding any of the activities under subsections (c)(i)–(c)(iii) where the funding source is connected to a federal officeholder, federal political appointee, foreign government, foreign person or entity under Section 22, or other actor whose interests would be served by distorting the body's composition; (v) Falsification or Solicitation of False Documentation. Coordinating the production, templating, or solicitation of falsified hardship documentation; this is in addition to (not a substitute for) Section 17.4.8 individual bad-faith liability for the citizen who knowingly submits false documentation; (d) Aggregate Pattern Detection by AIC. The Academic Integrity Commission (or during Phase One the AIC-Designate Forensic Consortium under Section 13B.7.1) shall conduct ongoing aggregate-pattern analysis of hardship petitions, declines, accommodations, and lottery-pool composition, applying the analytical methodology used in Section 13.8(c) voter roll auditing and Section 22.16.1 aggregate materiality analysis to detect: (i) demographic clustering of hardship petitions in patterns inconsistent with ordinary baseline rates; (ii) geographic clustering of hardship petitions in patterns inconsistent with ordinary baseline rates; (iii) professional clustering of hardship petitions in patterns inconsistent with ordinary baseline rates; (iv) temporal clustering of hardship petitions

correlated with specific Amendment proceedings; (v) similarity in supporting documentation suggesting common authorship or templating; (vi) financial flows funding hardship-related legal, medical, or caregiver services correlated with the demographic/geographic/professional patterns identified; (vii) other indicia of coordinated orchestration as distinguished from independent good-faith petition activity. Pattern detection shall expressly account for safe-harbor activity under subsection (b); patterns explainable by lawful safe-harbor activity (such as elevated petition rates among members of a labor union conducting member communications under (b)(ii)) shall not constitute prima facie evidence of prohibited orchestration; (e) Findings Threshold. Aggregate-pattern findings under this Section shall require clear and convincing evidence of coordination falling outside subsection (b) safe harbors, with the analytical standard articulated in Section 22.16.1 applying mutatis mutandis. Mere correlation between hardship petition rates and demographic characteristics shall not constitute coordination; specific evidence of orchestration is required, including: documented communications among coordinating actors evidencing intent to distort body composition; documented funding flows from sources enumerated in subsection (c)(iv); documented conditional or preferential resource provision under subsection (c)(ii); documented falsification or templating under subsection (c)(v); or other affirmative evidence beyond statistical pattern alone. Findings shall be published on the Franklin Ledger with full methodology disclosed; (f) Penalties. Where coordinated hardship-distortion campaigns are established under subsection (e), the orchestrating actors (not the individual citizens who filed good-faith petitions, and not actors operating within subsection (b) safe harbors) shall be subject to: (i) Section 13 interference prosecution with Senior Official multipliers under Section 13A.3 where the orchestrators are public officeholders; (ii) Section 13A.7 entity liability where the orchestration is conducted through corporations, political action committees, nonprofit organizations, or similar entities; (iii) Section 22.17 penalties where the funding source is foreign-linked under Section 22; (iv) the Section 13D asset recovery framework where orchestrators received financial benefit from the campaign; (v) Section 13.2 bar from public office; (g) No Penalty for Petitioning Citizens or Safe-Harbor Actors. Citizens who filed individual hardship petitions during a coordinated campaign — including citizens whose petitions might not have been filed but for the campaign's influence — shall not face Section 13 liability, retaliation, professional consequence, or social consequence. The citizen's individual hardship may have been real even if the campaign's influence brought it to the citizen's attention. Liability under this Section attaches exclusively to orchestrators outside subsection (b) safe harbors, not to petitioning citizens or to civic organizations operating within those safe harbors; (h) First Amendment Construction. This Section shall be construed consistently with the First Amendment to the United States Constitution. Where any application of this Section's prohibited-conduct provisions would, in the judgment of an adjudicating §17C panel, infringe protected speech, association, or petition rights, the panel shall apply the safe harbors of subsection (b) expansively and the prohibited-conduct provisions of subsection (c) narrowly to preserve constitutional protections. The Amendment does not displace First Amendment doctrine; this Section operates within and reinforces it; (i) Lottery Composition Remedy. Where a coordinated campaign is established under subsection (e) and is shown to have materially distorted lottery-drawn body composition, the Watchdog Tribunal may, by two-thirds (2/3) supermajority, order remedial actions including: (i) supplemental lottery draws targeting the distorted demographic, geographic, or professional categories to restore proportional representation under Section 17.8; (ii) extension of body terms by up to ninety (90) days to absorb supplemental draws without operational disruption; (iii) other remedial actions narrowly tailored to undoing the documented distortion. Remedial actions shall be published on the Franklin Ledger with full methodology and proportionality reasoning; (j) Federal Executive Non-Interference. No President, Vice President, Cabinet officer, federal agency head, or other federal executive officeholder shall direct, fund, influence, pressure, or impede AIC aggregate-pattern analysis under this Section, AIC-Designate Forensic Consortium operations during Phase One, or Watchdog Tribunal remedial actions. Any such interference shall constitute Section 13 interference with Senior Official multipliers, prosecutable through the Section 17C.15 framework; (k)

Privacy Preservation in Aggregate Analysis. Aggregate-pattern analysis under this Section shall be conducted with strict preservation of individual petitioner privacy. Statistical analysis shall use anonymized data; published findings shall report patterns at jurisdictional or category level without identifying individual petitioners; the Section 17.4.7 privacy protections apply with full force. Aggregate analysis is a tool to identify orchestrators, not a justification for surveillance of individual petitioners; (l) Article V Protection. The provisions of this Section shall be protected under the Article V protection established in Sections 18.6.1 and 18.6.2. 17.5 Members shall receive: (a) federally protected employment with no retaliation permitted; (b) full wage replacement at median

US household income, cost-of-living adjusted; (c) full housing, travel, dependent care, and medical coverage; (d) federal protection from harassment, intimidation, or surveillance, with violations a 10-year federal felony. 17.6 No member shall accept any gift or thing of value from any corporation, lobbyist, PAC, foreign national, or federal officeholder during service or for 4 years thereafter. Violation = removal and bribery prosecution. 17.7 Ineligible for service: current or former federal or state officeholders; federal employees within 10 years; registered federal lobbyists within 10 years; employees of federal political contributors within 10 years; immediate family of any of these. 17.8 The Board shall proportionally reflect age, geography, and profession of the People across all Participating Jurisdictions. The Academic Integrity Commission shall audit annually upon the Ledger. 17.8.1 Citizens' Oversight Board Training Requirements. Because the Citizens' Oversight Board consists of three hundred (300) registered voters drawn by randomized lottery from all walks of American life, and because these citizens exercise continuous oversight authority with Liberty Bell Initiative, Single-Body Compromise Declaration, and audit authorities over consequential federal matters, every newly-selected Board member shall complete the following training before exercising substantive Board authority: (a) Initial Training Program. A structured eighty (80) hour training program administered by the Academic Integrity Commission, to be completed within thirty (30) days of selection notification. Training shall occur before the member participates in any Liberty Bell Initiative vote, Single-Body Compromise Declaration vote, or other substantive Board authority. The program shall be accessible through in-person sessions, live-video sessions, and recorded modules to accommodate geographic diversity and scheduling constraints of ordinary citizens. (b) Curriculum Scope. Training shall cover: (i) the structure and purpose of this Amendment, including its foundational principles and history of the constitutional problem it addresses; (ii) the Board's specific authorities under Sections 17.2 through 17.8, 17.21 through 17.23 (continuous audit authority, Liberty Bell Initiative, real-time Ledger recording), and related provisions; (iii) the Board's specific limitations and prohibitions under Sections 17.6 (gift prohibition), 17.20 (federal contractor and foreign funding prohibitions applied mutatis mutandis), and Section 13 interference framework; (iv) the Liberty Bell Initiative mechanics under Section 17.22, including mutual-veto structure and concurrence requirements; (v) the Single-Body Compromise Declaration framework under Sections 17.22.1 through 17.22.5, including valid Declaration requirements, reciprocal scrutiny, and bad-faith consequences; (vi) interactions with the State Elections Council and Academic Integrity Commission; (vii) Watchdog Tribunal oversight and complaint procedures; (viii) the Section 17.7 ineligibility rules and ongoing disclosure obligations; (ix) practical exercises in Board deliberation, vote recording, and Ledger transparency requirements; (x) recognition of capture, intimidation, and manipulation attempts, and proper reporting thereof. (c) Training Administration. The Academic Integrity Commission shall develop and maintain the training curriculum with input from the State Elections Council, Watchdog Tribunal, and outgoing Board members. Training materials shall be published on the Franklin Ledger for public review. Curriculum shall be updated not less frequently than every two (2) years to reflect accumulated operational experience. (d) Pre-Training Limited Authority. During the training period before training completion, newly-selected Board members may observe Board proceedings, receive materials and briefings, and attend deliberations in non-voting capacity, but shall not vote on Liberty Bell Initiatives, Single-Body Compromise Declarations, or other substantive Board authorities until training completion. Incumbent members whose terms overlap with newly-selected members shall continue ordinary Board operations during training periods. (e) Training Completion Certification. Upon completion, each member shall affirm on the Franklin Ledger that they have completed the training program and understand their duties and limitations. Certification shall be ministerial; the Commission shall not withhold certification based on member policy views, political orientation, or ideological preferences. Only failure to complete the required training hours shall justify non-certification. (f) Refresh and Continuing Education. Board members shall complete annual refresher training of not less than sixteen (16) hours covering developments in Amendment operations, legal interpretation, and emergent capture threats. Refresher training shall be administered by the same framework as initial training. (g) Good-Faith Training Protection. Board members who undertake training in good faith and subsequently make decisions based on that training shall be protected from adverse legal consequence for decisions made within their authority, even where such decisions are subsequently criticized or reviewed. This protection does not extend to bad-faith action, corruption, or willful violation of duties.

(h) Compensation During Training. Members shall receive full Section 17.5(b) compensation during training, as training is an integral part of service. Training-related travel, housing, and dependent care shall be covered under Section 17.5(c). (i) Federal Executive Non-Interference with Training. No President, Vice President, Cabinet officer, federal agency head, or other federal executive officeholder shall direct, influence, fund, or interfere with Board training. Any attempt to do so shall constitute Section 13 interference with Senior Official multipliers where applicable. This includes attempts to add, remove, or modify curriculum content; attempts to pressure Commission trainers; and attempts to identify or retaliate against trainees. (j) Non-Compliance Consequences. A Board member who fails to complete initial training within the thirty (30) day window without documented hardship under Sections 17.4.1 through 17.4.11 shall be replaced through the ordinary lottery process under Section 17.2, with the replacement receiving the same training requirement. A Board member who refuses refresher training shall be subject to Watchdog Tribunal review and potential replacement. B. The State Elections Council 17.9 The chief election officer of each of the fifty states, the District of Columbia, and each of the five territories enumerated in Section 3.1.1, serving ex officio. The Council shall consist of fifty-six (56) members in total, one from each Participating Jurisdiction, each with equal voting authority. 17.10 Participation is mandatory. Refusal = removal from state, DC, or territorial office and 5-year federal prosecution. 17.11 No federal compensation. Members paid only by their states during Authority service. 17.12 During any active Authority process, members operate under a Federal Communications Firewall, prohibited from: (a) any federal communication or directive; (b) any federal funding; (c) any federal agreement. 17.13 Firewall violation = 10-year federal felony, removal, and lifetime disqualification from public office. All communications shall be logged upon the Ledger. 17.14 Members shall receive federal protection from harassment and intimidation equivalent to 17.5(d). 17.14.1 State Elections Council Training Requirements. Because the State Elections Council consists of fifty-six (56) state chief election officers serving ex officio, and because these officials bring extensive electoral administration expertise but exercise Amendment-specific duties (participation in Authority Liberty Bell Initiatives, Federal Communications Firewall obligations, nuclear vote coordination, emergency frameworks) that differ from their ordinary state roles, every Council member shall complete the following training upon assuming Council participation: (a) Initial Orientation Program. A structured forty (40) hour orientation program administered by the Academic Integrity Commission, to be completed within sixty (60) days of assuming ex officio Council membership. Orientation shall occur before the member participates in any Liberty Bell Initiative vote, substantive firewall-protected decision, or other Amendment-specific Council authority. The program shall accommodate ongoing state electoral duties through flexible scheduling and remote participation options. (b) Curriculum Scope. Orientation shall cover: (i) the structure and purpose of this Amendment, with particular focus on provisions affecting Council duties; (ii) the Council's Authority role under Sections 17.9 through 17.14, including Liberty Bell Initiative participation under Section 17.22 and Single-Body Compromise Declaration framework under Sections 17.22.1 through 17.22.5; (iii) the Federal Communications Firewall under Section 17.12, including permitted and prohibited federal communications, documentation requirements, and violation consequences under Section 17.13; (iv) the State Attorneys General Council coordination framework under Section 19.5.0.18; (v) the ninety percent (90%) Governor nuclear vote coordination under Section 16.7.1, including secure communications infrastructure; (vi) Emergency Nuclear Authorization Committee lottery and oversight interactions; (vii) Nuclear Authorization Vote administration under Section 16.8(b); (viii) election integrity obligations specific to Amendment mechanisms (No Confidence Referendums, Sunset Review votes, Emergency Elections); (ix) Section 11A Electoral Integrity provisions; (x) interactions with Citizens' Oversight Board and Academic Integrity Commission; (xi) recognition of federal interference attempts and proper reporting thereof. (c) Training Administration. The Academic Integrity Commission shall develop and maintain the orientation curriculum. The curriculum shall be developed with input from the Citizens' Oversight Board, Watchdog Tribunal, and experienced Council members. Materials shall be published on the Franklin Ledger for public review. Curriculum shall be updated not less frequently than every two (2) years. (d) Pre-Training Participation Limits. During the orientation period, newly-serving Council members may observe Council proceedings, receive materials and briefings, and attend deliberations, but shall not vote on Liberty Bell Initiatives, Single-Body Compromise Declarations, or Amendment-specific decisions until orientation completion. Ordinary state election duties are unaffected. (e) Ministerial Certification. Upon completion, each member shall affirm on the Franklin Ledger that they have completed the orientation program. Certification shall be ministerial; no substantive gatekeeping based on policy views or political orientation shall be permitted.

(f) Refresher Training. Council members shall complete annual refresher training of not less than twelve (12) hours covering developments in Amendment operations and emergent electoral integrity threats. (g) No Federal Compensation for Training. Consistent with Section 17.11, training shall occur without federal compensation. Travel, materials, and logistics costs shall be covered by each member's home Participating Jurisdiction. The Academic

Integrity Commission shall minimize cost burden by providing remote participation options and efficient curriculum design. (h) Federal Executive Non-Interference. No federal officeholder shall direct, influence, fund, or interfere with Council training. Attempts shall constitute Section 13 interference with Senior Official multipliers where applicable, prosecutable by State Attorneys General Council under Section 19.5.0.18. (i) Non-Compliance Consequences. A Council member who refuses orientation shall be treated as refusing Council participation under Section 17.10, with consequences specified therein (removal from state office and five (5) year federal prosecution). Refusal of refresher training shall trigger Watchdog Tribunal review. A Participating Jurisdiction whose chief election officer has been removed for orientation refusal shall fill the position under state law, with the successor completing the orientation requirement. C. The Academic Integrity Commission 17.15 50 representatives, one drawn by lottery from each of 50 universities randomly selected from a Pre-Certified Pool of 500+ institutions. 17.16 The Pool shall be recertified every 5 years by the Citizens' Oversight Board publicly. The Pool shall include qualifying universities and institutions from all Participating Jurisdictions, including the states, the District of Columbia, and the five territories enumerated in Section 3.1.1, to ensure geographic and institutional diversity of scholarly perspective. Qualifying universities must: (a) receive no more than 5% of operating budget from federal grants; (b) demonstrate academic independence for 10 years; (c) publish all federal contracts in a searchable manner; (d) have no foreign government control. 17.16.1 Pool Floor and Withdrawal Documentation. The Pre-Certified University Pool shall contain no fewer than two hundred (200) qualifying institutions at any time. If the Pool falls below two hundred (200) institutions at any point, the Citizens' Oversight Board (or during Phase One, the Washington Commission) shall investigate the cause and publish findings upon the Franklin Ledger or provisional public ledger within thirty (30) days. Any qualifying university that declines participation in the Pool, or that withdraws from the Pool after prior participation, shall within thirty (30) days of its decision publish upon the Ledger a written statement explaining its reasoning. A pattern of unexplained, coordinated, or plausibly-pressured withdrawals shall constitute a Section 13 interference trigger and shall prompt Hamilton Contingent investigation once operational, and shall prompt State Attorneys General Council investigation (acting by supermajority under Sections 19.5.0.5.2 and 19.5.0.18.9.1) prior to Hamilton Contingent operational status. If the geographic diversity requirements of Section 17.16 cannot be satisfied due to pressured withdrawals or other participation failures, the Pool shall be expanded to include accredited institutions meeting subsections (a) through (d) of Section 17.16 from adjacent Participating Jurisdictions, with priority given to state flagship universities, until geographic diversity is restored. No qualifying university shall face adverse federal action, investigation, audit, or funding consequence as retaliation for Pool participation; any such action shall itself constitute Section 13 interference. 17.16.2 Initial Pool Formation — Accreditation as Substrate. Recognizing that the Academic Integrity Commission cannot compile or certify the initial Pre-Certified University Pool (as the Commission itself is drawn from the Pool and therefore cannot exist prior to Pool formation), and recognizing that American higher education already possesses a comprehensive credentialing infrastructure through independent regional and specialized accreditation, the initial Pool shall be formed as follows, without requiring any new pre-Ratification body: (a) Accreditation as Substrate. The initial Pool shall be drawn from the universe of all accredited degree-granting institutions in the Participating Jurisdictions, including but not limited to: universities; colleges; law schools; medical schools; graduate schools; professional schools in engineering, business, public policy, or other disciplines; and accredited research institutes. Accreditation shall be as recognized by regional accrediting bodies (the Higher Learning Commission, the Middle States Commission on Higher Education, the New England Commission of Higher Education, the Northwest Commission on Colleges and Universities, the Southern Association of Colleges and Schools Commission on Colleges, the WASC Senior College and University Commission, and successors thereto) or by specialized accrediting bodies (the American Bar Association for law schools, the Liaison Committee on Medical Education for medical schools, ABET for engineering programs, and similar recognized accreditors). Accreditation serves as the substrate because it is an established, independent, and decentralized credentialing system that predates this Amendment, operates without federal executive control, and already verifies institutional legitimacy across all Participating Jurisdictions; (b) Qualification Self-Attestation. Any accredited institution in a Participating Jurisdiction may seek inclusion in the initial Pool by submitting to the Attorney General of its home jurisdiction written attestation that the institution meets the qualifying criteria of Section 17.16(a) through (d), with supporting documentation including: current-year federal grant receipts as a percentage of operating budget; documentation of academic governance independence for the preceding ten (10) years; public posting of all federal contracts in a searchable format; and certification of no foreign government control or ownership. Attestations may be submitted at any time during the ratification period and continuing through Day sixty (60) following Ratification; (c) State Attorney General Verification. The State Attorney

General of each Participating Jurisdiction shall verify attestations submitted by institutions in their jurisdiction as a ministerial matter, limited to confirming that documentation is complete and facially consistent with Section 17.16 criteria. Substantive re-investigation shall be required only where specific evidence suggests an attestation is materially false. Verified attestations shall be published on state government transparency infrastructure within fourteen (14) days of receipt, with public accessibility continuing through Washington Commission adoption of the initial Pool; (d) National Aggregation. The National Association of Attorneys General (or successor organization) shall aggregate state-verified attestations into a compiled initial Pool proposal, publishing the compiled proposal on state government transparency infrastructure no later than Day thirty (30) following Ratification. The compiled proposal shall identify each institution, its state AG verification date, and its documentation summary, with full documentation accessible through the state AG publication under subsection (c); (e) Washington Commission Formal Adoption. The Washington Commission shall formally adopt the initial Pool within thirty (30) days of receipt of the NAAG compiled proposal, subject to a concurrent thirty (30) day public comment period during which any United States citizen, professional association, or civic organization may submit comments regarding specific institutions' qualifications. Public comments may challenge specific institutions based on Section 17.16 criteria, but shall not require creation of new bodies or verification processes beyond those already established through accreditation and state AG verification. The Washington Commission shall resolve substantive challenges by majority vote within the comment period, with resolution reasoning published on the provisional public ledger; (f) Initial Pool Deemed Established. The initial Pool shall be deemed established on the later of: (i) Washington Commission formal adoption; or (ii) completion of the thirty (30) day public comment period under subsection (e). In no event shall the initial Pool be deemed established later than Day ninety (90) following Ratification, consistent with Section 19.19(c); (g) Minimum Pool Size Verification. At initial Pool establishment, the Pool shall contain not fewer than two hundred (200) qualifying institutions as required under Section 17.16.1. If the initial Pool falls below two hundred (200) institutions, the Washington Commission shall extend attestation and verification timelines by up to thirty (30) additional days and shall additionally reach out through accrediting bodies to qualifying institutions that have not yet submitted attestations, with outreach documented on the provisional public ledger. The initial Pool shall not be deemed established until the two hundred (200) institution floor is met; (h) Transition to Ongoing Pool Management. Upon Academic Integrity Commission full constitution on Day One Hundred Eighty (180), ongoing Pool management and the five (5) year recertification cycle under Section 17.16 shall commence under AIC authority. The initial Pool established under this subsection shall remain the operative Pool from establishment through the first five (5) year recertification, during which the Academic Integrity Commission shall conduct its initial recertification process under Section 17.16; (i) No New Federal Body Required. Nothing in this Section shall be construed to create a new federal body, federal agency, or federal bureaucracy. The initial Pool formation relies entirely on existing institutions — accredited colleges and universities, independent accrediting bodies, state Attorneys General, the National Association of Attorneys General, and the Washington Commission — all of which either existed before this Amendment or bootstrap directly from existing officials exercising ex officio responsibilities. 17.16.3 AIC Selection Lottery Administration. Because the Academic Integrity Commission cannot administer its own initial formation lottery (as the Commission does not exist until the lottery is complete), and because the Commission shall not administer its own subsequent formation lotteries (as self-administered selection enables self-perpetuation), the following lottery administration framework applies to all AIC formation under Section 17.15: (a) Two-Stage Lottery Structure. AIC selection shall proceed in two stages: Stage One consisting of the random selection of fifty (50) universities from the Pre-Certified Pool established under Sections 17.16, 17.16.1, and 17.16.2; and Stage Two consisting of the selection of one (1) representative from each of the fifty selected universities through that university's existing academic governance processes; (b) Initial Lottery Administration (Pre-Day-180). For the initial AIC formation following Ratification, Stage One lottery shall be administered by the Washington Commission under Section 19.5.0, applying the lottery integrity standards of Section 19.5.0.3.3, with operational support from the National Association of Attorneys General and the State Elections Council acting in its ex officio capacity. The initial Stage One lottery shall be conducted no later than Day One Hundred Thirty-Five (135) following Ratification to permit Stage Two university-internal selection and AIC swearing-in by Day One Hundred Eighty (180); (c) Ongoing Lottery Administration (Post-Day-180). For all subsequent AIC formation cycles under

Section 17.17, Stage One lottery shall be administered by the State Elections Council in coordination with the outgoing Academic Integrity Commission and the Citizens' Oversight Board, applying the same lottery integrity standards of Section 19.5.0.3.3. The Academic Integrity Commission itself shall not administer its own selection lottery, though it may provide technical support, historical data, and coordination assistance to the State Elections Council administering the lottery; (d) Stage Two University-Internal Selection. Within fourteen (14) days of notification by the lottery administrator that it has been selected in Stage One, each selected university shall select one representative to serve on the Academic Integrity Commission. Selection shall be through the university's existing academic governance processes, including faculty senate, academic council, provost designation, or equivalent, with the selection process documented and published on state government transparency infrastructure (during Phase One) or the Ledger (following full operation). The representative need not be a member of faculty; a university may select an administrator, researcher, senior staff member, or other affiliated person whose expertise serves the Amendment's purposes, provided the person meets Section 17.19 disclosure requirements and is not disqualified under Section 17.20 prohibitions; (e) Alternate University Draw. If a selected university declines participation or fails to produce a

representative within fourteen (14) days, the lottery administrator shall draw another university by lottery from the remaining Pool, with the alternate-draw process continuing until fifty (50) valid representatives are selected. Universities that decline participation shall publish their reasoning under Section 17.16.1, with pattern analysis of declined participations conducted by the State Attorneys General Council during Phase One and by the Watchdog Tribunal thereafter to detect pressured non-participation; (f) Lottery Integrity Standards. All AIC selection lotteries shall comply with the lottery integrity standards of Section 19.5.0.3.3, including multi-party seed generation, public livestream, cryptographic verification, and individual seed publication, and shall be subject to challenge and re-run under Section 19.5.0.3.4. The comprehensive integrity framework established for Commission lotteries and blockchain substrate selection applies to AIC lotteries without modification; (g) Geographic and Institutional Diversity. Lottery administrators shall ensure that Section 17.16 geographic and institutional diversity requirements are reflected in the final selection. Where a random draw produces substantial geographic concentration beyond statistical expectation (defined as any single Participating Jurisdiction receiving more than five (5) selections or as fewer than forty (40) distinct Participating Jurisdictions being represented among the fifty selected universities), the administrator shall re-conduct the Stage One lottery with documentation of the concentration concern and the re-draw process published on state government transparency infrastructure or the Ledger. Where the Pre-Certified Pool itself does not contain qualifying institutions from forty (40) or more Participating Jurisdictions — because certain Jurisdictions lack accredited institutions meeting Section 17.16 qualifying criteria — the forty (40) Jurisdiction diversity threshold shall adjust to the number of Jurisdictions actually represented in the Pool, with the re-draw requirement triggered only where the selection represents fewer Jurisdictions than the Pool itself contains. In no circumstance shall the geographic diversity requirement of this subsection block lottery completion where the Pool's own composition makes the ordinary threshold mathematically unachievable; the lottery shall proceed with the maximum Jurisdictional diversity the Pool permits, with documentation of the Pool's Jurisdictional composition published on state government transparency infrastructure or the Ledger to preserve public accountability; (h) Federal Executive Non-Interference. No President, Vice President, Cabinet officer, federal agency head, or other federal executive officeholder shall direct, fund, influence, or impede the AIC selection lottery or university internal selection processes under this Section. Any federal executive attempt to influence the lottery or university processes shall constitute Section 13 interference with Senior Official multipliers where applicable, shall be prosecutable by the State Attorneys General Council (acting by supermajority under Sections 19.5.0.5.2 and 19.5.0.18.9.1) during Phase One and by the Hamilton Contingent thereafter, and shall be grounds for enhanced penalties under Section 13A. 17.17 1-year terms. No consecutive service. No consecutive university selections. No individual shall serve more than two (2) terms on the Commission in their lifetime, whether or not consecutive.

17.18 No federal compensation. Paid by home university at institutional rate. 17.19 Pre-service public disclosure required of: federal and foreign grants; institutional affiliations; financial interests; personal relationships with federal officeholders. 17.20 Prohibited during service from federal contractor or foreign government funding, and from public political advocacy. 17.20.1 Academic Integrity Commission Training Requirements. Because the Academic Integrity Commission consists of fifty (50) representatives drawn from Pre-Certified Pool universities, and because these representatives bring academic expertise but exercise Amendment-specific duties (infrastructure certification, curriculum design for other bodies' training programs, lottery administration, security review, training administration itself) that differ from their ordinary academic roles, every newly-selected Commission member shall complete the following training before exercising substantive Commission authority: (a) Initial Training Program. A structured sixty (60) hour training program administered jointly by the outgoing Academic Integrity Commission and the Watchdog Tribunal, to be completed within forty-five (45) days of selection notification. Training shall occur before the member participates in any Liberty Bell Initiative vote, infrastructure certification decision, or training curriculum approval. The program shall accommodate academic scheduling through flexible modalities. (b) Curriculum Scope. Training shall cover: (i) the structure and purpose of this Amendment, with particular focus on the Commission's unique role as the Amendment's technical and educational backbone; (ii) the Commission's authorities under Sections 17.15 through 17.20, 17.21 through 17.23, and related provisions; (iii) the Commission's responsibility for training other Amendment bodies (Citizens' Oversight Board, State Elections Council, Watchdog Tribunal, Emergency Nuclear Authorization Committee, Hamilton Contingent personnel, Oversight Officers, Escort Roster, Interim Caretaker Council, and others), with emphasis on developing, maintaining, and updating curricula; (iv) infrastructure certification and security review under Sections 14 (Sovereign Voting Terminals), 14.21 (Infrastructure Evolution), and related provisions; (v) cryptographic review, lottery administration, blockchain substrate oversight, and audit authorities; (vi) Liberty Bell Initiative mechanics and Single-Body Compromise Declaration framework; (vii) the Pre-Certified University Pool under Sections 17.16 through 17.16.3, including recertification cycles; (viii) disclosure obligations under Section 17.19 and prohibited activities under Section 17.20; (ix) interactions with Citizens' Oversight Board, State Elections Council, and Watchdog Tribunal; (x) Section 13 interference framework and recognition of capture attempts; (xi) practical exercises in curriculum development, infrastructure review, and public accountability reporting.

(c) Training Administration. Training shall be administered jointly by the outgoing Academic Integrity Commission (which possesses institutional memory and operational experience) and the Watchdog Tribunal (which provides independent oversight of the training process itself to prevent outgoing-Commission capture of curriculum). For initial Commission formation under Section 17.16.2 and Section 17.16.3, where no outgoing Commission exists, initial training shall be administered by the Washington Commission under Section 19.5.0 with operational support from the Pre-Certified Pool institutions. Materials shall be published on the Franklin Ledger (or provisional public ledger during Phase One) for public review. Curriculum shall be updated not less frequently than annually. (d) Pre-Training Limited Authority. During the training period before completion, newly-selected Commission members may observe Commission proceedings, receive materials and briefings, and attend deliberations in non-voting capacity, but shall not vote on Liberty Bell Initiatives, infrastructure certifications, curriculum approvals, lottery administrations, or other substantive Commission authorities until training completion. Overlapping outgoing and incoming membership shall maintain Commission operations during training periods. (e) Ministerial Certification. Upon completion, each member shall affirm on the Franklin Ledger that they have completed the training program. Certification shall be ministerial; withholding based on policy views, academic discipline, or institutional origin shall be prohibited. (f) Refresher Training. Commission members shall complete semi-annual refresher training of not less than eight (8) hours covering developments in Amendment operations, technology evolution affecting certification duties, and emergent threats to infrastructure integrity. (g) No Federal Compensation for Training. Consistent with Section 17.18, training shall occur without federal compensation. Costs shall be covered by each member's home university at institutional rate. Where a home university cannot support training costs, the Academic Integrity Commission shall utilize Ratification Loan funds to ensure no qualified member is excluded from service due to institutional resource constraints. (h) Federal Executive Non-Interference. No federal officeholder shall direct, influence, fund, or interfere with Commission training. Attempts shall constitute Section 13 interference with Senior Official multipliers where applicable. (i) Non-Compliance Consequences. A Commission member who fails to complete initial training within the forty-five (45) day window without documented hardship under Sections 17.4.1 through 17.4.11 shall be replaced through the lottery process under Section 17.16.3, with the selecting university drawing a replacement representative. Refusal of refresher training shall trigger Watchdog Tribunal review and potential replacement.

(j) Self-Sustaining Training Excellence. Because the Academic Integrity Commission both administers training for other bodies and receives training itself, the Commission shall be particularly rigorous in developing, reviewing, and continuously improving its own training program. Substandard Commission training undermines training throughout the Amendment. The Watchdog Tribunal shall conduct annual review of Commission training adequacy, with findings published on the Franklin Ledger and recommended improvements considered by the Commission. D. Cross-Body Integrity 17.21 Each body possesses continuous audit authority over the other two. 17.22 No Authority decision is valid without a Liberty Bell Initiative — separate concurrence of all three bodies. This is the mutual-veto structure: any one body may block any action, regardless of what the other two decide. When all three ring together, the Initiative is complete and the action becomes Authority-certified. 17.22.1 The Single-Body Compromise Declaration — Purpose and Principle. When any one of the three bodies of the Authority has formed a supermajority conclusion that one or both of the other two bodies have been corrupted, captured, or compromised to a degree that renders ordinary Liberty Bell Initiative under Section 17.22 unworkable, that body may issue a Single-Body Compromise Declaration calling upon the People to exercise their sovereign authority over the oversight apparatus through an Expedited Compromise Referendum. This provision exists because the mutual-veto structure of Section 17.22 depends upon all three bodies operating in good faith, and because no effective alarm can be raised through ordinary Authority processes when two of the three bodies are themselves the subject of the alarm. The provision shall be construed as an emergency constitutional mechanism, available only where ordinary accountability pathways are foreclosed by the very capture that the Declaration alleges. 17.22.2 Requirements for a Valid Declaration. A Single-Body Compromise Declaration shall be valid only if all of the following requirements are met: (a) Supermajority Within the Declaring Body. The Declaration shall require the affirmative vote of not less than three-fourths (3/4) of the full membership of the declaring body, meaning: two hundred twenty-five (225) of the three hundred (300) members of the Citizens' Oversight Board; forty-two (42) of the fifty-six (56) members of the State Elections Council; or thirty-eight (38) of the fifty (50) members of the Academic Integrity Commission. Each member's vote shall be individually recorded and published upon the Franklin Ledger; (b) Specific Evidentiary Basis. The Declaration shall identify with specificity the conduct, pattern, or finding constituting the alleged corruption, capture, or compromise, supported by documented evidence published upon the Ledger at the time of Declaration. Policy disagreement among the three bodies, good-faith differences of judgment on Liberty Bell Initiatives, or objections to the other bodies' priorities shall not constitute grounds for Declaration; (c) Public Publication. The Declaration, the underlying evidence, and all individual member votes shall be published upon the Ledger simultaneously with the Declaration's issuance, with no delay, redaction, or suppression permitted except for narrow operational-security exclusions certified by unanimous vote of the declaring body and reviewable within thirty (30) days; and (d) No Self-Exemption. A Declaration may name one or two of the other Authority bodies as compromised, but shall not exempt the declaring body from reciprocal scrutiny under Section 17.22.3. A Declaration seeking to remove accountability from the declaring body shall be void ab initio. 17.22.3 Reciprocal Scrutiny, Suspension, and Good-Faith Safeguards. Upon issuance of a valid Declaration under Section 17.22.1: (a) Suspension of Declaring Body from Ordinary Liberty Bell Initiative. The declaring body shall be suspended from participation in ordinary Liberty Bell Initiatives under Section 17.22 during the pendency of the Compromise Declaration process, with the corresponding sub-council of the Rotating Tripartite State Council under Section 21.14 temporarily performing the declaring body's Liberty Bell function solely for ordinary Authority operations unrelated to the Declaration; (b) Expedited Review Authority. The two bodies named in the Declaration and the Watchdog Tribunal shall each have expedited review authority over the declaring body, including full access to the declaring body's records, communications, and individual member conduct during the period covered by the Declaration's evidentiary basis. Review findings shall be published upon the Ledger before the Expedited Compromise Referendum; (c) Bad-Faith Declaration Consequences. If the Watchdog Tribunal finds by two-thirds (2/3) supermajority, or if the People through Vote B of Section 17.22.4(c) determine, that the Declaration was issued in bad faith — meaning without credible evidentiary basis, for the purpose of extracting policy concessions, or to preempt accountability for the declaring body itself — the declaring body's members who voted for the Declaration shall be subject to individual Section 13 interference prosecution and immediate replacement under Section 21.7, and no renewed Declaration by the declaring body's reconstituted membership shall be permitted within eighteen (18) months; (d) Good-Faith Safe Harbor. Members who voted for a Declaration in good faith based on the evidentiary record available to them shall not face retaliation, prosecution, or adverse consequence if the Declaration ultimately fails at citizen vote, provided that the evidentiary basis was credible at the time of Declaration. Good-faith failed Declarations shall be treated as valuable civic engagement consistent with Section 23.12; (e) Cooldown After Good-Faith Failure. If a Declaration fails at citizen vote but the Tribunal and Vote B findings indicate good faith rather than bad faith, the declaring body shall not issue a renewed Declaration within twelve (12) months, provided that this cooldown shall not apply if new evidence of substantially different conduct from that alleged in the original Declaration emerges during the twelve-month period. 17.22.4 The Expedited Compromise Referendum. A valid Declaration shall automatically trigger an Expedited Compromise Referendum with the following

framework: (a) No Citizen Petition Required. The Declaration itself substitutes for the ordinary petition threshold under Section 17B.3, on the constitutional theory that one body of the Authority speaking with three-fourths supermajority voice already represents substantial deliberative consent for triggering citizen review; (b) Thirty-Day Public Comment Period. Immediately upon Declaration, a thirty (30) day public comment period shall open during which the declaring body's evidence shall be publicly reviewed; the accused bodies may publish responses upon the Ledger; citizens may submit comments and counter-evidence; and the Watchdog Tribunal shall publish its own findings on both the substance of the Declaration and the good faith of the declaring body; (c) Hybrid Two-Vote Ballot. Not later than ninety (90) days after the Declaration, a national Expedited Compromise Referendum shall be held, in which every eligible voter shall cast two (2) independent votes: Vote A: "Shall the Authority body or bodies named in the Declaration be removed and reconstituted under Section 17B?" — yes or no; and Vote B: "Shall the Authority body that issued the Declaration be removed and reconstituted under Section 17B?" — yes or no; (d) Threshold. For each Vote, a majority of more than fifty percent (50%) of ballots cast on that Vote, with a minimum turnout of forty percent (40%) of registered voters of the United States, shall determine the outcome of that Vote. The two Votes shall be tabulated independently. The outcomes shall be: (i) Vote A yes, Vote B no — the named body or bodies shall be removed under Section 17B.6 through 17B.10 and the declaring body shall continue; (ii) Vote A no, Vote B yes — the declaring body shall be removed under Section 17B.6 through 17B.10 and the named bodies shall continue, with Section 17.22.3(c) bad-faith consequences applying; (iii) Vote A yes, Vote B yes — all three Authority bodies shall be removed and full Restoration shall proceed under Section 17B; (iv) Vote A no, Vote B no — no body shall be removed, the suspension of the declaring body under Section 17.22.3(a) shall lift, and ordinary Liberty Bell Initiative shall resume; (e) Ballot Design. The ballot shall present Vote A and Vote B with equal prominence and in language accessible to all registered voters, with the Declaration text, accused bodies' responses, and Tribunal findings summarized on the ballot or accompanying voter information materials published upon the Ledger; (f) Certification and Effect. The State Elections Council shall certify the Referendum results within seven (7) days of the vote, and any removal shall take effect immediately upon certification, with reconstitution proceeding on the timelines of Section 17B.6 through 17B.10. 17.22.5 Integration with Existing Accountability Mechanisms. The Single-Body Compromise Declaration pathway of Sections 17.22.1 through 17.22.4 shall be available in addition to, not in place of, the citizen-initiated Restoration pathway under Section 17B.3, the Citizen Emergency Override under Section 21.10, the alternative trigger pathways under Section 17B.4, and the Reclamation mechanism under Section 1. The People, the Tribunal, and the Authority bodies may pursue any or all of these mechanisms concurrently. Nothing in this Section shall limit or suspend the ordinary operation of Section 17A accountability mechanisms, Section 17B Restoration pathways, Section 21 failsafes, or Section 23.13.1 mutual veto misuse safeguards. The Declaration pathway is an additional tool available when ordinary accountability is foreclosed by the very capture the Declaration alleges, not a replacement for any other pathway. 17.22.6 No Delay of Expedited Compromise Referendum Permitted. No act of Congress, executive order, presidential proclamation, judicial ruling, state action, emergency declaration, martial law declaration, or any other federal, state, or territorial action shall delay, postpone, modify, or prevent an Expedited Compromise Referendum triggered under Section 17.22.4. Any attempt to do so shall be void ab initio and shall have no legal force; officials administering the Referendum shall proceed notwithstanding any such purported order, declaration, ruling, or action. Any such attempt shall constitute interference under Section 13, triggering the full penalties thereof, including the fifteen (15) year minimum sentence and the lifetime bar from public office without possibility of pardon. The Section 5.12.1 officials' duty-to-proceed protections shall apply to Expedited Compromise Referendum administration without modification. Because this Referendum exists specifically to address scenarios where ordinary Authority processes have been compromised by capture, undelayability is essential; the compromised apparatus cannot be relied upon to permit its own evaluation. 17.23 All deliberations recorded upon the Ledger in real time. No secret sessions. 17.24 All members swear a constitutional oath to the Constitution and the sovereign authority of the People, taking no direction from any government, party, corporation, or foreign power. The oath shall be publicly recorded upon the Ledger. 17.25 Bribery, threats, blackmail, or corruption of any member = 20-year federal felony. Sponsoring entities forfeit federal charters, tax-exempt status, contracting ability, or diplomatic standing. 17.26 Funding flows automatically through the constitutional appropriation. Attempts to reduce or redirect are impeachable offenses and federal felonies.

Section 17A. Authority Administration — Staff, Procurement, and Anti-Waste Framework

Key terms in this Section: • "Covered Body" — For purposes of this Section: the Citizens' Oversight Board, the State Elections Council, the Academic Integrity Commission, the Watchdog Tribunal (including the Travel Division and all other divisions), the Hamilton Contingent (in addition to its own procurement rules under Section 13C), the Joint Implementation Command, the Washington Commission, the Constitutional Transition Committee when convened, and any other body established by this Amendment that has operational staff, procurement authority, or a budget under the constitutional appropriation. • "Approving Officer" — Any member of a Covered Body, senior staff member with delegated signing authority, or other person authorized to approve a hiring decision, contract, or expenditure above the micro-purchase threshold on behalf of a Covered Body. • "Pre-Certified Personnel Roster" — The roster of vetted candidates for employment by Covered Bodies, maintained by the Academic Integrity Commission under Section 17A.7. • "Authority Budget Year" — The twelve-month fiscal cycle for Covered Bodies, running from October 1 through September 30, aligning with the federal fiscal year for administrative convenience but operating under separate appropriation. • "Gross Waste" — Expenditure, hiring, or procurement that a reasonable Approving Officer, exercising ordinary professional judgment and acting in good faith, would have identified as: (a) unjustified by the Body's operational needs; (b) substantially above prevailing market cost for comparable goods, services, or labor; (c) approved through evasion of this Section's procedural safeguards; or (d) tainted by undisclosed conflict of interest of the Approving Officer. Good-faith judgment calls that later prove suboptimal shall not constitute Gross Waste. A. Operational Autonomy with Anti-Waste Discipline 17A.1 Foundational Principle. The Covered Bodies established by this Amendment shall possess the operational autonomy necessary to fulfill their constitutional functions, including the authority to hire staff, procure goods and services, enter contracts, lease facilities, and manage day-to-day operations without congressional or executive branch interference. This autonomy is essential to prevent capture through the appropriations process or administrative sabotage. However, operational autonomy is not a license for waste. The Covered Bodies operate as stewards of public funds drawn from the constitutional appropriation, and every dollar spent must serve the People's constitutional interest. This

Section establishes the framework for operational autonomy paired with strict anti-waste discipline. 17A.2 Independent Operational Authority. Each Covered Body shall have independent authority to: (a) hire and dismiss staff under Sections 17A.5 through 17A.9; (b) enter contracts and procure goods and services under Sections 17A.10 through 17A.15; (c) lease office space, equipment, and real property necessary for

operations; (d) maintain operational budgets, manage cash flow, and execute expenditures within approved budget lines; (e) engage outside counsel, consultants, auditors, and experts as needed for the Body's constitutional functions; and (f) establish internal administrative procedures, provided that all such procedures are consistent with this Section and published upon the Franklin Ledger. 17A.3 Prohibited Interference with Administration. No act of Congress, executive order, judicial ruling, state action, or federal agency action shall: (a) condition any Covered Body's funding on adoption of particular administrative procedures; (b) impose hiring freezes, procurement restrictions, or other operational limits on Covered Bodies outside of this Amendment's framework; (c) require Covered Body use of particular federal vendors, contractors, or service providers; (d) direct Covered Body hiring toward or away from particular candidates or categories of candidates except where this Amendment expressly so requires; or (e) otherwise interfere with Covered Body administration. Violations shall constitute Section 13 interference with full penalties thereof. B. Budget Process and Fiscal Discipline 17A.4 Annual Zero-Based Budgeting. Each Covered Body shall prepare an annual operating budget on a zero-based foundation, meaning that every line item shall be justified from zero each Authority Budget Year, without presumption that prior-year spending is automatically renewed. The budget shall be: (a) Published upon the Franklin Ledger no later than sixty (60) days before the Authority Budget Year begins; (b) Organized by operational function, with staff costs, facility costs, procurement costs, and special projects separately identified; (c) Benchmarked against prevailing market cost for comparable staff compensation, facility leases, and goods and services, with the benchmark methodology disclosed on the Ledger; (d) Reviewed in public hearing by the Watchdog Tribunal within thirty (30) days of publication, with a public report published on the Ledger; (e) Subject to citizen petition challenge under Section 17A.16 at any time during the Authority Budget Year; (f) Finalized by the Covered Body upon consideration of the Tribunal report and any citizen challenges, with final version published upon the Ledger no later than fifteen (15) days before the Authority Budget Year begins. The final budget shall note any material deviations from the Tribunal's review and the reasoning for such deviations; (g) Amendable mid-year only with public justification on the Ledger and Watchdog Tribunal notification, with amendments exceeding ten percent (10%) of any line item requiring a second round of public hearing;

(h) Subject to real-time expenditure publication under Section 17A.15. C. Staff Hiring Framework 17A.5 Pre-Certified Personnel Roster. The Academic Integrity Commission shall maintain a Pre-Certified Personnel Roster of vetted candidates eligible for employment by Covered Bodies. The Roster shall be organized by position type (legal counsel, forensic accountant, cryptographic specialist, administrative staff, communications staff, research analyst, investigator, security personnel, information technology specialist, and other functional categories as needed). Vetting shall include: (a) Verification of professional qualifications, including education, licensure, and relevant experience; (b) Background check appropriate to the position, including criminal history and relevant financial integrity review; (c) Disclosure of federal employment within the preceding ten (10) years, federal contracting relationships within the preceding ten (10) years, federal lobbying registration within the preceding ten (10) years, and federal political contributions within the preceding ten (10) years exceeding a minimal public-service threshold; (d) Disclosure of foreign ties, including foreign employment, foreign government connections, or foreign financial interests; (e) Ethical attestation consistent with the constitutional oath of Section 17.24; (f) Certification of eligibility published on the Ledger with appropriate privacy redactions for personal information while preserving public accountability for disqualifying relationships. 17A.6 Disqualifying Conditions for Staff Employment. No person shall be eligible for employment by any Covered Body who: (a) has held a federal officeholder or political appointee position within the preceding five (5) years (ten years for senior staff positions); (b) is a registered federal lobbyist or has been within the preceding five (5) years; (c) has been employed by a federal contractor within the preceding three (3) years (five years for senior positions); (d) has foreign government employment, foreign state-owned enterprise employment, or foreign political party employment within the preceding ten (10) years; (e) has an undisclosed conflict of interest with the work of the employing Covered Body; (f) has been found by a court of competent jurisdiction to have committed fraud, corruption, or breach of fiduciary duty; or (g) has failed a vetting procedure administered by the Academic Integrity Commission for reasons of integrity, reliability, or security. 17A.7 Hiring Process. Each Covered Body shall hire staff according to the following process:

(a) The Body shall publish the position description and qualifications on the Ledger, identifying the functional category, the responsibilities, the compensation range benchmarked against prevailing market rates for comparable work, and the application deadline; (b) The Academic Integrity Commission shall, within fourteen (14) days, identify all candidates on the Pre-Certified Personnel Roster qualified for the position and provide the list to the hiring Covered Body. The Body may additionally seek candidates outside the Roster, but such candidates must complete Roster vetting before hire; (c) The Body shall conduct interviews, reference checks, and such other evaluation as it deems necessary, with all process decisions documented for audit purposes; (d) The Body shall make the hiring decision by majority vote of its members (or by its delegated hiring authority, where the position is operational rather than senior), with the hiring decision published on the Ledger within seven (7) days of offer acceptance; (e) Compensation shall not exceed the applicable position benchmark by more than fifteen percent (15%) without public justification on the Ledger. Compensation below the benchmark is permitted and encouraged where candidate qualifications warrant. 17A.8 Compensation Benchmarking. The Academic Integrity Commission shall maintain a public Compensation Benchmark Table for each Pre-Certified Personnel Roster category, updated annually, reflecting prevailing market compensation for comparable roles. The Table shall be published on the Ledger. Covered Body compensation decisions shall be measured against this Table, with any compensation exceeding the benchmark subject to public justification requirements and possible citizen petition challenge under Section 17A.16. 17A.9 Staff Ethical Obligations and Post-Service Restrictions. All staff employed by Covered Bodies shall: (a) Swear an oath substantially equivalent to the constitutional oath of Section 17.24, adapted for the staff role; (b) Be bound by the gift, financial, and conflict-of-interest restrictions applicable to their employing Body; (c) Be prohibited from federal lobbying for a period of five (5) years following the end of their Covered Body service; (d) Be prohibited from federal contractor employment for a period of three (3) years following the end of their Covered Body service, where the contractor has received contracts from the Covered Body during the staff member's service; (e) Be entitled to the same whistleblower protections established in Section 13B.16, including federal protection from retaliation, federal legal representation, and the reward schedule of Section 13B.17 where a disclosure leads to recovery. D. Four-Tier Procurement Framework 17A.10 Procurement Tiers — Overview. Procurement of goods, services, and contracts by Covered Bodies shall proceed under a four-tier framework based on contract value, with scrutiny proportional to value: (a) Tier 1 — Micro-Purchase: under five thousand dollars ($5,000); (b) Tier 2 — Simplified Acquisition: five thousand dollars to fifty thousand dollars ($5,000 to $50,000); (c) Tier 3 — Major Contract: fifty thousand dollars to five hundred thousand dollars ($50,000 to $500,000); (d) Tier 4 — Strategic Contract: over five hundred thousand dollars ($500,000). (e) Dollar thresholds shall be adjusted annually for inflation by the Academic Integrity Commission using the Consumer Price Index for All Urban Consumers, with adjustments published on the Ledger. 17A.11 Tier 1 — Micro-Purchase Rules. Purchases under five thousand dollars ($5,000) shall follow simplified rules: (a) May be approved by any Approving Officer with budgetary authority; (b) Shall be posted on the Franklin Ledger within thirty (30) days of the transaction, including vendor, amount, and brief description; (c) Shall not be structured (deliberately split into multiple smaller purchases to evade Tier 2 scrutiny). Structured purchases shall be treated as Tier 2 or higher depending on aggregate value, and structuring shall constitute Gross Waste subject to Section 17A.17 personal liability; (d) Shall include conflict-of-interest disclosure by the Approving Officer where the vendor has any relationship with the Officer or immediate family. 17A.12 Tier 2 — Simplified Acquisition Rules. Purchases between five thousand dollars and fifty thousand dollars ($5,000 to $50,000) shall follow simplified-competition rules: (a) Three (3) written quotes shall be obtained from eligible vendors, with the selection reasoning documented; (b) Where three quotes cannot reasonably be obtained (for example, sole-source specialty items or urgent needs), the Approving Officer shall document the reason on the Ledger; (c) Approval by the Body or its delegated procurement officer shall be required;

(d) Posting on the Ledger within seven (7) days of contract execution, including vendor, amount, description, and summary of competitive process; (e) Conflict-of-interest disclosure by all approving personnel. 17A.13 Tier 3 — Major Contract Rules. Contracts between fifty thousand dollars and five hundred thousand dollars ($50,000 to $500,000) shall follow open-bid rules: (a) Open solicitation with not less than fourteen (14) days for bid submission, posted on the Ledger; (b) Clear and objective evaluation criteria established before solicitation; (c) Bid opening and evaluation recorded on the Ledger with vendor identities, bid amounts, and evaluation scoring; (d) Body approval by majority vote of members or delegated committee; (e) Academic Integrity Commission procurement integrity review before contract execution, confirming that the process followed the rules of this Section and that no disqualifying conflicts exist; (f) Full contract text posted on the Ledger within seven (7) days of execution; (g) Performance monitoring with deliverable tracking published on the Ledger. 17A.14 Tier 4 — Strategic Contract Rules. Contracts over five hundred thousand dollars ($500,000) shall follow strategic-procurement rules: (a) Open solicitation with not less than thirty (30) days for bid submission, posted on the Ledger; (b) Independent forensic auditor pre-review of the solicitation design, evaluation criteria, and vendor selection, with the auditor drawn by randomized lottery from the Academic Integrity Commission's pre-qualified auditor pool, rotating such that no auditor reviews consecutive contracts for the same Body; (c) Public bid opening with livestreamed session on the Ledger; (d) Body approval by majority vote, recorded on the Ledger with reasoning; (e) Liberty Bell Initiative concurrence of all three Authority bodies required before contract execution for strategic contracts awarded by the Authority. For strategic contracts of the Watchdog Tribunal, two-thirds (2/3) supermajority of the Tribunal shall substitute for Liberty Bell concurrence. For strategic contracts of the Hamilton Contingent, the procedures of Section 13C shall apply in parallel with this Section; (f) Full contract text posted on the Ledger within seven (7) days of execution, including all schedules, pricing, and performance terms; (g) Quarterly performance reviews published on the Ledger throughout the contract term;

(h) Automatic forensic audit at contract completion or annually for multi-year contracts, with audit findings published on the Ledger. 17A.15 Real-Time Expenditure Publication. All expenditures by Covered Bodies, regardless of tier, shall appear on a public Expenditure Ledger on the Franklin Ledger no later than thirty (30) days after the expenditure, including: vendor or recipient; amount; purpose; budget line; and approving officer. Staff compensation shall be published in aggregate by position category, with individual compensation published for positions above a senior threshold established by each Body and disclosed on the Ledger. Every citizen shall have the right to search, download, and analyze the Expenditure Ledger. E. Citizen Petition Right and Independent Auditor Rotation 17A.16 Citizen Petition Right to Challenge Expenditures. Any citizen may petition the Watchdog Tribunal for review of any specific expenditure, hiring decision, or contract by a Covered Body upon a showing that the challenged action may constitute Gross Waste, procedural violation, or conflict of interest. The petition process shall operate as follows: (a) A petition may be filed at any time using a standard form published on the Ledger, requiring only the citizen's identifying information, the specific challenged action, and a brief statement of the basis for challenge; (b) The Watchdog

Tribunal shall acknowledge receipt within seven (7) days and shall conduct initial review within thirty (30) days to determine whether the petition states a potentially meritorious challenge. The initial review determination shall be published on the Ledger with reasoning; (c) If the petition states a potentially meritorious challenge, the Tribunal shall open formal investigation, engaging the independent forensic auditor pool under Section 17A.17 as appropriate; (d) The Tribunal shall issue a formal finding within one hundred eighty (180) days of opening formal investigation, with findings published on the Ledger. Findings may include: no violation; procedural correction required; recovery of funds required; Approving Officer liability under Section 17A.18; referral to the Hamilton Contingent Prosecution Division for criminal investigation; or other appropriate remedy; (e) The filing citizen shall have the right to observe non-confidential portions of the investigation and to receive the final findings; (f) Frivolous or repetitive petitions filed in bad faith may result in limited restrictions on future petition filing by the offending citizen, subject to due process and review by the Authority. This limitation shall be applied narrowly and shall not chill good-faith citizen oversight.

17A.17 Independent Forensic Auditor Pool and Rotation. The Academic Integrity Commission shall maintain a pre-qualified pool of independent forensic auditors available for: (a) pre-review of Tier 4 contracts under Section 17A.14(b); (b) investigation of citizen petitions under Section 17A.16; (c) annual zero-based budget review support to the Watchdog Tribunal; (d) periodic comprehensive audits of Covered Bodies; (e) special investigations referred by the Watchdog Tribunal or Hamilton Contingent. The pool shall include: (a) Only Certified Public Accountants or equivalent credentialed professionals with demonstrated forensic accounting expertise; (b) Auditors unaffiliated with any of the Big Four accounting firms' federal contracting arms, to avoid capture by dominant market participants. Sole-practitioner forensic accountants, smaller firms, and academic forensic accountants shall be actively recruited; (c) No auditor who has provided services to any federal officeholder's campaign, personal businesses, or family members within the preceding ten (10) years; (d) Rotation requirements ensuring that no auditor conducts consecutive reviews of the same Covered Body, and that auditors rotate among Bodies over time to prevent capture; (e) Compensation at prevailing market rates for forensic accounting services, drawn from the constitutional appropriation without intermediate budgeting; (f) Public disclosure of auditor identities, engagements, and findings on the Ledger, with narrow redactions only where specific information would compromise ongoing investigations. F. Personal Liability for

Gross Waste 17A.18 Personal Liability Framework. Any Approving Officer who approves expenditure, hiring, or procurement constituting Gross Waste shall be subject to comprehensive personal liability, encompassing criminal prosecution, removal, federal office bar, and financial recovery: (a) Criminal Liability. Approval of Gross Waste by an Approving Officer, where the waste exceeds one hundred thousand dollars ($100,000) or occurs in a pattern, shall constitute a federal felony punishable by not less than five (5) years imprisonment. Where the waste is accompanied by personal enrichment, kickback receipt, or undisclosed conflict of interest, the penalty shall be not less than fifteen (15) years imprisonment, with the matter referred to the Hamilton Contingent Prosecution Division; (b) Removal and Federal Office Bar. An Approving Officer found to have approved Gross Waste shall be subject to removal from their Covered Body position by the Watchdog Tribunal through procedures consistent with Section 21, and shall face permanent bar from federal office and from service on any Amendment-established

Body. Removal and bar shall be separate from criminal proceedings and shall not require criminal conviction, although the standard shall be clear and convincing evidence; (c) Financial Recovery. Wasted funds shall be recoverable from the personal assets of the Approving Officer, including assets held individually, jointly, beneficially, or through trusts or intermediaries. Recovery shall proceed through civil action by the Hamilton Contingent Prosecution Division acting on behalf of the United States, with recovered funds returning to the constitutional appropriation; (d) Cumulative Application. The three liability provisions of this Section are cumulative, not alternative. Serious cases of Gross Waste may result in all three consequences applying simultaneously; (e) Protection for Good-Faith Judgment. Approving Officers who exercise good-faith professional judgment shall not face personal liability merely because an approval later proves suboptimal. Gross Waste requires the definitional elements in the Section Key above, including unjustified expenditure, substantially-above-market cost, procedural evasion, or undisclosed conflict of interest. Ordinary business-judgment calls are protected. 17A.19 Whistleblower Protections for Reporters of Waste. Any person, including Covered Body staff, vendors, citizens, or third parties, who reports suspected Gross Waste by a Covered Body to the Watchdog Tribunal, Academic Integrity Commission, Authority, Hamilton Contingent, or any federal Inspector General, shall be entitled to the full Protected Whistleblower Status of Section 13B.16 and the financial reward schedule of Section 13B.17 where the disclosure leads to recovery. F.1. Annual Comprehensive Audit

17A.19.1 Mandatory Annual Audit. Every Covered Body shall undergo a comprehensive annual audit conducted by independent forensic auditors drawn from the pool established under Section 17A.17. The audit is mandatory, not optional; no Covered Body may decline, delay, or restrict audit access. The audit shall examine: (a) Budget adherence — whether actual spending tracked the zero-based budget published under Section 17A.4, with line-item variance analysis; (b) Procurement compliance — whether contracts followed the four-tier rules of Sections 17A.10 through 17A.14, including scrutiny for structured micro-purchases, bypassed competitive processes, and conflicts of interest; (c) Hiring compliance — whether staff hiring followed Sections 17A.5 through 17A.9, including Pre-Certified Personnel Roster use, disqualifying-condition screening, and compensation benchmarking;

(d) Internal controls — the Body's systems for preventing fraud, misuse of funds, and procedural evasion; (e) Asset verification — physical, digital, and financial assets under the Body's control, including cryptographic keys, sensitive records, and equipment; (f) Performance against constitutional mandate — whether expenditures and activities served the Body's constitutional function under this Amendment; (g) Whistleblower and citizen-petition handling — whether reports under Sections 17A.16 and 17A.19 were processed appropriately; (h) Any other area the Watchdog Tribunal or Academic Integrity Commission designates for enhanced scrutiny based on prior findings, citizen petitions, or institutional risk factors. 17A.19.2 Fixed Annual Audit Schedule. Each Covered Body shall be assigned a fixed annual audit commencement date by the Academic Integrity Commission, published permanently on the Ledger, corresponding to the Body's fiscal year end. Audits shall commence within thirty (30) days of fiscal year end and shall complete within one hundred twenty (120) days of commencement. The schedule shall be published permanently so that every citizen knows when each Body's audit occurs. The Commission may stagger audit dates across Covered Bodies to manage auditor pool capacity, with stagger decisions published on the Ledger. 17A.19.3 Audit Scope and Access. Independent forensic auditors conducting annual audits shall have unrestricted access to: (a) All financial records, including bank statements, wire transfer records, credit card statements, cryptographic wallet records, and petty cash logs; (b) All procurement records, including solicitations, bids, evaluations, contracts, amendments, performance reports, and payment records; (c) All personnel records, including hiring files, compensation records, performance reviews, disciplinary records, and departure records; (d) All electronic communications relating to Body operations, subject to attorney-client privilege where specifically applicable to privileged legal counsel; (e) All physical assets, including real property, equipment, and secure storage; (f) All Body members and staff for interview under oath, with refusal to cooperate constituting grounds for immediate Section 13 interference referral; (g) Any other records or personnel the auditor reasonably requires to complete the audit. 17A.19.4 Audit Outcomes — Three-Tier Grading System. Annual audits shall result in one of three graded outcomes:

(a) Pass — the Body is operating within the requirements of this Amendment, with no material irregularities identified. Minor procedural observations may be noted for Body attention without affecting the Pass grade. A Pass result requires no remediation; (b) Fail — the Body has material compliance failures, including but not limited to: procurement procedures substantially evaded on multiple occasions; hiring done outside Pre-Certified Personnel Roster without appropriate justification; budget variance exceeding twenty-five percent (25%) on material line items without public justification; internal controls insufficient to prevent reasonably foreseeable fraud; or other substantial departures from this Section's requirements. A Fail result triggers the remediation process of Section 17A.19.6; (c) Criminal Referral Required — the audit has identified clear and convincing evidence of criminal activity by any Approving Officer, staff member, contractor, or other person in connection with Body operations, including fraud, embezzlement, bribery, kickbacks, Gross Waste under Section 17A.18, evidence destruction, or other federal crimes. A Criminal Referral Required result triggers immediate Hamilton Contingent Prosecution Division engagement under Section 17A.19.7, and the remediation process of Section 17A.19.6 applies concurrently with the criminal investigation. 17A.19.5 Audit Report Publication. Within thirty (30) days of audit completion, the full audit report shall be published upon the Franklin Ledger, including the grading outcome, supporting findings, auditor methodology, and auditor qualifications and compensation. Redactions shall be permitted only for specific classified information (national security details, active criminal investigation specifics, or personal privacy information of non-officials) certified as such by the Academic Integrity Commission with narrow reasoning published alongside the redaction. The redacted full report shall be held in secure Commission custody for ten (10) years and shall be automatically declassified after that period unless the narrow basis for redaction remains valid. 17A.19.6 Remediation Process for Failed Audits. A Covered Body receiving a Fail grade shall enter the following remediation process: (a) Remediation Plan Required. Within fifteen (15) days of audit report publication, the Body shall publish upon the Ledger a Remediation

Plan specifically addressing each identified material irregularity, with timelines, responsible officers, and success criteria. The plan shall be developed by the Body with technical assistance from the Academic Integrity Commission upon request; (b) Thirty-Day Correction Period. The Body shall have thirty (30) days from publication of the Remediation Plan to implement corrections. Progress reports shall be published on the Ledger at days ten (10) and twenty (20) of the correction period, identifying which remediation items have been completed and which remain outstanding;

(c) Retest Audit. Upon expiration of the thirty-day correction period, the same forensic auditor (or an equivalent auditor drawn by lottery from the pool if the original auditor is unavailable) shall conduct a Retest Audit focused on the material irregularities identified in the original audit and the remediation actions undertaken. The Retest Audit shall be completed within thirty (30) days and shall result in either a revised Pass grade or a Remediation Failure finding; (d) Retest Audit Report Publication. The Retest Audit report shall be published on the Ledger within fifteen (15) days of completion, with the same transparency standards as the original audit report; (e) If the Retest Audit results in a revised Pass grade, the annual audit process is complete and normal operations continue. If the Retest Audit results in a Remediation Failure finding, the escalation consequences of Section 17A.19.7 apply. 17A.19.7 Consequences of Failed Remediation or Criminal Referral. Where a Covered Body fails remediation under Section 17A.19.6, or receives a Criminal Referral Required grade under Section 17A.19.4(c), the following maximum accountability stack shall apply: (a) Leadership Removal. The senior leadership of the Covered Body responsible for the failed operations shall be removed from their positions by the Watchdog Tribunal through procedures consistent with Section 21.7, with the specific individuals identified based on the audit findings. Where the entire Body leadership is implicated, the Authority through Liberty Bell Initiative shall oversee succession under Section 17A.19.8; (b) Funding Freeze of Non-Essential Operations. The Academic Integrity Commission shall freeze funding for non-essential Body operations, maintaining only funding necessary for: (i) core constitutional functions that cannot be paused without violating this Amendment; (ii) legally required staff compensation through a transition period not exceeding sixty (60) days; (iii) facility security and data preservation. Non-essential operations include new procurement, new hiring, non-essential travel, and discretionary spending. The freeze shall continue until the Body achieves a Pass grade on a subsequent audit; (c) Hamilton Contingent Investigation. The matter shall be referred to the Hamilton Contingent

Prosecution Division for federal criminal investigation of any person implicated in the audit findings. The investigation shall proceed under Section 13C standards and shall result in criminal prosecution where evidence supports it. Prosecutions shall include consideration of Section 17A.18 Personal Liability (criminal penalties for Gross Waste), Section 13A corruption penalties, Section 13 interference penalties where remediation obstruction occurred, and any other applicable provisions of this Amendment or federal criminal law; (d) Public Hearing. The Watchdog Tribunal shall conduct a public hearing within sixty (60) days of the Remediation Failure finding or Criminal Referral Required grade, with full livestreamed proceedings on the Ledger. The hearing shall: (i) present the audit findings to the public; (ii) allow testimony from affected officials, staff, and citizens; (iii) document the corrective actions the Body will take going forward; (iv) publish a Tribunal finding on the Ledger with reasoning; (e) Forced Restructuring. If the Tribunal finds by clear and convincing evidence that the failed Body cannot be restored to compliance through leadership replacement alone, the Tribunal shall recommend to the Authority through Liberty Bell Initiative (or to the body-specific governance mechanism for non-Authority Bodies) a forced restructuring, which may include: complete replacement of senior leadership; reorganization of operational divisions; revised internal procedures; enhanced audit frequency for a period of not less than three (3) years; or other structural changes; (f) Citizen Emergency Override Eligibility. A Covered Body that has received consecutive Failed Audits with Remediation Failure, or a Criminal Referral Required grade where Hamilton Contingent investigation confirms systemic corruption, shall be eligible for the Citizen Emergency Override process established in Section 21.10. Citizens may initiate an Override petition under Section 21.11 to trigger simultaneous investigation of the Body's entire structure, with the audit failure serving as supporting documentation for the petition; (g) Maximum Stack Application. The remedies in (a) through (f) shall be cumulative, not alternative. A Covered Body with a Criminal Referral Required grade, for example, shall face leadership removal AND funding freeze AND criminal investigation AND public hearing simultaneously, with forced restructuring and Citizen Emergency Override eligibility as potential additional remedies. 17A.19.8 Leadership Succession After Removal. When senior leadership of a Covered Body is removed under Section 17A.19.7(a): (a) For Authority bodies (Citizens' Oversight Board, State Elections Council, Academic Integrity Commission), succession shall follow the body's normal replacement procedures under Section 17, accelerated as necessary to maintain operational continuity. During the gap, the remaining two Authority bodies shall jointly perform the removed body's functions to the extent possible; (b) For the Watchdog Tribunal, succession shall occur through accelerated selection under Section 21.3. If the Tribunal leadership as a whole is implicated, the State Council under Section 21.14 shall temporarily perform Tribunal functions until new Tribunal members are sworn; (c) For the Hamilton Contingent, succession shall follow the procedures of Section 13C, with the Authority through Liberty Bell Initiative overseeing Contingent Director and Division Chief replacement;

(d) For other Covered Bodies, succession shall follow the specific procedures applicable to that Body, with Authority Liberty Bell Initiative oversight where Body-specific procedures are insufficient; (e) In all cases, succession shall be expedited to minimize operational gap, with provisional leadership empowered to maintain core functions during full replacement proceedings. 17A.19.9 Audit Independence Protection. Forensic auditors conducting annual audits shall enjoy the following protections to ensure their independence from the bodies they audit: (a) No Covered Body member or staff member shall have authority to select, direct, evaluate, compensate, or dismiss the auditor conducting the annual audit of that Body. All such authority rests with the Academic Integrity Commission acting through the forensic auditor pool established in Section 17A.17; (b) Auditors shall have direct secure communication channels to the Watchdog Tribunal, the Academic Integrity Commission, and the Hamilton Contingent Prosecution Division, independent of the Body being audited; (c) Any attempt by Body personnel to intimidate, threaten, bribe, coerce, obstruct, or retaliate against an annual auditor shall constitute Section 13 interference with the penalties thereof, including the fifteen (15) year minimum sentence and lifetime office bar; (d) Auditors reporting suspected corruption during the audit process shall be entitled to full Protected Whistleblower Status under Section 13B.16 and the reward schedule of Section 13B.17 where the disclosure leads to recovery; (e) Auditors shall not be removable from their pool qualification status except for demonstrable professional misconduct, conflict of interest, or performance failure, determined by the Academic Integrity Commission through publicly reasoned procedures. 17A.19.10 Audit Evasion as Gross Waste. Any Approving Officer who knowingly obstructs, impedes, misdirects, or otherwise interferes with an annual audit, or who provides false information to an auditor, shall be deemed to have committed Gross Waste under Section 17A.18, subject to the triple-stack personal liability established therein. Obstruction includes but is not limited to: failure to produce requested records within reasonable timeframes; directing staff to withhold information from auditors; structuring transactions or personnel decisions to evade audit scrutiny; retaliation against staff who cooperate with auditors; or any other conduct calculated to impair audit completeness or accuracy. 17A.19.11 Consecutive Audit Failure. A Covered Body that receives Failed Audits in two (2) consecutive years, regardless of remediation outcomes in the intervening period, shall automatically trigger the full maximum accountability stack of Section 17A.19.7 regardless of whether the second-year remediation succeeds. The purpose of this provision is to prevent cycles of failure-and-remediation from masking systemic institutional dysfunction. A Body that fails twice, even if both failures are fully remediated, has demonstrated a pattern of inadequate controls that requires structural intervention. F.2. Anti-Corruption Audit Enhancements 17A.19.12 Anti-Auditor-Capture Provisions. To prevent corruption of forensic auditors through future employment, family ties, or social capture, the following protections apply to every auditor in the Academic Integrity Commission's pool: (a) Post-Audit Employment Ban. No forensic auditor who has conducted an annual audit or retest audit of any Covered Body shall accept employment, consulting engagements, contractor positions, board service, or any compensated role with that Body, its members, its contractors, or its significant vendors for a period of ten (10) years following completion of the audit. Violation shall constitute a federal felony punishable by not less than ten (10) years imprisonment, permanent bar from forensic accounting practice, and forfeiture of all compensation received from the prohibited engagement; (b) Family and Relationship Disclosure. Before beginning any audit engagement, the auditor shall publicly disclose upon the Ledger: all immediate family members (spouse, children, parents, siblings, in-laws) and any close personal relationships with any member, senior staff, vendor, or contractor of the Covered Body to be audited. The Academic Integrity Commission shall evaluate disclosed relationships and may disqualify the auditor where any relationship creates material appearance of conflict; (c) Social Contact Logging. During the audit engagement and for one (1) year following completion, the auditor shall log all social, professional, and personal contacts with any member, senior staff, vendor, or contractor of the Covered Body. The log shall be published on the Ledger quarterly in a format sufficient to identify patterns of contact while respecting legitimate privacy. Any attempt by Body personnel to cultivate social relationships with an assigned auditor shall be treated as audit interference under Section 13; (d) Anonymous Auditor Tipline. The Academic Integrity Commission shall maintain a secure anonymous tipline exclusively for forensic auditors to report threats, bribery offers, intimidation attempts, or suspicious contact from Body personnel. Reports shall be investigated by the Watchdog Tribunal within fourteen (14) days. The existence of any such report shall not be disclosed to the subject Body until the investigation is complete. Retaliation against auditors who use the tipline shall be prosecuted under Section 13 interference penalties; (e) Threat-Response Protection. Any auditor who reports being threatened, bribed, or coerced shall be entitled to: immediate reassignment to a different Body if desired; federal protection from retaliation under Section 13B.16; federal legal

representation; and relocation or identity protection if physical safety is at risk. Reports of threats shall never be treated as grounds for removal from the auditor pool. 17A.19.13 Surprise Mid-Year Audits. In addition to the fixed annual audit schedule of Section 17A.19.2, each Covered Body shall be subject to random surprise audits conducted at unpredictable times during the Authority Budget Year, as follows: (a) Surprise Audit Frequency. The Academic Integrity Commission shall conduct at least one (1) surprise audit per Covered Body per Authority Budget Year, in addition to the mandatory annual audit. High-risk Bodies (those with Fail grades in the prior two years, active Hamilton Contingent investigations, or elevated citizen petition activity under Section 17A.16) shall receive up to three (3) surprise audits per year; (b) No Advance Notice. Surprise audits shall be announced to the target Body no earlier than twenty-four (24) hours before commencement. The target Body shall receive no advance warning sufficient to alter records, postpone suspicious activities, or brief personnel on audit responses; (c) Random Selection. The timing of each surprise audit shall be determined by cryptographic randomization administered by the Academic Integrity Commission, with the randomization algorithm and seed source publicly verifiable on the Ledger. No person shall have advance knowledge of the randomization outcome; (d) Focused Scope. Surprise audits shall be narrower than annual audits, focusing on specific risk areas identified through ongoing oversight: recent large procurements, unusual hiring patterns, flagged expenditures, whistleblower reports, or citizen petition allegations. Scope shall be determined by the Academic Integrity Commission based on current intelligence; (e) Full Access Standard. Surprise auditors shall have the same unrestricted access rights as annual auditors under Section 17A.19.3. Any delay or obstruction shall be presumptively evidence of audit evasion under Section 17A.19.10; (f) Surprise Audit Report Publication. Surprise audit reports shall be published on the Ledger within thirty (30) days of completion, under the same transparency standards as annual audit reports. Findings may trigger the remediation process of Section 17A.19.6 or, in severe cases, direct application of the maximum accountability stack of Section 17A.19.7; (g) Leak Prevention. Any person who leaks advance information about a surprise audit, thereby compromising its surprise element, shall be subject to Section 13 interference penalties and shall forfeit any position or role in which they obtained the leaked information. 17A.19.14 Mandatory Record Retention for Covered Body Administrative Records. To prevent pre-audit document destruction, the following mandatory retention periods apply to all administrative records of Covered Bodies:

(a) Financial Records — Twenty (20) Years. All financial records, including bank statements, wire transfer records, credit card statements, cryptographic wallet records, petty cash logs, expense reports, receipts, and payment authorizations, shall be retained for not less than twenty (20) years from the date of the transaction; (b) Procurement Records — Twenty (20) Years. All procurement records, including solicitations, bids, evaluations, contracts, amendments, performance reports, inspection reports, and payment records, shall be retained for not less than twenty (20) years from the date of contract completion; (c) Personnel Records — Fifteen (15) Years. Personnel records, including hiring files, compensation records, performance reviews, disciplinary records, and departure records, shall be retained for not less than fifteen (15) years from the date of employment termination; (d) Electronic Communications — Seven (7) Years. Electronic communications relating to Body operations, including emails, instant messages, and electronic document transmissions, shall be retained for not less than seven (7) years from the date of communication; (e) Body Deliberations — Fifty (50) Years. All Body deliberations, meeting minutes, decision records, and vote records shall be retained for not less than fifty (50) years, reflecting the historical and constitutional significance of these records; (f) Cryptographic Integrity. All retained records shall be stored with cryptographic timestamping and integrity verification under Academic Integrity Commission standards, such that any subsequent modification, deletion, or tampering is detectable. Records not cryptographically protected shall be presumptively invalid for audit purposes; (g) Destruction Only by Protocol. No Covered Body record may be destroyed within the applicable retention period except pursuant to a formal destruction protocol approved by the Academic Integrity Commission, documented on the Ledger with specific reasoning, and conducted with forensic verification. Unauthorized destruction shall constitute evidence destruction under Section 13B, subject to its full penalties; (h) Post-Retention Disposition. Upon expiration of applicable retention periods, records shall be transferred to the

National Archives for permanent preservation of constitutional and historical significance, or destroyed pursuant to approved protocol if determined to have no continuing archival value. 17A.19.15 Beneficial Ownership Disclosure and Bid Collusion Detection. To prevent corruption through shell company bidding and bid rigging, the following requirements apply to all Tier 2, Tier 3, and Tier 4 procurement under Sections 17A.12 through 17A.14: (a) Beneficial Ownership Disclosure. Every vendor submitting a bid shall disclose upon the Ledger, as a condition of bid eligibility: all beneficial owners holding ten percent (10%) or more of the vendor entity; the full ownership chain through any intermediate entities to ultimate individual or governmental beneficial owners; all affiliated or commonly-controlled entities; and any individuals with directing authority over the vendor's operations. Disclosure shall be sworn under penalty of perjury. False disclosure shall result in immediate bid disqualification, five-year federal contracting bar, and referral to Hamilton Contingent for prosecution under Section 13A; (b) Anti-Rigging Screening. Before bid opening, the Academic Integrity Commission shall screen all bids against the beneficial ownership database to identify: common ownership among purportedly competing bidders; recent entity formations inconsistent with operational capability; geographic clustering of bidders without competitive explanation; and pricing patterns suggestive of bid rigging. Screening results shall be published on the Ledger at bid opening; (c) Specification-Tailoring Prohibition. No solicitation shall include specifications, certifications, experience requirements, or other criteria designed or reasonably likely to restrict competition to a single vendor or a small group of coordinated vendors. Each solicitation's criteria shall be reviewed by the Academic Integrity Commission before publication, with tailored specifications returned for broader drafting. Repeated tailoring by a Covered Body shall be treated as Gross Waste under Section 17A.18; (d) Anti-Structuring Detection. The Academic Integrity Commission shall monitor for deliberate structuring of procurements to land below tier thresholds and thereby evade more stringent scrutiny. Patterns including repeated purchases just below threshold breakpoints, related purchases artificially split across vendors or time periods, or budget-line-item manipulation shall be presumptive evidence of structuring. Confirmed structuring shall constitute Gross Waste under Section 17A.18; (e) Debarment Database. The Academic Integrity Commission shall maintain a public Debarment Database on the Ledger, listing all vendors barred from Covered Body contracting for corruption, false disclosure, bid rigging, or related misconduct. Debarment shall attach to beneficial owners, not merely entity names, preventing reconstitution of barred operations under new names. 17A.19.16 Body-Level Cryptocurrency and Digital Asset Operations. Where a Covered Body maintains or uses cryptocurrency or digital assets for operational purposes (such as paying international vendors, funding Academic Integrity Commission research, or facilitating blockchain infrastructure operations), the following requirements apply: (a) Authority Pre-Approval. No Covered Body may hold, transact in, or use cryptocurrency or digital assets for any purpose without prior approval of the Authority through Liberty Bell Initiative, establishing the specific operational need and approved asset categories. Approval shall be narrowly drawn to the actual

operational need; (b) Wallet Disclosure. Every cryptographic wallet address controlled by or beneficially held for a Covered Body shall be publicly disclosed on the Ledger, with the associated purpose and approved transaction types. All inbound and outbound transactions shall be publicly verifiable on the underlying blockchain; (c) Transaction Logging. Every cryptocurrency transaction by a Covered Body shall be logged on the Ledger within twenty-four (24) hours, including transaction hash, counterparty (where known), amount, purpose, and approving officer; (d) Prohibited Asset Classes. Covered Bodies shall not hold, transact in, or use: privacy coins or mixers designed to obscure transaction trails; non-fungible tokens except where directly related to operational need; decentralized finance positions for yield generation; or cryptocurrency derivatives or leveraged positions. Operational crypto usage shall be strictly for payment and settlement, not for investment or yield; (e) Audit Applicability. Annual and surprise audits shall include full review of cryptocurrency operations, with forensic auditors requiring specific qualification in blockchain forensic analysis as maintained by the Academic Integrity Commission; (f) Misuse Penalties. Misuse of Covered Body cryptocurrency operations shall constitute Gross Waste under Section 17A.18, with enhanced penalties reflecting the elevated difficulty of recovering misdirected digital assets. 17A.19.17 Pension and Retirement Account Integrity. To prevent corruption through pension or retirement account manipulation affecting Covered Body staff: (a) Defined Contribution Structure. Covered Body staff pension and retirement benefits shall operate exclusively through defined-contribution structures with individual account ownership by the staff member, using qualified retirement plans that prohibit political or patronage-based account management; (b) Prohibited Concentrations. No pension or retirement account shall be concentrated in assets of federal contractors, Covered Body vendors, or entities with material financial relationships to the Covered Body or its members. Diversification requirements shall be enforced by the Academic Integrity Commission; (c) Independent Trustees. Pension and retirement plans for Covered Body staff shall be administered by independent qualified trustees with no material relationship to the Covered Body, its members, or its vendors. Trustees shall be selected by randomized lottery from a pre-qualified pool maintained by the Academic Integrity Commission; (d) Annual Independent Audit. Pension and retirement plan operations shall be subject to annual independent audit separate from the Covered Body's general annual audit, with audit reports published on the Ledger;

(e) Prohibition on Patronage Hiring. Hiring, promotion, compensation, or pension decisions shall not be influenced by patronage relationships, political contributions, or kinship with Covered Body members or senior staff. Violations shall constitute Gross Waste under Section 17A.18. 17A.19.18 Cryptographic Record Integrity. To prevent data fabrication, backdating, and AI-generated document fraud, all Covered Body records subject to audit shall be cryptographically protected under standards established by the Academic Integrity Commission: (a) Real-Time Timestamping. Every administrative record created by a Covered Body shall be timestamped and hashed to a public blockchain (the Franklin Ledger or compatible infrastructure) at the moment of creation. The timestamp shall be verifiable by any auditor or citizen, establishing the record's existence at that specific moment and its unchanged state thereafter; (b) Integrity Verification. Auditors shall, as a standard procedure, verify the cryptographic integrity of records produced during audit, rejecting any record lacking verifiable timestamping or showing evidence of modification after creation; (c) AI-Generated Content Detection. The Academic Integrity Commission shall maintain current capabilities for detecting AI-generated or machine-fabricated documents, invoices, receipts, and other potential audit evidence, with the detection capabilities continuously updated as adversarial AI evolves. Detected AI-generated content shall be presumptively treated as fabricated unless the Body establishes legitimate AI use (such as translation) that was properly disclosed at creation; (d) Vendor Invoice Verification. For Tier 2, Tier 3, and Tier 4 procurement, vendor invoices above threshold amounts shall be independently verified through direct vendor communication by auditors, confirming invoice authenticity and payment accuracy. Fake invoice operations shall constitute federal fraud; (e) Backdating Detection. Any record showing timestamp inconsistency, metadata anomaly, or evidence of backdating shall be treated as potential evidence destruction under

Section 13B, with the creating or submitting party subject to prosecution; (f) Continuous Technology Evolution. Cryptographic record integrity standards shall be reviewed and updated annually by the Academic Integrity Commission to address evolving threats, with updates published on the Ledger and incorporated into audit methodology. F.3. Audit Fairness and Proportionality 17A.19.19 Scale-Adjusted Procurement Thresholds. To ensure audit and procurement requirements are proportional to Body size and budget, the Academic Integrity Commission shall maintain scale-adjusted threshold tables applied to each Covered Body based on:

(a) Body Size Classification. Bodies shall be classified as Small (fewer than twenty-five (25) total personnel), Medium (twenty-five to two hundred fifty (25-250) personnel), or Large (more than two hundred fifty (250) personnel), with classification based on headcount including both members and staff; (b) Scale Adjustment Factors. For Small Bodies, procurement thresholds of Section 17A.10 shall be reduced to: Tier 1 under two thousand dollars ($2,000); Tier 2 two thousand to twenty thousand dollars ($2,000-$20,000); Tier 3 twenty thousand to two hundred thousand dollars ($20,000-$200,000); Tier 4 over two hundred thousand dollars ($200,000). For Large Bodies, thresholds shall remain as stated in Section 17A.10. For Medium Bodies, thresholds may be adjusted upward by the Academic Integrity Commission based on demonstrated operational need, not to exceed fifty percent (50%) above the Section 17A.10 levels; (c) Annual Review. Scale adjustments shall be reviewed annually with adjustments published on the Ledger. No Body shall have thresholds adjusted upward based solely on growth where such growth itself is not adequately justified; (d) Fairness Principle. The purpose of scale adjustment is to ensure that audit and procurement overhead does not disproportionately burden smaller Bodies, not to provide larger Bodies with less scrutiny. Larger Bodies spend more money and warrant more scrutiny, not less. 17A.19.20 Graduated Fail Grades. To ensure proportionality in audit consequences, the Fail grade under Section 17A.19.4(b) shall be subdivided into three tiers based on severity of findings: (a) Technical Fail. Material compliance failures that are predominantly procedural or documentation-based, not indicative of financial loss, fraud risk, or structural dysfunction. Examples: hiring conducted outside Pre-Certified Personnel Roster without adequate documentation; minor procurement procedural errors without cost impact; delayed Ledger postings of non-sensitive information. Technical Fail triggers the standard remediation process of Section 17A.19.6, with a focused remediation period of thirty (30) days and light Tribunal oversight; (b) Material Fail. Substantial compliance failures involving meaningful financial impact, risk of fraud, or pattern of procedural evasion across multiple transactions. Examples: budget variance exceeding twenty-five percent (25%) on material line items without adequate justification; procurement structuring to evade tier thresholds; compensation substantially above benchmark without justified grounds; failure to investigate whistleblower reports. Material Fail triggers the standard thirty-day remediation plus enhanced Tribunal oversight including site visits during remediation; (c) Severe Fail. Compliance failures indicative of systemic institutional dysfunction or significant misuse of public funds, short of criminal conduct (which would trigger Criminal Referral Required). Examples: internal controls so insufficient that reasonably foreseeable fraud was undetected; pattern of beneficial ownership concealment by vendors without detection; failure of multiple internal checks simultaneously; significant cryptocurrency operations without proper controls. Severe Fail triggers the full maximum accountability stack of Section 17A.19.7, including potential leadership removal, even on first occurrence; (d) Grading Standard. The determination among Technical, Material, and Severe Fail shall be made by the forensic auditor with documented reasoning, subject to review by the Academic Integrity Commission and potential appeal to the Watchdog Tribunal by the affected Body within fifteen (15) days of audit publication. 17A.19.21 Good-Faith Reliance Protection. The good-faith protection of Section 17A.18(e) shall be explicitly extended to protect Approving Officers who relied in good faith on documentation, certifications, or representations prepared by staff, vendors, or third parties that subsequently prove false, where: (a) The Approving Officer had no actual knowledge of the falsity at the time of approval; (b) No reasonably apparent red flags (unusual cost patterns, internal inconsistency in documents, suspicious vendor characteristics, late or irregular submissions) were present that a reasonable Approving Officer would have investigated; (c) The Approving Officer followed the applicable procedural requirements of this Section, including any conflict-of-interest disclosures and documentation reviews; (d) The Approving Officer cooperated fully with subsequent investigation and did not attempt to conceal, destroy, or obstruct evidence after learning of the falsity; (e) Reliance Is Not Negligence. An Approving Officer who reviewed documents and had no reason to suspect fabrication is not liable for staff or vendor fraud, even where the approved transaction later proves to involve fraud. Holding Approving Officers personally liable for undetectable staff or vendor fraud would produce either paralytic over-review of every transaction or difficulty recruiting qualified individuals to serve as Approving

Officers. Liability attaches to knowing approval of waste, gross neglect of available red flags, or undisclosed conflicts — not to good-faith reliance on reasonably-appearing documentation. 17A.19.22 Whistleblower Identity Protection During Audit. To prevent inadvertent or intentional identification of whistleblowers during audit processes: (a) Confidential Auditor Interviews. Any staff member, vendor representative, or third party providing information to an auditor may request confidential treatment, obligating the auditor to protect the source's identity in all audit work products to the maximum extent consistent with audit integrity and due process for the accused; (b) Aggregation and Abstraction. Where a whistleblower's specific information would inevitably identify them in an audit report, the auditor shall aggregate information across multiple sources, use abstracted descriptions of concerns, and

defer identification until and unless legal proceedings require disclosure under court protection; (c) Separate Confidential Annex. Where whistleblower-specific information is essential to the audit finding but publication would identify the source, the auditor shall prepare a separate confidential annex available only to Watchdog Tribunal investigators, Hamilton Contingent prosecutors, and court proceedings under appropriate protection. The main audit report shall indicate the existence of the annex without revealing its contents; (d) Full Section 13B.16 Protections. Whistleblowers providing information during audits shall be entitled to the full Protected Whistleblower Status of Section 13B.16, including identity protection, retaliation protection, relocation if needed, and the reward schedule of Section 13B.17; (e) Retaliation Specifically During Audit Period. Any Covered Body action during or within one hundred eighty (180) days after an audit that adversely affects a staff member who provided information to auditors shall be presumptively retaliation, with the burden on the Body to demonstrate by clear and convincing evidence that the action was unrelated to the disclosure. 17A.19.23 Proportional Audit Scope for Small Bodies. To ensure audit requirements do not disproportionately burden smaller Covered Bodies: (a) Scoped Annual Audits. Small Bodies (as defined in Section 17A.19.19) shall receive annual audits proportionally scoped to their size and budget, with the Academic Integrity Commission establishing streamlined audit procedures that cover the full substantive areas of Section 17A.19.1 but with reduced documentation and testing requirements where low transaction volume permits; (b) Shared Audit Resources. Multiple Small Bodies may share audit resources, with a single auditor conducting parallel audits of related Small Bodies where coordination efficiencies exist without compromising audit independence; (c) Reduced

Surprise Audit Frequency. Small Bodies shall be subject to surprise audits under Section 17A.19.13 at minimum once per Authority Budget Year, rather than the up-to-three required for high-risk Large or Medium Bodies. High-risk Small Bodies with prior failures or active investigations may receive additional surprise audits at Commission discretion; (d) Equivalent Standards, Proportional Depth. Small Body audits shall apply the same substantive compliance standards as Large Body audits, with proportional depth of inquiry matched to Body size and transaction volume. Proportionality does not mean reduced integrity; it means appropriate scope for actual risk; (e) Cost Support for Small Body Compliance. The Academic Integrity Commission shall provide technical assistance, template procedures, and training resources to Small Bodies to help them achieve compliance without disproportionate overhead burden. Struggling Small Bodies shall receive support, not punishment, where their compliance challenges reflect capacity limitations rather than willful evasion. F.4. Accountability Chain — Auditing the Auditors 17A.19.24 Corrupt Auditor Penalties and Removal. Any forensic auditor who produces a false, fraudulent, or materially incomplete audit report; who accepts bribes, gifts, or promises of future employment from any Covered Body or related party in connection with an audit; who conspires with audited personnel to conceal findings; who destroys, alters, or fails to preserve audit evidence; or who otherwise corrupts the integrity of the audit process, shall face the following escalating consequences: (a) Criminal Prosecution. Corrupt audit conduct shall constitute a federal felony punishable by not less than fifteen (15) years imprisonment, with no pardon, commutation, or clemency possible. Where the corruption involves bribery, the minimum sentence shall be twenty (20) years. Prosecution shall proceed through the Hamilton Contingent Prosecution Division, with referral from the Watchdog Tribunal or from any person reporting the misconduct; (b) Permanent Pool Removal. Any auditor found by clear and convincing evidence to have engaged in corrupt audit conduct shall be permanently removed from the Academic Integrity Commission's forensic auditor pool, with the removal recorded on the Ledger. No such auditor shall ever again serve as a forensic auditor for any Covered Body, nor for any successor mechanism established under this Amendment; (c) Professional License Forfeiture. The Academic Integrity Commission shall coordinate with state Certified Public Accountant licensing authorities to ensure that corrupt audit conduct results in permanent forfeiture of professional licensure, and shall publish the findings in a manner supporting such forfeiture proceedings; (d) Compensation Forfeiture. All compensation received by the auditor for the corrupted audit shall be forfeited, and additional civil penalties of not less than three (3) times the compensation received shall be recoverable by the United States through the Hamilton Contingent Prosecution Division; (e) Voiding of Corrupt Audit. Any audit determined to have been corrupted shall be void, and the affected Covered Body shall be re-audited by a different auditor drawn from the pool, with the re-audit conducted under heightened scrutiny. The Body's prior Pass grade (if any) shall be rescinded, and any remediation undertaken in reliance on the voided audit shall be reviewed anew; (f) Whistleblower Standing. Any person, including other auditors, Covered Body staff, vendors, or citizens, who reports suspected auditor corruption shall be entitled to Protected Whistleblower Status under Section 13B.16, including the reward schedule of Section 13B.17 where recovery results.

17A.19.25 Cross-Check on Auditor Work Product. To prevent corruption through single-auditor capture or error, the Academic Integrity Commission shall implement the following cross-check mechanisms: (a) Random Secondary Review. A minimum of ten percent (10%) of all completed annual audits and surprise audits shall be subjected to random secondary peer review by a different auditor drawn from the pool. Secondary reviews shall examine the primary auditor's methodology, findings, and conclusions for accuracy, completeness, and freedom from bias. Selection of audits for secondary review shall be by publicly verifiable cryptographic randomization administered by the Commission; (b) Mandatory Secondary Review for Contested Findings. Any audit finding that results in a Fail grade or Criminal Referral Required grade shall be subject to mandatory secondary review before the grade becomes final, unless the affected Body waives this right in writing. The secondary review shall confirm or challenge the primary auditor's findings, with the final grade determined by the Watchdog Tribunal upon consideration of both audits; (c) Statistical Pattern Detection. The Academic Integrity Commission shall maintain statistical analytics across all audits in the pool, identifying unusual patterns that may indicate auditor bias or systematic manipulation: auditors whose grading is statistically inconsistent with peer auditors on similar Bodies; auditors whose clients consistently receive more favorable grades than statistical expectation; auditors with unusual timing patterns in report production; or any other detectable anomaly. Detected anomalies shall trigger enhanced review under Section 17A.19.24; (d) Public Peer Review. The full methodology and findings of every audit shall be available upon the Ledger for academic peer review by the broader forensic accounting community, law schools, public policy researchers, and journalists. Professional critique of audit methodology shall be welcomed and responded to by the Academic Integrity Commission in publicly posted responses, with methodological improvements incorporated as appropriate; (e) Rotating Pair Audits for High-Risk Bodies. For Covered Bodies under enhanced scrutiny (those with recent Fail grades, active investigations, or elevated citizen petition activity), audits shall be conducted by rotating pairs of auditors rather than single auditors. The two auditors shall work independently and file separate findings, with material disagreement between them triggering Watchdog Tribunal review. 17A.19.26 Academic Integrity Commission Circuit Break. When the Academic Integrity Commission is itself the Covered Body being audited, the potential for circularity — the AIC maintaining the pool of auditors who audit the AIC — creates an unacceptable conflict of interest. To break this circle:

(a) Alternate Auditor Source for AIC Audits. Audits of the Academic Integrity Commission shall not use auditors drawn from the AIC-maintained pool. Instead, the audit shall be conducted by forensic auditors drawn from an Alternate Roster maintained jointly by the Citizens' Oversight Board and the State Elections Council — the other two Authority bodies that do not have direct vetting authority over the primary auditor pool; (b) Alternate Roster Qualifications. The Alternate Roster shall include forensic auditors meeting equivalent professional qualifications, independence standards, and vetting procedures as the primary pool, but whose vetting and maintenance is administered by the joint authority of the Citizens' Oversight Board and State Elections Council under Liberty Bell Initiative. No Alternate Roster auditor shall have been vetted, credentialed, trained, or professionally connected to the Academic Integrity Commission in any material capacity within the preceding ten (10) years; (c) Heightened Scrutiny for AIC Audits. Audits of the Academic Integrity Commission shall apply heightened scrutiny including: mandatory rotating pair audits under Section 17A.19.25(e); automatic secondary review regardless of grade; and Watchdog Tribunal oversight throughout the audit process rather than only upon contested findings; (d) Symmetric Protection. The Citizens' Oversight Board and State Elections Council, when audited, shall likewise use auditors who do not have material conflicts of interest with those bodies, with the Academic Integrity Commission maintaining the primary pool for their audits. This symmetric structure prevents any one Authority body from becoming the sole gatekeeper of accountability for the others; (e) Circularity Monitoring. The Watchdog Tribunal shall annually review cross-body audit arrangements to identify and eliminate any circularity that develops over time. Where circularity is identified, the Tribunal shall recommend to the Authority through Liberty Bell Initiative appropriate restructuring. 17A.19.27 Watchdog Tribunal Itself as Covered Body. The Watchdog Tribunal, established under Section 21 as the primary oversight mechanism for the Authority, shall itself be a Covered Body under this Section 17A, subject to the annual and surprise audit framework in full. To prevent self-audit conflicts: (a) Tribunal Audit Source. The Watchdog Tribunal shall be audited by forensic auditors drawn jointly from the primary AIC-maintained pool and the Alternate Roster under Section 17A.19.26, with selection by randomized lottery from the combined rosters. This dual-source selection prevents any single Authority body from controlling Tribunal oversight; (b) Citizen Participation in Tribunal Audit. The annual audit of the Watchdog Tribunal shall include a Citizen Oversight component: a randomly selected panel of fifty (50) citizens, drawn by lottery from registered voters across all Participating

Jurisdictions, shall observe the audit process, submit questions to auditors, and publish their own citizen observations on the Ledger alongside the formal audit report. The citizen panel shall serve without the requirement to be professional auditors; their role is democratic participation in the accountability process; (c) Elevated Transparency. All Tribunal audit proceedings shall be livestreamed upon the Ledger, with the narrow exception of specific confidential operational security matters certified as such by the Academic Integrity Commission with narrow reasoning. The Tribunal's accountability to the People shall be maximally visible; (d) Tribunal Failure Consequences. Where the Watchdog Tribunal receives a Fail grade or Criminal Referral Required grade, the maximum accountability stack of Section 17A.19.7 shall apply, with the State Council under Section 21.14 automatically activating to perform Tribunal functions during reconstitution. This ensures oversight continuity even during Tribunal accountability proceedings; (e) No Tribunal Exemption. The Watchdog Tribunal shall not be exempt from any provision of this Section 17A, and shall face the same consequences for Gross Waste, audit evasion, and corruption as any other Covered Body. The Tribunal's essential constitutional role does not entitle it to reduced accountability; it heightens the accountability standard. 17A.19.28 Ultimate Circuit Breaker — Total Capture Scenario. In the extraordinary and catastrophic scenario in which the Authority, the Watchdog Tribunal, the Academic Integrity Commission, and the forensic auditor pool are all simultaneously corrupted, captured, or dysfunctional — such that the ordinary accountability mechanisms of this Section 17A have failed completely — the following ultimate circuit breaker mechanisms shall be available to the People: (a) Citizen Emergency Override Activation. The Citizen Emergency

Override established in Section 21.10 shall be activatable specifically on grounds of total accountability-chain capture, supported by evidence of: Authority body audit failures or refusals to audit; Tribunal dysfunction or corruption; Academic Integrity Commission audit-pool corruption; or simultaneous failures across multiple levels of the accountability chain. The Override petition shall require the standard supermajority and turnout thresholds of Section 21.11, but may be initiated on these grounds without requiring the ordinary predicates; (b) State-Level Emergency Audit. Upon certification of a Citizen Emergency Override petition, or upon determination by three-fifths (3/5) of the fifty-six Participating Jurisdiction Chief Election Officers acting collectively that the accountability chain has catastrophically failed, the State-Level Backstop under Section 21.14 shall automatically activate to conduct emergency audits of all Covered Bodies using state-based forensic resources independent of the federal accountability-chain structures. State audit findings shall be treated as authoritative pending reconstitution of the federal accountability mechanisms;

(c) Independent Emergency Auditor Recruitment. During total-capture scenarios, the State Council under Section 21.14, upon Liberty Bell-equivalent supermajority of its sub-councils, may recruit forensic auditors from: state government forensic accounting offices; international forensic accounting bodies acting as neutral observers; academic forensic accounting programs at universities not part of the corrupted Pre-Certified University Pool; and retired forensic professionals with no recent ties to federal or Authority body operations. Emergency-recruited auditors shall serve under the same oath, qualifications, and accountability standards as regular pool auditors; (d) Constitutional Convention Trigger. In the most extreme case, where the accountability chain failure is so comprehensive that no federal accountability mechanism remains functional, the Sunset Review under Section 18 may be accelerated by citizen petition: if citizens of thirty (30) or more Participating Jurisdictions submit petitions with the Section 3 threshold percentages of signatures alleging accountability-chain total failure, an accelerated Sunset Review shall be held within one hundred eighty (180) days, allowing the People to vote to Modify, Repeal, or Reconstitute the Amendment's accountability framework; (e) Reclamation Mechanism Itself. In the ultimate failure scenario, the People retain the Section 1 right of popular No Confidence against any Federal Government operating under a captured accountability framework. A No Confidence Referendum may be initiated even where the ordinary Authority-maintained infrastructure is compromised, using the State Council infrastructure and state-level mechanisms as substitutes until the accountability framework is restored. The People's sovereign authority to reclaim their government does not depend on the integrity of any intermediate body; (f) No Authority Over the People. The accountability chain established in this Amendment exists to serve the People's sovereignty, not to constrain it. No provision of this Section, this Amendment, or any implementing measure shall be construed to prevent the People from exercising their reserved constitutional powers of reclamation, override, reconstitution, or amendment. The accountability chain is a tool for the People's protection; when it fails, the People retain every power they possessed before it was created. G. Integration and Coordination 17A.20 Integration with Hamilton Contingent Framework. The Hamilton Contingent shall be a Covered Body subject to this Section, except that where the Hamilton Contingent's specific provisions under Section 13C establish additional or more specific procurement, hiring, or operational rules, those provisions shall apply in addition to this Section. Where conflict arises, the more stringent rule shall control. The Contingent's investigative and prosecutorial autonomy under Section 13C shall not be diminished by this Section.

17A.21 Integration with Sunset Review. The dollar thresholds, timelines, and procedural requirements of this Section shall be reviewed in each Sunset Review under Section 18. The People may, through a Modify vote, adjust specific numbers based on accumulated operational experience, while the foundational principles of this Section — operational autonomy, anti-waste discipline, citizen petition rights, personal liability for waste, and independent forensic oversight — shall be preserved. 17A.22 Emergency Procurement. In cases of genuine operational emergency (disaster response, active security threat, Amendment-operational failure requiring immediate correction), a Covered Body may execute emergency procurement without full compliance with the tier rules of Sections 17A.11 through 17A.14, subject to the following constraints: (a) emergency must be documented on the Ledger at the moment of invocation; (b) emergency procurement shall not exceed seventy-two (72) hours' duration absent ratification by the Body's voting process; (c) post-emergency compliance audit by the Watchdog Tribunal within thirty (30) days; (d) abuse of emergency procurement to evade tier rules shall constitute Gross Waste under Section 17A.18. 17A.23 Article V Protection. The provisions of this Section shall be protected under the Article V protection established in Sections 18.6.1 and 18.6.2. No act of Congress, executive order, judicial ruling, or state action shall evade, diminish, or nullify the operational autonomy, anti-waste framework, or personal liability provisions of this Section. 17A.24 Foundational Commitment. The People of the United States, in ratifying this Amendment, commit themselves to the principle that the institutions established herein to protect their sovereignty shall operate with both the freedom necessary to function and the discipline necessary to remain trustworthy. Operational autonomy without accountability becomes oligarchy; accountability without autonomy becomes paralysis. This Section establishes the balance: the Covered Bodies have what they need to act, and the People have what they need to watch. No Approving Officer may treat public funds as their own; no Body may be choked into dysfunction. The Framers of this Amendment recognized that institutions left unwatched become corrupt, and institutions watched too closely become ineffective, and they rejected both failure modes in favor of transparent, accountable operational autonomy.

Section 17B. Authority Restoration — Sovereign Reset When All Else Fails

Key terms in this Section: • "The Restoration" — The citizen-initiated constitutional mechanism by which the People simultaneously remove and replace the entire oversight apparatus of this Amendment — all three bodies of the Authority together with the Watchdog

Tribunal — in a single sovereign act when comprehensive capture has rendered the ordinary accountability mechanisms incapable of self-correction. • "The Oversight Apparatus" — For purposes of this Section: the collective of the Citizens' Oversight Board, the State Elections Council, the Academic Integrity Commission (together constituting the Authority under Section 17), and the Watchdog Tribunal (Section 21). Combined membership: five hundred six (506) persons. • "Restoration Referendum" — The national Referendum held pursuant to Section 17B.3 through which a citizen-initiated Restoration is ratified by the People. • "Washington Commission Restoration Expansion" — The automatic temporary expansion of the Permanent Washington Commission's authorities under Section 17D, triggered by certification of a Restoration under this Section, for the specific and limited purpose of overseeing the simultaneous reconstitution of all four bodies subject to Restoration. Because the Commission is a permanent body under Section 17D, this is an activation of additional authorities, not a reconvening of a dormant body. See Section 17B.5. • "Post-Restoration Disposition" — The procedural framework established in Section 17B.7 governing the status of members removed by a Restoration, including default barring from Amendment bodies with individual clearance available upon petition. A. Foundational Purpose and

Scope 17B.1 Foundational Purpose of the Restoration. The ordinary accountability mechanisms of this Amendment assume that at any given time, at least some portion of the oversight apparatus remains uncaptured and capable of correcting the rest. Individual removal processes, remediation cycles, and even the maximum accountability stack under Section 17A.19.7 presuppose functional oversight bodies to implement them. When the entire oversight apparatus — all three bodies of the Authority together with the Watchdog Tribunal — has been comprehensively captured, the ordinary mechanisms deadlock. The Restoration established in this Section is the citizen-initiated constitutional mechanism by which the People themselves simultaneously remove and replace the entire oversight apparatus in a single sovereign act, breaking the deadlock without relying on captured institutions.

17B.2 The Restoration — Scope. A certified Restoration under this Section shall simultaneously remove all members of: (a) The Citizens' Oversight Board established under Section 17.2 (three hundred (300) members); (b) The State Elections Council established under Section 17.9 (fifty-six (56) members); (c) The Academic Integrity Commission established under Section 17.15 (fifty (50) members); and (d) The Watchdog Tribunal established under Section 21 (one hundred (100) members). (e) Combined total: five hundred six (506) members removed in a single sovereign act. The Restoration shall be simultaneous and complete; partial Restorations of individual bodies are not authorized under the citizen-initiated pathway, as the purpose of the Restoration is to break deadlocked oversight where capture has spread across the entire apparatus. Limited Restorations of specific bodies are available only through the alternative pathways of Section 17B.4. B. Thresholds and Trigger Pathways 17B.3 Threshold for Citizen-Initiated Restoration. A citizen-initiated Restoration shall require the same threshold as a No Confidence Referendum under Section 3, reflecting the gravity of clearing the entire oversight apparatus: (a) Petition Phase. Signatures from fifteen percent (15%) of registered voters nationally, including fifteen percent (15%) in each of thirty (30) of the fifty-six (56) Participating Jurisdictions, collected within ninety (90) days. The petition shall allege comprehensive capture of the oversight apparatus with specific supporting evidence, including but not limited to: documented consecutive audit failures across multiple bodies; Watchdog Tribunal dysfunction or documented corruption; failure of the ordinary accountability mechanisms under Sections 17A.19.24 through 17A.19.28; or other patterns establishing that the apparatus cannot self-correct; (b) Referendum Phase. A national Restoration Referendum shall be held within ninety (90) days of petition certification, conducted through

Sovereign Voting Terminals under Section 14 and the Franklin Ledger under Section 4. The Referendum shall require sixty percent (60%) approval with minimum fifty percent (50%) turnout of registered voters across all Participating Jurisdictions, consistent with the No Confidence threshold under Section 5.2. Below the turnout threshold, the provisions of Section 18.3 regarding failed referenda shall apply by analogy, with a two-year retry permitted; (c) Certification and Effect. Upon certification of a Restoration Referendum achieving the required threshold, the Restoration shall take effect automatically and simultaneously at 12:00:01 Eastern Time on the seventh (7th) day following certification, with all five hundred six (506) removed members losing their positions and authorities at that instant. This seven-day delay permits orderly records transfer and Washington Commission expansion to Restoration oversight role under Section 17B.5, while preventing any removed member from attempting to take extraordinary action in anticipation of removal. 17B.3.1 Five-Year Protection Period for Citizen-Initiated Restoration. Citizens may initiate a Restoration petition under Section 17B.3 only after the three bodies of the Authority and the Watchdog Tribunal have been fully operational for at least five (5) years. This waiting period serves three purposes: (a) it gives the bodies time to establish themselves, complete initial annual audit cycles under Section 17A.19, and prove how they function; (b) it prevents opponents of this Amendment from weaponizing the Restoration mechanism to dismantle the oversight apparatus before it can demonstrate its legitimacy; and (c) it allows the ordinary accountability mechanisms of Sections 17A.19.24 through 17A.19.28 to operate first, reserving Restoration for when those ordinary mechanisms have clearly failed. 17B.3.2 Clock Commencement and Expiration. The five-year protection period shall commence on the date the Authority is certified as fully inaugurated under Section 19.19. Both the commencement date and the expiration date shall be published permanently on the Franklin Ledger. The clock shall not be paused, suspended, or reset for any reason short of a formal Amendment ratification under Article V. 17B.3.3 Emergency Triggering Events — Citizens May Petition Without Institutional Certification. The five-year protection period of Section 17B.3.1 may be waived upon the occurrence of any one of the enumerated emergency triggering events below, without requiring institutional certification. These are events so obviously serious that their occurrence is itself the emergency; no captured or compromised body's approval is required for citizens to recognize the emergency and initiate a Restoration petition. Citizens initiating a Restoration petition during the protection period shall reference the specific triggering event in their petition, with supporting documentation publicly verifiable. The Academic Integrity Commission, or in its absence the State Elections Council, shall accept petitions referencing any listed event. The enumerated emergency triggering events are: 17B.3.3.1 Emergency Category A — Criminal and Legal Triggers. Any of the following criminal or legal events shall waive the protection period: (a) Arrest of any senior Authority leadership member or Watchdog Tribunal leader on charges of bribery, corruption, interference (Section 13), evidence destruction (Section 13B), or foreign interference (Section 22); (b) Indictment by federal grand jury of any Authority body member or Watchdog Tribunal member for Amendment-related offenses; (c) Federal court finding of Authority misconduct at any level, published on public court records.

17B.3.3.2 Emergency Category B — Infrastructure and Operational Triggers. Any of the following operational failures shall waive the protection period: (a) Franklin Ledger compromise lasting seven (7) or more consecutive days, whether by cyberattack, infrastructure failure, or deliberate tampering; (b) Failure of any Authority body to meet voting quorum for thirty (30) or more consecutive days, as documented on the Ledger; (c) Failure of any annual audit under Section 17A.19 to complete within its statutory one-hundred-twenty (120) day timeline; (d) Documented interference with forensic auditor access to Authority body records, personnel, or facilities, where such interference is published on the Ledger or state-level infrastructure. 17B.3.3.3 Emergency Category C — Capture-Pattern Triggers. Any of the following capture-pattern events shall waive the protection period: (a) Audit Fail grade published under Section 17A.19.4(b) on any Authority body, without waiting for the ordinary remediation period to conclude; (b) Consecutive Fail grades across two (2) or more Authority bodies within any thirty-six (36) month period; (c) Hamilton Contingent Prosecution Division opens formal criminal investigation of any Authority body member, with investigation documented on the Ledger. 17B.3.3.4 Emergency Category D — Foreign and Adversarial Triggers. Any of the following foreign interference events shall waive the protection period: (a) Documented foreign interference in Authority operations under Section 22, triggered by credible intelligence or forensic evidence; (b) Cyberattack attributed to a hostile foreign power against Authority infrastructure, the Franklin Ledger, or Sovereign Voting Terminals. 17B.3.3.5 Emergency Category E — Transparency and Integrity Triggers. Any of the following integrity breakdown events shall waive the protection period: (a) Three (3) or more Protected Whistleblower reports under Section 13B.16 filed against members of the Authority bodies within any twelve (12) month period; (b) Evidence destruction under Section 13B attributed to Authority members, whether confirmed by Hamilton Contingent investigation or by independent forensic audit; (c) Missing or unaccounted-for Authority funds exceeding one million dollars ($1,000,000) in any fiscal year, as documented in the annual audit under Section 17A.19.

17B.3.3.6 Unforeseen Catastrophic Events Clause. In addition to the enumerated triggering events of Sections 17B.3.3.1 through 17B.3.3.5, the protection period may be waived upon the occurrence of sudden catastrophic events beyond the drafters' specific anticipation, limited to the following categories: (a) Natural disasters rendering the Authority bodies or Watchdog Tribunal unable to perform their constitutional functions for more than thirty (30) consecutive days; (b) Declaration of war or active armed conflict on United States territory that materially impairs Authority or Tribunal operations; (c) Catastrophic cyberattack against the United States critical infrastructure, including the Franklin Ledger, resulting in operational failure of the oversight apparatus; (d) Pandemic or mass-casualty public health event incapacitating more than one-third (1/3) of the combined membership of the Authority and Watchdog Tribunal; (e) Application of Subsection. This unforeseen catastrophic events clause shall not be used to expand the enumerated categories; it addresses only sudden catastrophic events meeting the above limited categories. The specific event shall be documented in any citizen petition invoking this subsection, with the nature of the catastrophic event and its impact on Authority operations specifically described. 17B.3.3.7 No Institutional Certification Required. Citizens may initiate a Restoration petition upon the occurrence of any enumerated triggering event or qualifying unforeseen catastrophic event, without waiting for any Amendment body, federal agency, or state body to certify that the event has occurred. The triggering event itself, once publicly documented, suffices. Frivolous petitions referencing triggering events that have not actually occurred shall be subject to Section 17B.9(d) Anti-Gaming Provisions, with clear-and-convincing-evidence standards applying to any finding of frivolous petitioning. 17B.3.4 What Remains Available During the Protection Period. The protection period of Section 17B.3.1 applies solely to citizen-initiated Restoration petitions under Section 17B.3. During the protection period: (a) the Alternative Trigger Pathways of Section 17B.4 (Tribunal-Initiated Authority Restoration, Authority-Initiated Tribunal Restoration, and State-Level Consensus Restoration) remain fully available without any waiting period, as each of those pathways has its own built-in institutional threshold difficult to manipulate politically; (b) the Reclamation mechanism of Section 1 remains fully available to the People at all times, as Reclamation targets the Federal Government rather than the oversight apparatus; and (c) all ordinary accountability mechanisms under Section 17A continue to operate, including citizen petitions challenging specific expenditures under Section 17A.16.

17B.4 Alternative Trigger Pathways. In recognition that bottom-up citizen initiation may be difficult if the captured apparatus is actively suppressing citizen petition activity, the Restoration may also be triggered through the following alternative pathways, any one of which suffices: (a) Tribunal-Initiated Authority Restoration. If by two-thirds (2/3) supermajority the Watchdog Tribunal finds, with supporting evidence published upon the Ledger, that the three bodies of the Authority are collectively captured beyond remediation, the Tribunal may initiate a Restoration limited to the three Authority bodies (not including itself). The Tribunal finding shall be subject to immediate citizen challenge by petition under Section 17A.16. If no challenge succeeds within thirty (30) days, the Tribunal-initiated Restoration shall proceed. The Tribunal shall not initiate a Restoration of itself; (b) Authority-Initiated Tribunal Restoration. If by Liberty Bell Initiative the three Authority bodies concur that the Watchdog Tribunal is captured beyond remediation, the Authority may initiate a Restoration limited to the Tribunal. The Authority finding shall be subject to immediate citizen challenge by petition. If no challenge succeeds within thirty (30) days, the Authority-initiated Restoration shall proceed. The Authority shall not initiate a Restoration of itself; (c) State-Level Consensus Restoration. If fifty (50) of the fifty-six (56) Chief Election Officers serving on the State Elections Council (accounting for the possibility that some Council members may themselves be the captured portion) jointly determine, meeting outside the captured Council and publishing their determination on state-level election infrastructure independent of the federal Ledger, that the entire oversight apparatus has failed, a Restoration of all four bodies shall proceed, subject to citizen ratification by a simple-majority fast-track Referendum within sixty (60) days; (d) Circuit-Breaker Limitation. No captured body may use these alternative pathways to initiate a Restoration of the body investigating it. An Authority body under investigation by the Tribunal cannot initiate a Tribunal Restoration; a Tribunal under investigation by the Authority cannot initiate an Authority Restoration. Where cross-accusations arise, only the citizen-initiated pathway under Section 17B.3 or the State-Level Consensus pathway shall apply. C. Washington Commission — Temporary Expansion for Restoration

Oversight 17B.5 Washington Commission — Temporary Expansion to Restoration Oversight Role. Upon certification of any Restoration under Sections 17B.3 or 17B.4, the Permanent Washington Commission established under Section 17D (transitioned from its Phase One role under Section 19.5.0.1) shall temporarily expand its authorities to oversee the replacement process. Because the Commission is a permanent body under Section 17D and does not dissolve, this expansion is an activation of additional limited authorities rather than a reconvening of a dormant body. The temporarily expanded Commission shall:

(a) Composition. Consist of seven (7) sitting Chief Justices of Participating Jurisdictions as defined in Section 3, selected by randomized lottery from among all Chief Justices of Participating Jurisdictions at the moment of Restoration certification, excluding any Chief Justice from a Jurisdiction whose chief election officer is among State Elections Council members subject to Restoration still under investigation. The selection shall be administered by state-level election infrastructure independent of the federal Ledger, to ensure that the captured apparatus cannot interfere with Commission selection; (b) Expansion Activation. The Commission's expanded Restoration oversight authorities shall activate automatically within seventy-two (72) hours of Restoration certification. Because the Commission is already permanently convened under Section 17D, no separate convening is required; rather, the Commission shifts from ordinary Permanent Oversight operations to the expanded Restoration oversight role. Sessions under the expanded authorities shall take place at State Supreme Court facilities on a rotating basis as originally provided in Section 11C.7. No act of Congress, executive order, judicial ruling, or state action shall delay, impede, or invalidate the Commission's expanded authorities under this Section; (c) Duties During Restoration. Oversee the simultaneous reconstitution of all four bodies subject to Restoration as provided in Sections 17B.6 through 17B.10. The Commission shall: (i) supervise the randomized lottery for new Citizens' Oversight Board members; (ii) notify state Chief Election Officers of their ex officio State Elections Council reconstitution; (iii) supervise the Pre-Certified University Pool lottery for new Academic Integrity Commission members; (iv) supervise Watchdog Tribunal reconstitution under the procedures of Section 21; and (v) certify completion of reconstitution upon the Ledger; (d) Limited Authorities During Restoration. During Restoration oversight, the Commission's expanded authorities shall be limited to the authorities necessary for the reconstitution process and to protect the institutions subject to Restoration's physical and digital infrastructure from tampering during the transition. The Commission shall not exercise governing authority beyond these reconstitution duties. All original limits of Section 19.5.0.6 and the permanent limits of Section 17D.8 shall continue to apply, with narrow modifications only to the extent necessary for the Restoration oversight function; (e) Return to Permanent Oversight Mode After Restoration. The Commission's expanded Restoration oversight authorities shall terminate automatically sixty (60) days after the last of the four reconstituted bodies is fully sworn in, with all Restoration-specific records transferred to the reconstituted Authority. The Commission itself shall NOT dissolve at that point; it shall return to its ordinary Permanent Oversight role under Section 17D, with only the authorities enumerated in Section 17D.7 continuing thereafter. The temporary expansion under this Section shall not create precedent for routine governance authority or expanded Commission powers.

D. Simultaneous Reconstitution 17B.6 Simultaneous Same-Day Replacement — Reconstitution Procedures. To prevent any governance vacuum during the Restoration transition, replacement members for all four bodies subject to Restoration shall be selected and sworn in on the same day as Restoration effect, such that the moment the removed members lose authority, their replacements simultaneously assume it. The replacement procedures for each body shall be: (a) Citizens' Oversight Board. Three hundred (300) new members selected by randomized lottery from the registered voter pool under the procedures of Section 17.2, with the lottery administered by the Washington Commission (operating under its temporarily expanded Restoration authorities per Section 17B.5) and conducted in a livestreamed ceremony on the Franklin Ledger (or, if the Ledger itself has been compromised as part of the capture scenario, on state-level public election infrastructure). The lottery shall complete within six (6) days of Restoration certification, permitting sworn-in status on Day 7; (b) State Elections Council. Fifty-six (56) new members consisting of the current chief election officers of the fifty states, the District of Columbia, and the five territories enumerated in Section 3.1.1, serving ex officio under Section 17.9. Because this body is ex officio, reconstitution is automatic upon Restoration certification — whoever holds the chief election officer position in each Participating Jurisdiction on Day 7 is the new State Elections Council member. Where a member subject to Restoration's capture arose from corruption of their state-level election office, succession within that state shall follow state law, with federal courts available to adjudicate contested succession on an expedited basis; (c) Academic Integrity Commission. Fifty (50) new representatives selected by randomized lottery from the Pre-Certified

University Pool under Section 17.16, with the same livestreaming and seven-day timeline provisions as the Citizens' Oversight Board. Where universities among the Pre-Certified Pool were themselves complicit in the capture scenario, the Washington Commission during Restoration oversight may exclude those institutions from the lottery by clear and convincing evidence of complicity, with excluded institutions eligible for re-certification review at the next Pool recertification cycle; (d) Watchdog Tribunal. One hundred (100) new members selected through the accelerated process of Section 21.3, with the Washington Commission supervising the Pre-Certified Personnel Roster draw under Section 17A.5 to ensure Tribunal candidates meet the enhanced qualification standards required for Tribunal service. Reconstitution shall complete within six (6) days of Restoration certification. Where capture of the outgoing Tribunal was connected to compromise of the Pre-Certified Personnel Roster itself, the Commission shall draw from the Alternate Roster established under Section 17A.19.26;

(e) Simultaneous Swearing. At 12:00:01 Eastern Time on Day 7 after Restoration certification, all five hundred six (506) new members shall simultaneously take the constitutional oath of Section 17.24 (and Section 21.24 for Tribunal members), with the ceremony livestreamed on the Franklin Ledger and state-level infrastructure. Upon oath completion, the new members assume full authority and the members subject to Restoration's authority terminates simultaneously. E. Post-Restoration Disposition and Transition 17B.7 Post-Restoration Disposition of Removed Members. Members removed by a Restoration shall be subject to the following: (a) Default Barring. All removed members shall be barred from future service in the Citizens' Oversight Board, State Elections Council, Academic Integrity Commission, Watchdog Tribunal, or any other body established by this Amendment, until individually cleared under subsection (b); (b) Individual Clearance Procedure. Any member subject to Restoration who asserts that they were not personally involved in the capture or corruption leading to the Restoration may petition the reconstituted Watchdog Tribunal for individual clearance. The procedure shall be: (c) Petition Requirements. The petitioning former member shall file with the Tribunal within one hundred eighty (180) days of the Restoration, establishing with clear and convincing evidence: (i) the petitioner did not participate in, facilitate, or knowingly tolerate the capture conduct; (ii) the petitioner took reasonable steps consistent with their position to oppose or report the capture; and (iii) the petitioner's continued participation in this Amendment's bodies would not present ongoing risk of recurrence; (d) Tribunal Review. The reconstituted

Tribunal shall review each petition with the forensic assistance of the Academic Integrity Commission, and shall publish its findings on the Ledger. Individual clearance decisions shall be subject to citizen petition challenge under Section 17A.16; (e) Upon Clearance. A cleared former member shall have the default barring lifted and shall be eligible for future service through the ordinary selection mechanisms, with no presumption in favor of selection. Clearance does not restore the vacated position; it only removes the categorical bar; (f) Criminal Liability Preserved. Individual clearance from the categorical Restoration bar shall not affect any individual criminal liability for corruption, bribery, evidence destruction, interference under Section 13, or other criminal conduct. Where the Hamilton Contingent Prosecution Division determines that individual prosecution is warranted, clearance from the categorical bar shall not prevent prosecution;

(g) No Retaliation. Cleared former members shall be protected from retaliation or adverse treatment as if they had never been among those subject to Restoration, and the clearance finding shall serve as authoritative. Clearance decisions shall be published on the Ledger for transparency, but subsequent attempts to use the Restoration-and-clearance record against the cleared person shall constitute retaliation subject to Section 13 penalties. 17B.8 Transition Governance During Restoration — Preventing Governance Vacuum. Because the Restoration removes the entire oversight apparatus simultaneously, ordinary governance functions that depend on these bodies — such as Liberty Bell Initiative approvals, Authority audits of federal operations, and Tribunal investigations — would otherwise halt. The following transition protections apply during the seven-day Restoration-to-reconstitution period: (a) Automatic Stays. All Authority approvals, audits, and proceedings scheduled during the seven-day period shall be automatically stayed until reconstitution is complete, without any requirement of individual stay orders. Parties shall not be prejudiced by delays caused by the Restoration; (b) Hamilton Contingent Continuity. The Hamilton Contingent Prosecution Division shall continue ordinary criminal prosecutions and investigations without interruption, as its constitutional authority derives from Section 13C independently of Authority oversight. Referrals to the Authority that would occur during the Restoration period shall be held in queue until reconstitution; (c) Emergency Override Available. The Reclamation mechanism of Section 1 remains available to the People throughout any Restoration period. A No Confidence Referendum against the existing Federal Government (which is a separate matter from a Restoration of the oversight apparatus) may be initiated or continued during a

Restoration if circumstances warrant; (d) Washington Commission Residual Authority. During the seven-day period, the Washington Commission (operating under its temporarily expanded Restoration authorities per Section 17B.5) possesses the authority to: (i) protect the physical and digital infrastructure of the institutions subject to Restoration from tampering; (ii) preserve records pending their transfer to the reconstituted bodies; (iii) issue emergency orders necessary for the safety of persons or preservation of evidence; and (iv) coordinate with state governments and the Hamilton Contingent on matters arising during the transition. These expanded authorities terminate upon reconstitution completion; the Commission itself continues in its Permanent Oversight role under Section 17D; (e) No New Initiatives. No party — removed members, replacement members, the Washington Commission, or other federal bodies — shall initiate new substantive policy, operational, or personnel decisions during the seven-day period beyond those strictly necessary for the reconstitution process. The seven-day period is for orderly transition, not for taking advantage of the transition.

F. Anti-Gaming and Foundational Framework 17B.9 Anti-Gaming Provisions. To prevent the Restoration mechanism from being weaponized politically or used to destabilize legitimate oversight: (a) Threshold Integrity. The threshold requirements of Section 17B.3 are minimum requirements and shall not be reduced by any authority. Attempts to lower the threshold through interpretation, implementing regulation, or judicial construction shall constitute interference under Section 13; (b) Mandatory Cooldown. Following any certified Restoration, no subsequent Restoration petition may be initiated for a period of three (3) years, absent extraordinary circumstances determined by the reconstituted Watchdog Tribunal with clear and convincing evidence of renewed capture. This cooldown prevents cycles of successive Restorations that could paralyze governance; (c) Retaliation Protection. No person involved in initiating a good-faith Restoration petition (whether it succeeds or fails) shall be subject to retaliation, adverse action, or investigation solely for petition activity. Retaliation shall constitute Section 13 interference. Good-faith petitioners are protected even if their evidence is ultimately insufficient to achieve the threshold; (d) Frivolous Petitions. Petitions knowingly filed without factual basis, for political harassment purposes, or as coordinated campaigns unconnected to genuine evidence of capture, shall not qualify for any protections of this Section, and the petition organizers may face prosecution under Section 13 where the coordinated activity meets interference standards. Frivolous-petition determinations shall require clear and convincing evidence of bad faith and shall be reviewable by the Authority through Liberty Bell Initiative (once reconstituted) or by the Hamilton Contingent in the interim; (e) No Restoration During Active Reclamation. A Restoration petition shall not be initiated during any active No Confidence Petition period, active Reclamation Referendum period, or during the seven (7) day period following No Confidence certification. The Reclamation and Restoration mechanisms are separate sovereign acts and shall not be conducted simultaneously to avoid confusion and prevent gaming of the sovereign electoral process. 17B.10 The Restoration as Ultimate Structural Failsafe. The Restoration established in this Section, together with the accountability-chain provisions of Section 17A.19.24 through 17A.19.28, the maximum accountability stack of Section 17A.19.7, and the Reclamation mechanism of Section 1, together constitute a graduated failsafe framework with increasing sovereign intensity: (a) Individual accountability — Personal Liability Triple-Stack (Section 17A.18); (b) Body-level accountability — Maximum Accountability Stack (Section 17A.19.7);

(c) Chain-level accountability — Accountability Chain Mechanisms (Sections 17A.19.24 through 17A.19.28); (d) Apparatus-level accountability — The Restoration (this Section); (e) Government-level accountability — Reclamation through No Confidence Referendum (Section 1). (f) The People retain every level of this framework. When any level proves insufficient, the next level is available. When all institutional levels fail, the People themselves act directly through Reclamation. This framework recognizes that no institutional design is perfect, no combination of procedural safeguards can anticipate every failure mode, and the ultimate protection against corruption is the preserved sovereign authority of the People themselves. Every provision of this Amendment, from the most technical procedural rule to the most profound constitutional principle, serves this single purpose: ensuring that the People retain the ability to reclaim their government when the institutions intended to serve them have failed to do so. 17B.11 No Delay of Restoration Vote Permitted. No act of Congress, executive order, presidential proclamation, judicial ruling, state action, emergency declaration, martial law declaration, or any other federal, state, or territorial action shall delay, postpone, modify, or prevent a Restoration Vote certified under this Section. Any attempt to do so shall be void ab initio and shall have no legal force; officials administering the Vote shall proceed notwithstanding any such purported order, declaration, ruling, or action. Any such attempt shall constitute interference under Section 13, triggering the full penalties thereof, including the fifteen (15) year minimum sentence and the lifetime bar from public office without possibility of pardon. The Section 5.12.1 officials' duty-to-proceed protections shall apply to Restoration Vote administration without modification. The Restoration mechanism addresses capture of the very oversight apparatus designed to prevent capture; its undelayability is essential because the captured apparatus itself cannot be relied upon to permit its own removal.

Section 17C. Authority Accountability — Independent State-Sovereign Prosecution and Judgment

Key terms in this Section: • "State Attorneys General Prosecution Panel" — A panel of five (5) State Attorneys General drawn by randomized lottery from the Attorneys General of all Participating Jurisdictions (as defined in Section 3), tasked with prosecuting criminal cases against members of the three Authority bodies, the Watchdog Tribunal, and senior Hamilton Contingent personnel under this Section. Also referred to in this Section as "the Prosecution Panel."

• "State Supreme Court Judicial Panel" — A panel of five (5) Justices of the highest courts of Participating Jurisdictions (as defined in Section 3) drawn by randomized lottery from the full complement of sitting justices of the highest courts of all Participating Jurisdictions, tasked with presiding over, adjudicating, and sentencing criminal cases against members of the three Authority bodies, the Watchdog Tribunal, and senior Hamilton Contingent personnel. Also referred to in this Section as "the Judicial Panel." • "Covered Official" — For purposes of this Section: any member of the Citizens' Oversight Board, the State Elections Council, or the Academic Integrity Commission; any member of the Watchdog Tribunal; the Hamilton Contingent Director or any Division Chief; or any other senior Amendment-body officeholder designated by the Authority through Liberty Bell Initiative for Section 17C protection and accountability. • "Appellate Panel" — A second panel of five (5) Justices of the highest courts of Participating Jurisdictions (as defined in Section 3), drawn by randomized lottery and excluding all Justices who served on the original Judicial Panel in any given case, tasked with hearing appeals of Judicial Panel verdicts and sentences under Section 17C.10. A. Foundational Principle and Structure 17C.1 Foundational Principle of Fair State-Sovereign Accountability. Members of the three Authority bodies, the Watchdog Tribunal, and senior Hamilton Contingent personnel occupy positions of unique constitutional responsibility — overseeing the Federal Government on behalf of the People. Criminal accountability for these Covered Officials must therefore come from sources independent of both the Federal

Government they oversee and the Amendment bodies to which they belong. Ordinary federal prosecution by the Department of Justice and ordinary federal judicial review present unacceptable risks of capture in both directions: federal prosecutors appointed by a captured executive could weaponize prosecution against honest Covered Officials, while federal judges appointed by the same captured government could bias proceedings. The state-sovereign framework established in this Section solves this problem by drawing prosecutorial and judicial authority from the governments of the Participating Jurisdictions — independent of the federal government being watched and independent of the Amendment bodies being investigated — producing multi-sovereign, lottery-selected, rotating accountability that is extraordinarily difficult to capture. The framework established in this Section is narrowly tailored to the specific scenario of criminal accountability for Covered Officials whose unique constitutional responsibilities create unique capture vulnerabilities on both sides; the federal judiciary retains its ordinary Article III authority over all matters outside this narrow scenario, and nothing in this Section shall be construed as a general displacement of federal judicial review or as reflecting generalized distrust of the federal judiciary. The Amendment addresses specific structural vulnerabilities with specific structural protections; it does not replace the federal judiciary in its ordinary constitutional role. 17C.2 Three-Phase Accountability Chain. Criminal accountability for Covered Officials under this Amendment shall proceed through three distinct phases, each handled by a structurally independent body: (a) Investigation Phase. The Hamilton Contingent Prosecution Division, established under Section 13C, shall conduct criminal investigations of Covered Officials under its existing investigative authority. The Division shall have the same powers and procedural protections against interference as in all other criminal investigations under this Amendment. The Watchdog Tribunal may assist investigations with its own authority, but shall not itself prosecute Covered Officials from Authority bodies it oversees; (b) Prosecution Phase. The State Attorneys General Prosecution Panel, established under Section 17C.3, shall conduct formal prosecution of Covered Officials. The Panel operates independently of the Hamilton Contingent, the Department of Justice, and the Authority, though the Contingent may refer investigation findings to the Panel and the Panel may request additional investigation; (c) Judgment and Sentencing Phase. The State Supreme Court Judicial Panel, established under Section 17C.6, shall preside over criminal trials, render verdicts, and impose sentences. The Panel operates independently of the federal judiciary, ordinary state judicial processes, the

Authority, and the Hamilton Contingent; (d) Appellate Phase. Appeals from Judicial Panel verdicts and sentences shall be heard by the Appellate Panel under Section 17C.10, drawn from different Justices of the highest courts of Participating Jurisdictions than served on the original Judicial Panel. B. The State Attorneys General Prosecution Panel 17C.3 Composition and Selection. The State Attorneys General Prosecution Panel shall consist of five (5) state Attorneys General drawn by randomized lottery from the Pre-Certified State AG Pool maintained by the Permanent Washington Commission under Section 17D.13.1, with the following selection parameters: (a) Pre-Certified Pool Requirement. Only sitting state Attorneys General included in the current Pre-Certified State AG Pool under Section 17D.13 shall be eligible for lottery draw. Attorneys General not in the Pool at the time of draw shall be

skipped and replaced by redraw from eligible Pool members; (b) Selection Administration. The lottery shall be administered by the Academic Integrity Commission using publicly verifiable cryptographic randomization, with the algorithm, seed source, and draw results posted upon the Franklin Ledger; (c) Case-Specific Selection. A new Panel shall be drawn for each case prosecuted under this Section. The same Attorney General shall not serve on consecutive Panels, rotating accountability across the full Pre-Certified Pool; (d) Disqualification. An Attorney General shall be excluded from a particular Panel where: (i) the Covered Official being prosecuted is from the Attorney General's home state; (ii) the Attorney General has a personal or professional relationship with the Covered Official disclosed under Section 17A.6 standards; (iii) the Attorney General's state has been party to litigation materially adverse to the prosecution in the preceding ten (10) years; or (iv) the Attorney General has publicly prejudged the matter. Disqualifications trigger immediate redraw from the remaining pool; (e) Voluntary Refusal. An Attorney General drawn for a Panel may decline service under the hardship framework established in Section 17.4.13(a), which applies the full Section 17.4 framework to multi-month case-specific panels, with privacy protections for medical, caregiver, and financial hardship under Section 17.4.7 and appeal to the Watchdog Tribunal. Refusals exceeding fifteen percent (15%) across any twelve-month period shall trigger Authority review of the Panel selection process, consistent with the pattern-analysis provisions of Section 17.4.13(j); (f) Compensation. Panel Attorneys General shall receive federal compensation from the constitutional appropriation for their service on the Panel, supplemental to their state compensation, in amounts benchmarked to federal prosecutorial rates under Section 17A.8. 17C.3.1 Collaborative Working Group Model. The five

Attorneys General drawn for a specific case shall function as a collaborative prosecutorial working group, not as five isolated individual prosecutors. The Panel shall operate under the following structural principles: (a) Lead Prosecutor. The five Panel members shall select from among themselves a Lead Prosecutor for the case, by simple majority vote. The Lead Prosecutor shall manage day-to-day case operations, coordinate investigative strategy with Hamilton Contingent, serve as public-facing spokesperson for the prosecution, and represent the Panel in courtroom appearances as the other members' schedules permit. The Lead Prosecutor's individual decisions on day-to-day matters (scheduling, routine motions, non-substantive responses) do not require concurrence of the other members; (b) Substantive Decision Authority. Substantive decisions — charge filing, plea agreements, case declination, major strategic choices, and sentencing recommendations — require majority vote of the Panel (3 of 5). The Lead Prosecutor has a single vote equal to each other member; (c) Shared Coordination Infrastructure. The Panel shall operate from a shared secure coordination platform administered by the Academic Integrity Commission, enabling joint strategy sessions, secure document review, coordinated witness preparation, and collaborative drafting of pleadings. The platform shall maintain auditable logs of access and activity to ensure integrity; (d) Preserved Individual Conscience. Notwithstanding the collaborative model, each Attorney General retains the right of individual conscience. An AG who disagrees with a Panel decision shall have the right to: (i) file a dissent on the Ledger stating their specific concerns; (ii) decline to sign specific pleadings or motions with which they personally disagree (provided the Panel majority's action is not impeded); and (iii) refuse to prosecute specific theories they consider legally unfounded (with such refusal handled by assignment within the Panel, not by Panel dissolution); (e) Coordination With Hamilton Contingent. The Panel shall coordinate closely with Hamilton Contingent investigators during case preparation, but shall retain ultimate prosecutorial discretion independent of Hamilton Contingent preferences. Disagreements between the Panel and Hamilton Contingent shall be resolved in favor of Panel decisions, with Panel reasoning published on the Ledger; (f) Case-Continuity Team. Where cases extend across Biennial Rotation boundaries of the Permanent Washington Commission or across standard 12-month periods, Panel continuity is preserved — the same five AGs serve through case conclusion unless disqualifying events require replacement. The full Panel is not re-drawn mid-case. 17C.4 Authority and Duties of the Prosecution Panel. The Prosecution Panel, operating as the collaborative working group under Section

17C.3.1, shall possess the following authorities: (a) Independent Prosecutorial Authority. The Panel has full independent prosecutorial authority to file charges, present evidence, examine witnesses, argue before the Judicial Panel, and take all other actions ordinarily within prosecutorial discretion. The Panel operates free from direction by the Department of Justice, the executive branch, the Authority, or the Hamilton Contingent; (b) Charge Filing and Declination Authority. The Panel shall review Hamilton Contingent investigation findings and independently determine whether to file charges. A majority vote of the five Panel members (3 of 5) shall be required to file charges, as specified in Section 17C.3.1(b). Declinations shall be published upon the Ledger with reasoning, subject to Watchdog Tribunal review where alleged conflicts of interest exist;

(c) Plea Agreement Authority. The Panel may enter into plea agreements with defendants, subject to Judicial Panel acceptance. Plea agreements shall be published upon the Ledger with terms and reasoning; (d) Witness Subpoena Authority. The Panel shall have authority to issue witness subpoenas enforceable by the Hamilton Contingent or, where necessary, by federal marshals; (e) Evidence Access. The Panel shall have unrestricted access to all evidence gathered by the Hamilton Contingent investigation, and may request additional investigation where warranted; (f) Public Accountability. All Panel decisions shall be published upon the Franklin Ledger with reasoning, with narrow redactions only for specific law enforcement methods, witness identity protection, or active investigation integrity. 17C.5 Protection of the Prosecution Panel. Prosecution Panel members shall enjoy the following protections: (a) Federal Protection from Retaliation. Any attempt to retaliate against a Panel member for their Panel service — whether by Federal Government officials, Authority members, or any other party — shall constitute interference under Section 13 and shall be prosecuted under Section 13's full penalties; (b) Interference With Panel Service. Any attempt to bribe, threaten, intimidate, or otherwise corrupt a Panel member shall constitute a federal felony punishable by not less than twenty (20) years imprisonment with no pardon possible; (c) Secure Communications and Support. Panel members shall have access to secure communications infrastructure, legal research staff, and administrative support drawn from the Hamilton Contingent Protection Division and funded from the constitutional appropriation; (d) State-Level Non-Interference Protection. The home state of each Panel member shall not take adverse action against the Attorney General in consequence of Panel service, including but not limited to: impeachment proceedings grounded in Panel decisions; reduction of state resources to the Attorney General's office; or state-level political targeting.

Violations constitute federal interference under Section 13; (e) Post-Service Protection. For ten (10) years following Panel service, no federal or state government shall retaliate against the former Panel member. Retaliation during this period constitutes Section 13 interference. 17C.5.1 AG Panel Whistleblower Protections. Because Panel Attorneys General occupy unique positions of access to prosecutorial information, corruption evidence, and the operations of Covered Accountability Bodies, they shall enjoy enhanced whistleblower protections tailored to the Panel context. These protections supplement and do not replace the general whistleblower framework of Section

13B.16: (a) Protected Reports. A Panel AG (or former Panel AG) is protected in making a report concerning any of the following: (i) corruption, bribery, or other criminal conduct by another Panel AG, by any member of the Judicial Panel, by any member of the Appellate Panel, by Hamilton Contingent personnel, or by any Covered Official being prosecuted; (ii) attempts by any person or entity to interfere with Panel service, including threats, bribes, or coercion; (iii) conduct by federal or state officials that appears intended to obstruct the Panel's prosecutorial work; (iv) weaknesses in the Pre-Certified Pool vetting framework that permit compromised individuals to serve on Panels; or (v) any other conduct materially affecting the integrity of the Section 17C accountability framework; (b) Protected Reporting Channels. A Panel AG may make a protected report through any of the following channels: (i) directly to the Permanent Washington Commission under Section 17D; (ii) directly to the Hamilton Contingent Protection Division under Section 13C; (iii) directly to the Watchdog Tribunal under Section 21; (iv) through the Section 13B.16 general whistleblower framework; or (v) publicly upon the Franklin Ledger where urgent and where internal channels are themselves compromised or suspected to be compromised; (c) Immediate Protection Upon Report. Upon making a protected report through any authorized channel, the reporting Panel AG shall be protected from retaliation by any party, and shall receive: (i) secure communications infrastructure if not already provided; (ii) physical protection through Hamilton Contingent Protection Division where credible threat exists; (iii) legal counsel funded from the constitutional appropriation; and (iv) expedited removal from the case-specific Panel if the report concerns fellow Panel members, with replacement drawn from the Pre-Certified Pool; (d) Criminal Penalties for Retaliation. Any person — state or federal official, Amendment-body member, private party, or other — who retaliates against a Panel AG for a protected report shall be guilty of a federal felony punishable by not less than twenty (20) years imprisonment, with no pardon possible.

Retaliation includes but is not limited to: employment consequences in the AG's home state; professional retaliation through bar associations; financial attacks; personal threats; political campaigns of personal destruction; or any other adverse action connected to the protected report; (e) Presumption of Good Faith. Panel AG reports are presumed made in good faith unless clear and convincing evidence establishes knowing falsity with malicious intent. Ordinary good-faith mistakes in reporting, or reports that ultimately prove unfounded but were made on reasonable belief, shall not subject the reporting AG to any penalty or adverse consequence; (f) Identity Protection. Where feasible consistent with due process requirements of any resulting investigation or prosecution, the Panel AG's identity as a whistleblower shall be protected, using techniques similar to those available under Section 13B.16(a) and (d). Where identity disclosure is ultimately required, the AG shall receive enhanced protection under subsection (c); (g) Post-Service Whistleblower Rights. Former Panel AGs retain full whistleblower protections for life regarding any matters they observed during their Panel service. Retaliation against former Panel AGs for post-service disclosures about Panel-era matters constitutes federal felony interference, prosecutable at any time without statute of limitations; (h) Cross-Panel Reporting. Panel AGs may report concerns about Judicial Panel or Appellate Panel conduct. Judicial Panel and Appellate Panel Justices shall have reciprocal whistleblower rights for reports about Prosecution Panel conduct, with the same protections applying to Justices as to AGs under this subsection. C. The State Supreme Court Judicial Panel 17C.6 Composition and Selection. The State Supreme Court Judicial Panel shall consist of five (5) Justices of the highest courts of Participating Jurisdictions (as defined in Section 3) drawn by randomized lottery from the Pre-Certified State Supreme Court Justice Pool maintained by the Permanent Washington Commission under Section 17D.13.1, with the following selection parameters: (a) Pre-Certified Pool Requirement. Only sitting Justices of the highest courts of Participating Jurisdictions included in the current Pre-Certified Pool under Section 17D.13 shall be eligible for lottery draw. Justices not in the Pool at the time of draw shall be skipped and replaced by redraw from eligible Pool members; (b) Selection Administration. The lottery shall be administered by the Academic Integrity Commission using publicly verifiable cryptographic randomization, with algorithm, seed source, and results posted upon the Franklin Ledger; (c) Case-Specific Selection. A new Judicial Panel shall be drawn for each case. No Justice shall serve on consecutive Panels, rotating accountability across the full Pre-Certified Pool; (d) Geographic Diversity Requirement. The five Justices selected shall represent five different states. Where two Justices from the same state are drawn, the later-drawn Justice shall be replaced by redraw until five distinct states are represented; (e) Disqualification. A Justice shall be excluded from a particular Panel where: (i) the Covered Official being tried is from the Justice's home state; (ii) the Justice has a personal or professional relationship with any Panel prosecutor, defense counsel, or the Covered Official; (iii) the Justice has publicly prejudged the matter; (iv) the Justice served on any prior Amendment-related panel involving the same underlying conduct. Disqualifications trigger redraw;

(f) Voluntary Refusal. Justices may decline service under the hardship framework established in Section 17.4.13(a), which applies the full Section 17.4 framework to multi-month case-specific panels, with privacy protections for medical, caregiver, and financial hardship under Section 17.4.7 and appeal to the Watchdog Tribunal; (g) Presiding Justice. The Justices drawn shall elect a Presiding Justice from among themselves for administrative purposes. The Presiding Justice's vote carries no extra weight in substantive decisions. 17C.7 Authority and Duties of the Judicial Panel. The Judicial Panel shall possess the authorities of an Article III trial court for Amendment-body prosecution cases, including: (a) Pre-Trial Authority. Rule on motions, set trial schedules, issue protective orders, manage discovery, approve or reject plea agreements, and conduct all other pre-trial functions ordinarily exercised by federal trial courts; (b) Trial Authority. Preside over trials, rule on evidentiary matters, instruct juries where juries are empaneled, accept verdicts, and conduct all other trial functions; (c) Jury Empanelment. Defendants retain the right to trial by jury under the Sixth Amendment. Juries shall be drawn from the pool of United States citizens residing in the jurisdiction where the alleged offenses occurred, through procedures equivalent to federal jury selection. Alternatively, defendants may waive jury trial in favor of panel-decided trial; (d) Verdict by Majority. Where the Panel sits as fact-finder (in jury-waived trials), verdicts shall be rendered by majority vote of the five Panel members (3 of 5). Where juries decide factual questions, the Panel rules on legal matters; (e) Sentencing Authority. Upon conviction, the Panel shall impose sentences within the ranges established by this Amendment (Sections 13, 13A, 13B, 17A.18, or other applicable sections) or by federal criminal law, whichever is applicable. Sentences shall be published upon the Ledger with written reasoning; (f) Post-Conviction Motions. The Panel shall rule on post-conviction motions, including motions for new trial, for judgment notwithstanding the verdict, and similar relief. 17C.8 Protection of the Judicial Panel. Judicial Panel Justices shall enjoy protections equivalent to those of the Prosecution Panel under Section 17C.5, including federal protection from retaliation, twenty-year felony penalties for interference, secure communications, state-level non-interference protection, and ten-year post-service protection. D. Procedural Framework 17C.9 Trial Procedural Standards. Trials before the Judicial Panel shall follow procedural standards ensuring fair process to defendants while protecting the integrity of Amendment prosecutions: (a) Defendant Rights. Covered Officials tried under this Section shall have full procedural rights equivalent to those enjoyed by defendants in federal criminal proceedings, including: (i) right to counsel, with court-appointed counsel provided at no cost where the defendant cannot afford private counsel; (ii) right to confront adverse witnesses; (iii) right to subpoena favorable witnesses; (iv) right against self-incrimination; (v) right to jury trial under subsection 17C.7(c); (vi) presumption of innocence and requirement of proof beyond a reasonable doubt; (vii) protection from double jeopardy; (b) Burden and Standards of Proof. The Prosecution Panel shall bear the burden of proving each element of charged offenses beyond a reasonable doubt. The Judicial Panel shall apply federal evidence rules adapted as necessary for Amendment-specific contexts; (c) Public Proceedings. All trial proceedings shall be public and livestreamed upon the Franklin Ledger, with narrow closure only for witness identity protection, national security matters certified as such under established procedures, or specific due process concerns requiring limited closure; (d) Venue. Trials shall be conducted at a venue selected by the Judicial Panel, typically at a highest-court facility of a neutral Participating Jurisdiction, with secure proceedings and public access; (e) Pre-Trial Detention. Pre-trial detention determinations shall apply federal bail standards, with the Panel determining risk of flight, danger to the community, and risk of evidence tampering. Covered Officials facing pre-trial detention shall not simultaneously retain their Authority, Tribunal, or Hamilton Contingent positions; suspension from position shall be automatic upon pre-trial detention order. 17C.9.1 Pre-Trial Detention Framework for Section 17C Prosecutions. Because Section 17C prosecutions involve defendants who may possess significant resources, political networks, and — in the case of federal officials prosecuted under Section 17C.15 — potential foreign connections implicating flight risk, and because fair administration of Amendment accountability requires clear pre-trial detention standards that protect both defendants' due process rights and the integrity of Amendment prosecutions, the following framework shall apply to all prosecutions conducted under this Section: (a) Presumption of Release. Every defendant charged under this

Section is presumed innocent and shall be released pending trial unless the Judicial Panel finds, by clear and convincing evidence at a detention hearing under subsection (d), that specific statutory grounds for detention under subsection (c) exist; (b) Release with Conditions. Where release is ordered, the Judicial Panel may impose conditions reasonably necessary to assure appearance at trial and protect the integrity of the prosecution, including but not limited to: (i) execution of a bail bond in an amount commensurate with the defendant's assets and the seriousness of the charges, with bail scaled to recovered

or recoverable assets under Section 13D where applicable; (ii) surrender of United States passport and all foreign passports to the Judicial Panel clerk, with notification to relevant foreign governments that the defendant's travel documents are surrendered; (iii) electronic monitoring through GPS or equivalent technology; (iv) home confinement, with permitted absences for medical care, counsel meetings, religious observance, and court proceedings; (v) restrictions on travel beyond a specified geographic area; (vi) prohibition on contact with specific witnesses, co-defendants, or potential co-conspirators; (vii) prohibition on use of classified or sensitive federal information systems; (viii) drug or alcohol testing where relevant; (ix) any other condition reasonably tailored to the specific risks presented; (c) Grounds for Pre-Trial Detention. The Judicial Panel may order pre-trial detention only upon clear and convincing evidence of one or more of the following: (i) Flight Risk. Substantial risk that the defendant will not appear at trial, considering factors including: access to private aircraft or other non-commercial transportation; foreign citizenship or residency rights; undisclosed foreign financial assets; prior pattern of non-appearance in other proceedings; specific evidence of flight planning; and for defendants in Section 22 foreign interference prosecutions, documented relationships with foreign governments or their agents. Flight risk shall not be presumed solely from the defendant's wealth or prominence; (ii) Danger to Community. Substantial risk that release would endanger specific identifiable persons or the community generally, considering the nature of the charges, prior pattern of violence or threats, access to weapons, and specific evidence of ongoing dangerous conduct. Political speech, advocacy, or criticism of the Amendment shall not constitute danger to community; (iii) Obstruction of Justice. Substantial risk that release would result in witness intimidation, evidence destruction or tampering, flight-assistance to co-defendants, or other obstruction of the prosecution, considering specific evidence of such conduct already undertaken or specifically planned; (iv) Active Refusal. The defendant is currently refusing to vacate federal office under Section 13E and has not voluntarily ceased Refusal as of the detention hearing. Release of an active Refusing Official pending trial would defeat the purpose of Section 13E enforcement. This ground sunsets upon the defendant's documented cessation of Refusal and vacation of contested office; (v) Foreign Sanctuary Risk. Specific evidence that the defendant has received or sought offers of foreign sanctuary, safe passage, or foreign citizenship from any foreign government or its agents, particularly where such offers come from governments implicated in Section 22 foreign interference investigations. This ground applies whether or not the defendant's foreign connections were previously disclosed; (d) Detention Hearing Procedures. A detention hearing shall be held within seventy-two (72) hours of the defendant's arrest or, where the defendant has not been arrested, within seventy-two (72) hours of the defendant's initial appearance before the Judicial Panel. The hearing shall provide: (i) right to counsel, with counsel of the defendant's choice or, where the defendant cannot afford counsel, appointed counsel compensated through the constitutional appropriation under Section 11.3; (ii) right to be present, with narrow exceptions for security circumstances documented and reviewable; (iii) right to present evidence, including witness testimony, documentary evidence, and character evidence; (iv) right to cross-examine prosecution witnesses; (v) right to written findings of fact and conclusions of law supporting any detention order; (vi) livestream of the hearing on the provisional public ledger or Franklin Ledger unless the Judicial Panel finds by majority vote that specific security considerations require narrow livestream redaction, with such redactions subject to review under Section 4A transparency standards; (e) Detention Review. Any pre-trial detention order shall be reviewed by the Judicial Panel no less frequently than every thirty (30) days, with the prosecution bearing continuing burden to establish that detention grounds under subsection (c) continue to exist. Any defendant held in pre-trial detention may petition for release at any time upon material change in circumstances, with the Panel ruling within seven (7) days of petition filing. Denial of release petitions shall be appealable to the Appellate Panel under Section 17C.10 procedures; (f) Speedy Trial Guarantee. Trials under this Section shall commence within the following timelines from the earlier of (A) the filing of formal charges by the Prosecution Panel, or (B) the initial appearance of the defendant before the Judicial Panel: (i) Detained Defendants: Within one hundred twenty (120) days, with Judicial Panel authority to extend by up to sixty (60) days upon written finding of good cause published on the Ledger and consented to by the defendant or determined necessary despite the defendant's objection based on specific documented prosecution complexity; (ii) Released Defendants: Within two hundred forty (240) days, with extensions available under the same good cause standard; (iii) Good Cause Factors: May include unusual case complexity, foreign evidence requirements, translation needs, defendant-requested continuance, unavailability of witnesses despite diligent effort, or case consolidation. Good cause shall NOT include prosecution inconvenience, resource constraints that could be addressed, or generalized policy concerns about pace of prosecutions; (iv) Consequences of Timeline Violation: Where a detained defendant's trial fails to commence within the applicable timeline including authorized extensions, the defendant shall be released pending trial with conditions under subsection (b), with the Prosecution Panel retaining authority to proceed with the trial and seek re-detention only upon specific new evidence of grounds under subsection (c). Where a released defendant's trial fails to commence within the applicable timeline, the defendant may petition for dismissal of charges, which the Judicial Panel may grant with prejudice where prosecution delay is found to prejudice the defense or to constitute willful failure to prosecute; (g) Conditions of Confinement. Defendants held in pre-trial detention under this Section shall be held under conditions meeting the following standards: (i) Facility. At state Department of Corrections facilities designated by the Judicial Panel under Section 17C.15(g), with federal Bureau of Prisons facilities excluded where federal executive control creates release-risk or access-risk concerns. Geographic dispersal across multiple facilities shall be preferred to prevent concentration of Amendment defendants at any single site; (ii) Humane Treatment. Conditions meeting all Eighth Amendment requirements, ordinary state DOC standards for pre-trial detainees, and

the following specific protections: adequate food, shelter, medical care, mental health care, hygiene, and exercise; protection from physical and sexual violence by staff or other inmates; protection against retaliation for filing grievances; (iii) Access to Counsel. Unrestricted access to defense counsel including confidential communications (telephone, video, in-person), confidential mail, and confidential review of evidence. Counsel access shall not be conditioned on facility convenience or staffing, and any denial of counsel access shall be immediately remediable through emergency Judicial Panel order; (iv) Family Contact. Reasonable visitation and communication with family members, subject only to specific security restrictions documented and reviewable. Defendants shall not be isolated from family contact as a form of pressure to plead or cooperate; (v) Safety from Retaliation. Because Amendment defendants may face unusual retaliation risks in general population — whether from other inmates politically opposed to the former official or from former political allies seeking to silence potential cooperators — the facility shall provide protective custody upon defendant request or Judicial Panel order, without such custody constituting punitive confinement; (vi) Access to Ledger. Defendants shall retain access to the Franklin Ledger and provisional public ledger for purposes of following their own proceedings and the proceedings of co-defendants, with such access not constituting ordinary "internet access" for purposes of any facility restriction on internet use; (vii) Preservation of Constitutional Rights. All constitutional rights not necessarily restricted by detention shall be preserved, including First Amendment rights (with reasonable facility restrictions), religious observance, voting (where state law permits for pre-trial detainees), and legal self-representation where chosen; (viii) Conditions Review. Any defendant may petition the Judicial Panel for relief from specific detention conditions violating subsection (g), with review within fourteen (14) days of petition; (h) Flight and Sanctuary Protocols. Where specific evidence indicates foreign government offers of sanctuary, safe passage, or citizenship to a defendant or potential defendant: (i) Enhanced Monitoring. The Judicial Panel may order enhanced monitoring including continuous GPS tracking, daily check-ins, and coordination with the State Department for passport and visa monitoring across all jurisdictions where the defendant holds travel documents; (ii) Extradition Framework. Where a defendant flees to foreign jurisdiction notwithstanding release conditions or detention, the State Attorneys General Council coordinating with Hamilton Contingent (upon operational capability) shall pursue extradition through existing treaties and, where necessary, the Authority may through Liberty Bell Initiative declare the foreign sanctuary to itself constitute foreign interference under Section 22, triggering diplomatic and economic consequences under applicable federal law; (iii) In Absentia Proceedings. Where a defendant who received proper notice and opportunity to appear flees the United States and cannot be extradited within a reasonable time, the Judicial Panel may, by majority vote and with specific written findings published on the Franklin Ledger, conduct trial in absentia. In absentia proceedings require the highest standards of procedural protection including: appointed counsel of the defendant's prior choice where known, or alternative appointed counsel; full evidentiary presentation; unanimous verdict requirement; and automatic right to re-trial upon the defendant's subsequent return to United States jurisdiction.

Asset recovery under Section 13D shall proceed independent of any in absentia criminal determination; (i) Capacity and Volume Management. Because Section 17C prosecutions may involve substantial simultaneous volume (particularly following No Confidence certification), the following capacity management shall apply: (i) Multiple Judicial Panels. Where case volume exceeds the capacity of a single Judicial Panel, additional Judicial Panels may be constituted under Section 17C.6 selection procedures, with each Panel conducting independent proceedings. Up to five (5) concurrent Judicial Panels may operate simultaneously under ordinary conditions. During Surge Periods — defined as the two (2) year period following any No Confidence Referendum certification under Section 5 or Inaugural Referendum passage under Section 19A, or any other period the Permanent Washington Commission under Section 17D certifies by majority vote requires expanded capacity based on documented case volume — up to ten (10) concurrent Judicial Panels may operate simultaneously. Where Surge Period capacity remains insufficient, the Permanent Washington Commission may by Liberty Bell Initiative equivalent (five (5) of seven (7) Chief Justices concurring) authorize additional Panels beyond ten (10) upon specific findings of continuing volume necessity, published on the Ledger, with Panel composition continuing to meet Section 17C.6 selection parameters including Jurisdictional diversity requirements. Case assignment across all concurrent Panels shall proceed by randomized allocation to prevent defendants from steering their cases; (ii) Multiple Prosecution Panels. Where case volume exceeds the capacity of a single Prosecution Panel, additional Prosecution Panels may be constituted under Section 17C.3 selection procedures, with case allocation coordinated to prevent duplicative prosecution; (iii) Case Prioritization. Prosecutions shall be prioritized by: (A) Refusing Officials under Section 13E; (B) Section 22 foreign interference defendants with flight risk; (C) Senior Officials with largest Benefit Received under Section 13A; (D) defendants facing most serious charges; (E) defendants whose evidence would materially assist other prosecutions if cooperation is offered. Prioritization shall be documented on the Franklin Ledger; (iv) State DOC Capacity. Where state DOC capacity is insufficient for volume of detained defendants, the Judicial Panel may designate alternative state-sovereign detention facilities, utilize private correctional facilities operated under state contract with Amendment-specific oversight, or establish temporary detention infrastructure through Ratification Loan funding under Section 13I.4. State DOC costs for housing Amendment defendants shall be reimbursed through the constitutional appropriation under Section 11.3 at rates no less than ordinary federal per-diem rates; (j) Federal Executive Non-Interference. No President, Vice President, Cabinet officer, federal agency head, or other federal executive officeholder shall direct, fund, influence, or impede detention determinations, conditions of confinement, or speedy trial administration under this Section. Any such interference shall constitute Section 13 interference with Senior Official

multipliers where applicable, prosecutable under the Section 17C framework itself; (k) Funding. All costs of pre-trial detention, conditions of confinement, detention hearings, and speedy trial administration under this Section shall be funded through the constitutional appropriation under Section 11.3 or through the Ratification Loan under Section 13I.4 during the Amendment's initial implementation period. No state shall bear financial burden for Amendment-related pre-trial detention; federal constitutional funding covers the full operational cost. 17C.10 Appeals. Verdicts and sentences of the Judicial Panel may be appealed to the Appellate Panel under the following procedures: (a) Appellate Panel Composition. The Appellate Panel shall consist of five (5) Justices of the highest courts of Participating Jurisdictions drawn by lottery, excluding all Justices who served on the original Judicial Panel in the case, and excluding all Justices from the same Participating Jurisdiction as any original Panel member. The Appellate Panel shall represent five different Participating Jurisdictions, none overlapping with the Jurisdictions of the original Judicial Panel; (b) Appeal Rights. The convicted defendant shall have full appellate rights including appeal of verdicts on grounds of: insufficient evidence; procedural error; legal error; ineffective assistance of counsel; prosecutorial misconduct; or other traditional appellate grounds; (c) Prosecution Appeals. The Prosecution Panel may appeal acquittals only on procedural or legal grounds, not on re-examination of factual findings, consistent with Double Jeopardy Clause protections; (d) Appellate Standards. The Appellate Panel shall apply federal appellate standards of review. Factual findings shall be reviewed for clear error; legal determinations de novo; sentencing for abuse of discretion; (e) Final Appellate Decisions. Appellate Panel decisions shall be final within the Amendment framework, with the sole further recourse being petition to the United States Supreme Court on federal constitutional grounds, subject to certiorari discretion. The Appellate Panel shall not itself be subject to appeal by state-supreme-court-panel review. E. Scope and Coordination 17C.11 Scope of Jurisdiction. The Section 17C framework governs criminal accountability of Covered Officials as defined in the Section Key. Covered Officials shall not be prosecuted under this Section for conduct outside their Amendment-body service, which shall continue to be handled by ordinary federal or state criminal processes. Conversely, ordinary federal and state criminal processes shall not prosecute Covered Officials for conduct within their Amendment-body service; such conduct falls exclusively within Section 17C jurisdiction. Where conduct is ambiguous, the Prosecution Panel and Judicial Panel shall, by majority vote, determine jurisdictional scope with published reasoning.

17C.12 Coordination with Other Accountability Mechanisms. The Section 17C criminal accountability framework operates in parallel with, not as a replacement for, the other accountability mechanisms of this Amendment: (a) Restoration Under Section 17B. The Restoration mechanism removes Covered Officials from their positions based on sovereign citizen action; Section 17C imposes criminal penalties based on individual guilt. Both mechanisms may proceed simultaneously or sequentially against the same Covered Official without constituting double jeopardy, as one addresses institutional replacement and the other addresses individual criminal culpability; (b) Personal Liability Triple-Stack Under Section 17A.18. The Section 17A.18 framework for Gross Waste operates in parallel with Section 17C. Gross Waste prosecutions under this Section follow §17C procedures; civil and administrative consequences under §17A.18 proceed on their own tracks; (c) Reclamation Under Section 1. Reclamation targets the Federal Government; Section 17C targets Covered Officials from Amendment bodies. These are mutually exclusive subject matters operating in parallel tracks; (d) Civil Recovery Under Sections 13A and 13D. Civil forfeiture and asset recovery under Sections 13A and 13D proceed independently of Section 17C criminal process. Civil and criminal proceedings against the same Covered Official for the same underlying conduct are permitted. 17C.13 Anti-Capture Protections for Section 17C Framework. Because the Section 17C framework itself is a potential target of capture attempts, the following protections apply to the framework as a whole: (a) Constitutional Appropriation. All funding for Prosecution Panel, Judicial Panel, Appellate Panel, and supporting infrastructure shall flow automatically through the constitutional appropriation under Section 11.3, without congressional control or executive intermediation; (b) No Federal Interference. No act of Congress, executive order, judicial ruling, or federal agency action shall: limit the jurisdiction of Section 17C; impose procedural restrictions outside this Amendment; condition funding on particular outcomes; direct Panel selection; or otherwise interfere with the framework's operation. Violations constitute interference under Section 13; (c) No Jurisdictional Interference. Where individual Participating Jurisdictions attempt to impede their Attorneys General or Justices of their highest courts from Section 17C service, such impediment constitutes federal interference under

Section 13. Jurisdictional governments shall be required to facilitate, not obstruct,

Panel service by their officers; (d) Article V Protection. The Section 17C framework shall be protected under the Article V protection established in Sections 18.6.1 and 18.6.2, beyond ordinary legislative, executive, or judicial alteration.

17C.14 Foundational Commitment. The fair accountability of Covered Officials is not a luxury of this Amendment; it is essential to the Amendment's legitimacy. Officials charged with overseeing the Federal Government must themselves face accountability when they violate their duties, and that accountability must come from sources independent of both the Government they oversee and the Bodies to which they belong. By drawing prosecution from the Attorneys General of the Participating Jurisdictions and judgment from Justices of the highest courts of Participating Jurisdictions through randomized lottery, this Section creates multi-sovereign accountability that protects both the People from corrupt watchdogs and the watchdogs from corrupt Government. No captured President can direct prosecution against honest Amendment officials; no captured Amendment body can shield its corrupt members from justice. The Framers of this Amendment understood that accountability machinery, to be just, must be difficult to weaponize, difficult to corrupt, and impossible to monopolize. This Section embodies that understanding. 17C.15 Extension to Federal Officials Prosecuted Under Amendment Provisions. Because this Amendment activates in response to federal corruption that may include captured federal judicial infrastructure, and because prosecution of corrupt federal officials in courts they may have influenced presents structural capture risk, the §17C framework shall extend to prosecutions of federal officials under the following framework: (a) Scope of Extended §17C Jurisdiction. The Prosecution Panel and Judicial Panel framework under Sections 17C.3 through 17C.10 shall apply to prosecutions of federal officials for: (i) Section 13 interference offenses, including all Senior Official multipliers; (ii) Section 13E Refusing Official offenses; (iii) Section 16.5 military oath violations; (iv) Section 22 foreign interference offenses; (v) Section 24 post-Amendment corruption offenses; and (vi) any other offense specifically created by this Amendment where the defendant is a sitting or former federal official; (b) Ordinary Federal Jurisdiction Preserved. Federal offenses unrelated to this Amendment (including conventional criminal offenses committed by federal officials that do not involve Amendment provisions) shall continue to be prosecuted through ordinary federal courts with ordinary federal procedures. The §17C extension under this Section is limited to Amendment-specific prosecutions and shall not displace ordinary federal jurisdiction over non-Amendment offenses; (c) Jurisdictional Determination. Where a prosecution involves both Amendment-related and ordinary federal offenses, the Prosecution Panel shall determine, by majority vote, whether the Amendment-related nexus is sufficient to warrant §17C jurisdiction over the entire case or whether the cases should be severed between §17C and ordinary federal courts. Determinations shall be published with reasoning on the provisional public ledger during Phase One or the Franklin Ledger thereafter; (d) Phase One Application. During Phase One, before the §17C framework is fully operational, State Attorneys General Council prosecutions under Section 19.5.0.5.2 may proceed in ordinary federal courts where judicial independence is demonstrably maintained, or may petition the Washington Commission for transfer to alternate venue at highest-court facility of a Participating Jurisdiction where federal court hostility is documented. The Washington Commission shall make venue transfer determinations by majority vote (four of seven Chief Justices), with supporting evidence published on the provisional public ledger; (e) Sunset and Restoration Clause. The extension of §17C jurisdiction under this Section shall remain in effect until such time as the Authority, through Liberty Bell Initiative, certifies that federal judicial infrastructure has been reliably restored such that ordinary federal prosecution of Amendment-related offenses can proceed without capture risk. Certification shall require clear and convincing evidence including: absence of systematic federal judicial loyalty to any prior captured administration; demonstrated independent decision-making in Amendment-related cases tried under §17C; and sustained operational independence of federal judiciary over a period not less than three (3) years. Upon certification, subsequent Amendment-related prosecutions may proceed in either §17C or ordinary federal courts, with Prosecution Panel discretion to select venue based on case-specific factors; (f) Defendant Protections During Transition. Defendants tried under extended §17C jurisdiction shall enjoy all due process protections of Section 17C.9, including right to counsel, jury trial, presumption of innocence, beyond-reasonable-doubt standard, and full appellate rights under Section 17C.10. No defendant shall be disadvantaged by the choice of §17C over ordinary federal jurisdiction; the protections and standards are equivalent or greater; (g) Pre-Trial Detention Venue. Pre-trial detention of

federal officials tried under extended §17C jurisdiction shall occur at secure state-sovereign facilities designated by the Judicial Panel, typically state Department of Corrections facilities operating under state constitutional protections. Federal Bureau of Prisons facilities shall not be used where federal executive control creates release-risk or access-risk concerns. Defendants shall have full legal representation access regardless of detention location; (h) Federal Executive Non-Interference. No President, Vice President, Cabinet officer, federal agency head, or other federal executive officeholder shall direct, fund, influence, or impede Section 17C.15 prosecutions, venue determinations, or pre-trial detention arrangements. Any such interference shall constitute Section 13 interference with Senior Official multipliers where applicable, prosecutable under the §17C framework itself and subject to enhanced penalties under Section 21.9 for interference with constitutional accountability mechanisms.
17C.16 Recusal and Disqualification Framework for §17C Panels. Recognizing that fair administration of §17C prosecutions requires explicit recusal procedures for the Justices and Attorneys General who serve on the State Supreme Court Judicial Panel under Section 17C.6, the State Attorneys General Prosecution Panel under Section 17C.3, the Appellate Panel under Section 17C.10, and other §17C bodies, and recognizing that the Amendment's silence on recusal would create litigation invitations and risk procedural reversals undermining §17C convictions, and recognizing further that the Amendment's commitment to randomized lottery selection of panel members under Section 17C.6 (Judicial Panel), Section 17C.3 (Prosecution Panel), and Section 17C.10 (Appellate Panel) reflects the

constitutional judgment that random draw from broad-Jurisdictional pools produces structurally impartial panels superior to party-selected panels, and that this lottery integrity must be protected against strategic veto over random composition through challenges-without-cause, the following recusal framework applies to all §17C panel proceedings: (a) Foundational Principle. §17C panel members shall recuse from any specific case or matter in which their impartiality might reasonably be questioned. The recusal standard is the ordinary federal judicial standard codified at 28 U.S.C. § 455 as it existed at Ratification, applied with attention to the specific structural realities of §17C panels. Recusal protects the Amendment's legitimacy; it is not a tool for case manipulation, party advantage, or strategic veto over lottery-drawn panel composition; (b) Mandatory Recusal Grounds. A panel member shall recuse, without need for motion, where any of the following apply: (i) Personal Bias or Prejudice. The panel member has a personal bias or prejudice concerning a defendant or material witness, or personal knowledge of disputed evidentiary facts concerning the proceeding; (ii) Prior Involvement. The panel member previously served as counsel to a defendant or material witness; previously served as a material witness; or participated as a judge in a prior phase of the same matter, including (for Judicial Panel members) any role in the underlying Hamilton Contingent investigation or Prosecution Panel charge filing; (iii) Family Relationship. The panel member, the panel member's spouse, or any individual within the third degree of relationship to either, is a party, defendant, witness, attorney, or other person whose interests would be substantially affected by the proceeding outcome; (iv) Financial Interest. The panel member or the panel member's spouse holds a financial interest in the proceeding outcome, including any holding affected by the proceeding's asset-recovery or sanction provisions, or any holding in an entity that is a defendant under Section 13A.7 entity liability or a related party; (v) Documented Public Statement. The panel member has, within the five (5) years preceding case assignment, made a documented public statement specifically expressing opinion about the merits of the proceeding, the credibility of the defendant, or the validity of the Amendment provision under which prosecution proceeds; ordinary scholarly commentary on legal questions does not constitute mandatory recusal grounds, but specific case-related public commentary does; (vi) Foreign Government Connection. The panel member has, within the five (5) years preceding case assignment, received compensation from, served as agent of, or maintained substantial financial interests connected to a foreign government implicated in the proceeding under Section 22; (c) Voluntary Recusal. Where a panel member becomes aware of circumstances that might reasonably cause others to question their impartiality but that fall short of mandatory recusal grounds, the panel member should disclose the circumstances and may voluntarily recuse. Voluntary recusal shall not constitute admission of disqualifying conflict; it shall reflect ordinary judicial caution; (d) Disclosure Obligation. Each panel member, upon assignment to a specific case, shall complete a written disclosure regarding the case identifying any potential recusal grounds known to the member. The disclosure shall be filed with the Permanent Washington Commission under Section 17D.13.1 and made available to the parties through ordinary discovery channels, with sealed disclosure of personal financial details under Section 17.4.7 privacy protections; (e) No Peremptory Challenges. Consistent with the Amendment's commitment to randomized lottery selection of panel members and recognizing the documented federal jurisprudential concerns regarding peremptory challenges as vehicles for discriminatory exclusion (see, by way of analogy, the line of authority beginning with Batson v. Kentucky, 476 U.S. 79 (1986), and its progeny addressing race-based, gender-based, and other invidious uses of peremptory challenges), no party shall have a right to peremptorily challenge any §17C panel member without cause. All challenges to panel composition must proceed under the for-cause framework of subsection (f), grounded in the recusal grounds enumerated in subsection (b). The structural impartiality of randomly-drawn panels is itself the protection against partial adjudication; superimposing party veto over random composition would partially defeat the lottery's anti-capture purpose; (f) For-Cause Challenge. Either party may challenge a panel member for cause based on the recusal grounds enumerated in subsection (b) at any point during proceedings, with such challenges to be resolved within seven (7) days of filing. For-cause challenges shall be filed in writing with specific factual basis. There is no numerical limit on for-cause challenges, but bad-faith for-cause challenges intended to delay proceedings or to achieve through procedural attrition what subsection (e) prohibits in direct form (peremptory challenge of disfavored members) shall be sanctionable under Section 17C.9 procedural standards, with the Permanent Washington Commission empowered under subsection (i) pattern analysis to identify and address such conduct; (g) Who Decides Recusal Challenges. Recusal challenges shall be decided as follows: (i) Self-Recusal. The challenged panel member may self-recuse upon any challenge, ending the matter without further inquiry; (ii) Initial Determination. Where the challenged member declines to self-recuse, the remaining members of the same panel shall determine the recusal challenge by majority vote of the non-challenged members. The challenged member shall not vote on their own recusal; (iii) Appeal of Recusal Determination. The losing party on a recusal challenge may appeal the determination to the Permanent Washington Commission under Section 17D, which shall rule within seven (7) days. Permanent Washington Commission rulings on recusal are final, subject only to subsection (h) review; (h) Watchdog Tribunal Review. The Watchdog Tribunal under Section 21 may, on its own motion or upon party petition, review any recusal determination it finds suggests bad-faith refusal to recuse, bad-faith granting of recusal as a tool for panel manipulation, or pattern of recusal practice that indicates structural capture of §17C panel composition. Tribunal review shall be conducted by majority vote with findings published on the Franklin Ledger; (i) Pattern Analysis. The Permanent Washington Commission shall conduct ongoing pattern analysis of recusal practice across all §17C panels, identifying: for-cause challenge patterns suggesting strategic use as a substitute for prohibited peremptory challenges (including challenges concentrated against panel members of specific demographic, geographic, or professional characteristics); recusal grants concentrated among

specific panel members suggesting either capture (selectively recusing favorable members) or harassment (forcing recusal of disfavored members); and other patterns warranting investigation. Pattern findings shall be published on the Franklin Ledger; (j) Replacement Process. When a panel member is recused (by mandatory ground, voluntary recusal, or for-cause grant), replacement shall proceed through the same lottery procedure that selected the original member, with: (i) the replacement drawn from the same Pre-Certified Pool under Section 17D.13.1; (ii) the replacement subject to the same recusal framework, including the parties' right to challenge the replacement for cause; (iii) panel proceedings paused pending replacement seating, with reasonable expedition consistent with Section 17C.9.1 speedy trial requirements; (iv) the replacement granted reasonable time to review case materials before resumption of proceedings, ordinarily not less than fourteen (14) days; (k) Cumulative Recusal Limit. To prevent recusal abuse, where cumulative recusals (mandatory plus voluntary plus for-cause) on a single panel reach three (3) total recusals across the panel's composition (in the case of a five-member Judicial Panel), the Permanent Washington Commission shall conduct mandatory review of the recusal pattern to determine whether good-faith fair-trial concerns justify continued recusal-driven panel reconstitution or whether the pattern indicates strategic abuse warranting Section 13 interference investigation. Where the Permanent Washington Commission finds the pattern to reflect good-faith concerns, recusal-driven reconstitution may continue; where the Commission finds strategic abuse, the underlying for-cause challenges driving the pattern shall be denied with reasoned explanation published on the Franklin Ledger, the proceedings shall continue with the panel as constituted, and the abusing party shall be subject to Section 17C.9 procedural sanctions. The cap of three (3) reflects the recognition that a five-member Judicial Panel reduced below three sitting members can no longer fairly conduct proceedings; the cap is not a procedural cliff but a trigger for Permanent Washington Commission resolution; (l) Privacy Protections. Recusal disclosures and challenge proceedings shall be conducted with privacy protections analogous to Section 17.4.7, with sensitive personal details (medical conditions, family circumstances, financial specifics) sealed from public view while the categorical fact of recusal is publicly recorded. Recusal records shall be permanently maintained in panel proceedings record but shall be subject to access controls reflecting privacy interests; (m)

Federal Executive Non-Interference. No President, Vice President, Cabinet officer, federal agency head, or other federal executive officeholder shall direct, influence, fund, or pressure recusal determinations under this Section. Any such interference shall constitute Section 13 interference with Senior Official multipliers, prosecutable under the §17C framework itself; (n) Funding. Costs of recusal administration, replacement panel-member orientation, and Permanent Washington Commission recusal review shall be funded through the constitutional appropriation under Section 11.3; (o) Article V Protection. The provisions of this Section shall be protected under the Article V protection established in Sections 18.6.1 and 18.6.2. Recusal procedure is essential to fair administration of §17C prosecutions; the

Amendment cannot rely on judicial improvisation of recusal rules in the first §17C cases.

Section 17D. The Permanent Washington Commission — Watcher of the

Watchers' Watchers

Key terms in this Section: • "The Permanent Commission" — The Washington Commission in its permanent ongoing role under this Section, distinct from its Phase One implementation role under Section 19.5. The Permanent Commission shall consist of seven (7) sitting Chief Justices of Participating Jurisdictions (as defined in Section 3), drawn by randomized lottery, serving staggered biennial terms with full refresh every two years as provided in Section 17D.5. • "Covered Accountability Body" — For purposes of this Section: the Hamilton Contingent (Section 13C); the State Attorneys General Prosecution Panel (Section 17C.3); the State Supreme Court Judicial Panel (Section 17C.6); and the Appellate Panel (Section 17C.10). The Covered Accountability Bodies are the bodies that prosecute and judge Covered Officials under Section 17C, and therefore require independent oversight to prevent the accountability mechanism itself from becoming captured. • "Oversight Finding" — A published determination by the Permanent Commission that a Covered Accountability Body, or a specific member thereof, has engaged in or may have engaged in conduct warranting further investigation, referral for prosecution, or recommendation of removal by the body with removal authority. • "Biennial Rotation" — The regular two-year cycle under Section 17D.5 in which all seven sitting Commission members rotate out and seven new Chief Justices are drawn by lottery, with a sixty (60) day transition overlap ensuring continuity. A. Foundational Purpose and Transition 17D.1 Foundational Purpose. The accountability framework of this Amendment creates a chain of watchers: the Authority watches the Federal Government; the Watchdog Tribunal investigates the Authority; the Hamilton Contingent investigates criminal violations; the State Attorneys General Prosecution Panel and State Supreme Court Judicial Panel prosecute and judge Covered Officials. Each link in this chain must itself be accountable, yet the chain cannot indefinitely extend without either concentrating power dangerously or collapsing under its own complexity. This Section establishes the Permanent Washington Commission as the terminal watcher — a narrow, transparent, rotating body of seven state supreme court Chief Justices who observe the Covered Accountability Bodies without themselves holding operational power. The Commission's role is to watch, document, refer, and recommend — never to execute, remove, or prosecute directly. The Framers of this Amendment recognized that at some point the chain must terminate, and the terminal watcher must therefore be the most constrained link in the chain. 17D.2 Transition from Phase One. The Washington Commission established under Section 19.5.0.1 for Phase One implementation shall, upon the full inauguration of the Authority under Section 19.19, transition from its Phase One protective role to its Permanent Oversight role under this Section. The transition shall be automatic, without requirement of ratification, affirmation, or action by any other body. The Phase One composition of seven (7) Chief Justices shall remain in place through the first Biennial Rotation under Section 17D.5, providing institutional continuity across the transition. The limits on Commission authority established in Section 19.5.0.6 shall continue to apply in the Permanent Oversight role, with additional limits specified in Section 17D.9. 17D.3 Scope of Permanent Oversight. The Permanent Commission's oversight authority under this Section extends to and is limited to: (a) The Hamilton Contingent established under Section 13C, including its Director, Division Chiefs, and senior personnel; (b) The State Attorneys General Prosecution Panel established under Section 17C.3, including Panel members during their service on specific cases; (c) The State Supreme Court Judicial Panel established under Section 17C.6, including Panel members during their service on specific cases; (d) The Appellate Panel established under Section 17C.10, including Panel members during their service on specific appeals; (e) The Commission's reactivation role during Restoration under Section 17B.5 is preserved and expanded by this Section, with the Permanent Commission serving as the reactivated body rather than requiring separate convening; (f) The Permanent Commission shall have NO oversight authority over the Authority bodies (Sections 17.2, 17.9, 17.15), the Watchdog

Tribunal (Section 21), or any other body. Those bodies remain subject to their own established accountability mechanisms. The Commission's oversight is specifically of the bodies that prosecute and judge other Covered Officials — the bodies that would otherwise be unwatched. B. Composition and Biennial Rotation

17D.4 Permanent Composition. The Permanent Commission shall consist of seven (7) sitting Chief Justices of Participating Jurisdictions as defined in Section 3, drawn by randomized lottery from among all Chief Justices of Participating Jurisdictions, with the following parameters: (a) Seven Different Jurisdictions. The seven Chief Justices shall represent seven different Participating Jurisdictions. Where two Chief Justices from the same Jurisdiction are drawn, the later-drawn Chief Justice shall be replaced by redraw until seven distinct Jurisdictions are represented; (b) Sitting Chief Justice Requirement. Only currently sitting Chief Justices of Participating Jurisdictions are eligible. Upon a Commissioner's departure from Chief Justice status (retirement, term expiration, promotion, removal from Jurisdictional office), the Commissioner shall complete the current Biennial Term unless disqualified under Section 17D.6; (c) Selection Administration. The lottery shall be administered by the Academic Integrity Commission using publicly verifiable cryptographic randomization, with algorithm, seed source, and results posted upon the Franklin Ledger. Selection results shall also be published on state-level judicial infrastructure independent of the federal Ledger, providing redundancy in case of federal infrastructure compromise. 17D.5 Biennial Rotation — Full Refresh Every Two Years. The composition of the Permanent Commission shall fully refresh every two (2) years through the following process: (a) Rotation Schedule. On the last business day of each second anniversary of the Permanent Commission's establishment, the sitting seven (7) Chief Justices shall rotate out and seven (7) new Chief Justices shall rotate in, drawn by lottery from the then-eligible pool; (b) Transition Overlap With Training. A sixty (60) day transition overlap shall precede each Biennial Rotation, during which both outgoing and incoming Commissioners shall serve concurrently (fourteen (14) members total during overlap). The overlap period shall include: (i) completion by incoming members of the training curriculum established under Section 19.5.0.2.2, typically requiring the first two to three (2-3) weeks of the overlap; (ii) briefing of incoming members by outgoing members on active oversight matters; and (iii) collaborative handoff of ongoing investigations, pending determinations, and institutional knowledge. During overlap, substantive oversight decisions shall require concurrence of at least four (4) outgoing and four (4) incoming members, ensuring both perspectives contribute to the transition. Training completion shall be certified on the Franklin Ledger before incoming members assume independent oversight authority; (c) Immediate Effective Date. Upon completion of the transition overlap, outgoing members' authorities cease and incoming members' authorities begin simultaneously, with the swearing-in ceremony livestreamed on the Franklin

Ledger; (d) Consecutive Service Barred. A Chief Justice who has served on the Permanent Commission may not be drawn again for at least ten (10) years following rotation out. This restriction ensures that no Chief Justice accumulates permanent oversight authority, and that the lottery draws rotate among the full pool over time; (e) Active Case Continuity. Where the Permanent Commission has active oversight matters at the time of Biennial Rotation, outgoing members shall brief incoming members in writing, with the briefing documents transferred to incoming members as part of the transition. Outgoing members may be recalled by incoming members to provide testimony or context on matters they participated in, with such recalls compensated at the same rates as active Commission service. 17D.6 Disqualification and Mid-Term Vacancies. (a) Disqualification. A drawn Chief Justice shall be disqualified from Commission service where: (i) they have served on a highest court of a Participating Jurisdiction that issued a substantive ruling on the Amendment in the preceding ten (10) years; (ii) they have a personal or professional relationship with any member of a Covered Accountability Body that would materially compromise independence; (iii) they have publicly prejudged matters likely to come before the Commission; or (iv) they have been subject to pending disciplinary proceedings in their Jurisdiction's judicial system in the past five (5) years; (b) Mid-Term Vacancies. Where a Commissioner dies, resigns, is removed from Chief Justice status by their state, or becomes incapacitated during a Biennial Term, a replacement shall be drawn by lottery within thirty (30) days. The replacement shall serve only the remainder of the current Biennial Term; (c) Voluntary Withdrawal. A Commissioner may withdraw upon good-faith grounds published on the Ledger. Withdrawals exceeding twenty percent (20%) within any twelve-month period shall trigger Authority review of the selection process. C. Limited Authorities (What the Commission Can Do) 17D.7 Authorized Oversight Activities. The Permanent Commission shall have the following authorities and only these authorities in the exercise of its permanent oversight role: (a) Ongoing Monitoring. Continuous review of Hamilton Contingent operations, including review of investigation openings, closings, plea agreements, declinations, asset seizures, and use of investigative authorities under Sections 13C and 13G; (b) Panel Conduct Review. Review of State Attorneys General Prosecution Panel decisions including charge filings, declinations, plea agreements, and sentencing recommendations; review of State Supreme Court Judicial Panel conduct including rulings, evidentiary decisions, and sentencing; and similar review of Appellate

Panel conduct; (c) Investigation of Specific Allegations. Upon receipt of credible allegation of misconduct by any member of a Covered Accountability Body — whether via whistleblower report under Section 13B.16, citizen petition under Section 17A.16, referral from another Amendment body, or the Commission's own observation — the Commission may open a specific investigation; (d) Subpoena Authority (Limited). In support of open investigations, the Commission may issue subpoenas for documents and testimony from members of Covered Accountability Bodies. Commission subpoenas shall be enforced by the Hamilton Contingent Protection Division, or where Hamilton Contingent itself is under investigation, by state law enforcement in the jurisdiction where service is required; (e) Publish Oversight Findings. Upon completion of investigation, the Commission shall publish Oversight Findings on the Franklin Ledger with full reasoning and supporting evidence (with narrow redactions only for witness protection, active investigation integrity, or classified national security matters); (f) Criminal Referral. Where Oversight Findings indicate potential criminal conduct, the Commission shall refer the matter to the State Attorneys General Prosecution Panel under Section 17C. Where the Prosecution Panel itself is under investigation, the Commission shall refer to a specially-drawn Panel excluding any member implicated in the matter; (g) Recommend Removal. Where Oversight Findings indicate conduct warranting removal short of criminal prosecution, the Commission may recommend removal to the body with removal authority — the Authority for the Hamilton Contingent Director under Section 13C.15, the home state government for a state AG or Justice, or the Panel itself for Panel members. Recommendations are advisory only; the body with removal authority retains its ordinary authority to act or decline; (h) Annual Report. Publish a comprehensive annual report on the Franklin Ledger describing oversight activities, findings issued, referrals made, recommendations made, and systemic observations about the health of the accountability framework. D. Strict Limits (What the Commission Cannot Do) 17D.8 Prohibited Actions — What the Permanent Commission Cannot Do. The Permanent Commission's authority is strictly limited to the activities enumerated in Section 17D.7. The Commission SHALL NOT: (a) Directly remove, suspend, or discipline any member of a Covered Accountability Body. Removal authority remains with the bodies specified in Section 17C, Section 13C.15, and state judicial systems; (b) Prosecute criminal cases directly. All criminal prosecution of Covered Officials shall be conducted through the State Attorneys General Prosecution Panel under

Section 17C. The Commission's role is referral, not prosecution;

(c) Adjudicate guilt or impose sentences. All criminal adjudication shall be conducted through the State Supreme Court Judicial Panel under Section 17C; (d) Enact rules with the force of law. The Commission may develop internal procedures for its own operations but shall not issue binding rules applicable to Covered Accountability Bodies or other Amendment bodies; (e) Direct Hamilton Contingent operations. While the Commission may investigate Hamilton Contingent conduct and refer criminal matters, it shall not direct specific investigations, compel Hamilton Contingent to open or close investigations, or otherwise substitute its judgment for Hamilton Contingent operational authority except where conduct is itself the subject of Commission investigation; (f) Interfere with ongoing Section 17C prosecutions. Once Prosecution Panel has filed charges or Judicial Panel has accepted a case, the Commission may observe and later review, but shall not intervene in the proceedings themselves. Commission intervention would substitute its judgment for the lawful constitutional process under Section 17C; (g) Exercise any authority listed in Section 19.5.0.6 as prohibited to the Phase One Commission. Those limits continue and apply to the Permanent Commission; (h) Seek or accept expansion of authority beyond this Section. The Commission shall not petition Congress, the President, or any other body for expanded powers. Any expansion of authority shall require formal Amendment of this Constitution under Article V; (i) Act outside the Biennial Term without emergency authorization. Upon completion of the Biennial Rotation, outgoing members have no residual authority and shall not act in any Commission capacity, except upon recall under Section 17D.5(e) to provide testimony. E. Transparency Requirements 17D.9 Full Ledger Transparency. All Permanent Commission activities shall be subject to complete transparency on the Franklin Ledger: (a) All Findings on Ledger. Every Oversight Finding under Section 17D.7(e) shall be published in full on the Ledger within fourteen (14) days of issuance. Findings shall include: the body or individual under review; the conduct investigated; the evidence considered; the Commission's conclusions; and the recommended action (if any); (b) Dissent Publication. Where

Commission decisions are not unanimous, dissenting Commissioners shall have the right to publish reasoned dissents on the Ledger alongside the majority Finding. This preserves the transparency principle even where the Commission itself is divided;

(c) Deliberation Records. Records of Commission deliberations — meeting minutes, vote tallies, analytical work product — shall be preserved for twenty (20) years and made available to the Academic Integrity Commission for audit under Section 17A.19. After the twenty-year period, deliberation records shall become part of the public constitutional archive; (d) Real-Time Docket. The Commission shall maintain a real-time docket on the Ledger listing all open investigations (with narrow redaction for witness protection), all pending referrals, all pending recommendations, and all completed matters with their dispositions; (e) Citizen Challenge. Any Commission Finding or recommendation shall be subject to citizen petition challenge under Section 17A.16, with the same threshold requirements and procedures applicable to challenges of other Amendment body decisions; (f) Compensation Disclosure. Compensation paid to Commissioners during their service shall be published on the Ledger, as shall any expense reimbursements. Commissioners shall also be subject to the financial monitoring provisions of Section 13F during their service and for two (2) years following rotation out. F. Accountability of the Commission Itself 17D.10 The Commission Subject to Its Own Accountability. The Permanent Commission is itself accountable: (a) Criminal Accountability Under Section 17C. Commissioners are Covered Officials under Section 17C and are subject to criminal prosecution through the State Attorneys General Prosecution Panel for corruption, bribery, interference, or other criminal conduct during or related to their Commission service. Because the Commission oversees the Section 17C panels, Section 17C proceedings against Commissioners shall use a specially-drawn Prosecution Panel and Judicial Panel that excludes any Attorneys General or Justices whose service on Commission oversight investigations gave rise to the charges, preventing circular conflicts; (b) Recall Mechanism. Any Commissioner found by the specially-drawn Section 17C proceeding to have committed misconduct warranting removal shall be removed immediately upon verdict, with the Biennial Rotation lottery drawing a replacement under Section 17D.6(b); (c) Citizen Petition for Commission Member Removal. Citizens may petition under Section 17A.16 for removal of a specific Commissioner upon clear and convincing evidence of misconduct. The petition process shall refer the matter to the Section 17C framework for full criminal proceeding, or to the Academic

Integrity Commission for administrative review where criminal conduct is not alleged; (d) Biennial Rotation as Primary Check. The Biennial Rotation under Section 17D.5 is itself the primary check on Commission authority — no Commissioner serves long enough to accumulate entrenched power, and every two years the entire composition changes. This structural check operates independently of individual accountability mechanisms. G. Operational Framework and Transition Preservation 17D.11 Operational Framework. The Permanent Commission shall operate under the following framework: (a) Headquarters. The Commission shall operate from facilities at the highest-court locations of Participating Jurisdictions on a rotating basis, with sessions held at the court facility of each serving Chief Justice on a rotation ensuring geographic diversity; (b) Staff (Minimal). The Commission shall have minimal permanent staff, consisting of: an executive director (one position); legal counsel (two positions); investigators (five positions drawn from the Hamilton Contingent Protection Division on rotational detail); and administrative support (three positions). Staff expansion beyond this structure shall require Liberty Bell Initiative approval and shall be strictly limited to the extent necessary for the Commission's narrow oversight mission; (c) Budget. The Commission's budget shall flow through the constitutional appropriation under Section 11.3 and Section 13I, benchmarked at a level sufficient for narrow oversight operations but not at levels supporting operational law enforcement (which is reserved to the Hamilton Contingent) or judicial proceedings (which is reserved to the Section 17C Panels). The Commission's annual budget shall be published on the Ledger; (d) No Separate Law Enforcement. The Commission shall have no independent law enforcement personnel beyond the rotational investigators detailed from Hamilton Contingent. The Commission is a watching body, not an enforcing body. 17D.12 Preservation of Restoration Reactivation Role. The Permanent Commission shall retain the Restoration reactivation role established in Section 17B.5. Upon certification of a Restoration under Section 17B, the Permanent Commission shall: (a) transition to Restoration oversight mode for the duration of the Restoration process (typically seven days plus up to sixty days for reconstitution completion); (b) exercise the expanded authorities specifically enumerated in Section 17B.5 for the limited purpose of Restoration oversight; and (c) return to ordinary Permanent Oversight role upon completion of Restoration reconstitution. The Permanent Commission's capacity to perform this reactivation role is enhanced by its permanent existence, as the body does not need to be convened from scratch but rather simply expands its authorities temporarily. 17D.13 Article V Protection. The provisions of this Section shall be protected under the Article V protection established in Sections 18.6.1 and 18.6.2. No act of Congress, executive order, judicial ruling, or state action shall evade, diminish, or

nullify the oversight role of the Permanent Commission or the limits upon its authority established in Section 17D.8. H. Pre-Certified Pool Vetting for Section 17C Panels 17D.13.1 Pre-Certified Pools for Section 17C Panels. To close the pre-vetting gap in the Section 17C framework while respecting the sovereignty of Participating Jurisdictions over the election and confirmation of their Attorneys General and Justices of their highest courts, the Permanent Commission shall maintain two Pre-Certified Pools from which the lottery draws under Sections 17C.3 and 17C.6 shall be conducted: (a) Pre-Certified State AG Pool. An ongoing list of sitting Attorneys General (or equivalent chief legal-executive officers) of Participating Jurisdictions who have been screened and determined eligible for Section 17C Prosecution Panel service; (b) Pre-Certified State Supreme Court Justice Pool. An ongoing list of sitting Justices of the highest courts of Participating Jurisdictions (including Chief Justices, except those currently serving on the Permanent Commission) who have been screened and determined eligible for Section 17C Judicial Panel and Appellate Panel service; (c) Lottery Draws Limited to Pre-Certified Pools. All lottery draws under Sections 17C.3 and 17C.6 shall draw only from the respective Pre-Certified Pool. Drawn individuals who are not in the current Pre-Certified Pool shall be replaced by redraw from the remaining pool members; (d) Ongoing Maintenance. The Permanent Commission shall review the Pre-Certified Pools annually and upon the occurrence of any event that could affect an individual's eligibility (new criminal charge, bar discipline, change of office, foreign agent registration, or similar disqualifying event). 17D.13.2 Eligibility Criteria — Objective Pass/Fail Standards. The Permanent Commission shall apply the following eligibility criteria to all Attorneys General and Justices of the highest courts of Participating Jurisdictions for Pre-Certified Pool inclusion. The Commission shall exercise no discretion beyond these objective criteria; each criterion is either met or not met: (a) No Disqualifying Criminal Conviction. The individual has not been convicted of a crime involving corruption, bribery, fraud, obstruction of justice, perjury, or similar offense bearing on fitness for prosecutorial or judicial service, whether in state or federal court; (b) Bar License in Good Standing. The individual holds an active bar license in at least one United States jurisdiction, not currently suspended, revoked, or under active disciplinary proceedings; (c) No Current Foreign Agent Status. The individual is not currently registered as a foreign agent under the Foreign Agents Registration Act (FARA), and has not been so registered within the preceding ten (10) years; (d) Constitutional Oath Compliance. The individual has maintained the constitutional oath under Section 19.5.0.3.2 and has not been found, in any state or federal proceeding, to have violated the constitutional order established by this Amendment; (e) No Active Hamilton Contingent Investigation. The individual is not currently the subject of an active Hamilton Contingent investigation for Amendment-related offenses; (f) Holds Relevant Office. The individual holds the office required for pool eligibility (Attorney General of a Participating Jurisdiction or Justice of the highest court of a Participating Jurisdiction), as verified by Jurisdictional records. 17D.13.3 Cooling-Off Periods — Time-Based Objective Disqualifications. In addition to the eligibility criteria of Section 17D.13.2, the following cooling-off periods apply as time-based objective disqualifications. An individual meeting any of these conditions shall be excluded from the Pre-Certified Pool for the specified period: (a) Campaign Funding from Interested Parties. An individual who received campaign contributions exceeding ten thousand dollars ($10,000) in aggregate from any single source during their most recent election cycle, where the contributing source is: (i) a party likely to be subject to Authority or Watchdog Tribunal oversight; (ii) a party with pending Hamilton Contingent investigation; or (iii) a party identified in Section 13F as subject to Post-Amendment Financial Monitoring. The disqualification shall last two (2) years from the date of receipt of the contribution; (b) Prior Employment by Interested Parties. An individual who was employed, within the preceding two (2) years, by any entity subject to pending Hamilton Contingent investigation or Section 13F financial monitoring, in a capacity involving substantive legal or business decisions affecting that entity's compliance with federal law; (c) Prior Professional Relationship With Covered Official. An individual who has, within the preceding five (5) years, served as counsel to, direct supervisor of, direct subordinate to, or business partner with any current Covered Official under Section 17C; (d) Public Prejudgment. An individual who has, within the preceding two (2) years, publicly prejudged material factual or legal issues likely to arise in Section 17C proceedings, such that an ordinary reasonable observer would conclude the individual could not approach those issues with impartiality. This criterion requires concrete evidence of prejudgment (public statements, writings, speeches), not mere political or ideological affiliation.

17D.13.4 Determination Process. The Permanent Commission shall determine eligibility through the following process: (a) Initial Screening Upon Office

Taking. When a new Attorney General of a Participating Jurisdiction or Justice of the highest court of a Participating Jurisdiction takes office, the Permanent Commission shall complete initial screening within thirty (30) days. During this thirty-day period, the individual shall be provisionally ineligible pending screening completion; (b) Annual Reassessment. The Permanent Commission shall reassess eligibility annually for all Pool members, completing reassessments within a rolling ninety-day window; (c) Event-Triggered Reassessment. Upon the occurrence of any event that could affect eligibility (new criminal charge, bar discipline, foreign agent registration, or Hamilton Contingent investigation opening), the Permanent Commission shall reassess within fourteen (14) days; (d) Published Reasoning. All Pool inclusion and exclusion determinations shall be published on the Franklin Ledger with specific reasoning tied to the objective criteria of Sections 17D.13.2 and 17D.13.3. Vague or discretionary reasoning shall not suffice; (e) Citizen Challenge. Both exclusions and inclusions shall be subject to citizen petition challenge under Section 17A.16. Challenges shall be resolved within forty-five (45) days, with the Pool status suspended during pending challenges only where the challenge presents serious probable grounds. 17D.13.5 Due Process Protections for Affected AGs and Justices. Because Pool exclusion affects the career opportunity of state-level officials, the following due process protections apply: (a) Right to Notice. An Attorney General of a Participating Jurisdiction or Justice whom the Commission has tentatively determined should be excluded from the Pool shall receive written notice with specific reasoning at least thirty (30) days before exclusion takes effect; (b) Right to Respond. The affected individual may submit a response to the tentative determination, including evidence and arguments. The Commission shall consider the response before finalizing the determination; (c) Right to Reapply. An individual excluded from the Pool may petition for re-inclusion at any time upon demonstrating that the disqualifying condition no longer exists; (d) No Jurisdictional-Office Effect. Pool exclusion shall not affect the individual's underlying Jurisdictional office or duties. The individual continues as Attorney General or Justice of the highest court of their Participating Jurisdiction under that Jurisdiction's law; only Section 17C Panel eligibility is affected;

(e) Retaliation Protection. State governments shall not retaliate against an Attorney General or Justice based on Pool inclusion or exclusion determinations. Such retaliation constitutes federal interference under Section 13. 17D.13.6 No Discretionary Exclusion. The Permanent Commission shall not exclude any state Attorney General or Justice from the Pre-Certified Pool based on: (a) political party affiliation; (b) ideological orientation; (c) prior judicial or prosecutorial decisions not involving misconduct; (d) expected voting pattern; or (e) any basis other than the objective criteria of Sections 17D.13.2 and 17D.13.3. Violations of this prohibition by Commissioners shall constitute Section 13 interference and shall be prosecuted accordingly. This restriction ensures the Commission's vetting role is eligibility screening, not selective exclusion based on expected outcomes. 17D.14 Foundational Commitment. The People of the United States, in establishing this Permanent Commission, commit themselves to the principle that every link in the accountability chain must itself be accountable, and that accountability is preserved not by creating ever-longer chains of watchers but by terminating the chain with a narrow, transparent, rotating body that observes without executing. The Permanent Commission watches the watchers of the watchers, publishing its observations so that the People themselves may judge. Its power is the power of daylight: what it documents on the Ledger, the People can see; what the People see, they can act upon through the mechanisms this Amendment establishes — through citizen petition under Section 17A.16, through Restoration under Section 17B, and through Reclamation under Section 1. The Permanent Commission does not replace citizen sovereignty; it illuminates the work of the accountability bodies so that citizen sovereignty remains meaningful. No body in this Amendment exists apart from the People's oversight; the Permanent Commission ensures that the bodies which prosecute and judge other officials are themselves visible to the People they serve.

Section 18. Sunset Review and the Right of Future Generations

Key terms in this Section: • "The Authority" — The Independent Tripartite Oversight Authority (three bodies, see Section 17). • "The Ledger" — The Sovereign Blockchain Voting Ledger (Section 4). • "Terminal" — A Sovereign Voting Terminal (Section 14). • "Sunset Review Vote" — The national vote held every twenty (20) years, in which the People vote to Retain, Modify, or Repeal this Amendment.

• "Constitutional Review Convention" — The 150-delegate body convened if the People vote to Modify this Amendment at a Sunset Review, with the power to draft proposed modifications for subsequent ratification. 18.1 Every 20 years, the People shall vote to Retain, Modify, or Repeal this Amendment. No generation may bind those that follow. 18.2 The Sunset Review Vote shall be a 30-day open vote upon the Ledger. 18.3 Turnout Requirement and Failure Procedures. Valid outcome requires fifty percent (50%) turnout of registered voters across all Participating Jurisdictions, consistent with the No Confidence threshold under Section 5.2 reflecting the principle that Amendment-scale decisions warrant majority engagement of the registered electorate. Below this threshold, the following procedures apply: (a) Automatic Retention: If turnout falls below fifty percent (50%), the Sunset Review shall be deemed FAILED, and this Amendment shall remain in force without modification. The outcome shall be equivalent to a Retain vote, and no Modification or Repeal shall take effect regardless of the vote distribution among those who participated; (b) Two-Year Retry: A second Sunset Review Vote shall be held within twenty-four (24) months of the failed Vote, under the same procedures of Sections 18.1 through 18.2 and the heightened public-awareness provisions of Section 18.3(d); (c) Consecutive Failure Protection: If two (2) consecutive Sunset Review Votes fail the fifty percent (50%) turnout threshold, the Amendment shall automatically continue in force, and the ordinary twenty-year (20-year) cycle shall resume with the next scheduled Vote twenty (20) years thereafter. Two consecutive failures shall constitute evidence of broad public acceptance of the Amendment as currently constituted, and shall not trigger any extraordinary process or emergency action; (d) Heightened Public Awareness on Retry: For any retry Vote following a failed Sunset Review, the Citizens' Oversight Board shall expand public outreach including mandatory civic education on Amendment provisions, expanded Ledger and media publication of the Board's 20-year comprehensive report, and increased Mobile Accessibility Team deployment. The retry Vote shall not be construed as an attempt to pressure a particular outcome, but as an effort to achieve meaningful civic participation in a constitutional review; (e) No Backdoor Modification: Under no circumstances shall a Sunset Review Vote with below-threshold turnout be interpreted as authorizing any change to this Amendment. Any attempt by any officeholder or body to treat a failed Sunset Review as a mandate for Modification or Repeal shall constitute interference under Section 13 and shall trigger the full penalties thereof.

18.4 Modify triggers a Constitutional Review Convention of 150 delegates (100 Citizens' Board by lottery + 25 state legislature appointees + 25 from Academic Pool), producing amendments ratified by supermajority. The composition is weighted toward lottery-drawn citizens to make the Convention itself maximally resistant to capture by long-horizon partisan organization; the smaller state-legislature and academic appointee shares retain democratic legitimacy contributions while reducing the Convention's exposure to the institutional capture vectors that twenty-year planning horizons enable. 18.5

Repeal triggers an orderly 2-year wind-down. The nuclear protections established in Section 16, Subsection B shall persist beyond Repeal as freestanding constitutional provisions, modifiable only through the Article V constitutional amendment process as specified in Section 18.14, and not subject to modification by Congress, executive order, judicial ruling, or any other ordinary federal action. 18.6 Structures of this Amendment cannot be dismantled between Sunset Reviews by any act of Congress, executive order, or judicial ruling. 18.6.1 Ratification and Article V Protection. No act of Congress, executive order, judicial ruling, state action, or other federal action shall: (a) Alter, question, or invalidate the ratification status of this Amendment; (b) Attempt retroactive amendment of the Article V process under which this Amendment was ratified; (c) Subject this Amendment to additional ratification procedures not specified in Article V of the Constitution itself; (d) Impose any new conditions, interpretations, requirements, or limitations upon the operation of this Amendment not contained within the text of this Amendment itself; or (e) Attempt to nullify, in whole or in part, the application of this Amendment through any legal maneuver, procedural challenge, or doctrinal innovation. 18.6.2 Any such attempt described in Section 18.6.1 shall be void ab initio, shall have no legal effect, and shall constitute interference under Section 13. Any officeholder, federal employee, or federal appointee who directs, authorizes, or materially participates in any such attempt shall be subject to the full Section 13 interference penalties: imprisonment of not less than fifteen (15) years; permanent lifetime bar from any federal, state, or local public office, appointed position, or government employment; without possibility of pardon, commutation, or clemency. No subsequent officeholder shall have authority to retroactively excuse or pardon such conduct. 18.7 The Citizens' Oversight Board shall publish a comprehensive 20-year public report 90 days before each Vote, detailing Authority history, Petition attempts, Nuclear Votes, identified weaknesses, and proposed modifications.

18.8 Ballot Design for Sunset Review. The Sunset Review Vote ballot shall present the three options clearly and without bias: (a) Three-Option Presentation. The ballot shall display three options: 'Retain' (continue the Amendment without modification); 'Modify' (continue the Amendment with proposed modifications developed through Constitutional Review Convention); and 'Repeal' (wind down the Amendment over two years). Voters shall select one option; no ranked-choice selection shall apply to the Sunset Review. (b) Consequence Summary Required. The ballot shall display, with each option, a brief summary (not more than one hundred (100) words per option) of the consequence of that option, prepared by the Academic Integrity Commission in neutral factual language. Voters at the moment of voting shall understand what they are choosing. (c) No Editorial Framing. Consequence summaries shall be factual descriptions of what each option produces, not advocacy for or against any option. The Watchdog Tribunal shall review summaries for neutrality before publication, with corrections ordered where advocacy is detected. (d) Multi-Language Display. Ballot content shall be available in English, Spanish, and the primary languages of Participating Jurisdictions with significant non-English-speaking populations, consistent with Section 12.12(c). (e) Uniform National Design. Ballot layout and content shall be identical across all Jurisdictions, with only translation variations for linguistic accessibility. 18.9 Voter Education Period. To enable informed Sunset Review voting: (a) Ninety-Day Education Period. A ninety (90) day voter education period shall precede the thirty (30) day Sunset Review Vote. During this period, the Academic Integrity Commission shall oversee preparation and distribution of non-partisan educational materials regarding: the Amendment's history; the twenty-year record of Authority operation; identified strengths and weaknesses; modifications that could be proposed under the 'Modify' option; and consequences of the 'Repeal' option. (b) Public Forums and Debates. During the education period, the Authority shall organize public forums in every Participating Jurisdiction, featuring advocates for each option (Retain, Modify, Repeal). Forums shall be livestreamed on the Franklin Ledger and shall preserve balanced representation of perspectives. (c) Media Coverage Requirements. Broadcast media shall provide minimum coverage of the Sunset Review during the education period, with equal-time principles applied to advocates for each option. Public broadcasting shall provide enhanced coverage funded through the Section 11.3 appropriation where necessary. (d) Academic Independence. Voter education materials shall be prepared with academic independence, drawing on analysis from multiple universities in the

Pre-Certified University Pool under Section 17.16. No single institution or political viewpoint shall control materials development. (e) Non-Partisan Standard. Educational materials shall not advocate for any specific option. They shall present factual analysis of the Amendment's operation, acknowledged strengths and weaknesses, and consequences of each Sunset Review outcome. Advocacy shall be left to civic organizations and option advocates, not to Authority-supervised education infrastructure. 18.10 Scope of the 'Modify' Option. The Modify option under Section 18.4 shall permit substantial amendment of this Amendment through Constitutional Review Convention, subject to the following limits: (a) Substantive Modifications Permitted. The Constitutional Review Convention may propose modifications to: signature thresholds under Section 3.1; Referendum thresholds under Section 5.2; Authority body composition under Section 17; oversight structures; operational procedures; and other substantive elements of the Amendment's operation. (b) Core Provisions Protected From Modification. The Convention shall not propose modifications that: (i) eliminate the People's right to issue a Declaration of No Confidence under Section 1.1; (ii) eliminate or substantially weaken the Authority's independence from federal executive control; (iii) eliminate the mutual-veto structure of the Authority; (iv) eliminate the Section 16 military oath protections or nuclear safeguards; (v) eliminate the Article V protections of Sections 18.6 and 18.6.1; (vi) eliminate the Sunset Review mechanism itself; or (vii) otherwise propose modifications that would functionally repeal the Amendment while nominally retaining it. (c) Distinction Between Modify and Repeal. The Modify option is for genuine substantive improvement of the Amendment based on twenty years of operational experience. Proposals that would functionally repeal the Amendment shall proceed through the Repeal option, not the Modify option. The distinction shall be enforced by the Watchdog Tribunal with authority to reject Convention proposals that cross the threshold. (d) Enhancement of Core Provisions Permitted. Nothing in subsection (b) shall prevent the Convention from proposing modifications that strengthen, clarify, or enhance the protection of core provisions. The limitation applies to elimination or substantial weakening, not to enhancement. (e) Good-Faith Modification Standard. The Watchdog Tribunal shall evaluate Convention proposals under a good-faith modification standard — modifications designed to improve the Amendment based on experience are presumptively valid; modifications designed to undermine the Amendment while claiming to modify it are void.

18.11 Constitutional Review Convention Structure. Where the Modify option prevails: (a) Composition Detail. The Convention's one hundred fifty (150) delegates shall consist of: (i) one hundred (100) delegates drawn by randomized lottery from the Citizens' Oversight Board (current members and alumni within the preceding ten years), with the lottery administered by the Academic Integrity Commission under Section 17.16.3; (ii) twenty-five (25) delegates appointed by state legislatures, with one (1) delegate appointed per Participating Jurisdiction selected by randomized lottery from the fifty-six (56) Participating Jurisdictions for each Sunset Review cycle. The selection lottery for the twenty-five Participating Jurisdictions shall be administered by the Permanent

Washington Commission under Section 17D using the same cryptographic methodology as Section 17.16.3, with the lottery seed published in advance and verifiable by independent researchers. Each selected Jurisdiction shall appoint its single delegate by method left to that Jurisdiction's law within sixty (60) days of selection notification. Geographic broad-distribution is preserved across cycles — over multiple Sunset Review cycles, every Jurisdiction receives appointee participation in approximate proportion to its share of the fifty-six — while concentration of capture surface in any single cycle is prevented because the specific twenty-five Jurisdictions selected for any given cycle cannot be predicted in advance; (iii) twenty-five (25) delegates drawn by randomized lottery from the Pre-Certified University Pool under Section 17.16, with selection proceeding through the Academic Integrity Commission's two-stage lottery under Section 17.16.3. Delegate selection shall complete within sixty (60) days of Sunset Review certification of the Modify outcome. The 100/25/25 composition reflects the constitutional judgment that lottery-drawn citizens bear primary responsibility for Amendment modification, with state legislature and academic appointee shares reduced from earlier 50/50/50 framing specifically to harden the Convention against twenty-year-planning capture campaigns; the appointee shares remain to preserve democratic and expert legitimacy contributions that lottery alone cannot supply, while the per-cycle Jurisdictional lottery for the twenty-five state-legislature seats prevents fixed-target capture of specific large-state legislatures across decades-long planning horizons. (b) Operating Procedures. The Convention shall adopt its own operating procedures by majority vote in its first session, subject to the following required procedures: (i) public livestreaming of all proceedings on the Franklin Ledger; (ii) public comment periods for proposed modifications; (iii) expert testimony from Authority bodies, the Watchdog Tribunal, and independent analysts; (iv) supermajority voting requirements for final modification proposals; and (v) minority dissent reporting in final output. (c) Operational Timeline. The Convention shall convene within ninety (90) days of Sunset Review certification and shall complete its work within eighteen (18) months, with a single six (6) month extension available upon Convention supermajority vote and Watchdog Tribunal approval. Extensions beyond twenty-four (24) months shall not be permitted. (d) Hardship Framework Applies. The hardship framework of Sections 17.4 through 17.4.13 shall apply to Convention delegates per Section 17.4.12, with Convention membership treated as comparable to other mandatory-service bodies. Delegates may request accommodation or excuse under the established framework. (e) Convention

Independence. The Convention shall operate independently of the sitting federal government, federal courts, and the Authority itself. No sitting federal official shall direct, influence, or interfere with Convention deliberations. Convention funding shall be through the Section 11.3 appropriation with a dedicated Sunset Review reserve. (f) Watchdog Tribunal Oversight. The Watchdog Tribunal shall maintain oversight of Convention proceedings for integrity (preventing corruption, foreign interference, or capture of the Convention), with findings published on the Franklin Ledger. Tribunal oversight shall not extend to substantive review of modification proposals except where those proposals would violate Section 18.10(b). 18.12 Supermajority Ratification of Modifications. Convention-proposed modifications shall not take effect until ratified as follows: (a) Supermajority Standard. Ratification shall require approval by three-fourths (3/4) of Participating Jurisdictions, consistent with the Article V supermajority standard applicable to original constitutional amendments. This reflects the constitutional weight of modifications to the Amendment. (b) Ratification Timeline. Ratification shall proceed over a seven (7) year period beginning upon Convention's final output, with each Jurisdiction's ratification pathway determined by Jurisdictional law. Jurisdictions may ratify through legislative vote, Jurisdictional referendum, or other method consistent with Jurisdictional constitutional process. (c) Package vs. Item-by-Item Ratification. The Convention may submit modifications as a package (requiring Jurisdictions to ratify all or none) or as separate items (requiring each to meet the three-fourths threshold independently). The Convention shall specify the submission method by supermajority vote. (d) Failure of Ratification. Modifications failing to reach three-fourths Jurisdictional approval within seven (7) years shall fail, with the Amendment continuing in its pre-Modify form. Failed modifications shall not be automatically re-submitted; proposing them again shall require a new Sunset Review Modify outcome. (e) Effective Date of Ratified Modifications. Ratified modifications shall take effect on the date of Jurisdictional certification of the three-fourths threshold, with implementation timelines for specific modifications determined by the modifications themselves as Convention-proposed.

(f) No Federal Court Review of Ratification. No federal court shall have jurisdiction to review, enjoin, or invalidate Jurisdictional ratification votes on Sunset Review modifications, consistent with the Article V framework and the Section 25 limits on federal judicial review of Amendment operations. 18.13 Repeal Wind-Down Procedures. Where the Repeal option prevails, the two-year wind-down under Section 18.5 shall proceed as follows: (a) Wind-Down Period Schedule. The wind-down shall commence upon Sunset Review certification of the Repeal outcome. During the first year, Authority bodies, the Watchdog Tribunal, and Hamilton Contingent shall continue operations at reduced capacity. During the second year, operations shall further reduce with orderly closure. At the end of year two, the Amendment's operational provisions shall cease to apply prospectively. (b) Pending Petitions Disposition. Petitions pending at the time of Repeal certification shall proceed to completion under the Amendment's framework, with their Referendum, if triggered, completed within the wind-down period. Petitions filed after Repeal certification shall not be accepted. (c) Active Prosecutions. Hamilton Contingent prosecutions active at Repeal certification shall proceed to completion through existing federal courts, with no loss of evidentiary or procedural protections. Convictions obtained shall remain in full effect. (d) Authority Bodies Dissolution. The Citizens' Oversight Board, State Elections Council, and Academic Integrity Commission shall dissolve at the end of year two, with all records transferred to the National Archives for permanent preservation under Federal Records Act standards. (e) Watchdog Tribunal Dissolution. The Watchdog Tribunal shall dissolve at the end of year two, with all findings, records, and institutional memory transferred to the National Archives. Tribunal-initiated investigations incomplete at dissolution shall be transferred to the Department of Justice for continuation under ordinary federal authority. (f) Hamilton Contingent Dissolution. The Hamilton Contingent shall dissolve at the end of year two, with all prosecutorial records, ongoing investigations, and asset recovery proceedings transferred to the Department of Justice for continuation. The Protection Division's protective protocols shall be maintained through the Department of Justice or its successor for persons covered by ongoing protection. (g) Office and Center Disposition. Citizens' Reclamation Offices and Centers shall be disposed of through sale, conversion to general public use, or transfer to Jurisdictional control, with funds from sales returning to the federal treasury. Terminal infrastructure shall be decommissioned and destroyed under secure procedures to prevent misuse.

(h) Records Preservation. All Amendment records — including all Ledger entries, all Authority findings, all prosecutorial records, all hardship documentation, all Convention records if applicable — shall be preserved through the National Archives with permanent public accessibility. The historical record of the Amendment's operation shall not be lost. 18.14 Nuclear Protections Persistence. Under Section 18.5, the nuclear protections established in Section 16, Subsection B remain in force pending alternatives. The following framework shall govern this persistence: (a) Post-Repeal Nuclear Framework. Upon completion of the Repeal wind-down, the nuclear protections of Section 16 shall continue in force as freestanding constitutional provisions. These provisions shall not be subject to modification, elimination, or replacement by any act of Congress, executive order, judicial ruling, or ordinary federal statute. The core principle of this Amendment — that no single individual or narrow body shall possess unilateral authority over nuclear first-use — shall persist beyond any Repeal of the Amendment's operational provisions. (b) Article V Modification Only. Modification of the nuclear protections shall be permitted only through the constitutional amendment process under Article V of the Constitution of the United States, requiring either a two-thirds supermajority of both houses of Congress proposing an amendment followed by ratification by three-fourths of the states, or a constitutional convention called by two-thirds of state legislatures followed by ratification by three-fourths of the states. No other pathway shall suffice. (c) Rationale for Article V Protection. The nuclear protections receive Article V protection because they address the most consequential power any government can exercise — authorization of weapons capable of ending civilization. That power must not be placeable in any single individual's hands, nor subject to elimination by a captured or corrupted legislature acting alone. Only the People themselves, acting through the supermajority consensus of Article V, may alter the nuclear framework. (d) Attempted Ordinary Legislation Void Ab Initio. Any act of Congress, executive order, judicial ruling, or other federal action purporting to modify, eliminate, weaken, or replace the Section 16 nuclear protections outside of the Article V process shall be void ab initio (meaning: invalid from the very beginning, as if it never existed legally). Federal officials who direct, authorize, or materially participate in such attempts shall be subject to Section 13 interference penalties with Senior Official multipliers, and Section 16.5 insurrection penalties where the attempt involves coordinated resistance to the nuclear framework. (e) Enhancement Permitted Without Article V. Notwithstanding subsections (a) through (d), Congress and federal executive agencies may adopt additional safeguards, protective procedures, or enforcement mechanisms that strengthen the Section 16 framework without diminishing any existing protection. Enhancement of the People's protection against unilateral nuclear authorization does not require

Article V; only elimination or weakening does. (f) International Notification. Upon Repeal of this Amendment, the State Department shall provide notification to allied nations and international organizations that the Section 16 nuclear protections persist as freestanding constitutional provisions and remain binding on the United States government, ensuring that the United States' nuclear posture remains clear to the international community and that no party is misled about the continuing constitutional constraints on U.S. nuclear authorization. (g) Judicial Review of Challenges. Federal courts shall have jurisdiction to review and enjoin any act challenging the Section 16 nuclear protections outside of Article V. Such review shall proceed under the framework of Section 18.6, with the persistence of nuclear protections treated as a core structural provision subject to the same void-ab-initio protection as other Amendment structures. (h) No Interpretation Permitting Congressional Modification. No interpretation of this Amendment or of Section 16 shall permit Congressional modification of nuclear protections outside of Article V, regardless of stated rationale (including emergency circumstance, international treaty obligation, technological change, or any other asserted justification). The prohibition on non-Article V modification is categorical. 18.15 Foreign Interference Protections During Sunset Review. The Section 22 foreign interference framework shall apply with heightened vigilance during the Sunset Review period: (a) Heightened Monitoring. From the commencement of the ninety-day education period through certification of the Sunset Review outcome, the Hamilton Contingent shall conduct heightened monitoring for foreign interference targeting the Sunset Review. Monitoring findings shall be published on the Franklin Ledger. (b) Education Material Protection. Foreign actor contributions to voter education materials, public forums, or debates shall be prohibited under Section 22, with violations prosecutable under the Section 22 framework. Funding of advocacy for any Sunset Review option by foreign actors shall be prohibited. (c) Convention Protection. If the Modify option prevails, Convention proceedings shall be specifically protected from foreign interference, with delegates subject to Section 22 disclosure obligations regarding foreign relationships and any foreign attempts to influence Convention output. (d) Social Media Monitoring. The Academic Integrity Commission, in coordination with the Hamilton Contingent, shall monitor social media and online forums during the Sunset Review period for coordinated inauthentic behavior, foreign information operations, and disinformation campaigns. Findings shall be published on the Franklin Ledger with attribution where possible.

(e) Expedited Prosecution. Foreign interference during the Sunset Review period shall be prosecuted under Section 22 with expedited timelines, recognizing that such interference attacks the Amendment's core intergenerational renewal mechanism. 18.16 Sunset Review Timing and Conflict Resolution. The twenty-year interval between Sunset Reviews shall be fixed, with the following rules for timing and conflict resolution: (a) Fixed Twenty-Year Interval. Sunset Review Votes shall occur every twenty (20) years from the first Sunset Review following Ratification, without deviation. The fixed interval preserves the Amendment's intergenerational framework and prevents manipulation through early or delayed reviews. (b) No Early Sunset Review. No mechanism shall exist for early Sunset Review before the twenty-year interval expires. This prevents the Sunset Review from being weaponized to destabilize the Amendment during crisis periods. (c) Sunset Review Priority Over Conflicting Processes. Where a Sunset Review Vote is scheduled during an active No Confidence Petition or Referendum process, the Sunset Review shall proceed on schedule. The two processes shall operate in parallel, with the People exercising both Amendment rights concurrently. (d) Exception for Genuine Emergency. Where a genuine emergency under Section 10.7 would materially prevent meaningful voter participation in the Sunset Review, the Authority may, by Liberty Bell Initiative, postpone the Sunset Review by up to ninety (90) days. Postponement beyond ninety days shall require Watchdog Tribunal approval. Pretextual emergency declarations used to manipulate Sunset Review timing shall constitute Section 13 interference with Senior Official multipliers. (e) No Indefinite Postponement. Under no circumstance shall the Sunset Review be postponed indefinitely or by more than one hundred eighty (180) days total across all postponements within a single review cycle. Persistent postponement attempts shall be treated as attempts to suspend the Amendment under Section 18.6. 18.17 Historical Record of Sunset Reviews. Each Sunset Review shall be preserved as part of the Amendment's historical record: (a) Permanent Ledger Publication. Results of every Sunset Review — including vote totals by option, Jurisdiction-by-Jurisdiction breakdown, turnout figures, and Authority certification — shall be permanently published on the Franklin Ledger, preserving the intergenerational record of the People's expressed will. (b) Convention Records Preservation. Where the Modify option prevails, Constitutional Review Convention proceedings, deliberations, proposed modifications, and final output shall be permanently preserved, providing historical reference for future Sunset Reviews.

(c) Ratification Records. Records of ratification votes on Convention modifications — including Jurisdiction-by-Jurisdiction votes, timing, and outcomes — shall be permanently preserved. (d) Twenty-Year Report Series. The Citizens' Oversight Board's twenty-year reports under Section 18.7 shall accumulate into a report series providing continuous historical analysis of Amendment operation across multiple generations. (e) Academic Integrity Commission Analysis. The Academic Integrity Commission shall publish, within five (5) years of each Sunset Review, a comprehensive analytic report examining: voter participation patterns; geographic and demographic patterns of support for each option; factors influencing the outcome; and comparison with prior Sunset Reviews. Analysis shall be non-partisan and shall inform future reviews. (f) No Manipulation of Historical Record. The historical record of Sunset Reviews shall not be altered, redacted, or destroyed. Any attempt to manipulate the historical record shall constitute Section 13B evidence destruction with enhanced penalties reflecting the constitutional weight of the intergenerational record. 18.18 No Delay of Sunset Review Vote Permitted. No act of Congress, executive order, presidential proclamation, judicial ruling, state action, emergency declaration, martial law declaration, or any other federal, state, or territorial action shall delay, postpone, modify, or prevent a Sunset Review Vote scheduled under Section 18.1. Any attempt to do so shall be void ab initio and shall have no legal force; officials administering the Vote shall proceed notwithstanding any such purported order, declaration, ruling, or action. Any such attempt shall constitute interference under Section 13, triggering the full penalties thereof, including the fifteen (15) year minimum sentence and the lifetime bar from public office without possibility of pardon. The Section 5.12.1 officials' duty-to-proceed protections shall apply to Sunset Review administration without modification. The Sunset Review is the People's intergenerational exercise of constitutional authority over this Amendment itself; no generation's sitting government shall obstruct the next generation's sovereign judgment on the Amendment's continuation, modification, or repeal.

Section 19. Implementation, Build-Out, and the Joint Implementation Command

Key terms in this Section: • "The Authority" — The Independent Tripartite Oversight Authority (three bodies, see Section 17) — fully operational after Year 1 of the Implementation Period. • "Liberty Bell Initiative" — Separate concurrence of all three bodies of the Authority.

• "The Ledger" — The Sovereign Blockchain Voting Ledger (Section 4), fully operational by Phase Three. A provisional public ledger operates from Day 1 of ratification until the full Ledger is activated. • "Terminal" — A Sovereign Voting Terminal (Section 14), deployed in Phase Three. • "The Washington Commission" — The 7-member civilian caretaker body (seven Chief Justices of

Participating Jurisdictions by lottery) that protects the Amendment from ratification through 60 days after the three Authority bodies are sworn in. Joint Chiefs serve as non-voting military advisors. Named for George Washington. • "Short-Term Civilian Review Board" — The 56-member citizen body (one per Participating Jurisdiction by lottery) that operates in parallel with the Washington Commission from Day 30 onward, holding military veto power over Commission actions. • "State Attorneys General Council" — The 56-member body comprising the Attorney General (or equivalent chief legal-executive officer) of each state, DC, and territory, serving as the third lock in the triple-authorization structure for military action during the Washington Commission's Phase One period. Role transfers to the Academic Integrity Commission upon the Commission's transition from Phase One to Permanent Oversight role under Section 17D (at sixty (60) days after Authority inauguration under Section 19.19). • "Triple-authorization / Triple-lock" — The requirement that any defensive military action after Day 30 be approved by ALL THREE of: the Washington Commission majority, the Short-Term Civilian Review Board majority, AND the State Attorneys General Council 2/3 supermajority (38 of 56). Three institutionally independent civilian checks. • "Implementation Director" — The executive officer elected on Day 180 who manages the 5-year build-out; serves until the Authority certifies full operational capability.

• "Joint Implementation Command" — The body comprising the Implementation Director plus the two senior Joint Chiefs who manage build-out security and construction. • "Citizens' Implementation Watch Board" — The 100-person citizen oversight body that monitors the Joint Implementation Command throughout the build-out. A. General Provisions 19.1 Upon ratification of this Amendment pursuant to Article V, the institutions, infrastructure, and mechanisms established herein shall be constructed, staffed, and brought to full operational capability over a phased five (5) year Implementation Period. During this Period, the provisions requiring in-person voting, blockchain infrastructure, and Sovereign Voting Terminals shall not yet be enforceable as operational requirements, but all protections for the build-out process itself shall have immediate constitutional force. 19.2 The Implementation Period shall commence on the date of certified ratification and shall conclude only upon certification by the Authority that all institutions and infrastructure required by this Amendment are fully operational. If this has not occurred by the end of year five (5), the Implementation Period shall continue, with mandatory public status reports issued quarterly upon the Ledger. B. The

Joint Implementation Command 19.3 There is hereby established the Joint Implementation Command ("the Command"), which shall exercise the authorities set forth in this Section and shall dissolve upon the Authority's certification of full operational capability. The Command shall consist of three (3) members, all of whom shall have co-equal authority within their respective spheres: (a) The Implementation Director, who shall lead all civilian build-out operations; (b) The Senior-Most Joint Chief of Staff confirmed to have maintained the constitutional oath, who shall lead all military security operations in support of the build-out; and (c) The Second Senior-Most Joint Chief of Staff confirmed to have maintained the constitutional oath, serving as the tiebreaker and integrity check on the other two members. 19.4 The Command shall act only by majority vote, publicly recorded upon a provisional public ledger maintained for this purpose until the full Sovereign Blockchain Voting Ledger comes online. No single member of the Command shall possess unilateral authority over civilian build-out operations or over the military security posture supporting them.

19.4.0 Provisional Public Ledger Substrate — Foundational Principle. The provisional public ledger established in Section 19.4 shall utilize not fewer than three (3) qualifying independent public blockchains operating simultaneously as cryptographic substrate. Records under this Amendment shall be written to all three blockchains as cryptographic hashes proving document existence and integrity, with full documents preserved on the mandatory mirror network established in Section 19.4.3. The use of three independent public blockchains, rather than infrastructure built anew at Ratification, recognizes that continuously-operated public blockchains provide superior immutability, tamper-resistance, geographic distribution, and verification capability compared to any system that could be constructed within the seventy-two (72) hour window of Section 19.4.1. The three-chain minimum ensures that simultaneous compromise of all blockchain substrates would require coordinated attack across structurally-distinct systems, which is computationally and organizationally infeasible under foreseeable technology. 19.4.0.1 Qualifying Blockchain Criteria. A public blockchain qualifies for selection as provisional public ledger substrate if it meets all of the following criteria at the time of its selection: (a) Continuous Operation. Operated continuously as a live public network for not less than ten (10) years preceding its designation, without successful fifty-one percent (51%) consensus attack or other catastrophic integrity failure affecting historical records; (b) Validator Distribution. Maintains a validator, miner, or node network consisting of not fewer than one thousand (1,000) independent nodes operated by not fewer than five hundred (500) distinct entities, geographically distributed across not fewer than fifteen (15) countries; (c) Independent Governance. Not controlled, majority-owned, directed, or materially influenced by any single government, corporation, or foreign power, with protocol upgrades requiring broad community consensus rather than unilateral executive authority by any single entity; (d) Open Source. All core protocol software is open-source under licenses permitting unrestricted review, audit, and independent implementation, with source code publicly accessible in perpetuity; (e) Permissionless Access. Permits any person to read and, upon payment of standard network fees, write to the blockchain, without gatekeeping or authorization requirements by any single authority; (f) Independent Security Audits. Core protocol has been reviewed by not fewer than three (3) independent professional cryptographic security audit firms, with audit reports publicly accessible; (g) No Single Point of Governance. No single entity possesses authority to freeze accounts, reverse transactions, censor records, or modify historical state without broad validator consensus; (h) Not Under Foreign Adversary Control. Not subject to Section 22 foreign adversary control determinations, with this criterion reassessed annually by the Academic Integrity Commission once constituted. 19.4.0.2 Joint Assembly of Governors and Attorneys General — Initial Selection Authority. The three (3) qualifying blockchains used during Days 0 through 180 shall be selected by a Joint Assembly of state Governors and state Attorneys

General convened within the first week following certified ratification, through the process established in this Section. The Joint Assembly mechanism is established because, at Day 0, no Amendment body is yet operational, and because the selection of cryptographic substrate for the provisional public ledger is a decision requiring the combined democratic legitimacy and professional judgment of state constitutional officers already operating under their state oaths. The use of both state Governors and state Attorneys General, voting in separate supermajorities, ensures cross-branch consensus and prevents capture by any single branch or faction. 19.4.0.2.1 Joint Assembly Composition. The Joint Assembly shall consist of: (a) the sitting Governor of each of the fifty states, the Mayor of the District of Columbia, and the Governor of each of the five territories enumerated in Section 3.1.1, totaling fifty-six (56) chief executives; and (b) the sitting Attorney General (or equivalent chief legal-executive officer) of each of the fifty states, the District of Columbia, and each of the five territories enumerated in Section 3.1.1, totaling fifty-six (56) chief legal officers. The Joint Assembly shall have one hundred twelve (112) members in total. All members shall serve ex officio by virtue of their existing state office, with no separate appointment, confirmation, term, or federal oath required. 19.4.0.2.2 Convening and Timeline. The Joint Assembly shall convene automatically upon certified ratification without requirement of any federal action. Logistics coordination shall be performed by the National Governors Association and the National Association of Attorneys General acting jointly, or successor organizations, operating under the supervision of the Washington Commission once convened under Section 19.5.0.2. The Assembly shall meet through secure video conferencing to enable full participation from all Participating Jurisdictions without requiring physical travel during the first week of Amendment implementation. The Assembly shall: (a) complete nomination submission, evidence review, and public comment during Days One (1) through Six (6) following certified ratification; (b) conduct the supermajority vote on Day Seven (7); (c) if supermajority thresholds are not achieved on Day Seven (7), continue deliberations for not more than seven (7) additional days, with a final vote no later than Day Fourteen (14). 19.4.0.2.3 Nomination Process. Any member of the Joint Assembly may nominate any public blockchain meeting the qualifying criteria of Section 19.4.0.1. Nominations shall be accompanied by documentation demonstrating how the nominated blockchain meets each of the eight criteria, with supporting public data sources cited. All nominations and supporting documentation shall be published on state government transparency infrastructure within twenty-four (24) hours of submission, enabling public review throughout the deliberation period. Any qualifying blockchain may be nominated; the Joint Assembly is not limited to a pre-identified list. 19.4.0.2.4 Public Comment Period. From the moment of the first nomination through Day Six (6), any United States citizen, cryptographic expert, academic institution meeting the Section 17.16 qualifying criteria, or internationally-recognized election integrity observer organization may submit comments, supporting evidence, technical analyses, or opposition regarding nominated blockchains. Comments shall be published alongside nominations on state government transparency infrastructure for Joint Assembly consideration. The public comment period provides accountability and independent expertise, recognizing that state Governors and Attorneys General may not themselves possess deep blockchain expertise but can integrate expert input in making their decisions. 19.4.0.2.5 Supermajority Vote Requirements. On Day Seven (7), or on such later day within the fourteen (14) day window of Section 19.4.0.2.2(c) as the Assembly may require, the Joint Assembly shall vote on the selection of three (3) blockchains from among nominated qualifying chains. Selection shall require both of the following independent supermajorities: (a) approval by not fewer than two-thirds (2/3) of sitting Governors voting, meaning thirty-eight (38) of the fifty-six (56) chief executives; AND (b) approval by not fewer than two-thirds (2/3) of sitting Attorneys General voting, meaning thirty-eight (38) of the fifty-six (56) chief legal officers. Both supermajorities must be achieved for a chain to be selected. This dual-supermajority requirement ensures cross-branch consensus — a chain approved by executives but not legal officers, or vice versa, shall not be selected, preventing single-branch capture of the selection process. 19.4.0.2.6 Tiebreakers and Insufficient Selection. Where more than three (3) chains meet both supermajorities, the three chains with the highest combined approval totals (Governor approval plus Attorney General approval) shall be selected, with tiebreakers resolved in favor of chains with longer continuous operation. If fewer than three (3) chains achieve both supermajorities on Day Seven (7), the Assembly shall continue deliberations through Day Fourteen (14). If the Assembly cannot select three chains within fourteen (14) days total, records shall be written to all qualifying chains that have received either supermajority (Governors or AGs) until the Academic Integrity Commission formalizes selection under Section 19.4.0.3. No Assembly action shall result in fewer than three (3) chains receiving provisional ledger records during this period; where necessary to maintain the three-chain minimum, the Assembly shall continue deliberations until three chains are selected or the AIC formalizes selection under Section 19.4.0.3. 19.4.0.2.7 Public Livestream and Individual Vote Recording. All Joint Assembly proceedings, deliberations, public comment discussions, and votes shall be livestreamed on state government transparency infrastructure and, once operational, on the provisional public ledger. No Assembly session shall be conducted in secret. Every member's vote on each nominated chain shall be individually recorded and publicly accessible, with the record identifying the voting member, the chain voted upon, and the vote cast (approval, disapproval, or abstention). This radical transparency prevents closed-door deals, undocumented pressure, and unaccountable decisions during a time-critical constitutional process.

19.4.0.2.8 Non-Participation Consequences. Any Governor or Attorney General who refuses without good cause to participate in Joint Assembly proceedings shall be subject to Section 13 interference investigation under Section 19.5.0.5.2 and, upon Hamilton Contingent operational commencement, under Section 13. Good cause shall be limited to: documented medical emergency preventing participation; documented state emergency requiring the Governor's or

Attorney General's direct executive presence and precluding video conferencing participation; or analogous circumstance published on state government transparency infrastructure with specific detail sufficient for public evaluation. Non-participation shall not count as either approval or disapproval for supermajority calculation, but shall trigger investigation of the non-participating official for possible interference with the Amendment's Phase One establishment. An official found to have refused participation in bad faith shall be subject to removal from state office under state law and Section 13 interference penalties with Senior Official multipliers where the non-participation materially affected Assembly outcomes. 19.4.0.2.9 Federal Executive Non-Interference. No President, Vice President, Cabinet officer, federal agency head, or other federal executive officeholder shall participate in, direct, fund, contact, lobby, threaten, or attempt to influence Joint Assembly proceedings, individual members, or member state offices regarding Assembly matters. Any federal executive attempt to influence the Joint Assembly shall constitute Section 13 interference with Senior Official multipliers where applicable, shall be prosecutable by the State Attorneys General Council under Section 19.5.0.18.9.1, and shall be grounds for enhanced penalties under Section 13A. The Joint Assembly's proceedings shall be state-sovereign, with no federal executive involvement whatsoever. 19.4.0.3 Academic Integrity Commission Formalization and Ongoing Review. Upon full constitution of the Academic Integrity Commission under Section 19.19(d) on Day One Hundred Eighty (180), the Commission shall within ninety (90) days: (a) Review Joint Assembly Selection. Verify that the Joint Assembly's selection remains qualifying under Section 19.4.0.1, with any chain that has failed to maintain criteria flagged for replacement; (b) Liberty Bell Formalization. Formalize the three-chain selection through Liberty Bell Initiative of the Authority. The Authority may retain the Joint Assembly selection, replace disqualified chains with qualifying alternatives, or expand the selection to more than three chains if operational experience warrants additional redundancy. The Commission shall give substantial weight to the Joint Assembly's democratic legitimacy and shall not lightly overturn Assembly selections absent documented qualification failure or substantial operational concern; (c) Annual Review. Review blockchain selection annually thereafter for continued compliance with Section 19.4.0.1 criteria. A chain failing to maintain criteria shall be replaced within sixty (60) days of the finding, with replacement requiring Liberty Bell Initiative of the Authority. Records written to a subsequently-disqualified blockchain retain their evidentiary value for their period of valid designation, with cryptographic verification artifacts preserved notwithstanding subsequent disqualification; (d) Sunset Review Integration. The qualifying criteria of Section 19.4.0.1, the three-chain minimum of Section 19.4.0, and the Joint Assembly selection mechanism of Section 19.4.0.2 shall be reviewed during each Sunset Review under Section 18. The People may, through the Modify procedure of Section 18.4, update the criteria, minimum chain count, selection process, or any other aspect of this Section to reflect technological evolution and accumulated operational experience. 19.4.0.4 Technical Implementation and Funding. Writing to the three selected blockchains shall be performed by open-source software tools, with reference implementations published on publicly-accessible repositories within thirty (30) days of Ratification. Any person or entity may operate such software; no single entity shall be the sole writer of records to the blockchains, and redundant writing by multiple independent operators shall be encouraged to ensure continuous availability and to prevent single-operator capture. Willing developers and open-source communities may prepare reference implementations during the ratification campaign period, but no pre-Ratification obligation is created by this Amendment. The Washington Commission during Days 0 through 180, and the Academic Integrity Commission thereafter, shall verify that records have been properly written to all three blockchains through independent cryptographic verification, with any discrepancy triggering investigation under Section 19.4.5. Transaction fees for writing records to the three selected blockchains, and costs of maintaining open-source reference software, shall be funded through the Ratification Loan under Section 13I.4 as Amendment implementation expenses, with publicly accessible accounting of all transactions written and fees paid published on the provisional public ledger and, after cutover, on the full Sovereign Blockchain Voting Ledger. Annual reports on blockchain transaction costs shall be published as part of the Academic Integrity Commission's ordinary reporting requirements. 19.4.1 Provisional Public Ledger — Activation and Operational Start. The provisional public ledger shall be operational no later than seventy-two (72) hours after certified ratification, coinciding with the convening of the Washington Commission under Section 19.5.0.2. If technical circumstances prevent full provisional ledger activation within seventy-two (72) hours, the Washington Commission shall record its proceedings upon any available cryptographically-verifiable public record-keeping system, including state government transparency infrastructure, Pre-Certified University Pool institutional servers, or multiple independent journalistic and civic records, with those records subject to subsequent cryptographic migration to the provisional ledger upon its activation. No Washington Commission action, Joint Chiefs oath certification, Commission lottery challenge, or Amendment accountability proceeding shall be invalidated, delayed, or suspended by virtue of delay in provisional ledger activation. Full operational status of the provisional ledger shall be certified upon the Ledger itself within twenty-four (24) hours of activation, with certification

visible to all citizens. 19.4.2 Provisional Public Ledger — Technical Integrity Standards. The provisional public ledger shall meet the following minimum technical integrity standards, consistent with the design principles of Section 4 applied to the provisional context: (a) Cryptographic Verifiability. Every entry shall be cryptographically hashed at the moment of publication, with the hash chain publicly verifiable by any citizen through open-source verification tools; (b) Tamper-Evidence. Any modification, deletion, or reordering of entries shall be cryptographically detectable through the hash chain structure, with detection triggering automatic alarm notifications to all mirror-site operators within one (1) hour of detection; (c) Open Source. All software administering the provisional public ledger shall be open-source, with complete code published at the moment of provisional ledger activation and all subsequent updates published with seventy-two (72) hours advance notice; (d) Public Read Access. Any citizen shall have unrestricted read access to the provisional ledger at all times, including the ability to download the full ledger state and independently verify the hash chain; (e) Cryptographic Standards Continuity. The provisional ledger shall use cryptographic standards compatible with the full Sovereign Blockchain Voting Ledger under Section 4, enabling seamless migration at cutover without loss of evidentiary value for any provisional-period record; (f) No Backdoors. No provisional ledger implementation shall contain administrative backdoors, key-escrow provisions accessible to any federal officeholder, or other mechanisms that would permit non-transparent modification. Any such mechanism discovered shall constitute Section 13B evidence destruction subject to the enhanced penalties of Section 19.4.5. 19.4.3 Provisional Public Ledger — Mandatory Mirror Network. The provisional public ledger shall be simultaneously mirrored in real time to no fewer than seven (7) independent mirror sites maintained by structurally distinct custodians, such that compromise of any single custodian cannot alter the authoritative record. The mandatory mirror network shall include: (a) National Archives and Records Administration. The National Archives and Records Administration shall maintain two (2) geographically-dispersed cryptographically-hashed mirror copies of the provisional ledger at facilities designated by the Archivist of the United States, with records subject to Federal Records Act preservation requirements supplemented by the penalties of Section 19.4.5. The National Archives shall additionally maintain physical paper backups of all constitutional-level actions including Commission orders, Declarations under Section 17.22.1, Override certifications, Restoration certifications, and Inaugural Referendum results. The National Archives shall serve as a preservation backbone and verification source, not as administrator or publication gatekeeper; (b) State Judicial Records Mirror. A mirror shall be maintained by the state judicial records system of not fewer than three (3) Participating Jurisdictions whose Chief Justices are not currently serving on the Washington Commission, rotated annually to distribute custodianship; (c) State Elections Authority Mirror. A mirror shall be maintained by the chief elections officer of not fewer than three (3) Participating Jurisdictions, rotated annually, drawn from the State Elections Council members once that body activates; (d) Pre-Certified University Pool Mirror. No fewer than three (3) mirrors shall be maintained by member institutions of the Pre-Certified University Pool under Section 17.16, once the Pool is established by Day ninety (90) pursuant to Section 19.19(c). Prior to Pool establishment, interim academic mirrors shall be maintained by any three (3) accredited research universities meeting the qualifying criteria of Section 17.16 subsections (a) through (d), selected by the Washington Commission; (e) International Observer Mirror. At least one (1) mirror shall be maintained by an internationally-recognized election integrity or democratic governance observer organization operating independently of the United States federal government, with custody agreement negotiated by the Washington Commission or, once convened, by the Academic Integrity Commission. Custody agreements shall specify that the observer organization acts solely as preservation custodian with no administrative authority. All mirror sites shall maintain identical cryptographically-hashed copies updated in real time, with any detected discrepancy between mirrors triggering automatic investigation by the Watchdog Tribunal once operational or the Washington Commission during Phase One. No federal officeholder, federal agency, or federal court shall have authority to alter, suspend, or direct the content of any mirror. 19.4.4 Provisional Public Ledger — Civilian Administration Authority. The provisional public ledger shall be administered under civilian authority throughout its operational period, notwithstanding the technical operations support role of the Interim Two-Member Command during Days 1-180. Administrative authority shall pass through the following sequence: (a) Days 1-30. From certified ratification through the convening of the Short-Term

Civilian Review Board, the Washington Commission shall exercise civilian administrative authority over the provisional ledger, with the Interim Two-Member Command providing technical operations support only and exercising no content-modification authority; (b) Days 30-180. Upon convening, the Short-Term Civilian Review Board shall exercise supervisory authority over provisional ledger administration in parallel with the Washington Commission, with power to publish dissenting findings, demand records, and flag integrity concerns without Commission approval; (c) Day 180 Forward. Upon the Academic Integrity Commission's full constitution under Section 19.19(d), primary administrative authority shall transfer to the Academic Integrity Commission, which shall retain administration through full Ledger cutover under Section 19.5. The Citizens' Oversight Board and State Elections Council shall exercise concurrent oversight authority consistent with their Section 17 roles; (d) State Attorneys General Council Audit Authority. The State Attorneys General Council under Section 19.5.0.18 shall have continuous audit authority over provisional ledger integrity throughout Phase One, with findings published directly to the provisional ledger without review by any federal body; (e) Hamilton Contingent Investigation Authority. Upon Hamilton Contingent constitution under Section 19.19(f), the Contingent shall have full investigation authority over any suspected

tampering, obstruction, or integrity failure affecting the provisional ledger, coordinated with the Academic Integrity Commission's administrative role; (f) No Federal Executive Override. No President, Vice President, Cabinet officer, federal agency head, or other federal executive officeholder shall have authority to modify, suspend, limit, or direct the provisional ledger during Phase One. Any attempted federal executive override shall constitute Section 13 interference and shall be void ab initio. 19.4.5 Provisional Public Ledger — Tampering as Enhanced Federal Felony. Any person who alters, deletes, corrupts, obstructs access to, or attempts to alter, delete, corrupt, or obstruct access to the provisional public ledger or any of its mandatory mirrors shall be subject to Section 13B evidence destruction penalties, with an enhanced minimum sentence of twenty-five (25) years reflecting the provisional ledger's singular importance as the sole evidentiary substrate during the Phase One and Phase Two build-out period. Any federal officeholder or employee who directs, funds, or coordinates such tampering shall additionally be subject to: (a) Section 13 interference penalties with Senior Official multipliers where applicable; (b) the Section 16.5 insurrection penalties where the tampering occurs in the context of coordinated resistance to Amendment implementation; (c) Federal

Records Act penalties where the tampering affects National Archives mirror copies; and (d) automatic Section 13D Tier Three maximum asset recovery upon conviction. These penalties shall apply cumulatively and shall not be subject to Presidential pardon under Section 24.5. 19.4.6 Provisional Public Ledger — Cryptographic Continuity and Preservation of Evidentiary Value. Upon the Section 19.5 cutover, the full Sovereign Blockchain Voting Ledger shall preserve not only the migrated records but also the cryptographic verification artifacts of the provisional ledger, enabling retroactive verification of provisional-period records by any citizen using the full Ledger's tools. No record originating on the provisional ledger shall lose its evidentiary value by virtue of the cutover. The Academic Integrity Commission shall publish, within ninety (90) days of cutover, a comprehensive public cryptographic audit comparing all seven mirror-site copies against the migrated full Ledger records, with any discrepancies documented and investigated under Section 19.4.5. Should any discrepancy suggest tampering with the provisional ledger during its operational period, retroactive prosecution under Section 19.4.5 shall proceed without statute of limitations, in recognition of the constitutional weight of Phase One and Phase Two records. 19.5 Upon activation of the full Sovereign Blockchain Voting Ledger, all prior records of the Command's provisional public ledger shall be cryptographically migrated to the Ledger and made permanently accessible to the People. The Academic Integrity Commission shall certify the full Sovereign Blockchain Voting Ledger as operational upon completion of Phase Three requirements, with the date of certification publicly recorded upon the provisional ledger immediately prior to cutover. The formal cutover from provisional ledger to full Ledger shall occur on a specific date certified by the Academic Integrity Commission no less than thirty (30) days after operational testing is complete. During the cutover period: (a) the provisional ledger shall continue recording new entries until the moment of cutover; (b) all records shall be cryptographically migrated with preservation of original timestamps, signatures, and cryptographic hashes; (c) any matter pending on the provisional ledger at the moment of cutover shall continue under identical cryptographic status on the full Ledger; (d) no records shall be lost, modified, or redacted in the migration process; and (e) a public cryptographic audit of the migration shall be published upon the full Ledger within ninety (90) days of cutover, verifying the integrity of all migrated records. B.0 The Washington Commission 19.5.0.1 There is hereby established the Washington Commission ("the Commission"), named in honor of George Washington, who first demonstrated that American leadership serves the Constitution and the

People rather than itself. From the moment of certified ratification of this Amendment until sixty (60) days after the three bodies of the Independent Tripartite Oversight Authority are fully selected and sworn in pursuant to Section 19.19, the Commission shall serve as the caretaker body protecting this Amendment, its build-out, and its infrastructure from interference, corruption, or capture by the then-existing Federal Government or any other actor. 19.5.0.2 The Commission shall convene automatically within seventy-two (72) hours of certified ratification. No act of Congress, executive order, judicial ruling, or state action shall delay, impede, or invalidate its convening. Any attempt to do so shall constitute interference under Section 13 and shall trigger the full penalties thereof. 19.5.0.2.1 Initial Training Week — Mission Preparation Before Substantive Operations. The first seven (7) consecutive days following the Commission's convening under Section 19.5.0.2 shall constitute a dedicated Initial Training Week, during which the Commission shall focus primarily on preparation for its mission rather than substantive operational decisions. This training week recognizes that Chief Justices drawn by lottery for Commission service, however distinguished in their state judicial work, require rapid orientation to the unique constitutional responsibilities of Phase One protection before being asked to exercise those responsibilities. The Initial Training Week operates as follows: (a) Curriculum Scope. The Initial Training Week curriculum shall cover: (i) the structure and purpose of this Amendment; (ii) the specific Phase One authorities established in Sections 19.5.0.2 through 19.5.0.5; (iii) the limits on Commission authority under Section 19.5.0.6; (iv) coordination protocols with the Hamilton Contingent, the Short-Term Civilian Review Board (once convened), and the State Attorneys General Council; (v) the Franklin Ledger systems and transparency requirements; (vi) emergency response procedures under Sections 19.5.0.16

through 19.5.0.22; (vii) ethics, conflict-of-interest, and anti-capture protocols; (viii) the military triple-lock authorization process under Section 19.5.0.18 (once fully operational at Day 31); and (ix) the Nuclear Authorization Panel substitution role under Section 19.5.0.12; (b) Training Administration. The Initial Training Week shall be administered by a pre-designated team of senior administrators of the highest courts of Participating Jurisdictions, selected from the Participating Jurisdictions' highest-court systems on a rotating basis, with curriculum materials prepared and maintained in advance pursuant to Section 19.5.0.2.2. Administration shall be Jurisdiction-sovereign and shall not depend on any federal agency or body, to ensure training can proceed even where federal infrastructure is compromised; (c) Limited Operational Authority

During Training. During the Initial Training Week, the Commission shall possess the following operational authorities and only these authorities: (i) response to true emergencies involving active armed attack, active military operations against Amendment personnel or infrastructure, or other imminent threats requiring immediate Commission action; (ii) essential administrative functions necessary to maintain the Commission's own continuity (security arrangements, secure communications setup, record-keeping establishment); (iii) coordination with the Joint Chiefs of Staff on the constitutional oath verification process under Section 19.5.0.3.2; and (iv) issuance of preservation orders under Section 13B to prevent evidence destruction pending full operational status; (d) Prohibited Actions During Training. The Commission shall NOT, during the Initial Training Week: (i) make substantive policy decisions not required by true emergency; (ii) authorize military actions beyond immediate defensive response to active attack; (iii) appoint personnel to positions not essential to Commission continuity; (iv) issue orders or findings on matters not requiring immediate action; or (v) take any action that could be reasonably deferred to the post-training operational period; (e) Transition to Full Operations. Upon completion of the seventh (7th) training day, the Commission shall automatically transition to full Phase One operational authority under Sections 19.5.0.4 and 19.5.0.5, with all authorities available from that moment forward. The transition shall be recorded on the Ledger with certification that the training week has concluded; (f) Continuing Education. Throughout the Commission's Phase One operation, members shall have access to ongoing educational resources, consultation with state judicial administrators, and periodic curriculum updates. The Initial Training Week provides the foundation, not the entirety, of Commission preparation. 19.5.0.2.2 Training Curriculum Preparation and Maintenance. The curriculum for the Initial Training Week under Section 19.5.0.2.1 shall be:

(a) Prepared in Advance. Within sixty (60) days of certified ratification of this Amendment, a standardized curriculum shall be developed by a working group consisting of: three (3) senior administrators of the highest courts of Participating Jurisdictions selected by lottery from among the chief administrative officers of the highest courts of Participating Jurisdictions; two (2) constitutional law scholars selected by the Academic Integrity Commission (once convened); and one (1) representative from the National Center for State Courts or equivalent judicial coordinating body. The curriculum shall be published on the Franklin Ledger upon completion; (b) Updated Biennially. The curriculum shall be reviewed and updated at least every two (2) years, coinciding with each Biennial Rotation under Section 17D.5, to reflect operational experience, new legal interpretations, and emerging oversight challenges. Updates shall be published on the Ledger with change logs; (c) Applied to Biennial Rotations. The same curriculum (as updated) shall be used for training new Commission members at each Biennial Rotation under Section 17D.5, provided through the 60-day transition overlap period. Future-rotation trainings may be more extensive than the initial seven-day training given the available transition window, but the core curriculum shall remain consistent; (d) Jurisdiction-Sovereign Administration. All curriculum development, maintenance, and delivery shall be conducted through Jurisdiction-sovereign infrastructure (highest-court administration, bar associations, and judicial training institutes of Participating Jurisdictions), with no federal agency controlling curriculum content or delivery. This Jurisdiction-sovereign character ensures training cannot be captured by a compromised federal government; (e) Public Availability. The curriculum shall be publicly available on the Franklin Ledger for citizen review, academic commentary, and transparency. Citizens may submit proposed curriculum improvements through the petition process under Section 17A.16, with the curriculum working group considering such submissions at each biennial update cycle. 19.5.0.3 The Washington Commission shall consist of seven (7) members, all civilian: (a) Seven (7) sitting Chief Justices of Participating Jurisdictions as defined in Section 3, selected by randomized lottery from among all Chief Justices of Participating Jurisdictions. Their service on the Commission shall be ex officio and shall not interfere with their continued duties in their home Jurisdictions. 19.5.0.3.1 The Joint Chiefs of Staff, confirmed to have maintained the constitutional oath under Section 16 pursuant to the process set forth in Section 19.5.0.3.2, shall serve as non-voting military advisors to the Washington Commission. They shall:

(a) Present professional military analysis, threat assessments, and proposed defensive responses to the Commission; (b) Advise on operational matters, logistical feasibility, and lawful military procedure; (c) Execute actions duly authorized by the Commission and its triple-lock process; (d) Retain the constitutional authority and duty established in Section 16.3 to refuse any order that violates the Constitution, this Amendment, the laws of war, or the laws of the United States; and (e) NOT vote on the authorization of any military action, treaty response, or use of force during the Washington Commission period. The separation of military advisory function from civilian authorization function is a structural safeguard against military self-authorization. 19.5.0.3.2 Within forty-eight (48) hours of convening, the Washington Commission shall, by majority vote of the seven Chief Justices, certify which members of the Joint Chiefs of Staff are oath-maintained for purposes of their advisory role under Section 19.5.0.3.1. Each Joint Chief shall publicly affirm the constitutional oath upon the provisional public ledger as part of this certification. Any Joint Chief who refuses to affirm the oath in writing, or whose conduct the Commission finds has materially violated the oath, shall be excluded from advisory service. The Commission shall proceed with oath-maintained successors in order of military seniority until a full advisory complement is established. 19.5.0.3.2.1 Joint Chiefs Phase One Assembly and Ongoing Access Infrastructure. Because the Washington Commission's Phase One operations depend on Joint Chief advisory service under Section 19.5.0.3.1, oath verification under Section 19.5.0.3.2, and Interim Two-Member Command functions under Section 19.5.1, and because Joint Chiefs are structurally embedded in federal executive infrastructure that may be captured or hostile during Phase One, the following framework ensures Joint Chief operational availability to the Washington Commission throughout Phase One: (a) Constitutional Right of Phase One Assembly. Each Joint Chief of Staff shall have the constitutional right to physically assemble and communicate with the Washington Commission for purposes of this Amendment during Phase One, notwithstanding any contrary order, directive, restriction, or obstruction from the sitting President, Vice President, Secretary of Defense, or any other federal executive officer. This right derives from the Joint Chief's Section 16.3 duty to refuse unlawful orders and is constitutionally superior to executive command authority for purposes of Phase One duties; (b) Primary Venue. Existing Department of Defense facilities under Section 11C.9 remain the primary venue for Joint Chief assembly and the Interim Two-Member Command, where such facilities remain accessible and uncompromised; (c) Alternate Venue Hierarchy. Where Department of Defense facilities are denied, obstructed, or compromised through access restrictions, communications denial, surveillance of

Joint Chief communications with the Washington Commission, or any other material interference, the Joint Chiefs are authorized to assemble and conduct Phase One duties at alternate venues in the following descending order of preference: (i) National Guard armories, aviation facilities, or installations under state Governor authority (Title 32 status), with host Participating Jurisdiction providing security and logistics; (ii) Highest-court facilities of Participating Jurisdictions, particularly where the Washington Commission is convening; (iii) Federal judicial facilities (Article III court buildings), which are under Article III judicial branch authority rather than federal executive authority; (iv) State capitol secure facilities under host Jurisdiction's emergency management authority; (v) Any other Jurisdiction-sovereign secure facility identified through the Day Zero activation coordination under subsection (i); (d) Alternate Communications Infrastructure. Where Department of Defense communications systems are denied, restricted, monitored in a manner interfering with candid advisory service, or compromised, Joint Chiefs are authorized to communicate with the Washington Commission through: (i) National Guard communications infrastructure under state authority; (ii) State judicial secure video conference systems and encrypted communications; (iii) Federal judicial communications systems under Article III authority; (iv) Jurisdictional emergency management communications systems; and (v) Any commercially available encrypted communications as a last-resort option; (e) Convening Authority. The Washington Commission, acting by majority vote of its seven Chief Justices, shall have authority to direct Joint Chief assembly at any alternate venue under subsection (c) or use of alternate communications under subsection (d). Before the Washington Commission is fully constituted, the senior-most Joint Chief of Staff who has not been credibly alleged to have violated the constitutional oath under Section 16 may self-convene the Joint Chiefs at an alternate venue where Department of Defense access is denied; (f) Assembly Timeline. Joint Chiefs shall be physically available for oath verification under Section 19.5.0.3.2 within thirty (30) days of Ratification, parallel to the Washington Commission convening timeline under Section 19.5.0.2. Where an individual Joint Chief cannot reach the assembly venue within thirty days due to genuine operational necessity (active deployment to a war zone, medical incapacity, or similar), that Joint Chief may affirm oath through the individual pathway under subsection (g); (g) Individual Oath Affirmation Pathway. Where a Joint Chief cannot assemble in person, oath affirmation shall be available through: (i) Secure video communication from the Joint Chief's current location using any alternate communications under subsection (d), witnessed by the Washington Commission via livestream; (ii) Sworn written affirmation executed before any sitting federal judge (Article III) or any sitting Chief Justice of a Participating Jurisdiction, transmitted to the Washington Commission with certification of authenticity; (iii) Video recording published directly to the provisional public ledger from state-sovereign infrastructure, subject to Washington Commission authentication verification within twenty-four (24) hours through live video confirmation by the affirming Joint Chief with the Washington Commission; (h) Ongoing Access

Protection During Phase One. Beyond initial assembly, the Washington Commission shall have authority throughout Phase One to direct Joint Chief attendance at advisory sessions, receipt of communications, and operational availability, using any venue and communications pathway authorized under subsections (b) through (d). Any pattern of denial, obstruction, or material interference with ongoing Joint Chief availability to the Washington Commission shall trigger: (i) an automatic finding of Section 13 interference by the Washington Commission upon majority vote (four of seven Chief Justices); (ii) activation of alternate venue and communications pathways under this Section; and (iii) publication of the denial pattern on the provisional public ledger; (i) Day Zero Activation of Alternate Venue Identification. Upon certified Ratification, the Washington Commission (once convened), the National Governors Association (or successor organization), the Conference of Chief Justices, and the National Guard Bureau (through the Chiefs of the National Guard, who hold state authority dual to federal authority) shall immediately coordinate to identify alternate assembly venues and alternate communications pathways in each Participating Jurisdiction, with initial identification completed within thirty (30) days of Ratification and published on state government transparency infrastructure and, upon activation, the provisional public ledger. Where the initial Joint Chief assembly under subsection (f) occurs before alternate venue identification is complete, assembly shall default to National Guard facilities in the Participating Jurisdiction where the Washington Commission is convening. Ongoing alternate venue identification shall continue throughout Phase One as a permanent operational capability. Willing state Governors, State Attorneys General, Chief Justices, and National Guard Adjutants General acting under their existing state authority may coordinate preparation during the ratification campaign period, but no pre-Ratification obligation is created by this Amendment; (j) National Guard Federalization Prohibition During Phase One. Because this Section contemplates use of National Guard facilities and communications under state authority, the President shall not, during the period from Ratification through Day One Hundred Eighty (180), federalize National Guard units (transfer to Title 10 federal status) where such federalization would materially impair Washington Commission operations, Joint Chief alternate venue access, or alternate communications availability under this Section. Any such federalization attempted during Phase One shall be void ab initio as to impairment of Phase One functions, with Governors retaining authority to treat such federalization orders as void ab initio for the duration of Phase One; (k)

Obstruction Consequence. Any President, Vice President, Cabinet officer (including Secretary of Defense, Deputy Secretary of Defense, Under Secretaries of Defense, and service Secretaries), federal agency head, military commander in federal executive chain of command, Secret Service Director or agent acting under federal executive direction, or any other federal executive officeholder or employee who denies, obstructs, surveilles to obstructive effect, or materially interferes with Joint Chief physical assembly, communications, logistics, or advisory service to the Washington Commission during Phase One shall be subject to Section 13 interference penalties with Senior Official multipliers, enhanced penalties under Section 21.9 for interference with a constitutional caretaker body, and forfeiture of any pension or deferred compensation associated with the federal office held. Obstruction by military personnel in violation of Section 16.3 shall additionally subject the offender to Section 16.12 penalties; (l) Protection from Military Legal Process for Phase One Duty Performance. No Joint Chief of Staff, and no other military officer or enlisted member, shall be subject to court-martial, non-judicial punishment, administrative discharge, loss of rank, pension forfeiture, or any other adverse military legal or administrative action for performance of duties under this Section, for attendance at Washington Commission sessions, for use of alternate venues or communications under subsections (c) and (d), for oath affirmation under subsections (f) or (g), or for refusal of orders obstructing such duties pursuant to Section 16.3. Any court-martial proceeding, administrative action, or punishment initiated in violation of this subsection shall be void ab initio, and all documentation and records of such proceedings shall be expunged upon Washington Commission finding of prohibited prosecution. The Washington Commission shall, upon majority vote, issue orders prohibiting continuation of such proceedings, and such orders shall bind military courts and commanders notwithstanding their position within federal executive chain of command. Where a military court or commander proceeds despite a Washington Commission prohibition order, the court or commander personally shall be subject to Section 13 interference penalties under subsection (k) of this Section, and any verdict or administrative action so rendered shall be void and automatically expunged; (m) Captured Jurisdiction Substitute Authority. Where a Participating Jurisdiction's Governor (or equivalent chief executive) refuses to honor this Amendment's authorization of alternate venues or communications under subsections (b) through (d), cooperates with federal executive obstruction of Joint Chief duties, or otherwise refuses to make state-sovereign infrastructure available for Phase One Joint Chief operations, the following substitute authority shall apply: (i) Any other Participating Jurisdiction's Governor may host Joint Chiefs at that Governor's Jurisdiction's Guard facilities, courthouses, capitol, or other secure facilities, with the hosting Governor's authority to provide security and logistics being fully sufficient under this Section; (ii) Within the non-compliant Jurisdiction, the Attorney General of that Jurisdiction (acting under Jurisdictional law authority independent of the Governor) may facilitate Joint Chief access to highest-court facilities under subsection (c)(ii), with the Chief Justice of the Jurisdiction's highest court providing security coordination; (iii) The Governor's refusal shall constitute material non-compliance under Section 20.15, triggering the consequences of that Section including funding cutoff and Congressional participation suspension, and individual gubernatorial obstruction shall constitute Section 13 interference with Senior Official multipliers under subsection (k); (iv) The substitute authority under this subsection is additional to, not in lieu of, the five-tier venue hierarchy under subsection (c) — Joint Chiefs may proceed under any available pathway without requiring exhaustion of others where delay would materially impair Phase One operations; (n) Safeguards Against Abuse

of Captured Jurisdiction Substitute Authority. Because subsection (m) creates substantial consequences for a Participating Jurisdiction's Governor, including Section 20.15 material non-compliance consequences that affect the entire Jurisdiction's federal relationship, the following safeguards shall apply before substitute authority is invoked against a Governor: (i) Good-Faith Presumption. Every Governor shall be presumed to act in good faith absent clear and convincing evidence of obstruction. Disagreement over venue selection, timing concerns, legitimate security questions, budget concerns, request for ordinary Jurisdiction-law authorization procedures, or other lawful exercises of gubernatorial authority shall not constitute obstruction; (ii) Written Request and Response Window. Before subsection (m) is invoked, the Washington Commission shall transmit a written request to the Governor specifying: the specific facility or infrastructure sought; the duration of proposed use; security and logistical arrangements; and the relevant Phase One duty being performed. The Governor shall have seventy-two (72) hours to respond with accommodation, alternative proposal, or specific objection. Response with alternative proposal or good-faith objection shall not constitute refusal triggering subsection (m); (iii) Supermajority Determination Required. A Governor shall not be deemed to have refused cooperation triggering subsection (m) consequences unless: the Washington Commission, acting by six-sevenths (6/7) supermajority (six of seven Chief Justices), formally finds that the

Governor has engaged in bad-faith obstruction rather than legitimate exercise of Jurisdictional authority; the finding is supported by specific documented evidence published on the provisional public ledger; and the Governor has been given the response window under subsection (ii); (iv) Governor Right of Rebuttal. Upon a preliminary six-sevenths finding under subsection (iii), the Governor shall have fourteen (14) days to submit rebuttal evidence and argument, which the Washington Commission shall consider before any determination of material non-compliance under Section 20.15 is finalized. During this rebuttal window, Joint Chiefs may proceed under alternate venues in willing Jurisdictions under subsection (m)(i) — substitute authority for operational continuity is not delayed by the rebuttal window, but Section 20.15 consequences are stayed pending rebuttal consideration; (v) Appeal to Emergency Panel. Where the Washington Commission makes a final determination of Governor bad-faith obstruction, the affected Governor may appeal to an Emergency Review Panel consisting of five (5) sitting Chief Justices of Participating Jurisdictions drawn by lottery from Chief Justices not serving on the Washington Commission and not from the appealing Governor's Jurisdiction. The Emergency Review Panel shall review under clear-error standard and may vacate the determination. Emergency Review Panel decisions shall be made within thirty (30) days of appeal filing and published on the provisional public ledger; (vi) No Retroactive Consequences for Good-Faith Errors. Where a Governor acted in good faith and is later determined (through subsections (iii) through (v) process) to have made a mistake in judgment, Section 20.15 consequences shall not be applied retroactively, and any interim operational workaround under subsection (m)(i) shall not trigger non-compliance findings against the Jurisdiction as a whole; (vii)

Protection Against Retaliatory Determination. Any Washington Commission finding against a Governor that is subsequently vacated by the Emergency Review Panel under subsection (v), or that is found by the Watchdog Tribunal (once convened) or by post-Phase-One Authority review to have been made in bad faith or without adequate evidence, shall subject the Washington Commission members who voted in favor of the finding to removal and Section 13 interference penalties personally. This safeguard prevents Washington Commission capture from being weaponized against legitimate Governors; (o) Ongoing Joint Chief Integrity Verification and Suspension Authority. Because Joint Chiefs are federally appointed by the President and may be corrupted before, during, or after oath verification under Section 19.5.0.3.2, and because the protective infrastructure of this Section (particularly subsections (a), (c), (d), (l), and (m)) could be misused by corrupt Joint Chiefs to shield themselves from accountability or facilitate corrupt coordination, the following ongoing integrity verification framework applies throughout Phase One and into Permanent Oversight: (i) Periodic Re-Verification. No less than every sixty (60) days throughout Phase One, and no less than every six (6) months during Permanent Oversight, the Washington Commission (or Permanent Commission) shall review the conduct of each oath-verified Joint Chief and either re-certify or suspend oath-maintained status. Re-certification shall require affirmative majority vote; silence or deadlock shall default to continuation of oath-maintained status only where no credible evidence of oath violation has emerged since prior certification; (ii) Credible Evidence Triggers. Any of the following shall trigger expedited Washington Commission review of a Joint Chief's oath-maintained status, with review completed within seventy-two (72) hours: (A) documented participation in any action facilitating federal executive interference with Amendment operations; (B) documented coordination with Refusing Officials under Section 13E; (C) documented failure to report known oath violations by subordinate military personnel; (D) undisclosed financial, professional, or personal relationships with individuals under investigation by the Hamilton Contingent or its predecessors; (E) pattern of votes or advisory positions inconsistent with the Joint Chief's prior professional record, suggesting possible coercion or corruption; (F) credible external intelligence (from allied nations, whistleblowers, or other sources) of compromise; (iii) Suspension Authority. Upon credible evidence under subsection (ii), the Washington Commission may, by majority vote (four of seven Chief Justices), immediately suspend a Joint Chief's oath-maintained status pending full review under subsection (iv). During suspension: (A) the suspended Joint Chief loses the protections of subsections (a), (l), and (m) of this Section; (B) the suspended Joint Chief may not participate in advisory sessions, Interim Two-Member Command functions, or any other Amendment-authorized military role; (C) the succession cascade under Section 19.5.5 proceeds; (D) the suspended Joint Chief retains ordinary federal legal rights including due process in any criminal or administrative proceeding; (iv) Full Review Process. Within thirty (30) days of suspension, the Washington Commission shall conduct full review with: (A) written specification of evidence supporting suspension published on the provisional public ledger; (B) opportunity for suspended Joint Chief to respond with rebuttal evidence and argument; (C) opportunity for suspended Joint Chief to be represented by counsel of their choice; (D) consideration of evidence from Hamilton Contingent (if operational) or AIC-Designate Forensic Consortium;

(E) final determination by supermajority vote (six of seven Chief Justices) to either revoke oath-maintained status permanently or restore it with documented reasoning published on the ledger; (v) Joint Chief Right of Appeal. A Joint Chief whose oath-maintained status is permanently revoked may appeal to an Emergency Review Panel consisting of five (5) sitting Chief Justices of Participating Jurisdictions drawn by lottery from Chief Justices not serving on the Washington Commission, reviewing under clear-error standard within thirty (30) days. Emergency Review Panel decisions shall be final and published on the provisional public ledger; (vi) Protection Against Abuse of Suspension Authority. Because suspension of a Joint Chief's oath-maintained status carries severe operational and reputational consequences, the Washington Commission shall not suspend without the specific evidentiary basis required under subsection (ii). Any Washington Commission member who votes to suspend a Joint Chief without adequate evidentiary basis, or in coordination with other Commission members to weaponize suspension authority against legitimate Joint Chiefs, shall be subject to removal from Washington Commission under the procedures of Section 17D.8 and to Section 13 interference penalties personally; (vii) Parallel Obligations Under Traditional Command. Nothing in this subsection shall impair the President's ordinary command authority over Joint Chiefs in non-Amendment matters, including removal for cause under existing law. A Joint Chief whose oath-maintained status is revoked under this Section may still continue to serve as a Joint Chief in ordinary military command functions unless separately removed through existing military legal processes, but shall not receive any Amendment-specific protection or authority; (p) Catastrophic Joint Chief Unavailability — Alternative Senior Military Officer Framework. Where the succession cascade under Section 19.5.5 and Section 19.5.6 exhausts without identifying any Joint Chief who can satisfy oath verification and civilian approval, or where the entire Joint Chiefs of Staff is credibly alleged to have materially violated the constitutional oath under Section 16, or where the Joint Chiefs cannot be physically located, contacted, or assembled within ninety (90) days despite all alternate venue and communications efforts under this Section, the following alternative senior military officer framework shall apply: (i) Qualifying Officer Pool. The pool of alternative senior military officers shall consist of: (A) active-duty four-star or three-star general and flag officers not in the Joint Chiefs seniority line; (B) retired four-star or three-star general and flag officers who retired within the preceding ten (10) years; (C) senior service academy superintendents (Commandants) not appointed during the administration alleged to have triggered the catastrophic unavailability; (D) Senior Staff Officers who held joint-command positions and retired within the preceding ten (10) years; (ii) Selection Authority. During Phase One before Washington Commission convening, selection shall be

made by the senior-most sitting Chief Justice of any Participating Jurisdiction not having declined or been excluded from the Washington Commission lottery, acting in consultation with the State Attorneys General Council and willing state Governors through National Governors Association infrastructure. After Washington Commission convening, selection shall be made by Washington Commission majority vote (four of seven Chief Justices), with recommendations permitted from Conference of Chief Justices, National Governors Association, and willing State Attorneys General; (iii) Verification Standards. Alternative senior military officers shall satisfy all the following before acting in any Phase One role: (A) oath affirmation under Section 19.5.0.3.2 procedures applied mutatis mutandis; (B) verification that no federal executive appointment during the administration alleged to have triggered the catastrophic unavailability contributed to the officer's current rank or position (to prevent captured-administration-appointed officers from claiming the role); (C) affirmation on the provisional public ledger of commitment to Amendment operations and civilian control of military; (D) public disclosure of any financial, professional, or personal relationships with officials under investigation; (iv) Legal Authority. An alternative senior military officer recognized under this subsection shall have, for Phase One Amendment purposes only: (A) full advisory authority under Section 19.5.0.3.1; (B) full Interim Two-Member Command authority under Sections 19.5.1 through 19.5.6 (if that role is vacant); (C) the constitutional protections of this Section 19.5.0.3.2.1 applied mutatis mutandis; (D) no command authority over ordinary military operations outside Amendment purposes, unless separately lawful through existing chain of command. This dual-track authority structure respects existing military command authority while providing Amendment-specific operational capacity; (v) Automatic Dissolution. The alternative senior military officer framework shall dissolve automatically upon identification of any Joint Chief (existing or newly appointed) who satisfies oath verification and civilian approval under the succession cascade of Sections 19.5.5 and 19.5.6. Upon dissolution, all records transfer and the alternative officer stands down; (vi) Good-Faith Civilian Coordination Protection. Any senior military officer who accepts an alternative role under this subsection in good-faith reliance on Washington Commission or Chief Justice certification shall not be subject to adverse military legal consequence for that service, consistent with subsection (l) of this Section. The protection extends to subordinate military personnel who support the alternative officer's Amendment functions; (vii) Limitation — Not a Coup Mechanism. Nothing in this subsection shall authorize military action beyond Amendment advisory and Phase One functions, and nothing shall authorize any military officer to assume civilian governing authority, command structure outside Amendment purposes, or any function not specifically enumerated. The purpose is narrow: ensuring Amendment-specific Joint Chief functions have qualified military advisors when the ordinary Joint Chiefs are catastrophically unavailable. 19.5.0.3.3 Commission Lottery Integrity. The lottery selecting the seven Chief Justices of Participating Jurisdictions for the Washington Commission shall be administered jointly by the Chief Justices of the five most populous Participating Jurisdictions whose Chief Justices are NOT among those ultimately selected, operating under the supervision of the National Center for State Courts or equivalent judicial coordinating body. The lottery shall use cryptographically-verifiable random number generation with multi-party seed contribution, with at least three (3) independent seed contributors drawn from distinct branches of Jurisdictional government (Jurisdictional judiciary, Jurisdictional elections administration, Jurisdictional auditor). Every step of the lottery shall be recorded upon the provisional public ledger within twenty-four (24) hours of selection, including: the seed values contributed; the algorithm used; the cryptographic verification data; and the full list of eligible Chief Justices considered. 19.5.0.3.4 Lottery Challenge and Re-Run Procedure. Any challenge to the integrity of the Commission lottery shall be filed within seven (7) days of selection by any sitting Chief Justice of a Participating Jurisdiction, any Attorney General of a Participating Jurisdiction, or any United States citizen submitting specific evidence of compromise. Challenges shall be resolved by a supermajority (two-thirds) vote of the Chief Justices of Participating Jurisdictions not selected in the original lottery, meeting within seventy-two (72) hours of the challenge filing by secure video conference, with the standard of review being whether the evidence raises substantial concern of lottery compromise. If the challenge succeeds, the lottery shall be re-run within forty-eight (48) hours using fresh seed values from new contributors, and all Commission actions between the original selection and the re-run shall remain in force as interim decisions subject to ratification by the newly-constituted Commission within fourteen (14) days of its re-convening. Any interim decision not ratified within the fourteen-day window shall be void ab initio. The original Commissioners shall continue to discharge their Phase

One duties during the challenge and any re-run period to prevent operational gap, but shall not take new non-emergency actions during the challenge pendency. Any person who files a challenge in bad faith specifically to delay or obstruct Commission convening shall be subject to Section 13 interference penalties. 19.5.0.3.5 Chief Justice Refusal Fallback — Extended Commission Lottery Pool. Because the Washington Commission's automatic convening under Section 19.5.0.2 requires sitting Chief Justices of Participating Jurisdictions willing to serve, and because coordinated intimidation, threats, retaliation, or capture could reduce the number of willing sitting Chief Justices below the seven required for Commission composition, the following cascading fallback pool expansion shall apply where the lottery under Section 19.5.0.3 cannot produce seven willing members within the seventy-two (72) hour convening window: (a) Fallback Trigger. The extended pool activates upon certification by the senior-most sitting Chief Justice willing to serve (or, if none willing, by the senior-most sitting Chief Justice of the highest-population Participating Jurisdiction) that the lottery under Section 19.5.0.3 cannot produce seven willing

members from the primary pool of sitting Chief Justices of Participating Jurisdictions within the convening window, with specific documented basis published on the provisional public ledger. (b) First Tier Extension — Retired Chief Justices. The lottery pool shall extend to include retired Chief Justices of Participating Jurisdictions who retired within the preceding ten (10) years and who remain eligible for judicial service under their home Jurisdiction's law. Retired Chief Justices who served prior to Ratification may participate in the lottery under this tier provided they affirm the constitutional oath upon the provisional public ledger. (c) Second Tier Extension — Senior Associate Justices of State Highest Courts. If the first tier extension does not produce seven willing members, the lottery pool shall further extend to include senior Associate Justices of the highest courts of Participating Jurisdictions, defined as the three (3) most senior Associate Justices of each Participating Jurisdiction's highest court (by continuous service on the court). For purposes of this extension, a senior Associate Justice serves in lieu of, not in addition to, the Chief Justice of the same Jurisdiction; the lottery shall select no more than one (1) member from any single Participating Jurisdiction. (d) Third Tier Extension — Federal Article III Judges. If the first and second tier extensions do not produce seven willing members, the lottery pool shall further extend to include senior Article III judges of federal courts of appeals and federal district courts, excluding any judge serving on the United States Supreme Court. For purposes of this extension, federal Article III judges shall serve in their personal judicial capacity rather than as representatives of the federal judiciary, and shall receive the same protections and authorities as state Chief Justices serving on the Commission. Federal Article III judges on the Commission shall recuse themselves from any Commission action affecting their ordinary federal judicial docket. (e) Cascading Time Windows. Each tier has an additional forty-eight (48) hours to produce seven willing members before the next tier activates. The cumulative window from initial convening deadline to third tier activation shall not exceed two hundred sixteen (216) hours (nine days) from certified Ratification. During the cumulative window, any willing sitting Chief Justices of Participating Jurisdictions shall continue to be drawn from the primary pool, with extension tiers filling only the remaining seats. (f) Mixed Commission Composition. A Commission constituted through any combination of tiers (primary pool sitting Chief Justices, retired Chief Justices, senior Associate Justices, federal Article III judges) shall function identically to a Commission constituted exclusively from the primary pool, with all members having equal voting rights and authorities. The mixed composition shall not affect the validity of any Commission action. (g) Documentation and Transparency. The certification under subsection (a), the rationale for each tier activation, the willingness confirmations from selected members, and the final Commission composition shall be published on the provisional public ledger in real time as events occur. Any interference with the fallback lottery process, intimidation of potential members, or bad-faith refusal by sitting Chief Justices designed to force reliance on extended tiers shall constitute Section 13 interference with Senior Official multipliers. (h) Automatic Restoration. If, during Phase One, conditions change such that sufficient sitting Chief Justices of Participating Jurisdictions become willing to serve, the Commission composition shall not be retroactively altered; members selected through extension tiers shall complete their Phase One service in ordinary course. However, at the first Biennial Rotation under Section 17D.5 following Commission composition through extended tiers, the primary pool shall be used exclusively unless circumstances requiring extended tiers persist. (i) Limitation — Narrow Emergency Scope. This subsection shall be invoked only when the primary pool genuinely cannot produce seven willing members, not for convenience, scheduling preference, or any other reason. Any certification under subsection (a) made without genuine basis shall be void, and the certifying official shall be subject to Section 13 interference penalties. The extended pool framework exists to ensure Phase One operability when coordinated attack has reduced Chief Justice willingness below sustainable levels, not to permit casual deviation from the constitutional design preference for sitting state Chief Justices. 19.5.0.4 The Commission shall act only by majority vote of the seven Chief Justices, with all decisions publicly recorded and livestreamed in real time pursuant to Section 19.5.0.10. The all-civilian composition guarantees civilian majority control at all times throughout the Commission's existence, and eliminates structural risk of military self-authorization. 19.5.0.5 The Commission shall possess the following limited authorities, and only these: (a) Override Power. The authority to override, suspend, or void any act, order, regulation, appropriation, directive, or other action of the existing Federal Government that is specifically designed to interfere with, obstruct, delay, defund, or prevent the Implementation of this Amendment, the establishment or operation of the three bodies of the Authority, the construction of any institution established by this Amendment, or the continued protection of its infrastructure. Overrides shall be by majority vote, publicly reasoned, and livestreamed; (b) Protective Authority. The authority to secure physical sites, personnel, equipment, and funds designated for the Implementation of this Amendment against seizure, destruction, defunding, or interference; (c) Referral Authority. The authority to refer any federal officeholder or employee found to have interfered with the Implementation to criminal prosecution under Section 13; and

(d) Nuclear Authorization Panel Oversight and Governor Vote Coordination. Authority to oversee the operational integrity of the 5-person Nuclear Authorization Panel established under Section 19.5.0.12 during the Washington Commission period, including: oath verification of Joint Chief members under Section 19.5.0.3.2; verification of State Attorneys General Council selection of the substitute member under Section 19.5.0.12(d); lottery integrity verification for the substitute Chief Justice member under Section 19.5.0.12(e); observation of Panel proceedings; coordination of the ninety percent (90%) Governor vote under Section 16.7.1 during the Washington Commission period, including secure communications coordination and vote publication oversight; oversight of the Emergency Nuclear Authorization Committee under Section 19.5.0.11.5; and referral of any Panel composition or procedural irregularities to the Watchdog Tribunal (upon operational) or to the State Attorneys General Council. The Commission does not itself sit on the Panel; its role is to ensure Panel composition integrity, Governor vote coordination, and Emergency Committee oversight during the Phase One substituted period. 19.5.0.5.1 Ratification Certification. For purposes of triggering the seventy-two (72) hour Commission convening clock under Section 19.5.0.2 and all other Amendment deadlines, Ratification shall be deemed certified upon the earliest of: (a) publication by the National Archives and Records Administration of certification that three-fourths of state legislatures have ratified pursuant to Article V of the Constitution; (b) joint declaration by not fewer than thirty-eight (38) state Attorneys General that three-fourths of state legislatures have ratified, published simultaneously upon each of their state websites and upon the provisional public ledger; or (c) Composite State Officer Declaration — joint declaration by any combination of state chief executive officers, state legislative chambers, state Chief Justices, and State Attorneys General representing thirty-eight (38) or more Participating Jurisdictions, where no single type of state officer need reach the thirty-eight (38) threshold alone but the combined total of Jurisdictions represented through any combination of officer types reaches thirty-eight (38) or more. For purposes of subsection (c), each Participating Jurisdiction may be represented by any of the following, with each Jurisdiction counted only once regardless of how many of its officers join: the sitting Governor or chief executive; the sitting Attorney General; the sitting Chief Justice of the highest court; a chamber of the state legislature acting by majority vote; or any combination thereof. The composite declaration shall be published simultaneously upon each participating state's government transparency infrastructure and upon the provisional public ledger, with identity and role of each declaring officer documented. If the National Archives declines to certify, delays certification beyond seven (7) days of the thirty-eighth state ratification, or purports to rescind certification after issuance, the State Attorneys General declaration under subsection (b) or the Composite State Officer Declaration under subsection (c) shall control. No federal official, court, or agency shall have authority to challenge, enjoin, or delay any declaration under subsections (b) or (c); any attempt to do so shall constitute Section 13 interference and shall be void ab initio. The Attorneys General making the declaration under subsection (b), and the state officers making the declaration under subsection (c), shall face no federal liability, investigation, or retaliation for their declaration, and any such action against them shall itself constitute Section 13 interference. Subsection (c) exists to address scenarios in which coordinated capture of a single type of state officer (for example, State Attorneys General) could otherwise block certification; by permitting Jurisdictions to be represented through any branch of state government, subsection (c) makes certification robust against single-branch capture across states. 19.5.0.5.1.1 Popular Sovereignty Foundation of Certification Pathways. The certification pathways under Section 19.5.0.5.1(b) and (c) do not themselves grant new authority to state Attorneys General, Governors, Chief Justices, or state legislative chambers; they record and document the constitutional fact of Ratification as established by the People of the several states acting through their legislatures under Article V. The authority to certify flows from the underlying ratification by three-fourths of state legislatures (the constitutional act), not from the certifying officials themselves. State officials performing certification under this Section act ministerially — recording what the People have accomplished — not substantively. This framework resolves any apparent circularity in self-executing ratification mechanisms: the Amendment becomes constitutionally operative when three-fourths of state legislatures ratify, and the certification pathways merely provide means of recording that constitutional fact when the traditional federal recording mechanism (National Archives) fails or refuses. Popular sovereignty — the fundamental authority of the People acting through their state legislatures — is the source of constitutional authority; state officer certifications are evidentiary, not constitutive. This principle draws from the original Constitution's ratification by state conventions acting on popular authority, which similarly preceded and established the constitutional framework that then recognized those conventions' authority. The constitutional act precedes and creates the framework that recognizes it. No court, agency, or official may invalidate certification under Section 19.5.0.5.1(b) or (c) on grounds that the certifying officials lacked authority; their authority is derivative and evidentiary, flowing from the People's ratification act itself, and challenges to their ministerial role do not reach the underlying constitutional act. 19.5.0.5.2 Federal Enforcement Coordination During Phase One. Until the Hamilton Contingent is fully operational on Day One Hundred Eighty (180) under Section 19.19(f), federal-level enforcement of Section 13 interference penalties shall be coordinated by the Commission through the State Attorneys General Council under Section 19.5.0.18.4. During this Phase One window: (a) the State Attorneys General Council shall have primary federal prosecution authority for Section 13 interference acts, with prosecution authorizations requiring two-thirds (2/3) supermajority of the Council (thirty-eight (38) of fifty-six (56)) consistent with Section 19.5.0.18.9.1. No individual State Attorney General shall exercise

federal prosecution authority under this subsection acting alone; all federal Section 13 prosecutions during Phase One shall proceed through Council supermajority authorization, with the State Attorney General of the Participating Jurisdiction in which the alleged act occurred designated by the

Council as lead prosecutor for each authorized case. Where an act occurred in multiple jurisdictions, the Council shall designate a lead jurisdiction and coordinating State Attorneys General by its authorizing vote; (b) State Attorneys General acting under Council authorization pursuant to this subsection shall have full federal authority for the authorized Section 13 prosecutions, and federal courts in their districts shall have jurisdiction over the resulting cases notwithstanding any assertion by the sitting Department of Justice to the contrary; (c) all such prosecutions shall be transmitted to the Hamilton Contingent upon its operational commencement for continuation, consolidation, or reconsideration as the Hamilton Contingent's own investigation warrants, with no prosecution terminated without published reasoning on the Ledger; (d) the Commission may additionally request the United States Marshals Service to execute arrest warrants issued by cooperating federal courts in connection with prosecutions under this subsection, and the Marshals Service shall comply pursuant to Section 13E.11(a); (e) the provisions of this subsection shall not limit the ordinary prosecutorial authority of any state Attorney General to prosecute under state law, which authority remains fully available to each State Attorney General without Council authorization; and (f) where credible evidence of imminent Section 13 interference is documented and Council supermajority cannot be obtained within the time available to prevent destruction or flight, the Council may authorize expedited prosecution by majority vote (twenty-nine (29) of fifty-six (56)) of members available within the expedited window, subject to the same ratification, publication, and judicial review protections established for emergency preservation orders under Section 19.5.0.18.9.3, and with ratification by full two-thirds (2/3) supermajority required within seventy-two (72) hours or the expedited authorization dissolves with pending charges reverting to ordinary Council supermajority process.
19.5.0.5.3 Ratification Rescission Framework. This subsection addresses rescission of state ratification at various stages of the Article V process, closing interpretive vulnerabilities that have historically created uncertainty about completed constitutional amendments. Ratification is a specific constitutional act under Article V; this framework specifies when and how rescission may operate, and when it may not. (a) Foundational Principle — Article V Completion Doctrine. Once three-fourths (3/4) of the States have ratified this Amendment as required by Article V of the Constitution of the United States, the Amendment is part of the Constitution and operates as the supreme law of the United States. Ratification is complete upon the thirty-eighth (38th) state's proper ratification action. Post-completion state action purporting to rescind

ratification does not unwind the completed Article V process. This principle is consistent with historical practice, including the Fourteenth

Amendment context in which Ohio and New Jersey purported rescissions were not recognized as affecting completed ratification. (b) Pre-Threshold Rescission — Narrow Availability. A state that has ratified may attempt rescission only before the three-fourths threshold is achieved. Pre-threshold rescission shall be effective only if: (i) the rescission is enacted through the same procedural pathway used for ratification (state legislature vote at the required supermajority, or state convention, per the state's own constitutional requirements for ratification procedure); (ii) the rescission is submitted to the National Archives in the same manner as ratification within the time period during which the three-fourths threshold remains unachieved; (iii) the rescission specifically identifies the Amendment being rescinded and articulates the state's grounds; and (iv) the rescission is not procured through any means described in subsection (e) Bad Faith Rescission Prohibition. (c) Post-Threshold Rescission Void. Any state action purporting to rescind ratification after the three-fourths threshold has been achieved — whether through state legislature resolution, state referendum, state constitutional amendment, state judicial ruling, or any other state-level mechanism — shall be void ab initio and shall have no effect on the Amendment's operation as supreme law. The completed Article V process cannot be retroactively unwound by individual state action; modification of the Amendment post-ratification requires either subsequent Article V amendment (prospective repeal or modification) or the Section 18 Sunset Review process (where Section 18.6 Amendment Protection boundaries permit). (d) Procedural Standards for Attempted Rescission. Any attempted rescission must meet the same procedural standards as ratification itself. A state legislature that ratified through a specific procedure cannot purport to rescind through a lesser procedure. If the state used a convention for ratification, rescission requires convention. If rescission attempt fails to meet procedural standards, the attempt is void without requiring further review. (e) Bad Faith Rescission Prohibition. Rescission procured through any of the following means is void regardless of procedural compliance: (i) bribery or other corruption of state legislators voting on rescission; (ii) foreign interference within the meaning of Section 22; (iii) coordinated multi-state scheme where rescission is part of a Section 20.25 coordinated multi-state obstruction pattern; (iv) threats, intimidation, or coercion directed at state legislators or state officials; (v) procedural manipulation such as mid-session rule changes designed to enable rescission without proper deliberation; (vi) fraudulent record-keeping regarding the rescission vote or proceedings. (f) National Archives Certification Authority. The Archivist of the United States shall certify ratification based on state ratifications properly submitted in the manner prescribed by Article V and this Amendment. The Archivist's certification authority does not extend to: (i) accepting post-threshold rescission attempts; (ii) withholding certification based on disputes about rescission when three-fourths of states have submitted proper ratifications; (iii) adjudicating the validity of pre-threshold rescission attempts beyond ordinary procedural review. Where rescission disputes arise, the Archivist shall certify based on facial compliance with Article V procedures, with dispute resolution through the frameworks established in this subsection. (g) State Attorneys General Council Joint Declaration Pathway. Consistent with Section 19.5.0.5.1, where the National Archives certification is obstructed, delayed, or withheld based on rescission disputes: (i) the State Attorneys General Council may, by two-thirds supermajority, issue Joint Declaration of Ratification based on proper state ratification submissions from three-fourths of Participating Jurisdictions; (ii) the Joint Declaration serves as dispositive certification equivalent to National Archives certification for Amendment operational purposes; (iii) rescission attempts shall be evaluated by the Council under subsections (b) through (e) standards, with bad-faith rescission excluded from the three-fourths calculation. (h) Judicial Review Framework. Federal courts have jurisdiction over justiciable controversies regarding rescission. Courts reviewing rescission matters shall apply the following standards: (i) political question doctrine under Coleman v. Miller (1939) provides substantial deference to congressional and constitutional ratification determinations, with courts disfavoring interference in the completed Article V process; (ii) Section 25A.27 interpretive rule (later constitutional provisions prevail) applies to any conflict between this Section and prior interpretation; (iii) Section 25A.29 judicial capture safeguard applies to any ruling that would effect functional repeal of this Amendment through retroactive rescission acceptance; (iv) Section 17C state-sovereign adjudication pathways remain available where federal courts are compromised. (i) Foreign Interference Detection. Rescission efforts showing evidence of foreign influence, coordination, or material support shall: (i) trigger Section 22 foreign interference framework against the foreign actors and any coordinating domestic actors; (ii) be presumed void under subsection (e) Bad Faith Rescission Prohibition unless affirmatively rebutted by clear and convincing evidence of independent state decision-making; (iii) activate Section 22 enhanced detection and prosecution frameworks. The Academic Integrity Commission shall conduct continuous monitoring for foreign-origin rescission campaigns during any active ratification dispute. (j) Amendment's Own Self-Defense. The Amendment's explicit textual treatment of rescission in this subsection constitutes binding constitutional construction. Any judicial ruling that contravenes the explicit framework — for example, accepting post-threshold rescission as effective, or permitting bad-faith rescission to count toward non-ratification — shall: (i) be void as contrary to the explicit constitutional text of this Amendment; (ii) trigger Section 13H alternative interpretive pathways because the ruling would effect functional repeal of the Amendment through interpretation rather than through Article V process; (iii) be treated as judicial

capture scenario activating alternative adjudication under Section 17C where applicable. (k) Distinction from Repeal and Sunset Review. Rescission is not repeal. The People retain sovereign authority to repeal or modify this Amendment through: (i) subsequent Article V amendment process (prospective modification through new amendment); or (ii) Section 18 Sunset Review where Section 18.6 Amendment Protection boundaries permit. These prospective mechanisms are preserved; rescission pretexts do not substitute for them. An attempt to repeal the Amendment must proceed through proper prospective constitutional procedure, not through retroactive rescission fiction. (l) State Sovereignty Preserved for Legitimate Domain. Nothing in this subsection limits state sovereignty in legitimate domains. States retain full authority over their own constitutions, their own laws, and their own governance not inconsistent with this Amendment. The limitation addressed here is narrow: post-completion rescission cannot retroactively unwind the completed Article V process that made this Amendment supreme law. States that did not ratify are under the Amendment's operational framework equally with states that did, consistent with the Supremacy Clause and Article V's historical operation. (m) Historical Record. All rescission attempts — successful, unsuccessful, and void — shall be publicly recorded on the Franklin Ledger as permanent constitutional historical record, providing transparency about the ratification process and any attempts to interfere with it. This historical record serves future Sunset Review consideration and constitutional scholarship, not any operational effect on the Amendment's supreme law status. (n) Individual Official Liability. State officials who direct, authorize, or materially participate in bad-faith rescission attempts under subsection (e) shall be subject to: (i) Section 13 interference prosecution with Senior Official multipliers; (ii) Section 20.14 personal consequences; (iii) Section 22 foreign interference framework where foreign coordination is present; (iv) Section 8 permanent federal office disqualification upon conviction. The individual liability attaches regardless of whether the rescission attempt succeeded in producing state action; bad-faith rescission efforts are independently prosecutable. (o) Sunset Review Consideration. Each Sunset Review under Section 18 shall include assessment of ratification rescission framework effectiveness — whether procedural standards are appropriately calibrated, whether bad-faith prevention is working, whether foreign interference detection is effective, and whether framework modifications would strengthen protection of the completed Article V process. The People retain authority to modify this framework through Sunset Review to improve its operation based on experience. (p) Ratification Validity Determined at Submission. To foreclose retroactive-invalidity claims that would functionally operate as post-threshold rescission through a different label: (i) the validity of a state's ratification shall be determined based on facial compliance with Article V procedures at the time of the state's ratification submission to the National Archives or State Attorneys General Council; (ii) challenges to previously-accepted ratifications on grounds that the original ratification was allegedly procedurally defective — raised months or years after submission — shall be treated under the same Coleman v. Miller political question framework as rescission attempts; (iii) the National Archives certification under subsection (f), or the State Attorneys General Council Joint Declaration under subsection (g), is dispositive as to facial compliance and forecloses retroactive-invalidity claims once certification or Joint Declaration has issued; (iv) this subsection applies regardless of the label attached to the challenge ("rescission," "void ab initio," "never validly ratified," "procedural nullity," or analogous framing); the substance of the claim controls, not its label; (v) bad-faith retroactive-invalidity claims are subject to the same subsection (e) and subsection (n) consequences as bad-faith rescission attempts, including individual official liability. 19.5.0.6 The Commission shall NOT, under any circumstances: (a) Enact, repeal, or amend any law, regulation, or statute; (b) Authorize any military deployment, action, or operation, except in direct and documented response to an active armed attack upon the members, personnel, physical sites, or infrastructure of the Implementation, or pursuant to the nuclear emergency provisions of Section 16.10 as modified in Section 19.5.0.12, and then only to the minimum extent necessary; (c) Exercise any domestic law enforcement authority beyond the referral authority in Section 19.5.0.5(c); (d) Enter into any treaty, binding contract, or long-term commitment; (e) Exercise any authority over the normal governing functions of the existing Federal Government that do not relate to the Implementation of this Amendment; (f) Direct, influence, or participate in the selection of Implementation personnel beyond those minimally necessary to initiate the Implementation Period; or (g) Remain in its Phase One implementation role beyond sixty (60) days after the three bodies of the Authority are fully selected and sworn in under Section 19.19. At the end of that sixty (60) day handover period, the Commission's Phase One protective role shall terminate, and all Phase One records, authorities, and oversight functions specific to implementation shall transfer to the three bodies of the Authority. The Commission itself shall NOT dissolve; rather, it shall automatically transition to its Permanent Oversight role under Section 17D, with the same seven (7) Chief Justices continuing in service through the first Biennial Rotation under Section 17D.5. The Phase One authorities enumerated in Sections 19.5.0.2 through 19.5.0.5 shall not survive the Phase One termination; the Commission's permanent

authorities thereafter shall be limited to those specified in Section 17D.7, subject to the limits of Section 17D.8 and the continuing limits of this Section 19.5.0.6. 19.5.0.7 There is hereby established the Short-Term Civilian Review Board ("the Review Board"), consisting of fifty-six (56) registered voters, one drawn by randomized lottery from registered voters of each Participating Jurisdiction, convened within thirty (30) days of certified ratification. The Review Board shall operate in parallel with the Washington Commission during the Phase One implementation period and shall dissolve at the end of the sixty (60) day handover period following the swearing-in of the three bodies of the Authority. The Review Board's dissolution is tied to the termination of the Commission's Phase One role, not to any dissolution of the Commission itself. The Commission transitions from Phase One to Permanent Oversight under Section 17D at that same moment, but the Review Board's Phase One-specific function does not continue into the Permanent Oversight period and therefore the Review Board dissolves. 19.5.0.8 The Short-Term Civilian Review Board shall possess the following authorities over the Washington Commission: (a) Observation. Unrestricted access to all meetings, deliberations, decisions, and records of the Commission, at any time, without prior notice; (b) Reporting. Authority to publish findings, concerns, and dissenting opinions directly upon the provisional public ledger without editorial review or approval by the Commission or any other body; (c) Emergency Military Veto. Authority to veto any proposed or executed military deployment or action by the Commission by majority vote of the Review Board. A veto under this subsection shall be immediate and self-executing. The Commission shall not override a Review Board veto of a military action under any circumstances; (d) Suspension of

Other Actions. Authority to suspend any other action of the Commission for seventy-two (72) hours by majority vote, pending review and resolution. The Commission may override such a suspension only by unanimous vote of all five members and a publicly reasoned finding that the action is necessary to prevent imminent and irreparable harm to the Implementation; and (e) Nuclear Authorization Parallel Oversight. Authority to observe all Nuclear Authorization Panel proceedings established under Section 19.5.0.12 and Emergency Nuclear Authorization Committee proceedings under Section 19.5.0.11.5 during the Washington Commission period with the same unrestricted access granted under subsection (a), publish findings on Panel and Committee operations and composition integrity on the provisional public ledger, and raise concerns about Panel composition, Committee composition, or procedural matters. Where a Panel or Committee nuclear authorization would proceed in violation of Section 16 restrictions or under improper composition, the Review Board may exercise its Emergency Military Veto under subsection (c) with respect to that authorization; such veto shall be immediate and self-executing and shall not be overridden. The Review Board does not itself sit on the Panel or Committee; it provides independent civilian oversight of Panel and Committee operations during Phase One. 19.5.0.9 Members of the Short-Term Civilian Review Board shall receive the same protections, compensation, and general eligibility standards as Citizens' Oversight Board members under Sections 17.5 through 17.7, adapted for the duration of the Washington Commission period. In addition to the disqualifications of Section 17.7, the following enhanced disqualifications shall apply to Review Board service given the Board's unique authorities (military veto, Nuclear Authorization Panel oversight, Emergency Nuclear Authorization Committee oversight, parallel oversight of the Washington Commission during a vulnerable transition period). 19.5.0.9.1 Foreign Interference Disqualifications. The following persons are ineligible for Review Board service, calibrated to address actual foreign interference risk without discriminating against the many loyal Americans with innocent international backgrounds: (a) Registered foreign agents under the Foreign Agents Registration Act (FARA), current or within the preceding ten (10) years; (b) Persons with direct financial relationships, compensation, or ownership interests tied to any government designated as a foreign adversary by the United States Department of State, within the preceding ten (10) years; (c) Persons who have served in a foreign nation's military within the preceding ten (10) years, except for United States citizens who served in allied forces under formal treaty obligation; (d) Persons convicted of espionage, treason, sedition, foreign interference, or violation of the Foreign Agents Registration Act; (e) Persons currently employed by or under contract with any foreign government, foreign government-controlled entity, or foreign intelligence service; (f) Persons with undisclosed foreign control interests in business entities, as defined under Section 22; (g) Persons with spouses or immediate family members currently holding senior policy positions in foreign adversary governments. 19.5.0.9.2 What Is Not Disqualifying. For clarity, and to prevent overreach, the following shall NOT disqualify a person from Review Board service: (a) Dual citizenship, whether by birth, descent, marriage, or lawful naturalization, except where the non-United States citizenship is held with a designated foreign adversary government and the person currently holds an active foreign government position;

(b) Foreign birth, ancestry, or heritage; (c) Past study abroad, academic fellowships, or educational funding from foreign governments (including Rhodes, Marshall, Fulbright, DAAD, and similar programs), so long as the funding did not come from a designated foreign adversary; (d) Past employment by foreign private-sector companies not controlled by foreign governments; (e) Foreign friends, acquaintances, or extended family; (f) Past service in the United States Peace Corps, Foreign Service, diplomatic corps, or similar international civilian service; (g) Past participation in international cultural, educational, or humanitarian exchanges. 19.5.0.9.3 Military and Defense Disqualifications. Given the Review Board's authority to veto military actions by the Washington Commission under Section 19.5.0.8(c), its oversight role over Nuclear Authorization Panel operations under Section 19.5.0.8(e), and its oversight role over the Emergency Nuclear Authorization Committee under Section 19.5.0.11.5, all during the Washington Commission period, the following disqualifications apply: (a) Active military service in the United States Armed Forces within the preceding ten (10) years; (b) Employment by, or substantial ownership interest in, a major federal defense contractor within the preceding ten (10) years; "major defense contractor" means any entity receiving more than one hundred million dollars ($100,000,000) in annual federal defense contracts in any year of the preceding ten; (c) Immediate family members (spouse, parents, children, siblings) currently holding senior operational positions within the United States Armed Forces or major defense contractors; (d) Past service in senior policy positions at the Department of Defense, Department of Homeland Security, or intelligence agencies within the preceding ten (10) years. 19.5.0.9.4 Integrity Disqualifications. The following additional disqualifications apply, structured in three felony tiers to balance public protection with fairness: (a) Tier One — Violent Felony Convictions (Automatic Disqualification). Any conviction for a violent felony at the federal or state level, at any time, regardless of recency, pardon, or expungement, shall automatically disqualify. "Violent felony" for purposes of this subsection means any felony offense involving the use, attempted use, or threatened use of physical force against another person, including but not limited to: murder; manslaughter; rape and other sexual assault offenses; robbery; aggravated assault; kidnapping; arson endangering persons; armed burglary; carjacking; domestic violence felonies; felony child abuse; felony elder abuse; human trafficking; and any federal or state offense classified as a crime of violence under 18 U.S.C. § 924(e)(2)(B) or its successor provision; (b) Tier Two — Public Trust and Corruption Felony Convictions (Automatic Disqualification). Any conviction for a public trust or corruption felony at the federal or state level, at any time, regardless of recency, pardon, or expungement, shall automatically disqualify. "Public trust or corruption felony" for purposes of this subsection means any felony offense involving corruption, breach of public trust, or misuse of public position, including but not limited to: bribery of public officials; embezzlement of public or private funds in excess of jurisdictional felony thresholds; public corruption; campaign finance felonies; treason; espionage; sedition; wire fraud, mail fraud, or securities fraud involving public officials or substantial public harm; felony tax evasion; perjury in official proceedings; obstruction of justice; racketeering; felony breach of fiduciary duty to public office; and any offense involving the corrupt use of federal or state power; (c) Tier Three — Other Felony Convictions (Case-by-Case Review). Any felony conviction not falling within Tiers One or Two shall not automatically disqualify, but shall trigger case-by-case review by the Washington Commission (or Watchdog Tribunal once operational), considering: (i) the nature of the offense; (ii) the recency of the offense; (iii) the person's conduct since the offense, including evidence of rehabilitation; (iv) whether the offense suggests ongoing risk relevant to Review Board duties; and (v) any mitigating circumstances including the person's age at the time of offense and circumstances surrounding the offense. Review shall be completed within twenty-one (21) days of disclosure, with written reasoning published upon the provisional public ledger; (d) Vacated Convictions Exception. A conviction in any of Tiers One, Two, or Three that has been vacated by a court of competent jurisdiction as wrongful — meaning the conviction has been overturned on its merits, not merely pardoned, expunged, or commuted — shall be treated as if it never occurred for purposes of this Section, in recognition that a wrongfully convicted person bears no moral culpability for the vacated offense; (e) Pending Felony Charges. Any pending felony charge for a crime of violence, public corruption, dishonesty, fraud, breach of public trust, espionage, or similar categories, where the person has been formally indicted by grand jury or where a court has found probable cause following a preliminary hearing, shall disqualify during the pendency of the charge. Disqualification under this subsection shall continue only for the duration of the pending charge; if charges are dismissed, dropped by prosecution, or the person is acquitted at trial, eligibility shall be automatically restored without further review or application, and the Washington Commission (or Watchdog Tribunal once operational) shall publish the restoration upon the Franklin Ledger or provisional public ledger within seven (7) days of dismissal;

(f) Misdemeanor Convictions — Case-by-Case Review. Misdemeanor convictions shall not automatically disqualify, but shall trigger case-by-case review by the Washington Commission (or Watchdog Tribunal once operational), which shall consider: (i) the nature of the offense; (ii) whether the offense involved dishonesty, fraud, violence, sexual misconduct, or breach of public trust; (iii) the recency of the offense; (iv) the person's conduct since the offense; and (v) the relationship of the offense to the duties of Review Board service. Review shall be completed within twenty-one (21) days of disclosure, with written reasoning published upon the provisional public ledger; (g) Pending Criminal Investigation. Any pending federal or state criminal investigation for a felony, where the investigation has been formalized through grand jury proceedings, prosecutorial filings, or equivalent procedural step indicating active prosecution. Informal inquiries, preliminary reviews, or ordinary administrative investigations shall not disqualify; (h) Anti-Democratic Advocacy. Public advocacy, within the preceding three (3) years, of interference with this Amendment's implementation, violent overthrow of the United States government, or refusal to recognize the outcomes of democratic processes; (i) Insurrection and Election Obstruction. Participation in insurrection, sedition, or organized efforts to obstruct certified elections. 19.5.0.9.5 Disclosure Requirement. Each selected Review Board member shall, within fourteen (14) days of notification of selection and before formally taking the oath, complete a comprehensive disclosure of: (a) All citizenships, national service, and military service; (b) All employment within the preceding ten (10) years; (c) All sources of income, financial interests, and substantial assets; (d) All foreign government relationships, contracts, or compensation; (e) All immediate family members' employment and government positions; (f) Any pending legal matters, investigations, or criminal charges. 19.5.0.9.6 Disclosure Review. The disclosure shall be reviewed by the Washington Commission within seven (7) days of submission. If the Commission finds potential grounds for disqualification, the Commission shall: (a) Notify the selected citizen of the specific concerns; (b) Provide a reasonable opportunity for response and clarification; (c) Issue a written determination within fourteen (14) days of the citizen's response; (d) If disqualification is confirmed, trigger replacement through state lottery under Section 19.5.0.9.8.

19.5.0.9.7 Mid-Service Disqualification. If a Review Board member is discovered to hold a disqualifying status after taking the oath, the following removal procedures apply based on the nature of the disqualification: (a) Immediate Removal (no review required) for clear-cut disqualifications: discovered foreign national status where no dual citizenship disclosed; active foreign agent registration not previously disclosed; criminal conviction during service; discovered undisclosed foreign adversary financial ties; discovered active foreign government employment; (b) Reviewed Removal (Washington Commission majority vote required) for ambiguous or disputed disqualifications: alleged undisclosed relationships; alleged ethics violations not rising to clear disqualification; disputed eligibility questions; alleged but unverified foreign interference; (c) Tribunal-Reviewed Removal (where the Watchdog Tribunal is operational under Section 21) for matters where the Washington Commission finds the question beyond its competence or where the member contests Commission removal, with Tribunal decision by two-thirds (2/3) supermajority within thirty (30) days; (d) Due Process in All Removals. Except in Immediate Removal cases under subsection (a), the member shall have opportunity to respond to allegations, present evidence, and be represented by counsel before removal takes effect. 19.5.0.9.8 Replacement Procedure. Upon disqualification or removal of a Review Board member, a replacement shall be selected as follows: (a) State-Based Lottery. A new member shall be drawn by randomized lottery from registered voters of the same state as the removed member, preserving the one-per-state allocation; (b) Enhanced Background Check. The replacement shall complete the full disclosure under Section 19.5.0.9.5 and Commission review under Section 19.5.0.9.6 before seating; (c) Timeline. Replacement shall be seated within fourteen (14) days of the removed member's vacating of their seat, absent exceptional circumstances; (d) Continuity. Pending replacement, the Review Board shall continue operating with the remaining members. Decisions requiring majority vote shall be calculated against the full fifty-six (56) member allocation, meaning a temporarily vacant seat effectively counts as an abstention until filled; (e) Arrangement Support. The replacement member shall receive the same arrangement stipend, thirty-day window for personal affairs, and seven-day no-fault refund window as other lottery-selected citizens under Section 19.14(a) through (d), adapted for the remaining duration of the Review Board's existence. 19.5.0.9.9 Constitutional Floor. The disqualifications in this Section shall not be weakened, narrowed, or evaded by any act of Congress, executive order, judicial ruling, or state action. However, the Authority through Liberty Bell Initiative, or future generations through Sunset Review under Section 18, may adopt additional disqualifications if circumstances warrant. Any modification shall be subject to the Article V protection of Section 18.6. 19.5.0.10 Every action, meeting, deliberation, and decision of the Washington Commission shall be livestreamed to the public in real time and recorded upon the provisional public ledger. This includes, without limitation, all overrides of federal action, all authorized military responses, all referrals for prosecution, and all routine deliberations. No Commission proceeding shall be conducted in secret. The existence, timing, and substance of all Commission actions shall never be classified. Narrow operational-security redactions of livestreamed military response footage may be imposed only by unanimous vote of all five Commission members AND approval by majority vote of the Short-Term Civilian Review Board, with all redactions subject to public review within thirty (30) days. 19.5.0.11 At the end of the sixty (60) day handover period following the swearing-in of the three bodies of the Authority, the Washington Commission's Phase One role shall terminate and the Short-Term Civilian Review Board shall dissolve. All Phase One records, decisions, and documentation shall be transferred to the three bodies of the Authority, and shall be preserved upon the provisional public ledger and, upon activation of the Sovereign Blockchain Voting Ledger, migrated to and permanently accessible upon the Ledger. The Washington Commission itself does NOT dissolve at this point; rather, it transitions automatically to its Permanent Oversight role under Section 17D, with only the narrow oversight authorities enumerated in Section 17D.7 continuing thereafter. The seven (7) Phase One Chief Justices shall continue in service until the first Biennial Rotation under Section 17D.5. 19.5.0.11.5 Emergency Nuclear Authorization Committee — Ramp-Up Period Interim Framework. Because the permanent nuclear authorization framework of Section 16 requires operational infrastructure that is not fully established until late in Phase One (including Governor voting infrastructure under Section

16.7.1(f), full Panel operability under Section 19.5.0.12 with oath-verified Joint Chiefs, and the public Nuclear Authorization Vote infrastructure under Section 14), an Emergency Nuclear Authorization Committee shall operate from the moment of certified Ratification until the full permanent framework is certified operational. The Committee addresses the timeline gaps that would otherwise leave the Republic without a functional non-emergency first-use authorization framework during the ramp-up period. (a) Composition. The Committee shall consist of seven (7) members drawn weekly by randomized lottery from a combined pool of: (i) the fifty-six (56) sitting Governors or chief executives of the Participating Jurisdictions; and (ii) the fifty-six (56) sitting Chief Justices of the highest courts of the Participating Jurisdictions, for a total combined pool of one hundred twelve (112) potential members. Members

shall not be drawn from the sitting Washington Commission membership (once the Commission is convened). Members shall not serve consecutive weekly rotations, ensuring continuous membership turnover that prevents consolidation of power or advance identification for corruption. (b) Lottery Administration — Pre-Commission Period. The first weekly lottery shall be conducted within forty-eight (48) hours of certified Ratification by joint action of the Conference of Chief Justices and the National Governors Association (or successor organizations), with results published upon the provisional public ledger. Pre-Ratification willingness by the Conference of Chief Justices and the National Governors Association to prepare operational infrastructure is encouraged but not required; no pre-Ratification obligation is created by this Amendment. Lottery procedures shall use cryptographically-verifiable random selection with multi-party seed contribution, with seed values, algorithm, and selection results published on the provisional public ledger. Where the Conference of Chief Justices and National Governors Association fail to conduct the first lottery within the forty-eight (48) hour window — whether through refusal, capture, intimidation, or inability to coordinate — the following cascading fallback authorities shall run the lottery, each acting if the prior tier has failed: (i) Any three (3) or more sitting Chief Justices of the highest courts of Participating Jurisdictions acting jointly; (ii) Any three (3) or more sitting Governors or chief executives of Participating Jurisdictions acting jointly; (iii) The State Attorneys General Council once organized under Section 19.5.0.18 (whether or not the Council has reached its own quorum thresholds, with any willing State Attorneys General acting jointly sufficient); (iv) Any combination of three (3) or more sitting state Chief Justices, sitting state Governors, and sitting State Attorneys General acting jointly. Each fallback tier has an additional forty-eight (48) hours to act before the next tier may proceed. The fallback authorities shall use cryptographically-verifiable random selection under the same standards as the primary authorities. Any fallback lottery shall be documented on the provisional public ledger with identity of the acting officials and evidence of the prior tier's failure to act. Once a valid lottery is conducted under any tier, its results are binding and the first Committee is operational. Federal executive, Congressional, or any other interference with fallback lottery administration shall constitute Section 13 interference with Senior Official multipliers. (c) Lottery Administration — Post-Commission Period. Upon Washington Commission convening under Section 19.5.0.2, weekly lotteries shall be conducted under Commission supervision using cryptographically-verifiable random selection with multi-party seed contribution under the same standards as Section 19.5.0.3.3, with results published upon the provisional public ledger. Commission members shall not participate in the Committee lottery pool while serving on the Commission. (d) Weekly Rotation. Members shall serve Sunday through the following Saturday. New members shall be drawn by noon Saturday each week for the following week's service, with the incoming Committee receiving briefing on pending matters from the outgoing Committee before Sunday service commencement. Rotation prevents consolidation of power and advance identification for corruption. Where a lottery-drawn member is unable to serve (due to incapacity, undisclosed conflict of interest, or refusal), a substitute shall be drawn immediately from the same pool. (e) Authority During Initial Ramp-Up (Day 0 through approximately Day 30). During the initial ramp-up period when Governor voting infrastructure is not yet operational and oath-verified Panel members are not yet fully available, the Committee may authorize emergency first-use or offensive nuclear action only under the following concurrence standard: (A) Default Unanimous Standard. Authorization requires unanimous seven-member concurrence. (B) Certified Unavailability Exception. Where one (1) Committee member is certified as genuinely unreachable, incapacitated, or non-responsive despite good-faith attempts to secure their participation within a two (2) hour window from authorization request, authorization may proceed upon unanimous concurrence of the remaining six (6) members, with certification made by Washington Commission majority vote (four of seven Chief Justices) and published on the provisional public ledger within twenty-four (24) hours with specific factual basis. In no case shall authorization proceed with fewer than six (6) concurring members. (C) Deliberate obstruction by a Committee member shall be prosecuted under Section 13 with Senior

Official multipliers; legitimate good-faith dissent is protected. Authorization may proceed under this subsection only where: (i) the action is demonstrably required to prevent catastrophic nation-threatening harm that cannot await full framework operability; (ii) the factual basis for the authorization is documented and published upon the provisional public ledger before authorization; (iii) the Washington Commission (if convened) has been notified and has not vetoed the authorization by majority vote within the time available; (iv) the Short-Term Civilian Review Board (if convened) has been notified and has not exercised Emergency Military Veto under Section 19.5.0.8(c); and (v) the Section 16.10 emergency override conditions under subsection (h) are not met (the Section 16.10 framework has priority over Committee authority where applicable). This initial authority recognizes the operational necessity of some nuclear authorization capacity during the period when the permanent framework is physically impossible to convene, while requiring near-unanimity, transparency, and multiple oversight layers. (f) Authority During Post-Governor-Vote Operability (Approximately Day 30 through Committee Sunset). Once Governor voting infrastructure is operational under Section 16.7.1(j), the Committee's emergency authorization authority under subsection (e) terminates, and Committee authority shall be limited to serving as a Panel-seat substitute within the full three-gate framework where specific Panel seats under Section 19.5.0.12 are not yet available or are temporarily unavailable. The Governor vote under Section 16.7.1 and public vote under Section 16.8(b) shall still be required. Committee members serving as Panel substitutes shall do so under oath-maintenance verification standards equivalent to those of Section 19.5.0.3.2,

conducted by the Washington Commission within seventy-two (72) hours of Committee member selection. (g) Washington Commission Oversight. The Committee shall operate under Washington Commission oversight once the Commission is convened. The Commission shall have authority to: (i) observe all Committee deliberations and decisions in real time through livestream pursuant to Section 19.5.0.10; (ii) review Committee lottery integrity and member eligibility; (iii) challenge Committee member eligibility where credible evidence of compromise exists; (iv) override any Committee authorization by six-sevenths (6/7) Commission supermajority where the Committee has acted outside its authority or contrary to Amendment principles. Commission override of a Committee authorization shall be published on the provisional public ledger with factual basis within twenty-four (24) hours. (h) Short-Term Civilian Review Board Oversight. Once convened on Day 30 under Section 19.5.0.7, the

Review Board shall have parallel oversight authority over the Committee equivalent to its oversight authority over the Washington Commission under Section 19.5.0.8, including Emergency Military Veto authority under Section 19.5.0.8(c) with respect to any Committee nuclear authorization. Review Board veto of a Committee authorization shall be immediate and self-executing, and shall not be overridden by the Committee or by the Washington Commission. (i) Federal Executive Non-Interference. No President, Vice President, Cabinet officer, federal agency head, military commander, or other federal executive officeholder shall direct, pressure, coerce, surveil, or interfere with Committee lottery administration, member selection, deliberation, or authorization processes. Any such interference shall constitute Section 13 interference with Senior Official multipliers and additional penalties under Section 22 where foreign coordination is present. Members of the Committee shall receive the same protections against adverse federal action as Short-Term Civilian Review Board members under Section 19.5.0.9 and Joint Chiefs under Section 19.5.0.3.2.1. (j) Operational Scope Transition — No Sunset. The Committee shall transition operational scope, but shall NOT dissolve, upon certification that the full permanent nuclear authorization framework is operational, including: (i) Governor voting infrastructure under Section 16.7.1(f); (ii) Panel operability under Section 19.5.0.12 (during Phase One) or under Section 16.8(a) (post-Phase-One); and (iii) public Nuclear Authorization Vote infrastructure under Section 14. Certification shall be made by the Washington Commission during Phase One (by majority vote of the seven Chief Justices), or by the Academic Integrity Commission upon Phase One termination. Certification shall be published on the provisional public ledger with specific operational verification of each framework component. Upon certification: (i) the Committee's ramp-up emergency authorization authority under subsection (e) terminates; (ii) the Committee's Panel-seat substitute authority under subsection (f) terminates; and (iii) the Committee's permanent role as default emergency nuclear response authority under Section 16.10(b) commences (or, where subsection (e) authorizations occurred before certification, continues). The Committee is a permanent standing body under this Section and Section 16.10; it does not dissolve. Weekly lottery rotation under subsection (d) continues in perpetuity. (k) Records Transfer. Upon dissolution, all Committee records, deliberations, authorization decisions, and member rosters shall transfer to the Authority for permanent preservation and Ledger publication, and shall remain accessible for Sunset Review consideration and constitutional scholarship. No Committee record shall be classified, redacted, or withheld beyond narrow operational-security redactions permitted under the same standards as Washington Commission records under Section 19.5.0.10. (l) Limitation — Not a Backdoor Authority. Nothing in this Section authorizes Committee action outside the narrow scope of filling timeline gaps in the permanent nuclear authorization framework. The Committee shall not: (i) authorize military action other than nuclear first-use under this Section; (ii) exercise any civilian governing authority; (iii) continue in existence beyond the operational certification sunset under subsection (j); (iv) expand its membership, authority, or duration through its own action; (v) coordinate with federal executive officers on any matter other than factual information relevant to specific pending authorization requests. Violation of these limitations by any Committee member shall subject the member to Section 13 interference penalties with Senior Official multipliers, removal from Committee service, and Section 8 permanent federal office disqualification upon conviction. (m) Sunset Review Consideration. The Committee framework shall be reviewed in each Sunset Review under Section 18, with the People retaining authority to modify the Committee's composition, authority, or sunset conditions based on operational experience — though ordinarily the Committee will have sunset before the first Sunset Review occurs, this subsection preserves the People's prospective authority over any future ramp-up framework that may be needed. (n) Training Requirements. Because the Committee exercises authority over nuclear first-use and emergency defensive response under Section 16.10, and because Committee members are drawn weekly from the combined pool of Governors and Chief Justices who may not have previously encountered Committee-specific duties, every newly-selected Committee member shall complete the following training before participating in substantive Committee decisions: (o) Rapid Orientation Protocol. Given the weekly rotation structure, training shall be delivered as a four (4) hour rapid orientation protocol completed immediately upon selection and before the member participates in any authorization vote. Orientation shall be deliverable through secure video conference to accommodate the short notification-to-service window. Orientation shall be administered by the Washington Commission during Phase One and by the Academic Integrity Commission thereafter, with Watchdog Tribunal oversight.

(p) Orientation Scope. Rapid orientation shall cover: (i) the Committee's role under Section 19.5.0.11.5 and Section 16.10, with particular focus on the differences between ramp-up authority under subsection (e) and permanent emergency authority under Section 16.10(b); (ii) the unanimity standard and certified-unavailability exception under subsection (e) and Section 16.10(b); (iii) Section 16.10(a) qualifying emergency conditions with independent verification requirements; (iv) scope limitations under Section 16.10(i), particularly proportionate defensive response limits; (v) documentation and Ledger publication requirements; (vi) mandatory post-action review under Section 16.10(l); (vii) falsification-as-treason penalties under Section 16.10(k) and Section 16.12; (viii) interactions with Washington Commission, Review Board, and Authority body oversight; (ix) obstruction accountability under Section 16.10(b)(iv) and protection for legitimate dissent; (x) recognition of capture attempts, fabricated emergency claims, and foreign interference indicators; (xi) secure communications infrastructure usage. (q) Pre-Orientation Limited Authority. Before completing rapid orientation, a Committee member may observe Committee proceedings and receive briefings but shall not participate in authorization votes. Given the weekly rotation, orientation must be prioritized to ensure the Committee is operational throughout the week. (r) Preparatory Pool Education. To minimize disruption from weekly orientation, the Academic Integrity Commission shall develop and distribute preparatory educational materials to all members of the Committee eligibility pool (all sitting Governors and all sitting Chief Justices of Participating Jurisdictions). These materials shall be made available in advance so pool members can familiarize themselves with Committee duties before potential selection. Preparatory materials shall not substitute for rapid orientation upon selection but shall reduce its cognitive load. Pool members shall not be required to complete preparatory education, but failure to do so shall not excuse any member from rapid orientation upon selection. (s) Orientation Records. Orientation completion shall be recorded on the provisional public ledger or Franklin Ledger for each Committee member's weekly service. Records shall be preserved for Watchdog Tribunal review and Sunset Review analysis. (t) Federal Executive Non-Interference. No federal officeholder shall direct, influence, or interfere with Committee orientation. Attempts shall constitute Section 13 interference with Senior Official multipliers. Orientation integrity is essential to Committee function; interference is a severe offense. (u) Non-Completion Consequences. A selected member who refuses orientation shall be treated as unavailable under subsection (e)(B) or Section 16.10(b)(ii), with the same certification and replacement process applicable. A selected member who claims orientation completion falsely shall be subject to Section 13 interference penalties and shall be subject to Section 16.10(k) fabrication treason penalties if any authorization proceeds based on their false certification.

B.0.1 Nuclear Authority During the Washington Commission Period 19.5.0.12 The permanent restrictions on nuclear weapons use established in Section 16.6 and the authorization process established in Section 16.7 shall take full effect immediately upon certified ratification of this Amendment. No nuclear weapon of the United States shall be launched, detonated, or deployed in a first-use or offensive capacity during the Washington Commission period except through the 5-person Nuclear Authorization Panel with substituted composition as follows: (a) the sitting President of the United States, serving in their ordinary capacity on the Panel; (b) the senior-most Joint Chief of Staff confirmed to have maintained the constitutional oath under Section 19.5.0.3.2; (c) the second senior-most Joint Chief of Staff confirmed to have maintained the constitutional oath under Section 19.5.0.3.2; (d) one chief legal-executive officer, selected by majority vote of the State Attorneys General Council from among its fifty-six members, standing in for the Citizens' Oversight Board seat; and (e) one sitting Chief Justice of a Participating Jurisdiction, selected by randomized lottery from among the forty-eight Chief Justices of Participating Jurisdictions NOT currently serving on the Washington Commission, standing in for the Academic Integrity Commission seat. Both substitute members shall rotate every ninety (90) days throughout the Washington Commission period, with no member serving consecutive rotations, to prevent the consolidation of power or advance identification for corruption. All other provisions of Section 16.7 shall apply without modification, including the requirement of unanimous Panel consent and the requirement of an affirmative vote of not less than sixty percent (60%) of ballots cast in a Nuclear Authorization Vote with minimum forty percent (40%) turnout over seventy-two (72) hours. 19.5.0.13 The emergency nuclear response framework of Section 16.10 shall apply during the Washington Commission period. Because Phase One occurs before the first successful No Confidence and Amendment-elected President can exist, the Committee framework under Section 16.10(b) applies exclusively during Phase One; the sitting President (whether pre-Amendment or post-Amendment-ratification but pre-first-No-Confidence) does not possess Presidential emergency authority under Section 16.10(d) during this period. Confirmed emergency circumstances under Section 16.10(a) shall trigger the Committee authorization process of Section 16.10(b) with Washington Commission majority concurrence as specified therein. 19.5.0.14 Upon the full swearing-in of the three bodies of the Authority pursuant to Section 19.19, and upon the conclusion of the sixty (60) day handover period, the substituted Nuclear Authorization Panel composition established in Section 19.5.0.12 shall automatically and immediately be replaced by the ordinary composition established in Section 16.7. All subsequent nuclear authorizations shall follow the ordinary process without substitution.

B.0.2 Military Freeze and Limited Defensive Action During the Washington Commission Period 19.5.0.15 Upon certified ratification of this Amendment, the following military authorities of the sitting President and the existing Federal Government shall be suspended for the duration of the Washington Commission period and shall not resume until the full operational capability of this Amendment has been certified under Section 19.21: (a) Authority to initiate any new offensive military operation, deployment, invasion, strike, or armed action; (b) Authority to commit United States forces to any new conflict, war, or armed engagement; (c) Authority to authorize any first-use or offensive nuclear action, except through the substituted process in Section 19.5.0.12; (d) Authority to enter into any new military alliance, defense pact, or binding mutual defense commitment; (e) Authority to authorize any new arms sale or weapons transfer to any foreign government, nongovernmental entity, or private party; and (f) Authority to expand, escalate, or increase in scope any existing military operation, deployment, or commitment. 19.5.0.16 Notwithstanding the suspension in Section 19.5.0.15, the following categories of military activity shall continue subject to the oversight and authorization requirements of this Section: (a) Existing troop positions and deployments as they existed at the moment of certified ratification shall be maintained in place. No new deployments shall be authorized, and no expansion of existing deployments shall occur. Ordinary rotation and resupply necessary to sustain existing positions shall continue; (b) Pure defensive response to direct armed attack on United States sovereign territory, United States forces, or United States citizens, subject to Section 19.5.0.17; (c) Response to mutual defense treaty obligations including NATO Article 5, subject to Section 19.5.0.17; (d) Protection of United States citizens abroad facing imminent threat, including embassy sieges, hostage situations, and mass evacuation scenarios, subject to Section 19.5.0.17; (e) Humanitarian and disaster response operations, including natural disasters, pandemic response, and evacuation of United States citizens from crisis zones, subject to Section 19.5.0.17; and

(f) Ongoing intelligence activities and alliance consultations existing at the moment of ratification, without expansion or escalation. 19.5.0.17 During the first thirty (30) days following certified ratification, before the convening of the Short-Term Civilian Review Board and before the State Attorneys General

Council has its first full session, any defensive military action under Section 19.5.0.16(b), (c), (d), or (e) shall be authorized as follows: (a) The Joint Chiefs of Staff, serving as non-voting military advisors to the Washington Commission, shall formally propose the defensive response based on their professional military judgment, in a written proposal documented upon the provisional public ledger in real time, specifying the threat, the proposed response, the objectives, the duration, the forces involved, and the operational scope; (b) The seven (7) Chief Justices of Participating Jurisdictions serving on the Washington Commission shall alone vote on whether to authorize the proposal. The Joint Chiefs shall not vote on any military action; (c) Authorization shall require the affirmative vote of at least six (6) of the seven (7) Chief Justices of Participating Jurisdictions (6/7 supermajority). Any two Chief Justices together may block any proposed action. The determination shall be publicly reasoned and livestreamed on the provisional public ledger; (d) Authorized defensive action shall be strictly defensive in nature. No offensive operations, territorial expansion, regime change, or escalation beyond the documented threat shall be permitted under this authorization; (e) No authorization under this subsection shall extend beyond seven (7) days without re-authorization through the full triple-authorization process under Section 19.5.0.18. If the Short-Term Civilian Review Board has not yet convened at the expiration of the seven-day window, the Review Board convening shall be expedited to the earliest possible date, and any continuing action shall terminate or be re-authorized within twenty-four (24) hours of the Review Board's convening; (f) Every deployment, engagement, and action taken pursuant to this subsection shall be livestreamed in real time, subject only to narrow operational-security redactions approved by supermajority of the Commission (six of seven Chief Justices) and by majority of the Short-Term Civilian Review Board once convened, with all redactions published and reviewed within thirty (30) days; and (g) Any officer or servicemember who acts beyond the scope of a duly authorized action, or who initiates military action without authorization under this Section, shall be subject to Section 16.5 insurrection penalties.
19.5.0.18 From the thirty-first (31st) day following certified ratification onward, through the termination of the Washington Commission's Phase One role (at sixty (60) days after Authority inauguration under Section 19.19), any defensive military action under Section 19.5.0.16 shall require full triple-authorization, consisting of ALL of the following three (3) institutionally independent civilian checks:

(a) Majority vote of the Washington Commission (four of seven Chief Justices); (b) Affirmation by majority vote of the Short-Term Civilian Review Board (twenty-six of fifty members); AND (c) Authorization by two-thirds (2/3) supermajority of the State Attorneys General Council (thirty-eight of fifty-six Attorneys General) established under Section 19.5.0.18.1. The Council shall review each proposed action for lawfulness, proportionality, compliance with international law, and defensive character. 19.5.0.18.1 There is hereby established the State Attorneys General Council ("the AG Council"), which shall serve as the third institutional check in the triple-authorization structure of Section 19.5.0.18. The AG Council shall consist of the sitting Attorney General (or equivalent chief legal-executive officer) of each of the fifty states, the District of Columbia, and each of the five territories enumerated in Section 3.1.1, serving ex officio for the duration of their office. The Council shall consist of fifty-six (56) members in total, one from each Participating Jurisdiction. No separate appointment, confirmation, or term shall apply. The AG Council shall be deemed convened and operational from the moment of certified ratification of this Amendment, with all fifty-six sitting chief legal-executive officers serving ex officio. The Council shall deliberate and vote upon any authorization matter referred to it within seventy-two (72) hours of referral, or within a shorter timeframe if the matter involves a confirmed imminent threat. 19.5.0.18.2 Participation on the AG Council shall be mandatory. A member may not decline, recuse, or delegate participation in any authorization matter under this Section. Failure or refusal shall result in automatic referral to the member's home state for removal from state office AND federal criminal prosecution for dereliction of constitutional duty, punishable by imprisonment of not less than five (5) years. 19.5.0.18.3 AG Council members shall receive no federal compensation and shall continue to be paid only by their respective states during Council service. The federal government shall have no financial or administrative leverage over any member. 19.5.0.18.4 During any active authorization matter, AG Council members shall operate under a Federal Communications Firewall identical to that applicable to the State Elections Council under Section 17.12. For purposes of this Firewall, an "active authorization matter" shall mean any referral pending before the AG Council from the moment of referral, and shall continue through thirty (30) days after the Council's final vote on that matter, to prevent post-vote lobbying, retaliation, or coordinated corruption. A member shall not: (a) Accept, solicit, or respond to any communication, directive, request, or instruction from any federal officeholder, federal agency, federal contractor, or any person acting under federal authority regarding the authorization matter;

(b) Accept any federal funding, grant, loan, or thing of value during the pendency of an authorization matter; (c) Enter into any agreement, memorandum, or understanding with any federal body during the pendency of an authorization matter. 19.5.0.18.5 Violation of the Firewall shall be a federal felony punishable by imprisonment of not less than ten (10) years, automatic removal from state office, and permanent lifetime disqualification from any federal, state, or local public office. All communications to and from AG Council members during an authorization matter shall be logged and published upon the provisional public ledger. 19.5.0.18.6 AG Council members shall be entitled to federal protection from harassment, intimidation, surveillance, or coercion equivalent to that provided to members of the Citizens' Oversight Board under Section 17.5(d), with violations constituting a federal felony punishable by imprisonment of not less than ten (10) years. 19.5.0.18.7 All proceedings, deliberations, and votes of the AG Council shall be recorded and published in real time upon the provisional public ledger. No AG Council business related to authorization matters under this Section shall be conducted in secret. 19.5.0.18.8 The AG Council shall dissolve at the same time the Washington Commission's Phase One role terminates (at sixty (60) days after Authority inauguration under Section 19.19). Upon dissolution of the AG Council, its role in the triple-lock shall transfer to the Academic Integrity Commission through a sixty (60) day structured handover process as follows: (a) Sixty-Day Overlap Period. For the sixty (60) days immediately following the full swearing-in of the three bodies of the Authority under Section 19.19 (which runs concurrent with the final sixty days of the Washington Commission period), both the AG Council and the Academic Integrity Commission shall participate in the triple-lock under Section 19.5.0.18. During this overlap period, the third-lock requirement shall be satisfied by concurrence of EITHER the AG Council by two-thirds supermajority (thirty-eight of fifty-six) OR the Academic Integrity Commission by majority vote (twenty-six of fifty). Either body's concurrence alone shall be sufficient to satisfy the third-lock requirement during the overlap, to prevent paralysis from institutional transition; (b) Records Transfer. On the first day of the overlap period, all AG Council investigations, pending matters, prior authorization determinations, investigative files, and institutional records shall be transferred to the Academic Integrity Commission, which shall preserve them as part of its permanent record. The AG Council shall provide full briefings to the Academic Integrity Commission on all pending matters and shall make its members reasonably available for consultation during the overlap period;

(c) Pending Matters in Progress. Any active authorization matter before the AG Council at the moment of the overlap commencement shall continue to completion under the AG Council's rules, typically within thirty (30) days. Matters newly arising during the overlap period shall be referred to both bodies simultaneously, with either body's concurrence sufficient per clause (a) above; (d) Final Dissolution. Upon the sixty-first (61st) day following the full swearing-in of the three bodies of the Authority, the AG Council shall dissolve completely. The Federal Communications Firewall applicable to AG Council members shall lift. The Academic Integrity Commission shall thereafter hold sole third-lock authority in the triple-lock, exercising that authority through its own internal majority-vote procedures; and (e) Continuity of Protection. Throughout the handover period and beyond, no defensive military action shall be authorized except through the full triple-authorization structure as it exists in that moment. The transition shall not create any gap in civilian oversight of military authorization. 19.5.0.18.9 Expanded Phase One Authorities of the State Attorneys General Council. In addition to the military triple-lock role established in Sections 19.5.0.18 through 19.5.0.18.8, the State Attorneys General Council shall exercise the following expanded Phase One authorities for the period from certified ratification through the Council's dissolution under Section 19.5.0.18.8. These authorities are specifically time-limited to the Phase One transition period and shall not continue beyond the Council's dissolution. The expansion is established because, during Phase One, the permanent federal enforcement apparatus (Hamilton Contingent, Watchdog Tribunal, Academic Integrity Commission) is not yet operational, and accountability matters cannot wait for those bodies to be fully constituted. The State Attorneys General, as sworn chief legal officers of their Participating Jurisdictions, serve as the collective transitional body best positioned to fill the enforcement gap, acting only by supermajority consensus and under the anti-abuse safeguards of this Section. 19.5.0.18.9.1 Federal Prosecution Authority. As provided in Section 19.5.0.5.2, the Council shall have primary federal prosecution authority for Section 13 interference acts during Phase One, acting collectively as a body. Prosecution authorizations shall require two-thirds (2/3) supermajority of the Council (thirty-eight (38) of fifty-six (56)), consistent with the military authorization threshold. Upon Council authorization, the State Attorney General of the Participating Jurisdiction in which the alleged act occurred shall serve as lead prosecutor for that authorized case, acting as the Council's designated prosecutor rather than under independent authority. No individual State

Attorney General shall initiate a federal Section 13 prosecution absent prior Council authorization, except through the expedited authorization pathway of Section 19.5.0.5.2(f) where imminent interference threatens destruction or flight before ordinary Council process can act. This collective-authorization requirement ensures that federal prosecution of federal officials during Phase One reflects broad multi-jurisdictional consensus rather than any single State Attorney General's individual judgment, protecting federal officials from politically-motivated prosecution while preserving the Council's ability to act decisively when necessary. Prosecutions so authorized shall be transmitted to the Hamilton Contingent upon its operational commencement for continuation, consolidation, or reconsideration as the Contingent's investigation warrants, with no prosecution terminated without published reasoning on the Ledger. Ordinary state-law prosecutorial authority of individual State Attorneys General under their respective state laws remains unaffected by this subsection. 19.5.0.18.9.2 Forensic Imaging Authorization. Where the Inspector General pathway under Section 13B.20 is denied, obstructed, or unavailable, the Council may authorize forensic imaging of federal devices by two-thirds (2/3) supermajority vote. Imaging authorizations shall: (a) specify particular federal devices or categories of devices to be imaged; (b) state specific findings of probable cause that evidence destruction has occurred or is imminent; (c) identify the Covered Persons or agencies whose devices are to be imaged; (d) be published upon state government transparency infrastructure and the provisional public ledger within twenty-four (24) hours of authorization; (e) be subject to judicial review by any federal or state court of competent jurisdiction, limited to Fourth Amendment particularity, probable cause, and scope review; and (f) be executable by the United States Marshals Service under Section 13E.3 or by state law enforcement under Section 13E.4, with the actual imaging work performed by the AIC-Designate Forensic Consortium under Section 13B.7.1. Imaging conducted under this subsection shall be transferred to the Academic Integrity Commission upon the Commission's full constitution. 19.5.0.18.9.3 Emergency Preservation Orders. Where imminent evidence destruction is credibly threatened and no other authorization pathway can act within the available window, the Council may issue an Emergency Preservation Order by majority vote (twenty-nine (29) of fifty-six (56)) of members available within the emergency window. Emergency orders shall be subject to: (a) full Council ratification by two-thirds (2/3) supermajority within seventy-two (72) hours, with failure to ratify causing the order to dissolve with no future effect and records of any preserved evidence returned to the custody from which seized, except where independent probable cause has subsequently developed; (b) automatic publication on state government transparency infrastructure within four (4) hours of issuance; (c) post-seizure judicial review within seventy-two (72) hours by any federal or state court of competent jurisdiction; and (d) limitation to evidence preservation only, with no investigative, prosecutorial, or punitive action permitted under the emergency order itself until the ordinary two-thirds supermajority threshold is met. 19.5.0.18.9.4 Whistleblower Reception. The Council shall serve as one of the authorized whistleblower reception channels under Section 13B.16 during Phase One, with reports received by any Council member treated as received by the Council collectively. Council members receiving whistleblower reports shall: (a)

preserve the report and all supporting evidence in Triple Custody under Section 13B.6, with Triple Custody partners being the AIC-Designate Forensic Consortium, the National Archives and Records Administration, and the receiving Council member's state archives; (b) maintain whistleblower anonymity and protection under Section 13B.16, with any Council member breaching anonymity subject to Section 13 interference penalties; (c) refer for investigation through the Temporary Evidence Destruction Task Force under Section 13B.7.3(b); and (d) transmit all reports, evidence, and investigation records to the Hamilton Contingent upon its operational commencement, with reports retaining full evidentiary value upon transfer without requirement of re-reporting for Section 13B.17 whistleblower reward eligibility. 19.5.0.18.9.5 Asset Freeze Authority. The Council may, upon clear and convincing evidence of suspicious asset transfers by Covered Persons under Section 13B.23 through Section 13B.25, authorize asset freezes by two-thirds (2/3) supermajority vote. Freezes shall: (a) be narrowly tailored to assets traceable to suspected evidence destruction, federal corruption, or the Section 13B.4 retroactive look-back period; (b) preserve due process rights through expedited hearing within fourteen (14) days of freeze imposition before any federal or state court of competent jurisdiction; (c) be published on state government transparency infrastructure and the provisional public ledger within twenty-four (24) hours; (d) be automatically reviewed by the Hamilton Contingent upon its operational commencement for continuation, modification, or termination as the Contingent's investigation warrants; and (e) transfer fully to Hamilton Contingent jurisdiction upon the Contingent's operational commencement, with the Council retaining no continuing asset freeze authority thereafter. 19.5.0.18.9.6 Coordination with Washington Commission. The Council shall operate in coordination with the Washington Commission established under

Section 19.5.0. Where Commission action under Sections 19.5.0.5 through 19.5.0.5.2 and Council action under Sections 19.5.0.18.9.1 through 19.5.0.18.9.5 concern the same subject matter, the bodies shall coordinate through joint proceedings livestreamed on the provisional public ledger, with neither body's action preempting the other's authority. Joint proceedings shall be preferred over parallel action to preserve institutional clarity and prevent duplicative or conflicting determinations. 19.5.0.18.9.7 Anti-Abuse Safeguards. All expanded Phase One authorities under Sections 19.5.0.18.9.1 through 19.5.0.18.9.5 shall be subject to the following safeguards, which shall not be weakened, narrowed, or evaded by any Council action, state action, or federal action: (a) No Unilateral Individual Action. No single Council member shall exercise any authority under Sections 19.5.0.18.9.1 through 19.5.0.18.9.5 alone. All actions require supermajority or, in emergency preservation orders under Section 19.5.0.18.9.3, majority vote of the full Council. No Council member acting individually possesses any authority under this Section; (b) Mandatory Public Livestream. All Council proceedings exercising authority under Sections 19.5.0.18.9.1 through 19.5.0.18.9.5 shall be livestreamed on the provisional public ledger per Section 19.5.0.18.7, with individual member votes recorded and publicly accessible; (c) Bad-Faith Authorization Consequences. Any Council member who votes for authorization in bad faith — meaning without credible evidentiary basis, for political retaliation, for the purpose of harassing federal officials for non-accountability reasons, or in coordination with private pressure — shall be subject to Section 13 interference penalties, removal from state office under state law procedures, and permanent lifetime disqualification from federal, state, or local public office; (d) Fourth Amendment Protections Preserved. All authorizations shall comply with Fourth Amendment particularity and probable cause requirements as applied through Section 13G. Nothing in this Section shall be construed to diminish constitutional protections against unreasonable searches and seizures; (e) Federal Executive Non-Interference. No President, Vice President, Cabinet officer, or other federal executive officeholder shall direct, fund, or attempt to influence Council proceedings under this Section, with interference constituting Section 13 interference with Senior Official multipliers where applicable; (f) Transfer Upon Dissolution. All Council authorities under Sections 19.5.0.18.9.1 through 19.5.0.18.9.5 shall transfer to the Hamilton Contingent and the Academic Integrity Commission upon the Council's dissolution under Section 19.5.0.18.8, with no gap in enforcement capacity. The transfer shall be governed by the sixty (60) day overlap period under Section 19.5.0.18.8(a), with either body's action sufficient to continue pending matters during the overlap. 19.5.0.18.9.8 Limited Duration — Cannot Be Extended. The expanded Phase One authorities of Sections 19.5.0.18.9.1 through 19.5.0.18.9.5 shall dissolve automatically with the Council under Section 19.5.0.18.8, at sixty (60) days after Authority inauguration under Section 19.19. The Council shall not possess these authorities beyond its dissolution. No act of Congress, executive order, judicial ruling, or state action shall extend these authorities beyond Phase One. No successor body shall inherit these specific Phase One authorities except through the transfer provisions to the Hamilton Contingent and Academic Integrity Commission under Section 19.5.0.18.9.7(f). This is a transitional body with transitional authority, and the time-limitation is constitutional in character and shall not be subject to emergency extension, implied extension through inaction, or retroactive restoration. 19.5.0.19 The Washington Commission shall, within sixty (60) days of its convening, review every existing mutual defense treaty, alliance commitment, military partnership, arms sale contract, and standing foreign operation of the United States, and shall categorize each into one of three categories, publicly reasoned and recorded upon the provisional public ledger: (a) Honor in Full — The commitment reflects a genuine defensive alliance serving the security of the United States and its allies, and shall continue to be honored under the authorization processes of Sections 19.5.0.17 and 19.5.0.18;

(b) Honor with Modified Approval — The commitment shall continue but any response shall require additional affirmative concurrence as follows: during the Washington Commission period, from the Short-Term Civilian Review Board by majority vote; from the moment the Citizens' Oversight Board is fully sworn in and operational under Section 19.19 onward, from the Citizens' Oversight Board by majority vote. Such affirmation shall be publicly reasoned and recorded upon the Ledger; or (c) Suspend During Transition — The commitment shall be suspended for the duration of the Washington Commission period, with notice provided to the counterparty, and shall be reviewed by the three bodies of the Authority upon their swearing-in. 19.5.0.19.1 Pending completion of the Treaty Review under Section 19.5.0.19, all existing mutual defense treaties shall be treated as "Honor in Full" category for purposes of any authorization matter arising during that period. Allies shall not be abandoned to armed attack merely because the Commission has not yet completed its categorization review. Once a treaty is formally categorized, the assigned category shall govern any subsequent authorization matter under that treaty. 19.5.0.20 All arms sales, weapons transfers, and military technology exports to foreign governments, nongovernmental entities, or private parties shall be suspended immediately upon certified ratification. Existing arms sales contracts shall be paused, not cancelled, pending review by the Washington Commission and later by the three bodies of the Authority. No new arms sales or transfers shall be authorized until the Authority certifies full operational capability under Section 19.21. The Washington Commission may, in narrowly defined cases of an allied nation under active armed attack and immediately dependent upon ongoing delivery of purely defensive weapons (including interceptors, armor, anti-air systems, and medical supplies) to prevent mass civilian casualties, authorize continued delivery on a per-shipment basis by unanimous vote of the three state Chief Justices on the Commission, with every shipment publicly recorded upon the provisional public ledger. 19.5.0.21 The ongoing drawdown of non-essential overseas operations shall be pursued with deliberate caution throughout the Washington Commission period, balanced against the need for alliance stability and orderly transition. The Commission shall publish a Foreign Posture Review every ninety (90) days upon the provisional public ledger, detailing the status of overseas deployments, any proposed drawdowns, any alliance consultations, and any corrective actions. The Commission shall not impose any drawdown schedule that materially destabilizes the United States' defensive posture or that abandons allies currently facing active armed attack. 19.5.0.22 Upon the termination of the Washington Commission's Phase One role pursuant to Section 19.5.0.6(g) (at sixty (60) days after Authority inauguration under Section 19.19), all the military freeze provisions of this subsection shall continue in full force under the oversight of the three bodies of the Authority, and shall not be lifted until the Authority certifies full operational capability under Section 19.21. Upon such certification, the military authorities suspended under Section 19.5.0.15 shall be restored under the ongoing permanent restrictions of Section 16 of this Amendment, which remain in effect at all times. The Washington Commission itself continues in existence under its Permanent Oversight role per Section 17D, but no longer exercises the Phase One military oversight authorities; those authorities transfer to the Authority. B.1 Interim Two-Member Command (Days 1-180) 19.5.1 Because the Implementation Director is elected on Day 180 of ratification pursuant to Section 19.6, and because the three-member Joint Implementation Command established in Section 19.3 cannot fully exist before the Director takes office, there is hereby established an Interim Two-Member Command for the period from certified ratification through the swearing-in of the Implementation Director. The Interim Two-Member Command shall consist solely of the two senior-most Joint Chiefs of Staff confirmed oath-maintained under Section 19.5.0.3.2. 19.5.2 The Interim Two-Member Command shall possess the following limited authorities, for preparatory work only: (a) Site selection planning, including survey of federal lands, identification of candidate locations, and preparatory coordination with state and territorial governments, subject to final decisions by the full Joint Implementation Command once the Director takes office; (b) Budget planning and coordination with the constitutional appropriation under Section 11.3; (c) Drafting of legal frameworks for construction, personnel hiring, procurement, and Terminal manufacture, in coordination with the Washington Commission; (d) Preparation for the Implementation Director election, including coordination with state chief election officers on ballot logistics, candidate filing procedures, and voter notification; (e) Coordination with the Academic Integrity Commission on the Pre-Certified University Pool established under Section 17.16; and (f) Design of personnel hiring frameworks for later Office, Center, and Authority staffing. 19.5.3 The Interim Two-Member Command shall NOT, under any circumstances: (a) Begin actual construction of any Office, Center, Terminal, or Network infrastructure; (b) Make any binding long-term decisions that would constrain the full Joint Implementation Command or the three bodies of the Authority;

(c) Hire construction personnel or sign construction contracts; (d) Set policy of any kind; (e) Exercise any authority reserved to the Washington Commission, the Implementation Director, the full Joint Implementation Command, or the three bodies of the Authority; or (f) Remain in existence beyond the swearing-in of the Implementation Director, upon which moment the Interim Two-Member Command shall dissolve automatically and all records, preparatory documents, and coordination work shall transfer immediately to the full Joint Implementation Command. 19.5.4 All actions of the Interim Two-Member Command shall require unanimous consent of both members, with each action livestreamed upon the provisional public ledger. The Interim Command shall provide weekly progress reports to the Washington Commission throughout its existence. The Watch Board, once convened pursuant to Section 19.14, shall exercise retroactive oversight authority over all Interim Command actions taken prior to the Watch Board's convening. If either Joint Chief on the Interim Command is found to have violated the constitutional oath, that member shall be replaced pursuant to Section 19.5.5. 19.5.5 Joint Chief Succession on the Command. In the event that any Joint Chief serving on the Interim Two-Member Command or the full Joint Implementation Command retires, dies, resigns, becomes incapacitated, or is found to have violated the constitutional oath, the next senior-most Joint Chief confirmed oath-maintained under Section 19.5.0.3.2 shall automatically ascend to the vacated seat provisionally, subject to two confirmation requirements: (a) Oath Verification. Within seven (7) days of provisional ascension, the ascending Joint Chief shall publicly affirm the constitutional oath upon the Ledger, with verification conducted by the Washington Commission (if still in existence), by the Watch Board (during the Implementation Period), or by the Authority through Liberty Bell Initiative (after the Implementation Period); and (b) Watch Board Approval. Within fourteen (14) days of provisional ascension, the Watch Board shall review and approve the succession by majority vote, or by the Authority through Liberty Bell Initiative if the Watch Board has dissolved. 19.5.6 If oath verification under Section 19.5.5(a) fails or Watch Board approval under Section 19.5.5(b) is denied, the ascending Joint Chief shall be removed from the seat, and the next senior-most Joint Chief confirmed oath-maintained shall ascend provisionally, with the confirmation process restarting. This cascade shall continue down the seniority list until a Joint Chief is both oath-verified and approved. In the extraordinary case where no Joint Chief in the seniority line can satisfy both requirements, the Watch Board shall petition the Washington Commission (if still existing) or the Authority through Liberty Bell Initiative to identify an alternative senior military officer who can satisfy both oath verification and civilian approval. B.2 The Interim Transition Council 19.5.7 From the date of certified ratification of this Amendment until the Implementation Director takes office under Section 19.6, the authorities that would otherwise vest in the Joint Implementation Command shall instead vest in an Interim Transition Council ("the Interim Council"), established to prevent any period of military-only authority over the build-out process. The Interim Council operates alongside and complementary to the Interim Two-Member Command under Sections 19.5.1 through 19.5.6, with the Two-Member Command handling narrow preparatory work under its limited authorities while the Interim Council exercises broader civilian-majority decision-making authority upon convening. 19.5.8 The Interim Council shall be convened no later than one hundred and twenty (120) days after certified ratification and shall consist of five (5) members: (a) The senior-most Joint Chief of Staff confirmed to have maintained the constitutional oath; (b) The second senior-most Joint Chief of Staff confirmed to have maintained the constitutional oath; (c) One sitting Governor or chief executive, elected by a vote of the fifty-six (56) Governors and chief executives of the Participating Jurisdictions, to represent executive experience and cross-jurisdictional coordination; (d) A second sitting Governor or chief executive, elected by a vote of the fifty-six (56) Governors and chief executives of the Participating Jurisdictions, who shall be of a different political party or political orientation than the Governor or chief executive selected under clause (c) to ensure bipartisan civilian leadership; and (e) One sitting Chief Justice of the highest court of a Participating Jurisdiction, selected by randomized lottery from among the Chief Justices of the highest courts of all Participating Jurisdictions, to provide an institutional check independent of executive and military authority. 19.5.9 The Interim Council shall act only by majority vote, with all decisions publicly recorded upon the provisional public ledger. The composition of the Council guarantees three (3) civilian votes to two (2) military votes at all times, ensuring civilian control of the build-out. 19.5.10 The Interim Council shall exercise only those authorities that are strictly necessary to prepare for, facilitate, and protect the build-out of the institutions established by this Amendment. The Interim Council shall NOT: (a) Authorize any military deployment or action except in direct response to a documented active attack on a build-out site, personnel, or infrastructure; (b) Exercise any domestic law enforcement authority;

(c) Enter into any treaty, long-term contract, or binding commitment that extends beyond the expected tenure of the Implementation Director; (d) Direct, influence, or participate in the selection, recruitment, training, or oversight of members of the three bodies of the Authority; (e) Exercise any authority reserved to the Implementation Director or Joint Implementation Command beyond those minimally required to initiate Phase One activities of Section 19.19; or (f) Take any action that would materially predetermine decisions properly reserved to the Implementation Director upon their election. 19.5.11 No member of the Interim Council shall be eligible to run for the position of Implementation Director in the election held under Section 19.6, nor shall any member be eligible to hold any federal office for a period of four (4) years following the conclusion of their service on the Interim Council. This prohibition prevents the Interim Council from being used as a political campaign platform or as a stepping stone to federal power. 19.5.12 During the period of the Interim Council, an Interim Watch Board shall convene alongside it, consisting of twenty-five (25) registered voters drawn by randomized lottery from all Participating Jurisdictions, in the same manner as the Citizens' Implementation Watch Board established in Section 19.14. The Interim Watch Board shall possess the same access, observation, and suspension authorities as the full Watch Board, scaled to the activities of the Interim Council. Upon the convening of the full one-hundred-member Watch Board, the Interim Watch Board shall be dissolved and its records preserved upon the provisional public ledger. 19.5.13 The Interim Council shall be dissolved automatically and immediately upon the Implementation Director taking office under Section 19.6. All records, decisions, and documentation of the Interim Council shall be transferred to the Joint Implementation Command and made permanently accessible upon the Ledger once it becomes operational. 19.5.14 No member of the Interim Council, and no person acting under the authority of the Interim Council, shall take any action during the Interim Period that obstructs, delays, or interferes with the election of the Implementation Director under Section 19.6. Any such action shall trigger the interference penalties established in Section 19.23. 19.5.15 Convening Failure Fallback. In the event that the Interim Transition Council fails to convene within the one hundred twenty (120) day window under Section 19.5.8, whether due to obstruction of Governor elections, Chief Justice lottery failure, Joint Chief refusal to serve, or any other cause: (a) Washington Commission Assumption of Council Role. The Washington Commission shall assume the Interim Council's authorities under Section 19.5.7 on an interim basis, exercising those authorities subject to the same limitations under

Section 19.5.10 that bind the Council itself. Commission assumption does not expand Commission authority generally; it narrowly extends Commission operational capacity to fill the Council gap. (b) Continued Convening Efforts. The Washington Commission shall continue active efforts to facilitate Council convening, including coordination with willing Governors, alternative Chief Justice lottery procedures under Section 20.13, Joint Chief succession cascades under Sections 19.5.5 through 19.5.6, and State Attorneys General Council facilitation under Section 19.5.0.18. Monthly progress reports on convening efforts shall be published on the provisional public ledger. (c) Transition Upon Successful Convening. Upon successful Council convening, full Council authorities shall transfer to the Council within fourteen (14) days, with Commission transition briefing providing records, pending matters, and operational context. The Commission's interim assumption of Council role shall end upon transfer, with the Commission returning to its ordinary Section 19.5.0 Phase One role. (d) Absolute Outer Limit. Convening failure shall not be permitted to extend beyond the Implementation Director's election under Section 19.6, at which point ordinary Joint Implementation Command authority vests regardless of Council status. If the Council never convenes before Director election, the Council authority simply terminates without retroactive effect, and the Director assumes full authority as ordinarily contemplated. (e) Documentation of Failure Causes. The Washington Commission shall publish on the provisional public ledger specific documentation of the cause(s) of convening failure, enabling future Sunset Review analysis and informing potential Amendment modifications. Documentation shall identify obstructing actors where identified, with Section 13 interference prosecution referrals as appropriate. 19.5.16 Tiebreaker Mechanism for Chief Justice Abstention. Where the Chief Justice member of the Interim Transition Council under Section 19.5.8(e) abstains on a matter due to conflict of interest, recusal, or other legitimate basis, and the remaining four members deadlock two-to-two (2-2): (a) Mediation Attempt. The Council shall first attempt resolution through non-binding mediation by the Washington Commission, with the Commission issuing an advisory opinion within seventy-two (72) hours of deadlock identification. The advisory opinion shall not bind the Council but shall inform further deliberation. (b) Substitute Chief Justice Lottery. If deadlock persists after mediation, a substitute Chief Justice shall be drawn by randomized lottery from the Participating Jurisdiction Chief Justices not previously excluded under Section 19.5.8(e), within forty-eight (48) hours of failed mediation. The substitute shall serve solely on the deadlocked matter; the original Chief Justice member retains membership on the Council for all other matters.

(c) Tiebreaker Vote. The substitute Chief Justice shall review the matter, including all Council deliberation record and the Washington Commission advisory opinion, and cast a tiebreaker vote within seven (7) days of selection. The substitute's vote shall break the deadlock. (d) Original Chief Justice Protection. The original Chief Justice member's abstention shall not be construed as membership failure, resignation, or grounds for replacement. Legitimate abstention on specific matters is a constitutional function of judicial independence, and this tiebreaker mechanism accommodates abstention without penalizing it. (e) Abuse Prevention. Patterns of abstention suggesting tactical rather than legitimate basis (for example, consistent abstention on politically significant matters) may be reviewed by the Watchdog Tribunal for Section 13 interference where abstention is being weaponized against Council operations. Legitimate judicial independence remains fully protected; tactical obstruction through strategic abstention is not. 19.5.17 Crisis-Period Compressed Succession Timeline for Joint Chief Vacancies. Where a Joint Chief vacancy occurs on the Interim Transition Council during an active crisis period — active armed attack on the United States, active No Confidence proceeding, active Caretaker Period under Section 6A, or analogous emergency — the ordinary succession cascade under Sections 19.5.5 and 19.5.6 shall be compressed as follows: (a) Compressed Oath Verification. Oath verification under Section 19.5.5(a) shall be completed within three (3) days rather than seven (7), with the Interim Watch Board under Section 19.5.12 or the full Watch Board (whichever is operational) conducting expedited verification. (b) Compressed Civilian Approval. Civilian approval shall be provided by the three (3) civilian Council members (two Governors and the state Chief Justice) within three (3) days, rather than by the fourteen-day Watch Board process ordinarily required. This compressed civilian approval reflects the operational necessity of Council function during crisis while preserving civilian authority over military succession. (c) Interim Operational Capacity. In the period before succession is complete, the remaining Council members may act by majority of available members (three (3) of the four (4) non-successor members) for time-sensitive matters requiring Council action. Non-time-sensitive matters shall await completed succession. (d) Retroactive Ordinary Review. Full ordinary timelines under Sections 19.5.5 and 19.5.6 shall apply retroactively for non-time-sensitive matters once crisis conditions subside. Succession validity confirmed under compressed timeline shall not be revisited unless affirmative evidence of procedural failure during compression is subsequently discovered.

(e) Crisis Certification. Compressed timeline activation shall require certification by either Washington Commission majority vote or Council majority vote (of remaining non-vacant members) upon specific factual finding of crisis conditions. Certification shall be published on the provisional public ledger within twenty-four (24) hours of activation. (f) Automatic Deactivation. Compressed timelines shall deactivate automatically upon cessation of the crisis conditions that triggered activation, with subsequent successions reverting to ordinary Sections 19.5.5 and 19.5.6 timelines. Deactivation shall be certified and published on the provisional public ledger. C. The Implementation Director 19.6 The Implementation Director shall be elected by popular national vote, held one hundred and eighty (180) days after certified ratification of this Amendment. Candidates shall meet the eligibility requirements set forth in Section 17.7 for the Citizens' Oversight Board, excluding the professional experience restrictions to permit qualified candidates with construction, civic infrastructure, or constitutional law backgrounds. 19.7 The Director shall serve until the Authority certifies the full operational status of all institutions and infrastructure established by this Amendment. No fixed term shall apply, but the Director shall be subject to recall by a majority vote upon a petition bearing the valid signatures of ten percent (10%) of registered voters. During the

Implementation Period, signatures may be collected at the voter's choice of venue — either (a) state election offices of the voter's Participating Jurisdiction, or (b) any operational Citizens' Reclamation Office or Center where such facilities exist. Both venues are equally valid, and no venue may be designated primary. This voter-choice approach prevents either venue from being manipulated or closed to suppress a legitimate recall effort. 19.8 The Director shall not simultaneously hold any other federal, state, or local office, nor shall the Director be eligible to hold any federal office for a period of four (4) years following the conclusion of their implementation service, to prevent use of this office as a political launching pad. 19.8.1 Director Death, Resignation, or Permanent Incapacitation. In the event that the Implementation Director dies, resigns voluntarily, or is found permanently incapacitated, the following succession shall apply: (a) Incapacitation Determination. A determination of permanent incapacitation shall require BOTH unanimous written certification by three (3) independent physicians selected by lottery from a pool maintained by the Academic Integrity Commission AND a majority vote of the Watch Board concurring with the medical certification, on the model of Section 6.9. The certification shall be published in full upon the Ledger;

(b) Acting Director from Watch Board. Within fourteen (14) days of the Director's death, resignation, or certified permanent incapacitation, the Watch Board shall elect one of its own members to serve as Acting Director by majority vote. The elected Watch Board member shall step down from their Watch Board seat upon accepting the role of Acting Director, with the vacated Watch Board seat filled through ordinary lottery replacement. This ensures no conflict of interest in having the overseer simultaneously serve as the overseen; (c) Special Election. A special Implementation Director election shall be held within ninety (90) days of the vacancy, conducted under the same rules as the original Director election pursuant to Section 19.6. The Acting Director may stand as a candidate in the special election if otherwise eligible; (d) Continuity of Command. During the interim from vacancy until the Acting Director takes office (up to fourteen days), the Joint Implementation Command shall operate under the temporary authority of the two Joint Chiefs of Staff serving on the Command, with authority limited to the preparatory and emergency matters set forth in Sections 19.5.2 and 19.5.3 — no new binding decisions, no new construction starts, no new long-term commitments. Upon the Acting Director taking office, the full Command authority resumes; and (e) Successor Eligibility. The elected special-election Director shall serve under the same terms as the original Director pursuant to Section 19.7, until the Authority certifies full operational capability of the Amendment. 19.9 The Director's compensation shall be fixed at the level of a federal judge of a United States Court of Appeals, adjusted for cost of living, and shall not be altered during the Director's service. Compensation shall be funded through the constitutional appropriation established in Section 11.3. 19.9.1 Implementation Director Training and Preparation. Because the Implementation Director coordinates all build-out operations across the five-year Implementation Period and serves as the senior civilian member of the Joint Implementation Command, and because the Director is elected through popular national vote rather than drawn from a pre-qualified professional pool, the following training framework ensures the Director has operational knowledge sufficient to discharge duties: (a) Candidate Preparation Materials. The Academic Integrity Commission (or during Phase One before the AIC is operational, the Washington Commission) shall publish comprehensive Implementation Director preparation materials on the Franklin Ledger or provisional public ledger not later than thirty (30) days before the Director election under Section 19.6. Materials shall cover: Joint Implementation Command structure and authorities under Sections 19.3 through 19.5; military security role under Section 19.10; Office and Center construction framework under Section 11; infrastructure activation under Section 14; three-body Authority structure under Section 17; all interactions between the Director and other Amendment bodies. All candidates are strongly encouraged but not required to study the materials before seeking the office. (b) Post-Election Orientation. Within seven (7) days of election certification, and before the Director assumes full operational authority, the Director-elect shall complete a comprehensive orientation program of not less than forty (40) hours administered by the Washington Commission (during Phase One when the AIC is not yet operational) with support from outgoing Amendment bodies. Orientation shall cover the full scope of materials listed in subsection (a) plus: specific ongoing build-out matters, current Command membership and working relationships, state-level construction coordination, budget and timeline status, and known operational challenges. (c) Limited Authority During Orientation. During the seven-day orientation period, the Director-elect shall observe but not direct operations. The outgoing Director (if applicable) or a senior Command member shall continue ordinary operations during orientation. Emergency decisions requiring Director authority during orientation shall be made by Command supermajority vote until orientation completes. (d) Ongoing Education. The Director shall receive quarterly briefings on build-out progress, legal developments affecting Amendment implementation, and emergent threats to Amendment operations. Briefings shall be documented on the Ledger for public transparency. (e) Recall Replacement Training. Where a Director is replaced through recall under Section 19.7, the successor Director shall complete the same orientation framework before assuming full authority. Continuity of operations during recall transition shall be maintained by Command supermajority. (f) Federal Executive Non-Interference. No federal officeholder shall direct, influence, fund, or interfere with Director preparation materials, orientation, or ongoing education. Attempts shall constitute Section 13 interference with Senior Official multipliers. (g) Public Transparency. Director orientation completion, quarterly briefing participation, and ongoing education shall be documented on the Ledger as part of public accountability for the office. D. The Military Security Role 19.10 During the Implementation Period, the Armed Forces of the United States, acting under the authority of the Joint Implementation Command, shall provide physical security for all Citizens' Reclamation Office construction sites, Sovereign Civic Network infrastructure, Terminal manufacturing facilities established by the Academic Integrity Commission, and all meeting locations of the three bodies of the Authority. 19.11 The military security role under this Section shall be strictly limited to:

(a) Physical protection of buildings, personnel, and equipment from sabotage, theft, destruction, or armed attack; (b) Cybersecurity protection of the provisional public ledger and the Sovereign Civic Network during construction and activation; and (c) Response to specific, credible, documented threats against the build-out process, with each such response authorized in advance by majority vote of the Joint Implementation Command and recorded publicly. 19.12 The military shall NOT, under any circumstances during the Implementation Period, exercise any of the following authorities: (a) Surveillance, investigation, or detention of any civilian except as specifically related to a documented threat against the build-out; (b) Direction, management, staffing, or operational control of any civilian build-out function; (c) Participation in the selection, recruitment, training, or oversight of members of the three bodies of the Authority; (d) Access to the substantive proceedings of the three bodies, except as required for physical security; (e) Interference with, or direction of, the design, manufacture, or certification of Sovereign Voting Terminals, which shall remain exclusively under the Academic Integrity Commission; or (f) Any action that would constitute domestic law enforcement, which shall remain the sole jurisdiction of civilian authorities. 19.13 The Joint Chiefs of Staff shall retain the constitutional authority and duty established in Section 16.3(c) to refuse any order that violates this Constitution, this

Amendment, or the laws of the United States, and shall apply this authority fully during the Implementation Period. Refusals shall be documented and published pursuant to Section 16.3. E. The Citizens' Implementation Watch Board 19.14 There is hereby established the Citizens' Implementation Watch Board ("the Watch Board"), consisting of one hundred (100) registered voters drawn by randomized lottery from all Participating Jurisdictions in the same manner as the Citizens' Oversight Board. The Watch Board shall be constituted according to the following timeline, designed to ensure citizen oversight from the earliest hours of ratification while respecting the real-world logistical needs of selected citizens: (a) Day 0 Lottery Commencement. Upon certified ratification, the randomized lottery selection process shall begin immediately and shall complete within seven (7) days;

(b) Thirty-Day Arrangement Window. Upon notification of selection (by Day 7), each selected citizen shall have a thirty (30) day window to arrange personal life matters, including childcare, employment notification, dependent care, temporary housing if relocation is needed, travel arrangements, and other real-world logistics. This window recognizes that citizens cannot be expected to drop their lives without proper notice; (c) Arrangement Stipend. Upon notification, each selected citizen shall receive an immediate arrangement stipend equal to the median monthly household income of their state or territory (cost-of-living adjusted for their specific Jurisdiction), disbursed automatically through the constitutional appropriation under Section 11.3. This stipend is intended to cover initial expenses including childcare setup, travel, lost income during onboarding, and temporary housing if needed; (d) Seven-Day No-Fault Refund Window. A selected citizen may decline service for any reason within seven (7) days of notification, with full refund of the arrangement stipend required. No reason need be given. Declination shall trigger the next randomized lottery selection for that seat; (e) Watch Board Convening. The Watch Board shall formally convene and take the constitutional oath no later than Day 30 of ratification, with all one hundred members sworn. The Board shall exercise retroactive oversight authority over any actions taken during Days 1-30 by the Interim Two-Member Command, the Washington Commission, or any other body acting under this Amendment during that period; and (f) Application to Other Lottery-Selected Bodies. The same Day 0 lottery commencement, thirty-day arrangement window, state-based arrangement stipend, and seven-day no-fault refund window shall apply to all other lottery-selected bodies established by this Amendment, including the Citizens' Oversight Board, the Watchdog Tribunal, the Foreign Interference Oversight

Board, Independent Investigation Panels, and any activation of State Council sub-councils. Citizens drawn into mandatory service deserve humane treatment; no citizen shall be expected to drop their life without notice and financial support. 19.15 The Watch Board shall exercise direct civilian oversight of all military security operations conducted under this Section. Watch Board members shall have: (a) Unrestricted access to all build-out sites, at any time, without prior notice; (b) Authority to observe all military security operations in person; (c) Authority to interview military personnel, civilian build-out personnel, and Command members regarding any security operation or build-out matter; (d) Authority to suspend, by majority vote of the Watch Board, any military security operation that the Board determines exceeds the authorities enumerated in Section 19.11 or violates the prohibitions in Section 19.12, pending review and resolution by the Joint Implementation Command; and

(e) Authority to publish findings and concerns directly upon the provisional public ledger without editorial review or approval by the Command or by military authorities. 19.16 Watch Board members shall receive the same protections, compensation, and eligibility standards as Citizens' Oversight Board members under Section 17.5 through Section 17.7, adapted for the Implementation Period. 19.17 All military security operations conducted during the Implementation Period shall be livestreamed or otherwise recorded in real time and made available upon the provisional public ledger, subject only to narrow operational security redactions certified as necessary by unanimous vote of the Joint Implementation Command and reviewable by the Watch Board. The existence, timing, and general nature of every security operation shall never be classified. 19.17.1 Full Oversight Scope. While Sections 19.15 through 19.17 establish the Watch Board's military oversight authority, the Watch Board's constitutional role extends beyond military security to encompass the entire Implementation Period. The Watch Board shall exercise civilian citizen oversight of: (a) Joint Implementation Command operations and decisions; (b) Implementation Phase One through Three milestone achievement under Section 19.18 and the specific phase deliverables under Sections 19.19 through 19.21; (c) Ratification Loan expenditures under Section 13I and related funding flows, including verification that funds are spent consistently with Section 13I.4 authorized uses and not for Section 13I.5 prohibited uses; (d) Office and Center construction progress and integrity under Section 11B; (e) Sovereign Voting Terminal procurement, testing, and deployment under Section 14; (f) Franklin Ledger and Sovereign Civic Network infrastructure development under

Sections 4 and 4A; (g) Academic Integrity Commission preparatory operations and Pre-Certified University Pool establishment; (h) State Attorneys General Council Phase One federal enforcement operations under Section 19.5.0.5.2; (i) Any other Amendment-related operation occurring during the Implementation Period. 19.17.2 Internal Governance. The Watch Board shall organize its own operations under the following framework: (a) Presiding Officers. Within five (5) days of convening, the Watch Board shall elect by majority vote from among its membership: a Presiding Chairperson; a Vice

Chairperson; and a Recording Secretary. Presiding officers shall serve one (1) year terms, with no member serving consecutive terms in any single role, preventing power consolidation. (b) Standing Subcommittees. The Board shall establish standing subcommittees to focus on specific oversight domains, including at minimum: a Military Oversight Subcommittee; a Funding Oversight Subcommittee; an Infrastructure Oversight Subcommittee (covering Offices, Terminals, Ledger, Network); and an Academic Integrity Commission Oversight Subcommittee. Each subcommittee shall have not fewer than seven (7) members drawn from the full Board. (c) Subcommittee Authority. Subcommittees shall prepare recommendations for full Board action, conduct focused investigations within their domains, and issue preliminary findings; substantive Board decisions require full Board vote, not subcommittee action. (d) Meeting Secretary Function. The Recording Secretary shall maintain official Board records, coordinate publication on the provisional public ledger, and ensure compliance with Section 13B evidence preservation standards for all Board proceedings. (e) Removal of Presiding Officers. Any presiding officer may be removed from that role (but retained as ordinary Board member) by two-thirds (2/3) supermajority of the full Board for documented cause including dereliction of duty, breach of confidentiality, or corruption. 19.17.3 Meeting Operations. To ensure effective oversight throughout the 780-day Implementation Period: (a) Continuous Session. The Watch Board shall maintain continuous working session throughout the Implementation Period, with formal voting sessions held not less than weekly and subcommittee working sessions held as determined by subcommittee operational needs. (b) Venue Rotation. Full Board meetings shall rotate among Pre-Certified University Pool institutions per Section 11C.8, preventing any single venue from becoming the Board's institutional capture target. (c) Secure Video Participation. Members physically unable to attend in person may participate through secure video conference meeting Academic Integrity Commission security standards. Given the geographically distributed nature of the

100-member Board and the 780-day duration, secure video participation is a legitimate ordinary mode, not solely emergency accommodation. (d) Public Observation. All Board meetings shall be livestreamed on the provisional public ledger under Section 19.14 transparency principles, ensuring citizen observation of oversight deliberation. Subcommittee working sessions shall be livestreamed except where the subcommittee certifies by majority vote that a specific session requires private deliberation (such as ongoing investigation integrity); private sessions shall be followed by public summary within seventy-two (72) hours. (e) Session Documentation. Every Board and subcommittee session shall be documented with: attendance; agenda; substantive discussion summary; votes taken with individual member positions recorded; and resulting actions. Documentation shall be published on the provisional public ledger within seventy-two (72) hours. 19.17.4 Voting Procedures. Watch Board action shall proceed under the following framework: (a) Ordinary Quorum. Ordinary quorum for Board action shall require the presence of not fewer than fifty-one (51) members (a majority of the one hundred member body), whether physically present or participating via secure video under Section 19.17.3(c). Ordinary action requires majority vote of those present and voting. (b) Supermajority Requirements. The following Board actions shall require two-thirds (2/3) supermajority of the full Board (sixty-seven (67) of one hundred (100)): (i) suspension of any military security operation under Section 19.15(d); (ii) publication of findings that specific Joint Implementation Command actions violate Amendment provisions; (iii) referral of specific persons to the State Attorneys General Council for Section 13 prosecution investigation; (iv) recommendation that specific Implementation Phase milestones be deemed unmet requiring corrective action; and (v) formal declaration that Implementation Period is at risk of material failure requiring Washington Commission intervention. (c) Individual Vote Recording. Every member's vote on every action shall be individually recorded and published on the provisional public ledger, ensuring member accountability to citizens observing oversight operations. (d) Abstention and Recusal. Members may abstain where they have specific conflicts of interest or personal involvement with the matter under consideration. Recusal shall be recorded with the specific basis. (e) Emergency Decision Protocol. For time-sensitive matters requiring action within seventy-two (72) hours, expedited procedures shall apply with compressed notice periods and abbreviated debate, while preserving quorum requirements and voting thresholds. 19.17.5 Investigation Authority. The Watch Board shall have robust investigation powers for effective oversight: (a) Document Access.

The Board shall have unrestricted access to documents, records, financial accounts, operational plans, and other materials held by the Joint Implementation Command, the Washington Commission, the Academic Integrity Commission, and other Amendment bodies operating during the Implementation Period. Claims of executive privilege, deliberative privilege, or similar doctrines shall not bar Board access to Amendment-related materials.

(b) Testimony Authority. The Board may compel testimony from: Joint Implementation Command personnel; Washington Commission members; career federal personnel (with full Section 13B.16 whistleblower protection); contractors performing Amendment build-out work; and other persons with material knowledge of Implementation Period operations. Testimony may be taken under oath with perjury liability for knowingly false statements. (c) Site Access. Board members shall have unrestricted access to all build-out sites, facility construction, Terminal manufacturing, infrastructure development, and other physical locations of Amendment implementation. Access shall be available at any time without prior notice, preventing staged compliance demonstrations. (d) Specialist Consultation. The Board may retain technical specialists (engineers, cybersecurity experts, financial auditors, construction specialists) to advise on specific oversight matters, funded through the Section 11.3 constitutional appropriation via the Watch Board's operating budget. (e) Cooperation Required. All federal personnel, contractors, and Amendment body members shall cooperate fully with Board investigations. Refusal to cooperate shall constitute Section 13 interference subject to Section 13 penalties, with refusal prosecuted regardless of asserted justification. (f) Subpoena Power. The Board may issue subpoenas for witnesses and documents, enforceable in federal courts or through Section 17C state-sovereign adjudication pathways where federal courts are obstructed. Subpoena enforcement shall proceed on accelerated timelines consistent with the Implementation Period's time-sensitive nature. 19.17.6 Staff and Operational Resources. To support effective oversight of the 780-day Implementation Period: (a) Professional Staff. The Board shall employ professional staff including: legal counsel independent of federal executive branch legal services; financial auditors with public-accounting credentials; policy analysts drawn from the Pre-Certified University Pool; records staff for Section 13B compliance; technical specialists as needed for ongoing subcommittee operations; and administrative personnel sufficient for Board operations. (b) Staff Size. Initial staff complement of not fewer than thirty (30) full-time equivalent professional staff positions, expandable upon Board supermajority vote with Washington Commission concurrence during Phase One. (c) Independence from Command. Staff shall report to the Recording Secretary under Board direction, not to the Joint Implementation Command. Command shall have no hiring, firing, compensation, or performance-evaluation authority over Board staff. (d) Funding. Staff compensation, operational expenses, and member support shall be funded through the Section 11.3 constitutional appropriation via a dedicated

Watch Board reserve under Section 13I.4, with specific line-item transparency on the provisional public ledger. 19.17.7 Member Security and Protection. Watch Board members overseeing a constitutionally critical period face elevated threats: (a) Federal Protection. Board members shall receive federal protection equivalent to sitting Members of Congress during their service, protecting against physical threats from actors opposed to Amendment implementation. (b) Residence and Family Security. Enhanced residence security during Board service; family member protection against harassment, intimidation, and retaliation; Section 13 interference prosecution for actors targeting Board families. (c) Communications Security. Secure communications infrastructure meeting Academic Integrity Commission standards, protecting Board communications from foreign intelligence collection, removed-official surveillance, and corrupt-federal-system interception. (d) Employment Protection. Board members' ordinary civilian employment protected under Section 17.5(a) framework, with employers required to hold positions or equivalent positions open for member return post-service. (e) Post-Service Protection. Protection shall continue for not less than three (3) years post-service, recognizing that adverse actors may seek retaliation after Board members return to ordinary civilian life. 19.17.8 Coordination with Other Bodies. The Watch Board shall coordinate with: (a) Washington Commission. The Board and Commission shall coordinate oversight functions, with the Board providing citizen oversight complementing the Commission's professional constitutional oversight. Commission decisions shall be subject to Board review and comment; Board findings shall be considered by the Commission in its decisions. (b) State Attorneys General Council. The Board shall refer matters requiring federal prosecution to the Council under Section 19.5.0.5.2, with Council supermajority vote determining prosecution proceeding. Board referrals are not self-executing; they initiate Council consideration. (c) Academic Integrity Commission. Coordination on technical oversight of Terminal development, Ledger infrastructure, Network security, and other technical build-out matters. Commission technical expertise supports Board oversight functions. (d) Joint Implementation Command. Ordinary coordination through regular Command briefings to the Board and Board communications to the Command. Coordination does not constitute Board deference; Board oversight of Command is independent.

(e) Authority Bodies Upon Formation. As the three Authority bodies stand up during Phase One to Two transition, the Board coordinates with emerging Authority on oversight handoff. Authority bodies, once operational, gradually assume oversight functions that the Board performed during earlier Implementation. 19.17.9 Public Reporting Obligations. Watch Board transparency shall include: (a) Monthly Public Reports. Not later than the fifteenth day of each month, the Board shall publish a comprehensive monthly report on the provisional public ledger covering: Implementation progress in each oversight domain; identified concerns requiring attention; Command response to prior Board concerns; financial oversight findings; and subcommittee findings during the reporting period. (b) Quarterly Phase Assessment. Not later than fifteen (15) days after the close of each calendar quarter, the Board shall publish quarterly assessment covering Implementation Phase progress relative to milestones, with specific findings on whether each phase is on track, at risk, or requires corrective action. (c) Findings Publication. Specific Board findings of concern, violation, or corruption shall be published immediately upon adoption rather than waiting for monthly or quarterly reports, ensuring time-sensitive matters receive timely public attention. (d) Annual Comprehensive Report. At the conclusion of each Implementation Year, a comprehensive annual report summarizing Board activity, findings, recommendations, and Implementation progress, providing permanent record accessible to citizens, researchers, and future Sunset Review consideration. (e) Real-Time Publication. Meeting minutes, votes, and substantive Board communications shall be published in real time on the provisional public ledger per Section 19.17.3(e), ensuring citizens can observe oversight activity as it occurs. 19.17.10 Member Replacement and Service Continuity. Given the 780-day service period and member life circumstances: (a) Replacement Triggers. Member replacement proceeds upon: (i) member resignation for hardship, health, or personal circumstance under Section 17.4 hardship framework adapted for Watch Board service; (ii) member removal for cause by Board two-thirds supermajority; (iii) member death or incapacity; or (iv) member ineligibility discovery under Section 17.7 standards. (b) Replacement Lottery. Replacements shall be drawn by randomized lottery from the Watch Board selection pool under Section 19.14, with new members receiving the same Day 0 arrangement benefits under Section 19.14(a)-(e) (adapted for their actual notification timing). (c) Replacement Timing. New members shall take constitutional oath within thirty (30) days of selection, following the Section 19.14(b) arrangement window. Board shall continue operations during replacement period with reduced membership, provided quorum per Section 19.17.4(a) remains achievable. (d) No Replacement Late in Service. Where Implementation Period is within ninety (90) days of conclusion, replacement may be deferred to the Authority formation process rather than separate Watch Board lottery, at Board discretion. (e) Hardship Framework Applies. The Section 17.4 through 17.4.13 hardship framework applies to Watch Board service, with Section 17.4.12 scaling provisions applicable to the 780-day duration placing Board service in the comprehensive tier of hardship consideration. 19.17.11 Handoff to Authority Oversight. Upon Authority bodies becoming fully operational around Day 180: (a) Gradual Transition. Watch Board oversight functions transition to Authority bodies and Watchdog Tribunal progressively as those bodies come online, with the Board continuing in support role until Implementation Period concludes at Day 780. (b) Continuing Implementation Focus. Even after Authority bodies operational, the Watch Board retains specific responsibility for Implementation-Period-specific oversight (build-out progress, milestone achievement, Ratification Loan expenditure, implementation-specific corruption) through Day 780, distinct from the Authority's broader constitutional oversight role. (c) Dissolution at Day 780. The Watch Board dissolves at the conclusion of the Implementation Period (Day 780), with final comprehensive report published within thirty (30) days of dissolution covering the complete Implementation Period. (d) Records Transfer. Upon dissolution, all Watch Board records transfer to the National Archives and the Franklin Ledger for permanent preservation. Records remain accessible for citizen review, academic research, and future Sunset Review consideration. (e) Former Member Post-Service. Former Watch Board members retain Section 19.17.7(e) post-service protections and Section 13B.16 whistleblower protections for matters within their Board knowledge for five (5) years post-dissolution, preserving their ability to speak publicly about Implementation Period observations without retaliation. (f) Institutional Memory. The Academic Integrity Commission shall, upon Board dissolution, coordinate creation of institutional memory documentation including: lessons learned; identified vulnerabilities corrected during Implementation; recommendations for future Sunset Review modification of Implementation framework. Institutional memory documents shall be published on the Franklin Ledger for future constitutional reference. F. The Phased Rollout

19.18 The Implementation Period shall proceed in three phases, with specific deliverables for each phase. Failure to meet a phase milestone shall trigger a mandatory public review by the Watch Board and a publicly recorded corrective action plan by the Command, but shall not void progress already made. 19.19 Phase One (Days 1 through 180 — Institutional Foundation). Within the first one hundred eighty (180) days following certified ratification, the core institutional bodies established by this Amendment shall be formed and made operational, in the following order and approximate timing: (a) the Washington Commission shall convene within seventy-two (72) hours of ratification pursuant to Section 19.5.0.2; (b) the Watch Board shall be constituted and convened by Day thirty (30) pursuant to Section 19.14; (c) the Pre-Certified Pool of universities shall be established by Day ninety (90) pursuant to Section 17.16; (d) the three bodies of the Authority shall be selected, sworn, and convened by Day one hundred eighty (180) pursuant to Section 17, with the State Elections Council activating immediately (its members being existing state chief election officers serving ex officio), the Citizens' Oversight Board completing lottery selection and convening, and the Academic Integrity Commission selected from the Pre-Certified Pool; (e) the Implementation Director shall be elected on Day one hundred eighty (180) pursuant to Section 19.6; (f) the Hamilton Contingent shall be constituted by Day one hundred eighty (180) pursuant to Section 13C; (g) the Watchdog Tribunal shall be constituted within ninety (90) days following the Authority's swearing-in, pursuant to Section 21.2, and shall be operational no later than Day two hundred seventy (270); (h) the provisional public ledger shall be established and operational; and (i) the legal framework for construction shall be finalized. All bodies required to administer the blockchain Testing Phase and the Inaugural Referendum shall exist before those activities begin. 19.20 Phase Two (Days 180 through 780 — Blockchain and Foundational Infrastructure). During months seven (7) through twenty-six (26) following ratification: (a) the Academic Integrity Commission shall conduct the seven-and-a-half-month blockchain Testing Phase under Section 4.5, commencing on Day one hundred eighty (180) and concluding on Day four hundred five (405); (b) selected chains shall enter the twelve-month setup period under Section 4.10, from Day four hundred five (405) to Day seven hundred sixty-five (765); (c) the Academic Integrity Commission shall certify the blockchain infrastructure as operationally ready no later than Day seven hundred fifty (750); (d) physical construction of Citizens' Reclamation Offices and Centers shall commence, prioritizing Priority Construction Zones under Section 11B; (e) Office and Center locations shall be determined by the Citizens' Oversight Board based on population distribution and accessibility, drawing on three independent cross-verified data sources: (i) the most recent decennial Census of the United States, which is constitutionally mandated and not subject to manipulation by any federal administration; (ii) current voter registration rolls provided by the chief election officer of each state, territory, and the District of Columbia through their positions on the State Elections Council; and (iii) an independent population-and-accessibility survey conducted by the Academic Integrity Commission during Phase One, with methodology and findings published upon the Ledger. No single data source shall be relied upon exclusively, and any material discrepancies among the three sources shall be resolved by Liberty Bell Initiative of the Authority with published reasoning; (f) Host Site agreements under Section 11B shall be executed to provide interim voting capacity pending full Office/Center construction; (g) Office and Center personnel recruitment and training shall commence, including professional Accessibility Officers under Section 11A.13; (h) Mobile Accessibility Teams under Section 11A.4 shall begin establishment; (i) the Inaugural Referendum shall be held on Day seven hundred eighty (780) pursuant to Section 19A. 19.21 Phase Three (Days 780 through Year 5 — Full Infrastructure Deployment and Certification). Following the Inaugural Referendum on Day seven hundred eighty (780), and extending through year five (5) after ratification: (a) construction of all fifty (50) Citizens' Reclamation Offices shall complete, one in each state; (b) all six (6) Citizens' Reclamation Centers shall complete construction, one in the District of Columbia and one in each of the five territories enumerated in Section 3.1.1; (c) the initial elections for Office and Center officers under Section 11.2 shall be held once sufficient infrastructure is in place; (d) the Sovereign Civic Network shall be designed, constructed, tested, and activated, including secure dedicated channels to United States embassies, major consulates, and major military installations abroad; (e) the Sovereign Voting Terminals shall be designed, manufactured, tested, and certified by the Academic Integrity Commission, including Accessible Terminals meeting the requirements of Section 11A.2; (f) Overseas Terminals shall be deployed pursuant to Section 14.9 for the participation of United States citizens and nationals residing abroad; (g) all legacy paper processes from the pre-Inaugural period shall be cryptographically migrated to the full Sovereign Blockchain Voting Ledger; (h) Mobile Accessibility Teams shall complete full deployment; (i) voter-verified paper ballot system under Section 14.10 through 14.20 shall be fully integrated. Upon successful completion and certification by the Authority, the Implementation Period shall conclude and the Joint

Implementation Command shall dissolve. If this has not occurred by the end of year five (5), the Implementation Period shall continue, with mandatory public status reports issued quarterly upon the Ledger pursuant to Section 19.2. G. Prohibitions and Penalties 19.22 During the Implementation Period, no officer of the existing Federal Government, no member of Congress, no sitting President or Vice President, no sitting federal judge, and no federal agency shall interfere with, delay, obstruct, underfund, or attempt to redirect the work of the Joint Implementation Command, the three bodies of the Authority, or the Watch Board. The constitutional appropriation established in Section 11.3 shall flow automatically and directly to

the Command and the Authority, bypassing the federal appropriations process entirely. F. The Inaugural Referendum as Exclusive No Confidence Mechanism During Implementation 19.23 Exclusive Mechanism. From Day Zero of Ratification through certification of the Inaugural Referendum under Section 19A, the Inaugural Referendum shall be the sole and exclusive mechanism for a No Confidence vote against the Federal Government in office at Ratification. No Petition under Section 3 shall be filed, certified, or advanced to Referendum during this period. This rule is established in Section 3.0 and further specified in Section 19A.26 through 19A.27.2. 19.24 No Delay of Inaugural Referendum. The Inaugural Referendum shall occur on Day Seven Hundred Eighty (780) regardless of the state of Implementation infrastructure, as provided in Section 19A.10 and Section 19A.10.1. A corrupt existing Federal Government shall not be permitted to delay, obstruct, or prolong Implementation in order to evade or postpone the Inaugural Referendum. Any attempt to do so shall constitute interference under Section 13 and shall trigger the full penalties thereof. 19.25 Activation of Regular Petition Mechanism After Inaugural. Following certification of the Inaugural Referendum, the regular Petition mechanism under Section 3 becomes available as provided in Section 3.0 and Section 19A.27.2. Any Petition initiated after Inaugural certification shall be conducted at the citizen's choice of Amendment-native venue, in priority order: (a) operational Citizens' Reclamation Offices, Centers, or Host Sites under Sections 11 and 11B where such facility has come online; (b) Authority-procured temporary venues under Section 11B.23 through 11B.28 operational in the citizen's Jurisdiction; (c) Mobile Participation Units under Sections 11A.21 through 11A.31, which continue deployment with priority to rural areas and Jurisdictions without fixed venue coverage; (d) Satellite Sites as needed. In extraordinary circumstances where Amendment-native infrastructure under subsections (a) through (d) cannot adequately cover a specific Jurisdiction, and only as a deep fallback with AIC certification that Amendment infrastructure is genuinely unavailable, state election offices may be used with heightened anti-capture protections. Signature verification shall proceed through the State Elections Council pursuant to Section 3.2. The Authority shall maintain temporary venue coverage under Section 11B.23 through 11B.28 until permanent Offices come online in each Jurisdiction, such that no citizen of any Jurisdiction — urban or rural — lacks access to the Petition mechanism during the permanent construction buildout. 19.26 Provisional Infrastructure for Post-Inaugural Referenda. If a Referendum under Section 5 is triggered after Inaugural Referendum certification but before the full Sovereign Blockchain Voting Ledger is operational, the vote shall be administered through the provisional public ledger established in Section 19.4, using paper-backed cryptographic signatures subject to subsequent migration to the full Ledger upon its activation. The Academic Integrity Commission shall certify the provisional system as sufficiently secure before any Referendum under this Section commences, with certification publicly recorded on the provisional public ledger. All other protections, procedures, and substantive provisions of this Amendment — including Sections 3, 5, 6, 6A, 7, 8, 9, 10, 13, 16, 22, and 23 — shall apply fully. The only modification shall be the provisional venue and infrastructure during the build-out of full operational capability. G. Penalties and Enforcement During Implementation 19.27 Any federal officeholder or employee who violates Section 19.22 shall be subject to the interference penalties established in Section 13, including the fifteen (15) year minimum sentence and the lifetime bar from public office without possibility of pardon. 19.28 Any military officer who exceeds the authorities enumerated in Section 19.11, violates the prohibitions in Section 19.12, or interferes with the Watch Board shall be immediately removed from command, subjected to public military tribunal pursuant to Section 16.5, and, upon conviction, imprisoned for not less than twenty-five (25) years for insurrection against the constitutional order. 19.29 The full operational provisions of this Amendment — including in-person-only voting, blockchain recording, Terminal-based ballot casting, and the 15% geographic-distribution petition requirement — shall become enforceable only upon the Authority's certification of full operational capability. Until such certification, petition and voting processes shall use interim paper-based methods approved by the three bodies of the Authority and subject to the security and transparency principles of this Amendment to the greatest extent practical.

Section 19A. The Inaugural Referendum

Key terms in this Section: • "Ratification" — The moment at which this Amendment is ratified by three-fourths of the several States pursuant to Article V of the Constitution of the United States. • "Day Zero" — The calendar date on which Ratification takes formal effect. • "Inaugural Referendum" — The automatic national vote held on Day Seven Hundred Eighty (780) following Ratification, in which the People directly vote whether to declare No Confidence in the Federal Government in office at the moment of Ratification.

• "The Authority" — The Independent Tripartite Oversight Authority (three bodies, see Section 17). • "Liberty Bell Initiative" — Separate concurrence of all three bodies of the Authority. • "The Ledger" — The Sovereign Blockchain Voting Ledger (Section 4), or the provisional public ledger established under Section 19.4 if the full Ledger is not yet certified operational at the time of the Inaugural Referendum. 19A.1 Foundational Principle. The People, in ratifying this Amendment, express their sovereign judgment that the existing constitutional order requires fundamental renewal. Ratification carries within it an implicit mandate for democratic renewal of federal leadership under the new constitutional framework. There is therefore hereby established the Inaugural Referendum, which provides the People with a direct, automatic opportunity to exercise their Section 1 right of popular No Confidence against the Federal Government in office at Ratification, without requiring them to meet Section 3 petition thresholds or to wait for a discretionary citizen initiation. A. Automatic Trigger and Timing 19A.2 Automatic Trigger. The Inaugural Referendum shall be triggered automatically by the act of Ratification itself. No petition, certification, initiation, or other procedural step shall be required. The Ratification of this Amendment shall be deemed, as a matter of constitutional law, the equivalent of a certified Petition under Section 3 for purposes of scheduling the Inaugural Referendum. 19A.3 Timing. The Inaugural Referendum shall be held on Day Seven Hundred Eighty (780) following Day Zero, providing twenty-six (26) months for the implementation build-out described in Section 19 and for the People to observe the existing Federal Government operating under this Amendment's new constraints. If Day Seven Hundred Eighty (780) falls on a Saturday, Sunday, or federal holiday, the Referendum shall be conducted on the following Monday that is not a federal holiday. 19A.4 No Delay Permitted. No act of Congress, executive order, judicial ruling, state action, emergency declaration, or any other federal, state, or territorial action shall delay, postpone, modify, or prevent the Inaugural Referendum. Any attempt to do so shall be void ab initio and shall constitute interference under Section 13, triggering the full penalties thereof, including the fifteen (15) year minimum sentence and the lifetime bar from public office without possibility of pardon. 19A.5 Public Notice. The Authority, or in Phase One the Washington Commission, shall publish notice of the Inaugural Referendum on the Ledger (or provisional public ledger) beginning on Day One (1) following Ratification, with continuous updates through Day Seven Hundred Eighty (780). Notice shall include: (a) the date, time, and venues of the Referendum; (b) the text of the ballot question; (c) the thresholds required for passage; (d) the consequences of passage and failure; and (e) the procedures for voting. B. Ballot Question and Thresholds 19A.6 Ballot Question. The ballot question for the Inaugural Referendum shall read substantially as follows, with final language certified by the Authority (or during Phase One, the Washington Commission): "Shall the People of the United States declare Inaugural No Confidence in the Federal Government in office on [Day Zero], thereby vacating all offices enumerated in Section 1.1 of this Amendment, triggering the Constitutional Transition Committee and Emergency Election under Sections 6 through 9?" The ballot shall offer the choices YES (declare Inaugural No Confidence) or NO (retain the existing Federal Government). 19A.7 Passage Thresholds. The Inaugural Referendum shall pass only upon: (a) the affirmative vote of not less than sixty percent (60%) of ballots cast; AND (b) participation of not less than fifty percent (50%) of registered voters across all Participating Jurisdictions. The sixty percent (60%) supermajority threshold and fifty percent (50%) turnout threshold are identical to the thresholds for regular No Confidence under Section 5.2, reflecting the principle that the People's judgment on governmental continuation — whether at the Inaugural moment or thereafter — should be subject to the same supermajority and majority-engagement standard. 19A.8 Close-Vote Procedures. Results falling within the automatic recount margin established in Section 23.3 shall trigger automatic recount procedures before certification. The recount shall be completed within fourteen (14) days of the initial vote tally, using the same forensic standards applicable to regular Referenda. C. Infrastructure and Administration 19A.9 Voting Venues. The Inaugural Referendum shall be administered through Amendment-native infrastructure at the following venues, in priority order: (a) all operational Citizens' Reclamation Offices and Centers built by Day Seven Hundred Eighty (780) under Section 11 and Section 19.15; (b) designated Host Sites under Section 11B.2 through 11B.22, utilizing existing public infrastructure; (c) Authority-procured temporary venues under Section 11B.23 through 11B.28, which shall be procured and operational in every Participating Jurisdiction by Day Seven Hundred Twenty (720) to serve the Inaugural Referendum; (d) Mobile Participation Units under Sections 11A.21 through 11A.31, which shall deploy with priority to rural areas and any Jurisdiction with insufficient fixed venue coverage; (e) Satellite Sites as needed. In extraordinary circumstances where Amendment-native infrastructure under subsections (a) through (e) cannot adequately cover a specific Jurisdiction, and only as a deep fallback, existing state and territorial election

offices may be used using paper ballots under Academic Integrity Commission supervision, with results subsequently migrated to the Ledger (or provisional public ledger) upon certification, and with explicit AIC certification that the state-office fallback is necessary and that adequate anti-capture protections are in place. The state-office fallback shall not be used as a convenience; it is a last resort when procurement and mobile deployment cannot reach a Jurisdiction. 19A.10 Ledger Infrastructure. The Inaugural Referendum shall be recorded upon the full Sovereign Blockchain Voting Ledger if operational by Day Seven Hundred Eighty (780), or upon the provisional public ledger established under Section 19.4 if the full Ledger is not yet certified operational. The Academic Integrity Commission shall certify the ledger infrastructure sufficient for the Inaugural Referendum no later than Day Seven Hundred Fifty (750), thirty (30) days before the Referendum. 19A.10.1 Certification Failure Backup. If the Academic Integrity Commission cannot certify full ledger infrastructure by Day Seven Hundred Fifty (750), the Inaugural Referendum shall nonetheless proceed on Day Seven Hundred Eighty (780) using the provisional public ledger under Section 19.4 and paper ballots at state election offices, with all votes cryptographically migrated to the full Ledger upon subsequent certification. The Authority (or Washington Commission) shall publish the fallback procedures upon the Ledger no later than Day Seven Hundred Fifty-Five (755). In no event shall infrastructure certification failure delay, postpone, or prevent the Inaugural Referendum. Failure of any person to administer the Referendum on Day Seven Hundred Eighty (780) for infrastructure reasons shall constitute interference under Section 13. 19A.11 Overseas and Territorial Participation. Sections 3.1.1 (territorial participation) and 14.9 (overseas Terminals at embassies) shall apply to the Inaugural Referendum. If overseas Terminals are not yet operational, overseas Americans shall vote by paper absentee ballot returned to U.S. embassies, with results cryptographically migrated to the Ledger upon infrastructure completion. 19A.12 Accessibility. All accessibility provisions of Section 11A shall apply to the Inaugural Referendum. Where Mobile Accessibility Teams are not yet fully deployed by Day Seven Hundred Eighty (780), state and territorial authorities shall cooperate with the Authority (or Washington Commission) to provide accessible voting options for homebound, elderly, disabled, and otherwise affected voters, subject to the same transparency and Ledger documentation standards. 19A.13 Oversight. The Inaugural Referendum shall be administered by the Authority through the Liberty Bell Initiative if the Authority is fully constituted and operational by Day Seven Hundred Eighty (780). If the Authority is not yet fully operational, the Washington Commission (Section 19.5.0) shall administer the Referendum with cooperation of the partially operational Authority bodies, subject to the oversight of the Watch Board and, where applicable, the Watchdog Tribunal. D. Consequences of Passage

19A.14 Immediate Vacation. If the Inaugural Referendum passes under Section 19A.7, all offices enumerated in Section 1.1 shall be vacated immediately upon certification, consistent with Section 5.3. The passage of the Inaugural Referendum shall have the same constitutional effect as passage of a regular Referendum under Section 5.2. 19A.14.1 Amendment Infrastructure Continuity. The Implementation Director under Section 19, the Citizens' Implementation Watch Board, the Joint Implementation Command (including its Interim Two-Member Command phase where applicable), and the three bodies of the Authority shall continue in their roles after Inaugural Referendum passage. Their work implementing the Amendment's infrastructure is independent of the political governance vacated by passage of the Referendum, and shall continue uninterrupted to ensure the new government elected through Emergency Election inherits fully operational Amendment infrastructure. The Watchdog Tribunal shall likewise continue its oversight functions. No person serving in these Amendment-specific roles shall be removed by operation of the Referendum. 19A.15 Caretaker Period and Committee. Upon certification of Inaugural Referendum passage, the Interim Caretaker Council under Section 6A shall convene within seventy-two (72) hours, Emergency Delegate Elections under Section 6.2 shall commence within ten (10) days, and the Constitutional Transition Committee under Section 6 shall convene upon completion of the Emergency Delegate Elections. All procedures of Sections 6, 6A, 7, 8, and 9 shall apply without modification. 19A.16 Grandfathering Provisions Voided. If the Inaugural Referendum passes, the grandfathering provisions of Sections 25.4 (Supreme Court term limits) and 26.6 (Congressional term limits) shall be deemed void, because the People have exercised their sovereign authority to remove the Federal Government in office at Ratification. The new government elected through the Emergency Election under Section 7 shall serve under the full application of Sections 25 and 26, without grandfathering protections.

19A.17 Supreme Court Reconstitution. If the Inaugural Referendum passes, all Justices of the Supreme Court in office at the moment of certification shall be subject to the vacation procedures of Section 1.1 and Section 5.3. Section 25.4 grandfathering shall be void by operation of Section 19A.16, and no Justice shall invoke Section 25.4 to retain their seat following Inaugural Referendum passage. The new Supreme Court Justices appointed by the new Federal Government following the Emergency Election shall serve staggered eighteen-year (18-year) terms under Section 25.2 and Section 25.3, with the staggered cycle initiated by the new appointments using the compression transition procedure of Section 25.3.1 to establish the full nine-Justice cycle. 19A.18 Agency Review. The 180-day Agency Review process under Section 15 shall proceed following Inaugural Referendum passage, subject to the same standards and timelines applicable to agency review following a regular No Confidence. 19A.19 Career Personnel Protection. The protections for career technical personnel under Section 1, Section 6A.10, and Section 15.2 shall apply with full force following Inaugural Referendum passage. Career federal employees shall continue operations during the Caretaker Period and Committee Period, ensuring that essential federal functions continue uninterrupted during the transition. 19A.20 Military Command Transition. The military chain of command transitions established in Section 16.14 shall apply following Inaugural Referendum passage, transitioning from the Interim Two-Member Command (if still in effect) to the Caretaker Council, then to the Constitutional Transition Committee Chairperson, and finally to the newly elected President upon swearing-in. E. Consequences of Failure 19A.21 Continued Operation. If the Inaugural Referendum fails to pass under Section 19A.7, either because the supermajority threshold is not met or because the turnout threshold is not met, the Federal Government in office at Ratification shall continue to serve out their respective terms, subject to the full application of this Amendment's constraints, including Sections 16, 24, 25, 26, and all other operative provisions. This Amendment shall continue to operate, and Implementation under Section 19 shall continue on schedule. 19A.22 Grandfathering Preserved. If the Inaugural Referendum fails, the grandfathering provisions of Sections 25.4 and 26.6 shall remain in force. Current Supreme Court Justices shall continue to serve under their original appointments. Current Members of Congress shall be subject to the transition grandfathering of Section 26.6. 19A.23 Regular No Confidence Remains Available. Failure of the Inaugural Referendum shall not preclude, delay, or inhibit the exercise of regular No Confidence under Sections 1 through 10. Citizens retain the full

Section 1 right of popular No Confidence from Day Zero onward, and may exercise it at any time subject to Section 3 petition thresholds. 19A.24 Cooldown Period. Following the failure of the Inaugural Referendum, no regular Section 5 Referendum shall be certified within two (2) years of the Inaugural Referendum date, to allow the Federal Government an opportunity to operate under the new constitutional constraints before facing another removal vote. The two-year cooldown of Section 10.3 shall apply to the Inaugural Referendum on the same terms as to regular Referenda. Petitions under Section 3 may be initiated and collected during the cooldown period but may not proceed to Referendum certification until the cooldown expires. This cooldown does not apply to emergency mechanisms of Sections 21 (Watchdog Tribunal), 22 (foreign interference), or other non-Section-5 removal or accountability procedures.

19A.25 Public Reasoning. The Authority (or Washington Commission) shall publish upon the Ledger (or provisional public ledger), within thirty (30) days of Inaugural Referendum failure, a comprehensive public report analyzing: (a) final vote totals by Jurisdiction; (b) turnout statistics; (c) any contested results or investigated irregularities; (d) the Government's conduct under the new constitutional constraints during the build-up period; and (e) any recommendations for Authority oversight going forward. This report shall be available for citizens exercising future Section 3 petition rights. F. Exclusivity of the Inaugural Referendum During Build-Up 19A.26 Exclusive Mechanism During Build-Up. During the twenty-six-month (26-month) period between Day Zero and Day Seven Hundred Eighty (780), the Inaugural Referendum shall be the sole and exclusive mechanism for a No Confidence vote against the Federal Government in office at Ratification. No Petition under Section 3 may be filed, certified, or advanced to Referendum during this period. The Petition mechanism under Section 3 becomes available only beginning on the day after the Inaugural Referendum has been certified, as provided in Section 3.0. 19A.27 Rationale for Exclusivity. Ratification itself expresses the People's judgment that constitutional renewal is needed. The Inaugural Referendum on Day Seven Hundred Eighty (780) provides the democratic mechanism to translate that judgment into leadership renewal. Permitting parallel petition-based referenda during the build-up period would create duplicative national votes on essentially the same question, confuse the Amendment's implementation schedule, and divert resources from building the infrastructure needed for both the Inaugural Referendum and subsequent democratic processes. Exclusivity during build-up is therefore essential to the orderly operation of this Amendment. 19A.27.1

Pre-Organization Permitted. Citizens may engage in advocacy, public debate, civic education, and political organization during the build-up period without limitation, subject only to the campaign finance provisions of Section 9 as they apply to Inaugural Referendum campaigning under Section 19A.28. Citizens may not, however, collect signatures, file Petitions, or initiate formal certification processes under Section 3 until after the Inaugural Referendum has been certified. 19A.27.2 Transition to Regular Petition Process. Upon certification of the Inaugural Referendum under Section 19A, the regular Petition mechanism under Section 3 becomes immediately available: (a) If the Inaugural Referendum passed: The Section 3 Petition mechanism becomes available against the newly-elected Federal Government immediately upon that government's swearing-in following the Emergency Election under Section 7. No cooldown applies, but the Section 10.3 two-year cooldown shall apply to any subsequent Referendum following an unsuccessful Section 5 Referendum initiated after that government takes office;

(b) If the Inaugural Referendum failed: The Section 3 Petition mechanism becomes available against the then-continuing Federal Government beginning on the day after Inaugural Referendum certification, subject to the two-year cooldown established in Section 19A.24. During the cooldown period, Petitions may be circulated and signatures collected, but may not proceed to Certification until the cooldown expires. 19A.28 Campaign Provisions. During the build-up period, the campaign finance provisions of Section 9 shall apply with full force to any advocacy, organizing, or campaigning related to the Inaugural Referendum. The Authority shall monitor and enforce Section 9 limits during this period, with particular attention to foreign interference under Section 22. G. Constitutional and Civic Significance 19A.29 Democratic Renewal Principle. The Inaugural Referendum reflects a fundamental constitutional principle: that Ratification of a substantial constitutional reform of this character carries with it a democratic imperative for leadership renewal under the new framework. The People, in ratifying this Amendment, express their judgment that the existing constitutional order requires fundamental change; the Inaugural Referendum provides the People with the opportunity to match that ratification with corresponding leadership change, should they so choose. 19A.30 No Precedent for Future Amendments. The Inaugural Referendum of this Section 19A is a one-time procedure specific to this Amendment, reflecting the unique scope and character of the constitutional reform effected by this Amendment. Nothing in this Section 19A shall be construed to require, authorize, or suggest an automatic No Confidence referendum upon the ratification of any other constitutional amendment, past, present, or future. 19A.31 Article V Protection. The provisions of this Section 19A shall be protected under the Article V protection established in Sections 18.6.1 and 18.6.2. No act of Congress, executive order, judicial ruling, or state action during the twenty-six-month (26-month) build-up period shall evade, diminish, nullify, delay, or prevent the Inaugural Referendum.

Section 20. State Non-Compliance and the Protection of Citizens

Key terms in this Section: • "The Authority" — The Independent Tripartite Oversight Authority (three bodies, see Section 17). • "Liberty Bell Initiative" — Separate concurrence of all three bodies of the Authority, required for any determination of material state non-compliance.

• "The Ledger" — The Sovereign Blockchain Voting Ledger (Section 4). • "Office / Reclamation Office" — A Citizens' Reclamation Office (Section 11). • "Emergency Delegate Election" — The citizen-level election under Section 6.2 to choose a state's delegate to the Constitutional Transition Committee. • "Three tiers of response" — The escalating federal response structure for states blocking Office construction: Tier One — federal civilian construction on federal land; Tier Two — Army Corps of Engineers unarmed construction; Tier Three — armed military protection (last resort, only against actual physical violence). 20.1 No state, state legislature, state executive, state court, or state agency shall refuse to comply with the requirements of this Amendment, obstruct its Implementation, interfere with its operation, or deny the citizens of that state access to the rights and mechanisms it establishes. The right of every citizen to participate in the processes of this Amendment shall not be abridged by any act or omission of any state government. A. Non-Compliant States Obstructing Delegate Elections 20.2 If a state fails to complete the Emergency Delegate Election required under Section 6.2 within the timeline established therein, or if state officials obstruct, delay, or interfere with the Election, the Authority shall immediately publish notice upon the Ledger and directly administer the Election in that state pursuant to Section 6.4, using mobile Citizens' Reclamation Offices as provided in Section 20.10. 20.3 Any state official who obstructs, delays, refuses to administer, or materially interferes with the Emergency Delegate Election shall be subject to the full interference penalties of Section 13, the non-compliance consequences of Section 20.14 and Section 20.15, and the personal financial liability provisions of this Section. 20.4 The Committee shall commence its work immediately upon convening with the delegates successfully elected, even if Emergency Delegate Elections remain pending in one or more states. No action of the Committee shall be invalidated by the absence or later arrival of delegates, and no non-compliant state shall be permitted to use its non-compliance to delay or invalidate Committee decisions. 20.5 When a delegate is elected in a state through Authority-administered Election under Section 6.4 due to state non-compliance, that delegate shall possess full and equal voting authority on the Committee, identical to delegates elected through ordinary State Elections Council administration.

B. Non-Compliant States Blocking Citizens' Reclamation Offices 20.6 If any state refuses to permit the construction of a Citizens' Reclamation Office within its borders, denies necessary permits or approvals, passes laws or regulations obstructing Office construction or operation, or otherwise interferes with the establishment of an Office in its state, the Authority shall proceed through the following three tiers of response, in order, and shall not resort to any subsequent tier until the preceding tier has proven insufficient. 20.7 Tier One — Federal Civilian Construction on Federal Land. The Implementation Director, or during the Interim Period the Interim Transition Council, shall order construction of the Citizens' Reclamation Office upon federal land located within the non-compliant state, including but not limited to: federal post offices, federal courthouses, national parks and monuments, Veterans Affairs facilities, non-operational portions of military installations, or other federal property. State permits, approvals, or authorizations shall not be required for construction on federal land. Construction shall be performed by civilian federal contractors and engineers, with no military personnel involved in construction activities. 20.8 Tier Two — Military Engineering Corps Construction. If federal land within the state is unavailable, insufficient, or physically blockaded such that Tier One construction cannot proceed, the Joint Implementation Command (or the active oversight body) may authorize the United States Army Corps of Engineers to construct the Office as a non-combat engineering mission. Army Corps personnel deployed under this Tier shall be unarmed except for standard duty equipment, shall wear engineering rather than combat uniforms, and shall conduct only construction activities. The deployment shall be authorized only by majority vote of the Joint Implementation Command and majority vote of the Citizens' Implementation Watch Board, with the deployment order, objectives, duration, and scope publicly recorded and livestreamed pursuant to Section 19.17. State National Guard forces shall not be federalized for this purpose. 20.9 Tier Three — Armed Military Protection (Last Resort). If, and only if, state officials, state agents, or private actors employ or credibly threaten physical violence against Office construction personnel, equipment, sites, or citizens attempting to access the Office, armed military protection may be authorized under the following strict conditions: (a) Authorization shall require BOTH majority vote of the Joint Implementation Command (or the active oversight body during the Washington Commission or Interim Period) AND majority vote of the Citizens' Implementation Watch Board (or the Short-Term Civilian Review Board during the Washington Commission Period); (b) The deployment shall be strictly defensive and limited to the minimum force necessary to protect persons, equipment, and the physical site of the Office;

(c) No offensive operations, no deployment beyond the Office site and its immediate approaches, and no interference with any other state function shall be permitted; (d) The deployment shall be livestreamed in real time pursuant to Section 19.17; (e) The deployment shall automatically terminate the moment the documented physical threat ends, and in no case shall continue for more than ninety (90) days without renewed authorization by the same two-body vote; and (f) No officer or servicemember shall remain at or near the Office site after the documented threat has ended. Any officer who does so shall be subject to Section 16.5 insurrection penalties. 20.10 While any Tier One, Tier Two, or Tier Three action under this Section is pending or underway, the Authority shall immediately deploy mobile Citizens' Reclamation Offices just across the state line in one or more neighboring compliant states, designated to serve the citizens of the non-compliant state. Such mobile Offices shall provide full petition and voting functionality identical to permanent Offices. Citizens of the non-compliant state shall never, at any moment, be denied the ability to exercise their rights under this Amendment. 20.11 No declaration of martial law, federal emergency, or federal receivership shall be imposed on a non-compliant state under this Section. The state's ordinary governing functions not related to this Amendment shall continue without federal interference. The federal action permitted under this Section is strictly and exclusively limited to establishing and protecting the Citizens' Reclamation Office, and shall not be used as a pretext for any broader federal occupation, intervention, or suspension of state authority. C. Non-Compliant Chief Election Officers and Highest Courts of Participating Jurisdictions 20.12 If a chief election officer of a Participating Jurisdiction refuses to serve on the State Elections Council, is removed by Jurisdictional authority for the purpose of evading Amendment compliance, or is prevented from serving by any Jurisdictional action, the Authority shall petition the highest court of that Participating Jurisdiction to appoint an Acting State Elections Council Member from among qualified election officials of that

Jurisdiction. If the highest court of that Participating Jurisdiction refuses to act within seventy-two (72) hours, the Authority shall select the Acting Member by randomized lottery from among that Jurisdiction's local-level election officials (such as county, parish, municipal, ward, village, or equivalent sub-jurisdictional election officials as the Jurisdiction's own structure provides). 20.13 If the highest court of a Participating Jurisdiction refuses to permit its Chief Justice to participate in any lottery required by this Amendment, the Authority shall substitute the Chief Justice of the next-most-senior appellate court of that Participating Jurisdiction. If no appellate court of that Participating Jurisdiction will permit participation, the Authority shall draw by lottery from the full pool of Chief Justices of compliant Participating Jurisdictions to fill the position on behalf of the non-compliant Jurisdiction. Such substitution shall not alter the legitimacy or authority of any body affected. D. Consequences for Non-Compliance — Personal, Institutional, and Federal 20.14 Any officer, official, employee, contractor, or member of the legislature, executive branch, court, or agency of a Participating Jurisdiction who directs, authorizes, orders, or materially participates in Jurisdictional non-compliance with this Amendment shall be subject to ALL of the following consequences, applied cumulatively: (a) Criminal Prosecution. Federal prosecution under Section 13 for interference with the operation of this Amendment, punishable by imprisonment of not less than fifteen (15) years and permanent lifetime bar from any federal, Jurisdictional, or local public office, appointed position, or government employment, without possibility of pardon, commutation, or clemency; (b) Personal Financial Liability. Personal civil liability for all costs incurred by the federal government in implementing Tier One, Tier Two, or Tier Three responses under this Section, to be assessed and collected in the same manner as federal tax obligations; and (c) Public Record. Permanent publication upon the Ledger of the officer's name, office, acts of non-compliance, and criminal and civil judgments rendered, accessible to the People without limitation. 20.15 Any Participating Jurisdiction whose officials, legislature, or agencies are found by the Authority to be materially non-compliant with this Amendment shall be subject to the following Jurisdiction-level consequences until compliance is certified by the Authority: (a) Federal Funding Cutoff. Suspension of all non-essential federal funding to the Jurisdictional government and to Jurisdictional agencies, EXCEPT for funds directly benefiting individual citizens or nationals including but not limited to Social Security payments, Medicare and Medicaid benefits, Veterans Affairs benefits, disaster relief, and federal education grants paid directly to students.

No federal funding to individual citizens or nationals shall ever be reduced or delayed on account of their Jurisdiction's non-compliance; (b) Loss of Congressional Participation. Suspension of the Congressional participation of the Jurisdiction's delegation in the United States House of Representatives and Senate, calibrated to the constitutional role the Jurisdiction's delegation holds: (i) For the fifty states, suspension of the voting rights of the state's delegation in both chambers until compliance is certified, with the delegation

retaining the right to speak and participate in debate but not to cast binding votes on legislation, appropriations, or confirmations; (ii) For the District of Columbia and the five territories enumerated in Section 3.1.1, suspension of the delegate's or Resident Commissioner's floor speaking privileges, committee memberships, committee voting rights, and authority to introduce legislation, until compliance is certified, with the delegate or Resident Commissioner retaining only their underlying office and salary but no participatory function in Congressional proceedings; (c) Territorial Proportionality Consequence. Because loss of Congressional voting under clause (b)(i) imposes substantially greater constitutional weight on the fifty states than loss of delegate privileges under clause (b)(ii) imposes on non-state Participating Jurisdictions, and because the consequences of this Section shall be proportional across Jurisdictions in aggregate weight, any non-state Participating Jurisdiction found materially non-compliant shall additionally face suspension of Jurisdiction-specific federal programs including but not limited to Compact of Free Association funding, Office of Insular Affairs discretionary funding, territorial capital improvement grants, Jurisdiction-specific Medicaid block grant enhancements, and similar programs unique to non-state Jurisdictions, until compliance is certified. This clause operates alongside clause (a) and shall not be construed to reduce protections for individual citizens and nationals established in clause (a); funds directly benefiting individuals shall remain uninterrupted. This clause is a proportionality consequence, not a punishment-enhancement, and is structured to ensure that non-compliance carries comparable aggregate weight across all Participating Jurisdictions regardless of their varying Congressional representation; (d) Mandatory Public Record. Continuous publication upon the Ledger of the Jurisdiction's non-compliance status, the specific violations found, the actions required for compliance, and the status of any federal response under Sections 20.7 through 20.9. 20.16 The consequences established in Sections 20.14 and 20.15 shall apply only to acts of material non-compliance directed at this Amendment and shall not be invoked for ordinary Jurisdiction-federal disagreements,

Jurisdictional policy choices not related to this Amendment, or Jurisdictional exercises of legitimate sovereign authority in other domains. The Authority shall, by Liberty Bell Initiative, make the determination of material non-compliance, with findings publicly reasoned and recorded upon the Ledger. 20.17 Upon certification by the Authority that a previously non-compliant Participating Jurisdiction has come into full compliance, all consequences imposed under Sections 20.14(b) and 20.15 shall be lifted immediately. Criminal convictions under Section 20.14(a) shall not be affected by later Jurisdictional compliance, as individual criminal liability attaches to the acts themselves. The Jurisdiction's full federal funding and Congressional participation rights shall be restored, and its delegation shall resume ordinary participation. E. State Bootstrap and Funding Non-Compliance Response 20.18 State Refusal to Contribute to Bootstrap. The Section 13I.29 state collective bootstrap contribution is voluntary; a Participating Jurisdiction's failure to contribute does not itself constitute material non-compliance under this Section. However, the following framework addresses affirmative state obstruction of bootstrap operations (distinct from mere non-contribution): (a) Non-Contribution Not Non-Compliance. A Jurisdiction's decision not to appropriate bootstrap funds is preserved as a matter of state fiscal sovereignty. Non-contribution shall be publicly recorded on the Franklin Ledger per Section 13I.29(c) but shall not trigger Section 20.14 personal consequences or Section 20.15 Jurisdiction-level consequences. (b) Affirmative Obstruction of Bootstrap. By contrast, Jurisdictional actions that affirmatively obstruct bootstrap operations beyond non-participation — including interfering with state-chartered bank hosting of escrow accounts under Section 13I.29(e), legislating against participation by the state's own financial institutions, targeting federal officials or Amendment personnel operating bootstrap infrastructure, or coordinating among Jurisdictions to prevent bootstrap from functioning — shall constitute material non-compliance subject to full Sections 20.14 and 20.15 consequences. (c) State-Chartered Bank Protection. State-chartered banks voluntarily hosting Section 13I.29(e) escrow accounts shall be protected from state retaliatory action. State banking regulatory action against such banks that is retaliatory in nature shall constitute Section 13 interference by the state officials directing the retaliation, with Section 20.14 personal consequences. (d) Federal Response Sequence. Where a Jurisdiction obstructs bootstrap operations: (i) initial response through federal engagement with state banking authorities; (ii) relocation of escrow accounts to Federal Reserve Banks per Section 13I.29(e)(ii) as primary fallback; (iii) international reserve component activation under Section 13I.29(g) if domestic pathways obstructed; (iv) Section 20 consequences for state officials directing obstruction. (e) No Jurisdiction Shall Face Consequences For Sovereign Non-Participation. To prevent this Section from being read to pressure states into contribution, the Authority shall not treat a Jurisdiction's documented non-participation decision as evidence of broader non-compliance, absent the affirmative obstruction described in subsection (b). 20.19 Citizens' Rights in Non-Contributing or Obstructing Jurisdictions. Citizens of a Jurisdiction that does not contribute to bootstrap, or that obstructs bootstrap, retain all Amendment rights without limitation:

(a) No Citizen Penalized. No citizen shall suffer any deprivation of Amendment rights, access, services, or benefits based on their Jurisdiction's funding participation decision or obstruction status. (b) Mobile Participation Continues. Mobile Participation Units under Section 11A.21 through 11A.31 continue operating in non-contributing and obstructing Jurisdictions, bringing Amendment participation to citizens regardless of their state's posture. (c) Office Establishment Independent. The Section 20.6 through 20.10 three-tier response applies to Office establishment independent of bootstrap contribution questions. (d) Distribution Rights Preserved. Section 13D citizen distributions flow to eligible citizens regardless of their Jurisdiction's compliance status, paid directly to citizens through federal pathways that do not require state cooperation. (e) Lottery and Authority Participation. Citizens of non-contributing or obstructing Jurisdictions remain eligible for all lottery-selected bodies (Citizens' Oversight Board, Watchdog Tribunal, Watch Board, Independent Investigation Panels) and all Amendment mechanisms on equal terms with citizens of contributing Jurisdictions. (f) Section 17C Access. Citizens in obstructing Jurisdictions retain Section 17C state-sovereign adjudication access through cooperating neighboring Jurisdictions where their own state courts are obstructed. F. Mixed State Compliance and Protection of Compliant Officials 20.20 Mixed State Compliance Scenarios. Recognizing that state-level compliance is not monolithic — Governor, legislature, Attorney General, judicial system, and local officials may have differing postures toward Amendment compliance — the following framework addresses mixed scenarios: (a) Individual Official Evaluation. Section 20.14 consequences apply to individual officials based on their own conduct, regardless of the compliance posture of other officials in the same Jurisdiction. A compliant Governor does not immunize an obstructing legislature; an obstructing Governor does not contaminate a compliant Attorney General. (b) Jurisdiction-Level

Determination. Section 20.15 Jurisdiction-level consequences apply based on whether the Jurisdiction as a whole is materially non-compliant. A Jurisdiction with mixed compliance is evaluated on net effect of the Jurisdiction's governmental actions on Amendment operations. (c) Partial Cooperation Credit. Where some state officials cooperate while others obstruct, cooperation shall be credited in the Section 20.15 evaluation, with Jurisdiction-level consequences potentially avoided or reduced where cooperation is material.

(d) Single-Branch Obstruction. Where obstruction is confined to one branch of state government (e.g., state legislature obstructing while Governor cooperates), Section 20 response may be tailored to address the obstructing branch without burdening compliant branches or the state generally. (e) Primary Pathway Through Compliant Officials. Where a compliant state official (Governor, Attorney General, Chief Justice) can facilitate Amendment operations despite obstruction elsewhere in the state, federal-state coordination shall proceed through the compliant official, with Section 20 action against obstructing officials running parallel. 20.21 Governor Compliance, Legislature Obstruction. Specific framework for this common scenario: (a) Gubernatorial Authority Preserved. A Governor who wishes to comply with Amendment operations may exercise gubernatorial authority to facilitate compliance, including ordering state agencies within gubernatorial control to cooperate, declining to enforce state laws that obstruct Amendment operations where constitutionally permissible, and serving fully in the Interim Caretaker Council under Section 6A.2. (b) Legislative Obstruction Individual Liability. Members of state legislatures who vote for or materially support obstructing legislation shall face Section 20.14 individual consequences regardless of Governor compliance. Legislative immunity under state constitutions shall not shield obstruction of federal constitutional operation — this is a parallel to Section 25A.3 federal Speech and Debate treatment. (c) State Appropriation Refusal. Where a state legislature refuses to appropriate state bootstrap funds (Section 13I.29 voluntary bootstrap) despite gubernatorial proposal, this is non-contribution under Section 20.18(a), not affirmative obstruction. The legislature's sovereign fiscal authority is respected. (d) Obstructing Legislation Void Where Contrary to Amendment. State laws that directly obstruct Amendment operations shall be void under the Supremacy Clause as modified by this Amendment, with the Governor authorized to so direct state executive officials. Federal courts with Section 17C alternative pathways are available to resolve disputes. 20.22 Legislature Compliance, Governor Obstruction. Specific framework for the reverse scenario: (a) Legislative Authority Preserved. A state legislature that wishes

Amendment compliance may pass enabling legislation, appropriate funds, or otherwise facilitate cooperation despite gubernatorial opposition, subject to ordinary state constitutional veto override procedures. (b) Lieutenant Governor or Acting Governor Role. Where a Governor's obstruction materially obstructs the state's participation in Amendment operations, state constitutional succession procedures apply if the state impeaches or otherwise removes the Governor. This Amendment does not authorize federal intervention in state gubernatorial removal, which remains entirely a matter of state constitutional law. (c) Interim Caretaker Council Succession. For Section 6A.2 Caretaker Council service, if a sitting Governor refuses to serve when Council convenes, Section 6A.2.1 succession applies with the state's acting chief executive serving. Gubernatorial refusal does not deprive the state of its Caretaker Council seat. (d) Governor Amendment Offense Prosecution. A Governor actively obstructing Amendment operations may be subject to federal prosecution under Section 13 interference with state-official-adaptation under Section 17C or Section 20A, in addition to the Governor's accountability under state law. 20.23 State Court Obstruction with Compliant Executive. Framework for judicial obstruction: (a) State Courts Not Amendment Bodies. State courts are not Amendment bodies; they have no affirmative Amendment duties beyond ordinary federal-law enforcement. Their obstruction would take the form of refusing to enforce Amendment requirements, refusing to participate in Section 17C adjudication, or ruling Amendment provisions unenforceable in state courts. (b) Section 17C Alternative Pathways. Where state courts are obstructing, Section 17C provides alternative adjudication pathways through cooperating Jurisdictions. The Amendment's architecture anticipates state judicial obstruction as a possibility. (c) Federal Court Supersession. Federal courts retain jurisdiction over Amendment matters regardless of state court rulings. State court rulings that Amendment provisions are unenforceable in state courts do not bind federal courts or Amendment bodies. (d) Chief Justice Substitution. For lottery pool participation requiring state Chief Justice service (State AG Prosecution Panel, Section 17C framework, etc.), the Section 20.13 substitution framework applies without modification — next-most-senior appellate court, or compliant-Jurisdiction substitute. (e) Individual Justice Liability. Individual state justices who engage in obstructive judicial conduct — such as pretextual rulings specifically designed to obstruct Amendment operations — may face Section 13 interference prosecution with Section 17C state-sovereign adjudication applicable. 20.24 Protection of Compliant State Officials from Obstructing State Actors. Essential counterpart to obstruction framework: (a) Federal Protection for Compliance. State officials who wish to comply with Amendment operations shall receive federal protection against state-level retaliation for their compliance conduct. Protection mirrors the Section 20A

framework but extends specifically to state-level adverse actions. (b) State-Level Retaliation Prohibited. State officials, agencies, legislators, or courts shall not retaliate against compliant state officials through: state employment action; state criminal prosecution for Amendment compliance activities; state civil litigation targeting compliance conduct; state regulatory action used pretextually; impeachment or removal proceedings based on Amendment compliance rather than ordinary state grounds. (c) Compliant Officials Section 13 Shield. Conduct by compliant state officials that constitutes Amendment compliance shall not be the basis for Section 13 liability, even if the conduct technically violates a state law found to be obstructing under Section 20.21(d) or analogous provisions. (d) Federal Employment Preservation. Where state-level retaliation costs a compliant official their state position, federal employment consideration (through Hamilton Contingent, Academic Integrity Commission, or other Amendment bodies) shall be available as restoration, at the Amendment body's discretion and consistent with Section 17 standards. (e) Personal Security. Compliant state officials facing credible threats due to their Amendment support shall have access to federal protection under Section 13 interference framework, with state officials or private actors targeting them subject to full federal prosecution. (f) Legal Defense Support. Compliant state officials facing state-level legal action for their Amendment compliance shall have access to federal legal support through a Defense Fund administered by Hamilton Contingent, covering reasonable legal expenses for defending against retaliatory state actions. G. Coordinated Multi-State Obstruction 20.25 Coordinated Multi-State Obstruction Framework. Where multiple Participating Jurisdictions coordinate obstruction of Amendment operations: (a) Individual Consequences Multiplied. Section 20.14 individual consequences apply to each participating official in each coordinating Jurisdiction, with enhanced penalties reflecting the coordinated nature of the obstruction. Coordination evidence supports conspiracy charging under existing federal criminal law. (b) Jurisdictional Consequences Compounded. Section 20.15 Jurisdiction-level consequences apply to each participating Jurisdiction, with no Jurisdiction shielded by coordination with others. Each Jurisdiction bears its own consequences regardless of joint action (c) Regional Compact Prohibition. Interstate compacts, agreements, coordination mechanisms, or formal/informal agreements among Jurisdictions to coordinate obstruction of Amendment operations are void under the Supremacy Clause as modified by this Amendment. Compacts that incidentally overlap with Amendment matters are not thereby voided; only compacts with obstruction purpose or effect. (d) Federal Enforcement Response. Federal response to coordinated multi-state obstruction may include: simultaneous Section 20 consequences across participating Jurisdictions; expanded Mobile Participation Unit deployment to serve citizens across all affected Jurisdictions; federal court preemption action against coordinated obstruction legislation; Section 13 conspiracy prosecution of coordinating officials. (e) Compliant Jurisdiction Partnership. Non-participating compliant Jurisdictions may partner with federal authorities to serve citizens of obstructing neighboring Jurisdictions through expanded mobile Office operations, cross-border adjudication cooperation, and other mutual aid. Such partnership shall not transfer compliance obligations to the assisting Jurisdiction. (f) Foreign Influence Detection. Multi-state obstruction with evidence of foreign influence or coordination shall trigger Section 22 foreign interference framework in addition to Section 20 framework. H. Expanded Federal Response Framework 20.26 Three-Tier Response Application Beyond Office Construction. The Section 20.7 through 20.9 three-tier response framework (federal civilian construction, Army Corps engineering, armed military protection as last resort) applies to Office establishment under Section 20.6. The following subsections apply analogous tiered response to other obstruction scenarios: (a) Election Obstruction Tiered Response. Where state obstructs ordinary elections or Section 7 Emergency Elections beyond the Section 20.2 delegate elections context, Authority may: (i) deploy mobile election infrastructure (Tier One); (ii) coordinate with neighboring compliant Jurisdictions for overflow capacity (Tier One-plus); (iii) establish federal election infrastructure on federal land (Tier Two); (iv) armed protection only where physical violence is employed or credibly threatened (Tier Three). (b) State AG Council Obstruction Response. Where a state attempts to prevent its Attorney General from participating in the State Attorneys General Council, Section 20.12 analogous response applies — substitute participant through state's own constitutional succession or, failing that, from compliant-Jurisdiction AGs. Extended enforcement authority under Section 13I.32 may activate where federal enforcement is itself obstructed. (c) State Court Obstruction of Section 17C. Where state courts refuse to host Section 17C state-sovereign adjudication, Section 17C itself provides alternative cooperating-Jurisdiction pathway. No military or forced-hosting response is contemplated; Section 17C relies on alternative venues rather than compelling hostile venues.

(d) State Legislature Obstruction. State legislatures cannot be compelled to pass legislation or appropriate funds. Federal response to legislative obstruction is through individual Member liability under Section 20.14, Jurisdiction-level consequences under Section 20.15, and citizen remedy through state electoral processes. I. Comprehensive Citizen Rights Preservation 20.27 Comprehensive Citizen Rights Framework in Obstructing Jurisdictions. Beyond the Section 20.10 mobile Office provision, citizens in obstructing Jurisdictions retain all Amendment rights through the following comprehensive framework: (a) Petition Rights Complete. Citizens may collect and submit petitions under Section 12 through Mobile Participation Units, mobile Offices, neighboring compliant Jurisdiction Offices, and federal infrastructure. No signature is invalidated based on the signer's Jurisdiction's compliance status. (b) Referendum Voting Complete. Citizens retain full Section 5 National No Confidence Referendum voting rights through Mobile Participation Units, neighboring-Jurisdiction Offices, and federal infrastructure. No vote is invalidated based on Jurisdictional compliance status. (c) Franklin Ledger Access. Citizens in obstructing Jurisdictions retain full access to the Franklin Ledger through internet infrastructure federally protected under Section 4A and, where state-level internet obstruction occurs, through federal backup access infrastructure including satellite connectivity. (d) Lottery Pool Participation. Citizens in obstructing Jurisdictions remain fully eligible for randomized selection to all lottery-selected bodies (Citizens' Oversight Board, Watchdog Tribunal, Watch Board, Foreign Interference Oversight Board, Independent Investigation Panels) on equal terms with citizens of compliant Jurisdictions. Selection cannot be frustrated by state obstruction; federal procedures ensure lottery participation. (e) Authority Body Elections. Citizens participate in all Authority body elections on equal terms, with voting infrastructure provided through Mobile Participation Units and federal facilities where state infrastructure is obstructed. (f) Section 13D Distribution Rights. Section 13D citizen distributions flow directly to eligible citizens through federal payment systems (Treasury, Federal Reserve, IRS direct deposit analog), not contingent on state participation in any way. (g) Section 17C Access Through Neighbors. Citizens facing Covered Official matters may access Section 17C adjudication through cooperating neighboring Jurisdictions when their own state's courts are obstructing. Venue accommodation shall be available.

20.28 Interstate Cooperation for Citizen Service. Compliant Jurisdictions adjacent to obstructing Jurisdictions shall have enhanced authority and federal support to serve citizens of obstructing neighbors: (a) Cross-Border Office Service. Compliant Jurisdictions' Offices shall serve eligible citizens of obstructing neighboring Jurisdictions on equal terms with their own citizens for Amendment functions. (b) Jurisdictional Cost Sharing. Where compliant Jurisdictions bear costs serving citizens of obstructing neighbors, federal cost reimbursement shall be available through Section 11.3 constitutional appropriation. (c) No Penalty for Compliant Jurisdictions. Compliant Jurisdictions that assist citizens of obstructing neighbors shall face no federal penalty, reduced funding, or other adverse consequence. Cross-jurisdictional cooperation is encouraged and supported. (d) Mutual Aid Coordination. State Attorneys General Council shall coordinate mutual aid among compliant Jurisdictions for citizen service in obstructing neighbors, with published coordination plans on Franklin Ledger. (e) Temporary Relocation Accommodation. Citizens of obstructing Jurisdictions who temporarily relocate to compliant Jurisdictions for Amendment participation (e.g., traveling to Mobile Unit deployments in compliant neighboring state) shall have their participation recognized without residency restrictions. 20.29 Re-Integration of Previously Obstructing Jurisdictions. Supplementing Section 20.17: (a) Phased Restoration. Where a previously obstructing Jurisdiction achieves compliance certification, consequence removal proceeds in phases over reasonable time frame: immediate restoration of federal funding and Congressional participation; restoration of State AG Council voting rights; restoration of lottery pool participation for state officials; gradual rebuilding of state-level Amendment infrastructure. (b) Institutional Rebuilding Support. Federal support for institutional rebuilding in previously obstructing Jurisdictions shall be available, including training for state officials taking up Amendment Duties, technical support for state infrastructure integration, and public education about restored rights and obligations. (c) Individual Liability Preserved. Individual officials who directed or materially participated in obstruction remain subject to their individual Section 13 and Section 20.14 consequences regardless of subsequent Jurisdictional compliance. Amnesty for individual officials is not available through this framework. (d) Trust Rebuilding. Recognition that post-obstruction trust rebuilding takes time. Jurisdictions may be fully compliance-certified but historical record of their obstruction period remains publicly accessible on the Franklin Ledger as constitutional historical record. (e) Preventive Oversight. Previously obstructing Jurisdictions may be subject to enhanced Authority oversight for a reasonable period post-certification (not exceeding five (5) years), ensuring sustained compliance and early detection of any renewed obstruction tendencies.

Section 20A. State Official Integrity and Transparency During Amendment

Operation

Key terms in this Section: • "The Authority" — The Independent Tripartite Oversight Authority (three bodies, see Section 17). • "Liberty Bell Initiative" — Separate concurrence of all three bodies of the Authority. • "The Ledger" — The Sovereign Blockchain Voting Ledger (Section 4). • "Covered State Official" — For purposes of this Section, any sitting state Governor (or equivalent chief executive), state Attorney General (or equivalent chief legal officer), Chief Justice of the state supreme court, or state chief election officer of any of the fifty-six Participating Jurisdictions. • "Amendment Duty" — Any responsibility arising under this Amendment, including but not limited to service on the State Elections Council, State Attorneys General Council, Caretaker Council, Authority lottery pools, or State Council sub-councils. • "Obstruction Registry" — The public registry established under Section 20A.8 tracking state officials whose conduct approaches but has not reached material non-compliance under Section 20. 20A.1 The operation of this Amendment depends upon cooperation from state officials whose ordinary duties intersect with federal electoral infrastructure, Amendment proceedings, and citizen protections. Passive obstruction, slow-rolling, selective compliance, and procedural foot-dragging are corruption pathways distinct from the active material non-compliance addressed in Section 20. This Section therefore establishes transparency mechanisms, fair-process protections, and early-warning accountability for state officials exercising or implicated in Amendment duties. All mechanisms in this Section operate under the fair due process protections of Section 20A.15 through 20A.17.

A. Public Affirmation Registry 20A.2 Within ninety (90) days of ratification of this Amendment, and within ninety (90) days of any subsequent assumption of office, every Covered State Official may file a public Affirmation of Constitutional Commitment upon the Ledger, stating their intent to uphold this Amendment in its operation. The Affirmation is voluntary and shall not be a condition of holding state office. 20A.3 The Ledger shall publicly display both the list of Covered State Officials who have filed Affirmations and the list of those who have not. Non filing shall not itself constitute obstruction, non-compliance, or misconduct, but citizens shall have transparent access to this information. Officials may file, update, or re-file at any time. No official shall be removed from state office, denied state salary, or subjected to federal penalty solely for non-filing. B. Mandatory Amendment Orientation 20A.4 Within one hundred eighty (180) days of assuming any state office carrying Amendment Duties, a Covered State Official shall complete a public Amendment Orientation administered by the Academic Integrity Commission. The Orientation shall cover only the official's specific duties under this Amendment, shall not inquire into political views or partisan affiliations, and shall not serve as a loyalty test of any kind. Completion shall be recorded upon the Ledger with date, topics covered, and certification of completion. 20A.5 An official who has not completed the Orientation within one hundred eighty (180) days of assuming office shall not exercise Amendment Duties — including voting on the State Elections Council, voting on the State Attorneys General Council, serving on the Caretaker Council, or being drawn from any Authority lottery pool — until completion. The official shall not be removed from their state office for failure to complete the Orientation; only their Amendment-specific duties are affected. Completion is one-time and not repeated. 20A.6 The Academic Integrity Commission shall ensure that Orientations are accessible, scheduled promptly, conducted in a professional manner consistent with the dignity of high state office, and completable within a reasonable time commitment not exceeding eight (8) hours total. Orientations may be conducted in person or via secure video, at the official's option. C. Cooperation Protocol Publication 20A.7 Within one hundred eighty (180) days of assuming any state office carrying Amendment Duties, a Covered State Official shall publish upon the Ledger their office's Cooperation Protocols, including: the designated staff member or members responsible for Amendment liaison; contact information for Amendment-related matters; standard response timeframes for Authority requests; and any special circumstances affecting coordination. Publication is ministerial and requires no approval; it exists solely to create transparency. Protocols shall be updated annually or upon material change. Failure to publish shall be a factor the Authority may consider in Section 20A.8 Registry determinations but shall not itself constitute material non-compliance under Section 20. D. Early Warning Obstruction Registry 20A.8 The Authority shall maintain upon the Ledger a public Obstruction Registry tracking Covered State Officials whose documented conduct approaches but has not reached material non-compliance under Section 20. Listing on the Registry is informational only and carries no automatic federal penalty, no loss of state office, and no loss of federal funding to the state. 20A.9 An official may be listed on the Registry only through the following fair process: (a) Concerning Pattern Notice. The Authority, by Liberty Bell Initiative publicly reasoned upon the Ledger, documents specific conduct giving rise to concern. Generic partisan accusations, political disagreements, or policy differences shall never support listing; (b) Thirty-Day Public Response Period. The Notice is published upon the Ledger, and the listed official shall have thirty (30) days to respond publicly upon the Ledger, presenting evidence, explanation, or correction; (c) Resolution Hearing. Following the response period, the Authority shall, by Liberty Bell Initiative, either remove the official from the Registry, continue the listing with updated findings, or refer the matter for formal Section 20 proceedings. The Resolution decision shall be publicly reasoned upon the Ledger; (d) Automatic Removal. Officials shall be removed from the Registry automatically when the concerning pattern resolves, upon the Authority's finding of resolution via Liberty Bell Initiative; and (e) Appeal Rights. Listed officials may appeal to a panel of three (3) Justices of the highest courts of Participating Jurisdictions drawn by randomized lottery from Chief Justices of Participating Jurisdictions NOT involved in the dispute, not currently serving on any Authority lottery pool, and not in the official's own Participating Jurisdiction. The appeal panel's decision is binding and published upon the Ledger within thirty (30) days. 20A.10 The Registry exists to create transparency and early warning. It shall not be used to harass officials for legitimate exercises of state authority, political viewpoints, or policy disagreements. Listings made in bad faith shall be removed upon appeal, and the Authority members responsible for a bad-faith listing may themselves be subject to Watchdog Tribunal review under Section 21.7. E. Citizens' Standing to Petition

20A.11 Any one thousand (1,000) registered voters of a state may petition the Authority to investigate whether a Covered State Official of that state is obstructing this Amendment. The petition shall: (a) Be filed in person at any Office or Center within the state, with all signatures verified by the State Elections Council; (b) Present concrete, specific, documented evidence of conduct approaching or constituting obstruction; generic accusations, partisan statements, or policy disagreements shall not be sufficient; (c) State with specificity the grounds alleged and the remedy sought; and (d) Be published in full upon the Ledger upon filing, including all filers' names and evidence presented. 20A.12 Within thirty (30) days of filing, the Authority shall determine the disposition of the petition through Liberty Bell Initiative: (a)

Investigation Opened. The Authority opens a formal inquiry under Section 20 with publicly reasoned basis, or a Registry listing under Section 20A.8; (b) Petition Dismissed. The Authority finds the evidence insufficient to support investigation, with publicly reasoned basis and no penalty to filers acting in good faith; or (c) Petition Frivolous. The Authority finds the petition was filed in bad faith, without concrete evidence, or for the purpose of harassment. Filers of frivolous petitions shall be subject to the bad-faith sanctions of Section 23.11, adapted for this context — including dismissal, a ten-year bar from named filer status on future Section 20A petitions, and civil fines not less than five thousand dollars ($5,000) per frivolous petition. 20A.13 Investigation results shall be published upon the Ledger in full regardless of outcome, including any exonerating findings. Citizens who in good faith raise concerns that prove unsupported shall not face sanctions; the bad-faith threshold is reserved for petitions demonstrably filed without concrete evidence or for demonstrable harassment. 20A.14 Covered State Officials subject to a petition filed under Section 20A.11 shall have the same appeal rights to a three-justice panel as are established in Section 20A.9(e), and all proceedings shall follow the fair due process standards of Sections 20A.15 through 20A.17. F. Fair Due Process Protections 20A.15 All mechanisms in this Section shall operate under the following fair process requirements:

(a) Public Notice. Any official subject to Registry listing, petition, investigation, or adverse finding shall receive public notice published upon the Ledger; (b) Opportunity to Respond. Every adverse proceeding shall include a public response period of no fewer than thirty (30) days during which the official may present evidence, explanation, or counterargument; (c) Publicly Reasoned Decisions. All decisions under this Section shall be publicly reasoned upon the Ledger with specific evidentiary basis; (d) Appeal Rights. Officials adversely affected by any decision under this Section may appeal to a three-justice panel drawn by randomized lottery from Chief Justices of Participating Jurisdictions meeting the independence criteria of Section 20A.9(e); (e) Clear and Convincing Evidence Standard. No adverse finding, Registry listing, or investigation opening under this Section shall be based on less than clear and convincing evidence of specific conduct; mere allegation, partisan accusation, or policy disagreement shall be insufficient; (f) No Retroactive Application. Conduct occurring before certified ratification of this Amendment shall not support any proceeding under this Section; and (g) No Punishment for Political Views. No proceeding under this Section shall be based on an official's political party affiliation, policy positions not involving Amendment obstruction, votes on state legislation, or lawful exercise of state authority in domains unrelated to this Amendment. 20A.16 Any Authority action under this Section that exceeds the fair process protections of Section 20A.15, or that targets officials for reasons unrelated to actual Amendment obstruction, shall itself constitute grounds for Watchdog Tribunal review under Section 21.7 and may result in replacement of the responsible Authority body members. 20A.17 Nothing in this Section shall be construed to authorize federal interference with a state's ordinary governing functions, state policy choices unrelated to this Amendment, or state exercises of legitimate sovereign authority in other domains. Federal authority under this Section is strictly limited to matters directly implicating the operation of this Amendment. G. Expanded Personal Financial Liability for Passive Obstruction 20A.18 The personal financial liability established in Section 20.14(b) for state officials causing federal expense through material non-compliance is hereby extended to cover passive obstruction as well. A Covered State Official whose documented passive obstruction — including but not limited to systematic slow-rolling of Authority requests, selective refusal to cooperate with Amendment operations, failure to meet reasonable response timeframes, or procedural foot-dragging causing federal expense — is found by the Authority through Liberty

Bell Initiative to have caused documented federal expense, shall be personally liable for that expense. 20A.19 Personal financial liability under this subsection shall be assessed and collected in the same manner as federal tax obligations under Section 20.14(b), with the same fair process protections, appeal rights, and publication requirements. The liability attaches to the individual official, not to the state, and shall not reduce any direct-to-citizen federal benefits within that state. 20A.20 This expanded liability is intended to create financial deterrence against passive corruption — the form of obstruction most likely to erode Amendment operation without triggering the dramatic consequences of Section 20's three-tier response. Officials acting in good faith, even if they make errors, shall not face liability; only documented patterns of obstruction producing federal expense trigger this provision.

Section 21. Anti-Corruption Failsafe — Protecting the Authority from Total

Capture

Key terms in this Section: • "The Authority" — The Independent Tripartite Oversight Authority (three bodies, see Section 17). • "The Ledger" — The Sovereign Blockchain Voting Ledger (Section 4). • "Watchdog Tribunal" —

The 100-member permanent body (50 randomly selected citizens + 50 retired federal judges by lottery) whose sole function is to monitor all three bodies of the Authority for corruption. Holds power of forced replacement, criminal referral, and full body dissolution by 2/3 supermajority. • "Citizen Emergency Override" — The direct-democratic failsafe allowing citizens themselves to trigger investigation of all oversight bodies (including the Tribunal), requiring 30% of registered voters nationally plus 30% in at least 30 states, with a 5-year cooldown between overrides. • "Independent Investigation Panel" — The 75-member body (25 state Chief Justices + 25 state AGs + 25 retired federal judges, all by lottery) convened upon certification of a Citizen Emergency Override petition. • "State Council / Rotating Tripartite State Council" — The dormant 150-member body (50 state Chief Justices + 50 state AGs + 50 state governors) that auto-activates whenever any Authority body is non-functional, temporarily performing that body's oversight functions until reconstitution. 21.1 Recognizing that no oversight structure is immune from corruption, however well-designed, this Section establishes three independent failsafe mechanisms to protect this Amendment against the catastrophic scenario in which all three bodies of the Authority are simultaneously corrupted, captured, or compromised. These mechanisms shall operate in concert with the mutual-veto structure of Section 17, and shall not replace the ordinary oversight functions of the three bodies when those bodies are operating lawfully. A. The Watchdog Tribunal (First Failsafe) 21.2 There is hereby established the Watchdog Tribunal ("the Tribunal"), a permanent independent body whose sole function is to monitor, audit, and safeguard the three bodies of the Authority against corruption, collusion, capture, or dereliction. The Tribunal shall convene no later than ninety (90) days after the three bodies of the Authority are sworn in under Section 19.19, and shall operate continuously thereafter. During Phase One of the Implementation Period, before the Tribunal is convened, the Washington Commission established in Section 19.5.0 shall perform equivalent oversight and safeguard functions over the Authority bodies as they are selected and sworn. Upon the convening of the Tribunal, all Washington Commission oversight records shall transfer to the Tribunal for continuity of accountability. The Tribunal is deemed established for reference purposes throughout this Amendment effective upon ratification, with operational capability effective upon its convening. 21.3 The Tribunal shall consist of one hundred (100) members: (a) Fifty (50) registered voters of the United States, drawn by randomized lottery in the same manner as the Citizens' Oversight Board, with distribution across all fifty-six (56) Participating Jurisdictions consistent with the proportional-plus-minimum formula of Section 17.2; and (b) Fifty (50) retired federal judges, drawn by randomized lottery from the full pool of retired Article III federal judges of the United States, who have not held federal judicial office within the preceding five (5) years and who are not actively engaged in any political advocacy, lobbying, or federal government service. 21.4 Tribunal members shall serve staggered three (3) year terms. No member may serve consecutive terms, and no person may serve more than two total terms on the Tribunal in their lifetime. Service shall be mandatory in the nature of federal jury duty for citizen members, and mandatory upon selection for retired judge members. Hardship excuse, accommodation, and mid-service hardship exit shall be governed by the hardship framework established in Sections 17.4 through 17.4.11, applied to the Tribunal through Section 17.4.12(a).

21.5 Tribunal members shall receive the same protections, compensation, and eligibility standards as Citizens' Oversight Board members under Sections 17.5 through 17.7, adapted for the Tribunal's specific role. No Tribunal member may be a current or former member of any of the three Authority bodies, nor may a Tribunal member subsequently serve on any Authority body for four (4) years after the end of their Tribunal service. 21.5.1 Watchdog Tribunal Training Requirements. Because the Watchdog Tribunal exercises oversight authority over all three Authority bodies, the Hamilton Contingent, the Washington Commission, and numerous other Amendment bodies, and because Tribunal members include retired judges, subject-matter experts, and drawn citizens whose ordinary backgrounds may not fully prepare them for the breadth of Tribunal responsibilities, every newly-selected Tribunal member shall complete the following training before exercising substantive Tribunal authority: (a) Initial Training Program. A structured seventy-two (72) hour training program administered by the Academic Integrity Commission, to be completed within forty-five (45) days of selection notification. Training shall occur before the member participates in any Tribunal review, investigation, replacement vote, or other substantive Tribunal authority. (b) Curriculum Scope. Training shall cover: (i) the full text and structure of this Amendment; (ii) the Tribunal's authorities under Section 21, including investigation, replacement, prosecution referral, action suspension, and review powers; (iii) oversight relationships with each Amendment body (Authority, Hamilton Contingent, Washington Commission, Caretaker Council, Emergency Nuclear Committee, Composite Authority, and others), including the scope and limits of Tribunal authority over each; (iv) Section 13 interference framework and enforcement responsibilities; (v) Section 22 foreign interference framework; (vi) evidentiary standards for

Tribunal findings; (vii) due process requirements for parties subject to Tribunal action; (viii) Tribunal Division specializations where applicable; (ix) coordination with State Attorneys General Council, Hamilton Contingent, and federal courts; (x) Tribunal record-keeping, Ledger publication requirements, and transparency obligations; (xi) recognition of capture attempts targeting the Tribunal itself. (c) Training Administration. The Academic Integrity Commission shall develop and maintain the curriculum with input from outgoing Tribunal members, the Authority bodies, and experienced prosecutors and judges from the Pre-Certified University Pool network. The curriculum shall be published on the Franklin Ledger for public review. Updates shall occur not less frequently than annually. (d) Pre-Training Limited Authority. During the training period, newly-selected Tribunal members may observe Tribunal proceedings, receive briefings, and attend deliberations in non-voting capacity, but shall not vote on findings, order replacements, suspend actions, refer prosecutions, or exercise other substantive Tribunal authority until training completion. Continuing members maintain ordinary Tribunal operations during training periods. (e) Ministerial Certification. Upon completion, each member shall affirm on the Franklin Ledger that they have completed the training program. Certification shall be ministerial; withholding based on member's prior judicial philosophy, subject-matter discipline, or political orientation shall be prohibited. (f) Refresher Training. Tribunal members shall complete semi-annual refresher training of not less than twelve (12) hours covering developments in Amendment case law (including Tribunal's own precedent), legal interpretation, and emergent threats to constitutional order. (g) Good-Faith Training Protection. Tribunal members who undertake training in good faith and subsequently make decisions based on that training shall receive the same good-faith protection as Citizens' Oversight Board members under Section 17.8.1(g). (h) Compensation and Cost Coverage. Members shall receive full compensation during training per Section 21.5 (applying Section 17.5(b) compensation). Training-related travel, housing, and dependent care shall be covered as part of service compensation. (i) Federal Executive Non-Interference. No federal officeholder shall direct, influence, fund, or interfere with Tribunal training. Attempts shall constitute Section 13 interference with Senior Official multipliers and shall be prosecutable through the Tribunal's own authority where applicable. (j) Non-Compliance Consequences. A Tribunal member who fails to complete initial training within the forty-five (45) day window without documented hardship shall be replaced through the ordinary selection process, with the replacement receiving the same training requirement. Refusal of refresher training shall trigger review by the remaining Tribunal members and potential replacement. 21.6 The Tribunal shall perform its oversight function through three parallel methods operating continuously and in combination: (a) Continuous Public Audit. The Tribunal shall review all proceedings, deliberations, decisions, and votes of all three bodies of the Authority within thirty (30) days of their occurrence. Audit findings shall be published upon the Ledger in full. (b) Reactive Investigation. The Tribunal shall investigate any credible allegation of corruption, collusion, foreign influence, bribery, coercion, or improper conduct by any Authority body member. Investigations may be triggered by: (i) a petition of not less than ten percent (10%) of registered voters; (ii) a referral from any Authority body against another Authority body; (iii) credible evidence discovered during continuous audit; or (iv) referral from law enforcement authorities.

(c) Random Deep Audits. The Tribunal shall conduct deep forensic audits of randomly selected Authority decisions no less than once per calendar quarter, with full investigative power including document review, member interviews, financial disclosure verification, and forensic analysis of communications occurring during the period under review. 21.6.1 Deep Audit Quality Standards. Each random deep audit under Section 21.6(c) shall meet the following minimum rigor standards, recognizing that audit frequency without audit quality produces only procedural compliance without substantive oversight: (a) Comprehensive Forensic Review. The audit shall include comprehensive forensic review of all financial transactions by the audited body during the audit period, including member compensation, reimbursements, vendor payments, and any cash flow touching Authority operations; (b) Individual Member Interviews. Each member of the audited body shall be interviewed regarding specific decisions within the audit period, with interviews recorded and transcripts preserved upon the Ledger subject to narrow operational-security redactions under Section 21.8; (c) Communications Review. The audit shall review all communications of audited body members related to Authority decisions during the audit period, subject to attorney-client privilege and narrow operational-security protections, with the Tribunal's access authority overriding ordinary privilege claims where the privileged communication is itself alleged evidence of corruption under Section 17.25; (d) Dual Sub-Team Verification. The audit shall be conducted by at least two (2) Tribunal sub-teams operating in parallel and independently, with findings compared at audit completion to detect inconsistency. Where sub-team findings differ materially, the Tribunal shall investigate the cause and may repeat the audit with fresh sub-teams; (e)

Published Findings with Specificity. Audit findings shall be published upon the Ledger with specificity sufficient for citizen review, including specific decisions examined, specific evidence gathered, specific findings reached, and specific reasoning supporting each finding. Vague or conclusory findings shall not satisfy this standard; (f) Academic Integrity Commission Quality Certification. Upon audit completion, the Academic Integrity Commission forensic auditors shall certify that the audit met the professional standards of this Section, with certification recorded upon the Ledger. Where the Academic Integrity Commission itself is the body being audited (under rotation or because of specific concerns), the certification shall be performed by forensic auditors from Pre-Certified Pool universities not then serving on the Commission, selected by lottery under Section 17.16; (g) Repeat of Failed Audits. An audit failing to meet any of the standards in subsections (a) through (f) shall be repeated by fresh Tribunal sub-teams within sixty (60) days, with the failed audit's findings not constituting the Tribunal's authoritative assessment of the audited body. Repeated audit quality failures (three or more failed audits within twelve months) shall themselves constitute Tribunal dereliction under Section 21.6(b) reviewable through Citizen Emergency Override under Section 21.10.

21.7 Upon finding credible evidence of corruption, collusion, capture, or material dereliction of duty by any Authority body member or members, the Tribunal may exercise the following powers, in combination or alone, by two-thirds (2/3) supermajority vote of the one hundred members (sixty-seven of one hundred): (a) Forced Replacement. Remove the corrupt member(s) from their Authority body and trigger immediate replacement by fresh lottery from the appropriate pool (citizens, state election officers, or academic institutions); (b) Criminal Referral. Refer the matter to federal criminal prosecution under Section 13 and Section 17.25, with the Tribunal's evidentiary findings serving as a prima facie basis for charges; and (c) Body Dissolution and Reconstitution. In cases of systemic corruption affecting a majority of a body, dissolve the affected Authority body and trigger complete re-selection by fresh lottery within thirty (30) days. During the dissolution period, the affected body's oversight functions shall be temporarily performed by the State-Level Backstop under Section 21.12. 21.7.1 Minority Findings and Public Record — Addressing Blocking Minorities. Recognizing that the two-thirds (2/3) supermajority threshold of Section 21.7 creates a mathematical vulnerability whereby thirty-four (34) or more captured or colluding Tribunal members could permanently block action despite credible evidence of corruption, the following safeguard applies: (a) Minority Findings Trigger. When a majority (fifty-one

(51) or more) of Tribunal members find credible evidence of corruption, collusion, capture, or material dereliction of duty but the 2/3 supermajority required for action under Section 21.7 is not achieved, the majority shall nonetheless publish a Minority Findings Report upon the Ledger within thirty (30) days of the failed supermajority vote; (b) Report Contents. The Minority Findings Report shall identify with specificity: (i) the Authority body or members investigated; (ii) the evidence supporting the majority's view, with citations to specific documents, testimony, or observable conduct; (iii) the members of the Tribunal who declined to concur and their stated reasons for non-concurrence; and (iv) any pattern of non-concurrence by specific Tribunal members over time, identifying members whose non-concurrence pattern deviates substantially from the Tribunal average; (c) Heightened Audit Trigger. A Minority Findings Report shall constitute a Section 21.6(b)(iii) credible-evidence trigger for heightened audit of the non-concurring Tribunal members themselves, with the Tribunal investigating whether the non-concurrence pattern reflects corruption, capture, or bad-faith obstruction rather than legitimate disagreement. The heightened audit shall be conducted by a sub-team composed entirely of Tribunal members who did vote with the majority, to prevent the accused members from participating in their own investigation; (d) Repeated Blocking Pattern. Where the same Tribunal members vote against majority findings three (3) or more times within twelve (12) months on matters where the Minority Findings Report identifies credible evidence, the blocking pattern shall automatically trigger Citizen

Emergency Override eligibility under Section 21.10 without regard to the ordinary five (5) year cooldown under Section 21.11(d), and shall additionally constitute grounds for criminal referral under Section 21.7(b) against the blocking members for potential violations of Section 17.25 bribery penalties or Section 13 interference penalties; (e) Preservation of Legitimate Dissent. Nothing in this Section shall be construed to penalize good-faith disagreement with majority findings. Tribunal members voting against majority findings shall retain full procedural protections and shall be subject to heightened audit only on the basis of pattern analysis and independent evidence of corruption, not on the basis of dissent alone. The purpose of this Section is to prevent captured blocking minorities from weaponizing the supermajority threshold, not to suppress legitimate minority views. 21.8 All Tribunal proceedings, investigations, findings, and decisions shall be recorded and published upon the Ledger in real time, subject only to narrow operational-security redactions during active investigations, certified as necessary by supermajority of the

Tribunal and reviewable within thirty (30) days of the investigation's conclusion. No Tribunal proceeding affecting an Authority body shall be conducted in secret. 21.9 Any person who attempts to bribe, threaten, blackmail, coerce, surveil, or otherwise corrupt any member of the Tribunal shall be subject to Section 17.25 bribery penalties, with an enhanced minimum sentence of twenty-five (25) years to reflect the Tribunal's role as the ultimate civilian safeguard. B. The Citizen Emergency Override (Second Failsafe) 21.10 Recognizing that even the Tribunal itself may theoretically be corrupted, the People of the United States shall retain an independent Citizen Emergency Override, by which citizens may directly trigger simultaneous investigation of all oversight structures. 21.11 A Citizen Emergency Override petition shall be initiated under the same in-person signature process as a No Confidence Petition in Section 12, and shall meet ALL of the following requirements: (a) National Threshold. Valid in-person signatures of not less than thirty percent (30%) of all registered voters of the United States; (b) Geographic Distribution. Valid signatures from at least thirty percent (30%) of registered voters within each of no fewer than thirty (30) of the fifty-six (56) Participating Jurisdictions; (c) Public Statement of Grounds. The petition shall state with specificity the grounds upon which the citizens believe all three Authority bodies have been corrupted, captured, or compromised, and these grounds shall be published upon the Ledger for public review throughout the signature collection period; and

(d) Frequency Limitation. No Citizen Emergency Override petition shall be initiated within five (5) years of the certification of a prior Override petition, whether the prior petition succeeded or failed. (e) Availability During All Periods. The Citizen Emergency Override petition mechanism of this Section shall be available throughout all periods of Amendment operation, including the twenty-six (26) month period between Ratification and Inaugural Referendum under Section 3.0. Because the Override is a failsafe specifically for the scenario of captured or compromised Authority bodies, its availability cannot be contingent on Authority cooperation or on completion of the initial buildout period. The Section 3.0 activation rule, which defers regular No Confidence Petitions under Section 12 until after the Inaugural Referendum, shall apply only to ordinary No Confidence Petitions and not to Emergency Override petitions under this Section. Where an Override petition is initiated during Phase One before the State Elections Council is fully constituted under Section 19.19(b), certification authority shall vest in the Emergency Chief Justices Panel under Section 21.12.1 through the same procedures applicable when the

State Elections Council refuses to certify. 21.12 Upon certification of a Citizen Emergency Override petition by the State Elections Council (or if the State Elections Council is itself alleged to be corrupt, by an emergency panel of fifty (50) Chief Justices of Participating Jurisdictions as defined in Section 3, drawn by lottery), the following three actions shall occur simultaneously: (a) Independent Investigation Panel. An Independent Investigation Panel shall be convened within thirty (30) days, consisting of twenty-five (25) Chief Justices of Participating Jurisdictions (as defined in Section 3) drawn by lottery, twenty-five (25) State Attorneys General of Participating Jurisdictions drawn by lottery, and twenty-five (25) retired federal judges drawn by lottery, totaling seventy-five (75) members. The Panel shall have full investigative power over all three Authority bodies, the Watchdog Tribunal, and any related federal officers, and shall publish its findings upon the Ledger within one hundred and twenty (120) days; (b) Tribunal Reconstitution. The entire Watchdog Tribunal shall be dissolved and reconstituted by fresh lottery within sixty (60) days, with all former members barred from re-selection for life. This ensures that if the Tribunal itself has been corrupted, the Override remedy is not blocked by the corrupted Tribunal itself; and (c) National Referendum. A national referendum shall be conducted upon the Ledger within one hundred and eighty (180) days of the Independent Investigation Panel's report, in which citizens shall directly vote on the action to be taken, including options for: retaining each Authority body unchanged, dissolving and reconstituting each body, structural amendments to the oversight framework, or referral to a Constitutional Review Convention under Section 18.4. The referendum shall require sixty percent (60%) supermajority approval with fifty percent (50%) minimum turnout, consistent with the No Confidence threshold under Section 5.2.

21.12.1 Emergency Chief Justices Panel — Convening Authority When State Elections Council Refuses. Where Section 21.12 provides for certification of a Citizen Emergency Override petition by an emergency panel of fifty (50) Chief Justices of Participating Jurisdictions as defined in Section 3, in lieu of the State Elections Council, the emergency panel shall be convened through the following automatic self-executing process: (a) Automatic Activation Triggers. The emergency panel shall be convened automatically within seventy-two (72) hours of any of the following triggers: (i) a formal finding by the Citizens' Oversight Board or the Academic Integrity Commission, by majority vote, that the State Elections Council has refused to certify an Override petition meeting the thresholds of Section 21.11; (ii) a joint declaration by not fewer than fifteen (15) state Attorneys General that the State Elections Council has refused to certify; or (iii) a formal finding by the Watchdog Tribunal by two-thirds (2/3) supermajority, or by the Section 23.13.1 extended mutual veto safeguard procedures, that the State Elections Council refusal constitutes corruption, capture, or bad-faith obstruction rather than legitimate concern; (b) Convening Authority. The Chief Justice of the most populous Participating Jurisdiction whose Chief Justice is not among the Chief Justices selected for the emergency panel shall serve as convening authority and shall administer the initial lottery, panel composition verification, and video conference logistics, with subsequent operations governed by the emergency panel's own procedures adopted by majority vote of seated members. If the designated convening authority Chief Justice is unavailable or declines, the role passes automatically to the next most populous Participating Jurisdiction's Chief Justice meeting the same criterion; (c) Lottery Composition. The emergency panel's fifty (50) Chief Justices of Participating Jurisdictions shall be drawn by randomized lottery from among Chief Justices of Participating Jurisdictions not currently serving on the Washington Commission under Section 19.5.0.3 and not currently serving on the Watchdog Tribunal, with each Participating Jurisdiction's Chief Justice having equal probability of selection. The lottery shall be conducted with the same integrity standards as the Commission lottery under Section 19.5.0.3.3 and subject to challenge under Section 19.5.0.3.4; (d) Narrow Authority. The emergency panel's authority shall be narrowly limited to Override petition certification under Section 21.12. The panel shall have no authority to alter the Override petition's grounds, adjudicate the petition's substantive merits, or exercise any other power beyond certification. The panel's certification decision shall be made by majority vote of its fifty members, published upon the Ledger within seven (7) days of convening; (e) Automatic Dissolution. The emergency panel shall dissolve immediately upon the earlier of: (i) issuance of its certification decision (whether certifying or declining certification); or (ii) subsequent certification of the Override petition by the State Elections Council itself, rendering the emergency panel's role unnecessary; (f) Anti-Obstruction Protections. Members of the emergency panel shall receive federal protection from intimidation, coercion, or surveillance equivalent to that provided to Citizens' Oversight Board members under Section 17.5(d). Any federal officeholder, federal agency, or private actor who attempts to interfere with the emergency panel's convening or certification decision shall be subject to Section 13 interference penalties with Senior Official multipliers where applicable, Section 17.25 bribery penalties where corruption is involved, and the enhanced penalties of Section 21.9 reflecting the emergency panel's role as ultimate citizen failsafe; (g) Federal Executive Non-Interference. No President, Vice President, Cabinet officer, federal agency head, or other federal executive officeholder shall direct, fund, contact, lobby, or attempt to influence emergency panel members, convening authority, or panel proceedings. Any such interference shall constitute automatic Section 13 interference and shall be void ab initio. 21.13 Throughout the Override process from petition certification through referendum resolution, the State-Level Backstop under Section 21.14 shall automatically activate to preserve constitutional continuity. No Authority body action shall be considered final or binding during the Override process until the referendum has resolved the status of that body. C. The State-Level Backstop (Third Failsafe) 21.14 There is hereby established the Rotating Tripartite State Council ("the State Council"), a dormant body that activates automatically whenever any of the three bodies of the Authority is non-functional, dissolved pending reconstitution, or whenever the Citizen Emergency Override under Section 21.12 is in progress. The State Council shall temporarily perform the oversight functions of whichever Authority body is non-functional, and shall dissolve automatically upon that body's full reconstitution and swearing-in, regardless of the elapsed time. 21.15 The State Council shall consist of one hundred and sixty-eight (168) members organized into three parallel sub-councils, each mirroring the function of the corresponding Authority body: (a) The Judicial Oversight Sub-Council. Fifty-six (56) sitting Chief Justices of the highest court of each Participating Jurisdiction — one from each of the fifty states, the District of Columbia, and the five territories enumerated in Section 3.1.1 — serving ex officio. This sub-council shall temporarily perform the functions of the Citizens' Oversight Board when that body is non-functional, exercising judicial integrity and civilian review on behalf of the People; (b) The Legal Oversight Sub-Council. Fifty-six (56) sitting Attorneys General (or equivalent chief legal officers) of the Participating Jurisdictions, serving ex officio. This sub-council shall temporarily perform the functions of the State Elections Council when that body is non-functional, exercising legal and electoral integrity review; and (c) The Executive Oversight Sub-Council. Fifty-six (56) chief executives of the Participating Jurisdictions — the Governor of each of the fifty states, the Mayor of the District of Columbia, and the Governor of each of the five territories

enumerated in Section 3.1.1, serving ex officio. This sub-council shall temporarily perform the functions of the Academic Integrity Commission when that body is non-functional, exercising executive and technical judgment on policy and administration matters. 21.16 Each State Council sub-council shall act only by two-thirds (2/3) supermajority vote of its fifty-six members (thirty-eight of fifty-six), with all deliberations and votes publicly recorded and livestreamed upon the Ledger. Any action requiring concurrence of multiple sub-councils shall require two-thirds supermajority within each participating sub-council. 21.17 State Council members shall serve under the same Federal Communications Firewall established in Section 19.5.0.18.4 for the State Attorneys General Council, prohibited from federal communications, federal funding, or federal agreements during active State Council operations. Violation shall be a federal felony punishable by not less than ten (10) years, automatic removal from state office, and permanent lifetime disqualification from any public office. 21.18 The State Council shall possess only those temporary oversight authorities strictly necessary to maintain constitutional continuity during Authority body reconstitution. The State Council shall NOT: (a) Make any permanent or long-term decisions that would bind the reconstituted Authority; (b) Alter the structural rules, selection processes, or authorities of the three bodies of the Authority or the Watchdog Tribunal; (c) Exercise any authority beyond the caretaker function of preserving ongoing processes and preventing lapse of essential oversight; or (d) Remain in existence one moment longer than necessary after the affected Authority body has been fully reconstituted and sworn in. 21.19 Upon full reconstitution and swearing-in of the affected Authority body, the corresponding State Council sub-council shall dissolve automatically and immediately. All records, pending matters, and documentation shall be transferred to the newly reconstituted body. The Authority body shall be bound to respect the caretaker decisions made by the State Council sub-council during the reconstitution period, but shall be fully empowered to modify or reverse such decisions going forward as appropriate to its ordinary duties. 21.20 The State Council as a whole shall dissolve automatically when all affected sub-councils have dissolved. The State Council shall not function as a standing body during ordinary operation of the three Authority bodies; its sub-councils activate only as needed and dissolve as soon as the need passes. 21.20.1 In the event that the Interim Caretaker Council under Section 6A is active simultaneously with the State Council Executive Oversight Sub-Council under

Section 21.15(c), the Caretaker Council shall take precedence and the Executive Oversight Sub-Council shall pause its operations for the duration of the Caretaker Period. This prevents governors from being required to serve in two federal caretaker capacities simultaneously. Upon convening of the Constitutional Transition Committee under Section 6.1 and dissolution of the

Caretaker Council, the Executive Oversight Sub-Council shall resume its functions if an Authority body remains non-functional. The Judicial Oversight Sub-Council and Legal Oversight Sub-Council under Sections 21.15(a) and (b) shall continue operating without interruption during any overlap, as Chief Justices and Attorneys General are not members of the Caretaker Council. D. Interlocking Protections and Prohibitions 21.21 The three failsafe mechanisms established in this Section — the Watchdog Tribunal, the Citizen Emergency Override, and the State-Level Backstop — shall operate independently and cumulatively. No mechanism shall be conditional upon any other mechanism, and the failure, corruption, or dysfunction of one mechanism shall not impair the operation of the others. 21.22 No act of Congress, executive order, judicial ruling, or state action shall diminish, suspend, or modify any of the three failsafe mechanisms established in this Section. Any attempt to do so shall constitute interference under Section 13 and shall trigger the full penalties thereof. 21.23 The funding of the Watchdog Tribunal, the Independent Investigation Panel, and any activation of the State Council shall flow automatically through the constitutional appropriation established in Section 11.3, bypassing the federal appropriations process entirely. Any attempt to defund or delay funding of these failsafe mechanisms shall constitute an impeachable offense and a federal felony. 21.24 Members of the Watchdog Tribunal, the Independent Investigation Panel, and the State Council shall all swear the same constitutional oath established in Section 17.24, taking no direction from any government, party, corporation, or foreign power and serving only the sovereign authority of the People of the United States. E. Travel Oversight Division 21.25 Establishment. There is hereby established within the Watchdog Tribunal a dedicated Travel Oversight Division ("the Travel Division") whose sole function is to administer the Steady-State Period travel approval framework of Section 13F.12 and to monitor Covered Officials during any approved International Travel. The Travel Division shall convene concurrent with the Watchdog Tribunal under Section 21.2 and shall operate continuously thereafter. 21.26 Composition. The Travel Division shall consist of twenty-five (25) members drawn from the one hundred Watchdog Tribunal members, selected by randomized lottery from among Tribunal members who affirmatively opt in to Travel Division service and who meet the additional qualifications of this Section. Members shall serve on the Travel Division for one (1) year rotations within their three-year Tribunal terms, with staggered rotations ensuring continuity of expertise. No Travel Division member may serve consecutive one-year rotations, and no more than one-third of the Travel

Division shall rotate in any given quarter. 21.27 Qualifications. Travel Division members shall possess, in addition to baseline Tribunal member qualifications under Section 21.5: (a) demonstrated understanding of international financial systems, sanctions frameworks, or anti-money-laundering law, established through professional experience or certified training provided by the Academic Integrity Commission; (b) no personal or business ties to the Covered Officials then in service in Section 1.1 positions; (c) no foreign ties within the prior ten (10) years that would create conflict of interest, disclosed publicly upon the Ledger at the time of Travel Division selection; and (d) security clearance at a level sufficient to review classified information bearing on foreign interference risks, as administered by the Academic Integrity Commission under Section 22. 21.28 Duties and Authority. The Travel Division shall: (a) Receive and review every International Travel approval request submitted by Covered Officials under Section 13F.12.4, conducting risk assessment and issuing a recommendation to the Authority for Liberty Bell Initiative action, within ten (10) days of request submission; (b) Evaluate each request against the approval criteria of Section 13F.12.5, with specific attention to destination risk, foreign-power connections, and accountability posture of the requesting Official; (c) Administer continuous monitoring of all approved travel pursuant to Section 13F.12.6, including receipt of daily check-ins, evaluation of itinerary deviations, and review of foreign meetings; (d) Operate the emergency approval process of Section 13F.12.7, with authority to grant expedited approval by majority vote of the twenty-five members within forty-eight (48) hours; (e) Maintain the public-facing Travel Ledger on the Franklin Ledger, documenting every request, approval, denial, and completed trip with searchable historical records; (f) Investigate any suspected violation of Section 13F travel provisions, referring violations to the Hamilton Contingent Prosecution Division under Section 13C for federal criminal action; (g) Publish quarterly reports on the Ledger analyzing patterns of travel requests, approval rates, denied requests, emergency invocations, and any trends suggesting abuse of the framework; and

(h) Recommend to the Authority, through the full Watchdog Tribunal, any modifications to the travel framework that experience reveals to be necessary, subject to Amendment procedures under Article V. 21.29 Independence and Protection. Travel Division members shall enjoy the same protections, compensation, and oath requirements as all Watchdog Tribunal members under Sections 21.5, 21.9, and 21.24. No Travel Division member shall be subject to retaliation by any Covered Official, the Authority, or any other federal body for Travel Division decisions. Bribery, threats, blackmail, or corruption of any

Travel Division member shall be treated as interference with the Watchdog Tribunal itself, subject to the twenty-five (25) year minimum penalty of Section 21.9. 21.30 Data Protection. The Travel Division shall maintain all travel-related data on secure, air-gapped systems under the cryptographic protection of the Academic Integrity Commission. Personal security information (precise residential addresses of family members, specific medical details, and similar sensitive information) shall be redacted from public disclosures where not essential to accountability. Information necessary for oversight — destinations, dates, purposes, funding sources, foreign contacts — shall remain publicly visible on the Ledger in perpetuity.

Section 22. Protection Against Foreign Interference in Petitions and Referendums

Key terms in this Section: • "The Authority" — The Independent Tripartite Oversight Authority (three bodies, see Section 17). • "Liberty Bell Initiative" — Separate concurrence of all three bodies of the Authority. • "The Ledger" — The Sovereign Blockchain Voting Ledger (Section 4). • "Foreign Person or Entity" — For purposes of this Section: any foreign government, foreign state-owned enterprise, foreign political party, foreign national, or any entity with ten percent (10%) or more foreign ownership or control. Naturalized United States citizens are NOT Foreign Persons and retain full civic participation rights under this Amendment and under the First Amendment to the Constitution. • "Detection Unit" — The Foreign Interference Detection Unit established by Section 22.5 — a joint operation of the State Elections Council and the Academic

Integrity Commission responsible for forensic detection of foreign interference. • "Oversight Board" — The Foreign Interference Oversight Board established by Section 22.7 — a 35-member civilian body watching over the Detection Unit to prevent abuse or targeting of protected civic activity. • "Material foreign interference" — Foreign involvement of sufficient scale, duration, or effect that the Authority, by Liberty Bell Initiative, determines may have meaningfully influenced petition signatures, Referendum outcome, or public understanding of either. 22.1 The mechanisms of this Amendment — particularly the ability to remove an entire Federal Government by No Confidence — constitute an unusually attractive target for foreign interference by hostile state actors. This Section therefore establishes comprehensive protections against such interference while preserving the full civic participation rights of United States citizens, including naturalized citizens and permanent residents acting on their own behalf. A. Comprehensive Ban on Foreign Money and Coordination 22.2 No Foreign Person or Entity shall, directly or indirectly, provide money, services, in-kind contributions, strategic direction, coordination, or material support to any person or organization engaged in: (a) Collection, verification, organization, or submission of signatures for any Petition under this Amendment; (b) Advocacy, advertising, social media operations, media placement, or paid messaging for or against any Petition, Referendum, Emergency Delegate Election, Emergency Election, or Sunset Review Vote; (c) Polling, messaging research, audience analysis, or strategic consulting relating to any of the above; (d) Training, compensation, or deployment of petition organizers, signature gatherers, Office or Center personnel, or campaign workers under this Amendment; or (e) Any other activity materially affecting the operation or outcome of any process established by this Amendment. 22.3 The prohibition in Section 22.2 applies regardless of whether the Foreign Person or Entity acts openly, through a United States-based intermediary, through a shell corporation, through a nonprofit organization, through a political action committee, or through any other means of laundering foreign origin or control. The substance of foreign involvement, not the form, controls.

22.3.1 Strategic Direction Equivalence and Willful Blindness. To close interpretive gaps that sophisticated foreign actors may attempt to exploit in the definition and application of this Section: (a) Strategic Direction Equivalence. An entity that is demonstrably receiving strategic direction, operational coordination, or decision-making authority from a Foreign Person or Entity — even where formal ownership is below the ten percent (10%) threshold in the definition of Foreign Person or Entity — shall be treated as a Foreign Person or Entity for purposes of this Section where clear, convincing, and publicly documented evidence establishes the substance of foreign control. The determination shall apply the same evidentiary standard as Section 22.16 and shall be made by Liberty Bell Initiative under Section 22.14 (from Day One Hundred Eighty (180) forward) or by the Phase One dual supermajority under Section 22.4.1(c) (during Phase One), with findings and supporting evidence published upon the Ledger; (b) Willful Blindness. For purposes of Section 22.17 criminal liability, the term "knowingly accepts" shall include reckless disregard of facts or circumstances that would cause a reasonable person in the defendant's position to inquire into foreign sources of funds, foreign strategic direction, or foreign coordination. United States persons who deliberately structure their arrangements, relationships, or communications to avoid inquiry into foreign sources of funds or direction shall not thereby avoid Section 22.17

liability. This subsection codifies the well-established federal criminal doctrine of willful blindness for explicit application to foreign interference offenses under this Section, removing any interpretive ambiguity that sophisticated actors might attempt to exploit. 22.3.2 Technological Neutrality, Broad Construction, and Future Technology. To close interpretive gaps that sophisticated foreign actors may attempt to exploit by using technologies or methods not explicitly enumerated in this Amendment at the time of Ratification, and to ensure durable constitutional protection of citizen decision-making across technological generations, the following framework applies: (a) Technological Neutrality Principle. The prohibitions of Section 22.2 apply to foreign interference conducted through any technology, method, platform, or medium — including those not in existence or not widely used at the time of Ratification. The substance of foreign interference (the effort to influence citizen decisions regarding Amendment processes through foreign money, direction, coordination, or material support) controls, regardless of the technological or operational form through which such interference is conducted. No foreign actor shall avoid Section 22 liability by conducting prohibited interference through emerging, novel, or technologically sophisticated methods rather than through methods traditionally associated with foreign interference; (b) Broad Construction of "Any Other Activity Materially Affecting." Section 22.2(e), which prohibits "any other activity materially affecting the operation or outcome" of Amendment processes, shall be construed broadly to cover any method by which foreign actors may seek to influence citizen decisions, including but not limited to: generation, distribution, or amplification of synthetic or artificially-generated content intended to represent real persons, events, or evidence; automated or coordinated inauthentic account activity designed to simulate organic public support, opposition, or engagement; anonymization, laundering, or obscuring of foreign-source funds through digital currencies, blockchain technologies, or other financial instruments; manipulation of content delivery, algorithmic amplification, or platform functionality of information platforms accessible to United States voters; and any other method by which foreign actors may seek to influence Amendment processes, whether currently in existence or developed subsequent to Ratification; (c) Not a Limitation on Existing Coverage. The enumeration in subsection (b) shall not be construed to limit the catch-all scope of Section 22.2(e). Activities not enumerated in subsection (b) remain prohibited where they meet the Section 22.2(e) standard. The enumeration is illustrative, not exhaustive, and is provided to prevent interpretive arguments that novel methods fall outside Section 22.2 coverage merely because those methods were not specifically named; (d) Protection of Legitimate United States Speech. Nothing in this subsection shall restrict, limit, or condition: (i) satire, parody, commentary, criticism, or other protected expressive activity by United States persons acting in their individual capacity; (ii) educational, academic, or research use of artificial intelligence, synthetic media, or similar technologies where such use does not constitute foreign interference under Section 22.2; (iii) authentic political speech, advocacy, or civic engagement by United States citizens, including naturalized citizens and lawful permanent residents acting on their own behalf; (iv) journalistic reporting on foreign interference, including demonstration or illustration of interference methods in the public interest; (v) legitimate business use of financial technologies, artificial intelligence, or communications platforms where such use does not involve prohibited foreign coordination. The protections of this subsection shall be construed broadly to preserve the full scope of First Amendment and civic participation rights of United States persons, consistent with Sections 22.11 through 22.13; (e) Technological Evasion Doctrine. Foreign actors who deliberately adopt technologies, methods, or operational structures specifically to evade Section 22 coverage — including by routing interference through newly-emerged technologies not explicitly named in this Amendment — shall not thereby avoid liability. The Willful Blindness doctrine of Section 22.3.1(b) shall apply to United States persons who coordinate with foreign actors using technologically novel methods; deliberate structuring to obscure the foreign character of coordination shall not defeat liability; (f) Detection Unit Methodology Authority. The Detection Unit under Section 22.5 (from Day One Hundred Eighty (180) forward) and the Phase One Detection function under Section 22.4.1(a) shall have explicit authority to develop detection methodologies appropriate to evolving foreign interference methods, including forensic analysis of synthetic content, pattern recognition of coordinated inauthentic activity, blockchain transaction analysis, and other evolving detection capabilities. Methodologies shall be subject to ordinary oversight under Section 22.7 through 22.10 (post-Day-180) or Section 22.4.1(b) (Phase One), with civil liberties protections under Section 22.11 through 22.13 applying fully regardless of detection methodology; (g) Materiality Standard Unchanged. The materiality

threshold under Section 22.14 and Section 22.16 shall apply to interference conducted through novel methods the same as to interference conducted through traditional methods. The use of sophisticated technology does not lower the evidentiary standard for material foreign interference determinations; clear, convincing, and publicly documented evidence remains required; (h) Future Technology Clause. The Framers of this Amendment recognize that this text is drafted at a specific moment in history, that technological capabilities available to foreign actors seeking to interfere with citizen decision-making will evolve in ways that cannot be anticipated at the time of Ratification, and that constitutional amendments cannot be revised rapidly enough to address each new interference method as it emerges. This subsection establishes that the prohibitions of Section 22.2, as interpreted through this Amendment's technological neutrality principles, extend to all methods of foreign interference regardless of whether those methods existed at the time of Ratification or emerge subsequently, including: (i) technologies existing at Ratification in forms or capabilities not yet widely recognized; (ii) technologies in early development at Ratification that reach widespread use subsequently; (iii) technologies not existing at Ratification but developed subsequently, whether through gradual evolution or sudden breakthrough; (iv) methods operating through psychological, cognitive, perceptual, behavioral, or other mechanisms seeking to influence citizen decisions regarding Amendment processes; (v) methods operating through mediums or platforms not currently recognized as venues for political communication, where foreign actors deliberately exploit such mediums to circumvent explicit coverage; (vi) any other method, technology, platform, capability, or mechanism — whether currently imaginable or not, whether currently existing or not — by which a Foreign Person or Entity may seek to influence citizen decisions regarding Amendment processes. The constitutional protection of citizen decision-making from foreign interference is a durable principle that transcends any specific technology of any particular era. No foreign actor shall evade Section 22 liability merely because the technology through which they conducted interference did not exist or was not explicitly named at the time of Ratification. This subsection's enumeration is illustrative, not exhaustive. 22.4 Every entity spending ten thousand dollars ($10,000) or more, adjusted quarterly for inflation, in any twelve (12) month period on activities enumerated in Section 22.2(a) through (e) shall publicly disclose upon the Ledger: all funding sources and amounts; all organizational affiliations and relationships; all foreign ties within the prior ten (10) years of any officer, director, controlling shareholder, or major funder; all contractual relationships with foreign entities; and quarterly updates during active Petition or Referendum periods. Disclosure shall be continuous, public, and machine-readable. Failure to disclose, or false disclosure, shall constitute material foreign interference under Section 22.14 if the failure conceals foreign involvement.

22.4.1 Phase One Foreign Interference Authority. Because the Detection Unit of Section 22.5, the Oversight Board of Section 22.7, and the Liberty Bell Initiative determination authority of Section 22.14 depend on bodies of the Authority (the State Elections Council, the Academic Integrity Commission, and the Citizens' Oversight Board) that are not fully constituted until Day One Hundred Eighty (180) following Ratification, and because foreign interference may be most attractive during Phase One when the Amendment's machinery is still being built, Phase One foreign interference protection shall function through the following substitute framework from Ratification through Day One Hundred Eighty (180): (a) Phase One Detection Function. During Phase One, the Detection function of Section 22.6 shall be performed jointly by: (i) the State Elections Council operating in its ex officio capacity from Day One under Section 19.5.0.18.1 framework; (ii) the State Attorneys General Council established under Section 19.5.0.18.1; (iii) the AIC-Designate Forensic Consortium established under Section 13B.7.1 for forensic financial analysis and pattern detection; and (iv) the Washington Commission under Section 19.5.0.3 for judicial authorization of subpoenas and investigative orders. These bodies shall coordinate through the Washington Commission as coordinating authority for Phase One foreign interference matters. The Phase One Detection function shall exercise all capabilities enumerated in Section 22.6(a) through (f), subject to the same limits on surveillance of private communications and individual political speech of United States persons; (b) Phase One Oversight Function. During Phase One, the Oversight function of Section 22.9 shall be performed jointly by: (i) the Short-Term Civilian Review Board established under Section 19.5.0.7 (all fifty-six (56) members), exercising authorities parallel to Section 22.9(a) through (e) with respect to Phase One Detection activities; and (ii) a Temporary Civil Liberties Panel of ten (10) members drawn by randomized lottery by the Washington Commission from the Pre-Certified Pool of civil liberties organizations under Section 22.7(c), operating alongside the Short-Term Civilian Review Board. The Temporary Civil Liberties Panel shall serve from activation through Day One Hundred Eighty (180) and shall dissolve upon the convening of the full Oversight Board under Section 22.7; (c) Phase One Materiality Determination. During Phase One, because Liberty Bell Initiative under Section 22.14 cannot occur (as the three Authority bodies are not yet constituted), a Phase One material foreign interference determination shall require BOTH: (i) six-sevenths (6/7) supermajority of the Washington

Commission (six of seven Chief Justices of Participating Jurisdictions); AND (ii) two-thirds (2/3) supermajority of the State Attorneys General Council (thirty-eight of fifty-six members) acting under Section 19.5.0.18.1. Both supermajorities shall be required; a determination approved by only one body shall not constitute a Phase One material foreign interference determination. Any determination shall apply the same "clear, convincing, and publicly documented evidence" standard required by Section 22.16 for Liberty Bell Initiative determinations, with all evidence published upon the provisional public ledger simultaneously with the determination, subject only to narrow redactions necessary to preserve active criminal prosecution; (d) Phase One

Consequences Unchanged. The consequences established in Sections 22.15, 22.17, 22.18, and 22.19 shall apply fully to Phase One determinations, including invalidation of tainted Petitions or Referendums in their entirety, one (1) year cooling-off periods, restoration of removed officials if applicable, criminal prosecution, foreign entity sanctions, and forfeiture of assets. The substitute determination under subsection (c) carries the same legal weight as a Liberty Bell Initiative determination under Section 22.14; (e) Transition to Full §22 Framework. On Day One Hundred Eighty (180), upon full constitution of the Academic Integrity Commission and Citizens' Oversight Board and operational commencement of the Detection Unit and Oversight Board, the Phase One substitute framework shall dissolve. All Phase One investigative records, forensic findings, pending investigations, and institutional memory shall transfer to the Detection Unit and Oversight Board for continuation under Sections 22.5 through 22.10. Phase One determinations of material foreign interference shall remain fully valid and binding after transition, with their consequences continuing unchanged; (f) Petitions or Referendums Spanning Transition. Where a Petition or Referendum is initiated during Phase One but concludes after Day One Hundred Eighty (180), foreign interference investigations opened under the Phase One framework shall continue under the permanent Detection Unit and Oversight Board, with the Phase One materiality determination standard of subsection (c) applying to any determination made before Day One Hundred Eighty (180) and the Section 22.14 Liberty Bell Initiative standard applying to any determination made after that date; (g) Federal Executive Non-Interference. No President, Vice President, Cabinet officer, federal agency head, or other federal executive officeholder shall direct, fund, influence, or impede the Phase One Detection function, Phase One Oversight function, or Phase One materiality determination. Any such interference shall constitute Section 13 interference with Senior Official multipliers where applicable, prosecutable by the State Attorneys General Council acting by supermajority under Sections 19.5.0.5.2 and 19.5.0.18.9.1 during Phase One and by the Hamilton Contingent upon its operational commencement. B. The Foreign Interference Detection Unit 22.5 There is hereby established the Foreign Interference Detection Unit ("Detection Unit") as a joint operation of the State Elections Council and the Academic Integrity Commission, reporting to both bodies jointly and NOT to any sitting federal officeholder, agency, or branch of the existing Federal Government. The Detection Unit shall operate continuously, not only during active Petition or Referendum periods. 22.6 The Detection Unit shall exercise the following capabilities, subject to oversight under Section 22.7 through 22.10: (a) Automated pattern detection of signature anomalies, including unusual geographic clustering, bot-like signature patterns, sudden spikes from specific origins, and inconsistencies with voter registration data;

(b) Pattern detection on social media amplification, coordinated inauthentic behavior, advertising spend concentration, and media coordination indicators; (c) Anomaly detection on the Ledger itself through blockchain analysis, funding pattern analysis, and real-time network forensics during active Petition and Referendum periods; (d) Investigation of suspected violations of Section 22.2, Section 22.3, or Section 22.4, with authority to subpoena records of disclosed entities, interview witnesses, and coordinate with state-level law enforcement; (e) Forensic financial analysis of petition and Referendum advocacy organizations, including tracing of funds through shell entities; and (f) Full continuous monitoring during any active Petition or Referendum period, including monitoring of the Ledger, publicly disclosed campaign spending, and publicly accessible indicators of coordinated influence operations. The Detection Unit shall not conduct surveillance of private communications or individual political speech of United States persons. C. The Foreign Interference Oversight Board 22.7 There is hereby established the Foreign Interference Oversight Board ("Oversight Board") to protect civil liberties and prevent the Detection Unit from becoming an instrument of political targeting, ideological discrimination, or suppression of legitimate civic participation. The Oversight Board shall consist of thirty-five (35) members: (a) Fifteen (15) registered voters, drawn by randomized lottery in the same manner as the Citizens' Oversight Board, proportionally distributed across the Participating Jurisdictions. Service is mandatory like federal jury duty, with the same protections, compensation, and eligibility standards applicable under Sections 17.5 through 17.7; (b) Ten (10) retired federal judges, drawn by randomized lottery from the full pool of retired Article III federal judges who have not held federal judicial office within the preceding five (5) years and who are not actively engaged in political advocacy, lobbying, or federal government service; and (c) Ten (10) civil liberties advocates, drawn by randomized lottery from certified civil liberties organizations maintained in a Pre-Certified Pool of at least fifty (50) qualifying organizations. The Pool shall include organizations representing both classically liberal and classically conservative civil liberties perspectives, specifically including but not limited to groups focused on speech rights, privacy rights, due process rights, minority and religious rights, and press freedom. The Pool shall be recertified every five (5) years by the Citizens' Oversight Board in public session upon the Ledger.

22.7.1 Anti-Capture Reinforcement for Pre-Publication Review Authority. Recognizing that Section 22.24 vests the Oversight Board with pre-publication review authority over Detection Unit findings, and recognizing that this authority is structurally upstream of subsequent oversight checks (Section 22.14 materiality determination, Section 21 Watchdog Tribunal review) such that capture of the Oversight Board itself would substantially undermine the framework before downstream remedies could attach, and recognizing further that the Oversight Board's composition requirements under Section 22.7 were drafted prior to the addition of pre-publication review authority and warrant proportionate hardening, the following anti-capture reinforcements apply to the Oversight Board specifically with respect to its Section 22.24 pre-publication review function: (a) Pre-Publication Review Sub-Quorum Requirement. Notwithstanding Section 22.7's thirty-five (35) member structure, no Section 22.24 pre-publication review determination shall be valid unless rendered by a sub-quorum of not fewer than seventeen (17) members, drawn by case-specific randomized lottery from the full thirty-five members for each pre-publication review matter, with the lottery administered by the Permanent Washington Commission under Section 17D.13.1 using the cryptographic methodology of Section 17.16.3. Random sub-panel composition prevents any captured subset of Oversight Board members from systematically dominating pre-publication review decisions across multiple matters; (b) Sub-Quorum Composition Floor. Each seventeen-member sub-quorum drawn under subsection (a) shall include not fewer than: seven (7) lottery-citizen members under Section 22.7(a); five (5) retired federal judges under Section 22.7(b); and five (5) civil liberties advocates under Section 22.7(c). Where the random draw fails to produce these category floors, additional draws shall continue until a complying sub-quorum is constituted, with the methodology published on the Franklin Ledger; (c)

Voting Threshold for Pre-Publication Review Outcomes. Section 22.24 outcomes shall require the following sub-quorum voting thresholds: (i) Approve Publication — majority of sub-quorum members present and voting; (ii) Approve with Modification — majority of sub-quorum; (iii) Defer Publication — majority of sub-quorum; (iv) Preclude Publication — two-thirds (2/3) supermajority of sub-quorum (twelve of seventeen members), reflecting the structural significance of preventing publication of an investigative finding; (d) Public Summary Documentation of Preclusion Decisions. Notwithstanding Section 22.24(e)(iv)'s internal documentation requirement, every preclusion decision under Section 22.24(e)(iv) shall be accompanied by a public summary published on the Franklin Ledger within seven (7) days of decision, including: the categorical type of finding precluded (e.g., "contact-pattern finding," "funding-flow finding") without identifying the subject of the precluded finding; the categorical reasoning for preclusion (e.g., "evidentiary insufficiency," "civil liberties violation," "scope exceeded statutory authority") without identifying specific evidence or subjects; and the sub-quorum vote breakdown by category. Public summary documentation makes preclusion patterns visible to citizens and the Watchdog Tribunal without compromising the confidentiality of subjects of unpublished investigations; (e)

Enhanced Pre-Service Disclosure for Pre-Publication Reviewers. Oversight Board members serving on Section 22.24 pre-publication review sub-quorums shall complete the Section 22.7 ordinary disclosure with additional categories tailored to pre-publication review risks, including: prior employment by entities that may be subjects of foreign-interference investigations; substantial financial interests in entities operating in regulatory categories the Detection Unit monitors; and relationships with federal officeholders or political organizations whose interests may be advanced or impeded by particular preclusion patterns. Disclosed information shall be sealed from public view by default with public release only upon Watchdog Tribunal finding of conflict warranting disclosure; (f) Watchdog Tribunal Pattern Review of Sub-Quorums. The Watchdog Tribunal under Section 21 shall conduct annual pattern review of Section 22.24 sub-quorum decisions, identifying: clustered preclusion decisions affecting findings about specific political actors, organizations, or coalitions; clustered approval decisions producing one-sided publication patterns; correlation between sub-quorum composition and outcome (suggesting that members of specific demographic, geographic, or ideological characteristics vote consistently for outcomes favoring one political coalition); and other patterns warranting investigation. Findings shall be published on the Franklin Ledger;

(g) Recusal of Sub-Quorum Members. Members drawn for a Section 22.24 pre-publication review sub-quorum shall recuse from the specific matter where any of the following apply: (i) personal financial interest in the outcome; (ii) family relationship with the subject of the finding under review; (iii) prior public statement specifically expressing opinion about the subject of the finding; (iv) any other circumstance that would constitute mandatory recusal grounds analogous to Section 17C.16(b). Recusal shall trigger replacement draw under subsection (a) procedures; (h) No New Substantive Authority. This Section creates no new substantive Oversight Board authority beyond what Section 22.7 and Section 22.24 establish; this Section adjusts only the procedural composition and voting requirements applicable to Oversight Board exercise of Section 22.24 pre-publication review authority specifically. Other Oversight Board functions under Section 22.7 and Section 22.9 continue to operate under their respective procedural frameworks; (i) Federal Executive Non-Interference. No President, Vice President, Cabinet officer, federal agency head, or other federal executive officeholder shall direct, fund, influence, pressure, or impede sub-quorum lottery administration, sub-quorum deliberations, preclusion summary documentation, or Watchdog Tribunal pattern review under this Section. Any such interference shall constitute Section 13 interference with Senior Official multipliers, prosecutable through the Section 17C.15 framework; (j) Funding. Costs of sub-quorum lottery administration, enhanced disclosure processing, and pattern review shall be funded through the constitutional appropriation under Section 11.3; (k) Article V Protection. The provisions of this Section shall be protected under the Article V protection established in Sections 18.6.1 and 18.6.2. The pre-publication review authority established in Section 22.24 is structurally significant; the Oversight Board's capacity to exercise that authority impartially requires composition and procedural protections proportionate to the authority's reach. 22.8 Oversight Board members shall serve staggered two (2) year terms. No member shall serve consecutive terms, and no person shall serve more than two total terms on the Oversight Board in their lifetime. All members shall swear the constitutional oath established in Section 17.24. 22.9 The Oversight Board shall exercise the following authorities over the Detection Unit: (a) Unrestricted access to all Detection Unit records, investigations, forensic analyses, personnel decisions, and automated-detection parameters at any time; (b) Authority to suspend any Detection Unit investigation, automated-detection function, or enforcement action by majority vote of the Oversight Board if the Board determines that it exceeds statutory authority, violates civil liberties, disproportionately targets United States persons or protected classes, or serves any improper purpose. Suspension shall be immediate and self-executing; (c) Authority to refer Detection Unit personnel for replacement, criminal prosecution under Section 13, or both, by two-thirds (2/3) supermajority vote (twenty-four of thirty-five members) if evidence establishes abuse of authority, improper targeting, or other misconduct; (d) Authority to publish findings, concerns, and dissenting opinions directly upon the Ledger without editorial review or approval by the Detection Unit or any other body; and (e) Authority to consult civil liberties organizations, academic experts, and other independent advisors as needed. Advisory consultations shall be disclosed upon the Ledger. 22.10 The Watchdog Tribunal established in Section 21.2 shall additionally monitor both the Detection Unit and the Oversight Board itself for corruption, capture, or dereliction, with the full powers enumerated in Section 21.7. This creates four independent layers of protection: Detection Unit specialists, Oversight Board civilian watchdog, Watchdog Tribunal meta-watchdog, and Citizen Emergency Override under Section 21.10. D. Protection of Naturalized Citizens and Permanent Residents 22.11 Nothing in this Section shall restrict, limit, or condition the First Amendment rights or civic participation rights of any United States citizen, including naturalized citizens, based upon national origin, country of birth, ethnic background, or language spoken. Naturalized United States citizens are United States citizens in full, with identical rights to participate in Petitions, Referendums, advocacy, donations under Section 9, and all other civic activities established by this Amendment or by the Constitution.

22.12 The Detection Unit shall not initiate or pursue any investigation of, maintain surveillance upon, or take adverse action against any United States person based solely, predominantly, or materially on national origin, country of birth, ethnic background, religious affiliation, language spoken, or membership in any protected class. Any pattern of Detection Unit activity that disproportionately affects protected classes without specific, articulable, non-discriminatory grounds shall be suspended by the Oversight Board pursuant to Section 22.9(b). 22.13 Lawful permanent residents (green card holders) and other lawful long-term residents may participate in civic discourse, public speech, and advocacy on their own behalf. The restrictions of this Section apply only to activity funded by, directed by, coordinated with, or on behalf of a Foreign Person or Entity as defined herein, not to the independent civic speech of non-citizen residents acting in their individual capacity. E. Consequences of Material Foreign Interference 22.14 Upon credible evidence of material foreign interference in any Petition, Referendum, Emergency Delegate Election,

Emergency Election, or Sunset Review Vote, the Authority shall, by Liberty Bell Initiative, determine the materiality of the interference within thirty (30) days of the evidence being presented. The determination shall be publicly reasoned and recorded upon the Ledger, with investigative details of ongoing criminal matters redacted as necessary to preserve prosecution. 22.15 Upon a Liberty Bell Initiative determination of material foreign interference, the tainted Petition, Referendum, or Election shall be invalidated in its entirety. A one (1) year cooling-off period shall apply before any new Petition on the same subject matter may be initiated. All removed officials under a Declaration of No Confidence found to be invalidated by material foreign interference shall be restored to their offices, unless already removed by other constitutional means. 22.16 A Liberty Bell Initiative determination of material foreign interference requires clear, convincing, and publicly documented evidence — not mere allegation, partisan accusation, or political dispute. The Authority shall not invalidate a Petition or Referendum on the basis of foreign interference unless the evidence meets this heightened standard. Failure to meet this standard shall result in the Petition or Referendum proceeding unchanged. 22.16.1 Aggregate Materiality Framework. To close the interpretive gap whereby sophisticated foreign actors may deliberately structure interference operations to remain individually below the materiality threshold while collectively producing material effect on Amendment processes, the following aggregate materiality framework applies: (a) Aggregate Materiality Principle. Material foreign interference under Section 22.14 and Section 22.16 may be established not only through single incidents meeting the materiality threshold, but also through patterns of multiple incidents that collectively meet the threshold, even where no single incident would individually qualify. The materiality standard applies to the aggregate effect, not merely to any single component; (b) Pattern Analysis Authority. The Detection Unit under Section 22.5 (post-Day-180) and the Phase One Detection function under Section 22.4.1(a) shall have explicit authority to conduct pattern analysis identifying aggregates of sub-threshold incidents. Pattern analysis may consider: (i) temporal concentration of multiple incidents during Petition, Referendum, or election periods; (ii) geographic concentration affecting specific Participating Jurisdictions or demographic groups; (iii) topical concentration on specific candidates, officials, ballot questions, or Amendment processes; (iv) methodological similarity suggesting common origin, funding, or direction; (v) financial pattern analysis showing common funding sources across apparently separate operations; (vi) platform or channel concentration suggesting coordinated access; (vii) any other pattern indicia the Detection Unit may identify with Oversight Board concurrence under Section 22.9; (c) Aggregate Materiality Determination. A finding of aggregate material foreign interference shall require: (i) identification of the specific incidents included in the aggregate, each supported by evidence of foreign involvement under Section 22.2 (even if below individual materiality threshold); (ii) analysis demonstrating the collective effect of the aggregated incidents meets the materiality standard, meaning the aggregate may have meaningfully influenced petition signatures, Referendum outcome, or public understanding of either; (iii) clear, convincing, and publicly documented evidence supporting both the constituent incidents and the aggregate analysis under Section 22.16; (iv) Liberty Bell Initiative determination under Section 22.14 (post-Day-180) or Phase One dual supermajority determination under Section 22.4.1(c) (Phase One); (v) publication on the Ledger of the constituent incidents, the pattern analysis methodology, and the aggregate determination reasoning; (d) Coordination Not Required for Aggregate Finding. An aggregate materiality finding does not require proof that the constituent incidents were coordinated with each other or orchestrated by a single foreign actor. Multiple independent foreign actors, or even uncoordinated but contemporaneous foreign operations, may collectively produce material effect warranting Section 22.14 and Section 22.15 consequences. However, where coordination is demonstrable, such coordination shall be separately documented and may constitute additional grounds for Section 22.17 criminal liability against any United States person found to have knowingly facilitated the coordinated activity; (e) Enhanced Scrutiny of Sub-Threshold Structuring. Evidence that foreign actors deliberately structured operations to remain individually below the materiality threshold — for example, by fragmenting a single intended operation into multiple smaller operations, rotating through different intermediaries, or staggering activities across time — shall be considered as evidence of willful evasion under Section 22.3.1(b) Willful Blindness doctrine and Section 22.3.2(e) Technological Evasion Doctrine, and shall support aggregate materiality determination; (f) Consequences of Aggregate Determination. Upon an aggregate material foreign interference determination, all consequences under Section 22.15, Section 22.17, Section 22.18, and Section 22.19 shall apply as fully

as for a single-incident material interference determination, including invalidation of tainted Petitions or Referendums, cooling-off periods, restoration of removed officials where applicable, criminal prosecution of participating United States persons, foreign entity sanctions, and asset forfeiture; (g) Protection Against Abuse of Aggregation. Because aggregate determinations could be abused to invalidate Petitions or Referendums based on accumulations of minor incidents that do not genuinely represent material interference, the following safeguards apply: (i) Constituent Incident Threshold. Only incidents with credible evidence of foreign involvement under Section 22.2 shall be includable in an aggregate; mere allegations, unverified reports, or partisan accusations shall not count toward aggregate materiality; (ii) Minimum Incident Count. An aggregate determination shall require not fewer than five (5) credibly documented incidents; aggregation of fewer than five incidents shall not satisfy this Section, though individual incidents remain prosecutable under the ordinary Section 22.14 framework; (iii) Materiality Nexus. The aggregate analysis must demonstrate, with clear and convincing evidence, a plausible causal nexus between the aggregated incidents and potentially meaningful effect on Amendment process outcomes. Mere accumulation of foreign-linked incidents without demonstrable effect nexus shall not satisfy the standard; (iv) Good-Faith Dispute Protection. Good-faith disputes regarding whether specific incidents qualify for aggregation, or whether aggregate analysis reaches the materiality threshold, shall be resolved in favor of allowing the Petition, Referendum, or election to proceed, consistent with Section 22.16's default that failure to meet heightened standard results in Petition or Referendum proceeding unchanged; (v) Watchdog Tribunal Review. Aggregate materiality determinations shall be subject to Watchdog Tribunal review under Section 21.7 on motion of any Authority body, any Participating Jurisdiction's Governor or Attorney General, or petition of ten thousand (10,000) registered voters. Tribunal review shall apply the same clear-and-convincing standard and shall be completed within thirty (30) days of motion filing; (h) Sunset Integration. The aggregate materiality framework shall be reviewed during each Sunset Review under Section 18 based on accumulated operational experience, with the People empowered through Modify vote to adjust the minimum incident count, pattern analysis factors, or other parameters of this Section. F. Criminal Penalties 22.17 Any United States person who knowingly accepts, solicits, coordinates, or directs money, services, in-kind contributions, strategic direction, or material support from a Foreign Person or Entity in violation of Section 22.2 shall be subject to ALL of the following, applied cumulatively: (a) Federal criminal prosecution with imprisonment of not less than twenty (20) years and permanent lifetime bar from any federal, state, or local public office or government employment, without possibility of pardon, commutation, or clemency;

(b) Prosecution as an agent of a foreign power under existing federal law, including applicable provisions of the Foreign Agents Registration Act, 18 United States Code § 951, and any successor statutes; and (c) Forfeiture of all assets, funds, property, and compensation derived from or connected to the foreign interference activity. 22.18 Any Foreign Person or Entity found to have engaged in prohibited interference under Section 22.2 shall be subject to: permanent barring of the foreign entity, its successor organizations, and its principal officers from any activity in the United States; sanctions applied to assets within United States jurisdiction; and diplomatic referral to the United States Department of State for appropriate action against the foreign sovereign sponsor, if any. 22.19 Knowing failure to disclose under Section 22.4, when the failure conceals foreign involvement, shall be treated as a prohibited act of interference subject to the penalties of Section 22.17. Negligent or reckless failure to disclose shall be punishable by civil fine of not less than ten times the undisclosed amount, plus criminal prosecution at the discretion of the Authority. G. Transparency and Continuous Improvement 22.20 The Detection Unit and the Oversight Board shall each publish quarterly public reports upon the Ledger detailing: the number and general nature of investigations opened and closed; aggregated statistics on detected anomalies and pattern matches; disciplinary actions and referrals; civil liberties concerns raised and addressed; and the demographic distribution of Detection Unit investigative activity, to enable public assessment of any disparate impact on protected classes. 22.21 Every five (5) years, the Academic Integrity Commission shall conduct a comprehensive review of the Detection Unit's methodology, detection algorithms, and civil liberties impact, with findings published upon the Ledger. The review shall specifically address: effectiveness of detection, rate of false positives, disparate impact on protected classes, and opportunities for methodological improvement. 22.22 Nothing in this Section shall authorize mass surveillance, warrantless monitoring of private communications of United States persons, or the suppression of lawful political speech by United States citizens or by lawful residents acting in their individual capacity. The Detection Unit's authority is strictly limited to publicly available information, disclosed funding records, and investigations grounded in specific, articulable, non-discriminatory evidence. 22.23 Foreign Sovereign Limits and Asymmetric Enforcement Framework. Recognizing that this Section establishes substantial penalties for foreign persons or entities found to have engaged in prohibited interference, and recognizing that foreign sovereign states are protected from civil liability in United States courts under the Foreign Sovereign Immunities

Act (28 U.S.C. §§ 1602–1611) and corresponding doctrines of customary international law, and recognizing that the Amendment cannot abrogate foreign sovereign immunity by domestic constitutional command alone, the People establish here an honest acknowledgment of the framework's asymmetric reach and the structural mechanisms through which the framework nevertheless retains substantial deterrent force: (a) Foundational Acknowledgment. The penalties of Sections 22.17 through 22.19 reach: (i) United States persons in full, including criminal prosecution, asset forfeiture, lifetime bars, and Section 13 interference penalties with Senior Official multipliers where applicable; (ii) foreign persons and entities in full where their assets, principals, or successor organizations are within or accessible to United States jurisdiction, including permanent barring, asset forfeiture, sanctions on originating entities, and personal sanctions on principals; (iii) foreign sovereign states only to the extent permitted by sovereign immunity doctrine and applicable treaties, which historically permits substantial sanctions, asset freezes against state-owned commercial property within United States jurisdiction, restrictions on diplomatic engagement, and other state-craft measures, but does not permit ordinary civil or criminal prosecution of the sovereign itself; (b) Asymmetric Enforcement Reality. The framework therefore operates with intentional asymmetry: it punishes the United States-side actors who collaborate with foreign interference (Section 22.17) at full domestic-criminal force; it punishes foreign actors operating within United States jurisdictional reach (Section 22.18) at the maximum extent permitted by international law and applicable treaties; it does not pretend to reach foreign sovereigns themselves with ordinary criminal prosecution. The People accept this asymmetry as the honest limit of what a domestic constitutional amendment can accomplish; (c) Sovereign-State Response Toolkit. Where Section 22.14 materiality determinations identify foreign-sovereign-state involvement in interference, the framework activates the following state-craft tools rather than ordinary prosecution: (i) Authority Certification. The Authority, through Liberty Bell Initiative, may certify the foreign-sovereign involvement to the Department of State, Department of the Treasury, and Office of Foreign Assets Control, with such certification triggering ordinary federal sanctions authority under existing statutes including the International Emergency Economic Powers Act (50 U.S.C. §§ 1701–1708) and successor statutes; (ii) Diplomatic Recommendation. The Authority may publish on the Franklin Ledger formal recommendations for diplomatic response, including expulsion of foreign agents, restriction of diplomatic engagement, and revocation of preferential trade or economic relationships. Recommendations are non-binding on the federal executive but create public record that informs subsequent democratic accountability; (iii) Asset Identification and Freezing. The Hamilton Contingent (or during Phase One the State Attorneys General Council) shall identify foreign-state-owned commercial assets within United States jurisdiction subject to freezing under existing federal authority, with Authority cooperation with Treasury and Department of State to effectuate freezing of identified assets; (iv) Treaty-Based Mechanisms. Where applicable mutual legal assistance treaties, extradition treaties, or other instruments provide pathways for foreign-state

cooperation in addressing interference, the Authority shall coordinate with Department of State to invoke such mechanisms; (v) Public Documentation. Foreign-sovereign involvement findings shall be published on the Franklin Ledger with full evidentiary basis, providing public record that informs both democratic accountability and subsequent international engagement; (d) Limit on Domestic-Side Asymmetry. The asymmetric reach of this framework shall not be invoked as defense by United States persons charged under Section 22.17. A United States person who knowingly accepts, solicits, coordinates, or directs material support from a foreign sovereign or its agents commits a Section 22.17 offense regardless of whether the foreign sovereign principal can itself be prosecuted. The reach over United States persons is comprehensive; the limit is only on prosecution of foreign sovereigns themselves; (e) Coordination with Federal Executive Foreign-Affairs Authority. Implementation of subsection (c) state-craft tools shall coordinate with ordinary federal executive foreign-affairs authority. The Authority shall not unilaterally conduct foreign relations; rather, the Authority shall provide certified evidentiary findings that activate existing federal authority under Department of State and Department of the Treasury. Where federal executive authority is itself implicated in the interference (because the executive officeholder being protected by the foreign-sovereign interference is the executive directing federal foreign-affairs response), the State Attorneys General Council under Section 19.5.0.18 may coordinate state-level economic and diplomatic measures to the extent permitted by Constitutional federalism, with the Permanent Washington Commission certifying the federal-executive conflict that justifies state-level response; (f) Honest Acknowledgment Requirement. Authority publications under this Section, including findings of foreign-sovereign involvement and recommendations for response, shall include explicit acknowledgment of the limits of domestic enforcement reach over foreign sovereigns. The Authority shall not represent that ordinary criminal prosecution will reach a foreign sovereign principal; representations of state-craft response shall accurately describe what the framework can and cannot accomplish. Honest acknowledgment is itself part of the framework's legitimacy; (g) Article V Protection. The provisions of this Section shall be protected under the Article V protection established in Sections 18.6.1 and 18.6.2. 22.24 Pre-Publication Review of Detection Unit Findings by Oversight Board. Recognizing that Section 22.7 establishes the Foreign Interference Oversight Board with civil liberties expertise, and recognizing that the Oversight Board's post-hoc review of Detection Unit findings does not prevent the political damage of premature, leaked, or pretextual preliminary findings during active Petition or Referendum windows, and recognizing that Detection Unit investigative authority operates structurally upstream of all subsequent checks (Section 22.14 materiality determination, Section 22.7 oversight, Section 21 Watchdog Tribunal review) such that by the time those checks weigh in the political damage from a leaked or premature finding has already occurred, the following Pre-Publication Review framework establishes upstream Oversight Board authority over Detection Unit publication decisions: (a) Foundational Principle. Detection Unit investigative authority remains intact under Sections 22.5 and 22.6. What this Section establishes is that the Detection Unit's decision to publish findings — not its decision to investigate — is subject to Oversight Board pre-publication review. Investigation may proceed without pre-publication review; publication may not. This distinction protects ongoing investigation while preventing publication-driven political damage; (b) Categories of Findings Subject to Pre-Publication Review. The following Detection Unit findings shall be subject to Oversight Board pre-publication review before any publication on the Franklin Ledger, the provisional public ledger, or any other Authority-controlled publication channel: (i) Preliminary Findings. Any finding characterized as "preliminary," "initial," "under investigation," or any equivalent characterization that suggests further investigation is required before final determination; (ii) Pattern Findings. Findings of patterns of foreign-linked activity that have not yet ripened into Section 22.14 materiality determinations; (iii) Identification Findings. Findings that specifically identify United States persons, organizations, or Petition/Referendum campaigns as subjects of investigation, regardless of whether prohibited conduct has been determined; (iv) Aggregate Findings. Findings drawing aggregate conclusions about foreign interference patterns affecting specific demographic, geographic, or political groups; (c) Findings Not Subject to Pre-Publication Review. The following findings are not subject to pre-publication review under this Section: (i) Final

Section 22.14 materiality determinations made by Liberty Bell Initiative concurrence, which carry their own three-body concurrence requirement and clear-and-convincing evidentiary standard; (ii) Section 22.18 enforcement actions against foreign persons or entities, which proceed under existing federal sanctions authority; (iii) Routine quarterly reports under Section 22.20 reporting aggregated statistics without specific subject identification; (iv) Court filings or prosecution charging documents in active cases, which proceed under ordinary judicial procedure; (d) Pre-Publication Review Standard. The Oversight Board shall review findings subject to pre-publication review for: (i) Evidentiary Sufficiency. Whether the finding's evidentiary basis meets the standards of Section 22.16 (clear and convincing, publicly documented), or whether the finding represents allegation, partisan accusation, or political dispute that has not ripened to publishable form; (ii) Civil Liberties Impact. Whether publication risks chilling lawful political speech, surveilling domestic political activity, or producing disparate impact on protected classes inconsistent with Section 22.22; (iii) Timing Considerations. Whether publication during an active Petition or Referendum window risks producing political damage disproportionate to the finding's evidentiary support — not as basis for indefinite suppression, but for evidentiary sufficiency assessment specifically informed by timing; (iv) Specificity. Whether the finding's articulation specifically identifies subjects beyond what evidentiary basis supports; (e) Pre-Publication Review Outcomes. Upon review, the Oversight Board shall, by majority vote, determine one of the following: (i) Approve Publication. The finding meets all applicable standards and may be published as proposed; (ii) Approve with

Modification. The finding may be published in modified form addressing specific Oversight Board concerns regarding evidentiary sufficiency, civil liberties impact, or specificity; (iii) Defer Publication. The finding lacks publishable evidentiary support at the present time; the Detection Unit may continue investigation and re-submit when evidentiary support is sufficient. Deferral is not suppression; deferred findings remain subject to Detection Unit continued investigation and subsequent re-submission; (iv) Preclude Publication. The finding fails fundamental publication standards (e.g., reflects allegation rather than evidence, presents civil liberties violations that cannot be remedied by modification) and shall not be published in its current form. Preclusion does not prevent the Detection Unit from re-investigating and submitting a fundamentally different finding based on new evidence; it only precludes the specific finding under review. Preclusion shall be documented internally with reasoning; the existence of preclusion (without specific finding details) shall be reported in quarterly reports under Section 22.20 to maintain accountability over Oversight Board preclusion authority itself; (f) Review Timing. Pre-publication review shall be completed within seven (7) days of submission of a finding for review, with expedited review within forty-eight (48) hours where the Detection Unit certifies time-sensitive necessity (e.g., active Referendum within thirty (30) days, identified ongoing interference requiring rapid response). Where Oversight Board fails to complete review within applicable timeline, the Detection Unit may publish without further review, with the failure-to-review documented on the Franklin Ledger; (g) Emergency Publication Pathway. Where the Detection Unit, by majority vote of its leadership, certifies imminent operational necessity for publication that cannot await pre-publication review (e.g., active interference operation requiring immediate public counter-disclosure), the Detection Unit may publish with simultaneous notice to the Oversight Board, which shall conduct retrospective review within seven (7) days. Bad-faith invocation of emergency publication — invocation in circumstances where ordinary review timelines could have been met — shall constitute Section 13 interference subject to enhanced penalties for misuse of emergency authority; (h) Detection Unit Investigation Authority Preserved. Nothing in this Section limits Detection Unit investigative authority under Sections 22.5 and 22.6. The Detection Unit may continue to investigate, gather evidence, and develop findings without pre-publication review; only the publication step is subject to Oversight Board review. This preserves the Detection Unit's ability to conduct effective investigation while preventing publication-driven political damage; (i) Oversight Board Composition for Pre-Publication Review. Oversight Board members exercising pre-publication review authority shall meet the civil liberties expertise requirements of Section 22.7. Where Oversight Board composition does not include adequate civil liberties expertise for specific review tasks, the Permanent Washington Commission may, by majority vote, supplement the review with additional Pre-Certified Pool civil liberties experts under Section 17.16, with the supplementation documented on the Franklin Ledger; (j) Watchdog Tribunal Oversight. The Watchdog Tribunal shall exercise oversight over Oversight Board pre-publication review authority itself, with authority to investigate allegations of bad-faith approval (where Oversight Board approves findings lacking evidentiary support), bad-faith preclusion (where Oversight Board precludes findings supported by adequate evidence), or pattern of preclusion practice that suggests structural protection of specific political interests. Tribunal findings shall be published on the Franklin Ledger; (k) Privacy Protections. Pre-publication review proceedings shall be conducted with privacy protections analogous to Section 17.4.7, with subjects of unpublished findings not identified during review proceedings. Where review results in publication, ordinary disclosure follows; where review results in deferral or preclusion, subjects shall not be identified by the review process itself; (l) Federal Executive Non-Interference. No President, Vice President, Cabinet officer, federal agency head, or other federal executive officeholder shall direct, fund, influence, or impede pre-publication review under this Section. Any such interference shall constitute Section 13 interference with Senior Official multipliers, prosecutable through the Section 17C.15 framework; (m) Funding. Costs of pre-publication review, Oversight Board operational support for the function, and Watchdog Tribunal oversight thereof shall be funded through the constitutional appropriation under Section 11.3; (n) Article V Protection. The provisions of this Section shall be protected under the Article V protection established in Sections 18.6.1 and 18.6.2. Pre-publication review converts the Oversight Board's civil liberties function from purely retrospective remedy to upstream prevention, capturing the difference between investigation that may occur and publication that may damage.

Section 23. Close-Vote Disputes, Recounts, and Contest Procedures

Key terms in this Section: • "The Authority" — The Independent Tripartite Oversight Authority (three bodies, see Section 17). • "Liberty Bell Initiative" — Separate concurrence of all three bodies of the Authority. • "The Ledger" — The Sovereign Blockchain Voting Ledger (Section 4), the cryptographically tamper-evident record of every vote. • "Terminal" — A Sovereign Voting Terminal (Section 14). • "Automatic Recount" — A recount triggered without any party needing to request it, occurring automatically when a result falls within the margin established by Section 23.3.

• "Contest" — A formal challenge to the result of a Petition, Referendum, or Election, filed under the procedures established in Sections 23.7 through 23.10. • "Certification" — The Authority's formal recording of a final vote result upon the Ledger after completion of all applicable recount and contest procedures. 23.1 Recognizing that the legitimacy of any outcome under this Amendment depends on public confidence in the accuracy of the count, this Section establishes uniform procedures for automatic recounts, contests, and final certification that protect the integrity of results while preventing weaponization of the contest process to delay legitimate outcomes. A. Automatic Recount

Procedures 23.2 The thresholds established in Section 5.2 are: a supermajority threshold of sixty percent (60%) of ballots cast and a turnout threshold of fifty percent (50%) of registered voters. These clean whole-number thresholds shall apply to all Referendums under this Amendment. 23.3 An Automatic Recount shall be triggered by the Authority, without any party needing to request it, whenever a certified preliminary count falls within either of the following margins: (a) Supermajority margin: the affirmative vote is between fifty-eight percent (58%) and sixty-two percent (62%) of ballots cast, inclusive, bracketing the sixty percent (60%) threshold of Section 5.2(a); OR (b) Turnout margin: the turnout is between forty-eight percent (48%) and fifty-two percent (52%) of registered voters, inclusive, bracketing the fifty percent (50%) threshold of Section 5.2(b). 23.4 Upon any Automatic Recount trigger, the Authority shall suspend certification of the preliminary result and commence recount procedures within seventy-two (72) hours. The recount shall be completed within fourteen (14) days of commencement, with findings published in full upon the Ledger. 23.5 The Automatic Recount procedure shall consist of: (a) Full blockchain re-verification of every vote recorded upon the Ledger, performed cryptographically by the Academic Integrity Commission with independent audit by the State Elections Council; (b) Physical forensic audit of every Terminal that recorded flagged anomalies during the original vote, including chain-of-custody review, hardware inspection, and software integrity verification; (c) Statistical analysis of voting patterns to detect any anomalies not caught by the automated systems; and

(d) Publication of the recount methodology, findings, and any discrepancies identified, upon the Ledger in full. 23.6 The recount result shall supersede the preliminary result upon certification by the Authority through Liberty Bell Initiative. If the recount reveals that the threshold was in fact met when originally miscounted, the Referendum shall pass; if the threshold was not met, the Referendum shall fail. Certification shall occur within fourteen (14) days of recount completion. B. Formal Contest Procedures 23.7 A formal Contest may be filed against any certified Petition, Referendum, Emergency Delegate Election, Emergency Election, or Sunset Review Vote under the following strict conditions: (a) Standing: No fewer than one hundred (100) registered voters banding together may file a single Contest. Individual Contests, filed by a single voter acting alone, shall not be permitted. The one hundred filers shall all sign the Contest in person at an Office or Center, with signatures verified by the State Elections Council; (b) Evidence: The Contest shall present concrete, specific, documented evidence of a claimed defect. Allegation without evidence, partisan opinion, or general suspicion shall not be sufficient. The evidence shall establish, at minimum, a reasonable probability that the defect, if proven, would have materially affected the outcome; (c) Grounds: The Contest shall state with specificity the grounds alleged, which may include: technical failure of Terminals or the Network; signature fraud; ballot manipulation; Ledger tampering; Authority misconduct; violation of civil liberties protections under Section 22; or material foreign interference under Section 22; (d) Timing: The Contest shall be filed within thirty (30) days of final Certification. After thirty days, results are final and may not be challenged, except upon discovery of material foreign interference as provided in Section 22, which follows its own separate timeline; and (e) Public Filing: The Contest, including all filers' names, the grounds alleged, and the evidence presented, shall be published upon the Ledger in full upon filing. 23.8 Upon receipt of a valid Contest meeting the requirements of Section 23.7, the Authority shall hear and decide the Contest within thirty (30) days. The decision shall require Liberty Bell Initiative to invalidate or modify any certified result. The evidentiary standard shall be clear and convincing evidence of material defect — not mere preponderance — to prevent minor procedural irregularities from overturning democratically expressed results. 23.9 If a Contest succeeds, the Authority shall determine the appropriate remedy by Liberty Bell Initiative, which may include: full re-vote of the Referendum or Election; invalidation of specific disputed ballots or signatures with the remainder counted normally; re-verification of affected signatures; replacement of affected Terminals followed by a re-vote of affected Offices; or such other remedy as the Authority finds just. The remedy shall be proportionate to the defect proven. 23.10 After the thirty-day Contest window closes and no Contest has succeeded, the Certification shall be final and irrevocable. No federal court, agency, officeholder, or other authority shall have jurisdiction to review, invalidate, or delay a final Certification. The only exception shall be discovery of material foreign interference under Section 22, which triggers its own invalidation procedure without time limitation but with the heightened evidentiary standard established therein. C. Sanctions Against Bad-Faith Contests 23.11 To prevent weaponization of the Contest process by removed officials, their supporters, or bad-faith actors seeking to delay legitimate outcomes, the following sanctions shall apply: (a) Contests presenting no concrete evidence, or evidence that on its face cannot meet the clear-and-convincing standard, shall be dismissed summarily by the Authority without full hearing, within seventy-two (72) hours of filing, with the dismissal published upon the Ledger; (b) Any person who files two (2) or more Contests dismissed as frivolous within a five (5) year window shall be barred from serving as a named filer on any future Contest for ten (10) years, and shall be liable for federal civil fines of not less than ten thousand dollars ($10,000) per frivolous Contest, adjusted for inflation; (c) Any person who organizes, funds, or coordinates a bad-faith Contest campaign specifically to delay removal of officials who have been lawfully declared removed under a valid Declaration of No Confidence, or to obstruct the operation of this Amendment, shall be subject to Section 13 interference penalties, including the fifteen (15) year minimum sentence and lifetime bar from public office; and (d) Any officeholder, former officeholder, or person acting on behalf of the removed government who directs, funds, or coordinates a bad-faith Contest shall additionally be subject to the insurrection penalties of Section 16.5. 23.12 A good-faith Contest that fails shall not expose its filers to any of the sanctions in Section 23.11. The sanctions apply only to Contests that are frivolous on their face, filed without concrete evidence, or demonstrably organized to delay a legitimate outcome. Legitimate concerns raised in good faith, even if ultimately unsuccessful, shall be treated as valuable civic engagement. D. Authority Body Refusal and Mutual Veto Misuse 23.13 Recognizing that any one of the three bodies of the Authority may theoretically refuse to participate in a Liberty Bell Initiative for improper reasons (corruption, capture, or political motivation), the following safeguard applies to

Certification specifically: if any one body refuses Certification of a Referendum result that the other two bodies independently find valid, the Watchdog Tribunal shall automatically investigate the refusing body within seven (7) days under its existing Section 21.7 authorities. 23.13.1 Extended Scope of Mutual Veto Misuse Safeguard. The safeguard procedures of Sections 23.13 through 23.15 shall apply to any Liberty Bell Initiative refusal by an Authority body where one body refuses Certification or concurrence that the other two bodies independently find valid, including but not limited to: (a) Petition Certification under Section 3.2, which is the Authority action that triggers a Referendum under Section 5; (b) Restoration Petition Certification under Section 17B.3; (c) Forced Restructuring recommendations under Section 17A.19.8(e); and (d) any other Authority action requiring Liberty Bell Initiative under Section 17.22. In each such case, the Watchdog Tribunal shall automatically investigate the refusing body within seven (7) days under its Section 21.7 authorities, and the remedies of Section 23.14 shall apply as if the refusal concerned a Referendum result. The purpose of this subsection is to close the structural gap whereby a captured or corrupted Authority body could block citizen-initiated Reclamation or Restoration by refusing at the Petition Certification stage before a Referendum is ever scheduled, defeating the will of the People without ever allowing that will to be measured at the ballot. 23.13.2 Expedited Timeline for Petition Certification Refusal. Where a refused Liberty Bell Initiative concerns Petition Certification under Section 3.2 or Restoration Petition Certification under Section 17B.3, the Watchdog Tribunal shall prioritize the investigation and shall complete its two-thirds (2/3) supermajority finding under Section 23.14 within thirty (30) days of opening the investigation, rather than the ordinary investigation timeline under Section 21.7. Throughout the investigation and any ensuing replacement proceedings under Section 23.14, all procedural timelines applicable to the Petition shall be tolled, and the Petition shall not be deemed lapsed, withdrawn, or otherwise defeated by virtue of delay occasioned by the refusal or the investigation. The urgency of citizen-initiated Reclamation and Restoration petitions, and the practical burden on citizens to maintain signature collection infrastructure indefinitely, require expedited resolution of Authority body obstruction at the Petition Certification stage. 23.14 If the Watchdog Tribunal finds by two-thirds (2/3) supermajority that the refusal constitutes corruption, capture, or bad-faith obstruction rather than legitimate concern, the Tribunal shall exercise its replacement, prosecution, or dissolution authority under Section 21.7 against the refusing body, and Certification shall proceed as if the replaced body had concurred. If the Tribunal finds the refusal to be in good faith based on legitimate concerns, the Certification remains blocked and the Authority's ordinary reconciliation procedures apply. 23.15 This safeguard ensures that the mutual-veto structure of Section 17 cannot be weaponized to block the legitimate will of the People, while preserving the genuine protective value of requiring all three bodies to concur on every action. E. Transparency and Public Confidence 23.16 All recount procedures, Contest filings, hearings, decisions, and sanctions under this Section shall be published in full upon the Ledger in real time. The forensic methodologies used by the Academic Integrity Commission in recount verification, and the statistical models used in anomaly detection, shall be publicly documented and subject to independent academic review. 23.17 The Authority shall publish a public Post-Vote Integrity Report within sixty (60) days of every Certification, detailing: vote totals, recount results if any, Contests filed and their disposition, Terminal and Network performance statistics, and any anomalies detected and investigated. The Report shall serve as the permanent public record of the integrity of each vote under this Amendment.

Section 24. Limits on Presidential Power

Key terms in this Section: • "The President" — The President of the United States, or Acting President, at any given time. • "The Watchdog Tribunal" — The body established under Section 21 for enforcement of anti-corruption provisions. • "The Ledger" — The Sovereign Blockchain Voting Ledger (Section 4). • "Executive Order" — Any Presidential directive, proclamation, memorandum, or similar instrument intended to have the force of law within the executive branch. 24.1 Concentration of power in any single officeholder creates the conditions for the corruption and tyranny this Amendment exists to prevent. The No Confidence mechanism is most effective when exercised rarely, because structural limits on power make it rarely necessary. The limits of this Section shall therefore apply to the President of the United States and to all Acting Presidents, without exception. 24.1.1 Application to Vice President and Acting Presidents. The provisions of this Section 24 shall apply to: (a) the elected President; (b) the Vice President when serving as Acting President under the Twenty-Fifth Amendment or any successor provision; (c) any person serving as Acting President through presidential succession; and (d) the Chairperson of the Constitutional Transition Committee when serving as acting Commander-in-Chief under Section 6.7. The Vice President in their ordinary role possesses no independent pardon or executive order authority; any attempt by a sitting Vice President to exercise such authority without serving as Acting President shall be void ab initio.

A. Pardon Power Reform 24.2 The pardon power established in Article II, Section 2 of the Constitution shall be subject to the following limitations. No provision of this Section shall be construed to expand the pardon power beyond its current scope; the purpose of this Section is solely to limit, not to augment, the pardon power. 24.3 Self-Pardon Prohibition. No President shall issue a pardon to himself or herself for any federal offense. Any purported self-pardon shall be void ab initio and shall have no legal effect. 24.4 Family and Associate Limitations. No President shall issue a pardon for any federal offense to: (a) any spouse, parent, child, sibling, grandchild, or in-law of the President; (b) any member of the President's campaign staff during the preceding presidential campaign; (c) any person who contributed, directly or through affiliated entities, to the top five hundred (500) financial contributors to the President's most recent campaign, transition, or inauguration; or (d) any person with whom the President or the President's family has a documented business or financial relationship. Any pardon issued in violation of this Section shall be void ab initio. 24.5 Corruption and Interference Carve-Out. No President shall issue a pardon for any offense under Section 13, Section 13A, Section 18.6, Section 22, or any provision of this Amendment establishing federal criminal liability. This restriction supplements and does not replace the existing no-pardon provisions throughout this Amendment. Any pardon issued in violation of this Section shall be void ab initio. 24.6 Final Ninety Days Prohibition. No President shall issue any pardon during the final ninety (90) days of the President's term of office, except in cases of demonstrably innocent persons supported by clear and convincing evidence of actual innocence or prosecutorial misconduct. Any pardon issued during this period shall be reviewed within thirty (30) days by the Watchdog Tribunal for compliance with this exception; pardons failing such review shall be void ab initio. This limitation prevents "midnight pardons" granted to avoid accountability to the incoming administration or the electorate. 24.7 Transparency Requirements for All Pardons. Every pardon issued by a President shall be accompanied by: (a) written justification published in full upon the Ledger within twenty-four (24) hours of issuance, stating the specific factual and legal basis; (b) disclosure of any personal, financial, or political relationship between the President and the pardoned person; (c) notification to the Watchdog Tribunal; and (d) opportunity for Authority review for compliance with this Section. Failure to publish the required justification within twenty-four (24) hours shall render the pardon voidable at the discretion of the Watchdog Tribunal. 24.8 Mass Pardon Restrictions. Any pardon order granting relief to more than ten (10) persons in a single action, or any series of coordinated pardons granting relief to more than ten (10) persons within any ninety-day (90-day) period, shall require ratification by a majority vote of both houses of Congress within thirty (30) days. Pardons not so ratified shall be void ab initio. This provision prevents the use of the pardon power to nullify large categories of federal criminal accountability without legislative concurrence. B. Executive Order Constraints 24.9 Statutory Authority Requirement. Every Executive Order shall cite the specific statutory provision or constitutional authority upon which it is based. Orders failing to cite such authority, or citing authority that does not support the action taken, shall be void ab initio. 24.10 Conflict with Statute. No Executive Order shall override, contradict, or effectively nullify any statute enacted by Congress. Orders conflicting with statute shall be void ab initio and shall have no legal effect. 24.11 Criminal Penalties Prohibition. No Executive Order shall create, modify, or expand any criminal offense, criminal penalty, or procedural rule affecting criminal liability. Only Congress may enact federal criminal law. Orders purporting to create criminal liability shall be void ab initio. 24.12 Publication and Transparency. All Executive Orders shall be published in full upon the Ledger within twenty-four (24) hours of issuance, including: (a) the full text of the Order; (b) the specific statutory or constitutional authority cited; (c) the date of issuance and effective date; and (d) any implementing regulations or directives. No Executive Order shall take effect until so published. 24.13 Congressional Nullification. Congress may nullify any Executive Order by simple majority vote of both houses within ninety (90) days of publication. Such nullification shall not be subject to Presidential veto. Orders nullified by Congress shall be void as of the date of the nullification vote. 24.14 Automatic Sunset. Every Executive Order shall automatically expire two (2) years after its effective date unless: (a) renewed by the President with new findings published on the Ledger; (b) codified by an act of Congress; or (c) expressly exempted from sunset by the Authority upon a finding of compelling ongoing operational necessity. Sunset provisions shall not apply to orders implementing specific statutory directives with fixed expiration dates, or to military orders during declared hostilities. 24.14.1 Transition Provision for Pre-Ratification Executive Orders. Executive Orders in effect at Ratification shall be subject to the two-year sunset under Section 24.14 beginning on Day One Hundred Eighty (180) following Ratification, providing the current President time to review, modify, or renew as appropriate. The Implementation Director, or where not yet elected the Interim Transition Council, shall publish a comprehensive list of all then-existing Executive Orders upon the Ledger (or provisional public ledger) within sixty (60) days of Ratification, including: (a) order number and date; (b) subject matter; (c) current

effect; (d) scheduled sunset date under this Section; and (e) statutory or constitutional authority. The President shall review each such Order and publish findings upon the Ledger before the scheduled sunset date indicating renewal, modification, or allowance of expiration. Orders not so reviewed before the sunset date shall expire. 24.15 Amendment Protection. No Executive Order shall infringe, limit, delay, or in any way impede the operation of this Amendment, the functioning of the Authority, the operation of the Ledger, Network, Offices, Centers, or Terminals, or the exercise of rights established by this Amendment. Orders attempting such infringement shall be void ab initio and shall constitute interference under Section 13. C. Emergency Power Reinforcement 24.16 Factual Findings Required. Every Presidential emergency declaration shall be accompanied by specific, documented factual findings establishing the nature, scope, and imminent character of the emergency. Such findings shall be published upon the Ledger within twenty-four (24) hours. Declarations lacking such findings shall be void ab initio. 24.17 Authority

Review. The Authority shall review every Presidential emergency declaration within forty-eight (48) hours of issuance for factual sufficiency and proper scope. If the Authority, by Liberty Bell Initiative, finds the declaration insufficiently supported or improperly scoped, the declaration shall be void as of the moment of the Authority's finding. 24.18 Reinforcement of Section 10. The cumulative one-hundred-twenty-day (120-day) cap on emergency declarations established in Sections 10.5 through 10.13 shall apply to all Presidential emergency powers under any statute or constitutional authority, not only those related to a No Confidence process. This Section 24.18 supplements and strengthens Section 10 by applying its limits universally to executive emergency authority. 24.18.1 Renewal of Emergency Declarations. After the initial one-hundred-twenty (120) cumulative days, emergency declarations may be renewed for additional one-hundred-twenty (120) day periods only upon: (a) Authority finding by Liberty Bell Initiative that the emergency continues to exist with factual sufficiency, published in full upon the Ledger; (b) Congressional concurrence by simple majority of both houses, or by joint resolution; or (c) Judicial concurrence by a panel of five (5) federal judges selected by lottery from a pool of senior federal judges maintained by the Chief Justice, making findings by at least four (4) judges concurring.

24.18.2 Limitation on Consecutive Renewals. No emergency declaration may be renewed more than six (6) consecutive times under Section 24.18.1, limiting the total duration of any single emergency declaration to approximately twenty-four (24) months even with continuous renewal. At the expiration of the sixth consecutive renewal, the emergency declaration terminates automatically and may not be re-issued on the same factual basis for at least one hundred eighty (180) days. This provision prevents the transformation of emergency powers into ordinary governance while accommodating genuine long-duration emergencies. 24.18.3 Public Review. Every renewal under Section 24.18.1 shall include: (a) specific factual findings of continuing emergency; (b) enumeration of emergency powers being exercised; (c) expected duration; and (d) conditions that would terminate the emergency. All findings shall be published in full upon the Ledger. 24.19 Prohibition on Amendment Bypass. No emergency declaration, emergency authority, or claim of emergency powers shall be used to bypass, suspend, override, or delay the operation of this Amendment. Any such attempt shall constitute interference under Section 13 and shall be subject to the full penalties thereof. D. Presidential Ethics Code 24.20 Divestiture Requirement. Within sixty (60) days of taking the oath of office, every President shall either: (a) divest all individual business holdings, stock positions, and direct ownership interests; or (b) place all such holdings into a qualified blind trust as defined by the Office of Government Ethics, with the trustee selected from a list maintained by the Academic Integrity Commission. The same requirement shall apply to the President's spouse and minor children. Failure to comply within the sixty-day period shall constitute a violation subject to Section 13A penalties. 24.21 Continuing Disclosure. Every President shall annually publish upon the Ledger: (a) complete federal tax returns for the preceding year for the President, the President's spouse, and dependent children; (b) all assets, including those held in blind trust in aggregate form; (c) all income from all sources; (d) all gifts received of value exceeding one hundred dollars ($100); and (e) all foreign contacts of substantial character. The first such disclosure shall be made within ninety (90) days of taking office and annually thereafter. 24.22 Prohibition on Self-Dealing. No President shall take any official action primarily for the purpose of benefiting personal financial interests, business holdings, family holdings, or the holdings of immediate associates. Violations of this Section shall constitute corruption under Section 13A and shall be subject to the full penalties thereof, including the enhanced Senior Official multiplier of fifty times (50×) benefit. 24.22.1 Evidentiary Standard. Violations of Section 24.22 shall be proven by clear and convincing evidence. Actions serving both legitimate public interests and incidental personal financial benefits shall not constitute violations unless the evidence establishes that the personal benefit was the primary motivating factor. The Watchdog Tribunal shall consider, among other factors: (a) whether the action would have been taken absent personal benefit; (b) whether the action departs materially from standard practice or career expert recommendations; (c) whether the action was advised against by career officials or ethics counsel; (d) the magnitude of personal benefit relative to public interest served; (e) contemporaneous statements, communications, or conduct of the President indicating motive; and (f) timing of the action relative to personal financial opportunities or liabilities. Ambiguous cases shall be resolved in favor of the President unless clear and convincing evidence overcomes the presumption of public purpose. 24.23 Watchdog Tribunal Jurisdiction. The Watchdog Tribunal established under Section 21 shall have jurisdiction over violations of this Section by the President, and may refer violations for criminal prosecution, impeachment, or (during an active No Confidence process) direct action under this Amendment. Presidential invocation of executive privilege shall not shield disclosures required by this Section from the Tribunal's jurisdiction. E. Appointment and Removal Authority Limits 24.24 Appointment Authority

Limits. Recognizing that Presidential appointments can effectively capture federal agencies independent of any specific Presidential action, the following limits shall apply: (a) Recess Appointment Restrictions. Recess appointments under Article II, Section 2 shall be strictly limited to genuine recess periods of the Senate exceeding ten (10) consecutive days. Recess appointments made during pro forma sessions or brief Senate pauses shall be void ab initio. Recess appointees shall serve only until the end of the Senate's next session, with no renewal without Senate confirmation. (b) Qualifications Required. Every Presidential nominee for Senate-confirmed position shall meet the qualifications established by statute and by professional standards applicable to the position. Nominations of persons lacking minimum statutory qualifications shall be void ab initio, with the nomination subject to Watchdog Tribunal review upon challenge by any Senator or registered voter. (c) Disclosure Before Nomination. Every nominee for Senate-confirmed position shall complete full financial disclosure under Section 13F.20 standards before the nomination is formally submitted, with disclosures published on the Franklin Ledger. Nominations submitted before disclosure completion shall be deemed incomplete and shall not proceed to Senate consideration. (d) Nominee Conflicts of Interest. Nominees with material conflicts of interest regarding the position shall either divest the conflict before nomination proceeds or withdraw from consideration. Conflicts include: financial interests in entities regulated by the position; personal relationships with persons subject to the position's authority; prior advocacy for or against the position's mission inconsistent with faithful execution; and analogous conflicts. The Watchdog Tribunal shall review conflict determinations upon challenge. (e) Acting Officers Time Limits. Acting officers serving in Senate-confirmed positions without confirmation shall not serve for more than two hundred ten (210) days in the position, consistent with existing Federal Vacancies Reform Act standards. Attempts to extend acting service beyond this limit through repositioning, reassignment, or technical devices shall be void ab initio. (f) No Anti-Confirmation Circumvention. The President shall not structure appointments, reassignments, or position descriptions to avoid Senate confirmation where the Constitution or statute requires it. Attempts to circumvent confirmation through such devices shall be void ab initio and shall constitute Section 13 interference where connected to Amendment operations. (g) Independent Agency Appointment Limits. For appointments to independent agencies (those with structural independence from ordinary executive direction), the President shall respect the agency's independence by: (i) selecting appointees meeting statutory qualifications; (ii) respecting partisan balance requirements where established by statute; (iii) not selecting appointees based on commitments to take specific decisions; and (iv) not pressuring appointees after confirmation to take specific decisions. Violations shall constitute Section 13 interference. (h) Judicial Nominations. Federal judicial nominations shall meet the qualifications standards of Section 24.24(b) with additional requirements: (i) the American Bar Association or equivalent body's qualifications rating shall be published on the Franklin Ledger; (ii) disclosure of the nominee's prior positions on matters likely to come before the court; (iii) no commitment to decide specific types of cases in specific ways; and (iv) genuine Senate advice-and-consent without manipulation of Senate rules to accelerate or delay consideration in bad faith. 24.25 Removal Authority Limits. Presidential removal authority shall be constrained to prevent its use for corruption: (a) Inspector General Removal. Consistent with Section 13B.20 protections, no Inspector General shall be removed except upon: (i) written notice to Congress thirty (30) days before removal; (ii) specific documented cause (material misconduct, incapacity, or gross dereliction); (iii) Senate majority concurrence in the cause finding; and (iv) publication of cause on the Franklin Ledger. Removal without these requirements shall be void ab initio, with the IG reinstated to office and the President subject to Section 13 interference penalties. (b) Special Counsel Removal. Special Counsels appointed to investigate specific matters involving the President, the President's family, the President's administration, or close associates shall be removable only upon: (i) the same requirements as Inspector General removal under subsection (a); (ii) transfer of the investigation to an alternative independent prosecutor without disruption of work; (iii) preservation of all investigation records under Section 13B standards; and (iv) Watchdog Tribunal review of the removal for improper motive. (c) Independent Agency Heads. Heads of independent agencies protected by statute from at-will Presidential removal shall retain that protection. Attempts to remove such officials outside statutory cause shall be void ab initio. Where statutes are ambiguous regarding removal protection, the ambiguity shall be resolved in favor of independence for agencies created to be insulated from political control (federal reserve banks, independent regulatory commissions, civil service protected officials, and analogous positions). (d) Career Civil Service Protection. Career civil service personnel shall retain full Merit Systems Protection Board and analogous protections against political removal. Reclassification of career positions to political positions (so-called 'Schedule F' devices) shall be reviewed by the Watchdog Tribunal for improper motive, with reclassifications found to be for political removal purposes deemed void ab initio. (e) No Mass Firing for Political Purpose. Removals of ten (10) or more federal employees in a single action or coordinated sequence shall be reviewed by the Watchdog Tribunal for evidence of political purpose. Mass removals found to serve political rather than legitimate administrative purposes shall be void ab initio with affected employees reinstated. (f) Retaliatory Removal as Interference. Removal of any federal employee in retaliation for: (i) whistleblower disclosure; (ii) Section 13 interference reporting; (iii) protected refusal under Section 16.19; (iv) cooperation with Watchdog Tribunal, Hamilton Contingent, or State Attorneys General Council investigations; or (v) testimony before Congress, the Authority, or the Tribunal shall constitute Section 13 interference with Senior Official multipliers applied to the President personally. F. Agency Direction Limits 24.26 Agency Direction Limits. Presidential direction of federal agencies shall be constrained as follows: (a) No Direction of Specific Cases. The President shall not direct, influence, or interfere with: (i) specific Department of Justice prosecutorial decisions regarding which cases to prosecute or decline; (ii) specific Internal Revenue Service decisions regarding specific taxpayer audits or enforcement; (iii) specific Securities and Exchange Commission decisions regarding specific enforcement targets; (iv) specific Environmental Protection Agency decisions regarding specific enforcement actions; (v) specific Federal Election Commission decisions regarding specific investigations; or (vi) specific decisions of other agencies with respect to specific parties under their jurisdiction. The President may set general enforcement policies

and priorities; specific case decisions rest with agency professionals. (b) Retaliatory Enforcement as Interference. Directing federal agencies to enforce law against specific persons on the basis of: (i) political affiliation; (ii) exercise of First Amendment rights; (iii) cooperation with investigations of the President or the President's allies; (iv) whistleblower disclosure; or (v) membership in classes politically disfavored by the President shall constitute Section 13 interference with Senior Official multipliers. Enhanced penalties shall apply where the targeted person was specifically identified by name to agencies. (c) No Impeding of Enforcement. Directing federal agencies to decline enforcement against specific persons on the basis of political or personal relationship with the President shall constitute Section 13 interference and corruption under Section 13A. (d) General Policy Permitted. The President retains authority to set general enforcement priorities, allocate agency resources, establish policy frameworks, and direct agency attention to categories of matters. General policy is within legitimate Presidential authority; specific case interference is not. (e) Documentation of Communications. All communications between the President (or White House officials acting on Presidential direction) and: (i) the Department of Justice regarding specific matters; (ii) independent regulatory agencies regarding specific matters; or (iii) Inspector Generals regarding ongoing investigations shall be documented, with documentation preserved under Section 13B standards and subject to Watchdog Tribunal review. Failure to document such communications shall create presumption of improper direction. (f) Protected Agency Refusal. Agency heads and career officials may refuse direction that would violate this Section, with refusal protected under Section 13B.16 whistleblower framework. Agency heads refusing improper direction shall not face removal for the refusal itself. G. Transition and Post-Term Restrictions 24.27 Presidential Transition Restrictions. During the final period of a Presidential term, the following restrictions shall apply: (a) Final 90 Days General Restriction. During the final ninety (90) days of any Presidential term (whether after election loss, term expiration, or pending resignation), the President shall not: (i) make personnel appointments to positions whose terms extend beyond the incoming administration except as necessary for operational continuity; (ii) issue pardons except as permitted by Section 24.6; (iii) enter into executive agreements with foreign governments of significant substantive content; (iv) issue executive orders with effect extending beyond the outgoing administration; or (v) take other actions designed to constrain the incoming administration.

(b) Transition Cooperation. The outgoing President shall cooperate with the President-elect transition team in good faith, including: providing access to transition briefings, facility arrangements, personnel information, and pending decisions; refraining from undermining the transition; and delivering functional government to the incoming administration on the constitutional transition date. (c) Preservation of Records. Outgoing Presidential administration shall preserve all records under the Presidential Records Act and Section 13B standards, with no destruction, alteration, or removal beyond that permitted by law. Violations shall constitute Section 13B.11 evidence destruction with enhanced penalties for the President personally. (d) No Sabotage of Incoming Administration. The outgoing President shall not take actions designed to impair the incoming administration's ability to govern, including: rewriting agency rules with short-term effect that consume transition period; classifying records to prevent incoming access; directing agencies to take actions the incoming administration would reverse at cost of resources; or similar sabotage. Such actions shall be subject to Section 13 interference review. (e) Post-Term Continuing Obligations. Former Presidents shall remain subject to: Section 13F financial monitoring for ten (10) years post-office consistent with Section 13F provisions; continued prohibition on foreign representation consistent with existing law; continued classification obligations regarding protected information; and Watchdog Tribunal jurisdiction over conduct during the Presidency for statute of limitations periods applicable to interference offenses. H. Federal Resources and Personal Benefit 24.28 Federal Resources for Personal or Political Use. Beyond the Section 24.22 self-dealing prohibition, the following specific limits shall apply: (a) White House Event Restrictions. The White House and official Presidential residences shall not be used for: (i) political campaign events, fundraisers, or partisan political rallies; (ii) personal business meetings regarding the President's private financial interests; (iii) events primarily benefiting the President's family financial interests; or (iv) events whose primary purpose is personal rather than official. Official events combining ceremonial and political elements shall be evaluated by the Watchdog Tribunal for primary purpose upon challenge. (b) Federal Aircraft and Travel. Federal aircraft (Air Force One, VC-25, and analogous) and associated travel resources shall be used for official travel, with campaign travel permitted only with full cost reimbursement to the federal government at published fair-market rates. Combining official and campaign travel in single trips shall require clear separation of official versus campaign portions with proportional reimbursement. (c) Federal Personnel for Personal Benefit. Federal personnel (White House staff, military aides, Secret Service, and others) shall not be used for personal or family benefit beyond ordinary Presidential security and official function. Directing federal personnel to attend to private business matters, family personal matters unrelated to Presidential security, or campaign matters shall constitute Section 13A corruption. (d) Presidential Residences for Commercial Promotion. Neither the White House nor official Presidential residences shall be used as marketing, branding, or commercial promotion platforms for the President's private businesses or those of the President's family. Consumer products, properties, or services shall not be displayed, promoted, or marketed using Presidential platforms. (e) Presidential Appearances for Private Benefit. Presidential appearances, speeches, and public activities shall not be structured primarily to generate financial benefit for the President, the President's family, or Presidential donors. Appearances at private properties owned by the President or family members shall be evaluated for primary purpose; where the primary purpose is commercial rather than official, the appearance shall be deemed Section 24.22 self-dealing. (f) Enforcement Through Ordinary Oversight. Violations of this Section shall be enforced through ordinary oversight mechanisms: General Accounting Office audit; Inspector General referral; Watchdog Tribunal investigation; and Section 13A corruption prosecution where benefit thresholds are met. I. Immunity and Accountability 24.29 Presidential Immunity Limits. Recognizing that immunity doctrines can shield corruption from accountability: (a) No Immunity for Amendment Offenses. The President shall not enjoy any form of civil or criminal immunity for offenses under this Amendment, including but not limited to: Section 13 interference; Section 13A corruption; Section 13E refusal to vacate office; Section 16 violations including Section 16.12 treason; Section 18.6 Article V violations; Section 22 foreign interference; Section 24 limits on Presidential power; and any other offense created by this Amendment. Prosecution may proceed during or after Presidential term without immunity as a bar. (b) Post-Term Prosecution. Former Presidents may be prosecuted for conduct during their Presidency for any offense under this Amendment, subject to applicable statutes of limitations. The fact of having been President shall not constitute a bar to prosecution, a basis for dismissal, or an enhanced proof burden beyond that applicable to other defendants. (c) Tolling During Office. Statutes of limitations for offenses committed by a sitting President shall be tolled during the President's term of office, recognizing that prosecution of a sitting President may be impractical. Tolling preserves prosecutorial opportunity post-term.

(d) Civil Liability for Amendment Violations. Sitting and former Presidents may be civilly liable for Amendment violations to affected parties, with liability extending to compensatory damages, restitution under Section 13D framework, and punitive damages where the violation was willful. Civil liability is in addition to criminal prosecution, not in lieu of it. (e) No Self-Pardon, No Successor Pardon for Amendment Offenses. Consistent with Sections 24.3 and 24.5, no self-pardon shall be effective and no successor President shall have authority to pardon Amendment offenses. Successor pardon attempts for Amendment offenses shall be void ab initio. (f) International Extradition Cooperation. Where a former President flees United States jurisdiction to avoid Amendment accountability, the United States shall seek extradition through existing treaty mechanisms and shall not intervene to block extradition. Refusal to cooperate with extradition proceedings shall itself constitute Section 13 interference by whichever officials obstruct cooperation. 24.30 Communications Restrictions During Investigations. To prevent improper

Presidential influence over investigations: (a) No Communications with Investigators on Specific Cases. Where the Watchdog Tribunal, Hamilton Contingent, Inspector General, Special Counsel, or other investigative body is investigating the President, the President's family, or Presidential allies, the President shall not communicate with the investigating body regarding the specific investigation. Communications regarding general policy, resource needs, or operational matters unrelated to the specific investigation are permitted. (b) Witness Tampering Prohibition. The President shall not communicate with witnesses, subjects, targets, or cooperators in investigations of the President or Presidential allies in any manner that: (i) offers inducement for favorable testimony or non-cooperation; (ii) threatens adverse consequence for unfavorable testimony or cooperation; (iii) coordinates testimony among witnesses; or (iv) otherwise interferes with the investigation. Witness tampering shall constitute Section 13 interference with Senior Official multipliers and shall independently constitute federal witness tampering under existing criminal law. (c) Presidential Commentary on Pending Cases. The President's commentary on pending investigations shall be subject to the following constraints: (i) factual statements about the President's own conduct are permitted; (ii) denial of wrongdoing is permitted; (iii) general criticism of investigations as process matters is permitted; but (iv) statements intended to intimidate witnesses, investigators, or jurors shall constitute Section 13 interference; and (v) false statements about material facts in pending investigations shall be subject to Section 13 framework. (d) Executive Privilege Limitations. Executive privilege shall not be invoked to shield: (i) evidence of crimes; (ii) evidence of Amendment offenses; (iii) communications demonstrating Presidential interference with investigations; (iv) communications with non-governmental parties regarding investigations; or (v) communications occurring outside official Presidential duties. Overbroad privilege claims shall be subject to Watchdog Tribunal review with adverse inferences permitted where privilege appears invoked in bad faith. (e) Document and Record Preservation During Investigations. Upon initiation of any investigation covered by this Section, the President and all White House staff shall be under immediate Section 13B preservation obligations with respect to documents, communications, and records potentially relevant to the investigation. Destruction or alteration shall constitute Section 13B.11 evidence destruction with enhanced penalties. (f) Private Counsel Communications. The President's communications with personal legal counsel regarding personal legal matters shall retain attorney-client privilege consistent with ordinary law.

However, communications with government counsel acting in official capacity do not carry personal attorney-client privilege and shall not be withheld from proper investigations on that basis. J. Presidential Self-Investigation Framework 24.31 Foundational Principle. A sitting President who is the target, subject, or person of interest in an investigation for Amendment offenses, federal crimes, or other misconduct cannot serve as a check on that investigation. The Amendment establishes the following comprehensive framework ensuring investigation proceeds regardless of the sitting President's use or attempted use of executive authority to obstruct. No Confidence under Section 5 remains the primary ultimate remedy for a corrupt sitting President, but investigation operates during the process leading to No Confidence, and investigation does not await removal. This Section supplements, without displacing, the Communications Restrictions of Section 24.30 and the general Pardon and Executive Order limits elsewhere in this Section 24. 24.32 Hamilton Contingent Authority Independent of Department of Justice. To ensure investigation capacity cannot be eliminated through Executive control of DOJ: (a) Full Investigation Authority. The Hamilton Contingent, once operational, shall have full authority to investigate sitting Presidents for Amendment offenses, with authority operating independently of Department of Justice direction, Presidential direction, or Attorney General supervision. (b) No DOJ Supervision. The Hamilton Contingent shall not be subject to Department of Justice supervision for Amendment-related investigations. Attorney General directives, Solicitor General positions, and Office of Legal Counsel opinions do not bind Hamilton Contingent prosecutorial decisions on Amendment matters. Directives contrary to Hamilton Contingent authority shall be void ab initio.

(c) Phase One State AG Council Authority. During Phase One before the Hamilton Contingent is operational, the State Attorneys General Council under Section 19.5.0.5.2 exercises comparable authority for investigating sitting Presidents, with two-thirds (2/3) supermajority Council authorization required for sitting-President investigations reflecting the gravity of the inquiry. (d) Independent Grand Jury Authority. The Hamilton Contingent may convene federal grand juries to investigate a sitting President for Amendment offenses, with grand jury authority operating outside the ordinary DOJ grand jury framework for these investigations. Grand jury secrecy rules apply without modification; presentment decisions rest with the grand jury. (e) Subpoena Enforcement. Hamilton Contingent subpoenas to a sitting President or to Executive Branch personnel carry the same legal force as any federal subpoena, enforceable through federal courts with Section 17C and Section 13H alternative pathways available where federal courts are captured. No Presidential directive may instruct subordinates to disregard properly issued subpoenas. (f) No Self-Recusal Gate. Investigation does not require Attorney General recusal, Special Counsel appointment, or any other Executive Branch gating process. The Hamilton Contingent (or State AG Council during Phase One) operates directly, without requiring Executive permission. 24.33 Career Investigator and Staff Insulation. To protect investigators from Presidential retaliation: (a) Career Personnel Tenure. Career federal investigators (Federal Bureau of Investigation agents, Inspectors General, career Department of Justice attorneys, and analogous career personnel) working on investigations involving the sitting President shall have Section 1.2 career personnel protection against Presidential removal, reassignment, demotion, or retaliation during the active investigation period and for three (3) years thereafter. (b) Hamilton Contingent Staff Protection. Hamilton Contingent staff working on investigations of the sitting President are not subject to Presidential removal, budget reduction, reassignment, or other adverse action during active investigation. Staffing decisions rest with the Contingent's Director per Section 13C. (c) Attorney General and Senior DOJ Direction. The Attorney General and senior DOJ officials may be directed by the President in ordinary Executive matters, but Presidential direction to terminate, reduce, or redirect an investigation involving the President, Presidential family, or Presidential allies shall constitute Section 13 interference. Attorney General or senior DOJ cooperation in such direction shall be separately prosecutable with Senior Official multipliers. (d) Whistleblower Protection Enhanced. Career personnel disclosing Presidential obstruction of investigation receive full Section 13B.16 whistleblower protection with enhanced protections reflecting the constitutional-scale nature of sitting-President investigation integrity. Disclosure may be made to the Watchdog Tribunal, Hamilton Contingent, State AG Council, or congressional oversight committees. (e) Protected Refusal. Career personnel may refuse unlawful Presidential or Attorney General directives regarding investigations under the Section 17 protected refusal framework. Career employment shall be protected; adverse action for protected refusal shall constitute Section 13 interference. (f) No Chilling Effect Through Investigation of Investigators. Using investigative tools (surveillance, leak investigations, polygraph mandates, security clearance reviews) against career investigators as retaliation for their investigation of the sitting President shall constitute Section 13 interference with doubled Senior Official multipliers reflecting the meta-obstruction character. 24.34 Executive Privilege — Narrow

Application in Self-Investigation. Supplementing Section 24.30(d): (a) Review Authority. Assertions of executive privilege in investigation of sitting President shall be reviewed by the Watchdog Tribunal, not by the Executive Branch itself. Where Tribunal is not yet operational, review proceeds through federal courts with Section 17C alternative pathways. (b) In Camera Review. Where privilege is asserted for specific documents, the reviewing authority may conduct in camera review to determine applicability without exposing privileged material unnecessarily. Where documents are determined non-privileged, they shall be produced without further delay. (c) Overbroad Claims. Overbroad privilege claims intended to shield Amendment offense evidence shall result in: (i) categorical rejection with adverse inference; (ii) Section 13 interference prosecution for those directing the claims; (iii) Section 13B.11 evidence concealment treatment where claims obstruct evidence access. (d) No Blanket Immunity. Executive privilege is a qualified, document-specific doctrine requiring particularized justification. Blanket refusals to cooperate with investigation under asserted privilege shall be rejected as facially invalid. Each document or communication requires specific privilege basis. (e) Precedent Honored. This Section operates consistently with United States v. Nixon (1974) and progeny, with Amendment-specific narrowing to foreclose hostile expansion of privilege beyond established bounds. 24.35 Classification and National Security Response. To prevent misuse of classification to shield corruption: (a) No Unilateral Classification of Corruption Evidence. A sitting President under investigation shall not unilaterally classify evidence of personal conduct, corruption, or Amendment offenses. Classification actions during active investigation affecting such evidence shall be void ab initio unless supported by: (i)

specific documented national security findings independent of personal concealment motive; (ii) Academic Integrity Commission independent verification of national security basis; or (iii) Watchdog Tribunal concurrence. (b) Declassification Authority. The Watchdog Tribunal may declassify material improperly classified to shield corruption, with declassification authority operating regardless of Presidential objection. Declassification decisions published on Franklin Ledger with factual basis. (c) National Security Tools Protection. National security letters, Foreign Intelligence Surveillance Act applications, and other national security investigative tools shall not be used to investigate, surveil, or otherwise target persons cooperating with investigations of the sitting President. Such use would constitute Section 13 interference with Senior Official multipliers. (d) Classified Evidence Access for Investigators.

Hamilton Contingent investigators and State AG Council prosecutors shall have access to classified information relevant to sitting-President investigation, with security clearance processing not subject to Presidential approval for this purpose. Watchdog Tribunal clearance-issuance authority applies where Executive Branch clearance processes are obstructed. (e) Classified Proceedings Framework. Criminal proceedings involving classified evidence against sitting or former Presidents may proceed under Classified Information Procedures Act procedures adapted for Amendment proceedings, with classification review by Watchdog Tribunal rather than by Executive Branch. The President cannot self-invoke the state secrets privilege to bar his or her own prosecution. (f) Pre-Classification Evidence. Evidence that existed before any classification action cannot be retroactively classified to bar investigation access. Classification actions with such apparent purpose shall be void ab initio. 24.36 Enhanced Evidence Preservation. Supplementing Section 24.30(e): (a) Automatic Preservation at Investigation Opening. Upon opening of any investigation into sitting President's conduct, automatic preservation orders attach without requiring separate judicial issuance to: all Presidential records; all White House staff communications; all Executive Branch documents potentially relevant to the investigation; all communications between the President and any person regarding matters within investigation scope. (b) Independent Archival. Critical evidence in Presidential self-investigation shall be archived independently of Executive Branch control through: (i) backup copies at Academic Integrity Commission; (ii) Franklin Ledger cryptographic timestamps of document existence; (iii) State AG Council coordinated independent storage; (iv) Hamilton Contingent independent storage. Independent archival prevents single-point evidence destruction.

(c) Escalated Destruction Penalties. Destruction of evidence in Presidential self-investigation shall constitute Section 13B.11 evidence destruction with enhanced penalties. Where destruction affects national security matters, foreign corruption evidence, or evidence of grave crimes, destruction may be charged as Section 16 treason where the destruction aids foreign adversary or constitutes insurrection against constitutional order. (d) Presidential Records Act Coordination. This Section supplements the Presidential Records Act. Any PRA disputes during active investigation shall be resolved in favor of preservation and investigation access. PRA custody disputes shall not delay investigation. (e) Staff Preservation Obligations. White House staff, Executive Branch personnel, contractors, and other persons with access to potentially relevant evidence have individual preservation obligations under Section 13B. Compliance by subordinate personnel shall not be directed by the sitting President; Presidential direction to subordinates to destroy evidence shall create personal liability for both the President and any complying subordinate. 24.37 Enhanced Witness Protection. Supplementing Section 24.30(b): (a) Federal Protection Extended. Witnesses in sitting-President investigations receive federal protection equivalent to Congressional witnesses, with protection extending during investigation and for not less than three (3) years after conclusion. (b) Employment Protection Enhanced. Federal employee witnesses protected against Presidential removal, reassignment, or retaliation under Section 1.2 framework with enhanced protections reflecting sitting-President investigation stakes. Protected Refusal framework applies where witnesses must refuse unlawful Presidential directives. (c) Family and Associate Protection. Immediate family members and professional associates of witnesses protected against retaliation by Presidential direction. Retaliation constitutes Section 13 interference with enhanced penalties. Retaliation through federal agency action (tax audits, security clearance revocation, regulatory investigation, business contract cancellation) receives the same treatment as direct personal retaliation. (d) Non-Federal Witness Protection. Witnesses not covered by federal employment shall have access to witness protection programs, accommodations for cooperation without retaliation, and legal protection against retaliation lawsuits brought by those allied with the sitting President. Civil litigation designed to harass witnesses shall be subject to heightened scrutiny with fee-shifting authority. (e) International Witnesses. Foreign witnesses providing evidence against sitting President protected against Presidential use of State Department, intelligence, or diplomatic pressure to intimidate or silence. Such pressure constitutes Section 13 interference and may constitute Section 22 foreign interference framework violations where the Presidential action coordinates with foreign powers to target witnesses. (f) Anonymous Tip Protection. Anonymous tips to Hamilton Contingent or State AG Council regarding Presidential conduct protected from disclosure pressure; Presidential efforts to identify anonymous tipsters constitute Section 13 interference. 24.38 Interim Protective Measures by Watchdog Tribunal. Short of No Confidence or impeachment removal: (a) Tribunal Order Authority. The Watchdog Tribunal shall have authority to issue interim orders during active investigation of sitting President, including: (i) specific prohibitions on Presidential conduct that would obstruct investigation; (ii) required preservation of evidence beyond automatic preservation; (iii) required compliance with subpoena; (iv) required cooperation by Executive Branch personnel; (v) limitations on specific Presidential actions related to the investigation matter (for example, halt on pardons of co-conspirators pending investigation conclusion). (b) Federal Court Enforcement. Watchdog Tribunal orders are enforceable in federal courts through ordinary injunctive framework, with Section 17C and Section 13H alternative pathways where federal courts are captured. (c) Suspension from Specific Duties. Where conduct is so grave and evidence so clear that continued exercise of specific Presidential authority would constitute ongoing interference, the Watchdog Tribunal may order temporary suspension from specific Presidential duties narrowly scoped to prevent ongoing obstruction. Such suspensions do not constitute removal; they are protective measures against specific ongoing obstruction pending resolution through No Confidence, impeachment, or investigation conclusion. (d) Narrow Scope Required. Section 24.38(c) suspensions shall be narrowly tailored to the specific obstruction concern. Blanket suspensions from Presidential authority generally are not authorized; removal from all Presidential authority requires No Confidence, impeachment, or 25th Amendment procedures. (e) No 25th Amendment Displacement. Nothing in this Section shall supplant Article II, Section 1 succession or the Twenty-Fifth Amendment operation. Section 24.38 suspensions are narrow protective measures, not invocations of the 25th Amendment's incapacity procedures. (f) Public Publication. Interim measures shall be published on the Franklin Ledger with factual basis and scope, ensuring transparency of the protective framework in operation. Confidentiality exceptions only for narrowly defined active investigation integrity concerns. (g) Tribunal Composition Protection. Tribunal members issuing protective orders against sitting President protected under Section 21 framework, with enhanced security during active Presidential investigation matters.

24.39 International Investigation Coordination. For Amendment offenses with foreign elements: (a) Foreign Evidence Preservation. Foreign evidence of Presidential Amendment offenses shall be preserved through: (i) Hamilton Contingent foreign law enforcement coordination; (ii) State AG Council international coordination; (iii) Academic Integrity Commission international partners; (iv) preservation requests through established Mutual Legal Assistance Treaties. (b) Foreign Jurisdiction Cooperation. United States cooperation with foreign investigations of current or former Presidents shall proceed under established treaty frameworks, with the sitting President disabled from using State Department, Attorney General, or diplomatic authority to obstruct legitimate foreign investigation requests regarding personal Presidential conduct. (c) International Witness Protection. Foreign witnesses subject to

Presidential retaliation pressure (State Department visa actions, diplomatic pressure, economic sanctions affecting the witness's country unfavorably, intelligence operations targeting witnesses) protected through Section 22 foreign interference framework adapted to shield witnesses from Presidential rather than foreign-actor harm. (d) Interpol and Foreign Law Enforcement. Hamilton Contingent and State AG Council may coordinate directly with Interpol, foreign law enforcement agencies, and foreign judicial authorities regarding sitting-President investigations, with Presidential Attorney General or State Department direction not binding on such coordination. (e) Extradition Availability. Former Presidents shall be available for extradition to foreign jurisdictions for Amendment-relevant foreign crimes consistent with United States treaty obligations, with no sovereign immunity claims available for personal criminal conduct. 24.40 Pardon Limitations During Active Investigation. Supplementing Section 24.5: (a) Co-Conspirator Pardons Voidable. Pardons issued during active investigation to persons who are, or may reasonably be, co-conspirators, witnesses, subjects, or targets in the same investigation shall be voidable by Watchdog Tribunal within thirty (30) days of issuance where the pardon would obstruct the investigation. Review standard: whether the pardon's reasonably foreseeable effect was obstruction of investigation rather than genuine exercise of clemency. (b) Pattern Pardons Enhanced Scrutiny. Patterns of pardons issued during active investigation creating apparent obstruction shall be reviewed under this Section with enhanced scrutiny. Multiple pardons of related persons create presumption of obstructive intent, rebuttable by specific showing of genuine clemency basis. (c) Pre-Resignation Pardons. Pardons issued by a President in connection with resignation or impending removal to avoid investigation or to shield allies from investigation shall be subject to this Section. Resignation or removal does not launder the intent behind prior pardon actions. (d) Dangling Pardons. Communications with potential witnesses suggesting future pardon in exchange for non-cooperation or favorable testimony shall constitute Section 13 interference and witness tampering, regardless of whether the pardon is ultimately issued. Promises not fulfilled remain prosecutable. (e) No Self-Pardon. The Section 24.3 self-pardon prohibition applies absolutely; no sitting or former President may self-pardon for Amendment offenses, federal crimes, or otherwise. Purported self-pardons void ab initio. 24.41 Parallel Proceedings Framework. Consistent with Section 25A.8: (a) Investigation and No Confidence Parallel. Investigation of sitting President proceeds in parallel with any No Confidence proceeding under Section 5. Neither proceeding pauses the other. No Confidence does not require completed investigation; investigation does not require completed No Confidence or await its conclusion. (b) Investigation and Impeachment Parallel. Investigation proceeds in parallel with any impeachment proceeding. Investigation findings may inform impeachment; impeachment findings may inform investigation; neither is bound by or waiting for the other. (c) Multiple Simultaneous Proceedings. Where multiple proceedings are simultaneously active (investigation, impeachment, and No Confidence), each proceeds under its own procedures. Coordination is encouraged but not required. Each proceeding's conclusion is its own event, not triggering or mooting others except as specifically provided. (d) Evidence Sharing Across Proceedings. Evidence developed in one proceeding is available for use in others where relevant and consistent with procedural protections. Classification restrictions, witness confidentiality, and other protections apply consistently across proceedings. (e) No Forum Shopping. Multiple parallel proceedings do not permit the sitting President to shop for favorable forum; each proceeds on its own terms. 24.42 Post-Removal Continuation. To prevent Presidential removal from constituting escape from accountability: (a) Investigation Continues Post-Removal. Investigation of a President for Amendment offenses continues after removal through any means — No Confidence, impeachment, resignation, end of term, or 25th Amendment procedures. Removal does not moot investigation. (b) Hamilton Contingent Retained Jurisdiction. The Hamilton Contingent retains jurisdiction over investigation of former Presidents for Amendment offenses occurring during their Presidency, with no Presidential immunity claims available

post-removal for Amendment offenses. The Section 24.29 immunity limits apply in full post-removal. (c) Criminal Prosecution Available. Post-removal criminal prosecution for Amendment offenses proceeds under ordinary statute of limitations extended where investigation was actively obstructed by Presidential action during tenure. Section 8 permanent disqualification flows from conviction. (d) Asset Recovery Available. Section 13D asset recovery proceeds against former Presidents for assets obtained through Amendment offenses, with family member and trust vehicle treatment per Section 13D. Post-removal wealth transfers to shield assets constitute Section 13B evidence obstruction and Section 13D fraudulent transfer analysis applies. (e) No Self-Pardon Rescue. A former President shall not have self-pardon shield under Section 24.3. Purported self-pardons are void; investigation and prosecution proceed without impediment. (f) Cooperation in Foreign Prosecution. Former Presidents shall be extradited or otherwise made available to foreign prosecutors for Amendment-relevant foreign crimes, consistent with treaty obligations and Section 24.39. Post-removal flight to non-extradition jurisdictions may itself constitute Section 13B flight from prosecution with enhanced penalties upon any subsequent return. (g) Succession Consequences. Successor Presidents shall not have authority to pardon former Presidents for Amendment offenses under Section 24.5. Attempts to do so are void ab initio and constitute Section 13 interference by the successor. (h) Historical Accountability. Investigation findings, prosecution outcomes, and consequence impositions shall be published on the Franklin Ledger as permanent historical record, ensuring that constitutional accountability has lasting public documentation regardless of political shifts in subsequent administrations.

Section 25. Limits on the Supreme Court and Federal Judiciary

Key terms in this Section: • "Senior Justice" — A Supreme Court Justice who has completed an eighteen-year term of active service and has transitioned to senior status, with rights to sit by designation on Courts of Appeals and other lower federal courts. • "Shadow Docket" — The practice of the Supreme Court issuing emergency orders, stays, injunctions, or similar rulings without full briefing, oral argument, or signed written opinions.

• "The Watchdog Tribunal" — The body established under Section 21 for enforcement of anti-corruption provisions. 25.1 Foundational Principle. The Supreme Court of the United States holds a foundational constitutional role as the ultimate interpreter of federal law and as a coequal branch of the constitutional order established by Article III of the Constitution. This Amendment preserves that role in full. The provisions of this Section address specific structural concerns identified through operational experience — lifetime tenure without term limits, evolving ethical standards, and accountability mechanisms that have not kept pace with the Court's expanded role — and establish reforms that strengthen rather than diminish the Court's essential function. The Supreme Court's ethical standards shall match or exceed those of lower federal courts. The following provisions shall therefore apply to the Supreme Court of the United States and, where specified, to the federal judiciary generally, to ensure that the Court serves the constitutional order and the People from whom its authority ultimately derives. A. Supreme Court Term Limits 25.2 Eighteen-Year Terms. Every Justice of the Supreme Court appointed after the ratification of this Amendment shall serve a single term of eighteen (18) years of active service. Upon completion of an eighteen-year active term, a Justice shall transition to Senior Justice status pursuant to Section

25.5. 25.3 Staggered Cycle. Appointments to the Supreme Court shall be staggered to produce one new appointment every two (2) years, resulting in nine Justices serving staggered eighteen-year terms. The first new appointment following ratification shall occur upon the next vacancy on the Court, and subsequent appointments shall follow the staggered cycle. If multiple vacancies occur simultaneously during the transition period, appointments shall be made in staggered order with overlapping but distinct eighteen-year terms to restore the cycle. 25.3.1 Transition Cycle Establishment. The staggered cycle shall formally commence with the first appointment made after Ratification. During the grandfathering period under Section 25.4, as current Justices retire or transition to Senior status, their replacements shall be appointed to terms designed to achieve the target steady-state cycle of one appointment every two (2) years. Specifically: (a) The first post-Ratification appointment shall be made to an eighteen (18) year term; (b) Subsequent appointments during the transition shall be made to compressed initial terms, in a sequence determined by the Authority upon Liberty Bell Initiative and published upon the Ledger, with terms of approximately sixteen (16), fourteen (14), twelve (12), ten (10), eight (8), six (6), four (4), and two (2) years respectively, adjusted as necessary to synchronize with actual vacancy dates;

(c) Once all nine (9) seats have turned over at least once following Ratification, the full eighteen-year (18-year) staggered cycle shall take effect, with each seat thereafter holding an eighteen-year term; (d) If the Inaugural Referendum under Section 19A passes, causing all Supreme Court seats to be vacated simultaneously, the staggered cycle shall commence with the new nine appointments receiving terms of eighteen (18), sixteen (16), fourteen (14), twelve (12), ten (10), eight (8), six (6), four (4), and two (2) years respectively, with seat-term assignments made by lottery at the time of initial appointment and published upon the Ledger; (e) This compression transition ensures the staggered cycle achieves steady-state regardless of how the Court is initially reconstituted, and prevents any Justice appointed during the transition from disadvantage relative to subsequent appointees with full eighteen-year terms. 25.4 Grandfathering of Current Justices. Justices serving on the Supreme Court at the moment of ratification shall not be subject to the eighteen-year term limit and shall continue to serve under the terms of their original appointments. The staggered-cycle transition of Section 25.3 shall operate only with respect to appointments made after ratification. 25.5 Senior Justice Status. A Justice who completes an eighteen-year active term shall automatically assume Senior Justice status, with the following rights and obligations: (a) continued receipt of full Justice salary for life, protecting judicial independence; (b) the right to sit by designation on any United States Court of Appeals or District Court, subject to assignment by the Chief Justice or by the Judicial Conference; (c) recusal from all Supreme Court cases; (d) continued ethical obligations and Watchdog Tribunal jurisdiction; and (e) voluntary transition to full retirement at any time. Senior Justice status preserves judicial experience for the federal bench while opening Supreme Court seats for regular turnover. 25.5.1 Chief Justice Transition. The Chief Justice of the United States shall be subject to the same eighteen-year (18-year) term limit and Senior Justice transition as Associate Justices under Sections 25.2 and 25.5. Upon the Chief Justice's transition to Senior Justice status, the senior-most remaining active Supreme Court Justice by date of appointment shall serve as Acting Chief Justice until a new Chief Justice is nominated by the President and confirmed by the Senate pursuant to Article II of the Constitution. The Senior Justice status of a former Chief Justice shall carry the same rights and obligations as Senior Associate Justices, with no special privileges or additional authority. Assignment authority for Senior Justices to sit on lower courts shall pass to the new Chief Justice upon confirmation. 25.6 Protection from Term-Length Manipulation. No Congress, President, or other body shall alter the eighteen-year term, the staggered cycle, or the Senior Justice provisions of this Section. Any attempt to do so shall be void ab initio and shall constitute interference under Section 13.

B. Authority Integrity Review of Supreme Court Nominations 25.6.1 Foundational Principle. Supreme Court Justices serve eighteen-year terms and shape constitutional interpretation for generations. The ordinary Article II process — Presidential nomination and Senate confirmation — is preserved in full under this Amendment. However, because the corruption that necessitated this Amendment demonstrated that both the Presidency and the Senate can be captured by corrupt interests, this Section establishes a final integrity backstop: the three bodies of the Authority shall conduct an independent integrity review of every Supreme Court nominee after Senate confirmation, providing a last line of defense against the elevation of corrupt or compromised individuals to the nation's highest court. This review is strictly limited to integrity grounds and shall not become a mechanism for ideological screening. 25.6.2 Scope of Review. Authority Integrity Review under this Section shall apply exclusively to nominees for: (a) Associate Justice of the Supreme Court of the United States; (b) Chief Justice of the United States. 25.6.3 Non-Applicability to Other Federal Judges. Authority Integrity Review shall not apply to nominees for any other federal judicial office, including United States Courts of Appeals, United

States District Courts, the Court of International Trade, the Court of Federal Claims, Bankruptcy Courts, Magistrate Judges, or any other Article I or Article III tribunal. Nominees to these courts shall proceed under ordinary Article II procedures without Authority involvement. 25.6.4 Timing. Authority Integrity Review shall commence automatically upon the United States Senate's vote to confirm a Supreme Court nominee. The Review Window shall be thirty (30) calendar days from the date of Senate confirmation. 25.6.5 Silence as Approval. If the Authority has not affirmatively rejected a confirmed nominee within thirty (30) days of Senate confirmation, the nominee shall be deemed approved by operation of this Section and shall be commissioned by the President in accordance with Article II, Section 3 of the Constitution. Silence is treated as approval to prevent indefinite delay of judicial appointments. 25.6.6 Full Investigative Authority. During the Review Window, the Authority shall have full investigative authority with respect to the nominee, including: (a) Financial review, including review of tax returns, asset disclosures, and financial transactions consistent with standards applied to other Covered Persons under Section 13F; (b) Background investigation into the nominee's professional history, relationships, affiliations, and public record;

(c) Compulsion of testimony from the nominee, witnesses, or other relevant persons, subject to ordinary privileges including Fifth Amendment protections; (d) Review of documents and records, subject to ordinary privileges and protections; (e) Public hearings on integrity concerns raised during the Review Window, conducted with due process protections for the nominee; (f) Access to existing federal investigative files on the nominee, subject to classification protocols; (g) Coordination with the Hamilton Contingent for specialized corruption investigation support where relevant. 25.6.7 Strictly Limited Grounds for Rejection. The Authority may reject a nominee only upon clear and convincing evidence of one or more of the following integrity grounds: (a) Corruption: evidence of corrupt conduct, including bribery, self-dealing, abuse of prior office, or unjust enrichment; (b) Conflicts of Interest: undisclosed or unresolvable material conflicts of interest that would compromise judicial impartiality; (c) Foreign Influence: evidence of inappropriate foreign government influence, foreign financial entanglement, or foreign loyalty that would compromise independent judgment; (d) Integrity Violations: serious ethical violations in prior legal or professional conduct, including dishonesty under oath, fraud, or material misrepresentation; (e) Material Failure to Disclose: knowing failure to disclose material information during the nomination and confirmation process; (f) Prior Conduct Disqualifying Under

This Amendment: conduct that would disqualify the nominee under Section 8 Special Eligibility Panel standards applied to Removed Officials. 25.6.8 Prohibited Grounds for Rejection. The Authority shall NOT reject a nominee based on: (a) Judicial philosophy, legal ideology, or constitutional interpretation methodology (originalist, textualist, living constitutionalist, pragmatist, or otherwise); (b) Political party affiliation or political views; (c) Policy positions or views expressed in scholarship, advocacy, or prior judicial opinions; (d) Religious beliefs, practices, or affiliations, consistent with Article VI religious test prohibition;

(e) Race, ethnicity, national origin, sex, gender, sexual orientation, or other protected characteristics; (f) Association with particular political movements, ideologies, or interest groups absent evidence of corrupt conduct; (g) The President or Senate majority that selected or confirmed the nominee. 25.6.9 Liberty Bell Initiative Standard. Any rejection by the Authority under this Section shall require Liberty Bell Initiative — separate concurrence of all three bodies under Section 17.22. Unless all three bodies of the Authority independently conclude that integrity grounds for rejection exist by clear and convincing evidence, the nominee shall be deemed approved. This high bar reflects the serious nature of rejecting a Senate-confirmed Supreme Court nominee and prevents any single body from unilaterally blocking appointments. 25.6.10 Published Reasoning Required. Any rejection under this Section shall be accompanied by: (a) A public written determination, published upon the Franklin Ledger within seventy-two (72) hours of the rejection decision; (b) Detailed findings of fact supporting each ground for rejection; (c) Identification of the specific integrity grounds under Section 25.6.7 relied upon; (d) Explanation demonstrating that rejection is based on Section 25.6.7 grounds and not on prohibited grounds under Section 25.6.8; (e) Dissenting statements from any bodies or members not concurring; (f) All evidence relied upon, subject to appropriate redaction of classified or genuinely privileged material. 25.6.11 Effect of Rejection. Upon Authority rejection of a confirmed nominee: (a) The nominee shall not receive a Presidential commission and shall not assume the office of Justice; (b) The President may nominate a new candidate for the vacancy, restarting the Article II process; (c) The rejected nominee may be re-nominated for the same or different vacancy only upon the Authority's affirmative finding that the grounds for prior rejection have been resolved; (d) The vacancy shall remain open until a new nominee successfully completes both Senate confirmation and Authority Integrity Review. 25.6.12 Review of Authority Determinations. A rejected nominee may challenge an Authority rejection on the grounds that it was based on prohibited grounds under Section 25.6.8, or on clearly erroneous factual findings, through the following review: (a) Petition for review filed with the Watchdog Tribunal within thirty (30) days of the rejection determination; (b) Tribunal review under a clear-error standard for factual findings and de novo review for the question whether rejection was based on prohibited grounds; (c) Tribunal determination by two-thirds (2/3) supermajority within sixty (60) days of petition filing; (d) Tribunal authority to either affirm the rejection, remand to the Authority with specific direction, or void the rejection upon finding that it was based on prohibited grounds; (e) Tribunal determination shall be final and published upon the Franklin Ledger. 25.6.13 No Retroactive Application. This Section shall apply only to nominees confirmed by the Senate after ratification of this Amendment. Sitting Justices at the moment of ratification shall not be subject to Authority Integrity Review, consistent with the grandfathering provisions of Section 25.4. 25.6.14 Protection Against Abuse. To prevent weaponization of this Section: (a) Liberty Bell Initiative requirement (Section 25.6.9) ensures no single body can block appointments; (b) Strict limitation to integrity grounds (Section 25.6.7) and prohibition of ideological grounds (Section 25.6.8) prevents ideological screening; (c) Thirty-day silence-as-approval default (Section 25.6.5) prevents indefinite delay; (d) Watchdog Tribunal review (Section 25.6.12) provides check against Authority overreach; (e) Published reasoning requirement (Section 25.6.10) ensures accountability for rejection decisions; (f) Any Authority member found to have participated in rejection based on prohibited grounds shall be subject to removal under Section 17 procedures and potential prosecution under Section 13. 25.6.15 Article V Protection. The provisions of this Section shall be protected under the Article V protection established in Sections 18.6.1 and 18.6.2. No act of Congress, executive order, judicial ruling, or state action shall evade, diminish, or nullify the Authority Integrity Review framework established herein. 25.6.16 Foundational Commitment. The People, in ratifying this Amendment, affirm that the Supreme Court of the United States shall be staffed by Justices of unimpeachable integrity. The Authority Integrity Review exists not to substitute the Authority's judgment for the President's or the Senate's on matters of judicial

philosophy or political preference — those matters remain entirely within the ordinary democratic process — but to provide a final, focused check against corruption, foreign influence, and integrity violations that the ordinary process might miss, might overlook, or might itself be corrupted to ignore. The highest court must be held to the highest integrity standard. C. Age Limits for the

Federal Judiciary 25.7 Supreme Court Appointment Age Limit. No person shall be appointed to active service on the Supreme Court of the United States after reaching the age of sixty-eight (68) years. A person appointed before reaching age sixty-eight may complete the eighteen-year term notwithstanding reaching age sixty-eight or higher during such term, subject to the mandatory health evaluation provisions of Section 25.7.1 through 25.7.9 and the mandatory Senior Status provisions of Section 25.8. 25.7.1 Mandatory Annual Health Evaluations. Beginning on the sixtieth (60th) birthday of any active Justice of the Supreme Court, and annually thereafter until the Justice transitions to Senior Justice status, retirement, or leaves office by any means, the Justice shall undergo a comprehensive annual health evaluation administered under the authority of the three bodies of the Independent Tripartite Oversight Authority. The evaluation shall be scheduled within thirty (30) days of the Justice's birthday each year. 25.7.2 Scope of Evaluation. Each annual evaluation shall comprehensively assess the Justice's fitness for the duties of active Supreme Court service, including: (a) Cognitive evaluation: assessment of memory, executive function, reasoning ability, language comprehension, attention, and decision-making capacity, administered by a licensed clinical neuropsychologist or equivalent specialist using standard validated instruments; (b) Physical evaluation: comprehensive medical examination assessing general health, cardiovascular function, neurological function, mobility, stamina, and any conditions materially affecting the physical capacity to perform judicial duties; (c) Mental health evaluation: assessment by a licensed psychiatrist or clinical psychologist of mental and emotional capacity to perform judicial duties, including evaluation for conditions that may affect judgment, temperament, or capacity to deliberate impartially. 25.7.3 Authority Responsibility. The three bodies of the Authority shall jointly administer the annual health evaluation program through Liberty Bell Initiative, with the following divisions of responsibility: (a) The Academic Integrity Commission shall identify, vet, and maintain a roster of qualified evaluating physicians from accredited academic medical centers, with no fewer than five (5) qualified evaluators per specialty (cognitive, physical, mental health) at any time;

(b) The Citizens' Oversight Board shall coordinate scheduling, logistics, and administrative compliance, and shall ensure citizen oversight of the evaluation process without access to specific medical findings; (c) The State Elections Council shall provide budget oversight and geographic coordination for evaluations conducted outside Washington, D.C.; (d) Evaluator assignment for each Justice shall be made by randomized selection from the qualified roster, with the Justice receiving reasonable notice and opportunity to object for conflict-of-interest reasons (for example, prior doctor-patient relationship creating a conflict). Objections shall be resolved by the Authority through Liberty Bell Initiative, with a new randomized assignment if the objection is sustained. 25.7.4 Evaluator Independence. Evaluating physicians shall: (a) Be licensed in good standing in their state of practice; (b) Be board-certified in their specialty; (c) Have no current or recent (within five years) professional or personal relationship with the Justice being evaluated; (d) Have no current or recent (within ten years) employment by the federal government or any federal political party, campaign, or political entity; (e) Disclose all potential conflicts of interest to the Authority before accepting the assignment; (f) Sign a confidentiality commitment protecting the Justice's medical privacy consistent with this Section; (g) Receive compensation at a rate set by the Authority, funded from the constitutional appropriation under Section 11.3. 25.7.5 Confidentiality of Medical Results. The detailed medical findings of each annual evaluation shall remain strictly confidential, with access limited to: (a) The Justice being evaluated, who shall receive the complete report; (b) The evaluating physicians, maintaining ordinary medical privacy standards; (c) A designated secure repository maintained by the Academic Integrity Commission, accessible only upon specific findings of unfitness under Section 25.7.7; (d) The Watchdog Tribunal, upon Tribunal initiation of unfitness review under Section 25.7.7. 25.7.6 Public Reporting. Following each annual evaluation, only the following shall be published upon the Ledger: (a) The fact that the evaluation occurred on the required date;

(b) A binary fitness determination: "Fit for Active Service" or "Referred to Watchdog Tribunal Review under Section 25.7.7"; (c) No specific medical findings, diagnoses, test results, or health information of any kind shall be published unless the Justice is ultimately transitioned to Senior Status or medical leave under Section 25.7.7 and such publication is necessary to explain the transition. 25.7.7 Watchdog Tribunal Review Upon Failed Evaluation. If the evaluating physicians conclude by majority concurrence that the Justice is unable to perform the duties of active Supreme Court service due to any combination of cognitive, physical, or mental health factors, the matter shall be referred to the Watchdog Tribunal for formal review. The Tribunal shall: (a) Convene a Fitness Review Panel of not fewer than seven (7) Tribunal members within thirty (30) days of referral; (b) Review the complete medical findings under strict confidentiality protections; (c) Hear the Justice's response, including any alternative medical opinion the Justice wishes to present; (d)

Consider, at the Justice's request, whether the condition is temporary (likely to resolve with treatment) or persistent; (e) Issue a determination by two-thirds (2/3) supermajority of the Fitness Review Panel within sixty (60) days of convening. 25.7.8 Outcomes of Fitness Review. The Fitness Review Panel shall select from the following outcomes: (a) Continued Active Service: If the Panel finds by two-thirds (2/3) supermajority that the Justice remains fit for active service notwithstanding the physicians' concerns, the Justice shall continue in office, with re-evaluation scheduled at the Panel's discretion (not less frequently than six (6) months); (b) Medical Leave: If the Panel finds that the Justice's condition is likely temporary and treatable, the Justice shall be placed on medical leave for a period of not less than three (3) months and not more than twelve (12) months, during which the Justice shall retain full salary and title but shall not participate in deliberations or decisions. Medical leave shall be followed by mandatory re-evaluation under Section 25.7.1 through 25.7.7; (c) Transition to Senior Justice Status: If the Panel finds that the Justice's condition is persistent, materially impairing, or otherwise incompatible with continued active service, the Justice shall transition to Senior Justice status under Section 25.5, with all associated rights and obligations, effective immediately upon the Panel's determination.

25.7.9 Justice's Rights and Protections. A Justice subject to health evaluation under this Section shall have the following rights: (a) Advance notice of evaluation date, location, and scope; (b) Reasonable accommodation of scheduling needs, subject to the annual timing requirement; (c) The right to submit additional medical opinions from physicians of the Justice's choosing, for Panel consideration during Fitness Review; (d) The right to legal representation during Fitness Review at federal expense; (e) Complete medical privacy except as strictly necessary for the fitness determination; (f) No public disclosure of medical conditions except as authorized by this Section; (g) Protection from public speculation, harassment, or prejudgment during the evaluation and review process; (h) Dignity of transition: if transition to Senior Status is determined, the Justice shall be entitled to a dignified announcement of transition without disclosure of specific medical details, with reasonable time to prepare personal and professional affairs. 25.7.10 Failure to Participate. A Justice who refuses to undergo the annual health evaluation without medically-justified cause shall be: (a) Referred to the Watchdog Tribunal for review; (b) Subject to automatic transition to Senior Justice status upon Tribunal finding that refusal was without adequate cause, by two-thirds (2/3) supermajority; (c) Such transition shall be treated as a voluntary transition for all purposes of compensation and benefits under Section 25.5. 25.7.11 Interaction with Mandatory Senior Status. The health evaluation provisions of this Section operate independently of, and in addition to, the mandatory Senior Status age of eighty (80) under Section 25.8. A Justice may transition to Senior Status through either: (a) completion of the eighteen-year term; (b) reaching age eighty; or (c) failed fitness determination under this Section, whichever occurs first. 25.7.12 Lower Federal Court Judges. The health evaluation provisions of Section 25.7.1 through 25.7.11 shall apply with equal force to active federal District Court and Courts of Appeals judges beginning on each judge's sixtieth (60th) birthday, administered under the same Authority framework. 25.8 Mandatory Senior Status. Every Justice of the Supreme Court shall transition to Senior Justice status upon the earlier of: (a) completion of the eighteen-year term under Section 25.2; or (b) reaching the age of eighty (80) years. Reaching age eighty shall operate as a mandatory transition regardless of term length, with any unfulfilled portion of the term filled by a new appointment serving only the remainder of the term before the staggered cycle resumes. 25.9 Lower Federal Court Age Limit. No person shall be appointed to active service as a federal District Court or Courts of Appeals judge after reaching the age of sixty-eight (68) years. Federal judges reaching the age of eighty (80) years during active service shall transition to senior status under existing statutory senior status provisions, or shall retire, within one (1) year of reaching age eighty. Federal judges are also subject to the annual health evaluation provisions of Section 25.7.12 beginning at age sixty (60). D. Enforceable Judicial Ethics Code 25.10 Application of Ethics Code. The ethical standards applicable to lower federal court judges under the Code of Conduct for United States Judges, as maintained by the Judicial Conference of the United States, shall apply with full force to Justices of the Supreme Court, supplemented by the specific requirements of this Section. Supreme Court Justices shall not enjoy lesser ethical obligations than lower federal judges. 25.11 Financial Disclosure. Every Supreme Court Justice shall annually publish upon the Ledger: (a) complete federal tax returns for the preceding year; (b) all assets, investments, and business interests valued at five thousand dollars ($5,000) or more; (c) all income from all sources; (d) all reimbursed or complimentary travel, lodging, or hospitality valued at one hundred dollars ($100) or more; (e) all gifts received of value exceeding one hundred dollars ($100); and (f) all outside speaking fees, book advances, consulting income, or similar outside compensation. The same disclosure shall apply to the Justice's spouse and minor dependents. First disclosure shall be made within ninety (90) days of oath-taking and annually thereafter. 25.12 Mandatory Recusal (meaning: a judge or official stepping aside from a specific case or decision because of a conflict of interest or bias). Every Justice shall recuse from any case in which: (a) the Justice, the Justice's spouse, or the Justice's minor dependents have a direct financial interest in the outcome; (b) the Justice has a close personal, familial, or business relationship with a party, counsel, or interested party of substantial character; (c) the Justice has previously served as counsel, witness, or advisor in the matter or closely related matters; (d) the Justice has made public statements indicating prejudgment of the specific issues in the case; or (e) any other circumstance would cause a reasonable person to question the Justice's impartiality. 25.13 Recusal Transparency. Every recusal decision shall be published upon the Ledger with written reasoning identifying the basis for recusal. Every denial of a motion to recuse shall be published with written reasoning addressing each asserted ground for recusal.

25.14 Recusal Review. Any party to a case before the Supreme Court, or any member of the public with standing (a legal concept meaning: the person has a sufficient personal stake or interest in the matter to be entitled to bring it before a court), may petition the Watchdog Tribunal for review of a denied recusal motion. The Tribunal shall decide such petitions by majority vote within thirty (30) days; if the Tribunal orders recusal by majority vote, the Justice shall recuse, and the Court shall proceed without that Justice. This procedure supplements and does not replace existing judicial recusal procedures. 25.14.1 Standing Requirements. Standing under Section 25.14 requires one of: (a) Direct party to the case before the Supreme Court; (b) Direct financial or legal interest in the outcome of the case of substantial character; (c) Membership in a class of persons likely to be directly and materially affected by the ruling, with an interest exceeding general public concern; (d) Legal representative of any of the persons described in subsections (a) through (c); or (e) Amicus organization (from Latin 'amicus curiae' meaning 'friend of the court' — an outside organization that isn't a party to a case but has expertise or interest and submits a brief to help the court understand the issues) with documented interest in the case that has filed an amicus brief in the matter. 25.14.2 Frivolous Petitions. Members of the general public without demonstrable interest under Section 25.14.1 shall not have standing to petition for recusal review. The Watchdog Tribunal may dismiss petitions failing the standing requirement, and may impose sanctions on bad-faith petitioners, including filing bars and costs, to prevent harassment of Justices through frivolous recusal petitions. 25.15 Gift and Travel Restrictions. No Justice shall accept any gift, favor, meal, lodging, travel, or thing of value exceeding one hundred dollars ($100) from any person or entity with interests before the Court or likely to have interests before the Court. Exceptions are permitted for: (a) official judicial business with full disclosure; (b) academic or educational events open to public attendance with full disclosure of sponsors and value; and (c) personal gifts from close family members unrelated to judicial functions. Violations shall constitute corruption under Section 13A. E. Shadow Docket Reform 25.16 Written Reasoning Requirement. Every order, stay, injunction, or other substantive ruling issued by the Supreme Court, whether through the merits docket, the emergency docket, or any other procedural path, shall be accompanied by a written opinion or order stating: (a) the specific legal basis for the ruling; (b) the factual record considered; (c) the legal standard applied; and (d) the names of

Justices joining and dissenting. No Supreme Court ruling shall be issued without written reasoning. 25.17 No Unsigned Rulings. No ruling of the Supreme Court shall be issued anonymously. The authoring Justice, or the Court as a whole with named concurrences and dissents, shall be identified in every ruling. 25.18 Consideration Period. Except in circumstances of genuinely imminent harm requiring emergency intervention, the Supreme Court shall not issue rulings on shadow-docket or emergency-docket matters within forty-eight (48) hours of receiving the application, to ensure adequate consideration and adversarial briefing. Emergency rulings bypassing this period shall include written findings identifying the imminent harm and why expedited consideration was necessary. 25.19 Ledger Publication. All Supreme Court decisions, including shadow-docket and emergency rulings, shall be published upon the Ledger in full within twenty-four (24) hours of issuance, including all written reasoning, dissents, concurrences, and recusals. F. Enforcement 25.20 Watchdog Tribunal Jurisdiction over the Supreme Court. The Watchdog Tribunal shall have jurisdiction to investigate violations of this Section by Justices of the Supreme Court and to recommend removal under existing constitutional procedures, prosecution under Section 13A, or other appropriate remedies. This jurisdiction supplements, and does not replace, the impeachment process under Article II of the Constitution. 25.21 Corruption Penalties. Violations of this Section by Justices shall constitute corruption under Section 13A and shall be subject to the full penalties thereof, including the Senior Official multiplier of fifty times (50×) benefit.

Section 25A. Constitutional Amendment Effects on Prior Provisions

25A.1 Foundational Principle. This Amendment, ratified under Article V, operates as a constitutional amendment to certain prior constitutional provisions where the prior provisions would, if unamended, create functional repeal of this Amendment's protective framework through hostile judicial interpretation. The amendments set forth in this Section are narrow, specific, and limited to Amendment-related contexts; they do not modify prior provisions for non-Amendment purposes. Each subsection identifies the specific prior provision, the narrow scope of modification, and the general operation that continues unaffected. This Section follows the same architectural principle as Section 13I.30 (Article I Section 9 supersession for Amendment appropriations), extending that principle to other prior provisions where necessary to protect Amendment operation against hostile interpretation. A. Speech and Debate Clause (Article I, Section 6, Clause 1)

25A.2 Speech and Debate Clause — General Operation Preserved. The Speech and Debate Clause continues in ordinary constitutional operation, protecting legitimate legislative speech, debate, voting, and committee proceedings of Members of Congress from civil or criminal liability in non-legislative tribunals. Legitimate legislative conduct — voting on bills, speaking in debate, participating in committee proceedings, conducting oversight hearings, proposing legislation — remains fully protected. 25A.3 Speech and Debate Clause — Narrow Exception for Amendment Interference. Notwithstanding the Speech and Debate Clause, conduct by Members of Congress that constitutes any of the following is not shielded by the Clause: (a) Section 13 interference with Amendment operations undertaken through coordinated legislative obstruction schemes; (b) Section 13A corruption involving Amendment-related matters, including bribery, receipt of things of value, or quid-pro-quo arrangements connected to Amendment operations; (c) Section 13I.23 funding obstruction offenses, including coordinated conspiracy to defund Amendment operations; (d) Coordinated conspiracy to functionally repeal this Amendment through sustained obstruction rather than through the Article V or Section 18 Sunset Review processes constitutionally provided for Amendment modification; (e) Conduct that would constitute Section 13 interference if performed outside legislative venues and that is performed in legislative venues solely to seek Speech and Debate immunity as a litigation shield. 25A.4 Speech and Debate Clause — Rationale. The Speech and Debate Clause's purpose is protecting legislative function from Executive or judicial intimidation of ordinary legislative conduct. Its purpose is not enabling coordinated constitutional sabotage. Where legislative conduct is itself an attack on the constitutional order — seeking functional repeal of a ratified constitutional amendment — the Clause's protective purpose inverts, and its protection does not extend. This is consistent with pre-Amendment Speech and Debate jurisprudence recognizing that bribery, receipt of things of value, and non-legislative criminal conduct are not shielded even when occurring in connection with legislative activity. 25A.5 Speech and Debate Clause — Legitimate Opposition Preserved. Nothing in this Section shall be construed to criminalize ordinary legislative opposition to Amendment operations. Members of Congress retain full constitutional authority to: vote against proposed Amendment-related legislation; speak in opposition to Amendment provisions in debate; propose Amendment modifications through Article V or Section 18 Sunset Review; conduct ordinary oversight hearings of Amendment bodies; introduce legislation affecting Amendment operations within permitted scope. Criminal liability attaches only to conduct meeting Section 13,

13A, 13I.23, or coordinated-conspiracy elements — not to ordinary legislative disagreement with the Amendment. 25A.6 Speech and Debate Clause — Interpretive Rule. In cases of asserted Speech and Debate immunity for Amendment-interference conduct, courts shall apply heightened scrutiny, requiring specific demonstration that the conduct falls within legitimate legislative function rather than within the Section 25A.3 exception. Ambiguity shall be resolved consistent with the preamble's ambiguity interpretation rule favoring preservation of the People's sovereign authority and prevention of accountability-structure capture. B. Impeachment Provisions (Article I, Sections 2–3; Article II, Section 4) 25A.7 Impeachment — General Operation Preserved. The impeachment framework continues in ordinary constitutional operation. The House of Representatives retains impeachment power under Article I, Section 2, Clause 5. The Senate retains trial authority under Article I, Section 3, Clauses 6 and 7. The Chief Justice of the United States continues presiding over Presidential impeachment trials. Civil officers of the United States remain removable for high crimes and misdemeanors under Article II, Section 4. 25A.8 Impeachment — Parallel Operation with No Confidence. Impeachment and No Confidence under this Amendment operate in parallel, not in sequence, and not in mutual exclusion: (a) Impeachment proceedings may continue during an active No Confidence Petition window or Referendum window without suspension or modification; (b) A No Confidence Petition may proceed during ongoing impeachment proceedings without suspension or modification; (c) Failed impeachment does not bar subsequent No Confidence proceedings — these are different constitutional procedures with different evidentiary standards, different political character, and different consequences; (d) Failed No Confidence does not bar subsequent impeachment — same reasoning; (e) Successful impeachment removal of an individual does not moot an ongoing No Confidence, because the Section 1.1 No Confidence is directed at the office-holding class (sitting President, Vice President, all Members of Congress, and the Supreme Court), not solely at the individual removed through impeachment. 25A.9 Impeachment — Disqualification Effects and Section 8. Officials removed from office by impeachment for conduct involving Section 13 interference, Section 13A corruption, or Section 13I.23 funding obstruction shall face Section 8 permanent federal office disqualification on the same terms as officials removed through No Confidence. Senate impeachment-disqualification findings under Article I, Section 3, Clause 7, when accompanying removal for Amendment-related conduct, carry Section 8 permanent disqualification weight.

25A.10 Impeachment — Amendment Bodies Not Ordinarily Impeachable. Amendment-established bodies — the Washington Commission, the three Authority bodies (Citizens' Oversight Board, State Elections Council, Academic Integrity Commission), the Watchdog Tribunal, the Hamilton Contingent, the Interim Caretaker Council, the Constitutional Transition Committee, the Watch Board, and their members — are not "civil officers of the United States" within the meaning of Article II, Section 4 for impeachment purposes. These are constitutionally established bodies under this Amendment with their own internal removal procedures: (a) Citizens' Oversight Board members: removal procedures under Section 17; (b) State Elections Council members: removal procedures under Section 17; (c) Academic Integrity Commission members: removal procedures under Section 17; (d) Watchdog Tribunal members: removal procedures under Section 21; (e) Hamilton Contingent Director and staff: removal procedures under Section 13C; (f) Watch Board members: removal procedures under Section 19.17.10 and Section 19.17.2(e); (g) Interim Caretaker Council members: removal through their state-level authority or per Section 21 oversight; (h) Constitutional Transition Committee delegates: removal procedures under Section 6. 25A.11 Impeachment — No Interference Through Impeachment. Using impeachment proceedings as a pretextual vehicle to obstruct Amendment operations — for example, initiating impeachment of Amendment body officials on pretextual grounds to disable Amendment operation — shall constitute Section 13 interference with Senior Official multipliers for the Members of Congress directing or participating in the pretextual impeachment. The constitutional impeachment power cannot be used as a tool for Amendment sabotage. 25A.12 Impeachment — Presidential Impeachment During No Confidence. Where a sitting President faces both impeachment and No Confidence: (a) The more procedurally advanced proceeding completes first without the other being extinguished; (b) If No Confidence completes first (resulting in Section 1.1 removal), impeachment is mooted as to removal but the Senate may still render disqualification judgment under Article I, Section 3, Clause 7; (c) If impeachment completes first (removal and disqualification), No Confidence may continue as to the other Section 1.1 officials, with the removed President considered already removed;

(d) Nothing in this framework shall delay or impede either proceeding; each proceeds on its own timeline under its own procedures. C. Due Process and Bill of Attainder Provisions (Fifth Amendment; Article I, Section 9, Clause 3) 25A.13 Due Process — General Operation Preserved. The Fifth Amendment Due Process Clause and the Bill of Attainder prohibition continue in ordinary constitutional operation. All persons retain Fifth Amendment due process protections in federal criminal and civil proceedings outside the narrow Amendment-specific contexts addressed here. The bill of attainder prohibition continues to bar Congressional legislation targeting specific persons for punishment without judicial process. 25A.14 Due Process — Amendment-Specific Framework. With respect to Amendment-established procedures, the Amendment establishes its own comprehensive due process framework: (a) Section 8 procedural protections for eligibility determinations, including notice, opportunity to be heard, access to evidence, right to counsel, and appeal rights; (b) Section 13 prosecution procedures with grand jury indictment, trial rights, and beyond-reasonable-doubt standard for criminal conviction; (c) Section 13D asset recovery procedures with clear and convincing evidence standard, innocent third-party protections, and adjudicative review; (d) Section 17C state-sovereign adjudication framework for Covered Officials with procedural protections specified therein; (e) Watchdog Tribunal oversight of Amendment-body procedural integrity; (f) Judicial review through ordinary federal courts, with Section 17C and Section 13H alternative pathways where federal courts are captured or compromised; (g) Appeal rights within Amendment-established frameworks. 25A.15 Due Process — Constitutional Amendment Status for Amendment Matters. To the extent that the Fifth Amendment Due Process Clause would require different or additional procedures beyond those established in this Amendment for Amendment-related matters, this Amendment operates as a constitutional amendment to the Due Process Clause, narrowly limited to Amendment-related contexts. The Amendment-specific procedures constitute the "due process of law" for Amendment matters. For non-Amendment matters, the Fifth Amendment Due Process Clause continues unaffected. 25A.16 Due Process — Protections Preserved Within Amendment Framework. Fundamental due process protections apply within the Amendment-specific framework:

(a) Notice of specific charges, allegations, or adverse determinations with adequate particularity; (b) Opportunity to be heard with reasonable preparation time; (c) Access to evidence used in determinations, subject to narrow operational-security protections; (d) Right to counsel, with appointed counsel for indigent persons in criminal and significant civil contexts; (e) Right to appeal adverse determinations to higher-tier Amendment bodies or to federal courts; (f) Innocent-until-proven-guilty presumption for criminal liability; (g) Clear and convincing evidence standard for eligibility determinations and significant civil consequences; (h) Beyond-reasonable-doubt standard for criminal convictions; (i) Fifth Amendment self-incrimination protection in criminal contexts (preserved without modification). 25A.17 Bill of Attainder — This Amendment Not a Bill of Attainder. This Amendment does not constitute a bill of attainder within the meaning of Article I, Section 9, Clause 3: (a) The Amendment does not name any specific person or group for punishment; (b) The Amendment establishes general legal standards applicable to any person whose conduct meets the defined elements; (c) The Amendment provides adjudicative procedures (Section 13 prosecution, Section 8 eligibility determinations, Section 17C adjudication) before consequences are imposed; (d) The Amendment's prospective application to future Senior Officials, future Covered Officials, and any future federal officeholder confirms its general-law character; (e) The Amendment's Section 1.1 immediate removal of sitting officials upon Ratification is not a bill of attainder because (i) it is effected through a constitutional amendment ratified by the sovereign People, not through ordinary legislation; (ii) it is general in application to the class of Section 1.1 officials, not targeted at specific named individuals; (iii) it is a structural constitutional remedy analogous to constitutional changes throughout American history that have altered office-holding, not a punitive bill of attainder; and (iv) individual sitting officials may run in Emergency Elections and be re-elected by the People, consistent with the Amendment being structural rather than punitive.

D. Ex Post Facto Provision (Article I, Section 9, Clause 3) 25A.18 Ex Post Facto — General Operation Preserved. The Ex Post Facto Clause continues in ordinary constitutional operation, prohibiting retroactive criminalization of conduct that was lawful when committed and retroactive enhancement of punishment for past conduct. 25A.19 Ex Post Facto — Prospective Application of Amendment Offenses. This Amendment is prospective in its substantive offense creation. Section 13 interference offenses, Section 13A corruption offenses, Section 13I.23 funding obstruction offenses, Section 16 nuclear-protection offenses, Section 20A state official targeting offenses, and all other Amendment-created criminal offenses apply only to conduct occurring after Ratification. No new substantive criminal liability is created for pre-Ratification conduct. 25A.20 Ex Post Facto — Permissible Contextual Use of Pre-Ratification Conduct. The Amendment uses pre-Ratification conduct in specific limited contexts that do not constitute retroactive criminalization under established Ex Post Facto jurisprudence: (a) Section 8 eligibility determinations consider past conduct as evidence of current trustworthiness for future office-holding — this is a prospective eligibility rule, not retroactive criminalization. The conduct is not newly criminalized; it is used as evidence for a forward-looking determination about fitness for future office; (b) Section 13F financial monitoring establishes post-Ratification monitoring obligations with pre-Ratification wealth patterns as investigative context — the monitoring obligations are prospective; pre-Ratification wealth is context for identifying suspicious patterns in post-Ratification monitoring; (c) Section 13D asset recovery targets assets obtained through conduct that was illegal when committed (bribery, fraud, corruption under pre-Ratification law) — the Amendment provides new procedural recovery mechanisms for pre-existing substantive crimes, not new substantive criminal law; (d) Section 17C state-sovereign adjudication addresses Covered Official conduct occurring after Ratification, with pre-Ratification conduct providing adjudicative context only for post-Ratification conduct determinations. 25A.21 Ex Post Facto — Calder v. Bull Framework Applies. Federal courts reviewing Ex Post Facto challenges to Amendment operations shall apply the established Calder v. Bull framework distinguishing: (i) laws making criminal conduct that was innocent when done (prohibited retroactive criminalization — not present in this Amendment); (ii) laws aggravating a crime or making it greater than it was when committed (prohibited — not present); (iii) laws changing the punishment and inflicting greater punishment than attached at commission (prohibited — not present); and (iv) laws altering legal rules of evidence and requiring less or different testimony to convict (analyzed case-by-case —

Amendment procedures do not lower evidentiary standards below constitutional minimums). Amendment operations fall within the regulatory, prospective, and procedural uses historically permitted consistent with the Ex Post Facto Clause. 25A.22 Ex Post Facto — No Retroactive Criminal Liability. For clarity: this Amendment does not create retroactive criminal liability for conduct that was lawful when committed. Every substantive criminal offense established by this Amendment applies to conduct occurring after Ratification. Arguments to the contrary based on contextual uses of pre-Ratification conduct for prospective eligibility, prospective monitoring, or procedural recovery mechanisms shall be foreclosed. E. Takings Clause (Fifth Amendment) 25A.23 Takings Clause — General Operation Preserved. The Takings Clause continues in ordinary constitutional operation, requiring just compensation for federal takings of private property for public use. Amendment provisions do not affect Takings protection for ordinary private property held in ordinary ways. 25A.24 Takings Clause — Section 13D Asset Recovery Not a Taking. Section 13D asset recovery of assets obtained through corruption does not constitute a Takings Clause taking: (a) Assets obtained through illegal conduct are not private property entitled to Takings Clause protection under established jurisprudence (Bennis v. Michigan framework and progeny); (b) Section 13D recovery proceeds through established civil and criminal forfeiture authority, applied through Amendment-specific procedures with due process protections under Section 25A.14 through 25A.16; (c) Innocent third-party interests are protected through Section 13D procedural safeguards, with recovery limited to assets substantively owned by the corrupt official; (d) Public use requirement is satisfied — recovered assets fund constitutional-accountability operations and benefit the People whose government was corrupted. 25A.25 Takings Clause — Family Member and Trust Assets. Where Section 13D recovery extends to family members or trusts: (a) Recovery targets only assets that are, in substance, the corrupt official's assets (nominally held by family members or trust vehicles but substantively owned or controlled by the corrupt official); (b) Genuinely independent family or trust assets are not subject to Amendment recovery;

(c) Fact-finding procedures under Section 13D establish the substantive ownership determination with clear and convincing evidence standard; (d) Innocent spouses, family members, and independent trust beneficiaries retain Takings Clause protection for their genuinely independent property. 25A.26 Takings Clause — Narrow Supersession for Corruption-Recovery Context. To the extent that specific Section 13D recovery of corruption-related assets would otherwise face Takings Clause challenges, this Amendment operates as a narrow constitutional amendment to the Takings Clause for corruption-recovery contexts. General Takings Clause protection for ordinary private property held in ordinary ways remains unaffected. The narrow supersession extends only to assets substantively obtained through, or substantively owned by persons who obtained them through, corruption within the meaning of this Amendment. F. Interpretive Rules and Judicial Construction 25A.27 Interpretive Rule — Later Constitutional Provisions Prevail. Consistent with established principles that later-ratified constitutional provisions prevail over earlier provisions where irreconcilable, courts interpreting apparent conflicts between this Amendment and prior constitutional provisions shall give effect to this Amendment's provisions to the extent they are clear, narrow, and specifically addressed to the conflict. Prior provisions continue to operate in full for all other contexts. 25A.28 Interpretive Rule — Ambiguity Resolution. In cases of ambiguity about whether specific Amendment operations conflict with prior constitutional provisions, courts shall apply the preamble's ambiguity interpretation rule favoring: (i) preservation of the People's sovereign authority expressed through Article V ratification; (ii) prevention of capture of accountability structures; (iii) protection of the Amendment's operational integrity; and (iv) narrow construction of the Amendment's modifications to prior provisions to limit effects to Amendment-specific contexts. 25A.29 Interpretive Rule — Judicial Capture Scenarios. Any judicial ruling that the narrow supersessions in this Section are themselves unconstitutional, or that prior provisions foreclose Amendment operation in ways contrary to the specific text of this Section, shall trigger Section 13H alternative interpretive pathways. Such ruling would effect functional repeal of the Amendment's protective framework contrary to its explicit constitutional text, and thus contrary to the People's sovereign authority expressed through Article V ratification. 25A.30 Interpretive Rule — Sunset Review and Future Amendment. Nothing in this Section shall preclude future Amendment modification through Article V or Section 18 Sunset Review. The narrow supersessions established here are themselves subject to the People's continuing constitutional authority. If operational experience reveals that specific supersessions are too broad, too narrow, or otherwise imperfect, the Sunset Review process under Section 18 provides the People's mechanism for refinement. 25A.31 Interpretive Rule — Non-Exhaustive List. The prior provisions addressed in this Section (Speech and Debate Clause, Impeachment, Due Process and Bill of Attainder, Ex Post Facto, Takings Clause) are the prior provisions identified at Ratification as requiring specific supersession clarification. Where other prior provisions are asserted in litigation as foreclosing Amendment operation, courts shall apply the Section 25A.1 foundational principle (narrow and specific supersession where the prior provision would functionally repeal Amendment protection) and the Section 25A.27 interpretive rule (later provisions prevail where irreconcilable), without this Section's non-exhaustive treatment implying that unlisted provisions foreclose Amendment operation. 25A.32 Relationship to Section 13I.30. The Article I, Section 9 supersession for Amendment appropriations established in Section 13I.30 remains in full force. This Section supplements but does not replace that provision, and the two sections operate together to address the different prior-provision contexts where supersession is necessary for Amendment operation.

Section 26. Term Limits, Age Limits, and Ethics for Congress

Key terms in this Section: • "Member of Congress" — A United States Senator or Representative, and where the context so requires, a Delegate or Resident Commissioner. • "Consecutive Terms" — Terms of office served in succession without an intervening period of service out of that particular office. • "The Watchdog Tribunal" — The body established under Section 21 for enforcement of anti-corruption provisions. 26.1 Career incumbency in federal elected office concentrates power, entrenches interests against the People, and creates the conditions for corruption this Amendment exists to prevent. The following term limits, age limits, and ethical obligations shall therefore apply to Members of Congress. A. Term Limits 26.2 House of Representatives Term Limit. No person shall be elected to more than six (6) terms of service in the United States House of Representatives. Terms served need not be consecutive; the lifetime cap is six (6) terms, equivalent to twelve (12) years of House service. 26.2.1 Partial Terms — House. Service of more than fifty percent (50%) of a House term, whether through special election, appointment where applicable, or other means, shall count as one full term for purposes of Section 26.2. Service of fifty percent (50%) or less shall not count toward the term limit but shall be disclosed in all campaign materials and on the Member's Ledger profile. For purposes of this calculation, a 'term' is measured from the statutory commencement date to the statutory expiration date. 26.3 Senate Term Limit. No person shall be elected to more than two (2) terms of service in the United States Senate. Terms served need not be consecutive; the lifetime cap is two (2) terms, equivalent to twelve (12) years of Senate service. 26.3.1 Partial Terms — Senate. Service of more than fifty percent (50%) of a Senate term, whether through appointment, special election, or other means, shall count as one full term for purposes of Section 26.3. Service of fifty percent (50%) or less shall not count toward the term limit but shall be disclosed in all campaign materials and on the Member's Ledger profile. For purposes of this calculation, a 'term' is measured from the statutory commencement date to the statutory expiration date. 26.4 Combined Federal Elected Service Cap. No person shall serve more than twenty-four (24) years in combined federal elected service across the House of Representatives, Senate, Vice Presidency, and Presidency. Time served in each office shall count cumulatively toward this cap. 26.4.1 Lifetime Cap Application. The twenty-four (24) year cumulative cap under Section 26.4 is a lifetime maximum. No person who has reached this cap may be elected or appointed to any federal office requiring constitutional oath for federal elected service, regardless of intervening time periods, cooling-off periods, or subsequent changes in political affiliation or party. This preserves the principle that federal service is a temporary public trust, not a lifelong career. This lifetime cap does not apply to: (a) appointed positions such as ambassadorships, cabinet positions, or judicial appointments that do not involve federal elected office; (b) state or local elected office; (c) Constitutional Transition Committee delegate service under Section 6; or (d) service on Authority bodies by ex officio, lottery, or other non-elected selection. 26.5 Cooling-Off Requirement. A Member of Congress who has served the maximum number of terms in one chamber under Sections 26.2 or 26.3 shall wait six (6) years before seeking election to any federal office, including the other chamber, the Presidency, or the Vice Presidency. 26.6 Grandfathering Transition. Members of Congress serving at the moment of ratification shall be subject to the following transition: (a) the current term may be completed without limitation; (b) Members may be elected to a maximum of one (1) additional term after ratification, regardless of prior service; (c) thereafter, the term limits of Sections 26.2 and 26.3 shall apply without grandfathering. This transition balances ratifiability against the urgent need for turnover in federal elected office.

B. Age Limits 26.7 Maximum Age for Swearing-In. No person shall be sworn into a new term of office as Member of Congress, President, or Vice President after reaching the age of seventy-five (75) years. This provision shall not remove from office any person already sworn into a term, but shall prevent election to new terms commencing after age seventy-five. 26.7.1 Interaction with Grandfathering. The age limit of Section 26.7 shall apply to all persons, including those subject to the grandfathering provision of Section 26.6. A

Member who is subject to Section 26.6 grandfathering but who would be over age seventy-five (75) at the commencement of the 'one additional term' permitted by Section 26.6 shall not be eligible for that additional term. The age limit is a hard constitutional ceiling that cannot be evaded through grandfathering. This ensures that the democratic principle of age-appropriate leadership applies uniformly, without creating exceptions that would undermine the purpose of Section 26.7. 26.8 Minimum Age Preservation. The minimum ages for service established in Article I, Section 2 (age 25 for House) and Article I, Section 3 (age 30 for Senate) of the Constitution shall remain in force. This Section establishes only the maximum age for new swearing-in. 26.9 Grandfathering for Age Limits. Members of Congress reaching age seventy-five during a current term may complete that term. The age-limit restriction applies only to election to new terms commencing after ratification. C. Ethics Code for Members of Congress 26.10 Enforceable Ethics Code. Every Member of Congress shall be subject to an enforceable Code of Ethics, administered by the Watchdog Tribunal in cooperation with existing House and Senate ethics committees. Where the Watchdog Tribunal finds violations by two-thirds (2/3) supermajority, such findings shall be binding upon the Member and shall be published upon the Ledger. 26.11 Mandatory Recusal. Every Member shall recuse from legislative votes, committee actions, or official actions where: (a) the Member has a direct financial interest in the outcome exceeding five thousand dollars ($5,000); (b) the Member has a business or familial relationship with a substantially interested party; or (c) any other circumstance would cause a reasonable person to question the Member's impartiality. 26.12 Gift Restrictions. No Member shall accept any gift, favor, meal, lodging, travel, or thing of value exceeding fifty dollars ($50) from any lobbyist, lobbyist organization, or person with interests before Congress. Exceptions are permitted for academic, educational, or non-partisan civic events with full disclosure. Aggregate gifts from a single source exceeding one hundred dollars ($100) in a calendar year shall be prohibited without supermajority Ethics Committee approval.

26.13 Watchdog Tribunal Enforcement. Violations of this Section shall constitute corruption under Section 13A and shall be subject to the full penalties thereof, including possible removal from office where the violation is sufficiently serious. D. Stock Trading Ban 26.14 Individual Stock Trading Prohibition. No Member of Congress, nor the spouse or minor dependents of a Member, shall own individual stocks, trade individual stocks, or hold substantial direct ownership interests in specific corporations during the

Member's term of service and for a period of five (5) years thereafter. 26.14.1 Mid-Term Acquisition. If a Member, spouse, or minor dependent acquires individual stock during the Member's term through inheritance, gift, divorce settlement, trust distribution, or other involuntary means, the stock must be converted pursuant to Section 26.15 within ninety (90) days of acquisition. Failure to convert shall constitute a violation subject to Section 26.17 penalties, unless the Member can demonstrate impossibility of conversion (for example, closely-held family corporation stock with no public market, or stock subject to legal restrictions on immediate sale) and petitions the Watchdog Tribunal for a specific exception within thirty (30) days of acquisition. The Tribunal may grant exceptions upon clear showing, subject to: (a) full Ledger disclosure; (b) mandatory recusal from all legislative matters materially affecting the entity; (c) divestiture upon any opportunity to do so; and (d) sunset of exception upon departure from Congress. 26.15 Conversion Requirement. Within ninety (90) days of taking the oath of office, every Member shall convert all individual stock holdings to one or more of: (a) diversified index funds or exchange-traded funds (ETFs) tracking broad market indices; (b) qualified blind trust managed by an independent trustee; (c) mutual funds not concentrated in specific sectors subject to active congressional regulation; or (d) United States Treasury securities or municipal bonds. 26.16 Spousal and Family Application. The stock trading ban applies equally to the Member's spouse and minor dependents. Adult children not financially dependent on the Member are not subject to the ban but shall be subject to disclosure requirements for any stock trading during the Member's service. 26.17 Violations. Violations of the stock trading ban shall result in: (a) automatic disgorgement of all profits from prohibited trades; (b) imposition of Section 13A penalties at the Senior Official multiplier of fifty times (50×) benefit; (c) referral for prosecution under insider trading or securities fraud statutes as applicable; and (d) referral to the House or Senate for potential expulsion proceedings. E. Post-Service Lobbying Ban 26.18 Ten-Year Lobbying Prohibition. No former Member of Congress shall engage in paid lobbying of the federal government, including direct lobbying, strategic lobbying advisory services, or lobbying-firm partnerships, for a period of ten (10) years following the conclusion of the Member's federal service. 26.18.1 Definition of 'Paid Lobbying.' For purposes of Section 26.18, 'paid lobbying' shall mean any activity for which the former Member receives compensation, direct or indirect, of more than one thousand dollars ($1,000) per year from any source, where the activity involves direct or substantially coordinated indirect communication with a covered federal official (as defined under the Lobbying

Disclosure Act or successor statute), intended to influence official action, legislation, regulation, or federal policy. Public commentary, speaking engagements, writing, media appearances, academic work, authorship, and general advocacy that does not involve direct or substantially coordinated indirect official communication is not prohibited, regardless of compensation. The Watchdog Tribunal shall publish guidance interpreting this definition within ninety (90) days of Ratification, and shall resolve contested cases by majority vote published upon the Ledger. 26.19 Scope of Prohibition. The lobbying ban applies to: (a) direct lobbying of current Members of Congress; (b) direct lobbying of federal executive branch officials above a specified threshold; (c) provision of strategic advisory services to entities engaged in federal lobbying; (d) partnership in or executive positions at registered lobbying firms; and (e) any activity substantially equivalent to lobbying under the Lobbying Disclosure Act or successor statutes. 26.20 Exceptions. The lobbying ban shall not prohibit: (a) public advocacy, commentary, or speaking on matters of public concern; (b) service as an academic, author, or non-lobbying consultant; (c) representation of constituents on constituent-service matters without compensation; or (d) service in elected or appointed government positions. 26.21 Enforcement. Violations of this Section shall constitute corruption under Section 13A and shall be subject to the full penalties thereof, including disgorgement of all lobbying-related compensation received during the prohibited period. F. Financial Disclosure 26.22 Annual Disclosure Requirements. Every Member of Congress shall annually publish upon the Ledger: (a) complete federal tax returns for the preceding year for the Member, the Member's spouse, and minor dependents; (b) all assets, investments, and business interests valued at one thousand dollars ($1,000) or more; (c) all income from all sources including speaking fees, book advances, and outside compensation; (d) all gifts received of value exceeding fifty dollars ($50); (e) all foreign travel and substantial foreign contacts; and (f) any ownership or financial interest of any family member in any entity with business before Congress.

26.23 Real-Time Transaction Disclosure. All financial transactions by Members, their spouses, and minor dependents, including but not limited to purchase or sale of index funds, real estate transactions, and significant financial events, shall be disclosed upon the Ledger within twenty-four (24) hours of the transaction. This real-time disclosure supplements, and does not replace, annual disclosure requirements. G. Application and Enforcement 26.24 Article V Protection. The term limits, age limits, ethics requirements, stock trading ban, lobbying ban, and disclosure requirements of this Section shall be protected under the Article V protection established in Sections 18.6.1 and 18.6.2. No act of Congress, executive order, judicial ruling, or state action shall evade, diminish, or nullify these requirements. 26.25 Watchdog Tribunal Primary Jurisdiction. The Watchdog Tribunal shall have primary jurisdiction over violations of this Section, with authority to: (a) conduct investigations upon complaint or on its own initiative; (b) issue findings of violation by two-thirds (2/3) supermajority vote; (c) impose Section 13A penalties; (d) refer violations for criminal prosecution; and (e) refer serious violations to the House or Senate for expulsion consideration. 26.26 Sunset Review Consideration. The provisions of this Section shall be reviewed in each Sunset Review under Section 18. The People may, through a Modify vote, adjust the specific term lengths, age thresholds, or ethical standards established herein, while preserving the general principle of congressional accountability.

Section 27. Amendment Operational Clarifications

27.1 Purpose of This Section. This Section consolidates operational clarifications addressing matters of definitional consistency, Congressional collective inaction, military command integrity beyond Section 16, and interpretive hierarchy. These clarifications supplement rather than displace the Amendment's substantive provisions; they provide navigation for actors applying the Amendment in edge cases and foreclose interpretive vulnerabilities that might otherwise invite hostile constructions. Each subheader below addresses one operational domain. A. Definitional Consistency 27.2 Unified Definitions for Core Terms. To ensure consistent interpretation across the Amendment, the following unified definitions apply unless a specific provision expressly provides otherwise. Where a specific provision provides a context-specific definition, that provision's definition controls for that provision's application, but this Section's definitions control for cross-provision interpretation and for any provision lacking specific definition.

(a) "Corruption" defined. For purposes of this Amendment, corruption means: any use of public office for private gain or for the benefit of any party, faction, foreign power, or private interest at the expense of the public; any quid-pro-quo arrangement exchanging official action or inaction for personal, political, or financial benefit; any solicitation, acceptance, or offer of bribes, gratuities, kickbacks, or improper things of value in connection with official duties; any misuse of federal resources, information, or authority for personal enrichment; any coordination with foreign powers against United States constitutional interests; and any pattern of official conduct demonstrating that the officeholder is acting against the public interest they are sworn to serve. Section 13A establishes specific prohibited conduct; Section 8 establishes eligibility consequences; Section 13 establishes prosecution framework; Section 17A establishes anti-corruption standards for Amendment bodies. All reference this unified definition of corruption unless a specific element of those provisions expressly modifies the core meaning for specific application. (b) "Capture" defined. For purposes of this Amendment, capture means: the substantial compromise, control, or co-optation of an institution, office, or body by actors whose interests are adverse to the institution's constitutional purpose; the functional rather than formal substitution of institutional decision-making by external direction; the condition in which an institution cannot perform its constitutional function because corrupt or adverse actors have succeeded in controlling its operations, personnel, or outputs. Section 13H addresses judicial capture; Section 17B addresses total accountability-chain capture; Section 17.22 addresses single-body compromise of Authority bodies. These specific provisions apply capture concept to their specific domains with their specific elements; this unified definition provides the underlying meaning. Capture is distinguished from mere political disagreement — it requires substantial functional compromise beyond ordinary institutional dispute. (c) "Emergency" defined. For purposes of this Amendment, emergency means: a time-limited, factually-grounded situation requiring rapid response that cannot be adequately addressed through ordinary governmental processes within necessary timeframes. Genuine emergencies involve specific, documented, factually-verifiable threats or circumstances; pretextual emergencies lack such grounding. Section 10 addresses emergency declarations during No Confidence processes; Section 16.10 addresses imminent nuclear attack; Section 24.16 through 24.18 addresses Presidential emergency declarations. These specific provisions define their particular emergency scopes; this unified definition provides the underlying requirement that emergency declaration requires factual grounding, temporal limitation, and necessity. Ordinary political circumstances, routine operational matters, and foreseeable governance needs do not constitute emergencies regardless of how urgent responsible officials claim them to be. (d) "Federal officeholder" defined. For purposes of this Amendment, federal officeholder means any person holding any federal position, whether elected, appointed, or career, including but not limited to: elected federal officials (President, Vice President, Senators, Representatives); Senate-confirmed appointees; Presidential appointees; career federal employees (Senior Executive

Service, General Schedule, uniformed services); federal judges (Article III and Article I); federal officers of any Executive agency, independent agency, or federal corporation; Members of federal commissions and boards. Context-specific provisions may expand or narrow this definition for specific purposes (e.g., Section 13's Senior Official multiplier focuses on specified senior positions; Section 1.2 career personnel protection has specific scope). This unified definition controls cross-provision interpretation. (e) "Covered Official" defined. For purposes of Section 17C state-sovereign adjudication, Covered Official bears the meaning assigned in Section 17C itself. For purposes of Section 20A state official integrity framework, Covered State Official bears the meaning assigned in Section 20A. These specific definitions are retained. Where this Amendment references "Covered Official" without Section 17C or Section 20A context, the relevant definition shall be determined by the most contextually appropriate specific definition, with ambiguity resolved under Section 27.11 interpretive hierarchy. (f) "Amendment body" defined. For purposes of this Amendment, Amendment body means any body established by or operating under this Amendment, including: the three Authority bodies (Citizens' Oversight Board, State Elections Council, Academic Integrity Commission); the Watchdog Tribunal; the Hamilton Contingent; the Constitutional Transition Committee; the Interim Caretaker Council; the Washington Commission; the Citizens' Implementation Watch Board; the Joint Implementation Command; the State Attorneys General Council; the Foreign Interference Oversight Board; and any successor, specialized, or subordinate body established under these primary bodies' authority. Amendment bodies operate under the Amendment's framework with the powers, limitations, and protections established in their respective governing provisions. (g) "Participating Jurisdiction" defined. For purposes of this Amendment, Participating Jurisdiction means any of the fifty (50) States, the District of Columbia, and the five (5) territories of the United States (Puerto Rico, Guam, American Samoa, the U.S. Virgin Islands, and the Northern Mariana Islands), totaling fifty-six (56) Participating Jurisdictions. This expansive definition recognizes that citizens of these Jurisdictions participate in this Amendment's mechanisms notwithstanding their varying status under other constitutional provisions. For Article V ratification purposes, ratification by three-fourths of the fifty (50) States remains the constitutional requirement; territorial and District ratification is not required for Amendment ratification validity. 27.3 Definitional Hierarchy. In cases of apparent conflict between a Section 27.2 unified definition and a provision-specific definition: (a) provision-specific definitions control for their specific provision's application; (b) unified definitions

control for cross-provision interpretation and gap-filling; (c) ambiguity is resolved under Section 27.11 interpretive hierarchy. No definition in this Amendment shall be construed to conflict with the explicit text of any substantive provision. B. Congressional Collective Inaction Framework 27.4 Foundational Principle. This Amendment anticipates that a corrupt or obstructive Congress may attempt to defeat Amendment operations not only through affirmative acts (addressed elsewhere) but also through collective inaction — refusing to confirm appointments, refusing to conduct required oversight, refusing to provide information, refusing to process legislation, and similar passive obstructions. The individual-officeholder frameworks of Sections 13, 25A.3, and 26 address individual Member conduct; this Section addresses collective inaction as a distinct obstruction vector. 27.5 Collective Inaction as Obstruction. Where Congress, or either house of Congress, collectively fails to perform required constitutional functions related to Amendment operations, the following framework applies: (a) Collective Inaction Defined. Collective inaction means: sustained failure of Congress or either house to exercise specific constitutional functions that Amendment operations depend upon, including but not limited to: failing to confirm Senate-required appointments to Amendment-related positions; failing to process Amendment-related oversight responsibilities; failing to respond to required information requests from Amendment bodies; failing to appropriate funds required under Section 13I.7 national budget integration; failing to pass implementing legislation where Amendment operations require Congressional action. (b) Duration Threshold. Collective inaction triggering this framework requires sustained failure over reasonable period, typically: (i) ninety (90) days for time-sensitive matters; (ii) one hundred eighty (180) days for non-time-sensitive matters; (iii) shorter periods where emergency conditions warrant (such as during active No Confidence processes). (c) Documentation Requirement. Collective inaction shall be documented through: (i) Watchdog Tribunal findings; (ii) State Attorneys General Council findings by two-thirds supermajority; (iii) Authority Liberty Bell Initiative finding; or (iv) any combination of these. Documentation shall identify the specific function not performed, the duration of non-performance, the opportunities Congress had to perform, and the impact on Amendment operations. 27.6 Consequences for Collective Inaction. Upon documented collective inaction: (a) Alternative Authorization Pathways. Where Amendment operations require Congressional action that Congress has failed to provide, alternative pathways shall activate: (i) for funding, Section 13I self-executing appropriation framework operates regardless of Congressional appropriation failure; (ii) for Senate confirmation failures affecting Amendment bodies, acting or interim appointments shall be authorized through Amendment-body-specific mechanisms (e.g., Watchdog Tribunal interim appointment authority); (iii) for information requests, Watchdog Tribunal subpoena authority applies with Section 13H alternative pathways; (iv) for oversight failures, Amendment bodies' own oversight mechanisms operate independently. (b) Individual Member Consequences. Members of Congress who direct, coordinate, or materially participate in collective inaction schemes shall face Section 13 interference prosecution. Collective inaction that is the product of coordinated scheme shall be evaluated for conspiracy liability regardless of each individual Member's specific actions. Individual Members may not shield themselves from accountability by pointing to the collective nature of the inaction. (c) Emergency Legislation Substitutes. Where Congressional failure to pass implementing legislation materially impairs Amendment operations, the Washington Commission during Phase One, and the Authority thereafter, may promulgate Temporary Implementing Standards that operate with force of federal regulation until Congress acts. Temporary Implementing Standards shall: (i) be strictly limited to matters where Congressional failure is documented; (ii) be narrowly tailored to preserve Amendment operations without broader policy-making; (iii) be subject to Watchdog Tribunal review; (iv) sunset upon Congressional legislative action; (v) be published on the Franklin Ledger with factual basis. (d) Public Accountability. Collective inaction findings shall be published on the Franklin Ledger with Member-specific voting records (where roll calls exist) or Member-specific position documentation (where votes were avoided). The public has standing to know which Members contributed to collective inaction, providing informational basis for electoral accountability through ordinary Congressional elections. (e) Sunset Review. The Congressional collective inaction framework and its application shall be reviewed in each Sunset Review under Section 18, with the People retaining authority to modify thresholds, procedures, and consequences based on operational experience. (f) Amendment Operations Continue During Broader Congressional Dysfunction. Where Congressional dysfunction extends beyond Amendment-specific inaction to include broader institutional paralysis — inability to convene, sustained quorum failure, complete legislative stoppage, or analogous institutional crisis — Amendment operations shall continue uninterrupted through the alternative authorization pathways established in subsection (a). The Amendment's framework is designed to function independently of Congressional operational status for its core protections: (i) Section 13I self-executing appropriation continues regardless of Congressional appropriations failure; (ii) Amendment body operations continue under their respective governing provisions; (iii) acting and interim appointments

authorized under Amendment body-specific mechanisms proceed; (iv) Watchdog Tribunal, Authority, Hamilton Contingent, and State Attorneys General Council functions continue; (v) Emergency Election processes under Section 7 operate to replace Congressional Members where applicable; (vi) Temporary Implementing Standards under subsection (c) substitute for Congressional legislation during extended dysfunction. Recognizing that broader Congressional institutional crisis is beyond this Amendment's scope to resolve — such matters fall under Article I and established constitutional practice — Amendment operations shall not themselves fail merely because Congress has failed. Constitutional remedies for broader Congressional dysfunction operate according to their own established frameworks, and this Amendment's alternative pathways ensure Amendment protections remain operational during such periods. C. Military Command Integrity Framework 27.7 Foundational Principle. Section 16 addresses military personnel compliance with Amendment operations, nuclear protections, and individual servicemember conduct. This Section addresses the distinct scenario of military command leadership itself — Joint Chiefs, combatant commanders, service chiefs, and senior command — attempting order-imposition outside the Amendment's chain of command during sensitive constitutional moments. Individual servicemember protections under Section 16 are preserved; this Section addresses the command-level coup scenario. 27.8 Military Command Limitations During Sensitive Periods. During the following sensitive constitutional periods, military command shall exercise only defensive authority in strict coordination with Amendment constitutional structures: (a) Periods Covered. Sensitive periods include: (i) the seventy-two (72) hour Caretaker Period under Section 6A; (ii) the Constitutional Transition Committee's active deliberations under Section 6; (iii) active No Confidence Petition and Referendum windows under Sections 5 and 12; (iv) Emergency Election processes under Section 7; (v) any period in which military command leadership is itself under Amendment investigation; (vi) periods of documented foreign attack or threatened attack where constitutional continuity is at risk. (b) Defensive Authority Only. During sensitive periods, military command authority is limited to: (i) response to confirmed armed attack on United States sovereign territory or armed forces; (ii) coordination with Amendment constitutional structures for defensive needs; (iii) nuclear authorization procedures under Section 16.8 (which apply without modification); (iv) emergency defensive actions meeting Section 16.10 imminent attack or nation-threatening invasion standards. Military command shall not: (i) impose order through military force absent confirmed armed attack; (ii) substitute military command judgment for constitutional authority; (iii) authorize military actions to enforce any political outcome; (iv) take the national guard force or military command center actions that bypass Amendment constitutional structures. (c) Joint Chiefs Advisory Role. The Joint Chiefs of Staff advise Amendment constitutional structures on defensive necessity and operational feasibility during sensitive periods; they do not decide on authorization. Authorization authority during sensitive periods flows through the Section 6A Caretaker Council, the Section 6 Constitutional Transition Committee, or whichever Amendment body is operational for the specific period, as provided in each body's governing provisions. (d) Combatant Commander Authority. Combatant Commanders retain operational authority for confirmed defensive missions authorized through proper channels. They shall not: (i) initiate new offensive operations during sensitive periods; (ii) respond to orders from persons purporting to exercise authority outside the Amendment's chain of command; (iii) authorize use of military force for domestic political purposes. (e) Service Chief Limitations. Service Chiefs maintain administrative authority over their services during sensitive periods. They shall not: (i) mobilize forces for purposes beyond defensive necessity; (ii) direct personnel or material in ways that impede Amendment operations; (iii) conduct coordinated service-level actions supporting any unauthorized command imposition. 27.9 Command-Level Coup Scenario Response. Where military command leadership (Joint Chiefs, combatant commanders, service chiefs, or any combination) attempts order-imposition outside Amendment constitutional structures: (a) Individual Servicemember Response. All servicemembers retain their Section 16.3(c) constitutional duty to refuse unlawful orders, extending to any order from military command leadership purporting to impose order outside Amendment structures. The refusal protection framework of Section 16 applies fully; servicemembers refusing coup-adjacent orders shall receive enhanced protection. (b) Chain of Command Integrity. Where senior command attempts to bypass or override Amendment constitutional structures, chain of command integrity shall be protected through: (i) Section 16.20 authentication protocols applied with compressed timeframes; (ii) two-person verification for all command actions affecting constitutional periods; (iii) immediate notification to Watchdog Tribunal (or Washington Commission or State AG Council if Tribunal is not operational) of suspicious command activity. (c) Criminal Liability. Military command leadership attempting order-imposition outside Amendment structures shall be subject to: (i) Section 16.5 insurrection charges with Senior Official multipliers; (ii) Section 13 interference prosecution; (iii) military justice proceedings through Uniform Code of Military Justice coordinated with civilian prosecution; (iv) Section 8 permanent disqualification from federal office. Command leadership cannot shield subordinate participants

through purported authority; subordinates who comply with coup-adjacent orders face their own Section 16 liability, with diminished but not eliminated individual responsibility under ordinary military justice principles. (d) Succession in Command. Where senior command is implicated in coup-adjacent conduct, succession in command proceeds through Uniform Code of Military Justice procedures adapted for constitutional-emergency context. The principle is continuity of lawful command; the specific succession follows established military law. (e) Civilian Authority Preserved. Civilian authority over military, established in Article II of the Constitution of the United States, remains fundamental. This Amendment operates within that constitutional tradition, reinforcing rather than diminishing civilian authority. Command-level coup scenarios are extraordinary; the ordinary operation of civilian-military relations under Article II and established military law continues undisturbed. (f) Public Transparency. Any Watchdog Tribunal finding or State AG Council finding of command-level coup-adjacent conduct shall be published on the Franklin Ledger with factual basis, ensuring public knowledge of command-integrity matters while respecting legitimate operational security regarding active defensive operations. D. Interpretive Hierarchy 27.10 Need for Interpretive Hierarchy. This Amendment establishes multiple bodies with interpretive authority over Amendment operations: federal courts (subject to Section 25 limits), the Authority bodies (through Liberty Bell Initiative), the Watchdog Tribunal, the Hamilton Contingent (for prosecution matters), the State Attorneys General Council (for coordinated state-level matters), the Washington Commission (during Phase One), and the People themselves (through Sunset Review under Section 18). To prevent interpretive chaos while preserving checks and balances, this subheader establishes the hierarchy among these interpretive authorities. 27.11 Interpretive Hierarchy. In cases of Amendment interpretation, the following hierarchy applies: (a) The

People's Sovereign Authority Supreme. The People, acting through Sunset Review under Section 18 (Affirm, Modify, Repeal) and through subsequent Article V amendment processes, possess supreme interpretive authority. Their determinations through these mechanisms control over all other interpretive bodies. (b) Watchdog Tribunal Primary for Amendment Body Matters. For matters regarding Amendment body operations, personnel, conduct, and internal disputes, the Watchdog Tribunal has primary interpretive authority, reviewable by federal courts under Section 25 constraints and by the People through Sunset Review.

(c) Federal Courts for Civilian Adjudication. Federal courts retain ordinary jurisdiction over civilian criminal prosecutions, civil cases, and constitutional challenges to Amendment applications, subject to: (i) Section 25 limits on Supreme Court authority; (ii) Section 17C state-sovereign adjudication alternative pathways where federal courts are captured; (iii) Section 13H alternative interpretive pathways; (iv) Section 25A supersession provisions narrowing federal court interpretive discretion for specific matters. (d) Authority Liberty Bell Initiative for Policy Interpretation. For matters of Amendment operational policy, procedural implementation, and forward-looking interpretation, the three Authority bodies acting through Liberty Bell Initiative may issue interpretive guidance. Such guidance binds Amendment bodies and provides interpretive context for federal courts, but does not bind federal courts in civilian adjudication. (e) Hamilton Contingent for Prosecution Decisions. For Section 13 prosecution decisions, the Hamilton Contingent (or State AG Council during Phase One or extended authority periods) has ordinary prosecutorial discretion, reviewable through appeal of specific prosecutions and through Watchdog Tribunal review of patterns. This is prosecution-specific interpretive authority, not general constitutional interpretation. (f) Washington Commission Phase One. During Phase One, the Washington Commission has interpretive authority for operational matters within its constitutional mandate under Section 19.5. This authority transfers to permanent Amendment bodies upon their operational commencement. (g) State AG Council for State-Federal Interface. For matters involving state-federal interface, coordinated state action, and Phase One/extended authority federal prosecution, the State AG Council has interpretive authority within its specific framework under Sections 19.5.0.5.2, 19.5.0.18, 13I.32, and related provisions. 27.12 Conflict Resolution Among Interpretive Bodies. Where interpretive bodies reach conflicting conclusions on the same matter: (a) Cooperation First. Initial response shall be inter-body consultation through the Washington

Commission (during Phase One) or the Watchdog Tribunal (thereafter), seeking cooperative resolution. (b) Judicial Resolution When Ripe. Where a justiciable civilian controversy presents the interpretive conflict, federal courts may resolve under ordinary Article III jurisdiction, subject to Section 25 constraints and Section 17C alternative pathways. (c) People's Resolution Through Sunset Review. Where interpretive conflicts persist or concern fundamental Amendment operation, Sunset Review under Section 18 provides the People's mechanism for clarification. Sunset Review Modify votes may include specific interpretive guidance addressing identified conflicts. (d) No Unilateral Interpretive Supremacy. No single interpretive body possesses absolute interpretive supremacy over all Amendment matters. The hierarchy in Section 27.11 establishes domain-specific primary authorities with checks through other bodies and ultimately through the People. This distribution of interpretive authority is itself protected under the Amendment's structural integrity. 27.13 Interpretive Rules Application. The specific interpretive rules established throughout this Amendment continue to apply, including: (a) Section 25A.27 (later constitutional provisions prevail where irreconcilable); (b) Section 25A.28 (ambiguity resolved per preamble interpretation rule); (c) Section 25A.29 (judicial capture scenarios trigger Section 13H alternative pathways); (d) Section 18.6 Amendment Protection boundaries; (e) provision-specific interpretive rules where established. This Section's hierarchy supplements rather than displaces these specific rules. 27.14 Sunset Review Consideration. The definitional consistency framework, Congressional collective inaction framework, military command integrity framework, and interpretive hierarchy shall be reviewed in each Sunset Review under Section 18, with the People retaining authority to modify these operational clarifications based on experience. Modifications shall remain consistent with Section 18.6 Amendment Protection boundaries. E. Amendment Scope and Congressional Enforcement Authority 27.15 Amendment Scope — Operational Detail as Structural Necessity. The operational detail contained in this Amendment — including specific procedural rules, timing windows, cryptographic lottery specifications, body composition rules, and similar particulars — is not conventional constitutional draftsmanship, and this departure from tradition is structurally necessary. The Amendment addresses a circumstance the original constitutional framework did not contemplate: coordinated capture of multiple federal branches simultaneously, rendering the traditional model (where constitutional amendments set broad principles for subsequent legislation, judicial interpretation, and executive enforcement to elaborate) inadequate.

Where Congress, the federal judiciary, and the executive branch may each be compromised, the Amendment cannot assume any of them will implement in good faith; it must therefore be self-executing in operational detail. 27.16 Precedent for Constitutional Detail. Prior constitutional amendments of similar structural significance contain detail proportionate to their purpose. The Fourteenth Amendment contains extensive procedural and substantive provisions across five sections. The Twenty-Second Amendment contains detailed Presidential eligibility rules. The Twentieth Amendment contains specific date specifications for transitions. Constitutional amendments address the problems they must address at the level of detail those problems require. The detail of this Amendment reflects the complexity of the capture scenarios it addresses, not a departure from constitutional

form. 27.17 Congressional Enforcement Authority Preserved. Consistent with the Section 5 enforcement authority patterns of the Thirteenth, Fourteenth, and Fifteenth Amendments, Congress retains authority to enact legislation for routine administrative elaboration of this Amendment's provisions, provided that such legislation: (a) does not diminish, limit, or functionally repeal any provision of this Amendment; (b) does not frustrate the operational purpose of Amendment bodies; (c) does not create delay, obstruction, or burden on Amendment implementation; and (d) is consistent with Section 18.6 Amendment Protection boundaries. Congressional legislation meeting these criteria is welcomed as elaboration; legislation failing any criterion shall constitute Section 13 interference and shall be void ab initio under Section 27.4 through Section 27.6. This preserves Congress's traditional elaborative role while ensuring that elaboration cannot become circumvention. 27.18 Self-Executing Operational Detail — Not a Departure from Constitutional Form. The self-executing operational provisions of this Amendment (including §13I self-executing appropriation, the Washington Commission's automatic convening, the Committee's lottery administration, and similar mechanisms) operate automatically upon Ratification without requiring Congressional enabling legislation. This self-executing character is not a departure from constitutional form but rather a necessary adaptation to the Amendment's purpose: addressing institutional capture scenarios where implementing legislation cannot be relied upon. Precedent for self-executing constitutional provisions includes the Thirteenth Amendment's immediate abolition of slavery (effective upon Ratification without enabling legislation), the Nineteenth Amendment's immediate grant of women's suffrage (effective without further action), and the Twenty-Sixth Amendment's immediate establishment of the eighteen-year-old voting age. The Amendment continues this tradition while extending it to operational detail where capture scenarios require it. 27.19 Response to Traditionalist Objection. Any objection that this Amendment is "too detailed" or "not in the traditional form" of constitutional amendments is respectfully addressed as follows: every constitutional amendment that has significantly restructured the constitutional order was unprecedented at the time of its drafting. The original Constitution was unprecedented. The Bill of Rights was unprecedented. The Reconstruction Amendments were unprecedented. The Nineteenth Amendment was unprecedented. The form of a constitutional amendment must be proportionate to the substance it addresses; where substance requires detail, form provides detail. This Amendment addresses the substantive problem of institutional capture with the detail that problem requires, consistent with the constitutional tradition of adapting form to purpose. The objection proves too much: it would invalidate every significant constitutional restructuring that has ever occurred.

Proposed for ratification by the legislatures of three-fourths of the several States, pursuant to Article V of the Constitution of the United States. "Whenever any Form of Government becomes destructive of these ends, it is the Right of the People to alter or to abolish it, and to institute new Government." — Declaration of Independence, July 4, 1776 A NOTE ON THE DRAFTER This proposed amendment — The People's Reclamation Amendment — was drafted across sixty-eight iterations by Shawn Theis, with detailed structural, legal, and procedural development conducted in collaboration to stress-test its mechanisms against edge cases, timeline errors, and corruption vectors. The Amendment reflects a considered judgment: that the authority of government must always rest, ultimately and reclaimably, with the People who consent to be governed. Every mechanism herein — the three-body Authority, the Liberty Bell Initiative, the Interim Caretaker Council, the Watchdog Tribunal, the strict limitations on nuclear first-use, and the comprehensive financial penalties for corruption — serves that single principle. This document is offered as a proposed framework for public discussion, civic education, and constitutional debate. It is not legal advice, nor does it presume to replace the democratic process of amendment under Article V. It is an exercise in seriously imagining what a mechanism of citizen-initiated government reconstitution might look like if designed today, with the tools of cryptographic verification, structured oversight, and explicit anti-corruption safeguards we did not possess in 1787. Shawn Theis DRAFTER

•

THE

PEOPLE'S

RECLAMATION

AMENDMENT

Proposed by: ________________________________ Date:
______________ Witnessed by: ________________________________ Date:
______________ Attested by: _________________________________ Date:
______________ —

END

OF

PROPOSED

AMENDMENT —

◆ ◆ ◆

Chapter Eight

Postscript

If you have read this far, you have read more about the proposed People's Reclamation Amendment than nearly anyone in the country, including most of the people who will eventually be asked to vote on it.

What you do with that is your business. There is no obligation in any direction. The Amendment is a tool. Tools are useful when used and harmless when set down. The People who decide whether to use this one are the People — which is you, by the way, and everyone you know — and the People will make that decision when the time comes. Two things are worth saying before the back matter starts. The first is that this book exists because, somewhere along the way, a citizen looked at the country and concluded that the existing tools were not going to be enough. That conclusion may be wrong. The Amendment may be unnecessary. The country may right itself through ordinary politics, the way it usually does. If so, this book becomes a curiosity — a thoughtful overreaction by a person who paid more attention than they had to. That is a fine outcome. Better than the alternative. The second is that if the conclusion turns out to be right — if the existing tools fail in a way that ordinary politics cannot repair — then having an extraordinary tool already drafted, already debated, already explained at this level of detail is meaningfully better than starting from scratch in a crisis. Constitutional amendments take years to draft well. They take longer to ratify. The work of building a peaceful, structured, legitimate way to remove a federal government has to be done in advance of needing one. There is no other way to do it. Whichever turns out to be the case — the Amendment used or unused, ratified or unratified, vindicated or rendered unnecessary — the work was worth doing. The country deserves to know that this kind of constitutional remedy is possible. That fact alone changes the calculus for any actor who might otherwise assume that no peaceful remedy exists. What follows is reference material. The Amendment's full text is in the previous chapter. The glossary defines the major terms. The indexes will help you find specific provisions when you need them. The maps belong to whoever needs them. Thank you for reading.

◆ ◆ ◆

Reference

Glossary

Definitions for the major terms used in the book and the Amendment. Where a term is formally defined in the Amendment text, the relevant section reference is included. Terms are listed alphabetically.

◆ ◆ ◆

A

Academic Integrity Commission

One of the three bodies of the Authority. Fifty academics drawn from the Pre-Certified University Pool, with required specialties in statistics, computer security, constitutional law, political science, and election administration. Established in §17.15. The Commission's role is technical rigor — auditing the math, identifying methodological flaws, and detecting fraud that would not be visible to non-specialists.

Aggregate-Pattern Coordinated Hardship Detection

The §17.4.14 framework for detecting coordinated third-party campaigns that orchestrate hardship petitions among drawn citizens of specific demographic, geographic, professional, or political characteristics — to distort the composition of Amendment lottery-drawn bodies. Liability attaches to orchestrators, not to individual citizens who file good-faith hardship petitions. Includes explicit safe harbors for civic education, member communications by civic organizations, legal aid, public commentary, and ordinary social-network communications. Construed consistently with the First Amendment.

Articles of No Confidence

The public document a citizen files to initiate a Petition under §3. The Articles state, in plain language, what the federal government is alleged to have done that warrants removal. Anyone may file — there is no requirement to be a lawyer, an elected official, or a person of any particular standing. Filed at any Citizens' Reclamation Office, posted to the Franklin Ledger upon registration.

Authority, the

Short for the Independent Tripartite Oversight Authority. The institution established by §17 that administers the Petition and Referendum process. Composed of three independent bodies — Citizens' Oversight Board, State Elections Council, and Academic Integrity Commission — that act jointly through the Liberty Bell Initiative. The Authority is not a government; it administers the process by which the People decide.

B

Bad Faith Determination

A formal finding under §13 that a particular act of interference with the §3 process was committed knowingly and in concert with others. A Tier 3 violation requires bad-faith findings. Determinations are made by §17C panels and require clear, convincing evidence published on the Franklin Ledger.

C

Citizens' Oversight Board

One of the three bodies of the Authority. Three hundred ordinary Americans, selected by lottery from the registered voter rolls, serving two-year staggered terms with one hundred fifty members rotating off each year. No consecutive terms; no person may serve more than two total terms in their lifetime. Established in §17.2–17.7. Members receive federally protected employment, full wage replacement at median U.S. household income (cost-of-living adjusted), full housing, travel, dependent care, and medical coverage, and federal protection from harassment, intimidation, or surveillance — violations of which are a 10-year federal felony. The Board is the People's voice within the institution and is, by design, the body least susceptible to capture by any organized political faction.

Citizens' Reclamation Offices

The dedicated buildings where citizens file Articles of No Confidence, sign Petitions, and vote in Referendums. Established in §11 and §11C. Each office contains Sovereign Voting Terminals and is open to the public during established hours. Offices are physically present in every congressional district.

Composite State-Sovereign Authority

The body that exercises emergency authority under §16.10's Reclamation-Earned Trust Framework when the regular Authority is unavailable. Composed of state Attorneys General and state Supreme Court Chief Justices in defined proportions, drawn by lottery, sworn to the Constitution. Its powers are bounded — it can administer, certify, and prosecute, but cannot legislate or suspend rights.

D

Day Zero

The moment of ratification — when three-quarters of state legislatures (or conventions) have ratified the Amendment. From Day Zero, §13F asset and travel restrictions on federal officials begin immediately, the Washington Commission convenes within 72 hours, and the phased activation timeline begins.

Defense in Depth

The architectural principle that no single section of the Amendment carries the load alone. To defeat the Amendment, an attempt must defeat §3 (the trigger), §17 (the administration), §13 (the prosecution), §22 (foreign-actor controls), §16 (the military oath), and §17C (the venue) — simultaneously. Coordinated defeat of all six is not a defeat of the Amendment but a description of a country that has stopped functioning.

Delay-Equals-Refusal Presumption

The §13I.36 framework converting Treasury slow-walking of Amendment funding into prosecutable refusal under §13I.23. Establishes specific timing categories — 7 days for operational funding, 72 hours for time-sensitive funding, 48 hours for Ratification Loan tranches, 14 days for procurement, 30 days for asset-recovery distribution. Failure to disburse within applicable timing creates a rebuttable presumption of refusal. Treasury may rebut by showing genuinely uncontrollable circumstances; ordinary administrative inconvenience does not rebut. Personal officeholder liability attaches to Treasury Secretary, Deputy Secretaries, Bureau of the Fiscal Service Commissioner, and others who direct or materially participate in delay. Emergency Direct Disbursement pathway via Permanent Washington Commission with Federal Reserve and State AG Council fallbacks.

E

Emergency Election

The federal election held within 90 days after a passing No Confidence Referendum, governed by §7. The President, Vice President, Congress, and other federal political leaders are elected by ranked-choice voting. The Caretaker Council holds administrative authority during the 90-day window.

F

Federalization of State Assets

The §16.7.1 procedure by which state-controlled buildings, vehicles, or personnel actively used to obstruct the §3 process can be brought under federal authority. Requires a 90% supermajority of other governors and is reserved for serious obstruction — the high threshold reflects that state sovereignty is real and that federalization is a serious step.

Forcible Removal

The §13E procedure that activates when a removed official refuses to vacate office after a passing Referendum. The 24-hour compliance window, the lapse of facilities access and security clearance, the Hamilton Contingent's arrest authority, and the immediate seating of the Interim Caretaker Council. Removal is a legal status; refusing to leave physically is trespassing, not a competing claim to authority.

Foreign Sovereign Limits

The §22.23 framework's honest acknowledgment that the Amendment's foreign-interference penalties operate asymmetrically. The Amendment reaches U.S. persons in full and reaches foreign persons and entities to the extent permitted by U.S. jurisdiction, but cannot prosecute foreign sovereign states themselves due to the Foreign Sovereign Immunities Act (28 U.S.C. §§ 1602–1611) and customary international law. Where foreign-sovereign involvement is established, §22.23 activates a state-craft response toolkit: Authority Certification to State and Treasury, formal Diplomatic Recommendations, Asset Identification and Freezing, treaty-based mechanisms, and public documentation. The Amendment is honest about what domestic constitutional law can and cannot reach.

Franklin Ledger

The cryptographically secured public record of all Amendment activity, established in §4A. Named for Benjamin Franklin. Includes a public website, mobile app, telephone information line, and physical print and broadcast distribution. Mirrored across at least seven independent custodians. Every Authority action, every Tribunal investigation, every Hamilton Contingent prosecution, and every dollar of recovered corrupt assets is published in real time.

H

Hamilton Contingent

The federal prosecution body established by §13C, named for Alexander Hamilton. Independent of the Department of Justice — the President cannot stand it down. Its only job is to prosecute interference with the §3 process. Has four divisions: Prosecution, Protection, Public Response, and Preservation. All cases tried before §17C state-level panels.

I

Inaugural Referendum

The first No Confidence Referendum, held automatically on Day 780 without requiring a Petition. Established in §19A. The People's first guaranteed opportunity to use the Amendment they ratified. If the Inaugural Referendum fails, normal operation begins; future Referendums require Petition initiation.

Independent Tripartite Oversight Authority

The full formal name of the Authority. See Authority, the.

Initial Comprehensive Voter Roll Audit

The §13.9 framework establishing the first cycle of post-Ratification AIC voter roll audit operations under the §13.8(c) continuous audit authority, with explicit retrospective evidentiary scope examining the inherited state of voter rolls and the administrative history that produced them. Conducted by the AIC-Designate Forensic Consortium during Phase One (Days 0–180) and the Academic Integrity Commission thereafter. Initial findings published by Day 300, final findings by Day 600. State remediation window of 180 days. Creates no preconditions on Section 3 Petitions or the Inaugural Referendum — its value is informational and remediative, not gatekeeping. Subsequent comprehensive audits every ten years. Includes a No Single-Point Failure backstop ensuring that capture of, or interference with, the audit administering body cannot prevent any Amendment process from proceeding.

Interim Caretaker Council

The fifty-six-member body established in §6A that holds limited emergency administrative authority during the Caretaker Period — the window between a passing No Confidence Referendum and the convening of the Constitutional Transition Committee. The Council consists of the sitting Governor (or equivalent chief executive) of each of the fifty states, the Mayor of the District of Columbia, and the Governor of each of the five territories — all serving ex officio. No election or appointment is required; the moment a Referendum is certified, sitting Governors automatically convene as the Council within seventy-two hours. The Council pays bills, honors treaties, signs routine documents, and ensures the country does not fall apart during the transition. It does not pass laws, start wars, appoint judges, or sign new treaties. Any action requires a two-thirds supermajority of all members. The Council dissolves automatically when the Constitutional Transition Committee convenes.

J

Jurisdiction Strip

The §3.3 provision that removes federal court subject-matter jurisdiction over the Petition-and-Referendum process. Surgical, not categorical — federal courts retain jurisdiction over criminal cases, civil rights cases, ordinary federal-question cases. What is removed is the power to halt or invalidate the §3 process as a whole.

L

Liberty Bell Initiative

The procedural mechanism by which the Authority's three bodies act jointly. Each body deliberates independently; all three must concur for an action to proceed; if any one dissents, the action fails. Established in §17. Named for the Liberty Bell at Independence Hall. The default is no action — the Authority must reach unanimous concurrence before anything happens.

M

Materiality Determination

A formal finding under §22.14 that foreign interference in a Petition or Referendum was material — significant enough to affect the outcome. Requires Liberty Bell Initiative concurrence (all three Authority bodies) and clear, convincing, publicly documented evidence. Triggers invalidation of the tainted Petition or Referendum.

Mutual Veto

The structural rule under which any one of the three Authority bodies may block any Authority action by declining to concur, regardless of what the other two bodies decide. Defined explicitly in §17. The mutual veto is the heart of the Liberty Bell Initiative's anti-capture design.

N

No Confidence Referendum

The 30-day national vote that follows successful Petition certification. Voters return to Sovereign Voting Terminals and vote yes or no on removing the federal government. Requires 60% of votes cast AND 50% turnout of registered voters to pass. Established in §5.

P

Participating Jurisdictions

The fifty-six units that participate as equals under the Amendment: the fifty states, the District of Columbia, and the five U.S. territories. Defined in §3.1.1. Petition signature thresholds require both 15% nationally AND 15% within at least thirty of these fifty-six jurisdictions.

Petition

The citizen-initiated formal request to trigger a No Confidence Referendum. Requires verified in-person signatures from 15% of registered voters nationally AND 15% in at least thirty of the fifty-six Participating Jurisdictions, collected within a 180-day window. Established in §3.

Pre-Certified Universities

The pool of universities certified in advance under §17.16 to host backup voting infrastructure. Vetted before any crisis arises against published criteria covering accreditation, governance independence, security capability, and conflict-of-interest disclosure. Provides redundancy if state-controlled venues are unavailable.

Pre-Inaugural Vulnerability Monitoring

The §13F.28 transparency-and-disclosure framework covering specific non-federal channels during the Pre-Inaugural Period (Days 0–780, spanning both Phase One and Phase Two). Reaches sitting Chief Justices in the Washington Commission lottery pool, sitting State Attorneys General on the State AG Council, senior administrators of Pre-Certified Universities, AIC-Designate Forensic Consortium members, Short-Term Civilian Review Board members, and Citizens' Implementation Watch Board members. Disclosure-only — does not impose travel restriction, asset freezing, or other §13F coercive measures. Administered by the AIC-Designate Forensic Consortium during Phase One and the Academic Integrity Commission thereafter. Includes monthly automatic enforcement-trigger reviews, external oversight by Short-Term Civilian Review Board and Watchdog Tribunal, and explicit negative enumeration of what monitoring cannot do. Sunsets automatically upon Inaugural Referendum certification.

Pre-Publication Review

The §22.24 framework giving the Foreign Interference Oversight Board upstream authority over Detection Unit findings before publication, converting the Oversight Board's civil liberties function from purely retrospective remedy to upstream prevention. Covers preliminary findings, pattern findings, identification findings, and aggregate findings. Four outcome categories: Approve Publication, Approve with Modification, Defer Publication, Preclude Publication. Standard 7-day review timeline with 48-hour expedited option and emergency-publication pathway with retrospective review. Detection Unit investigation authority is fully preserved — only publication is gated. Final §22.14 materiality determinations are exempt from pre-publication review. Hardened against capture by §22.7.1 sub-quorum lottery composition requirements (17 of 35 randomly drawn per matter), 2/3 supermajority required for preclusion, and public summary documentation of all preclusion patterns.

R

Reclamation-Earned Trust Framework

The §16.10 emergency authority structure that activates when the regular Authority cannot operate. Three-gate activation requires Washington Commission certification, 90% gubernatorial concurrence, and a fixed sunset. Reserved for genuine institutional unavailability — designed to be hard to activate.

Referendum

Short for No Confidence Referendum. See above.

S

Senior Official Multiplier

The §13A enhancement applied when an interference or corruption offense is committed by a public official wielding public authority. Sets the fine at no less than fifty times (50×) the benefit received, raises maximum prison sentences from 5 years to 15 years, and triggers permanent ban from federal office on conviction. Reflects the principle that interference by officeholders is more dangerous than interference by ordinary citizens — and that they should pay accordingly.

Single-Body Compromise Declaration

The §17.22.1 mechanism by which any single Authority body can publish a Declaration calling out a federal interpretation of the Amendment as bad-faith. Triggers Watchdog Tribunal review and procedural advantages for any subsequent Petition initiated on the issue. The Amendment's defense against being read into nothing by future Courts.

Sovereign Blockchain Voting Ledger

The cryptographically secured underlying data store for all Petition signatures and Referendum votes, established in §4. Distinct from the Franklin Ledger (which is the public-facing transparency layer). The Voting Ledger uses dual-chain primary plus standby architecture with voter-verified paper backup.

Sovereign Voting Terminals

The physical machines used to sign Petitions and cast Referendum votes, established in §14. Use cryptographic signatures, hardware security modules, and dual-chain blockchain ledger with voter-verified paper backup. In-person, ID-verified — no online signing, no online voting, no mail-in component. Universally accessible by §14.7's accessibility standards.

State Elections Council

One of the three bodies of the Authority. Fifty-six officials, one from each Participating Jurisdiction, serving ex officio while in their state role. Established in §17.10. Brings election expertise the other Authority bodies cannot — state elections officers have careers running actual elections.

Sunset Review

The §18 process by which the Amendment reviews itself every twenty years. Conducted by a body structurally separate from the Authority, drawing on state-level institutions. Can recommend Retain, Modify, or Repeal. Modify triggers a Constitutional Review Convention of 150 delegates — 100 drawn by lottery from the Citizens' Oversight Board, 25 appointed by state legislatures (with the 25 Participating Jurisdictions selected by per-cycle randomized lottery from all 56 to prevent fixed-target capture), and 25 drawn by lottery from the Pre-Certified University Pool. Recommendations require supermajority ratification by the People to take effect. Cannot be skipped or advanced — the clock runs at its own pace.

T

Tier 1 Interference

Under §13, the baseline interference penalty applied to any person who knowingly interferes with §3 processes. Maximum: 5 years federal prison, fines, civil damages. Includes harassment of signers, vandalism of terminals, spreading of verifiable fraud.

Tier 2 Interference

Under §13, the enhanced interference penalty applied to public officials with the Senior Official Multiplier. Maximum: 15 years federal prison, fines of 50× the benefit received, permanent ban from office. Includes elected officials ordering interference, judges issuing void §3.3 orders.

Tier 3 Interference

Under §13, the most severe interference penalty — applied to coordinated, bad-faith action and is unpardonable. Maximum: 25 years federal prison, fines up to 75× the benefit received under combined Senior Official and Repeat Offender multipliers, treble damages on actual harm, full asset forfeiture, no presidential pardon. Includes coordinated capture attempts, foreign-linked actors, officials acting in concert against the Amendment.

W

Washington Commission (Permanent)

The ongoing oversight body established in §17D — the watcher-of-watchers' watchers. Seven sitting Chief Justices of Participating Jurisdictions, with biennial rotation under §17D.5. Oversees the Hamilton Contingent, the §17C State Attorneys General Prosecution Panels, the §17C State Supreme Court Judicial Panels, and the §17C Appellate Panels. Has limited subpoena authority over Covered Accountability Bodies. Cannot direct prosecutions, but can investigate and publish Oversight Findings on the Franklin Ledger. The structurally distinct ongoing role of the Washington Commission, separate from its Phase One implementation role.

Washington Commission (Phase One)

The interim convening authority during the Amendment's first 180 days, established in §19.5.0 and named for George Washington. Seven sitting Chief Justices of Participating Jurisdictions, all civilian, drawn by randomized lottery from the highest courts. Convenes within 72 hours of certified ratification. Operates with the Joint Chiefs of Staff serving as non-voting military advisors. Bridges the gap before the three Authority bodies are fully constituted. Dissolves 60 days after Authority inauguration.

Watch Board

The 100-member lottery citizen body activated by Day 30 of Phase One, established in §19.14. Provides oversight during the activation period before the full Authority is constituted. Approves international travel of federal officials under §13F restrictions during Phase One.

Watchdog Tribunal

The §21 oversight body that investigates the Authority itself — and members of all other Amendment institutions. One hundred citizens selected by lottery, serving staggered three-year terms with no consecutive terms and no more than two total terms in a lifetime. Has full subpoena authority. Can remove members of any Amendment institution by two-thirds supermajority. Watches the watchers.

Whereas Clause

Each numbered statement in the Amendment's preamble, beginning with 'WHEREAS.' The Whereas clauses establish the constitutional principles and findings that motivate the operative sections. Not binding law in themselves, but interpretive guides — the Amendment's preamble functions like a contract's recitals, framing how the binding text should be read.

§ Section Symbol

The symbol used throughout the Amendment and this book to denote Section references. §3 means Section 3; §3.1.1 means Section 3, subsection 1, sub-subsection 1; §17C means Section 17C (a lettered subsection of Section 17). The symbol is standard in legal writing.

◆ ◆ ◆

www.ingramcontent.com/pod-product-compliance
Lightning Source LLC
LaVergne TN
LVHW071411210926
848486LV00004B/249
9798234092762